THE FAMILY CIRCLE
RECIPE
ENCYCLOPEDIA

THE FAMILY CIRCLE
RECIPE
ENCYCLOPEDIA

MURDOCH BOOKS®

Sydney • London • Vancouver • New York

Published by Murdoch Books®, a division of Murdoch Magazines Pty Ltd,
213 Miller Street, North Sydney NSW 2060

Editorial Director: Susan Tomnay
Creative Director: Marylouise Brammer
Project Editor: Sue Wagner
Photo Librarian and Manuscript Research: Dianne Bedford
Editors: Deirdre Blayney, Wendy Stephen, Amanda Bishop
Copy Editor: Elaine Myors
Dictionary Entries: Margaret McPhee
Additional Recipes: Barbara Lowery
Additional Text: John Fenton Smith
Murdoch Books® Food Editors: Kerrie Ray, Tracy Rutherford
Family Circle® Food Editor: Jo Anne Calabria

Publisher: Anne Wilson
Publishing Manager: Catie Ziller
International Sales Director: Mark Newman
General Manager: Mark Smith
Managing Editor: Jane Price

National Library of Australia
Cataloguing-in-Publication Data
The Recipe encyclopedia.
Includes index.
Cased edition ISBN 0 86411 401 X.
Limp edition ISBN 0 86411 559 8.
1. Cookery - Encyclopedias. 2. Food - Encyclopedias.
641.503

Printed by Leefung-Asco Printers Ltd, China

Cased edition first printed 1995, reprinted 1996 (twice).
Limp edition first printed 1996.

COVER ILLUSTRATIONS, FROM TOP: BRAISED OXTAIL (PAGE 43), MONTE CREAMS (PAGE 54), APPLE CHARLOTTES (PAGE 19)
AND SPAGHETTI PUTTANESCA (PAGE 226).
PAGE 2 ILLUSTRATION, FROM LEFT: PENNE WITH ARTICHOKE HEARTS (PAGE 22) AND OLIVE AND ROSEMARY FOCACCIA (PAGE 297).
PAGE 6 ILLUSTRATION, FROM TOP: HOT CARAMEL MANGO (PAGE 258) AND CHOCOLATE GLACÉ APRICOTS (PAGE 21).

CONTENTS

ALPHABETICAL LISTING

A 8-27
B 28-63
C 64-127
D 128-149
E 150-159
F 160-185
G 186-201
H 202-213
I 214-227
J 228-237
K 238-239
L 240-257
M 258-283
N 284-289
O 290-303
P 304-361
Q 362-365
R 366-379
S 380-443
T 444-461
U,V 462-473
W 474-477
Y 478-483
Z 484-485

SPECIAL FEATURES

ANTIPASTO	16
BEANS & BROCCOLI	40
CABBAGE & CAULIFLOWER	64
CAKE DECORATING	80
CARVING	86
CHEESECAKES	92
COFFEE	112
FINGER FOOD	166
FOCACCIA	176
FREEZING	182
HERBS	202
ICE-CREAMS & SORBETS	220
JAMS & MARMALADES	228
MICROWAVE	270
MUFFINS	276
NOODLES	288
ONIONS	294
PASTA	308
PASTRY	320
PEAS & POTATOES	330
PICKLES & CHUTNEYS	338
SALAD DRESSINGS	390
CLASSIC SAUCES	398
SOUFFLES	420
ASIAN VEGETABLES	466
YOGHURT & FRESH CHEESES	482
INDEX	486
ACKNOWLEDGEMENTS	496

THE RECIPE ENCYCLOPEDIA

Find a good cook and you find someone who *enjoys* food, someone for whom every stage of producing a meal—buying, preparing and ultimately serving—can be a source of pleasure. Such enthusiasm comes with an understanding of the ingredients, a knowledge of cooking techniques and, of course, inspiring recipes.

With this in mind we have created *The Recipe Encyclopedia*, a complete reference to food and cooking. The comprehensive dictionary of ingredients helps you make the most of everyday foods as well as giving an insight into more exotic fare. It covers cookery terms, famous dishes, national cuisines and the colourful history of food. Guidelines on choosing and using foods are given throughout the book, and 26 special sections will tempt you to try out new techniques.

The book is packed with recipes—more than 800 of them—all tried and tested in *Family Circle's* famous kitchens. There are 1500 colour photographs to whet your appetite and a star rating to help you choose recipes that suit your cooking expertise.

This beautifully crafted book is a pleasure in its own right; as your companion in the kitchen, *The Recipe Encyclopedia* will ensure that good food and cooking remain a constant delight.

HOW TO USE THIS BOOK

Both metric and imperial measurements are used. 1 cup is equal to 250 ml (8 fl oz). The recipes are classified according to their main ingredient (for example, strawberries), the sort of dish (for example, cakes) or the way they are cooked (for example, barbecue cookery). If in doubt, consult the Index. The food dictionary is in alphabetical order and covers ingredients, national cuisines, cookery terms, and famous dishes. There are special features which provide helpful information on the topics listed above.

 Easy   A little care needed   More care needed

A

Abalone A large sea snail with a shallow, ear-shaped shell. It lives close to the shoreline, clinging to the underside of rock ledges with a broad, fleshy foot. Found throughout the world, abalone at one time became so rare in California that it was not allowed to be canned, dried or sent out of the state; the advent of farm-raised abalone eased these restrictions. In the Channel Islands, when seasonal low tides temporarily exposed the abalone's rocky haunts, the locals once took part in a frenzied race to gather as many as possible before the waters rolled back in, leading to a decline in abalone numbers. In Australia, divers harvest them in southern waters.

The flesh is tough and must be tenderised by pounding before it can be eaten.

Abbacchio The Italian term for meat from an unweaned baby lamb. Dishes based on it have been a specialty of central and southern Italy since the time of the ancient Romans. Roasted with garlic and

ALMOND AND COCONUT LAMB CURRY

⭐⭐ **Preparation time:** 25 minutes
Total cooking time: 50 minutes
Serves 4

8 lamb forequarter or chump (rib) chops, each about 140 g (4½ oz)
¼ cup (2 fl oz) olive oil
1 medium onion, sliced
1 medium cooking apple, peeled and chopped
2 medium carrots, chopped
1 tablespoon fresh coriander leaves
3 dried curry leaves
½ teaspoon garam masala
½ teaspoon ground cumin
½ teaspoon turmeric
155 g (5 oz) can coconut cream
1 tablespoon ground almonds
1¼ cups slivered almonds, toasted

1 Trim chops of bone and excess fat and sinew. Cut meat evenly into 3 cm (1¼ inch) cubes.
2 Heat 2 tablespoons of the oil in a heavy-based pan. Cook meat quickly in small batches over medium-high heat until well browned; drain on absorbent paper.
3 Heat remaining oil in pan. Add onion, stir over medium heat for 5 minutes or until soft. Add meat, apple, carrot, herbs, spices and coconut cream; bring to boil. Reduce heat to a simmer and cook, covered, for 35 minutes or until the meat is tender. Stir in ground almonds just before serving. Serve curry sprinkled with toasted slivered almonds.

ABOUT ALMONDS

■ To blanch almonds, place them in a small bowl, cover with boiling water and stand for 4 minutes. Use a spoon to remove each nut, then press nut between finger and thumb: the skins should slip away easily.

■ To toast almonds, place them in a single layer on a baking tray; bake in a moderate oven 180°C (350°F/Gas 4) for 4 minutes (for flaked almonds) to 8 minutes (for whole almonds), checking regularly to prevent burning. Take care during the last minutes of cooking as the nuts tend to darken quickly.

■ Ground almonds are best purchased. It can be difficult to achieve the right texture by grinding in a food processor—over-processing can result in a paste. If you wish to grind your own, work in short bursts with small batches only.

■ Store almonds in an airtight container in the refrigerator for up to two months.

RIGHT: ALMOND AND COCONUT LAMB CURRY

rosemary, it is traditional Easter fare.

Aberdeen Sausage
A beef sausage that is wrapped in a cloth, boiled, and then coated in dry breadcrumbs.

Acidulated water
Water with a little lemon juice or vinegar added, sprinkled on cut raw fruit such as apples, bananas and pears to prevent browning.

Agar-agar A white, semi-translucent, tasteless and odourless setting agent made from various Asian seaweeds. Agar-agar sets without refrigeration and is used in Asian cookery to thicken soups and to make jellies.

Aïoli A garlic mayonnaise from Provence which is sometimes called the 'butter of Provence'. In Marseilles it is said that aïoli should contain at least two cloves of garlic per person. Traditionally associated with poached salt cod, aïoli is also served with other fish, meat and vegetables, and is also added to soup.

À la French for 'in the style or manner of', eg *à la Niçoise*, typical of the

cooking style of the Nice region; *à la vigneronne*, prepared with grapes (in the manner of the wine grower).
See individual entries.

Al dente An Italian cooking term, literally 'to the tooth', which is used to describe food, particularly pasta, that is cooked until firm to the bite rather than soft.

Alfalfa Sprouts The fine, short sprouts of alfalfa seeds, with pale stalks and deep green tips, used in salads and sandwiches. The sprouts have a nutty taste and a particular affinity for cheese. The alfalfa (or lucerne) plant was first grown by Arabs as food for their horses because its high protein and calcium content helped develop strong animals.

Allemande, à l'
A French term for food cooked in the German style: traditionally, dishes containing smoked sausages or garnished with sauerkraut and pork. It is also used to describe dishes served with allemande sauce, a white sauce made with veal or poultry stock.

Allspice A spice made from the berries of a tropical tree which grows throughout Central America and is especially abundant in Jamaica. Its aroma and flavour is similar to a blend of cloves, cinnamon and

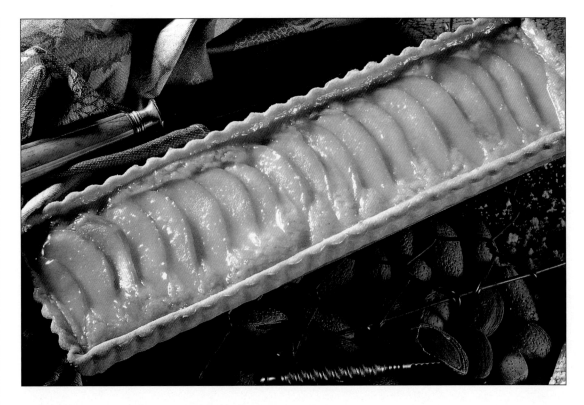

ALMOND AND PEAR TART

⋆⋆ ***Preparation time:*** 35 minutes + 20 minutes refrigeration
Total cooking time: 40 minutes
Serves 4–6

1¼ cups plain (all-purpose) flour	50 g (1¾ oz) butter
¼ cup icing (confectioners) sugar	¼ cup caster (superfine) sugar
90 g (3 oz) butter, chopped	1 egg, lightly beaten
1 egg yolk, lightly beaten	1 teaspoon vanilla essence
1–2 tablespoons iced water	2 teaspoons plain (all-purpose) flour
	50 g (1¾ oz) ground almonds
Filling	2 tablespoons apricot jam, warmed and sieved
2 large pears	

1 Place flour, sugar and butter in food processor bowl. Using the pulse action, press button for 15 seconds or until the mixture is fine and crumbly Add egg yolk and almost all the water, process for 20 seconds or until mixture comes together, adding more water if necessary. Turn onto a lightly floured surface, press mixture together until smooth. Brush a 35 x 11 cm (14 x 4½ inch) oblong flan tin with melted butter or oil. Roll out pastry to cover base and sides of tin. Ease pastry into tin; trim. Cover with plastic wrap; refrigerate for 20 minutes.
2 Preheat oven to moderate 180°C (350°F/Gas 4). Cut a sheet of greaseproof paper large enough to cover pastry-lined tin. Place over pastry and spread a layer of dried beans or rice evenly over the paper. Bake for 10 minutes, remove from oven and discard paper and beans. Return to oven for 10 minutes or until pastry is lightly golden. Leave to cool.
3 To make Filling: Peel pears, cut in half and remove the cores. Place in a small pan of boiling water and cook over medium heat for 10 minutes or until just tender. Drain, cool and slice thinly.
4 Using electric beaters, beat butter and sugar until light and creamy. Add the beaten egg gradually, beating well after each addition. Add essence and beat until combined. Using a metal spoon, fold in flour and almonds. Spread into pastry case and arrange slices of pear on top. Bake for 20 minutes, or until set and golden. While still warm, brush the pears with jam.

SPICY ALMONDS

Heat 2 tablespoons olive oil in a heavy-based frying pan. Add ½ teaspoon each ground cumin, ground coriander, garlic powder and chilli powder, and ¼ teaspoon each ground ginger and ground cinnamon. Stir over low heat for 2 minutes. Remove pan from heat, add 2 cups whole blanched almonds and stir until almonds are coated with spice mixture. Spread almonds on oven tray, place in a preheated oven 150°C (300°F/Gas 2), cook 15 minutes. Remove from oven, sprinkle with a little salt; cool.

A L M O N D   M A C A R O O N S

 Preparation time: 30 minutes
Total cooking time: 15–20 minutes
Serves 6

1 cup icing (confectioners)
  sugar, sifted
1 egg, beaten
2 cups ground almonds
2 teaspoons finely grated
  lemon rind

1 teaspoon vanilla essence
¼ teaspoon ground
  cinnamon
extra icing (confectioners)
  sugar, for sprinkling

1 Place icing sugar and egg in a large mixing bowl, beat until mixture turns white.
2 In another bowl, combine ground almonds, lemon rind, essence and cinnamon. Gradually mix into beaten sugar and egg mixture.
3 Knead dough in bowl for 5 minutes, or until pliable. Cover with a tea-towel, leave 15 minutes.
4 Preheat oven to moderate 180°C (350°F/Gas 4). On a lightly floured surface, roll dough to a long 4 cm (1½ inch) thick sausage shape. Cut into 24 pieces, roll each into an even-sized ball.
5 Lightly oil palms of hands and flatten each ball into a round about 4 cm (1½ inches) in diameter. Place on greased baking tray, leaving plenty of room for spreading; sprinkle with icing sugar. Bake for 15–20 minutes or until golden. Cool on wire rack. Store in an airtight container.

OPPOSITE PAGE: ALMOND AND PEAR TART
ABOVE: ALMOND MACAROONS

A L M O N D   B R E A D

 Preparation time: 10 minutes
Total cooking time: 45 minutes
Makes about 36

4 egg whites
pinch of cream of tartar
½ cup caster (superfine)
  sugar

1 cup plain (all-purpose)
  flour, sifted
¾ cup unblanched whole
  almonds
few drops almond essence

1 Preheat oven to 200°C (400°F/Gas 6); grease small loaf tin. Beat egg whites with cream of tartar until stiff peaks form. Gradually add sugar, beating constantly until stiff. Lightly fold in flour, almonds and essence.
2 Spoon mixture into prepared tin; bake for 30–35 minutes. Cool in tin for 5 minutes, then turn out onto a wire rack to cool completely.
3 Cut loaf into wafer-thin slices with a sharp, thin-bladed knife. Place on ungreased baking tray. Reduce oven temperature to 150°C (300°F/Gas 2) and bake slices for 10–12 minutes. Cool and store in an airtight container.

Note: Try a combination of macadamias, pecan, walnut and pistachio nuts for a delicious alternative to almonds. Partially cooked loaf can be frozen; bake as many slices as required at a time, straight from the freezer. These are excellent biscuits to serve with tea, coffee, after dinner or as an accompaniment to soft desserts.

nutmeg. The berries are picked while green and dried in the sun until dark red. Whole berries are used to flavour stews, pot roasts and chutney; the ground spice is added to apple dishes, milk puddings, gingerbread and tomato sauce. It is sometimes also called pimento or Jamaica pepper.

Almond The oval-shaped seeds of a tree closely related to the peach and apricot. Originally from the Middle East, the almond is one of the most widely used and longest cultivated nuts in the world. It was eaten in ancient Babylon, is mentioned in Hittite writings and in the Bible, and by Minoan times had spread west as far as the island of Crete. The ancient Greeks mixed the crushed nut with honey to make marzipan and it was popular with the Romans, who called it 'the Greek nut'. The prevalence of the almond in medieval cooking is thought to be connected to religious fast days when it replaced forbidden meat and milk.
   There are two types of almond: the sweet almond, from a pink-flowering tree, the form most widely used; and the strongly

flavoured bitter almond, from a white-flowering tree, a broader and shorter nut which contains prussic acid and is poisonous if consumed in more than minute amounts. In some styles of cooking the two are mixed, in

proportions of about one bitter to fifty sweet almonds.

California is the world's largest producer of almonds, followed by Italy and Spain, where the trees grow well on the poor soils of the Mediterranean hills. Almonds are eaten raw, roasted, or grilled and salted; pounded or ground, they are used in savoury stuffings and a variety of desserts, cakes and confectionery.

Almond Paste A mixture of finely ground almond, sugar and egg which is rolled out and used to cover rich fruit cakes with a smooth and even surface before they are iced. It also helps to preserve the cake and to stop it from discolouring the icing. It is used to make

marzipan confectionery and fillings for Danish pastries.

Alum An astringent mineral salt used in pickling to maintain the crispness of cucumbers

AMERICAN CLASSICS

CRUNCHY FRIED CHICKEN

 ✯ ✯ **Preparation time:** 10 minutes
Total cooking time: 16 minutes
Serves 6

12 chicken drumsticks (about 1.5 kg/3 lb)	1 teaspoon onion salt
¼ cup finely crushed cornflakes	2 tablespoons chicken stock powder
1¼ cups plain (all-purpose) flour	½ teaspoon garlic powder
1 teaspoon celery salt	½ teaspoon ground white pepper
	oil for deep frying

1 Place chicken drumsticks in a large pan of boiling water; reduce heat and simmer, uncovered, 8 minutes or until chicken is almost cooked through. Drain.
2 Combine cornflakes, sifted flour, celery salt, onion salt, stock powder, garlic powder and white pepper in a medium bowl. Place chicken drumsticks in large bowl, cover with cold water.
3 Dip wet drumsticks, one at a time, into the seasoned flour mixture; shake off excess.
4 Heat oil in deep heavy-based pan. Gently add drumsticks and cook a few at a time over medium-high heat for 8 minutes, or until chicken is golden and cooked through. Drain on paper towels; keep warm. Repeat with remaining pieces. Serve hot.

CORNED BEEF HASH

✯ **Preparation time:** 20 minutes
Total cooking time: 15 minutes
Serves 2

50 g (1¾ oz) butter	1 medium onion, chopped
4 medium potatoes, cooked, peeled and cubed	salt and pepper to taste
	tomato ketchup or chilli sauce
375 g (12 oz) cooked corned beef, cubed	2 poached or fried eggs (optional)

1 Melt butter in a heavy-based pan. Add potatoes, corned beef, onion, salt and pepper. Cook, stirring, for 1 minute.
2 Press mixture evenly over the pan, patting it down firmly with a spatula or egg slice. Cook over medium heat, uncovered, for about 15 minutes, or until the hash mixture forms a brown crust on its underside.
3 Serve hash hot, accompanied by ketchup or chilli sauce. It can be topped with poached or fried eggs, if desired.

Note: Use any variety of potatoes to make Corned Beef Hash. They can be prepared by whatever method you prefer: boiled, baked or cooked in a microwave oven.

ABOVE: CRUNCHY FRIED CHICKEN
OPPOSITE PAGE: CORNBREAD

BOSTON BAKED BEANS

Preparation time: 10 minutes
Total cooking time: 30 minutes
Serves 4

*30 g (1 oz) salt pork or
  bacon, chopped
880 g (28 oz) can baked
  beans in tomato sauce
1 large onion, chopped*

*3 tablespoons molasses
2 teaspoons dry mustard
1 tablespoon chilli or
  worcestershire sauce*

1 Preheat oven to 180°C (350°F/Gas 4). Grease an 8-cup heatproof dish.
2 Cut salt pork or bacon into 2 cm (¾ inch) pieces and cook in a dry pan until crisp. Drain.
3 Combine undrained beans with salt pork or bacon and add remaining ingredients. Spoon mixture into prepared dish; bake for 30 minutes or until bubbly. Serve hot.

CORNBREAD

Preparation time: 10 minutes
Total cooking time: 45 minutes
Makes 1 loaf

*1½ cups plain (all-
  purpose) flour
3 teaspoons baking powder
1 teaspoon salt
1 cup yellow cornmeal
  (maize flour)
2 tablespoons caster
  (superfine) sugar*

*2 eggs, beaten
1½ cups (12 fl oz)
  buttermilk
¼ cup (2 fl oz) vegetable
  oil
50 g (1¾ oz) butter,
  melted*

1 Preheat oven to 180°C (350°F/Gas 4). Heat a 30 x 20 cm (12 x 8 inch) shallow oblong baking tin in preheated oven for about 5 minutes.
2 Sift flour, baking powder and salt into a large bowl; stir in cornmeal and sugar. Make a well in the centre. Combine eggs, buttermilk and oil in a small bowl and mix thoroughly. Stir mixture into dry ingredients and mix well.
3 Brush heated baking tin with butter and pour in the batter. Smooth top. Bake for 25 minutes. Brush extra melted butter evenly over top and bake for another 15 minutes or until firm.
4 Cut cornbread into squares and serve hot.

PECAN PIE

Preparation time: 40 minutes
Total cooking time: 1 hour 15 minutes
Serves 6-8

*1¼ cups plain (all-purpose)
  flour
¼ teaspoon baking powder
90 g (3 oz) butter, cut
  into pieces
3–4 tablespoons water*

Filling
¼ cup soft brown sugar

*¼ cup plain (all-purpose)
  flour
375 ml (11½ fl oz)
  dark corn syrup
4 eggs, lightly beaten
30 g (1 oz) butter, melted
1½ teaspoons vanilla
  essence
1 cup pecan halves*

1 Sift flour and baking powder into a bowl. Rub in butter with fingertips until mixture resembles fine breadcrumbs. Add 3 tablespoons water to make a firm dough, adding remaining water if necessary. Turn dough onto a lightly floured surface, knead for 1 minute or until smooth. Store, covered in plastic wrap, in the refrigerator for 15 minutes.
2 Preheat oven to moderately hot 210°C (415°F/Gas 6–7). Roll out pastry between 2 pieces of plastic wrap until large enough to fit a deep, 23 cm (9 inch) quiche dish. Trim edges. Prick pastry evenly all over with a fork.
3 Bake for 15 minutes or until pastry is lightly golden; remove pie from oven. Reduce oven temperature to moderately slow 160°C (325°F/Gas 3).
4 To make Filling: Stir sugar and sifted flour together in a bowl. Using electric beaters, gradually beat in syrup, eggs, butter and vanilla essence. Stir in pecans, mix well. Pour mixture into prepared pastry case. Bake for 1 hour or until filling is evenly risen. Do not over-bake—filling should be firm but still custardy. Cool on wire rack (filling will sink slightly as it cools). Serve pie with cream or ice-cream.

and onions and as a whitening agent in flour.

Amaretti A crisp almond macaroon from Italy, where it was originally made with bitter almonds. The name

comes from the Italian word *amaro*, meaning bitter.

Ambrosia A semi-soft, cow's milk cheese, originally from Sweden, with a slightly tart taste and a number of small, irregular holes in the interior.

  Ambrosia is also the name of a chilled dessert made with layers of fruit, usually sliced orange, banana and fresh pineapple, and a mixture of desiccated (shredded) coconut and icing sugar.

Américaine, à l'
A French term for meat, seafood, eggs or vegetables served with a spicy, tomato-based sauce and often garnished with grilled bacon and tomatoes. The name was originally applied to a dish, created in the 1860s in Paris by a chef who had worked in North America, in which a cut lobster cooked in a tomato and wine mixture was served with a sauce made from the stock. Some say the term 'américaine' is a mistranslation of 'armoricaine', referring to Armorica, the ancient

name for Brittany, and that this style of cooking originated there.

American Food The cuisine of North America marries the diversity and abundance of the ingredients harvested from its vast lands (stretching from the tropics to the Arctic and along the coasts of two oceans) with the cooking styles and food habits of the many cultures from which its peoples are drawn. The style which has emerged was born in the basic kitchens of the early European settlers, where the frying pan and cooking pot ruled (today most dishes are still either stewed or fried). It is characterised by numerous variations on a simple theme—the apple pie, for example, has several distinct regional forms, each reflecting local ingredients as well as cultural backgrounds.

Americans like iced water on the table and a salad (often with a choice of several dressings) before the main course which, following the British tradition, usually consists of a relatively plain meat dish with two vegetables. Corn, native to the continent, features prominently in

DEEP DISH APPLE PIE

★ ★   *Preparation time:* 1 hour
Total cooking time: 50 minutes
Serves 6-8

1 cup self-raising flour
1 cup plain (all-purpose) flour
125 g (4 oz) chilled butter, chopped
2 tablespoons caster (superfine) sugar
1 egg
1–2 tablespoons milk
1 egg, extra, lightly beaten

Filling
8 large green apples, peeled, each cut into 12 wedges
2 thick strips lemon rind
6 whole cloves
1 cinnamon stick
2 cups (16 fl oz) water
½ cup sugar

1 Preheat oven to moderate 180°C (350°F/Gas 4). Brush a deep, 20 cm (8 inch) round springform tin with melted butter or oil. Line base with paper; grease paper. Dust tin lightly with flour, shake off excess.

2 To make Filling: Combine apples, lemon rind, cloves, cinnamon stick, water and sugar in large pan. Cover and simmer for 10 minutes or until apples are only just tender. Remove from heat, drain well. Discard rind, cloves and cinnamon stick. Set aside.

3 Place flours and butter in a food processor bowl; add sugar. Using pulse action, process for 15 seconds or until mixture has a fine, crumbly

texture. Add egg and almost all the milk; process for another 15 seconds until mixture comes together, adding more liquid if necessary. Turn dough onto a lightly floured surface; knead for 2 minutes or until smooth. Store, covered in plastic wrap, in the refrigerator for 15 minutes.

4 Roll two-thirds of the pastry between 2 sheets of plastic wrap until large enough to cover base and side of tin. Carefully spoon apple into pie shell. Roll remaining pastry into a circle large enough to cover top of pie. Brush pastry edge with a little of the extra beaten egg to seal. Trim excess pastry with a sharp knife and press around edge with a fork; brush top of pie with beaten egg. Bake for 50 minutes or until pastry is golden and cooked through. Leave pie in tin for 10 minutes before removing to a serving plate. Serve hot or cold with cream, ice-cream or custard.

Note: Apple pie is traditionally served, warm or cold, with a wedge of aged cheddar cheese.

VARIATIONS

■ Add ¾ cup cooked rhubarb or fruit mince to apple pie filling.
■ Use any combination of ground cinnamon, nutmeg, cloves mace or allspice to flavour.
■ If apples are very sweet, sprinkle with a little lemon juice for extra tartness.

ANCHOVIES

PAN-ROASTED POTATOES WITH ANCHOVIES

 Preparation time: 10 minutes
Total cooking time: 30 minutes
Serves 4–6

750 g (1½ lb) old potatoes	salt and freshly ground black pepper to taste
⅓ cup olive oil	2 cloves garlic, peeled and finely chopped
2 tablespoons butter	
4 flat anchovy fillets	2 tablespoons chopped fresh rosemary

1 Peel poatoes and cut into 1 cm (½ inch) thick slices; soak potatoes in cold water for at least 5 minutes. Drain; pat dry thoroughly with paper towels. Heat oil and melt butter in a large frying pan. Add chopped anchovies and cook for 1 minute, mashing slightly with a wooden spoon.
2 Add potatoes to frying pan and cook over high heat for 2–3 minutes until potatoes are crisp on the outside and well coated with butter-oil mixture. Reduce heat; cover pan with lid and cook a further 7 minutes, turning occasionally. Remove lid from pan and cook another 15 minutes or until potatoes are tender. Season with salt and pepper. Add garlic and rosemary. Cook 1 minute and combine well. Serve immediately as an accompaniment to roast meat, or serve as a light meal with bread and salad.

OPPOSITE PAGE: DEEP DISH APPLE PIE
ABOVE: PISSALADIÈRE

PISSALADIERE

 Preparation time: 15 minutes
Total cooking time: 35 minutes
Serves 6–8

1 sheet ready-rolled puff pastry	2 medium tomatoes, sliced
2 teaspoons olive oil	¼ cup grated cheddar cheese
2 medium onions, thinly sliced	45 g (1½ oz) can anchovy fillets
¼ teaspoon dried thyme	¼ cup black pitted olives, halved
½ teaspoon dried oregano	1 egg, lightly beaten

1 Preheat oven to moderate 180°C (350°F/Gas 4). Brush baking tray with oil or melted butter. Place pastry on prepared tray.
2 Heat oil in a frying pan and cook onions and herbs over medium heat for 10 minutes or until soft. Spread on top of pastry, leaving a 2 cm (¾ inch) border. Arrange tomato slices over onion mixture; sprinkle with cheese.
3 Drain anchovies and cut each fillet in half lengthways. Arrange in a lattice pattern over filling. Place an olive half in the centre of each diamond. Brush edges of pastry with beaten egg. Bake for 25 minutes or until pastry is golden brown. Serve warm.

ABOUT ANCHOVIES

■ To de-salt anchovies soak them in cold milk for 5 minutes. Use fingers to prise the soft backbone from each fillet.
■ Store canned anchovies, once opened, in their oil in an airtight glass container for up to 5 days in the refrigerator.

its cuisine, as does squash and rice. America gave the world the cocktail and is also the home of convenience foods and fast foods such as popcorn, the hot dog and fried chicken. It has the highest per capita consumption of hamburgers in the world.

Anchovy A small, slender, herring-like saltwater fish with a slightly oily flesh and a strong, sardine-like taste. Although anchovies are eaten fresh in the regions in which they occur, they are probably known to most in their preserved form. Traditionally the whole fish, packed in brine in kegs, was used for flavouring and

salting meat dishes. In Renaissance Italy a dish of anchovy fillets marinated in olive oil and vinegar was a popular first course, and for centuries salted anchovy fillets have been an important ingredient in the cooking of Provence. Today it is widely available as salted fillets marinated in oil and sold in jars or cans.

Sadly, pollution has largely banished the anchovy from its home in Mediterranean waters, although it is still netted off the coasts of France and Spain in May. In the English Channel on

ANTIPASTO

Shopping at a good deli is often the only thing you need to do to put together an impressive antipasto platter. It makes a lively and appetising start to an Italian meal, or add a bottle of wine and some crusty bread for an ideal summer lunch.

MARINATED OLIVES

Use cracked green or uncracked black olives. (To crack olives, tap lightly with a meat mallet. Alternatively you can make small slits in the olive with a sharp knife.) Place 250 g (8 oz) olives into a bowl. Pour over 3 tablespoons olive oil, add 1 tablespoon each of finely chopped fresh oregano and chives, 1/2–1 teaspoon chilli flakes, 1 clove crushed garlic, 1 teaspoon grated lemon rind and 1 teaspoon cracked black pepper. Mix together, making sure the olives are well coated. Heat 1 extra tablespoon olive oil in a small pan. Add 1 finely sliced onion and cook over medium heat until soft; cool. Stir into olive mixture.

Marinated olives will keep for a month in an airtight jar. If storing in the refrigerator, remove about 10 minutes before serving to soften the olive oil. Serve marinated olives on pizzas and in salads. They are also delicious sliced and served with cheese on herb bread.

FRESH PEARS AND PARMESAN

Prepare the pears just before serving, otherwise they will turn brown. Choose ripe pears with unblemished skin. Wash and dry them, cut in half, remove cores and slice pears thinly. Using a vegetable peeler make fine shavings of parmesan cheese and scatter over the pears.

MELON WITH PROSCIUTTO

Use cantaloupe or honeydew melon for this dish. Peel it, remove seeds and slice into long, thin wedges. Wrap paper-thin slices of prosciutto around the wedges.

FROM LEFT: MARINATED OLIVES, FRESH PEARS AND PARMESAN, MELON WITH PROSCIUTTO, TOMATO SALAD, COPPA AND SALAMI, MARINATED ARTICHOKES, CHAR-GRILLED RED PEPPER (CAPSICUM), CHILLI GARLIC OCTOPUS.

TOMATO SALAD

Cut 1–2 bocconcini (fresh baby mozarella) into thin slices. Choose tomatoes of about the same diameter as cheese and thinly slice. Arrange bocconcini and tomato in alternate slices on serving platter. Drizzle with olive oil, sprinkle with balsamic vinegar and scatter with shredded basil leaves.

COPPA AND SALAMI

An antipasto selection should always include a variety of sausage-type meats. Paper-thin slices of salami or coppa (cured pork, served raw) are ideal. There are many types of salami—some spicy, some with crusted coatings. Arrange in cornets, fans, folds or simply in overlapping slices.

MARINATED ARTICHOKES

Fresh artichokes may be used but canned artichoke hearts are simpler to prepare. Drain and rinse well to remove brine. Cut into quarters. Place in a bowl and, for 400 g (14 oz) artichokes, pour over 6 tablespoons olive oil, add 1 clove crushed garlic, 1 teaspoon grated lemon rind, 2-3 tablespoons finely chopped fresh herbs, and, if desired, a finely chopped fresh chilli. Toss gently but well, cover and set aside. Artichokes will keep in an airtight container for a week, if covered in oil.

CHAR-GRILLED RED PEPPER (CAPSICUM)

Cut red peppers in half, remove seeds and membranes. Place peppers, skin-side up, under a hot grill, or rotate over a gas flame, until skin blisters and blackens. Wrap in damp tea-towel for a few minutes, then peel off blackened skin. Cut peppers into wide strips and drizzle with olive oil and a few drops of balsamic vinegar.

CHILLI-GARLIC OCTOPUS

Mix together, in a large bowl, 3 tablespoons olive oil, 1 tablespoon soy sauce, 2 tablespoons each chopped fresh oregano and parsley, and 1 finely chopped fresh red chilli. Wash 500 g (1 lb) baby octopus, dry well. Slit open the head and remove the gut. Grasp body firmly and push the beak out with your index finger. Place octopus in the bowl with the marinade and toss well to coat. Drain octopus and reserve marinade. Cook on a hot barbecue flatplate 3–5 minutes until flesh turns white. Turn octopus frequently, brush with reserved marinade during cooking.

A

moonless nights large numbers are lured by artificial lights. The anchovy is caught in the Atlantic, and off the Pacific coasts of the Americas, and a similar species occurs in the coastal waters of Australia.

Preserved anchovy fillets are used in hors d'oeuvre, pizza toppings, in salads and as a garnish; boned anchovies are pounded into a paste which is the basis for many sauces.

Angel Cake A white-coloured cake with an airy texture resulting from the high proportion of beaten egg white in the mixture. The angel cake originated in North America, where it has been known since the late nineteenth century.

Angelica A herb best known for its candied stalks, used to flavour and decorate cakes and desserts. It was once eaten raw, like celery, and its fresh leaves can

be used in salads. In parts of Iceland and Norway the dried root is ground into flour and made into a form of bread. Angelica seeds are used in the preparation of vermouth and chartreuse.

Originally from

APPLES

BAKED APPLES

 Preparation time: 20 minutes
Total cooking time: 1 hour 15 minutes
Serves 4

4 green apples	1/2 cup brown sugar
1/2 cup finely chopped dates	30 g (1 oz) butter
1 tablespoon chopped walnuts	1/4 teaspoon ground cinnamon
1 tablespoon grated lemon rind	1/4 teaspoon ground nutmeg
1/2 cup (4 fl oz) water	ice-cream or whipped cream, to serve

1 Preheat oven to 180°C (350°F/Gas 4). Cut core neatly out of apples; peel skin from top quarter only of each apple.
2 Combine dates, walnuts and rind, mix well. Press mixture into centres of apples.
3 Place apples into baking pan or loaf tin. Put water, brown sugar, butter, cinnamon and nutmeg in small pan. Bring to boil; pour mixture over the apples. Bake for about 1¼ hours, basting apples occasionally with the liquid. Serve hot with vanilla ice-cream or whipped cream.

APPLE CHUTNEY

 Preparation time: 30 minutes
Total cooking time: 2 hours
Makes about 1.75 litres (7 cups)

10 small green apples	1 cup raisins
5 large ripe tomatoes, chopped	1/2 cup (4 fl oz) orange juice
3 large onions, chopped	1/3 cup (2 1/2 fl oz) lemon juice
1 tablespoon grated green ginger	3 cups soft brown sugar
4 cloves garlic, crushed	2 cups (16 fl oz) cider vinegar
2 small chillies, chopped	

1 Peel, core and chop apples. Combine with tomatoes, onions, ginger, garlic, chilli, raisins, juices, brown sugar and vinegar in large, deep heavy-based pan. Stir over low heat until sugar is completely dissolved.
2 Increase heat, stirring occasionally until mixture boils. Simmer, uncovered, 2 hours or until fruit and vegetables are tender and chutney is thick. Stir mixture occasionally.
3 Allow to stand 5 minutes. Using a jug, pour into warm, sterilised jars and seal immediately. Label and date jars when cool. Store in a cool, dark place for up to 12 months.

APPLE SAUCE

 Preparation time: 20 minutes
Total cooking time: 30 minutes
Makes 2 cups

4 large green apples, peeled and cored	2 teaspoons grated lemon rind
30 g (1 oz) butter	1/4 cup (2 fl oz) water
1/4 cup white sugar	

Place apples, butter, sugar, lemon rind and water in a heavy-based pan. Cook over low heat, stirring frequently, until apples become soft and pulpy. Serve sauce warm with roast pork, roast duck or goose.

Note: Apple Sauce may be made up to 3 days in advance and stored, covered, in the refrigerator.

ABOUT APPLES

■ Buy apples with blemish-free skin and no bruises. As a guide, the lighter the ground colouring, the crisper the apple is.
■ To avoid discolouration after cutting apples, brush with lemon juice diluted with a little water, or place cut or peeled apples in a bowl of water containing 2 tablespoons lemon juice.
■ To stew apples peel, core and thickly slice green cooking apples, place in a pan with a little water or apple juice and a few whole cloves. Bring to boil, reduce heat and simmer covered for 15 minutes, stirring occasionally.
■ To prevent apples bursting during baking score skin around centre with tip of a sharp knife.

ABOVE: BAKED APPLE. OPPOSITE PAGE, ABOVE: APPLE CRUMBLE; BELOW: APPLE CHARLOTTE

APPLE CHARLOTTES

⭐⭐ **Preparation time:** 30 minutes
Total cooking time: 25 minutes
Serves 6

5 cooking apples, peeled, cored and sliced
2 tablespoons soft brown sugar
1/4 teaspoon ground cinnamon
1 loaf day-old white bread, crusts removed
100 g (3 1/2 oz) butter, melted

Jam Sauce
1 cup strawberry jam
1 cup (8 fl oz) water
1 teaspoon grated lemon rind
1/2 cup caster (superfine) sugar

1 Preheat oven to 180°C (350°F/Gas 4). Brush six 1-cup capacity ovenproof dishes with oil or melted butter. Place apple in pan with sugar, cinnamon and enough water to cover. Cook until tender; drain and cool.
2 Using a biscuit cutter, cut 12 rounds from bread slices to fit top and base of each dish. Cut remaining slices into fingers 2 cm (3/4 inch) wide; trim to fit height of dish. Dip 6 rounds into melted butter and place in base of dishes. Dip each finger of bread into melted butter and press around sides of dish vertically, overlapping a little.
3 Fill each bread-lined dish with cooked apple; top with last rounds of butter-dipped bread, . Place on baking tray; bake 20 minutes. Turn onto plates. Serve warm with Jam Sauce and cream.
4 To make Jam Sauce: Place sauce ingredients in small pan; bring to boil and simmer for 15 minutes. Strain and serve hot.

APPLE CRUMBLE

⭐ **Preparation time**: 30 minutes
Total cooking time: 25–30 minutes
Serves 4–6

4 large green cooking apples, peeled and sliced
1 tablespoon soft brown sugar
2 tablespoons golden syrup (light corn syrup)
2 tablespoons lemon juice

Topping
3/4 cup self-raising flour
1/2 cup desiccated coconut
1/2 cup rolled oats
1/2 cup soft brown sugar
100 g (3 1/2 oz) butter

1 Brush a shallow 6-cup capacity casserole dish with melted butter or oil. Place apples, sugar, golden syrup and lemon juice in a large pan; cover with tight-fitting lid and cook over low heat for 10 minutes or until apples soften. Spoon apple mixture into dish. Preheat oven to moderate 180°C (350°F/Gas 4).
2 To make Topping: In a bowl combine flour, coconut, rolled oats and sugar; mix well. Make a well in the centre. Melt butter and pour into bowl with dry ingredients. Mix to form a crumble. Scatter crumble mixture over apples.
3 Bake for 25–30 minutes or until top is crisp and golden. Serve with whipped cream or ice-cream.

Note: Apple Crumble can be eaten hot or cold. Other fruits such as peaches, apricots, cherries or nectarines can be stewed and substituted for apples. Canned peaches or apricots, well drained, can also be used.

Anise The European anise (from which aniseed is derived) is a member of the parsley family and has a distinctive licorice-like flavour and fragrance. The plant is native to Egypt, where it still grows wild, and to Greece and parts of south-west Asia. The aromatic seeds are sprinkled on some types of bread, and are used to flavour coffee cakes, fruit salads, cooked cabbage, and chicken and veal dishes; oil extracted from them is used as a flavouring in confectionery and some alcoholic drinks, such as pernod and anisette.

The Romans ate anise cakes at the end of a meal as an aid to digestion. They also hung the plant near their beds in the belief that it would prevent bad dreams.

Antipasto The Italian term for appetisers, literally 'before the meal'. The antipasto course was probably created during the Renaissance when it was customary to begin and end a meal with a series of cold dishes served from the sideboard. There are three main categories of traditional antipasto:

A P R I C O T S

APRICOT VEAL BIRDS

★ ★ **Preparation time:** 30 minutes
Total cooking time: 30 minutes
Serves 4–6

8 thin veal steaks, about 105 g (3½ oz) each
1 cup cooked rice
125 g (4 oz) finely chopped dried apricots
1 tablespoon finely chopped glacé ginger
¼ cup chopped fresh coriander
2 tablespoons oil

30 g (1 oz) butter

Sauce
1 onion, sliced in rings
1 cup (8 fl oz) apricot nectar (juice)
½ cup (4 fl oz) good quality white wine
¼ cup French onion soup mix

1 Preheat oven to a moderately slow 160°C (325°F/Gas 3). Trim meat of any excess fat or sinew. Using a meat mallet or rolling pin, flatten steaks, between plastic wrap, to an even thickness.
2 Combine rice, apricots, ginger and coriander in a small mixing bowl; mix well. Place steaks on a flat surface. Place spoonful of filling along one end of each steak; roll and tie up securely with string at regular intervals.
3 Heat oil and butter in a heavy-based frying pan. Cook meat rolls quickly in a single layer over medium-high heat until well browned; drain on paper towels. Arrange rolls in casserole dish.
4 To make Sauce: Remove excess oil and butter from pan, leaving about 1 teaspoonful. Add onion and cook for 2–3 minutes over medium heat until well browned. Add combined apricot nectar, wine and soup mix. Stir over low heat until the mixture boils and thickens. Remove from heat and pour over meat rolls in casserole dish. Cover and bake for 25 minutes or until the meat is cooked through and tender. Remove string from rolls before serving. Apricot Veal Birds may be served with salad greens or steamed vegetables.

APRICOT AND LEMON JAM

★ ★ **Preparation time:** 15 minutes + overnight soaking
Total cooking time: 1 hour
Makes 2.5 litres (10 cups)

500 g (1 lb) dried apricots
1.25 litres (5 cups) water
5 lemons
1 kg (2 lb) sugar, warmed

1 Soak apricots in half the water for 24 hours. Boil lemons in remaining water until soft.
2 When lemons are cold, slice thinly, removing but not discarding the pips.
3 Boil apricots in soaking water until tender. Add the sugar and sliced lemons, together with the water in which they were boiled and the pips, tied in a small muslin (cheesecloth) bag. Boil jam mixture until it gels (see JAMS). Discard the muslin bag.
4 Ladle jam into warm, sterilised jars and seal. When cool, label and date.

ABOUT APRICOTS

■ Buy apricots that are heavy for their size, firm and plump with a bright colour. Store in a cool place. To ripen immature fruit, store in a brown paper bag in a dark place. Fully ripe fruit will deteriorate quickly at room temperature.
■ To cook fresh apricots halve fruit and remove stones, if desired. Place in a pan, cover with water, add 2 tablespoons sugar. Bring to the boil, reduce heat and simmer until tender.
■ To quickly process dried apricots place in pan, cover with cold water, bring to boil. Reduce heat and simmer, covered, until tender.
■ Apricot jam can be heated, sieved and used as a glaze for fruit tarts and cakes. To make it into a sauce for baked fruits and ice-cream, heat ¾ cup apricot jam with 4 tablespoons water. Sieve into a sauce boat and stir in 1 tablespoon apricot brandy. Serve warm.

ABOVE: APRICOT VEAL BIRDS. OPPOSITE PAGE, ABOVE: APRICOT PIE; BELOW: CHOCOLATE GLACE APRICOTS

APRICOT PIE

★★ **Preparation time:** 40 minutes
Total cooking time: 35 minutes
Makes one 23 cm (9 inch) round pie

2½ cups plain (all-
purpose) flour
¼ cup self-raising flour
⅔ cup cornflakes
250 g (8 oz) unsalted
(sweet) butter, chopped
2 tablespoons caster
(superfine) sugar

½ cup (4 fl oz) milk
1 egg, lightly beaten
2 x 425 g (13½ oz)
cans apricot pie filling
¼ cup brown sugar
1 egg yolk
1 tablespoon water
1–2 tablespoons sugar

1 Brush 23 cm (9 inch) round pie plate with melted butter or oil. Place flours, cornflakes and butter in food processor bowl; add sugar. Using pulse action, process for 15 seconds or until mixture is fine and crumbly. Add combined milk and egg, process 15–20 seconds or until mixture comes together. Leave, covered with plastic wrap, in refrigerator for 10 minutes. Roll ⅔ of pastry between 2 sheets of plastic wrap or baking paper, to cover the base and sides of prepared plate.
2 Preheat oven to moderate 180°C (350°F/Gas 4). Sprinkle brown sugar over pastry base, top with apricot; smooth surface. Roll remaining pastry to fit over top of pie. Brush pastry edges with combined yolk and water, press to seal. Trim edges. Brush top of pie with yolk mixture.
3 Roll leftover pastry out evenly. Using a 2 cm (¾ inch) fluted cutter, cut enough rounds to cover the entire rim of pie.
4 Place overlapping rounds around pie edge. Sprinkle with sugar, make 3 steam holes in top.

Bake 35 minutes or until pastry is golden. Stand 5 minutes before cutting. Serve with vanilla-flavoured whipped cream or vanilla ice-cream.

CHOCOLATE GLACE APRICOTS

★ **Preparation time:** 45 minutes
Total cooking time: 5–10 minutes
Makes about 24

250 g (8 oz) glacé
apricots
100 g (3¼ oz) dark
(semi-sweet) or milk
chocolate melts

50 g (1¾ oz) white
chocolate melts

1 Line a tray with greaseproof paper or foil. Cut each apricot into three pieces.
2 Place dark chocolate melts in a small heatproof bowl. Stand bowl over a pan of simmering water and stir until chocolate has melted and is smooth. Cool slightly. Dip apricot pieces one at a time into chocolate, coating half of each. Drain excess chocolate. Place on prepared tray. Set aside.
3 Place white chocolate melts in a small heatproof bowl. Stand over pan of simmering water, stir until chocolate has melted and is smooth. Cool slightly. Spoon chocolate into small paper icing bag, seal open end. Snip off piping bag tip. Pipe chocolate in squiggles, lines, initials or other design onto dark chocolate. Allow to set.

Note: Chocolate Glacé Apricots can be made up to 3 weeks ahead. Store in an airtight container.

BC, had planted orchards in the Nile delta. The Api variety (still available today, and known in the United States as the Lady Apple), was developed by Etruscans more than 2000 years ago.

The apple was the first introduced crop to flourish in North America, and during the eighteenth and nineteenth centuries was an important staple for European settlers in the northwest. Nineteenth century folk hero Johnny Appleseed, credited with spreading the fruit across North America, did so by establishing a chain of apple orchards from Pennsylvania west to Indiana, and not, as popularly depicted, by randomly scattering seed.

In Australia, Tasmania has long held the title 'Apple Isle'. Orchards planted in the south-east in the early 1840s supplied markets in India and New Zealand. The 1850s population boom caused by the gold rushes on the Australian mainland meant an increased demand for the fruit, and at one time some 500 varieties of apple were grown. Today this has diminished to fewer than ten varieties.

There are both eating and cooking varieties of apple. They are cooked in a range of sweet and savoury dishes, can be

ARTICHOKES

ARTICHOKE AND ASPARAGUS SALAD

Preparation time: 20 minutes
Total cooking time: 10 minutes
Serves 4

1 bunch fresh asparagus
130 g (4½ oz) green beans
155 g (5 oz) button mushrooms
5 canned or marinated artichoke hearts
30 g (1 oz) butter
½ teaspoon ground sweet paprika
2 cloves garlic, sliced thinly
2 tablespoons olive oil
2 tablespoons lemon juice
¼ teaspoon black pepper
2 tablespoons finely chopped mint

1 Cut the asparagus spears into 5 cm (2 inch) lengths. Trim the tops off the beans, leaving the tails on. Cut the mushrooms and artichoke hearts into quarters.
2 Half fill a medium saucepan with water; bring to boil. Place asparagus and beans into boiling water for 1–2 minutes or until they turn bright green. Remove from heat. Plunge into a bowl of iced water and leave until chilled; drain.
3 Heat butter in a small pan. Add paprika and garlic, cook for 1 minute. Add mushrooms, cook 2–3 minutes; remove from heat.
4 Combine oil, lemon juice, pepper and mint in a small bowl. Mix well. Place asparagus, beans, mushrooms and artichokes in a medium bowl. Pour over oil mixture and toss well. Transfer salad to serving bowl.

PENNE WITH ARTICHOKE HEARTS

Preparation time: 10 minutes
Total cooking time: 15 minutes
Serves 8

500 g (1 lb) penne
1 tablespoon olive oil
2 leeks, thinly sliced
2 medium red peppers (capsicum), cut into 1 cm (½ inch) strips
2 garlic cloves, crushed
410 g (13 oz) can artichoke hearts, drained and quartered
1 tablespoon lemon juice
30 g (1 oz) butter
½ cup fresh parmesan cheese

1 Cook pasta in a large pan of boiling water until just tender. Meanwhile, heat oil in a medium heavy-based pan, add leeks and cook, stirring, on medium heat for 3 minutes.
2 Add pepper and garlic and cook, stirring, for 3 minutes. Stir in artichoke hearts and lemon juice.
3 Drain pasta and return to large pan. Add butter and stir through to coat pasta, then add artichoke mixture and combine well. Serve immediately, with shavings of fresh parmesan.

ABOUT ARTICHOKES

■ To prepare artichokes, trim stalks, remove hard outer leaves and wash well under cold water. Artichokes may be steamed or baked (see specific recipes); cook only until centre leaves can be easily pulled out.

LEFT: ARTICHOKE AND ASPARAGUS SALAD; ABOVE: PENNE WITH ARTICHOKE HEARTS. OPPOSITE PAGE: ARTICHOKES WITH TARRAGON MAYONNAISE

ARTICHOKES WITH TARRAGON MAYONNAISE

★ ★ ***Preparation time:*** 30 minutes
Total cooking time: 30 minutes
Serves 4

4 medium globe artichokes	*1 egg yolk*
¼ cup (2 fl oz) lemon juice	*½ teaspoon French mustard*
	⅔ cup (5 fl oz) olive oil
Tarragon Mayonnaise	*salt and white pepper to taste*
1 tablespoon tarragon vinegar	

1 Trim stalks from base of artichokes. Using scissors, trim points from outer leaves. With a sharp knife, cut top from artichoke. Brush all cut areas with lemon juice to prevent discoloration.
2 Steam artichokes for 30 minutes, until tender. Top up pan with boiling water if necessary. Remove from heat and set aside to cool.

3 To make Tarragon Mayonnaise: Place vinegar, egg yolk and mustard in a medium mixing bowl. Using a wire whisk, beat for one minute. Begin to add the oil a teaspoon at a time, whisking constantly until the mixture is thick and creamy. As mayonnaise thickens, continue to add oil by pouring in a thin, steady stream. Keep whisking until all the oil has been added; season to taste. Place a cooled artichoke on each plate and top with a little Tarragon Mayonnaise.

Note: Cooked artichokes can be eaten with the fingers; pull leaves off one at a time, dip the base of the leaf into sauce or melted butter and scrape the fleshy part off with the teeth (the leaves at the centre of the artichoke are more tender, and more of each is edible). When the furry centre or 'choke' is reached, it should be removed and discarded. Use a fork to eat the tender base of the artichoke. Finger bowls should be provided, as well as a bowl for the discarded leaves.

1

2

3

dried, and are made into apple juice and cider.

Apricot The apricot was first cultivated in China more than 4000 years ago. It grew in Nebuchadnezzar's hanging gardens of Babylon and was an expensive delicacy in ancient Rome. The Persians called the soft golden fruit 'eggs of the sun'. The apricot was taken to Britain from Italy in the mid-1500s by the gardener of Henry VIII.

Fresh ripe apricots are eaten raw or cooked as a dessert, made into jams, and in savoury dishes are teamed with lamb and with chicken. Dried, canned and glacé apricots are available year-round.

Arborio Rice A variety of rice, originally grown in the Po Valley in Italy. It has a short, plump, oval shape and is used in both sweet and savoury dishes, notably in risotto.

Arrowroot A fine white powder obtained from the root of the maranta, a white-flowered plant of the Caribbean. An easily digestible starch, it is used as a thickener in sweet and savoury sauces. Because it

thickens at a lower temperature than either flour or cornflour, arrowroot is often used in delicate sauces that should not be boiled.

Arroz con Pollo
A Spanish or Mexican dish consisting of rice, chicken, garlic, olive oil, and herbs and spices. Saffron gives it its characteristic yellow colour.

Artichoke Two vegetables carry the name artichoke: the globe artichoke, which is the silvery-grey leafy bud of a large thistle-like plant; and the Jerusalem artichoke, the white-fleshed root of a relative of the sunflower.

The globe artichoke probably originated on the coasts of the western Mediterranean. It was not widely eaten until the fifteenth century, when, under the

patronage of the Medicis of Florence, it emerged as a culinary aristocrat with a reputation as an aphrodisiac. By the sixteenth century the globe artichoke was well established in Italy and France, where it remains popular today. In North America it is not mentioned until the late 1800s when, introduced by Italian settlers in California, it was called

A S P A R A G U S

A S P A R A G U S
H O L L A N D A I S E   R O L L S

 Preparation time: 30 minutes
Total cooking time: 15 minutes
Makes about 30

1 bunch fresh asparagus
30 slices fresh white bread

Hollandaise Sauce
1 tablespoon white vinegar
5 peppercorns

½ teaspoon dried
  tarragon
2 egg yolks
125 g (4 oz) unsalted
  (sweet) butter, melted
2 teaspoons lemon juice

1 Cut asparagus spears in half. Place in medium pan with a small amount of water. Cook over low heat until just tender. Plunge into cold water, drain. Pat dry with absorbent paper.
2 Cut a round from each bread slice with an 8 cm (3 inch) cutter.
3 Place a piece of asparagus across each bread round. Spoon a teaspoonful of Hollandaise Sauce on top. Fold in half, secure edges with toothpick.
4 To make Hollandaise Sauce: Combine vinegar, peppercorns and tarragon in small pan. Bring to boil and simmer until liquid has reduced to one teaspoonful. Place egg yolks in a food processor. Add strained vinegar liquid, process. Add melted butter in a thin, steady stream through chute in the food processor lid, with machine running. Process until mixture is thick; stir in lemon juice.

B E E F   A N D   A S P A R A G U S

✦ **Preparation time:** 15 minutes +
30 minutes marinating
Total cooking time: 10 minutes
Serves 4

500 g (1 lb) rump steak
2 tablespoons soy sauce
1 tablespoon dry sherry
2 teaspoons finely grated
  ginger
1 teaspoon sesame oil
1 clove garlic, crushed

1 medium red chilli, cut
  into fine strips
12 spears fresh asparagus
2 tablespoons peanut oil
1 teaspoon cornflour
  (cornstarch)

1 Trim meat of any fat and sinew. Slice across the grain evenly into long, thin strips. Combine soy sauce, sherry, ginger, sesame oil, garlic and chilli; add meat, stirring to coat. Leave for 30 minutes. Drain the meat, reserving marinade.
2 Cut woody ends off asparagus; cut spears into 5 cm (2 inch) pieces. Heat 1 tablespoon oil in wok or heavy-based frying pan, swirling gently to coat base and side. Add asparagus; stir-fry over medium heat for 2 minutes. Remove from wok; keep warm. Heat remaining oil in wok, cook meat quickly in small batches over high heat until browned but not cooked through. Remove and drain on absorbent paper.
3 Blend cornflour with the reserved marinade until smooth. Return asparagus and meat to wok with marinade mixture. Stir-fry over high heat until meat is cooked through and sauce has thickened. Serve at once.

ASPARAGUS IN LEMON SAUCE

Preparation time: 20 minutes
Total cooking time: 10 minutes
Serves 6

3 bunches fresh
  asparagus, trimmed
30 g (1 oz) butter
1 tablespoon plain (all-
  purpose) flour
3/4 cup (6 fl oz) water
1 egg yolk

1/3 cup (2 1/2 fl oz) lemon
  juice
2 teaspoons finely grated
  lemon rind
1/3 cup whole blanched
  almonds, toasted

1 Place prepared asparagus in a large shallow pan of simmering water and cook uncovered until just tender, about 8–10 minutes. Drain on absorbent paper.
2 Melt butter in small pan. Add flour; cook, stirring, for one minute. Remove from heat and gradually add water. Return to heat and stir constantly until mixture boils and thickens. Remove from heat and whisk in combined egg yolk, lemon juice and rind. Return to heat and stir over gentle heat for 3–4 minutes.
3 Arrange asparagus on one large platter or individual serving plates; pour over lemon sauce. Garnish with toasted almonds and serve.

ASPARAGUS WITH THAI DRESSING

Preparation time: 8 minutes
Total cooking time: 6 minutes
Serves: 6–8

2 bunches fresh asparagus
1 small onion, sliced
1/2 cup chopped mint
1/2 cup chopped coriander
1/4 cup (2 fl oz) vegetable
  oil

1 tablespoon lime or
  lemon juice
1 tablespoon nuoc mam
pinch red chilli flakes
lettuce cups for garnish

1 Trim and diagonally slice asparagus into 8 cm (3 inch) lengths. Steam over simmering water in covered saucepan until just tender, about 4–6 minutes. Refresh under cold running water. Drain thoroughly on paper towels.
2 Toss asparagus with onion slices, mint and coriander. Cover; chill 2–3 hours before serving.
3 Blend together oil, citrus juice, nuoc mam and chilli flakes; pour over asparagus mixture and arrange on lettuce-lined plates.

OPPOSITE PAGE: BEEF AND ASPARAGUS
RIGHT: CREAMY ASPARAGUS SOUP

CREAMY ASPARAGUS SOUP

Preparation time: 5 minutes
Total cooking time: 5 minutes
Serves 4

2 x 345 g (11 oz) cans
  green asparagus spears
1 cup (8 fl oz) chicken
  stock
3/4 cup (6 fl oz) cream
2 egg yolks

freshly ground white
  pepper
1 tablespoon finely
  chopped chives

1 Place asparagus spears, liquid from cans and chicken stock in electric blender or food processor and blend until smooth. Pour mixture into a saucepan and bring to the boil. Remove from heat.
2 Beat cream lightly with egg yolks and stir slowly into soup, season with pepper. Reheat soup without boiling.
3 Serve soup sprinkled with chives.

ABOUT ASPARAGUS

■ Select crisp, straight stems of similar size for even cooking.
■ To store, keep refrigerated, wrapped in damp paper towels and a plastic bag. To prepare, scrape stalks to remove small nibs; remove hard sections from base of stalk.
■ To steam asparagus without a steamer, tie asparagus together and stand bundle in a large pan containing a small amount of simmering water. Cover and cook over low heat until just tender.

the French artichoke. Globe artichokes can be pickled whole when small; both heart and bases are sold canned or frozen.

Despite its name, the Jerusalem artichoke has nothing at all to do with the Middle Eastern city: 'Jerusalem' is a corruption of *girasole*, the Italian word for sunflower, to which this plant is closely related. It comes, in fact, from North America, where it was cultivated by Native Americans (in that part of the world it is also known as Canadian artichoke). In the early 1600s, Samuel de Champlain, the founder of Quebec, noted in his diary that the roots had a taste somewhat like the heart of the European globe artichoke, hence the name.

By 1620 the vegetable was available in the street markets of Paris. It was first grown and eaten in England at about the same time and not long afterwards appeared in Italy. Its reception was generally subdued, many regarding it as fit only for swine, its usual role in Europe today.

Arugula See Rocket.

Asafoetida A bitter, garlic-smelling condiment, prepared

since the time of ancient Rome, and now used mainly in Indian and Middle Eastern cooking. The dried and powdered resin of a plant native to Afghanistan and Iran, it has been used medicinally for many centuries to treat flatulence.

Asparagus The edible, delicately flavoured young shoots of a member of the lily family. There are two basic types: the slender-stalked green asparagus, harvested when the stems are about 20 centimetres (8 inches) above ground; and white asparagus, of the same variety as the green, but pale because it is harvested while the stalk is still below ground. Although asparagus has been known since ancient times—the Egyptians thought it a suitable offering for their gods and Julius Caesar liked his served with melted butter—it was not widely used until the seventeenth century, when it became popular in France. By the

eighteenth century it was well established in North America.

Aspic A clear, savoury jelly, prepared from clarified stock made from the gelatinous parts of meat, chicken or fish and

A V O C A D O S

HOT AVOCADO SALAD

 Preparation time: 20 minutes
Total cooking time: 15 minutes
Serves 6 as a side dish

3 medium avocados	*1 stick celery, finely chopped*
1 medium tomato	*2 teaspoons sugar*
4 rashers bacon, optional	*2 teaspoons sweet chilli*
1 medium red onion,	* sauce*
* finely chopped*	*2 tablespoons balsamic*
1 red pepper (capsicum),	* vinegar*
* finely chopped*	*1 cup grated cheddar cheese*

1 Preheat oven to moderate 180°C (350°F/Gas 4). Brush a 25 cm (10 inch) pie plate with oil or melted butter. Cut avocados in half lengthways and remove seeds. Scoop out two-thirds of flesh, roughly chop. Retain shells.

2 Peel, seed and finely chop tomato. Trim bacon and place on cold grill tray. Cook under medium-high heat until crisp; let cool slightly and chop finely. Combine avocado, tomato, bacon, onion, pepper and celery in medium bowl. Combine sugar, chilli sauce and vinegar in a small screw-top jar; shake well. Pour over ingredients in bowl and mix well.

3 Spoon filling into avocado halves; sprinkle with cheese. Place in prepared dish. Bake 7–10 minutes or until heated through. Serve immediately with corn chips, crackers or thin slices of white toast.

AVOCADO WITH LIME AND CHILLIES

 Preparation time: 20 minutes
Total cooking time: nil
Serves 6

1 teaspoon finely grated	*1 tablespoon olive oil*
* lime rind*	*2–3 jalapeno chillies,*
2 tablespoons lime juice	* seeded, sliced*
1 teaspoon brown sugar	*2 ripe avocados, peeled,*
1 tablespoon chopped	* sliced*
* fresh parsley*	

1 Thoroughly combine lime rind and juice, sugar, parsley, oil and chillies in a small bowl. Pour over sliced avocado.

2 Serve as a tangy side salad to fish, shellfish, chicken or meat dishes.

ABOUT AVOCADOS

■ Buy avocados 3 to 7 days before use. Choose even-coloured fruit that is slightly soft at the stem end. To hasten ripening, store at room temperature in a brown paper bag with a banana. Ripe avocado flesh will yield to gentle pressure. Freezing will cause the flesh to turn black and ruin its texture.

■ Cut avocado in half lengthways around stone; twist knife to separate halves; remove stone. Pull or cut skin off, beginning at narrow (stem) end. Brush surface of cut avocados with lemon juice to prevent discolouration.

usually flavoured with vegetables and herbs. It is used to glaze cold dishes, and to coat savoury moulds.

Avgolemono A soup made from chicken stock flavoured with lemon juice and thickened with egg yolk, popular in Greece and the Balkans. The name also refers to a sauce based on the same ingredients which is served with poached fish or steamed vegetables.

Avocado A leathery-skinned fruit with a large seed and pale, buttery flesh with a slightly nutty flavour. The avocado comes from a tree originating in Central America. Avocado was once called 'midshipman's butter' by the English, a name probably dating from its use as crew food on far-flung sailing ships. Avocado is the main ingredient of guacamole and is used in many other Mexican dishes. Usually served raw in salads, sandwiches and as a first course, it can be cooked—it is mashed onto a piece of toast with crumbled grilled bacon, sprinkled with grated cheddar and heated.

AVOCADO, TOMATO AND HAM FLAN

Preparation time 15 minutes
Total cooking time: 40 minutes
Serves 6

8 slices bread, crusts removed	4 large cherry tomatoes, sliced
40 g (1½ oz) butter, softened	½ large ripe avocado, sliced
	1 cup grated cheddar cheese
Filling	3 eggs
90 g (3 oz) leg ham, sliced	⅓ cup (2½ fl oz) sour cream
	⅓ cup (2½ fl oz) milk

1 Preheat oven to moderately hot 210°C (415° F/ Gas 6–7). Flatten bread with a rolling pin. Spread both sides of slices with butter, cut each in half diagonally. Press into a 23 cm (9 inch) round pie plate, evenly covering base and sides. Bake for 10 minutes or until lightly browned but crisp.
2 To make Filling: Reduce oven to moderate 180°C (350°F/Gas 4). Arrange ham, tomatoes, avocado and cheese in cooked base. Combine eggs, sour cream and milk in a bowl; mix well, pour over pie filling. Bake for 30 minutes, or until filling is lightly browned and set.

OPPOSITE PAGE: HOT AVOCADO SALAD
ABOVE: AVOCADO WITH LIME AND CHILLIES

AVOCADO AND PRAWN SALAD WITH CITRUS DRESSING

Cut 2 large avocados in half and remove the stones. Pile 155 g (5 oz) small cooked and peeled school prawns (shrimps) into the cavities, scooping out a little flesh to make room if necessary. Arrange watercress on serving plates, place avocados on top. Place 3 tablespoons olive oil, 1 tablespoon lemon juice, 1 tablespoon orange juice, ½ teaspoon honey and 1 teaspoon chopped parsley in a small screw-top jar; shake well. Drizzle dressing over prawns. Serve immediately. Serves 4 as a first course.

AVOCADO VINAIGRETTE

Arrange 4 lettuce leaves (cos, mignonette or butter lettuce) on individual serving plates. Peel 2 avocados, halve lengthways, remove the seeds and place on top of lettuce leaves. Beat 1 tablespoon white wine or tarragon vinegar with 1 teaspoon French mustard, ¼ teaspoon caster (superfine) sugar, salt and some freshly ground pepper. Add 4 tablespoons light olive oil, one drop at a time, beating continuously so that dressing is thick.

Spoon dressing into the avocado cavities. Sprinkle with chopped chives or parsley and serve immediately. Serves 4 as a first course.

B

Baba (au Rhum) A dessert cake made of yeast dough containing raisins, which is soaked in rum or Kirsch syrup after cooking. The cake has its origin in the sweetened yeast cakes, called *gugelhupf,* of central Europe. The Polish King Stanislaus enlivened his cakes with a liberal splash of rum and Malaga wine and called his invention Baba, for the hero of his favourite work of literature, *The One Thousand and One Nights.*

Baba Ghannouj A dish from the Middle East, consisting of pureed eggplant (aubergine) flavoured with tahini, garlic and lemon juice, served as a dip.

Babaco The cylindrical fruit of a bush native to tropical America. It has soft yellow flesh that tastes like a mixture of banana and pineapple. The babaco is related to the pawpaw (papaya) and is similarly used to tenderise meat and aid digestion.

Bacon Fat and lean meat, from the side and back of the pig, which has been preserved by dry

BACON

BACON, LETTUCE AND TOMATO SANDWICH

 Preparation time: 10 minutes
Total cooking time: 5 minutes
Serves 2

2-4 rashers bacon, rind removed
1 firm ripe tomato
4 slices white or rye bread
2 large lettuce leaves
mayonnaise for serving

1 Cut bacon rashers in half. Cook in a frying pan over medium heat until crisp; drain bacon. towel.
2 Thinly slice tomato. Lightly toast bread slices. Spread with butter if desired.
3 Place one slice of bread on serving plate. Top with lettuce, bacon, tomato slice and a dollop of mayonnaise. Place remaining bread on top. Cut in half and serve hot.

Note: This is known throughout the world (and particularly in international hotels) as a BLT. It is traditionally served with potato crisps.

VARIATIONS:

■ Add thin slices of cooked chicken and turkey breast for a club sandwich.
■ Lay a slice of cheddar cheese on top of a toast slice and grill until melted. Place remaining ingredients on top (omit mayonnaise). Serve hot.

BACON AND CHEESE BURGER

 Preparation time: 30 minutes +
30 minutes standing
Total cooking time: 12 minutes
Makes 8 burgers

500 g (1 lb) rindless bacon, chopped
250 g (8 oz) lean pork, trimmed and chopped
1/2 cup shredded cheddar cheese
1/4 cup grated parmesan cheese
1/2 cup fresh breadcrumbs
pinch cayenne pepper
seasonings to taste
wholegrain bread or buns

1 Place bacon, pork, cheeses, breadcrumbs and seasonings in a food processor or blender. Process until finely chopped. Shape the mixture and chill.
2 Cook on oiled grill 6 minutes each side. Serve on wholegrain bread or bun, garnished as desired.

ABOUT BACON

■ Snip edges of bacon rind to prevent curling while cooking, or trim off rind if preferred.
■ To grill (broil), place on a cold grill tray, cook under a moderately high heat for 2–3 minutes each side. To pan-fry, place in a cold pan without oil or fat, cook over a low heat turning often. For really crisp bacon, drain fat from pan as bacon cooks.
■ To cook bacon in microwave, cook on 100% power until almost done. Stand for 1–2 minutes (bacon will continue to cook slightly).

B A N A N A   S P I C E   L O A F

 Preparation time: 15 minutes
Total cooking time: 1 hour
+ 5 minutes standing
Makes one 20 x 15 cm
(8 x 6 inch) loaf

1¹/₂ cups self-raising flour	³/₄ cup caster (superfine)
1 teaspoon ground mixed	sugar
spice	2 eggs, lightly beaten
125 g (4 oz) unsalted	¹/₃ cup plain yoghurt
(sweet) butter, chopped	²/₃ cup mashed ripe banana

1 Preheat oven to moderate 180°C (350°F/Gas 4).
Brush a 20 x 15 x 7 cm (8 x 6 x 2³/₄ inch) loaf tin
with melted butter or oil. Line base and sides
with paper; grease paper. Place flour, spice, butter
and sugar in food processor. Using pulse action,
process for 20 seconds or until mixture is fine and
crumbly. Add combined eggs, yoghurt and
banana, process 10 seconds or until mixture is just
combined; do not overbeat.
2 Spoon mixture into tin; smooth surface. Bake
1 hour or until skewer comes out clean when
inserted in centre of cake. Leave cake in tin
5 minutes before turning onto wire rack to cool.

*OPPOSITE PAGE: BACON, LETTUCE AND TOMATO
SANDWICH. ABOVE: BANANA SPLIT*

B A N A N A   S P L I T

 Preparation time: 5 minutes
Total cooking time: 10 minutes
Serves 4

Butterscotch Sauce
¹/₂ cup soft brown sugar
¹/₂ cup (4 fl oz) cream
55 g (1³/₄ oz) butter

Split
4 large ripe bananas

8 small scoops vanilla
  ice-cream
250 g (8 oz)
  strawberries, hulled
12 small white
  marshmallows
¹/₄ cup chopped pecan nuts

1 To make Butterscotch Sauce: Combine the
brown sugar, cream and butter in a saucepan and
stir over medium heat until mixture boils.
Reduce heat and simmer for 3 minutes, then cool
mixture to room temperature.
2 Peel bananas and cut in halves lengthways.
Arrange each banana in a long serving dish and
top with two scoops of ice-cream. Spoon sauce
over and top with strawberries, marshmallows
and pecans. Serve immediately.

A B O U T   B A N A N A S
■ Allow bananas to ripen at room temperature.
Once ripe, they can be stored in the refrigerator:
the skins will turn black, but the fruit inside will
not be affected. To avoid discoloration (the flesh
will turn brown when exposed to the air), toss
sliced bananas in lemon juice.

salting (curing) and is
usually smoked as well.
Bacon is sold in thin
slices called rashers.
Middle cut or prime
bacon is cut from the
middle rib area and
contains a large eye of
lean meat; streaky bacon,
with alternating strips of
lean and fat, is cut

from the
tail end of the loin.
Canadian bacon, in
England called back
bacon, is cut from the
loin and is leaner than
other cuts.
See also Gammon; Speck.

Bagel A ring of non-
sweet, baked yeast dough
with a characteristic
shiny, hard crust, the
result of being boiled in
water before baking. The
bagel originated in
eastern Europe in the

sixteenth
or seventeenth century,
and became popular with
the Jewish community in
Vienna, which began
producing it
commercially. The name
comes from a Yiddish
word meaning 'ring'.

Bagna Cauda A garlic
and anchovy flavoured
sauce served hot as a dip
for raw vegetables.

Originally from Piedmont, in Italy, the sauce is associated with the grape harvest and the rituals and celebrations that accompany winemaking. Its name means 'hot bath'.

Baguette (French Bread) A long, thin crusty loaf of bread made of bleached white flour. The baguette

originated in Paris and is the everyday bread of France—it appears on the table at every meal and its price is set by law.

Bake Blind To partially or fully bake a pie shell before filling with a mixture which would otherwise make the bottom soggy, or with fruit that does not need to be cooked. The pastry should be weighted with dried beans, rice or macaroni to prevent it rising during baking.

Baking Powder A raising agent consisting of bicarbonate of soda (baking soda), an acid (usually cream of tartar), and starch or flour, used for cooking cakes and biscuits. The bicarbonate of soda reacts with the acid to produce bubbles of carbon dioxide, causing the mixture to rise and become porous.

BANANA PEANUT BUTTER CAKE

⭐ **Preparation time:** 10 minutes
Total cooking time: 1 hour
Makes one 20 cm (8 inch) oblong cake

125 g (4 oz) unsalted (sweet) butter
1/2 cup soft brown sugar
1/4 cup honey
2 eggs, lightly beaten
1/3 cup crunchy peanut butter
1 cup mashed banana
2 cups wholemeal self-raising flour

1 Preheat oven to moderate 180°C (350°F/Gas 4). Brush a deep 21 x 14 x 7 cm (8½ x 5½ x 2¾ inch) loaf tin with melted butter or oil. Line the base and sides with paper; grease the paper. Using electric beaters, beat butter, sugar and honey in small mixing bowl until light and creamy. Add eggs gradually, beating thoroughly after each addition. Add peanut butter; beat until combined.
2 Transfer mixture to large mixing bowl; add banana. Using a metal spoon, fold in sifted flour, including husks. Stir until just combined and the mixture is almost smooth.
3 Spoon mixture into prepared tin; smooth surface. Bake for one hour or until skewer comes out clean when inserted in centre of cake. Leave cake in tin for 10 minutes before turning onto a wire rack to cool. Serve sliced and spread with butter, if desired.

HOT BANANAS WITH CINNAMON COCONUT SAUCE

⭐ **Preparation time:** 5 minutes
Total cooking time: 10 minutes
Serves 4

4 large bananas

Cinnamon Coconut Sauce
1 tablespoon plain (all-purpose) flour
2 tablespoons sugar
1/2 teaspoon ground cinnamon
1⅓ cups (10½ fl oz) canned coconut milk

1 Rinse bananas and remove ends. Place bananas into a covered steamer over a pan of boiling water; cook for 5 minutes. Use tongs and a knife to peel off banana skins (skins will be black but the fruit inside will be golden).
2 To make Cinnamon Coconut Sauce: Place flour, sugar and cinnamon in a pan and stir until well combined. Add coconut milk and blend until smooth. Stir constantly over medium heat until mixture boils and thickens. Simmer for 2 minutes. Serve with hot bananas.

BANANA SMOOTHIE

Combine in a blender or food processor 1/2 cup (4 fl oz) chilled milk, 1 banana, 1/4 cup plain or fruit yoghurt, 1 teaspoon honey, 1–2 scoops vanilla ice-cream and a pinch of ground nutmeg. Process or blend until smooth. Pour into a long tall glass. Sprinkle with extra nutmeg to serve.

BANANA AND PASSIONFRUIT SMOOTHIE

Place in blender 1 banana, pulp of 2 passionfruit and 1/2 cup frozen passionfruit yoghurt. Blend until smooth.

VARIATIONS

■ Add 1–2 tablespoons choc bits (chocolate chips) to banana smoothie mixure before blending.
■ Add 1–2 tablespoons wheatgerm to banana smoothie mixture before blending for a high protein hunger assuager.
■ Crushed ice, added before blending, produces a much thicker drink. This applies not only to banana smoothies but to all blended drinks.

ABOVE: HOT BANANAS WITH CINNAMON COCONUT SAUCE. OPPOSITE PAGE: STEAK WITH SPEEDY BARBECUE MARINADE

 BARBECUE COOKERY

STEAK WITH SPEEDY BARBECUE MARINADE

Preparation time: 5 minutes +
2 hours marinating
Total cooking time: 6-12 minutes
Serves 4

1 kg (2 lb) rump steak
1 cup (8 fl oz) red wine
2 tablespoons olive oil
1 tablespoon balsamic
  vinegar

1 tablespoon tomato paste
1 tablespoon Dijon mustard
1 clove garlic, crushed
2 teaspoons soft brown
  sugar

1 Trim meat of excess fat and sinew. Combine wine, oil, vinegar, tomato paste, mustard, garlic and sugar in a small bowl, whisk for one minute or until well combined. Place the meat in a large dish; pour marinade over. Store in the refrigerator, covered with plastic wrap, for 2 hours or overnight, turning occasionally. Drain the meat, reserving the marinade.
2 Place meat on lightly oiled grill or flat plate. Cook over a high heat for 2 minutes on each side, turning once. For a rare result, cook a further minute on each side. For medium and well done results, move the meat to a cooler part of the barbecue, continue to cook a further 2-3 minutes on each side for medium and 4-6

minutes on each side for well done; brush meat with the reserved marinade during cooking.
3 Leave the meat in a warm place, covered with foil, for 2-3 minutes. Cut it across the grain into 2 cm (¾ inch) thick slices for serving.

SKEWERED GINGER PORK

Preparation time: 20 minutes +
1 hour marinating
Total cooking time: 10 minutes
Serves 6

500 g (1 lb) pork fillets
2 tablespoons grated fresh
  ginger
½ teaspoon ground
  pepper

1 teaspoon sesame oil
1 tablespoon lemon juice
1 small onion, grated
salt and pepper to taste

1 Cut the pork fillets into cubes. In a small bowl, combine grated ginger, pepper, sesame oil, lemon juice and onion. Pour mixture over pork cubes and marinate for 1 hour.
2 Thread pork onto skewers and barbecue on flat plate for 5 minutes each side, or until cooked to taste. Serve with a salad and hot bread rolls.

Note: Pork fillets are a delicate cut with little fat visible. If they are not available, substitute with another lean cut.

ABOUT BARBECUING
■ Give the barbecue plenty of time to heat. A good way to find out if the heat is right is to hold the palm of your hand about 10 cm (4 inches) above the glowing coals. If you pull it away in two seconds, you know the barbecue is ready for the food. Likewise, when cooking over a wood fire, make certain that the flames have died down completely to leave glowing coals covered with ash before starting to cook.
■ Cooking times depend on the thickness of the meat and the efficiency of the barbecue.
■ To test meat for doneness, press with blunt tongs. If it feels springy, it is rare; if slightly resistant, it is medium cooked; if firm to the touch, it is well done.
■ When barbecuing kebabs, oiled metal skewers are ideal because it is easier to remove the cooked meat from them. Or use bamboo skewers that have been soaked in water for an hour—this will prevent them burning.
■ You can give food a smoked flavour with the addition of water-soaked mesquite or hickory chips just before cooking.

Baking Soda See Bicarbonate of Soda.

Baklava A cake, consisting of alternate layers of filo pastry and chopped nuts, which is doused in syrup while still hot and then cut into triangular pieces. Of Greek or Turkish origin, baklava first appeared during the time of the Ottoman Empire, about AD 1300. It is popular in the Middle East.

Balsamic Vinegar A richly flavoured, dark-coloured vinegar. It has a bitter-sweet taste, is almost syrupy in consistency and is used in salads, on berries, or as a meat marinade. The vinegar is made from unfermented sweet Trebbiano grapes, which are slowly boiled to a thick syrup, to which a strong wine vinegar is added. The mixture is aged in a series of aromatic hardwood casks for at least five years and sometimes a century or more. It is a specialty of the Italian Modena region. Less expensive products attempt to imitate the flavour by adding caramel to red wine vinegar.

Bamboo Shoots The young, tender and slightly crunchy cone-shaped shoots of an edible bamboo plant found throughout tropical Asia. Their use as a food dates from sixth century China and they are also an important ingredient in Japanese and Korean cooking.

Banana The yellow-skinned, crescent-shaped fruit of a tall, long-leaved plant (actually a giant herb, not a tree) cultivated throughout the tropics and probably native to the region between India and the island of New Guinea. By the fourteenth century they grew in Africa.

Bananas have been grown in tropical America since their introduction by the Spanish and Portuguese in the sixteenth century. However, only with improved transport methods in the mid-twentieth century did the fruit become common in Europe and North America.

As a general rule, the smaller the banana variety, the sweeter the flesh.

BARBECUED PORK SPARE RIBS

 Preparation time: 15 minutes +
3 hours marinating
Total cooking time: 30 minutes
Serves 4–6

1 kg (2 lb) American-style pork spare ribs
2 cups (16 fl oz) tomato sauce (ketchup)
½ cup (4 fl oz) sherry
2 tablespoons soy sauce
2 tablespoons honey
3 cloves garlic, crushed
1 tablespoon grated fresh ginger

1 Trim spare ribs of excess fat and sinew. Cut racks of ribs into pieces, so that each piece has three or four ribs. Combine tomato sauce, sherry, soy sauce, honey, garlic and ginger in a large pan; mix well.
2 Add ribs to mixture. Bring to the boil. Reduce heat and simmer, covered, for 15 minutes. Move ribs occasionally to ensure even cooking. Transfer ribs and sauce to a shallow non-metal dish; allow to cool. Refrigerate, covered with plastic wrap, for several hours or overnight. Prepare and heat barbecue 1 hour before cooking.
3 Place ribs on a hot, lightly oiled barbecue grill or flatplate. Cook over the hottest part of the fire for 15 minutes, turning and brushing with sauce occasionally. Serve with barbecued corn on the cob and potato salad, if desired.

RIGHT: GARLIC KING PRAWNS;
ABOVE: BARBECUED PORK SPARE RIBS;
OPPOSITE PAGE: CHICKEN SATAY WITH
PEANUT SAUCE

GARLIC KING PRAWNS (SHRIMPS)

 Preparation time: 10 minutes +
3 hours marinating
Total cooking time: 3-5 minutes
Serves 4

500 g (1 lb) green (uncooked) king prawns (shrimps)

Marinade
2 tablespoons lemon juice
2 tablespoons sesame oil
2 cloves garlic, crushed
2 teaspoons grated fresh ginger

1 Remove heads from prawns, peel and devein, leaving tails intact (reserve heads and shell for fish stock, if you like). Make a cut in prawn body, slicing three-quarters of the way through the flesh from head to tail.
2 To make Marinade: Combine juice, oil, garlic and ginger in jug; mix well. Place prawns in bowl; pour on marinade and mix well. Cover and refrigerate several hours or overnight. Prepare and light barbecue 1 hour before cooking.
3 Cook prawns on hot, lightly greased flatplate for 3–5 minutes or until pink in colour and cooked through. Brush frequently with marinade while cooking. Serve immediately.

CHICKEN SATAY WITH PEANUT SAUCE

 Preparation time: 30 minutes +
2 hours marinating
Total cooking time: 10 minutes
Makes 12

1 kg (2 lb) chicken thigh fillets
¼ cup (2 fl oz) soy sauce
1 tablespoon honey
2 tablespoons oil

¾ cup crunchy peanut butter
½ cup (4 fl oz) coconut cream
1 tablespoon soy sauce
2 tablespoons sweet chilli sauce
½ cup (4 fl oz) water
salt, to taste

Peanut Sauce
1 tablespoon oil
2 teaspoons dried onion flakes

1 Trim chicken of excess fat and sinew. Cut chicken into 2 cm (¾ inch) strips, thread onto skewers. Place in a shallow glass dish. Combine soy sauce, honey and oil, pour over chicken. Cover with plastic wrap, refrigerate 2 hours.
2 To make Peanut Sauce: Heat oil in a small heavy-based pan. Add onion flakes, cook over low heat 30 seconds. Add peanut butter, coconut cream, soy sauce, sweet chilli sauce, water and salt; combine well. Cook until heated through.
3 Drain chicken, reserve marinade. Cook satay sticks over medium-high heat 8 minutes on lightly greased grill. Turn often and brush with marinade. Serve immediately with Peanut Sauce.

Note: Soak bamboo skewers in cold water for at least 30 minutes to prevent scorching. Alternatively, cover the ends with foil.

SWEET AND SPICY SPATCHCOCKS

 Preparation time: 40 minutes +
24 hours standing
Total cooking time: 30 minutes
Serves 8

4 spatchcocks, halved and cleaned

Marinade
825 g (1 lb 11 oz) can plums, drained and stoned
1 onion, roughly chopped

2 cloves garlic, crushed
¼ cup (2 fl oz) red wine
¼ cup (2 fl oz) teriyaki sauce
2 tablespoons chilli sauce
juice of 1 lemon
1 teaspoon sesame oil
freshly ground pepper

1 Make several deep slashes in the flesh of each spatchcock half. Set aside.
2 To make Marinade: Place all ingredients in a food processor or blender. Process until smooth. Place spatchcocks cut-side down in a non-metal dish. Pour over marinade. Cover. Marinate in the refrigerator, turning and basting frequently, for at least 24 hours.
3 Drain spatchcocks. Cook over hot coals for 15 minutes each side, basting frequently with marinade.

The fruit can be eaten raw or used in a variety of cooked sweet and savoury dishes. A relative, the green-skinned plantain, contains less sugar and more starch and is cooked as a vegetable

accompaniment to West Indian, South American and African dishes.

Banbury Tart A small tart consisting of puff or flaky pastry filled with mincemeat (finely chopped dried and fresh fruit) and sometimes flavoured with rum and grated nutmeg. The cake originated in the seventeenth century in the English market town of Banbury.

Bannock A flat cake, originating in Scotland, made with oatmeal, barley or wheat flour and cooked on a griddle or in a frying pan.

Bap A light, white bread roll with a soft, floury crust. It is split open and spread with butter and a filling while still hot. The bap originated in Scotland where it has been known since the sixteenth century.

Barbecue Cookery Roasting or grilling (broiling) food over an open fire is the oldest form of cookery. Meat, poultry, fish, shellfish, vegetables and even fruit can be cooked in this

way. Flavours can be enhanced by basting with marinades and sauces during cooking, and by the fragrant smoke from aromatic woods and herbs thrown on the coals.

Barley A grain related to wheat, barley originated in the hilly areas of the Middle East. It was the chief grain of the ancient Greeks and in Rome was used to make bread as well as being the main food of the gladiators. Pearl barley, the shiny grains that have been hulled and milled until they resemble small pearls, has been used in cooking since ancient times, probably moistened with oil and water and flavoured with the juices from cooked poultry or lamb; it is still used in soups and stews. Barley water, prepared from the grain, was a favourite beverage of the Greek physician Hippocrates and is still a popular health drink. Today, barley is mostly used to make malt for beer brewing and as a stock food.

Barley Sugar A brittle confectionary (candy), traditionally made with water in which barley has been simmered for several

TERIYAKI STEAKS WITH BLUE CHEESE AND HERB BUTTER

 Preparation time: 20 minutes + 2 hours marinating + 4 hours refrigeration
Total cooking time: 6-16 minutes
Serves 8

8 rib eye steaks, about
200 g (6½ oz) each,
or 8 boneless sirloin
(loin) steaks
¼ cup (2 fl oz) teriyaki
sauce
2 cloves garlic, crushed

Blue Cheese and Herb Butter
125 g (4 oz) blue vein
cheese, chopped

125 g (4 oz) butter,
softened
1 tablespoon dry white
wine
1 teaspoon finely chopped
fresh mint
½ teaspoon dried rosemary
leaves
½ teaspoon dried oregano
leaves

1 Trim meat of excess fat and sinew. Combine steaks with teriyaki sauce and garlic. Refrigerate, covered, for 2 hours or overnight, turning occasionally. Drain meat, reserving marinade.
2 Place steaks on lightly oiled grill or flat plate. Cook over high heat 2 minutes each side to seal, turning once. For rare meat, cook another minute on each side. For medium and well done, move meat to cooler part of barbecue and cook

each side another 2–3 minutes (medium), or 4–6 minutes (well done); brush with remaining marinade in last minutes of cooking. Serve with slices of Blue Cheese and Herb Butter on top.
3 To make Blue Cheese and Herb Butter: Using electric beaters, beat cheese and butter in a small mixing bowl until light and creamy. Add wine and herbs; beat until just combined. Spoon mixture onto a large sheet of foil. Use foil to wrap, roll and shape cheese mixture into a log measuring 4 x 16 cm (1½ x 6½ inches). Refrigerate 4 hours or overnight.

FISH CAKES IN CORN HUSKS

 Preparation time: 30 minutes +
10 minutes standing
Total cooking time: 20 minutes
Serves 4

foil for wrapping
4 corn cobs, complete with
husks
500 g (1 lb) firm white
fish fillets, diced
2 cloves garlic, crushed
2 teaspoons Mexican
chilli powder (see Note)
⅓ cup finely chopped
fresh coriander

1 tablespoon chopped
canned jalapeño chillies
1 egg beaten
½ teaspoon ground black
pepper
1 tablespoon lemon juice
2 tablespoons chopped
spring onions (scallions)
1 teaspoon ground cumin

1 Cut foil into eight 16-cm (6½ inch) squares. Remove only four husks from each corn cob and set these aside. Turn back the remaining husks (being careful not to detach them) and remove the thread-like cornsilk. Pull husks back into position to enclose corn. Soak cobs in cold water for 10–15 minutes.
2 Puree fish fillets in a food processor until just smooth. Add garlic, chilli powder, coriander, chillies, beaten egg, pepper, lemon juice, spring onions and cumin to the food processor and blend until all ingredients are well combined. Divide mixture into eight equal portions.
3 Wrap each portion in two of the reserved corn husks, making eight parcels. Wrap each parcels in a square of foil.
4 Grill corn cobs on barbecue for 20 minutes, turning once or twice during cooking.
5 Place wrapped fish cakes on medium hot flat plate for last 8 minutes of corn cob cooking time.

Note: Mexican chilli powder, containing a mixture of paprika, chillies, cumin and oregano, is available from most large supermarkets.

BASIL

MOZZARELLA, BASIL AND TOMATO SALAD

 Preparation time: 10 minutes
Total cooking time: nil
Serves 6

6 medium, ripe tomatoes
3–4 fresh small
  mozzarella (bocconcini)
  cheeses
1 tablespoon lemon juice

4 tablespoons virgin
  olive oil
shredded basil leaves
freshly ground black
  pepper

1 Slice the tomatoes thickly; slice the mozzarella thinly. Arrange on a serving plate, alternating between the slices of tomato and the slices of mozzarella.
2 Combine lemon juice and olive oil in a small bowl. Mix well using a wire whisk. Drizzle dressing over salad. Sprinkle with basil leaves and black pepper.

Note: This salad is best made just before serving. Have tomatoes at room temperature to make the most of their flavour.

OPPOSITE PAGE: TERIYAKI STEAKS WITH BLUE CHEESE AND HERB BUTTER. ABOVE: MOZZARELLA, BASIL AND TOMATO SALAD

PESTO

 Preparation time: 10 minutes
Total cooking time: nil
Makes 2 cups (16 fl oz)

4 cloves garlic, peeled
2 cups fresh basil leaves
1 cup parsley sprigs
2/3 cup pine nuts

1½ cups grated parmesan
  cheese
1½ cups (12 fl oz) olive
  oil

1 Place garlic, basil, parsley, pine nuts and parmesan cheese in a food processor or blender. Blend at medium speed, adding oil in a thin stream until smooth.
2 Place in a clean jar, cover with a thin layer of oil, store in the refrigerator for up to 2 weeks. Pour away oil before using.

ABOUT BASIL

■ Of the many types now grown, sweet basil is the most widely used; other varieties include an extravagantly ruffled purple version, often used as a garnish, the small-leaved, spicier Greek or perennial basil and dark opal, which is a decorative red-leafed variety.
■ Store fresh basil in the refrigerator standing upright in a bottle or jar of water up to 3 days. Cover the leaves loosely with a plastic bag.
■ Dried basil has a stronger flavour than ground basil. Store in airtight jars in a cool, dark place.

hours (barley water) and sugar. Today it is made of boiled sugar, without barley and with various flavourings.

Barquette A small, boat-shaped tart made of either shortcrust or puff pastry, shaped in a small tin mould and baked blind before being filled with sweet or savoury ingredients.

Basil A pungent herb related to mint. Its flavour combines particularly well with tomatoes, zucchini (courgettes) and spinach; it is also used in salads, sauces and stuffings and as a garnish for pasta. The Greeks, who used it for

cooking in the third century BC, regarded basil as a royal herb, as reflected in the specific scientific name for sweet basil, *basilicum*, derived from the Greek word for king. Basil originated in tropical Asia.

Basmati An aromatic, long-grained textured rice much used in India. It has been grown for thousands of years in the Himalayan foothills.

Baste To moisten food while it is cooking by spooning over or brushing with pan juices, melted fat or a marinade.

fish before they are fried. The practice of dipping fish in batter before deep frying probably originated in China. In North America the term is also used for a cake mixture. The word comes from the French *battre*, to beat.

Bavarois (Bavarian Cream) A dessert made from egg custard and whipped cream, flavoured with pureed fruit, chocolate, coffee or liqueur. Its name may be linked to the numbers of French chefs who worked at the Bavarian (German) court during the time of the Wittelsbach kings (1806 to 1918).

Bay The bay tree, also known as the laurel, is a native of the Mediterranean region. In ancient Greece, wreaths of its aromatic leaves crowned victors in both cultural and sporting endeavours (the term 'laureate'

BEAN CURD

HONEY-BRAISED VEGETABLES WITH BEAN CURD

 Preparation time: 30 minutes
Total cooking time: 15 minutes
Serves 6

8 dried Chinese mushrooms	*1 tablespoon honey*
3 thin slices ginger	*2 teaspoons sesame oil*
20 dried lily buds (optional)	*2 teaspoons cornflour (cornstarch)*
2 tablespoons peanut oil	*4 spring onions (scallions) cut into 4 cm (1½ inch) lengths*
250 g (8 oz) sweet potato, halved and sliced	
2 tablespoons soy sauce	*410 g (13 oz) can baby corn*
45 g (1½ oz) fried bean curd, cut into 1 cm (½ inch) strips	*230 g (7½ oz) canned water chestnuts, drained*

1 Cover mushrooms with hot water and soak for 30 minutes. Drain, reserving ¾ cup liquid (6 fl oz). Squeeze mushrooms to remove excess liquid. Remove stems. Slice the mushrooms thinly. Slice ginger thinly. Soak the lily buds, if using, separately in warm water for 30 minutes; drain.
2 Heat the oil in a wok or heavy-based frying pan, swirling gently to coat base and sides. Add ginger and stir-fry over medium heat for one minute. Add the mushrooms and lily buds and

stir-fry for 30 seconds. Add sweet potato with soy sauce, fried bean curd, honey, sesame oil and mushroom liquid. Simmer, uncovered, for 15 minutes.
3 Dissolve cornflour in a little water, add to pan. Stir until liquid thickens. Add the spring onions, corn and water chestnuts; simmer for one minute.

Note: Dried lily buds may be found in Chinese food stores. Used for their texture and subtle flavour, they have no substitute, but may be omitted without radically altering the dish.

ABOUT BEAN CURD
■ Fresh bean curd or tofu is sold in plastic containers, packaged in water, in the refrigerator section of some supermarkets, Asian and health food stores; it will keep after opening, refrigerated, for 4 days; change water daily. Firm (pressed) bean curd comes in square cakes and is best for slicing, cubing and stir-frying; silken (soft) bean curd is good for blending with other ingredients and for enriching dishes. Fried bean curd (aburage) is sometimes available, vacuum packed; if not, firm bean curd can be deep fried in oil.
■ Longlife bean curd will last for up to 6 months unrefrigerated.
■ Powdered bean curd is also available.

ABOVE: HONEY-BRAISED VEGETABLES WITH BEAN CURD. OPPOSITE PAGE: CHINESE CHICKEN AND NOODLES

BEAN SPROUTS

CHINESE CHICKEN AND NOODLES

★ **Preparation time:** 10 minutes
Total cooking time: 15 minutes
Serves 4

6 chicken thigh fillets,
 about 660 g (1 lb 6 oz)
1/3 cup (2 1/2 fl oz) satay
 sauce
2 tablespoons soy sauce
2 tablespoons sherry
2 tablespoons oil
1 onion, cut into eighths
2 medium carrots, thinly
 sliced
125 g (4 oz) snow peas
 (mange tout)

4 cups chopped bok choy
 or Chinese cabbage
2 cups bean sprouts
2 tablespoons cornflour
 (cornstarch)
1 cup (8 fl oz) light
 chicken stock
salt, to taste
105 g (3 1/2 oz) fresh
 Chinese egg noodles

1 Trim chicken of excess fat and sinew. Cut into 2 cm (3/4 inch) cubes. Combine with satay sauce, soy sauce and sherry in a large mixing bowl.
2 Heat oil in a heavy-based frying pan. Add onion and carrot and cook over high heat for 2 minutes, stirring occasionally. Add snow peas and bok choy and cook, stirring, over high heat for 1 minute. Remove from pan; set aside.

3 Add chicken mixture to pan. Cook, stirring occasionally, over high heat for 4 minutes or until chicken is tender and cooked through.
4 Return vegetables to pan. Add bean sprouts and blended cornflour and stock. Add salt, stir 2 minutes or until sauce boils and thickens. Cook noodles in a medium pan of rapidly boiling water until just tender, about 2 minutes. Drain. Place noodles in individual deep serving plates, spoon chicken and vegetables over. Serve immediately.

ABOUT BEAN SPROUTS

■ To grow sprouts: Place 1/4 to 1/2 cup mung beans in a large glass jar (beans will take up to 10 times the volume once sprouted). Rinse well, then soak in cold water for 12 hours. Drain water off, cover mouth of jar with a piece of loosely woven fabric held in place with string, or an elastic band. Lay the jar on its side in a warm, well-lit place (not direct sunlight); rinse and drain beans twice a day for 3–4 days. Do not let sprouting beans dry out or they will die. Sprouts are ready to eat when they are about 2.5 cm (1 inch) long.
■ Place sprouts in a large bowl of water and swish to release the husks. Remove husks with a slotted spoon (the husks are edible, but bean sprouts look more appetising without them).
■ Alfalfa and other legumes can also be sprouted.

comes from this practice). In the Middle Ages bay leaves were used as a strewing herb to banish stale odours and it is only in later centuries that their culinary qualities have been appreciated. The leaves can be used fresh or dried, crushed or powdered, to enliven soups and casseroles; they are always a component of a bouquet garni.

Bean Curd A processed extract of the soy bean obtained by soaking, boiling and sieving the beans to produce a liquid which, after the addition of a coagulant, is similar in appearance and texture to fresh cheese. It takes on the flavour of what it is cooked with, and is valued for its high nutritional content. The use of bean curd is believed to date from the Han dynasty in China (about 206 BC to about AD 220); it was introduced into Japan by Buddhist priests in the eighth century. Bean curd is also known by its Japanese name, tofu. In Japan, it is added to sweet and sour sauces, used in soups, sukiyaki and seafood dishes and diced or crumbled with noodles and other vegetables.

Bean Sprouts The sprouts of the mung bean and, less commonly, the soy bean, used in salads or as a stir-fry vegetable. Bean sprouts are very low in kilojoules (calories).

Beans, Dried The dried seeds of various beans, which, with dried peas and lentils, are usually classified as pulses. There are many varieties of dried beans—haricot,

cannellini, lima, borlotti, red kidney beans, black-eyed peas or beans, chickpeas, broad beans, mung beans and soya beans. All are highly nutritious; all contain soluble dietary fibre which helps to control the level of cholesterol in the blood. The Romans made cakes from ground dried beans in times of cereal shortage, as did the peasants of western Europe in later centuries. Traditionally dried beans have played an important role in the diet of the peoples of Central and South America and the Middle East, providing low-cost high protein meals. Dried beans require slow cooking.

Beans, Green Green beans are the edible pods of a number of bean varieties which actually range in colour from pale yellow to deep purple.

BEANS
DRIED AND CANNED

HEARTY BACON AND BEAN STEWPOT

★ **Preparation time:** 25 minutes
Total cooking time: 40 minutes
Serves 4–6

200 g (6½ oz) piece of speck (see Note)
2 tablespoons oil
2 small leeks, thinly sliced
2 tablespoons plain (all-purpose) flour
2 cups (16 fl oz) chicken stock
3 large carrots, cut into 1 cm (½ inch) cubes

4 medium potatoes, about 800 g (1 lb 10 oz), peeled and cut into 1 cm (½ inch) cubes
410 g (13 oz) can red kidney beans, rinsed and drained
½ cup finely chopped parsley
½ teaspoon freshly ground black pepper

1 Remove rind from speck. Cut speck into 1 cm (½ inch) cubes. Place in a large pan; cook over low heat until crisp. Remove from pan and drain on paper towels. Remove excess fat from pan.
2 Heat oil in pan, add leeks and cook for 5 minutes until soft. Add the flour to pan. Stir over low heat for 2 minutes or until the flour mixture is lightly golden.
3 Add chicken stock gradually to pan, stirring until mixture is smooth. Stir constantly over medium heat for 3 minutes or until mixture boils

and thickens; boil for another 1 minute. Reduce heat; simmer.
4 When mixture is at simmering point, add the potatoes, carrots and drained speck; cover and cook gently over medium heat for 20 minutes or until potatoes and carrots are tender.
5 Add beans, parsley and pepper and stir to combine. Cook over low heat for 5 minutes. Serve with a green vegetable such as steamed broccoli or green beans.

Note: Speck is available from butchers and delicatessens. If you do not like its strong taste, thick bacon rashers with rind removed can be used as a substitute.

SWEET BEAN SALAD

★ **Preparation time:** 35 minutes
Total cooking time: 15 minutes
Serves 4

500 g (1 lb) frozen broad beans (fava beans)
2 cloves garlic, crushed
1 leek, sliced
1 large carrot, sliced

½ cup (4 fl oz) olive oil
⅓ cup (2½ fl oz) cider vinegar
¼ cup soft brown sugar
¼ cup chopped parsley

1 Cook beans in boiling water till tender. Drain.
2 Return beans to saucepan, add garlic, leek, carrot and olive oil; cook gently for 5 minutes. Add vinegar and brown sugar and cook 5 minutes longer, making sure brown sugar is dissolved.
3 Chill well. Garnish with chopped parsley.

ABOUT DRIED BEANS

■ Soak dried beans overnight in cold water, or cover with boiling water and stand for 2 hours; drain and rinse well. Place in a large pan, cover with water and cook over low heat for 40–50 minutes or until tender. (Some beans, such as soy beans, take much longer to cook.) To test beans, remove one or two from the water and press between thumb and finger—beans should feel soft but not mushy. If the centre is still hard, cook for a little longer. Dried beans are much more economical than canned beans, but take a long time to prepare and cook. Canned beans can be substituted in all recipes that call for dried beans. They require no special preparation, needing only to be heated through.
■ Around 500 g (1lb) or 2½ cups dried beans yields 6 cups of cooked beans.

ABOVE: HEARTY BACON AND BEAN STEWPOT.
OPPOSITE PAGE: COUNTRY BEAN SALAD

COUNTRY BEAN SALAD

 Preparation time: 15 minutes + 1 hour standing + 1 hour refrigeration
Total cooking time: 45 minutes
Serves 4

1 cup dried cannellini beans	**Dressing**
2 tomatoes	1/4 cup (2 fl oz) olive oil
1 onion, thinly sliced	1 tablespoon lemon juice
3 spring onions (scallions), chopped	2 teaspoons finely chopped fresh dill
1/3 cup coarsely chopped continental parsley	salt and freshly ground black pepper, to taste
1/2 red pepper (capsicum), cut into strips	5 canned anchovy fillets, drained

1 Place beans into a medium pan; cover with water. Bring to boil, remove from heat; leave, covered, for one hour. Drain and rinse. Return beans to pan; cover with water. Bring to boil, reduce heat. Cover and simmer 40 minutes or until tender; drain.
2 To peel tomatoes, make a small cross on the top, place in boiling water for 1–2 minutes, then plunge immediately into cold water. Remove and peel down skin from the cross. Cut tomatoes in half; gently squeeze to remove seeds and roughly chop the flesh.
3 Place beans into a large bowl. Add tomato, onions, spring onions, parsley and pepper; mix well.
4 To make Dressing: Combine oil, juice, dill, salt and pepper and pour over salad; mix well. Cover salad and refrigerate for one hour.
5 Cut anchovies into long thin strips and arrange over salad just before serving.

PORK AND BEAN SOUP

 Preparation time: 30 minutes
Total cooking time: 1 hour 40 minutes
Serves 4–6

1 tablespoon olive oil	1 carrot, chopped
2 cloves garlic, crushed	1/2 small cabbage, shredded
1 large onion, chopped	1/2 fennel bulb, chopped
6 rashers lean bacon, chopped	2 teaspoons fresh thyme or 1/2 teaspoon dried thyme
250 g (8 oz) boneless pork, fat removed, diced	1.5 litres (6 cups) chicken stock
2 large ripe tomatoes, peeled and chopped	2 x 315 g (10 oz) cans mixed beans, drained
1 stick celery, chopped	

1 Heat oil in a large pan, add the garlic and onion and fry for one minute.
2 Add bacon and pork and cook over medium heat until the pork is well browned. Add tomatoes, celery, carrot, cabbage, fennel, thyme and chicken stock. Cover pan, bring to the boil, reduce heat and simmer for 1¼ hours.
3 Add the mixed beans and cook for another 15 minutes. Serve soup hot with some fresh, crusty bread or rolls.

They include the French bean (called *haricot vert* in France and string bean in North America), the yellow wax bean, and the runner bean, which has purple pods that turn green when cooked. Green beans can be steamed, boiled, stir-fried (on their own or with other food) or cooked for salads.

The green bean is native to tropical America where it has been cultivated for many thousands of years. By the time of European contact it had spread both north and south, and was often found planted with corn. At first only its seeds were used, but by the late eighteenth century whole pods were eaten.

The long, deep green Chinese or snake bean has been cultivated and eaten since ancient times and features in South-East Asian cooking.

Béarnaise Sauce A creamy sauce made of

B BEANS & BROCCOLI

If you overcook beans they lose their bright green colour. When quickly cooked (they don't have to be hard, but they should never be flabby) beans are among the sweetest tasting vegetables. When preparing broccoli, include the stems, too. Don't overcook broccoli.

MINTED TOMATO AND BEANS

Cut 20 beans in half. Heat 1 teaspoon oil in frying pan. Add 1 clove crushed garlic, 1 teaspoon grated ginger, ½ teaspoon each of ground coriander, cumin and garam masala, 2 chopped ripe tomatoes. Cook, stirring, for 1 minute. Add beans, cook 2–3 minutes or until just tender.

Garlic and basil beans

BEAN AND WALNUT SALAD

Shred 20 green beans. Combine with ¼ cup fresh coriander leaves, 4 torn red oak leaf lettuce leaves, ¼ shredded red pepper (capsicum), ¼ cup walnut halves, 2 tablespoons tarragon vinegar, 1–2 tablespoons peanut oil and 2 tablespoons chopped fresh mint. Mix well. Serve immediately.

BEAN BUNDLES

Top and tail 20 beans. Divide beans into bundles of five. Tie together with the green end of a spring onion (scallion), or chives. Steam or microwave until just tender. Sprinkle with lemon pepper. Serve hot.

GARLIC AND BASIL BEANS

Top and tail 20 beans. Heat 1 tablespoon olive oil in frying pan or wok. Add 1 clove crushed garlic and beans. Cook, stirring, 2–3 minutes or until beans are just tender. Stir in 1 tablespoon shredded basil leaves. Serve hot.

Bean bundles

Minted tomato and beans

Bean and walnut salad

40

*BROCCOLI
AND ONION
STIR-FRY*

BROCCOLI AND ONION STIR-FRY

Cut 250 g (8 oz) broccoli into small florets. Slice a medium onion into 8 wedges. Heat 2 teaspoons sesame oil and 2 teaspoons vegetable oil in pan. Add broccoli and onions, cook until just tender. Stir in 2 teaspoons soy sauce and 3 teaspoons sweet chilli sauce. Sprinkle with herbs.

BROCCOLI AND MUSHROOMS

Cut 250 g (8 oz) broccoli into small florets. Heat 30 g (1 oz) butter and 1 clove crushed garlic in heavy-based frying pan. Add 4 sliced button mushrooms. Cook over medium heat 2 minutes or until tender. Remove from pan, set aside. Add broccoli, stir-fry 3–4 minutes until tender. Return mushrooms to pan, and stir until just heated through.

BROCCOLI WITH BACON AND PINE NUTS

Cut 250 g (8 oz) broccoli into small florets. Heat 2 teaspoons oil in wok or heavy-based frying pan. Add 2 rashers thinly sliced bacon. Cook over medium heat 2 minutes. Add broccoli, stir-fry 3–4 minutes until just tender. Stir in 2 tablespoons toasted pine nuts and 1 tablespoon chopped fresh chives. Serve hot.

BROCCOLI WITH MUSTARD BUTTER

Cut 250 g (8 oz) broccoli into medium florets. Steam broccoli until just tender. Combine 60 g (2 oz) softened butter, 2 teaspoons Dijon mustard and ground black pepper to taste. Mix well. Serve over hot broccoli.

*BROCCOLI WITH
MUSTARD BUTTER*

*BROCCOLI WITH BACON
AND PINE NUTS*

*BROCCOLI AND
MUSHROOMS*

butter and egg yolk that is served hot with grilled and roast meat, fish and chicken. It appeared in France during the reign of Henri IV and is named after his birthplace, Béarn, in the Pyrenees.

Béchamel Sauce A creamy sauce made with flour, butter and milk and served hot. The original Béchamel sauce was

named for the Marquis de Béchameil, a French financier, noted art lover and gourmet, who in the late 1600s became chief steward in the household of Louis XIV. The sauce was a marked departure from the coarse mixtures in use at the time, and has since become the basis of many other sauces. Béchamel is also known as white sauce.

Beef The meat from cattle raised for food. Although the domestication of cattle began some 10,000 years ago, they were bred primarily as working animals (in India the cow is sacred and

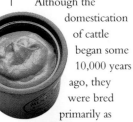

BEEF

ROAST BEEF WITH YORKSHIRE PUDDING

★★ *Preparation time:* 15 minutes
Total cooking time: 1½–2 hours
Serves 6

2 kg (4 lb) piece of sirloin on the bone	**Yorkshire Pudding**
½ teaspoon dry mustard	*¾ cup plain (all-purpose) flour*
½ teaspoon ground black pepper	*salt, to taste*
salt, to taste	*1 egg, lightly beaten*
60 g (2 oz) dripping or oil	*¼ cup (2 fl oz) water*
	½ cup (4 fl oz) milk
	30 g (1 oz) dripping or butter, melted

1 Preheat oven to moderate 180°C (350°F/Gas 4). Trim meat; score fat and rub surface with a mixture of mustard, pepper and salt. Heat dripping in frying pan until hot; place meat in pan, fat side down, seal quickly. Brown all sides.
2 Place meat on a roasting rack in a baking dish, fat side up. Roast meat for 25–30 minutes per 500 g (1 lb) for medium roast beef, or follow times indicated below. Allow the meat to stand for 15 minutes before carving.
3 To make Yorkshire Pudding: Sift flour and salt into a bowl. Add combined egg and water, and mix to a paste. Heat milk and pour into mixture; beat until smooth. Set aside. Pour dripping into 12-cup deep patty tray; heat in 210°C (415°F/Gas 6-7) oven for 5 minutes. Remove from oven. Spoon pudding batter into patty cups in tray; bake for 10–15 minutes or until puddings are puffed.

ABOUT ROASTING BEEF

Roast beef according to how well done you want it to be, using the following times as a guide (times given are per 500 g/1 lb of meat):
■ **Rare:** 20–25 minutes (60°C/140°F internal temperature on a meat thermometer);
■ **Medium:** 25–30 minutes (70°C/160°F internal temperature);
■ **Well done:** 30–35 minutes (75°C/170°F internal temperature).
■ If using a meat thermometer, insert it in the thickest part of the meat, away from fat or bone.

BRAISED OXTAIL

⭐ **Preparation time:** 15 minutes
Total cooking time: 2 hours 20 minutes
Serves 6

¼ cup (2 fl oz) oil	2 tablespoons plain (all-purpose) flour
16 small pieces oxtail, about 1.5 kg (3 lb)	3 cups (24 fl oz) beef stock
4 baby potatoes, peeled and quartered	1 teaspoon dried marjoram leaves
1 large onion, chopped	2 tablespoons worcestershire sauce
2 medium carrots, sliced	
250 g (8 oz) baby mushrooms, halved	

1 Preheat oven to moderate 180°C (350°F/Gas 4). Heat 2 tablespoons of oil in heavy-based pan. Cook the oxtail quickly in small batches over medium-high heat until well browned; place in a deep casserole dish; add potato.
2 Heat remaining oil in pan. Add onion and carrot, stir over medium heat 5 minutes. Place in casserole dish. Add mushrooms to pan, stir over medium heat 5 minutes. Stir in flour. Reduce heat to low and stir for 2 minutes.
3 Add stock gradually, stirring till liquid boils and thickens. Add marjoram and sauce. Pour mixture over ingredients in casserole dish. Transfer to oven. Cook, covered, for 1 hour 30 minutes. Stir, then cook, uncovered, for another 30 minutes.

OPPOSITE PAGE: ROAST BEEF WITH YORKSHIRE PUDDING. ABOVE: BRAISED OXTAIL

BEEF STOCK

Place about 500 g (1 lb) stewing beef, including bones, in a large heavy-based saucepan, add 2 litres (8 cups) water and bring very slowly to the boil without stirring (stirring will make the stock cloudy). Cover pan, reduce heat and simmer for 3–4 hours. Occasionally remove any scum that rises to the top with a slotted spoon. In last hour of cooking, add large pieces of carrot, leek, celery, whole onions and unpeeled whole garlic cloves (peeled garlic cooks to a puree and clouds stock). If desired, add a bouquet garni of bay leaf, thyme and parsley. When the stock has cooked, carefully strain the liquid through a fine sieve and into a large bowl. Remove any fat from surface with absorbent paper; cover and refrigerate (remaining fat will solidify on top and can be removed easily). Makes about 1.5 litres (6 cups).

ABOUT BEEF STOCK

◼ Good stock must be made from the finest fresh ingredients. It is a mistake to think that any meat and vegetables, or even leftover cooked meat, will give the same results.
◼ Stock will keep for one week in refrigerator, and for up to 4 months if frozen. To freeze, decide how stock will be used. If you are using it as the basis of a soup, freeze in a plastic container with a screw-top lid. For small quantities to flavour sauces or casseroles, or to cook vegetables in, freeze stock in ice-cube trays, remove when frozen and store in plastic bag in the freezer. Don't forget to label and date the bag.

its meat is not eaten). In the Middle Ages roast beef made its appearance in the banquet halls of England; the term 'Beefeater', now used for the Yeomen of the Guard in the Tower of London, originally described a well-fed live-in servant. In France, the eating of grilled beef seems to date from when English troops crossed the Channel for the Battle of Waterloo. The French today are the greatest per capita eaters of beef in Europe, while the Americans hold the world record for both production and consumption.

Good quality beef has a rich red colour, a fairly fine texture, shiny appearance, is firm to the touch and in the thicker parts has flecks of fat (marbling). Cuts vary from country to country. In general, the most tender meat comes from the upper back, and cuts requiring longer cooking come from the more heavily muscled areas of the legs and rear.

Beef Tea A nutritious drink prepared by slowly heating minced (ground) lean beef in water then straining off the juice.

Beef Wellington A cut of tender beef that is browned, topped with pâté, wrapped in pastry and baked. A popular dish for dinner parties.

BEEF WELLINGTON

⭐⭐ **Preparation time:** 25 minutes
Total cooking time: 50 minutes –
1 hour 35 minutes
Serves 6–8

1 kg (2 lb) beef fillet (tenderloin) or rib eye in one piece
freshly ground black pepper
1 tablespoon oil

2 tablespoons brandy
125 g (4 oz) peppercorn pâté
2 sheets frozen puff pastry, thawed
1 egg, lightly beaten

1 Preheat oven to moderately hot 210°C (415°F/Gas 6–7). Trim meat of excess fat and sinew; fold tail end under. Tie meat securely with string at regular intervals to help hold its shape; rub with pepper.

2 Heat oil in large, heavy-based pan. Add meat and cook over high heat, browning well all over to seal in juices. Remove pan from heat. Add brandy and ignite carefully, using a long match or taper. Shake pan until flames subside. Remove meat from pan and leave to cool. Remove string. Spread pâté over top and sides of beef.

3 Place pastry sheets on a lightly floured surface. Brush one edge with a little beaten egg and overlap the edge of the other sheet, pressing well to join. Place the beef on the pastry and fold pastry over to enclose the meat completely; trim excess pastry and use to decorate top, if desired. Brush edges of pastry with egg and seal; cut a few slits in top to allow steam to escape. Brush the top and sides with egg.

4 Transfer to a baking dish; cook for 45 minutes for a rare result, 1 hour for medium and 1 hour 30 minutes for well done. Remove from oven. Leave in a warm place for 10 minutes, lightly covered with foil. Cut into 2 cm (3/4 inch) thick slices and serve with horseradish cream made by combining 1 tablespoon bottled horseradish with 1 cup light sour cream.

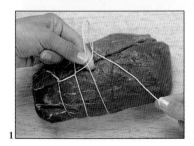

STEAK, ONION AND TOMATO PIES

⭐ ⭐ **Preparation time:** 10 minutes
Total cooking time: 2 hours
Makes 4

750 g (1¹/2 lb) chuck
  steak
plain (all-purpose) flour
2 tablespoons oil
1 large onion, thinly
  sliced
1¹/2 cups (12 fl oz) beef
  stock
1 teaspoon soy sauce

2 teaspoons cornflour
  (cornstarch)
1 tablespoon water
2 sheets ready-rolled
  shortcrust pastry
1 tomato, sliced
1 egg, lightly beaten
2 sheets ready-rolled puff
  pastry

1 Trim meat of excess fat and sinew. Cut meat
into 1 cm (¹/2 inch) cubes. Toss with flour in
plastic bag, shake off excess. Heat oil in a heavy-
based pan. Cook meat quickly in small batches
over medium-high heat until well browned; drain
on paper towels.
2 Add onion to pan, cook over medium heat
until soft. Return meat to pan. Add stock and soy
sauce. Bring to boil; reduce heat. Simmer,
covered, 1¹/4 hours, stirring occasionally, or until
tender. Blend cornflour and water in small jug or
bowl until smooth; add to pan. Simmer, stirring,
until thickened. Remove from heat, cool slightly.
3 Preheat oven to moderately hot 210°C
(415°F/Gas 6–7). Cut each pastry sheet in half
daigonally. Line four 12 cm (4³/4 inch) individual
pie tins with shortcrust pastry, trim edges. Place
one-quarter of the filling in each pastry case. Top

with tomato slices. Brush edges with a little
beaten egg, top with puff pastry, seal and trim
edges. Cut the remaining pastry scraps into leaf
shapes. Place on pies. Brush tops with egg, bake
for 25 minutes or until pastry is golden. Remove
pies from tins, place them on an oven tray and
bake for another 5 minutes or until the pastry
base is cooked through.

ROAST BEEF FILLET WITH EASY BEARNAISE SAUCE

⭐ **Preparation time:** 10 minutes
Total cooking time: 45 minutes –
1 hour 10 minutes
Serves 6

1.5 kg (3 lb) whole beef
  fillet (tenderloin)
freshly ground black
  pepper, to taste
1 tablespoon oil
30 g (1 oz) butter
1 clove garlic, crushed
1 cup (8 fl oz) water

Easy Béarnaise Sauce
2 bay leaves

¹/2 cup (4 fl oz) tarragon
  vinegar
2 teaspoons black
  peppercorns
4 spring onions
  (scallions), chopped
5 egg yolks, lightly
  beaten
250 g (8 oz) butter,
  melted

1 Preheat oven to moderately hot 210°C
(415°F/Gas 6-7). Trim beef fillet of excess fat and
sinew. Tie fillet securely with string at regular
intervals to retain its shape. Rub meat all over
with pepper.
2 Heat oil, butter and garlic in a deep baking dish
on top of the stove, add meat; brown it all over
on high heat. Place a rack in the dish and put the
meat on top; add the water to dish. Transfer to
oven. Roast meat for 45 minutes for a rare result,
1 hour for a medium result and 1 hour 10
minutes for well done. Baste meat occasionally
with pan juices. Remove from oven. Leave in a
warm place for 10 minutes, covered with foil.
Remove string from the meat before slicing.
3 To make Easy Béarnaise Sauce: Combine
bay leaves, vinegar, peppercorns and spring
onions in a small pan. Bring to boil, reduce heat
to a simmer and cook, uncovered, until liquid has
reduced to 2 tablespoonsful. Strain, reserving the
liquid. Place liquid and egg yolks in a food
processor or blender and process for 30 seconds.
With the motor constantly running, add melted
butter slowly in a thin stream, processing until all
butter is added. Serve Easy Béarnaise Sauce with
the sliced meat.

leaves, and not the root,
that were eaten (they can
be cooked in the same
way as spinach). The
present varieties are
thought to have been
developed by German
gardeners. By the
fifteenth century it was
known in France and
England. It is the chief
ingredient in the Eastern
European soup borscht
and is also used as a salad
vegetable.

Beignet Soufflé Small,
fluffy fritter made of
deep-fried choux pastry,
usually served with a
sweet sauce. The term
'beignet' also

refers
to food that has been
coated in batter and fried,
such as beignets
d'aubergines, eggplant
fritters, and beignets de
pommes, apple fritters.

Bel Paese A soft,
creamy, mild-tasting,
cow's milk cheese first
made in the Lombardy
area of Italy in the 1920s
and now produced in
other European countries
and in North America.
The name comes from
the Italian for 'beautiful
country'.

Besan Flour A pale
yellow flour made from
dried chick peas
(garbanzo beans) and
used in Indian cooking.
Besan flour is a source of
protein and is most often
used to make a batter for

pakoras, the Indian vegetable fritters.

Beurre Manié A paste of butter and flour, kneaded together, used to thicken soups, stews and sauces by whisking it in pellets into simmering liquid.

Bicarbonate of Soda (Baking Soda) A fine white powder that is the alkaline component of baking powder. When used on its own it has no leavening properties, but when combined with an acid or acid salt (such as cream of tartar, the other main ingredient of baking powder) and then moistened, it produces carbon dioxide.

Bigarade, Sauce An orange-flavoured sauce served with roast duck. Bigarade is French for the bitter Seville orange.

Bind To make a dry mixture hold together by moistening it with egg, milk, cream or sauce.

Biryani (Biriani) A Mongol dish from India consisting of layers of pilau rice and spicy lamb or chicken.

Biscuit (Cookie) A dry, flat cake, either sweet or savoury. The name comes from the French *bis* twice, *cuit* cooked, because they were originally returned to the oven to make them crisper and thus improve their keeping

BEEF IN BLACK BEAN SAUCE

Preparation time: 10 minutes
Total cooking time: 10 minutes
Serves 4

2 tablespoons canned salted black beans
1 medium onion
1 small red pepper (capsicum)
1 small green pepper (capsicum)
2 teaspoons cornflour (cornstarch)
½ cup (4 oz) beef stock

2 teaspoons soy sauce
1 teaspoon sugar
2 tablespoons oil
1 teaspoon finely crushed garlic
¼ teaspoon ground black pepper
410 g (13 oz) rump or fillet (tenderloin) steak, finely sliced

1 Rinse black beans in several changes of water. Drain and mash black beans. Cut the onion into wedges. Halve the capsicum, discard seeds and cut into small pieces. Dissolve cornflour in stock, add soy and sugar.

2 Heat one tablespoon of the oil in a wok or heavy-based frying pan, swirling gently to coat base and side. Add garlic, pepper, onion and pepper and stir-fry over high heat for one minute; remove to a bowl.

3 Add remaining tablespoon of oil, swirling gently to coat base and side of wok. Add beef and stir-fry over a high heat for 2 minutes, until it changes colour. Add black beans, cornflour mixture and vegetables. Stir until sauce boils and thickens. Serve with steamed rice.

BEEF POT ROAST WITH EGGPLANT (AUBERGINE) AND SWEET POTATO

Preparation time: 20 minutes
Total cooking time: 1 hour 15 minutes
Serves 4

1 kg (2 lb) piece topside (top round) beef
2 tablespoons oil
1 cup (8 fl oz) beef stock
1 medium onion, sliced
1 clove garlic, crushed
4 large tomatoes, peeled, seeded and chopped
1 teaspoon ground cumin
1 teaspoon turmeric
1 teaspoon finely grated lemon rind

2 tablespoons lemon juice
1 medium eggplant (aubergine), cut into 3 cm (1¼ inch) cubes
1 medium sweet potato, halved, cut into 3 cm (1¼ inch) cubes
2 tablespoons plain (all-purpose) flour
3 tablespoons water
1 tablespoon chopped fresh coriander

1 Trim meat. Heat oil in deep, heavy-based pan, add meat and brown over medium-high heat.
2 Remove pan from heat, add stock, onion, garlic, tomato, cumin, turmeric, lemon rind and juice. Return pan to low heat. Cover, slowly bring to simmering point and simmer 45 minutes.
3 Add eggplant and sweet potato, cook for 30 minutes, uncovered, until meat and vegetables are tender. Remove meat from sauce. Cover with foil for 10 minutes before slicing. Add combined flour and water to sauce with coriander, stir over medium heat until sauce boils and thickens. Cook 3 minutes. Pour over sliced meat to serve.

PIQUANT COUNTRY BEEF WITH HERB SCONES (BISCUITS)

 ★★ **Preparation time:** 30 minutes
Total cooking time: 2 hours
10 minutes
Serves 4

1 kg (2 lb) chuck steak	2 teaspoons sweet chilli sauce
¼ cup plain (all-purpose) flour	
3 tablespoons oil	**Herb Scones (Biscuits)**
4 medium onions, roughly chopped	2 cups self-raising flour
	30 g (1 oz) butter
2 cloves garlic, crushed	2 tablespoons chopped fresh chives
⅓ cup plum jam	
⅓ cup (2½ fl oz) brown vinegar	2 tablespoons chopped fresh parsley
1 cup (8 fl oz) beef stock	¾ cup (6 fl oz) milk

1 Preheat oven to moderate 180°C (350°F/Gas 4). Trim meat of excess fat and sinew. Cut into 3 cm (1¼ inch) cubes. Toss in flour. Heat 2 tablespoons oil in a heavy-based pan. Cook meat quickly, in small batches, over medium-high heat until well browned. Drain meat on absorbent paper.

2 Heat remaining oil in pan, add onion and garlic and cook, stirring, for 3 minutes or until soft. Combine onion mixture and meat in large bowl.

3 Add jam, vinegar, stock and chilli sauce, mix well. Transfer to ovenproof dish. Cover and bake for 1 hour 30 minutes or until meat is tender.

4 Uncover dish, turn oven up to hot 240°C (475°F/Gas 9). Place Herb Scones on top of meat, bake, uncovered, for 30 minutes or until scones are golden brown.

5 To make Herb Scones: Sift flour into a bowl, rub in butter until mixture resembles fine breadcrumbs. Stir in chives and parsley. Add milk, stir until just combined. Turn onto a lightly floured surface, knead until smooth. Press dough out to a 4 cm (1½ inch) thick round; using a pastry cutter, cut into 5 cm (2 inch) rounds.

Note: Casserole can be cooked 2 days ahead without the scones and refrigerated, or frozen for up to 2 weeks.

VARIATION

■ CHEESE SCONES: Reduce flour by ¼ cup and replace with the same quantity of grated parmesan cheese. Add 2 finely chopped spring onions.

OPPOSITE PAGE: BEEF POT ROAST.
ABOVE: PIQUANT COUNTRY BEEF

properties. In the United States the term biscuit is used for small, light, bread-like cakes (similar to plain scones) which are served warm, split open and spread with butter. Savoury biscuits are called crackers in the United States and some other parts of the world. Biscuits have come a long way since their early use as a staple (but apparently barely edible) item in the provisions of soldiers and sailors (Pliny felt that those issued to the Roman legions would last for centuries and in the army of Louis XIV biscuit rations were called *pain de pierre* 'stone bread').

Bisque A rich, thick soup made of pureed shellfish, stock and cream. Originally bisques were made of boiled game or fowl, and it was only after the seventeenth century that shellfish became the principal ingredient of the dish. The most popular bisques are crab, lobster, prawn (shrimp) and, especially in the United States, clam. They are served as a first course, not a main meal.

parboiled before being added to stir-fry dishes; it is often cooked with beans or meat to off-set its somewhat bitter flavour.

Blackberry The black, juicy berry of a prickly shrub. Freshly picked, they can be eaten with a dusting of sugar and a little cream, or can be cooked as jams, jellies, preserves and fillings for tarts and pies. The blackberry is also known as a bramble.

Black Bread See Rye Bread.

Blackcurrant The black, rather sour, juicy fruit of a northern European shrub. The blackcurrant is the basis of the French liqueur cassis, flavours cordials and syrups, and is cooked as jams, jellies and fillings for tarts.

Black Forest Cake A rich chocolate cake moistened with kirsch, filled and topped

with whipped cream and decorated with cherries and shaved chocolate.

BEETROOT (BEETS)

SPICED BAKED BEETROOT (BEETS)

 Preparation time: 15 minutes
Total cooking time: 1 hour 25 minutes
Serves 6

12 small beetroot (beets), about 1.2 kg (2½ lb)	½ teaspoon ground cardamom
2 tablespoons olive oil	½ teaspoon nutmeg
1 teaspoon ground cumin	3 teaspoons sugar
1 teaspoon ground coriander	1 tablespoon red wine vinegar

1 Preheat oven to moderate 180°C (350°F/Gas 4). Brush a baking tray with oil or melted butter. Trim leafy tops from beetroot, wash thoroughly. Place on tray and bake 1 hour 15 minutes, until very tender. Cool slightly. Peel away skins, trim tops and tails.
2 Heat oil in a large pan. Add spices and cook one minute, stirring constantly, over medium heat. Add sugar and red wine vinegar, stir for 2–3 minutes, until sugar dissolves.
3 Add beetroot to pan, reduce heat to low and stir gently for 5 minutes, until beetroot is well glazed. Serve warm or cold with hot or cold roast meats or poultry.

Note: This dish can be cooked up to 2 days ahead. Store in a covered container in the refrigerator until needed.

BEETROOT (BEET) SALAD

 Preparation time: 25 minutes
Total cooking time: nil
Serves 4-6

3 whole fresh beetroot (beets), peeled and grated	2 teaspoons grated orange rind
2 large carrots, peeled and grated	1 tablespoon tahini paste
⅓ cup (2½ fl oz) orange juice	½ small red chilli, finely chopped
	1 tablespoon toasted sesame seeds

1 Combine the grated beetroot and carrot in a large bowl.
2 For dressing, combine orange juice, rind, tahini paste and chilli in a small bowl. Mix ingredients well, using a wire whisk.
3 Pour dressing over beetroot mixture. Toss well and serve sprinkled with sesame seeds.

BORSCHT

 Preparation time: 5 minutes
Total cooking time: 1 hour 15 minutes
Serves 8

1 kg (2 lb) shin (shank) of beef	2 carrots, peeled, cut into thin strips
2 litres (8 cups) water	750 g (1½ lb) beetroot (beets), cut into thin strips
1 onion, chopped	
3 bay leaves	2 teaspoons vinegar
1 teaspoon whole allspice	freshly ground pepper
2 tomatoes, peeled and chopped	¼ cup chopped parsley
2 potatoes, peeled, cut into thin strips	2 tablespoons snipped fresh dill
1 small cabbage, shredded	

1 Put beef, water, onion, bay leaves and allspice into a large saucepan; bring to boil. Skim if necessary and simmer, covered, for one hour or until tender.
2 While meat is cooking, use a sharp knife to cut vegetables rather than grating them (this would make soup cloudy). When meat is cooked, remove from pot. Cut thick strips of meat from bone, return them to pot. Add vegetables; boil, uncovered, for about 15 minutes (if lid is left on, soup will not retain its bright attractive colour).
3 Stir in vinegar, pepper, parsley and dill. Serve hot with black bread and a spoonful of whipped cream with horseradish cream if desired.

ABOVE: SPICED BAKED BEETROOT. OPPOSITE PAGE: SUNFLOWER AND PARMESAN BISCUITS

BISCUITS
SAVOURY (CRACKERS)

SUNFLOWER AND PARMESAN BISCUITS

Preparation time: 30 minutes
Total cooking time: 10–15 minutes
Makes 30

150 g (5 oz) unsalted
(sweet) butter
3/4 cup grated parmesan
cheese
1/3 cup grated cheddar
cheese

1 1/4 cups plain (all-
purpose) flour
2–3 teaspoons lemon-
pepper seasoning
1/4 cup sunflower seeds
1/4 cup grated parmesan
cheese, extra

1 Preheat oven to moderate 180°C (350°F/Gas 4). Line 2 oven trays with baking paper. Using electric beaters, beat butter until light and creamy. Add parmesan and cheddar cheeses and beat until combined.

2 Using a metal spoon, fold in sifted flour and lemon pepper seasoning. Add sunflower seeds. Combine with well-floured hands. Turn onto a lightly floured surface and knead for 2–3 minutes or until smooth.

3 Roll dough between two sheets of baking paper to a thickness of 5 mm (1/4 inch). Cut into 4 cm (1 1/2 inch) squares. Place on prepared trays, allowing room for spreading. Sprinkle with parmesan cheese. Bake for 10–15 minutes or until golden. Cool on trays.

ABOUT BISCUITS

■ Have ingredients at room temperature unless otherwise stated. Do not open oven door until at least two-thirds of the way through baking.

minutes, or until golden. Cool on trays for 2–3 minutes. Transfer to a wire rack to cool completely. Store in an airtight container.

SAVOURY STRIPS

Preparation time: 25 minutes
Total cooking time: 15–20 minutes
Makes about 60

1/2 cup plain (all-
purpose) flour, sifted
1/2 cup self-raising flour,
sifted
1 egg
1/4 cup (2 fl oz) beer
1/2 teaspoon salt
1/4 teaspoon paprika
1/4 teaspoon cayenne
1 1/2 cups grated, matured
cheddar cheese
extra beer, for brushing
coarse salt, for sprinkling

1 Combine sifted flours in a mixing bowl with salt, paprika, cayenne and cheese. Beat egg lightly in a small bowl and stir in beer. Pour over dry ingredients and mix to a firm dough.
2 Knead dough lightly on a floured surface. Roll out thinly and cut into 1 x 5 cm (1/2 x 2 inch) wide strips. Place on an ungreased baking tray. Brush lightly with extra beer. Sprinkle with salt.
3 Bake at 180°C (350°F/Gas 4) for 15–20 minutes, or until golden. Cool on trays for 2–3

HERBED PRETZELS

Preparation time: 25 minutes
Total cooking time: 10–15 minutes
Makes about 25

40 g (1 1/2 oz) butter,
softened
2 sheets ready-rolled puff
pastry, thawed
1 tablespoon each
chopped parsley, chives
and rosemary
1 clove garlic, crushed
pepper to taste
20 g (1/2 oz) extra butter,
melted
2 tablespoons poppy seeds

1 Combine butter, herbs, garlic and pepper in a small bowl, and mix well.
2 Spread mixture evenly over one sheet of pastry, coating completely. Top with remaining pastry. Press edges to seal. Brush top with melted butter. Sprinkle with poppy seeds.
3 Cut pastry into 2 cm (3/4 inch) wide strips. Twist each strip from both ends to make a spiral. Place on an ungreased baking tray.
4 Bake at 230°C (450°F/Gas 8) for 10–15 minutes, or until golden brown. Store in an airtight container. Serve warm or cold.

Blanch To lightly cook food in boiling water. This is done to preserve the colour of green vegetables before home freezing; to remove excess salt, fat, strong tastes and odours; or to remove bacteria. The term is also used for the process of covering fruit and nuts with boiling water in order to loosen skins for peeling.

Blancmange A dessert made from a mixture of cornflour (cornstarch) and milk that has been cooked, sweetened and flavoured, and set in a mould.

Blanquette A stew, usually of veal, lamb or chicken, in which braised meat is covered in a white sauce and enriched with milk or cream and egg yolk.

Blend To combine two or more ingredients into a smooth mixture.

Black Pudding (Blood Sausage) A sausage traditionally made of seasoned pig's blood and fat mixed with finely ground cereals, cooked, and then either re-boiled or sliced and grilled (broiled), or fried. It dates from the time of ancient Greece.

Blini A small, thick pancake made from a yeast dough containing buckwheat flour. Originating in Russia, traditionally it is served topped with sour cream and caviar or smoked salmon.

Blintz A pancake with either a savoury or sweet filling. It is first cooked on one side until just set, the filling is placed in the centre, and the pancake is folded over and the edges pressed together before the whole is refried. Blintzes are a traditional Jewish food.

Blueberry The small, dark, purplish-blue berry of an evergreen shrub related to heather, native to North America. It is also known as a huckleberry and can still be collected in the wild. North America produces some 75 per cent of the world's blueberry crop. They can be eaten raw, cooked as a pie filling or added to muffin batter.

Blue Vein Cheese A soft, usually cow's milk, cheese with veins of blue-green mould culture criss-crossing the interior. It is made by adding mould spores to

BISCUITS (COOKIES)

MELTING MOMENTS

★

Preparation time: 15 minutes
Total cooking time: 15 minutes
Makes 45

*180 g (5³/4 oz) unsalted
(sweet) butter
¹/3 cup icing (confectioners)
sugar
1 teaspoon vanilla essence*

*¹/3 cup cornflour (cornstarch)
1 cup plain (all-purpose)
flour
105 g (3¹/2 oz) glacé
cherries*

1 Preheat oven to moderate 180°C (350°F/Gas 4). Line a 32 x 28 cm (13 x 11 inch) biscuit (oven) tray with baking paper. Using electric beaters, beat butter, sugar and essence in a small mixing bowl until light and creamy. Using a flat-bladed knife, stir in sifted flours until just combined and mixture is smooth.
2 Spoon mixture into a piping bag fitted with a 1 cm (¹/2 inch) fluted nozzle and pipe 4 cm (1¹/2 inch) rosettes of mixture onto prepared tray.
3 Top each rosette with a half a cherry. Bake for 15 minutes or until lightly golden and crisp. Transfer biscuits onto wire rack to cool.

Note: Sandwich together two Melting Moments with raspberry jam. Decorate biscuits by dusting with icing (confectioners) sugar. Soft butter icing can be piped onto biscuits to decorate, or they can be sandwiched with butter icing as well as jam. Drizzle melted chocolate on top or dip biscuits in chocolate.

FLAKED ALMOND TUILES

★
★★

Preparation time: 8 minutes + 2 hours standing
Total cooking time: 5 minutes each tray
Makes 22

*²/3 cup plain (all-purpose)
flour
¹/2 cup caster (superfine)
sugar
60 g (2 oz) unsalted
(sweet) butter, melted*

*2 egg whites, lightly
beaten
¹/4 teaspoon almond
essence
¹/2 cup toasted flaked
almonds*

1 Brush two 32 x 28 cm (13 x 11 inch) biscuit trays with oil or melted butter, line base with paper; grease paper. Sift flour into medium mixing bowl; add sugar. Make a well in the

ABOVE: MELTING MOMENTS.
OPPOSITE PAGE: FLORENTINES

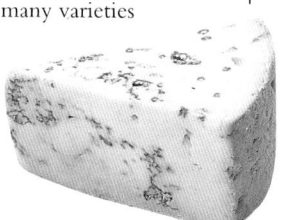

centre. Add butter, egg whites and essence to bowl. Using a wooden spoon, stir until well combined. Cover mixture with plastic wrap; allow to rest for 2 hours.

2 Heat oven to moderate 180°C (350°F/Gas 4). Drop 2 level teaspoons of mixture at a time onto prepared trays. Spread mixture to form rounds 10–12 cm (4–4¾ inch) in diameter. Sprinkle each round with flaked almonds.

3 Bake biscuits for 5 minutes or until lightly golden. Remove from oven; stand on tray for 30 seconds. Carefully loosen and lift biscuits from tray and drape over a bottle or rolling pin to curl.

FLORENTINES

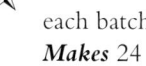 **Preparation time:** 25 minutes
Total cooking time: 7 minutes each batch
Makes 24

¼ cup plain (all-purpose) flour

2 tablespoons chopped walnuts

2 tablespoons chopped flaked almonds

2 tablespoons finely chopped glacé cherries

2 tablespoons finely chopped mixed peel

75 g (2½ oz) unsalted (sweet) butter

¼ cup soft brown sugar

185 g (6 oz) dark (semi-sweet) chocolate, chopped

1 Preheat oven to moderate 180°C (350°F/Gas 4). Line a 32 x 28 cm (13 x 11 inch) biscuit (oven) tray with baking paper. Sift flour into medium mixing bowl. Add walnuts, almonds, cherries and mixed peel. Stir to combine. Make a well in the centre. Combine butter and sugar in a small pan. Stir over low heat until butter has melted and sugar has dissolved; remove from heat.

2 Add butter mixture to the dry ingredients. Using a wooden spoon, stir until just combined; do not overbeat. Drop heaped teaspoonsful of mixture onto prepared trays, leaving about 8 cm (3 inches) between them. Press the mixture into neat 5 cm (2 inch) rounds. Bake for 7 minutes. Remove tray from oven. While biscuits are still soft, use a flat-bladed knife to push them into neat rounds. Cool on tray for 5 minutes before transferring to a wire rack and allowing to cool thoroughly.

3 Place chocolate in heatproof bowl. Stand over simmering water and stir until chocolate is melted and smooth. Using a flat-bladed knife, spread chocolate on the underside of Florentines. Draw the tines of a fork across the chocolate to make the characteristic wavy pattern. Place biscuits chocolate-side up on a wire rack to set.

Note: These are best made on the day of serving and are perfect to serve with after-dinner coffee.

maturing curds, and then aiding their spread by salting and perforating the curds. This type of cheese was first made in the tiny French village of Roquefort some two thousand years ago. The many varieties

include Gorgonzola, Danish Blue, Roquefort and Stilton.

Bok Choy A leafy vegetable with thick, fleshy white stalks. It is native to southern China, where it has been cultivated for more than 3000 years. Bok choy is used there as the staple green accompaniment for meat, poultry and bean curd

dishes. Its name comes from the Chinese words *bok,* white, and *choy,* vegetable; it is also known as Chinese white cabbage.

Bolognaise Sauce A thick meat and tomato sauce, served with pasta (usually spaghetti), originally from the city of Bologna in northern Italy. In Italy the sauce is known as *ragù* and traditionally contains

GINGERBREAD FAMILIES

★★ ***Preparation time:*** 30 minutes +
15 minutes refrigeration
Total cooking time: 10 minutes
Makes 16

125 g (4 oz) unsalted
(sweet) butter
1/3 cup soft dark brown or
soft brown sugar
1/4 cup golden syrup
(light corn syrup)
1 egg, lightly beaten
2 cups plain (all-purpose)
flour
1/4 cup self-raising flour
1 tablespoon ground ginger
1 teaspoon bicarbonate of
soda (baking soda)
1 tablespoon currants

Icing
1 egg white
1/2 teaspoon lemon juice
1 1/4 cups icing
(confectioners) sugar,
sifted
assorted food colourings

1 Preheat oven to moderate 180°C (350°F/Gas 4). Line 2 or 3 oven trays with baking paper. Using electric beaters, beat the butter, sugar and syrup in a small mixing bowl until light and creamy. Add egg gradually, beating mixture thoroughly after each addition.

2 Transfer mixture to large bowl. Sift dry ingredients onto butter mixture. Mix with a knife until just combined. Combine dough with well-floured hand. Turn onto a well-floured surface and knead for 1–2 minutes or until smooth.

3 Line a large chopping board with baking paper. Roll out dough on board to 5 mm (1/4 inch) thickness. Refrigerate (on board) for 15 minutes so dough is firm enough to cut.

4 Cut dough into shapes with 13 cm (5 1/4 inch) gingerbread people cutter. Press remaining dough together and re-roll; cut out shapes. Place biscuits on prepared trays. Use currants for eyes and noses on the gingerbread figures. Bake for 10 minutes or until they are lightly browned. Remove from oven and cool on trays.

5 To make Icing: Place egg white in small dry mixing bowl. Using electric beaters, beat egg white until foamy. Add lemon juice and icing sugar gradually. Beat until thick and creamy. Divide icing into several bowls. Tint mixture with desired food colourings. Spoon into small paper icing bags, seal open ends. Snip tips off piping bags; pipe faces and clothing onto gingerbread people.

Note: When the icing is completely dry, gingerbread families may be stored in an airtight container for up to 3 days.

chopped ham, beef, lean pork, chicken livers, several vegetables and white wine.

Bombay Duck A variety of fish found in the Arabian Sea, particularly in the waters off Bombay. It is a predatory shoal fish caught in large numbers during the monsoon season, when it swims close to the surface (a habit said to be the origin of the 'duck' in its name). In India it is eaten fresh; in the West it is best known in its dried and salted form, deep-fried and served as a curry accompaniment.

Bombe A frozen dessert set in a mould, usually consisting of an outer layer of ice-cream and a centre of custard, mousse, fruit puree or cream. It is named after the spherical mould in which the dessert was originally made.

Borage A herb with long, pointed, greyish-green leaves, native to the Middle East and the

Mediterranean region, where it still grows wild. Borage has a cucumber-like taste. Young leaves are added to drinks and used in spring salads; more mature leaves are cooked like spinach. The blue, star-shaped flowers are often used as a garnish.

Bordelaise, à la A French term for a dish of roasted or grilled (broiled) meat served with a sauce made from a reduction of red wine, bone marrow, chopped shallots, thyme, bay leaf and pepper; a sauce made with white wine is served with seafood. The cooking style originated in the Bordeaux region of France.

Börek A pastry with a savoury filling, traditionally a cheese mixture, served hot as an appetiser. Böreks are usually in small cigar-shapes and tiny half moons, and are originally from Turkey.

Borlotti Bean A dried bean, slightly kidney-shaped and pale brown in colour with darker speckled markings. It has a smooth texture and ham-like flavour when cooked, and is used in soups, stews or casseroles, or cooked, dressed and mixed with onion rings or tuna and served as a salad.

CHOCOLATE CHIP COOKIES

Preparation time: 10 minutes
Total cooking time: 15 minutes
Makes 24

150 g (4¾ oz) unsalted (sweet) butter
¼ cup soft brown sugar
⅓ cup caster (superfine) sugar
1 egg yolk
1 teaspoon vanilla essence
1½ cups self-raising flour
1 cup choc bits (chocolate chips)

1 Preheat oven to moderate 180°C (350°F/Gas 4). Line an 32 x 28 cm (13 x 11 inch) oven tray with baking paper. Using electric beaters, beat butter, sugars and yolk in small mixing bowl until light and creamy. Add essence, beat until combined.

2 Transfer mixture to large mixing bowl; add flour and two-thirds of the bits. Using a metal spoon, stir until ingredients are just combined.

3 Using fingers, press mixture together to form a soft dough. Roll one tablespoon of mixture at a time into a ball.

4 Press remaining chocolate bits firmly on top of balls. Arrange on prepared tray, allowing room for spreading. Bake 15 minutes or until crisp and lightly browned. Cool biscuits on trays.

MONTE CREAMS

Preparation time: 30 minutes
Total cooking time: 15–20 minutes
Makes 25

125 g (4 oz) unsalted (sweet) butter
½ cup caster (superfine) sugar
¼ cup milk
1½ cups self-raising flour, sifted
¼ cup custard powder, sifted
⅓ cup desiccated coconut

Filling
75 g (2½ oz) unsalted (sweet) butter
⅔ cup icing (confectioners) sugar
2 teaspoons milk
⅓ cup strawberry jam

1 Preheat oven to 180°C (350°F/Gas 4). Line two 32 x 28 cm (13 x 11 inch) biscuit (oven) trays with baking paper. Using electric beaters, beat butter and sugar in a medium mixing bowl until light and creamy. Add milk, beat until combined. Add flour, custard powder and coconut and mix to form a soft dough.

2 Roll two teaspoonsful of mixture at a time into a ball. Place on prepared trays. Press with a fork. Dip fork in custard powder occasionally to prevent sticking. Bake for 15–20 minutes, until just golden. Transfer to a wire rack to cool completely before filling.

3 To make Filling: Using electric beaters, beat butter and icing sugar until light and creamy. Add milk and beat until combined. Spread one biscuit with about half a teaspoon of the butter mixture, and one with about half a teaspoon of jam; sandwich together.

ABOVE: MONTE CREAMS;
RIGHT: CHOCOLATE CHIP COOKIES.
OPPOSITE PAGE: CHOC-MINT SWIRLS

Borscht A beetroot (beet) soup, originally from eastern Europe, which became popular in France following the arrival of Russian émigrés in the 1920s. Served hot or chilled, traditionally it is topped with sour cream.

Bouchée A small, round, puff or choux pastry case, filled shortly before serving with a hot or cold savoury or sweet mixture.

Bouillabaisse A soup made from a variety of fish (traditionally white-fleshed rock fish) and shellfish and usually containing tomato, onion, garlic, herbs, wine and saffron. The name of the dish refers to the rapid cooking method used and comes from the French bouillir, to boil, and abaisser, to reduce: 'when it boils, lower the heat'. It was originally served as two courses: first the broth, usually poured over dried home-made bread, then the seafood.

Bouillon An unclarified stock or broth made by

CHOC-MINT SWIRLS

 **Preparation time:** 30 minutes
Total cooking time: 15 minutes
Makes 22

65 g (2¼ oz) unsalted
    (sweet) butter
¼ cup caster (superfine)
    sugar
½ cup plain (all-purpose)
    flour
⅓ cup self-raising flour
2 tablespoons cocoa powder
1–2 tablespoons milk

1⅓ cups icing
    (confectioners) sugar
few drops peppermint
    essence
22 choc bits (chocolate
    chips)
1 teaspoon icing
    (confectioners) sugar,
    extra
1 teaspoon cocoa powder

Topping
100 g (3⅓ oz) unsalted
    (sweet) butter, extra

1 Preheat oven to 180°C (350°F/Gas 4). Line two 32 x 28 cm (13 x 11 inch) biscuit (oven) trays with baking paper. Beat butter and sugar in until light and creamy. Add sifted flours, cocoa and milk. Stir with a flat-bladed knife until mixture forms a soft dough. Turn onto a piece of baking paper; knead 1 minute or until smooth.
2 Roll dough out to 5 mm (¼ inch) thickness. Cut into rounds, using a 4 cm (1½ inch) plain biscuit cutter. Place on prepared tray and bake for 15 minutes. Transfer to a wire rack to cool.
3 To make Topping: Beat butter until soft. Add icing sugar and beat until creamy and light. Add essence; beat until combined. When biscuits are cool, use a piping bag fitted with a large fluted nozzle to pipe a flower of peppermint cream onto each biscuit. Place a choc bit in the centre of each flower. Dust with one teaspoon each of icing sugar and cocoa powder, sifted together.

GINGERNUTS

 **Preparation time:** 15 minutes
Total cooking time: 15 minutes
Makes 55

2 cups plain (all-purpose)
    flour
½ teaspoon bicarbonate of
    soda (baking soda)
1 tablespoon ground
    ginger
½ teaspoon mixed spice

125 g (4 oz) unsalted
    (sweet) butter
1 cup soft brown sugar
¼ cup (2 fl oz) boiling
    water
1 tablespoon golden syrup
    (light corn syrup)

1 Preheat oven to moderate 180°C (350°F/Gas 4). Line two 32 x 28 cm (13 x 11 inch) biscuit (oven) trays with baking paper. Sift flour with remaining dry ingredients into a large mixing bowl; add chopped butter and sugar. Using fingertips, rub butter into flour for 3 minutes or until mixture is fine and crumbly.
2 Place boiling water in a small jug, add golden syrup and stir until dissolved. Add to flour mixture and mix to a soft dough.
3 Roll 2 teaspoonsful of mixture one at a time into a ball. Place on prepared trays and flatten out slightly with fingertips. Bake for 15 minutes. Cool biscuits on trays for 10 minutes before transferring to a wire rack to cool.

simmering meat, chicken, fish or vegetables in water. The strained liquid may be served as is, or used as a base for soups and sauces.

Bouquet Garni A bundle of herbs, either tied together or enclosed in a small muslin (cheesecloth) bag, used to flavour soups, stews and casseroles and removed after cooking. It usually contains thyme, bay leaf and parsley; other ingredients can include rosemary, garlic, leek, fennel or sage.

Bourguignonne, à la French term for a dish slowly cooked with red wine, onions and mushrooms, as *boeuf bourguignonne*.

Bourride A thick soup made with white-fleshed fish and flavoured with aïoli, originally from Provence, in France.

Boysenberry The large, juicy, purplish-black fruit of a hybrid of the blackberry, loganberry and raspberry developed in California in the 1920s by Rudolph Boysen. It is cultivated in North America, Australia and New Zealand. Boysenberries can be eaten fresh, cooked as jam or as a filling for pies and tarts.

Brains A white offal or variety meat, usually

BISCUITS

Bran The husk or inner casing of wheat and other cereal grains, removed during the refining of white flour. Bran is a source of dietary fibre and has a high vitamin B and phosphorus content.

Brandade A puree of salt cod, olive oil and milk, eaten hot; it was a specialty of the town of Nîmes, in southern France. Garlic is added to the mixture in some regions. Its name comes from a Provençal word, *brandar, to stir.*

Brandy A spirit distilled from wine and used in cooking to flavour a variety of sweet and savoury dishes including sauces, casseroles, pâtés and terrines, consommés, fruit cakes and fruit desserts, and in flambés.

Brawn A mixture of stewed boned meat flavoured with seasonings and spices, and set in aspic, prepared from the cooking liquid. It is sliced and served

lamb and calf brains, which provide a soft pale meat with a high fat

---

AMARETTI

★ ★ **Preparation time:** 15 minutes +
1 hour standing
Total cooking time: 15–20 minutes
Makes 40

1 tablespoon plain (all-purpose) flour
125 g (4 oz) ground almonds
1 tablespoon cornflour (cornstarch)
1 teaspoon ground cinnamon
2 egg whites
¼ cup icing (confectioners) sugar

1 teaspoon grated lemon rind
⅔ cup caster (superfine) sugar

1 Line a 32 x 28 cm (13 x 11 inch) biscuit (oven) tray with baking paper. Sift plain flour, cornflour, cinnamon and half the sugar into a large bowl; add lemon rind and ground almonds.

2 Place the egg whites in small, dry mixing bowl. Using electric beaters, beat egg whites until firm peaks form. Add reserved one-third cup sugar gradually, beating constantly until mixture is thick and glossy and all the sugar has dissolved. Using a metal spoon, fold white mixture into dry ingredients. Stir until ingredients are just combined and mixture forms a soft dough.

3 Roll 2 level teaspoons of mixture at a time with oiled or wet hands into a ball. Arrange on prepared tray, allowing room for spreading. Set tray aside, uncovered, for 1 hour before baking.

4 Heat oven to moderate 180°C (350°F/Gas 4). Sift icing sugar liberally over biscuits. Bake for 15–20 minutes or until crisp and lightly browned. Transfer biscuits to wire rack to cool.

BRANDY SNAPS WITH COFFEE LIQUEUR CREAM

★ **Preparation time:** 12 minutes +
★ ★ 1 hour standing
Total cooking time: 6 minutes each tray
Makes 25

60 g (2 oz) unsalted (sweet) butter
2 tablespoons golden syrup (light corn syrup)
⅓ cup soft brown sugar, lightly packed
¼ cup plain (all-purpose) flour
1½ teaspoons ground ginger

Coffee Liqueur Cream
⅔ cup (5 fl oz) cream
1 tablespoon icing (confectioners) sugar, sifted
1 teaspoon instant coffee granules
1 tablespoon coffee liqueur
80 g (2½ oz) dark (semi-sweet) chocolate, melted for decorating

1 Preheat oven to moderate 180°C (350°F/Gas 4). Line two 32 x 28 cm (13 x 11 inch) biscuit (oven) trays with baking paper. Combine butter, syrup and sugar in a small pan. Stir over low heat until butter has melted and sugar has dissolved; remove from heat. Add sifted flour and ginger to pan. Using a wooden spoon, stir until well combined; do not overbeat.

2 Bake in batches. Drop three or four level teaspoonful of mixture, about 13 cm (5 inches) apart, onto trays. Spread into 8 cm (3 inch) rounds. Bake 6 minutes or until lightly browned.

3 Stand biscuits on trays for 30 seconds. Carefully lift a biscuit from tray and wrap it around the handle of a wooden spoon while still hot; leave to cool. Repeat process with remaining biscuits.

4 To make Coffee Liqueur Cream: Combine all ingredients in a small mixing bowl; stir until just combined. Cover with plastic wrap and refrigerate for one hour. Using electric beaters, beat until mixture is thick and forms stiff peaks. Fill brandy snaps with Coffee Liqueur Cream and pipe or drizzle with melted chocolate.

Note: Store brandy snaps in an airtight container for up to 2 days, or freeze for up to one month without filling. To fill, spoon cream into a small paper icing bag. Seal open end and snip off tip. Pipe into brandy snaps.

ABOVE: ANZAC BISCUITS.
OPPOSITE PAGE: LEBKUCHEN

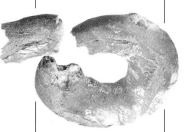

Brawn was originally made solely from the meat from a pig's head (excluding the brain)—hence its French name *fromage de tête*, head cheese.

Brazil Nut The hard-shelled, creamy-fleshed, nut of a tall tree native to tropical South America. Most of the world's supply comes from trees growing in the wild along the Amazon. Brazil nuts can be eaten fresh.

Bread A food made of a kneaded mixture of flour and water, usually with the addition of a leaven (raising agent), which is then baked. Flat cakes of grain pastes cooked on hot stones (unleavened bread) are the oldest known form of prepared food, dating from more than 10,000 years ago; varieties of unleavened bread are still made in India and the Middle East. The Egyptians are thought to have been the

---

LEBRUCHEN

 Preparation time: 25 minutes
Total cooking time: 25 minutes
Makes 35

2½ cups plain (all-purpose) flour
½ cup cornflour (cornstarch)
2 teaspoons cocoa powder
1 teaspoon mixed spice
1 teaspoon ground cinnamon
½ teaspoon ground nutmeg

105 g (3½ oz) unsalted (sweet) butter
¾ cup golden syrup (light corn syrup)
2 tablespoons milk
155 g (5 oz) white chocolate melts
¼ teaspoon mixed spice, extra

1 Preheat oven to moderate 180°C (350°F/Gas 4). Line a 32 x 28 cm (13 x 11 inch) biscuit (oven) tray with baking paper. Sift flours, cocoa and spices into large bowl. Make well in centre.
2 Combine butter, syrup and milk in small pan. Stir over low heat until butter is melted and mixture smooth; remove from heat.
3 Add butter mixture to dry ingredients. Stir well with a knife to form soft dough. Knead on lightly floured surface 1 minute. Shape dough into a ball.
4 Roll dough to 1 cm (½ inch) thickness. Cut into heart shapes using a 6 cm (2½ inch) biscuit cutter. Place on prepared tray; bake 25 minutes or until lightly browned. Cool on wire rack.
5 Place chocolate in small heatproof bowl. Stand over pan of simmering water and stir until melted. Remove from heat.

ANZAC BISCUITS

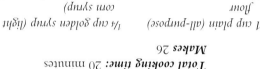 **Preparation time:** 12 minutes
Total cooking time: 20 minutes
Makes 26

1 cup plain (all-purpose) flour
⅔ cup sugar
1 cup rolled oats
1 cup desiccated coconut
¼ cup golden syrup (light corn syrup)
125 g (4 oz) unsalted (sweet) butter
1 tablespoon boiling water
½ teaspoon bicarbonate of soda (baking soda)

1 Preheat oven to moderate 180°C (350°F/Gas 4). Line a 32 x 28 cm (13 x 11 inch) biscuit (oven) tray with baking paper. Sift flour and sugar into bowl. Add oats and coconut; make well in the centre.
2 Combine butter and golden syrup in small pan. Stir over low heat until butter has melted and mixture is smooth; remove from heat. Dissolve soda in water, add immediately to butter mixture. Add butter mixture to dry ingredients. Using a wooden spoon, stir until well combined.
3 Drop one level tablespoon of mixture at a time onto tray. Flatten gently, allowing room for spreading. Bake 20 minutes or until just browned. Remove from oven; transfer to wire rack to cool.

6 Dip one side of biscuits into chocolate. Place biscuits onto greaseproof paper until chocolate has set. Sprinkle with mixed spice.

BRAN

BANANA BRAN MUFFINS

★ **Preparation time:** 20 minutes + 1 hour standing
Total cooking time: 15–20 minutes
Makes 12

1 cup (8 fl oz) boiling water
1 cup natural bran
1 teaspoon vanilla essence
1 cup plain (all-purpose) flour
1/3 cup skim milk powder
1 1/2 teaspoons baking powder
1 1/2 teaspoons bicarbonate of soda (baking soda)
1/2 cup mashed ripe banana
1 egg, beaten
2 tablespoons vegetable oil
1/3 cup firmly packed brown sugar

1 Pour boiling water over bran in medium bowl. Stir and let stand for 1 hour.

2 Preheat oven to 200°C (400°F/Gas 6). Brush oil into bottoms only of 12 muffin tins.

3 Sift flour, milk powder, baking powder and bicarbonate of soda in a medium bowl. Add banana, egg, oil, brown sugar and vanilla essence to bran mixture and mix well.

Stir gently with fork until all ingredients are just moistened.

4 Spoon batter evenly into each muffin tin, filling them only two-thirds full. Bake 15–20 minutes, until golden. Serve warm with butter.

BRAN AND FRUIT LOAF

★ **Preparation time:** 15 minutes
Total cooking time: 50 minutes
Serves 8

1 1/2 cups plain (all-purpose) flour
3/4 cup (6 fl oz) milk
2 teaspoons baking powder
2 teaspoons mixed spice
1 cup unprocessed bran
1/2 cup soft brown sugar
1/2 cup (4 fl oz) vegetable oil
2 eggs, beaten
1/2 cup chopped, dried apricots
1/2 cup sultanas
2 apples, peeled and grated

1 Preheat oven to moderate 180°C (350°F/Gas 4). Brush a 20 x 15 x 7 cm (8 x 6 x 2¾ inch) loaf tin with melted butter or oil. Line base with paper; grease paper. Sift flour, baking powder and spice into a large mixing bowl; stir in bran and sugar. Make a well in the centre. In a small bowl combine oil, eggs and milk.

2 Pour liquids onto dry ingredients. Using a wooden spoon, stir until well combined; do not overbeat. Stir in sultanas, apricots and apple.

3 Pour mixture into the prepared tin. Bake for 50 minutes or until a skewer comes out clean when inserted in centre of cake. Leave cake in tin 10 minutes before turning out.

Note: This loaf is best eaten within 1 or 2 days.

ABOVE: BRAN AND FRUIT LOAF.
OPPOSITE PAGE: WHITE BREAD.

first to make leavened bread, discovering the aerating effects of fermentation on dough. In the Middle Ages bread became common throughout Europe.

shape and is cut into wedges for serving. The cheese has been made since the eighth century when Charlemagne ate it in the priory of Reuil-en-Brie and pronounced it 'one of the most marvellous of foods'.

Brine A strong salt solution used for pickling and preserving meat, fish and vegetables.

Brioche A slightly sweet bread roll with a soft, spongy texture made from a yeast dough enriched with butter and eggs. Brioche is a popular breakfast in France, where it is eaten warm, spread with butter and jam. It is often baked in the shape of a plump cup-cake with a smaller 'head' on top—the *brioche à tête* of Paris.

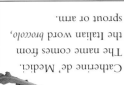

B R E A D

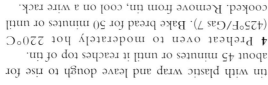

BREAD (WHITE LOAF)

✳ **Preparation time:** 30 minutes +
standing time
Total cooking time: 50 minutes
Makes 1 loaf

15 g (1/2 oz) dry yeast
400–500 ml
(12–16 fl oz) water
500 g (1 lb) plain (all-purpose) flour, white or wholemeal
2 teaspoons salt

1 Combine yeast and 2–3 tablespoons of cold or tepid water in a small bowl. Dissolve salt in remainder of water. Sift flour into a large bowl. Make a well in the centre and add yeast mixture, sprinkling flour over yeast. Add salt and water mixture and combine with hands or a wooden spoon.

2 Gently knead on a lightly floured surface, adding more flour if necessary, about 10 minutes. Shape dough into a ball, place in a large, lightly oiled mixing bowl. Stand, covered with plastic wrap, in a warm place for 1½ hours or until dough doubles in volume.

3 Brush a 1 litre (4-cup) capacity tin with oil or melted butter. Remove dough from the bowl, knead for 2–3 minutes until smooth. Press dough down into tin, sprinkling top with flour. Cover

tin with plastic wrap and leave dough to rise for about 45 minutes or until it reaches top of tin.

4 Preheat oven to moderately hot 220°C (425°F/Gas 7). Bake bread for 50 minutes or until cooked. Remove from tin, cool on a wire rack.

V A R I A T I O N S

■ OLIVE AND HERB ROLLS: Add ⅓ cup sliced black olives and 2–3 tablespoons chopped fresh herbs (oregano, lemon thyme, parsley or chives) to flour mixture in step 1. Follow recipe to kneading stage in step 3. Divide dough into 8–10 portions (depending on size of roll required). Knead each portion. Shape into rounds, flat rounds, sausage shapes or knots. Place on greased oven trays. Brush tops with milk and sprinkle with flour if desired. Cover with plastic wrap and leave to rise for 40 minutes or until rolls are well-risen. Bake in preheated oven for 40–50 minutes or until rolls are golden and cooked through.

■ HERB AND CHEESE SCROLL: Follow bread recipe to step 3. Remove dough from bowl and knead for 2–3 minutes. Press dough into a flat rectangular shape, about 20 x 25 cm (8 x 10 inches). Combine ½ cup grated cheese, 2 tablespoons fresh chopped parsley and pepper and sprinkle on top of dough. Roll up dough from the shortest side, as for a swiss roll (jelly roll). Place dough in prepared tin. Continue baking as for bread recipe.

Broccoli A member of the cabbage and cauliflower family. The most common variety, sprouting or heading broccoli, has deep green heads of tightly clustered buds and thick, juicy stalks. It was known to the ancient Romans, and was taken to France in the sixteenth century by Catherine de' Medici. The name comes from the Italian word *broccolo*, sprout or arm.

Broad Bean A bean with a flat green pod containing large, pale green seeds. The broad bean was a staple of the poor in ancient Egypt, usually as a bean cake called *tamia*, forerunner of the *tamiya* of Egypt today; the ancient Greeks ate the beans green, in the pod, and also used the large dried seeds as voting tokens in the election of magistrates; in Italy bean dishes were eaten as part of the funeral ceremony. During the Middle Ages when grain was scarce the beans were ground into a flour to make bread. The broad bean has been grown in China for more than 4000 years and China is now the main producer.

WHOLEMEAL BREAD

★★ **Preparation time:** 30 minutes + standing
Total cooking time: 35–40 minutes
Makes 1 loaf

1 teaspoon soft brown sugar
15 g (1/2 oz) fresh (compressed) yeast or 7 g (1/4 oz) sachet dried yeast
1 1/4 cups (10 fl oz) warm water or milk
3 1/4 cups wholemeal plain (all-purpose) flour
1 teaspoon salt

1 Brush a deep loaf tin with oil or melted butter. Combine sugar and yeast in a medium bowl. Gradually add water or milk; blend until smooth. Stand covered with plastic wrap in a warm place for about 10 minutes or until foamy.

2 Sift flour and salt into large mixing bowl. Make a well in the centre. Add yeast mixture using a flat-bladed knife, mix to a soft dough.

3 Turn onto lightly floured surface, knead for 5–10 minutes or until smooth. Shape dough into a ball, place in large, lightly oiled mixing bowl. Leave covered with plastic wrap in warm place for 15–20 minutes or until well risen. Punch air out of dough using your fist. Knead dough again for 3–5 minutes or until smooth. Place dough in prepared tin. Leave covered with plastic wrap in warm place until well risen and dough has doubled.

4 Preheat oven to moderately hot 210°C (415°F/Gas 6–7). Brush loaf with a little milk. Make slits or patterns in the top with a sharp knife and/or sprinkle with a little extra flour if desired. Bake for 35–40 minutes or until well browned and cooked through. Stand bread in tin 5 minutes before transferring to wire rack to cool.

VARIATIONS

■ After punching air from dough and kneading again, divide into portions for individual rolls. Shape into sausage shapes and tie in knots, or divide dough into three; roll in sausage lengths and plait together. Place rolls or decorative loaves on greased baking trays. Leave room for spreading. Brush with milk and sprinkle with poppy seeds, sesame seeds or dried herbs and rock salt. Bake until golden and cooked through.

■ For a lighter wholemeal loaf use half plain (all-purpose) white flour and half plain (all-purpose) wholemeal flour.

■ CHEESE, BACON AND CHIVE LOAF: Combine 1/2 cup grated cheddar cheese, 2 rashers finely chopped bacon and 1/4 cup finely chopped chives with the sifted flour; proceed as recipe indicates.

■ After punching air from dough and kneading again, press into a rectangle 1 cm (1/2 inch) thick. Sprinkle 1/2 cup chopped fresh mixed herbs, 1–2 cloves crushed garlic, salt and pepper on top. Roll dough from shortest end. Place seam-side down in prepared tin. Continue recipe as indicated.

ABOVE: WHOLEMEAL BREAD.
OPPOSITE: GARLIC FOCACCIA

Broth The clear liquid in which meat, fish or vegetables have been cooked. It can be eaten as a clear soup or thickened with vegetables, meat and grain.

Brownie A rich, chocolate cookie popular in North America. It ranges in texture from heavy and chewy to light and cake-like.

Brown Sauce A sauce made from meat stock thickened with flour and butter and flavoured with onions, mushrooms and tomatoes. Also known as Sauce Espagnole, it is the basis of a number of sauces such as Bordelaise, Madeira and Périgueux.

Brussels Sprout A green vegetable that resembles a tiny cabbage. Although its name suggests a Belgian origin, the Belgians themselves believe it was brought to their country in ancient times by the Romans. In Britain it was not widely grown or eaten until the mid-nineteenth century.

Bubble and Squeak A dish made from cooked leftover meat and vegetables, named for the sound it makes while sizzling in the pan.

Buckwheat The triangular seeds of a plant native to Central Asia. It

GARLIC FOCACCIA

✹

Preparation time: 20 minutes + 50 minutes standing
Total cooking time: 25 minutes
Serves 4–6

7 g (1/4 oz) dry yeast	2 tablespoons olive oil
1 teaspoon sugar	1 tablespoon cornmeal
2 1/3 cups plain (all-purpose) flour	(maize flour) or semolina
3/4 cup (6 fl oz) lukewarm water	1 tablespoon olive oil, extra
1 teaspoon salt	2 teaspoons finely crushed sea salt
3 cloves garlic, crushed	
sea salt	

1 Combine yeast, sugar, 1 teaspoon flour and water in small mixing bowl. Stand, covered with plastic wrap, in a warm place 10 minutes or until foamy.

2 Sift remaining flour and salt into a large mixing bowl. Add garlic and stir with a knife to combine. Make a well in the centre, stir in yeast mixture and olive oil. Using a flat-bladed knife, mix to a firm dough.

3 Turn dough onto lightly floured surface, knead for 10 minutes. Shape dough into a ball, place in a large, lightly oiled mixing bowl. Stand, covered with plastic wrap, in a warm place 40 minutes or until well risen.

4 Preheat oven to moderately hot 210°C (415°F/Gas 6–7). Sprinkle base of an 18 x 28 cm (7 x 11 inch) shallow tin with cornmeal or

semolina. Knead dough again 2 minutes or until smooth. Press dough into tin; prick deep holes with a skewer. Sprinkle lightly with water and place in oven. Bake 10 minutes, sprinkle again with water. Bake a further 10 minutes, brush with extra olive oil, sprinkle with sea salt, then bake 5 more minutes. Serve warm or at room temperature, cut into squares.

VARIATIONS

■ CHEESE AND CHIVE Add 1/3 cup finely grated parmesan cheese and 1/4 cup finely chopped chives to mixture in step 2.

■ CHEESE AND BACON Sprinkle 3/4 cup grated cheddar cheese, 2–3 rashers finely chopped bacon and 1 small finely sliced onion over focaccia after pricking holes on surface with a skewer. Bake as required. Omit sprinkling with water.

■ OLIVE, PEPPER (CAPSICUM) AND ANCHOVY Sprinkle 1/2 cup sliced black olives, 1/2 small red pepper, finely chopped, and a 45 g (1 1/2 oz) can drained and finely sliced anchovy fillets over focaccia after pricking holes on surface with a skewer. Bake as required. Omit water sprinkling.

OLIVE AND ONION FLAT BREAD

 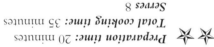 ✹✹

Preparation time: 20 minutes
Total cooking time: 35 minutes
Serves 8

1 tablespoon olive oil	2 cups plain (all-purpose)
2 medium onions, finely	flour
sliced	1 teaspoon sugar
15 g (1/2 oz) dried yeast	1/2 cup (4 fl oz) warm milk
3 cups wholemeal plain	1 egg, beaten
(all-purpose) flour	1/2 cup (4 fl oz) olive oil,
1 tablespoon caraway seeds	extra
1 3/4 cups (14 fl oz) warm	1 cup pitted black olives
water	

1 Preheat oven to moderately hot 210°C (415°F/Gas 6–7). Oil a 35 x 25 cm (14 x 10 inch) shallow baking dish. Heat oil in pan, add onions and cook for 10 minutes or until golden. Cool.

2 Combine sugar and milk, sprinkle with dried yeast. Mix and stand 5 minutes. Sift flours into a bowl, add caraway seeds.

3 Combine yeast mixture, water, extra oil and egg. Add to flours, mix well—mixture will be tacky. Spread into tin; smooth with oiled hands.

4 Sprinkle with cooked onions and olives, patting them firmly into top of dough. Bake for 35 minutes or until golden and firm.

---

did not appear in Europe until the Middle Ages, probably introduced by the Arabs, for in many regions it was known as 'Saracen wheat'. The seeds are roasted and made into a flour used in pancakes (especially the Russian blini), crisp thin cakes, and Asian soba noodles.

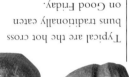

Bun A small, round, yeast roll, usually slightly sweetened and sometimes containing spices and dried fruit.

Typical are the hot cross buns traditionally eaten on Good Friday.

Burghul Cracked wheat, made by cooking wheat then drying and cracking it. It absorbs twice its volume in water when soaked or briefly re-cooked before use. Burghul includes the wheat germ, and so is rich in protein. It is much used in Middle Eastern cooking, notably in the salad dish tabouli.

Burrito A dish consisting of a flat bread (tortilla) made of wheat flour, wrapped around a filling of shredded meat,

beans and sometimes cheese, which, after the ends have been turned in to seal it, is either eaten immediately or baked. The burrito is of Mexican origin; its name comes from burro, a small pack donkey, because the modest tortilla wrapping can accommodate a generous load of filling. A deep-fried burrito is called a *chimichanga*.

Butter A dairy product made by churning cream into a solid fat. In most countries, by law, butter must contain at least 80 per cent fat and not more than 16 per cent water. Butter is used as a spread, as a cooking medium and as an ingredient in a wide range of savoury and sweet dishes. It is salted to improve its keeping qualities; unsalted (sweet) butter is also available. Clarified butter has been heated to remove the water content by evaporation and then strained to remove any non-fat solids.

The first to make butter from cow's milk were probably the Sumerians, although most early butter was made from the milk of goats and sheep, as cattle

FRUIT AND NUT BREAD

★ ★ **Preparation time:** 35 minutes + standing
Total cooking time: 40–50 minutes
Makes 1 loaf

375 g (12 oz) plain (all-purpose) flour
60 g (2 oz) soft brown sugar
pinch of salt
1/4 teaspoon ground cinnamon
1/4 teaspoon grated nutmeg
1/4 teaspoon powdered ginger
1/4 teaspoon allspice
15 g (1/2 oz) fresh yeast

150 ml (5 fl oz) warm milk
60 g (2 oz) butter, melted but not hot
90 g (3 oz) sultanas
75 g (2 1/2 oz) currants
60 g (2 oz) candied peel
125 g (4 oz) brazil nuts, chopped

Glaze
150 ml (5 fl oz) milk
6 tablespoons sugar

1 Combine flour, sugar, salt and spices in a large bowl. Dissolve the yeast in a little of the milk. Make a well in the centre of the dry ingredients, add the milk and yeast mixture. Add the butter and remaining milk and use a flat-bladed knife to mix to a soft dough, adding more flour or warm water if necessary.
2 Turn dough onto a lightly floured surface and knead for about 4 minutes or until the dough is soft and elastic. Return to bowl and leave to stand, covered with plastic wrap, in a warm place for about 1 1/2 hours or until well-risen.

3 Preheat oven to 200°C (400°F/Gas 6). Brush a small loaf tin with butter or oil. Add fruit, peel and nuts to dough and knead again until well mixed, add to tin. Leave covered with plastic wrap in a warm place for about 30 minutes, until the dough rises to top of tin. Bake for 35 to 45 minutes or until it has shrunk slightly in tin and is brown on top. Turn onto wire rack, tap and if loaf is very soft return to oven, upside down without the tin, for a further 5 minutes.
4 When cooked and still hot, paint with Glaze. Leave on wire rack to cool.
5 To make Glaze: Combine milk and sugar in saucepan and bring to boil, stirring constantly until sugar has dissolved. Boil for 3–5 minutes until glaze thickens slightly.

VARIATIONS

■ Fruit and Nut Bread can be formed into twists or made into individual rolls.
■ For hot cross buns, place a shortcrust pastry cross on top of each bun before baking. Brush with glaze as usual.
■ Bread is lighter if made with all white flour and much denser if made with all wholemeal.
■ Use different fruit and nuts: chopped hazelnuts, and glacé cherries make a lovely tea bread.

ABOVE: FRUIT AND NUT BREAD.
OPPOSITE PAGE, ABOVE: WHOLEMEAL RYE SOURDOUGH BREAD; BELOW: OLIVE DAMPER

OLIVE DAMPER

★ *Preparation time:* 20 minutes
Total cooking time: 25 minutes

Serves 8

2 cups self-raising flour	1 tablespoon chopped
1 teaspoon salt	fresh rosemary
30 g (1 oz) butter, chopped	1/2 cup (4 fl oz) milk
1/2 cup shredded parmesan	1/4 cup (2 fl oz) water
cheese	1 tablespoon milk, extra
1/2 cup black pitted olives,	2 tablespoons shredded
sliced	parmesan cheese, extra

1 Preheat oven to moderately hot 210°C (415°F/Gas 6–7). Brush a baking tray with melted butter or oil and sprinkle lightly with flour. Sift self-raising flour and salt into a mixing bowl. Add chopped butter. Using fingertips, rub butter into flour until mixture is fine and crumbly.

2 Add parmesan, olives and rosemary; stir. Combine milk and water and add to dry ingredients. Mix to a soft dough with a flat-bladed knife.

3 Turn out onto a lightly floured surface and knead briefly until smooth. Shape dough into a ball, then flatten out to a round approximately 2 cm (3/4 inch) thick.

4 Place dough on prepared baking tray. Using a large knife, score dough deeply to mark into eight portions. Brush with extra milk and sprinkle with extra cheese. Bake for 25 minutes or until golden brown and crusty.

WHOLEMEAL RYE SOURDOUGH BREAD

★★ *Preparation time:* 50 minutes
Total cooking time: 40 minutes
Makes 1 large or 2 small loaves

Sourdough Starter

2 teaspoons soft brown	1 cup wholemeal plain
sugar	(all-purpose) flour
5 g (1/4 oz) fresh yeast	1 cup (8 fl oz) warm
1 cup wholemeal plain	water
(all-purpose) flour	2 1/2 cups rye flour
	1 teaspoon salt
Bread Dough	2 teaspoons caraway seeds
30 g (1 oz) fresh yeast	extra rye flour for
1 1/2 cups (12 fl oz) water	kneading

1 To make Sourdough Starter: Dissolve yeast in warm water. Sift in flour, mix until smooth. Cover and leave at room temperature for 2 days.

2 To make Bread Dough: Combine water, yeast and brown sugar. Leave to stand in warm place until mixture starts to bubble.

3 Place wholemeal and rye flours in a large basin with salt. Make a well in the centre of flours and add yeast mixture and 1/2 cup Sourdough Starter. Mix until well combined. Knead until dough is smooth and elastic. Place in lightly oiled basin and leave in warm position until dough has doubled in bulk.

4 Preheat oven to 200°C (400°F/Gas 6). Punch dough down, place on floured work surface and knead for 10 minutes. Shape into one or two long loaves.

5 Place loaves on greased oven tray, allow to prove for 10 minutes. Glaze with water, sprinkle tops with caraway seeds. Bake for 30–40 minutes until golden.

Butter Bean See Lima Bean

Buttermilk Originally the thin liquid left after cream has been churned into butter. Today buttermilk is made from pasteurised skim milk, to which a culture has been added to thicken it and increase its lactic acid content. It is used as a drink (usually mixed with fruit juice), in baking and confectionery, and it can be added to hot soups and casseroles or used as a low-fat substitute for oil or cream in salad dressings.

Butternut Pumpkin (Squash) A member of the marrow family, shaped like a long pear. It has smooth buff-coloured skin and bright orange flesh and is widely used as a cooked vegetable.

Butterscotch A slightly cloudy boiled sweet (candy) made with water, sugar and butter. See index for recipes.

(B) Greeks and Romans did not use butter in their cooking, preferring olive oil, but appreciated its medicinal properties as an ointment. Butter was produced by the Gauls, and its use was spread throughout northern Europe by the Normans.

...as draught animals gave little milk. The ancient which were worked hard

C

CABBAGE & CAULIFLOWER

abbage, so often overcooked, has not always been kindly looked upon. One of the most nutritious vegetables, it can be delicious if imaginatively prepared. Cauliflower has also suffered by being buried under thick white sauce. Here are some tasty alternatives.

QUICK COLESLAW

Finely shred ½ small green cabbage. Combine with 2 grated carrots, 1 stick finely chopped celery, 1 finely chopped onion, 1 finely chopped small green or red pepper (capsicum) and ½ cup prepared coleslaw dressing in a large bowl. Toss well to combine. Add ¼ cup mixed freshly chopped herbs if desired. Chill before serving.

SWEET RED CABBAGE WITH CARAWAY SEEDS

Finely shred ½ small red cabbage. Heat 30 g (1 oz) butter, 1 teaspoon caraway seeds, 1 teaspoon balsamic vinegar and 1 teaspoon soft brown sugar in pan. Add cabbage, cook, stirring, for 2–3 minutes or until just tender. Serve hot.

GARLIC PEPPER CABBAGE

Finely shred ½ small green cabbage. Heat 30 g (1 oz) butter and 1 teaspoon oil in heavy-based frying pan or wok. Add 2 teaspoons garlic pepper seasoning and cabbage. Stir-fry 2–3 minutes or until tender. Serve hot.

CABBAGE AND POTATO CAKES

Combine 1 cup cooked shredded cabbage, ½ cup roughly mashed potato, 1 finely chopped spring onion (scallion), 2 lightly beaten eggs and salt and freshly ground pepper to taste and mix well. Heat some oil or butter in a frying pan. Cook spoonfuls of the mixture in small batches for about 2 minutes each side or until it is golden. Drain on paper towels. Serve hot.

GARLIC PEPPER CABBAGE

CABBAGE AND POTATO CAKES

SWEET RED CABBAGE WITH CARAWAY SEEDS

QUICK COLESLAW

HOT CHILLI CAULIFLOWER

CAULIFLOWER WITH TOMATO SAUCE

PARMESAN CAULIFLOWER

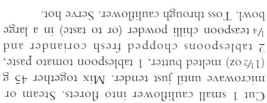
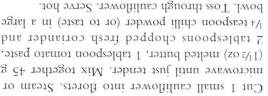
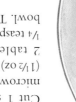

CAULIFLOWER WITH BACON

CAULIFLOWER WITH TOMATO SAUCE

Cut 1 small cauliflower into medium florets. Steam or microwave cauliflower until just tender. Heat 1 tablespoon oil in medium pan. Add ½ teaspoon cracked pepper, 1 teaspoon mixed Italian herbs and 1 clove crushed garlic. Cook 1 minute. Add one 440 g (14 oz) can crushed tomatoes. Bring to boil, reduce heat, simmer 5 minutes or until reduced slightly. Pour sauce over vegetables and serve hot.

HOT CHILLI CAULIFLOWER

Cut 1 small cauliflower into florets. Steam or microwave until just tender. Mix together 45 g (1½ oz) melted butter, 1 tablespoon tomato paste, 2 tablespoons chopped fresh coriander and ¼ teaspoon chilli powder (or to taste) in a large bowl. Toss through cauliflower. Serve hot.

PARMESAN CAULIFLOWER

Cut 1 small cauliflower into florets. Combine, in a bowl, ¼ cup plain (all-purpose) flour, 2 tablespoons finely grated parmesan cheese and 1 teaspoon dried mixed herbs. Toss florets in this mixture. Heat 2 tablespoons oil and 45 g (1½ oz) butter in a heavy-based frying pan. Gently cook cauliflower in batches until just tender. Drain on paper towels. Serve hot.

CAULIFLOWER WITH BACON

Cut 1 small cauliflower into florets. Steam or microwave until just tender. Heat 1 teaspoon of oil in a medium pan. Add 2 rashers of finely shredded bacon; cook until browned. Add cauliflower and 2 finely chopped spring onions (scallions); stir to combine. Serve hot.

CAJUN CLASSICS

CAJUN SPICES

Mix together 1 tablespoon garlic powder, 1 tablespoon onion powder, 2 teaspoons white pepper, 2 teaspoons cracked black pepper, 1½ teaspoons cayenne pepper, 2 teaspoons dried thyme and ½ teaspoon dried oregano. Store the mixture in a spice jar.

CAJUN VEGETABLES

Peel, trim and finely chop 1 large onion, 1 green pepper (capsicum) and 2 short celery sticks.
Makes 3–3½ cups.

ROUX

Roux is one of the most important elements in Cajun cooking. To make it, use equal parts oil and flour. Heat a heavy pan (preferably cast-iron as high heat can damage a non-stick surface) and add the oil. When oil is very hot, sprinkle on one-quarter of the flour and whisk in briskly. Add remaining flour gradually, whisking constantly until the desired colour is reached. The mixture should be on a slow boil with tiny bubbles constantly breaking the surface. Light roux needs about 2 minutes cooking on high heat, red-brown roux about 5 minutes. For best results, keep the heat reasonably high, sliding the pan off the heat for 30 seconds every so often. Whisking must be constant and fast to avoid scorching, which will make the roux bitter. Be careful not to allow hot roux to splash on your skin—it is a good idea to wear long rubber gloves when preparing it. Store roux in the refrigerator and heat gently to room temperature before use.

BLACKENED FISH

★ Preparation time: 5 minutes
Total cooking time: 6–8 minutes
Serves 6

125 g (4 oz) unsalted (sweet) butter
2 tablespoons Cajun spices
6 large white fish fillets
2 teaspoons sweet paprika

1 Melt the butter in a small pan.
2 Brush each fish fillet generously with melted butter. Mix together Cajun spices and paprika and sprinkle thickly over the fish.
3 Place fish fillets, one or two at a time, in the hot pan to cook for 1–2 minutes on high heat. Turn and cook a few minutes more until done. The surface should be well charred on each side. Add a little extra butter if needed. Cook remaining fillets. Serve hot with remaining melted butter and plain white rice.

ABOVE: BLACKENED FISH
OPPOSITE PAGE: PRAWN GUMBO

Cabanossi A thin, spicy, precooked sausage made from seasoned minced (ground) pork or beef, or a mixture of the two. Cabanossi originated in Poland as a snack for hunters far from home. It can be served as finger food and packed in lunches.

Cabbage A vegetable with pale green leaves formed into a tightly packed head. It can be eaten raw finely chopped in salads, or thinly sliced and steamed, boiled or microwaved and served as a vegetable, or added to soups, stews and casseroles; the smooth, curved outer leaves are used as wrappings for savoury fillings. Native to Europe and western Asia, cabbage is one of the oldest cultivated vegetables. Ancient Greeks and Romans believed it could prevent drunkenness. Cabbages were first eaten for the stems, rather than the leaves; from the Middle Ages cabbage leaf dressings were applied to wounds and open fractures. The high vitamin C content of cabbage was recognised by eighteenth-century navigators who carried

crates of cabbages on board to prevent scurvy among their crews.

Cabécou A soft-textured goat's milk cheese made in small cakes, originally produced on farms in the Quercy region of south-western France. It can be eaten fresh, or at varying stages of ripening. Its flavour becomes more intense with age.

Cabinet Pudding A pudding made from cubed bread or cake, and butter and raisins. It is either steamed in a mould or baked, and served hot with custard.

Caerphilly A crumbly, semi-hard, cow's milk cheese with a mild, slightly salty flavour. It is almost white in colour and takes only two weeks to mature. Caerphilly takes its name from the Welsh town and, perhaps because of its easy digestibility or because it stayed fresh and moist, it was a popular ingredient in the packed lunches of local coal miners.

Caesar Salad A salad of cos or romaine lettuce, croutons, parmesan cheese and sometimes anchovies, dressed with olive oil, vinegar and coddled egg. The salad is named after its inventor.

DIRTY RICE

★★ **Preparation time:** 15 minutes
Total cooking time: 30 minutes
Serves 6

2½ cups chopped Cajun vegetables
¼ cup red-brown roux
½ teaspoon Tabasco sauce
2 teaspoons Cajun spice mix
60 g (2 oz) butter
2 cloves garlic, chopped
185 g (6 oz) chicken livers, chopped
250 g (8 oz) minced (ground) pork
2 cups long grain white rice
3 cups (24 fl oz) chicken stock
1½ teaspoons chicken stock powder
black pepper

1 Cook vegetables in half the butter until tender; add garlic, cook briefly. Remove from pan.

2 Cook livers and pork for about 2–3 minutes, breaking up lumps in mince with a fork as it cooks. Add vegetables, cook for 2–3 minutes.

3 Stir in the chicken stock powder, roux and Tabasco sauce, Cajun spices, pepper, rice and stock and bring to the boil. Reduce heat and simmer for about 20 minutes.

4 Check seasoning, stir well and serve.

Note: Stir in chopped spring onions (scallions) if liked. Wedges of hard-boiled egg, cubes of cooked chicken or ham, cooked prawns (shrimps) and red kidney beans can be added to make a substantial main course dish.

PRAWN GUMBO

★★ **Preparation time:** 20 minutes
Total cooking time: 1 hour
Serves 6

315 g (10 oz) canned okra (ladies' fingers), rinsed and drained
425 g (13½ oz) can tomatoes
2 cups chopped Cajun vegetables
60 g (2 oz) butter
2 cloves garlic, chopped
2 teaspoons tomato paste
2 teaspoons Cajun spices
2 bay leaves
¼ teaspoon ground allspice

2 teaspoons chilli flakes
1 teaspoon worcestershire sauce
pepper, to taste
2 cups (16 fl oz) seafood stock
600 g (1¼ lb) medium green prawns (shrimps), peeled and deveined
1 teaspoon filé powder, optional

1 Combine okra and crushed tomatoes in a pan. Bring to the boil, reduce heat, cover and simmer gently for 15 minutes.

2 Cook the Cajun vegetables in butter for 2–3 minutes, add garlic and cook for 20 minutes.

3 Add okra and tomato mixture to Cajun vegetables, with tomato paste, Cajun spices, bay leaves, allspice, chilli, worcestershire sauce and pepper. Stir for 2 minutes, then add stock and roux and cook a further 15 minutes.

4 Add the prawns and simmer gently until just cooked. Season to taste and stir in the filé powder if using.

Caesar Cardini, who served it in his Tijuana, Mexico, restaurant in the 1920s. It became popular with the fashionable Hollywood set and soon appeared on menus in Los Angeles. It is now considered a classic American dish.

Café au Lait Hot black coffee mixed with scalded milk, usually in equal proportions. A traditional breakfast beverage in many other European countries, it came to France in the seventeenth century. It was reputedly the favourite drink of Marie Antoinette.

Café Latte An Italian style of coffee in which very strong espresso coffee is combined in a glass with very hot milk. It is generally drunk at breakfast.

Cajun Food Cajun country takes in the bays, bayous and hinterland of southern Louisiana. In the mid-1750s it was refuge to the French Huguenots expelled by the English from Arcadia, in Nova Scotia, Canada ('Cajun' is derived from 'Arcadian'). Cajun food is earthy and robust; its roots are in the peasant

---

CHICKEN AND SMOKED HAM JAMBALAYA

★ *Preparation time:* 45 minutes
Total cooking time: 1¾ hours
Serves 6

2 tablespoons vegetable oil	*1 kg (2 lb) chicken pieces, deboned*
2 cups chopped Cajun vegetables	*1 small carrot, chopped*
1 small onion, chopped	*2 sprigs parsley*
6 peppercorns	*1 sprig fresh thyme*
2 cloves garlic, chopped	*4 cups (32 fl oz) water*
425 g (13½ oz) can peeled tomatoes, chopped	*500 g (1 lb) tasso (smoked ham), cubed*
2½ cups long-grain white rice	
2 teaspoons Cajun spice mix	

1 Place chicken bones and skin, carrot, onion, peppercorns, parsley and thyme in a pan, add 4 cups water. Bring to the boil, reduce heat and simmer, uncovered, for 30 minutes. Strain, reserving stock.

2 Cut the chicken meat into cubes and cook with the ham in the oil for about 6 minutes. Add chopped Cajun vegetables and garlic and cook until golden. Add tomatoes, rice, 3 cups (24 fl oz) of reserved chicken stock and the Cajun spice mix; bring to the boil.

3 Pour into a greased casserole dish and bake, uncovered, at 180°C (350°F/Gas 4) for about 1 hour. The rice should be slightly crisp on top.

ABOVE: HUSHPUPPIES ; LEFT: CHICKEN AND SMOKED HAM JAMBALAYA
OPPOSITE PAGE: BASIC BUTTER CAKE

HUSHPUPPIES

★ *Preparation time:* 10 minutes
Total cooking time: 10 minutes
Makes 24–36

1 cup fine cornmeal (maize flour)	*1 teaspoon Cajun spices*
½ cup self-raising flour	*1 clove garlic, finely chopped*
2 tablespoons cornflour (cornstarch)	*2 tablespoons grated onion*
1 tablespoon baking powder	*2 eggs, lightly beaten*
½ teaspoon onion salt	*¾ cup (6 fl oz) milk*
¼ teaspoon chilli powder	*1 tablespoon lard*
	oil, for deep frying

1 In mixing bowl combine cornmeal, flour, cornflour, baking powder, onion salt, chilli powder and spices. Add garlic, onion and eggs.

2 Place milk and lard in a small pan. Cook over low heat until lard has melted and mixture is warm. Pour over the dry mixture; stir well. Cool.

3 Heat oil in deep, heavy pan until moderately hot. Carefully spoon tablespoonsful of mixture into oil. Cook only four or five at a time; fry until puffy and lightly golden, turning once or twice.

4 Remove from oil with a slotted spoon or strainer. Drain on absorbent paper. Serve warm.

CAKES BUTTER

BASIC BUTTER CAKE

⭐ **Preparation time:** 20 minutes
Total cooking time: 45 minutes
Makes one 20 cm (8 inch) round cake

125 g (4 oz) unsalted
  (sweet) butter
¾ cup caster (superfine)
  sugar
2 eggs, lightly beaten
1 teaspoon vanilla essence
2 cups self-raising flour
½ cup (4 fl oz) milk

Lemon Glacé Icing
1 cup icing (confectioners)
  sugar
15 g (½ oz) unsalted
  (sweet) butter, melted
3–4 teaspoons lemon juice

1 Preheat oven to moderate 180°C (350°F/Gas 4). Brush a deep, 20 cm (8 inch) round cake tin with melted butter or oil; line the base and side with paper, grease paper. Using electric beaters, beat butter and sugar in a small mixing bowl until light and creamy. Add the eggs gradually, beating thoroughly after each addition. Add essence; beat until combined.
2 Transfer the mixture to a large mixing bowl. Using a metal spoon, fold in the sifted flour alternately with the milk. Stir until just combined and the mixture is almost smooth. Spoon mixture into the prepared tin and smooth the surface. Bake for 45 minutes or until a skewer comes out clean when inserted in the centre of the cake.

Leave the cake in its tin for 10 minutes before turning onto a wire rack to cool.
3 To make Lemon Glacé Icing: Combine sifted icing sugar, melted butter and sufficient lemon juice in a small bowl to form a firm paste. Stand bowl in a pan of simmering water, stirring until icing is smooth and glossy; do not overheat or the icing will be dull and grainy. Remove from heat. Spread icing over cake using a flat-bladed knife.

Note: Sugar assists with incorporating air into fat in cake making, so it is important to use the type of sugar appropriate to the recipe. Caster (superfine) sugar is ideal for butter cakes because of the size of the granules: the finer the crystals, the more numerous the air cells that can be created in the mixture and the lighter the finished cake will be.

MARBLE CAKE

Divide basic butter cake mixture equally into three separate bowls. Add 2 tablespoons sifted cocoa powder and an extra 1 tablespoon of milk to first bowl; mix well. Add enough red food colouring to second bowl to tint the mixture pink. Leave the third bowl plain. Drop spoonfuls of alternating colours into prepared tin until all mixture has been used. Draw a skewer or knife through to swirl colours. Bake as directed.

cooking of rural France, but its distinctive style comes from a combination of Native American uses of local herbs and roots, ingredients introduced by African slaves (okra, sesame seeds, melons and hot spices) and the culinary legacy of earlier Spanish settlers. Cajun cooking features simple, one-pot meals using fresh farm produce— onion, peppers (capsicum), both hot and sweet, okra, celery, chicken and pork, bacon and ham (pigs were easier to raise than sheep or cattle), as well as the bounty of both the brackish bayous and the waters of the Gulf of Mexico—crayfish (always called crawfish in Louisiana), prawns, lobster, crab, oysters and fish. Many dishes are based on a brown roux; rice or beans are served at most meals. Filé powder, made from dried sassafras leaves, adds a distinctive flavour. Cajun specialties include spicy gumbos, peppery jambalayas (fragrant rice, pork, sausage, ham and shellfish), étouffée (shellfish cooked in a seasoned sauce and served over rice) and custard tarts.

Cake A term that covers a variety of sweet, baked foods with a texture similar to bread, usually made from flour, sugar,

eggs and a liquid. Cakes are grouped according to the relative proportions of these basic ingredients and the method by which they are made. Many cakes have a ceremonial or symbolic significance, such as that of the rich Christmas cake

(originally part of a religious feast), the wedding cake (which dates from the time of ancient Greece), christening cakes and birthday cakes.

Cake Decorating
The technique of covering cakes with icing (frosting) and other sweet, edible trimmings, usually for a festive occasion, such as a wedding, birthday or christening.

Calamari The Italian name for squid, a saltwater mollusc related to the octopus and cuttlefish and prized for its delicately flavoured flesh.

FAIRY CAKES

⭐⭐ **Preparation time:** 30 minutes
Total cooking time: 10–15 minutes
Makes 36 patty cakes

150 g (4¾ oz) unsalted (sweet) butter
¾ cup caster (superfine) sugar
2 eggs, lightly beaten
1 teaspoon vanilla essence
2 teaspoons lemon juice

2 cups self-raising flour
½ cup (4 fl oz) milk
½ cup raspberry jam
1¼ cups (10 fl oz) cream, whipped
icing (confectioners) sugar, for decoration

1 Preheat oven to moderate 180°C (350°F/Gas 4). Line two 12-cup, deep patty tins with paper patty cases. Using electric beaters, beat butter and sugar in small mixing bowl until light and creamy. Add eggs gradually, beating well after each addition. Add essence and juice; beat until combined.
2 Transfer to large mixing bowl. Using a metal spoon, fold in sifted flour alternately with milk. Stir until just combined and mixture is almost smooth. Spoon level tablespoonsful of mixture into patty cases. Bake 10–15 minutes or until golden. Leave in tins 5 minutes then place on wire rack to cool.
3 Line tins again with patty cases, repeat procedure with remaining mixture. When cakes are cold, cut a small circle from top, to a depth of about 2 cm (¾ inch), to allow for the filling. Reserve tops.
4 Spoon half a teaspoon of jam into each patty cake, top with a teaspoon of cream, replace reserved tops. Dust with sifted icing sugar.

MADEIRA CAKE

⭐ **Preparation time:** 20 minutes
Total cooking time: 55 minutes
Makes 1 loaf cake

155 g (5 oz) butter
¾ cup caster (superfine) sugar
3 eggs, lightly beaten
2 teaspoons finely grated orange or lemon rind

½ cup ground almonds
1¾ cups self-raising flour
icing (confectioners) sugar, for dusting

1 Preheat oven to moderate 180°C (350°F/Gas 4). Brush a 23 x 13 x 7 cm (9 x 5 x 2¾ inch) loaf tin with melted butter or oil. Line base and sides with baking paper. Using electric beaters, beat butter and sugar in a small mixing bowl until light and creamy. Add the eggs gradually, beating thoroughly after each addition. Add rind; beat until combined.
2 Transfer the mixture to a large mixing bowl. Using a metal spoon, fold in ground almonds and sifted flour. Stir until just combined and mixture is smooth.
3 Spoon mixture into prepared tin; smooth surface. Bake 55 minutes, until a skewer comes out clean when inserted in centre of cake. Leave in tin 10 minutes before turning onto wire rack to cool. Dust top of cake lightly with icing sugar.

ABOUT CAKES

■ For successful cake baking, read the recipe entirely beforehand and assemble all ingredients and equipment. Preheat oven to correct temperature, prepare baking tins.
■ Measure ingredients accurately—do not guess quantities. Use standard measuring cups, spoons and kitchen scales. Have eggs and butter at room temperature. Pre-sift dry ingredients.
■ Butter and sugar should be thoroughly creamed. Beat in a small glass bowl with electric beaters until mixture is light and creamy—it should almost double in volume and have no trace of sugar granules. Fold in ingredients carefully, mixing lightly yet evenly (over-beating can result in a heavy, coarse-textured cake).
■ Check oven temperature. Avoid opening oven door until two-thirds of the way through baking. Total cooking times given are approximate and may vary according to oven accuracy. Stand cake in tin for the specified time before turning onto a wire rack to cool.

ABOVE: FAIRY CAKES
OPPOSITE PAGE: PANFORTE

CAKES CHOCOLATE

PANFORTE

★ **Preparation time:** 30 minutes
Total cooking time: 50 minutes
Makes one 20 cm (8 inch) round cake

2 tablespoons cocoa powder
2/3 cup plain (all-purpose) flour
1 1/2 cups mixed dried fruit
2/3 cup chopped walnuts
2/3 cup chopped macadamia nuts
2/3 cup slivered almonds
1 teaspoon ground cinnamon
60 g (2 oz) dark (semi-sweet) chocolate, chopped
60 g (2 oz) unsalted (sweet) butter
1/3 cup caster (superfine) sugar
1/4 cup honey
icing (confectioners) sugar

1 Preheat oven to 180°C (350°F/Gas 4). Brush a shallow 20 cm (8 inch) round cake tin with oil or melted butter. Line base with paper; grease. Combine nuts and dried fruit in a large mixing bowl. Add sifted flour, cocoa and cinnamon, stir until combined. Make a well in the centre.

2 Stir the chocolate, butter, sugar and honey in a small pan over low heat until melted and well combined; remove from heat. Add the butter mixture to the dry ingredients. Using a wooden spoon, stir until all ingredients are well combined; do not over-beat.

3 Spoon into prepared tin; smooth surface. Bake 50 minutes until cake is firm to touch in the centre. Allow to cool in the tin before turning out. Decorate with icing (confectioners) sugar. Serve thin wedges with coffee or liqueur.

EASY CHOCOLATE CAKE

★ **Preparation time:** 20 minutes
Total cooking time: 35 minutes
Makes one 20 cm (8 inch) double layer cake

125 g (4 oz) butter
3/4 cup caster (superfine) sugar
1 egg
1 1/2 cups self-raising flour, sifted
1 teaspoon vanilla essence
1/2 cup (4 fl oz) cream, whipped
1/4 cup (2 fl oz) hot water
1/4 teaspoon bicarbonate of soda (baking soda)
1 tablespoon cocoa, sifted
icing (confectioners) sugar
strawberries
1/2 cup (4 fl oz) milk

1 Preheat oven to 180°C (350°F/Gas 4). Brush two shallow 20 cm (8 inch) round cake tins with melted butter or oil, line the base and sides with paper; grease. Beat butter and sugar with electric beaters in small bowl until light and creamy. Add egg and beat thoroughly. Add vanilla essence; beat until combined.

2 Transfer mixture to large mixing bowl. Using a metal spoon, fold in sifted ingredients alternately with milk. Stir until just combined and mixture is almost smooth. Dissolve bicarbonate of soda in hot water. Fold into mixture.

3 Spoon into prepared tins; smooth surface. Bake 35 minutes or until skewer comes out clean when inserted in centre of cakes. Stand cakes in tins 5 minutes before turning onto wire rack to cool. Sandwich cakes together with whipped cream. Dust with icing sugar, decorate with strawberries.

Camembert A cow's milk cheese, produced in small, flat disc shapes with a tangy, creamy flavour. Like brie, camembert is ripened from the outside by surface moulds that form a soft white skin encasing the creamy centre. Originally from Normandy, it has been known since the seventeenth century, but the modern cheese is credited to Marie Harel, a farm woman who during the French Revolution is said to have sheltered a fugitive priest from the Brie region and learned cheese-making methods which she combined with local techniques to produce an improved version. In the 1890s the cheese came to a wider audience when packaging in small wooden boxes allowed it to be sent without the risk of spoilage into new markets far afield.

Camomile (Chamomile) A plant of the daisy family, native to western Europe. It has been used since the days of ancient Egypt, either eaten or applied, to treat sprains, muscle strain, cramps and colic. In the Middle Ages the aroma of its crushed leaves was used to rid homes of foul odours. Camomile tea, made from flower heads, is a soothing drink.

Canapé

A bite-sized piece of bread, covered with a savoury butter or spread to which is added a topping such as crab, caviar, smoked salmon, ham or asparagus tips and a garnish such as stuffed olives, pimiento, capers or gherkin. Canapés are served either hot or cold as finger food. The name comes from the French word for couch, because canapés were originally eaten before the evening meal, while sitting in the drawing room.

Candy See Confectionery recipes.

Cannellini Bean A

dried bean, white, slightly kidney-shaped and larger than the haricot. It is mild flavoured and fluffy when cooked and is used in soups, stews, casseroles or cooled for salads. The cannellini bean is from tropical America; it was taken to Europe by the Spanish in the sixteenth century and is now the most popular white bean in Italy. It is available dried or canned.

Cannelloni

An Italian dish consisting of long tubes of pasta filled with meat, vegetables or cheese and served topped with cheese or a sauce.

MUD CAKE

★ ★

Preparation time: 40 minutes
Total cooking time: 2–2¼ hours
Serves 8–10

300 g (9⅔ oz) butter, melted
1¼ cups plain (all-purpose) flour
1 cup self-raising flour
½ cup cocoa powder
½ teaspoon bicarbonate of soda (baking soda)
4 eggs, lightly beaten
1 cup (8 fl oz) buttermilk
1 teaspoon vanilla essence
pinch salt

Icing
200 g (6½ oz) dark (semi-sweet) chocolate, chopped
⅓ cup (2½ fl oz) cream

2 cups sugar
300 g (9⅔ oz) dark (semi-sweet) chocolate, finely chopped
white chocolate for serving

1 Preheat oven to slow 150°C (300°F/Gas 2). Brush a deep 23 cm (9 inch) round cake tin with oil or melted butter; line the base and sides with baking paper.

2 Place sugar in large mixing bowl. Add sifted flours, cocoa and soda. Make a well in centre. Using a metal spoon, fold in combined eggs, buttermilk, essence and salt. Combine well.

3 Add butter and chocolate, mix well. Pour mixture into prepared tin and smooth surface. Bake for 2–2¼ hours or until a skewer comes out clean when inserted in centre of cake. Leave cake in tin until cold, then turn onto a wire rack (cake will crack on top). Using a serrated-edged knife, cut a dome off the top of the cake horizontally.

Turn the cake upside down and stand it on a wire rack over a paper-lined tray. Pour icing completely over the cake, smoothing top and sides with a flat-bladed knife. Allow to set. Transfer the cake carefully to a serving plate. Serve in wedges with whipped cream, garnished with shavings of white chocolate.

4 To make Icing: Combine chocolate and cream in a small pan. Stir over low heat until chocolate has melted and the mixture is smooth. Remove from heat. Cool slightly.

ABOUT MELTING CHOCOLATE

■ Chop chocolate into even-sized pieces and place in a glass bowl. Place bowl over a pan of simmering water; stir gently until chocolate has melted. Do not allow any water to fall into the chocolate or it will immediately stiffen and be unworkable. Cool chocolate slightly before use.

■ Melting chocolate in the microwave is easy. Chop the chocolate for your recipe into even sized pieces and place in a microwave-safe bowl. Microwave on Medium (50% power), using short bursts of power to avoid 'hot spots'. Remove the bowl from the microwave and stir the chocolate gently until it is quite smooth. Chocolate will hold its shape when melted in the microwave—in order to avoid scorching it is essential to stir it before microwaving again.

ABOVE: CHOCOLATE MUD CAKE
OPPOSITE PAGE: WHOLEMEAL FRUIT AND NUT CAKE

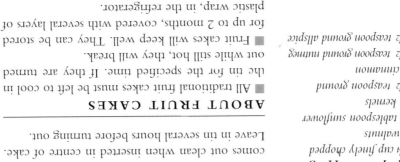

CAKES
FRUIT AND NUT

WHOLEMEAL FRUIT AND NUT CAKE

★ *Preparation time:* 45 minutes
Total cooking time: 2½–3 hours
Makes one 20 cm (8 inch) square cake

180 g (5¾ oz) unsalted (sweet) butter
¾ cup soft dark brown sugar
3 eggs, lightly beaten
200 g (6½ oz) figs, chopped
200 g (6½ oz) dried apricots, chopped
105 g (3½ oz) currants
105 g (3½ oz) sultanas
105 g (3½ oz) walnut pieces
½ cup sunflower kernels
1½ cups plain (all-purpose) flour
½ cup wholemeal flour
½ cup self-raising flour
1 teaspoon ground cinnamon
1 teaspoon ground nutmeg
1 teaspoon ground allspice
½ cup (4 fl oz) apricot nectar (juice)

Spicy Nut Topping
¼ cup finely chopped walnuts
1 tablespoon sunflower kernels
½ teaspoon ground cinnamon
½ teaspoon ground nutmeg
½ teaspoon ground allspice

1 Preheat oven to moderately slow 160°C (325°F/Gas 3). Brush a deep 20 cm (8 inch) square cake tin with melted butter or oil. Line base and sides with paper; grease paper. Using electric beaters, beat butter and sugar in small mixing bowl until light and creamy. Add the eggs gradually, beating thoroughly after each addition.

2 Transfer mixture to a large mixing bowl; add fruit, walnuts and kernels. Using a metal spoon, fold in sifted dry ingredients alternately with apricot nectar. Stir until mixture is almost smooth. Spoon evenly into tin; smooth surface.

3 To make Spicy Nut Topping: Combine all topping ingredients. Spoon mixture onto top of the cake, pressing down firmly with the back of the spoon.

4 Bake cake for 2½ to 3 hours until a skewer comes out clean when inserted in centre of cake. Leave in tin for several hours before turning out.

ABOUT FRUIT CAKES

■ All traditional fruit cakes must be left to cool in the tin for the specified time. If they are turned out while still hot, they will break.

■ Fruit cakes will keep well. They can be stored for up to 2 months, covered with several layers of plastic wrap, in the refrigerator.

Canola Oil
Also known as rapeseed or colza oil, the pale yellow, almost colourless and odourless oil extracted from the seed of the rape or colza plant. It is used as a salad oil, a cooking oil and in the manufacture of table margarine. Canola oil is a mainly mono-unsaturated fat and a source of vitamin E.

Cantaloupe Another name for rockmelon, derived from Cantalupo, near Rome, the summer residence of the popes, where monks developed the melon in Renaissance times.

Cape Gooseberry
The edible berry of a tropical plant native to Peru, but widely grown in warm countries throughout the world, especially in the Cape region of South Africa, hence its common name. Golden in colour, the fruit is the size of a cherry and is encased in a gauzy sac which must be removed before use. The Cape gooseberry has a tart flavour and may be eaten as a fresh

fruit, puréed and added to sorbets and ice-creams, or cooked in syrups and jams. It is also known as golden berry, strawberry tomato, winter cherry and ground cherry.

Caper The unopened, olive-green flower bud of a prickly shrub native to the Mediterranean, the Middle East and northern Africa, preserved in jars of seasoned vinegar or packed in salt in wooden boxes. The buds range in size from very tiny to pea size and, because the flower will open with the sun, must be gathered before sunrise.

Capers have been used as a condiment since the time of ancient Greece. Their sharp, sour taste adds flavour to fish, cheese and creamed dishes as well as white sauces, salads and mayonnaise. They are also used as a garnish on appetisers, pizzas and open sandwiches. Salted capers must be rinsed thoroughly in cold water before use.

Capon A male chicken that has been neutered to produce tender flesh. It has a higher proportion of white breast meat to darker meat.

Cappuccino Espresso coffee topped with milk which has been frothed by passing steam through it.

FESTIVE FRUIT CAKE

★ *Preparation time:* 30 minutes
Total cooking time: 1–1½ hours
Makes two bar tin cakes

125 g (4 oz) unsalted (sweet) butter
¼ cup soft brown sugar
2 eggs, lightly beaten
¼ cup golden syrup (light corn syrup)
125 g (4 oz) whole macadamia nuts
125 g (4 oz) whole brazil nuts
125 g (4 oz) whole hazelnuts
¼ cup self-raising flour
¼ cup plain (all-purpose) flour

200 g (6½ oz) whole red glacé cherries
125 g (4 oz) glacé pineapple, cut into 2 cm (¾ inch) pieces
250 g (8 oz) dates, pitted
125 g (4 oz) glacé apricots, cut into 2 cm (¾ inch) pieces
2 tablespoons port or brandy

1 Preheat oven to slow 150°C (300°F/Gas 2). Line bases and sides of two 26 x 8 x 4.5 cm (10½ x 3 x 1¾ inch) bar tins with greaseproof paper. Using electric beaters, beat butter and sugar in small mixing bowl until light and creamy. Add eggs gradually, beating thoroughly after each addition. Add syrup; beat until combined.

2 Transfer mixture to large bowl; add fruit and nuts. Using a metal spoon, fold in the sifted ingredients alternately with the liquid. Stir until just combined and mixture is almost smooth.

3 Spoon mixture evenly into prepared tins; smooth surface. Bake for 1¼ hours or until skewer comes out clean when inserted in centre of cakes. Leave in tin in 1 hour before turning out.

DUNDEE CAKE

★ *Preparation time:* 30 minutes
Total cooking time: 2–2¼ hours
Makes one 20 cm (8 inch) round cake

250 g (8 oz) unsalted (sweet) butter
1 cup soft brown sugar
4 eggs, lightly beaten
1½ cups plain (all-purpose) flour
½ cup self-raising flour
2 tablespoons rum
1 cup sultanas
¼ cup glacé cherries, chopped

1⅓ cups currants
1 cup almond meal
¾ cup slivered almonds
⅓ cup combined orange and lemon peel
1 cup raisins
½ cup whole almonds, for decoration

1 Preheat oven to slow 150°C (300°F/Gas 2). Brush deep 20 cm (8 inch) round cake tin with oil or melted butter. Line base and side with greaseproof paper. Using electric beaters, beat butter and sugar in a small mixing bowl until light and creamy. Add eggs gradually, beating thoroughly after each addition.

2 Transfer to large mixing bowl, add peel, fruits and nuts. Using a metal spoon, fold in sifted dry ingredients alternately with liquid. Stir until combined and mixture is almost smooth.

3 Spoon into tin; smooth surface. Arrange almonds on top. Bake 2–2¼ hours or until skewer comes out clean when inserted in centre. Leave in tin several hours before turning out.

ABOVE: DUNDEE CAKE
OPPOSITE PAGE: ORANGE SPONGE

CAKES SPONGE AND ANGEL FOOD

BASIC SPONGE SANDWICH

✳ *Preparation time:* 25 minutes
Total cooking time: 20–25 minutes
Makes one 20 cm (8 inch) cake

3 eggs, separated
3/4 cup caster (superfine) sugar
1 cup self-raising flour, sifted
2 tablespoons icing (confectioners) sugar
1/2 cup strawberry jam (or any favourite jam)
300 ml (9 fl oz) carton thick cream, whipped
3 tablespoons very hot water

1 Preheat oven to 180°C (350°F/Gas 4). Grease and flour two 20 cm (8 inch) sandwich cake tins. Place egg whites in a clean, dry bowl. Beat until stiff peaks form. Gradually beat in sugar. Beat until thick and glossy.

2 Fold through egg yolks then flour and water.

3 Divide mixture evenly between prepared tins. Bake for 20–25 minutes or until cake springs back when touched.

4 Remove both cakes from tins. Cool on a tea-towel placed on a cake rack. When cakes are cool, spread with jam then cream. Sandwich layers together. Decorate top of cake with sifted icing sugar.

VARIATIONS

■ **Chocolate Sponge:** Replace 1 cup self-raising flour with 3/4 cup self-raising flour, sifted with 1/4 cup cocoa; replace 3 tablespoons water with 3 tablespoons boiling milk.

■ **Coffee Sponge:** Sift 2 teaspoons instant coffee with the self-raising flour.

■ **Lemon Sponge:** Add 2 teaspoons grated rind with the sugar; ice with lemon icing.

■ **Orange Sponge:** Add 2 teaspoons grated rind with the sugar. Fill with orange liqueur flavoured cream, ice with orange flavoured glacé icing and decorate with orange segments.

■ **Nut Sponge:** Fold in 1/4 cup finely ground almonds, hazelnuts, walnuts or pecans. Cut sponge in half, fill with coffee-flavoured cream.

ABOUT SPONGE CAKES

■ Eggs are the most important ingredient in sponge making. To ensure success, use fresh eggs from the refrigerator. Separate each egg over two small bowls, before transferring to a larger bowl for mixing. Bring to room temperature before use. Add sugar to egg white or whole eggs gradually, about 1 tablespoon at a time, and beat well after each addition. The folding technique for dry ingredients is also critical: use a large metal spoon, running it along the bottom of bowl and up in one sweeping action. Cut down through the bowl, rotating the bowl as you fold.

Capsicum see Sweet Pepper

Carambola The fruit of a tree originally from Indonesia and Malaysia and now grown throughout South-East Asia, China, India, the Caribbean and parts of South America. The small, oval, golden-yellow fruit has five prominent ribs which result in star-shaped slices when the carambola is cut crosswise—hence its common names, star fruit and five corner fruit. It has a sharp, sour-sweet taste, and can be eaten fresh, added to fruit and savoury salads, served with cheese, used as a garnish, pureed for use in sorbets and ice-creams, or cooked in South-East Asian dishes.

Caramel
Sugar heated until it melts into a brown syrup. It is used in cakes, sweet sauces and puddings, to line moulds for puddings and custards, as a sweet, brittle coating for fruit such as strawberries, and

to colour soups, stews and gravies.

The term caramel is also used for a rich, chewy confectionery (candy) made from sugar, butter, and cream or milk.

Caraway A plant related to parsley and native to southern Europe, the Mediterranean and parts of western Asia. Its highly aromatic, hard, brown, crescent-shaped seeds were used by the ancient Egyptians to treat stomach complaints and flatulence; they were first used as a flavouring by the Arabs, and for centuries have been added to cakes, rye bread, cheeses, casseroles, potatoes, salads and sauerkraut. Oil from the seed flavours the liqueur known as kümmel.

Carbonnade de Boeuf Thin slices of beef, browned quickly over a high heat, then cooked with beer and onions. The dish is originally from Belgium, but its name comes from the Italian word *carbonata*, charcoal-grilled. In France the name carbonnade is also given to grilled (broiled) pork loin, and

CITRUS GENOISE SPONGE

★
Preparation time: 40 minutes
Total cooking time: 20 minutes
Makes one 20 cm (8 inch) round layer cake

1 cup self-raising flour
4 eggs, lightly beaten
1/2 cup caster (superfine) sugar
60 g (2 oz) unsalted (sweet) butter, melted and cooled
2 teaspoons finely grated orange rind
1 teaspoon finely grated lemon rind

Lemon Curd Filling
6 teaspoons cornflour (cornstarch)
1/3 cup caster (superfine) sugar
3/4 cup (6 fl oz) milk
1/3 cup (2 1/2 fl oz) lemon juice
2 eggs, lightly beaten

1 Preheat oven to moderate 180°C (350°F/Gas 4). Brush two shallow, 20 cm (8 inch) round sandwich tins with melted butter or oil. Line bases with paper; grease the paper. Dust the tins lightly with flour, shake off excess. Sift the flour three times onto greaseproof paper. Combine eggs and sugar in medium heatproof mixing bowl. Place bowl over pan of simmering water. Beat until mixture is thick and pale yellow. Remove from heat, continue to beat until mixture has cooled slightly and increased in volume.

2 Add flour, melted butter, lemon and orange rind. Using metal spoon, fold quickly and lightly until ingredients are just combined. Spread mixture evenly into prepared tins. Bake for 20 minutes or until the sponges are lightly golden and shrink from sides of tins. Leave sponges in tins for 5 minutes before turning onto wire rack to cool.

3 To make Lemon Curd Filling: Combine cornflour, sugar, milk, lemon juice and eggs in small pan, mix well. Stir over low heat until mixture boils and thickens, cook for 1 minute longer. Remove from heat. Transfer to a small bowl, cover with plastic wrap and allow to cool before using.

4 Cut each cake in half horizontally. Place a cake layer on a serving plate. Spread the cake evenly with the filling. Continue layering with remaining cake and filling, ending with a cake layer on top. Dust the top with sifted icing (confectioners) sugar, if desired.

ANGEL FOOD CAKE

★ ★
Preparation time: 15 minutes
Total cooking time: 45 minutes
Serves 8

1 cup plain (all-purpose) flour
1/4 teaspoon salt
1 teaspoon cream of tartar
1 teaspoon vanilla essence
1/4 teaspoon almond essence
1 cup caster (superfine) sugar
10 eggs
egg whites (use about 300 ml (9 fl oz))
icing (confectioners) sugar
strawberries for serving

1 Preheat oven to 170°C (340°F/Gas 3–4). Sift flour with half the sugar three times. Place egg whites in a large dry mixing bowl with salt and cream of tartar. Using electric beaters, beat egg whites until stiff but not dry in texture. Add remaining sugar gradually, beating until mixture is thick and glossy and the sugar is dissolved.

2 Stir in the vanilla and almond essence lightly. Sift flour and sugar mixture again over the egg whites in three or four lots, folding in gently after each addition.

3 Pour mixture into an ungreased angel cake pan or a 23 cm (9 inch) tube pan. Tap tin gently on bench to release any air bubbles. Bake on centre shelf in oven for 45 minutes, or until a skewer comes out clean when inserted in cake. Remove from oven and invert tin. Allow cake to cool completely before turning out by loosening edges gently with a spatula.

ABOVE: ANGEL FOOD CAKE
OPPOSITE PAGE: FROSTED CHRISTMAS CAKE

in the south of France to a beef stew prepared with red wine.

Cardamom The aromatic, rounded seed pod from a shrub native to tropical Asia, but also present from ancient times in parts of Europe, used

as a spice. The pods, containing tiny black seeds, are picked before they ripen, and dried. They should be stored, unopened, in an airtight container, and the seeds ground as required. Cardamom is one of the ingredients in curry powder and is also used in pickles, rice and sweet dishes. Seeds have been found in Neolithic lake settlements in Switzerland. In Arab countries, seeds are often added to coffee beans before grinding. As each pod has to be picked by hand, it is the most expensive spice in the world after saffron.

Cardoon Native to southern Europe and related to the artichoke, cardoon's celery-like stalk is eaten as a vegetable, boiled, steamed or fried, usually served with a sauce. Most tender and delicate in flavour are those that have been wrapped in paper as they grow, to produce white stalks.

Carob The fruit of the carob tree, native to the Mediterranean region.

CAKES CELEBRATION

FROSTED CHRISTMAS CAKE

★ *Preparation time:* 1 hour
Total cooking time: 3–3½ hours
Makes one 20 cm (8 inch) square cake

250 g (8 oz) unsalted (sweet) butter
1 cup soft brown sugar
4 eggs, lightly beaten
1 teaspoon vanilla essence
1 tablespoon orange marmalade
1 tablespoon golden syrup (light corn syrup)
1.25 kg (2½ lb) mixed dried fruit
2 cups plain (all-purpose) flour
½ cup self-raising flour
2 teaspoons mixed spice

1 teaspoon ground cinnamon
½ cup (4 fl oz) rum, brandy or port

Royal Icing
4 egg whites
5½ cups pure sifted icing (confectioners) sugar
2 teaspoons lemon juice

Decorations
1 metre (1 yard) ribbon
selection of small suitable ornaments

1 Preheat oven to slow 150°C (300°F/Gas 2). Line the base and sides of a deep, 20 cm (8 inch) square cake tin with greaseproof paper. Beat the butter and sugar in a small mixing bowl until light and creamy. Add the eggs gradually, beating well after each addition. Add essence, orange marmalade and golden syrup; beat until ingredients are combined.

2 Transfer mixture to a large mixing bowl; add fruit. Using a metal spoon, fold in the sifted flours and spice alternately with liquid. Stir until ingredients are just combined and mixture is almost smooth. Spoon into prepared tin; smooth the surface with wetted hand.

3 Tap the tin gently on a benchtop to settle mixture. Wrap double thickness of brown paper around tin; secure with paper clip. Bake 3–3½ hours or until skewer comes out clean when inserted in centre. Leave cake overnight before turning out.

4 To make Royal Icing: Using electric beaters, beat egg whites in clean, dry mixing bowl for 30 seconds. Add icing sugar a tablespoon at a time, beating continuously on slow speed until mixture is very stiff and forms peaks. Blend in lemon juice. Cover with a damp cloth or plastic wrap.

5 Place cake on large plate or cake board. Using a flat-bladed knife, cover with icing, reserving 2 tablespoons for decoration. Use knife to work icing into fluffy peaks. Allow to harden 2 hours.

6 Wrap ribbon around cake, secure with small amount of icing. Trim excess ribbon, tie into a bow, trim edges. Place a small amount of icing on back of bow, place over ribbon join, secure with a pin; remove pin when icing is firm. Secure ornaments on cake with a small amount of icing.

Note: Royal Icing sets very quickly so it is important to work fast. If desired, icing can be coloured with food colouring.

The long, leathery pod contains hard, reddish seeds in a brown pulp. Both the fresh pods and pulp can be eaten raw and have a sweet, chocolate-like taste. A powder made from the dried and ground pod and pulp can be used in cooking in the same way as cocoa powder.

Carpaccio A dish of paper-thin slices of raw meat, usually beef, dressed with oil and lemon juice or a creamy vinaigrette made with olive oil, and served as a first course. It was named by its inventor, the proprietor of Harry's Bar in Venice, after Vittore Carpaccio, a fifteenth-century Venetian painter.

Carpetbag Steak A thick piece of tender steak with a pocket cut into it which is filled with raw oysters. The steak is then pan-fried or grilled (broiled).

Carrot A root vegetable, related to parsley, parsnip and celery, with crisp, orange flesh, that is eaten raw in salads or cooked in both savoury and sweet dishes. Its ancestor was a wild plant. It was introduced to Europe by the Dutch during the Middle Ages. Baby carrots (sometimes known as Dutch carrots) and young carrots need only be scrubbed clean

BLACK FOREST CAKE

★★

Preparation time: 1 hour 15 minutes
Total cooking time: 40–50 minutes
Makes one 23 cm (9 inch) round cake

200 g (6½ oz) unsalted (sweet) butter
¾ cup caster (superfine) sugar
3 eggs, lightly beaten
1 teaspoon vanilla essence
1⅔ cups self-raising flour
⅓ cup plain (all-purpose) flour
¾ cup cocoa powder
1 tablespoon instant coffee powder
½ teaspoon bicarbonate of soda (baking soda)
½ cup (4 fl oz) buttermilk

Chocolate Mock Cream
200 g (6½ oz) dark (semi-sweet) chocolate, chopped
250 g (8 oz) unsalted (sweet) butter
⅓ cup (2½ fl oz) milk
1¼ cups (10 fl oz) cream, whipped
425 g (13½ oz) can pitted cherries, drained
white and dark (semi-sweet) chocolate curls, for decoration

1 Preheat oven to moderate 180°C (350°F/Gas 4). Brush a deep, 23 cm (9 inch) round cake tin with oil or melted butter, line the base and side with paper; grease paper. Beat butter and sugar in small mixing bowl until light and creamy. Add eggs gradually, beat thoroughly after each addition. Add essence, beat to combine. Transfer to a large bowl. Using a metal spoon, fold in sifted flours, cocoa, coffee and soda alternately with combined buttermilk and milk. Stir until just combined.

2 Pour mixture evenly into tin; smooth surface. Bake 40–50 minutes or until a skewer comes out clean when inserted in centre. Leave cake 20 minutes before turning onto wire rack to cool.

3 To make Chocolate Mock Cream: Place chocolate in a glass bowl. Stir over barely simmering water until melted; remove from heat. Beat butter in a small mixing bowl until light and creamy. Add chocolate, beating for 1 minute or until mixture is glossy and smooth.

4 Turn cake upside down; cut into 3 layers horizontally. Place first layer on serving plate. Spread with half whipped cream, top with half cherries. Continue layering with remaining cake, cream and cherries, ending with cake on top.

5 Spread Mock Cream over top and sides, using a flat-bladed knife. Pipe stars of remaining mixture around cake rim. Decorate with chocolate curls if desired.

6 To make Chocolate Curls: Spread 250 g (8 oz) melted chocolate onto a marble slab or cool work surface to a depth of 1 cm (½ inch); smooth surface lightly. Allow chocolate to cool until almost set. Hold a sharp, flat-bladed knife horizontally against the surface of the chocolate. Applying constant pressure to the blade with both hands, pull the knife towards you. Varying the pressure will determine the thickness of the curls.

ABOVE: BLACK FOREST CAKE
OPPOSITE PAGE, ABOVE: HONEY AND COCONUT CAKE; BELOW: CHERRY TEACAKE

CAKES TEACAKES

CHERRY TEACAKE

★ *Preparation time:* 15 minutes
Total cooking time: 30 minutes
Makes one 20 cm (8 inch) round cake

60 g (2 oz) unsalted (sweet) butter
1/3 cup cornflour (cornstarch)
2/3 cup caster (superfine) sugar
1 1/2 cups icing (confectioners) sugar
1/2 teaspoon coconut essence
3 eggs, lightly beaten
1/3 cup chopped glacé cherries
1/4 cup desiccated coconut
1 1/4 cups self-raising flour

Pink Icing
1 teaspoon unsalted (sweet) butter
2 teaspoons boiling water
2–3 drops pink food colouring

1 Preheat oven to moderate 180°C (350°F/Gas 4). Brush deep, 20 cm (8 inch) round cake tin with oil or melted butter. Line base with paper; grease paper. Using electric beaters, beat butter, sugar and essence in small bowl until light and creamy.

2 Add eggs and beat for 3 minutes or until just combined. Transfer to a large mixing bowl. Add cherries, coconut, sifted flour and cornflour, beat for 1 minute or until mixture is almost smooth. Spoon evenly into tin; bake 30 minutes or until skewer comes out clean when inserted in centre. Leave cake in tin for 10 minutes before turning onto wire rack to cool.

3 To make Pink Icing: Combine sifted icing sugar, butter and water in small bowl to form a firm paste. Stand bowl in pan of simmering water, stir until icing is smooth and glossy; remove from heat, tint with colouring. Spread over top of cake.

HONEY AND COCONUT CAKE

★ *Preparation time:* 40 minutes
Total cooking time: 30 minutes
Makes one 28 cm (11 inch) oblong cake

125 g (4 oz) unsalted (sweet) butter
2/3 cup raw sugar
2 eggs, lightly beaten
1 teaspoon vanilla essence
1/4 cup honey
1/4 cup desiccated coconut
1 3/4 cups self-raising flour
1 teaspoon ground nutmeg
1/4 teaspoon ground cinnamon

1/4 teaspoon ground allspice
1/2 cup (4 fl oz) milk

Honey and Cream Cheese Icing
125 g (4 oz) cream cheese, softened
1/2 cup icing (confectioners) sugar
1 tablespoon honey

extra ground nutmeg, for decoration

1 Preheat oven to moderate 180°C (350°F/Gas 4). Brush shallow, 28 x 18 x 3 cm (11 x 7 x 1 1/4 inch) oblong cake tin with oil or melted butter, line base and sides with paper; grease paper. Using electric beaters, beat butter and sugar in small mixing bowl until light and creamy. Add eggs gradually, beating well after each addition. Add essence and honey; beat until combined.

2 Transfer to large mixing bowl; add coconut. Using a metal spoon, fold in sifted flour and spices alternately with milk. Stir until just combined and mixture is almost smooth. Pour mixture into prepared tin; smooth surface.

3 Bake 30 minutes or until skewer comes out clean when inserted in centre of cake. Leave cake in tin 10 minutes before turning onto wire rack.

4 To make Honey and Cream Cheese Icing: Using electric beaters, beat cream cheese in small bowl until creamy. Add sifted icing sugar and honey, beat 3 minutes or until mixture is smooth and fluffy. Spread on cake; sprinkle with nutmeg.

Cashew Nut
The creamy, kidney-shaped nut of a tall tree native to South America. The hard-shelled nut develops inside an apple-shaped, fleshy fruit (used to make a liquor) and protrudes from the end of the fruit when ripe. The shell contains caustic oils which must be rendered harmless by heating before the nut can be extracted. Cashew nuts are sold shelled. They are eaten roasted and salted, and used to make cashew nut butter. The raw nuts are added to curries or other Asian dishes. They can also be used in stuffings for chicken, or as a salad ingredient. The cashew nut has a high fat content (46 per cent).

for salads and sandwiches or cut into strips for dips.

with a stiff brush before use. Tiny carrots can be cooked whole. Older carrots should be scraped or peeled and then sliced, diced or cut into julienne strips for cooking. If carrots are to be used raw, grate

CAKE DECORATING

Sprinkle a simple sponge cake with sifted icing (confectioners) sugar, or cover a chocolate cake with rich buttercream, pipe with rosettes of chocolate cream, and decorate with chocolate curls and fanned strawberries. The way you decorate a cake depends on the type of cake, your level of skill and, most of all, your own taste.

TECHNIQUES

Always work with completely cooled cakes when decorating, unless the recipe states otherwise. If the cake is even slightly warm, the icing will be difficult to handle and there is every possibility that it will crack or break when sliced.

When baked, some cakes may have a slight dome which can be trimmed to give a better appearance when the cake is iced. Use a long, sharp, serrated knife to slice off the dome—only trim enough cake to obtain an even surface. Cut with a gentle sawing motion, using your other hand to steady the cake while you slice. Turn the cake over onto a serving plate, base side up, before icing.

Many cakes are cut in half, or in one or more layers, horizontally before they are filled. To make the job easy, mark the mid-point round the side of the cake with toothpicks. Use a long, sharp, serrated knife for slicing the cake; cut with a gentle sawing action. Repeat the marking and cutting procedure for each layer of cake.

HOW TO ICE A CAKE

Use a pastry brush to brush off any loose crumbs. For a smoothly iced surface, spread icing over the cake using a flat-bladed knife. To assemble layers, slice the cake as described above.

Place a dab of icing or filling on a serving plate

COOLING THE CAKE

A cake is quite fragile when just removed from the oven. It is best to leave it in the tin for the specified time before turning it onto a wire rack to cool. Leave the cake on the wire rack until it is completely cold.

If a cake seems to be stuck to its tin, run a flat-bladed knife around the sides to release it. Cakes lined with paper are easiest to release: gently lever with a thin spatula or knife before turning upside down; remove paper lining immediately. Spray wire racks with vegetable oil to prevent sticking.

ICINGS AND FILLINGS

Buttercreams make excellent fillings or coverings for cakes. Cakes that are covered in either butter-cream or another type of icing will keep moist and fresh for far longer than cakes that have not been iced.

Buttercreams can range from a fairly simple mixture of icing (confectioners) sugar, butter and flavourings, to rich combinations of butter, egg yolks and sugar syrups which result in smooth, velvety fillings. The secret of making a good buttercream is to use unsalted (sweet) butter and to beat the mixture thoroughly until it reaches a light, creamy consistency.

and centre on it the first layer (the icing stops it moving). Brush with jam if specified in recipe, then evenly spread the filling mixture. Using a flat-bladed knife or spatula, spread filling to within about 5 mm (1/4 inch) of the edge of the cake. Warming the knife or spatula by dipping it into hot water as you spread the filling will make it easier to work; wipe knife with a clean cloth before continuing.

Place the second layer on top and spread with filling mixture, as described above. Place the final layer, base side up, on top. Spread a thin layer of cream or frosting around sides and top of cake to seal in any crumbs and to fill any gaps.

Spread a final layer of cream or frosting evenly around the sides and then on top of the cake, blending at the edges. Use even strokes.

VANILLA BUTTERCREAM

In a bowl, beat together 250 g (8 oz) unsalted (sweet) butter and 2 tablespoons icing (confectioners') sugar until the mixture is light, fluffy and

VIENNA BUTTERCREAM

Beat 100 g (3½ oz) unsalted (sweet) butter in a bowl until soft. Gradually add 250 g (8 oz) sifted icing (confectioners') sugar, beating until mixture is light and fluffy. Add 2 tablespoons of hot water and 1 teaspoon of vanilla essence and stir in well. This can be used as a filling for cakes and biscuits (cookies) as well as an icing.

CREAM CHEESE ICING

Using electric beaters, beat 100 g (3½ oz) cream cheese and ¾ cup sifted icing (confectioners') sugar together in a small bowl until the mixture becomes light and creamy. Add the flavourings of your choice, and a little milk if necessary. Beat for 2 minutes or until mixture takes on a smooth and fluffy consistency. Spread the icing thickly over the cake, using a wide, flat-bladed knife.

■ **LEMON ICING:** to the cream cheese and the sugar, add 1–2 teaspoons finely grated lemon rind and 2 teaspoons milk.

■ **ORANGE ICING:** to the cream cheese and the sugar, add 1–2 teaspoons finely grated orange rind and 2 teaspoons milk.

■ **HONEY ICING:** to the cream cheese and the sugar, add 1–2 teaspoons warmed honey and 2 teaspoons milk.

■ **PASSIONFRUIT ICING:** to the cream cheese and sugar, add 1 tablespoon passionfruit pulp.

GLACE ICING

This is a thin, shiny icing poured onto the centre of the cake as soon as it reaches a coating consistency. Allow icing to run down the sides, guiding it with a flat-bladed knife.
In a heatproof bowl, mix together 1 cup icing (confectioners') sugar, 2 teaspoons butter, the flavouring of your choice, and sufficient liquid to make a smooth firm paste. Stand the bowl over a pan of simmering water and stir until the icing has become smooth and glossy.

■ **LEMON GLACE ICING:** to the sugar and the butter, add 1 teaspoon finely grated lemon rind and 1–2 tablespoons lemon juice.

■ **ORANGE GLACE ICING:** to the sugar and the butter, add 1 teaspoon finely grated orange rind and 1–2 tablespoons orange juice.

■ **PASSIONFRUIT GLACE ICING:** to sugar and butter, add 1–2 tablespoons passionfruit pulp.

■ **COFFEE GLACE ICING:** to the sugar and the butter, add 1 teaspoon instant coffee powder and 1–2 tablespoons water.

■ **CHOCOLATE GLACE ICING:** to the sugar and the butter, add 1 tablespoon cocoa powder and 1–2 tablespoons hot milk.

pale. Add, a little at a time, another 1¼ cups of icing (confectioners') sugar, beating well between each addition. Then add 2 beaten egg yolks and 2 teaspoons boiling water. Whisk the mixture thoroughly until it reaches a smooth and even consistency. Add vanilla essence to taste.

MAKING PIPING BAGS Here is a quick and easy way to make a small paper piping bag. Cut a 25 cm (10 inch) square of strong greaseproof paper and fold it in half diagonally to form a triangle.

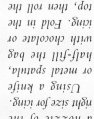

Working with the long side at the bottom, roll a corner to the centre and tape it into place. Wrap the other corner to the back and tape that in place. Use scissors to trim the tip of the bag to suit the size of your decorating. You can also insert into the bag a nozzle of the right size for icing.
Using a knife or metal spatula, half-fill the bag with chocolate or icing. Fold in the top, then roll the top down to the level of the icing to seal the bag. Grip the bag at the top with the full end resting in your palm. Use pressure from the palm of your hand to push the icing out through the hole.

CAKE DECORATING

CHOCOLATE DECORATIONS

Chocolate provides an easy way of dressing up a simple cake or a batch of biscuits (cookies). It can be used not only for making icing and fillings, but for scrolls, curls and leaves to decorate the top of the cake. Melted chocolate may be used to drizzle over biscuits in decorative patterns. While good eating chocolate is superior in flavour, compound chocolate is much easier to work with. It sets at room temperature and melts easily over a bowl of hot water.

CHOCOLATE SHAPES

Line a flat, cold baking tray with greaseproof paper, brush lightly with oil. Break dark (semi-sweet) or milk chocolate into small pieces, place in a bowl over a pan of gently simmering water. Make sure that no water or steam gets into the bowl. Stir chocolate until it has just melted. Using a flat-bladed knife to guide it, pour chocolate over oiled paper to form a thick, even coating. Leave in a cool place until chocolate is almost set.

Using a knife or a shaped cutter (star, flute, round, etc), cut chocolate into desired shapes. Chill chocolate before lifting off the cut-out shapes. The shapes should be stored in a cool, dry place. Chocolate shapes are useful not only as cake decorations, but also make very attractive garnishes for desserts such as ice-cream.

CHOCOLATE PETALS

Cut foil into several squares in the sizes of your choice. Melt dark (semi-sweet) or milk chocolate in a bowl over a pan of hot water and cool slightly. Hold a square of foil in the palm of your hand. With a palette knife or a spoon, thinly spread melted chocolate onto the foil in the shape of a flower petal. While the chocolate is still soft, lift your fingers under the foil to slightly bend the petal into a natural shape. Leave aside until set. Repeat procedure with remaining chocolate. Peel off foil before using. Petals can be formed into the shape of a flower using melted chocolate to join them together.

CHOCOLATE WEDGES

Cover the base of a 20 cm (8 inch) round tin with foil. Melt about 150 g (5 oz) dark (semi-sweet) or milk chocolate in a bowl over a pan of hot water.

CHOCOLATE CURLS

Melt dark (semi-sweet) or milk chocolate in a bowl over a pan of hot water. Spread thinly over a smooth board using a palette knife. Set aside until chocolate is almost set. Using a large flat-bladed knife, pull the blade towards you along the length of the chocolate to make long curls.

CHOCOLATE SHAVINGS

Use a vegetable peeler to shave off curls from the flat side of a large block of chocolate. Work over greaseproof paper or a plate, using long, even strokes. Leave chocolate in a warm spot for 10–15 minutes before shaving. For best results chocolate should be warmed, but only sufficiently to enable you to work it. Spoon or shake the shavings onto the iced cake.

Wedges are an ideal decoration for the top of a 20 cm (8 inch) round cake. Spread melted chocolate in an even layer over foil and refrigerate until semi-set. Using a sharp, flat-bladed knife, carefully mark the chocolate into 12 wedges of equal size. Return to refrigerator until chocolate is completely set. Peel away foil.

SQUARES

These are an easy and impressive way to decorate the sides of a cake or a special dessert. Using a 32 x 28 cm (13 x 11 in) oven tray, cover the base with foil. Spread 200 g (7 oz) of melted chocolate evenly over it and swirl a fork lightly through the chocolate to create a wavy effect; make sure you do not push the fork right down to the base of the oven tray. Refrigerate until chocolate is semi-set. Using a sharp, flat-bladed knife and a ruler, mark off the chocolate into squares of about 6 cm (2½ inches). Return oven tray to the refrigerator until chocolate has cooled and completely set. Peel away the foil. Carefully press the chocolate squares around the edges of the iced cake to decorate. Squares can also be used as garnishes for ice-cream desserts.

OTHER DECORATIONS

Cakes can look marvellous when decorated with crystallised (candied) fruit and flowers, marzipan fruit, spun sugar, silver cachous or coloured sprinkles.

CRYSTALLISED (CANDIED) FLOWERS

Lightly beat an egg white until it is broken up and foamy. Pour 1 cup caster (superfine) sugar into a shallow bowl. Using small fresh flowers such as violets or rosebuds, or the petals of large flowers such as roses, brush petals with egg white (use a small paintbrush) then dip them into sugar, making sure petals are well coated. Place flowers on a rack to dry. Store in an airtight container.

MELTING CHOCOLATE

Use the best chocolate you can for decorations and icing. Compound chocolate is easier to work with, although it does not have the flavour of good quality eating chocolate. Chop the chocolate into even-sized pieces and place in a glass bowl. Place bowl over a pan of simmering water; stir gently until chocolate has melted. Do not allow even a drop of water to fall on the chocolate or it will immediately stiffen dramatically and be unworkable for decoration purposes. Cool the chocolate slightly before using.

SUGAR PATTERNS

Cut greaseproof paper into long thin strips and place in a criss-cross or other pattern on top of a plain cake. Dust with sifted icing (confectioners) sugar. Carefully remove paper strips to reveal a sugar pattern. A simpler way to make a sugar pattern is to lay a paper doily on top of the cake. Sift sugar over the doily and then remove it. This will leave a pretty, lacy pattern.

SPUN SUGAR

Combine 1 cup of sugar and ½ cup (4 fl oz) of water in a pan. Place over medium heat and stir constantly until sugar has dissolved. Make sure you do not bring the mixture to the boil until the sugar has dissolved completely. Then bring to the boil, and boil rapidly without stirring until the mixture is a light golden brown colour. Remove the pan from the heat and, using a metal spoon, drizzle toffee in a thin stream backwards and forwards over lightly oiled baking trays. When set, break the toffee up into small pieces and place on the cake. The toffee may also be spun over an iced cake. Place two forks back to back and dip them into the toffee mixture. Carefully pull the toffee in thin strands over the cake.

FLAKED ALMOND DECORATION

Scatter 180 g (6 oz) flaked almonds over an ungreased baking tray. Bake almonds at 180°C (350°F/Gas 4) for about 5 minutes or until they are light golden brown. Take a generous tablespoon of the roasted almonds in the palm of your hand and press them lightly and evenly onto the icing on the side of a cake, before the icing has completely set. Roasted flaked almonds are a popular way of finishing off cake decorations as they are easy to place on the icing around the sides and impart a wonderful flavour and texture to the cake.

CANAPES

Canapés are usually served with drinks before dinner, or at a cocktail party. They should be small enough to allow them to be held in one hand and eaten in a single bite.

QUICK BASES AND TOPPINGS

- Spread crisp bread croûtes with pesto and top with halved cherry tomatoes.
- Fill tiny cooked pastry cases with a mixture of light cream cheese, finely chopped smoked salmon and finely chopped chives.
- Top freshly cooked mini wholemeal blinis or pikelets with thick sour cream and caviar.
- Top thick slices of unpeeled cucumber with blue cheese and walnuts, or slices of smoked salmon and a spoonful of sour cream.
- Top crisp bread croûtes with tapenade and sliced hard-boiled egg or poached quail egg.
- Spread crisp bread croûtes with thick garlic-flavoured mayonnaise. Top with a green asparagus tip and garnish with a strip of roasted red pepper (capsicum).
- Top tiny wedges of spinach frittata with fine strips of ham.
- Top fresh oysters on the shell with thick mayonnaise containing finely chopped herbs.

CRISP BREAD CROUTES

Trim crusts from sliced white or brown bread. Using a biscuit cutter, cut 4 x 4 cm (1½ x 1½ inch) circles from each slice. Brush both sides of bread with melted butter, place on tray and bake at 180°C (350°F/Gas 4) for 10 minutes until golden. Cool, store in an airtight container.

- Spread crisp bread croûtes with chicken liver or salmon pâté and top with sliced dill cucumber.
- Spread pumpernickel circles with Blue Castello cheese and top with sliced stuffed olives.
- Wrap slices of fresh pear or cubes of cantaloupe (rockmelon) in wafer-thin slices of prosciutto.
- Spread crisp bread croûtes or pumpernickel circles with seeded mustard, top with sliced rare roast fillet of beef and top with a piece of mango.
- Fill fresh white button mushrooms with a mixture of chopped ham and cream cheese. Top with toasted pine nuts and finely chopped fresh parsley.
- Fill tiny uncooked pastry cases with chopped sundried tomato, chopped basil and crumbled fresh goats cheese. Bake until cheese melts.
- Make mini pizza bases, top with sautéed onion, chopped anchovy fillets and parmesan cheese.

ABOVE: A SELECTION OF CANAPES
OPPOSITE PAGE: CARROT CAKE

Cassata An iced dessert of Italian origin usually consisting of layers of ice-cream, at least one of which contains chopped nuts and glazed fruit, and sometimes also a layer of sweetened, whipped cream. Sicilian cassata consists of strips of sponge cake soaked in a liqueur or sweet dessert wine, encasing ricotta cheese mixed with nuts and glazed fruit and then chilled. Both types are traditionally made in a rectangular mould—hence the name, which is derived from the Italian word for 'little brick'.

Cassava (Manioc) A plant native to tropical America and grown throughout the Pacific Islands, Indonesia, the Philippines and parts of Africa. The starchy, tuberous roots can be prepared and cooked in the same way as the potato, the tender leaves cooked like spinach and the larger tougher ones used as wrappings for food to be baked. A powder prepared from the dried root is used as a thickener in the cooking of South-East Asia.

Casserole A selection of meat, poultry or fish, and vegetables, herbs, seasonings and liquid.

CARROTS

CARROT CAKE

★ **Preparation time:** 15 minutes
Total cooking time: 35 minutes
Serves 8

125 g (4 oz) butter	1½ teaspoons baking
1 cup sugar	powder
1¼ cups plain (all-	pinch salt
purpose) flour	¼ cup (2 fl oz) warm
(wholemeal or white or	water
half and half)	grated rind of 1 orange
pinch of cinnamon,	2 eggs
nutmeg and allspice	1 large carrot, grated
	60 g (2 oz) unblanched
	almonds, chopped
	(about ⅔ cup)

1 Preheat oven to 180°C (350°F/Gas 4). Brush a 20 cm (8 inch) square cake tin with butter or oil. Line base and sides with paper, grease paper.

2 Beat butter in an electric mixer or with wooden spoon until it is light and fluffy. Add sugar and mix until combined. Add spices and orange rind and mix well. Add eggs, one at a time, and stir until well mixed, then add carrot and nuts. Add sifted flour, baking powder and salt. Add the warm water a little at a time until the consistency is smooth without overbeating.

3 Spoon mixture into prepared tin; smooth surface. Bake for 35 minutes or until a skewer comes out clean when inserted in centre of cake. Leave cake in tin for 10 minutes before turning out onto wire rack to cool. Decorate with lemon icing or a thick buttery frosting.

CARROT SOUP

★ **Preparation time:** 12 minutes
Total cooking time: 35 minutes
Serves 4

30 g (1 oz) butter	4 cups (32 fl oz) chicken
6 carrots, sliced	stock
1 clove garlic, crushed	¾ cup (6 fl oz) sour
1 onion, chopped	cream or yoghurt
2 medium potatoes, diced	2 tablespoons chopped
	herbs to garnish

1 Melt butter in a large saucepan, add carrot, garlic and onion and cook for 2–3 minutes. Stir in potato, reduce heat to low, cover and sweat vegetables for 4–5 minutes.

2 Pour in stock and bring to the boil. Season to taste. Reduce heat and allow soup to simmer, covered, for 25 minutes.

3 Puree soup in food processor or blender. Serve garnished with a spoonful of sour cream or yoghurt and sprinkled with herbs.

GRATED CARROT SALAD

★ **Preparation time:** 15 minutes
Total cooking time: nil
Serves 6

10 large carrots	1 teaspoon ground
2 small cucumbers	cinnamon
100 g (3 oz) raisins	1 tablespoon lemon juice
100 ml (3 fl oz) olive oil	½ teaspoon ground ginger
½ cup flaked almonds	ground pepper
	1 tablespoon honey

1 Peel and coarsely grate carrots. Cut cucumbers in quarters lengthways, then cut into thick slices. Place carrots and cucumber in a bowl, add raisins and mix through.

2 Combine the lemon juice, ginger, cinnamon, honey, olive oil and pepper in a small bowl or screw-top jar. Shake the jar well to combine ingredients.

3 Place flaked almonds in a small pan, stir over low heat until lightly golden.

4 Pour dressing over salad, garnish with almonds and serve.

ABOUT CARROTS

■ Buy carrots which are firm and smooth and a deep orange colour. To prepare, wash and lightly scrape or peel, if desired. Young carrots will not need peeling.

■ The flavours of ginger, cloves, dill, honey and marjoram team well with carrots.

Sidebar:

...cooked slowly in a covered dish in the oven. It is usually served from the dish at the table. The term is also used both for the covered utensil and for the cooking method. It comes from the French *casse*, meaning pan or ladle.

Cassoulet A hearty bean and meat stew originally from Languedoc in southern France. Recipes vary, but the essential ingredient is haricot beans, to which various meats are added.

Cauliflower A member of the cabbage family with a large head of tight flower buds that range in colour from creamy white, to green and purple. Cauliflower can be eaten raw, cut into small sprigs and dipped in various dressings, or it can be steamed, boiled or stir-fried. It was first grown in western Asia.

Caviar The roe (eggs) of the sturgeon fish, salted and served as a delicacy. Caviar ranges in colour from grey to yellowy-brown to shiny black, and in size from eggs as small as pinheads (Sevruga) to the highly prized pearl-sized seed-eggs of the

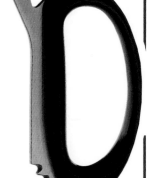

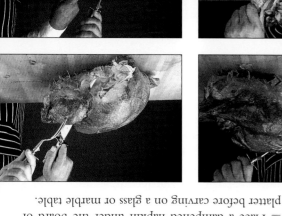

CARVING

Skilful carving makes the most of roast dishes, and leaves them attractive enough to serve cold. Always allow roast meat and poultry to rest for 15 minutes, loosely covered with foil, before carving. Carve with a light slicing rather than sawing action to avoid tearing the flesh.

TO CARVE A TURKEY

1 Use a sharp carving knife and a carving fork to steady the bird. Cut into the turkey where the ball joint of the wing meets the breast, and loosen the meat.

2 Continue cutting around the wing, until the wing can be separated from the rest of the body.

3 Tilt the bird to see the angle of separation between the breast and thigh. Starting at the top, cut down through skin and meat to hip joint.

4 Continue cutting through the hip socket until the thigh and leg section can be loosened and removed from the body. Place section on carving board.

5 Separate thigh from leg (drumstick) by cutting through joint. Cut meat from thigh into long, thin slices. Serve legs whole or sliced, according to size and individual preference.

6 The breast is now ready to be carved. Start at the top of the breast, carving at an angle into thin, even slices.

■ Repeat all steps to carve the other side. The wishbone can be removed by snipping the sinews on either side. Serve a piece of leg with a piece of breast and a portion of the stuffing.

■ Place a dampened napkin under the board or platter before carving on a glass or marble table.

TO CARVE HAM

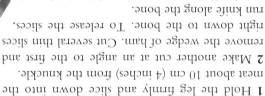

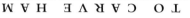

Ham can be sliced on a board or a ham stand. The important thing is that it's kept steady as you slice. Use a clean tea-towel or napkin to firmly grasp the bone while ham carving. A ham knife is a good investment if you eat ham often. Otherwise, use the sharpest knife, sharpening beforehand with a steel.

1 Hold the leg firmly and slice down into the meat about 10 cm (4 inches) from the knuckle.

2 Make another cut at an angle to the first and remove the wedge of ham. Cut several thin slices right down to the bone. To release the slices, run knife along the bone.

3 Lift off slices on the flat of the knife and arrange attractively on a serving platter.

TO CARVE A DUCK

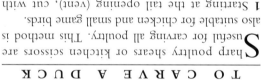

Sharp poultry shears or kitchen scissors are useful for carving all poultry. This method is also suitable for chicken and small game birds.

1 Starting at the tail opening (vent), cut with poultry shears through breast and up to the neck.

2 Turn the bird over; cut with the shears on one side of the backbone and separate into halves.

3 Place each half skin-side up and, following the natural line between breast and thigh, cut crossways into quarters.

Note: Duck may also be carved Chinese fashion, by removing legs and wings, separating thigh from drumstick, and chopping the duck into small pieces with a cleaver.

TO CARVE A STANDING RIB ROAST

Carving will be easier if you have the backbone removed by the butcher and the rib bones cut short. Usually a rib roast is carved into slices, as shown here, but hearty eaters may like a whole rib.

If the roast has been left to stand for 15 minutes before carving, the meat will settle and very little of the juices will be lost during carving.

1 Place the roast on a board with rib side down and bone ends to the left of the board. Using the tip of the knife, release the meat from the base of the rib bone.

2 Slice meat parallel to rib bones, from top to rib; cut into thick slices.

3 Using the tip of the knife, cut along each rib bone, close to the bone, to release slices.

CAULIFLOWER

CAULIFLOWER FRITTERS WITH TOMATO RELISH

✷✷

Preparation time: 35 minutes
Total cooking time: 30 minutes
Serves 4–6

1 small cauliflower
1/2 cup peasemeal (see Note)
1/4 cup self-raising flour
1 teaspoon ground cumin
1/4 teaspoon bicarbonate of soda (baking soda)
2/3 cup (5 fl oz) water
1 egg
200 g (6½ oz) plain yoghurt
vegetable oil for deep frying

Tomato Relish
2 tablespoons vegetable oil
1 medium onion, finely chopped
410 g (13 oz) tomatoes, peeled and chopped
1/2 cup (4 fl oz) white wine vinegar
3/4 cup sugar
1 clove garlic, crushed
1 teaspoon ground cumin
1/2 cup sultanas
3/4 cup finely chopped fresh coriander

1 Cut cauliflower into large florets. Remove as much stem as possible without breaking florets. Wash and drain, pat dry with paper towels. Combine peasemeal, flour, cumin and soda in medium mixing bowl; make a well in centre. Beat together water, egg and yoghurt; pour onto dry ingredients. Stir with wooden spoon until batter is smooth. Leave for 10 minutes.

2 Heat oil in deep heavy-based pan. Dip florets in batter, drain off excess. Using a metal spoon or tongs, gently lower cauliflower into hot oil in small batches. Cook until golden brown, 3–5 minutes. Lift out with a slotted spoon and drain on paper towels. Serve hot with Tomato Relish.

3 To make Tomato Relish: Place oil, onion, tomato, vinegar, sugar, garlic, cumin and sultanas in a pan. Bring to boil, reduce heat; simmer, covered, 20 minutes. Increase heat and cook, stirring occasionally, until mixture thickens. Remove from heat. Stir in coriander.

Note: Peasemeal is a flour made from yellow split peas; it is available from health food stores.

CAULIFLOWER SOUP

Melt 45 g (1½ oz) butter in a pan, add 1 medium onion, chopped, and cook gently until just softened. Add 500 g (1 lb) trimmed cauliflower, chopped, 2 cups (16 fl oz) milk, 2 cups (16 fl oz) chicken or vegetable stock and 1 small bay leaf; bring to boil. Cover soup and simmer for 15–20 minutes, until cauliflower is tender. Remove bay leaf, cool. Place mixture in a food processor or blender and blend until smooth. Return to rinsed saucepan. Heat gently until boiling and stir in 1/2 cup (4 fl oz) cream. Serve hot or cold, sprinkled with 1 tablespoon chopped chives. Serves 4–6.

ABOVE: CAULIFLOWER FRITTERS WITH TOMATO RELISH. OPPOSITE PAGE: BRAISED CELERY

Celery A vegetable valued primarily for its long, juicy stem, although the leaves and stem are served in salads (raw, grated and mixed with dressing), or steamed or boiled and served hot with a sauce.

Celeriac The bulbous, white-fleshed root of a variety of celery. It became popular in Italy in Renaissance times, and by the eighteenth century had spread to France, Germany and Italy. Peeled like a potato, it can be

Cayenne Pepper A fiery spice made from the dried and powdered pod and seeds of several varieties of small red chilli peppers, used exceedingly sparingly to flavour cheese and fish dishes.

Beluga sturgeon. Pressed caviar is made from ripe eggs, salted and pressed into a block. Commercial quantities of caviar are harvested in the Caspian Sea. Salmon and lumpfish roe are sometimes called 'red caviar'. It should be well chilled and served on a bed of crushed ice for spreading on thin triangles of toast.

CELERY

BRAISED CELERY

Preparation time: 15 minutes
Total cooking time: 40 minutes
Serves 6

1 head celery
30 g (1 oz) butter
2 cups (16 fl oz) chicken stock
2 teaspoons finely grated lemon rind
1/4 cup (2 fl oz) lemon juice
1/2 teaspoon ground mace

1 tablespoon cornflour (cornstarch)
2 egg yolks
1/4 cup (2 fl oz) cream
1/4 cup chopped parsley
white pepper and salt to taste

1 Lightly brush a 6-cup capacity shallow heatproof dish with melted butter or oil. Preheat oven to moderate 180°C (350°F/Gas 4). Trim celery and cut into 5 cm (2 inch) lengths. Melt butter in a large pan. Add the celery, toss to coat evenly in butter. Cover and cook for 2 minutes.

2 Pour over the stock, lemon rind and juice; cover and simmer for 10 minutes. Remove the celery with a slotted spoon and place into prepared dish. Reserve 1/4 cup (2 fl oz) of cooking liquid.

3 Blend cream, egg yolks and cornflour. Whisk in reserved cooking liquid. Return to heat and cook until the mixture boils and thickens. Add parsley, pepper, salt and mace.

4 Pour the sauce over the celery in a heatproof dish. Cook in the oven for 15–20 minutes or until the celery softens.

CURRIED CHICKEN, APPLE AND CELERY SALAD

Preparation time: 30 minutes
Total cooking time: 20 minutes
Serves 8

2 kg (4 lb) chicken thighs
1 cup (8 fl oz) orange juice
2 cups (16 fl oz) water
2 medium red apples
2 celery sticks
220 g (7 oz) green seedless grapes
3/4 cup walnuts, roughly chopped

Curry Mayonnaise
60 g (2 oz) butter
1 small onion, finely chopped
3 teaspoons curry powder
1/3 cup mayonnaise
1/2 cup (4 fl oz) sour cream
1/3 cup (2 1/2 fl oz) cream
2 tablespoons lemon juice
2 teaspoons soft brown sugar
sugar
salt, to taste

1 Trim chicken of excess fat and sinew and place in a large heavy-based pan. Add orange juice and water. Cover and bring to the boil. Reduce heat; gently simmer, covered, until tender. Remove from heat, drain and cool. Discard bones; cut meat into 2 cm (3/4 inch) pieces.

2 Halve apples, remove cores and cut into 1 cm (1/2 inch) cubes. Slice celery. Combine chicken, apples, celery, grapes and walnuts in a large bowl.

3 To make Curry Mayonnaise: Melt butter in a small pan. Add onion, cook 2 minutes or until onion is soft. Stir in curry powder, cook 30 seconds. Transfer mixture to a small bowl. Add mayonnaise, creams, juice, sugar and salt; mix well. Gently fold through chicken mixture.

CELERY

seeds are also eaten. The ancient Egyptians gathered shoots of wild celery from seaside marshes, the Greeks used it as a seasoning. In seventeenth-century France, celery was used to flavour soups and stews; the technique of 'blanching' (heaping earth against growing stems to make them paler) dates from the time of Louis XIV and was first used in the royal gardens at Versailles, outside Paris. The stringless salad vegetable popular today was developed in Utah, in the United States.

Celery can be eaten raw, cooked in soups, stews and casseroles, or boiled, steamed or braised to be served as a vegetable.

Cep A large, wild, edible mushroom of south-western Europe. It has a bulbous stalk and fleshy brown cap, and is gathered in autumn from the leaf litter around oak and chestnut trees. Highly prized in France for its subtle, earthy flavour, it is available dried or canned.

Cereal Plants cultivated for their edible grains and seeds, such as wheat, rye, oats, corn (maize) and barley. Cereals provide protein, vitamins and minerals and have a

CHEESE

HERBED CHEESE CRACKERS

Preparation time: 20 minutes ★★
Total cooking time: 8 minutes each tray
Makes 20

Biscuit Pastry
1 cup plain (all-purpose) flour
½ teaspoon baking powder
60 g (2 oz) butter, chopped
1 egg, lightly beaten
1 tablespoon iced water
½ cup grated cheddar cheese
¼ teaspoon lemon pepper
1 tablespoon chopped fresh chives
1 tablespoon chopped fresh parsley

Cheese Filling
75 g (2½ oz) cream cheese
25 g (¾ oz) butter
1 tablespoon chopped fresh chives
1 teaspoon chopped fresh parsley
¼ teaspoon lemon pepper
¾ cup grated cheddar cheese

1 Preheat oven to moderately hot 210°C (415°F/Gas 6–7). Line 2 oven trays with baking paper.
2 Place flour and baking powder in food processor; add butter. Process 30 seconds or until mixture is fine and crumbly. Add egg, water and cheese to bowl and process 40 seconds or until mixture comes together. Turn out onto floured surface, and knead in herbs until smooth.
3 Roll pastry between sheets of baking paper to 2.5 mm (⅛ inch) thickness. Cut into rounds, using a 5 cm (2 inch) fluted cutter. Place on prepared trays. Bake 8 minutes or until lightly browned. Transfer rounds to wire rack to cool.

CHEESE TOAST

Preparation time: 10 minutes ★
Total cooking time: 10 minutes
Serves 6

1 cup grated cheddar cheese
2 tablespoons chutney
30 g (1 oz) butter
1 teaspoon worcestershire sauce
1 tablespoon grated onion
6 thick slices wholegrain bread
1 tablespoon tomato sauce

1 Put the grated cheese into a mixing bowl. Add chutney, onion and sauces.
2 Melt butter and add to mixing bowl; stir.
3 Turn grill on to high. Toast bread on one side. Spread cheese mixture on untoasted side. Put it back under the grill until cheese is melted. Slice and serve immediately.

CHEESE STRAWS

Preparation time: 10 minutes ★
Total cooking time: 10 minutes
Makes 36

1 cup plain (all-purpose) flour
2 tablespoons grated parmesan cheese
½ teaspoon salt
½ teaspoon dry mustard
60 g (2 oz) firm butter, diced
½ cup shredded cheddar cheese
1 egg yolk
2 teaspoons lemon juice

1 Preheat oven to moderate 180°C (350°F/Gas 4). Place flour, salt, mustard, cheddar and parmesan cheeses in a food processor fitted with a metal blade. Process for a few seconds to combine ingredients.
2 Add butter and process until mixture resembles fine breadcrumbs.
3 Beat egg yolk and lemon juice in a small bowl and add to dry ingredients while machine is running. Process only until mixture begins to form a ball around the blade. Remove dough and form ball.
4 Roll out dough to 5 mm (¼ inch) thickness on a lightly floured board. Cut into 6 x 1 cm (2½ x ½ inch) strips. Place on a greased baking tray and bake for 10 minutes, until golden. Cool on tray, then store in an airtight container.

4 **To make Cheese Filling:** Using electric beaters, beat cream cheese and butter in bowl until light and creamy. Add herbs, pepper and cheese. Beat until smooth. Spread filling on half the biscuits, sandwich together with other half.

high carbohydrate content. In one form or another they are the basic food of most of the world's people.

Ceviche A dish of raw fish or raw scallops marinated in lemon or lime juice until the flesh becomes opaque. It is often served with raw onion rings and tomatoes. Ceviche is popular in South America and the South Pacific.

Champignon The cultivated common mushroom, picked when very young before the gills are visible. Also known as a button mushroom, the champignon is valued for its delicate flavour. It is available throughout the year. Champignons can be eaten raw, in salads or with dips; or, sliced or whole, they can be fried, stir-fried, grilled (broiled), baked or microwaved.

Chapatti A flat unleavened bread from India. It is made from wholewheat flour and cooked on a hot griddle. Chapattis are served with curries and other savoury dishes, and are sometimes used like edible plates to hold the food eaten with them.

OPPOSITE PAGE: *HERBED CHEESE CRACKERS*
ABOVE: *WARM GOATS CHEESE SALAD*
RIGHT: *CHEESE PUDDING*

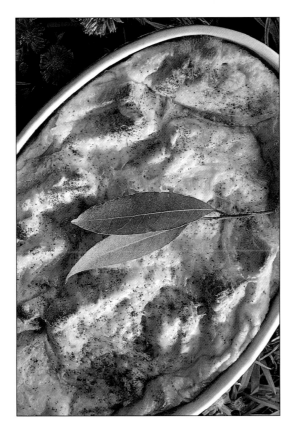

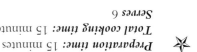

WARM GOATS CHEESE SALAD

✳ **Preparation time:** 15 minutes
Total cooking time: 15 minutes
Serves 6

6 slices wholemeal bread
2 x 105 g (3½ oz) rounds goats cheese
105 g (3½ oz) mixed salad leaves

Dressing
1 tablespoon tarragon vinegar
3 tablespoons olive oil
½ teaspoon grain mustard

1 Preheat oven to moderate 180°C (350°F/Gas 4). Using a biscuit cutter, cut a round out of each slice of bread that will just fit the round of goats cheese. (The bread must not extend out from the cheese or it will burn.) Place bread onto a baking tray, and cook for 10 minutes.

2 Slice each cheese round into three discs. Place a disc of cheese onto each bread round. Arrange a bed of salad leaves on small serving plates.

3 Cook cheese under hot grill 5 minutes or until golden and bubbling. Drizzle salad leaves with dressing, place a cheese round on top and serve.

4 **To make Dressing:** Combine vinegar, oil and mustard in a small jar. Screw lid on tightly; shake vigorously for 1 minute or until well combined.

CHEESE PUDDING

✳ **Preparation time:** 20 minutes + 30 minutes standing
Total cooking time: 30 minutes
Serves 4

8 slices stale bread
60 g (2 oz) softened butter
155 g (5 oz) cheddar cheese, grated
4 eggs
1 cup (8 fl oz) chicken stock
½ cup (4 fl oz) cream
freshly ground pepper

1 Preheat oven to 150°C (300°F/Gas 2). Remove crusts from bread, butter each slice one side only. Sprinkle two-thirds of the grated cheese onto four slices, sandwich with remaining bread. Cut cheese sandwiches in half diagonally.

2 Grease a shallow ovenproof dish with remaining butter. Arrange sandwiches over base.

3 Beat the eggs, stock and cream; pour mixture over the sandwiches, moistening each. Stand for 30 minutes.

4 Sprinkle remaining cheese on top and season with ground black pepper. Bake until pudding is set and golden.

Note: Cheese Pudding is a traditional Irish dish, economical and comforting. It's the perfect Sunday night supper and needs only a green salad and a loaf of crusty bread to accompany it.

Charlotte A dessert consisting of puréed fruit (usually apple) cooked in a mould lined with thin slices of buttered bread. It is served warm with cold custard. Charlotte russe is a cold dessert made by lining a mould with sponge fingers, then filling it with bavarois (bavarian cream), creamy mousse or whipped cream.

Chateaubriand A thick slice of beef fillet steak, grilled (broiled) or sautéed, and served with sauces, traditionally béarnaise. It was reputedly the favourite dish of the eighteenth-century French statesman, writer and gourmet, Vicomte Francois René de Chateaubriand, for whom it is named.

Chayote See Choko.

Cheddar A semi-hard cow's milk cheese with a close, creamy texture and rich, nutty flavour that can range from mild to very sharp, depending on the age of the cheese. It varies in colour from near white for young cheeses, to deep yellow for mature, full-flavoured cheddars. Traditionally made in a large cylindrical shape, cheddar takes its name from the Somerset.

CHEESECAKES

Creamy, luscious cheesecakes are always a popular dessert. Here you'll find easy recipes for both baked and unbaked versions, with suggestions for ringing changes in the bases, fillings and toppings to produce some spectacular versions of this favourite.

BAKED CHEESECAKE WITH SOUR CREAM TOPPING

Baked cheesecake is delicious served simply with its sour cream topping, but it also lends itself to a variety of rich fruit, nut and cream extravaganzas. The sour cream topping can be omitted if you prefer and the fruit and cream piled straight onto the plain baked cheese-cake once it has cooled.

■ Crush 250 g (8 oz) butternut cookies in a food processor and add 1 teaspoon mixed spice. Melt 100 g (3½ oz) butter and add to the crushed biscuits, processing until all the crumbs are moistened. Line the base of a 20 cm (8 inch) round springform cake tin with foil, brush oil. Press cookie crumbs over base and sides of tin. Refrigerate for 20 minutes.

To make filling: Preheat oven to 180°C (350°F/Gas 4). Using electric beaters, beat 500 g (1 lb) cream cheese until smooth. Add 2/3 cup caster (superfine) sugar, 1 teaspoon vanilla essence and 1 tablespoon lemon juice. Beat until smooth. Add 4 whole eggs, one at a time, beating well after each addition. Pour mixture into chilled biscuit base, bake for 45 minutes or until cheesecake is just firm to the touch.

To make topping: Put 1 cup of sour cream in a bowl and add 1/2 teaspoon vanilla essence, 3 teaspoons lemon juice and 1 tablespoon caster (superfine) sugar. Beat well. Spread over the hot cheesecake, sprinkle with nutmeg and return cheesecake to the oven for 7 minutes. Cool in the oven and then refrigerate.

VARIATIONS

BLUEBERRY AND STRAWBERRY CHEESECAKE
Beat 3/4 cup cream until firm. Spread over cheesecake, top with fresh blueberries and strawberry halves. Dust lightly with sifted icing (confectioners) sugar.

BRAZIL NUT CHEESECAKE
Using a vegetable peeler, finely peel 1/4 cup whole Brazil nuts in thin strips. Beat 1 cup cream until stiff peaks form. Decorate cheesecake with whipped cream and Brazil nut shavings. Sprinkle with ground nutmeg if desired.

MANGO CHEESECAKE
Thinly slice 1–2 fresh mangoes. Arrange slices decoratively over cheesecake. Heat 1/3 cup apricot jam and 2–3 teaspoons brandy in small pan. Stir over heat until melted. Strain through a sieve. Brush warmed jam mixture over mango slices. Cool and serve in wedges.

KIWIFRUIT AND COCONUT CHEESECAKE
Beat 1 cup cream until stiff peaks form. Spread cheesecake with cream, arrange 1–2 peeled and thinly sliced kiwifruit on top and sprinkle with 1/4 cup toasted baked coconut.

NEW YORK CHEESECAKE

This is a dense cheesecake with a pastry base instead of the usual crumb crust. It often contains sultanas. This version has a citrus-flavoured filling and a candied rind topping.

■ Place in a food processor 1/2 cup self-rising (all-purpose) flour, 1 cup plain flour, 1/4 cup caster (superfine) sugar, 1 teaspoon grated lemon rind and 75 g (2½ oz) cubed butter. Process until

TRIPLE CHOCOLATE CHEESECAKE

This is an example of an unbaked cheesecake, made with gelatine and set in the refrigerator before serving. Much simpler recipes are available, but this one shows just how spectacular a gelatine-based cheesecake can be.

■ Line the base of a 20 cm (8 inch) springform cake tin with greased foil.

Place 125 g (4 oz) plain chocolate biscuits in a food processor and crush. Add ½ teaspoon ground cinnamon and 60 g (2 oz) melted butter. Blend well. Press biscuit crust into base of tin. Refrigerate for 20 minutes.

To make filling: Sprinkle 1 tablespoon gelatine over ¼ cup (2 oz) water in a small bowl. Stand the bowl in a pan of hot water and stir until gelatine is dissolved; cool slightly. Beat 375 g (12 oz) cream cheese in a bowl with electric beaters until smooth. Beat in ½ cup (4 fl oz) milk and ½ cup caster (superfine) sugar. Divide the mixture into three equal portions in three separate bowls. Fold 60 g (2 oz) melted white chocolate into one portion, the same quantity of milk chocolate into the second, and the same quantity of dark chocolate into the third portion. Fold one-third of the gelatine mixture into each portion. Whip 1 cup cream until stiff, divide into three and gently fold one-third of it into each portion. Spread the white chocolate mixture over the biscuit base. Cover carefully with the milk chocolate mixture, then the dark chocolate mixture. Refrigerate for 3 hours, or until filling has set. Decorate top of the cheesecake with whipped cream, halved chocolate discs and curls. Sprinkle with icing (confectioners) sugar.

To make chocolate curls: Spread 250 g (8 oz) melted chocolate onto a marble board to a depth of about 1 cm (½ inch), smoothing the surface lightly. Allow to cool until almost set. Use a sharp, flat-bladed knife and hold it horizontally. Applying constant pressure to the blade with both hands, pull the knife towards you. The pressure applied to the blade will determine how thick or thin the curls will be. Chocolate curls take time, practice and patience to master, but they look splendid as a decoration on chocolate cakes, desserts and cheesecakes.

ALL CHEESECAKES ARE SHOWN FROM ABOVE AS WELL AS IN CROSS SECTION. FROM TOP LEFT, OPPOSITE PAGE: BAKED CHEESECAKE WITH BLUEBERRY AND STRAWBERRY TOPPING, WITH BRAZIL NUT TOPPING AND WITH MANGO TOPPING; NEW YORK CHEESECAKE; TRIPLE CHOCOLATE CHEESECAKE, AND BAKED CHEESECAKE WITH KIWIFRUIT AND COCONUT TOPPING.

mixture just comes together. Knead gently, form into a ball and store, wrapped in plastic, in the refrigerator for 20 minutes.

Roll pastry out, ease into a 22 cm (9 inch) round springform cake tin and trim edges. Bake blind in a preheated oven 210°C (415°F/Gas 6–7) for 10 minutes; remove paper and beans or rice. Bake 5 minutes more. Cool. Place 750 g (12 oz) cream cheese in a large bowl. Beat with electric beaters until smooth. Add ¼ cup plain (all-purpose) flour, and 2 teaspoons each of grated orange and lemon rind; beat until smooth. Add 4 eggs, one at a time, beating well after each addition. Add ⅓ cup cream; beat well. Pour filling into pastry case; bake at 150°C (300°F/Gas 2) for 1 hour 35 minutes or until set. Cool; chill until firm.

To make candied rind: Combine 1 cup sugar and ¼ cup water in a medium pan. Stir over heat without boiling until the sugar has dissolved. Add the shredded rind of 3 limes and 3 oranges. Bring to the boil, reduce heat, simmer, uncovered, for 10 minutes. Remove from heat and cool. Drain rind and reserve syrup. Beat 1 cup cream until stiff peaks form. Spread it over the cooled cheesecake and decorate with candied rind. Serve in wedges with reserved syrup, if desired.

village of Cheddar, where it was first made; today it is duplicated in factories around the world; most of the cheese produced in the United States is of the cheddar type. Cheddar is an all-purpose cheese, used for cooking, in sandwiches and snacks.

Cheese A nutritious food prepared from curdled milk that has separated into curds (milky white solids) and whey (a cloudy liquid). Most of the world's cheese is made from cow's milk, but it can be made from the milk of sheep, goats, buffaloes, reindeer, camels and other domesticated grazing animals. The type of milk used (skimmed, partly skimmed, whole or enriched with cream) is the main determinant of texture and flavour; other factors include the additive used to curdle the milk, the culture used in the fermentation process, and the methods of processing the curd. If categorised by texture, cheese falls into four main types: fresh, unripened cheeses (cottage cheese, cream cheese, mozzarella and ricotta); soft, briefly ripened cheeses, spreadable and with a high moisture and fat content (brie,

CHERRIES

CHERRIES JUBILEE

✪ **Preparation time:** 20 minutes
Total cooking time: 15 minutes
Serves 4

1/2 cup (4 fl oz) water	1 tablespoon arrowroot or
3/4 cup sugar	cornflour (cornstarch)
2 strips lemon rind	vanilla ice-cream for
500 g (1 lb) sweet red or	serving
black cherries, pitted	1/4 cup (2 fl oz) brandy

1 Heat water in a pan, add sugar and stir to dissolve. Bring syrup to the boil, add lemon rind and cherries and simmer until cherries are tender.
2 Remove cherries from syrup with a slotted spoon, discard lemon rind and boil syrup rapidly for 3 minutes. Blend arrowroot with a little extra cold water in a small bowl and stir in some of the cherry syrup. Return mixture to pan and stir until it boils and thickens. Add cherries.
3 Spoon ice-cream into heatproof serving dishes. Have cherries at boiling point. Heat brandy, add to cherries and carefully ignite. Pour flaming cherries and sauce over ice-cream and serve immediately.

Note: A 425 g (13½ oz) can sweet cherries in syrup can be used if desired. It is then unnecessary to make a syrup. Simply add 1–2 tablespoons sugar and lemon rind to syrup from can of cherries.

BLACK CHERRY JAM

✫ ✫ **Preparation time:** 35 minutes +
overnight standing
Total cooking time: 1 hour
Makes 1 litre (4 cups)

1 kg (2 lb) black cherries	1 cup (8 fl oz) water
juice of 2 lemons	2½ cups sugar

1 Rinse cherries, drain well and remove stones. Put lemon juice and water in a bowl; add some of the sugar, then a layer of cherries. Continue with remaining sugar and cherries. Cover and leave overnight.
2 Next day, strain the syrup into a large saucepan or boiler and stir over medium heat until sugar has dissolved. Bring to boil, add cherries and boil for 45 minutes or until setting point is reached (see Jams & Marmalades). Stir frequently to prevent the mixture burning.
3 Remove from heat and stand 5 minutes. Pour jam into warm, sterilised jars and seal immediately. When cool, label and date.

CHERRY CLAFOUTIS

✪ **Preparation time:** 25 minutes
Total cooking time: 50 minutes
Serves 8

500 g (1 lb) cherries,	pinch salt
stalks removed	1/3 cup caster (superfine)
30 g (1 oz) unsalted	sugar
(sweet) butter	4 eggs, lightly beaten
2 tablespoons sugar	1½ (12 fl oz) cups milk
2 tablespoons plain (all-	30 g (1 oz) unsalted
purpose) flour	butter, melted, extra
1/2 teaspoon baking	2 tablespoons brandy
powder	

1 Preheat oven to 180°C (350°F/Gas 4). Melt butter in large frying pan and add cherries. Cook 2-3 minutes. Sprinkle over sugar, cook over medium heat 5 minutes or until juices form. Remove from heat; cool.
2 Sift flour, baking powder and salt into a medium bowl. Add sugar. Whisk eggs and milk. Stir into flour mixture. Stir in combined butter and brandy. Place the cherries in a shallow ovenproof dish. Pour batter over the top. Bake 40 minutes or until puffed and just set when tapped in the centre. Serve hot or warm, dusted with sifted icing (confectioners) sugar.

ABOVE: CHERRIES JUBILEE
OPPOSITE PAGE: CHOCOLATE CHESTNUT MOUSSE

CHESTNUTS

CHESTNUT STUFFING FOR TURKEY

✷✷ Preparation time: 30 minutes
Total cooking time: 30 minutes
Serves 10

20–25 large chestnuts
500 g (1 lb) pork sausage meat
60 g (2 oz) butter
1 cup fresh white breadcrumbs
1 medium onion, chopped
½ cup finely chopped celery
1 green cooking apple, peeled and chopped
2 teaspoons dried marjoram
salt
freshly ground pepper
1 egg, beaten

1 With a sharp knife, make a slit down one side of each chestnut. Place in a pan of cold water, bring to the boil, cover and simmer for 20 minutes or until chestnuts are tender. Leave chestnuts in water until just cool enough to handle, then peel outer and inner skins away. Chop chestnuts coarsely.

2 Melt butter in a pan and cook onion, celery and apple slowly until tender. Transfer to a large mixing bowl and allow to cool. Add the chopped chestnuts, eggs, sausage meat, breadcrumbs, marjoram, salt and pepper and mix ingredients to combine well.

3 Use Chestnut Stuffing for turkey, chicken or duck. The quantity given is sufficient to stuff one turkey, or two chickens or ducks.

CHOCOLATE CHESTNUT MOUSSE

✷✷ Preparation time: 30 minutes
Total cooking time: 25 minutes
Serves 6

250–300 g (8–9 oz) fresh chestnuts, or ½ cup (4 fl oz) canned unsweetened chestnut puree
155 g (5 oz) dark (semi-sweet) chocolate
4 eggs, separated
2 tablespoons brandy
2 tablespoons caster (superfine) sugar
whipped cream for decoration
strawberries for serving

1 To prepare chestnuts: With a sharp knife, make a slit down one side of each chestnut, place chestnuts in a pan of cold water, bring to boil, cover and simmer for 20 minutes or until tender. Leave chestnuts in water until just cool enough to handle, then peel off outer and inner skins. Grind chestnuts in a food processor until fine; measure 1 cup lightly packed ground chestnuts.

2 Break chocolate into even-sized pieces in large, clean, dry bowl; melt in microwave or over a pan of gently simmering water. Beat in egg yolks and brandy, making a smooth mixture. Add ground chestnuts.

3 Using electric beaters, beat egg whites until stiff peaks form, then add caster sugar gradually while beating. Stir one tablespoon of egg white into chocolate mixture, to lighten, then fold in remaining whites.

4 Spoon into six individual dishes. Refrigerate until mousse is set. Decorate with whipped cream and strawberries before serving.

Note: If fresh chestnuts are unavailable, canned whole chestnuts in water, or dried chestnuts that have been soaked in cold water overnight and cooked for 15 minutes in chicken stock, may be substituted.

ABOUT CHESTNUTS

■ Chestnuts do not keep well at room temperature and should be stored in a vented plastic bag in the refrigerator. Whole shelled chestnuts can be blanched in water and frozen for up to 1 month.

■ Roast chestnuts by making a slit in the pointed end and with a small sharp knife; roast in a moderately hot 210°C (415°F/Gas 6–7) oven for about 20 minutes, or in hot coals until the shells split open and chestnuts are golden.

■ Chestnuts contain more starch and less oil than other nuts, so are often used like vegetables.

camembert, feta and the blue cheeses); semi-hard or firm cheeses matured with less moisture (cheddar, colby and gruyère); and hard cheeses, dry, long-matured and sharp-tasting (parmesan, pecorino and romano). Curd cheese has been made for thousands of years. Nomadic peoples in the Middle East may have discovered the cheese-making process when milk carried in containers made of animal stomachs turned to curds. In Europe until the Middle Ages, curds were drained in wicker baskets and then compressed into a wooden box (the mould was called a forma, the origin of fromage, the French word for cheese).

Cheesecake A rich dessert in the form of an open pie. The sweet, crumbly pastry shell is filled with a custard-like mixture based on a fresh, unripened cheese, such as cottage cheese, ricotta or cream cheese. There are two types of cheesecake: in one the cheese mixture is baked in a cool oven; in the

CHICKEN

ROAST CHICKEN WITH BREADCRUMB STUFFING

★★ *Preparation time:* 25 minutes + 5 minutes standing
Total cooking time: 1 hour 30 minutes
Serves 6

1.4 kg (2 lb 13 oz) chicken
salt and freshly ground black pepper to taste
45 g (1½ oz) butter, melted
1 tablespoon oil
1 tablespoon soy sauce
1½ cups (12 fl oz) water
1 clove garlic, crushed
1 tablespoon plain (all-purpose) flour

3 rashers bacon, finely chopped
6 slices wholegrain bread, crusts removed
3 spring onions (scallions), chopped
2 tablespoons chopped pecan nuts
2 teaspoons currants
¼ cup finely chopped parsley
1 egg, lightly beaten
¼ cup (2 fl oz) milk

1 Preheat oven to moderately hot 210°C (415°F/Gas 6-7). Cook bacon in a small pan over high heat 5 minutes or until crisp. Chop bread into 1 cm (½ inch) squares; place into a large mixing bowl. Add bacon, spring onions, nuts, currants, parsley and combined egg and milk; season to taste and mix well.

2 Remove the giblets and any large deposits of fat from the chicken. Wipe chicken and pat dry with paper towels. Spoon stuffing into chicken cavity; close cavity with a skewer or toothpick. Tie wings and drumsticks securely in place with string. Rub chicken all over with salt and pepper.

3 Place on roasting rack in deep baking dish. Brush with combined butter, oil and soy sauce; pour leftover butter mixture, half the water and garlic into baking dish. Roast chicken for 1 hour and 15 minutes or until browned and tender. Baste occasionally with pan juices during cooking. Transfer chicken to a serving dish. Leave, loosely covered with foil, in a warm place for 5 minutes before carving. Serve with gravy and vegetables.

4 To make Gravy: Transfer baking pan to stovetop. Add flour to pan juices; blend to a smooth paste. Stir constantly over low heat for 5 minutes or until mixture browns. Add remaining water, stir until mixture boils and thickens. (Add extra water if necessary.) Season to taste; strain into a serving jug. Serve hot.

other the cheese mixture is chilled in the refrigerator.

Chelsea Bun A bun made from a rich yeast dough rolled out, spread with butter, sprinkled with currants and sugar, then rolled up and cut into slices.

Cherimoya See Custard Apple.

Cherry The small, juicy fruit with a single stone (pit) of several species of tree related to the plum. It probably originated in Asia, but in prehistoric times spread to Europe and North America and was introduced to Britain by the Romans. From medieval times the cherry fair marked the start of summer and was a time of general merry-making. Cherries are available for a very short season in early summer. Raw, they are best eaten as fresh as possible.

Chervil A small herb, similar in appearance to parsley, with lacy, bright green leaves and a delicate aniseed flavour. In ancient Rome it was valued not only as a

COQ AU VIN

Preparation time: 20 minutes
Total cooking time: 1 hour
Serves 6

2 kg (4 lb) chicken pieces	1 1/2 cups (12 fl oz) good quality red wine
plain (all-purpose) flour	1 1/2 cups (12 fl oz) chicken stock
salt and pepper	250 g (8 oz) small button mushrooms
2 tablespoons oil	4 bacon rashers, chopped
1 tablespoon oil, extra	10 small pickling onions
1/4 cup tomato paste	1 clove garlic, crushed

1 Coat chicken in seasoned flour, shake off excess. Heat oil in heavy-based pan. Cook chicken quickly in small batches until well browned; drain on paper towels.

2 Heat extra oil in deep heavy-based pan. Add bacon, onions and garlic; cook, stirring, until onions are browned. Add chicken, wine, stock and paste. Bring to boil and reduce heat and simmer, covered, 30 minutes.

3 Add the mushrooms, stir to combine and simmer, uncovered, for a further 10 minutes, or until the chicken is very tender and the sauce has thickened slightly. Coq au Vin is traditionally served sprinkled with finely chopped fresh herbs.

OPPOSITE PAGE: ROAST CHICKEN WITH BREADCRUMB STUFFING. ABOVE: COQ AU VIN

CHICKEN AND CORN SOUP

Remove skin and meat from one cooked chicken and shred the meat. Heat 3 cups (24 fl oz) chicken stock in a medium pan. Add chicken meat, 440 g (14 oz) can creamed corn, 270 g (8 1/2 oz) can corn kernels, and 1/2 teaspoon soy sauce to the chicken stock and mix well. Bring to the boil, reduce heat and simmer gently for 4 minutes. Stir in 2 finely sliced spring onions (scallions). Season to taste. Serves 4.

CHICKEN STOCK

Place 500 g (1 lb) chicken bones and 1 large onion, chopped, into a baking dish and bake in 180°C (350°F/Gas 4) oven for 50 minutes or until well browned. Transfer to a large pan or stockpot. Wrap 2 bay leaves and 6 peppercorns in a piece of muslin (cheesecloth) to make a bouquet garni.

Chop 1 carrot and 1 stick of celery (leaves included) and add to pan with bouquet garni and 5 cups (1.25 litres) of water. Bring to boil, reduce heat and simmer, uncovered, for 40 minutes, adding a little more water if necessary. Strain stock. Discard bones and vegetables. Cool stock quickly and refrigerate, then skim any hard fat that may have risen to the surface. Refrigerate or freeze. Use stock as indicated in recipes. Makes 4 cups (1 litre).

---

seasoning but also as a remedy for hiccoughs. An important ingredient in *fines herbes*, it flavours many sauces, such as béarnaise. Chopped chervil leaves are added to egg dishes, poultry, fish, salads, mashed potatoes, sauces, soups and mornays. Best used fresh; it loses its flavour if cooked.

Cheshire Cheese A hard, crumbly, slightly salty cow's milk cheese, similar to cheddar. It can be either red, white or blue in colour. The oldest of the English cheeses, it has been made in Cheshire since the twelfth century.

Chestnut A round, heavy, whitish-fleshed nut covered with a thin brown skin and encased in a glossy brown shell. When cooked the nut has a sweet, floury taste. The chestnut tree is thought to be native to southern Europe and western Asia, and since prehistoric times the easily gathered nutritious nuts have been valued as a food. Unlike most nuts, which are rich in fat and low in starch, the chestnut kernel contains less than 3 per cent fat and has a high carbohydrate content. Roasted in the shell, they are a traditional winter snack. The shelled kernels can be simmered in stock and

CHICKEN WITH TARRAGON AND MUSHROOMS

Preparation time: 10 minutes
Total cooking time: 50 minutes
Serves 6

6 large chicken breast fillets, about 750 g (1½ lb), skin removed
¼ cup (2 fl oz) olive oil
3 rashers bacon, cut into strips
315 g (10 oz) button mushrooms, sliced
½ cup (4 fl oz) white wine
2 tablespoons tomato paste
1 teaspoon dried tarragon
3 spring onions (scallions), finely chopped
½ cup (4 fl oz) cream
salt and freshly ground black pepper, to taste

1 Trim chicken of excess fat and sinew. Preheat oven to moderate 180°C (350°F/Gas 4). Heat oil in a large heavy-based pan; add chicken. Cook over medium-high heat 2 minutes each side, turning once. Remove from pan; drain.

2 Add bacon to pan. Stir over heat 2 minutes; add mushrooms. Cook 5 minutes; add wine, tomato paste and tarragon. Stir until mixture boils. Reduce heat; add cream; simmer 2 minutes. Remove from heat, stir in spring onions. Season to taste. Arrange the chicken over the base of a shallow ovenproof dish and pour sauce over it. Bake, covered, for 30 minutes or until the chicken is very tender.

CHICKEN CACCIATORE

Preparation time: 15 minutes
Total cooking time: 55 minutes
Serves 6

125 g (4 oz) button mushrooms
12 chicken drumsticks, about 1.2 kg (2½ lb)
½ cup (4 fl oz) white wine
1 tablespoon oil
1 medium onion, chopped
1 clove garlic, crushed
410 g (13 oz) can tomatoes, puréed
1 teaspoon dried oregano
1 teaspoon dried thyme
salt and pepper to taste
½ cup (4 fl oz) chicken stock

1 Preheat oven to moderate 180°C (350°F/Gas 4). Cut mushrooms into quarters.

2 Heat oil in a heavy-based frying pan. Cook drumsticks in small batches over medium-high heat until well browned; transfer to a large ovenproof casserole dish.

3 Place the onion and garlic in a pan; cook over medium heat until golden. Spread over chicken. Add remaining ingredients to the pan; season to taste. Bring to boil, reduce heat and simmer for 10 minutes. Pour mixture over chicken. Bake, covered, for 35 minutes or until the chicken is very tender.

ABOVE: CHICKEN CACCIATORE. RIGHT: CHICKEN WITH TARRAGON AND MUSHROOMS. OPPOSITE PAGE: GRILLED GARLIC AND ROSEMARY MARYLANDS

served as a vegetable, pureed and used in soups, stuffings and cakes, or sweetened and mixed with cream as a dessert. They are also used for the French dish marrons glacés (glazed or candied chestnuts). Available dried and canned.

Chèvre The French term for cheese made from goat's milk. Fresh chèvre is soft and mild in flavour; more mature cheeses are harder and have a sharp, biting taste.

Chick Pea (Garbanzo Bean) The round, pale-golden, pea-like seed of a bushy plant of southern Europe and western Asia. The chick pea has a nutty flavour and is much used in soups and stews. Boiled and then ground to a paste, it is the basic ingredient in the Middle Eastern dip, hummus. In India it is ground to make besan flour, or dry roasted and seasoned with spices as a

snack food. The Phoenicians are said to have introduced it to Spain where it has been a staple food ever since. Chick peas can be added to stews or, cooked and cooled, tossed in salad.

Chicken The flesh of the domestic hen, one of

GREEN CHICKEN CURRY

Preparation time: 10 minutes
Total cooking time: 45 minutes
Serves 4

8 chicken thigh cutlets,
about 1.5 kg (3 lb)
2 tablespoons peanut oil
3 cloves garlic, crushed
3 green chillies, finely
chopped
1 tablespoon grated ginger
3 spring onions
(scallions), finely
chopped
3 curry leaves

1/2 teaspoon ground cumin
1/2 teaspoon ground
coriander
1 cup (8 fl oz) water
155 g (5 oz) can coconut
cream
1/2 cup finely chopped
fresh coriander
3 teaspoons Thai fish
sauce (nam pla)
2 medium tomatoes,
seeded, chopped
salt, to taste

1 Trim chicken of excess fat and sinew. Heat oil in medium heavy-based pan; add garlic, chillies, ginger, spring onions and curry leaves. Stir over medium heat 1 minute.
2 Add chicken and spices to pan. Cook over medium heat 5 minutes each side, turning once. Add water to pan, bring to boil. Reduce heat and simmer gently, covered, for 15 minutes, turning chicken once.
3 Stir in coconut cream, coriander, fish sauce, tomato and salt. Simmer, uncovered, for 10 minutes or until the chicken is tender and cooked through. Do not cover the pan after adding coconut cream or milk as the milk may separate.
Serve with steamed rice.

GRILLED GARLIC AND ROSEMARY MARYLANDS

Preparation time: 10 minutes +
3 hours marinating
Total cooking time: 20 minutes
Serves 4

4 chicken maryland pieces,
about 1.75 kg (3 1/2 lb)
2 tablespoons chopped
fresh rosemary
1 orange
1/2 cup (4 fl oz) orange juice
2/3 cup (5 fl oz) olive oil
3 cloves garlic, crushed

1 tablespoon chopped
fresh thyme
1 teaspoon Dijon mustard
salt, to taste

1 Trim chicken of excess fat and sinew. Line an oven tray with foil. Brush foil with melted butter or oil. Using a sharp knife, make 3 or 4 deep cuts into the thickest section of chicken pieces.
2 Using a vegetable peeler, peel long strips from half the orange.
3 Combine orange rind and juice, oil, garlic, rosemary, thyme, mustard and salt in a small bowl. Place chicken in a large shallow dish and pour garlic-herb mixture over. Cover with plastic wrap, refrigerate 3 hours or overnight, turning occasionally. Drain chicken and reserve marinade.
4 Place chicken onto prepared oven tray. Grill under medium heat 10 minutes each side or until tender and cooked through, brushing with reserved marinade several times during cooking. Garnish with orange slices and sprigs of rosemary.

ABOUT CHICKEN

■ Chicken must be stored and handled carefully to avoid the possibility of food poisoning. Store fresh, uncooked chicken in the coldest part of the refrigerator for 1 or 2 days only; do not allow its liquid to drip onto other foodstuffs. Keep chicken away from strong-smelling items.

■ Frozen chickens or chicken portions must be fully defrosted in the refrigerator, or use the microwave oven for chicken pieces; separate pieces as they soften. Microwave defrosting is not recommended for whole frozen chickens because of uneven defrosting.

■ Never leave chicken to defrost on the kitchen bench—harmful bacteria can multiply rapidly. Poultry purchased frozen should be placed in the freezer only if it is still rock hard. If it has begun to defrost, defrost fully in refrigerator, then cook, cool and freeze. After chopping raw chicken flesh, wash work surfaces and utensils in very hot water; scrub chopping boards.

■ Chicken must be thoroughly cooked: pierce the thickest part of flesh with a knife and if juices run pink, continue cooking until they run clear.

the most widely used of meats, featuring in national cuisines around the world. All breeds are descended from the red jungle fowl of India (where the bird is still found in the wild). It was domesticated some 5000 years ago and taken by humans to every part of the world, first to China and then to the Pacific Islands and the Mediterranean. At first it was kept for its eggs rather than its flesh, which was considered tough, but the Romans discovered that hand-fed birds had tender and tasty meat.

The basic cuts are breast, thigh, drumstick and wing. The breast contains the most tender meat; breast fillet is the thin strip of meat next to the breastbone. Thigh meat, although more fatty, can sometimes be used as a substitute for breast. The drumstick is the upper part of the leg; a maryland is the thigh and drumstick.

Chicken Kiev *A boned and flattened chicken breast wrapped around a mixture of butter and*

CHICKEN AND HAM PIE

✳ ✳ **Preparation time:** 30 minutes
Total cooking time: 1 hour 15 minutes

Serves 6

---

375 g (12 oz) packet
frozen shortcrust pastry
6 chicken thigh fillets,
about 600 g (1¼ lb)
2 tablespoons oil
60 g (2 oz) butter
1 medium onion, chopped
⅓ cup plain (all-purpose)
flour
1½ cups (12 fl oz) milk
1 tablespoon seeded
mustard
1 cup grated cheddar cheese

155 g (5 oz) lean leg
ham, chopped
3 spring onions
(scallions), finely
chopped
½ large red pepper
(capsicum), chopped
salt and freshly ground
black pepper, to taste
2 hard-boiled eggs,
quartered
375 g (12 oz) packet
frozen puff pastry
1 egg, beaten

1 Preheat oven to moderately hot 210°C (415°F/Gas 6–7). Brush a deep, 22 cm (8¾ inch) round fluted flan tin with melted butter or oil. On lightly floured surface, roll shortcrust pastry out to cover base and sides of prepared tin. Ease pastry into tin. Cut a sheet of greaseproof paper large enough to cover pastry-lined tin. Spread a layer of dried beans or rice evenly over paper. Bake for 7 minutes. Remove from oven; discard paper and beans. Return pastry to oven for another 8 minutes or until lightly golden; cool.

2 Trim chicken of excess fat and sinew. Cut into 2 cm (¾ inch) pieces. Heat oil in a heavy-based frying pan. Add chicken and cook in small batches over medium heat until lightly browned and cooked through; drain on paper towels.

3 Heat butter in medium heavy-based pan. Add the onion and cook for 2 minutes or until onion is soft. Add flour and stir over low heat for 1 minute or until mixture is lightly golden. Add milk gradually to pan, stirring until mixture is smooth. Stir constantly over medium heat until sauce boils and thickens; remove from heat. Stir in mustard and cheese; cool slightly. Add the ham, pepper spring onions and chicken to the sauce mixture, season to taste; stir gently until well combined. Spoon half the mixture into the prepared pastry case. Top with quartered eggs, then remaining chicken mixture. Shape mixture with a large spoon, forming a rounded top.

4 Roll puff pastry out on a lightly floured surface, large enough to cover top of pie. Brush edge of cooked pastry shell with beaten egg. Top with puff pastry and press down edge to seal; trim. Brush top with egg. Decorate pie with trimmings from pastry, if liked. Reduce oven temperature to moderate 180°C (350°F/Gas 4). Bake 45 minutes or until pastry is golden brown. Serve hot.

Note: Pie can be assembled one day ahead up to final baking. Store, covered with plastic wrap, in the refrigerator. Bake 45 minutes as directed.

ABOVE: CHICKEN AND HAM PIE. OPPOSITE PAGE:
BARBECUED HONEY CHICKEN WINGS

Chicory Also known as Belgian endive and witloof, chicory (Cichorium intybus) is a vegetable with compact, cone-shaped heads of long, pale, yellow-tipped leaves which are eaten cooked, or raw and sliced as a salad vegetable. It was first cultivated for its roots, which when roasted and ground are used as a coffee substitute. There is much confusion attached to the use of the terms 'endive' and 'chicory' in different parts of the world. In Belgium and Australia, chicory or Belgian endive is often called witloof. In the United States the term chicory is used for the salad vegetable, curly endive. See Endive, Curly.

Chilli The small, smooth-skinned, elongated pods of a plant of the capsicum family. Chillies are smaller and far hotter in taste than sweet peppers; the

chives, dipped in egg and breadcrumbs and then fried until crisp and golden.

hundreds of species vary greatly in size, shape, colour, and most importantly, in their fierceness. Domesticated chillies were present in Peru from 8000 BC. They are an important ingredient in the cooking of Mexico, and following their introduction to Africa and Asia in the late sixteenth century are now also closely identified with the dishes of those regions.

Chilli con Carne A spicy dish of cubed or minced (ground) meat, red kidney beans and thinly sliced onions, seasoned with chilli peppers. Chilli con Carne has its origins in the cooking of the Incas, Mayas and Aztecs, who were aware of the preservative properties of hot peppers on meat. Today it is a popular dish, especially when served with corn chips.

Chilli Powder A blend of dried chilli peppers and seasonings. It has a hot, spicy, peppery taste, and is most commonly used to flavour chilli con carne. Available commercially, it is best purchased in small quantities as it rapidly loses its flavour and becomes unusable. Chilli powder should not be confused with paprika, which looks similar but is mild in flavour.

CHICKEN CHOW MEIN

Preparation time: 20 minutes
Total cooking time: 10 minutes
Serves 4

60 g (2 oz) dried Chinese mushrooms	2 cups shredded cabbage
500 g (1 lb) chicken breast fillets, cut into thin strips	1/2 cup chopped spring onions (scallions)
1 tablespoon dry sherry	1 cup chopped green beans
2 teaspoons cornflour (cornstarch)	1 cup sliced celery
1/3 cup (2 1/2 fl oz) peanut oil	1 cup bean sprouts
1 clove garlic, crushed	1/2 cup (4 fl oz) chicken stock
2 teaspoons grated fresh ginger	2 teaspoons soy sauce
	1 teaspoon sugar
	crisp fried noodles for serving

1 Soak mushrooms in water for 20 minutes. Combine chicken, sherry and half the cornflour in a bowl; toss and allow to stand for 10 minutes.

2 Heat half the oil in a wok or heavy-based pan. Add chicken and stir-fry until meat is almost cooked. Remove chicken and set aside.

3 Add remaining oil to wok and fry garlic and ginger for a few seconds; add prepared vegetables and drained, sliced mushrooms; stir-fry until crisp but tender. Blend remaining cornflour with stock, soy and sugar, add to wok. Stir until mixture boils and thickens. Return chicken to wok and stir-fry until heated through. Serve Chow Mein over crisp fried noodles.

BARBECUED HONEY CHICKEN WINGS

Preparation time: 10 minutes +
2 hours marinating
Total cooking time: 15 minutes
Serves 4

12 chicken wings (about 2 1/2 lb)	1/4 cup (2 fl oz) soy sauce
2 tablespoons sherry	1 clove garlic, crushed
2 tablespoons oil	
2 tablespoons honey	

1 Wipe and pat dry chicken wings with paper towels. Tuck wing tips to underside. Place in shallow glass or ceramic dish. Combine soy sauce, garlic, sherry and oil in a small jug; pour over chicken wings.

2 Cover with plastic wrap, and refrigerate for 2 hours, turning occasionally. Drain chicken wings and place on preheated lightly oiled grill or flatplate. Place honey in a small heatproof cup or jug on a cool part of the grill to warm and thin down a little. Cook chicken wings for 12 minutes or until tender and cooked through, turning occasionally.

3 Brush wings with honey and cook for 2 minutes more. Serve immediately.

Chinese Broccoli / Chinese Food

Chinese Broccoli A vegetable related to the broccoli of Europe and the Middle East, with long, smooth stems, larger leaves than its Western cousins and clusters of small, white flowers. Stem, leaves

and flower-heads are eaten, either steamed or boiled until they are only just tender and served with oyster sauce; or used in stir-fry dishes.

Chinese Food The cooking and presentation of food is a central part of Chinese culture. It requires a harmonious combination of colour, aroma, flavour and texture, and

the balancing of the five basic flavours—sweet, sour, salty, bitter and piquant. A Chinese meal starts with a soup course, followed by dishes of rice, meat, fish, poultry and vegetables all placed on the table at the same time; each diner has a small eating bowl and a pair of chopsticks. Dessert is usually fruit; dairy products are rarely eaten. Tea is the main drink.

Regional cuisines

CHICKEN PROVENCALE

PRE-COOKED CHICKEN

★ Preparation time: 15 minutes
Total cooking time: 15 minutes
Serves 4

1 large barbecued
chicken
1 tablespoon olive oil
1 medium onion,
chopped
2 cloves garlic, crushed
2 large red peppers
(capsicums), thinly
sliced
1 tablespoon tomato paste
1/4 cup (2 fl oz) sherry
1/2 teaspoon sugar
1/3 cup shredded fresh
basil leaves
1/2 cup pitted black olives,
halved
salt and freshly ground
black pepper, to taste
425 g (13 1/2 oz) can
tomatoes, undrained

1 Preheat oven to moderately slow 160°C (325°F/Gas 3). Cut chicken into eight serving pieces. Keep warm.

2 Heat the oil in a medium heavy-based pan. Add onion, garlic and red pepper. Cook over medium heat until onion is just soft. Add crushed tomatoes with their juice, tomato paste, sherry and sugar. Bring to boil, reduce heat and simmer gently, uncovered, 10 minutes or until sauce thickens.

3 Add chicken pieces, basil and olives. Stir until heated through. Season to taste; serve immediately with green salad and crusty bread rolls.

ABOVE: CHICKEN PROVENCALE
OPPOSITE: PORT AND PEPPER PATE

WARM CHICKEN SALAD

★ Preparation time: 35 minutes
Total cooking time: 10 minutes
Serves 4

1 small onion, thinly
sliced
2 tablespoons olive oil
2 large peppers
(capsicums) seeded, cut
into thin strips
1 kg (2 lb) cooked
chicken, skinned and
cut into pieces
1/4 teaspoon Chinese five-
spice powder
pinch sugar
freshly ground black
pepper

Dressing
1 tablespoon vinegar
1/4 cup blanched almonds,
toasted
1 tablespoon soy sauce

1 In a pan, cook onion in half the oil until golden. Add pepper strips and cook until crisp-tender, about 5 minutes.

2 Stir in chicken pieces, soy sauce, five-spice powder, sugar and seasonings (to taste). Heat through. Transfer to serving bowl or individual plates.

3 To make Dressing: Combine vinegar and remaining oil; drizzle over salad. Serve garnished with almonds.

SMOKED CHICKEN SALAD WITH SWEET AND SOUR DRESSING

★ Preparation time: 25 minutes
Total cooking time: nil
Serves 4–6

155 g (5 oz) tub salad
sprouts
1 carrot, peeled and cut
into thin strips
155 g (5 oz) oyster
mushrooms
155 g (5 oz) snow peas
(mange tout)
1/4 cup cashews
1 kg (2 lb) smoked
chicken, flesh removed
and cut into chunks

Dressing
1/4 cup (2 fl oz) olive oil
2 tablespoons white wine
vinegar
2 tablespoons prepared
sweet and sour sauce
few drops Tabasco sauce

1 Spread a layer of sprouts on a serving plate. Top with carrot, mushrooms, snow peas, cashews and smoked chicken.

2 To make Dressing: Place all ingredients in a screw-top jar. Shake well.

3 Pour over salad just before serving. Serve salad with boiled new potatoes.

Chinese Gooseberry See Kiwi Fruit.

Chinese Parsley See Coriander.

Chipolata A small sausage, about finger length, made from pork or a mixture of pork and beef. It is often served as a garnish for roast meat or poultry, or as a cocktail snack.

Chive A herb related to the onion and leek with hollow, grass-like stems, thought to have originated in north-eastern Asia. Chives are used fresh and finely chopped to impart a delicate onion flavour to vegetable, cheese and egg dishes, to salads and savoury dips; they are also an ingredient in *fines herbes*. Chopped chives

have been shaped by the diversity in terrain and climate over the vast lands, dictating not only local ingredients but also, because of a general lack of fuel, cooking techniques: most food is chopped into small pieces and quickly cooked, either stir-fried in a wok or steamed. Cantonese cooking, the style best known outside China, uses stir-fried pork, fish or shellfish, crisp vegetables, steamed dumplings with fragrant dipping sauces and rice as an accompaniment to every meal.

CHICKEN LIVERS

PORT AND PEPPER PATE WITH MOON TOASTS

★ **Preparation time:** 40 minutes + overnight refrigeration
Total cooking time: 20 minutes
Serves 8

60 g (2 oz) can green peppercorns
1/3 cup (2 1/2 fl oz) port
90 g (3 oz) butter
1/3 cup (2 1/2 fl oz) cream
470 g (15 oz) chicken livers, chopped
1 tablespoon chopped chives
1 medium onion, chopped
2 cloves garlic, crushed

Moon Toasts
10 slices bread
lemon pepper seasoning

1 Preheat oven to moderate 180°C (350°F/Gas 4). Line an oven tray with foil. Drain peppercorns. Heat butter in a large, heavy-based pan. Add livers, onion, garlic and port. Stir over medium heat until liver is almost cooked and onion is soft. Bring to boil; simmer 5 minutes. Remove from heat. Cool slightly.

2 Place mixture in food processor. Using the pulse action, process 30 seconds or until mixture is smooth. Add cream, process further 15 seconds.

3 Transfer mixture to medium mixing bowl. Stir in chives and peppercorns. Spoon mixture into individual or one large ramekin dish. Refrigerate overnight or until firm.

4 To make Moon Toasts: Using a moon-shaped cutter, cut shapes out of bread. Place on

PASTA WITH CHICKEN LIVERS

★ **Preparation time:** 15 minutes
Total cooking time: 20 minutes
Serves 4–6

250 g (8 oz) pasta (penne, twists or rigatoni)
1/4 cup (2 fl oz) olive oil
1 large onion, chopped
1–2 cloves garlic, crushed
1/2 cup finely chopped lean bacon
500 g (1 lb) chicken livers, trimmed
1 tablespoon chopped parsley
1 tablespoon chopped marjoram or oregano
2 tablespoons red wine vinegar
2 cups torn spinach leaves
freshly ground pepper

1 Cook pasta in large pan of rapidly boiling water until just tender; drain.

2 Heat oil in a large pan and cook onion until soft but not brown. Add garlic, bacon and chicken livers and while stirring cook quickly until livers are almost cooked; they should still be faintly pink inside.

3 Add herbs and vinegar, spinach, pepper and warm pasta and toss ingredients over medium heat until spinach has wilted. Serve immediately.

prepared tray. Sprinkle with pepper. Bake 5 minutes or until crisp. Cool on wire rack.

Note: Make pâté one day ahead. Moon Toasts can be made one week ahead and stored in an airtight container.

CHINESE CLASSICS

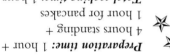

MINI SPRING ROLLS

★ ★ **Preparation time:** 45 minutes
Total cooking time: 30 minutes
Makes 20

4 dried Chinese mushrooms
3 cups finely shredded Chinese cabbage
2 large carrots, grated
1 tablespoon oyster sauce
1 tablespoon soy sauce

155 g (5 oz) pork mince
1 teaspoon grated ginger
1/2 teaspoon crushed garlic
2 teaspoons salt
6 teaspoons oil
3 teaspoons cornflour (cornstarch)
2 tablespoons water
10 large spring roll wrappers
oil for deep-frying
1/4 teaspoon ground black pepper

1 Soak mushrooms in hot water to cover for 30 minutes. Drain, squeeze to remove excess liquid. Remove stems and chop caps finely. Place cabbage in colander, sprinkle with salt, leave 10 minutes to draw out excess liquid. Rinse under cold, running water, squeezing to remove liquid.

2 Heat oil in wok or heavy-based frying pan, swirling gently to coat base and side. Add garlic and ginger, cook until pale golden. Increase heat to high, add mince and stir-fry, breaking up lumps, until meat changes colour. Stir in pepper and sauces. Add mushrooms, cabbage and carrot; continue stir-frying 3 minutes. Mix cornflour with water, add to meat mixture. Cook, stirring, until liquid is clear and thick. Leave to cool.

PEKING DUCK WITH MANDARIN PANCAKES

★ ★ **Preparation time:** 1 hour + 4 hours standing + 1 hour for pancakes
Total cooking time: 1 hour
Serves 4

1 x 1.75 kg (3 1/2 lb) duck
3 litres (12 cups) boiling water
1 tablespoon honey
1/2 cup (4 fl oz) hot water

Mandarin Pancakes
2 1/2 cups plain (all-purpose) flour
2 teaspoons caster (superfine) sugar
1 cup (8 fl oz) boiling water
1 tablespoon sesame oil

1 thin-skinned cucumber
12 spring onions (scallions)
2 tablespoons hoisin sauce

3 Cut spring roll wrappers diagonally in half. Work with one triangle at a time, keeping remainder covered with clean, damp tea-towel. Place 2 teaspoonsful of filling on a triangle. Fold in two side points, then roll up towards last point, forming a log. Seal point with a little flour and water paste. Repeat with remaining wrappers.

4 Heat oil in wok and deep-fry rolls four at a time until golden—about 3 minutes. Drain on absorbent paper. Serve with sweet and sour sauce.

Note: Prepare rolls 1 day ahead; refrigerate. Store uncooked in freezer for up to 1 month. Deep-fry frozen rolls in moderately hot oil for 5 minutes.

Chocolate A food made from the seeds of the cacao tree native to Central America. The white seeds grow in a pod and are fermented to develop the flavour, dried, roasted and ground to a dark brown paste which is solidified into blocks of pure chocolate, also called bitter or unsweetened chocolate. More than half the weight of pure chocolate is the vegetable fat known as cacao butter; cocoa powder is ground from the solids left if this fat is extracted.

The Maya people of Central America were the first to cultivate the cacao tree and to process its seeds. Columbus knew of the beans but not the preparation methods needed to rid it of its bitterness. The Spanish explorer Cortez brought back the beans as well as the knowledge of how to treat them. They were ground to a paste and mixed with cane sugar to produce a

freeze well and can be used in the same way as fresh chives. Chives are available fresh and freeze-dried.

OPPOSITE PAGE: MINI SPRING ROLLS

ABOVE: PEKING DUCK WITH MANDARIN PANCAKES

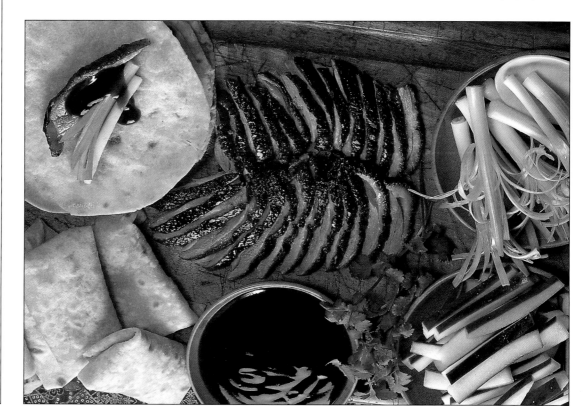

1 Wash duck, remove neck and any large pieces of fat from inside carcass. Hold duck over the sink and slowly pour boiling water over, rotating duck so that water scalds all skin. You may need another kettle of boiling water.

2 Put duck on a cake rack over a baking dish. Mix honey and hot water to make a glaze and brush two coats over duck, covering completely. Dry duck, preferably by hanging up in a cool, airy place. Alternatively, use an electric fan on a cool setting, positioned 1 metre (1 yard) away. Skin is sufficiently dry when papery to touch.

3 Remove seeds from cucumber and slice flesh into matchsticks. Take an 8 cm (3 inch) section from each spring onion and make fine parallel cuts from the centre towards the end. Place in iced water: spring onions will open into 'brushes'.

4 Preheat oven to moderately hot 210°C (415°F/Gas 6–7). Roast duck on the rack over baking pan for 30 minutes. Turn over carefully without tearing the skin and roast another 30 minutes. Remove from oven and let stand a minute or two. Place on a warm dish.

5 To make Mandarin Pancakes: Place flour and sugar in a medium bowl, pour over boiling water. Stir mixture a few times and leave until lukewarm. Knead on a lightly floured surface to make a smooth dough. Stand 30 minutes. Take two level tablespoons of dough and roll each into a ball. Roll out 2 circles, 8 cm (3 inches) in diameter. Lightly brush one circle with sesame oil and place the other on top. Re-roll to make a thin pancake about 15 cm (6 inches) in diameter. Repeat with remaining dough and oil to make about 10 'double' pancakes. Heat frying pan and cook pancakes one at a time in the ungreased pan. When small bubbles appear on the surface, turn over and cook the second side, pressing surface with a clean tea-towel. The pancake should puff up when done.

6 Remove to a plate. When cool enough to handle, peel two pancakes apart. Stack on a plate and cover at once to prevent them drying out.

7 To serve, arrange cucumber sticks and spring onion brushes on a serving plate. Place the hoisin sauce in a small dish. Place pancakes and finely sliced duck on separate plates. Each guest takes a pancake, spreads a little sauce on it and adds a couple of pieces of cucumber, a spring onion brush and finally a piece of crisp duck skin. The pancake is then folded over into a neat envelope shape for eating with the fingers. Follow the same procedure with the pancakes and duck meat when all the skin has been used.

Note: Traditionally, these pancakes should be paper-thin. Once you have mastered the technique of making them, use one level tablespoon of dough for each and proceed as before.

Choko (Chayote) The pale green, pear-shaped fruit of a climbing vine related to the gourd. It is peeled and boiled as a vegetable or used as an ingredient in chutney. The plant originated in Central America.

Chop Suey A dish developed by immigrant Chinese cooks in the United States and often served in Chinese restaurants in Western countries. It consists of a mixture of bean sprouts and finely sliced vegetables and meat (usually chicken or pork), stir-fried then simmered in sauce. The name is from the Chinese and means 'mixed bits'.

Chorizo A coarse-textured, dried, spicy sausage of Spanish origin, heavily flavoured with garlic and chilli. It is added to many Spanish dishes, such as cocido (Spanish stew) and paella. Any spicy salami may be used in its place.

Choux Pastry Also called choux paste, a light pastry used for making éclairs, cream puffs, profiteroles and croquembouche. It is cooked twice: first in the saucepan, where water,

pour simmering stock over and serve.

WONTON SOUP

★★ *Preparation time:* **40 minutes**
Total cooking time: **5 minutes**
Serves 6

4 dried Chinese mushrooms
250 g (8 oz) pork mince
125 g (4 oz) raw prawn (shrimp) meat, finely chopped
1 teaspoon salt
1 tablespoon soy sauce
1 teaspoon sesame oil
2 spring onions (scallions), finely chopped

1 teaspoon grated ginger
2 tablespoons finely sliced water chestnuts
250 g (8 oz) packet wonton wrappers
1.25 litres (5 cups) chicken or beef stock
4 spring onions (scallions), very finely sliced, for garnish

1 Soak mushrooms in hot water to cover for 30 minutes. Drain, squeeze to remove excess liquid. Remove stems and chop caps finely. Thoroughly combine mushrooms, pork, prawn meat, salt, soy, sesame oil, spring onion, ginger and water chestnuts. Work with one wonton wrapper at a time, keeping remainder covered with a clean, damp tea-towel. Place a heaped teaspoonful of mince mixture on the centre of a square wrapper.
2 Moisten edges of pastry, fold in half diagonally and bring two points together. Place wontons on a plate dusted with flour to prevent sticking.
3 Cook wontons in rapidly boiling water for 4–5 minutes. Bring stock to boil in separate pan. Remove wontons from water with slotted spoon, place in bowl. Garnish with extra spring onion, pour simmering stock over and serve.

FRIED RICE

★ *Preparation time:* **15 minutes**
Total cooking time: **10 minutes**
Serves 4

2 eggs, lightly beaten
1 medium onion
4 spring onions (scallions)
1/4 cup cooked peas
2 tablespoons soy sauce
250 g (8 oz) ham in the piece
2 tablespoons peanut oil

2 teaspoons lard, optional
4 cups cold, cooked rice
250 g (8 oz) cooked small prawns (shrimps), peeled

1 Season eggs with salt and pepper. Peel onion and cut into wedges about 1.5 cm (5/8 inch) wide. Cut spring onions into short lengths on the diagonal. Cut ham into very thin strips. Heat 1 tablespoon oil in a wok or large frying pan and add eggs, pulling set egg towards the centre and tilting the pan to let unset egg run to the edges.
2 When egg is almost set, break into large pieces resembling scrambled eggs. Transfer to a plate.
3 Heat remaining oil and lard in wok, swirling to coat base and side. Add onion and stir-fry over high heat until almost transparent. Add ham and stir-fry for 1 minute. Add rice and peas, stir-fry for 3 minutes until rice is heated through. Add eggs, soy sauce, spring onion and prawns. Heat through and serve.

ABOVE: FRIED RICE; BELOW: WONTON SOUP
OPPOSITE PAGE, ABOVE: EASY CHOCOLATE FUDGE; BELOW: CLASSIC CHOCOLATE MOUSSE

flour, butter and sugar—for sweet choux—are mixed before the eggs are whisked in to produce a smooth, shiny paste; the mixture is piped onto greased trays and cooked for a second time in the oven. The egg causes the mixture to swell, resulting in almost hollow logs or balls. When cool, they are split open and filled with custard or cream.

Chow Mein A Chinese dish consisting of strips of meat (usually chicken, pork or seafood) and vegetables, stir-fried and served with fried noodles. The name comes from the Cantonese dialect and means 'fried noodles'.

Chowder A thick soup, usually milk-based, made with seafood, fish, vegetables or chicken. The name comes from the French chaudière, a copper pot in which fishermen's wives cooked a communal soup from a share of each man's catch to celebrate the safe return of the fishing fleet from the sea.

Churro A fritter made of deep-fried choux pastry, sprinkled with sugar and served as a dessert. The churro originated in Spain where it is often also served at breakfast with a large cup of hot chocolate or coffee.

CHOCOLATE

CLASSIC CHOCOLATE MOUSSE

★ *Preparation time:* 25 minutes + 2 hours refrigeration
Total cooking time: 5 minutes
Serves 6

200 g (6½ oz) dark (semi-sweet) chocolate, chopped
45 g (1½ oz) unsalted (sweet) butter
1 tablespoon brandy, cognac or orange liqueur
1 tablespoon icing (confectioners) sugar
1 teaspoon vanilla essence

4 eggs, separated
⅔ cup (5 fl oz) cream, whipped
whipped cream, extra, for serving

1 Place chocolate in heatproof bowl. Stand over pan of simmering water and stir until chocolate has melted and is smooth. Remove from heat. Cool slightly.

2 Using electric beaters, beat butter, sugar and essence until light and creamy. Add yolks, one at a time, beating well after each addition. Add chocolate, beat until smooth. Fold in a third of the cream.

3 Place egg whites in small, dry mixing bowl. Beat until stiff peaks form. Using a metal spoon, fold egg whites, remaining cream and liqueur into chocolate mixture. Pour mixture into individual glasses. Refrigerate for 2 hours or until set. Serve with cream.

CHOCOLATE SAUCE

Break 155 g (5 oz) dark (semi-sweet) chocolate into small pieces and place in a pan with ½ cup (4 fl oz) cream. Heat gently until the chocolate melts, stirring until smooth. Serve warm or at room temperature. Makes about 1 cup (8 fl oz).

EASY CHOCOLATE FUDGE

★ *Preparation time:* 10 minutes
Total cooking time: 5 minutes
Makes 64

125 g (4 oz) dark (semi-sweet) chocolate, chopped
125 g (4 oz) unsalted (sweet) butter
1½ cups icing (confectioners) sugar, sifted
2 tablespoons milk
½ cup coarsely chopped pecans, almonds, walnuts or hazelnuts

1 Line base and sides of a shallow 17 cm (6¾ inch) square cake tin with aluminium foil. Brush foil with oil or melted butter. Combine chocolate, butter, sugar and milk in a medium heavy-based pan. Stir over low heat until chocolate and butter have melted and mixture is smooth. Bring to boil; boil for 1 minute only. Remove from heat; beat with a wooden spoon until mixture is smooth. Fold in chopped nuts.

2 Pour mixture into the prepared tin; smooth surface with the back of a metal spoon. Stand tin on wire rack to cool. When fudge is firm, remove from tin. Carefully peel off the foil and cut into squares. Store Easy Chocolate Fudge in an airtight container in a cool, dark place for up to 7 days.

Chutney A sweet-and-sour condiment of fruits and vegetables cooked with sugar, spices and vinegar until thick. Chutney is served as an accompaniment to hot and cold meat, with cheese platters, with fish dishes and with Indian curries.

Cider An alcoholic drink made from the fermented juice of apples (sometimes pears); it can be still or sparkling. Cider is used in cooking to flavour meat, poultry and fish dishes, and in desserts.

Cilantro See Coriander.

Cinnamon The light brown, aromatic, flaky bark of a small, evergreen tree native to Sri Lanka. The inner bark is taken from thin branches and dried in the sun to form curled tubes called 'quills'. The palest, from young shoots, are superior.

Cinnamon Sugar A combination of equal parts of sugar and cinnamon sprinkled on coffee cakes and buttered toast.

DATE AND CHOCOLATE FUDGE SLICE

Preparation time: 25 minutes
Total cooking time: 35 minutes
Makes one 30 x 20 cm (12 x 8 inch) oblong slice

1 cup self-raising flour, sifted
2 tablespoons golden syrup (light corn syrup)
1/2 cup dates, chopped
1 egg, lightly beaten
1 teaspoon grated lemon rind
125 g (4 oz) butter
2 tablespoons cocoa
1/2 cup walnuts, chopped
60 g (2 oz) dark (semi-sweet) chocolate, chopped
1 cup brown sugar

1 Preheat oven to 180°C (350°F/Gas 4). Brush a shallow 30 x 20 cm (12 x 8 inch) oblong cake tin with oil or melted butter. Cover base with paper extending over two sides; grease paper. Combine flour, dates, walnuts and lemon rind in large mixing bowl. Make a well in the centre.
2 Combine butter, brown sugar, cocoa and golden syrup in small pan. Stir over low heat until butter has melted and sugar has dissolved; remove from heat. Cool slightly and whisk in egg.
3 Add mixture to dry ingredients. Stir with metal spoon until well combined. Spoon into tin; smooth surface. Bake 25 minutes or until skewer comes out clean when inserted into centre; cool.
4 Place chocolate in glass bowl. Stir over barely simmering water until melted; remove from heat. Drizzle over slice. Cut into slices to serve.

CHOCOLATE-DIPPED FRUIT OR PETALS

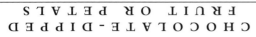

Chocolate-dipped petals make very attractive decorations for cakes and desserts, and chocolate-dipped fruit is a delicious way to end a meal. Melt 125 g (4 oz) dark (semi-sweet) chocolate in a small bowl over a pan of simmering water; cool slightly. Carefully separate the petals of small roses or other edible flowers. Working with one petal at a time, dip it into the chocolate to half-coat only—this gives a lovely effect. Drain excess chocolate. Place the coated petals on a foil-lined tray and set aside to harden.
Dip strawberries or glacé fruit pieces in the same way; dip them fully, or half-dip for a different effect. Serve with coffee and liqueur.

Above: SOUR CREAM AND CHOCOLATE SLICE, with DATE AND CHOCOLATE FUDGE SLICE
Opposite, above: PISTACHIO PRALINE TRUFFLES; below: CHOCOLATE AND CREAMY BERRY ROULADE

SOUR CREAM AND CHOCOLATE SLICE

Preparation time: 15 minutes
Total cooking time: 40 minutes
Makes one 30 x 20 cm (12 x 8 inch) oblong slice

100 g (3½ oz) dark (semi-sweet) chocolate, chopped
2/3 cup (6 oz) sour cream
3 eggs
1 cup caster (superfine) sugar
155 g (5 oz) butter, melted
1 cup plain (all-purpose) flour
100 g (3½ oz) milk chocolate, chopped

Icing
1/4 cup cocoa
2 tablespoons sour cream

1 Preheat oven to 180°C (350°F/Gas 4). Brush a shallow 30 x 20 cm (12 x 8 inch) oblong tin with melted butter or oil, line the base and sides with paper; grease paper.
2 Place chocolate in glass bowl. Stir over barely simmering water until melted; remove from heat.
3 Place all ingredients into a food processor. Process for 10 seconds or until mixture is smooth. Pour into prepared tin and smooth surface. Bake for 35 minutes or until skewer inserted in centre comes out clean. Stand for 10 minutes before turning onto wire rack to cool.
4 **To make Icing:** Combine chocolate and sour cream in small pan. Stir over low heat until smooth; cool slightly. Spread evenly over slice using a palette knife. Cut into slices to serve.

Clam A saltwater shellfish with edible flesh protected by two large hinged shells marked by fine circular ridges. Clams are opened like oysters, and, like oysters, the flesh can be eaten fresh on the half shell, dressed with a squeeze of lemon juice. The east coast of North America is famous for its summer clambakes and its New England clam chowder. In Italy, tiny clams (*vongole*) are often part of pasta sauces; in Japan clam broth is served at wedding banquets.

Citrus Fruit A family of tropical fruits that includes the orange, lemon, grapefruit, lime, tangerine, mandarin, clementine and cumquat.

Citron A pear-shaped citrus fruit resembling a lemon, but larger and with a thicker, fragrant rind. A native of China, it is grown mainly for its peel, which is candied or preserved and used in the making of fruit cakes. It is the traditional topping to Madeira cake.

CHOCOLATE AND CREAMY BERRY ROULADE

★★ *Preparation time:* 30 minutes
Total cooking time: 20 minutes
Makes 1 roulade

60 g (2 oz) dark (semi-sweet) chocolate, chopped
2 tablespoons cold water
1/2 teaspoon bicarbonate of soda (baking soda)
4 eggs
3/4 cup caster (superfine) sugar
1/2 cup plain (all-purpose) flour, sifted
1/2 teaspoon baking powder, sifted
1 teaspoon vanilla essence
icing (confectioners) sugar, sifted

Filling
1 cup (8 fl oz) cream, whipped
250 g (8 oz) fresh raspberries, sliced in half

1 Preheat oven to 200°C (400°F/Gas 6). Grease a shallow 30 x 25 x 2 cm (12 x 10 x 3/4 inch) swiss roll (jelly roll) tin. Line base and two sides with paper; grease paper. Stir chocolate in a bowl, over a pan of simmering water until melted; remove from heat. Beat eggs with electric beaters in mixer bowl until thick and pale. Add sugar gradually, beating until mixture is pale and glossy and sugar dissolved. Stir in essence. Using a metal spoon, lightly fold in flour and baking powder.

2 Stir water and bicarbonate of soda into cooled chocolate. Fold into flour mixture. Spread evenly in prepared tin. Bake 15 minutes or until springy to touch. Turn onto tea-towel covered with greaseproof paper. Using tea-towel to guide, roll cake up with paper; stand 5 minutes or until cool. Unroll cake; discard paper.

3 Spread with cream and cover with fruit; re-roll. Trim ends of roll; dust with icing sugar.

PISTACHIO PRALINE TRUFFLES

★★ *Preparation time:* 50 minutes + 15 minutes refrigeration
Total cooking time: 20 minutes
Makes 55

250 g (8 oz) dark (semi-sweet) chocolate, chopped
1/3 cup shelled pistachio nuts
1/2 cup sugar
1/4 cup (2 fl oz) water
1/3 cup (2 1/2 fl oz) cream
45 g (1 1/2 oz) unsalted (sweet) butter, chopped
2 teaspoons brandy or cognac
1/3 cup cocoa powder, sifted

1 Preheat oven to moderate 180°C (350°F/Gas 4). Place shelled pistachios in shallow cake tin. Bake 5–10 minutes or until nuts are lightly roasted; cool. Combine sugar and water in medium pan. Stir over low heat without boiling until sugar has dissolved. Brush sugar crystals from side of the pan with a wet pastry brush. Bring to boil, reduce heat and simmer 8–10 minutes or until syrup turns golden. Remove from heat, stir in nuts. Pour mixture onto an oiled, foil-lined tray.

2 Place butter and chocolate in medium heatproof bowl. Stand over pan of simmering water until mixture has melted and is smooth. Remove from heat; cool slightly. Add the cream and brandy, mix well; cool completely.

3 Using a meat mallet or rolling pin, finely crush hardened toffee. Add to chocolate mixture, mix well. Cover and refrigerate for 45 minutes or until firm enough to handle.

4 Roll teaspoonsful of mixture into small balls. Place on paper-lined tray and refrigerate for 15 minutes. Roll in sifted cocoa and serve.

Clarify To clear a liquid from impurities or sediments. Stocks and broths are clarified for use as clear soups by whisking egg white into the cold liquid; as the mixture is heated the egg white coagulates, trapping any opaque particles in a scum on the top which can then be strained off.

Clove The fragrant, sun-dried flower-bud of an aromatic evergreen tree native to the Moluccas, or Spice Islands, of Indonesia. Cloves have a sweet, peppery aroma and a warm, fruity, slightly bitter flavour. Its use, both medicinal (it was believed to ward off the plague) and culinary (as a preservative of meat and a flavouring for a wide range of dishes), was widespread in the Middle Ages. Cloves are used in stewed fruit, spiced cakes and breads, in pork and ham dishes, and sauces, chutneys, marinades, wines and liqueurs. They are available whole or ground as a powder.

Cock-a-Leekie A thick Scottish soup consisting of chicken pieces simmered in stock with chopped leek, thickened with barley and traditionally served with stewed prunes.

Cocktail An alcoholic drink usually made from a mixture of spirits and liqueurs, often with fruit or vegetable juice, sometimes sweetened, and blended either by shaking the ingredients in a closed container or by stirring. A cocktail is usually served chilled as a pre-dinner drink. Non-alcoholic versions combine juices and aerated drinks. The cocktail is probably an American invention.

Cocoa A dark brown, powder made from seeds of the cacao, a tree native to tropical America. The seeds are roasted and ground into a paste of pure chocolate. Cocoa powder is ground from the dry solids left when the vegetable fat known as cacao butter is removed.

Coconut A large nut, the fruit of the coconut palm. Grown throughout the tropics, it is an important food, providing oil-rich white flesh and a refreshing liquid. The soft pulp of a young coconut can be

CHUTNEYS

BANANA DATE CHUTNEY

 ★

Preparation time: 45 minutes
Total cooking time: 45 minutes
Makes 2 litres (8 cups)

1 kg (2 lb) bananas	1 cup (8 fl oz) orange
500 g (1 lb) onions	juice
375 g (12 oz) pitted dates	½ cup (4 fl oz) lemon
2 cloves garlic, crushed	juice
1½ cups (12 fl oz) malt	1 tablespoon yellow
vinegar	mustard seeds
1½ cups sultanas	5 whole cloves
⅔ cup drained preserved	1 teaspoon salt
ginger, chopped	¼ teaspoon hot chilli flakes

1 Peel and mash bananas; chop the onions and dates coarsely.
2 In a large, heavy saucepan or boiler combine the bananas, onions, dates, garlic and vinegar. Mix well and heat until boiling. Reduce heat, cover and simmer for 20 minutes. Add sultanas, ginger, orange and lemon juice, mustard seeds, cloves, salt and chilli flakes. Heat until boiling. Reduce heat and simmer, stirring frequently until thickened, 15–20 minutes more.
3 Ladle into warm, sterilised jars and seal. When cool, label and date.

APPLE, TOMATO AND MINT CHUTNEY

★ ★ **Preparation time:** 1 hour
Total cooking time: 2½ hours
Makes 1.5 litres (6 cups)

1 kg (2 lb) green apples	1 cup raisins
1 kg (2 lb) tomatoes	⅓ cup (2½ fl oz) lemon
3 onions	juice
⅔ cup mint leaves	3 cups brown sugar
½ cup parsley	2 teaspoons salt
½ cup (4 fl oz) orange	2 cups (16 fl oz) cider
juice	vinegar

1 Wash, peel and finely chop apples, tomatoes and onions. Finely chop fresh herbs.
2 Place all ingredients in a large saucepan or boiler. Bring slowly to boil and simmer for about 2½ hours or until mixture is thick, stirring occasionally.
3 Remove cooked chutney from the heat and stand 5 minutes. Spoon into warm, sterilised jars and seal immediately. When cool, label and date.

Note: Chutneys are delicious served with cold sliced meats, especially in sandwiches.

ABOVE: BANANA DATE CHUTNEY, APPLE, TOMATO AND MINT CHUTNEY. OPPOSITE, ABOVE: COCONUT MACAROONS; BELOW: COCONUT FISH CURRY

COCONUTS

COCONUT FISH CURRY

Preparation time: 20 minutes
Total cooking time: 20 minutes
Serves 4–6

650 g (1 lb 5 oz) thick
white fish fillets
2 cm (¾ inch) piece
ginger, chopped
1 medium-sized onion
¾ teaspoon turmeric
2 teaspoons tamarind
concentrate (see Note)
2 tablespoons butter
1½ cups (12 fl oz) water
2 tablespoons chopped
coriander

2 cloves garlic
2 dried red chillies,
soaked for 15 minutes
in hot water
½ cup desiccated coconut
½ teaspoon fennel seeds
1 teaspoon cumin seeds
2 teaspoons lemon juice

1 Cut across the fillets to make thick slices. Sprinkle with lemon juice and set aside.

2 Toast cumin, fennel seeds and coconut in a dry pan until lightly golden and aromatic. Grind to a powder in a spice grinder or mortar.

3 Grind chillies, garlic, ginger and onion to a paste; add ground spices, turmeric and tamarind.

4 Fry mixture in butter for 1½–2 minutes, stirring. Add water, bring to boil. Simmer for 6 minutes.

5 Add fish with half the coriander. Simmer gently until fish is tender, about 6 minutes. Serve with rice, garnishing with the remaining coriander.

Note: If tamarind concentrate is not available, use a tablespoon of lemon juice for tartness.

COCONUT MACAROONS

Preparation time: 15 minutes
Total cooking time: 15–20 minutes
Makes 60

3 egg whites
1¼ cups caster (superfine)
sugar
1 teaspoon grated lemon
rind
2 tablespoons cornflour
(cornstarch), sifted
3 cups desiccated coconut
125 g (4 oz) dark (semi-
sweet) chocolate melts,
melted

1 Preheat oven to moderately slow 160°C (325°F/Gas 3). Line two 32 x 28 cm (13 x 11 inch) biscuit (oven) trays with baking paper. Place egg whites in a small, dry mixing bowl. Using electric beaters, beat egg whites until firm peaks form. Add sugar gradually, beating constantly until mixture is thick and glossy and sugar has completely dissolved. Add rind; beat until just combined.

2 Transfer mixture to a large mixing bowl; add cornflour and coconut. Using a metal spoon, stir until just combined.

3 Drop heaped teaspoonful of mixture onto prepared trays about 3 cm (1¼ inch) apart. Bake on top shelf for 15–20 minutes or until golden.

4 Cool macaroons on trays. Dip half of each into melted chocolate. Allow to set before serving.

ABOUT COCONUT

■ Traditionally coconut milk was made by grating fresh coconut into a bowl, adding hot water and straining it. It is much easier to use desiccated coconut (make sure it's unsweetened) and easiest of all is to open a can of coconut milk.
■ Coconut cream is the thick layer that forms on top of the milk after it has been left to stand in the refrigerator. You can buy it in compressed blocks which, once opened, will keep for several years in the refrigerator.

Coddle To cook an egg in the shell just below boiling point, until the white turns opaque and the yolk is heated.

Cod A fish with moist, creamy-white, firm flesh that when cooked separates into large flakes. An inhabitant of cold waters, it is known especially in the northern Atlantic. Cod has been eaten since prehistoric times; in its dried form it provisioned the Vikings on their sea voyages. It was the first fish to be caught and salted commercially.

Coconut Milk The liquid pressed from coconut flesh. It is used in many Asian dishes, especially curries. Coconut cream is obtained by chilling coconut milk then scooping off the oily surface 'cream' and is used similarly. Both are available canned.

coconut is used in cakes, biscuits (cookies) and confectionery (candy).

eaten with a spoon and in some areas is the first solid food given to an infant. The coconut probably originated in Melanesia but this is uncertain because the huge nut can float across oceans and then take root wherever it is beached. Desiccated

COFFEE

Coffee, with its incomparable aroma, is one of the world's favourite beverages. It can be roasted, blended and brewed in a variety of ways, and served either hot or cold, black or enriched with milk or cream, sweetened with sugar or flavoured with spices or alcohol.

BLENDS AND ROASTS

The type of bean, and the region, climate and soil in which it was grown, all affect coffee's flavour. Specialist coffee merchants select and blend beans from many parts of the world to produce subtle differences in flavour. The temperature at which the beans are roasted affects both the aroma and the taste of the coffee.

■ Light or pale roast enhances delicate, subtle flavours; this coffee is good with milk.

■ Medium roast gives a more distinctive flavour and aroma—good for daytime drinking, with or without milk.

■ Dark or full roast produces a strong aroma and flavour, suitable for after-dinner drinking and usually served black.

■ Double or continental roast has a powerful, smoky aroma. The beans are glossy and very dark in colour and the coffee has an almost bitter taste. It is served black.

GRINDING COFFEE

Coffee can be bought as whole beans or ready-ground, with a choice of coarse, medium, fine or superfine grinds; the latter is sometimes labelled 'Espresso' or 'Turkish' coffee. The type of grind depends on the brewing method to be used. Ground beans lose flavour faster than whole ones and should be ground just before use.

COFFEE FROM LEFT:
CAFFÈ LATTE;
CAPPUCCINO; ICED
COFFEE; LONG BLACK;
CAFFÈ MACCHIATO

BREWING COFFEE

Despite the wide variety of equipment available, there are two basic methods of brewing coffee—infusion and boiling.

■ PERCOLATOR: Steam pressure forces boiling water up a central tube and over the grounds. This takes about 15 minutes. Use coarse grind.

■ PLUNGER POT (*Cafetière*): Water is boiled, allowed to go just off the boil, then poured over grounds in a pot. A lid with attached plunger is put on and coffee allowed to infuse for several minutes before the plunger is slowly pushed down; grounds are held in the bottom of the pot while the coffee is poured. Use a medium grind.

■ FILTER POTS: A filter paper is folded to fit into a holder on top of the pot (or cup); coffee is placed in the paper and just-past-boiling water is poured slowly over the grounds. The coffee filters down into the pot. Some have their own heating device. Use a fine grind.

INTERNATIONAL FAVOURITES

■ ESPRESSO This very strong coffee (its name is Italian for 'pressed out') is made in a machine which forces a combination of steam and water through very finely ground coffee. A high proportion of coffee is used—about 2 tablespoons of coffee to 6 tablespoons water. Traditionally served in a small cup with sugar to taste.

■ CAPPUCCINO This, too, is made in an espresso machine. The coffee is not quite as strong and is served in a larger cup, and topped with hot milk which has been frothed by having steam passed through it. Grated chocolate, powdered chocolate or cinnamon is often sprinkled on top.

■ **CAFFE MACCHIATO** Another Italian favourite. Fill a 90 ml (3 fl oz) glass with espresso to within 5 mm (¹/₄ inch) of the rim. Add a small dash of cold milk by pouring down the side of the glass, forming a lighter, coffee-coloured layer above the espresso. Place the filled glass on a saucer, accompanied by a small paper napkin.

■ **CAFFE LATTE** Italian breakfast coffee. A 250 ml (8 fl oz) glass is half-filled with espresso and topped up with hot milk, which forms a slight froth on top. Serve on a saucer with a white paper napkin tied around the glass so it can be held without burning the hands.

■ **CAFÉ AU LAIT** An essential part of breakfast in France, this is strong black coffee and hot milk in equal proportions (sometimes 2 or 3 parts milk to 1 of coffee). The two are poured simultaneously into a large cup or bowl.

■ **TURKISH COFFEE** In Turkey, the Middle East and in Greece, rich, dark, sweet coffee is made in an *ibrik*, a small brass or copper pot with a long handle. For each small cup, place 1 heaped teaspoon of dark-roast coffee (pulverised to a fine powder), 60 ml (2 fl oz) cold water and 1 teaspoon sugar into the pot. Bring to boil over medium heat; remove from heat as soon as it froths up. Pour a little coffee into each cup, bring coffee back to the boil and again pour some into each cup; repeat a third time, making sure each cup has foam on top. Turkish coffee is traditionally drunk from tiny, stemmed cups; often a glass of iced water is offered with it.

■ **IRISH COFFEE** For each person, place 2 lumps (1 teaspoon) sugar and 1 measure (45 ml/ 1¹/₂ fl oz) Irish whiskey in a warm, tall stemmed glass, and fill two-thirds of the glass with hot, strong black coffee. Stir briefly and carefully add cream, pouring it over the back of a spoon so that it floats on the surface. Do not mix—drink the coffee and whiskey through the layer of cream.

■ **SPICED VIENNA COFFEE** Place 3 cups hot strong coffee, 2 cinnamon sticks, 4 cloves and 4 allspice berries in a pan; simmer over low heat for 10-15 minutes. Strain and pour into warmed wine glasses or mugs. Top with whipped cream, sprinkle with nutmeg. Sugar can be added. Or serve cold; omit cream and garnish with lemon.

■ **ICED COFFEE** Prepare strong black coffee and sweeten to taste while still hot. Cool and refrigerate. Pour some coffee into an ice-cube tray. To serve, pour chilled coffee into tall glasses, add a coffee ice cube, top with whipped cream.

■ **GRANITA DI CAFFE** This soft water ice, also known as *café frappé*, is a summer favourite in Europe. Prepare strong black coffee, sweeten to taste, cool and strain through a filter paper. Pour into a shallow tray, freeze until solid, then process briefly in a blender. Transfer the frozen granita to tall glasses, top with whipped cream and sprinkle with powdered chocolate.

■ **HOT MOCHA JAVA** Mocha is a very strongly flavoured coffee, often combined with chocolate. Here, anise gives it a new twist. Combine the zest of 1 orange and 1 lemon, 4 cinnamon sticks, ¹/₄ cup chocolate syrup, 4 drops of oil of anise and 8 cups strong, hot coffee. Steep mixture over low heat for 15 minutes; strain and pour into demitasses. Add a lemon twist to each cup, top with whipped cream. Serves 12.

POINTS FOR SUCCESS

■ *Black coffee should be strong, clear and very hot. Use 1 to 1¹/₂ tablespoons of coffee per 200 ml (6 fl oz) of water. If weaker coffee is required, brew at normal strength, then dilute with hot water to taste.*

■ *Coffee kept for too long after brewing loses its flavour due to the formation of astringent and bitter residues.*

■ *Clean coffee pots thoroughly after use; oily residues can collect inside and turn rancid, tainting subsequent brews.*

■ *Buy coffee in quantities to last you not more than 2 weeks. Store it in a sealed container in the refrigerator.*

Coffee The roasted and ground beans of a tropical tree, made into a beverage and also used as a flavouring. The 'beans' are the seeds of a red berry (two to each fruit); when roasted they develop the characteristic coffee aroma and flavour. The coffee tree, native to Ethiopia and the Sudan, is now cultivated in New Guinea, the Americas and Africa. Drinking coffee did not become fashionable in Europe until the seventeenth century. Coffee is available as whole or ground beans, and as instant powder or granules.

Colby A soft-textured cow's milk cheese similar to cheddar. It has a mild, sweetish flavour, is yellow in colour and has tiny holes.

Colcannon A dish of Irish origin consisting of chopped cooked cabbage, chopped onion

Coeur à la Crème A dessert of unripened fresh cheese, such as cream cheese or fromage blanc, mixed with fresh cream and sometimes sugar, and drained in a perforated mould, traditionally heart-shaped—hence its name. It is served chilled with fresh fruit.

CONFECTIONERY (CANDY)

PEANUT BRITTLE

★ ★ *Preparation time:* 20 minutes
Total cooking time: 15 minutes
Makes about 500 g (1 lb)

2 cups sugar	½ cup (4 fl oz) water
1 cup brown sugar, lightly packed	60 g (2 oz) butter
2½ cups roasted unsalted peanuts	½ cup golden syrup (light corn syrup)

1 Line base and sides of a shallow 30 x 25 x 2 cm (12 x 10 x ¾ inch) swiss roll (jelly roll) tin with foil or greaseproof paper. Brush foil with oil or melted butter. Combine sugars, syrup and water in a large, heavy-based pan. Stir over medium heat without boiling until sugar has completely dissolved. Brush sugar crystals from side of pan with a wet pastry brush. Add butter, stir until melted. Bring to boil, reduce heat slightly, boil without stirring 15–20 minutes; OR until a teaspoon of mixture dropped into cold water reaches soft-crack stage; OR, if using a sugar thermometer, until mixture reaches 138°C (271°F). Remove pan from heat immediately.

2 Fold in peanuts. Pour into tin. Stand tin on wire rack to cool; break into pieces when almost set.

TIPSY FUDGE

★ *Preparation time:* 10 minutes
Total cooking time: 25 minutes
Makes 36 pieces

¾ cup sultanas	2 tablespoons glucose syrup
2 tablespoons rum	
3 cups sugar	90 g (3 oz) unsalted butter (sweet)
1 cup (8 fl oz) milk	

1 Brush a 20 cm (8 inch) square cake tin with melted butter or oil. Line base and sides with foil; grease foil. Combine sultanas and rum, set aside.

2 Combine sugar, milk and glucose syrup in a large, heavy-based pan. Stir over medium heat without boiling until sugar has completely dissolved. Brush sugar crystals from sides of pan with a wet pastry brush. Bring to boil, reduce heat slightly and boil without stirring for about 20 minutes; OR boil until a teaspoon of mixture dropped into cold water reaches soft-ball stage; OR if using a sugar thermometer, until the mixture reaches 115°C (239°F). Remove from heat immediately.

3 Add butter to pan without stirring. Stand 5 minutes, add sultanas and beat until thick and creamy. Pour into prepared tin, leave to cool. Cut into squares when cold. Store in airtight container in a cool dark place for up to 1 week.

CARAMELS

★ ★ *Preparation time:* 10 minutes + 30 minutes refrigeration
Total cooking time: 25 minutes
Makes 36

125 g (4 oz) butter	1 cup caster (superfine) sugar
410 g (13 oz) can condensed milk	½ cup golden syrup (light corn syrup)

1 Line base and sides of shallow 17 cm (6¾ inch) square cake tin with foil, leaving edges overhanging. Brush foil with oil or melted butter. Combine butter, condensed milk, caster sugar and golden syrup in medium, heavy-based pan. Stir over low heat without boiling until sugar has completely dissolved. Bring to boil; reduce heat slightly. Stir constantly (to prevent burning) 15–20 minutes, until mixture turns dark golden caramel colour (do not undercook or it will not set).

2 Pour into prepared tin; smooth surface. Mark into squares. Refrigerate 30 minutes or until firm. Remove from tin; cut through. Store in airtight container in the refrigerator for up to 3 weeks.

TURKISH DELIGHT

★★ **Preparation time:** 30 minutes + overnight setting
Total cooking time: 20 minutes
Makes 50

rind of 1 medium lemon	2 tablespoons gelatine
rind of 1 medium orange	1 cup (8 fl oz) water, extra
¼ cup (2 fl oz) orange juice	⅔ cup cornflour (cornstarch)
2 tablespoons lemon juice	3–4 drops orange or rose flower water
3 cups caster (superfine) sugar	red food colouring
½ cup (4 fl oz) water	½ cup icing (confectioners) sugar

1 Line base and sides of a deep 17 cm (6 ¾ inch) square cake tin with aluminium foil, leaving edges overhanging. Brush foil with oil or melted butter. Remove white pith from rinds.
2 Combine rinds, juices, sugar and water in large heavy-based pan. Stir over medium heat without boiling until sugar has completely dissolved. Brush sugar crystals from side of pan with a wet pastry brush. Bring to boil, reduce heat slightly and boil without stirring for about 5 minutes; OR boil until a teaspoon of mixture dropped into cold water forms long threads; OR if using a sugar thermometer it must reach 105°C (221°F).

3 Combine gelatine with ½ cup (4 fl oz) extra water in bowl. Stir over hot water until dissolved. In separate bowl combine cornflour with remaining water; mix until smooth.
4 Add gelatine and cornflour mixtures to sugar syrup. Stir over medium heat until mixture boils and clears. Stir in flower water and a few drops of red food colouring. Strain mixture into tin; refrigerate overnight. When set peel off foil and cut into squares. Roll in icing sugar.

HONEYCOMB

Line the base and sides of a 27 x 18 cm (10¾ x 7 inch) oblong tin with aluminium foil; brush foil with melted butter or oil. Combine 1¾ cups sugar, ¼ cup (2 fl oz) liquid glucose and ½ cup (4 fl oz) water in a large, heavy-based pan. Stir over medium heat without boiling until sugar has completely dissolved. Brush sugar crystals from sides of pan with a wet pastry brush. Bring to boil, reduce heat slightly, boil without stirring for about 8 minutes or until mixture just begins to turn golden. Remove from heat immediately. Sift 2 teaspoons bicarbonate of soda (baking soda) into sugar mixture. Using a wooden spoon, stir until bubbles begin to subside and there is no soda visible on surface. Pour carefully into tin and leave to set for about 1½ hours. Remove from tin, peel away foil and cut into pieces. Store in an airtight container in a cool dark place for up to seven days. Makes about 28 pieces.

OPPOSITE PAGE: PEANUT BRITTLE AND CARAMELS
ABOVE: TURKISH DELIGHT, HONEYCOMB AND TIPSY FUDGE

SPICED FRUIT AND NUT BARS

★★ **Preparation time:** 20 minutes
Total cooking time: 40 minutes
Makes 32

2/3 cup blanched almonds
2/3 cup walnuts
1/2 cup mixed peel
1/3 cup mixed dried fruit
2 tablespoons cocoa
2 tablespoons plain (all-purpose) flour
250 g (8 oz) dark (semi-sweet) chocolate, chopped
1/4 teaspoon ground nutmeg
1/3 cup caster (superfine) sugar
1/4 cup honey
1/4 cup (2 fl oz) water
1/2 teaspoon ground cinnamon
1/4 teaspoon ground cloves

1 Preheat oven to moderate 180°C (350°F/Gas 4). Line a 20 cm (8 inch) square cake tin with aluminium foil; grease foil. Spread almonds and walnuts on an oven tray and bake for 5 minutes or until just golden. Remove from tray to cool and chop finely. Combine nuts, peel, dried fruit, cocoa, flour and spices in a large mixing bowl.

2 Combine sugar, honey and water in a heavy-based pan. Stir over medium heat without boiling until sugar has dissolved. Brush sugar crystals from sides of pan with wet brush. Bring to boil, reduce heat slightly, boil 10 minutes without stirring. Remove from heat, pour onto fruit mixture and combine well. Press into prepared tin with back of oiled spoon and bake 20 minutes. Cool in tin. Remove from tin and peel away foil. Cut crusts from edges and discard. Cut cake into four long bars, then each bar into eight short fingers.

3 Line an oven tray with foil. Place chocolate in a heatproof bowl. Stir over a pan of simmering water until chocolate has melted and is smooth. Cool slightly. Dip each bar into melted chocolate. Using a spoon, coat in chocolate, then lift out on a fork. Drain and place onto prepared tray to set.

CHERRY CHOCOLATES

★★ **Preparation time:** 30 minutes
★★ **Total cooking time:** 10 minutes
Makes about 40

125 g (4 oz) unsalted (sweet) butter
2 cups icing (confectioners) sugar
1/3 cup (2 1/2 fl oz) thick cream
2 cups desiccated coconut
pink food colouring
220 g (7 oz) glacé cherries
105 g (3 1/2 oz) dark (semi-sweet) chocolate, chopped
30 g (1 oz) white vegetable shortening
60 g (2 oz) white cooking chocolate

1 Heat butter in a small pan until lightly browned then remove from heat. Add sifted icing sugar, cream, coconut and few drops of food colouring. Stir until combined.

2 Take about 2 teaspoons of mixture and press evenly around each cherry.

3 Place dark chocolate and shortening in a small heatproof bowl. Stand over a pan of simmering water, stir until the chocolate and shortening have melted and the mixture is smooth.

4 Place a wire rack over an oven tray. Using two forks, dip cherries into chocolate; drain excess. Place on wire rack and allow to set.

5 Place white chocolate in small heatproof bowl. Place over a pan of simmering water until chocolate has melted. Cool mixture slightly; spoon into a small paper icing bag. Seal the open end and snip off tip of bag. Drizzle white chocolate over cherry chocolates to decorate; allow to set.

Consommé A rich, clear soup made of meat or chicken stock which has been reduced and clarified. It can be served hot or cold, often with the addition of finely sliced meat or vegetables or pasta shapes.

Coq au Vin Chicken cooked in red wine. As the dish was traditionally made with a rooster which was at least twelve months old, the wine was needed to tenderise the meat; nowadays a chicken or boiling fowl may be substituted.

Coquilles St Jacques A dish in which scallops poached in white wine are returned to their shells and served topped with a rich sauce.

Coriander An annual herb, a member of the carrot family, which has green, lacy leaves and a pungent aroma and flavour. The leaves, also known as cilantro and Chinese parsley, are used fresh; the roots, finely chopped, have a similar but stronger flavour. Both are important ingredients in the cooking of South-East Asia, China, Central America and the Middle East. The roasted and ground seeds are used in curries; in northern Europe coriander seeds are used in pickling, chutneys and marinades.

ABOUT CORIANDER

■ The chopped leaves of this pungent herb add a delightful freshness and fragrance to chicken, lamb and vegetable dishes.

SPICY TORTILLA TRIANGLES

★★ **Preparation time:** 20 minutes
Cooking time: 10 minutes
Makes 24

2 x 23 cm (9 inch) flour tortillas
¼ cup (2 fl oz) oil, approximately

Topping
1 tablespoon oil
1 onion, finely chopped
2 small red chillies, finely chopped
2 cloves garlic, crushed
425 g (13½ oz) can pinto beans, drained, mashed roughly
1 cup bottled thick and chunky salsa
2 tablespoons chopped coriander
½ cup grated cheddar cheese

1 Cut tortillas into quarters. Cut each quarter into 3 triangles. Heat 2 tablespoons of the oil in frying pan. Add a few triangles to pan, cook 30 seconds each side or until crisp and golden. Remove from pan, drain on paper towel. Repeat with remaining triangles, adding oil if necessary.
2 To make Topping: Heat oil in a shallow pan, add onion, garlic and chilli, stir over medium heat 3 minutes or until onion is tender. Stir in beans, salsa and coriander. Remove from heat and cool.
3 Spread topping on triangles, sprinkle with cheese. Cook under preheated grill for 1 minute or until the cheese has melted.

Note: Triangles can also be cooked in oven. Place on baking tray in preheated moderate 180°C (350°F/Gas 4) oven 5 minutes or until crisp. Add topping, cook 3–5 minutes or until cheese melts.

POTATO AND CORIANDER (CILANTRO) SALAD

Cut 6 large potatoes, about 2 kg (4 lb), into thick slices and cook in a large pan of boiling water until just tender; drain and place in a bowl. In a small bowl, whisk together ½ cup (4 fl oz) white wine vinegar, ⅓ cup (2½ fl oz) olive oil, 1 clove garlic, crushed, 1 tablespoon finely shredded fresh ginger and 1 teaspoon finely sliced fresh red chilli for 2 minutes or until well combined. Pour mixture over potato, top with ½ cup chopped coriander and serve immediately. Serves 4–6.

CORIANDER (CILANTRO)

SPICY CORIANDER (CILANTRO) LAMB

★ **Preparation time:** 10 minutes
Total cooking time: 1 hour 10 minutes
Serves 6

1 kg (2 lb) chump lamb chops
1 tablespoon olive oil
2 small onions, chopped
2 cloves garlic, crushed
⅓ cup finely chopped fresh coriander
1 teaspoon turmeric
2 teaspoons ground cumin
freshly ground black pepper to taste
2 cups (16 fl oz) chicken stock
1 tablespoon ground ginger
1 tablespoon ground coriander

1 Trim meat of excess fat and sinew. Heat oil in a large heavy-based pan. Cook meat quickly, in small batches, over medium-high heat for two minutes or until well browned; drain the meat on absorbent paper.
2 Add onions and garlic to pan and cook two minutes or until browned. Stir in the remaining ingredients except chicken stock.
3 Return meat to pan with stock; bring to the boil. Reduce heat and simmer, covered, 1 hour or until meat is tender. Serve with steamed rice.

Corn (Maize, Sweet Corn) The round, yellow kernels borne on long, cone-shaped 'ears', encased in a green husk and growing on a plant native to the Americas. First domesticated more than 7000 years ago in Mexico, it was a staple throughout the Americas. Native Americans showed English settlers in North America how to plant and use it.

Corn Bread A bread, leavened with baking powder, made from cornmeal (polenta) and flour.

Corned Beef A cut of beef which has been preserved (cured) by soaking and injecting it with brine. The treatment causes the flesh to turn pink. Cooked corned beef can be served hot, with vegetables and an onion sauce; or cold, sliced as a salad meat.

Cornflour (Cornstarch) A fine, white powder obtained from corn kernels. It is used as a thickening agent for sauces, gravies and puddings, and is the main ingredient in blancmange.

CORN AND CRABMEAT SOUP

⁕ Preparation time: 20 minutes
Total cooking time: 10 minutes
Serves 4–6

2 cups frozen or canned corn kernels
105 g (3½ oz) crabmeat
1 spring onion (scallion), finely chopped
3 tablespoons cornflour (cornstarch)

3½ cups (28 fl oz) water
1½ tablespoons soy sauce
2 teaspoons chicken stock powder
2 tablespoons chopped spring onion (scallion) greens to garnish

1 Thaw or drain corn. Chop the corn in a food processor until partially ground.
2 Mix corn, crabmeat and white parts of the spring onion in a saucepan, add stock powder, water, and cornflour. Bring to the boil and simmer, stirring, until thickened.
3 Season with soy sauce. Pour into soup bowls and garnish with the spring onion greens.

1 Cook bacon in its own fat until browned. Remove from pan. Add onion and garlic to pan and cook for a few minutes. Stir in undrained tomatoes, sliced potatoes, pepper to taste and the bacon. Cook gently with the lid on 10–15 minutes.
2 Slice the corn cobs and press into the hotpot, adding a small amount of vegetable stock if necessary. Cover pot and cook until corn is tender, about 10 minutes.

CORN

HOT CHILLI CORN

⁕ Preparation time: 30 minutes
Total cooking time: 10 minutes
Serves 6

3 whole corn cobs, sliced in 3 cm (1¼ inch) rounds
30 g (1 oz) butter, melted
1 tablespoon tomato paste

2 tablespoons chopped fresh coriander
¼ teaspoon chilli powder, or to taste
sour cream, to serve

1 Half fill a large pan with water. Bring to the boil and add corn. Reduce heat, simmer until corn is soft. Drain.
2 Combine butter, tomato paste, coriander and chilli in a large bowl. Add hot corn. Mix well. Serve immediately with a dollop of sour cream.

CORN AND BACON HOTPOT

⁕ Preparation time: 20 minutes
Total cooking time: 30 minutes
Serves 4

250 g (8 oz) bacon, cut into wide strips
2 onions, sliced
1 clove garlic, crushed
410 g (13 oz) can tomatoes
4 small potatoes, sliced
pepper
4 fresh or frozen corn cobs

Cornish Hen A specially bred small chicken valued for its tender meat.

Cornish Pasty A mixture of finely chopped meat and vegetables in a turnover of shortcrust pastry. It originated in Cornwall as a meal for tin miners.

Cornmeal A yellow-white flour made from finely ground dried corn kernels. Cornmeal is an important food in northern Italy, where it is called polenta, and in the United States and Latin America. It is used to make cornbread, muffins and as a coating for fried food.

Cornstarch See Cornflour.

Corn Syrup See Corn Syrup.

Cottage Cheese A soft, fresh, usually low-fat cheese made from milk curds. It was first made using soured milk. Creamed cottage cheese is made from washed curds.

Cottage Pie See Shepherd's Pie.

CORNED BEEF

CORNED BEEF WITH ONION SAUCE AND HORSERADISH CREAM

★ *Preparation time:* 5 minutes
Total cooking time: 1 hour 45 minutes
Serves 6–8

1.5 kg (3 lb) piece corned
silverside (brisket)
1 tablespoon oil
1 tablespoon white vinegar
1 tablespoon soft brown
sugar
4 whole cloves
4 whole black peppercorns
2 bay leaves
1 clove garlic, crushed
1 large sprig parsley
4 medium carrots
4 medium potatoes,
about 750 g (1½ lb)
6 small onions

Onion Sauce
30 g (1 oz) butter
2 medium white onions,
chopped
2 tablespoons plain (all-
purpose) flour
1⅓ cups milk

Horseradish Cream
3 tablespoons horseradish
relish
1 tablespoon white vinegar
freshly ground black
pepper, to taste
½ cup cream, whipped

1 Trim meat of excess fat and sinew. Heat oil in a deep, heavy-based pan. Add meat, cook over medium-high heat, turning until browned on all sides. Remove pan from heat; add vinegar, sugar, cloves, peppercorns, bay leaves, garlic and parsley.

2 Pour over enough water to cover. Return to heat. Reduce heat, cover pan and bring slowly to simmering point. Simmer for 30 minutes. Cut carrots and potatoes into large pieces; add to pan with onions and simmer, covered, for 1 hour or until tender. Remove vegetables with a slotted spoon and keep warm. Reserve ½ cup liquid to make Onion Sauce.

3 Remove meat from pan and discard remaining liquid and spices. Carve the meat into slices and serve with vegetables, Onion Sauce and Horseradish Cream.

4 To make Onion Sauce: Heat butter in a small pan. Add the onion and cook gently for 10 minutes or until soft but not browned. Transfer onion to a bowl. Add flour to the butter left in pan; stir over low heat for 2 minutes or until the flour is lightly golden. Gradually add milk and the ½ cup of reserved liquid to the pan; stir until sauce boils and thickens. Boil for 1 minute; remove from heat and stir in the cooked onion. Season to taste.

5 To make Horseradish Cream: Combine all ingredients until smooth.

ABOUT CORNED BEEF

■ Corned beef or silverside is a cured meat with a strong, rosy pink colour. It is sold, ready to cook, by butchers or the meat department of most supermarkets. The meat is usually simmered in a clove- and onion-flavoured stock.

■ Cooked silverside can also be purchased from the deli counter as a cold cut of meat and is ideal for sandwiches and salads.

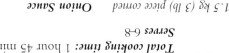

OPPOSITE, ABOVE: HOT CHILLI CORN; BELOW: CORN AND BACON HOTPOT. ABOVE: CORNED BEEF WITH ONION SAUCE AND HORSERADISH CREAM

Coulibiac A pie of Russian origin filled with salmon, rice, mushrooms, eggs and seasonings.

Coulis A liquid purée of cooked vegetables or of cooked or fresh fruit.

Courgette See Zucchini.

Court Bouillon An aromatic mixture of water or stock, and a dash of vinegar, wine or lemon juice and chopped herbs and vegetables, in which fish or shellfish is poached.

Couscous A cereal made from semolina and wheat flour pressed into tiny grains. It is cooked in water or stock until soft, butter is added and it is served hot as a side dish (in much the same way as steamed or boiled rice), or as part of a dish of stewed meat. Couscous is a staple in the cooking of North Africa.

Crab Species vary in colour when alive, but when cooked all turn red-orange; the flesh is white, moist and sweet. Found in sheltered coastal waters around the world, crabs can be purchased fresh, frozen or in cans.

CRAB

CRAB IN BLACK BEAN SAUCE

✳ **Preparation time:** 40 minutes
Total cooking time: 10 minutes
Serves 4

4 crabs
1 medium onion
1/2 red pepper (capsicum)
1/2 green pepper (capsicum)
2 spring onions (scallions)
1/2 cup (4 fl oz) oil
3 teaspoons finely chopped salted black beans

1 teaspoon finely chopped garlic
1 teaspoon finely chopped ginger
1 teaspoon sugar
1 tablespoon soy sauce
1/3 cup (2 1/2 fl oz) water
2 teaspoons cornflour (cornstarch)

1 Remove back flap from each crab's underbelly.

2 Remove shell from front of crab; remove grey fibrous tissue. Wash crabs and cut them in half.

Crack the large nippers with a meat mallet. Cut the vegetables into 8 cm (3 inch) strips.

3 Heat the oil in a wok. Cook crab pieces in oil for 3 minutes. Drain on absorbent paper. Strain oil and return 2 tablespoons to the wok. Stir-fry black beans, garlic and ginger for 30 seconds. Add the sugar and vegetables. Stir-fry for 2 minutes.

4 Add the crab. Combine soy sauce, water and cornflour and add to wok. Cook until sauce boils and thickens. Remove from heat. Serve immediately.

ABOUT CRAB

■ Crabs can be purchased uncooked and cooked. Blue swimmer crabs (sand crabs or Atlantic blue crabs), can be sold dead and uncooked; most other crabs sold raw should be sold live—the flesh deteriorates quickly after death. Cooked crabs should have intact limbs with no discoloration at the joints, and a pleasant, sweet sea smell.

Crabapple A small, sour tasting apple, grown mainly for its ornamental qualities. Crabapples are used to make jellies and preserves.

Cracked Wheat Whole wheat grains that have been soaked, cooked, dried and then crushed into small pieces.

Cranberry A small, round, red berry too tart to eat raw, but best known for cranberry sauce, the traditional accompaniment to roast turkey.

Crayfish A freshwater crustacean that looks like a miniature lobster. Most of the meat is in the tail and when cooked is white, sweet and moist.

Cream The fatty part of milk which rises to the top when milk is allowed to stand. It is made into butter and many varieties of cheese, and used on its own as an accompaniment to fruits and desserts, as a filling for cakes and pastries, or to add richness to sauces, soups and custards. Whipping, double or heavy cream is the richest form, with a fat content of 48 per cent; it is used as a rich pouring cream, or is whipped. Fresh, pure cream or light whipping cream has a minimum fat content

CHILLI CRAB AND SOFT NOODLES

Preparation time: 20 minutes
Total cooking time: 7–10 minutes
Serves 4–6

10–12 large Chinese cabbage leaves
2 tablespoons oil
200 g (6½ oz) egg noodles, cooked and cooled
2 teaspoons grated ginger
1 clove garlic, chopped
200 g (6½ oz) crabmeat pieces
1 bunch asparagus, cut into 4 cm (1½ inch) lengths, cooked
1 cup bamboo shoots
1 red pepper (capsicum), thinly sliced into strips
1 tablespoon oil
2 tablespoons soy sauce
1 teaspoon chilli sauce

1 Plunge cabbage leaves one at a time into boiling water for 30 seconds, remove and place into iced water. Remove and pat dry on a clean tea-towel.
2 Heat oil in large pan, add noodles and cook for 3–4 minutes, remove and set aside. Remove oil from pan, add ginger, garlic and crabmeat, stir 2–3 minutes. Remove, add to noodles.
3 Add asparagus, bamboo shoots and red pepper to mixture. Combine oil, soy sauce and chilli, add to noodle mixture, toss well to combine.
4 Place cabbage leaves on a large serving dish, with crab and noodle mixture in serving bowl. Guests can fill and roll their own cabbage leaves. Serve with Asian Sweet Chilli Sauce if desired.

CRAB CAKES WITH HOT SALSA

Preparation time: 30 minutes + 30 minutes refrigeration + 1 hour standing
Total cooking time: 5–6 minutes each batch
Serves 6

105 g (3½ oz) vermicelli, broken into 8 cm (3 inch) lengths
600 g (1¼ lb) crab meat
2 tablespoons finely chopped fresh parsley
1 small red pepper (capsicum), chopped
¼ cup finely grated parmesan cheese
¼ cup plain (all-purpose) flour
2 spring onions (scallions), finely chopped
2 tablespoons sweet chilli sauce

Hot Salsa
2 large ripe tomatoes
1 medium onion, finely chopped
2 cloves garlic, crushed
1 teaspoon dried oregano leaves
2 tablespoons sweet chilli sauce

freshly ground black pepper
2 eggs, lightly beaten
2–3 tablespoons oil, for frying

1 Cook vermicelli in boiling water until just cooked; drain. In a large bowl, combine noodles, crab meat, parsley, red pepper, parmesan cheese, flour, onions and pepper. Add egg and mix well.
2 Shape mixture into 12 flat patties. refrigerate 30 minutes. Heat oil in large heavy-based pan; cook crab cakes a few at a time over medium-high heat until golden brown. Serve with Hot Salsa.
3 **To make Hot Salsa:** Combine all ingredients in small bowl. Stand at room temperature 1 hour.

...of 35 per cent and will double its volume when whipped. Reduced or light cream (known in Britain as single cream) has a fat content of between 18 and 25 per cent and cannot be whipped; it is used in coffee and with desserts.

Cream Cheese A soft, white, fresh cheese made from cream or a mixture of milk and cream. It is smoother in texture and has a higher fat content than cottage cheese.

Cream of Tartar A white powder obtained by the fermentation of grape juice and used as one of the raising agents in baking powder. Cream of tartar is often added when whipping egg whites.

Crème Brûlée A rich baked custard topped with a shell of hard, caramelised sugar.

Crème Caramel A vanilla-flavoured baked custard coated with thick caramel sauce.

Crème Chantilly Sweetened whipped fresh cream which has been flavoured with vanilla.

Crème Fraîche A mature cream with a nutty, slightly sour flavour. It is available in cartons or can be made by mixing pure fresh cream with

CUCUMBER AND FENNEL WITH DILL

★ **Preparation time:** 20 minutes
Total cooking time: 10 minutes
Serves 4–6

1 tablespoon olive oil
1 fennel bulb, washed, trimmed and sliced
60 g (2 oz) roasted hazelnuts, roughly chopped
1 large cucumber, peeled, halved, seeds removed and sliced
⅓ cup chopped dill
freshly ground pepper

1 Heat oil in a large shallow pan. Add the sliced fennel, then cover and cook over a gentle heat until fennel is just tender.
2 Add the cucumber and cook over gentle heat for 3–4 minutes. Scatter dill over top, and some freshly ground pepper. Shake the pan to combine ingredients.
3 Place on a serving plate and garnish with roasted hazelnuts. Serve.

CUCUMBER RELISH

★ **Preparation time:** 15 minutes + overnight standing
Total cooking time: 1 hour
Makes 1 litre (4 cups)

1 kg (2 lb) yellow apple cucumbers
1 cup (8 fl oz) white vinegar
1½ cups sugar

315 g (10 oz) can corn kernels, drained
2 small green cucumbers
2 teaspoons brown mustard seeds
2 tablespoons salt
1 red pepper (capsicum)
1 green pepper (capsicum)
1 medium onion
2 teaspoons celery seeds

1 Slice cucumbers thinly. Place in a large bowl, sprinkle with salt, cover with dry cloth and stand overnight. Dice peppers and chop the onion finely. Drain cucumbers, rinse in cold water then drain again.
2 Place marinated cucumbers, peppers, onion, celery seeds, corn kernels, mustard seeds, vinegar and sugar in a large saucepan or boiler. Bring to boil, reduce heat and simmer for 1 hour or until mixture is thick, stirring occasionally.
3 Remove from heat. Spoon into warm, sterilised jars and seal. When cool, label and date.

Note: Store relish in a dry place for up to 1 month. Refrigerate after opening.

ABOVE: BREAD AND BUTTER CUCUMBERS
Opposite page: Quick Chicken Curry

BREAD AND BUTTER CUCUMBERS

★ **Preparation time:** 30 minutes + overnight standing
Total cooking time: 10 minutes
Makes 2 litres (8 cups)

3 long, thin-skinned cucumbers
2 teaspoons salt
2 teaspoons mustard seeds
2 cups (16 fl oz) white vinegar
3 tablespoons sugar
1 red pepper (capsicum), thinly sliced
½ cup (4 fl oz) hot water

1 Cut washed, unpeeled cucumbers into very thin slices. Layer cucumbers in large bowl and sprinkle lightly with salt between layers. Cover and stand overnight.
2 Rinse cucumbers under cold water; drain well. Place vinegar, sugar, hot water, salt and mustard seeds in large saucepan or boiler. Bring to the boil, stirring until sugar is dissolved. Simmer, uncovered, for 5 minutes.
3 Add cucumber slices to pan and bring back to the boil. Remove from heat.
4 Using tongs, pack cucumber slices into warm, sterilised jars. Add a few strips of pepper to each jar. Pour hot vinegar mixture into jars to cover cucumbers. Seal; cool. Label and date.

Note: Serve Bread and Butter Cucumbers with salads, or add to sandwich fillings or dips. They are also good served on crackers with cheese and can be used with chicken or steak as a relish.

---

sour cream, yoghurt or cultured buttermilk. Crème fraîche is used in savoury sauces for game, poultry, fish and vegetables; in salad dressings; as a garnish for soups; and in confectionery (candy).

Crème Pâtissière A stirred custard lightened with whipped egg whites. Flavoured with coffee or chocolate, it is

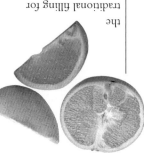

the traditional filling for éclairs; flavoured with vanilla or orange, it is used to fill cream puffs.

Crêpe A light, thin pancake made with a batter of milk, eggs and flour, fried on each side until golden. They can be eaten with a topping of lemon juice and sugar, or rolled around sweet and savoury fillings or topped with sauces.

Cress Any of several plants of the mustard family. Eaten while still seedlings, their tiny leaves and slender stems give a peppery flavour to salad and sandwich fillings, and can be used as a garnish for meat.

Croissant A soft, flaky, buttery, crescent-shaped roll of yeast milk dough, baked until crisp and golden and served warm.

CURRIES

BEEF CURRY WITH POTATOES

✳ *Preparation time:* 15 minutes
Total cooking time: 1 hour 30 minutes
Serves 4

1 kg (2 lb) chuck steak
2 tablespoons oil
¾ cup (6 fl oz) coconut
 cream
½ cup (4 fl oz) water
1 tablespoon tamarind sauce
500 g (1 lb) baby
 potatoes, halved

Spice Paste
2 medium onions,
 chopped

2 cloves garlic, chopped
2 teaspoons grated lemon
 rind
2 small red chillies,
 chopped
2 teaspoons ground
 coriander
2 teaspoons ground cumin
1 teaspoon turmeric
½ teaspoon ground
 cardamom
1 teaspoon garam masala

1 Trim meat of excess fat and sinew. Cut meat evenly into 3 cm (1¼ inch) cubes. Heat oil in a heavy-based pan. Cook the meat quickly in small batches over medium-high heat until well browned; drain on absorbent paper.
2 **To make Spice Paste:** Combine all ingredients in food processor or blender, process one minute or until very finely chopped.
3 Add Paste to pan, stir over medium heat 2 minutes. Return meat to pan with coconut cream, water and tamarind sauce; bring to boil. Reduce heat, simmer, covered, for 30 minutes, stirring occasionally.
4 Add potato, cook for another 30 minutes or until the meat is tender and liquid has almost evaporated.

QUICK CHICKEN CURRY

✳ *Preparation time:* 10 minutes
Total cooking time: 50 minutes
Serves 4

750 g (1½ lb) boned
 chicken thighs
2 cloves
2 cardamoms
3 tablespoons ghee or oil
1 large onion, halved and
 thinly sliced
1 teaspoon mashed garlic
1½ teaspoons grated
 ginger
1 cinnamon stick
2 bay leaves

2 dried chillies
1 tablespoon ground
 coriander
2 teaspoons garam masala
½ teaspoon turmeric
pepper
lemon juice
lemon slices, for garnish

1 Brown chicken pieces in ghee or oil, set aside.
2 Fry the onion until golden brown, add garlic, ginger, cinnamon, bay leaves, cloves, cardamoms and chillies and fry for 2 minutes, stirring. Add ground spices and pepper.
3 Return chicken to pan and add water to barely cover. Cover pan and simmer for about 40 minutes until the chicken is very tender.
4 Add lemon juice to taste. Garnish with lemon slices and serve with rice and chutney.

Note: This curry is delicious when first made, but improves in flavour if made a day ahead. Store, covered, in the refrigerator.

ACCOMPANIMENTS

■ Curries, particularly Indian curries, are complemented with chutneys, relishes or pickles: sweet to go with hot, fiery to pep up a mild dish, and crunchy with smooth dishes. Try the ideas below, or any of the great Indian relishes, such as mango chutney or lime pickle, available bottled.

■ Peel a large cucumber, halve vertically and scoop out seeds. Coarsely grate cucumber into a bowl, sprinkle on about 1 teaspoon salt, stand 5 minutes. Drain off accumulated liquid. Stir in ½ cup plain yoghurt and 1 tablespoon finely chopped mint. Add a sprinkling of cumin seeds.

■ Combine 1 cup plain yoghurt with ½ cup cream, stir in ½ teaspoon finely chopped red chilli and a pinch of salt. Peel and chop two bananas into small pieces, stir into yoghurt mixture.

■ Finely chop 1 red onion, chop 2 ripe tomatoes, combine with onion. Add salt, chilli powder and fresh chopped coriander.

■ Deep fry papadams, or cook in a microwave by first brushing each pappadam lightly with oil on one side, then cooking one at a time on High (100%) power for about 1 minute.

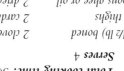

as part of a traditional French breakfast. Croissants can be eaten either on their own or split open and spread with butter and jam or preserves. They can also be filled with ham, cheese, mushrooms or chicken.

Croque Monsieur A hot sandwich of gruyère or emmenthal cheese and ham between slices of toasted bread.

Croquembouche An elaborate pastry made up of a number of individual choux puff pastries, each filled with cream, piled into a cone shape, glazed with toffee and topped with sugar.

Croquette A small patty of minced (ground) meat, poultry, fish or shellfish, bound with a thick white sauce, coated with breadcrumbs and deep-fried until crisp.

Crostini Slices of bread that have been toasted, or quickly fried, or dipped in broth, and then spread with a savoury topping such as pâté.

Croustade A case made out of fried, hollowed bread, puff pastry or duchess potato which is

used to hold preparations of cooked meat or vegetables.

Croûte A small, thick slice of bread, fried in butter or oil or dried in the oven, which is served with soup, casseroles or mornays.

Croûte, en A French term for food cooked, wrapped or encased in pastry or dough.

Croûtons Small cubes of bread, fried or toasted and served as a crisp accompaniment to soup or salads.

Crown Roast Two racks of lamb curved around and secured in the shape of a crown. The centre is usually filled with stuffing.

Crudités Raw vegetables cut into strips or grated, served as finger food accompanied by dips and cold sauces.

Cucumber The crisp, juicy, pale-fleshed fruit of a vine of the melon family. Cucumbers can be used raw, as a salad vegetable, as well as cooked or pickled.

CREAMY PRAWN (SHRIMP) CURRY

Preparation time: 20 minutes
Total cooking time: 18–20 minutes
Serves 4

1 kg (2 lb) medium green prawns (shrimps)
1 teaspoon chopped garlic
1 medium onion, finely chopped
1 teaspoon ground coriander
1 teaspoon turmeric
1 teaspoon vegetable shrimp paste
400 ml (12 fl oz) coconut cream
1 teaspoon tamarind concentrate
2 tablespoons fish sauce (nuoc mam)
1 bunch fresh coriander

3 tablespoons vegetable or peanut oil
1 teaspoon chopped ginger
1 large red chilli, chopped
1 tablespoon finely chopped lemon grass root

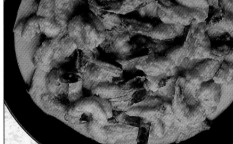
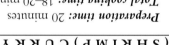

1 Peel prawns, leaving tail and last section of shell in place. Remove heads. Cut deeply along the back of each prawn, remove the dark vein and press the prawns flat as if preparing prawn cutlets.
2 Cook onion in oil until well coloured. In a spice grinder, food processor or mortar, grind onion, ginger, chilli, lemon grass and garlic to a smooth paste. Add ground coriander, turmeric and shrimp paste, grind again to a paste, adding a little coconut cream if necessary.
3 Cook ground seasonings in pan used to fry onions, about 5 minutes. Add coconut cream and tamarind. Bring almost to boil, reduce heat, simmer, stirring constantly for 5 minutes.
4 Add ¾ cup (6 fl oz) water and the prawns with fish sauce and cook for 3 minutes.

VEGETABLE CURRY

Preparation time: 10 minutes
Total cooking time: 35 minutes
Serves 6

1 tablespoon oil
2 onions, chopped
1 tablespoon grated fresh ginger
2 cloves garlic, crushed
2 teaspoons curry powder
2 teaspoons green curry paste
1 teaspoon ground cumin
2 x 440 g (14 oz) cans tomatoes, crushed
¼ cup tomato paste
½ cup sweet fruit chutney
¼ cup crunchy peanut butter

400 ml (12 fl oz) can coconut cream
375 g (12 oz) pumpkin, chopped
1 medium carrot, chopped
125 g (4 oz) fresh beans, sliced
125 g (4 oz) yellow or green squash, chopped
125 g (4 oz) cauliflower florets
2 medium potatoes, peeled and chopped
315 g (10 oz) can butter (lima) beans

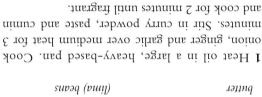
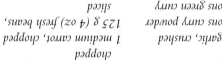
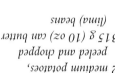
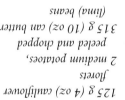
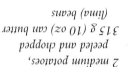
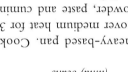
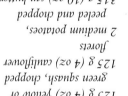
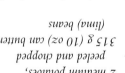
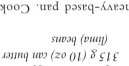
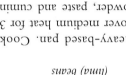
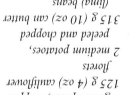
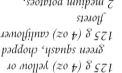
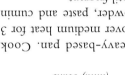
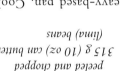
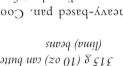
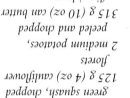
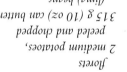

1 Heat oil in a large, heavy-based pan. Cook onion, ginger and garlic over medium heat for 3 minutes. Stir in curry powder, paste and cumin and cook for 2 minutes until fragrant.
2 Add all remaining ingredients and stir to combine; bring to boil. Reduce heat to simmer and cook, covered, for 30 minutes. Serve with steamed rice.

Note: Shrimp paste gives a much better flavour if 'roasted' before use. Wrap in a piece of aluminium foil and cook for 2 minutes on each side in a dry wok. Always store shrimp paste in a tightly sealed jar in a dark corner of your spice cupboard.

5 Pick off the coriander leaves, add to the curry and serve at once with rice.

124

C U S T A R D S

BAKED VANILLA CUSTARD

Preparation time: 10 minutes
Total cooking time: 40 minutes
Serves 4

2 cups (16 fl oz) milk	1/4 teaspoon vanilla essence
3 eggs	ground nutmeg for sprinkling
1/4 cup caster (superfine) sugar	

1 Preheat oven to moderate 180°C (350°F/Gas 4). Brush ovenproof dish with oil. Whisk milk, eggs, sugar and vanilla in mixing bowl for 2 minutes.

2 Pour mixture into prepared dish and sprinkle top with nutmeg.

3 Put the custard dish into a larger baking dish. Pour enough cold water into the baking dish to come halfway up the sides. Bake for 20 minutes, then turn oven down to moderately slow 160°C (325°F/Gas 3). Bake for 20 minutes more or until custard is set and a knife comes out clean when pushed into the centre. Remove dish from water bath immediately. Serve warm or cold, with fruit if desired.

RICH CUSTARD

★ ★

Preparation time: 10 minutes
Total cooking time: 12 minutes
Makes 2 1/2 cups

2 cups (16 fl oz) milk	1/4 cup sugar
4 egg yolks	1 teaspoon vanilla essence

1 Scald milk in the top of a double boiler. Beat the egg yolks and sugar together and slowly beat into hot milk.

2 Place custard over a pan of simmering water, and beat with a rotary beater until it thickens sufficiently to coat the beater. Remove from heat and beat again from time to time until custard cools. Stir in vanilla and chill.

Note: If you do not have a double boiler, make custard by scalding the milk in a saucepan, then transferring it to a heatproof bowl that will fit comfortably on top of another saucepan. Take care not to let the bowl of milk touch the simmering water.

OPPOSITE PAGE, ABOVE: CREAMY PRAWN CURRY; BELOW: VEGETABLE CURRY
THIS PAGE: BAKED VANILLA CUSTARD

ABOUT CUSTARD

■ There are two types of custard: stirred and baked. Each uses the same cooking principles and similar ingredients.

■ Both types of custard are cooked over, or with, a controlled application of gentle heat (over simmering water or in a water bath). This is important if the characteristic velvety smoothness is to be achieved. The exception is when cornflour is added. This custard can be cooked over direct heat with no danger of curdling it.

■ Also important to success is the correct beating of the eggs, sugar and milk for the custard; depending on the recipe, they should be whisked until the mixture has an even colour and consistency.

■ A stirred custard has reached the correct consistency when it coats the back of a metal spoon. If the custard curdles, remove from heat immediately and pour it into a cold dish sitting in a bowl of ice cubes; beat vigorously—you may have some success in restoring smoothness.

■ If a stirred custard is removed from heat immediately it will thin on standing. Applying intense heat to a baked custard will cause it to separate and weep on standing; this cannot be rectified.

125

Cumberland Sauce A sauce, made with redcurrant jelly and port, which is served cold with ham, lamb, beef or game.

Cumin A spice made from the seeds of a plant, similar in appearance to parsley; the long, aromatic, yellow-brown seeds have a pungent flavour (similar to caraway) and are used whole or ground in a range of savoury Middle Eastern or Indian dishes.

Cumquat A berry-sized, orange-coloured citrus fruit with bitter flesh and sweet-tasting, edible, thin skin. Native to China, it is used to make marmalade, or preserved in sugar syrup or brandy.

Currant A small, round, smooth-skinned, tart berry; there are red, white (rare) and black varieties. Redcurrants can be eaten fresh, with sugar and cream or in salads; redcurrants and blackcurrants are used in jams, jellies and sauces; blackcurrants are used in cordials and the liqueur cassis. They are not related to dried currants.

Currant, Dried The dried fruit of a small, purple, seedless grape; used in cake, biscuit (cookie) and pastry mixtures for stuffings in

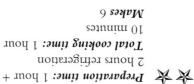
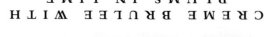

CREME BRULEE WITH PLUMS IN LIME

★★

Preparation time: 1 hour + 2 hours refrigeration
Total cooking time: 1 hour
Makes 6

3 cups (24 fl oz) cream
2 vanilla beans
8 egg yolks
1/2 cup caster (superfine) sugar
1 teaspoon vanilla essence
3 teaspoons sugar

Plums in Lime
825 g (27 oz) can pitted plums
1/3 cup (2 1/2 fl oz) lime juice
1/3 cup sugar
zest of 2 limes, finely grated

1 Place cream and vanilla beans in a large, heavy-based pan. Bring to boil; remove from heat. Set aside to infuse. Remove vanilla beans, rinse and retain to use again. Beat or whisk egg yolks and sugar in a large heatproof bowl until mixture is thick and pale. Place bowl over a pan of simmering water; beat constantly until mixture is just warmed through. Add cream gradually to egg mixture, beating for about 10 minutes. Continue to stir until mixture thickens slightly and coats the back of a wooden spoon. Remove from heat, stir in essence. Spoon mixture into six 2/3-cup capacity heatproof dishes. Refrigerate until set, about 2 hours.

2 To make Plums in Lime: Combine all ingredients in medium, heavy-based pan. Stir over low heat until sugar has completely dissolved. Bring to boil, reduce heat and simmer, stirring occasionally, keeping plums whole, for 40 minutes or until liquid has reduced and thickened. Remove from heat, set aside to cool.

3 Thirty minutes before serving, sprinkle 1/2 teaspoon sugar over each custard. Place in large ice-packed baking dish. Place under pre-heated hot grill until sugar caramelises—about 10 minutes. Serve immediately, with Plums in Lime.

CREME PATISSIERE

Beat 3 egg yolks with 1/4 cup caster (superfine) sugar, 1 tablespoon plain (all-purpose) flour, 1 tablespoon cornflour (cornstarch) in mixing bowl until pale. Heat 1/2 cup (4 fl oz) milk in pan until almost boiling; remove from heat. Add milk gradually to egg mixture, beating constantly. Strain into pan. Stir constantly over medium heat until mixture boils and thickens. Remove from heat; add 1 teaspoon vanilla essence. Place plastic wrap over surface to prevent skin forming; cool. Makes 1 1/2 cups. Use to fill choux puffs or cakes. For a richer mixture, fold in whipped cream.

Curry A savoury dish of meat, poultry, fish or vegetables, flavoured with tangy spices and served with rice, pappadams or Indian bread and a variety of accompaniments. Curries, most strongly identified with India, are also part of the cooking of Thailand, Malaysia, Indonesia and the West Indies.

Curry Leaves The small, shiny, aromatic leaves from a tree native to South-East Asia, used whole in much the same way as bay leaves. Available fresh, dried or fried in oil, they add a curry-like flavour.

Curry Paste and Curry Powder Blends of ground spices used to flavour savoury dishes. A basic Indian curry powder includes ground dried red chillies, coriander, mustard, black peppercorns, fenugreek, cumin and turmeric; other spices that can be included are cardamom, cloves, cinnamon, allspice, ginger and

game or fish; and in savoury sauces and rice dishes.

OPPOSITE PAGE: CREME BRULEE WITH PLUMS IN LIME; ABOVE: CREME CARAMEL

CREME CARAMEL

✹✹ *Preparation time:* 25 minutes +
6 hours refrigeration
Total cooking time: 40–45 minutes
Serves 8

Caramel
1 litre (4 cups) milk,
    warmed
1 cup sugar
1/4 cup (2 fl oz) water
6 eggs

Custard
1 1/2 teaspoons vanilla
    essence
1/2 cup sugar

1 To make Caramel: Preheat oven to moderate 180°C (350°F/Gas 4). Brush eight 1/2 cup (4 fl oz) capacity ovenproof ramekins with melted butter. Place sugar and water in medium pan. Stir over low heat until sugar dissolves. Bring to boil, reduce heat and simmer 5–10 minutes or until mixture turns caramel. Remove from heat. Pour a little hot mixture over base of each prepared dish and swirl to cover base.

2 To make Custard: Place the sugar and milk in a pan and stir over low heat until sugar has dissolved. Whisk together eggs and vanilla for 2 minutes, stir in warm milk. Strain into jug.

3 Divide egg and milk mixture between the moulds and place in a baking dish. Pour in hot water to come halfway up the side. Bake for 30 minutes until custard is set and a knife comes out clean when inserted. Cool and refrigerate for at least 6 hours before serving.

4 To unmould, run a knife around the edge of each custard and gently upturn onto the serving plate. Shake gently if necessary. Serve with whipped cream and strawberries, if desired.

CUSTARD TARTS

✹✹ *Preparation time:* 30 minutes +
20 minutes refrigeration
Total cooking time: 45 minutes
Makes twelve 10 cm (1 inch) tarts

2 cups plain (all-purpose)
    flour
1/3 cup rice flour
1/4 cup icing (confectioners)
    sugar
120 g (3 3/4 oz) butter
1 egg yolk
1/4 cup (2 fl oz) iced water
1 egg white, lightly beaten

Filling
3 eggs
1 1/2 cups (12 fl oz) milk
1/4 cup caster (superfine)
    sugar
1 teaspoon vanilla essence
1/2 teaspoon nutmeg

1 Place flours, icing sugar and butter in a food processor. Press pulse button for 20 seconds or until mixture is fine and crumbly. Add yolk and almost all the water and process for 30 seconds or until mixture comes together, adding more water if necessary. Turn onto a lightly floured surface and press together until smooth. Divide dough into 12 equal portions. Roll out to line twelve 10 cm (4 inch) fluted tart tins. Refrigerate for 20 minutes.

2 Preheat oven to moderate 180°C (350°F/Gas 4). Cut sheets of greaseproof paper to cover each pastry-lined tin. Spread a layer of dried beans or rice evenly over the paper. Place tart tins on a large flat baking tray and bake for 10 minutes. Remove from oven; discard baking paper and beans or rice. Return to oven and bake for 10 minutes more or until pastry is lightly golden; cool. Brush the base and sides of each pastry case with beaten egg white.

3 To make Filling: Reduce oven to low 150°C (300°F/Gas 2). Place eggs and milk in a medium mixing bowl and whisk to combine. Add sugar gradually, whisking to dissolve completely. Stir in essence. Strain mixture into a jug, then pour into pastry cases. Sprinkle with nutmeg and bake for 25 minutes or until filling is just set. Serve tarts at room temperature.

---

garlic. The addition of oil, vinegar or water gives a curry paste, or wet masala. The green and red curry pastes of Thai cooking are both based on a blend of fresh coriander leaves, chillies, garlic and other spices and fresh herbs.

Custard A mixture of egg and milk, sweetened, cooked and served hot or cold as a dessert. Baked custard is cooked in the oven; stirred custard, cooked over simmering water, is often used as a sweet sauce and is also the basis of many other desserts.

Custard Apple Also known as cherimoya, the large, round, green-skinned fruit of a tree native to Peru and now cultivated in many tropical regions. Its sweet-scented, creamy-white flesh tastes like a combination of banana, pineapple and strawberry and is scooped out and eaten with a spoon.

Cuttlefish A saltwater mollusc closely related to squid, but with a broader, thicker oval body. It has been eaten for centuries around the shores of the Mediterranean, either stuffed or cut into rings and fried in batter.

STEAMED DATE AND PECAN PUDDING

⋆ Preparation time: 30 minutes
Total cooking time: 2 hours
Serves 6-8

125 g (4 oz) butter
1 cup caster (superfine) sugar
4 eggs
2 cups dates, chopped
1 teaspoon ground cardamom
1/4 cup (2 fl oz) milk
1 cup plain (all-purpose) flour
1 cup self-raising flour
3/4 cup chopped pecans

Cardamom Sauce
30 g (1 oz) unsalted (sweet) butter
2 tablespoons soft brown sugar
1 teaspoon ground cardamom
3/4 cup (6 fl oz) orange juice

1 Grease a 6-cup capacity pudding steamer with melted butter. Line base with greaseproof paper, grease paper. Beat butter and sugar in a small mixer bowl until light and creamy. Add eggs gradually, beating thoroughly after each addition.

2 Transfer mixture to a large bowl, fold in dates, pecans and milk. Stir in cardamom and sifted flours. Spoon into prepared steamer, cover with greased round of foil, secure with lid and string.

3 Carefully place steamer on a trivet in a large pan with simmering water to come halfway up side of steamer. Cover and cook for 2 hours. Do not allow pan to boil dry; replenish simmering water during cooking if necessary.

4 To make Cardamom Sauce: Combine butter, soft brown sugar and cardamom in a small pan; cook over low heat, stirring until the butter melts and mixture is smooth. Stir in orange juice and blend well. Serve warm.

DATE AND WALNUT LOAF

Preheat oven to moderate 180°C (350°F/Gas 4). Cream 125 g (4 oz) butter and 1 cup soft brown sugar in a medium bowl. Add 2 eggs, one at a time, beating well after each addition. Blend in 1 cup (8 fl oz) milk, 1 1/2 cups chopped dates and 1 cup chopped walnuts. Lightly fold in 3 cups sifted self-raising flour. Pour mixture into two greased 14 x 21 cm (5 1/2 x 8 1/2 inch) loaf tins. Bake for 35–40 minutes. Remove cakes from tins and leave on a cake rack to cool. Serve sliced, warm or cold, with butter. Store in an airtight container. Makes 2 loaves.

ABOVE: STEAMED DATE AND PECAN PUDDING.
OPPOSITE PAGE: PINEAPPLE UPSIDE-DOWN PUDDING AND BUTTERSCOTCH PUDDINGS.

DATES

WARM DATE AND MASCARPONE TART

⋆ Preparation time: 25 minutes
Total cooking time: 25 minutes
Serves 6-8

4 sheets filo pastry
125 g (4 oz) mascarpone cheese
40 g (1 1/4 oz) unsalted (sweet) butter, melted
1/4 cup caster (superfine) sugar
1/4 cup ground almonds
225 g (7 1/4 oz) fresh dates, pitted and sliced
1/2 cup (4 fl oz) cream
2 eggs
2 tablespoons flaked almonds
2 teaspoons custard powder

1 Preheat oven to moderate 180°C (350°F/Gas 4). Brush a shallow 10 x 35 cm (4 x 14 inch) fluted rectangular flan tin with oil or melted butter. Brush a sheet of filo pastry sparingly with melted butter, sprinkle with ground almonds. Fold sheet in half lengthways. Carefully line flan tin lengthways with pastry. Repeat process with remaining pastry, butter and nuts.

2 Spread dates evenly over the pastry base. Combine eggs, custard powder, cheese, sugar and cream in a medium bowl; whisk until smooth. Pour mixture over dates. Sprinkle with flaked almonds. Bake for 25 minutes or until custard is set and golden. Leave for 10 minutes before slicing. Serve warm with whipped cream.

D

Daikon A variety of radish grown in Japan with a long, almost cylindrical, fleshy white root and a mild, peppery taste. It is eaten raw (either grated or sliced in salads), cooked (steamed or stir-fried) as a vegetable and, in its pickled form (takuan) is served with almost every meal. Spicy-tasting daikon sprouts (kaiware) are used in salads and as a garnish. Daikon is also known as Japanese radish and mooli.

Daiquiri A cocktail made from white rum, lemon or lime juice and sugar, served in a chilled glass. The drink is named after a small village near Santiago, on the Cuban coast. Fruits such as peaches, strawberries or kiwi fruit are sometimes added.

Damper Unleavened bread made from a simple dough of flour and water. It was a staple food for early European settlers in outback Australia. Traditionally the dough was cooked directly in the hot ashes of an open fire (with this method the encrusting ashes must be knocked off before the bread can be eaten), or wound around a green stick which was placed over the fire (the result was known as a johnny cake). In later years camp ovens were used and, after they became available, baking powder and powdered milk were added to the mixture. Today the term damper refers to leavened bread, round in shape, with a crunchy crust and a taste and texture similar to white bread. The name comes from a British dialect word meaning 'something that takes the edge off the appetite'.

Damson A small, dark purple variety of European plum with a thick skin. It is also known as a prune plum. The fruit is too tart to eat raw but is delicious cooked in compotes, jams, jellies and as a pie filling. The name is a contraction of 'Damascene,' from Damascus.

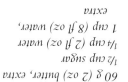

DESSERTS BAKED PUDDINGS

PINEAPPLE UPSIDE-DOWN PUDDING

✿✿ *Preparation time:* 15 minutes
Total cooking time: 45 minutes
Makes one 20 cm (8 inch) round cake

7 g (1/4 oz) butter, melted
1 tablespoon desiccated coconut
1/2 cup caster (superfine) sugar
2 eggs, lightly beaten
1 teaspoon vanilla essence
1 cup self-raising flour
1/3 cup (2 1/2 fl oz) coconut milk

90 g (3 oz) butter
1/4 cup soft brown sugar
440 g (14 oz) can sliced pineapple, drained

1 Preheat oven to moderate 180°C (350°F/Gas 4). Brush a 20 cm (8 inch) ring tin with melted butter or oil and sprinkle with coconut and sugar. Cut pineapple slices in half, arrange over coconut.

2 Beat butter and sugar in small bowl until light and creamy. Add eggs gradually, beating well after each addition. Add vanilla essence.

3 Transfer to large bowl. Using a metal spoon, fold in sifted flour alternately with coconut milk. Stir until ingredients are just combined and mixture is almost smooth. Carefully spoon into prepared tin; smooth surface. Bake 45 minutes or until skewer comes out clean when inserted in centre. Leave cake in tin 5 minutes before turning onto serving plate. Serve with custard or cream.

DESSERTS BAKED PUDDINGS

BUTTERSCOTCH SELF-SAUCING PUDDINGS

✿ *Preparation time:* 15 minutes
Total cooking time: 45 minutes
Serves 6

90 g (3 oz) butter, chopped
1 cup soft brown sugar
1 1/2 cups self-raising flour
1 teaspoon mixed spice
3/4 cup (6 fl oz) milk

60 g (2 oz) butter, extra
1/2 cup sugar
1/4 cup (2 fl oz) water
1 cup (8 fl oz) water, extra

1 Preheat oven to moderate 180°C (350°F/Gas 4). Brush six 1-cup capacity ovenproof dishes with oil or melted butter. Using electric beaters, beat butter and sugar in small mixing bowl until light and creamy. Transfer to a large mixing bowl. Using metal spoon, fold sifted flour and mixed spice into butter mixture alternately with milk. Spoon evenly into dishes. Place on a baking tray.

2 Place extra butter, sugar and 1/4 cup (2 fl oz) water in small pan. Stir over low heat until butter has melted and sugar has dissolved. Bring to boil, reduce heat and simmer gently, uncovered, until golden brown. Remove from heat. Very carefully stir in extra water. Stir over low heat until smooth; cool slightly.

3 Pour an equal amount of mixture over each pudding. Bake for 35 minutes, or until skewer comes out clean when inserted in centre. Loosen edges of each pudding by running a knife around the edge. Invert onto serving plates.

INDIVIDUAL BUTTER PUDDINGS

★ **Preparation time:** 20 minutes
Total cooking time: 20 minutes
Serves 8

125 g (4 oz) butter
3/4 cup caster (superfine) sugar
2 eggs, lightly beaten
1 teaspoon vanilla essence
1 1/2 cups self-raising flour
1/2 cup (4 fl oz) milk

Golden Syrup Cream
60 g (2 oz) butter, extra
1/2 cup golden syrup (light corn syrup)
1 1/4 cups (10 fl oz) cream

1 Preheat oven to moderate 180°C (350°F/Gas 4). Brush eight 1-cup capacity ovenproof ramekins or moulds with melted butter. Using electric beaters, beat butter and sugar in a small mixing bowl until light and creamy. Add eggs gradually, beating thoroughly after each addition. Add essence; beat until combined. Transfer to a large mixing bowl. Using a metal spoon, fold in sifted flour alternately with milk. Stir until just combined and mixture is almost smooth.

2 Spoon into prepared tins; place on large oven tray, bake for 20 minutes or until a skewer comes out clean when inserted in centre. Leave in tins for 5 minutes then turn onto a wire rack to cool.

3 **To make Golden Syrup Cream:** Melt the butter in a small heavy-based pan. Add golden syrup and stir over medium heat until well combined. Add cream and bring to the boil, stirring constantly. Transfer to a jug. To serve, place a pudding on each plate and drizzle with Golden Syrup Cream. Serve with cream or vanilla ice-cream.

Note: Puddings can be made up to 2 hours in advance. Store at room temperature, covered with a clean tea-towel. Make Golden Syrup Cream just before serving.

CREME CHANTILLY

Serve baked puddings, macerated fruit and sweet tarts with Crème Chantilly. Pour 2 cups (16 fl oz) cream into a large bowl, add 1 tablespoon vanilla sugar and beat until soft peaks form—take care not to over-beat.

Vanilla sugar is made by placing 2 or 3 vanilla pods in a jar of caster (superfine) sugar. Refill the jar as you use the sugar. The vanilla will continue to flavour the sugar for a year.

ABOVE: INDIVIDUAL BUTTER PUDDING.
OPPOSITE PAGE: FRUIT BREAD AND APPLE PUDDING.

Dandelion A flowering plant well known as a weed. Its young leaves can be added to mixed green salad; their peppery bite also combines well with beetroot and with bacon. The leaves should be picked before the plant flowers (otherwise they can be tough and bitter); cut them off at the root crown. Dandelions can also be blanched by covering the growing plant with an inverted flowerpot; the result is a crisp pale leaf with a milder flavour.

Danish Blue A soft, creamy white, cow's milk cheese with fine blue veining and a sharp, sometimes salty, taste. It has a buttery texture and can be either spread or sliced. Modelled on the blue-veined Roquefort cheese of France, it was developed in Denmark in the early 1900s to compete in the United States with Roquefort sales. The cheese is also known as Danablu.

Danish Open Sandwich A thin slice of bread, buttered right to each edge to seal the

DESSERTS
BREAD PUDDINGS

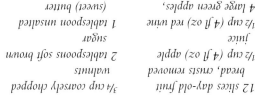

FRUIT BREAD AND APPLE PUDDING

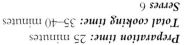

Preparation time: 25 minutes
Total cooking time: 35–40 minutes
Serves 6

12 slices day-old fruit bread, crusts removed
1/2 cup (4 fl oz) apple juice
1/2 cup (4 fl oz) red wine
4 large green apples, peeled, cored and sliced into thin wedges
1 teaspoon cinnamon
3/4 cup coarsely chopped walnuts
2 tablespoons soft brown sugar
1 tablespoon unsalted (sweet) butter
1 cup (4 fl oz) sour cream
3 tablespoons soft brown sugar, extra

1 Put bread into bowl, pour over half combined juice and wine, stand for 5 minutes. Remove bread, place 4 slices in base of greased ovenproof dish. Preheat oven to 180°C (350°F/Gas 4).

2 Combine apples, cinnamon, walnuts and sugar. Place half mixture over bread. Top with 4 bread slices, and rest of apple mixture. Cover with remaining bread, pour over rest of juice and wine. Dot with butter, bake for 35–40 minutes.

3 Combine sour cream and extra brown sugar. Leave pudding for 10 minutes then serve warm, topped with a spoonful of sour cream mixture.

BREAD AND BUTTER PUDDING

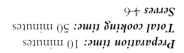

Preparation time: 10 minutes
Total cooking time: 50 minutes
Serves 4–6

30 g (1 oz) butter, softened
6 thin slices day-old white or brown bread, crusts removed
3/4 cup mixed dried fruit
3 tablespoons caster (superfine) sugar
1 teaspoon mixed spice
2 eggs, lightly beaten
1 teaspoon vanilla essence
2 1/2 cups (20 fl oz) milk

1 Preheat oven to moderate 180°C (350°F/Gas 4). Grease a medium, shallow, ovenproof dish. Butter bread and cut slices in half diagonally. Layer bread into the dish, sprinkling each layer with dried fruit, sugar and spice.

2 Beat the eggs, essence and milk together. Pour mixture over the bread and set aside for 5 minutes to soak.

3 Bake pudding for 50 minutes, or until it is set and top is browned.

bread from the topping, which can include generous mounds of fresh salad vegetables, cold meats, smoked fish, cheese, mayonnaise, pickles, gherkins and relishes, garnished with fresh herbs such as parsley, dill, chervil and cress. A Danish open sandwich is best eaten with a knife and fork. The Danish word is *smørbrød*, meaning buttered bread.

Danish Pastry A sweet, light pastry consisting of a buttery yeast dough encasing a filling such as stewed fruits, custard, preserves, nuts and cheese. The dough is shaped into rolls and twists, then glazed with spices and sprinkled with coarse sugar before being baked. Danish pastries are usually served with coffee.

Dariole The name given to both a small, steep-sided mould and the preparation cooked in it. Dariole moulds are used to make pastries, individual fruit cakes and puddings. They can also be lined with aspic jelly, filled with a savoury mixture and topped with more jelly. When the mixture has set, it is turned out onto a platter for serving.

Dashi A fish and kelp stock which gives Japanese cooking its distinctive 'sea' flavour. It is made by heating konbu (large leaf kelp) in water to boiling point then removing the kelp and adding hano-katsuo (flakes of dried bonito, a member of the mackerel family never used fresh); the mixture is stirred until the flakes sink and then strained. Dashi is also eaten as a clear soup and is used as a dipping sauce and marinade. It is available from Asian food stores in small, ready-to-use infusion bags (dashi-no-moto), as a liquid concentrate and in granule form.

Date The oblong, amber to dark brown, sweet-fleshed fruit of the date palm. A French author described it as being 'to the people of the Sahara what wheat is to the

French and rice to the Chinese'. In the hot deserts of western Asia and northern Africa, the date palm is the tree of life, fringing every oasis and thriving in conditions where virtually nothing else can grow. Date palms have been known to bear fruit for up to a century.

Dates travel well and were exported (mostly

Left: BERRY CHERRY CRUMBLE (TOP) AND BREAD AND BUTTER PUDDING (BOTTOM)

DESSERTS
CRUMBLES, CRISPS AND COBBLERS

BERRY CHERRY CRUMBLE

★ **Preparation time:** 10 minutes
Total cooking time: 15 minutes
Serves 6

250 g (8 oz) strawberries, hulled
200 g (6½ oz) blueberries
425 g (13½ oz) can pitted black cherries, strained, ½ cup (4 fl oz) juice reserved
½ teaspoon cornflour (cornstarch)

Topping
90 g (3 oz) butter
¼ cup golden syrup (light corn syrup)
2 cups rolled oats
1 tablespoon icing (confectioners) sugar

1 Preheat oven to moderate 180°C (350°F/Gas 4). Cut strawberries in half. Place in an ovenproof dish with blueberries and cherries. Mix well. Blend cornflour with reserved cherry juice until smooth. Pour over fruit. Sprinkle on sifted icing sugar. Set aside.

2 **To prepare Topping:** Melt butter and golden syrup in a small pan over low heat. Remove from heat; stir in rolled oats until combined. Spoon the oat mixture over the berries. Bake crumble for 15 minutes, or until topping is golden and crunchy. Serve hot.

APRICOT BETTY

★ **Preparation time:** 10 minutes
Total cooking time: 30 minutes
Serves 6

2 x 425 g (13½ oz) cans apricot halves, drained, ⅓ cup (2½ fl oz) juice reserved
¼ cup caster (superfine) sugar
2 cups fine, fresh white breadcrumbs
60 g (2 oz) butter, melted

1 Preheat oven to moderate 180°C (350°F/Gas 4). Brush 20 cm (8 inch) pie dish with melted butter. Place half the apricots into the prepared dish.

2 Sprinkle with half the caster sugar and half the breadcrumbs. Pour half the melted butter and half the juice over crumbs.

3 Repeat procedure with remaining ingredients. Bake 30 minutes. Serve hot.

---

from Egypt) to ancient Greece and Rome where they were sold on the streets and in the theatres as a sweet snack food, as they were again fifteen hundred years later in medieval Europe. The fruit is available

fresh or dried. Iraq is the main exporter of dried dates; Israel, Lebanon and the United States export 'fresh' frozen dates. The name comes from the Greek *daktylos*, meaning finger.

Daube, en A French term for a method of cooking meat by braising it in red wine seasoned with herbs.

Deep Fry To cook pieces of food by immersing them in very hot fat or oil. Deep frying creates a crust around the food which seals in the flavour and juices. Food should be cooked in small batches so as not to lower the temperature of the frying medium. Fish, chicken, croquettes or soft vegetables should be protected with a coating of batter or breadcrumbs before being fried. Peanut and corn (maize) oils have a high smoking point and so are most suitable for deep frying.

D E S S E R T S   **C H R I S T M A S**   **P U D D I N G S**

Déglaze To add water, stock or wine to the cooking juices and cooked-on sediments left in the pan after roasting or frying meat. The mixture is then heated, stirred and reduced to make a sauce or gravy. The name comes from the French *déglacer*, to dissolve into liquid.

Dégorger A French term (meaning 'disgorge') for the process of soaking meat, poultry, offal or fish in cold water to free it of impurities and blood, or to eliminate any 'muddy' flavour from freshwater fish. The term is also used for the process of removing excess water and strong flavours from certain vegetables.

Demerara Sugar A white cane sugar treated with molasses to produce large, slightly sticky, pale brown crystals. It is often served with coffee and is used for making biscuits (cookies), cakes and confectionery. Brown confectionery sugar or raw sugar can be substituted. It was first produced in the Demerara region of Guyana, West Indies.

Demi-glace A basic brown or espagnole sauce reduced to a rich, thick, glossy syrup. It is used to coat meat and game dishes as well as to enrich other sauces.

D E S S E R T S
C H R I S T M A S   P U D D I N G S

ICE-CREAM CHRISTMAS PUDDING

★ *Preparation time:* 20 minutes + 20 minutes standing + overnight freezing
Total cooking time: 4 minutes
Serves 8–10

2 litres (8 cups) vanilla ice-cream, softened
1/4 cup choc bits
1/2 cup chopped pecan nuts

Chocolate Sauce
1/2 cup (4 fl oz) water
1/4 cup cocoa powder,
2 tablespoons soft brown sugar
60 g (2 oz) butter
105 g (3 1/2 oz) dark (semi-sweet) chocolate, chopped
1 tablespoon brandy

2 cups mixed dried fruit
90 g (3 oz) glacé cherries, cut into quarters
45 g (1 1/2 oz) glacé apricots, chopped
45 g (1 1/2 oz) glacé pineapple, chopped
2 teaspoons finely chopped glacé ginger
2 teaspoons grated orange rind
2 tablespoons Grand Marnier
1 tablespoon brandy

1 Mix fruits, rind, liqueur and brandy in a large mixing bowl. Set aside for 20 minutes, uncovered; stir occasionally.

2 Using a metal spoon, break up ice-cream in a large mixing bowl. Add fruit mixture, choc bits and nuts to ice-cream; stir until well mixed.

3 Line a 9-cup capacity pudding basin or bowl with plastic wrap. Spoon in ice-cream mixture; smooth surface. Cover with plastic wrap; freeze overnight. To serve, unmould and cut into wedges. Serve with Chocolate Sauce.

4 To make Chocolate Sauce: Place water, cocoa, butter and sugar in small pan. Stir over low heat 4 minutes or until mixture boils and sugar is dissolved. Remove from heat; add chocolate. Stir until chocolate has melted and mixture is smooth; stir in brandy.

STEAMED CHRISTMAS PUDDING

★ *Preparation time:* 30 minutes
Total cooking time: 6–7 hours
Serves 8–10

2 cups sultanas
1 1/2 cups raisins
3/4 cup currants
1 tablespoon finely chopped mixed peel
1/4 cup (2 fl oz) brandy
1/4 cup (2 fl oz) rum
250 g (8 oz) butter
1 cup soft brown sugar

5 eggs
1 cup plain (all-purpose) flour
1/2 teaspoon bicarbonate of soda (baking soda)
1 1/2 teaspoons mixed spice
125 g (4 oz) fresh breadcrumbs
1/4 cup chopped almonds

1 Combine fruits, peel, brandy and rum in a bowl. Beat butter and sugar together until pale. Add eggs, one at a time, beating well after each addition. Gradually add sifted flour, bicarbonate of soda and spice. Fold in undrained fruit, breadcrumbs and chopped almonds.

2 Spoon mixture into a well-greased 8-cup pudding basin. Allow room for rising. Cover with greased greaseproof paper, then foil. Tie with string, leaving a loop handle for lifting. Place on a trivet in a large saucepan. Pour in hot water to come two-thirds up sides of pudding basin. Bring to boil, boil rapidly for 5–6 hours. Check water occasionally; refill as needed. Cool pudding completely; refrigerate.

3 To serve: Reheat pudding by cooking in the same way for 1 hour before needed. Serve with hot Brandy Butter.

BRANDY BUTTER

Beat together 250 g (8 oz) butter, 1/3 cup firmly packed soft brown sugar and 1 cup sifted icing (confectioners) sugar until mixture is smooth. Add 1/4 cup (2 fl oz) brandy gradually, beating continuously. Store in the refrigerator for up to a week. Makes about 1 cup.

DESSERTS FRUIT

SUMMER PUDDING

⁂ ⁂ **Preparation time:** 20 minutes + 1 hour standing + overnight refrigeration
Total cooking time: 13 minutes
Makes one 20 cm pudding

425 g (13½ oz) can raspberries
300 g (10 oz) raspberries
boysenberries
425 g (13½ oz) can blackberries
15 slices thick bread, crusts removed
fresh strawberries, blueberries, raspberries and blackberries, for decoration
¾ cup sugar
1 medium apple, peeled and coarsely grated

1 Drain berries and set aside. Pour syrup into pan, add sugar. Stir over low heat 3 minutes or until sugar dissolves. Bring to boil, reduce heat. Simmer uncovered 10 minutes; remove from heat.
2 Combine canned berries with apple and raspberries in large mixing bowl, mix well.
3 Cut bread diagonally in half. Arrange half of the bread over base and sides of a deep 20 cm cake tin. Brush with a little syrup. Spoon half the fruit onto bread; pour ⅓ of syrup over fruit. Arrange a layer of bread over fruit. Top with remaining fruit and ⅓ of syrup. Arrange remaining bread over fruit and cover with remaining syrup.
4 Stand tin in a plate with a lip. Cover with plastic wrap, top with a plate and a weight. Stand 1 hour. Remove plate and weight. Refrigerate overnight. Turn onto serving plate; decorate with berries.

MOROCCAN-STYLE FRESH FRUIT SALAD

✶ **Preparation time:** 20 minutes
Total cooking time: 5 minutes
Serves 6

2 apples
2 pears
250 g (8 oz) strawberries, hulled and halved lengthways
1 tablespoon lemon juice
2 bananas
2 tablespoons orange flower water

icing (confectioners) sugar
¾ cup (6 fl oz) orange juice
fresh mint leaves
rind of 1 orange

1 Core apples and pears and cut into thin slices. Place in serving bowl and add orange and lemon juices to prevent apples and pears discolouring.
2 Peel and cut bananas thinly. Add to fruit in bowl and toss gently. Add orange flower water and sprinkle with icing sugar to taste. Add strawberry halves to fruit salad. Sprinkle with fresh mint leaves.
3 Remove bitter white pith from orange rind. Slice orange rind into thin matchsticks and cook in water or light sugar syrup for 5 minutes, drain. Arrange over fruit salad and serve.

Note: This fruit salad is best served plain without cream or ice-cream.

OPPOSITE PAGE: ICE-CREAM CHRISTMAS PUDDING.
ABOVE: MOROCCAN-STYLE FRESH FRUIT SALAD;
LEFT: SUMMER PUDDING

Dessert A sweet course eaten at the end of a meal. It can range from a simple compote of fresh fruit to ice-creams, jellies, custards, sweet pies, steamed puddings and elaborate cakes. In ancient times a meal was likely to have been rounded off with fruit, honey or cheese. In medieval Europe it was customary at banquets to serve jellies and sweet tarts between meat courses. In the seventeenth century, sweet ices and sherbets (which originated in Spain and Sicily) made an appearance, as did chocolate, brought back from the Americas. Ideally, a light, fruit-based dessert should follow a heavy meal, while a sweet pie or rich pudding is appropriate after a light meal. Nowadays, dessert can also mean cheese and biscuits. The word comes from the French *desservir*, to remove all that has been served: at a formal dinner, everything, including the tablecloth, was removed and the table re-laid for dessert.

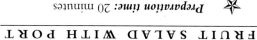

TRIFLE

Preparation time: 20 minutes +
50 minutes refrigeration
Total cooking time: 10 minutes
Serves 6–8

1 sponge cake, 16 cm
(6½ inches) diameter x
3 cm (1¼ inches) deep
2½ cups (20 fl oz) milk
1 teaspoon vanilla essence
1 egg
2 x 425 g (13½ oz)
cans peach slices,
drained
1 cup (8 fl oz) cream
¼ cup icing (confectioners)
sugar
¾ cup (6 fl oz) cold
water

90 g (3 oz) red jelly
¾ cup (6 fl oz) boiling
water
sherry or port
¾ cup (6 fl oz) cream
¼ cup sugar
water
250 g (8 oz)
strawberries, hulled and
halved
¼ cup custard powder

1 Cut sponge into 2 cm (¾ inch) cubes and place in an 8-cup capacity serving dish. Drizzle sherry over the cake.

2 Pour boiling water over jelly and stir until dissolved. Add cold water. Pour into a 28 x 18 cm (11 x 7 inch) tin and refrigerate for 30 minutes or until set.

3 Place sugar and custard powder into a medium pan, gradually blend in milk. Stir over medium heat with a wooden spoon until custard boils and thickens. Remove from heat. Add essence and egg, mix well. Cover surface with plastic wrap, cool to room temperature.

4 Using a plastic spatula, cut jelly into cubes. Place in a layer on top of sponge. Add fruit for the next layer, then pour custard over top. Refrigerate for 20 minutes or until custard has set. Whip cream with icing sugar until thick, pipe or spoon onto trifle and garnish with strawberries.

FRUIT SALAD WITH PORT

Preparation time: 20 minutes
Total cooking time: nil
Serves 6

½ cup caster (superfine)
sugar
¼ cup lemon juice
¼ cup (2 fl oz) port
250 g (8 oz) raspberries
1 kiwi fruit (Chinese
gooseberry), peeled and
sliced
1 pawpaw (papaya),
peeled and sliced
other seasonal fruit

1 Combine sugar, lemon juice and port in a screw-top jar. Shake well.

2 Combine pawpaw, raspberries, kiwi fruit and other fruit in a serving bowl. Pour over dressing. Cover. Refrigerate until required. Serve with lashings of whipped cream.

Dessert Wine A sweet, full-bodied wine served at the end of a meal and with the dessert. Dessert wines include muscat, madeira, sauternes and tokay; champagne can also be served with the dessert course.

Devilled The term applied to food, such as meat, poultry, fish and shellfish, with a sharp flavour that has been imparted by using seasonings or marinades before grilling (broiling) or frying. Flavourings (which are often brushed on during cooking) can include mustard, Tabasco or worcestershire sauce, cayenne pepper and lemon juice.

Devilled Butter Softened butter mashed with Tabasco sauce, worcestershire sauce or dry mustard, and chopped onion and parsley, formed into a roll and then chilled. Serve sliced on grilled (broiled) meat or fish.

Devil on Horseback An hors d'oeuvre consisting of stoned prunes wrapped in bacon which is grilled until the bacon is crisp.

ICE-CREAM FRUIT BOMBE

⭐ **Preparation time:** 20 minutes + overnight soaking + overnight freezing
Total cooking time: nil
Serves 8

315 g (10 oz) jar fruit mince	4 eggs
½ cup dried figs, finely chopped	1 cup caster (superfine) sugar
¼ cup (2 fl oz) rum	1½ cups (12 fl oz) cream
1 cup (4 oz) flaked almonds	¾ cup (6 fl oz) buttermilk

1 Combine fruit mince, figs and rum in small mixing bowl. Cover and soak overnight. Toast almonds on a tray under hot grill until golden.
2 Using electric beaters, beat eggs in large mixing bowl 5 minutes or until thick and pale. Add sugar gradually, beat until sugar dissolves and mixture is pale and glossy. Gradually add combined cream and buttermilk; beat for another 5 minutes.
3 Using a metal spoon, fold in fruit mixture and almonds. Pour into deep 8-cup capacity pudding bowl, cover with foil. Freeze overnight.
4 Push a flat-bladed knife down between bowl and pudding and gently ease onto serving plate.

OPPOSITE PAGE: TRIFLE.
ABOVE: MANGO ICE-CREAM

MANGO ICE-CREAM

⭐⭐ **Preparation time:** 25 minutes + freezing time
Total cooking time: 10 minutes
Makes 1 litre (4 cups)

4 egg yolks	½ cup (4 fl oz) coconut cream
¾ cup icing (confectioners) sugar	½ cup (4 fl oz) cream
2 cups (16 fl oz) mango puree	brandy baskets, fresh mango and shredded coconut for serving
1 tablespoon lemon juice	

1 Place egg yolks and icing sugar in a medium heatproof bowl. Stand bowl over a pan of simmering water, beating until mixture is thick and creamy. Remove from heat, continue beating for 1 minute longer or until cool.
2 Place mango puree, lemon juice, coconut cream and cream into a large bowl, mix well. Using a metal spoon, gently fold in egg mixture.
3 Spoon into an 18 x 28 cm (7 x 11 inch) or 1-litre (4-cup) capacity rectangular tin. Store, covered with foil in freezer for 3 hours, or until the mixture is almost frozen.
4 Transfer to large mixing bowl. Using electric beaters, beat on high speed until smooth. Return mixture to tin or container, store, covered with foil, in freezer for 5 hours or overnight. Scoop into brandy baskets and top with slices of fresh mango and shredded coconut.

Note: Buy brandy baskets from gourmet delicatessens and major department stores.

Devonshire Tea Scones, jam and clotted cream served with a pot of tea as a light mid-morning or mid-afternoon meal. Clotted cream, also known as Devonshire cream, was originally made by slowly warming fresh cream in an earthenware bowl which was then left on a cold stone floor to cool, allowing the cream to thicken. The process originated in the county of Devon, in south-western England.

Dhal An Indian dish of lentils cooked with garlic, ginger and seasonings and then pureed. It has a consistency similar to porridge and can be eaten on its own, served with boiled rice or Indian breads, or as an accompaniment to a meat dish.

Diable A cooking vessel consisting of two unglazed clay pots, one of which fits the other as a lid. It is used for cooking foods such as potatoes, onions, beetroot and chestnuts without water; halfway through cooking the diable is turned upside down. The vessel can be used in the oven or, with a heat diffuser, on an electric hotplate or gas ring. A diable should never be washed.

Dibs A chocolate-flavoured syrup made from the carob pod. In Syria and Lebanon it is mixed with tahini and used as a spread.

Dibs Roman Also known as grenadine molasses, a thick, dark, purple-red syrup with a strong, sour-sweet flavour. Made from concentrated pomegranate juice, it is used in the cooking of the Middle East to sharpen the flavour of lamb fillings for pies, as a marinade for lamb and to add a tart sweetness to soups and stews. It is also the basis of a drink. The name is derived from the Arabic word for 'pomegranate sugar'.

Dijonnaise French term for a dish prepared with Dijon mustard, one of the traditional French mustards. This creamy condiment, paler than some mustards, is made from mustard seeds that have been soaked in the acidic, fermented juice of unripened grapes. *Dijonnaise* is also the name given to a mustard-flavoured mayonnaise served with cold meats. Both are called after Dijon, capital of the Burgundy region of France, an ancient city famous for its castles and museums, an annual International Food Fair, and the blackcurrant syrup cassis.

EASY ORANGE MOUSSE

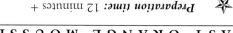

Preparation time: 12 minutes +
10 minutes standing
Total cooking time: nil
Serves 8

1 cup (8 fl oz) orange
  juice
2 tablespoons lemon juice
2/3 cup caster (superfine)
  sugar
1 tablespoon gelatine

1/4 cup (2 fl oz) water
1 tablespoon orange
  liqueur
3 egg whites
3/4 cup (6 fl oz) cream,
  whipped until stiff

1 Combine orange and lemon juice in a bowl; add the sugar. Leave for 10 minutes until sugar has softened.

2 Sprinkle gelatine over water in a small bowl. Stand in boiling water, stirring until the gelatine has dissolved. Add to juices, with orange liqueur. Mix well. Refrigerate until mixture is the consistency of unbeaten egg white.

3 Beat orange and lemon jelly base until fluffy and light. Using electric beaters, beat egg whites until stiff peaks form. Using a metal spoon, fold the cream and egg whites together. Fold gelatine mixture into egg white mixture. Spoon into eight individual dessert dishes or wine glasses. Decorate with an orange segment, orange rind and a little whipped cream, if desired.

ABOVE: ORANGE MOUSSE; RIGHT: PASSIONFRUIT AND CITRUS FLUMMERY. OPPOSITE PAGE: BLUEBERRY CHEESE TART (LEFT) AND BUTTERMILK NUTMEG TART.

PASSIONFRUIT AND CITRUS FLUMMERY

Preparation time: 35-40 minutes +
4 hours chilling
Total cooking time: 10 minutes
Serves 8

1 tablespoon plain (all-
  purpose) flour
1/4 cup (2 fl oz) lemon
  juice
2/3 cup (5 fl oz) orange
  juice

1 cup (8 fl oz) warm
  water
1 tablespoon gelatine
1/4 cup (2 fl oz) cold
  water
3/4 cup caster (superfine)
  sugar
pulp of 5 passionfruit

1 In a medium pan, blend the flour and a little warm water to a paste, adding remaining water a little at a time. Bring the mixture to boil, stirring or whisking constantly. Boil for 1 minute, remove from heat.

2 Sprinkle gelatine over combined cold water and lemon juice in a small bowl. Whisk, standing bowl in pan of warm water, until gelatine has dissolved and there are no lumps.

3 Add juices, gelatine mixture, sugar and passionfruit pulp to pan. Return to heat; bring to the boil. Transfer mixture to a large heatproof bowl.

4 Place the bowl over ice cubes and beat mixture with electric beaters until thick and light. Transfer mixture to clean bowl and set aside until beginning to set. Whisk again lightly to distribute the passionfruit seeds evenly. Spoon mixture into individual parfait glasses. Chill for about 4 hours or until lightly set. Serve with cream and extra passionfruit pulp if desired.

BLUEBERRY CHEESE TART

Serves 6

★

Preparation time: 30 minutes
Total cooking time: 45 minutes

2 sheets ready-rolled
shortcrust pastry
125 g (4 oz) cream
cheese
2 tablespoons caster
(superfine) sugar
2 teaspoons lemon juice
1 egg, lightly beaten

500 g (1 lb) fresh or
frozen blueberries
2 tablespoons seedless
blackberry jam
1 teaspoon vanilla essence
1 egg, extra, lightly beaten

1 Preheat oven to moderate 180°C (350°F/Gas 4).
Line a 23 cm (9 inch) fluted flan tin with pastry;
trim edges. Cut remaining pastry sheet into long
thin strips. Brush with extra beaten egg.

2 Using electric beaters, beat cream cheese and
sugar in a small mixing bowl until light and
creamy. Add the egg gradually, beating
thoroughly. Beat in vanilla essence.

3 Spread cheese mixture over pastry, top with
blueberries. Heat jam and juice together in a
small pan until jam has melted. Gently spoon
over top of blueberries. Lay pastry strips in a
lattice pattern over tart; gently press edges to base.
Trim excess pastry. Bake for 45 minutes, or until
cheese mixture has set. Leave to cool in tin for 10
minutes. Serve warm or cold with ice-cream.

BUTTERMILK NUTMEG TART

Serves 6

★ ★

Preparation time: 30 minutes
Total cooking time: 50 minutes

1 sheet ready-rolled
shortcrust pastry

Filling
2 teaspoons custard
powder
3 eggs, lightly beaten

1/3 cup caster (superfine)
sugar
1 teaspoon vanilla essence
1/2 cup (4 fl oz) cream
1 cup (8 fl oz) buttermilk
1 teaspoon ground
nutmeg

1 Preheat oven to moderate 180°C (350°F/Gas 4).
Brush a shallow 20 cm (8 inch) round ovenproof
pie plate with oil or melted butter.

2 Ease pastry sheet into prepared pie plate; trim
around edge. Using fingertips, pinch a fluted
pattern around the edge of the pastry.

3 **To make Filling:** Whisk the custard powder,
eggs and sugar together in a medium bowl. Add
vanilla essence, cream and buttermilk and mix
until well combined. Pour mixture into the pie
shell and sprinkle with nutmeg.

4 Place tart on a baking tray. Bake 50 minutes or
until custard is set and a sharp knife comes out
clean when inserted in centre. Leave 10 minutes
before serving. Serve warm or cold with cream.

Note: Custard tarts need cooling before serving
to allow the filling to set to a perfect consistency.

Dill An aromatic herb,
similar in appearance and
related to fennel, that is a
native of southern
Europe and western
Asia. Both its feathery
green leaves and small
brown seeds are used as a
flavouring (the leaves in
soups, egg dishes, salads,
soft cheeses and sauces to
accompany fish; the
seeds in
breads,
pickles and for flavouring
vinegar and cooked
cabbage). Dill is widely
used in the cooking of
northern Europe, where
it flavours sauerkraut and
potato salad, fish and
vegetable dishes and
pickled gherkins. Dill
water was for many years
given to babies to soothe
them to sleep. The
leaves are also known
as dillweed.

Dim Sim A tiny parcel
of finely chopped meat
and cabbage wrapped in
a wonton wrapper (a
thin sheet of dry pasta
dough) and
then either
deep fried
until crisp
and golden,
or steamed. The
name comes
from the
Cantonese
word *tim-sam*.
Dim sim are
sometimes applied to a
range of similar bite-
sized morsels such as
gow gee and spring rolls.

Dip A dish of pureéd or finely chopped food blended with a moist or oily base to form a creamy mixture; it is served as a snack or appetiser. Bread, crackers, corn chips or crisp raw vegetables cut into pieces are eaten with dips. Popular for entertaining, dips are often thought of as a recent invention; however the practice of using a firm food to scoop up a softer food is far from new and is found in all parts of the world. The ancient Romans snacked on pieces of coarse bread dipped in goat's milk; the chick pea mixture hummus has been made for thousands of years in the Middle East; taramasalata, a paste of mullet roe, has a long history around the Aegean; the Mayas of Central America enjoyed guacamole for many centuries before the arrival of the Spanish in the sixteenth century; and in India, dhal, made from pureéd lentils, is often eaten with chapattis, roti or one of the many other types of flat bread. Nowadays a variety of commercially prepared dips can be found on the shelves of most large supermarkets.

DESSERTS STEAMED PUDDINGS

DARK CHOCOLATE PUDDING WITH MOCHA SAUCE

★ **Preparation time:** 30 minutes
Total cooking time: 1 hour 30 minutes
Serves 6

1¼ cups self-raising flour
1 cup plain (all-purpose) flour
2 eggs, lightly beaten
1 teaspoon vanilla essence
¾ cup (6 fl oz) buttermilk
¼ cup cocoa powder
¼ teaspoon bicarbonate of soda (baking soda)
155 g (5 oz) butter
½ cup caster (superfine) sugar
¼ cup soft dark brown sugar
105 g (3½ oz) dark (semi-sweet) chocolate, chopped

Mocha Sauce
55 g (1¾ oz) butter
155 g (5 oz) dark (semi-sweet) chocolate, chopped
1½ cups (12 fl oz) cream
1 tablespoon instant coffee powder
1–2 tablespoons chocolate liqueur

1 Brush an 8-cup capacity pudding basin or steamer with oil or melted butter. Line the base with paper, grease paper. Grease a large sheet of aluminium foil and a large sheet of greaseproof paper. Lay paper over foil, greased side up. Pleat paper and foil down the centre. Set aside.

2 Sift flours, cocoa and soda into large mixing bowl. Make a well in centre. Combine butter, sugars, chocolate and essence in pan. Stir over low heat until butter and chocolate have melted and sugars have dissolved; remove from heat. Add butter mixture, beaten eggs and buttermilk to dry ingredients. Using a wooden spoon, stir until well combined; do not overbeat.

3 Spoon mixture into prepared basin. Cover with the greased foil and paper, greased side down. Place lid over foil and secure clips. If you have no lid, lay a pleated tea-towel over foil and tie securely with string under lip of basin. Knot ends of tea-towel together—this will act as a handle to help lower the basin into the pan.

4 Place basin on a trivet in a large, deep pan. Carefully pour boiling water into pan to come half-way up side of basin. Bring to boil; cover and cook for about 1 hour and 15 minutes. Do not allow to boil dry—replenish pan with boiling water if necessary. When cooked, uncover, invert onto plate. Serve hot with Mocha Sauce.

5 To make Mocha Sauce: Combine butter, chocolate, cream and coffee powder. Stir over low heat until the butter and chocolate have melted and mixture is smooth. Add chocolate liqueur, combine well; remove from heat.

Above: **DARK CHOCOLATE PUDDING WITH MOCHA SAUCE.** *Opposite page:* **FRUIT MINCE PUDDING WITH CITRUS SAUCE**

FRUIT MINCE PUDDING WITH CITRUS SAUCE

★ ★ *Preparation time:* 15 minutes
Total cooking time: 1 hour 40 minutes
Serves 6

125 g (4 oz) butter	1 cup (8 fl oz) water
3/4 cup caster (superfine) sugar	1 cup (8 fl oz) orange juice
2 eggs, lightly beaten	1/2 cup (4 fl oz) lemon juice
2 teaspoons finely grated orange rind	1 tablespoon finely grated orange rind
1/2 cup fruit mince	1 tablespoon cornflour (cornstarch)
1 1/2 cups self-raising flour	2 teaspoons finely grated lemon rind
1/4 cup (2 fl oz) milk	1 teaspoon butter
1/4 cup (2 fl oz) orange juice	1 egg yolk
Citrus Sauce	1 tablespoon sugar

1 Brush an 18 cm (7 inch), 6-cup capacity pudding basin or steamer with melted butter or oil. Line the base with paper; grease paper. Grease a large sheet of aluminium foil and a large sheet of greaseproof paper. Lay paper over foil, greased side up, and pleat in the centre. Set aside.

2 Using electric beaters, beat butter and sugar in mixing bowl until creamy. Add eggs gradually, beating well after each addition. Stir in rind.

3 Transfer mixture to large mixing bowl; add fruit mince. Using a metal spoon, fold in sifted flour alternately with liquids. Stir until mixture is just combined and almost smooth.

4 Spoon mixture into prepared basin. Cover with the greased foil and paper, greased side down. Place lid over foil and secure clips. If you have no lid, lay a pleated tea-towel over foil, tie securely with string under the lip of the basin. Knot the ends of the tea-towel together—this will act as a handle to help lower the basin into the pan.

5 Place the basin on a trivet in a large, deep pan. Carefully pour boiling water down the side of pan to come halfway up side of basin. Bring to the boil, cover and cook for 1 hour 30 minutes. Do not let pudding boil dry; replenish pan with boiling water if necessary as the pudding cooks. Once it is cooked, leave pudding in tin for 5 minutes before uncovering and inverting onto a plate. Serve warm with Citrus Sauce.

6 To make Citrus Sauce: Combine sugar and all but 1 tablespoon of water in small pan. Heat gently, stirring, until sugar dissolves. Add orange and lemon juice and rinds. Combine the cornflour with reserved water to make a smooth paste. Bring sugar and juice mixture to boil and add cornflour paste; stir until sauce thickens and clears. Stir in butter. Remove pan from heat, cool slightly, then beat in egg yolk. Strain through a fine sieve into a serving jug.

STEAMED JAM PUDDING

★ *Preparation time:* 10 minutes
Total cooking time: 1 hour
Serves 6

1/2 cup strawberry jam	1 1/2 cups plain (all-purpose) flour
60 g (2 oz) butter	1 teaspoon baking powder
1/2 cup caster (superfine) sugar	1/2 cup (4 fl oz) milk
1 egg	

1 Grease a 4-cup pudding bowl. Spread jam in the base. Beat butter, sugar and egg until smooth and creamy.

2 Sift in flour and baking powder. Add milk and mix well. Spread mixture carefully on top of the jam in the bowl.

3 Make a foil lid for the bowl; press the edges to seal tight. Make a string handle for the bowl and lower it onto a trivet in a large pan filled with boiling water to a depth of about 5 cm (2 inches). Cover the pan with a lid. Simmer over low heat for 1 hour, taking care not to let pan boil dry—refill with boiling water if necessary. Run a knife around edge of pudding, turn onto serving plate.

Dolmades Small

cylindrical packages consisting of rice, minced (ground) lamb, finely chopped onion, nuts and seasonings wrapped in partially cooked grapevine leaves, braised in a little stock or wine and then sprinkled with olive oil and lemon juice. The mixture can also be wrapped in cabbage leaves. Dolmades are usually eaten cold as a first course. Of Middle Eastern origin, the dish is served throughout Greece, Turkey and Lebanon. The name comes from the Persian *dolmeh*, meaning stuffed.

Doner Kebab Lamb

slices and salad sprinkled with a tahini-based sauce and wrapped in a piece of unleavened bread to form a meal that can be eaten in the hand. Even-sized rounds of boneless lamb, marinated for up to 24 hours in a mixture of olive oil, salt, pepper, onion, rigani (a variety of oregano), thyme, parsley and sometimes mint, are threaded, tightly packed and interspersed with fat from the tail, onto a heavy spit. Traditionally the spit was turned over a charcoal fire; today it is usually a vertical motor-driven rotisserie. When the surface of the lamb cooks to a warm brown

SALMON DIP

★
Preparation time: 10 minutes
Total cooking time: nil
Makes about 3½ cups

410 g (13 oz) can pink
  salmon, drained
250 g (8 oz) packet
  cream cheese, softened
¼ cup (2 fl oz) sour
  cream
3-4 gherkins, chopped
1 tablespoon chopped
  chives
½ cup (4 fl oz) prepared
  mayonnaise
juice of 1 lemon
freshly ground black pepper

1 Place all ingredients for dip in a food processor or blender. Process until mixture is smooth.
2 Transfer dip to a serving dish. Refrigerate until required. Serve with crackers.

LIVERWURST COTTAGE DIP

1 Place 250 g (8 oz) cottage cheese, 125 g (4 oz) liverwurst, ½ cup (4 fl oz) mayonnaise, 2 chopped dill cucumbers, 1 chopped onion, 1 tablespoon capers (optional) and 1 tablespoon prepared mustard in a food processor or blender. Process until the mixture is smooth.
2 Transfer mixture to a serving dish. Cover and refrigerate. Serve dip with corn chips and a selection of crackers. Serves about 10.

Note: The flavour of this dip is best appreciated if it is served at room temperature.

SUN-DRIED TOMATO DIP WITH GRISSINI AND CRUDITÉS

★
Preparation time: 10 minutes
Total cooking time: nil
Serves 6

155 g (5 oz) sun-dried
  tomatoes
2 tablespoons grated
  parmesan cheese
2 cloves garlic
1 tablespoon mango
  chutney
6 slices prosciutto
12 grissini
2 spring onions
  (scallions), chopped
6 anchovy fillets
2 tablespoons chopped
  fresh basil leaves
1 cup (8 fl oz) sour cream
vegetables for crudités—
  baby carrots, celery,
  broccoli, cucumber, red
  pepper (capsicum)

1 Drain sun-dried tomatoes and combine them with garlic, chutney, spring onions, anchovies, basil, parmesan and sour cream in a food processor. Process for 40 seconds or until mixture is smooth.
2 Cut each slice of prosciutto in half lengthways. Wrap a half-slice around each grissini.
3 Cut carrots, celery, cucumber, pepper or other vegetables for crudités into sticks or slices; separate the broccoli into small florets. Transfer the dip mixture to a serving bowl and surround with grissini and vegetables arranged attractively on a serving platter.

ABOVE: SUN-DRIED TOMATO DIP.
OPPOSITE: ROCKET AND PINE NUT DIP

it is removed in thin slices; the remaining meat continues to cook. The salad usually consists of tabouli, raw onion rings, lettuce and tomato; the sauce can be hummus bi tahini, chilli or barbecue sauce. The doner kebab originated in Turkey and is very popular throughout the Middle East; it is known as *chawarma* in Lebanon and *grass* in Iraq.

Double Gloucester
A firm-textured, straw-yellow cow's milk cheese, with a mellow, cheddar-like flavour. It is also available layered with stilton cheese. Originally made in England from the milk of the now virtually extinct Gloucester cattle, it has more recently been made with full cream milk from the herds of adjoining counties such as Somerset, Dorset and Wiltshire. The cheese almost became a casualty of the disruptions caused in Britain by World War II. When peace returned it seemed that traditional methods for making Double Gloucester had been lost, and the situation was saved only by the appearance of an ancient farm woman who before her death was able to instruct cheese factory workers in the craft and so keep the cheese alive.

The ring doughnut

Dough A mixture of flour and liquid, usually water, to which other ingredients (butter, margarine, seasonings or sweeteners) are often added before it is baked into bread or pastry. Although the ingredients are basically the same as for batter, the proportions are different (dough has far less liquid and is thick enough to be kneaded). There are two main types of dough: soft dough, with a slightly higher liquid content, is used for scones and doughnuts; stiff dough, with less liquid, is used for pastry, pie crusts and biscuits (cookies). Fermented dough, called sourdough, was originally used instead of yeast as a raising agent when baking bread. The word probably comes from the Anglo-Saxon *deawian*, meaning to wet or moisten.

Doughnut A small, usually ring-shaped cake, made of deep-fried yeast dough, which is dusted with spiced sugar or iced (frosted). It has a moist, bread-like texture. Doughnuts can also be made in twisted and round shapes, and are sometimes filled with jam or custard. The ring doughnut

AVOCADO DIP

Blend 1 large ripe peeled and seeded avocado in food processor until smooth. Add 1/2 teaspoon finely grated lemon rind, 1 small clove garlic, crushed, 1 cup plain yoghurt, salt and freshly ground black pepper. Blend until smooth, stir in 1/4 cup of finely chopped Spanish (large red) onion and 2 teaspoons finely chopped parsley. Serve with crackers, corn chips, cooked baby potatoes, cooked peeled prawns (shrimps), raw button mushrooms, crisp celery, carrot or pepper (capsicum) sticks or baby tomatoes.

ROCKET (ARUGULA) AND PINE NUT DIP

Place 3/4 cup (6 fl oz) light sour cream and 1/4 cup mayonnaise in a food processor. Add 1 cup rocket (arugula) leaves and process until rocket is chopped, but not too finely. Season with salt and freshly ground pepper. Stir in 2 tablespoons pine nuts. Serve with cooked peeled prawns (shrimps), baked chicken wings, dolmades, raw button mushrooms, red pepper (capsicum) sticks or fried eggplant (aubergine) fingers.

SMOKED SALMON DIP

Beat 250 g (8 oz) light cream cheese until smooth. Stir in 1/4 cup (2 fl oz) cream, 1/4 cup finely chopped smoked salmon, 1 tablespoon finely chopped chives and freshly ground white pepper. Serve dip with crackers, grissini sticks, crisp cucumber or celery sticks, baby tomatoes, cooked warm baby potatoes, raw button mushrooms, cooked asparagus spears or canned artichoke hearts.

FRAGRANT COCONUT DIP

Mix 1 cup plain yoghurt with 1/4 cup instant coconut powder. Stir in 1 tablespoon sweet chilli sauce, 1 tablespoon lime juice and 1 tablespoon chopped coriander. Chill dip for 30 minutes and serve with fresh oysters, grilled sea scallops, cooked peeled prawns (shrimps), grilled fish pieces, chicken or lamb satay sticks, snow peas (mange tout), blanched baby beans, celery sticks, melon or mango wedges.

MEDITERRANEAN DIP

Mix 250 g (8 oz) light cream cheese with 1/2 cup plain yoghurt and stir until smooth. Add 1 small clove of garlic, crushed, 1 tablespoon sliced black olives, 1 tablespoon sliced stuffed olives, 2 tablespoons grated parmesan cheese, 1 tablespoon finely chopped fresh basil or oregano, and some freshly ground black pepper. Mix all ingredients to combine. Serve dip with grissini sticks, crisp crackers, mini meatballs, canned artichoke hearts, cooked asparagus spears, or raw celery, carrot, pepper (capsicum) or zucchini (courgette) sticks.

is of modern North American origin and is attributed to John Blondel, who in the 1870s patented a doughnut cutter which cut a hole in the centre.

Drambuie A liqueur, made from whisky and honey, which originated in Scotland.

Dredge To coat food (by dusting, sprinkling or rolling) with a dry ingredient, such as flour or sugar.

Dresden Sauce A cold sauce made from sour cream, mustard and horseradish. It is generally served with smoked or boiled fish.

Dressing A liquid used to moisten and flavour a variety of foods, from salads or cooked vegetables to raw meat or fish dishes. Dressings can be based on olive oil, wine or vinegars, with lemon juice, various flavourings, or contain richer ingredients such as eggs (as in mayonnaise), cream or yoghurt.

Dried Fruit See Fruit, Dried

Dripping The fat that drips from beef or lamb during roasting. Dripping should be strained from the roasting pan and left to

---

DRINKS COCKTAILS

MARTINI

Stir ice, 75 ml (2½ fl oz) gin and 15 ml (½ fl oz) dry vermouth in a mixing glass. Strain into a martini glass and garnish with an olive. Serves one.

MARGARITA

Shake ice, 45 ml (1½ fl oz) tequila, 30 ml (1 fl oz) Cointreau and 15 ml (½ fl oz) lemon juice, with a dash of beaten egg white in shaker. Strain into salt-frosted glass. Garnish with lemon peel. Serves one.

JAPANESE SLIPPER

Combine ice, 30 ml (1 fl oz) each Midori, Cointreau and lemon juice in a shaker; shake well. Strain, serve in a chilled glass. Garnish with a lemon slice and a sprig of flowers. Serves one.

PINA COLADA

Place ice, 45 ml (1½ fl oz) light rum, 30 ml (1 fl oz) coconut cream, 15 ml (½ fl oz) cream, 15 ml (½ fl oz) sugar syrup and 90 ml (3 fl oz) pineapple juice in shaker; shake well. Strain into serving glass and garnish with a slice of fresh pineapple and a maraschino cherry. Serves one.

BRANDY ALEXANDER

Place ice, 30 ml (1 fl oz) brandy, 30 ml (1 fl oz) crème de cacao and 60 ml (2 fl oz) cream in a shaker; shake well. Strain into a serving glass and garnish with a sprinkling of nutmeg and a strawberry. Serves one.

LONG ISLAND ICED TEA

Place crushed ice, 15 ml (½ fl oz) light rum, 15 ml (½ fl oz) vodka, 15 ml (½ fl oz) gin, 15 ml (½ fl oz) tequila and 15 ml (½ fl oz) Cointreau and 15 ml (½ fl oz) juice. Top with cola and dash of lemon juice. Garnish with lemon slice. Serves one.

FROZEN STRAWBERRY DAIQUIRI

Blend 45 ml (1½ fl oz) light rum, 15 ml (½ fl oz) strawberry liqueur, 15 ml (½ fl oz) lime juice, 6 strawberries and some crushed ice in a blender. Pour into a glass, garnish with a strawberry. Serves one.

ABOVE, LEFT TO RIGHT: MARGARITA, PINA COLADA, FROZEN STRAWBERRY DAIQUIRI, JAPANESE SLIPPER.
OPPOSITE PAGE, LEFT TO RIGHT: RED SANGRIA, PIMMS PUNCH, PINEAPPLE AND PASSIONFRUIT PUNCH

DRINKS
FRUIT CUPS AND PUNCHES

CHAMPAGNE PUNCH

Place 250 g (8 oz) strawberries in a bowl, sprinkle with ⅓ cup sugar, and add ½ bottle Sauternes and ½ cup (4 fl oz) brandy. Place in refrigerator and chill for at least 1 hour. Just before serving, pour in 3 bottles of champagne slowly and mix all ingredients gently. Serves 18–20.

RED SANGRIA

Mix 3 bottles dry red wine, ¾ cup (6 fl oz) Grand Marnier (or other orange-flavoured liqueur) and 3 tablespoons caster (superfine) sugar in a large container such as a punch bowl, or in two or three jugs. Cut 3 oranges and 3 lemons into 24 wedges each. Add wedges to sangria and chill for up to 24 hours. Just before serving, add 3 cups (24 fl oz) soda water and ice cubes. Serves 18–20.

PINEAPPLE AND PASSIONFRUIT PUNCH

Combine 2 cups strong hot black tea with ¼ cup demerara sugar in a medium bowl. Stir until sugar has dissolved. Cool. Place ¾ cup lemon juice, 4 cups pineapple juice, 1–2 tablespoons lime cordial, 1.25 litre (40 fl oz) bottle soda water, two 1.25 litre (40 fl oz) bottles lemonade, 425 g (13½ oz) can crushed pineapple, the cooled tea and the pulp of 5 passionfruit in a large punch bowl. Mix well. Add crushed ice, shredded fresh mint and orange slices before serving. As a variation, a few drops of Angostura bitters may be added to the recipe. Serves 18–20.

BRANDY ALEXANDER PUNCH

Combine 3 cups (24 fl oz) brandy, 1½ cups (12 fl oz) crème de cacao and 2⅓ cups (19 fl oz) cream in a large bowl or jug. Whisk until well combined. Add crushed ice to a large punch bowl, pour over cream mixture. Sprinkle with nutmeg and decorate with strawberry slices to serve. Serves 10–15.

PIMMS PUNCH

Place ice into large punch bowl or jug. Add 1½ cups (12 fl oz) each Pimm's No 1 and Southern Comfort, ¾ cup (6 fl oz) each sweet vermouth and dark rum (not overproof), 1½ cups (12 fl oz) orange juice, 3 cups (24 fl oz) champagne, 250 g (8 oz) hulled and sliced strawberries, and orange, lime and lemon slices. Add freshly sliced mango for a tropical touch. Mix well. Serve immediately. Serves 10–15.

---

set so that the jellied meat juices can be removed from the bottom. Dripping can also be purchased, packaged in solid blocks, from the butcher or supermarket.

Duchess Potatoes
A purée of potatoes blended with butter, egg yolk and seasonings and piped into various individual shapes. Used as a garnish for roasts or as a decorative border for fish

and savoury dishes, the mixture is glazed with beaten egg yolk, then browned in a hot oven or under the grill. It is said to have been created especially for the Duchess of Bedford.

Duck A large, long-bodied waterbird with dark, moist, richly flavoured flesh. Duck has been part of the human diet since the time of the earliest hunters. Always in plentiful supply on rivers, lakes, ponds and marshlands around the world, the bird and its eggs were there for the

ROAST DUCK WITH MANDARIN SAUCE

★

Preparation time: 30 minutes
Total cooking time: 1 hour 50 minutes

Serves 8

3 x 1.6 kg (3¹/₄ lb) ducks	***Mandarin Sauce***
60 g (2 oz) butter, melted	315 g (10 oz) can mandarin segments
	2 tablespoons cornflour (cornstarch)
Stuffing	4 cups (32 fl oz) light chicken stock
90 g (3 oz) butter	¹/₂ cup (4 fl oz) orange juice
12 spring onions (scallions), chopped	2 tablespoons lemon juice
3 garlic cloves, crushed	1 tablespoon honey
3 teaspoons grated ginger	1 tablespoon soy sauce
8 cups fresh white breadcrumbs	2 teaspoons grated ginger
¹/₄ cup fresh chopped coriander	1 tablespoon sugar
2 eggs, lightly beaten	

1 Preheat oven to moderate 180°C (350°F/Gas 4). Rinse ducks, pat dry with paper towel.

2 To make Stuffing: Heat butter in medium pan, add spring onions, garlic and ginger. Stir-fry for 3 minutes or until soft, add breadcrumbs, coriander and eggs and stir until combined.

Remove from heat. Spoon stuffing into ducks, ensuring each has the same amount.

3 Tie wings and drumsticks securely in place. Place ducks on roasting rack over a shallow baking dish and brush with butter. Roast for one hour, basting ducks occasionally with pan juices. While ducks are roasting, prepare Mandarin Sauce.

4 To make Mandarin Sauce: Process undrained mandarin segments to a smooth texture in blender or food processor. Place cornflour in small pan, add a little stock and stir until smooth. Add remaining stock, orange and lemon juice, honey, soy sauce, ginger, sugar and mandarin puree. Stir over medium heat until sauce boils and thickens.

5 Remove ducks from oven, drain pan juices, place ducks in baking dish, and pour over Mandarin Sauce. Roast for another 40 minutes. To test if duck is cooked, insert skewer into the thigh. If juice runs clear, duck is ready. Strain sauce and serve with ducks.

ABOUT DUCK

■ To prepare ducks for cooking, remove the fat sac at the base of the tail, rinse thoroughly in cold water and dry with absorbent paper. Prick the duck all over with a fine metal skewer. For roasting, skewer the neck skin to the back, tie the legs to the tail and turn the wing tips underneath.

taking. It was the first fowl to be domesticated, probably by the Chinese some 4000 years ago, although some claim the first duck farmers were the Incas of South America.

Domesticated breeds are now kept in all parts of the world; even so, some of the duck eaten today is, by preference, still taken from the wild. Ducks bred for the table include the large and lean Barbary duck of Europe; the English Aylesbury and Gadwell; the French Nantais, which is often reared semi-wild, and the Rouenais; and the Peking duck of China. In Australia the most common breed is a cross between the Peking and the Aylesbury.

The ancient Egyptians ate the ducks of the Nile. The Romans feasted on the breast and brains of wild duck and throughout Europe until medieval times the bird, although eaten regularly, seems always to have been caught in the wild and not reared in the fowl yard.

Duck is a favourite in the cooking of France and China. The art of drying duck meat (to preserve the flesh and intensify its flavour) has been practised in China for more than 2000 years

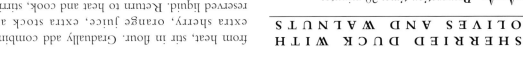

SHERRIED DUCK WITH OLIVES AND WALNUTS

✹ ✹ *Preparation time:* 20 minutes
Total cooking time: 1 hour 45 minutes
Serves 4–6

2 tablespoons olive oil
2 kg (4 lb) duck, cleaned and trussed
2 onions, halved
2 carrots, cut into large pieces
1/4 cup (2 fl oz) medium dry sherry
1/2 cup (4 fl oz) fresh orange juice
1/2 cup (4 fl oz) chicken stock or water, extra
1/2 cup stuffed green olives, warmed in brine
1/2 cup walnut halves, warmed in oven

2 tablespoons plain (all-purpose) flour
1/4 cup (2 fl oz) medium dry sherry
1/4 cup (2 fl oz) chicken stock or water
40 g (1 1/2 oz) butter

1 Preheat oven to 180°C (350°F/Gas 4). Heat olive oil in large baking dish on top of stove. Add duck, onions and carrots. Gently turn duck to brown all over, being careful not to split the skin. Pour over combined dry sherry and stock or water. Cover with aluminium foil. Bake in oven for 1 hour, basting occasionally with juices (for crisp skin, uncover during last 15 minutes).

2 Remove duck and vegetables from baking dish. Reserve any remaining liquid. Discard vegetables.

3 Place baking dish on top of stove over medium heat, add butter, allow to melt and brown. Remove scraping pan; do not allow to burn. Remove from heat, stir in flour. Gradually add combined extra sherry, orange juice, extra stock and reserved liquid. Return to heat and cook, stirring constantly, until mixture boils and thickens.

4 Put duck back in pan and spoon over sauce. Cover and bake at 180°C (350°F/Gas 4) for 15–20 minutes or until duck is tender. Place on heated serving dish, pour over sauce. Garnish with warm stuffed olives and walnut halves.

WARM DUCK SALAD

✹ *Preparation time:* 15 minutes
Total cooking time: nil
Serves 4

Oriental Dressing
1/4 cup (2 fl oz) peanut oil
1 tablespoon cider or white wine vinegar
1 tablespoon honey, warmed
2 teaspoons grated fresh ginger
1 teaspoon soy sauce
1/4 teaspoon five-spice powder

1 large Chinese barbecued duck, chopped
315 g (10 oz) can mandarin segments, drained
105 g (3 1/2 oz) snow peas (mange tout), trimmed
1 cup bean sprouts
1/2 cup canned water chestnuts, sliced
1/2 cup sliced spring onions (scallions)

1 Half an hour before serving, place dressing ingredients in a small jar, shake well for 1 minute.

2 Place duck, drained mandarins, snow peas, bean sprouts, water chestnuts and spring onions in a large bowl. Add dressing, toss gently and serve.

(traditionally the flattened, deboned, salted and seasoned carcases were suspended from bamboo racks to dry in the sun).

Because of its fattiness (it has more fat and, weight for weight, provides less meat than chicken) duck should be roasted or braised. It is often served with fruit to offset its greasiness, as in the famous French dish, duck à l'orange. Very little of the bird need go to waste. The carcase can be used to make stock and the liver to make pâté. In France there is an increasing market for foie gras made from duck liver to supplement the traditional product made from goose liver. Duckling, a young duck aged between six weeks and two months, is best grilled (broiled) or roasted and does not need stuffing. Older ducks are more strongly flavoured. Duck is available fresh or frozen.

Dumpling A small ball of dough, either savoury or sweet, poached and served as an accompaniment to meat dishes.

DUCK

ABOVE: *Soup with Chicken Dumplings.*
OPPOSITE: *Beef Goulash with Caraway Dumplings*

---

and desserts. Savoury dumplings simmered in meat stock or stew are traditionally served with roast or boiled beef. In Asian cooking, mixtures of finely chopped pork or beef and vegetables wrapped in dough and steamed are called dumplings. Sweet dumplings are simmered in either a dessert sauce or fruit juice. The name is also given to a piece of fruit encased in a sweet pastry dough and baked.

Dundee Cake A butter cake flavoured with dried fruit and nuts. Before baking the top is closely covered with blanched and halved almonds. The cake is named for Dundee, a seaport on the east coast of Scotland.

Durian A large, ovoid fruit covered with an armour of close-set, short, hard spikes. The durian is native to South-East Asia, where it is grown mainly in Malaysia, the Philippines and Vietnam. In Thailand it is so highly regarded that some orchardists employ security guards to deter fruit thieves. The sticky, cream-coloured pulp of the durian is noted especially for the contrast between its putrid odour and delicious taste. In this respect its appeal has been compared by both

---

DUMPLINGS

SOUP WITH CHICKEN DUMPLINGS

★ ★

Preparation time: *25 minutes*
Total cooking time: *15 minutes*
Serves 6

1 chicken breast fillet
1 teaspoon dried thyme
2 cups fresh white breadcrumbs
1 tablespoon chopped parsley
3 cups (24 fl oz) rich chicken stock
chopped parsley, extra

2 eggs
1/2 cup finely chopped leek
1/2 cup finely chopped onion
1/2 cup finely chopped carrot
1 teaspoon pepper

1 Cut chicken into small pieces. Process eggs in food processor until thick and creamy. Add leek, process until smooth, add onion and carrot, process until smooth. Add chicken, blend until mixture is thick and smooth; transfer to bowl.
2 Add pepper, thyme, breadcrumbs and parsley. Shape dumplings between two spoons dipped in water. Place on lightly greased tray and cover.
3 Bring stock to boil in medium pan, lower heat. Gently spoon dumplings into simmering stock, cook until they float. Cover, simmer for 10 minutes. Divide dumplings between six soup bowls and pour 1/2 cup (4 fl oz) of chicken stock over each. Sprinkle with chopped parsley.

DUMPLINGS (BASIC RECIPE)

★

Preparation time: *5 minutes*
Total cooking time: *15–20 minutes*
Serves 4

1 cup self-raising flour
1/4 teaspoon salt
ground white pepper
1 egg, beaten
1/4 cup (2 fl oz) milk
30 g (1 oz) butter, or grated suet

1 Sift flour, salt and pepper into a bowl. Rub in butter until mixture resembles fine breadcrumbs. Combine egg and milk and add to flour, mixing to a soft dough.
2 Using lightly floured hands, shape dumplings into balls about 3 cm (1 1/4 inches) in diameter. About 20 minutes before stew or casserole is cooked, arrange dumplings in a layer on top, leaving space between them.
3 Cover and cook until dumplings are light and fluffy, about 15–20 minutes.
Note: If desired, dumplings can be steamed in a perforated steamer for 30–40 minutes.

HERB DUMPLINGS
Add 1 tablespoon chopped parsley and 1 teaspoon chopped thyme to basic dumpling recipe. Good with veal, chicken, beef or vegetable stews.

ZUCCHINI (COURGETTE) CHEESE DUMPLINGS
Add 1/4 cup grated zucchini (courgette) and 1 tablespoon grated parmesan cheese to basic dumpling recipe. Serve with chicken, lamb or beef stews.

ORANGE DUMPLINGS
Add 1 teaspoon finely grated orange rind and 2 teaspoons chopped parsley to basic dumpling recipe. Good with pork, veal or lamb stews.

HIGH FIBRE DUMPLINGS
Use wholemeal self-raising flour in basic dumpling recipe and add 1 tablespoon finely chopped chives to dry ingredients. Good with beef, lamb or vegetable stews.

BEEF GOULASH WITH CARAWAY DUMPLINGS

✷✷ **Preparation time:** 1 hour
Total cooking time: 1 hour 15 minutes
Serves 6

1.5 kg (3 lb) round or topside (top round) steak	1/4 teaspoon ground black pepper
1/3 cup (2 1/2 fl oz) red wine	1/3 cup (2 1/2 fl oz) olive oil
1/2 cup plain (all-purpose) flour	1 clove garlic, crushed
1/2 teaspoon dried mixed herbs	2 medium onions, sliced
2/3 cup (5 fl oz) bottled chunky tomato sauce	1 teaspoon ground sweet paprika
1 large red pepper (capsicum)	1/2 teaspoon ground cinnamon
	1/2 cup (4 fl oz) beef stock

Caraway Dumplings

1 1/2 cups self-raising flour
65 g (2 1/4 oz) butter
1/2 cup (4 fl oz) milk
1 teaspoon caraway seeds
1 tablespoon milk, extra

1 Preheat oven to moderate 180°C (350°F/Gas 4). Trim the meat and cut into 3 cm (1 1/4 inch) cubes. Combine flour and pepper on greaseproof paper. Toss meat in seasoned flour, shake off excess.

2 Heat 2 tablespoons of the oil in a heavy-based pan. Cook the meat quickly in small batches over medium-high heat until well browned; drain on paper towel.

3 Heat remaining oil. Add garlic and onion, stir over medium heat for 2 minutes or until soft.

4 Return meat to pan with spices, stock, wine, mixed herbs and tomato sauce; bring to boil. Remove from heat, transfer to a deep casserole dish. Cook, covered, for 45 minutes. Increase oven temperature to hot 240°C (475°F/Gas 9).

5 Cut pepper into halves lengthways; remove seeds. Place on cold, greased oven tray, skin side up. Place under a hot grill for 10 minutes or until skin burns and blisters. Remove and cool. Carefully peel off skins, discard. Cut pepper into 2 cm (3/4 inch) wide strips. Arrange over meat.

6 To make Caraway Dumplings: Place flour and butter in food processor. Process 10 seconds or until mixture is fine and crumbly. Add milk. Process 10 seconds or until mixture forms a soft dough. Turn onto lightly floured surface. Add caraway seeds, knead 1 minute or until smooth. Press out to 1 cm (1/2 inch) thickness. Cut into 4 cm (1 1/2 inch) rounds with a fluted cutter. Top meat with dumplings; brush with extra milk. Return to oven, cook, uncovered, 15 minutes or until dumplings are puffed and golden.

Note: Thickly sliced potatoes can be added to the goulash at Step 4 instead of dumplings, OR slice potatoes thinly and place, overlapping, over surface. Dab with small pieces of butter. Cook until golden and crisp.

---

the French and English to that of cheese. The flesh of the durian is eaten raw, as a dessert, either on its own or with sugar and cream or ice-cream. Chilling the fruit reduces its smell. In Java the durian is made into fruit jelly. The seeds can be roasted and eaten like nuts. Canned durian pulp is also available.

Durum Wheat A variety of wheat milled to produce semolina flour, a more durable flour than that used to make bread. It is ideal for pasta making. The wheat is noted for its extreme hardness and yellow colour.

Duxelles The French name for a mixture of mushrooms finely chopped with a little spring onion (scallion), then sautéed in butter until soft and dry. Duxelles add a strong mushroom flavour to stuffings, gravies and sauces and they can also be used as a garnish.

E

Eccles Cake A traditional English small cake of currants, chopped peel, brown sugar and spices encased in puff pastry. The cakes were originally made to sell during the Eccles Wakes, festival days once held in the Lancashire town of Eccles.

Eclair A finger-shaped bun made by piping lengths of choux pastry onto greased baking trays and baking them until crisp. The cooked pastry is split open and filled with cream or custard and topped with chocolate or coffee icing (frosting).

Edam A semi-hard cow's milk cheese of mellow flavour, made from a combination of full cream and skim milk. Edam is made in the shape of a sphere and coated in red wax. In Holland ripening cheeses are assessed by rapping knuckles.

EGGS

EGG, SALMON AND RICE PIE

★ ★ **Preparation time:** 50 minutes
Total cooking time: 1 hour
Serves 8

3/4 cup (6 fl oz) fish stock
1/4 cup short-grain rice
40 g (1 1/3 oz) butter
2 tablespoons plain (all purpose) flour
2/3 cup (5 fl oz) milk
1 egg, lightly beaten
1/4 cup finely chopped fresh parsley

2 x 200 g (6 1/2 oz) cans pink salmon, drained
4 hard-boiled eggs, quartered
1 egg, extra, lightly beaten
1/2 cup fresh or frozen peas
2 sheets ready-rolled puff pastry

1 Preheat oven to moderately hot 210°C (415°F/Gas 6–7). Line two oven trays with baking paper. Place stock in medium heavy-based pan. Bring to boil. Add rice, reduce heat. Simmer, covered, for 10 minutes or until rice has absorbed all the liquid. Remove from heat.

2 Heat butter in medium pan; add flour. Stir over low heat for 2 minutes or until flour is lightly golden. Add milk gradually to pan, stirring until mixture is smooth. Stir constantly over medium heat for 5 minutes or until mixture boils and thickens; boil for 1 minute, remove from heat. Cool slightly, stir in egg, parsley and peas.

3 Carefully lay pastry sheets on a work surface. Place salmon in small bowl, flake with a fork. Spread evenly in an oblong shape down centre of each pastry sheet, leaving a 3 cm (1 1/4 inch) gap on all sides. Place the quartered eggs on top.

4 Combine rice and pea mixture in medium bowl. Mix well. Spoon mixture evenly over salmon. Brush pastry edges with extra egg. Fold in edges like a parcel. Turn over and place on tray seam-side down. Make three diagonal slits in top of pie. Brush with egg. Bake for 30 minutes or until pastry is puffed and golden. Cut each pie into four to serve. Serve with fresh green salad.

ABOUT EGGS

■ Use eggs as quickly as possible after purchase (although eggs will last for up to five weeks); store in the carton in refrigerator with pointed ends downward. Discard eggs that are broken or cracked as they may be infected with harmful bacteria. In some countries, infants, pregnant women and the elderly are advised to avoid eating raw or lightly cooked eggs. This is because of the danger of salmonella. Dishes made with raw eggs (or almost raw eggs) such as mayonnaise, mousses or Caesar salad dressing should be eaten within two days.

■ White or brown eggs have the same nutritional value. The type of poultry feed causes variations in yolk colour; some say it also affects the taste.

■ For cooking, eggs should be at room temperature. Eggs separate more easily if fresh and cold; bring to room temperature after separating. Whites can be stored for up to a week and frozen for up to nine months. Unbroken yolks can be refrigerated for up to three days, covered with water in a small bowl.

ABOVE: EGG, SALMON AND RICE PIE. OPPOSITE PAGE: CREAMY EGGS WITH RED PEPPER

QUICK EGGS FLORENTINE

Tear 2 bunches spinach into pieces. Steam or microwave until tender. Combine spinach with 30 g (1 oz) butter, nutmeg and salt to taste. Divide into two ramekin dishes. Top each with a poached egg; sprinkle with grated cheddar cheese. Bake in a moderate oven 180°C (350°F/Gas 4) for 5–10 minutes until cheese melts and browns.

CREAMY EGGS WITH RED PEPPER

★ *Preparation time:* 10 minutes
Total cooking time: 10 minutes
Serves 4–6

1 tablespoon butter or olive oil
6 eggs
1/2 cup (4 fl oz) cream
freshly ground black pepper
chopped parsley or dill, optional
2 onions, sliced
2 small red peppers (capsicum)

1 Heat butter or oil in a heavy-based frying pan. Add onion and cook slowly until golden brown. Cut peppers into thin strips; add to pan and cook until soft.
2 Combine eggs, cream and pepper; beat well.
3 Pour mixture over onion and peppers. Stir gently until eggs are creamy and soft.
4 Serve immediately. Sprinkle with chopped parsley or dill if desired.

Note: Do not allow the mixture to overcook or the eggs will become tough and 'weep'.

TO SCRAMBLE EGGS

■ Whisk the required number of eggs in a bowl with a small amount (1 tablespoon per egg) of milk or cream. Melt 30 g (1 oz) of butter in a pan. Pour eggs into pan and stir over very low heat until eggs begin to thicken and bubble. (Add herbs or flavourings at this stage, but do not salt.) Remove from heat and continue stirring another minute. Serve immediately.

TO POACH EGGS

■ For best results, use eggs less than a week old. Half fill a shallow pan with cold water, bring to the boil over medium high heat then reduce heat slightly so water is just simmering. Break 1 egg into a cup, slip the egg into simmering water and slide the egg into the water by tilting the cup. Repeat with remaining eggs, allowing each an equal amount of space. Cover pan and cook for 3 minutes for soft eggs and up to 5 minutes for firmer ones. Remove pan from heat. Lift poached egg from water with slotted spoon or egg slice; rest spoon or slice on paper towel to remove any water. Transfer egg to a slice of hot toast.

HUEVOS RANCHEROS

★ *Preparation time:* 1 hour
Total cooking time: 35 minutes
Serves 6

2 small red peppers (capsicum), halved and seeded
1 medium green pepper (capsicum), finely chopped
2 teaspoons olive oil
2 teaspoons olive oil, extra
1 small onion, finely chopped
2 tablespoons tomato paste
1 teaspoon ground oregano
2 jalapeño chillies, finely chopped
6 x 15 cm (6 inch) tortillas
6 eggs, fried or poached
1/2 cup grated cheddar cheese

1 Brush small red peppers with oil. Grill for 12–15 minutes or until skin is black. Cover with damp tea-towel until cool; peel off the skin. Cut pepper flesh into small pieces and place in a food processor. Process for 30 seconds or until smooth. Set aside.
2 Heat extra oil in a medium pan. Add onion, tomato paste, oregano and green pepper. Cook until soft. Stir in red pepper puree and chillies. Heat gently, stirring for 1 minute.
3 To serve, place a fried or poached egg onto a tortilla. Top with a tablespoon of pepper sauce and sprinkle with grated cheddar cheese.

---

against the sphere (a dull thump is the sign of a well-cured cheese ready for eating).

Eel A long, snake-like fish with a smooth, slippery, olive green or silvery skin, found throughout the world. Most commonly eaten are freshwater varieties; saltwater eels are larger and include the moray and the conger. The eel has firm, white, fatty flesh which deteriorates rapidly and so must be cooked as quickly as possible after killing. For this reason, in many parts of the world, eels are kept in large tanks and sold live. Smoked eel is also available, and in Britain and northern Europe is a popular appetiser, served either in thin slices or as fillets lifted off the bone, dressed with lemon juice on a round of rye bread. The matchstick-thin, finger-length, transparent young are called elvers or glass eels and are a delicacy in parts of Italy, France and Belgium.

Egg A roundish reproductive body enclosed in a protective shell. Most commonly eaten by humans is the egg of the domestic hen, but duck, goose, quail, pheasant, guinea fowl, partridge, plover, ostrich and emu eggs are also used. In some parts of

the world the fish-flavoured, soft-skinned egg of the sea turtle is an important food. The egg is a highly nutritious and well-balanced package: two eggs provide half of the body's total daily protein and vitamin needs. The yolk, about 30 per cent of the total weight of the egg, contains more than 80 per cent of its protein.

Most eggs are from hens caged in large, temperature-controlled and artificially lit sheds. Free-range eggs are from birds with access to outside runs and are reckoned by many to have a better flavour. Eggs are best used as fresh as possible. Two simple, age-old methods of testing freshness are based on the fact that the little weight and moisture lost each day by evaporation through the porous shell is replaced by air in the sac at the round end of the egg. To assess the freshness of an egg either put it in a bowl of water (a fresh egg will sink to the bottom) or hold it up to a strong light (the larger the air sac the older the egg). Alternatively, a fresh egg broken onto a plate will have a well-rounded yolk centred in a thick, sticky white; in an older egg the white is runny and the yolk flattened.

EGGS VINDALOO

Preparation time: 25 minutes
Total cooking time: 30 minutes
Serves 4-6

8 eggs
1 teaspoon vinegar
3 tablespoons ghee or butter
1 large onion, coarsely grated
1 teaspoon mashed garlic
1/2 teaspoon grated ginger
1 green chilli, seeded and chopped

2 tablespoons vindaloo or other hot curry paste
3 tablespoons coconut cream
1/3 cup water
vegetable oil for deep frying
1 tablespoon chopped coriander or mint leaves
lemon juice

1 Boil the eggs in enough water to cover, with 1 teaspoon vinegar added, for 8-9 minutes. Remove to a large dish of cold water; when eggs have cooled, peel them and prick evenly all over with a fork. Dry well.

2 Melt the ghee or butter and cook onion, garlic, ginger and chilli until onions have softened and turned golden. Add the vindaloo or curry paste and cook over medium heat for another 2 minutes. Add the coconut cream and water. Cook, stirring, until sauce thickens.

3 Heat the oil and deep-fry the eggs until they turn golden on the surface. Transfer eggs to pan containing vindaloo mixture. Add coriander and lemon juice to taste and simmer in the sauce for 8-9 minutes. Serve with rice.

CARROT PARSNIP FRITTATA

Preparation time: 10 minutes
Total cooking time: 20 minutes
Serves 2-4

60 g (2 oz) butter
1 clove garlic, crushed
2 parsnips, peeled and grated
2 carrots, peeled and grated
4 eggs
3 tablespoons chopped flat-leaf parsley
freshly ground black pepper
2 teaspoons olive oil

1 Melt butter, add the garlic and fry for one minute without browning. Add the parsnip and carrot and cook gently with the lid on the pan for 10 minutes. Allow to cool.

2 Beat the eggs just enough to combine them. Add parsley and freshly ground black pepper and stir in the cooled parsnip and carrot.

3 Heat olive oil in an omelette pan or other small pan. Pour in the egg mixture to cover the base of the pan. Lift the edges of the frittata with a spatula to allow uncooked egg to run underneath. When the frittata is set on top, turn it over, or brown it under a hot grill. Serve frittata warm sprinkled with parsley if desired. Serve with a crisp green salad and slices of crusty French bread.

Note: For extra flavour, freshly grated cheddar or parmesan cheese can be added to the frittata. Stir in with the parsnip and carrot or sprinkle on top before grilling. This recipe makes a delicious, light main meal.

LEFT: EGGS VINDALOO; ABOVE: CARROT PARSNIP FRITTATA. OPPOSITE PAGE: SCOTCH EGGS

EGGS

Other eggs besides that of the hen are also used. The more richly flavoured duck egg is eaten in England, Holland and Belgium and in parts of Asia. The famous 'thousand-year' or 'hundred-year' eggs of China are usually raw duck eggs, kept for several months buried in

a mixture of salt, lime, ash and tea leaves until the shell is marbled black, the white firm and pale brown, and the yolk green-veined with a texture of creamy cheese.

The Egyptians ate both ostrich (a single ostrich egg, about twenty times the size of a hen egg, can make an omelette for ten people) and pelican eggs. Peahen eggs were eaten in ancient Rome. In modern times pheasant, quail, partridge and plover eggs are used hard-boiled in salads, pickled in brine or preserved in aspic. Many rites and

traditions are associated with the egg. From the time of ancient Rome eggshells were crushed to prevent evil spirits from hiding in them. The egg

---

SCOTCH EGGS

✳ **Preparation time:** 15 minutes
Total cooking time: 8 minutes
Makes 4

4 hard-boiled eggs
250 g (8 oz) sausage
mince
1 small onion, grated
2 tablespoons dried
breadcrumbs
1 egg, separated

1 tablespoon chopped
fresh parsley
salt and pepper
pinch nutmeg
1/2 cup dried breadcrumbs,
extra
oil for deep-frying

1 Remove shells from eggs. Place mince, onion, breadcrumbs, egg yolk, parsley, salt, pepper and nutmeg in a medium bowl. Stir to combine. Divide mixture into four. Using wet hands, press one portion of mince, large enough to cover egg, into palm of hand. Press around egg to enclose. Repeat with remaining mince and eggs.

2 Coat Scotch Eggs in lightly beaten egg white, then coat with breadcrumbs.

3 Heat oil in a heavy-based pan. Lower eggs into oil, cook over medium heat for 8 minutes until golden and crisp. Remove from oil. Drain.

EGGS BENEDICT

✳ **Preparation time:** 10 minutes
Total cooking time: 10 minutes
Serves 2

**Quick Hollandaise
Sauce**
125 g (4 oz) butter
4 egg yolks
3 teaspoons lemon juice
cayenne pepper to taste

Ham and Eggs
30 g (1 oz) butter
4 thick slices leg ham
2 English muffins
4 eggs
2 teaspoons red caviar
(optional)

1 To make Sauce: Heat butter slowly in pan until it begins to bubble. Place egg yolks, lemon juice and cayenne in electric blender, blend for 5 seconds. Slowly pour hot butter onto yolk mixture in a steady stream until it is all added. Transfer sauce to a bowl, cover and keep warm.

2 Melt butter in a pan and heat ham slices through. Split muffins, toast, then place a slice of ham on each muffin half. Keep muffins warm.

3 Poach eggs, drain, place one on each ham slice.

4 Spoon warm Hollandaise Sauce over the eggs. Garnish with red caviar and serve.

Eggplant (Aubergine) A fruit used as a vegetable with smooth, shiny, purple skin and creamy white, pithy flesh studded with numerous tiny, soft, pale brown edible seeds. It may be egg-shaped (from which it takes its common name), round, or long and thin; some varieties are white-skinned. The eggplant originated in South-East Asia, where varieties still grow wild, and in antiquity was cultivated in India, China and Turkey. By the fifteenth century it was known in Italy and by the seventeenth century had reached France. The eggplant is widely used in Mediterranean cookery and in the Middle East, particularly by the Syrians and Turks. It can be steamed, boiled, grilled

Egg Noodle A type of pasta made from wheat flour, egg and water and cut into long strips.

has long been a symbol of fertility and renewal. The brightly wrapped Easter egg of modern times has its origins in the coloured eggs that were a feature of spring festivals of medieval Europe.

CLASSIC SOUFFLE OMELETTE

★ *Preparation time:* 5 minutes
Total cooking time: 10 minutes
Serves 2

4 eggs, separated
salt and freshly ground
pepper
1 tablespoon milk or
cream
30 g (1 oz) butter

1 Beat egg yolks in medium bowl until thick. Add milk or cream, salt and pepper. Whisk whites in medium bowl with electric beaters until soft peaks form. Fold whites into yolk mixture.
2 Heat butter in pan until it covers base of pan and foams. Pour in omelette mixture and cook over medium heat until base of omelette sets and it turns lightly golden underneath.
3 Cook top of omelette under a hot grill until puffed and lightly golden, or bake in a moderate oven 180°C (350°F/Gas 4) for 5 minutes. Souffle omelette is usually served flat, not folded.

Note: For a sweet soufflé omelette, omit salt and pepper; add 1 tablespoon of caster (superfine) sugar to egg yolks before beating.

CLASSIC FRENCH OMELETTE

★ *Preparation time:* 2 minutes (unfilled)
Total cooking time: 1 minute
Serves 1

3 eggs
freshly ground pepper
salt
1 tablespoon water
30 g (1 oz) butter

1 Beat eggs in small bowl until yolks and whites are just combined. Stir in water, salt and pepper.
2 Heat butter in a pan until it covers base of pan and foams. Pour eggs into pan. Over moderate heat, draw outside edges of mixture into centre with a spatula until eggs are lightly set.
3 Add a hot prepared filling if desired. Tilt the pan away from you so that the omelette can be folded or rolled easily. Carefully tip omelette onto a warmed plate. Serve.

Note: Use 2 eggs for each filled omelette and 3 eggs for each plain omelette. Suitable fillings would include grated cheese, chopped ham, cooked asparagus, mushrooms or seafood.

CLASSIC SOUFFLE OMELETTE (RIGHT); CLASSIC FRENCH OMELETTE (LEFT)

(broiled), sautéed or stuffed, added to salads or made into dips. It is the basic ingredient in classic dishes such as the French ratatouille and the Greek moussaka.

Eggs Benedict A dish consisting of a poached egg, a slice of ham and a dollop of Hollandaise sauce, all perched on an English muffin.

Eggs Florentine A light luncheon dish consisting of two soft poached eggs in a nest of cooked spinach topped with mornay sauce and grated cheese.

Emmenthal A hard, pale yellow, cow's milk cheese, with a mild, nutty flavour. Made in huge, flat wheels and with characteristic, large, regularly spaced, spherical holes, it is the cheese most identified with Switzerland.

Empanada A pie or pastry shell filled with meat or fish. The dish originated in Spain where empanadas are now usually made with flaky pastry and are often eaten cold. The dish is now also popular in parts of Central and South America, where it often features a spicy meat filling and is served hot as an appetiser.

Enchilada A dish of Mexican origin consisting of a corn or wheat flour tortilla, dipped in a chilli and tomato sauce, wrapped around a meat, vegetable or cheese filling and then topped with more sauce. In Mexico they are sometimes served at breakfast. The name comes from *enchilar*, to cover, wrap or coat with chilli.

Endive, Belgian Also known as chicory (in England and some other parts of Europe) and witloof (in Belgium and Australia), Belgian endive (*Cichorium intybus*) is a vegetable with compact, cone-shaped heads of long, pale leaves which are eaten cooked (steamed or boiled) or raw (either whole leaves or thinly sliced) as a salad vegetable. See also Chicory.

Endive, Curly Curly endive (*Cichorium endivia*) is a salad vegetable with frilly, dark green leaves and a mildly bitter taste. It is a native of the

EGGPLANT (AUBERGINE)

EGGPLANT (AUBERGINE) AND CORIANDER SALAD

★★

Preparation time: 25 minutes
Total cooking time: 6 minutes
Serves 6

2 small eggplant
(aubergine), halved
lengthways
salt
3 small zucchini
(courgettes)
2 tablespoons olive oil
1/2 cup chopped fresh
coriander
1 tablespoon lemon juice
1 tablespoon orange juice
1/2 teaspoon ground
pepper

1 Cut the eggplant into thin slices. Place in a colander and sprinkle with salt. Allow to stand for 15–20 minutes.

2 Using a vegetable peeler, cut zucchini lengthways into thin slices. Wash eggplant and pat dry with paper towels. Brush both sides of eggplant lightly with olive oil and place on a baking tray. Cook under preheated grill or until lightly browned on both sides. Remove and allow to cool.

3 Place the eggplant, zucchini, oil, coriander, juices and pepper in a bowl and toss to combine. Serve the salad as a first course or as a side salad to a main meal.

ABOVE: EGGPLANT AND CORIANDER SALAD.
OPPOSITE PAGE: CHELSEA BUNS

STUFFED WHOLE EGGPLANT (AUBERGINE)

★

Preparation time: 15 minutes +
30 minutes standing
Total cooking time: 1 hour
Serves 6

3 small to medium
eggplant (aubergine)
1 tablespoon salt
2 tablespoons chopped
fresh parsley
2 cloves garlic, crushed
2–3 tablespoons lemon
juice
3 medium onions, thinly
sliced
4 ripe tomatoes, chopped
freshly ground black
pepper
1/2 cup (4 fl oz) olive oil
1/2 teaspoon sugar
1/3 cup (2 1/2 fl oz) water

1 Cut stems from eggplant and cut in half lengthways. Cut a long deep slit into each half, leaving 1.5 cm (5/8 inch) at each end. Sprinkle eggplant with salt and stand in a bowl of iced water for 30 minutes. Drain and squeeze dry with paper towels.

2 Heat half the oil in a frying pan and cook the garlic and onions over medium heat for 5 minutes or until onions are soft. In a small bowl, combine onion and garlic mixture with tomato, pepper, and parsley. Mix well.

3 Preheat oven to moderately slow 160°C (325°F/Gas 3). Heat the remaining oil in pan. Cook the eggplant over medium heat until lightly browned.

4 Remove from pan and place in an ovenproof dish. Spoon onion mixture into slits. Add combined lemon juice, sugar and water to dish. Cover; bake 45–50 minutes, basting occasionally with pan juices. To serve, sprinkle with parsley; spoon cooking juices over top of eggplant.

ABOUT EGGPLANT (AUBERGINE)

■ Choose firm eggplant, heavy for their size, with a uniform, deep aubergine colour. Wilted or shrivelled fruit will be bitter and poorly flavoured.

■ The bitter juices of the eggplant are generally 'degorged' or extracted before the flesh is used in cooking. Cut off the stem end, slice or cube the flesh, place in a colander, sprinkle with salt and stand for 15–30 minutes. Rinse eggplant well and dry with paper towels before use.

■ Sliced degorged eggplant make a crunchy side vegetable if coated in flour and fried in olive oil.

■ There are small varieties of eggplant which are less bitter and do not need degorging.

ENGLISH CLASSICS

CHELSEA BUNS

★★ **Preparation time:** 35 minutes
Total cooking time: 30–35 minutes
Makes 12

2 cups self-raising flour
1 tablespoon soft brown sugar
1/4 cup caster (superfine) sugar
1 cup dried mixed fruit
30 g (1 oz) butter, chopped
1/3 cup (2 1/2 fl oz) milk
1 egg

Glaze
1/4 cup sugar
1/4 cup (2 fl oz) water

Filling
30 g (1 oz) butter, softened
1 teaspoon ground mixed spice

1 Preheat oven to moderately hot 210°C (415°F/Gas 6–7). Brush a 20 cm (8 inch) square cake tin with oil or melted butter. Line base of tin with baking paper. Sift flour and sugar into a bowl; add chopped butter. Using your fingertips, rub butter into flour until the mixture is fine and crumbly.

2 Whisk milk and egg together, pour onto sifted ingredients and mix to form a soft dough. Turn onto a sheet of baking paper and roll into a rectangle 35 x 22 cm (14 x 8 3/4 inch).

3 Spread the dough with softened butter, sprinkle with sugar, mixed fruit and mixed spice. Roll up to make a long roll; cut into 12 evenly-sized pieces. Place pieces in prepared tin with sides touching. Reduce oven temperature to moderate 180°C (350°F/Gas 4). Bake 25–30 minutes until brown and cooked through. Remove; place on wire cooling rack.

4 **To make Glaze:** Place sugar and water in a small pan. Stir over medium heat without boiling until sugar dissolves. Bring to the boil and boil without stirring for 2–3 minutes. Remove pan from heat and brush Glaze over the buns while still warm. When ready to serve, split bun and serve with butter if desired.

CORNISH PASTIES

★ **Preparation time:** 30 minutes + 30 minutes refrigeration
Total cooking time: 50 minutes
Makes 6 pasties

Shortcrust Pastry
2 1/2 cups plain (all-purpose) flour
125 g (4 oz) butter, chopped
1/2 teaspoon dry mustard
1–3 tablespoons water

Filling
250 g (8 oz) round or blade steak, finely chopped
2 small old potatoes, peeled, finely chopped
1 medium brown onion, peeled and finely chopped
1/4 cup chopped fresh parsley
1/4 cup (2 fl oz) beef or chicken stock
white pepper
salt to taste
1/4 teaspoon English mustard
1 teaspoon grated horseradish
beaten egg to glaze

1 Brush baking tray with oil or melted butter. Place flour, mustard and butter in food processor. Process until mixture is fine and crumbly. Add almost all the water, process 20 seconds or until mixture comes together; add more water if needed. Remove pastry, form into a ball, cover with plastic wrap; refrigerate 30 minutes.

2 **To make Filling:** Combine steak, potatoes, onion and parsley. Add stock and season with pepper, salt, mustard and horseradish. Mix well.

3 Preheat oven to moderately hot 210°C (415°F/Gas 6–7). Roll pastry out to 5 mm (1/8 inch) thickness. Cut out six circles, 16 cm (6 1/2 inch) in diameter, using a saucer as a guide. Divide filling between circles, placing in centre of each.

4 Glaze edge of circle with egg and bring two sides together to form a half circle. Pinch edge to form a frill. Brush with egg and place on a baking tray in preheated oven for 10 minutes. Reduce heat to moderate 180°C (350°F/Gas 4) and cook for another 40 minutes. Serve hot.

English Food The food of England has a reputation for being stodgy and uninteresting, but the best English food is peerless. Poached salmon with cucumber salad and mayonnaise, steak and kidney pie, baked ham, summer pudding and chelsea buns are a few examples. An 'English breakfast' has always meant bacon and eggs with grilled tomato, and perhaps sausage or kippers, with toast and marmalade and a cup of tea. The ploughman's lunch, another famous English meal, consists of good country bread, a piece of cheddar or local cheese, and some pickled onions. Tea is an English institution and usually takes place at 4 pm. A 'proper' tea starts with bread and butter and homemade jam, or little sandwiches. A fruitcake or rich gateau, an iced teacake, or little iced cakes.

Mediterranean. It can be used in salads in the same way as lettuce, or cooked like spinach. In the United States and France curly endive is called chicory (the term used in England and some other parts of Europe for the cone-shaped, pale-leaved winter vegetable also known as Belgian endive and witloof).

SHEPHERD'S PIE

⭐ **Preparation time:** 15 minutes
Total cooking time: 1 hour

Serves 6

750 g (1¹/₂ lb) lean cooked roast lamb	¹/₂ teaspoon ground pepper
25 g (³/₄ oz) dripping or butter	salt to taste
2 medium brown onions, thinly sliced	2 tablespoons worcestershire sauce
¹/₄ cup plain (all-purpose) flour	**Potato Topping**
¹/₂ teaspoon dry mustard	4 large old potatoes, cooked and mashed
1¹/₂ cups (12 fl oz) chicken stock	¹/₄–¹/₃ cup (2–2¹/₂ fl oz) hot milk
¹/₄ cup chopped fresh mint	30 g (1 oz) butter
¹/₄ cup chopped fresh parsley	salt and pepper to taste

1 Brush an 8-cup capacity casserole with melted butter or oil. Preheat oven to moderately hot 210°C (415°F/Gas 6–7). Trim meat and cut into small cubes, or mince. Melt dripping or butter in a large pan. Add onions and cook until golden.

2 Sprinkle in the flour and mustard. Gradually add stock and blend, stirring until smooth. Bring gravy to boil, reduce heat, simmer for 3 minutes. Stir though meat, mint, parsley, pepper, salt and sauce. Remove from heat and spoon into dish.

3 To make Potato Topping: Combine potato, milk, butter, salt and pepper. Mix until smooth and creamy. Spread evenly over meat; rough up the surface with fork. Bake for 40–45 minutes until pie is heated through and potato topping is golden.

BANGERS AND MASH

⭐ **Preparation time:** 25 minutes
Total cooking time: 25 minutes

Serves 4

8 thick sausages	**Mash**
1 tablespoon oil	4 medium potatoes
2 medium onions, sliced	2 tablespoons milk
2 tablespoons gravy powder	30 g (1 oz) butter
1¹/₂ cups (12 fl oz) water	salt and pepper
	finely chopped parsley, for garnish

1 Prick the sausages with a fork. Heat oil in a large heavy-based frying pan; add sausages. Cook over medium heat for 10 minutes until sausages are brown and cooked through. Transfer to a plate covered with paper towel.

2 Pour off most of the fat from pan, leaving about a tablespoonful. Add onions and cook over a medium heat for 5 minutes until soft and golden.

3 Combine gravy powder with water in a jug, stir until smooth. Add to pan, stir to combine with onions. Stir gravy constantly over a medium low heat for 2 minutes or until mixture boils and thickens. Return sausages to pan. Combine with gravy and serve immediately with mash.

4 To make Mash: Cook potatoes in large pan of boiling water until tender; drain well. Mash with a potato masher until free from lumps. Add milk and butter, blend with a fork until smooth and creamy. Add salt and pepper to taste. Sprinkle parsley over potatoes to serve, and accompany with a green vegetable, such as beans or peas.

---

may also be served, with plenty of hot tea. Nowadays, eating a 'proper' tea would probably eliminate the need for dinner. The English dinner often starts with soup, followed by a main course of meat or fish with vegetables, a dessert and then cheese. (The English, in contrast to the French, eat cheese at the end of the meal, rather than before the dessert.) A 'savoury'—anchovy toast or devils on horseback— often finishes a meal, although they are generally only offered nowadays at old-fashioned clubs.

English Muffin A round, flat, unsweetened yeast bun served split and toasted, buttered and spread with jam or honey or a savoury topping.

Entrecôte A piece of beef from between the ribs, a tender and flavoursome cut.

Entrée Generally regarded as the first course of a meal, traditionally a dish served with sauce. In the United States the term refers to the main course of a meal.

OPPOSITE PAGE, ABOVE: BANGERS AND MASH;
BELOW: SHEPHERD'S PIE. ABOVE: ECCLES CAKES

SPOTTED DICK

✳ ✳

Preparation time: *15 minutes*
Total cooking time: *2½ hours*
Serves 4

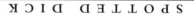

1⅓ cups plain (all-purpose) flour	¾ cup currants
1½ teaspoons baking powder	125 g (4 oz) shredded suet
½ cup sugar	2 teaspoons finely grated lemon rind
1½ teaspoons ground ginger	2 eggs, lightly beaten
2 cups soft breadcrumbs	1 cup (8 fl oz) milk
½ cup sultanas	custard or cream to serve

1 Brush a 1.5 litre (2½ pint) capacity pudding steamer with oil or melted butter. Line the base with baking paper; grease paper. Grease a large sheet of aluminium foil and a large sheet of greaseproof paper. Lay paper over foil, greased side up, and pleat in centre. Sift flour, baking powder, sugar and ginger into a bowl. Add breadcrumbs, fruit, suet and rind. Mix well with a wooden spoon.
2 Combine egg and milk, add to dry ingredients, mix well. Spoon into pudding steamer. Cover with foil and paper, greased side down. Place lid over foil, bring clips up, secure firmly with string.
3 If you have no lid, lay pleated tea-towel over foil, tie firmly with string under basin lip. Knot tea-towel ends, forming a handle to lower basin into pan.
4 Place basin on a trivet in a large, deep pan. Carefully pour boiling water down side of pan to come halfway up side of basin. Bring to boil, cover and cook for 2½ hours. Do not allow to boil dry—replenish with boiling water as pudding cooks. Unmould onto a serving plate, slice and serve with warm custard or cream.

ECCLES CAKES

✳

Preparation time: *20 minutes*
Total cooking time: *15–20 minutes*
Makes 27

1 cup currants	1 tablespoon sugar
½ cup mixed peel	1 tablespoon brandy
3 sheets ready-rolled puff pastry	½ teaspoon ground cinnamon
1 egg white	2 teaspoons sugar, extra

1 Preheat oven to moderately hot 210°C (415°F/Gas 6–7). Brush 2 oven trays with melted butter. Combine currants, peel, brandy, cinnamon and sugar in a bowl.
2 Cut nine 8 cm (3 inch) circles from each sheet of pastry. Place 2 level teaspoons filling on each circle. Bring edges together, pinch; turn seam side down, roll out to 1 cm (½ inch) thick rounds.
3 Place cakes on trays. Brush with egg white, sprinkle with sugar. Make 3 slashes across top of each cake. Bake for 15–20 minutes, until golden.

Note: Use home-made puff pastry for even better eccles cakes.

Escabèche A spicy marinade used to preserve fish.

Escalope A thin piece of boneless white meat, usually from veal or pork. Slices are beaten until thin, then usually coated with breadcrumbs before frying. Known in Italy as scallopine, and in Germany as schnitzel.

Escargot The French name for snail.

Escarole A vegetable with long, flat, irregularly shaped, pale green leaves. It has a slightly bitter taste and is used either in salads, mixed with milder-flavoured lettuces; warmed and served in wilted salads, or as a cooked vegetable. It is part of the endive family and is also known as broadleaf endive and Batavian endive.

Espagnole, Sauce Another name for brown sauce. See SAUCES for recipe.

Espresso Coffee Made by forcing steam under pressure through finely-ground coffee beans; served in small cups.

Estouffade A dish which is slowly stewed, most usually applied to beef in wine sauce. The name is also used for beef stock.

FENNEL

F

Falafel Deep-fried balls of ground and spiced chick pea, a snack of Middle Eastern origin.

Feijoa An oval, green-skinned, egg-sized tropical fruit. The pale yellow flesh is similar in flavour to a mixture of pineapple and strawberry. Sometimes called pineapple guava, the feijoa is now cultivated in New Zealand, California and Australia. It can be eaten raw (when fully ripe), scooped from the skin with a teaspoon or served with cheese boards; poached for use in fruit salads; or used to make jellies, jams and sorbets.

Fennel A tall, feathery, aromatic plant; its finely divided, blue-green leaves have a slightly bitter anise taste and are similar in appearance to dill. Fresh leaves can be used as a stuffing for baked fish, or wrapped around seafood to be grilled (broiled), or

CRUNCHY FENNEL SALAD

✶ **Preparation time:** 15 minutes
Total cooking time: 3 minutes
Serves 4

4 thin slices prosciutto
1 bunch spinach
1 medium fennel bulb
2 oranges, peeled and segmented
1 tablespoon finely chopped chives
1/4 cup chopped walnuts

Dressing
1/2 cup (4 fl oz) olive oil
2 tablespoons orange juice
2 teaspoons seeded mustard
freshly ground pepper

1 Cook prosciutto in a heated dry pan or grill until crisp. Cool and crumble coarsely. Set aside.

2 Remove green tops and outer stems from fennel. Trim top and base; cut bulb in quarters and slice thinly across ribs. Wash spinach well, dry thoroughly and tear into bite-size pieces.

3 Place fennel, spinach, orange segments, chives and walnuts in a large bowl. Add dressing and toss ingredients lightly to combine. Transfer to a salad bowl and sprinkle with crumbled prosciutto. Serve salad immediately.

4 **To make Dressing:** Whisk all ingredients in a small bowl until combined.

ABOVE: CRUNCHY FENNEL SALAD;
RIGHT: CREAMED FENNEL SOUP.
OPPOSITE PAGE: BAKED FENNEL PARMESAN

CREAMED FENNEL SOUP

✶ **Preparation time:** 10 minutes
Total cooking time: 20–25 minutes
Serves 4

1 medium fennel bulb
60 g (2 oz) butter
2 medium potatoes, peeled and chopped
2 cups (16 fl oz) chicken stock
salt
freshly ground black pepper
125 g (4 oz) cream cheese, chopped
1 tablespoon chopped fresh chives
1 tablespoon lemon juice

1 Trim and slice fennel. Heat butter in a medium pan; add fennel. Cook, covered, over low heat for 10 minutes, stirring occasionally. Do not allow fennel to colour. Add potatoes and stock to pan, stir. Bring to boil, reduce heat to low. Cover and cook 10 minutes or until vegetables are tender. Season to taste. Remove from heat; cool slightly.

2 Transfer mixture to a food processor; add cheese. Process until mixture is smooth and creamy. Return soup to pan. Add chives and juice, stir over low heat until just heated through. Soup can be made one day ahead. Store in refrigerator.

ABOUT FENNEL

■ The principal edible part of the fennel is the white bulb at the base of the green stem. The bulb should be crisp and white; trim the base and separate the sections and slice each section before use. Use the bulb as you would celery. It has a slight aniseed flavour and is delicious in salads, stir-fries and soups, or you can simply braise or steam and serve it with butter and freshly ground black pepper. The leafy foliage can be finely chopped and used to garnish and flavour dishes; trim away any tough stalks.

Fettuccine Pasta cut into long flat ribbons. It can be made at home from an egg-rich pasta dough or bought fresh, frozen or dried. Sometimes coloured and flavoured with

Feta A soft, white, crumbly cheese originally made from ewe's or goat's milk, but now often made from cow's milk. Feta has been known in Greece since ancient times, and was probably first made by shepherds in the mountain regions outside Athens. It is an important ingredient in Greek salads and savoury pastries.

Fenugreek A small plant of the pea family. Its tiny, squarish, brown, aromatic seeds have a spicy, slightly bitter flavour; they are very hard and can only be ground with a mortar and pestle or a special grinder. Lightly roasted and powdered, they are an essential ingredient in curry powders and pastes.

added to court bouillon. Chopped leaves are used in sauces, stuffings, dressings and seafood salads. The small brown seeds, also tasting of anise, are also used.

BAKED FENNEL PARMESAN

✦ **Preparation time:** 15 minutes
Total cooking time: 20–25 minutes
Serves 4

2 medium fennel bulbs
freshly ground black pepper
45 g (1 1/2 oz) butter
1 clove garlic, crushed
1/2 cup freshly grated parmesan cheese

2 tomatoes, peeled, seeded and chopped
2 tablespoons black pitted olives, sliced
2 teaspoons chopped fresh oregano

1 Preheat oven to moderate 180°C (350°F/Gas 4). Remove green tops and outer stems from fennel. Trim bulbs at the top and base. Cut each bulb in half and slice across ribs.

2 Cook fennel in boiling water for about 7 minutes and drain. Combine with tomatoes, olives, oregano and pepper. Place in a shallow heatproof dish.

3 Melt butter in a small pan and cook garlic gently for 30 seconds. Spoon garlic butter over fennel and top with cheese. Bake for 15–20 minutes until top is golden.

FISH BARBECUED WITH FENNEL

✦ **Preparation time:** 10 minutes + 1 hour marinade
Total cooking time: 8–10 minutes
Serves 4

4 white-fleshed whole fish
large bunch fresh fennel stalks
juice of 1 lemon
4 tablespoons cognac or brandy
salt and freshly ground black pepper to taste
2 cloves garlic, crushed

Marinade
1/2 cup (4 fl oz) olive oil

1 Scale, gut and clean fish. Score fish on each side. Place one fennel stalk inside each fish.

2 Combine marinade ingredients. Place fish in shallow dish, pour over marinade, cover and refrigerate for 1 hour. Dry remaining fennel stalks in a slow oven at 100°C (200°F/Gas 1/4). Place fennel on hot barbecue. Place fish and marinade in foil, with ends folded up to form a boat, on top of the fennel on the barbecue. Cook for 5 minutes each side or until the fish flakes easily when tested. The fennel will burn, giving an aromatic taste to the fish.

Varieties of fig tree grow in warm climates throughout the world. Fig is the sweetest of all fruits. When in season, in summer, it is served raw wrapped in prosciutto slices as a first course, in fruit salad, on cheese boards or baked as a dessert. The dried fruit, its sugar concentrated and sweetness intensified by the preservation process, can be stewed or used in cakes and puddings. The fig probably originated in the Middle East, where it has been eaten for 5,000 years or more. Figs were grown in the hanging gardens of Babylon; ripe figs were covered with hot desert sands to dry and preserve

Fig A small, soft, pear-shaped fruit with sweet, pulpy flesh studded with small, edible seeds.

tomato or spinach, fettuccine is especially identified with Rome and the surrounding region; its name is the Roman word for 'noodles'.

FIGS

STICKY FIG PUDDING WITH QUICK BRANDY CUSTARD

★★

Preparation time: 15 minutes
Total cooking time: 1 hour 35 minutes
Serves 8

1½ cups self-raising flour
¾ cup plain (all-purpose) flour
2 teaspoons mixed spice
½ teaspoon bicarbonate of soda (baking soda)
¼ cup powdered milk
1 cup dried figs, chopped
¾ cup (6 fl oz) water
2 eggs, lightly beaten

Quick Brandy Custard
2½ cups (20 fl oz) prepared custard
1¼ cups (10 fl oz) cream
¼ cup (2 fl oz) brandy

¾ cup soft brown sugar
150 g (5 oz) butter

1 Brush a 21 cm (8½ inch), 8-cup capacity pudding basin or steamer with oil or melted butter. Line base with paper, grease paper. Grease a large sheet of aluminium foil and a large sheet of greaseproof paper. Lay the paper over the foil, greased side up, and pleat in the centre. Set aside.
2 Sift the flours with the remaining dry ingredients into a large mixing bowl. Make a well in the centre. Combine butter, sugar, figs and water in a small pan. Stir over low heat until butter has melted and sugar has dissolved.
3 Add butter mixture and eggs to dry ingredients. Stir until just combined—do not overbeat mixture.

---

4 Spoon mixture into the prepared basin. Cover with the greased foil and paper, greased side down. Place lid over foil and secure clips. If the pudding basin has no lid, lay a pleated tea-towel over the foil and tie it securely with string under the lip of the basin. Knot the four ends of the tea-towel together to make a handle for lowering the basin into the pan.
5 Place the basin on a trivet in a large, deep pan. Carefully pour boiling water down the side of the pan to come halfway up the side of the basin. Bring to the boil, cover, cook for 1½ hours. Do not let the pudding boil dry. Remove covering, invert onto a plate. Serve warm with Quick Brandy Custard.
6 To make Quick Brandy Custard: Place all the ingredients in a small pan. Stir over a low heat until warmed through. Do not allow the mixture to boil.

ABOUT FIGS

■ Choose fresh figs that are fully coloured and firm with no skin breaks. They should be sweet-smelling with no sign of sweating or sour odour (this suggests over-ripeness). Figs range in colour from greenish yellow to purple/black. They are extremely perishable and should be stored in the refrigerator. Guard against any bruising from other produce, and enjoy them as soon as possible. Eat figs fresh, lightly poach them, or cut in half, sprinkle with sugar and briefly place under a hot grill.

them. Dried figs were sold in the markets of Paris from the fourteenth century.

Filé Powder The ground dried leaves of the sassafras shrub used in Cajun cooking as a thickener and to add a thyme-like flavour to gumbos. Filé should not be cooked in the pot (as it will turn stringy), but added at the table or just before serving.

Filet Mignon A small, tender steak cut from the narrow end of a fillet of beef. It is often cut thick and then gently beaten to the required thickness and width. The name comes from the French for 'little fillet'.

Fillet A piece of boneless meat, poultry or fish, with little or no fat. Beef fillet, also known as tenderloin, is prized for its tenderness and delicate flavour. A chicken fillet is the small strip of flesh near the breast bone. A fish fillet is the side of the fish cut along the length of the body; it contains few if any bones.

Filo Pastry Also known as phyllo, pastry made with a dough of high-gluten flour, water and oil that is stretched until tissue-thin, then cut into sheets. Filo is widely used in the cooking of

FIGS IN SYRUP

✳ **Preparation time:** 30 minutes +
3 hours soaking
Total cooking time: 25 minutes
Serves 6

500 g (1 lb) dried figs
3 cups (24 fl oz) cold tea
3/4 cup sugar
1 1/2 cups (12 fl oz) water
1 whole cinnamon stick
thin strip orange rind
1/4 cup honey
1/2 cup (4 fl oz) orange juice
1/3 cup slivered almonds
200 g (6 1/2 fl oz) plain yoghurt
1 teaspoon orange flower water

1 Wash figs, cover with cold tea and leave to soak for 3 hours. Remove figs and discard tea.
2 Heat sugar, water and orange juice in heavy-based saucepan, stirring occasionally until sugar has dissolved. Add honey, orange rind and cinnamon stick. Bring to the boil.
3 Add figs, boil gently for 5 minutes. Reduce heat and simmer uncovered 20 minutes until figs are tender and syrup is reduced. For a thicker syrup, remove figs and allow syrup to cook longer. Remove orange rind and cinnamon stick. Stir in orange flower water.
4 Pour syrup over figs in serving bowl, sprinkle with almonds and serve with yoghurt.

OPPOSITE PAGE: STICKY FIG PUDDING WITH QUICK BRANDY CUSTARD. ABOVE: FIGS IN SYRUP

FIG AND PROSCIUTTO SALAD

Cut 4 fresh figs in halves, wrap each half in a thin slice of prosciutto. Arrange 2 halves per person on serving plates on a bed of rocket (arugula) leaves. Sprinkle with ground black pepper and drizzle with virgin olive oil and balsamic vinegar. Serves 4.

SPICED FIGS AND ORANGES

Combine 1 cup (8 fl oz) orange juice, 1/4 cup sugar and 1/2 teaspoon mixed spice in pan, bring to boil. Simmer 3 minutes; cool. Slice 6 fresh, unpeeled figs and 4 peeled oranges. Place in serving dish, pour syrup over. Chill 1 hour. Sprinkle with 1 tablespoon pine nuts. Serves 4.

FIGS WITH RICOTTA

Combine 1 cup ricotta cheese with 1 tablespoon finely chopped mixed peel, 1 tablespoon chopped ginger and 1/4 cup chopped toasted almonds. Cut 4–5 fresh figs into halves and arrange around ricotta. Serves 4.

FILO PASTRY

SWEET CUSTARD ROLLS

★★ **Preparation time:** 15 minutes +
10 minutes standing
Total cooking time: 50 minutes
Serves 6-8

1 lemon
3 cups (24 fl oz) milk
1/2 cup coarse semolina
1/4 cup rice flour
2/3 cup caster (superfine) sugar
2 eggs, lightly beaten
1 teaspoon vanilla essence

14 sheets filo pastry
2 tablespoons unsalted (sweet) butter, melted
1 tablespoon oil
2 tablespoons icing (confectioners) sugar
1/2 teaspoon ground cinnamon

1 Preheat oven to moderate 180°C (350°F/Gas 4). Grease a 32 x 28 cm (13 x 11 inch) oven tray. Peel lemon rind into three strips 1 x 5 cm (1/2 x 2 inches) long. Combine rind with milk in small heavy-based pan. Stir over low heat until almost boiling. Reduce heat and simmer, covered, for 10 minutes. Remove pan from heat, leave to cool for 10 minutes. Remove peel.

2 Using electric beaters, beat semolina, rice flour, sugar and eggs on low speed 2 minutes or until smooth. Add milk gradually, beating thoroughly after each addition. Return mixture to pan. Stir over medium heat 10 minutes or until mixture boils and thickens. Remove and stir in essence.

3 Cover surface of custard with plastic wrap to prevent skin forming; cool. Place filo sheets onto work surface. Cut widthways into three even pieces. Brush one with combined butter and oil, top with a second piece. Brush one narrow end.

4 Place 2 tablespoons of custard 2 cm (3/4 inch) in from opposite end. Roll pastry over filling, fold ends in, roll to end. Repeat with remaining pastry and custard.

5 Arrange rolls on prepared tray about 2 cm (3/4 inch) apart. Brush with remaining butter mixture. Bake 30 minutes or until pastry is puffed and lightly golden. Serve warm, dusted with combined icing sugar and cinnamon.

ABOUT FILO PASTRY

■ Filo pastry can be purchased frozen or chilled. Chilled filo stores well for up to two months; once frozen filo is thawed, unused sheets can be refrigerated for up to one month (do not re-freeze). Cold filo is very brittle; leave it in its packaging until fully thawed (about 2 hours). Count out and remove the number of sheets needed, re-roll and store the remainder in their wrapping. Work quickly with one sheet at a time; cover reserved unrolled sheets with a clean, damp tea-towel.

■ Brush each sheet of filo with melted unsalted (sweet) butter or olive oil, or spray with olive or canola oil.

ABOVE: *SWEET CUSTARD ROLLS.*
OPPOSITE PAGE: *SEAFOOD PARCELS*

---

the Middle East, Turkey, Greece, Austria and Hungary. Each sheet is lightly brushed with oil or melted butter before being topped with another. The layered sheets can be twisted or wrapped around a sweet or savoury filling; baking results in light, crisp, flaky layers. Filo can be made at home, but as it requires skill and time, commercially made filo, available chilled or frozen, is most often used.

Fines Herbes A mixture of finely chopped, subtly flavoured fresh herbs, usually parsley, tarragon, chives and chervil, used to flavour omelettes, sauces and fish. Fines herbes mixtures are commercially available in dried form.

Finger Food Small portions of hot or cold savoury food that can easily be eaten held in one hand. Finger food is served at drinks and cocktail parties. See also Hors d'oeuvre.

Finnan Haddie Haddock that has been gutted, split, flattened and immersed in brine before being smoked (traditionally over peat smoke) until the flesh is pale golden. Finnan

SEAFOOD PARCELS

★★ **Preparation time:** 25 minutes
Total cooking time: 25 minutes
Serves 4

250 g (8 oz) boneless
white fish fillets
105 g (3½ oz) scallops
200 g (6½ oz) peeled,
cooked prawns
(shrimps)
1 tablespoon plain
(all-purpose) flour
1 tablespoon lemon juice
½ cup grated cheddar
cheese

1 tablespoon chopped
fresh chives
1 tablespoon chopped
fresh dill
30 g (1 oz) butter
1 cup (8 fl oz) milk
10 sheets filo pastry
60 g (2 oz) butter,
melted
2 teaspoons poppy seeds

1 Preheat oven to moderate 180°C (350°F/Gas 4). Line an oven tray with baking paper. Cut fish into 1 cm (½ inch) wide strips. Wash scallops, remove brown vein, leaving corals intact.

2 Heat butter in heavy-based pan. Add fish, scallops and juice. Cook over medium heat for 1 minute or until tender. Remove fish and scallops from pan with slotted spoon and keep warm.

3 Stir flour into pan. Add the milk gradually to flour and butter mixture, stirring constantly over medium heat for 3 minutes or until mixture boils and thickens. Simmer for another minute, stirring constantly. Remove pan from heat. Stir in cheese, chives, dill, cooked fish, prepared scallops and prawns. Cover surface with plastic wrap and set aside while preparing pastry.

4 Place two sheets of pastry on a work surface. Brush each sheet with melted butter. Place one sheet of pastry on top of the other. Cut pastry in four equal strips using a sharp knife or scissors. Place two tablespoons of mixture on one short end of each pastry strip. Fold in edges and roll up. Repeat with remaining pastry and mixture. Place seam-side down on prepared tray. Brush with butter, sprinkle with poppy seeds. Bake for 20 minutes or until golden.

ASPARAGUS STRUDEL

★★ **Preparation time:** 20 minutes
Total cooking time: 35 minutes
Serves 4

2 bunches fresh asparagus
2 tablespoons freshly
grated parmesan cheese
2 small onions
1 tablespoon oil
125 g (4 oz) can corn
kernels, drained
1 egg
6 sheets filo pastry

45 g (1½ oz) butter,
melted
2 tablespoons chopped
parsley
2 tablespoons chopped
fresh basil
2 tablespoons grated fresh
parmesan cheese, extra
⅔ cup grated cheddar
cheese

1 Preheat oven to moderately hot 210°C (415°F/Gas 6–7). Cut asparagus into 3 cm (1¼ inch) lengths. Trim any woody stems with a vegetable peeler. Place in a pan of boiling water. Stand for 1 minute, then drain and plunge into iced water. Drain well.

2 Chop onions finely. Heat oil in large heavy-based pan. Add onions. Cook, stirring, over medium heat for 3 minutes or until soft. Add asparagus, corn, parsley, basil, parmesan and cheddar cheese. Mix well; remove from heat. Cool to room temperature, then add egg; stir well to combine.

3 Brush pastry sheets with melted butter. Layer sheets on top of each other. Place asparagus mixture along one long end of pastry, leaving a 3 cm (1¼ inch) border.

4 Form into log shape with hands. Roll pastry tightly, enclosing filling, folding in short ends to form a parcel. Brush with any remaining melted butter.

5 Place parcel on greased oven tray. Sprinkle with extra parmesan cheese. Bake for 25 minutes or until pastry is lightly browned and filling is cooked through. Serve sliced as a first course or main meal.

Fish Fish is valued especially for its low kilojoule (calorie) and cholesterol counts, its high protein content and its easy digestibility. Fresh fish deteriorates quickly and is best cooked on the day of purchase. It can be grilled (broiled) and baked; poached in water or stock; battered and deep-fried; steamed; cooked wrapped in foil or buttered paper; or microwaved. Fish is cooked when the flesh becomes opaque and flakes easily and the juices are milky white.

Some dishes, such as ceviche (from Mexico and the South Pacific) and sashimi (from Japan) feature raw fish. Fish is preserved in several ways. Smoked fish is first soaked in brine and then hung or put on a rack in a compartment filled with smoke produced by smouldering sawdust. Cold smoking is a slow process performed at low temperatures; the smoke has cooled down before it reaches the fish. In hot

haddie can be grilled (broiled), poached or baked before being baked with a rich egg sauce, or flaked and used as an omelette filling; it is also an ingredient of the fish and rice dish kedgeree.

FINGER FOOD

Finger food is the perfect party food and makes entertaining easy. Going beyond canapés or appetisers, it needs to be substantial, but the name says it all. Finger food should be manageable—no runny fillings, precarious toppings or unwieldy sizes.

GOATS CHEESE AND ARTICHOKE TARTS

Spread some goats cheese or ricotta cheese into base of cooked shortcrust pastry cases. Top with plain or marinated artichoke hearts, drained and quartered, and a sprinkling of black or red caviar.

FINGER SANDWICHES

Cut avocado in half and remove the seed. Cut the flesh into thin slices, squeeze a little lemon juice over slices to prevent discolouration. Lay avocado slices side-by-side on a slice of brown bread and sprinkle with salt and pepper. Place a slice of white bread on top. Spread white bread with some canned pink or red salmon, mashed and drained. Top with shredded spinach or basil leaves. Place another slice of brown bread on top. Press down firmly but do not squash filling. Cut crusts from bread and cut sandwich into small fingers. Repeat process to make several more sandwiches. Substitute your own favourite fillings, varying colours and textures. Avoid ingredients that will make the bread soggy.

WONTON FRILLS

Mix together in a small bowl 155 g (5 oz) pork and veal mince, 1 tablespoon finely chopped fresh coriander, 1 clove crushed garlic, 2–3 teaspoons soy sauce, salt, pepper and 1 tablespoon plum sauce. Place 1 teaspoon of mixture towards corner of a square wonton wrapper. Brush around corner edge with water. Fold corner over, press to seal, leaving a large filled edge. Continue with remaining mixture and wrappers. Deep-fry wontons in oil until crisp. Drain on paper towel. Serve with sweet chilli sauce for dipping.

PRAWN (SHRIMP) AND MELON SKEWERS

Scoop 12 balls from a honeydew or cantaloupe (rockmelon). Peel 12 cooked medium king prawns (shrimp), leaving tails intact. Thread prawns, melon balls and slices of avocado onto bamboo skewers. Squeeze over a little lemon or orange juice. Serve.

CLOCKWISE, FROM LEFT: WONTON FRILLS, PRAWN AND MELON SKEWER, GOATS CHEESE AND ARTICHOKE TART, FINGER SANDWICH, RICOTTA AND ONION BOAT, YAKITORI, PIZZA WEDGE, TARAMASALATA PASTRY, CAVIAR OYSTER, CORN FRITTERS, AND A SALMON AND CHEESE SQUARE.

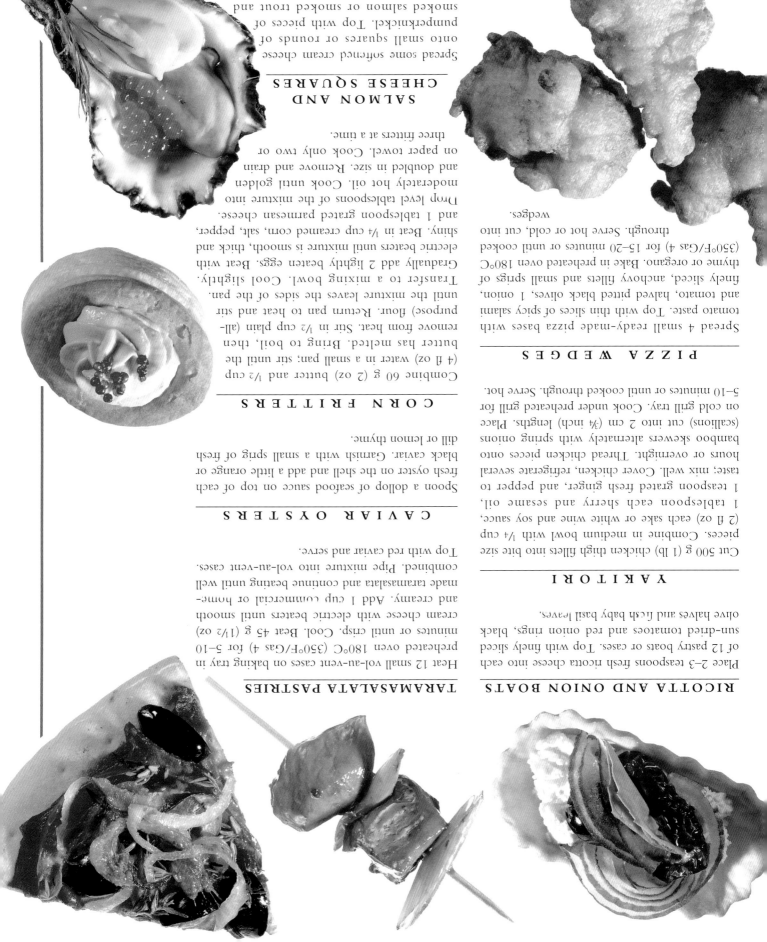

SALMON AND CHEESE SQUARES

Spread some softened cream cheese onto small squares or rounds of pumpernickel. Top with pieces of smoked salmon or smoked trout and decorate with small sprigs of fresh dill. Sprinkle the squares with a little freshly ground pepper, if desired.

CORN FRITTERS

Combine 60 g (2 oz) butter and 1/2 cup (4 fl oz) water in a small pan; stir until the butter has melted. Bring to boil, then remove from heat. Stir in 1/2 cup plain (all-purpose) flour. Return pan to heat and stir until the mixture leaves the sides of the pan. Transfer to a mixing bowl. Cool slightly. Gradually add 2 lightly beaten eggs. Beat with electric beaters until mixture is smooth, thick and shiny. Beat in 1/4 cup creamed corn, salt, pepper, and 1 tablespoon grated parmesan cheese. Drop level tablespoons of the mixture into moderately hot oil. Cook until golden and doubled in size. Remove and drain on paper towel. Cook only two or three fritters at a time.

CAVIAR OYSTERS

Spoon a dollop of seafood sauce on top of each fresh oyster on the shell and add a little orange or black caviar. Garnish with a small sprig of fresh dill or lemon thyme.

TARAMASALATA PASTRIES

Heat 12 small vol-au-vent cases on baking tray in preheated oven 180°C (350°F/Gas 4) for 5–10 minutes or until crisp. Cool. Beat 45 g (1 1/2 oz) cream cheese with electric beaters until smooth and creamy. Add 1 cup commercial or home-made taramasalata and continue beating until well combined. Pipe mixture into vol-au-vent cases. Top with red caviar and serve.

PIZZA WEDGES

Spread 4 small ready-made pizza bases with tomato paste. Top with thin slices of spicy salami and tomato, halved pitted black olives, 1 onion, finely sliced, anchovy fillets and small sprigs of thyme or oregano. Bake in preheated oven 180°C (350°F/Gas 4) for 15–20 minutes or until cooked through. Serve hot or cold, cut into wedges.

YAKITORI

Cut 500 g (1 lb) chicken thigh fillets into bite size pieces. Combine in medium bowl with 1/4 cup (2 fl oz) each sake or white wine and soy sauce, 1 tablespoon each sherry and sesame oil, 1 teaspoon grated fresh ginger, and pepper to taste; mix well. Cover chicken, refrigerate several hours or overnight. Thread chicken pieces onto bamboo skewers alternately with spring onions (scallions) cut into 2 cm (3/4 inch) lengths. Place on cold grill tray. Cook under preheated grill for 5–10 minutes or until cooked through. Serve hot.

RICOTTA AND ONION BOATS

Place 2–3 teaspoons fresh ricotta cheese into each of 12 pastry boats or cases. Top with finely sliced sun-dried tomatoes and red onion rings, black olive halves and fresh baby basil leaves.

smoking, the smoke reaches the fish at temperatures high enough to cook it. Salt-cured fish are split and gutted and packed in coarse salt. Unsalted dried fish are gutted and hung in an air current for about six weeks.

Fish Sauce See Nuoc Mam.

Five Spice Powder A fragrant spice mixture used in Chinese and Vietnamese cooking, consisting of ground star anise, Szechwan pepper, cinnamon, cloves and fennel seeds.

Flambé To ignite a spirit, such as brandy to burn off its alcohol content and at the same time create delicate flavours. The spirit must be warmed to release sufficient fumes to set alight; then ignited with a taper and poured over the food. Alternatively, cooking juices containing a spirit can be flambéed in a shallow pan. Sometimes fresh fruit is sautéed in butter and sugar, then flambéed with brandy or rum.

Flan A shallow, open, round pastry case. The pastry, usually shortcrust, can be either baked blind or with a filling (sweet or savoury) and served hot or cold. Flan tins, with fluted sides and a removable base, are available.

FISH FRESH

FISH AND CHIPS

★ *Preparation time:* 15 minutes + 10 minutes standing
Total cooking time: 30 minutes
Serves 6

2 tablespoons white
   vinegar
1 kg (2 lb) white fish
   fillets
5 large old potatoes
oil for deep frying
lemon wedges, for serving

Batter
1 1/2 cups plain
   (all-purpose) flour
1/2 cup self-raising flour
salt to taste
2/3 cup (5 fl oz) water
3/4 cup (6 fl oz) milk
1 egg, lightly beaten

1 To make Batter: Sift flours and salt into large bowl; make a well in the centre. In jug, whisk together water, milk, egg and vinegar. Gradually pour liquid into flour well. Stir with a wooden spoon until mixture forms a smooth batter; stand for 10 minutes before using.

2 Trim the fish, removing any skin and/or bones; cut into serving-sized pieces. Peel potatoes and cut into 1 cm (1/2 inch) slices, then into chip lengths 1 cm (1/2 inch) wide. Place cut potatoes into water until ready to use.

3 Heat oil in deep pan. Drain and dry chips with paper towels. Lower a few at a time into moderately hot oil, cook over medium heat 4 minutes or until pale golden. Drain on paper towels. Reheat oil; cook chips again in batches until crisp. Drain; keep warm to serve with fish.

4 Reduce oil temperature. Dip fish into batter, coating evenly. Deep-fry for 4–5 minutes until batter is crisp and golden. Drain on paper towels.

ABOUT FISH
■ Whole fresh fish should have bright, bulging eyes, red gills, shiny skin, close-fitting scales and firm, resilient flesh. Look for a pleasant sea smell and be wary of ammonia or musty odours. Fillets and cutlets should have moist, resilient flesh with no discolouration or dryness. Fillets should not be waterlogged, cutlets should be firmly attached to the bones. Smoked fish should have a fresh smoky smell—do not buy any with a sweaty appearance or a rancid smell.
■ Store fresh and smoked fish in the refrigerator and use within 2–3 days. Freeze fish, in a single layer, only when very fresh. Defrost overnight in refrigerator.

Above: Fish and chips. Opposite page:
Moroccan fish with fresh tomato sauce

MOROCCAN FISH WITH FRESH TOMATO SAUCE

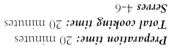

Preparation time: 30 minutes +
3 hours standing
Total cooking time: 5–10 minutes
Serves 6

750 g (1½ lb) white
fleshed fish fillets
2 tablespoons chopped
fresh coriander
1 clove garlic, crushed
⅓ cup chopped flat-leafed
parsley
½ teaspoon sweet ground
paprika
¼ teaspoon chilli powder
⅓ cup (2½ fl oz) olive oil
2 tablespoons lemon juice

Tomato Sauce
4 large, red, ripe
tomatoes, peeled,
seeded and chopped
2 small red chillies cut in
half, seeded and finely
shred
4 spring onions
(scallions), including
some green, finely sliced
½ bunch fresh coriander,
chopped finely
½ cup (4 fl oz) olive oil,
extra virgin
ground pepper
lemon or lime juice
(optional)
1 red onion, finely
chopped (optional)

1 Cut fish fillets across grain into 2 x 2 cm (¾ x ¾ inch) squares. Combine onion, garlic, coriander, parsley, paprika, chilli powder, olive oil and lemon juice and spoon over fish. Mix to coat fish

squares well. Marinate for 2 hours or overnight.
2 Place fish on metal skewers and grill (broil), turning frequently until browned on all sides.
3 To make Tomato Sauce: Combine tomatoes, chillies, spring onions and coriander in a bowl; add olive oil and pepper to taste. Add lemon or lime juice and chopped onion, if using.
4 Allow Tomato Sauce to stand for at least an hour in the refrigerator before serving with fish.

Note: Fish could be barbecued instead of grilled (broiled). This type of tomato sauce or 'salsa' makes a very good quick sauce for fish. Allow tomatoes to drain in a strainer for at least 30 minutes to get rid of excess water.

PAN FRIED FISH WITH SPICY VINEGAR SAUCE

Preparation time: 20 minutes
Total cooking time: 20 minutes
Serves 4–6

½ cup plain (all-purpose)
flour
½ teaspoon ground pepper
6 x 90 g (3 oz) small
white fish fillets
3 eggs
1 clove garlic, crushed
1 teaspoon ground sweet
paprika, extra
½ cup (4 fl oz) olive oil

Spicy Vinegar Sauce
1 cup (8 fl oz) white
wine vinegar
¼ cup fresh thyme leaves
1 spring onion (scallion),
chopped
1 teaspoon caster
(superfine) sugar
1 teaspoon ground sweet
paprika

1 To make Spicy Vinegar Sauce: Combine the vinegar, thyme, onion, sugar and paprika in a small pan. Simmer, uncovered, for about 10 minutes.
2 Combine flour and pepper in a medium bowl. Toss fish lightly in seasoned flour; shake off any excess. In a medium bowl, lightly beat the eggs with garlic and paprika until frothy. Dip each fillet into egg mixture and hold up to drain off any excess.
3 Heat oil in a medium pan; add fish. Cook on medium-high heat 3–4 minutes each side until golden brown and cooked through. Remove from pan; drain on paper towels.
4 Serve fish immediately, accompanied by Spicy Vinegar Sauce.

Note: The egg coating on the fish results in a fine, slightly crisp coating. Fish should be served as soon after cooking as possible, otherwise the coating will become soggy.

Flapjack A thick pancake. Buttered, stacked in a pile and topped with maple syrup, flapjacks are a popular breakfast food in North America. They are also known as griddle cakes, flannel cakes, hot cakes and wheat cakes. In Britain the term is also used for a mixture of rolled oats, brown sugar and melted butter pressed into a shallow tin, baked, and while still warm, then cut into fingers or squares.

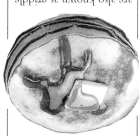

Fleuron Small pieces of puff pastry, traditionally crescent-shaped but also made in oval or diamond shapes, used as decoration on pie crusts or to garnish fish and chicken dishes served in a rich sauce. The shapes are cut from thinly rolled trimmings of puff pastry, glazed and baked or fried.

Florentine Very thin biscuits (cookies) containing dried fruit and nuts and coated on one side with melted chocolate that has been decorated with the tines of a fork to create wavy lines on its surface.

Florentine, à la A French term for a dish featuring fish, poultry or eggs, served on a bed of spinach, sometimes with a mornay sauce.

Flour Finely ground cereals, seeds or roots. Cereals commonly ground into flour include wheat, corn (maize), barley, oats, rye and rice; in Western countries the term generally refers to wheat flour. Dried chick peas are ground into besan flour; arrowroot is ground from the tuber of a plant; and soy beans are also ground into flour.

Flower, Edible Fresh whole flowers or petals bring a bright touch to salads, sorbets and drinks; when crystallised (candied) they are used to decorate cakes and desserts.

Not all flowers are edible; if in doubt, check with the local poisons centre or agriculture department. Make sure that flowers have not been treated with pesticides or other harmful chemicals.

Flowers commonly added to salads include the petals of yellow and white chrysanthemums,

---

FISH PIE

★★ **Preparation time:** 45 minutes
Total cooking time: 50 minutes
Serves 4–6

750 g (1½ lb) firm white fish fillets
½ cup chopped spring onions (scallions)
1 large leek, chopped
1 kg (2 lb) potatoes, cooked and mashed
2 strips lemon rind
¼ teaspoon ground nutmeg
1 teaspoon ground sweet paprika, optional
ground pepper

Sauce
30 g (1 oz) butter
1 clove garlic, crushed
1 chopped leek, extra
2½ cups (20 fl oz) milk
6 parsley stalks
2 bay leaves
8 peppercorns
2 strips lemon rind
¼ teaspoon ground nutmeg
2 tablespoons plain (all-purpose) flour
extra milk or cream

1 Preheat oven to 200°C (400°F/Gas 6). Place fish in pan, add leek, lemon rind, peppercorns, bay leaves and parsley stalks. Add milk. Simmer, uncovered, over low heat for 15 minutes or until fish is cooked (cooking time depends on thickness of fillets). Remove fish, strain liquid and reserve for sauce.

2 Melt butter in pan, add garlic, leeks and spring onions. Cook over low heat 7 minutes, or until leeks soften. Remove half mixture and reserve.

3 To make Sauce: Sprinkle flour over remaining mixture in pan, blend until smooth. Measure reserved liquid and make up to 1½ cups (12 fl oz) with extra milk or cream. Add to flour, stir until mixture boils and thickens. Cook 1 minute more.

4 Cut fish into chunks, fold gently through sauce. Add reserved leek and spring onion mixture to mashed potatoes. Season both mixtures with pepper. Pour sauce into a greased shallow casserole dish. Top with potatoes, sprinkle with paprika. Bake 20 minutes or until topping browns.

ROLLMOPS

★★ **Preparation time:** 20 minutes + 5 days marinating
Total cooking time: 10 minutes
Serves 6

12 herrings or fresh sardines, gutted and rinsed
2 cups (16 fl oz) white wine or cider vinegar
2 cups (16 fl oz) water
12 black peppercorns
6 allspice berries, crushed
6 whole cloves
1 tablespoon mustard seeds
2 bay leaves
2–3 pickled cucumbers, chopped
¼ cup chopped spring onions (scallions)
2 tablespoons chopped capers
2 medium onions, sliced

1 Fillet fish, leaving tails on. Lay flat on a board, skin side down. Sprinkle with cucumbers, spring onions and capers, roll up firmly from tail end. Secure each fillet with wooden cocktail sticks; arrange in glass jar alternating with sliced onions.

2 Place remaining ingredients in pan, bring to boil. Simmer, uncovered, 10 minutes; cool. Pour over fish. Cover, refrigerate for at least five days. Serve, drained, with salad and bread.

STEAMED FISH WITH GINGER

Preparation time: 45 minutes+ refrigeration
Total cooking time: 12 minutes
Serves 4

1 x 750 g (1½ lb) snapper (sea bass), cleaned and scaled
2 spring onions (scallions), finely sliced diagonally
2 tablespoons finely grated ginger
2 teaspoons dry sherry
2 tablespoons soy sauce
2 tablespoons peanut oil

2 teaspoons sesame oil
½ cup pine nuts, toasted
1 rasher bacon, diced and cooked until crisp, optional

1 Wash fish, removing any remaining loose scales; pat dry with paper towels. Place on a large heatproof dish; sprinkle with ginger, sherry and soy. Leave for 30 minutes in the refrigerator.

2 Place a round cake-cooling rack in a wok; balance the fish dish on top. Carefully pour 6–8 cups (1.5–2 litres) of boiling water into wok. Cover, steam fish over a rolling boil for 10 minutes.

3 Test if cooked by flaking a little flesh from the thickest part of the fish with a fork—fish is ready when it flakes easily and is milky white. Turn off heat and keep the dish covered.

OPPOSITE PAGE: FISH PIE.

ABOVE: STEAMED FISH WITH GINGER

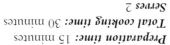

BAKED FISH WITH SPICES

Preparation time: 15 minutes
Total cooking time: 30 minutes
Serves 2

2 x 300 g (10 oz) whole white fish
lemon rind
1 onion, chopped
2 tablespoons tamarind sauce
1 clove garlic, crushed
1 teaspoon chopped fresh ginger

1 teaspoon chopped ginger
1 tablespoon soy sauce
1 tablespoon peanut oil

1 Place fish onto 2 large sheets of foil. Make 3 deep incisions on each side of the fish.

2 In a food processor, combine onion, garlic, ginger, lemon rind, tamarind sauce, soy sauce and peanut oil; blend until mixture is smooth.

3 Spread the mixture on both sides, and on the inside, of the fish.

4 Wrap foil around the fish and secure firmly. Place in a baking dish and bake at 180°C (350°F/Gas 4) for 30 minutes, or until the fish is just cooked through.

Carefully remove fish on its dish from wok. Sprinkle the spring onions over the fish and very carefully pour on the hot oil. Garnish with nuts and bacon, if desired. Serve at once with stir-fried vegetables and steamed rice.

4 Heat the oils in a small pan until very hot.

---

whole nasturtiums, marigold and calendula petals, whole blooms of violet, heartsease, pansy, honeysuckle and cornflower, and herb flowers such as borage and chive. A salad dressing, light in vinegar or lemon juice should be used, and the flowers strewn across the top after the greens have been tossed as the dressing will affect their colour. Pumpkin, zucchini (courgette) and squash flowers can be stuffed or dipped in batter and fried. Crystallised candied petals (rose and violet are most commonly used) can be made by dipping petals into beaten egg white and then into sugar until evenly coated; dry on a cake rack and store in an airtight container.

Flummery A dessert of fruit, fruit juice and cream or milk, thickened with gelatine and whipped until fluffy, then poured into a wetted mould and chilled until set. It is of Welsh origin and was originally thickened with oatmeal.

Focaccia A flat bread made

from yeasted dough, sprinkled with coarse salt and baked in a shallow, well-oiled pan. It is originally from Italy. Flavourings and baked toppings (such as herbs, tomatoes, onions, garlic and olives) vary according to the region. Warmed and filled with salads and cheese or meat, focaccia is popular as a snack or light meal.

Foie Gras Literally, 'fat liver', the enlarged liver of a specially fattened goose or duck. Foie gras, seasoned, poached and often studded with truffles, is served cold at the beginning of a meal or is made into a smooth paste, pâté de foie gras.

Fondant A sweet, smooth confectionery (candy), made from sugar, water and a pinch of cream of tartar. Fondant, with flavourings added, is used for many chocolate centres and and to make moulded fruits, flowers and icings.

Fondue Food that is cooked at the table by being immersed in simmering sauce or oil kept hot in a specially designed fondue pot. Diners using individual long-handled forks dip or retrieve the food

SMOKED FISH FLAN

 Preparation time: 20 minutes
Total cooking time: 45 minutes
Serves 4

250 g (8 oz) smoked fish fillets
1 small onion, sliced
4 tablespoons water
4 tablespoons sherry
4 sheets filo pastry
75 g (2½ oz) butter
2 tablespoons plain (all-purpose) flour

1 cup (8 fl oz) milk
lemon juice to taste
1 egg, beaten
½ teaspoon anchovy essence
1 tablespoon chopped fresh parsley
salt and pepper to taste

1 Preheat oven to 180°C (350°F/Gas 4). Place fish, onion, water and sherry in a pan. Bring to the boil, reduce heat and simmer for 10 minutes or until fish flakes when tested. Remove fish and flake, discarding any bones and skin.
2 Brush all pastry sheets with 45 g (1½ oz) melted butter. Fold each sheet in half. Layer pastry, one folded piece on top of the other, to give eight layers. Using a 20 cm (8 inch) flan ring as a guide, cut out a circle from the pastry sheets, 1 cm (½ inch) larger than the flan. Lift all the layers into flan tin carefully, leaving pastry standing up around edge of flan tin.
3 Melt the remaining 30 g (1 oz) butter in a pan. Add flour and cook, stirring continuously, for 2 minutes. Off the heat, gradually add milk and bring to the boil, stirring. Reduce heat and simmer for 5 minutes. Stir in lemon juice, beaten egg, anchovy essence and parsley. Season to taste.
4 Spread fish and onion over base and pour over sauce. Bake for 20 minutes. Serve hot or cold.

SMOKED HADDOCK IN WHITE SAUCE

 Preparation time: 12 minutes
Total cooking time: 20 minutes
Serves 4

1 large onion, thinly sliced
500 g (1 lb) smoked haddock
1⅔ cups (13 fl oz) milk
½ teaspoon cracked black pepper
1½ teaspoons mustard powder

25 g (¾ oz) butter, softened
2 teaspoons plain (all-purpose) flour
1 spring onion (scallion), finely chopped

1 Spread onion over base of large pan. Cut haddock into 2 cm (¾ inch) wide pieces. Arrange over onion.
2 Blend milk, pepper and mustard; pour over fish. Bring slowly to the boil. Reduce heat to low, simmer covered for 5 minutes. Uncover and simmer for another 5 minutes.
3 Remove fish to serving dish; keep warm. Simmer mixture in pan 5 minutes more, stirring.
4 Combine butter and flour, add to pan with spring onions. Stir over low heat until mixture boils and thickens. Pour over fish.

OPPOSITE PAGE: SMOKED HADDOCK IN WHITE SAUCE. ABOVE: SMOKED SALMON AND DILL CREPES

SMOKED SALMON AND DILL CREPES

⋆⋆ *Preparation time:* 50 minutes
Total cooking time: 25 minutes
Makes 9 crepes

Crêpes
1 cup plain (all-purpose) flour
1 egg, lightly beaten
1½ cups (12 fl oz) milk

Filling
155 g (5 oz) cream cheese, softened
1 tablespoon sour cream
1 tablespoon chopped dill
2 teaspoons chopped mint
1 tablespoon lemon juice
1 small avocado, mashed
200 g (6½ oz) smoked salmon, thinly sliced
sprigs of dill, for garnish

1 Sift flour into a medium mixing bowl; make a well in the centre. Using a wooden spoon, gradually stir in combined egg and milk. Beat until all liquid is incorporated and batter is free of lumps. Transfer mixture to jug; cover with plastic wrap and leave for 30 minutes.

2 To make Filling: Using electric beaters, beat cream cheese in a small mixing bowl until creamy. Add sour cream, dill, mint, juice and avocado, beat 30 seconds or until mixture is smooth and creamy. Cover with plastic wrap. refrigerate until needed.

3 Pour 2–3 tablespoons batter onto lightly greased 20 cm (8 inch) crêpe pan, swirl evenly over base. Cook over medium heat one minute or until underside is golden. Turn over; cook other side. Transfer to a plate; cover with tea-towel. Repeat with remaining batter; grease pan when necessary.

4 Spread each crêpe evenly with filling, top with salmon slices. Stack crêpes, cut into eight wedges. Garnish with dill sprigs. Serve with green salad.

SMOKED TROUT MOUSSE

⋆ *Preparation time:* 20 minutes + overnight setting
Total cooking time: nil
Serves 4

750 g (1½ lb) smoked trout
2 teaspoons French mustard
1½ tablespoons gelatine
½ cup (4 fl oz) cold water
¾ cup mayonnaise
½ cup very finely chopped celery
1 tablespoon white wine vinegar
pinch cayenne pepper

1 Skin and fillet trout. Place in bowl, mash finely.
2 To the trout add mayonnaise, celery, vinegar, and mustard. Mix well. Add gelatine combined with water. Season with cayenne pepper.
3 Put mixture into individual wetted moulds. Set in refrigerator. Unmould onto serving plates.

---

from the communal pot. There are several types of fondue: cheese fondue (originally from Switzerland), a mixture of melted cheeses and white wine into which pieces of crusty bread are dipped; meat fondue, in which cubes of meat, poultry or fish, as well as vegetables, are cooked in oil or stock; and dessert fondue, where pieces of cake, pastries, fruit or marshmallow are dipped into a sweet sauce, often made from chocolate.

Fool A dessert of fresh or cooked fruit, which has been puréed,

sweetened, chilled and, just before serving, mixed with whipped cream or custard.

Forcemeat A mixture of finely chopped or minced (ground) meat, herbs and seasonings, used as a stuffing.

Four Spices (*Quatre Épices*) A spice mixture of ground white peppercorns, nutmeg, cloves and ginger, used to flavour pâtés, terrines, and some slowly cooked meat and poultry dishes.

Frankfurter A lightly smoked sausage made from

SALMON PATTIES

CANNED FISH

Preparation time: 20 minutes
Total cooking time: 6 minutes
Serves 4

200 g (6½ oz) can pink
salmon, drained
2 tablespoons mayonnaise
4 spring onions
(scallions), chopped

500 g (1 lb) potatoes
1 egg
plain (all-purpose) flour
¾ cup packaged
breadcrumbs
¼ cup (2 fl oz) oil
lemon wedges for serving

1 Peel and chop potatoes. Cook in boiling water until tender; drain. Mash until smooth.

2 Put salmon, mayonnaise and spring onions in bowl with potatoes. Stir with wooden spoon until well mixed. Divide mixture into eight portions. Roll each portion into a smooth patty.

3 Dust patties lightly in flour. Beat egg in small bowl, and use to brush patties. Coat in breadcrumbs.

4 Heat oil in frying pan. Put in patties in a single layer; cook over medium heat for 3 minutes or until underside is golden. Use an egg slice to turn patties over and cook 3 minutes or until golden. Drain on paper towels. Serve with lemon wedges.

Note: If preferred, drained, canned tuna can be used to replace the pink salmon in this recipe.

TUNA MORNAY

Preparation time: 15 minutes
Total cooking time: 30 minutes
Serves 4-6

45 g (1½ oz) butter
2 spring onions (scallions),
finely chopped
2 tablespoons plain
(all-purpose) flour
1½ cups (12 fl oz) milk
¼ cup grated cheddar
cheese, extra

2 x 425 g (13½ oz)
cans tuna, drained
¼ cup fresh breadcrumbs
2 tablespoons finely
chopped fresh parsley
¾ cup grated cheddar
cheese

1 Preheat oven to moderately hot 210°C (415°F/Gas 6-7). Heat butter in a medium pan; add spring onions and cook over a low heat for 2 minutes until soft. Add flour, stir over low heat 2 minutes, until mixture is lightly golden.

2 Add milk gradually to pan, stirring until mixture is smooth. Stir constantly over medium heat 4 minutes or until mixture boils and thickens; boil for another minute, remove from heat. Cool slightly, stir in grated cheese.

3 Add tuna to pan and fold through gently, taking care not to break up pieces too much. Transfer mixture to 1.25 litre (5-cup) capacity casserole dish. Sprinkle with combined breadcrumbs, extra cheese and parsley. Bake for 20 minutes, or until golden brown.

ABOVE: SALMON PATTIES.
OPPOSITE PAGE: BAGNA CAUDA (TOP) AND CHEESE FONDUE (BELOW)

FETTUCCINE AND TUNA WITH CAPERS

Preparation time: 10 minutes
Total cooking time: 15 minutes
Serves 4-6

500 g (1 lb) fettuccine
⅓ cup (2½ fl oz) lemon
juice
¼ cup (2 fl oz) olive oil
2 cloves garlic, crushed
2 tablespoons chopped
capers
225 g (7 oz) can tuna,
drained
½ teaspoon chopped chilli
60 g (2 oz) butter

1 Place fettuccine in a pan of boiling water and cook until just tender.

2 Heat oil in pan, add garlic, cook 1 minute, add tuna and cook 2 minutes longer. Add butter, lemon juice, capers and chilli, stir into tuna and cook on low until heated through. Drain fettuccine, add to sauce and mix to combine.

French Food French cooking is still seasoned with salt and freshly ground black pepper.

French Dressing Also called vinaigrette, a salad dressing consisting of one part vinegar to three parts olive oil.

Freezing A method of preserving food by storing it at or below the freezing point. Freezing halts the growth of bacteria, yeasts and moulds.

Frappé The French term for 'iced'. It is used to describe both a drink that is poured over crushed ice and a refreshing dessert made of partially frozen sweetened fruit juice.

Frankfurters spiced meat, either pork, a beef and pork mixture, or poultry meat. Frankfurters are sold contained in a casing, or skinless; they are precooked and need only to be reheated in simmering water (boiling may split them), or by making several slashes in the skin and grilling (broiling), or barbecuing until they are lightly browned. Frankfurters range from the tiny cocktail to bun-length hot dog franks.

ABOUT FONDUES

■ To eat fondue spear chunks of bread or fruit with long-handled fondue forks, twirl into cheese or sweet fondue mixture and carefully tip bread or fruit directly into the mouth.

CHEESE FONDUE

Preparation time: 20 minutes
Total cooking time: 10 minutes
Serves 10–15

2 cups grated mild cheddar cheese
2 cups grated vintage cheddar cheese
2 cups (16 fl oz) white wine
1/4 cup plain (all-purpose) flour

2 teaspoons mustard powder
1 cup grated parmesan cheese
2 teaspoons Dijon mustard
cubes French bread

1 Combine cheeses, flour and mustard powder. Pour the wine into the fondue pot, slowly bring to simmering point. Add heaped tablespoonsful of cheese mixture at a time, stirring after each one until it has melted.

2 Continue process until all the cheese has melted and mixture is thick. Stir in Dijon mustard, season with pepper to taste.

3 Stir until fondue is bubbling and smooth. Keep hot over burner. Supply fondue forks or skewers for dipping cubes of French bread. Fondue can be made in a pan a day ahead. Keep covered in refrigerator. Reheat gently in fondue pot just before serving.

BAGNA CAUDA

Preparation time: 20 minutes
Total cooking time: 10 minutes
Serves 6

5 cloves garlic, crushed
45 g (1 1/2 oz) can anchovies, drained and chopped
90 g (3 oz) unsalted (sweet) butter
2 egg yolks
selected raw vegetables, cut into 5 cm (2 inch) long sticks

1 Cook anchovies, unsalted butter and garlic in a medium pan until butter has melted. Transfer mixture to a food processor. Add egg yolks. Process until thick.

2 Pour into fondue pot, slowly bring to simmering point. Serve at once with selected vegetables and skewered crusty bread. Bagna Cauda may also be served in a bowl and passed around on a platter with the bread and vegetables.

FONDUES

CARAMEL TOFFEE FONDUE

Preparation time: 30 minutes
Total cooking time: 20 minutes
Serves 6

1/2 cup caster (superfine) sugar
1/2 cup demerara sugar
1/2 cup (4 fl oz) cream
1/2 cup (4 fl oz) condensed milk

2 teaspoons cornflour (cornstarch)
1 cup (8 fl oz) thick cream
seasonal fruits

1 Combine the sugars in a large pan. Heat gently over a low heat until sugars dissolve. Remove from heat. Combine a small amount of the condensed milk with the cornflour and blend until smooth.

2 Add the cornflour mixture, cream and the remaining condensed milk to the sugars. Return the pan to heat until a toffee lump forms. Continue stirring over a low heat until the lump dissolves. The fondue should be a dark, rich caramel colour.

3 Transfer the mixture to a fondue pot. Stir often to prevent burning. Serve caramel toffee immediately with a selection of skewered fresh fruit. Fondue may also be served in a bowl and passed around on a platter with skewered fruit.

---

considered by many to be the finest in the world. It has become so universally accepted that many dishes we take for granted are French in origin: the humble omelette, pâté, mayonnaise, quiche, fruit tart.

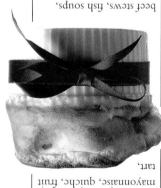

beef stews, fish soups, and soufflés. Over the past decade, classic French food has given way to a more casual style of eating. Conscious of weight and health, people are eschewing rich egg- and cream-based sauces in favour of simpler French food, brasserie style. The essence of French food has not changed, but a cheese soufflé is now more likely to be served as a main course with a salad and a chunk of bread than as a first course to a big dinner. There will always be a place for

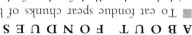

French desserts such as profiteroles, tarts, crêpes and gateaux. Croissants, served with café au lait, are fast becoming an international breakfast.

FOCACCIA

Focaccia is a light yeast flatbread from Italy, traditionally brushed with oil and sprinkled with flavouring like herbs, onions, olives, rock salt or even nuts. Nowadays, it is popular split and served as a sandwich with hot or cold fillings. It can be toasted, grilled or even pan-fried in variations limited only by your imagination.

Focaccia has become a popular alternative to ordinary sliced bread. It is flatter and drier in texture than the familiar fresh white loaf from the bakery, and is made in large squares or rounds as well as in small rounds like flattened bread rolls. The close texture and hard crust of traditional focaccia make it perfect for carrying moist foods such as marinated vegetables and cheeses.

APHRODITE

Combine some thinly sliced marinated feta or goats cheese, 4–5 sun-dried tomatoes in oil, drained, and 4–5 green or purple basil leaves. Sprinkle with freshly cracked black pepper and parmesan cheese shavings, if desired.

To marinate cheese: In a bowl, combine ¼ cup (2 fl oz) olive oil, ½ teaspoon grated lemon rind, 1 crushed clove garlic, 1 teaspoon each chopped parsley, chives and thyme, ¼ teaspoon dried chilli flakes, and freshly ground black pepper. Mix well. Place cheese slices in the bowl and toss gently to coat with marinade. Cover the bowl and refrigerate for up to 2 hours.

COPENHAGEN

Plunge slender baby asparagus spears into boiling water for 1 minute or until they turn bright green, then plunge them into a bowl of iced water; drain well. Split focaccia and fill with some finely sliced red or brown onion rings, slices of fresh smoked salmon, baby asparagus spears and tiny capers. Top with a dollop of horseradish cream or crème fraîche, if desired. Sprinkle with freshly cracked black pepper and serve.

MEDITERRANEAN MEDLEY

Halve 1 red pepper (capsicum); remove seeds and membrane. Brush skin with olive oil. Cook under hot preheated grill, cut-side down, until skin blisters and blackens. Cover with a damp tea-towel until cool. Peel and discard skin. Cut flesh into strips. Slice 1–2 small slender eggplant (aubergine) lengthways. Fry the slices in 2–3 tablespoons olive oil, with 1 clove crushed garlic, 2–3 minutes each side; drain. Layer peppers, eggplant and thin slices of provolone cheese on focaccia. Lightly toast, if desired.

ROCKET EXPRESS

Wash some rocket (arugula) or lettuce leaves. Layer onto focaccia with 2–3 slices chilli-, pepper- or herb-crusted salami and thinly sliced baby bocconcini. Drizzle with virgin olive oil and good balsamic vinegar. If you prefer, use thin slices of mozzarella cheese instead of bocconcini.

POMPEII

Halve 1 red pepper (capsicum); remove all the seeds and membrane. Brush skin with olive oil. Cook under hot preheated grill, cut-side down, until skin blisters and blackens. Cover with damp tea-towel until cool. Peel off skin; discard. Cut flesh into strips. Split focaccia, spread with olive paste. Top with strips of pepper, halved pitted green and black olives, halved marinated artichokes and thin slices of mortadella.

NAPOLI

Thinly slice 1–2 egg (plum) tomatoes, or use ripe vine tomatoes. Arrange on split focaccia. Top with fresh green or purple basil leaves and thin slices of coppa or prosciutto. Sprinkle with crushed rock salt, cracked black pepper and drizzle with olive oil. Add some fresh grated parmesan or pecorino cheese, if desired.

OPPOSITE, FROM TOP TO BOTTOM: APHRODITE, COPENHAGEN, MEDITERRANEAN MEDLEY, ROCKET EXPRESS, POMPEII AND NAPOLI.

FRENCH CLASSICS

CASSOULET

★★ *Preparation time:* 25 minutes
Total cooking time: 2 hours
Serves 6

315 g (10 oz) chicken thigh fillets	1 cup (8 fl oz) white wine
315 g (10 oz) lean lamb	1 teaspoon fresh thyme leaves
315 g (10 oz) lean pork loin	2 bay leaves
60 g (2 oz) lard	3 cloves
2 medium onions, chopped	ground pepper, to taste
2 cloves garlic, crushed	410 g (13 oz) can white cannellini beans, drained
2 sticks celery, chopped	200 g (6½ oz) chopped pickled pork
1 tablespoon plain (all-purpose) flour	90 g (3 oz) salami, chopped
440 g (14 oz) can tomatoes, drained, juice reserved	

1 Trim the meat of excess fat and cut into 2 cm (¾ inch) cubes. Heat lard in a large pan. Cook the chicken until brown and remove from pan. Add lamb to pan and cook until brown; remove. Cook the pork until brown, and remove. Add onions to remaining fat in pan and cook until they are well browned. Add garlic and celery, stir for one minute and remove from pan.

2 Sprinkle flour over base of pan. Add chopped tomatoes, tomato juice and wine; stir until sauce boils and thickens. Add thyme, bay leaves, cloves and pepper. Bring to boil, reduce heat and simmer uncovered for 10 minutes.

3 Add meat, onion mixture and cannellini beans, cover and simmer for one hour. Remove the lid, add pickled pork and salami; cover and cook for 30 minutes.

FRENCH ONION SOUP

★★ *Preparation time:* 15 minutes
Total cooking time: 55 minutes
Serves 4–6

45 g (1½ oz) butter	425 g (13½ oz) can beef consommé
1 tablespoon olive oil	1¼ cups (10 fl oz) water
4 large brown onions, thinly sliced	2 tablespoons olive oil, extra
1 clove garlic, crushed	1 clove garlic, crushed, extra
1 tablespoon sugar	1 small French bread stick, cut into 2 cm (¾ inch) slices
2 tablespoons red wine vinegar	½ cup grated parmesan cheese
⅓ cup plain (all-purpose) flour	thyme, to garnish
½ cup (4 fl oz) dry sherry	
1 cup (8 fl oz) dry white wine	

food; in some countries they're served for lunch with ham and cheese.

French Fries Also known as potato chips, thin strips of potato which are deep-fried until pale golden. They are a very popular vegetable accompaniment in France, where they are known as pommes frites.

French Toast Slices or fingers of bread, dipped in an egg and milk mixture and fried in butter until crisp and golden-brown on both sides. French toast is served hot, topped with sugar and cinnamon, syrup or jam for breakfast or dessert.

Fricassée A dish of meat or poultry (usually veal or chicken) first fried in butter without browning, then cooked slowly in white stock thickened with flour; cream is added just before serving. A fricassée is usually garnished with small glazed onions and lightly cooked mushrooms.

Frikadell A small fried meat ball, usually served hot, garnished with sour cream or a tomato-based sauce.

OPPOSITE PAGE: CASSOULET.
ABOVE: FRENCH ONION SOUP;
RIGHT: BEEF BOURGUIGNON

Note: It is important that the onions used for making French Onion Soup are well browned to give the soup an authentic flavour. The sugar assists by caramelising the onions. Start with full heat for a few minutes, then reduce to a medium heat to brown the onions slowly.

1 Heat the butter and olive oil together in a large frypan. Add onions, cook for about 20 minutes until brown.

2 Add the garlic and sugar and stir through until the sugar has browned. Add the vinegar and cook for 2 minutes. Sprinkle flour over the onions; cook, stirring, for 1 minute. Stir in the sherry, white wine, consommé and water. Continue stirring until the mixture boils and thickens. Reduce heat and simmer the soup uncovered for about 25 minutes.

3 Preheat the oven to 210°C (415°F/Gas 6–7). Combine the extra olive oil and garlic in a small bowl. Brush the mixture over both sides of the bread, then sprinkle one side with parmesan cheese. Bake for 5 minutes or until bread slices are crisp and golden.

4 To serve, place a slice of bread at the bottom of each soup bowl, pour over the soup and garnish with thyme. Alternatively, lay a slice of thinly sliced Swiss cheese, such as gruyère, on the slice of bread. Float on top of soup and place under a hot grill for 1–2 minutes or until cheese melts.

BEEF BOURGUIGNON

Preparation time: 25 minutes
Total cooking time: 1 hour 30 minutes
Serves 6

1 kg (2 lb) blade steak
2 rashers bacon
2 tablespoons olive oil
12 small pickling onions, peeled
2 cloves garlic, crushed
1/3 cup plain (all-purpose) flour
2 cups (16 fl oz) red wine
1 teaspoon fresh thyme leaves
1 tablespoon grated or bottled horseradish
30 g (1 oz) butter
375 g (12 oz) button mushrooms, quartered
fresh thyme, to garnish

1 Trim meat of excess fat, cut into 1.5 cm (5/8 inch) cubes. Cut bacon into 1 cm (1/2 inch) strips.

2 Heat oil in large pan; add bacon, cook until brown, remove. Add onions to pan and cook in bacon fat until well browned; remove. Add garlic, cook one minute. Brown meat pieces in remaining fat; stir through flour. Add red wine, thyme and horseradish, stir until mixture boils and thickens. Return onions and bacon to pan; reduce heat, cover and simmer for one hour.

3 Heat butter in small pan; add mushrooms, cook until soft. Stir mushrooms and juices through casserole, cook uncovered a further 30 minutes.

4 Serve casserole garnished with fresh thyme, accompanied with fresh vegetables.

Frittata A dish using beaten eggs, frittata is similar to an omelette but the filling (diced vegetables, cheese, meat, chicken and seafood) is stirred into the egg mixture before it is cooked.

Fritter Food dipped in or mixed with a batter of flour, and liquid and egg and then deep-fried until crisp and golden.

Fritto Misto Literally 'mixed fry', a dish of Italian origin consisting of assorted vegetables, seafood or meat, dipped in a light batter, deep-fried, served piping hot. Perhaps best known is the mixed seafood fritto misto, a Neapolitan specialty, which usually includes baby squid and calamari rings; a version of the dish from Florence consists of chicken, rabbit and vegetables such as artichokes and zucchini (courgette); in the Piedmont region of northern Italy savoury fritters (brain, sweetbreads and veal) are popular.

Fromage Blanc A soft, white, unripened fresh cheese. It has a slightly sour, tangy taste and in France is widely used in sauces, as a topping for steamed or boiled vegetables, a dressing for

salad vegetables, a dip for crudités and a topping for fresh fruit.

Frosting A cooked topping for cakes, consisting of water, sugar, cream of tartar and egg white. In North America the term covers all sweet cooked and uncooked toppings for cakes and cookies.

Fruit Botanically, a fruit is the pulp that covers the seeds of various flowering plants. This includes nuts and some fruits principally eaten as vegetables, such as the eggplant (aubergine), tomato, corn, olive and avocado. In general usage the term is restricted to fruits that are fleshy, sweet and sometimes juicy. Low in fat and high in fibre, fruit is an essential part of a healthy diet. It is eaten fresh, but can also be cooked.

Fruit, Dried Fruit that is preserved by having its natural water content reduced by exposure to the sun in the open air or by heating. Such dehydration slows the growth of bacteria, allowing most dried fruits to be stored for up to a year. Fruits most commonly

CREPES SUZETTE

★★

Preparation time: 30 minutes
Total cooking time: 35 minutes
Serves 4–6

Crêpe Batter
1 cup plain (all-purpose) flour
1 tablespoon grated orange rind
1 tablespoon grated lemon rind
2 teaspoons caster (superfine) sugar
2 eggs, lightly beaten
1 cup (8 fl oz) milk
15 g (½ oz) butter, melted
1 tablespoon brandy

Suzette Sauce
60 g (2 oz) butter
¼ cup sugar
1 tablespoon grated orange rind
1 cup (8 fl oz) orange juice
¼ cup (2 fl oz) lemon juice
½ cup (4 fl oz) Grand Marnier
cream or ice-cream, to serve

1 To make Batter: Place all ingredients into the bowl of a food processor. Using the pulse action, press button for 40 seconds or until ingredients are combined and the mixture is free of lumps. Transfer mixture to bowl or jug and stand covered with plastic wrap for one hour. The crêpe batter should be the consistency of pouring cream—if it thickens on standing, thin with extra milk or water.

2 To cook Crêpes: Pour 2–3 tablespoons of batter onto a lightly greased 10 cm (4 inch) crêpe pan; swirl evenly over base. Cook over medium heat 1 minute or until underside is golden. Turn crêpe over, cook other side. Transfer to plate; cover with tea-towel and keep warm. Repeat process with the remaining batter, greasing pan when necessary.

3 To make Sauce: Heat butter in a pan, add sugar and stir over a medium heat until caramelised. Add the rinds, juices and Grand Marnier; simmer uncovered 10 minutes.

4 To assemble: Preheat oven to 210°C (415°F/Gas 6–7). Fold crêpes into quarters and arrange across base of ovenproof dish, overlapping to form a pattern. Pour over Sauce. Bake for 10–15 minutes and serve warm with cream or ice-cream. This crêpe batter can be used for all sweet crêpe recipes.

Note: Crêpes can be flambéed at the table. Heat 2 tablespoons Grand Marnier, brandy or orange liqueur in small pan or Turkish coffee pot. Carefully light at the table and pour over crêpes.

ABOVE: *CREPES SUZETTE.*
OPPOSITE PAGE, ABOVE: *SPINACH FRITTATA; BELOW:*
CHICKEN AND ASPARAGUS FRITTATA

dried include apples, apricots, bananas, dates, figs, grapes (as currants, raisins and sultanas), and peaches, pears and plums (as prunes). Dried fruit mixtures, for use in rich fruit cakes, fruit minces and boiled fruit puddings, are also available.

Fruit Cake A rich, moist cake containing dried and crystallised (candied) fruit, crystallised fruit peel, nuts and spices. Well wrapped in muslin (cheesecloth), soaked in brandy, rum or fruit juice and stored in an airtight container, a fruit cake will keep for several months, its flavour deepening and maturing with each passing day. Fruit cakes are traditional holiday and celebration fare (weddings, christenings and Christmas). Forms of fruit cake have been made since ancient times, when the Greeks and Romans baked cakes containing honey, walnuts, pine nuts and dried figs.

Fruit Cocktail A mixture of fruit chunks, doused with lemon juice and sprinkled with a little sugar, chilled and served as a first course or dessert. Use fruits that contrast in colour and

---

FRITTATA

CHICKEN AND ASPARAGUS FRITTATA

Preparation time: 10 minutes
Total cooking time: 20 minutes
Serves 4

30 g (1 oz) butter
4 spring onions (scallions), finely chopped
8 canned asparagus spears, drained
6 eggs, lightly beaten
1 cup (8 fl oz) milk
3/4 cup grated Swiss cheese

freshly ground black pepper to taste
2 teaspoons wholegrain mustard
1 1/2 cups chopped, cooked chicken

1 Heat butter in a large pan. Add spring onions and cook, stirring, for one minute or until soft. Whisk together the eggs, milk and mustard.
2 Stir in chicken and pepper to taste. Pour egg mixture over spring onions and cook over low heat for 15 minutes or until frittata is set.
3 Preheat grill. Arrange asparagus on top of frittata and sprinkle with cheese. Place under hot grill for 2 minutes, or until the cheese is melted and golden. Serve with a crisp garden salad.

Note: Frittata can be served hot or cold. Cut into wedges for lunchbox or picnics.

SPINACH FRITTATA

✳ *Preparation time: 2 minutes*
Total cooking time: 30 minutes
Serves 4

6 eggs, lightly beaten
1/2 cup grated parmesan cheese
1 cup (8 fl oz) milk
250 g (8 oz) packet frozen spinach, thawed
1 onion, chopped
1/2 cup grated cheddar cheese

1 clove garlic, crushed
1 tablespoon chopped fresh parsley
freshly ground black pepper to taste

1 Preheat oven to moderate 180°C (350°F/Gas 4). Whisk together eggs and milk. Squeeze all water from thawed spinach.
2 Stir spinach, onion, cheeses, garlic, parsley and pepper to taste into the egg mixture.
3 Pour into a greased 23 cm (9 inch) pie plate. Bake for 30 minutes or until set and golden. Serve hot or cold, cut into wedges. Serve with crusty wholemeal bread.

ABOUT FRITTATAS

■ Frittatas are similar to omelettes, except that the filling and the beaten eggs are combined. They can be fried and the uncooked side browned under the grill, or baked. When frying, use a heavy-based, non-stick frying pan with a long, heat-resistant handle. Pour mixture into pan and cook over moderate heat until the underside is golden. Place the frittata under a hot grill until the top is puffed and golden or you can turn it like an omelette if you prefer.

■ Experiment with fillings—any combination of meat, fish or vegetables which are suitable for an omelette or quiche can be incorporated into a frittata. Herbs can also be added.

FREEZING

Freezing is an excellent way of preserving food; it allows economical shopping in bulk, meals or school lunches can be prepared in advance, leftovers can be stored, and favourite produce enjoyed out of season. As long as the food is carefully prepared and packaged, it will retain its colour, texture, taste and nutritional value.

EQUIPMENT

■ Plastic freezer bags. Flatten contents to a thin layer, expel air and seal with masking tape.

■ Sturdy plastic containers with tight-fitting lids. Useful for liquids. Allow about 1 cm (1/2 inch) space for expansion.

■ Foil containers. Cooked food can be reheated in the same container.

■ Microwave cookware, which allows food to go from freezer to microwave, and even to the table.

■ Aluminium foil, for wrapping and padding.

■ Freezer wrap for interleaving. The double layers allow easy separation of frozen foods.

■ Labels or tags and a waterproof pen or wax pencil. Label frozen items with name, number of serves, date frozen, any reminders, and 'use by' date.

■ A double-edged freezer knife for cutting food frozen into solid blocks.

UNCOOKED MEAT

■ Meat purchased on styrofoam trays should be repackaged and the trays discarded. As a general rule, uncooked meat can be frozen for up to 6 months. Do not refreeze meat which has partially thawed—cook it first.

■ Steaks and chops: Wrap individually in plastic wrap, expelling air; pad bones with foil to prevent the wrap tearing. Pack number of steaks or chops required in a strong plastic freezer bag; extract air, twist the top and seal with masking tape. Label and freeze for up to six months.

■ Cubes or strips for stewing or braising: Store meal-sized portions in strong plastic bags, filling to the corners with meat. Flatten packages for quick thawing, expel air, twist top, seal and label. Freeze for up to 2 months.

■ Roasting joints and corned joints can be kept frozen in a strong freezer bag for 6 months.

■ Chicken: Uncooked, home-frozen chicken (without giblets) will keep for up to 9 months. The giblets can be frozen separately for 8 weeks. Stuffed poultry should never be frozen as harmful bacteria can develop.

■ Sliced processed meats: Bacon, ham, salami and other delicatessen meats can be frozen, well wrapped, for up to one month without the flavour deteriorating.

■ Liver, kidneys and brains do not freeze well and are best purchased as needed.

FRUIT AND VEGETABLES

■ Vegetables must be blanched before they are frozen and most fruit are frozen in a sugar syrup or dry sugar pack. Contact your local health authority for information on the most up-to-date method of freezing fruit and vegetables.

■ The exception is berries, which can be frozen without any preliminaries. Line baking trays with freezer wrap and spread out the washed and dried fruit so that pieces do not touch. Set freezer at coldest setting and freeze fruit until hard, about 2 hours. Remove, pack in freezer bags, expel air, seal and label. Keep for up to 3 months.

FREEZER SAFETY HINTS

■ Make sure that meat or chicken bought frozen is completely enclosed in its package.

■ Defrost frozen chicken in refrigerator—allow 2–3 hours per 500 g (1lb)—to prevent bacterial growth. Microwave defrosting of whole chickens is not recommended because of uneven thawing.

■ Thaw frozen meat in refrigerator or on defrost setting in microwave, never at room temperature. If frozen meat is accidentally defrosted (e.g. in a power failure), do not re-freeze.

■ Remove frozen meat from wrapping before defrosting. Separate items as they defrost.

HERBS

■ Freeze whole sprigs of thyme or rosemary in freezer bags.

■ Mint, basil, marjoram and oregano can be chopped, mixed with a little water and set in ice-cube trays. Seal frozen cubes in plastic bags. Label cube trays (one frozen herb purée looks just like another).

■ Basil, dill, chervil, parsley or tarragon can be chopped, mixed with butter and stored as a frozen cylinder for up to 2 months. Slice and serve with grilled meat or fish.

BAKED GOODS

■ Sliced sandwich bread over-wrapped in a freezer bag will freeze for one month.

■ Home-baked bread or rolls, sealed in plastic bags, can be frozen for 3 months.

■ Cakes without filling or icing can be frozen for 3 months. Iced cakes lose quality after about 2 months—freeze them, unwrapped, until icing sets, then wrap in foil and pack in containers.

■ Biscuits (cookies) are best frozen unbaked and will keep for up to 6 months. Freeze cooked biscuits (cooled and without icing) in layers, interleaved with greaseproof paper, in an airtight container.

■ Croissants and Danish pastries (baked) will keep for 1–2 months in freezer bags.

■ Sandwiches freeze well for up to 1 month. Avoid fillings with cooked egg whites, raw vegetables, mayonnaise or jam.

COOKED MEAT

■ Quickly reduce the temperature of cooked items by placing in refrigerator in a shallow container, or by plunging base of dish into cold water, then cooling completely in refrigerator.

■ Stews, casseroles, curries, soups: line suitable containers with heavy-gauge plastic bags and ladle an individual serve or meal-sized portion into each; place containers in freezer. When contents are frozen, remove bags, expel air, label and seal. Freeze for 2 months.

■ Meat sauce, meatballs in sauce and savoury minced (ground) meat dishes can be three-quarters cooked, then frozen for up to a month.

■ Slices of roast meat should be covered with gravy before freezing to prevent moisture loss. Reheat gently to avoid tough, stringy meat. Whole cooked roasts do not freeze well. They tend to become waterlogged and when they are defrosted, they lose much of their goodness.

texture, such as grapes and rockmelon (cantaloupe), strawberries and orange.

Fruit Cup A refreshing drink made of a mixture of fresh fruit pieces and fruit juices, sometimes mixed with iced water, soda, lemonade or alcohol and sweetened to taste. Serve in a stemmed glass garnished with a slice of lemon and a sprig of mint.

Fruit Leather A chewy confectionery (candy) made by boiling down pureed fruit (such as apricot, peach, apple, plum, strawberry or raspberry) and sugar until it forms a thick paste. This is spread on a lightly greased flat surface to dry and then cut into strips. Fruit leather has a sweet, tangy taste; it can be served after a meal with coffee or included in a packed lunch.

Fruit Salad A combination of chopped, sliced or small whole fruits served as a dessert accompanied by cream, ice-cream or custard. Fresh fruit (raw or poached and cooled) or canned fruit can be used. The fruit is generally first sprinkled with sugar (for canned fruit use the syrup instead of sugar) and steeped in fruit juice.

FRITTERS

ONION FRITTERS

★ Preparation time: 20 minutes
Total cooking time: 15 minutes
Makes 18–24

4 large onions
4 cloves garlic
1½ teaspoons bicarbonate of soda (baking soda)
¾ cup besan flour (see Note)
½ cup plain (all-purpose) flour
1 teaspoon chilli powder (or sweet paprika for a milder taste)
1 egg
vegetable oil for shallow frying

1 Peel and halve the onions and then slice very thinly. Finely chop garlic.
2 Mix the flours with egg, soda, chilli powder or paprika and enough water to make a smooth creamy batter. Add the onion and garlic.
3 Heat oil, about 2 cm (¾ inch) deep, in a wide flat pan. Add tablespoonsful of the batter and press into patties. Fry on both sides until golden brown and cooked through. Remove to a rack covered with absorbent paper to drain.
4 Serve fritters hot accompanied by chilli sauce or hot mango chutney.

Note: Besan flour is a soft, golden flour milled from dried chick peas (garbanzo beans).

ABOVE: ONION FRITTERS;
RIGHT: FRITTERS WITH STRAWBERRY SAUCE.
OPPOSITE PAGE: DRIED FRUIT SALAD.

FRITTERS WITH STRAWBERRY SAUCE

★ Preparation time: 30 minutes
Total cooking time: 35 minutes
Serves 6–8

Fritters
1 cup (8 fl oz) water
60 g (2 oz) butter
¼ cup caster (superfine) sugar
½ cup currants
1 teaspoon grated orange rind
1 cup plain (all-purpose) flour
3 eggs, lightly beaten
oil, to deep-fry
icing (confectioners) sugar, to dust
whipped cream, to serve

Strawberry Sauce
¼ cup caster (superfine) sugar
¼ cup (2 fl oz) water
250 g (8 oz) strawberries
2 tablespoons brandy or strawberry liqueur

1 To make Fritters: Place water, butter, sugar, currants and rind in a small pan; bring to the boil. Stir in flour and beat until smooth using a wooden spoon; cool slightly. Gradually add the eggs, beating well after each addition. Set aside.
2 To make Strawberry Sauce: Heat sugar and water until sugar dissolves. Add strawberries, simmer, uncovered, 5 minutes. Process in food processor for 30 seconds or until smooth. Flavour with brandy or strawberry liqueur, to taste.
3 Heat oil in deep pan. Lower tablespoons of batter into hot oil, cook over medium heat until fritters puff and turn golden brown. Drain on absorbent paper, dust with icing sugar.
4 Serve with Strawberry Sauce and whipped cream. As a variation, kiwi fruit (Chinese gooseberries), mangoes, passionfruit or other berries can be used instead of strawberries.

DRIED FRUIT SALAD

Preparation time: 20 minutes +
2 hours chilling time
Total cooking time: 15 minutes
Serves 6

12 cardamom pods
90 g (3 oz) dried figs
90 g (3 oz) dried pears
90 g (3 oz) dried apples
200 g (6 1/2 oz) dried apricots
90 g (3 oz) muscatel raisins
90 g (3 oz) pitted dessert prunes
1 teaspoon orange flower water

Yoghurt Cardamom Cream
1 cup toasted slivered almonds
3/4 cup (6 fl oz) plain yoghurt
3/4 cup (6 fl oz) sour cream
2 tablespoons soft brown sugar
1/4 teaspoon ground cardamom

1 Tie cardamom pods in piece of muslin (cheesecloth); lightly roll with a rolling pin to bruise.

2 Cut figs and pears into halves. Combine fruits in large saucepan, cover with water to 2 cm (3/4 inch) over fruit. Bring to boil, add cardamom pods. Simmer 10 minutes, then allow to cool.

3 Remove cardamom pods, spoon fruit into a serving dish and stir through orange flower water. Chill well; serve with Yoghurt Cardamom Cream and sprinkle with toasted almonds.

4 To make Yoghurt Cardamom Cream: Combine yoghurt, sour cream, brown sugar and ground cardamom; chill before serving.

DRIED FRUIT COBBLER

Preparation time: 20 minutes
Total cooking time: 30 minutes
Serves 6

500 g (1 lb) mixed dried fruit, chopped
2 cups (16 fl oz) hot water
1/3 cup soft brown sugar
1/2 teaspoon cinnamon
1/4 teaspoon ground ginger
1/4 teaspoon ground cloves

Topping
2 cups self-raising flour
1 teaspoon baking powder
55 g (1 3/4 oz) butter, chopped
1 tablespoon caster (superfine) sugar
3/4 cup (6 fl oz) milk, extra
soft brown sugar, extra

1 Preheat oven to moderate 180°C (350°F/Gas 4). Grease a 23 cm (9 inch), 6-cup capacity ovenproof dish. Soak dried fruit in hot water for 10 minutes. Drain well; mix sugar and spices through and spoon into dish. Cover with aluminium foil and bake in oven 10 minutes.

2 To make Topping: Sift flour and baking powder into bowl. Using fingertips, rub butter into flour until the mixture is a crumbly texture; stir in sugar. Add almost all the liquid, mix to a soft dough, adding more liquid if necessary. Turn onto a floured surface, and knead 2 minutes or until smooth. Roll dough out to 1 cm (1/2 inch) thickness. Using a 5 cm (2 inch) round cutter, cut out about 17 rounds. Remove dish from oven and uncover. Arrange rounds of dough on top of fruit, brush with a little milk and sprinkle lightly with sugar. Return to oven; bake for 20 minutes.

Fudge A soft, sweet confectionary (candy) made with sugar and milk or cream to which other flavourings, such as chocolate and coffee, are added. The mixture is poured into a shallow tin and when cold, it is cut into squares. Fudge originated in the nineteenth century.

Fry To cook a food in very hot vegetable oil or fat over a direct heat. This cooking method usually results in a crisp, golden-brown crust. Deep frying requires sufficient fat to immerse the food. Shallow frying involves enough fat or oil to cover the bottom of a shallow pan and is often used for foods coated with batter. Pan frying uses less fat again, and is suitable for foods that have a light coating of flour or breadcrumbs.

liqueur or sweet wine, and is served chilled with the flavoured juices poured over. Fruit salad as a desert was developed in France, in the early nineteenth century, prompted by the appearance in the Paris markets of numbers of new, exotic fruits.

G

Gado Gado A salad from Indonesia consisting of a mixture of cooked and raw vegetables garnished with sliced, hard-boiled eggs and dressed with a thick, spicy peanut sauce.

Galangal The spicy root of two plants closely related to ginger and used in the cooking of South-East Asia. Greater galangal, the more delicately flavoured, is a knobbly root with creamy white flesh. The lesser galangal has  orange-red flesh, a stronger flavour and is cooked as a vegetable.

Game Animals traditionally hunted for their meat, though many are now bred for the table. Often classified as: game birds (wild duck, grouse, partridge, pheasant and quail); small game (rabbit and hare); and large game (buffalo, deer, wild boar, kangaroo and emu). In

---

GAME

VENISON PIE

★★ **Preparation time:** 35 minutes
Total cooking time: 45–55 minutes
Serves 6–8

1 kg (2 lb) boneless venison
60 g (2 oz) butter
3 rashers bacon, rind removed, diced
2 large onions, chopped
3 tablespoons plain (all-purpose) flour
1/2 teaspoon dried mustard
1/4 cup (2 fl oz) port
1/2 cup (4 fl oz) red wine
6 juniper berries

1 cup (8 fl oz) chicken or beef stock
30 g (1 oz) dried mushrooms, soaked in water for 10 minutes
1/2 tablespoon fresh thyme leaves
pepper
1/4 cup chopped parsley
375 g (12 oz) puff pastry
1 egg, lightly beaten

1 Cut venison into 2 cm (3/4 inch) pieces, heat butter and fry meat quickly to brown; remove from pan, drain on paper towels. Add bacon to pan, cook until crisp, remove, drain. Add onion and fry until golden. Sprinkle flour over onion and stir until brown.

2 Add mustard, port, red wine, berries, stock, mushrooms and thyme leaves to pan and stir until mixture comes to the boil. Add venison and simmer gently until tender, about 30–40 minutes. Preheat oven to 210°C (415°F/Gas 6–7).

3 Using a slotted spoon, transfer meat to a large, greased casserole dish. Continue simmering the sauce until it thickens. Season with pepper. Pour sauce over the meat and sprinkle with parsley.

4 Roll pastry out large enough to cover top of casserole dish. Brush edge of dish with a little egg and cover casserole with pastry. Brush top of pastry with egg and make a couple of slits to allow steam to escape. Bake in preheated oven 10–15 minutes or until pastry is golden.

Note: It is important not to overcook venison as it will become tough.

ABOVE: VENISON PIE AND RABBIT WITH DIJON MUSTARD. OPPOSITE PAGE: QUAILS WITH TARRAGON AND PANCETTA

RABBIT WITH DIJON MUSTARD

Preparation time: 35 minutes ✷ ✷
Total cooking time: 1 hour 40 minutes
Serves 6

2 rabbits, about 1 kg
(2 lb) each
1/4 cup plain (all-purpose)
flour
freshly ground pepper
1/2 teaspoon dry mustard
60 g (2 oz) butter
2 cloves garlic, crushed
250 g (8 oz) small
mushrooms
1 tablespoon olive oil
5 rashers bacon, rind
removed, chopped

2 onions, chopped
2 carrots, diced
1 parsnip, diced
1 cup (8 fl oz) white wine
1/2 cup (4 fl oz) chicken
stock
6 whole allspice
4 teaspoons Dijon
mustard
2 tablespoons chopped
fresh parsley
2 tablespoons cream

1 Preheat oven to moderate 180°C (350°F/Gas 4). Clean rabbits, cut each into 6 portions. Place flour, pepper and mustard in a plastic bag, add rabbit pieces a few at a time. Toss to coat with flour.

2 Heat butter in pan, add garlic and rabbit pieces, cook until browned on both sides. Transfer rabbit to ovenproof dish. Add mushrooms to pan, cook 1 minute, remove. Heat oil in pan. Add bacon, onion, carrot and parsnip. Stir for 3 minutes.

3 Add vegetables, wine, stock, allspice and mustard to rabbit in dish. Cover, cook 1 1/2 hours or until rabbit is tender. Stir in parsley and cream. Serve.

QUAILS WITH TARRAGON AND PANCETTA

Preparation time: 20 minutes ✷
Total cooking time: 40 minutes
Serves 4

8 small quails
1/2 cup (4 fl oz) chicken
stock
1/2 cup plain (all-purpose)
flour
1 tablespoon redcurrant
jelly
1/4 cup (2 fl oz) olive oil
2 onions, chopped
315 g (10 oz) button
mushrooms
105 g (3 1/2 oz) pancetta
1 1/2 cups (12 fl oz) red
wine
pepper, to taste
1 teaspoon chopped fresh
tarragon

1 Tie quails into neat shapes. Place flour in plastic bag. Toss quails in flour, remove excess. Heat oil in a heavy-based pan and cook quails, turning until brown on all sides. Remove from pan. Drain on paper towels.

2 Add onion to pan and cook 1 minute. Add mushrooms and pancetta; cook until mushrooms soften. Add wine and chicken stock and stir until mixture comes to the boil. Add redcurrant jelly, pepper and tarragon.

3 Add quails to sauce and simmer gently, turning quails occasionally until they are tender and sauce has thickened, about 20–30 minutes.

4 Serve quails on a warm serving plate with fried polenta wedges and vegetables in season.

general game meat has a darker colour, stronger flavour and less fat than the meat from domesticated animals. Cuts of large game are often marinated before cooking, otherwise methods are the same as for similar cuts of beef or poultry. Tougher older game is braised, stewed or casseroled and made into pies and pâtés. Young game birds can be roasted. Small game is braised, stewed or casseroled.

Gammon The lower end of a cured side of bacon. Gammon is eaten hot, either boiled and served with parsley sauce, or sliced into thick steaks and grilled (broiled) or gently fried.

Garam Masala A spice mixture of northern Indian origin used to flavour curries and other dishes. The basic ingredients are cumin, coriander, cardamom, cinnamon, pepper and cloves.

Garlic A member of the onion family. Its strongly scented bulb provides a distinctive flavouring integral to the cooking of Asia, the Middle East and the Mediterranean. Each bulb is made up of a number of segments called cloves. The

GARLIC

pungent flavour is released when a clove is cut, if it is crushed or pounded greater quantities are released and the flavour is even more powerful.

Garnish An edible trimming added to a dish before serving to enhance its visual appeal and complement its flavour. Garnishes used on savoury dishes include sprigs of parsley (fresh, fried or chopped) and coriander; dill and fennel (in sprigs or finely chopped); small bunches of watercress; leaves of basil; celery curls and young leaves; raw carrot in long, fine strips; onion rings, curls of spring onion (scallion) and finely chopped chives; slices of hard-boiled egg; small wedges of tomato; edible flowers, such as nasturtiums; slices of lemon, orange or cucumber. Croutons and small bits of bacon, as do pastries often garnish soups and stews. Crystallised (candied) flower petals, fruit and fruit rind are used on sweet dishes.

Gâteau A rich, elaborately decorated cake, often a liqueur-flavoured sponge layered with cream. A gâteau can be served as dessert.

HERB AND GARLIC CORNBREAD SLICES

★ Preparation time: 20 minutes
Total cooking time: 50 minutes
Makes about 16 slices

Herb and Garlic Butter
125 g (4 oz) butter, softened
1 tablespoon chopped fresh parsley
1 tablespoon chopped fresh chives
2 cloves garlic, crushed

2/3 cup self-raising flour
2 teaspoons baking powder
1/2 teaspoon chilli powder
1 1/2 cups polenta (fine)
90 g (3 oz) butter, melted
3 eggs, lightly beaten
3/4 cup (6 fl oz) milk

1 Preheat oven to moderate 180°C (350°F/Gas 4). Brush a 21 x 14 x 7 cm (8½ x 5½ x 2¾ inch) loaf tin with melted butter or oil; line the base and sides with baking paper. Sift flour, baking powder and chilli into bowl. Add polenta and stir until combined. Make a well in the centre. Add butter, eggs and milk to dry ingredients. Using a wooden spoon, stir until just combined; do not overbeat the mixture.

2 Pour mixture into tin. Bake for 45 minutes or until bread is firm in the centre and beginning to brown around the edges. Turn bread out onto a wire rack; leave at least 10 minutes or until cool. Using a sharp knife, cut loaf into thin slices.

3 To make Herb and Garlic Butter: Combine butter, parsley, chives and garlic. Spread on cornbread slices. Place slices on an oven tray; bake for another 5 minutes or until slightly crispy.

ABOUT GARLIC

■ Look for firm compact heads of garlic. Avoid any with greyish loose papery bulbs or those which have begun to sprout. Store fresh garlic bulbs and heads in a cool, dry, dark place for about 2–3 weeks.

■ Garlic loses flavour the longer it is cooked. A whole head of garlic roasted in the oven will yield soft flesh which is surprisingly sweet, whereas a freshly crushed single clove raw will give a distinct bite to a salad. If you like garlic, add it at the end of the cooking process, rather than—as stated in most recipes—at the beginning.

■ One of the most prevalent herbs in cooking, garlic is also available powdered, dried or minced, but it is much more delicious fresh.

■ The easiest way to prepare garlic is to crush the peeled clove in a garlic press. In the absence of a press, crush the clove with the flat part of a knife, press down firmly, and work to a paste.

■ Keep aside one chopping board for processing garlic. The smell of garlic can be removed from hands by rubbing with salt or a cut lemon.

ABOVE: HERB AND GARLIC CORNBREAD SLICES.
OPPOSITE PAGE: GARLIC SOUP

GARLIC SOUP

★ **Preparation time:** 15 minutes
Total cooking time: 35–40 minutes
Serves 4–6

1/4 cup (2 fl oz) olive oil
6 cloves garlic, crushed
1 1/2 cups fresh white breadcrumbs
3 medium ripe tomatoes, peeled and chopped
2 eggs, lightly beaten
1/4 cup chopped fresh parsley
1 litre (4 cups) water
1 teaspoon ground sweet paprika
1/2 teaspoon chilli powder

1 Heat oil in large pan; add garlic. Cook over gentle heat 1–2 minutes until soft but not brown. Add breadcrumbs and cook over medium heat 3 minutes or until they turn a light golden brown.
2 Add chopped tomatoes, chilli powder, paprika and water. Bring to the boil; simmer, covered, for 30 minutes.
3 Add eggs in a thin stream to simmering soup. Cook over low heat for another 2 minutes.
4 Pour into serving bowl, sprinkle parsley over and serve. Serve hot and heavily seasoned.

GARLIC BREAD

■ Traditionally made with a long French bread stick, garlic bread can also be made with any type of crusty bread. Slice the bread almost all the way through, spread with garlic-flavoured butter and bake until hot.

WALNUT AND GARLIC SAUCE

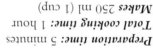 **Preparation time:** 10 minutes
Total cooking time: 5 minutes
Makes 250 ml (1 cup)

105 g (3 1/2 oz) walnut halves
4 cloves garlic, peeled
1/3 cup (2 1/2 fl oz) white wine vinegar
salt
2 cups (16 fl oz) olive oil

1 Place walnuts on a baking tray, bake at 180°C (350°F/Gas 4) for 5 minutes. Cool.
2 Place walnuts and garlic in a food processor, process until finely ground. Add oil in a slow stream until thick and creamy. Add vinegar and salt to taste.
3 Place in a small clean jar, cover with a thin layer of oil, store in the refrigerator for up to one week. Pour away oil before using. Use as a dip for fresh bread and raw celery, or as a sauce for cold veal and pork.

ROASTED GARLIC PASTE

 Preparation time: 5 minutes
Total cooking time: 1 hour
Makes 250 ml (1 cup)

10 bulbs garlic
2 tablespoons olive oil
1/3 cup (2 1/2 fl oz) water

1 Preheat oven to moderate 180°C (350°F/Gas 4). Remove the loose papery skin from garlic bulbs. Place garlic in a greased baking dish, pour over oil and water.
2 Cook garlic in oven for about 1 hour or until garlic is very soft. Spoon oil and water from baking dish over garlic cloves as they cook, add a little more water to baking dish if it dries out. Remove garlic from oven and cool.
3 Separate the garlic cloves, press the cooked garlic out of their skins into a small bowl. Mash garlic with a fork until smooth.
4 Spread on toasted slices of French bread.

ROAST GARLIC

The next time you are cooking a roast, try roasting a head of garlic at the same time. Using a sharp knife, cut off the top of the head. Place in a moderate oven for 30–45 minutes. Serve 1 or 2 cloves to each individual. The soft, sweet flesh can be squeezed over the rest of the food, or spread on toasted slices of French bread.

G

for a special celebration or with coffee. Gâteau is the French word for 'cake'.

Gazpacho A spicy, chilled soup of Spanish origin. It varies from region to region, but usually contains ripe red tomatoes, red peppers (capsicum), cucumber, olive oil and bread crumbs or garlic croutons.

Gefilte Fish Poached fish balls, a traditional Jewish dish made from chopped fish fillets, finely diced onion, breadcrumbs or matzo meal, egg and seasonings. The mixture is formed into balls and cooked in simmering fish stock. Gefilte fish can be eaten warm or chilled.

Gelatine A setting agent prepared from a natural animal protein, collagen, extracted from the bones and cartilage of animals. Available as powdered granules or thin leaves, gelatine is odourless, virtually tasteless and creamy white in colour. When mixed with hot water it forms a viscous liquid which sets as a jelly as it cools. Gelatine is used in sweet and savoury dishes, and can be used with almost all foods apart from some raw fruits which contain an enzyme

which prevents setting. These include pineapple, kiwi fruit (Chinese gooseberry) and pawpaw (papaya).

Gelato Italian ice-cream, made with sweetened milk or cream, egg yolks and flavourings. It is firmer and less sweet than British and American ice-creams.

Genoise Cake A light sponge cake. Eggs and sugar are whisked over a low heat until warm and thick; flour and melted butter are added after

the mixture has cooled. Genoise cake is used for layered cakes, sponge fingers and bombe Alaska.

Ghee Clarified butter, much used in the cooking of northern India. Because the milk solids have been removed, it can be heated to a much higher temperature than butter without burning. To make ghee, melt butter until frothy, scoop off the foam, then gently pour the liquid butter into a heatproof glass container, leaving milk solids in the pan. When set, discard any solids from the base, reheat and repeat the process, straining through fine muslin (cheesecloth).

GELATINE

AVOCADO ASPIC MOUSSE

⭐⭐ **Preparation time:** 30 minutes
Total cooking time: 10–15 minutes
Serves 6

Aspic
light olive oil
1 cup (8 fl oz) chicken stock (see Note)
1 tablespoon gelatine
garnish (pink peppercorns, finely sliced lemon and sliced avocado)

1 tablespoon gelatine
2 ripe medium avocados
2 tablespoons lemon juice
1½ cups mayonnaise
1 teaspoon finely grated white onion
salt and white pepper
½ cup (4 fl oz) cream, whipped

Avocado Mousse
½ cup (4 fl oz) chicken stock

1 To make Aspic: Lightly brush a 4-cup capacity mould with a small amount of light olive oil. Place chicken stock in a small pan and sprinkle with gelatine. Stir over low heat until gelatine is dissolved; cool and pour half of the mixture into base of the mould. Chill in refrigerator until almost set, add garnish and carefully spoon over remaining mixture. Chill until set.

2 To make Avocado Mousse: Place stock in a small pan and sprinkle with gelatine. Heat gently and stir until gelatine is dissolved; allow mixture to cool to lukewarm.

3 Peel avocados, cut in half and remove stones. Chop avocados and place in food processor. Add lemon juice, mayonnaise, onion, salt and pepper and process until smooth. Transfer mixture to a medium bowl. Stir dissolved gelatine into avocado mixture and leave until partially set.

4 Fold whipped cream into mixture and pour mousse over aspic in mould. Refrigerate until set. To unmould, gently loosen sides of mousse to create an air space and invert mousse onto a serving plate.

Note: For the aspic, chicken stock must be well flavoured, clear and free from fat. Commercial aspic powder can be substituted.

FRUITS IN CHARDONNAY JELLY

⭐ **Preparation time:** 30 minutes
Total cooking time: 5 minutes
Serves 4

2 tablespoons gelatine
½ cup (4 fl oz) water
2 cups (16 fl oz) chardonnay
½ cup sugar
¼ cup blanched slivered almonds

2 cups prepared fruit (strawberries, melon balls, seedless grapes, chopped apricots)
ice-cream or whipped cream, for serving

1 Sprinkle gelatine over water in a small bowl. Place chardonnay in a medium pan with sugar and heat gently while stirring to dissolve sugar. Remove from heat, add gelatine mixture and stir until dissolved.

2 Cool jelly until it begins to thicken slightly. Place a few tablespoons of jelly in a 5- or 6-cup capacity mould which has been rinsed with cold water. Arrange a layer of fruit and almonds on jelly, allow to set and repeat until all fruits and almonds have been used.

3 Chill the jelly in refrigerator for several hours or until firmly set. Unmould and serve plain or with ice-cream or whipped cream. Extra chopped fresh fruit may be served with the jelly.

Note: Clear apple juice with a tablespoon lemon juice can be used instead of chardonnay.

ABOVE: FRUITS IN CHARDONNAY JELLY.
OPPOSITE PAGE: COLD LEMON SOUFFLE

COLD LEMON SOUFFLE

Preparation time: 35 minutes
Total cooking time: nil
Serves 4–6

5 eggs, separated
1 cup caster (superfine) sugar
2 teaspoons finely grated lemon rind
3/4 cup (6 fl oz) strained lemon juice
1 tablespoon gelatine

300 ml (9 fl oz) cream, lightly whipped
1/4 cup (2 fl oz) water
chopped pistachio nuts or toasted ground almonds
whipped cream, extra, for decoration

1 Cut a piece of aluminium foil 5 cm (2 inches) longer than the circumference of a deep 16 cm (6½ inch) 1.25 litre (5-cup capacity) soufflé dish. Fold foil in half lengthways. Wrap foil around the outside of soufflé dish extending 5 cm (2 inches) above the rim. Secure foil with string.

2 Using electric beaters, beat egg yolks, sugar and lemon rind in a bowl 3 minutes until sugar has dissolved and mixture is thick and pale. Heat lemon juice and gradually add to yolk mixture, while beating, until well mixed.

3 Combine gelatine with water in a small bowl. Stand bowl in hot water and stir until gelatine has dissolved. Add gradually to lemon mixture, with beaters on low, until combined. Transfer mixture

to a large bowl, cover with plastic wrap and refrigerate 15 minutes, until thickened but not set.

4 Using a metal spoon, fold whipped cream into lemon mixture. Using electric beaters, beat egg whites in a clean, dry mixing bowl until soft peaks form. Fold whites quickly and lightly into lemon mixture until just combined and all lumps of egg white have dissolved. Pour gently into prepared dish and chill until set. Remove foil collar, sprinkle nuts around edge of soufflé and decorate top with extra whipped cream.

ABOUT GELATINE

■ Extracted from animal bones and cartilage, gelatine is sold in powdered form, or as sheets or leaves. Gelatine has no taste so it can be used as a setting agent in foods from pâtés to desserts.

■ Follow any recipe calling for gelatine exactly. Measure water and gelatine carefully, as incorrect amounts will cause the gelatine to set at the wrong consistency. Use a metal teaspoon to remove any undissolved crystals or threads.

■ Take care that when adding dissolved gelatine to the mixture to be set, both are at the same temperature (slightly warm), otherwise gelatine may form into clumps called roping which can't be dissolved. Add dissolved gelatine slowly, stirring constantly until mixture begins to thicken.

Gherkin The small, rough-skinned fruit of a variety of cucumber pickled for use as a condiment to accompany hot boiled beef, cold meats, pâtés and cheese, and as a cocktail savoury.

Giblets The edible inner parts of poultry (the heart, liver and gizzard, and sometimes also the neck). Giblets can be used for stock, gravy, soup or stuffings.

Ginger A spicy tasting root much used in Asian cooking in

both savoury and sweet dishes. The length of the root indicates its maturity (older roots tend to be hotter and more fibrous). Fresh ginger root is peeled, then grated, finely sliced or crushed to season meat, poultry, fish and vegetable dishes. Ground dried ginger is used in desserts. Ginger is also available pickled, preserved and crystallised.

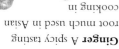

Ginger Beer A sweet, aerated drink made by fermenting sugar, water, ginger and yeast.

Gingerbread An aromatic, sticky cake flavoured with ginger, treacle (light molasses) and cinnamon.

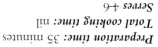

GINGER

Glacé A term applied to food that has been coated with a sugar syrup that hardens into a hard, glossy surface. Glacé cakes, such as petit fours, have a smooth, thin layer of shiny icing.

Glacé Fruit Fruit that has been preserved in syrup; it is moist and sticky on the inside and has a glazed surface achieved by a final dipping in a very strong syrup. Glacé fruit has four times as many kilojoules (calories) as its fresh equivalent.

Glaze A thin glossy surface on a food which enhances its visual appeal and stops it from drying out. Glazes are used on both sweet and savoury dishes; some are applied before cooking, others are brushed onto cold food. Pastry can be glazed with egg white before cooking and biscuits (cookies), cakes and breads are often sprinkled with a sugar and milk mixture before going into the oven. Hot vegetables are glazed with sugar and melted butter. Cold savoury food can be brushed with aspic jelly, and fruit flans are coated with a glaze made of jam or jelly.

Globe Artichoke See Artichoke.

GINGER

GINGER-CHILLI DRUMSTICKS WITH CUCUMBER YOGHURT

Preparation time: 10 minutes +
3 hours marinating
Total cooking time: 16 minutes
Serves 6

12 chicken drumsticks
(about 1.3 kg/
2 lb 10 oz)
1 tablespoon grated fresh
ginger
2 teaspoons bottled
crushed chilli
1/4 teaspoon ground tumeric
1 teaspoon lemon juice
1 teaspoon grated lemon
rind
1 cup plain yoghurt
1 1/2 teaspoons soft brown
sugar

Cucumber Yoghurt
1 cup plain yoghurt
1 teaspoon bottled
crushed chilli
1 small cucumber, finely
chopped
salt, to taste
1/2 teaspoon caster
(superfine) sugar

1 Wipe chicken and pat dry. Line a grill tray with foil. Lightly brush tray with melted butter or oil. Combine ginger, chilli, turmeric, lemon juice and rind, yoghurt and sugar in a large bowl; mix well. Add chicken, stir well to coat with marinade. Store, covered with plastic wrap, in refrigerator 3 hours or overnight, stirring occasionally. Drain chicken; reserve marinade.

2 Place drumsticks on prepared tray and grill, brushing frequently with marinade, under medium heat 8 minutes on each side or until cooked through. Serve hot or cold with Cucumber Yoghurt.

3 To make Cucumber Yoghurt: Combine all ingredients in small bowl and mix well.

GINGER CHOCOLATES

Preparation time: 10 minutes
Total cooking time: 5 minutes
Makes about 24

100 g (3 1/3 oz) dark
(semi-sweet) chocolate
125 g (4 oz) crystallised
ginger pieces

1 Line a 32 x 28 cm (13 x 11 inch) oven tray with aluminium foil. Place chocolate in a medium heatproof bowl. Stand over a pan of simmering water, stir until chocolate has melted and is smooth. Cool slightly.

2 Add ginger to chocolate, stir to combine, making sure ginger pieces are completely coated in chocolate.

3 Place heaped teaspoonful of mixture onto prepared tray. Leave on tray until set. Serve with coffee or liqueur.

Note: Ginger Chocolates can be made 4 weeks ahead. Store in an airtight container in a cool, dark place, or refrigerate in hot weather.

LEFT: GINGER CHOCOLATES; ABOVE: GINGER-CHILLI DRUMSTICKS WITH CUCUMBER YOGHURT. OPPOSITE PAGE: GINGERBREAD

ABOUT GINGER

■ Fresh ginger is used extensively in Asian cooking, with fish, chicken, duck, prawns (shrimps) or vegetables. To prepare fresh ginger, scrape the tough skin from the root and either grate or thinly slice the flesh. Bruise dried ginger root to open its fibres and release its flavours.

■ Leftover peeled fresh ginger can be stored for several months if packed tightly into a clean glass screw-top jar. Pour in enough sherry to completely cover the ginger, seal the jar and store in the refrigerator.

■ Powdered ginger is traditionally used in ginger biscuits, brandy snaps or gingerbread. It can also be sprinkled on melons—offering a surprising, but pleasant contrast between hot and cool.

GINGER APPLE MARMALADE

✴ **Preparation time:** 30 minutes
Total cooking time: 45 minutes
Makes 1.25 litres (5 cups)

1 kg (2 lb) cooking apples	2 tablespoons grated fresh
4 cups sugar, warmed	ginger
2 large lemons	1 cup (8 fl oz) water
	grated rind and juice of

1 Peel, core and chop the apples finely.

2 Place sugar and water in large pan and bring to the boil, stirring until sugar has dissolved. Add the grated fresh ginger, lemon juice and chopped apples. Reduce heat, simmer, stirring occasionally, until setting point is reached.

3 Spoon into warm, sterilised jars, seal, label and date the jars.

GINGERED GREEN BEANS

✴ **Preparation time:** 5 minutes
Total cooking time: 7–8 minutes
Serves 6

1 cm (1/2 inch) piece fresh	2 tablespoons finely
ginger, finely grated	chopped fresh mint
500 g (1 lb) green beans,	1 teaspoon ground
trimmed and sliced	fenugreek
	2 tablespoons olive oil

1 Pour enough water into a pan to cover the bottom and heat. Add ginger and fenugreek and cook for 2 minutes.

2 Add mint and beans and toss lightly. Cook over low heat until beans are just tender.

3 Remove from pan and refrigerate until chilled. Toss in olive oil before serving.

GINGERBREAD

✴ **Preparation time:** 15 minutes
Total cooking time: 30–40 minutes
Makes one 20 x 30 cm (8 x 12 inch) square cake

250 g (8 oz) butter	2 tablespoons boiling
1/2 cup demerara sugar	water, extra
1/2 cup treacle	2 eggs, lightly beaten
1/2 cup golden syrup	3 1/2 cups plain
(light corn syrup)	(all-purpose) flour
1 cup (8 fl oz) water	1 tablespoon ground
1 cup sultanas	ginger
2 teaspoons bicarbonate of	2 teaspoons ground allspice
soda (baking soda)	1/2 teaspoon salt

1 Preheat oven to 180°C (350°F/Gas 4). Brush a deep 20 x 30 cm (8 x 12 inch) oblong cake tin with melted butter or oil, line the base and sides with paper; grease paper. Place the butter, demerara sugar, treacle, golden syrup and water in a large pan. Cook over a low heat until butter melts and sugar dissolves, add sultanas and cook slightly.

2 Blend bicarbonate of soda with extra water, add to butter mixture with lightly beaten eggs.

3 Sift flour, ground ginger, allspice and salt into a large bowl. Make a well in centre and add butter mixture; stir until ingredients are just combined and moistened. Spoon into tin; bake 30 minutes, or until gingerbread is cooked through.

4 May be served warm with whipped cream, or cold, dusted with icing (confectioners) sugar; or serve spread with butter.

Golden Syrup (Light corn syrup) A smooth, clear syrup derived from the processing of sugar cane, used in cooking and as a sweetener for porridge and desserts.

Goats Milk Milk from goats is whiter and sweeter than cow's milk. Used mainly to make cheese, it is more easily digestible than cow's milk and can be used by those allergic to cow's milk. Available from health food shops.

Goats Cheese See Chèvre.

Gnocchi Small savoury dumplings made with potato, semolina flour or puff pastry. Gnocchi are poached and served with a sauce or melted butter and grated cheese as a first course, accompanied by a salad as a main course or served as a side dish to roast meat or grilled (broiled) chicken. The word is Italian for 'lumps'; similar dumplings knödel, noques and knepfe are found in the cooking of Austria, Hungary and north-eastern France.

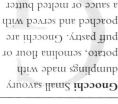

GNOCCHI

POTATO GNOCCHI WITH RICH TOMATO SAUCE

Preparation time: 40 minutes
★★
Total cooking time: 45 minutes
Serves 4–6

3 medium potatoes
(700 g/1 lb 5 oz),
peeled and chopped
1 large onion, finely
chopped
1 clove garlic, crushed
425 g (13½ oz) can
tomatoes, undrained
2 teaspoons capers, finely
chopped
4 anchovy fillets, chopped
1 tablespoon finely
chopped fresh basil
shavings parmesan cheese,
extra, for serving

Sauce
1 tablespoon olive oil
freshly ground pepper
¼ cup freshly grated
parmesan cheese
30 g (1 oz) butter, melted
2 cups plain (all-purpose)
flour, sifted

1 Cook potato in large pan of boiling water until just tender; drain and mash. Transfer to large bowl. Add flour, butter, parmesan and pepper. Mix until well combined. Turn onto a lightly floured surface. Knead 4 minutes or until smooth.
2 Form dough into a long roll; divide into 2.5 cm (1 inch) pieces. Form into small rounds. Indent with fingertips or fork prongs to shape.
3 Heat a large pan of water until boiling. Gently lower batches of gnocchi into the boiling water and cook for 5 minutes or until gnocchi float to the top. Drain and keep warm.
4 To make Sauce: Heat oil in a medium pan and cook onion over low heat 5–8 minutes or until soft. Add garlic, cook for another minute.

add crushed tomatoes and their juice. Cook for 15 minutes, uncovered, add capers, anchovy fillets and fresh basil. Cook 1 minute. Pour sauce over gnocchi and serve with parmesan.

SPINACH GNOCCHI

Preparation time: 40 minutes
★★
Total cooking time: 45 minutes
Serves 4

750 g (1½ lb) spinach or
young silverbeet (Swiss
chard), cleaned, trimmed
and very finely chopped
410 g (13 oz) ricotta
cheese
1 cup freshly grated
parmesan cheese
pinch pepper
pinch ground nutmeg
plain (all-purpose) flour
for rolling
2 eggs
90 g (3 oz) butter, melted

1 Place spinach in a bowl with ricotta, eggs, half the parmesan, pepper and nutmeg. Mix well.
2 With flour-dusted hands, shape spinach mixture into 5 cm (2 inch) balls; lightly coat with a little flour to prevent sticking. Set aside on greaseproof paper until required. Preheat oven to 200°C (400°F/Gas 6).
3 Heat a large pan of water to boiling. Drop gnocchi 3–4 at a time into water. Simmer until they float to the surface. Remove with a slotted spoon and drain briefly.
4 Transfer gnocchi to a buttered shallow baking dish. Top with remaining parmesan, drizzle with melted butter. Bake 15 minutes until browned.

Above: POTATO GNOCCHI WITH RICH TOMATO SAUCE. Opposite page: PUMPKIN GNOCCHI WITH SAGE BUTTER

Goose A large waterbird with sweet-tasting gamey flesh; compared with other poultry, goose has a lot of fat and a low meat yield. Gosling (young goose) is usually roasted; older birds are best braised or casseroled. Goose liver is used to make pâté de foie gras.

Gooseberry A small, firm, tart-flavoured fruit; skin colour can be yellow, green or red-black, depending on the variety. The gooseberry originated in the cooler parts of northern Europe; the American gooseberry comes from the east coast of North America. Gooseberries can be served fresh or stewed; they are also available frozen and canned.

Gorgonzola A semi-soft, creamy textured, blue-veined cow's milk cheese with a rich, strong flavour; its veining is more green than blue. Named after the northern Italian village where it was first produced more than a thousand years ago, gorgonzola can be served with

PUMPKIN GNOCCHI WITH SAGE BUTTER

Preparation time: 30 minutes + 5 minutes standing
Total cooking time: 1 hour 45 minutes
Serves 4

500 g (1 lb) pumpkin
1½ cups plain (all-purpose) flour
¼ cup freshly grated parmesan cheese
freshly ground black pepper

Sage Butter
90 g (3 oz) butter
2 tablespoons chopped fresh sage
¼ cup freshly grated parmesan cheese, extra

1 Preheat oven to moderate 180°C (350°F/Gas 4). Brush a baking tray with oil or melted butter. Cut pumpkin into large pieces and place on prepared tray. Bake for 1½ hours or until very tender. Allow to cool slightly. Scrape flesh from skin, avoiding any tough or crispy parts.

Place pumpkin flesh in a large mixing bowl. Sift flour into bowl, add parmesan cheese and pepper. Mix until well combined. Turn onto a lightly floured surface and knead for 2 minutes or until smooth.

2 Divide dough in half. Using floured hands, roll each half into a sausage about 40 cm (16 inches) long. Cut into 16 equal pieces. Form each piece into an oval shape and indent with fork prongs.

3 Heat a large pan of water until boiling. Gently lower small batches of gnocchi into water. Cook until gnocchi rise to the surface, and then cook for another 3 minutes. Drain in a colander and keep warm.

To make Sage Butter: Melt butter in small pan, remove pan from heat and stir in the chopped sage. Set pan aside for 5 minutes; keep warm. To serve, place equal portions of gnocchi in individual serving bowls, drizzle with Sage Butter and sprinkle with extra parmesan cheese.

Gouda A semi-hard Dutch cow's milk cheese with a mild, buttery flavour that deepens as the cheese matures. Gouda is made in wheel shapes which are coated with red or yellow wax; the interior of the cheese is dotted with small unevenly shaped holes.

Gougère Choux pastry flavoured with cheese, baked in a ring shape and served either sliced as a finger food with drinks (in Burgundy it is traditional in wine-tasting cellars) or, with a chicken or meat mixture, as a first course or light luncheon dish.

Goulash A rich meat stew of Hungarian origin containing beef or veal and onions and seasoned with paprika. It is served topped with chopped parsley and accompanied by sour cream.

Granadilla See Passionfruit.

Granita A sorbet made with fruit juices, soft fruit, coffee, wine or liqueur, sweetened with a little sugar, and frozen until grainy crystals form. It is served between courses or as a dessert.

Grape A small, sweet-fleshed, smooth-skinned fruit that grows in tight

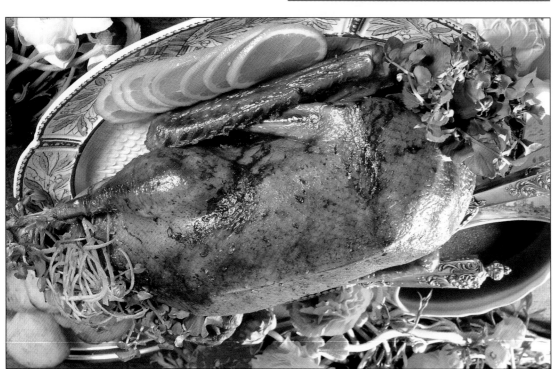

GOOSE

ROAST GOOSE

✷✷ **Preparation time:** 40 minutes
Total cooking time: 2 hours 45 minutes
Serves 6

3 kg (6 lb) goose	2 teaspoons grated lemon
30 g (1 oz) butter	rind
1 onion, finely chopped	1/2 cup chopped fresh
2 green apples, peeled,	parsley
cored and chopped	2 tablespoons plain (all-
1 1/2 cups chopped, pitted	purpose) flour
prunes	2 tablespoons brandy
3 cups small cubes of bread	1 1/2 cups chicken
	stock (12 fl oz)

1 Remove all loose fat from goose. Using a fine skewer, prick the skin across the breast. Set aside.

2 Melt butter in pan, add onion and cook, stirring, until golden. Combine butter and onion with apples, prunes, bread, rind and parsley; mix thoroughly. Spoon stuffing loosely into cavity of goose, then join edges of cavity with skewer. Tie legs together.

3 Preheat oven to 200°C (400°F/Gas 6). Sprinkle 1 tablespoon of flour over goose. Place goose on a rack in a baking dish and bake for 15 minutes. Remove and discard any fat from baking dish. Prick skin of goose to remove excess fat. Cover with foil. Reduce oven temperature to 180°C (350°F/Gas 4) and return goose to oven and bake for 2 hours, basting occasionally. Discard fat as it

accumulates in baking dish. Remove foil, bake a further 15 minutes or until goose is golden. Remove goose from baking dish. Allow to stand for 15 minutes before carving; keep warm.

4 Drain all but 2 teaspoons of fat from baking dish and place dish over a low heat. Add remaining flour and stir well to incorporate all the sediment. Cook, stirring constantly, over medium heat until well browned, taking care not to burn. Gradually stir in brandy and stock. Heat, stirring constantly, until gravy boils and thickens. Serve the goose with gravy, roast potatoes and creamed onions.

Note: During roasting, baste goose with its own, plentiful fat. This helps crisp the skin.

ABOUT GOOSE

■ Geese usually weigh from 3 to 5 kg (6 to 10 lb) making goose a meal for at least six people; one serve is approximately 500 g (1 lb). Choose a young bird in the mid-weight range and, if possible, a hen.

■ Always baste the goose as it cooks. Scattering flour over the top of the bird will coat the skin in dark, crusty speckles. Alternatively, increase heat of the oven for a few minutes, then splash the bird with a few drops of cold water; this will leave the skin crisp.

ABOVE: ROAST GOOSE.
OPPOSITE PAGE, ABOVE: GRAPEFRUIT WATERCRESS
SALAD; BELOW: GRAPEFRUIT MARMALADE

caraway-flavoured.
Traditionally served with sugar, salt and dill.
Gravlax Salmon fillets cured in a marinade of sugar, salt and dill. Traditionally served with caraway-flavoured.

Gratin The crisp, golden crust formed when breadcrumbs and/or grated cheese are spread over already cooked food, dotted with butter, and then browned.

as marmalade and grapefruit juice is used in cooking and as a drink.

Grapefruit A large round citrus fruit with juicy segmented flesh and yellow to golden-pink skin. It is a popular breakfast fruit, cut in half crossways and served in the skin (the segments can be loosened from the membrane with a special knife). It is cooked

dried as raisins, sultanas and currants, and used in wine-making.

clusters on vines. Varieties range in colour from pale green to dark purple-black, some with seeds, others seedless. Grapes are eaten fresh as a dessert fruit or with cheese;

GRAPEFRUIT

GRAPEFRUIT WATERCRESS SALAD

⁂ **Preparation time:** 20 minutes
Total cooking time: nil
Serves 6

220 g (7 oz) watercress
1 large orange
1 tablespoon raspberry vinegar
1 medium grapefruit
3 tablespoons olive oil

1 Wash and dry watercress thoroughly. Tear into large sprigs, discarding thick stems. Place in a serving bowl.
2 Cut a slice off each end of orange to where the flesh starts. Using a small knife cut the skin away from the orange in a circular motion, cutting only deep enough to remove all white membrane. (Reserve a 4 cm (1½ inch) long piece of orange peel.) Separate segments by cutting between the membrane and flesh. Repeat process with the grapefruit and scatter segments over watercress.
3 With a sharp knife, cut away white pith from reserved peel. Cut peel into long strips.
4 Drizzle oil over salad, then vinegar. Toss lightly to combine. Garnish with strips of orange peel.

Note: Raspberry vinegar can be made by mixing ⅔ cup crushed raspberries with 2 cups white wine vinegar. Place in a glass bottle with a cork or plastic (not metal) lid. Leave 3 days in cool dark place, shaking occasionally. Strain before use.

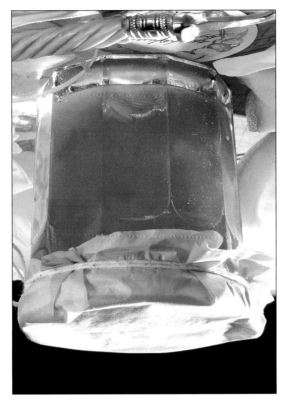

GRAPEFRUIT MARMALADE

⁂ **Preparation time:** 35 minutes
Total cooking time: 1 hour 40 minutes
Makes 1 litre (4 cups)

750 g (1½ lb) grapefruit
2 litres (8 cups) water
2 medium lemons
6 cups sugar, warmed

1 Peel grapefruit and lemons thinly. Cut the peel into very fine strips and place in a large saucepan. Remove pith from fruit and cut flesh into small pieces, reserving seeds.
2 Tie seeds and some pith in a piece of muslin (cheesecloth) and add to the peel with the water. Bring water to boiling point then simmer until peel is tender and liquid reduced by half.
3 Add sugar, stir until dissolved then boil rapidly until setting point is reached. Leave 10 minutes. Skim gently, turn into warm, sterilised jars and seal. When cool, label and date.

ABOUT GRAPEFRUIT

■ Grapefruit come as large yellow or smaller pink fruit. In either case, choose ones which are evenly coloured and unblemished. They will keep well, for several weeks, in a cool place because of their thick skin.
■ Grapefruit are popular as a breakfast dish; simply cut in half and sprinkle lightly with sugar. Special double-sided serrated grapefruit knives help loosen segments from the membrane.

Scandinavian spirit aquavit. (Gin, vodka or brandy can be substituted).

Gravy A sauce made in the pan from the juices released by roasting meat or poultry, thickened with flour, diluted with stock, wine or water and served over meat, poultry or vegetables.

Grecque, à la A French term for food cooked in a marinade flavoured with olive oil and lemon juice and served cold.

Greek Food In the early evening, sitting in outdoor cafes, the Greeks enjoy a glass of ouzo and a selection of little morsels, collectively called *mezze*. The selection may include taramasalata, tzatziki (a mixture of yoghurt, cucumber and garlic), dolmades, marinated vegetables, cold meats, octopus and fish. It is served with pitta bread. Greek yoghurt, thick and creamy, is often eaten for breakfast with honey. And feta, the famous goats milk cheese, is crumbled over many dishes, not just the familiar Greek salad. Lamb (or more often mutton) plays an important role in Greek cooking, especially in the north of the country. It is slowly roasted until very tender and served

GRAPES

GRAPE AND CURLY ENDIVE (CHICORY) SALAD

Preparation time: 15 minutes
Total cooking time: nil
Serves 4–6

Dressing

1/2 head curly endive (chicory)	3 tablespoons red wine vinegar
220 g (7 oz) seedless green grapes	3 tablespoons olive oil
220 g (7 oz) black grapes	1 teaspoon French mustard
1 Spanish (large red) onion, chopped	freshly ground black pepper

1 Wash and dry curly endive. Shred leaves. Place endive, grapes and onion in a large salad bowl.

2 **To make Dressing:** Mix vinegar, olive oil, mustard and black pepper in a small jar. Shake well until combined. Pour dressing over salad and toss gently to combine. Serve.

FROSTED GRAPES

Lightly whisk 1 egg white in medium bowl. Gently wash and pat dry grapes (either singly or in small bunches) with paper towel. Carefully dip or brush grapes with egg white, then sprinkle or lightly roll in caster (superfine) sugar, covering all sides. Shake off excess. Place on a paper-lined tray to dry. Repeat process. Use to decorate cakes, desserts or drinks.

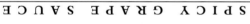

SPICY GRAPE SAUCE

Preparation time: 15 minutes
Total cooking time: 40–50 minutes
Makes 1 litre (4 cups)

2 kg (4 lb) grapes, washed	1 teaspoon ground ginger
2 cups (16 fl oz) vinegar	2 cloves garlic
2 cups soft brown sugar	1/4 teaspoon chilli powder
1/2 teaspoon ground cloves	
6 peppercorns	

1 Place grapes and vinegar in a large saucepan or boiler and squash grapes with a wooden spoon. Simmer gently 20 minutes or until grape skins are tender. Strain and push grapes through a coarse sieve. Discard skins and seeds.

2 Return to saucepan and add remaining ingredients. Stir until boiling and simmer another 20–30 minutes. Remove from heat and strain again. Pour into warm, sterilised jars and seal. When cool, label and date.

Note: White or black grapes may be used for this recipe. Serve Spicy Grape Sauce with pork, duck or goose.

GRAPES WITH CHEESE

Make a very simple but elegant cheese board with black grapes and a soft cheese. Choose goats cheese, brie or camembert, or cream cheese mixed with sour cream or whipped fresh cream. Serve with slices of fruit bread and walnuts or pecans.

Gremolata A mixture of finely chopped parsley, finely grated lemon zest, crushed garlic and sometimes chopped anchovy, traditionally sprinkled over the veal dish osso bucco just before

Green Pepper See Peppers.

Green Goddess An anchovy-flavoured mayonnaise used on fish and shellfish. It gets its green colour from the addition of finely chopped parsley.

Greengage A variety of plum with pale yellowy-green skin and sweet, fragrant yellow flesh. It is eaten fresh, cooked as jam or stewed as a filling for tarts.

with baked potatoes. The Greeks like to serve their food tepid rather than hot. Greek vegetables are often marinated: the most common are eggplant (aubergine), zucchini (courgette) and artichokes. Vegetables à la grecque are among the most delicious of summer vegetable dishes. Greek desserts are rich and sticky. Pastries filled with nuts and honey (baklava) are traditionally served with a glass of cold water and a cup of very strong sweet coffee.

OPPOSITE PAGE: GRAPE AND ENDIVE SALAD.
ABOVE: TARAMASALATA;
RIGHT: TZATZIKI

GREEK CLASSICS

TARAMASALATA

⋆ Preparation time: 20 minutes +
2 hours refrigeration
Total cooking time: 20 minutes
Makes 1½ cups

2 large old potatoes, peeled
125 g (4 oz) cod's roe or tarama
⅓ cup (2½ fl oz) lemon juice
2 tablespoons fresh parsley
⅔ cup (5 fl oz) olive oil

1 Cut potatoes into 2 cm (¾ inch) cubes. Place into small pan; cover with water. Bring to boil, reduce heat and simmer, covered, for 15 minutes or until tender. Drain well. Mash potato with a fork until almost smooth; cool.

2 Using electric beaters, beat roe in small mixing bowl on high speed 2 minutes. Add potato gradually, beating thoroughly after each addition.

3 Add oil and juice gradually, beating thoroughly after each addition. When all the oil and juice has been added, beat mixture on high speed for 5 minutes or until light and fluffy.

4 Refrigerate for 2 hours. Finely chop parsley. Transfer puree to serving dish; sprinkle with parsley. Serve at room temperature with bread and olives.

TZATZIKI

⋆ Preparation time: 15 minutes +
2 hours refrigeration
Total cooking time: 20 minutes
Serves 6

3 small cucumbers, coarsely grated
500 g (16 oz) thick natural yoghurt
3 cloves garlic, crushed
1 teaspoon finely chopped fresh dill
1 tablespoon olive oil
salt and freshly ground black pepper, to taste
2 pitta breads
2 tablespoons olive oil, extra

1 Line a fine strainer with muslin (cheesecloth). Spoon cucumber into strainer, cover with cloth to enclose. Press and squeeze firmly to remove the moisture from the cucumber. Place cucumber in mixing bowl.

2 Add yoghurt, garlic, dill and oil; mix well to combine. Season to taste. Cover with plastic wrap; refrigerate for at least 2 hours or overnight.

3 Preheat oven to moderate 180°C (350°F/Gas 4). Cut through the centre of pitta breads with a sharp knife. Brush rough side with oil. Cut each round into eight wedges. Bake bread on ungreased tray 20 minutes or until crisp. Serve cool with chilled yoghurt dip.

Note: If preferred, you can serve tzatziki with savoury crackers or crisps instead of pitta bread. It is a very refreshing dip.

---

serving; a specialty of the Italian city of Milan.

Gribiche Sauce A cold sauce similar to mayonnaise, but using the yolk of a hard-boiled egg instead of a raw egg yolk; capers, gherkin, chopped egg white and fines herbes can be added; serve with fish and cold meat.

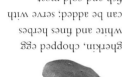

Griddle Cake Small flat cakes, either sweet or savoury, cooked on a griddle (a thick, flat iron plate), but now also cooked on a hot plate or in a frying pan.

Grill (Broil) To cook food quickly by direct heat either under a griller (broiler) or on a barbecue; only one side of the food at a time is exposed to the heat source.

Grissini Long, thin sticks of crisp, rusk-like bread. In Italy bread sticks are served along with bread at a meal; they are often to be seen bunched in tumblers on restaurant tables.

Grouse A small, mostly ground-dwelling game bird. Young birds can be

CHEESE TRIANGLES ✦✦

Preparation time: 35 minutes
Total cooking time: 20 minutes
Serves 4–6

200 g (6½ oz) feta cheese
1 egg, lightly beaten
white pepper to taste
105 g (3½ oz) ricotta cheese
2 tablespoons olive oil
¼ cup grated mozzarella cheese
15 sheets filo pastry
2 tablespoons butter, melted

1 Preheat oven to moderate 180°C (350°F/Gas 4). Place feta in medium mixing bowl; mash with a fork. Add ricotta, mozzarella, egg and pepper; mix well.

2 Place one sheet of pastry lengthways on work surface. Brush all over with combined oil and butter. Fold into thirds lengthways.

3 Place 1 tablespoon cheese mixture on corner of pastry strip. Fold this corner over the filling to edge of pastry to form a triangle. Continue to fold until filling is enclosed and end of pastry is reached. Repeat process with remaining pastry and filling.

4 Place triangles on lightly greased oven tray. Brush with oil and butter mixture. Bake for 20 minutes or until crisp and golden.

Note: While working with filo, keep it covered with a clean, damp tea-towel to prevent drying out. Cooked triangles can be frozen for up to 3 months.

SOUVLAKIA ✦

Preparation time: 20 minutes + overnight refrigeration
Total cooking time: 10 minutes
Serves 4

1 kg (2 lb) leg of lamb, boned
1 green pepper (capsicum), cut into 2 cm (¾ inch) squares
1 red pepper (capsicum), cut into 2 cm (¾ inch) squares
⅔ cup (5 fl oz) olive oil
1 tablespoon white wine vinegar
2 cloves garlic, crushed
3 teaspoons dried oregano leaves
2 bay leaves, crumbled
salt and freshly ground black pepper, to taste
⅓ cup (2½ fl oz) lemon juice

1 Trim lamb of excess fat and sinew. Cut lamb evenly into 3 cm (1¼ inch) cubes.

2 Thread the meat and red pepper pieces alternately onto oiled skewers; place in a shallow non-metal dish.

3 Combine juice, oil, vinegar, garlic, oregano, bay leaves, salt and pepper. Pour over meat on skewers. Cover with plastic wrap and refrigerate overnight, turning occasionally. Drain skewers and reserve marinade.

4 Place skewers on lightly greased grill. Cook over medium heat 10 minutes or until tender, brushing with reserved marinade several times during cooking. Serve Souvlakia with warm pitta bread and Greek salad or Tzatziki (cucumber yoghurt dip).

roasted or grilled (broiled); older birds are best casseroled or braised. In Scotland roast grouse is traditionally served with bread sauce and redcurrant jelly.

Gruel A thin porridge made by boiling meal, usually oatmeal, in water, vegetable broth or milk. It is one of the oldest forms of cooked food—the Egyptians made millet, barley and wheat gruel.

Gruyère A Swiss hard cow's milk cheese, pale in colour and with a sharp but creamy nutty flavour. The curd is 'cooked' in heated whey and then pressed into wheel-shaped moulds to mature; its interior is dotted with small holes. Gruyère is served on the cheeseboard at the end of a meal or is cooked in fondues and quiches.

Guacamole A Mexican dish consisting of mashed ripe avocado, finely chopped onion, lime or lemon juice, coriander and sometimes tomato, and seasoned with chilli. It is served with corn chips or as a dip.

MOUSSAKA

Preparation time: 20 minutes
+ 1 hour standing
Total cooking time: 1 hour 45 minutes
Serves 6

3 medium eggplants (aubergines)
1 tablespoon salt
1/2 cup (4 fl oz) olive oil

Meat Sauce
2 tablespoons olive oil
1 large onion, finely chopped
500 g (1 lb) minced (ground) beef
2 tablespoons dry white wine
425 g (13 1/2 oz) can tomato puree
1 tablespoon finely chopped fresh flat-leaf parsley
2 teaspoons finely chopped fresh mint leaves
1/2 teaspoon ground cinnamon
1/4 teaspoon ground white pepper

Cheese Sauce
90 g (3 oz) butter
1/3 cup plain (all-purpose) flour
2 cups (16 fl oz) milk
2 eggs, lightly beaten
2/3 cup grated romano cheese

1 Cut unpeeled eggplant into 1 cm (1/2 inch) slices. Sprinkle both sides with salt; stand in a colander 1 hour. Rinse in cold water; drain well. Squeeze out excess moisture with paper towels.

2 To make Meat Sauce: Heat oil in pan. Add onion and beef. Stir over high heat 10 minutes or until well browned and all liquid has evaporated. Add wine, tomato puree, herbs, cinnamon and pepper; bring to boil. Reduce heat, simmer, covered, 20 minutes, stirring occasionally. Remove lid and simmer 10 minutes.

3 To make Cheese Sauce: Heat butter in small pan; add flour. Stir over low heat for 2 minutes. Add milk gradually to pan, stirring until smooth. Stir over medium heat for 5 minutes or until mixture boils and thickens. Cook for 1 minute; remove pan from heat. Add eggs and cheese; beat until smooth.

4 Preheat oven to moderate 180°C (350°F/Gas 4). Heat oil in heavy-based pan. Cook eggplant a few slices at a time until golden; remove from pan, drain on paper towels. Divide eggplant into three. Arrange one portion over base of shallow ovenproof dish. Spread half with half the mince sauce. Spread Cheese Sauce over eggplant; second layer of eggplant, remaining mince and eggplant. Spread Cheese Sauce over eggplant. Bake 45 minutes or until golden. Leave in dish for 5 minutes before serving.

OPPOSITE PAGE, ABOVE: SOUVLAKIA; BELOW: CHEESE TRIANGLES. ABOVE: BAKLAVA

BAKLAVA

Preparation time: 15 minutes
Total cooking time: 40 minutes
Serves 4-6

375 g (12 oz) walnuts, finely chopped, not ground
155 g (5 oz) almonds, finely chopped
1/2 teaspoon ground cinnamon
1/2 teaspoon ground mixed spice
1 tablespoon caster (superfine) sugar
2 tablespoons butter, melted
1 tablespoon olive oil
16 sheets filo pastry

Syrup
1 cup sugar
2/3 cup (5 fl oz) water
3 whole cloves
3 teaspoons lemon juice

1 Preheat oven to moderate 180°C (350°F/Gas 4). Brush sides and base of shallow 18 x 28 cm (7 x 11 inch) ovenproof dish with oil. Combine walnuts, almonds, spices and sugar in a bowl; divide into three.

2 Sprinkle one portion walnut mixture over pastry. Repeat process with another three sheets of pastry. Place one sheet of pastry on work surface. Brush half the sheet with combined butter and oil; fold in half widthways. Trim edges to fit dish. Place in dish. Repeat process using four sheets of pastry at a time and walnut mixture in between. When final four sheets of pastry are on top, trim edges.

3 Brush top of pastry with remaining butter and oil mixture. Cut the slice in four lengthways. (Do not cut through the base). Bake 30 minutes.

4 Pour cooled syrup over hot slice. When cold, cut slice into squares or diamonds.

5 To make Syrup: Stir ingredients in pan over low heat until mixture boils and sugar dissolves. Reduce heat, simmer without stirring 10 minutes.

Gugelhopf (Kugelhupf) A yeast cake containing almonds with sultanas, currants or raisins, and the cherry liqueur kirsch, and baked in a high, fluted ring mould.

Guava The fruit of a tree native to Central America and the Caribbean. It is about the size and shape of a small apple with a thin green to yellow skin and a pulpy flesh that ranges in colour from off-white to red, is studded with tiny edible seeds and has a flavour reminiscent of pineapple and lemon. Guavas can be eaten fresh (scooped from the skin with a teaspoon), added to fruit salad, pureed for use in ice-creams and sorbets or cooked as jam and jelly. Guava juice is a popular drink in Hawaii.

Gumbo A thick, spicy soup-stew. It is made from vegetables and seafood, meat, poultry or sausage and is often served with rice. The dish is named for the gombo, or okra (ladies' fingers), an African vegetable introduced into the Americas in the days of slavery. Okra thickens and gives a distinctive, slightly gelatinous texture to the stew, but is not used in all gumbos; filé powder is also frequently added. The gumbo is a specialty of the Louisiana region.

HERBS

Herbs, especially fresh ones, can lift dishes from out of the ordinary into the realms of the exceptional. You can be generous with them, although it is wise to be discreet when using dried herbs—their flavour is concentrated and too much can ruin a dish.

BASIL: Bright-green herb with distinctive taste and aroma. Staple ingredient in Italian cuisine. Essential to pesto sauce. **BUY:** fresh, store in water 5 days; or dried. **USE:** whole or chopped leaves as ingredient or garnish. Cooking diminishes flavour. **FOODS:** tomato, eggplant (aubergine) or zucchini (courgette), green salads, pasta dishes.

BAY: Glossy, dark-green leaves essential to bouquet garni and many marinades. **BUY:** dried (whole leaves); fresh not usually available. **USE:** whole leaves for flavour. Cooking makes the flavour more pronounced; discard before serving. **FOODS:** meat and chicken dishes, baked fish, pickling mixtures. **VARIETIES:** Bay Laurel, Sweet Laurel.

CHIVES: Thin, grassy herb with delicate flavour suggestive of onions. **BUY:** fresh, keep in water 5 days; or dried, use a third less than fresh. **USE:** chopped or whole stalks for garnishing, or chopped as an ingredient. Cooking diminishes flavour, add just before serving. **FOODS:** egg dishes, green salads, potato salad, tomato dishes, soups, yoghurt dips.

CORIANDER: Light-green herb with delicate leaves and distinctive flavour. **BUY:** fresh (in bunches, roots attached), store in water 2 days; or minced in jars. **USE:** whole leaves as garnish, or chopped leaves or roots as ingredient; use sparingly. Cooking diminishes flavour. **FOODS:** stir-fries, salads, seafood, salsa chutneys. **OTHER NAMES:** Chinese parsley, cilantro.

DILL: Fern-like herb with slightly aniseed flavour and aroma. **BUY:** fresh, store in water 2–3 days; or dried. **USE:** fresh as garnish, whole sprigs or chopped just before serving; dried, use one third quantity of fresh. **FOODS:** potatoes, egg dishes, creamy sauces, pickled cucumbers, rice dishes, salads and seafood.

GARLIC: Strongly flavoured aromatic bulb used in many savoury dishes. **BUY:** fresh (in bulbs), store for 2–3 weeks; dried, as powder, flakes or minced. **USE:** peeled cloves, chopped or crushed. **FOODS:** chicken and meat dishes, pasta sauces, pizza, garlic bread, curries, shellfish, salad dressings.

GARLIC CHIVES: Flat, dark, grass-like herb with taste of garlic. Much used in Asian dishes. **BUY:** fresh, store 5 days in refrigerator. **USE:** chopped green parts as garnish or ingredient, add 2–3 minutes before serving; cooking diminishes flavour. **FOODS:** soups, scrambled eggs, dips.

LEMON GRASS: Long, thick grass-like plant with a strong citrus flavour. Used in Asian cooking. **BUY:** fresh, store in water for 2–3 days; dried powder form (1 teaspoon equals one stalk). **USE:** first 10 cm (4 inch) only of chopped and bruised stem, as ingredient. Cooking enhances flavour; do not use uncooked. **FOODS:** fish, chicken, curries. **OTHER NAMES:** Serai.

MARJORAM: Small, dark-green herb related to oregano but less strongly flavoured. **BUY:** fresh, store in water 5 days; or dried. **USE:** chopped leaves as ingredient or as a garnish. Cooking will diminish the flavour. **FOODS:** savoury scones or dumplings, savoury pies, meatloaf, fish.

PARSLEY (FLAT-LEAF): Dark-green herb with a stronger flavour than curly variety. **BUY:** fresh, store in water for 7 days. **USE:** chopped or whole leaves as garnish, chopped as ingredient. Cooking diminishes flavour, although it withstands heat better than the curly leafed variety. **FOODS:** salads, soups, omelettes, chicken, tabouli, fish, shellfish, pasta dishes, vegetables and soft cheeses.

PARSLEY: Curly-leafed herb with mild, crisp flavour. **BUY:** fresh, refrigerate 2 weeks; or dried. **USE:** chopped leaves as ingredient or garnish. Cooking will diminish flavour. Part of bouquet garni with thyme and bay leaf. **FOODS:** all savoury dishes, especially egg dishes, casseroles, mornays, soups, salads, fish and shellfish, chicken, tomatoes, eggplant (aubergine).

OREGANO: Small-leafed aromatic plant with strong flavour used widely in Greek and southern Italian dishes. **BUY:** fresh, store in water for 5 days; or dried. **USE:** chopped leaves as ingredient or garnish. Cooking diminishes flavour. **FOODS:** pizza, Greek salad, moussaka, salad dressings, tomato-based sauces, risotto, casseroles, pasta dishes.

MINT: Dark-green herb with strong, fresh flavour. Many varieties, of which spearmint is the most common. **BUY:** fresh, store in water 5 days; or dried. **USE:** whole leaves as garnish, chopped leaves as ingredient. Cooking diminishes flavour. **FOODS:** peas, potatoes, lamb dishes, roast duck, Asian-style salads, fruit drinks. **VARIETIES:** Peppermint, Apple, Vietnamese, Pineapple.

THYME: Fragrant herb with tiny leaves and strong flavour. **BUY:** fresh, store in water for 7 days, or dried. **USE:** whole sprigs as a garnish or whole or chopped leaves as ingredient. Cooking will enhance flavour. Discard whole sprigs before you serve. **FOODS:** roast meats, pâtés, terrines, herb breads, marinades, stuffings. **VARIETIES:** Lemon, Orange.

TARRAGON: Thin-leafed, dark green herb with distinctive flavour and aroma. Used widely in French cuisine. **BUY:** fresh, store in water for 2–3 days; or dried, use a third of the quantity of fresh. **USE:** chopped as ingredient or garnish. Cooking diminishes flavour. **FOODS:** chicken dishes, omelettes, fish, salad dressings, Béarnaise sauce. **VARIETIES:** French (the best), Russian.

SORREL: Large-leafed herb, closely resembling young spinach, with a slightly bitter taste and lemony aroma. **BUY:** fresh, store in water 5 days. **USE:** whole leaves as ingredient or (used sparingly) as garnish. Cooking diminishes flavour. **FOODS:** soup, omelettes, salads. **VARIETIES:** Garden, Wild.

SAGE: Greenish-grey, long-leafed plant with a savoury, dry aroma and strong taste. Traditionally used to counteract oily, rich meats. **BUY:** fresh, store in water 5 days; or dried, use half quantity of fresh. **USE:** whole or chopped leaves as an ingredient. Cooking will enhance its flavour; discard whole leaves before serving. **FOODS:** in stuffing mixtures for chicken, goose, duck; with veal, liver, sausages, oily fish. **VARIETIES:** Purple, Golden.

ROSEMARY: Dark-green herb with spiny leaves and a strong taste and aroma. Traditional affinity with lamb. **BUY:** fresh, store 5 days in refrigerator; or dried, use third quantity of fresh. **USE:** whole sprigs or leaves or finely chopped leaves as ingredient. Cooking enhances flavour. Discard whole sprigs or leaves before serving. **FOODS:** lamb dishes, roast chicken, veal, pork, beef, fish.

Haddock A fish of northern Atlantic waters, related to the cod. Fresh haddock has firm, white, delicately flavoured flesh. It can be baked whole or its fillets braised, poached, grilled (broiled) or fried. Smoked haddock is usually poached in milk (this is a traditional breakfast dish in Britain) but can also be baked, grilled or gently fried. Haddock is the main ingredient in the Anglo-Indian classic kedgeree.

Haggis A traditional Scottish dish, served on Burns Night and Hogmanay, and considered by many to be the national dish of Scotland. The minced (ground) heart, liver and lungs of a sheep are mixed with minced beef or mutton, suet and oats, seasoned with cayenne pepper and finely chopped onion, and boiled in the stomach of the sheep. It is served hot, scooped out of its casing, and accompanied by pureed turnips and potatoes. Made from animal parts which might otherwise be discarded, haggis is nevertheless enjoyed by many as a great delicacy.

Halloumi A sheep's milk cheese with a firm texture and a sharp, creamy taste similar to feta. Made in Cyprus, Syria and Lebanon for at least 2000 years.

HAM

HAM STEAKS IN WHISKEY SAUCE

Preparation time: 20 minutes
Total cooking time: 35 minutes
Serves 4

4 x 1.5 cm (5/8 inch) thick ham steaks
15 g (1/2 oz) butter
1 large onion, thinly sliced
15 g (1/2 oz) butter, extra
2 green apples, peeled, cored and cut into 5 mm (1/4 inch) slices
1 tablespoon brown sugar
2 tablespoons Irish whiskey
1 tablespoon plain (all-purpose) flour
3/4 cup (6 fl oz) chicken stock
ground pepper
2 tablespoons cream

1 Trim ham steaks and snip edges to prevent curling during cooking. Heat butter until foaming, then quickly cook steaks on both sides until brown, remove and keep warm. Add onion to pan, cook until golden, remove and keep warm.

2 Heat extra butter in pan, add apple, cook until tender, remove and keep warm. Sprinkle sugar over juices in pan and cook until sugar dissolves. Add whiskey and swirl it with pan juices.

3 Blend in flour, cook 1 minute, add chicken stock and stir until mixture is smooth. Cook until sauce boils and thickens, season with pepper. Add cream just prior to serving.

4 Arrange ham steaks on a serving plate, pour sauce over meat. Arrange cooked onion and apple slices on top. Serve with mashed potatoes and steamed cabbage.

ABOUT HAM

■ Ham is an ideal food for large-scale entertaining, particularly over the Christmas and New Year period. Your butcher will be able to help you choose the appropriate cut and size for the number of guests—generally, a half a leg serves 5–10 people, and a whole ham up to 20 people.

■ Ham can be roasted in the oven or cooked on a kettle-style barbecue. Remove the rind and most of the fat, score the skin in a criss-cross pattern and flavour. Traditionally, ham is coated with fruit glaze, such as orange or cherry, and studded with whole cloves. Carve thickly and serve warm or cold with a variety of sauces.

■ Store ham in the refrigerator, covered loosely with a clean cloth—a small tablecloth or pillowcase, for example, changing the cloth every 2–3 days. Stored carefully, ham will last for up to 3 weeks. Serve cold slices with fried eggs, chop and toss into fried rice or pasta sauces, or simply make up into sandwiches. The bone can be frozen for up to a month and is an excellent base for soup.

ABOVE: HAM STEAKS IN WHISKEY SAUCE
OPPOSITE PAGE: ORANGE-GLAZED HAM

ORANGE-GLAZED HAM

✳ ✳ **Preparation time:** 10 minutes +
1 hour standing
Total cooking time: 3 hours 45 minutes
Serves 20

1 x 7 kg (14 lb) leg ham	1 teaspoon yellow
1 large orange	mustard seeds
2 cups (16 fl oz) water	whole cloves
6 whole cloves	
1¼ cups soft brown sugar	**Mustard Cream**
1 tablespoon mustard	2 tablespoons French
powder	mustard
1 cup golden syrup (light	½ cup (4 fl oz) sour cream
corn syrup)	½ cup (4 fl oz) cream

1 Preheat oven to moderate 180°C (350°F/Gas 4).
Remove rind from ham by running a thumb
around the edge, under the rind. Begin pulling
from the widest edge. When rind has been
removed to within 10 cm (4 inches) of the shank
end, cut through the rind around the shank.
Using a sharp knife, remove excess fat from ham
and discard. Squeeze juice from the orange
and reserve juice. Peel the orange rind into
long, thin strips. Place ham on a roasting rack in
deep baking dish; add water, rind and cloves to
dish. Cover ham and dish securely with foil;
cook for 2 hours.

2 Remove baking dish from oven. Drain meat
and reserve 1 cup (8 fl oz) of the pan juices.
Using a sharp knife, score across the fat with deep
cuts crossways and then diagonally to form a
diamond pattern. Combine the sugar, mustard
powder and golden syrup in a medium bowl; mix
to a thick paste. Spread half the paste thickly over
the ham. Return to a moderately hot oven
210°C (415°F/Gas 6–7), and cook, uncovered,
30 minutes.

3 Combine reserved orange juice and mustard
seeds with remaining brown sugar paste to make
a glaze; stir until smooth. Remove ham from the
oven; brush with a little of the glaze. Press a clove
into each diamond, return to oven. Roast,
uncovered, for another hour, brushing with the
glaze every 10 minutes. Place reserved pan juices
and any remaining orange and brown sugar glaze
in small pan. Stir mixture over low heat until it
boils. Allow to boil, without stirring, for 3
minutes. Serve ham sliced, warm or cold with
glaze and Mustard Cream.

To make Mustard Cream: Place French
mustard, sour cream and cream in a bowl. Stir to
combine. Leave, covered, 1 hour.

Note: Ham will keep in the refrigerator for about
3 weeks. Cover ham with a damp cloth; change
cloth regularly.

cook for 2 hours.

Cover ham and dish securely with foil;

Ham Meat from the
hind leg of a pig, salted,
usually smoked and
sometimes aged to
intensify the flavour.
The many forms include:
the strongly flavoured,
salt-cured raw hams such
as Parma, prosciutto and
Westphalian, which are
often served thinly sliced
as a first course; and the
cooked hams which can
be baked and served hot,
but are also served cold
in salads, sandwiches or
cooked in a variety of
other dishes. York ham,
lightly smoked, is a
British specialty; also
known as country hams,
Virginia (sugar-cured and
smoked) and
Kentucky (smoked over
hickory and apple
wood), are firmer than
other hams and very salty
and need to be soaked
and simmered before
they are baked.

Halva A sweetmeat
from the Middle East
made with tahini, butter,
sugar, honey and nuts
and flavoured with rosewater
or saffron.

haloumi is available fresh
or vacuum-packed.

Hamburger A flat, round cake of minced (ground) meat, usually beef, seasoned, fried and served with salad vegetables and condiments on a soft

bun, usually lightly toasted. The hamburger evolved in the United States in the early years of the twentieth century.

Hare An animal similar to the rabbit, but larger, with darker flesh and a rich and gamey flavour. Young hare can be roasted. Older meat is usually 'jugged' (marinated overnight in red wine then slowly casseroled with bacon and mushrooms).

Haricot Bean (Navy Bean) Fresh haricot beans are eaten green, pod and all. The small, white dried seed is used in casseroles, soups and stews and is processed into canned baked beans.

Harissa A fiery paste from Morocco served as an accompaniment for couscous and saffron-flavoured soups; used as a marinade for

 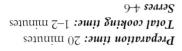

HAM AND MUSHROOM CROQUETTES

★
Preparation time: 15 minutes + refrigeration
Total cooking time: 10 minutes
Serves 4

45 g (1½ oz) butter	1 teaspoon lemon juice
⅓ cup plain (all-purpose) flour	salt and freshly ground pepper, to taste
1 cup (8 fl oz) hot milk	1 tablespoon cream
125 g (4 oz) ham, finely chopped	1 tablespoon chopped parsley
15 g (½ oz) butter, extra	dry breadcrumbs
105 g (3½ oz) button mushrooms, chopped	1 egg, beaten lightly
	light olive oil for frying

1 Melt butter in a small pan, remove from heat. Stir in flour and add hot milk. Return pan to heat and stir continuously until mixture boils and thickens, add ham and simmer 1 minute.

2 In a separate pan melt extra butter and toss mushrooms over high heat for 2 minutes; add lemon juice. Add mushrooms to hot ham sauce, beat in salt, pepper, cream and parsley. Spread mixture into a shallow dish and refrigerate until firm, preferably overnight.

3 Form mixture into 8 cylinder shapes. Roll in breadcrumbs, dip in beaten egg, roll in breadcrumbs again. Refrigerate croquettes for at least 1 hour. Heat oil in a pan and fry croquettes until golden. Serve.

HAM SALAD

★
Preparation time: 20 minutes
Total cooking time: 1–2 minutes
Serves 4–6

200 g (6½ oz) mixed green lettuce leaves or salad mix (mesclun)	3 eggs, hard-boiled
8 slices smoked leg ham	
1 red onion, finely sliced	vinaigrette dressing, mayonnaise or chutney, optional
1 bunch fresh thin asparagus spears	

1 Wash lettuce leaves or salad mix (mesclun) thoroughly and pat dry gently with paper towels. Combine lettuce in large bowl with onion. Set aside.

2 Trim any woody ends from the asparagus. Plunge into medium pan of boiling water 1–2 minutes or until bright green in colour and just tender. Drain and plunge into bowl of iced water. Drain well.

3 Peel eggs and cut into quarters. Arrange salad leaves, onion, asparagus, eggs and ham slices on individual serving plates. Drizzle with vinaigrette or a thin mayonnaise dressing, or serve with a fruity chutney if desired.

ABOVE: HAM SALAD. OPPOSITE PAGE, ABOVE: BEEF BURGERS WITH CARAMELISED ONIONS; BELOW: CHICKEN BURGERS

HAMBURGERS

BEEF BURGERS WITH CARAMELISED ONIONS

Preparation time: 25 minutes
Total cooking time: 46 minutes
Serves 6

1 kg (2 lb) beef mince
1/4 cup (2 fl oz) sour cream
1 teaspoon dried rosemary
1 teaspoon dried basil
1 teaspoon dried thyme
3 medium red onions, sliced into rings

Caramelised Onions
1 tablespoon olive oil
1 tablespoon balsamic vinegar
2 teaspoons honey

1 Place beef mince, sour cream and herbs in a large mixing bowl and combine thoroughly. Divide mixture into six equal portions and shape into 1.5 cm (⅝ inch) thick patties. Refrigerate, covered, until required.

2 **To make Caramelised Onions:** Heat oil in a large pan, add onion and cook over medium-low heat for 20 minutes. Onions should be very soft and golden brown. Add vinegar and honey and cook, stirring, for another 10 minutes.

3 While onions are cooking, heat grill or frying pan and brush lightly with oil. Cook burgers over medium-high heat for 8 minutes each side, turning once only. When burgers are cooked through, remove from pan and serve with salad and warm Caramelised Onions.

CHICKEN BURGERS WITH GRAINY MUSTARD CREAM

Preparation time: 12 minutes +
20 minutes standing
Total cooking time: 10 minutes
Makes 6

500 g (1 lb) chicken mince
2/3 cup packaged breadcrumbs
1 tablespoon mild curry powder
2 tablespoons mango chutney
2 tablespoons finely chopped flat-leaf parsley
1 egg, lightly beaten

Grainy Mustard Cream
1/4 cup (2 fl oz) sour cream
1 tablespoon seeded mustard
1 tablespoon mango chutney
1/4 cup (2 fl oz) olive oil

1 Place chicken mince, breadcrumbs, curry powder, chutney, parsley, egg, salt and pepper into mixing bowl.

2 Using hands, press the mixture together until ingredients are well combined. Cover mixture with plastic wrap and refrigerate for 20 minutes.

3 Divide mixture into six equal portions. Shape each portion into a patty with lightly oiled hands and flatten slightly. Place the patties on a lightly oiled grill or flatplate. Cook over medium-high heat for 5 minutes each side or until the burgers are well browned and cooked through, turning once. Serve hot with Grainy Mustard Cream.

4 **To make Grainy Mustard Cream:** Place cream, mustard and chutney in a bowl. Using a wire whisk, stir to combine. Add oil a few drops at a time, beating until all the oil has been added.

---

chicken, lamb or fish. Available from specialty shops. The main ingredients are chillies and olive oil.

Hash A fried mixture of diced vegetables and meat, originally a way to use up leftovers.

Havarti A semi-hard cow's milk cheese with a tangy flavour that deepens with age; usually made in a loaf shape; the interior has small, irregularly shaped holes.

Hazelnut A small round hard-shelled nut with mild sweet flavour; it can be eaten fresh, or  roasted and salted. The filbert is a large cultivated hazelnut.

Head Cheese See Brawn.

Heart Dark red lean muscle surrounded by fatty tissue. Lamb and calf heart are preferred. Heart requires long slow cooking such as stewing or braising.

Heart of Palm The tender, pale-coloured interior of certain palm trees.

Herb The leaves and stems of various aromatic

CARPETBAG BURGERS WITH HORSERADISH CREAM

★

Preparation time: 20 minutes
Total cooking time: 16 minutes
Serves 6

750 g (1½ lb) beef
mince
6 hamburger buns
shredded lettuce
1 cup fresh white
breadcrumbs

Horseradish Cream
½ cup (4 fl oz) sour
cream
½ teaspoon finely grated
lemon rind
5 drops Tabasco sauce
2 teaspoons horseradish
relish
1 egg, lightly beaten
6 oysters

1 Place beef mince, breadcrumbs, lemon rind, Tabasco and egg in a large mixing bowl and combine thoroughly. Divide mixture into six equal portions and shape into patties 1.5 cm (⅝ inch) thick. With your thumb, make a cavity in the top of each burger. Place an oyster in each cavity and smooth the mince over the oyster to enclose completely. Refrigerate until required.

2 **To make Horseradish Cream:** Place sour cream and horseradish relish in a small bowl, stir to combine. Refrigerate until required.

3 Heat grill or a frying pan and brush lightly with oil. Cook prepared mince patties on medium-high heat for about 8 minutes on each side, turning once only. Halve the hamburger buns and lightly toast and butter if desired. Place bases of buns on individual serving plates. Spread shredded lettuce over buns and add a cooked mince patty to each. Add Horseradish Cream and finish with bun top.

ABOVE: CARPETBAG BURGERS WITH HORSERADISH CREAM. OPPOSITE: COFFEE HAZELNUT BISCUITS

VEGEBURGER WITH CHICK PEA SAUCE

✻

Preparation time: 20 minutes +
2 hours refrigeration
Total cooking time: 20 minutes
Serves 4

½ cup (4 fl oz) olive oil
1 medium onion, finely
chopped
1 tablespoon curry powder
½ cup fresh or frozen peas
½ cup finely chopped
carrot
½ cup finely chopped
pumpkin
1 ripe tomato, peeled and
chopped
¾ cup fresh white
breadcrumbs
1 egg
salt and pepper
315 g (10 oz) can chick
peas (garbanzo beans),
drained
4 wholemeal rolls

lettuce
1 small cucumber, thinly
sliced lengthways
1 tomato, thinly sliced
1 red onion, cut in thin
rings

Hummus
315 g (10 oz) can chick
peas (garbanzo beans),
extra, drained
2 cloves garlic, crushed
2 tablespoons lemon juice
2 tablespoons sour cream
1 tablespoon peanut
butter
1 teaspoon ground cumin
2 tablespoons toasted
sesame seeds

1 Heat 2 tablespoons oil in medium pan, add onion and curry powder. Cook over medium heat 3–4 minutes or until softened. Stir in peas, carrot and pumpkin; cook for another 2 minutes. Add chopped tomato, reduce heat, cover and cook 3–5 minutes or until vegetables are soft. Remove from heat, cool slightly. Stir in breadcrumbs, egg, salt and pepper. Transfer mixture to bowl.

2 Place chick peas in food processor. Process until smooth. Add to vegetable mixture and mix well.

Cover; refrigerate 2 hours. Divide mixture into four portions. Shape each portion into a flat round patty.

3 Heat remaining oil in frying pan. Cook patties over medium heat 3–4 minutes each side or until golden and cooked through. Cut rolls in half horizontally. Lightly toast if liked. Place bases of rolls on serving plates. Top with lettuce, cucumber, tomato, onion rings and cooked patties. Spoon over Hummus mixture. Place remaining roll halves on top. Serve.

4 **To make Hummus:** Place chick peas, garlic, lemon juice, sour cream, peanut butter, cumin and sesame seeds in food processor. Process for 20–30 seconds or until smooth.

plants used in cooking to enhance the flavour and colour of food. Among the most often used herbs are parsley, mint, thyme, rosemary, sage, basil, dill, marjoram, tarragon, oregano and bay leaf. Some herbs have a particular affinity with certain foods.

Herring A saltwater fish of the north Atlantic with dark, richly flavoured, soft-textured, oily flesh. Fresh herring, sold whole or in fillets, is best grilled (broiled) or fried, but can also be baked and poached. Because of its high fat content the herring is well suited to smoking and pickling.

Hoisin Sauce A sweet and spicy, red-brown sauce made from a paste of fermented soy beans, flour, salt, sugar, garlic and red rice, a natural colouring responsible for the red glaze of many meat dishes in Chinese cooking. Hoisin is used when cooking pork and chicken, as a seasoning for braised dishes and, sparingly, in stir-fried dishes.

Hollandaise Sauce A rich, golden yellow sauce made with butter, egg yolk, lemon juice or

COFFEE HAZELNUT BISCUITS

★★ **Preparation time:** 15 minutes + 30 minutes freezing
Total cooking time: 15 minutes
Makes 25

1 1/4 cups plain (all-purpose) flour
100 g (3 1/2 oz) unsalted (sweet) butter, chopped
1/3 cup caster (superfine) sugar
3 teaspoons instant coffee granules
2 teaspoons boiling water
1 egg yolk
1/3 cup ground hazelnuts

2/3 cup finely chopped hazelnuts
13 whole hazelnuts, halved

Coffee Glacé Icing
1/2 cup pure icing (confectioners) sugar
1/2 teaspoon instant coffee
10 g (1/2 oz) butter, softened
2 teaspoons milk

1 Preheat oven to 180°C (350°F/Gas 4). Brush two 32 x 28 cm (13 x 11 inch) biscuit (oven) trays with melted butter or oil. Line the base with paper; grease paper. Sift flour into large bowl; add butter and sugar. Using your fingertips, rub butter into the flour for 2 minutes or until the mixture is fine and crumbly. Make a well in the centre.

2 Dissolve coffee in water. Add egg, cooled coffee and ground hazelnuts to bowl. Mix with fingers until mixture is soft and almost smooth.

3 Turn dough onto a lightly floured surface. Knead for 1 minute or until smooth; shape dough into a log 30 cm (12 inch) long x 4 cm (1 1/2 inch) wide. Roll log in chopped hazelnuts. Cover and place in the freezer for 30 minutes. Using a sharp knife, cut the log evenly into 25 slices. Place slices on prepared trays about 3 cm (1 1/4 inches) apart. Bake for 15 minutes or until golden. Cool on trays.

4 **To make Icing:** Sift icing sugar into bowl; stir in coffee, butter and milk. Stand bowl over warm water; mix until smooth. Spread a little in centre of each biscuit; top with half a hazelnut.

ABOUT HAZELNUTS

■ Hazelnut meal is frequently used as a substitute for flour in biscuits and cakes. However, the mild sweetness of hazelnuts also suits savoury food. Chop nuts coarsely and combine with melted butter, then scatter over trout or lobster; toss through a green salad or sprinkle over mushroom or vegetable soup.

■ Hazelnuts are difficult to shell (the nut needs to be roasted and the skin rubbed off with a towel) so are probably best bought shelled. Hazelnuts are available whole, chopped or ground; purchase the form that best suits the recipe. Ground hazelnuts can be used as a substitute for ground almonds in many recipes.

■ Hazelnut oil is rare and expensive, but makes a delicious salad dressing.

---

vinegar and seasonings. It is served warm with poached or steamed chicken and fish, with egg dishes and with steamed or boiled vegetables.

Hominy Dried corn kernels that have been hulled and the germ removed—this is done by soaking in slaked lime or lye. Ground hominy is called grits or hominy grits; coarsely ground hominy is sometimes called pearl hominy. Hominy can be served as a vegetable, added to casseroles, soups and stews or, mixed with egg and flour, fried as cakes.

Honey A sweet viscous fluid made by bees from flower nectar and stored sealed in wax

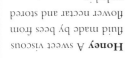

honeycombs. Colour and flavour depends upon the species of flower the nectar came from—in general, the darker the colour, the stronger the flavour. Thyme honey is clear and dark golden and ranked by some as the finest in the world; orange blossom yields an amber-coloured citrus-flavoured honey. Clover honey, the most common in North

America, is pale, clear and mild.

Liquid honey is the honey as extracted from the honeycomb. Candied, creamed or whipped honey has some of the moisture removed and is finely crystallised (all honeys will crystallise and harden with age).

Honey is used as a spread, in baking, as a sweetener for beverages and cereals and in the making of confectionery.

Honeycomb A waxy structure made by bees consisting of rows of adjacent hexagonal cells in which they store honey, lay eggs and allow larvae to develop. Resembling this in its structure is a brittle confection (candy) with an aerated interior

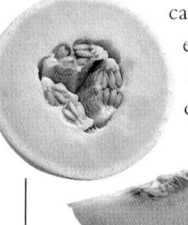

made by adding bicarbonate of soda (baking soda) to a boiling syrup of honey and sugar.

Honeydew Melon A round, pale-skinned melon with honey-scented, juicy, pale green flesh and slender, pale seeds. The flesh can be eaten raw on its own,

HAZELNUT CHOCOLATE ROLL

✦ **Preparation time:** 35 minutes
Total cooking time: 12 minutes
Makes one Swiss roll (jelly roll)

½ cup self-raising flour
3 eggs
⅓ cup caster (superfine) sugar
100 g (3½ oz) chocolate, finely chopped
½ cup ground hazelnut meal
1 tablespoon strong black coffee
1¼ cups (10 fl oz) cream
1 tablespoon strong black coffee, extra
⅓ cup icing (confectioners) sugar
2 tablespoons cocoa powder

1 Preheat oven to moderately hot 210°C (415°F/Gas 6–7). Brush shallow, 30 x 25 x 2 cm (12 x 10 x ¾ inch) Swiss roll (jelly roll) tin with oil. Line the base and two sides with paper; grease paper. Sift the flour three times onto greaseproof paper. Using electric beaters, beat eggs in small mixing bowl 5 minutes or until thick and pale. Add sugar gradually, beating constantly until dissolved and mixture is pale yellow and glossy. Transfer to a large mixing bowl.
2 Using a metal spoon, fold in chocolate, hazelnut, coffee and flour quickly and lightly. Spread mixture evenly in prepared tin; smooth surface. Bake 12 minutes or until golden. Beat cream and extra coffee liquid in small bowl until stiff peaks form. Refrigerate until required.
3 Turn cake onto a dry tea-towel covered with greaseproof paper which has been dusted with sifted icing sugar and cocoa; leave for 1 minute. Using tea-towel as a guide, roll up cake with paper; leave 5 minutes or until cool. Unroll, discard paper. Spread with coffee cream filling; re-roll. Trim ends of roll with a serrated knife.

SPICED HAZELNUTS

✦ **Preparation time:** 6 minutes
Total cooking time: 30 minutes
Makes 4–5 cups

1 egg white
¼ cup caster (superfine) sugar
3 teaspoons ground cinnamon
¼ teaspoon ground nutmeg
¼ teaspoon ground cloves
250 g (8 oz) roasted hazelnuts

Preheat oven to 160°C (325°F/Gas 3). Beat egg white until stiff; fold in sugar, cinnamon, nutmeg and cloves. Toss nuts in mixture to coat. Spread on greased baking tray. Bake for 30 minutes. Cool completely. Cut into bite-size bits.

HAZELNUT SHORTBREAD

✦ **Preparation time:** 30 minutes
Total cooking time: 15 minutes
Makes about 30

250 g (8 oz) butter, softened
½ cup sugar
1 egg, plus 1 egg yolk, extra
1 teaspoon vanilla essence
1½ cups plain (all-purpose) flour
½ teaspoon baking powder
¼ teaspoon bicarbonate of soda (baking soda)
½ cup finely ground hazelnuts
about 30 whole hazelnuts

1 Preheat oven to 180°C (350°F/Gas 4). Beat butter and sugar in a bowl with electric beaters until light and fluffy. Beat in egg, egg yolk and vanilla. Sift in flour, baking powder and soda. Add ground hazelnuts and mix well.
2 Lightly roll level tablespoonsful of mixture into rounds, place on greased oven trays, allow room for spreading. Flatten slightly, place a hazelnut on each.
3 Bake 15 minutes or until golden. Cool on trays for 2–3 minutes. Transfer to wire rack to cool.

HONEY

HONEY MINT ROASTED CHICKEN

Preparation time: 15 minutes
Total cooking time: 1 hour 10 minutes
Serves 4–6

1.6 kg (3¼ lb) chicken
juice of 1 lemon
2 cloves garlic, crushed
2 tablespoons finely chopped fresh mint
60 g (2 oz) butter

¼ cup honey
1½ cups (12 fl oz) water
preserved ginger, to serve
chopped almonds, to serve

1 Preheat oven to 180°C (350°F/Gas 4). Remove excess fat from chicken. Wash chicken and pat dry with paper towels.
2 Combine crushed garlic and mint. Using your fingers or a spoon, spread mixture under the chicken skin. Heat butter, lemon juice and honey in a medium pan, stirring well to combine.
3 Brush chicken all over with honey mixture; tie wings and drumsticks securely in place. Place chicken on a roasting rack in a baking dish. Pour water into dish.
4 Bake 1 hour or until golden, brushing with honey mixture. Serve with preserved ginger and chopped almonds.

OPPOSITE, PAGE, ABOVE: HAZELNUT CHOCOLATE ROLL; BELOW: HAZELNUT SHORTBREAD.
ABOVE: HONEY MINT ROASTED CHICKEN; RIGHT: BARBECUED HONEY SEAFOOD.

ABOUT HONEY

■ Honeys range in colour from light and clear to thick and opaque. Each offers a distinct flavour and taste, depending on the flower the honey is harvested from. Usually, the paler the honey, the milder its taste.

■ Cooking honey will caramelise its sugars and diminish its flavour, so choose darker, more strongly flavoured honeys for cooking.

BARBECUED HONEY SEAFOOD

Preparation time: 15 minutes + 3 hours marinating
Total cooking time: 5 minutes
Makes 8 skewers

500 g (1 lb) medium uncooked prawns (shrimps)
250 g (8 oz) fresh scallops, with corals intact

¼ cup honey
2 tablespoons soy sauce
¼ cup (2 fl oz) bottled barbecue sauce
2 tablespoons sweet sherry

1 Soak 8 wooden skewers in water. Remove heads from prawns. Peel and devein prawns, keeping tails intact. Clean scallops, removing brown thread.
2 Thread prawns and scallops alternately onto the 8 skewers (about 3 of each per skewer). Place in the base of a shallow non-metal dish. Combine honey, soy sauce, barbecue sauce and sherry in a jug and pour over the skewers. Cover and refrigerate several hours or overnight. Prepare and heat barbecue 1 hour before cooking.
3 Remove skewers from dish and cook on a hot lightly greased barbecue flatplate for 5 minutes or until cooked through. Brush frequently with marinade while cooking.

Hors d'Oeuvre A French term meaning 'outside the main body of work', used to describe small portions of hot or cold savoury foods served with drinks prior to a meal. Cold hors d'oeuvres can range from olives and nuts to pâtés, spreads, dips and crudités, vegetables à la grecque, marinated and smoked seafood and caviar. Hot hors d'oeuvres include croquettes, fritters, vol-au-vents, tiny pizzas and bacon-wrapped tidbits.

Horseradish A plant of the mustard family native to eastern Europe and now cultivated around the world for its pungent hot-flavoured root, which is grated to flavour sauces (such as those served with roast beef and seafood dishes) and soups. Grate horseradish just before use, as it quickly loses its bite. Fresh horseradish is available from specialist greengrocers and is also sold preserved or as a relish. Horseradish cream is a preparation of grated horseradish root, oil, white vinegar and sugar. The young leaves of the horseradish plant can be added to salads.

added to fruit salads or served with prosciutto as a first course.

HONEY

Hot Cross Bun A small bun made with a yeast dough flavoured with spices and dried fruits. It is slashed on top with a cross and glazed with a sugar syrup. Nowadays it is traditionally eaten on Good Friday, but the hot cross bun was originally baked to honour the pagan goddess of spring—the round shape representing the moon and the cross the four seasons.

Hot Dog A hot frankfurter served on a split soft bread roll of the same length and garnished with mustard,

sauce, pickles, relish, chopped onion, or cheese (or a mixture of any of these). The frankfurter is said to have been brought to St Louis, in the United States, in the 1880s where it was served on a bread bun for the first time at the 1904 St Louis World Fair.

Hotwater Pastry A pastry made with hot water, lard, flour and salt that even before baking sets into a shell firm enough to stand by itself. The pastry must be used while still warm, as it becomes brittle when cold. Hotwater pastry is used for traditional English raised pies such

HONEY DATE CAKE

★ **Preparation time:** 10 minutes + 10 minutes standing
Total cooking time: 35 minutes
Makes one 20 cm (8 inch) round cake

340 g (10¾ oz) packet buttercake cake mix
½ cup (4 fl oz) buttermilk
20 g (½ oz) unsalted (sweet) butter
¼ cup honey
½ cup finely chopped fresh dates
1 teaspoon mixed spice
1 tablespoon water
1 egg

1 Preheat oven to moderate 180°C (350°F/Gas 4). Brush a shallow 20 cm (8 inch) round cake tin with melted butter or oil, line the base and side with paper; grease paper.
2 Place contents of packet mix, dates, mixed spice, egg and buttermilk in a small bowl. Using electric beaters, beat ingredients together on low speed for 1 minute or until just combined. Beat on medium speed 2 minutes or until mixture is smooth.
3 Spread mixture in prepared tin. Bake for 35 minutes or until a skewer comes out clean when inserted in centre of cake. Leave cake in tin for 10 minutes before carefully turning out onto a wire rack.
4 Combine honey, unsalted butter and water in a small pan. Stir over low heat 1 minute or until butter has just melted. Brush warm honey mixture over warm cake. Serve warm with custard or ice-cream. Decorate cake with sifted icing (confectioners) sugar, if desired.

HONEY PEANUT BUTTER COOKIES

★ **Preparation time:** 15 minutes
Total cooking time: 10 minutes
Makes about 30

1 cup plain (all-purpose) flour
½ cup self-raising flour
1 cup rolled oats
1 cup roasted unsalted peanuts, finely chopped
⅓ cup honey
125 g (4 oz) unsalted (sweet) butter
½ cup caster (superfine) sugar
2 tablespoons peanut butter

Topping
¾ cup icing (confectioners) sugar
25 g (¾ oz) butter, softened
1 tablespoon warm water

1 Preheat oven to moderate 180°C (350°F/Gas 4). Brush 2 oven trays with melted butter or oil. Sift flours into a large mixing bowl; stir in oats.
2 Combine butter, sugar, peanut butter and honey in pan, stir over medium heat until melted. Add to flour mixture. Using metal spoon, stir to combine. Roll teaspoonful of mixture into balls. Arrange on trays, with room for spreading, press lightly. Bake 10 minutes or until golden. Cool on trays.
3 **To make Topping:** Combine icing sugar, butter and water in small bowl. Stir until smooth. Dip tops of cookies into topping, then into nuts.

ABOVE: HONEY DATE CAKE
OPPOSITE PAGE: BARBECUED TROUT WITH HORSERADISH CREAM AND LEMON SAUCE

BARBECUED TROUT WITH HORSERADISH CREAM AND LEMON SAUCE

Preparation time: 20 minutes
Total cooking time: 15 minutes
Serves 4

1/4 cup chopped fresh dill
2 tablespoons chopped fresh rosemary
1/3 cup coarsely chopped fresh flat-leaf parsley
2 teaspoons chopped fresh thyme
6 teaspoons crushed green peppercorns
1/3 cup (2 1/2 fl oz) lemon juice
salt and pepper, to taste
2 lemons
4 whole fresh trout
1/3 cup (2 1/2 fl oz) dry white wine

Horseradish Cream
1 tablespoon horseradish
1/2 cup (4 fl oz) sour cream
2 tablespoons cream
salt and pepper, to taste

Lemon Sauce
2 egg yolks
155 g (5 oz) butter, melted
3–4 tablespoons lemon juice
salt and pepper, to taste

1 Prepare and heat the barbecue. Lightly grease four large sheets of foil, each double-thickness. Place herbs, peppercorns, juice, salt and pepper in a bowl and mix well. Cut each lemon into eight slices, cut each slice in half. Place 2 of the lemon pieces in each fish cavity. Spoon equal portions of the herb mixture into each fish cavity.

2 Place each fish on foil layers, sprinkle each with 1 tablespoon of wine. Seal fish in foil to form neat parcels. Cook fish on barbecue 10–15 minutes or until fish is just cooked through. (Test fish for doneness by gently flaking back flesh with a fork.) Stand fish, still wrapped in foil, 5 minutes, then serve with Horseradish Cream and Lemon Sauce.

3 **To make Horseradish Cream:** Combine creams, salt and pepper in bowl; mix well.

4 **To make Lemon Sauce:** Place yolks in food processor. Process 20 seconds or until blended. With motor constantly running, add butter slowly in a thin, steady stream. Continue processing until all butter has been added and mixture is thick and creamy. Add juice, season with salt and pepper.

FRESH HORSERADISH

Preparation time: 5 minutes
Total cooking time: nil
Makes 200 ml (6 fl oz)

6 tablespoons grated horseradish roots
2 tablespoons raw sugar
3 tablespoons vinegar
2 teaspoons salt

Place horseradish in a small bowl and stir in salt, sugar and vinegar to taste. Pack in sterilised jars and refrigerate until required.

Note: Horseradish is delicious as an accompaniment for roast beef, oily fish and grilled meats. Add to cream cheese or cottage cheese and use as a spread or dip.

ABOUT HORSERADISH

■ Grated horseradish in salt and vinegar is available in jars from most supermarkets and delicatessens.

■ When buying fresh horseradish, look for firm roots without sprouting or traces of green—these will be very bitter. Peel the roots thoroughly and grate or process the flesh finely. Prepare only the quantity you need as grated horseradish loses its pungency very quickly.

■ Plants should be stored in a cool, dark place to prevent the roots turning green. (Alternatively, use a commercially prepared grated horseradish or powdered dried horseradish, which is reconstituted with liquid.)

■ Grated horseradish can be combined with softly whipped cream, a good mayonnaise, sour cream or a good white vinegar for use as a relish or a sauce.

Huckleberry See Blueberry.

Huevos Rancheros Eggs served on tortillas topped with a tomato salsa, a traditional breakfast throughout the south-west of the United States. Traditionally, the eggs are poached in the salsa; they can also be fried or scrambled. The name is Spanish for 'ranch-style' or country-style eggs.

Hummus bi Tahini A dip of Middle Eastern origin made from cooked and ground chick peas (garbanzo beans), tahini (a paste of ground roasted sesame seeds), garlic and lemon juice. Hummus can be served with pita bread or chopped vegetables as a dip, topped with olive oil mixed with paprika or cayenne pepper.

Hushpuppy A deep-fried dumpling or fritter made from a cornmeal batter, often served with fried fish. It is said to have originated in the south of the United States, from the practice of tossing fried batter to the dogs to keep them from barking.

I

Ice-cream A frozen dessert made of sweetened cream or rich milk, sometimes thickened with egg or gelatine, variously flavoured and churned while partially frozen until of a smooth consistency. Ice-cream is available commercially in many forms and flavours (including low-fat versions) or it can be made at home. It can be flavoured with vanilla, chocolate, caramel, honey, coffee, spirits or liqueurs; pieces of honeycomb, chopped nuts, puréed fruit can be stirred through.

A home-made ice-cream will freeze harder than a commercial one; if too hard, move it from the freezer to the refrigerator half an hour before serving; home-made ice-cream is best eaten within 48 hours of being made.

Ice-cream is descended from the flavoured ices eaten in China some 3000 years ago, the semi-solid iced fruit drinks of ancient Persia (the word 'sherbet' comes from

BEEF SAMOSAS WITH MINT CHUTNEY DIP

★ **Preparation time:** 50 minutes
Total cooking time: 30–40 minutes
Makes 20

2 tablespoons oil
1 medium onion, finely chopped
2 teaspoons finely chopped fresh ginger
410 g (13 oz) beef mince
1 tablespoon curry powder
1 teaspoon salt
1 medium tomato, peeled and chopped
1 medium potato, cubed
¼ cup (2 fl oz) water
1 teaspoon garam masala
1 tablespoon finely chopped fresh mint
1 kg (2 lb) packet ready-rolled puff pastry sheets

Mint Chutney Dip
1 cup fresh mint sprigs
4 spring onions (scallions)
1 red chilli, seeded
¼ teaspoon salt
1 tablespoon lemon juice
2 teaspoons caster (superfine) sugar
¼ teaspoon garam masala
¼ cup (2 fl oz) water

1 egg yolk, lightly beaten
1 tablespoon cream

1 Heat oil in a pan, add the onion and ginger. Cook until onion is soft and golden. Add meat and curry powder. Stir over high heat until beef has browned. Add salt and tomato, cook, covered, 5 minutes. Add potato and water, cook 5 minutes. Remove from heat, cool. Stir in mint.

2 Preheat oven to moderately hot 210°C (415°F/Gas 6–7). Cut pastry into circles of 13 cm (5 inch) diameter; cut in half. Form cones by folding each of the semi-circles in half and pinching the sides together.

3 Spoon 2 teaspoonsful of mince mixture into each cone. Pinch edges together to seal. Place puffs on a lightly greased baking tray. Beat egg yolk with cream and brush over puffs. Cook 10 to 15 minutes.

4 To make Mint Chutney Dip: Roughly chop the mint sprigs, spring onions and chilli and place in a food processor or blender with all the remaining ingredients; process the mixture thoroughly. Serve dip with the hot samosas.

VEGETABLE PAKORAS

★★ **Preparation time:** 30 minutes
Total cooking time: 20 minutes
Makes about 40

1 large potato
1 small cauliflower
1 medium onion
2 cabbage or 5 spinach leaves
½ cup sweet corn kernels, parboiled
2 teaspoons ground coriander
1 small red pepper (capsicum)
1½ cups besan (chick pea/garbanzo bean) flour
3 tablespoons plain (all-purpose) flour
1 teaspoon bicarbonate of soda (baking soda)
1 teaspoon chilli powder
1 tablespoon lemon juice
2 teaspoons garam masala
¾–1 cup cold water
vegetable oil for deep frying

BEEF VINDALOO

✹ *Preparation time:* 15 minutes
Total cooking time: 1 hour 15 minutes
Serves 6

1 kg (2 lb) round steak	1 large onion
3–5 tablespoons vindaloo paste (to taste)	2 tablespoons toasted flaked almonds
1/2 cup ghee	

1 Trim meat of excess fat and sinew. Cut meat into 2 cm (3/4 inch) cubes. Place the beef cubes and vindaloo paste in a bowl. Stir until beef is coated on all sides.

2 Heat ghee in heavy-based pan. Finely chop the onion, add to pan and cook until quite dark in colour. Add the meat and cook until brown.

3 Add water to cover, partially cover the pan and cook for 40 minutes. Remove lid from pan and cook until the meat is tender and the sauce is well reduced.

4 Serve vindaloo garnished with the flaked almonds and accompanied by boiled rice.

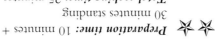

1 Boil potato until just tender, peel and chop finely.

2 Finely chop cauliflower, pepper and onion. Shred the cabbage or spinach.

3 Make a creamy batter with the water and remaining ingredients. Stir until smooth. Add the vegetables and mix in evenly.

4 Heat the oil. Drop tablespoonsful of mixture into oil, about eight at a time; fry until golden. Remove to a rack covered with paper towels.

5 Serve hot with sweet mango chutney or sweet chilli sauce if desired.

YOGHURT AND CUCUMBER RAITA

✹ *Preparation time:* 10 minutes
Total cooking time: nil
Serves 4–6

1 large cucumber	3 teaspoons chopped fresh mint
1 1/4 teaspoons salt	1/2 cup plain yoghurt

1 Peel cucumber, cut in halves, and scoop out seeds with a teaspoon. Coarsely grate the cucumber into a bowl, sprinkle with the salt, and leave for 5–6 minutes. Drain off the accumulated liquid.

2 Stir yoghurt and mint into the cucumber. Serve in small containers with curry meals.

CHAPATTIS

✹ ✹ *Preparation time:* 10 minutes + 30 minutes standing
Total cooking time: 25 minutes
Makes 12

1 cup plain (all-purpose) flour	1 cup wholemeal or atta flour (see note)
1/2 teaspoon salt	2/3 cup (5 fl oz) water
1 tablespoon ghee	

1 Sift flours into a mixing bowl. Using fingertips, rub in ghee until well incorporated. Dissolve salt in water, pour into the flour mixture and mix immediately to form a ball. Knead on a lightly floured board for 5 minutes to make a smooth dough. Leave for 30 minutes in a cool place.

2 Divide dough into 4 pieces; divide each quarter into 3 to make 12 small balls. Roll out each ball to about 15 cm (6 inch) diameter, keeping the others covered with a damp tea-towel.

3 Heat a non-stick frying pan to moderate and cook chapattis one at a time for about 1 minute. Turn and cook for another minute, pressing the edge of the chapatti with a clean, dry tea-towel to make it puff slightly.

Note: Atta flour is wheat flour used for making chapattis. It is available from health food shops.

---

sharbia, the Arab word for 'drink') and the ice sorbets of the Mongol emperors of sixteenth century India. Thirteenth-century Venetian traveller Marco Polo returned from China with tales of a frozen sweet cream dish; kulfi is an ancient Indian dish made with milk boiled until thick and then frozen. In the sixteenth century the Florentine cooks of Catherine de'Medici, bride of France's Henri II, introduced the French to the frozen cream confection gelati; it was quickly taken up by fashionable Parisian cafés who served it in small silver bowls. The ice-cream churn, invented by American Nancy Johnson in 1846, enabled good quality ice-cream to be made at home; it is also made possible to mass produce ice-cream and sell it commercially. The best ice-cream churns are electric or hand operated with salt and ice placed around the outside of the bucket containing the ice-cream. When the paddles stop, the ice-cream is ready.

Iced Coffee

Strong black coffee, sweetened, chilled and served in a tall glass with milk or topped with Chantilly cream. If required, the coffee can be sweetened before being chilled; alternatively, a small jug of cooled sugar syrup (made by dissolving sugar in an equal quantity of hot water) can be served with it. Iced coffee is said to have been first concocted in Vienna in the seventeenth century, following a windfall booty of coffee beans left behind by the vanquished Turkish army which had unsuccessfully besieged the city.

Iced Tea

Tea brewed extra strong, stirred, sweetened to taste, strained and chilled. Serve in a tall glass, pour over ice cubes and garnish with a slice of lemon and a sprig of mint. For a stronger mint taste, add bruised mint leaves to the brewing tea, sweeten, strain and chill; serve with ice cubes in a tall glass. Iced tea originated in St Louis, in the United States, as a cool and refreshing drink for patrons of the 1904 World Fair.

LAMB KORMA

Preparation time: 15 minutes
Total cooking time: 35–45 minutes
Serves 4

1 kg (2 lb) leg of lamb, boned
2 large onions, chopped
2 teaspoons grated ginger
3 teaspoons chopped garlic
3 large dried chillies, or to taste
3 tablespoons ghee or oil
3/4 teaspoon turmeric
2 teaspoons ground cumin
3 teaspoons ground coriander
1/2 cup tomatoes, peeled and chopped
1/4 teaspoon ground cloves
1/2 teaspoon ground cinnamon

Onion and Mint in Yoghurt
1 medium white onion, very finely sliced
2 tablespoons white vinegar
1/4 teaspoon salt
1 tablespoon coarsely chopped fresh mint
2 tablespoons plain yoghurt

Yoghurt
1/4 teaspoon ground cardamom
1/4 teaspoon ground black pepper
1/3 cup (2 1/2 fl oz) water
1/2 cup (4 fl oz) cream

1 Trim lamb of excess fat and sinew. Cut lamb in 3 cm (1 1/4 inch) cubes and set aside. Place onion, ginger, garlic and chillies in a food processor or blender and process until smooth. Add a little water to make blending easier, if necessary.

2 Heat the ghee or oil in a pan and add the onion mixture. Add the turmeric, cumin and coriander and cook, stirring, until the moisture has evaporated. Add the meat and stir over high heat until browned all over.

3 Reduce heat, add the remaining ingredients and simmer gently, covered, for 30–40 minutes. Stir occasionally to prevent the mixture sticking to the base of the pan. Serve with steamed long-grain rice and Onion and Mint in Yoghurt.

4 **To make Onion and Mint in Yoghurt:** Place the onion in a small glass or ceramic bowl. Pour on the white vinegar and leave for 30 minutes. Drain off the vinegar and rinse onion twice in cold water. Drain well, return to bowl; add the salt, chopped mint and yoghurt. Stir to combine. Refrigerate. Serve well chilled.

Note: Lamb Korma can be cooked three days ahead and refrigerated. It can also be frozen for up to one month.

TANDOORI CHICKEN KEBABS

Preparation time: 10 minutes + 5 hours marinating
Total cooking time: 10 minutes
Serves 4–6

500 g (1 lb) chicken breasts
2 tablespoons ghee, melted
1/2 cup plain yoghurt
1/2 teaspoon mashed garlic
1 1/2 teaspoons garam masala
1 tablespoon tandoori or vindaloo paste
2 small limes

1 Cut the chicken into 3 cm (1 1/4 inch) cubes. Thread cubes onto oiled skewers, using about three or four pieces on each skewer. Arrange side by side in a flat dish.

2 Place yoghurt, garlic and tandoori or vindaloo paste in a bowl. Mix thoroughly to form a paste and spread evenly over the chicken. Refrigerate, covered with plastic wrap, for 4–5 hours, turning several times.

3 Line a grill tray with aluminium foil and brush with ghee. Grill (broil) the kebabs for about 4 minutes on each side or until the surface is flecked with brown and the chicken tender. Brush with melted ghee when kebabs are half cooked to keep the meat moist.

4 Arrange on serving plates. Serve with steamed rice, several small wedges of lime, and sprinkle with garam masala.

ABOVE: TANDOORI CHICKEN KEBABS
OPPOSITE PAGE, BELOW: SEAFOOD LAKSA;
ABOVE: PANDANG CHICKEN

SEAFOOD LAKSA

✴ **Preparation time:** 25 minutes
Total cooking time: 10 minutes

Serves 4

500 g (1 lb) medium-sized uncooked prawns (shrimps)
1 tablespoon curry paste
1 teaspoon sambal oelek
1 teaspoon shrimp paste
1 teaspoon ground turmeric
500 g (1 lb) white fish fillets
155 g (5 oz) vermicelli
1.5 litres (6 cups) fish stock
1 cup (8 fl oz) coconut milk
1½ cups finely shredded lettuce
4 spring onions (scallions), chopped
2 tablespoons chopped mint
stem of lemon grass, 10 cm (4 inches) long

1 Peel and devein prawns, cut fish fillets into 2 cm (¾ inch) cubes.
2 Place vermicelli in large bowl. Pour over hot water to cover. Stand 10 minutes; drain.
3 Combine fish stock in a pan with spring onions, lemon grass, curry paste, sambal oelek, shrimp paste and turmeric, bring to the boil. Reduce heat to low, simmer for 3 minutes.
4 Add prawns, fish and coconut milk, simmer for 3 minutes. Remove lemon grass.
5 To serve, place lettuce and vermicelli in bowls, add soup, sprinkle with mint.

PANDANG CHICKEN

✴ **Preparation time:** 15 minutes +
1 hour standing
Total cooking time: 40–50 minutes

Serves 4

1 kg (2 lb) chicken thigh
fillets, cut into
3 cm (1¼ inch) cubes
½ cup (4 fl oz) lime juice
250 g (8 oz) ripe tomatoes
1 cup (8 fl oz) water
3 small red chillies,
seeded and sliced in
short, thin strips

2 teaspoons grated fresh
ginger
2 cloves garlic, crushed
1 teaspoon ground
turmeric
stem of lemon grass,
10 cm (4 inches) long
1 cup (8 fl oz) coconut
cream

1 Place prepared chicken cubes in a bowl. Add lime juice, stir to combine and allow to stand for about 1 hour.
2 Peel and chop tomatoes and combine in a bowl with water, mix until smooth; strain into a pan.
3 Add the sliced chillies, grated ginger, crushed garlic, turmeric, lemon grass and undrained chicken. Bring to the boil, reduce heat, cover and simmer for 30 minutes.
4 Stir in the coconut cream and simmer, uncovered, for approximately 10 minutes. Using tongs or a fork, remove lemon grass before serving. May be served with boiled rice.

Icing A sweet coating, usually made with icing (confectioners) sugar and butter, used to decorate cakes and biscuits (cookies).

Icing Sugar (Confectioners Sugar) Finely powdered granulated sugar used to make icings and frostings and in confectionery. Icing sugar mixture has a small amount of cornflour added to prevent it from drying out and turning lumpy during storage.

Ile Flottante (Floating Island) A dessert consisting of a rich custard topped with an island of baked meringue coated in toffee or caramel. It is sometimes decorated with crushed praline (a confection of nuts and caramelised sugar) or toasted slivered almonds.

Indian Food Although most people think of hot curries when they think of Indian food, many Indian dishes are not hot at all (although those from the south generally are). Some curries and rice dishes, especially from the northern regions, have a rich deep flavour and are spicy but not at all pungent. Indian food differs according to the region it originates from and according to the religious practices of its

people. Hindus will not eat beef. Muslims will not eat pork. Southern Indians are for the most part vegetarian; this is partly because they are poorer, partly because vegetables grow very well in the hot climate. Rice is eaten in the south, chapattis (made from wheat flour) in the north. Delhi is famous for its tandoori dishes, Kashmir for its lamb, Madras for its vegetarian dishes and Bombay for its fish.

Curry powder is never used in traditional Indian cooking: fresh spices are ground into a powder, mixed together and fried. Nearly every family cherishes its own recipes for spice mixtures.

In India, meals are eaten with the fingers—of the right hand only. Chapattis are always torn with the fingers and used to scoop up small quantities of food. When serving an Indian meal, be generous with the rice—an Indian meal uses a lot more rice and less meat or vegetables than a Western meal would. Snacks are popular, especially fried dishes. They are served as a first course or sometimes at teatime.

Indonesian Food In an Indonesian meal, all the food is laid out at once.

NASI GORENG

Preparation time: 15 minutes
Total cooking time: 8 minutes
Serves 4 as a main course

500 g (1 lb) medium-sized uncooked prawns (shrimps)
2 chicken thigh fillets
2 eggs
3 tablespoons peanut oil
1 large carrot, cut into fine julienne strips
1 clove garlic, crushed
1 teaspoon sambal oelek

1 tablespoon soy sauce
4 cups cooked rice (see note)
4 spring onions (scallions), sliced on diagonal
1 large spring onions (scallions) and red pepper (capsicum), for garnish

1 Peel and devein prawns. Slice chicken fillets into thin strips.

2 Beat eggs with a fork until blended. Heat 1 tablespoon of oil in a frying pan, pour in eggs, cook over low heat until eggs have set, lift out. When omelette is cold, roll it up, slice thinly.

3 Heat remaining oil in frying pan, add prawns, chicken, carrot and garlic, stir until browned.

4 Add sambal oelek, soy sauce, rice and spring onions, stir-fry until heated through. Serve garnished with omelette strips and spring onion and red pepper curls.

5 To make spring onion and pepper curls: Cut into fine strips and place in iced water; refrigerate.

Note: You will need to cook 1 1/2 cups of raw rice for this recipe. Cooked rice should be cooled before using for fried rice to prevent glugginess.

BEEF RENDANG

Preparation time: 15 minutes
Total cooking time: 2 hours
Serves 4

1 kg (2 lb) rump steak
2 onions, chopped
4 cloves garlic, chopped
1 teaspoon ground turmeric
10 curry leaves
1 tablespoon chopped fresh ginger
4 small red chillies, 10 cm (4 inches) long
1/2 cup (4 fl oz) water
2 teaspoons ground coriander
2 tablespoons tamarind sauce
stem of lemon grass
4 cups (32 fl oz) coconut milk

1 Remove excess fat and sinew from steak, cut meat into 3 cm (1 1/4 inch) cubes, place in a bowl.

2 In food processor, combine onions, garlic, ginger, chillies and water; blend until smooth. Add the mixture to steak.

3 Add coriander, tamarind sauce, turmeric, curry leaves and lemon grass, stir until combined. Transfer to a pan. Stir in coconut milk. Slowly bring to the boil, reduce heat to medium, simmer, uncovered, for 1 hour, stirring occasionally. Reduce heat to very low, simmer for 30 minutes, stirring frequently, until the meat is very tender and liquid has been absorbed. Remove lemon grass before serving.

Note: Stir Beef Rendang often during last 30 minutes of cooking to prevent coconut milk from separating, and to avoid sticking.

INDONESIAN CHICKEN IN COCONUT MILK

Preparation time: 15 minutes + 1 hour marinating
Total cooking time: 50 minutes
Serves 4

8 large or 12 small chicken drumsticks
2 teaspoons crushed garlic
1 teaspoon salt
1/2 teaspoon ground black pepper
2 teaspoons ground cumin
2 teaspoons ground coriander
1/2 teaspoon ground cinnamon

3 tablespoons oil
1/2 teaspoon ground fennel
2 medium onions, finely sliced
3/4 cup (6 fl oz) coconut milk
1 cup (8 fl oz) water
1 tablespoon lemon juice, malt vinegar or tamarind liquid

1 Wash chicken and pat dry with paper towels. Combine garlic, salt, pepper, cumin, coriander, cinnamon, fennel and 2 tablespoons oil. Rub mixture over chicken; refrigerate, covered, for about 1 hour.

2 Heat remaining oil in a large pan. Add onion, cook, stirring, until soft and golden. Add the chicken, cook quickly over medium-high heat until well browned.

3 Combine coconut milk, water and lemon juice. Pour over chicken, cover, simmer 40 minutes or until chicken is tender and sauce is well reduced.

OPPOSITE PAGE, ABOVE: NASI GORENG BELOW: BEEF RENDANG. ABOVE: GADO GADO WITH PEANUT SAUCE

GADO GADO

Preparation time: 20 minutes
Total cooking time: 25 minutes
Serves 6

3 eggs
2 medium orange sweet potatoes (yams)
2 medium potatoes
125 g (4 oz) yellow squash
250 g (8 oz) cabbage
2 medium carrots, cut into 1 cm (1/2 inch) thick strips
1 thin-skinned cucumber, thinly sliced lengthways
125 g (4 oz) fresh bean sprouts, tails removed,
watercress sprigs, for garnish
2/3 cup (5 fl oz) Peanut Sauce (recipe below)
2/3 cup (5 fl oz) coconut milk

1 Place eggs in a pan, cover with water. Bring to the boil, reduce heat, simmer 10 minutes. Drain, run eggs under cold water to cool. Bring a large pan of water to the boil. Cut sweet potato into 1 cm (1/2 inch) thick slices. Cut potatoes in half, then into 1.5 cm (5/8 inch) thick slices. Halve the squash. Cut cabbage into large pieces.

2 Blanch sweet potato, potato, squash, cabbage and carrot separately in boiling water until firm but not overcooked. The sweet potato and potato will take 8–10 minutes; the squash, 1 minute; carrot 2 minutes; cabbage 2 minutes. Remove from water with a slotted spoon, plunge into a bowl of iced water. Drain vegetables; dry on clean tea-towel.

3 Shell eggs and cut in halves or quarters. Arrange vegetables in decorative groups and garnish with the sliced eggs, bean sprouts and watercress sprigs.

4 Heat Peanut Sauce and coconut milk in a small pan. Serve in a bowl.

PEANUT SAUCE

Preparation time: 5 minutes
Total cooking time: 5–10 minutes
Makes 2 cups

250 g (8 oz) roasted unsalted peanuts
1 small onion, chopped
1 clove garlic, chopped
1 teaspoon chopped fresh ginger
1 teaspoon shrimp paste
1 teaspoon sambal oelek
1 tablespoon soy sauce
1 tablespoon lemon juice
1/2 cup mango chutney
1 cup (8 fl oz) water

1 Chop peanuts and onions roughly. Combine all ingredients in a food processor, blend until smooth.

2 Pour mixture into a pan, bring to the boil. Reduce heat to low and simmer, stirring occasionally, for about 5 minutes, or until sauce has reduced and thickened.

Rice is the most important part of the Indonesian diet: it is eaten with every meal. Indonesians make good use of fresh, aromatic seasonings such as chillies, galangal, lemongrass, turmeric (both root and leaves), basil, mint and curry leaves. The food is a ready mixture of spicy and salty, pungent and sweet. The sweetness of the dishes comes from fresh coconuts and sweet soy sauce: sourness from limes and tamarinds, and texture from candlenuts and peanuts. Indonesian cuisine is also characterised by its Dutch-Indonesian dishes the most famous are rijsttafel and nasi goreng.

Tempeh is a typically Indonesian ingredient which is gaining popularity in the West. Made from soy beans, it is cut into thin matchsticks and fried with peanuts, onions, chillies and tamarind.

The soup, if there is one, is not eaten first, but sipped between mouthfuls of other food.

ICE-CREAMS & SORBETS

Home-made ice-cream, sorbet or gelato are among the most elegant desserts. Ice-cream and gelato can be made in an ice-cream machine, as well as by hand. Sorbets are made in freezer trays.

ICE-CREAM

Old-fashioned vanilla ice-cream will complement most desserts, and fruit, nut, chocolate or other flavoured ice-creams are delicious by themselves. Home-made ice-cream freezes much harder than commercial ice-cream. Remove it from the freezer half an hour before serving time.

BASIC VANILLA ICE-CREAM

Place in a medium bowl ¾ cup caster (superfine) sugar and 2 vanilla beans, split lengthways. Stir in 1 cup (8 fl oz) milk, place bowl over a pan of simmering water and stir until sugar has dissolved and mixture starts to simmer.

Warm 6 egg yolks in a large bowl and gradually whisk in hot milk. Place bowl over simmering water, stir constantly (never allow it to boil) until mixture coats the back of the spoon. Set bowl aside to cool with a piece of plastic wrap over the surface of the custard to prevent a skin forming.

Stir 2 cups (16 fl oz) cream into the custard and chill for 2 hours. Remove the vanilla beans and scrape the seeds into the custard, discarding the pods. Pour the custard into an ice-cream machine and churn for about 30 minutes or until the ice-cream has become firm and thick.

VARIATIONS

Other ingredients may be added to the custard mixture before chilling. These include:

■ **COFFEE:** Add 2 tablespoons instant coffee dissolved in 1 tablespoon hot water.

■ **COCONUT:** Add 2 cups (16 fl oz) coconut cream or 1 cup desiccated coconut.

■ **CHOCOLATE CHIP:** Add 250 g (8 oz) finely chopped semi-sweet chocolate with 2 tablespoons orange juice or liqueur.

■ **BANANA:** Add 3 small ripe bananas, mashed or pureed with 1 tablespoon lemon juice.

■ **BERRY:** Add 250 g (8 oz) pureed fresh strawberries, blackberries or raspberries.

■ **PASSIONFRUIT:** Place the pulp of 8 passionfruit in a sieve placed over a bowl to extract as much juice as possible. Discard seeds. Add 1 teaspoon lemon juice to the passionfruit juice, and fold into the ice-cream mixture before churning.

■ **MACADAMIA OR PISTACHIO NUTS:** Before starting to churn ice-cream, add 2 cups roughly chopped nuts to the mixture.

To make by hand: Pour the custard into metal freezer trays and freeze for 2–3 hours or until just solid around the edges. Transfer to a medium bowl and beat with electric beaters until smooth.

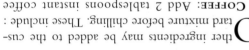

FROM LEFT TO RIGHT: BASIC VANILLA ICE-CREAM, LEMON SORBET, BLACKBERRY AND RASPBERRY SORBET, AND RICH CHOCOLATE GELATO

A sorbet is a water ice served to refresh the palate between courses or as a light dessert. Fruit sorbets are the simplest and freshest-tasting, but tea, coffee, champagne, wine, spirits, liqueur or spices are also used as flavourings. Gelato is slightly richer and is always served as a dessert.

LEMON SORBET

Pour 1/2 cup (4 fl oz) cold water into a medium pan, sprinkle with 1 tablespoon gelatine. Stand for 10 minutes. Pour 1/2 cup boiling water over gelatine mixture, stirring over low heat until gelatine is dissolved. Add 1 cup sugar and stir over low heat without boiling until sugar is dissolved. Remove from heat. Add 1 cup (8 fl oz) cold water and 1 cup strained lemon juice. Cool, then pour into freezer trays. Freeze 2-3 hours or until just firm. Scrape into chilled dessert dishes.

BLACKBERRY AND RASPBERRY SORBET

Place 6 cups fresh or frozen blackberries and 2 cups raspberries in a large pan with 1 cup (8 fl oz) water. Bring to the boil, reduce heat and simmer for 2 minutes. Strain through a fine muslin sieve. Return mixture to pan; add 1 cup water. Add 1 1/2 cups sugar and 1 tablespoon lemon juice, stir over low heat until sugar dissolves. Set aside to cool. Pour mixture into freezer trays and freeze until sorbet is mushy. Transfer to a bowl. Beat 2 egg whites until stiff. Using a metal spoon, fold egg whites into berry mixture.

Return to freezer trays and freeze, stirring occasionally to ensure egg whites are evenly distributed. Scrape mixture into serving dishes.

RICH CHOCOLATE GELATO

Place 1 litre (4 cups) milk, 1 1/4 cups sugar and 1/2 teaspoon vanilla essence into a large pan. Stir over low heat until sugar has dissolved but don't allow to boil. Remove pan from heat and stir in 1/4 teaspoon instant coffee powder and 155 g (5 oz) of chopped dark (semi-sweet) chocolate. Continue to stir until chocolate has melted and mixture is smooth. Pour the mixture into an ice-cream machine and churn for about 30 minutes or until gelato is firm.

To make by hand: Pour the chocolate mixture into metal freezer trays and freeze until mixture is set around the edges. Transfer mixture to a large bowl. Beat with electric beaters until thick. Return to freezer trays and freeze 3-4 hours or until firm.

POINTS FOR SUCCESS

■ Most ice-cream and sorbet mixtures taste over-sweet before freezing. This compensates for the numbing effect coldness has on our tastebuds. Ices with too little sweetening are flat-tasting and bland. As fruits differ in the amount of sugar and water they contain, the proportions of sugar to water in the sugar syrup vary. It is important to dissolve the sugar completely by stirring over direct heat—undissolved crystals give a grainy texture to frozen mixtures.

■ Working utensils such as bowls, freezer trays or containers should be icy cold. The mixture should always be chilled before freezing. If using an ice-cream machine, refrigerate prepared mixture for at least 4 hours, preferably overnight, before churning, for a smoother result. Freeze hand-made ice-creams at the coldest setting of your freezer, especially when freezing in trays—slow freezing can produce coarse crystals. To avoid crystallisation in sorbets and hand-made ice-creams and gelatos, beat the mixture at least twice, at hourly intervals, during the freezing process.

Tempeh is used in the same way as tofu and added to many dishes – vegetable, meat and fish. Satay is made by threading small pieces of meat onto a skewer, cooking them over coals and serving with a peanut sauce. Sambal, a fiery mixture of ground fresh chillies, salt and sometimes lime juice, tomatoes or brown sugar, is served with almost every meal. In poorer families a meal might consist of just rice and sambal.

Irish Coffee A mixture of Irish whiskey and freshly brewed coffee, sweetened with sugar, topped with a layer of chilled cream and served at the end of an evening meal. It should be served in a tall coffee cup or a heatproof glass. Do not stir once the cream has been added: the hot beverage should be sipped through the layer of cream. The drink is said to have been invented in the 1950s by a barman at Dublin's Shannon Airport.

Irish Food The traditional cooking of Ireland is more functional than fancy and is intended to sustain rather than excite. The style is straightforward and has been little influenced by the cuisines of France or other European countries. Nonetheless,

---

BROWN SODA BREAD

Preparation time: 10 minutes
Total cooking time: 20–30 minutes
Serves 4–6

2 cups self-raising unbleached flour	1 teaspoon bicarbonate of soda (baking soda)
2 cups self-raising wholemeal flour	2–3 cups (16–24 fl oz) buttermilk

1 Preheat oven to 190°C (375°F/Gas 5). Grease a baking tray with melted butter or margarine. Sift flours and bicarbonate of soda into a large mixing bowl. Use sufficient buttermilk to moisten the ingredients and form a soft dough — the amount of buttermilk required will depend on the strength of the flour.

2 Turn dough onto a floured surface and knead lightly until smooth. Press into a 20 cm (8 inch) round. Place round on a greased baking tray. With a floured knife score a deep cross, one-third of the depth of dough. Brush with water and sprinkle with a little flour. Bake for 20–30 minutes, or until bread sounds hollow when tapped with the fingers.

Note: No yeast is used in this bread. Bicarbonate of soda and buttermilk give rise, texture and flavour. If buttermilk is unavailable, use sour milk. This is made by adding a teaspoon of lemon juice or vinegar to a cup (8 fl oz) of milk. Allow to stand for about 15 minutes before using.

COLCANNON

Preparation time: 15 minutes
Total cooking time: 20 minutes
Serves 4

4 medium potatoes	⅔ cup (5 fl oz) warm milk
315 g (10 oz) shredded cabbage	ground pepper
60 g (2 oz) butter	1 tablespoon chopped parsley, for garnish
½ cup chopped spring onions (scallions)	

1 Peel potatoes, cut into quarters and cook in boiling water for 15 minutes, or until tender. Drain, mash with a fork.

2 Cook cabbage in boiling water for 10 minutes, remove from pan with tongs, drain well. Melt butter in a large pan, add cabbage and stir in spring onions, cook for 1 minute.

3 Combine cabbage mixture with mashed potatoes. Add enough warm milk to give a creamy consistency. Season with pepper and serve, garnished with chopped parsley. Drizzle over extra melted butter for a richer dish.

Note: This is a kind of Irish Bubble and Squeak. Leftover vegetables can be added or substituted.

LEFT: BROWN SODA BREAD; ABOVE: COLCANNON.
OPPOSITE PAGE, BELOW: GUINNESS BEEF STEW;
ABOVE: DUBLIN CODDLE

the sheer quality of many of its ingredients (salmon fresh from the streams, high quality dairy products, succulent lamb and excellent bacon) are a delicious compensation for any lack of culinary sophistication. In Ireland the day begins with a substantial cooked breakfast of

porridge, bacon and eggs or fish, followed by toast and marmalade and tea or coffee. The midday meal, known as dinner, is the main meal of the day. A light supper is eaten in the evening.

The history of Ireland has been greatly influenced by the potato, the humble 'pratie', said to have been introduced to the island by Sir Walter Raleigh in the late sixteenth century. It was a godsend to a country constantly on the edge of famine, for when planted with potato, Ireland's poor soils yielded up to six times as much nourishment as when sown with grain. Ireland became a one crop country, with both people and stock dependent for

DUBLIN CODDLE

Preparation time: 40 minutes
Total cooking time: 1 hour 15 minutes
Serves 4

8 thick pork sausages
4 rashers bacon, 5 mm (1/4 inch) thick
2 large brown onions, chopped
2 cloves garlic, crushed
30 g (1 oz) dripping
4 medium-sized potatoes
1/4 teaspoon dried sage
ground pepper
3/4 cup (6 fl oz) chicken stock
2 tablespoons chopped fresh parsley

1 Preheat oven to 180°C (350°F/Gas 4). Place sausages in a pan, cover with cold water and bring to boil. Reduce heat, simmer uncovered for 7 minutes, drain and cool. Cut the bacon into 2 cm (3/4 inch) strips.

2 Heat dripping in pan, cook bacon for 1 minute. Add onion and cook until golden. Add garlic and cook for 1 minute. Remove bacon, onion and garlic, drain on paper towels. Add sausages to pan and cook on all sides until well browned, remove and drain on paper towels.

3 Peel the potatoes and cut into 2.5 mm (1/8 inch) slices. Arrange potato slices in base of large heatproof dish, top with bacon, onion and garlic. Sprinkle sage and pepper over dish and add the chicken stock. Place drained sausages on top, cover and cook in preheated oven for 1 hour. Serve garnished with the chopped parsley.

Note: Prunes add sweetness to this dish and balance the characteristic bitterness of Guinness.

chopped parsley.

30 minutes of cooking. Serve garnished with the final thickened. If using prunes, add to pan in the cook uncovered until sauce is reduced and occasionally to prevent catching. Remove lid and

4 Cover and simmer gently for 1 1/2 hours, stirring carrots, herbs and pepper, stir until combined. comes to simmering point. Add onion and garlic, smooth sauce. Add Guinness and stir until mixture

3 Add stock, stir until mixture forms a thick, Reduce heat, stir in flour until all meat is coated. meat and cook quickly to brown on all sides.

2 Heat remaining dripping in a large pan, add minute. Remove from pan, drain on paper towels. cook onion until golden. Add garlic, cook for another 1 cm (1/2 inch) cubes. Heat half the dripping in a pan,

1 Remove excess fat from meat, cut meat into

1 cup (8 fl oz) beef stock
flour
1/4 cup plain (all-purpose)
2 cloves garlic, crushed
chopped
2 large brown onions,
2 tablespoons dripping
1 kg (2 lb) rump steak

1 cup (8 fl oz) Guinness
2 large carrots, sliced
2 bay leaves
1 sprig fresh thyme
ground pepper
1/2 cup prunes, halved and pitted (optional)
chopped parsley, for garnish

Serves 4-6
Total cooking time: 2 hours
Preparation time: 20 minutes

GUINNESS BEEF STEW

IRISH MIST CREAM

★★ **Preparation time:** 30 minutes +
1 hour 30 minutes setting
Total cooking time: 10 minutes
Serves 8

2¼ cups (18 fl oz) milk
4 eggs, separated
4 tablespoons caster
(superfine) sugar
½ cup (4 fl oz) cream,
whipped
extra whipped cream
chocolate, for decoration

⅓ cup (2½ fl oz) Irish
Mist liqueur
2 tablespoons gelatine
¼ cup (2 fl oz) boiling
water

1 Bring milk to boil in a pan. Remove from heat. In a bowl, whisk egg yolks and 2 tablespoons caster sugar. Add milk and whisk to combine. Pour mixture back into pan, cook over low heat for 7 minutes; do not boil.
2 Dissolve gelatine in boiling water, add to hot milk mixture, stir well. Pour in Irish Mist, refrigerate for 40 minutes, or until mixture begins to set.
3 Beat egg whites until soft peaks form, sprinkle with remaining sugar and beat until it dissolves. When milk and egg mixture begins to set, fold through whipped cream and beaten egg whites. Pour even portions into eight glass serving dishes and refrigerate until set.
4 Decorate each portion with whipped cream and chocolate curls. Sprinkle with grated chocolate.

Note: Prepare Irish Mist Cream one day ahead.

IRISH STEW

★ **Preparation time:** 20 minutes
Total cooking time: 1 hour 15 minutes
Serves 4

8 lamb neck chops
4 rashers bacon
2 cups (16 fl oz) beef
stock
1 tablespoon dripping
1 kg (2 lb) potatoes, cut
into thick slices
3 carrots, sliced
diagonally
3 medium onions, thickly
sliced
ground pepper
1 teaspoon chopped fresh
thyme
chopped fresh parsley, for
garnish

1 Trim chops, removing excess fat. Cut bacon into 2 cm (¾ inch) strips. Heat dripping in a pan, add bacon and cook until crisp and brown, remove from pan, drain on paper towels. Cook chops until brown on both sides, remove from pan, drain.
2 Arrange half the potato, carrot and onion in the base of a deep, heavy-based pan. Season with pepper, and add half the bacon. Place chops over this layer. Cover the chops with remaining potato, carrot, onion and bacon.
3 Add stock and thyme. Cover, bring to boil, reduce heat, simmer for 1 hour or until lamb is very tender. Serve garnished with chopped parsley.

ABOVE: IRISH STEW; *BELOW:* IRISH MIST CREAM.
OPPOSITE PAGE: CARPACCIO

sustenance upon the vegetable. The failure of the blight-infested 1845 potato harvest triggered a national disaster, and families across the land faced starvation. It was a time when many of Ireland's people, her greatest export, were forced to flee to more fruitful soils. Potatoes remain a staple throughout rural Ireland. There are many traditional potato dishes—pratie cakes are scones made from mashed potato cooked on a griddle and served, buttered, for supper; champ is fluffy mashed potatoes enriched with milk and butter and sprinkled with chopped spring onions (scallions).

The potato is also a basic ingredient in soups, stews, breads and pastry, and is predominant in Irish stew, traditionally made from a neck of mutton or lamb, onions and potatoes. Soda bread, made with buttermilk and raised with bicarbonate of soda, is found throughout Ireland. A fine array of seafood can be had in the fishing villages and the fish markets of the coastal towns; delicious smoked mackerel is available throughout the year. Regional specialties include crubeen, pig's feet, from Cork and

The potato

ITALIAN CLASSICS

MINESTRONE

Preparation time: 20 minutes
Total cooking time: 1 hour 30 minutes
Serves 6–8

1/3 cup (2 1/2 fl oz) olive oil
2 cloves garlic, finely chopped
2 onions, chopped
1/2 cup chopped bacon or salt pork
2 carrots, chopped
3 sticks celery, sliced
2 potatoes, peeled and diced
2 zucchini (courgettes), diced
125 g (4 oz) green beans, chopped

250 g (8 oz) savoy cabbage, shredded
410 g (13 oz) can peeled tomatoes, chopped
1 teaspoon dried oregano
2 litres (8 cups) chicken or beef stock
1 cup elbow macaroni
315 g (10 oz) can cannellini beans, drained
1 tablespoon chopped fresh basil
freshly grated parmesan cheese for serving

1 Heat oil in a large pan and cook garlic, onions and bacon until onions are soft but not brown. Add carrot and celery and cook for 3 minutes, stirring occasionally. Add remaining vegetables, tomato and tomato juice from the can.

2 Stir in oregano and stock, bring to the boil and simmer soup for 1 hour. Add macaroni, cook for 10 minutes; add cannellini beans and basil and simmer for 5 minutes.

3 Serve minestrone liberally sprinkled with parmesan cheese. May be served with thick, crusty bread or warm bread rolls.

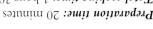
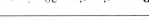

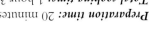

VEAL SCALOPPINE WITH EGGPLANT (AUBERGINE)

Preparation time: 25 minutes
Total cooking time: 30 minutes
Serves 4

4 large pieces veal scaloppine
plain (all-purpose) flour for dusting
60 g (2 oz) butter
2 teaspoons dried oregano leaves
4 slices fontina cheese
1 large tomato, thinly sliced
1 small eggplant (aubergine), thinly sliced
freshly ground black pepper

1 Dust veal with flour. Heat butter in a frying pan until it begins to brown. Add veal in a single layer. Brown quickly on both sides for about 30 seconds; remove from pan.

2 Add eggplant slices to pan. Fry on both sides until brown; remove, drain on paper towels.

3 Lay each veal slice on a separate sheet of foil; top each with eggplant, tomato and cheese. Sprinkle with oregano and pepper.

4 Bring foil loosely up around veal to make a secure package; seal at the top, leaving space between the foil and cheese. Place packages on a baking tray; bake in moderate oven 180°C (350°F/Gas 4) for 20 minutes or until vegetables are tender. Serve with sautéed potatoes.

CARPACCIO

Preparation time: 20 minutes +
2 hours refrigeration
Total cooking time: nil
Serves 4

410 g (13 oz) beef eye fillet (tenderloin) in one piece
salt (optional)
lemon juice
olive oil
freshly ground black pepper
fresh parmesan cheese
lemon wedges

1 Place beef eye fillet in the freezer for about 2 hours or until firm but not frozen solid. Using a sharp knife, trim away any fat. Slice fillet into wafer thin slices. Lay slices in single layer over serving plates.

2 Drizzle beef with oil. Using a vegetable peeler, shave shreds of parmesan cheese from a block; sprinkle over beef. Sprinkle with pepper and salt and drizzle lemon juice over the meat. Serve with lemon wedges.

Note: Choose high quality beef with low fat and sinew content for this recipe.

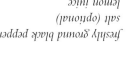

---

coddle, pork sausage and potato, from Dublin. Ireland is also known for its rich black stout, introduced to the world in 1759 by Arthur Guinness. A favourite in the pub, it is also features in the kitchen as a slightly bitter flavouring for beef stew and a rich fruit cake.

Irish whiskey, made from barley malt and wheat or oats and matured for seven years, is the secret to a successful Irish coffee. The Irish were the first to make whiskey, which they called uisge breatha, 'blessed water'. Legend has it they were taught the art of distilling, in which alcohol is produced from cereal grain instead of grapes, by St Patrick, patron saint of Ireland, in the fifth century; it seems certain that Irish monks were busy at their stills long before they began selling the warming spirit outside the monasteries in the eleventh century.

Irish Soda Bread

Irish Soda Bread made with buttermilk or sour milk and leavened with bicarbonate of soda (baking soda). Currants, raisins and caraway seed are often added. Soda bread is a specialty of Ireland and is

baked in homes and bakeries throughout the country.

Irish Stew A hearty stew in which mutton or lamb is arranged in alternate layers with sliced potatoes and onions, moistened with water and simmered. It is called a 'white stew' because the meat is not browned before being cooked with the vegetables. There should be more potato than meat; during the long, slow cooking the potatoes break up and thicken the gravy. To serve, first lift out the potatoes, place the meat on top, cover with the gravy and garnish with chopped parsley.

Italian Food Italy produces some of the best loved food in the world. The culinary differences between northern and southern Italy have become hazier—with pizza napoletana eaten not only in Naples but also in the north and all over the world, and risotto alla milanese being enjoyed in Sicily as well as Milan. But it is the fact that Italian food is regional—and that it uses fresh local produce—that has made it so popular. From the south

SPAGHETTI PUTTANESCA

Preparation time: 15 minutes
Total cooking time: 20–25 minutes
Serves 4

4 large ripe tomatoes
(about 750 g/1½ lb)
1 tablespoon olive oil
2 cloves garlic, crushed
2 small red chillies,
chopped
½ cup (4 fl oz) water
12 green or black pitted
olives, sliced
8 anchovy fillets, chopped

2 teaspoons chopped
capers
2 tablespoons chopped
fresh parsley
1 tablespoon chopped
fresh basil
315 g (10 oz) spaghetti
freshly shredded parmesan
cheese (optional)

1 Peel tomatoes and remove seeds; chop roughly.
2 Heat oil in a pan. Add garlic and chilli; cook over medium heat for 1 minute. Add tomato and water; cover. Reduce heat to low and simmer for 10 minutes or until tomato becomes soft and pulpy; add a little extra water if sauce starts to stick to the pan.
3 Add olives, anchovies, capers, parsley and basil; simmer for 3 minutes.
4 Bring a large pan of water to the boil; add spaghetti and cook 10–12 minutes or until tender. Drain thoroughly in a colander. Return to pan, add sauce and toss over low heat until combined. Serve Spaghetti Puttanesca sprinkled with freshly shredded parmesan if desired.

TRADITIONAL CRISPY PIZZA

Preparation time: 30 minutes
Total cooking time: 30 minutes
Serves 4

Crust
7 g (¼ oz) dried yeast
2 teaspoons sugar
¾ cup (6 fl oz) warm
water
2½ cups plain (all-
purpose) flour
pinch salt

Topping
¾ cup (6 fl oz) bottled
tomato sauce
125 g (4 oz) Italian
salami, sliced and cut
into strips

2 tablespoons chopped
fresh basil
125 g (4 oz) small cap
mushrooms, sliced
1 onion, sliced into thin
wedges
½ green pepper
(capsicum), sliced
12 pitted black olives,
halved
6 anchovy fillets
1 cup grated mozzarella
cheese
¼ cup freshly grated
parmesan cheese

1 To make Crust: Combine yeast and sugar in a bowl; stir in warm water. Sift flour and salt into a bowl; add yeast mixture and stir until combined.
2 Knead dough on a lightly floured surface for 10 minutes or until smooth and elastic. Roll dough out to a circle large enough to fit a 30 cm (12 inch) pizza tray.
3 Preheat oven to 190°C (375°F/Gas 5). Spread pizza with tomato sauce and top with salami, basil, mushrooms, onion, pepper and olives. Lay anchovies over top; sprinkle with mozzarella and parmesan cheeses. Bake for 30 minutes.

come olive oil, olives, tomatoes and wheat. The cooking reflects this: pizza with tomato sauce, mozzarella, olives, anchovies; pasta with rich tomato sauce, olives and fresh oregano. Eggplant (aubergine) dishes are popular as are red peppers (capsicum) and artichokes. Seafood is prepared simply, usually grilled or fried. The food of the north is more sophisticated. More meat is eaten, especially beef—the charcoal-grilled bistecca of Florence is thought to be the best beef dish in Italy—and while pasta is popular all over Italy, rice in the form of risotto is a northern speciality. In northern Italy butter is used in preference to olive oil, and many cheeses are made there, notably gorgonzola, mascarpone, and bel paese. The most famous cheese of the south, mozzarella, is made from ewe's milk. Polenta is a batter made from cornmeal and is one of the favourite accompaniments of northern Italy. It is cooked, cooled, cut into squares, fried and served with quail and other meat and poultry dishes.

VEAL CHOPS WITH SAGE AND LEMON

Preparation time: 10 minutes
Total cooking time: 10 minutes
Serves 4

4 veal loin chops
3/4 cup dried breadcrumbs
30 g (1 oz) butter
1 tablespoon olive oil
1 clove garlic, crushed
lemon wedges
2 tablespoons milk
1 egg, beaten
plain (all-purpose) flour for dusting
1 tablespoon finely chopped fresh sage or
2 teaspoons dried sage

1 Trim excess fat from the veal chops; curl up tails of chops and secure in place with toothpicks.

2 Place the flour in a plastic bag. Place chops, one at a time, in the bag and coat thoroughly with flour, shake off excess. Place egg and milk in a shallow bowl and stir to combine. Combine sage and breadcrumbs on a plate. Dip the floured chops in egg mixture, then press lightly in the breadcrumb mixture coating thoroughly.

3 Heat butter, oil and garlic in a large frying pan. Add chops in single layer; fry on both sides over medium heat until cooked through. Serve with lemon wedges.

LEMON ZABAGLIONE

Preparation time: 5 minutes
Total cooking time: 5 minutes
Serves 4

3 egg yolks
1/2 cup (4 fl oz) white wine
1/4 cup sugar
4 teaspoons Marsala
8 almond biscuits
1/4 cup (2 fl oz) lemon juice

1 Whisk egg yolks and sugar in a heatproof bowl until light and creamy. Add Marsala, lemon juice and wine. Whisk until combined.

2 Place bowl over a pan of simmering water. Using a wooden spoon, stir over heat for 5 minutes or until mixture has thickened.

3 Spoon into serving glasses and serve with almond biscuits.

Note: Zabaglione can be served on its own or as a topping for fruit or ice-cream. It is quite rich so only small amounts are served.

JAMS & MARMALADES

J am (jelly) and marmalade are made by boiling together sugar and fruit in a concentration high enough to preserve the mixture and prevent spoilage. While jam does not store indefinitely, it usually has a shelf life of about two years.

JAM (JELLY)

J am should set to a firm consistency and have a good, clear colour characteristic of the fruit used to make it. The flavour should be that of the fruit without being excessively sweet or acidic. What makes jam set is the combination of pectin and acid (naturally occurring in fruit) and added sugars. Because pectin and acid are present to varying degrees in different fruits, two or more fruits are often combined in one jam. Alternatively, lemon juice or commercial pectin may be added. Pectin is highest in slightly under-ripe fruit: it is concentrated in the core and skin, and in the white pith and pips of citrus fruit.

FROM LEFT: ORANGE
MARMALADE, LIME
MARMALADE, APRICOT
JAM; RIGHT:
STRAWBERRY JAM.

PECTIN CONTENT

The pectin content of fruits varies considerably. Some fruits are rich in pectin and acid and make jam which sets easily, while others contain less pectin. Pectin levels of some common fruits are:

High	Medium	Low
citrus fruits	apricots	bananas
cooking apples	blackberries, early	blackberries, late
crab apples	greengages	cherries
cranberries	loganberries	figs
currants (red & black)	mulberries	guavas
damsons	raspberries	melon
gooseberries	sweet apples	nectarines
grapes	peaches	
plums (some varieties)	pears	
quinces	pineapple	
	rhubarb	
	strawberries	
	tomatoes	

STEPS IN MAKING JAM

1 PREPARING THE FRUIT

Choose slightly under-ripe fruit. Wash fruit thoroughly, drain, remove leaves and stalks, and cut off any bruised or damaged sections. Peel, cut or slice fruit according to recipe.

2 RELEASING THE PECTIN

Cook fruit with or without water (see individual recipes) to soften it and to release the pectin. Place in a large pan, add water as specified, bring to boil, reduce heat and simmer, covered, until fruit has softened.

To test for pectin: Place 1 teaspoon of liquid from pan in a glass. Cool, add 3 teaspoons methylated spirits (grain alcohol), leave for 3 minutes. If pectin is high, liquid will form a firm, jelly-like clump. If jelly is only partially set, pectin level is not enough to set jam. Boil mixture a little longer, adding 1 tablespoon lemon juice per 1 kg (2 lb) fruit; test again. If it still does not jell, use commercial pectin.

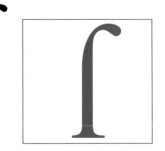

3 COOKING WITH SUGAR

Use amount of sugar specified in recipe. For best results, warm sugar in oven before adding to fruit—this minimizes the amount of scum on the surface during cooking. Bring fruit to boil, add sugar; stir until sugar has fully dissolved. Bring to boil, boil without stirring for time specified. (Check with a wooden spoon that mixture is not burning.) Setting point of jam is reached when correct concentration of sugar is achieved. If testing with a sugar thermometer, it should reach 105°C (221° F).

Alternatively, spoon a little jam onto a cold plate; cool. When setting point has been reached, the jam holds its shape and wrinkles when it is pushed gently with the finger. If this does not happen the first time, continue to cook jam and test again at frequent intervals.

4 BOTTLING

Before bottling, remove any scum from surface of jam with a metal spoon. Allow jam to stand for 10 minutes to prevent fruit sinking to the bottom of the jar. Ladle hot jam into warm sterilised jars, filling to within 1 cm (½ inch) of top, and seal immediately. Plastic or plastic-coated metal lids are suitable, or seal jars with wax or special cellophane-like jam covers (follow directions on packet).

MARMALADE

Marmalade is essentially jam made from citrus fruit, and methods are the same. However, because citrus rind is tough, prepared fruit is often soaked overnight, and the initial cooking period is longer, with more water used. It is important to boil the peel until it is soft enough before adding sugar, as no further softening will be achieved once sugar has been added.

The cutting of citrus fruit takes time, but this can be minimised by using a food processor or a vegetable slicer.

Citrus fruits are high in pectin and acid, so it is not necessary to test for pectin.

1 Slice citrus fruit thinly. Place fruit and water in a large bowl. Cover and set aside for fruit to soak overnight.

2 Place fruit and water in a large pan and bring to the boil. Simmer until the citrus rind has softened.

3 Add warmed sugar to the pan, stirring until sugar has completely dissolved.

4 Boil without stirring until mixture reaches setting point 105° C (221° F). Use a sugar thermometer to check temperature.

5 Carefully pour the marmalade into warm jars that have been sterilised.

6 To seal, carefully pour melted wax over marmalade. When cool, label and date.

TO STERILISE JARS

Wash jars thoroughly, rinse in very hot water and invert them on a rack to drain. Place jars upright in a slow oven 150°C (300°F/Gas 2) for 30 minutes. Use the jars straight from the oven to minimise the risk of them cracking when filled with hot mixture. Lids should be boiled or rinsed in very hot water. To avoid burns, use cotton gloves when handling hot jars.

SLICE CITRUS FRUITS THINLY. PLACE IN A BOWL, COVER WITH WATER AND SOAK OVERNIGHT.

WARM SUGAR IN A LOW OVEN AND ADD IT TO THE SOFTENED FRUIT IN THE PAN.

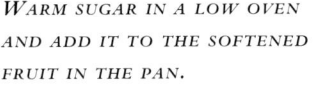

SPOON MARMALADE INTO WARMED STERILISED JARS. USE COTTON GLOVES TO HOLD JARS.

Jalapeño Chilli A small, tapered, thick-fleshed, fiery-tasting chilli, the most common variety in North America. Fresh jalapeño chillies are usually sold green, but bright red, fully ripe and slightly sweeter tasting forms can also be found; both green and red are available pickled in brine.

Jackfruit A large, barrel-shaped fruit with yellow–green knobbly skin and sweet, pungent-smelling creamy white flesh and numerous large white seeds. A relative of the breadfruit and native to the rainforests of tropical India and Malaysia, it is now grown throughout tropical Asia and Africa. The crunchy flesh can be eaten fresh on its own, added to fruit salad or puréed for use in ice-cream; it can also be boiled, deep fried or added to curries. The seeds can be cooked in the same way as chestnuts; in Africa they are ground into flour. Jackfruit is in season in summer; it is also available canned or preserved.

JAPANESE CLASSICS

SUNOMONO (CUCUMBER AND PRAWN/SHRIMP SALAD)

★ **Preparation time:** 20 minutes + 1 hour standing
Total cooking time: 5 minutes
Serves 4

1 long cucumber	1 tablespoon caster (superfine) sugar
salt	¼ cup (2 fl oz) rice
375 g (12 oz) medium uncooked prawns (shrimps)	vinegar
¼ teaspoon soy sauce	1 tablespoon toasted
¼ teaspoon fresh ginger finely grated	sesame seeds

1 Halve cucumber lengthways and remove seeds with a teaspoon. Cut into thin slices, sprinkle with salt and allow to stand for 5 minutes. Gently squeeze moisture from cucumber.
2 Place prawns in a pan of lightly salted boiling water and simmer for 2 minutes or until just cooked. Drain and plunge into cold water. Allow prawns to cool; peel and devein prawns.
3 Place vinegar, sugar, soy sauce and ginger in a large bowl and stir until sugar dissolves. Add prepared prawns and cucumber and leave to stand for 1 hour.
4 Drain prawn mixture in a colander. Place on serving plates and sprinkle with sesame seeds.

MISOSHIRU (MISO SOUP)

★ **Preparation time:** 10 minutes
Total cooking time: 10 minutes
Serves 4

1 litre (4 cups) dashi (bonito stock)	105 g (3½ oz) red miso
125 g (4 oz) tofu, diced	2 spring onions (scallions)
	1 tablespoon mirin
	4 button mushrooms

1 Place dashi in a medium pan and bring to the boil. Blend miso with mirin and add to hot stock.
2 Simmer soup gently, uncovered, for 2 minutes. Add diced tofu to soup and simmer for another 5 minutes.
3 Trim mushroom stems level with caps and finely slice mushrooms. Finely slice spring onions. Pour soup into warmed bowls and sprinkle mushrooms and spring onions on top.
Note: Instant dashi is available in powdered form or as a concentrated liquid in specialist Japanese food stores. Add boiling water as directed on the pack.

Note : To toast sesame seeds quickly, place in a small dry pan and toss over low heat until seeds are golden brown. Remove to a plate to cool.

SUSHI ROLLS

✻✻ *Preparation time:* 45 minutes
Total cooking time: 10–15 minutes
Makes about 30

1 cup short-grain white rice	2 cups (16 fl oz) water
125 g (4 oz) smoked salmon, trout or fresh sashimi tuna	2 tablespoons rice vinegar
	1 tablespoon sugar
1/2 long thin cucumber, peeled	1 teaspoon salt
1/2 small avocado	3–4 sheets nori
1/4 cup pickled ginger	1–2 teaspoons wasabi
soy sauce for dipping	

1 Wash rice in cold water, drain well. Place rice and water in medium pan. Bring to boil, reduce heat, simmer uncovered 4–5 minutes or until water is absorbed. Cover, reduce heat to very low and cook for another 4–5 minutes. Remove pan from heat, cool. Stir combined vinegar, sugar and salt into rice. Place 1 sheet of nori onto a piece of greaseproof paper on a flat work surface. Place a quarter of the rice along one end of the nori, leaving a 2 cm (3/4 inch) border around the three sides. Spread a very small amount of wasabi evenly down centre of the rice.

2 Cut the fish into thin strips, and the cucumber and the avocado into small pieces. Place the pieces of fish, cucumber, avocado and ginger over the wasabi.

3 Using the paper as a guide, roll up firmly from the bottom, enclosing in the rice the ingredients placed in the centre. Press nori to seal edges. Using a sharp flat-bladed or electric knife, cut roll into 2.5 cm (1 inch) rounds. Repeat the process with remaining ingredients. Serve sushi rolls with small shallow bowls of soy sauce or extra wasabi mixed with soy sauce, for dipping.

Jalousie A pastry dessert of French origin consisting of a layer of thinly rolled puff pastry spread with a sweet filling such as marzipan (almond paste), stewed fruit or jam, then topped with a second layer of pastry which is glazed with beaten egg yolk and milk and cut into fine slats before baking.

Jam (Jelly) A sweet spread made by cooking fruit in sugar and water until set. The setting power depends on the pectin content of the fruit (pectin occurs naturally in many ripe fruits, but commercial pectin can be added if there is insufficient in the mixture). The fruits that are abundant in pectin include apples, blackberries, lemons, oranges, quinces and redcurrants. One of these can be combined with a strong-flavoured fruit which is low in pectin to produce a good-setting jam. Jam is made from whole fruit that is either crushed or chopped and so differs from conserve, in which the fruit or fruit pieces remain intact, and from fruit jelly, which is made from fruit juice strained to remove all other matter and then boiled with sugar.

Marmalade is similar in preparation to other jams, but only citrus fruit (either a single fruit or a mixture) is used.

Jambalaya A peppery Cajun dish featuring rice, chicken, prawn (shrimp) and ham and derived from the Spanish paella. It is a specialty of Louisiana: the name is thought to come from *jamón*, the Spanish word for 'ham'.

Japanese Food Rice is the staple of Japanese food and a meal without rice is not considered a meal — it is a snack.

The three major ingredients used in Japanese cooking are fish stock, rice and soy bean products.

Sashimi (raw fish) is a delicacy considered the high point of any Japanese meal. The fish must be absolutely fresh, it is sliced and served with a dipping sauce into which a little wasabi (green horseradish paste) is mixed.

Sushi are little rolls of vinegared rice wrapped in seaweed with a filling of fish and vegetables.

Tempura is probably the best-loved Japanese food in the West. It is made by dipping prawns (shrimps) and vegetables in a very light batter, deep frying and serving immediately.

Miso soup can be sipped immediately through the meal or at the beginning or the end. One-pot

VEGETABLE TEMPURA

★ **Preparation time:** 30 minutes + 1 hour refrigeration
Total cooking time: 5 minutes per batch
Serves 6

1¼ cups plain (all-purpose) flour
1 egg
1¼ cups (10 fl oz) iced water
125 g broccoli
1 small onion
1 small red pepper (capsicum)
1 small green pepper (capsicum)
1 medium carrot
60 g (2 oz) green beans
light vegetable oil for deep frying

Dipping Sauce
3 tablespoons soy sauce
2 tablespoons mirin

1 Sift flour into a large mixing bowl. Make a well in the centre, add egg and water and whisk until combined. Cover, refrigerate 1 hour.

2 Cut broccoli into small florets. Finely slice onion, and cut peppers and carrot into thin strips about 6 cm (2½ inches) long. Cut beans to about 6 cm (2½ inches) long, and halve lengthways. Add vegetables to batter and mix.

3 Heat oil in a medium pan. Using tongs, gather a small bunch of batter-coated vegetables (roughly two pieces of each vegetable) and lower into oil. Hold submerged in oil for a few seconds until batter begins to set and vegetables hold together. Release from tongs and cook until crisp and golden. Drain on paper towels. Repeat until all vegetables are cooked. Serve immediately with dipping sauce.

4 To make Dipping Sauce: Place soy sauce and mirin in a small bowl and combine.

CHICKEN TERIYAKI

★ **Preparation time:** 20 minutes + 2 hours marinating
Total cooking time: 6 minutes
Makes 12

750 g (1½ lb) chicken tenderloins
¼ cup (2 fl oz) soy sauce
2 tablespoons mirin
2 tablespoons sherry
2 tablespoons soft brown sugar
2 teaspoons grated fresh ginger
1 medium red pepper (capsicum), cut into 2 cm (¾ inch) squares
4 spring onions (scallions), cut into 3 cm (1¼ inch) lengths
2 tablespoons oil

1 Trim chicken of excess fat and sinew. Soak bamboo skewers in water to prevent burning. Place chicken in a shallow glass or ceramic dish. Combine soy sauce, mirin, sherry, brown sugar and ginger in a small bowl. Stir to dissolve sugar; pour over chicken. Cover and refrigerate for up to 2 hours, turning occasionally. Drain and cut tenderloins in half lengthways.

2 Thread chicken onto skewers alternating with pepper and spring onion pieces.

3 Brush kebabs with oil and place on a lightly oiled grill or flat plate. Cook over medium-high heat 6 minutes or until tender, turning and brushing with oil occasionally. Serve immediately, with steamed rice or egg noodles and stir-fried or grilled vegetables.

OPPOSITE PAGE, ABOVE: VEGETABLE TEMPURA;
BELOW: CHICKEN TERIYAKI.
THIS PAGE, ABOVE: GUAVA JELLY;
RIGHT: ROSEMARY, TOMATO AND APPLE JELLY

JELLIES

GUAVA JELLY

Preparation time: 30 minutes +
overnight standing
Total cooking time: 45 minutes
Makes 3½ cups

1 kg (2 lb) slightly under-ripe guavas	1 litre (4 cups) water
½ cup (4 fl oz) lemon juice	sugar
1 green apple, peeled and cored	

1 Cut guavas and apple into thick slices.
2 Combine guava, apple, lemon juice and water in large pan. Bring to the boil and boil slowly, uncovered, for 10 minutes. Break up guava and apple with a wooden spoon and boil slowly for another 10 minutes.
3 Strain mixture through muslin (cheesecloth) suspended over a bowl and leave to stand overnight. Measure strained juice and return to pan. Add 1 cup of warmed sugar for each cup (8 fl oz) of juice; stir over heat until sugar is dissolved. Bring to boil; boil rapidly until setting point is reached.
4 Remove from heat and pour into warm, sterilised jars. When cool, seal jars, label and date. Serve on toast or muffins.

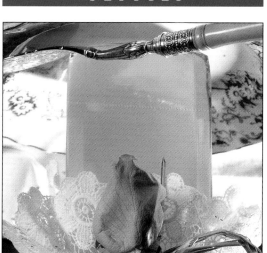

ROSEMARY, TOMATO AND APPLE JELLY

Preparation time: 25 minutes
Total cooking time: 1 hour 45 minutes
Makes 1.75 litres (7 cups)

7 medium green apples	⅔ cup (5 fl oz) lemon juice
2 medium pears	sugar
1 ripe tomato	
1 cup fresh rosemary leaves	

1 Wash the apples, pears and tomato; drain. Finely chop apples, pears and tomato; coarsely chop rosemary.
2 Combine apple, pear (including cores and seeds), tomato and rosemary in a large pan and cover with water. Bring to the boil and simmer, covered, for about 1 hour or until fruit is soft and pulpy.
3 Strain fruit mixture through a muslin (cheesecloth) bag suspended over a bowl. Measure juice and return to pan with lemon juice. Heat until boiling. Add ¾ cup warmed sugar per cup (8 fl oz) of juice. Return to boil, stirring until sugar dissolves. Boil rapidly, uncovered, for ¾ hour or until setting point is reached.
4 Remove cooked jelly from heat; allow to stand for 5 minutes. Skim any scum off surface of jelly with a metal spoon. Pour into warm, sterilised jars and cool before sealing. When almost set, a sprig of fresh rosemary may be suspended in the jelly using a clean bamboo skewer. When cool, label and date. Serve with roast lamb.

dishes such as sukiyaki are favourite restaurant dishes, where everyone cooks their own meat and vegetables in a central pot of stock. Food cooked on a teppan is also popular in the West. In teppan bars you sit at the bar and watch the chef cook the food for you on a hot griddle. He usually shows wonderful skill with his knife as he slices through vegetables and omelette rolls, so it's a bit of a show as well as a feast. Japanese food is among the most visually beautiful in the world. Appearance is rated as highly as taste.

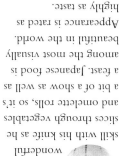

Jarlsberg A deep yellow, semi-hard, cow's milk cheese with a sweet nutty flavour. It is made by the hard cooked process (curd 'cooked' in heated whey is pressed into a wheel-shaped mould to mature). The interior is dotted with large irregularly shaped holes sometimes called 'eyes'; the rind is covered with yellow wax. Jarlsberg is a good eating cheese (let it reach room temperature before serving) and can be used on cheeseboards.

MINT JELLY

★ **Preparation time:** 30 minutes + overnight standing
Total cooking time: 45 minutes
Makes 3½ cups

1 kg (2 lb) green apples	2 cups fresh mint leaves
1 litre (4 cups) water	sugar
½ cup (4 fl oz) lemon juice	green colouring, optional

1 Cut the apples into thick slices but do not peel or core.

2 Combine apples, water, lemon juice and mint leaves in a large pan. Bring to the boil and boil slowly, uncovered, for about 10 minutes. Break up apples with a wooden spoon and boil slowly for another 15 minutes or until apples are soft and pulpy.

3 Strain mixture through muslin (cheesecloth) suspended over a bowl and stand overnight. Measure strained juice and return to pan. Add 1 cup of warmed sugar for each cup (8 fl oz) of juice and stir over heat until sugar is dissolved. Bring to the boil and boil rapidly until setting point is reached. Add a few drops of colouring to mixture until it is the desired colour.

4 Remove pan from heat; stand for 2 minutes. Pour into warm, sterilized jars. Seal when cold. Label and date jars. Serve with roast lamb.

SAGE JELLY

★★ **Preparation time:** 35 minutes + 3 hours standing
Total cooking time: 1 hour 50 minutes
Makes 2 litres (8 cups)

8 medium green apples	⅔ cup (5 fl oz) lemon juice
2 medium red apples	sugar
40 fresh sage leaves	
2 teaspoons grated lemon rind	

1 Wash and dry fruit. Finely chop fruit and coarsely chop sage leaves.

2 Combine fruit including cores and seeds, leaves and rind in a large saucepan or boiler. Cover with water, bring to boil and simmer, covered, for 1 hour or until fruit is soft and pulpy.

3 Strain fruit through muslin (cheesecloth) bag suspended over a bowl and stand for 3 hours. Measure juice and return to saucepan. Add ¾ cup warmed juice and heat until boiling. Add ¾ cup sugar per cup (8 fl oz) of juice. Return to the boil, stirring until sugar dissolves. Boil rapidly for 45 minutes or until setting point.

4 Remove jelly from the heat and allow to stand for 5 minutes. Pour into warm, sterilised jars. Allow to cool completely. When almost set, sage leaves may be suspended in the jelly using a clean bamboo skewer. Seal jars. When cool, label and date the jars. Serve with roast pork.

in sandwiches and salads; it is also cooked in fondues and sauces. The cheese was developed in the late 1950s at the Jarlsberg estate in Norway.

Jelly A clear or semi-clear food preparation with a soft elastic consistency due to the presence of gelatine or pectin.

There are several types of jelly: a spread made from fruit juice boiled with sugar to which commercial pectin is often added; a cold dessert made with sugar and fruit juice, sometimes flavoured with a liqueur, then set with gelatine, often in a mould; aspic, made from meat, fish or vegetable stock set with gelatine and used as a garnish and glaze; and jellied confectioneries (candies) such as marshmallow, Turkish delight and jujubes, made from thick syrup set with gelatine.

Jerky Meat, usually beef, which is cut into thin strips, salted and then cured by being smoked or dried. It is one of the earliest methods of transforming meat into a non-perishable and easily transportable food.

JEWISH CLASSICS

OPPOSITE PAGE, ABOVE: MINT JELLY; BELOW: SAGE JELLY. THIS PAGE, ABOVE: CHICKEN SOUP WITH MATZO BALLS; RIGHT: CHOPPED LIVER

JEWISH CLASSICS

CHICKEN SOUP WITH MATZO BALLS

✷✷ Preparation time: 30 minutes +
1 hour refrigeration
Total cooking time: 2 hours 30 minutes
Serves 6

Soup
1.75 kg (3½ lb) chicken
4 litres water
3 onions, sliced
4 carrots, chopped
4 stalks celery, chopped
1 leek, chopped
2 large parsley sprigs
1 bay leaf
8 peppercorns
1 tablespoon salt

Matzo Balls
2 tablespoons chicken fat or vegetable oil
1 medium onion, finely chopped
1 cup matzo meal (coarse)
2 eggs, beaten
1 tablespoon chopped fresh parsley
salt and pepper
almond meal

1 Remove excess fat from chicken and reserve. Cut chicken into 8 or 9 pieces, place in large pan with water and remaining soup ingredients. Bring to boil slowly; skim the surface. Reduce heat, simmer 2 hours or until chicken meat leaves the bone. Strain and return soup to the rinsed pan and bring to the boil. Reserve chicken meat for soup.

2 Add Matzo Balls and simmer, uncovered, for 15 minutes. Return shredded chicken meat to pan and simmer for another 5–10 minutes.

3 To make Matzo Balls: Heat fat or oil in a medium pan, cook onion until golden. Transfer contents of pan to a bowl. Add matzo meal, eggs and parsley. Season mixture with salt and pepper; mix. If necessary, add sufficient almond meal to bind mixture. Cover, refrigerate 1 hour. With hands dipped in cold water, roll mixture into 2 cm (¾ inch) balls.

CHOPPED LIVER

✷ Preparation time: 15 minutes
Total cooking time: 10 minutes
Serves 4

1 tablespoon chicken fat
1 medium onion, chopped
1 clove garlic, crushed
250 g (8 oz) chicken livers, trimmed
2 hard-boiled eggs
1 tablespoon fresh white breadcrumbs
extra chicken fat
salt
freshly ground black pepper
nutmeg

1 Melt chicken fat in a pan and cook onion and garlic until onion is soft. Add livers and cook quickly until tender. Do not overcook.

2 Allow mixture to cool for a few minutes; place in a food processor with hard-boiled eggs and breadcrumbs. Process until mixture is fine, adding a little more chicken fat if necessary to make a smooth paste.

3 Season mixture with salt, pepper and nutmeg.

Jerusalem Artichoke
See Artichoke.

Jewish Food Although Jewish food comes from many different countries, and has been influenced by the local produce of these diverse regions, a surprising number of the dishes are quite similar. Jewish cooking is closely linked to religious feast days. Plaited bread (challah), honey and eggs are all parts of feast-day food, and they all have biblical connotations. All fruit and vegetables are kosher (permitted) but there are strict rules regarding meat, fish and dairy products. Pork is forbidden, as is game, shellfish and fish without scales. Dairy products may not be eaten in the same meal as meat dishes, nor prepared using the same equipment. Many Jewish traditions have been taken up by non-Jews. For example the cooking of fish in olive oil. The oil must be fresh and hot, the fish is dusted with flour and cooked until brown on both

sides. Even non-orthodox Jews eat traditional dishes on feast days: soup with matzo balls and charoseth (fruit and nut with red wine) at Passover and teiglach (honey cake) at Rosh Hashanah (Jewish New Year).

Johnny Cake In North America the term refers to a flat, round, unleavened bread made from a dough of cornmeal, water or milk and salt and cooked on a griddle; eggs and butter are sometimes added. In Australia, johnny cakes are made from a flour, water and salt dough either cooked as small flat cakes on the embers of a camp fire or formed into strips, wound around a green stick and cooked over the fire.

Julienne Food, especially vegetables such as carrot, turnip, celery, leek, cut into thin, matchstick-sized pieces; they can be used raw in salads or lightly cooked to serve as a garnish in soup or as a vegetable with main courses. Cooked meat for salads can be cut

the same way, as can citrus peel.

Juniper Berry The aromatic, slightly resinous-flavoured dark berry of a small

LATKES

⭐ **Preparation time:** 35 minutes
Total cooking time: 30 minutes
Serves 4

1.5 kg (3 lb) medium potatoes	salt and freshly ground pepper
1 tablespoon oil	2 tablespoons plain (all-purpose) flour
1 egg, beaten	vegetable oil for frying

1 Scrub potatoes well. Peel and coarsely grate potatoes; rinse and drain. Squeeze out excess moisture using paper towels. Place in a bowl.
2 Add oil and beaten egg to potatoes, mixing well. Season with salt and pepper and stir in flour.
3 Shape into round flat cakes with floured hands. Heat oil and shallow fry potato cakes until golden brown on both sides.

ROAST BRISKET OF BEEF

In a baking dish, brown a 2.5 kg (5 lb) lean brisket of beef in oil on both sides. Remove from pan. Fry 3 sliced onions in the same oil and baking dish until onion is transparent. Add brisket and 1 cup (8 fl oz) of water. Sprinkle meat with 1 tablespoon of flour, salt and garlic, to taste, and bake in preheated moderately slow oven 160°C (325°F/Gas 3) for 3½ hours.

GEFILTE FISH

⭐ ⭐ **Preparation time:** 5 minutes
Total cooking time: 1 hour 45 minutes
Serves 4

1 kg (2 lb) cod, bream or haddock, with skin and bones for stock	1 tablespoon chopped parsley
2 stalks celery, chopped	2 tablespoons ground almonds
2 onions, chopped	2 eggs, beaten
2 medium carrots, sliced	salt and ground white pepper
3 cups (24 fl oz) water	matzo meal

1 Remove skin and bones from fish and place in a large pan with celery, half of the onion and half of the carrot. Add water, bring to the boil and simmer for 30 minutes. Strain stock.
2 Chop fish roughly and place in a food processor with remaining onion and parsley. Process until fine, add ground almonds, eggs, salt and pepper and sufficient matzo meal to bind. Roll mixture into 8 balls with floured hands.
3 Simmer remaining sliced carrot in fish stock for 10 minutes and remove. Add fish balls to stock, cover and simmer gently for 1 hour. Remove fish balls with a slotted spoon to a serving plate and top each with a slice of carrot.
4 Strain fish stock and spoon a little over each fish ball. Chill remaining stock which will set to a jelly. Chop jelly and use to garnish fish balls.

COTTAGE CHEESE BLINTZES

★★ *Preparation time:* 15 minutes + 1 hour standing
Total cooking time: 30 minutes
Serves 4–6

1 cup plain (all-purpose) flour	2 tablespoons sour cream
1/2 teaspoon salt	2 egg yolks
3 eggs	2 tablespoons caster (superfine) sugar
1/4 cup (2 fl oz) milk	1 lemon finely grated rind of
45 g (1 1/2 oz) butter, melted	1/2 teaspoon vanilla essence
Filling	1/4 cup sultanas (seedless raisins)
375 g (12 oz) cottage cheese	

1 Sift flour and salt into a medium bowl. Make a well in the centre. Add eggs one at a time, beating well after each addition. Stir in milk and melted butter. Cover and allow to stand for 1 hour.

2 Heat an 18–20 cm (7–8 inch) crêpe pan and brush with oil. Pour 2–3 tablespoons batter into pan; swirl evenly over base. Cook on medium heat until underside is golden. Turn pancake over and cook the other side. Place pancakes on a plate and cover with a tea-towel. Repeat process with remaining batter, brushing pan with oil when necessary.

3 Place a heaped tablespoon of filling on one side of each pancake and roll up firmly, tucking sides in to form a parcel.

4 Place pancakes in a shallow, greased heatproof dish and bake in a hot oven 220°C (425°F/Gas 7) for 10 minutes. Dust blintzes with sifted icing (confectioners) sugar and serve hot.

5 **To make Filling:** Place cottage cheese in a medium bowl and stir in sour cream and egg yolks. Add caster sugar, lemon rind, vanilla essence and sultanas to bowl and mix thoroughly to combine.

Opposite page, above: LATKES;
below: GEFILTE FISH.
This page, above: COTTAGE CHEESE BLINTZES

CHAROSETH

★ *Preparation time:* 15 minutes + 1 hour refrigeration
Total cooking time: nil
Serves 6

2 medium red apples	1 teaspoon cinnamon
1/4 cup finely chopped blanched almonds or walnuts	2 tablespoons red wine
	1 tablespoon honey

1 Halve and core apples, leaving the skin on. Chop very finely and place in a small bowl.

2 Add almonds or walnuts, cinnamon, wine and honey to bowl and mix well. Chill for 1 hour before serving.

Note: Charoseth should be eaten on the day it is made, as it does not keep well. If the wine that you use is sweet, you may wish to reduce the amount of honey.

BAGELS AND LOX

Slice bagels in half horizontally (allow 1 per person). Spread both sides of bagels with softened cream cheese. Top with 2–3 slices of fresh smoked salmon (lox) and bring bagel together. Capers and onion slices can also be added.

Note: This is the classic bagel combination, although there are many ways to serve them. Any sandwich filling can be used on a bagel. Traditionally, they are served unfilled and lightly toasted with scrambled eggs. Bagels can be purchased white or pumpernickel, with poppy seed, onion, garlic or cinnamon toppings.

Jus, au A French term applied to meat served in its own juice or gravy. Water or stock is added to pan juices and it is boiled until reduced and concentrated. *Au jus* means 'with the juice'.

Junket is easily digested and is often served to invalids.

Junket A sweet milk pudding, often flavoured with chocolate or vanilla, that is set by the curdling action of the enzyme rennet and served topped with grated nutmeg or cinnamon or garnished with crystallised (candied) lemon rind.

Juniper The juniper berries are used to flavour gin (the word 'gin' comes from the Dutch *jenever*, 'juniper') and other spirits. Dried berries are added to marinades for wild boar, pork and venison; used in stuffings for poultry and game birds and in the curing of hams; and often add flavour to slowly cooked meat dishes and sauerkraut. Crush berries before cooking to release the spicy pine aroma. Juniper berries are sold in small jars. Juniper evergreen tree.

K

Kale A strong-flavoured leaf vegetable native to the Mediterranean. It is prepared and cooked in the same way as silver beet (Swiss chard).

Kangaroo A lean, dark, high-protein meat similar in taste to venison. Kangaroo meat can be pan fried, roasted, barbecued or casseroled.

Kasha An eastern European dish made from buckwheat, butter and milk.

Kebab Small pieces of meat, poultry or seafood (often marinated), threaded on a skewer and grilled (broiled) or barbecued.

Kedgeree A mixture of rice and flaked white or smoked fish. Of Indian origin.

Kibbi A Middle Eastern dish made from lean lamb, burghul (cracked wheat) and minced onion.

Kidney Classed as offal, the kidneys of lamb, calf, beef and pig vary in colour from light to

KEBABS

GRILLED TERIYAKI BEEF KEBABS

★

Preparation time: 15 minutes + 2 hours marinating
Total cooking time: 6–14 minutes
Serves 6

6 topside (top round) steaks, about 345 g (11 oz) each
1 cup (8 fl oz) beef stock
1/4 cup (2 fl oz) teriyaki sauce
2 tablespoons hoisin sauce
2 tablespoons lime juice
1 tablespoon honey
2 spring onions (scallions), finely chopped
2 cloves garlic, crushed
1 teaspoon finely grated fresh ginger

1 Trim meat of excess fat and sinew. Slice meat across the grain into long, thin strips. Thread meat onto skewers, 'weaving' them in place.

2 Combine stock, teriyaki and hoisin sauces, lime juice, honey, spring onion, garlic and ginger in a small bowl, whisk for 1 minute or until well combined. Place skewered meat in a shallow dish, pour marinade over. Store in refrigerator, covered with plastic wrap, for 2 hours or overnight, turning occasionally. Drain, reserving marinade.

3 Place skewered meat on a cold, lightly oiled grill tray. Cook under high heat for 2 minutes each side to seal, turning once. For a rare result, cook for another minute each side. For medium and well done results, lower the grill tray or reduce heat, and cook for another 2–3 minutes

FISH AND CUMIN KEBABS

★

Preparation time: 10 minutes + 3 hours marinating
Total cooking time: 5–6 minutes
Serves 4

750 g (1½ lb) firm white fish fillets
1 tablespoon chopped fresh coriander
1 clove garlic, crushed

Marinade
2 tablespoons olive oil
2 teaspoons ground cumin
1 teaspoon ground pepper

1 Cut fish fillets into 3 cm (1¼ inch) cubes. Thread onto oiled skewers and set aside.

2 To make Marinade: Combine oil, garlic, coriander, cumin and pepper in a small bowl. Brush fish with marinade. Cover with plastic wrap and refrigerate several hours or overnight.

3 Place skewers on cold, lightly oiled grill. Cook under medium-high heat 5–6 minutes or until tender, turning once and brushing with reserved marinade several times during cooking. Serve with pitta bread and lime wedges.

each side for medium and 4–6 minutes each side for well done. Brush occasionally with the reserved marinade during cooking.

ABOVE: FISH AND CUMIN KEBABS.
OPPOSITE PAGE, BELOW: GREEK LAMB KEBABS;
ABOVE: GARLIC CHICKEN KEBABS

ORIENTAL VEAL STICKS

Preparation time: 6 minutes
Total cooking time: 6–8 minutes
Serves 4

750 g (1½ lb) veal strips
1 clove garlic, crushed
½ cup (4 fl oz) plum sauce
½ teaspoon grated fresh ginger
2 teaspoons soy sauce
¼ teaspoon minced chilli

1 Thread meat onto 8 bamboo skewers.
2 Combine plum and soy sauces, garlic, ginger and chilli. Brush kebabs with chilli-plum mixture. Barbecue kebabs over hot coals 3–4 minutes each side, brushing constantly with sauce.
3 Serve veal sticks with brown rice and salad. Any leftover baste may be used as a dipping sauce.

GREEK LAMB KEBABS

Preparation time: 20 minutes + 2 hours marinating
Total cooking time: 12 minutes
Makes 20 kebabs

1.5 kg (3 lb) boned leg of lamb
2 tablespoons soy sauce
1 teaspoon dried oregano leaves
⅓ cup (2½ fl oz) olive oil
¼ cup (2 fl oz) lemon juice
2 tablespoons dry white wine
2 cloves garlic, crushed
1 large onion, finely chopped
½ teaspoon ground black pepper
¼ cup finely chopped fresh parsley

1 Trim meat of excess fat and sinew. Cut meat evenly into 3 cm (1¼ inch) cubes. Thread cubes onto oiled skewers. Place oil, juice, wine, garlic, sauce, oregano and pepper in a bowl. Whisk for 2 minutes or until well combined. Pour over meat.
2 Refrigerate, covered with plastic wrap, 2 hours or overnight. Drain meat, reserving the marinade.
3 Place meat on a cold, lightly oiled grill tray. Cook under high heat 12 minutes or until tender, turning once. Brush with reserved marinade several times during cooking. Combine onion and parsley; serve sprinkled over the kebabs.

GARLIC CHICKEN KEBABS

Preparation time: 20 minutes
Total cooking time: 12 minutes
Makes 12

6 (750 g/1½ lb) chicken thigh fillets
½ cup (4 fl oz) oil
2 cloves garlic, crushed
1 tablespoon chopped fresh chives
1 tablespoon chopped fresh mint
1 tablespoon chopped fresh thyme
½ teaspoon seasoned pepper
1 medium red pepper (capsicum), cut into 3 cm (1¼ inch) pieces
1 medium green pepper (capsicum), cut into 3 cm (1¼ inch) pieces
1 large red onion, cut into 12 wedges

1 Soak bamboo skewers in water for several hours. Trim chicken of excess fat and sinew. Cut chicken into 3 cm (1¼ inch) cubes.
2 Thread chicken, peppers and onion alternately onto skewers. Combine oil, garlic, herbs and pepper in a small bowl.
3 Place kebabs on lightly oiled grill. Cook skewers under medium-high heat 6 minutes each side or until cooked through, brushing with herb mixture several times during cooking.

---

deep red-brown. Lamb kidney can be cut in half and grilled (broiled); calf kidney can be cubed and braised and pork kidney is best slowly casseroled.

Kidney Bean, Dried, red-brown, kidney-shaped seed of the haricot bean, used in Mexican cooking and salads.

Kipper A herring, split, gutted and soaked in brine then dried and smoked. They are a favourite British breakfast.

Kiwi Fruit Also known as Chinese gooseberry, an egg-shaped, hairy fruit with sweet, juicy flesh and tiny black seeds. Eat fresh, peeled and sliced or cut in half; add to fruit salads or puree; ice-creams and sorbets.

Kofta A dish popular in Asia and the Middle East consisting of ground meat or chicken balls cooked in a spicy sauce.

Korma An Indian dish consisting of lean meat or chicken braised in a spicy yoghurt or cream sauce.

Ladies' Fingers A term used for several different foods, all slender and finger-shaped. Okra, a vegetable much used in North African and Caribbean dishes is known in some places as ladies' fingers, as is a small sweet variety of banana. A small, finger-shaped, crisp sponge biscuit (cookie) also carries the name. In Middle Eastern cooking the name can refer to thin rolls of filo pastry filled with either a spicy meat mixture or crushed nuts and honey.

Lamb Meat from a sheep under one year old; milk-fed or baby lamb is under 3 months old; spring lamb, 3–9 months. Lamb should be firm with fine-grained, reddish-pink meat with an even edge of white fat; it is generally succulent and is suitable for roasting, grilling (broiling) and barbecuing. It features in the cuisines of many countries. In Greece it is slow-roasted in *kleftico*; in the Middle East kebabs are cubes of lamb

LAMB

CROWN ROAST OF LAMB WITH ROSEMARY STUFFING

✸✸ **Preparation time:** 20 minutes
Total cooking time: 45 minutes
Serves 6

1 crown roast (minimum 12 cutlets)
2 medium brown onions, peeled and chopped
1 green or cooking apple, peeled and chopped
15 g (1/2 oz) butter
2 cups (about 125 g/4 oz) fresh breadcrumbs

2 tablespoons chopped fresh rosemary
1 tablespoon chopped fresh parsley
1/4 cup (2 fl oz) unsweetened apple juice
2 eggs, separated

1 Preheat the oven to moderately hot 210°C (415°F/Gas 6–7). Trim meat of excess fat and sinew. Cook onion and apple in butter until soft. Remove from heat and stir in breadcrumbs and herbs. Whisk apple juice and egg yolks together. Stir into breadcrumb mixture.

2 Place egg whites in a small, dry mixing bowl. Using electric beaters, beat egg whites until soft peaks form. Fold lightly into stuffing mixture.

3 Place crown roast in a baking dish. Place a sheet of lightly greased foil underneath the roast to hold stuffing. Spoon stuffing into cavity. Roast meat for 45 minutes, or until cooked to your liking. Use a sharp knife to cut between cutlets to separate.

Note: Order the crown roast in advance and ask your butcher to shape and tie it with string. Wrap foil around the ends of the cutlet bones to prevent them burning; discard before serving.

ABOUT LAMB

■ In recent years, the variety of boneless and fat-free cuts of lamb has increased its popularity at the table. A flavoursome and nutritious alternative to beef, lamb steaks and fillets are usually cooked quickly and served rare, or medium. (To test for doneness, press the meat gently with tongs—rare lamb will be very soft, and medium slightly firm.) Minced (ground) lamb is an alternative to recipes that usually use beef, such as hamburgers.

■ More traditional (and just as delicious) is the practice of cooking lamb until it is almost ready to fall apart or away from the bone. Lamb curries, stews and casseroles should be cooked very slowly until the meat almost melts in the mouth.

ABOVE: CROWN ROAST OF LAMB WITH ROSEMARY STUFFING. OPPOSITE PAGE, BELOW: ROAST LEG OF LAMB; ABOVE: LAMB NAVARIN WITH VEGETABLES

ROAST LEG OF LAMB WITH SAGE AND TARRAGON

✳ *Preparation time:* 15 minutes
Total cooking time: 1 hour 30 minutes
Serves 6

2 kg (4 lb) leg of lamb
1/4 cup roughly chopped fresh sage leaves
2 tablespoons roughly chopped fresh tarragon leaves
1 cup (8 fl oz) white wine
2 tablespoons plum sauce
1 tablespoon oil
1 medium onion, chopped
1/4 cup (2 fl oz) chicken stock
1 clove garlic

1 Preheat oven to moderate 180°C (350°F/Gas 4). Using a small, sharp knife, trim meat of excess fat and sinew. Combine sage, tarragon, garlic, onion, oil and plum sauce in food processor. Process for 30 seconds or until mixture is smooth.

2 Place meat in a deep baking dish. Rub meat all over with sage mixture. Add a little water to base of dish to prevent burning. Bake, uncovered, for 1 hour 15 minutes. Remove from oven, place on carving platter. Cover loosely with foil and leave in a warm place for 10 minutes before slicing.

3 Place baking dish on top of stove. Add wine and stock to pan juices, stirring well to incorporate browned bits off the bottom of the pan. Bring to boil, reduce heat, simmer for 5 minutes. Pour over sliced lamb when serving.

LAMB NAVARIN WITH VEGETABLES

✳ *Preparation time:* 20 minutes
Total cooking time: 1 hour 45 minutes
Serves 6

1 kg (2 lb) lamb leg chops
30 g (1 oz) butter
1/4 cup (2 fl oz) olive oil
2 medium onions, chopped
1 clove garlic, crushed
2 parsnips, sliced
2 carrots, sliced
2 sticks celery, sliced
1/4 cup plain (all-purpose) flour
440 g (14 oz) can tomatoes, drained, juice reserved
1/2 cup (4 fl oz) water

1 cup (8 fl oz) chicken stock
2 tablespoons chopped fresh mint
1/2 cup frozen green beans
1 tablespoon chopped fresh parsley
1 teaspoon fresh thyme leaves
ground pepper, to taste
1 tablespoon French mustard
1/2 cup chopped fresh parsley, extra

1 Preheat oven to 150°C (300°F/Gas 2). Trim meat of bones and excess fat, cut into 2 cm (3/4 inch) cubes. Heat butter and oil in a large pan. Cook meat in batches over medium heat until well browned; drain on paper towels.

2 Cook onion until golden, add garlic, parsnip, carrot and celery; cook until all vegetables are lightly browned. Stir through flour, add roughly chopped tomatoes and reserved juice, water, stock, mint, beans, parsley, thyme, pepper and mustard, to taste. Stir until sauce thickens.

3 Add meat, place in casserole dish, cover. Cook 1 1/2 hours. Garnish with extra chopped parsley.

Lancashire Hot Pot A warming stew of lamb, onions and potatoes, topped with a crust of overlapping potato slices. It originally also contained mushrooms and oysters and was cooked in a special earthenware pot.

marinated and grilled and the feast dish *mansaf* is lamb simmered in a spicy yoghurt sauce; *mechoui*, eaten in North Africa and the Middle East, is whole lamb roasted on the spit; in France roasting joints of lamb are basted with buttery stock; in Iran lamb is stewed; spicy-sauced Mongolian lamb is a Chinese favourite; and in the British Isles lamb is the essential ingredient in Irish stew and Lancashire hot pot. In Muslim India lamb is the main meat.

Lamington A small cube of sponge or butter cake dipped in thin chocolate icing and then coated in desiccated coconut. The lamington originated in Australia and is said to be named after Lord Lamington, governor of Queensland from 1895 to 1901.

Langue de Chat A crisp, flat, oblong biscuit (cookie) served with iced desserts, fruit salad, dessert wines and champagne. Its name is French for 'cat's tongue', a reference to its shape.

Lard Rendered pork fat, pure white in colour and virtually odourless, used to make pie-crusts and biscuits or as a frying and roasting medium. It is sold from the refrigerator section of supermarkets.

Larding The process of inserting strips of pork or bacon fat into cuts of lean meat and game to give it additional juiciness and flavour during cooking. The strips, called lardoons, are inserted with a larding needle, a hollow stainless steel skewer.

Lasagne A variety of Italian pasta. It is flat and wide with either straight or wavy edges. Lasagne sheets are boiled in water, drained, then combined with various sauces, topped with cheese and baked. There is a pre-cooked

---

MONGOLIAN LAMB

★

Preparation time: 15 minutes + 1 hour marinating
Total cooking time: 10 minutes
Serves 4

750 g (1½ lb) lamb fillets
3 teaspoons cornflour (cornstarch)
2 cloves garlic, crushed
1 teaspoon grated fresh ginger
1 tablespoon soy sauce
¼ cup (2 fl oz) dry sherry
1 tablespoon sesame oil
2 tablespoons peanut oil
4 medium onions, cut in wedges
1 tablespoon toasted sesame seeds (see note)

1 Trim meat of any fat and sinew. Slice meat across the grain evenly into thin slices. Combine garlic, ginger and sesame oil; add meat, stirring to coat. Store in refrigerator, covered with plastic wrap, 1 hour or overnight, turning occasionally.

2 Heat peanut oil in wok or heavy-based frying pan, swirling gently to coat base and side. Add onion, stir-fry over medium heat for 4 minutes or until soft, remove from wok; keep warm. Reheat wok, cook the meat quickly in small batches over high heat until browned but not cooked through. Remove from wok; drain on paper towels.

3 Combine cornflour, soy sauce and sherry to make a smooth paste. Return meat to wok with cornflour mixture, stir-fry over high heat until meat is cooked and sauce has thickened. Remove from heat, top with onion and sprinkle with toasted sesame seeds.

Note: To toast sesame seeds, place in a dry pan and stir over low heat until golden.

LAMB CUTLETS WITH TOMATO-MINT SAUCE

★

Preparation time: 20 minutes + 1 hour standing
Total cooking time: 15 minutes
Serves 6

12 lamb cutlets, about 75 g (2½ oz) each
1 tablespoon olive oil

Tomato–Mint Sauce
3 medium tomatoes
1 teaspoon cider vinegar
1 spring onion (scallion), finely chopped
2 teaspoons finely chopped fresh mint
2 teaspoons soft brown sugar

1 Trim excess fat and sinew from each cutlet. Scrape bone clean, and trim meat to a neat disc. Heat oil in pan. Cook cutlets over high heat 2 minutes each side to seal, then another minute each side. Serve with Tomato-Mint Sauce.

2 To make Tomato-Mint Sauce: Mark a small cross on the top of each tomato. Place in boiling water for 1–2 minutes, then plunge immediately into cold water. Remove and peel skin down from the cross. Cut tomatoes in half and gently squeeze seeds out. Remove any remaining seeds with a teaspoon. Chop tomatoes finely.

3 Combine tomato, vinegar, sugar, and onion in a pan over medium heat. Bring to boil, reduce heat, simmer 5 minutes. Remove from heat, transfer to a bowl, leave at room temperature for at least 1 hour. Stir in mint just before serving.

OPPOSITE PAGE, ABOVE: LAMB CUTLETS WITH TOMATO-MINT SAUCE; BELOW: MONGOLIAN LAMB. ABOVE: LANCASHIRE HOT POT.

LANCASHIRE HOT POT

✶✶ **Preparation time:** 20 minutes
Total cooking time: 2 hours
Serves 8

8 lamb forequarter chops,
　2.5 cm (1 inch) thick
1/4 cup plain (all-purpose)
　flour
45 g (1 1/2 oz) dripping
　or butter
2 large brown onions, sliced
2 sticks celery, chopped
1 large parsnip, peeled
　and sliced
4 medium old potatoes,
　peeled and very thinly
　sliced
1 3/4 cups (14 fl oz)
　chicken or beef stock
200 g (6 1/2 oz)
　mushrooms, sliced
1/2 teaspoon white pepper
　salt to taste
2 teaspoons dried mixed
　herbs
1 tablespoon
　worcestershire sauce

1 Preheat oven to moderately slow 160°C (325°F/Gas 3). Brush a large 6-cup capacity heatproof casserole dish with melted butter or oil. Trim meat of excess fat and sinew. Place flour in a plastic bag and toss chops in flour to coat thoroughly. Shake off excess and reserve for later use. Heat dripping or butter in frying pan. Add chops and cook until both sides are brown. Remove chops and place in a casserole dish.

2 Add onion, celery and parsnip to pan, cook until slightly softened. Place mixture on top of chops in casserole dish.

3 Sprinkle reserved flour over base of pan and cook, stirring, until dark brown. Gradually pour in stock and stir until mixture comes to the boil. Add mushrooms, pepper, salt, herbs and worcestershire sauce, simmer for 10 minutes. Remove from heat and pour over chops.

4 Place overlapping slices of potato on top to completely cover the meat and vegetables. Cover casserole dish with lid and place in preheated oven. Cook for 1 1/4 hours. Remove lid and continue cooking for another 30 minutes or until potatoes are brown and crisp.

JHAL FARAZI

Heat a little oil in a pan and cook 1 sliced onion for 8 minutes. Add 1/2 teaspoon grated ginger and cook for another minute. In a bowl mix 1/2 teaspoon ground turmeric, 1/2 teaspoon garam masala, 1/4 teaspoon chilli powder and 1/2 teaspoon salt. Add a little cold water and mix to a paste. Add this to the pan and cook, stirring for another minute, being careful not to allow mixture to burn. Add 200 g (6 1/2 oz) sliced leftover roast lamb and toss well. Add a sliced cooked potato and toss gently, moistening with 2–3 tablespoons water. Cover pan and cook over low heat until heated through. Sprinkle with lemon juice and chopped mint just before serving.

---

lasagne which does not need boiling.

Lassi A refreshing yoghurt drink popular in India and the Middle East. It is made by blending plain yoghurt with iced water and traditionally is seasoned to taste with salt and pepper, although for a sweetened version this can be replaced by sugar. Serve in a tall glass with ice cubes.

Lebanese Food The ingredients that predominate in Lebanese cooking are sesame seeds, pistachios, burghul (cracked wheat), filo pastry, chick peas and yoghurt. Outside of the country, the most famous Lebanese dishes are tabouli—a salad made from burghul, parsley, mint and tomatoes; falafel—little balls of crushed chick peas and

hummus, a dip made from pureed chick peas, sometimes with tahini (sesame seed paste) added. These three are often rolled into a round of pitta bread, the result of which is universally known as a falafel sandwich. And that's about as much as many Westerners know about Lebanese food.

L In fact, like the food of many Middle Eastern countries, it is a subtle and elegant cuisine. Kibbeh, one of Lebanon's most famous meat dishes, is made from lamb and there are many varieties of lamb pastries too. The most common vegetables in Lebanese cooking are those of the Mediterranean: eggplant (aubergine), zucchini (courgette) and tomatoes. But okra features as well, as do broad beans (fava beans) and cucumbers. The Lebanese are fond of sweet, fragrant desserts and use orange flower water and rose water and honey, nuts and spices.

Leek A member of the onion family valued for its fleshy, mild-flavoured stem. When preparing leeks, remove the outer layers; cut off roots and base and tough dark green tops; thoroughly wash to remove all dirt and grit. Leeks can be steamed, boiled or braised as a hot vegetable; cooked in soups, pies, tarts and stir-fries; or served cold, as a salad with a mayonnaise or vinaigrette dressing. They are in season in winter.

ROGHAN JOSH

✸✸ *Preparation time:* 25 minutes
Total cooking time: 1 hour 10 minutes
Serves 6

1 tablespoon coriander seeds	1/2 teaspoon ground nutmeg
4 whole cloves	1/2 teaspoon ground cardamom
3/4 cup plain yoghurt	1 cup (8 fl oz) water
1/2–1 1/2 teaspoons chilli flakes	3 teaspoons garam masala
1 kg (2 lb) boneless lamb, cut into 3 cm (1 1/4 inch) cubes	1/4 teaspoon powdered saffron
1/2 teaspoon grated fresh ginger	1/2 cup (4 fl oz) cream
4 tablespoons ghee or unsalted (sweet) butter	

1 In a dry pan, toast the coriander seeds until they are very aromatic. Add the chilli flakes and cook very briefly. Remove from pan and grind both to a fine powder.

2 Season the meat with ginger, and brown in the ghee or butter with the cloves. Sprinkle with the coriander and chilli. Add yoghurt, nutmeg and cardamom to the pan and cook for 8 minutes, stirring occasionally.

3 Add the water, cover pan and simmer for about 50 minutes until meat is very tender. Uncover halfway through cooking to reduce the sauce if a drier curry is preferred. Add the garam masala.

4 Stir saffron into the cream and add to the pan. Cook gently, stirring, for 3–4 minutes. Serve with steamed white rice.

LAMB SHANKS WITH ROASTED GARLIC

✸ *Preparation time:* 20 minutes
Total cooking time: 1 hour 40 minutes
Serves 6

6 large lamb shanks	1 medium sprig rosemary (branches)
2 medium leeks, sliced	1 cup (8 fl oz) dry white wine
freshly ground black pepper, to taste	1 head garlic
1 tablespoon oil	

1 Preheat oven to moderate 180°C (350°F/Gas 4). Season shanks with pepper. Heat oil in a heavy-based pan. Cook shanks quickly in batches over medium-high heat until well browned; drain on paper towels. Place in a heatproof casserole dish.

2 Add leek and cook in pan until tender. Add to casserole with rosemary and wine.

3 Cut whole garlic through the centre horizontally. Brush cut surfaces with a little oil. Place cut side up in casserole, but not covered by liquid. Cover pan and bake for 1 hour. Remove lid and cook for another 15 minutes. Discard rosemary before serving. Serve with steamed vegetables and crusty bread on which to spread the roasted garlic.

LEFT: ROGHAN JOSH; ABOVE: LAMB SHANKS WITH ROASTED GARLIC. OPPOSITE PAGE, BELOW: LADIES' FINGERS; ABOVE: HUMMUS.

LADIES' FINGERS

Preparation time: 25 minutes
Total cooking time: 30–35 minutes
Makes 24

2 tablespoons olive oil
1 onion, finely chopped
⅓ cup pine nuts
500 g (1 lb) minced (ground) lamb
¼ cup raisins, chopped
1 cup grated cheddar cheese
2 tablespoons chopped fresh coriander
1 teaspoon ground pepper

Yoghurt Sauce
¼ small cucumber
¾ cup plain yoghurt
1 tablespoon chopped fresh coriander
2 tablespoons chopped fresh mint
375 g (12 oz) filo pastry
90 g (3 oz) butter, melted

1 Preheat oven to 190°C (375°F/Gas 5). Line a 32 x 28 cm (13 x 11 inch) oven tray with baking paper. Heat oil in heavy-based pan. Cook onion and pine nuts over medium heat 5 minutes until golden brown. Add lamb and cook over medium heat 5–10 minutes until well browned and almost all liquid has evaporated. Use a fork to break up any large lumps of lamb as it cooks.

2 Remove from heat, cool slightly. Add raisins, cheese, coriander, pepper and mint; mix.

3 Place 10 sheets of pastry on work surface. Using a sharp knife or scissors, cut pastry lengthways into 4 strips. Cover pastry strips with a dry tea-towel. Brush two strips with melted butter, place one on top of the other. Place a tablespoon of lamb mixture at one end of top sheet. Fold in ends and roll into a finger shape. Repeat process with remaining filo pastry and filling.

4 Place pastries on prepared tray and brush with remaining butter. Bake for 15–20 minutes or until golden brown. Serve warm or cold with Yoghurt Sauce if desired.

5 To make Yoghurt Sauce: Peel skin from cucumber. Scoop out the seeds. Chop the flesh and place in a bowl. Add yoghurt and coriander and mix to combine.

HUMMUS

Preparation time: 10 minutes +
4 hours soaking
Total cooking time: 1 hour
Serves 8–10

1 cup chick peas (garbanzo beans)
3 cups (24 fl oz) water
¼ cup (2 fl oz) lemon juice
¼ cup (2 fl oz) olive oil
2 cloves garlic, roughly chopped
2 tablespoons water, extra
½ teaspoon salt
ground sweet paprika, to garnish

1 Soak chick peas in water for 4 hours or overnight. Drain chick peas, place in a pan, add water and bring to the boil. Simmer, uncovered, for 1 hour, drain.

2 Place chick peas, lemon juice, olive oil, chopped garlic, water and salt into a food processor, process for 30 seconds or until the mixture is smooth. Sprinkle with paprika and serve as a dip with pitta bread.

The leek was grown in ancient Egypt, and 3500 years ago was mentioned in a Chinese food guide. The emperor Nero is said to have supped daily on leek soup, believing it would strengthen his voice for delivering orations. In Celtic Britain the vegetable patch was called a *leactun*, 'leek enclosure'; it has a particular association with Wales and is that country's national emblem. On St David's Day, pieces of leek are worn in the buttonhole to commemorate the famous seventh century victory over the Saxons by the Welsh warriors of King Cadwallader.

Legumes A group of plants which bear their seeds in pods, especially beans, peas and lentils. Legumes are a good source of protein in meatless diets. They have been used since the earliest times, from the soy bean of Asia to the lentils of ancient Egypt and the beans of the Americas.

Leicester A semi-hard cow's milk cheese with a moist, crumbly texture and mellow flavour; its deep orange colour comes from annatto dye. A good snack and

FALAFEL WITH TOMATO RELISH

★★ **Preparation time:** 25 minutes +
30 minutes standing + 4 hours soaking
Total cooking time: 20–25 minutes

Serves 6

Falafel

2 cups chick peas
(garbanzo beans)
3 cups (24 fl oz) water
1 small onion, finely
chopped
2 cloves garlic, crushed
2 tablespoons chopped
fresh parsley
1 tablespoon chopped
fresh coriander
2 teaspoons ground cumin
1 tablespoon water, extra
1/2 teaspoon baking powder
oil for deep-frying

Tomato Relish

2 medium tomatoes, peeled
and finely chopped
1/4 small cucumber, finely
chopped
1/2 green pepper (capsicum),
finely chopped
2 tablespoons chopped
fresh parsley
2 teaspoons chilli sauce
1 teaspoon sugar
1/2 teaspoon ground black
pepper
grated rind and juice of
1 lemon

1 To make Falafel: Soak chick peas in water
4 hours or overnight. Drain, place chick peas in
food processor. Process until finely ground.
2 Add onion, garlic, parsley, coriander, cumin,
extra water and baking powder, process for
10 seconds or until mixture resembles a rough
paste. Leave to stand for 30 minutes.
3 To make Tomato Relish: Place all
ingredients in a bowl, mix to combine; set aside.
4 Shape heaped tablespoons of Falafel mixture
into balls. Squeeze out excess liquid using your

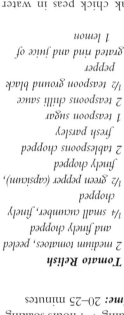

hands. Heat oil in a deep heavy-based pan. Lower
Falafel balls on a large spoon into moderately hot
oil. Cook in batches of five at a time, for about
3–4 minutes each batch. When balls are well
browned, carefully remove from the oil with a
large slotted spoon. Drain Falafel on paper towels.
Serve hot or cold on a bed of Tomato Relish or
in pitta bread with relish and hummus.

BABA GHANNOUJ

★ **Preparation time:** 20 minutes
Total cooking time: 20 minutes
Serves 6–8

2 small eggplants
(aubergines), halved
lengthways
salt, extra, to taste
1 tablespoon olive oil
1/4 cup tahini
2 cloves garlic, crushed
1 tablespoon finely
chopped fresh mint
2 tablespoons lemon juice

1 Preheat oven to 190°C (375°F/Gas 5). Sprinkle
eggplant flesh with salt. Stand for 10–15 minutes
then rinse off salt and pat dry with paper towels.
2 Place eggplant, flesh-side-up, on a baking tray.
Bake for 20 minutes or until flesh is soft. Peel off
the skin and discard.
3 Place eggplant flesh, garlic, lemon juice, tahini
and olive oil in a food processor. Process
for 30 seconds or until smooth. Season to taste
with salt. Garnish with fresh mint and serve with
pitta bread wedges.

LMowbray, in
Leicestershire, England.

Lemon An oval,
yellow-skinned citrus
fruit with pale yellow,
tart-tasting flesh.
Although not usually
eaten on its own,
it is the most
versatile and widely used
of all fruits as its acid
juice and fragrant rind
are used to flavour a
wide range of sweet and
savoury dishes, and in
drinks, marinades, sauces
and icings. Slices and
wedges of lemon are a
common garnish. Its
juice stops cut fruit from
turning brown when
exposed to the air. The
lemon is a good source
of vitamin C. Fresh
lemons are available
throughout the year;
lemon juice can be
bought frozen or as a
concentrate.
The lemon
probably originated in
northern India, from
where it spread to
China and to the
Middle East.

Lemon Balm A
member of the mint
family with crinkle-

sandwich cheese, it goes
well with fruits and salad
vegetables and is an
excellent cooking
cheese. It originated near
the village of Melton

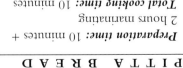

TABOULI

Preparation time: 20 minutes
Total cooking time: nil
Serves 6-8

1 cup medium burghul (cracked wheat)
2 cups (16 fl oz) water
2 medium tomatoes, finely chopped
4 spring onions (scallions), finely chopped
3/4 cup chopped flat-leaf parsley
3/4 cup chopped fresh mint
2 tablespoons lemon juice
1 tablespoon olive oil
1 teaspoon ground pepper

1 Soak the cracked wheat in water for 10 minutes, drain and squeeze remaining water from wheat in a sieve, pressing down hard with the back of a spoon.
2 Place wheat, parsley, mint, spring onions, tomato, lemon juice, oil and pepper in a bowl and mix to combine. Serve as a first course with small crisp lettuce leaves to scoop up the Tabouli or as a side salad to a main meal.
Note: Tabouli can be stored for up to 2 days, covered in plastic wrap, in the refrigerator but is best eaten soon after making.

OPPOSITE PAGE, ABOVE: FALAFEL WITH TOMATO RELISH; BELOW: BABA GHANNOUJ. THIS PAGE, ABOVE: TABOULI; BELOW: SPICY LAMB IN PITTA

SPICY LAMB IN PITTA BREAD

Preparation time: 10 minutes + 2 hours marinating
Total cooking time: 10 minutes
Serves 6

2 lamb loins
Marinade
2 teaspoons olive oil
2 cloves garlic, crushed
2 teaspoons onion powder
1 teaspoon grated fresh ginger
1 teaspoon ground pepper
1 tablespoon finely chopped fresh coriander
1/2 cup (4 fl oz) red wine

4 large pitta breads
2 medium tomatoes, sliced
hummus, to serve
tabouli, to serve

1 **To make Marinade:** Combine all of the ingredients in a medium bowl.
2 Trim lamb of excess fat or sinew. Add lamb to marinade, toss to coat well; refrigerate, covered with plastic wrap, several hours or overnight. Drain; reserve marinade.
3 Heat oil in medium pan; add lamb. Cook over medium-high heat for 5 minutes each side. Add the reserved marinade during the last 3 minutes and reduce to 2 tablespoons over high heat. Slice the lamb thinly.

4 Place lamb on warmed, opened-out pitta bread. Place tomato slices over top followed by hummus and tabouli. Roll bread to encase filling; serve.

edged, heart-shaped, lemon-scented leaves. The leaves can be added to almost any dish using lemon juice. They are also used to make a soothing tea. The sweet-scented flowers are the basis of the cordial eau des Carmes. Lemon balm is easy to grow and is best used fresh.

Lemon Butter Also known as lemon curd and lemon cheese, a sweet spread made from lemon juice, lemon rind, egg, butter and sugar. It is also used as filling for tarts, cakes and biscuits (cookies).

Lemon grass A tall, tufted, sharp-edged grass with a strong citrus flavour, common in tropical South-East Asia. The whitish, slightly bulbous base of the stem is used especially in the cooking of Thailand and Vietnam; it flavours curries, soups, stews and casseroles, particularly those made with chicken and seafood. To prepare lemon grass for adding to a dish either pound the stem to bruise the flesh and release the fragrant juices, or make cuts down the stem, leaving the bottom intact; remove the stalk before serving. Lemon grass is available fresh from greengrocers and Asian food stores; dried ground and shredded stalks are

also available (ground stalks can be added directly to the dish, shredded stalks must first be soaked). Lemon grass is very easy to grow. Grated lemon rind and a pinch of finely shredded ginger can be substituted for fresh lemon grass.

Lentil The tiny, flat disc-shaped seed of an annual plant of the legume (pod-bearing) family. Lentils are a good source of vegetable protein and have been used as a food since prehistoric times. The brown lentil (sometimes called the continental lentil) has a bland, nutty flavour when cooked; it is often added to stews and casseroles, and can be used in salads. Red lentils (which can be yellow or orange and are also known as split lentils) are much used in Asian cooking; they have a subtle spicy flavour and are used for the Indian dish dhal. Both brown and red lentils are used to make vegetarian loaves and patties. Lentils are sold in dried form or pre-cooked in cans; they are also processed into flour. In ancient Egypt, lentils were grown, eaten and exported in large quantities, mainly to Greece and Rome, where they provided protein in the diets of the poor.

LEEKS

LEEK TART

★★ **Preparation time:** 30 minutes + 30 minutes refrigeration
Total cooking time: 40–50 minutes
Makes one 23 cm (9 inch) flan

Pastry
2½ cups plain (all-purpose) flour
150 g (4¾ oz) butter, chopped
2 tablespoons lemon juice
1 tablespoon water

1 tablespoon white wine vinegar
¼ cup plain (all-purpose) flour
1 cup (8 fl oz) milk
2 eggs, lightly beaten
1 cup grated cheddar cheese
1 teaspoon ground black pepper
beaten egg, for glaze
fresh herbs, to garnish

Filling
30 g (1 oz) butter
2 rashers bacon, finely chopped
4 leeks, finely sliced

1 Preheat oven to 210°C (415°F/Gas 6–7). Brush a shallow 23 cm (9 inch) round fluted flan tin with melted butter or oil.
2 **To make Pastry:** Place flour and chopped butter in a food processor. Process for 30 seconds or until mixture has a fine crumbly texture. Add the lemon juice and almost all the water, process for 30 seconds or until mixture is smooth, adding remaining water if necessary. Refrigerate the dough, covered with plastic wrap, for about 30 minutes.

3 **To make Filling:** Heat butter in a medium pan, add bacon, cook until crisp. Add leek, cook for 5 minutes or until leek is soft. Stir through vinegar and flour. Remove from heat. Add milk gradually, stir until smooth. Return to heat, stir until sauce boils and thickens. Allow filling to cool slightly. Stir in eggs, cheese and pepper.
4 Roll two-thirds of the pastry out to line flan tin. Spoon filling over pastry base. Roll out remaining pastry to cover top of the pie. Trim and decorate edges, glaze with beaten egg. Cut three deep slits in pastry to allow steam to escape. Bake for 30–40 minutes or until crust is golden brown and crisp. To serve, cut Leek Tart into wedges and garnish with fresh herbs.

LEEKS IN HERB SAUCE

Cut off and discard green tops of 12 baby leeks. Wash leeks thoroughly and simmer them in salted water for about 10 minutes or until they are tender. Drain and place on a serving dish. Make a sauce by mixing together 5 tablespoons olive oil, 1 tablespoon white wine vinegar, l finely chopped large spring onion (scallion), 2 teaspoons finely chopped capers, 1 teaspoon chopped parsley, ½ teaspoon chopped fresh tarragon, ½ teaspoon chopped fresh chervil and 125 ml (4 fl oz) of cream. Pour sauce over the leeks and put them aside until they cool. Serve at room temperature.

ABOVE: LEEK TART.

OPPOSITE PAGE: FROZEN LEMON TART

LEMONS

FROZEN LEMON TART

✷✷ **Preparation time:** 40 minutes +
30 minutes refrigeration +
overnight refrigeration
Total cooking time: 25 minutes
Serves 6

1 cup plain (all-purpose) flour	½ cup (4 fl oz) lemon juice
75 g (2½ oz) butter	2 tablespoons iced water
1 tablespoon finely grated lemon rind	1½ cups sugar
2 medium lemons	¼ cup cornflour (cornstarch)
30 g (1 oz) butter, extra	1¼ cups (10 fl oz) water
4 egg yolks, lightly beaten	½ cup sugar, extra
	½ cup (4 fl oz) water, extra

1 Sift the flour into a large mixing bowl; add chopped butter. Using fingertips, rub butter into flour for 2 minutes or until mixture is a fine crumbly texture. Add almost all the water and mix to a firm dough, adding more liquid if necessary. Turn onto a lightly floured surface, knead 1 minute or until smooth. Roll pastry until it is large enough to cover base and sides of a 23 cm (9 inch) flan tin. Line tin with pastry, trim edge. Cover with plastic wrap and refrigerate for 30 minutes. Preheat oven to moderate 180°C (350°F/Gas 4). Cut a sheet of greaseproof paper large enough to cover pastry-lined tin. Spread a layer of dried beans or rice evenly over paper.

Bake for 10 minutes, remove from oven. Discard paper and beans. Return pastry to oven for another 5 minutes or until lightly golden. Set aside to cool.

2 Combine sugar, cornflour and water in a medium pan and stir until smooth. Add lemon juice and rind and cook, stirring, over medium heat until mixture boils. Reduce heat slightly, add egg yolks, whisking to combine, and cook for 1 minute. Remove from heat and stir in butter. Set aside to cool.

3 Slice lemons very finely, being careful to retain round shape. Combine sugar and water in a small heavy-based pan. Stir over medium heat without boiling until sugar has completely dissolved. Bring to the boil, reduce heat slightly, add lemon slices and boil for 1 minute without stirring. Remove lemon slices from syrup and drain thoroughly. Spread cold lemon mixture into cold pastry shell and cover top with overlapping lemon slices. Freeze overnight. Stand for 5 minutes at room temperature before serving. Cut into wedges and serve with whipped cream.

ABOUT LEMONS

■ Lemons do not ripen after picking, so choose fruit with deep yellow skins.

■ There is no need to cut a whole lemon if all you require is a tablespoon of juice. Simply pierce the skin with a sharp metal skewer and squeeze out the required amount. (Microwave on 50% power for 20 seconds first, if possible.) An average lemon yields about 3 tablespoons of juice.

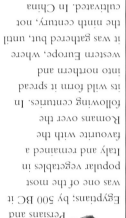

Lettuce A plant valued for its large, succulent leaves which are mainly used in salads, although they are sometimes braised or steamed and served as a hot vegetable. Today's lettuces descend from loose-leafed plants native to the Middle East and they have been cultivated there since ancient times. Lettuce was eaten by the Greeks, Persians and Egyptians; by 500 BC it was one of the most popular vegetables in Italy and remained a favourite with the Romans over the following centuries. In its wild form it spread into northern and western Europe, where it was gathered but, until the ninth century, not cultivated. In China lettuce has been cultivated since the fifth century; Christopher Columbus introduced it into the Americas. There are three main types of lettuce: butterhead (including the mignonette and butter) with soft-textured, loosely packed leaves; crisphead (including the iceberg

and bibb) with crisp, tightly packed leaves; and cos (romaine), with long dark green leaves. Lettuce, either a single variety or a mixture, can be made into a green salad or can be used as the basis of a number of other salad dishes.

Leyden A semi-hard cow's milk cheese with a tangy taste and a dark-yellow, dryish texture. It is usually spiced with caraway seeds; varieties flavoured with cumin and cloves or a mixture of the three spices are also available. Leyden is made in cylinder shapes, is coloured with annatto dye, and has a dark yellow rind covered in red wax stamped with two crossed keys, the symbol of the Dutch city of Leyden.

Lima Bean A bean with pale green or white slightly kidney-shaped seeds. They are mainly used in

their dried form (added to soups and casseroles or served in salads), although they can also be cooked fresh as a vegetable. The lima bean does not come from Lima (in Peru) but from Guatemala. It is available fresh, dried, canned and frozen.

Limburger A semi-soft cow's milk cheese with a

CHINESE LEMON CHICKEN

★ **Preparation time:** 15 minutes
Total cooking time: 1 hour 10 minutes
Serves 4

1.6 kg (3¼ lb) chicken
1 tablespoon soy sauce
1 tablespoon dry sherry
1 tablespoon lemon juice
2 teaspoons soft brown sugar

½ cup caster (superfine) sugar
2 teaspoons dry sherry
1 teaspoon soy sauce
1 tablespoon cornflour (cornstarch)
½ cup (4 fl oz) water
salt and white pepper, to taste

Lemon Sauce
2 spring onions (scallions)
½ cup (4 fl oz) lemon juice

1 Preheat oven to moderate 180°C (350°F/Gas 4). Remove giblets and any large deposits of fat from the chicken. Wipe chicken, pat dry with paper towels. Tie wings and drumsticks securely in place. Place chicken on a rack in a baking dish. Brush with combined soy sauce, sherry, juice and sugar.
2 Bake chicken 1 hour or until juices run clear when flesh is pierced with a skewer. Baste occasionally with remaining soy mixture. Remove from oven, leave covered with foil 10 minutes. Remove string before serving hot with Lemon Sauce.
3 To make Lemon Sauce: Cut onions into long thin strips; place in iced water until curly. Combine juice, sugar, sherry and sauce in pan. Blend cornflour with water in bowl until smooth. Add to pan. Stir over medium heat 4 minutes or until sauce boils and thickens slightly. Season to taste; stir in spring onions.

LEMONADE

★ **Preparation time:** 15 minutes
Total cooking time: 15 minutes
Serves 6

6 lemons
1½ cups sugar
1.5 litres (6 cups) water

ice cubes, for serving
lemon slices, for serving

1 Wash and dry lemons. Using a potato peeler remove the peel very thinly from three of the lemons. Place peel in a medium pan, add sugar and half of the water. Cover and simmer gently for 15 minutes. Allow to cool.
2 Squeeze juice from all of the lemons and strain into a large jug. Strain syrup over lemon juice and add remaining water stirring to combine. Cover and chill.
3 Serve lemonade in glasses, over ice cubes. Float lemon slices on top.

LEMON BUTTER

★ **Preparation time:** 10 minutes
Total cooking time: 15 minutes
Makes about 500 ml (2 cups)

3 eggs, beaten
1 cup sugar
1 tablespoon grated lemon rind

½ cup (4 fl oz) lemon juice
60 g (2 oz) butter, chopped

1 Combine all ingredients in a heatproof bowl. Whisk constantly over simmering water until mixture thickens and coats the back of a metal spoon.
2 Remove from heat and pour into warm, sterilised jars. When cool, label and date. Store in the refrigerator until required.

SEMOLINA CAKE WITH LEMON SYRUP

✴ *Preparation time:* 30 minutes
Total cooking time: 1 hour
Serves 6–8

250 g (8 oz) unsalted (sweet) butter
3/4 cup desiccated coconut
1 1/4 cups self-raising flour
1 cup caster (superfine) sugar
3 eggs, lightly beaten
1 teaspoon vanilla essence
1 cup fine ground semolina

Lemon Syrup
3/4 cup sugar
1 cup (8 fl oz) water
1 lemon, thinly sliced

1 Preheat oven to moderate 180°C (350°F/Gas 4). Brush a deep 23 cm (9 inch) springform tin with melted butter or oil. Line base and sides with paper; grease paper. Using electric beaters, beat butter and sugar in small mixing bowl 10 minutes. Add eggs gradually, beating thoroughly after each addition. Add essence and semolina; beat 5 minutes.

2 Transfer mixture to large mixing bowl; add coconut. Using a metal spoon, fold in sifted flour. Stir until just combined and mixture is smooth.

3 Spoon mixture evenly into tin; smooth surface. Bake 1 hour or until a skewer comes out clean when inserted in centre of cake. Pour cold syrup over hot cake in pan. When cold, remove paper. Serve cake with the lemon slices and cream.

4 **To make Lemon Syrup:** In a pan, stir sugar and water constantly over low heat until sugar dissolves; add lemon. Bring to boil, reduce heat, simmer uncovered, without stirring 15 minutes.

CHOCOLATE LEMON SWIRLS

✴ *Preparation time:* 10 minutes
Total cooking time: 12 minutes
Makes 60

125 g (4 oz) unsalted (sweet) butter
2/3 cup icing (confectioners) sugar
1 egg, lightly beaten
2 teaspoons grated lemon rind
1 1/4 cups plain (all-purpose) flour
1/4 cup cocoa powder
2 tablespoons finely chopped mixed peel

1 Preheat oven to moderate 180°C (350°F/Gas 4). Line a 32 x 28 cm (13 x 11 inch) oven tray with baking paper. Using electric beaters, beat butter and sugar until light and creamy. Add egg and rind, beat until well combined.

2 Add sifted flour and cocoa. Using a metal spoon, stir until ingredients are just combined and mixture is almost smooth.

3 Spoon mixture into a piping bag fitted with a fluted 1 cm (1/2 inch) wide piping nozzle; pipe swirls about 3 cm (1 1/4 inch) in diameter onto prepared tray. Top each swirl with mixed peel. Bake for 12 minutes; cool on tray.

Note: Chocolate Lemon Swirls may be stored in an airtight container for up to two days.

OPPOSITE PAGE, BELOW; ABOVE: LEMON BUTTER; ABOVE: CHOCOLATE LEMON SWIRLS
CHINESE LEMON CHICKEN. LEFT: SEMOLINA CAKE;

powerful aroma, distinctive, tangy taste, and a yellow, creamy textured interior covered by a thin, red-brown rind. It should be served at room temperature on the cheeseboard, accompanied by dark bread and strong-flavoured vegetables such as onion and radish.

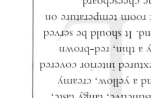

Lime A green-skinned citrus fruit about the size of a small lemon with tart greenish-yellow pulp. Its juice and grated zest adds a piquant flavour to both sweet dishes (ice-creams, sorbets, mousses, soufflés and pie fillings) and savoury dishes (curries and stews, especially chicken and fish), it is cooked as marmalade and its juice is used in cordial and other drinks. The lime is native to the tropics and is much used in the cooking of those regions; the Spanish introduced it to the Caribbean in the sixteenth century. In South America and the Pacific Islands lime juice is used to 'cook' raw fish in the dish ceviche. Its sharpness in key lime pie (named for the Florida keys) gives an

LEMON MERINGUE PIE

★★

Preparation time: 40 minutes + 1 hour standing
Total cooking time: 35 minutes
Serves 6

Pastry
1½ cups plain (all-purpose) flour
1 tablespoon caster (superfine) sugar
125 g (4 oz) butter or margarine, chopped
1 egg yolk
1 tablespoon cold water

Filling and Meringue
½ cup sugar
⅓ cup cornflour (cornstarch)
1 cup (8 fl oz) water
grated rind of 2 lemons
½ cup (4 fl oz) lemon juice
3 eggs, separated
1 tablespoon butter
½ cup caster (superfine) sugar, extra

1 To make Pastry: Combine flour and caster sugar. Rub in butter until crumbly. Beat together egg yolk and cold water, add to flour mixture and mix to a firm dough. Refrigerate, covered with plastic wrap, for 1 hour. Preheat oven to 220°C (425°F/Gas 7). On lightly floured surface, roll out dough to line a 23 cm (9 inch) flan tin. Trim, decorate rim as desired. Pierce pastry well with a fork. Bake blind (see Note) for 15 minutes, or until cooked through and golden brown. Cool.

2 To make Filling: Combine ½ cup sugar with cornflour in a pan. Stir in water, lemon rind and juice. Cook, stirring constantly, over moderately low heat until thickened and bubbly. Reduce heat and simmer for 2–3 minutes. Remove from heat.

3 Beat egg yolks in small bowl. Stir in a little of the hot filling, then return all to pan. Cook, stirring, for another 2–3 minutes. Stir in butter, then pour into pastry case.

4 To make Meringue: Beat egg whites until stiff. Gradually add extra caster sugar, beating constantly until meringue forms stiff, glossy peaks. Swirl meringue to completely cover the filling.

5 Bake at 220°C (425°F/Gas 7) for about 10 minutes or until topping is golden brown. Cool pie in tin on a wire rack. Serve cold.

Note: To bake a flan 'blind', line pierced pastry with baking paper, greaseproof paper or foil. Fill with dry beans, rice or ceramic baking beads to weigh down pastry. Bake pastry until firm, then remove weights and paper. Return flan to oven and continue baking until pastry is evenly browned.

ABOVE: LEMON MERINGUE PIE. OPPOSITE PAGE, BELOW: WARM LENTIL AND RICE SALAD; ABOVE: SPICY CREAMED LENTILS

---

agreeable bite to the sweet creamy filling. Pickled lime is served with meat and fish dishes; the peel can be crystallised (candied) for a garnish. Fresh limes are in season in spring and autumn.

Linzer Torte A rich jam tart consisting of a cinnamon and nut-flavoured shortbread base filled with raspberry jam and covered with a lattice of pastry strips. It is served in thin wedges. The linzer torte takes its name from the Austrian town of Linz.

Liqueur An alcoholic syrup distilled from wine or brandy and flavoured with fruit, herbs or spices. Liqueurs are available in a wide variety of flavours and alcoholic content. Crème de cacao is made from the cocoa bean. Kümmel is flavoured with caraway seed and ouzo with aniseed. Cointreau gets its strong orange tang from orange peel, while many other fruit liqueurs are made by macerating the fruit with spirit and adding sugar. Some liqueurs are flavoured

LENTILS

WARM LENTIL AND RICE SALAD

★ ★ **Preparation time:** 15 minutes
Total cooking time: 50 minutes
Serves 6

1 cup brown lentils
1 cup Basmati rice
4 large red onions, finely
  sliced
2 teaspoons ground cumin
2 teaspoons ground
  coriander
3 spring onions
  (scallions), chopped
4 cloves garlic, crushed
1 cup (8 fl oz) olive oil
45 g (1½ oz) butter
2 teaspoons ground
  cinnamon
2 teaspoons ground sweet
  paprika
ground pepper

1 Cook lentils and rice in separate pans of water until grains are just tender; drain.
2 Cook the onion and garlic in oil and butter for 30 minutes, on low heat until very soft.
3 Stir in cinnamon, paprika, cumin and coriander and cook for another few minutes.
4 Combine onion and spice mixture with well-drained rice and lentils. Stir in chopped spring onions until combined and add ground pepper, to taste. Serve warm.

Note: Do not use red lentils, which become mushy very quickly and do not retain their shape. Rinse brown lentils thoroughly before cooking.

SPICY CREAMED LENTILS

★ **Preparation time:** 5 minutes
Total cooking time: 45 minutes
Serves 4

1 cup red lentils
½ teaspoon turmeric
2 tablespoons ghee or oil
1 large onion, finely
  sliced
2 teaspoons finely
  chopped garlic
1 teaspoon finely chopped
  ginger
2½ cups (20 fl oz) water
½ teaspoon salt
1 teaspoon garam masala
fresh coriander sprigs, for
  garnish

1 Wash lentils and drain thoroughly. Heat ghee in a pan. Add the onion, garlic and ginger and cook until soft and golden. Add turmeric and drained lentils, cook 1–2 minutes.
2 Add water and bring to the boil, reduce heat to a simmer. Add the salt and cook lentil mixture, uncovered, for 15 minutes.
3 Add the garam masala and cook for another 15 minutes until lentils are soft and most of the liquid has evaporated. Garnish with sprigs of fresh coriander and serve with rice or bread.

ABOUT LENTILS

■ Red lentils are sold split and require no soaking. They will soften and become mushy after 20 minutes or so, and are used in soups, purees and casseroles.
■ Green and brown lentils (sometimes known as continental lentils) take longer to cook than red lentils—up to 1½ hours depending on their age—and can be soaked in cold water for 2 hours before using to shorten the cooking time.

---

with herbs or spices. Liqueurs are used to flavour a range of sweet dishes and savoury dishes; they are also served in special small glasses to be sipped with coffee after a meal.

Liver Classed as offal, the liver of lamb, sheep, calf, ox (beef), pig, poultry and game are eaten. Liver is the organ that purifies the blood of an animal. It is a red-brown meat with a distinctive flavour. To prepare liver for cooking, first wash and pat dry; remove the thin outer skin and cut away any fat, gristle and veining. Slice thinly and cook uniformly and until the pink colour disappears (care should be taken not to overcook as the meat toughens easily). Liver can be fried, grilled (broiled), braised or casseroled. Calf liver or lamb's liver (sometimes called lamb's fry) sautéed with bacon is a popular breakfast. Goose and chicken liver are used to make pâté.

Liverwurst A soft sausage containing a smooth mixture of liver, ground pork, onion and seasonings. Liverwurst is used as a spread on bread or savoury biscuits (crackers) and can also be added to stuffings. It has a long

Lobster A large saltwater crustacean related to the crayfish and crab. The shell of the living lobster is bluish green to pinkish-brown, depending on the species; the shell of the cooked lobster is bright red. The lobster has a pair of huge pincers or claws (actually modified legs) and uses its tail to move through the water in quick, backward movements. Lobster can be boiled or grilled (broiled). The cooked meat is firm-textured, white, sweet and moist; it is usually served in the shell with various sauces. The coral—coloured roe (sometimes called coral) present in female lobsters is considered a delicacy and should either be served with the meat or added to the sauce. Most of the meat is in the claws and the tail; use a nutcracker to break open the claws. Live lobsters are available throughout the year (keep live lobsters in a damp hessian bag until

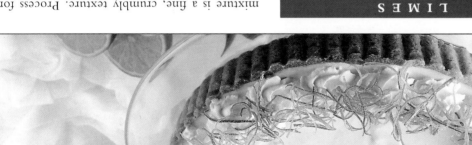

history in many regions of Europe and was often used to garnish roast meats on festive occasions.

LIMES

LEMON-LIME PIE

★★

Preparation time: 1 hour + overnight standing
Total cooking time: 1 hour
Makes one 23 cm (9 inch) round flan

1/4 cup rice flour
1/2 cup plain (all-purpose) flour
2 tablespoons caster (superfine) sugar
125 g (4 oz) chilled unsalted (sweet) butter, chopped
1/2 cup ground almonds
1/4 cup desiccated coconut
2 teaspoons caster (superfine) sugar
2 tablespoons icing (confectioners') sugar

Filling
2 tablespoons custard powder
2 tablespoons caster (superfine) sugar
1/4 cup (2 fl oz) lemon juice
1/4 cup (2 fl oz) lime juice
1/2 cup (4 fl oz) sour cream
1 cup (8 fl oz) cream, whipped

Candied Rind
1 cup caster (superfine) sugar
1/4 cup (2 fl oz) water
rind of 3 lemons
rind of 3 limes

1 Preheat oven to moderate 180°C (350°F/Gas 4). Brush the inside of a shallow, 23 cm (9 inch) round fluted flan tin with melted butter. Coat base and sides with flour; shake off excess. Place flours, sugars, coconut, almonds and butter in food processor. Process for 20 seconds or until mixture is a fine, crumbly texture. Process for another 10–15 seconds. Turn pastry onto lightly floured surface, knead for 5 minutes or until smooth. Refrigerate, covered, for 15 minutes.

2 Roll pastry between 2 sheets of plastic wrap until large enough to cover base and sides of prepared tin. Trim pastry with a flat-bladed knife. Cover pastry with a sheet of greaseproof paper. Spread a layer of dried beans or rice evenly over paper. Bake for 15 minutes. Remove from oven; discard paper and beans or rice. Return to oven for another 10–15 minutes or until very lightly golden. Stand pastry in tin on a wire rack to cool.

3 To make Filling: Combine custard powder, sugar, juices and sour cream in medium, heavy-based pan. Cook over low heat, stirring constantly, until mixture boils and thickens; remove from heat. Cool slightly. Transfer mixture to a bowl. Using a metal spoon fold in cream. Stir until mixture is smooth. Pour mixture into pastry shell; smooth surface. Refrigerate overnight.

4 To make Candied Rind: Combine sugar and water in heavy-based pan. Stir over low heat without boiling until sugar has dissolved. Add rind, bring to boil, reduce heat, simmer for 10 minutes. Remove from heat, cool. Drain rind and reserve syrup. Decorate outer edge with whipped cream, place candied rind over cream. Serve with syrup.

ABOVE: LEMON-LIME PIE.
OPPOSITE PAGE: CEVICHE

254

KEY LIME PIE

✸✸ **Preparation time:** 40 minutes +
20 minutes standing
Total cooking time: 30–35 minutes
Serves 6–8

1¹⁄₃ cups plain (all-purpose) flour	4 eggs, separated
1 teaspoon icing (confectioners) sugar	¹⁄₂ cup condensed milk
100 g (3¹⁄₂ oz) butter, chopped	finely grated rind of 4 limes
1 egg yolk	¹⁄₃ cup (2¹⁄₂ fl oz) lime juice
1–2 tablespoons iced water	

Filling

1 Place flour, sugar and butter in food processor. Process 30 seconds or until mixture is fine and crumbly. Add egg yolk and almost all the water and process 20 seconds or until the water comes together when squeezed. Add more water if necessary. Turn onto lightly floured surface and knead gently to form a smooth dough. Cover with plastic wrap and refrigerate for 20 minutes.

2 Preheat oven to moderate 180°C (350°F/Gas 4). Brush a 23 cm (9 inch) fluted round flan tin or dish with melted butter or oil. Roll pastry between two sheets of baking paper large enough to cover the base and sides of prepared tin. Ease pastry into tin; trim edges with rolling pin or sharp knife. Cut a sheet of greaseproof paper to cover pastry-lined tin. Line tin with paper and spread a layer of dried beans or rice evenly over paper. Bake for 10 minutes, remove from oven and discard paper and beans or rice. Bake for another 7 minutes or until lightly golden; cool.

3 To make Filling: Using electric beaters, beat egg yolks in large bowl until thick and creamy. Gradually add condensed milk in a thin stream. Continue beating until mixture is thick and pale. Add rind; mix well. Gradually beat in juice until combined. Beat egg whites in separate bowl until soft peaks form. Using a metal spoon, fold egg whites into yolk mixture. Stir until smooth. Spoon mixture into prepared pastry base. Bake 15–20 minutes or until filling is set and top is lightly golden. Serve cool or chilled, with whipped cream. Dust pie with sifted icing (confectioners) sugar to serve, if preferred.

CEVICHE

✸ **Preparation time:** 20 minutes +
2 hours marinating
Total cooking time: nil
Serves 4

750 g (1¹⁄₂ lb) white fish fillets	3 tomatoes, sliced
1 teaspoon freshly ground pepper	1 large green pepper (capsicum), chopped
3 onions, thinly sliced	³⁄₄ cup (6 fl oz) lime juice
3 cloves garlic, crushed	1 teaspoon salt
1 small red chilli, finely chopped	4 hard-boiled eggs, quartered

Garnish

1 Wash and skin fillets. Cut fillets into thin strips. Place in a bowl. Add onion, garlic and chilli.

2 Place juice, salt and pepper in a small bowl; whisk to combine. Pour over fish. Marinate for 2 hours, covered, in refrigerator. The fish is ready when the flesh turns white.

3 Serve the fish accompanied by sliced tomato, chopped pepper and quartered hard-boiled eggs.

ABOUT LIMES

■ Buy limes with dark green skins—yellowish limes are over-mature and without tang. Limes will perish quickly; store at room temperature for a week, then keep in the refrigerator.

■ Use limes in sweet or savoury dishes as a sweeter, milder substitute for lemons. Lime juice may be used as a marinade for meat and fish. Grated lime peel is delicious in sherbets, sorbets and ice-cream.

■ Make curls, knots or spirals from the rind to use as a decoration for summer drinks.

---

ready to use) or frozen whole or as tails. Pre-cooked whole lobsters should have bright eyes, a curled tail that springs back when raised and all limbs intact; pre-cooked tails are also available. Cooked meat is available frozen or in cans.

Loganberry A large, soft, pink to red berry fruit. The loganberry is a hybrid between the blackberry (from which it takes its shape) and raspberry (from which it takes its flavour). It was developed in the 1880s by Scottish-born Californian judge and amateur horticulturist James H. Logan and was first exhibited in England in 1897. The loganberry can be eaten fresh, served whole as a dessert topped with cream, ice-cream or liqueur; puréed for use in ice-cream, sorbets, soufflés, mousses or fools; or cooked as a filling for pies and tarts or as jam.

Longan An oval-shaped fruit of Asian origin. It is similar to the lychee, but smaller, and has dull, red-brown skin and sweet, firm, translucent flesh surrounding a dark brown stone. The longan can be eaten fresh, added to fruit salad or savoury salad, or poached for use in sweet and savoury dishes. Longan is in season in late summer and

LOBSTERS

LOBSTER MORNAY

★ **Preparation time:** 15 minutes
Total cooking time: 20 minutes
Serves 2

1 medium cooked lobster or crayfish, halved	¼ cup (2 fl oz) cream
1¼ cups (10 fl oz) milk	½ cup grated cheddar cheese
1 bay leaf	salt and ground white pepper
1 onion, chopped	15 g (½ oz) butter, melted, extra
6 peppercorns	½ cup fresh white breadcrumbs
30 g (1 oz) butter	
2 tablespoons plain (all-purpose) flour	

1 Remove tail meat from lobster and reserve shells. Cut lobster into cubes and set aside.

2 Place milk in a pan with bay leaf, onion and peppercorns. Heat slowly to boiling point. Remove from heat; leave, covered, 10 minutes.

3 In a separate pan, melt butter and remove from heat. Stir in flour and blend in strained, hot milk. Return pan to heat and stir continuously until sauce boils and thickens. Simmer sauce for 1 minute. Remove from heat, add cream, cheese, salt and pepper. Stir sauce until cheese melts and add lobster to sauce.

4 Divide lobster mixture between shells and place shells in a shallow heatproof dish. Melt extra butter in a small pan and add breadcrumbs, stirring lightly to combine. Scatter crumbs over filling and cook under a medium hot grill until crumbs are golden brown and filling is hot.

CHILLED LOBSTER WITH HOME-MADE SEAFOOD SAUCE

★ **Preparation time:** 20 minutes + chilling time
Total cooking time: nil
Serves 4

2 x 1 kg (2 lb) cooked lobsters	1½ cups good quality mayonnaise
2 tablespoons tomato paste	1 teaspoon creamed horseradish
	1 tablespoon worcestershire sauce
	½ cup (4 fl oz) sour cream
	¼ teaspoon dry mustard

1 Cut lobsters in half lengthways. Wash inside lightly and remove tail meat.

2 Cut tail meat into medallions and return to each tail shell. Cover and place in refrigerator to chill well before serving.

3 Combine remaining ingredients for sauce. Serve half a lobster with sauce to each person.

ABOVE: LOBSTER MORNAY, OPPOSITE PAGE, BELOW: LOBSTER MEDALLIONS IN HOISIN MARINADE; ABOVE: BARBECUED LOBSTER TAILS WITH AVOCADO SAUCE

---

early autumn, it is also available canned (preserved in syrup) and dried. Dried longan can be eaten as it is, as you would other dried fruit, or added to braised and sweet and sour Chinese dishes. The fruit's Chinese name *lung-yen* means 'dragon's eye'.

Loquat The pear-shaped fruit of a small evergreen tree native to Asia and now widely grown in the lands of the Mediterranean. It is the size of a small plum with glossy yellow-orange skin and crisp, juicy, tart-sweet yellow flesh. It can be eaten fresh on its own, added to fruit salads or other desserts (in Asia it is often set in a jelly of agar agar) or cooked as jellies and jam.

Lotus A type of water lily native to China and India. All parts of the plant are edible, but it is the crunchy, reddish-coloured root that is most widely used: stir-fried, braised, coated in batter and deep-fried or simmered in stock. The root is perforated with holes and when sliced in cross-section makes an attractive garnish, much utilised in Japanese cooking. Lotus seeds can be eaten raw, boiled or grilled (broiled) or, cooked, sweetened and mashed, used as a filling

BARBECUED LOBSTER TAILS WITH AVOCADO SAUCE

★★

Preparation time: 15 minutes +
3 hours marinating
Total cooking time: 10 minutes
Serves 4

1/4 cup (2 fl oz) dry white wine
1 tablespoon honey
1 teaspoon sambal oelek (bottled chopped chillies)
2 tablespoons sour cream
3 teaspoons lemon juice
1 clove garlic, crushed
1 tablespoon olive oil
1 small tomato, chopped finely
4 fresh green lobster tails, about 410 g (13 oz)
salt and pepper, to taste

Avocado Sauce
1 medium ripe avocado, mashed

1 Combine wine, honey, sambal oelek, garlic and olive oil in a jug; mix well. Using a sharp knife or kitchen scissors, cut along the soft shell on the underside of the lobster. Gently pull shell apart and ease raw flesh out with fingers.

2 Place the lobster flesh in a shallow non-metal dish. Pour marinade over lobster and stir well. Cover and refrigerate for several hours or overnight. Prepare and light the barbecue 1 hour before cooking. Cook lobster tails on hot lightly greased barbecue grill or flatplate for 5–10 minutes, turning frequently. Brush with marinade until cooked through. Slice into medallions and serve with Avocado Sauce and a green salad if desired.

3 **To make Avocado Sauce:** Combine avocado, juice and sour cream in bowl; mix well. Add tomato and mix to combine with avocado mixture; add salt and pepper, to taste.

LOBSTER MEDALLIONS IN HOISIN MARINADE

★

Preparation time: 20 minutes +
1 hour marinating
Total cooking time: 15 minutes
Serves 4

1.5 kg (3 lb) cooked lobster or crayfish tails
1 bunch asparagus, cut into 4 cm (1 1/2 inch) lengths

Marinade
1/2 cup (4 fl oz) hoisin sauce
3 tablespoons tomato paste
2 tablespoons lemon juice
2 tablespoons honey
2 tablespoons soy sauce

1 Preheat oven to 180°C (350°F/Gas 4). Remove flesh from lobster tails. Discard shells. Cut tails into medallions approximately 1 cm (1/2 inch) thick.

2 Place medallions in a shallow ovenproof dish. Combine marinade ingredients and pour over the lobster. Cover and refrigerate for 1 hour.

3 Cook the asparagus until just tender. Add to lobster.

4 Place dish in oven and cook 10 minutes or until heated through. Serve immediately.

---

for Japanese and Chinese pastries and cakes. Dried lotus leaves are used as food wrappers (they impart a leafy flavour to food, but are tough and not meant to be eaten). Lotus root is available fresh and canned; lotus seeds are available dried and canned.

Lychee (Litchi) A small oval fruit about the size of a large cherry with sweet, pale pink flesh similar in flavour to a grape, and thin, knobbly, reddish skin. The flesh surrounds a shiny brown stone. Lychees can be eaten fresh on their own, added to fruit salads and to savoury salads or served as a dessert with cream or ice-cream; poached, they can be added to both sweet and savoury dishes. Lychees are in season in summer; the fruit is also available canned and dried. The lychee is native to southern China and has been cultivated there for some 4000 years.

Lyonnaise, à la A French term for food cooked with chopped and sautéed onions, a style characteristic of the Lyonnaise region of eastern France.

M

MANGOES

Macadamia Nut The round, hard-shelled, creamy-fleshed nut of a tree native to Australia. Fresh or roasted nuts are eaten as a snack; crushed nuts can be added to ice-cream or used in biscuits (cookies), cakes or breads; whole nuts are coated with chocolate as a confectionary (candy).

Macaroni Pasta in the form of short, dried, hollow tubes.

Macaroon A small, flat, round biscuit (cookie), crunchy on the outside and moist on the inside, made from ground almonds mixed with sugar and egg white. Macaroons originated in France and are a specialty of the Nancy region.

Mace The fibrous, lacy skin that envelopes the nutmeg, but which has its own distinctive flavour and is used as spice. It is made up of numerous tendrils called blades; the spice is also sold in ground form.

Blade

CHICKEN CURRY WITH MANGO AND CREAM

Preparation time: 10 minutes
Total cooking time: 20 minutes
Serves 4

750 g (1½ lb) chicken breast fillets
2 tablespoons ghee or oil
2 large onions, finely sliced
2 red chillies, seeded and sliced
1 teaspoon grated fresh ginger
¼ teaspoon saffron strands
1 tablespoon hot water
½ teaspoon salt
¼ teaspoon ground white pepper
½ teaspoon ground cardamom
½ cup (4 fl oz) cream
2 ripe mangoes or
1 x 425 g (13½ oz) can mango slices, drained

Mint and Yoghurt Raita
1 cup plain yoghurt
¼ cup finely chopped fresh mint leaves
1 green chilli, seeded and chopped
1 teaspoon finely chopped ginger
½ teaspoon salt

1 Wash chicken under cold water. Pat dry with paper towels. Cut chicken into 3 cm (1¼ inch) wide strips. Heat ghee in a pan, add onion, chilli and ginger and cook until onion is soft.

2 Heat saffron strands in a dry pan over low heat until crisp. Place strands in a bowl, crush with the back of a spoon. Add hot water to dissolve. Add chicken strips. Add pepper and cardamom to onion mixture in pan and stir to coat chicken with spices. Add saffron and cream to pan. Simmer, uncovered, for 10 minutes.

3 Peel mangoes and slice flesh from the stone. Add to the pan and cook for another 4 minutes until mango is heated through and slightly softened.

4 To make Mint and Yoghurt Raita: Mix ingredients together. Serve chilled.

HOT CARAMEL MANGO

Preparation time: 20 minutes
Total cooking time: 5 minutes
Serves 6

3 large mangoes
¾ cup (6 fl oz) cream
1 tablespoon caster (superfine) sugar
2 tablespoons soft brown sugar

1 Peel mangoes. Cut mango flesh into thin slices. Arrange slices in six individual ramekin dishes. Pour cream evenly over each dish. Sprinkle with combined sugars.

2 Preheat grill to hot. Place dishes under grill for 5 minutes or until the sugar has caramelised and mango is warm. Serve immediately, with a wafer biscuit or tuille.

ABOUT MANGOES

■ Mangoes continue to ripen after picking so, unless using immediately, choose fruit that are slightly green and firm.

LEFT: HOT CARAMEL MANGO; ABOVE: CHICKEN CURRY WITH MANGO AND CREAM. OPPOSITE PAGE, BELOW: SPLIT PEA SOUP WITH MEATBALLS; ABOVE: HERB MEATBALLS WITH RICH TOMATO SAUCE

HERB MEATBALLS WITH RICH TOMATO SAUCE

★ *Preparation time:* 40 minutes
Total cooking time: 10–15 minutes
Makes about 45

1 medium onion, finely chopped
750 g beef mince
1 egg, lightly beaten
2 cloves garlic, crushed
2 teaspoons cracked black pepper
1/4 teaspoon salt
2 tablespoons plum sauce
1 tablespoon worcestershire sauce
2 tablespoons finely chopped fresh rosemary
1–2 tablespoons finely chopped fresh mint or sweet basil
oil for frying

Rich Tomato Sauce
1 1/2 cups red wine
1 clove garlic, crushed
3/4 cup tomato puree
1/3 cup chunky bottled tomato sauce
2–3 teaspoons Dijon mustard
30 g butter, chopped

1 Combine onion, beef, egg, garlic, pepper, salt, sauces and herbs in a bowl. Use hands to combine well. Shape level tablespoons of mixture into balls.

2 Heat oil in a large frying pan. Cook meatballs in batches over medium heat for 5 minutes or until browned. Shake pan during cooking to prevent sticking. Drain on paper towels. Keep warm.

3 To make Rich Tomato Sauce: Drain oil from pan, add wine and garlic to pan juices. Bring

SPLIT PEA SOUP WITH MEATBALLS

★ *Preparation time:* 1 hour 30 minutes
Total cooking time: 1 hour 30 minutes
Serves 6

2 cups green split peas
1.5 litres (6 cups) chicken stock or water
1/2 cup chopped celery
1 large onion, chopped
1/2 teaspoon dried marjoram
1/4 teaspoon pepper
500 g (1 lb) pork and veal mince

2 rashers bacon, chopped
2 tablespoons chopped fresh parsley
2 teaspoons grated lemon rind
3 potatoes, peeled and diced
juice of 1 lemon

1 Wash peas in cold water. Drain, place in large pot, add stock or water, celery, onion, marjoram and pepper. Bring to boil. Reduce heat, cover, simmer 1 hour or until peas are tender. Do not drain.

2 Combine pork and veal mince, bacon, parsley, lemon rind and sage. Mix well with hand. Using wet hands, shape into walnut-sized balls.

3 Gently drop meatballs and potatoes into the soup mixture. Return soup to boiling. Reduce heat, cover and simmer for 20–30 minutes or until meatballs and potatoes are cooked. Add lemon juice to taste before serving.

to boil, reduce heat, simmer to reduce liquid by half. Strain into medium pan. Add tomato puree, sauce and mustard. Bring to boil, reduce heat and reduce liquid by half. Gradually whisk in butter.

mace is used to flavour clear soups, jellies and pale sauces; ground mace is used to season English potted meats, pork dishes and béchamel sauce.

Mackerel A saltwater fish with oily, dark, firm-textured flesh. It is suitable for baking, grilling (broiling), pan-frying and poaching.

Madeira Cake A rich cake flavoured with lemon or orange juice and baked with a slice of citron peel on top. In Victorian England the cake was traditionally served with a glass of madeira wine.

Madeleine Small cake baked in shell-shaped mould and often served dusted with finely powdered sugar. They are a specialty of the town of Commercy, in north-eastern France.

Madrilène A clear soup (chicken or vegetable) thickened and flavoured with tomato pulp and usually served chilled.

Maître d'Hôtel Butter Softened butter mixed with chopped parsley, lemon juice and freshly ground white pepper, then chilled until firm. It is served on top of grilled (broiled) steak and fish.

Maize See Corn.

MEATBALLS IN SHERRY SAUCE

★

Preparation time: 35 minutes
Total cooking time: 30 minutes
Serves 4–6

500 g (1 lb) minced (ground) pork and veal
1 teaspoon ground sweet paprika
1/2 cup fresh white breadcrumbs
1 tablespoon plain (all-purpose) flour
1/4 cup chopped fresh parsley
1/2 cup (4 fl oz) dry or sweet sherry
1 cup (8 fl oz) chicken stock
2 cloves garlic, crushed
2 teaspoons ground sweet paprika
2 tablespoons olive oil
30 g (1 oz) butter
10 small new potatoes
1/4 cup chopped fresh parsley, extra
1 medium onion, finely chopped

1 Combine mince, breadcrumbs, parsley, garlic and paprika in a medium bowl. Mix well. Using wet hands, roll the mixture into meatballs the size of walnuts.

2 Heat oil and butter in medium pan; add meatballs. Cook over medium-high heat 3–4 minutes until well browned. Remove from pan; drain.

3 Add onion, paprika and flour to pan and cook, stirring, for 2 minutes. Add sherry and stock gradually to pan, stirring until mixture is smooth. Stir constantly over medium heat 2 minutes or until sauce boils and thickens.

4 Return meatballs to pan, add potatoes. Cover, cook over low heat 20 minutes. Serve with parsley.

SPAGHETTI AND MEATBALLS

★★

Preparation time: 25 minutes
Total cooking time: 50 minutes
Serves 6

Sauce
1 tablespoon oil
1 small onion, chopped
425 g (13 1/2 oz) can tomatoes
4 tablespoons tomato paste
1/2 cup (4 fl oz) water
1/2 cup (4 fl oz) dry red wine
1 small clove garlic, crushed
1 bay leaf
pinch black pepper

Meatballs
1/2 cup (4 fl oz) milk
1 cup soft breadcrumbs
500 g (1 lb) minced (ground) steak
1 small onion, very finely chopped
1 tablespoon grated parmesan cheese
1 egg, beaten
1 tablespoon chopped fresh parsley
pinch black pepper
1/4 teaspoon dried oregano leaves
4 tablespoons oil
500 g (1 lb) spaghetti
grated parmesan cheese to serve

1 To make Sauce: Heat oil in a pan. Add onion and fry until soft. Add remaining ingredients and simmer for 20 minutes until thick, stirring occasionally.

2 To make Meatballs: Add the milk to breadcrumbs, leave for 5 minutes. Combine soaked breadcrumbs with remaining meatball ingredients. Form into balls, brown on all sides in 3 tablespoons hot oil. Add to sauce and simmer gently for about 15 minutes. Remove bay leaf.

3 Bring a large pan of water to the boil, add remaining oil. Add spaghetti, cook 10–12 minutes. Drain. Spoon meatballs and sauce over spaghetti and serve with grated parmesan cheese.

Malt The term given to a grain, usually barley, which has been soaked, sprouted, roasted and crushed. During this process the starch content of the grain is converted by partial fermentation into sugar. Further processing of malt produces beer; distillation results in whisky. Malt extract, which comes in syrup or dried form, can be added to drinks, cakes, puddings and bread dough.

Mandarin A small, loose-skinned citrus fruit with sweet, juicy, easily separated segments. It can be eaten as a fruit.

Mango A tropical fruit with juicy, sweet, golden flesh clinging to a large seed. Mangoes are delicious eaten fresh; perhaps the least messy way is to slice a

Mange tout See Snow Pea.

MEATLOAVES

GOURMET MEATLOAF

Preparation time: 20 minutes ✦

Total cooking time: 1 hour 20 minutes

Serves 6

500 g (1 lb) pork and veal mince	1 tablespoon green peppercorns, drained, chopped
250 g (½ lb) sausage mince	2 tablespoons chopped fresh mint
1½ cups fresh white breadcrumbs	2 teaspoons ground sweet paprika
1 small green pepper (capsicum), chopped	1 tablespoon toasted sesame seeds
1 medium onion, finely chopped	
2 cloves garlic, crushed	***Tomato Cream Sauce***
½ cup (4 fl oz) bottled tomato pasta sauce	1½ cups (12 fl oz) bottled tomato pasta sauce
½ cup fruit chutney	½ cup (4 fl oz) cream
1 egg, lightly beaten	3 teaspoons seeded mustard
½ cup chopped dried apricots	

1 Grease a 23 x 13 cm (9 x 5 inch) loaf pan. Preheat oven to moderate 180°C (350°F/Gas 4). Combine both minces in a bowl. Add breadcrumbs, onion, garlic, tomato sauce, chutney, egg, apricots, peppercorns, mint and paprika, mix.

2 Press prepared mixture into loaf pan, bake, uncovered, 1 hour 15 minutes. Carefully pour off the juices. Turn out the meatloaf, sprinkle with

3 To make Tomato Cream Sauce: Combine all the ingredients in a pan. Bring to boil. Reduce heat, simmer 3 minutes stirring occasionally.

sesame seeds. Slice meatloaf and serve with Tomato Cream Sauce.

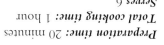

BEEF AND PIMIENTO LOAF WITH CHEESE

Preparation time: 20 minutes ✦✦

Total cooking time: 1 hour

Serves 6

1 kg (2 lb) beef mince	2 cups fresh white breadcrumbs
1 egg, lightly beaten	¼ cup tomato paste
1 cup chopped pimiento	1 tablespoon dry mustard powder
⅓ cup chopped fresh basil	2 tablespoons chopped black olives
2 garlic cloves, crushed	250 g (8 oz) ricotta cheese
2 teaspoons dried mixed herbs	125 g (4 oz) feta cheese

1 Preheat oven to moderate 180°C (350°F/Gas 4). Line a 12 x 14 x 7 cm (4¾ x 5½ x 2¾ inch) loaf tin with aluminium foil. Combine mince in a large bowl with breadcrumbs, garlic and egg, mustard, tomato paste, mixed herbs, basil and olives. Divide into 3 portions.

2 Combine pimiento, basil and olives.

3 Press 1 portion of mince mixture evenly over base of tin. Top with half the pimiento mixture. Top with another portion of mince, then with remaining mince, then pimiento mixture. Drain off liquid, stand loaf for 5 minutes, turn out, serve sliced. Bake 1 hour or until cooked through. Drain off

4 Combine ricotta cheese and crumbled feta cheese; serve as an accompaniment to sliced loaf.

ABOVE: GOURMET MEATLOAF

MEATBALLS, BELOW: MEATBALLS IN SHERRY SAUCE.

OPPOSITE PAGE, ABOVE: SPAGHETTI AND

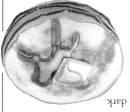

Mango A tropical fruit, about the size and shape of an apple, with a shiny, thick, purple skin containing four to six segments of soft, white, lychee-like flesh. It is eaten fresh as a fruit. To prepare, cut in half, then scoop out the flesh with a teaspoon.

Manioc See Cassava.

Maple Syrup The sap of various species of maple tree, boiled down into a syrup that varies in colour from pale amber (considered the finest) to dark amber (used mainly in cooking). Maple syrup is poured over pancakes, waffles, ice-cream and other desserts. Maple-flavoured syrup is a blend of pure maple syrup and corn syrup.

Mango is sometimes cooked in curries and other savoury dishes (it goes especially well with chicken). It is also made into chutney and pickles which are often served with curries. Mango pulp can be used in ice-cream, mousse and sorbet. Mangoes are in season in summer; they are also available canned.

check from each side of the seed, score the flesh into small squares, then push the skin upwards so that the cubes bristle like a porcupine.

MELONS

MELON WITH GINGER SYRUP

Preparation time: 40 minutes
Total cooking time: 5 minutes
Makes about 25 skewers

1 cantaloupe (rockmelon), halved
1 honeydew melon, halved
half a small watermelon

Ginger Syrup
1 cup caster (superfine) sugar
1 cup (8 fl oz) water
2 tablespoons brandy
2 tablespoons preserved ginger syrup or green ginger wine

1 Remove seeds from each of the melons. Using a melon baller, scoop the flesh of each melon into balls. Place balls in a large bowl. Cover with plastic wrap. Chill well.

2 To make Ginger Syrup: Place sugar and water in a small saucepan. Heat gently until sugar has dissolved. Simmer until slightly thickened.

3 Stir in brandy and ginger syrup or green ginger wine. Allow the mixture to cool before pouring over the melons. Cover with plastic wrap and return to refrigerator until well chilled.

4 For serving, skewer one of each type of melon ball onto a bamboo skewer. Repeat until all the fruit is used. May be served with dollops of freshly whipped cream or ice-cream.

SUMMER MELON SALAD

Preparation time: 15 minutes
Total cooking time: nil
Serves 6

345 g (11 oz) honeydew melon
345 g (11 oz) cantaloupe (rockmelon)
345 g (11 oz) watermelon (optional)
2 small red onions
1 tablespoon chopped fresh parsley
2 tablespoons lemon juice

1 Cut melon flesh into pieces roughly 4 cm (1½ inches) square and 1 cm (½ inch) thick. Slice the onions into very thin rings.

2 Place onion, parsley and lemon juice in a small bowl; toss to combine.

3 Layer melons and onion in a glass bowl, pour over juice mixture. Serve immediately.

ABOUT MELONS

■ The tough skin of a melon (which belies its soft, sweet interior) can make judging its ripeness difficult. Choose melons which have a sweet smell and are slightly soft at the stalk end.

■ Once cut, melons should be used quickly. Even well wrapped in the refrigerator, melons can quickly taint the flavour of other foods.

ABOVE: MELON WITH GINGER SYRUP.
OPPOSITE PAGE: APRICOT AND ALMOND VACHERIN

Maraschino A liqueur made from a bitter black cherry called *marasca*. Maraschino cherries are sweet cherries that have been bleached, stoned, then steeped in a sugar syrup flavoured with maraschino liqueur; they are used in baking and as a garnish for cocktails.

Marble Cake A cake which, when sliced, has a marble-like appearance, achieved by colouring the portions of the batter (pink, chocolate and plain) then mixing them in the pan before baking.

Marengo A dish of chicken cooked with tomato, mushroom, garlic and wine. It was created for Napoleon in 1800, following his victory over the Austrians at the battle of Marengo, and cooked for him on the battlefield.

Margarine A butter-like spread made from vegetable oil or a combination of vegetable and animal oils. In most recipes margarine can be substituted for butter. Polyunsaturated and monounsaturated margarines are made from a refined and purified vegetable oil and have a smooth, easy-to-spread consistency. Cooking or block (stick)

MERINGUES

APRICOT AND ALMOND VACHERIN

★★

Preparation time: 40 minutes
Total cooking time: 50 minutes
Serves 8–10

4 egg whites
1 cup caster (superfine) sugar
1½ teaspoons vanilla essence
1½ teaspoons white vinegar
1 cup ground almonds

Filling
200 g (6½ oz) chopped dried apricots

1 cup (8 fl oz) water
½ cup caster (superfine) sugar
30 g (1 oz) butter

Topping
1½ cups (12 fl oz) cream, whipped
½ cup chopped dried apricots, extra
½ cup toasted flaked almonds

1 Preheat oven to slow 150°C (300°F/Gas 2). Line 2 oven trays with baking paper, mark 22 cm (9 inch) circle on each. Place egg whites in small dry mixing bowl. Using electric beaters, beat egg whites until soft peaks form. Gradually add sugar, beating constantly after each addition. Beat for 5–10 minutes or until thick and glossy and sugar has dissolved. Gently fold in essence, vinegar and almonds.

2 Divide mixture between trays, spread evenly over marked circles. Bake for 45 minutes or until

meringues are pale and crisp. Turn off oven and cool meringues in oven with door ajar.

3 To make Filling: Place apricots and water in small pan, stir over medium heat until apricots are just tender. Add sugar and simmer, uncovered, over low heat for 3–5 minutes or until nearly all the liquid has been absorbed. Transfer apricot mixture into food processor, process until smooth. Add butter, process until smooth and the mixture is smooth. Cool.

4 To assemble: Place one meringue disc on serving plate, spread with apricot mixture, top with half the whipped cream, then other meringue disc. Spread top with rest of cream, decorate with extra apricots and almonds. Refrigerate until required for serving.

MERINGUE NESTS WITH KAHLUA CREAM AND STRAWBERRIES

★★

Preparation time: 40 minutes
Total cooking time: 30 minutes
Serves 4

3 egg whites
¾ cup caster (superfine) sugar

Filling
¾ cup (6 fl oz) cream
1 tablespoon sugar
2 teaspoons instant coffee powder

1 teaspoon water
1 tablespoon Kahlua or coffee liqueur
250 g (8 oz) strawberries
60 g (2 oz) dark (semi-sweet) cooking chocolate, melted

1 Preheat oven to very slow 120°C (250°F/Gas ½). Line 2 oven trays with baking paper. Mark two 10 cm (4 inch) circles on each tray. Place egg whites in small dry mixing bowl. Using electric beaters, beat egg whites until soft peaks form. Gradually add the sugar, beating constantly after each addition. Beat 5–10 minutes until thick and glossy and sugar has dissolved.

2 Place meringue mixture into piping bag fitted with a 1.5 cm (⅝ inch) star-shaped nozzle. Pipe some of the meringue over marked rounds to form a base. Pipe remaining mixture around edge of base to form a wall (or nest). Bake for 30 minutes or until meringue nests are pale and crisp. Turn off oven, cool nests in the oven with door ajar.

3 To make Filling: Using electric beaters, beat cream with the sugar until soft peaks form. Fold in blended coffee powder, water and Kahlua and beat until firm peaks form. Divide cream between nests, top with whole strawberries, drizzle with melted chocolate.

Margarine is firmer. Margarine contains saturated animal fats and vegetable oils and is used like butter for frying and baking.

Marinade A seasoned mixture in which raw meat, poultry, fish or seafood is steeped (or marinated) before cooking, both to tenderise by softening the fibres and to add flavour.

Marjoram Also known as sweet marjoram, an aromatic herb with spicy flavoured. small grey-green leaves which are used in meat, poultry, egg, cheese, cabbage, green bean and tomato dishes. Oregano, a similar but more strongly flavoured herb, is also known as wild marjoram.

Marmalade A thick, jam-like spread made from citrus fruit and peel (either a single fruit or a

Marrow, Bone A fatty tissue found in the centre of animal bones. It is usually eaten at breakfast, on hot buttered toast. It is

MERINGUE NESTS WITH KAHLUA CREAM (LEFT) AND
PAVLOVA WITH FRUIT SALAD TOPPING

PAVLOVA WITH FRUIT SALAD TOPPING

★ Preparation time: 15 minutes
Total cooking time: 40 minutes
Serves 6-8

4 egg whites
1 cup caster (superfine) sugar
3 teaspoons cornflour (cornstarch)
1 teaspoon white vinegar
1 cup (8 fl oz) cream, whipped

250 g (8 oz) strawberries, sliced
2 kiwi fruit (Chinese gooseberries), sliced
1 banana, sliced
2 passionfruit

1 Preheat oven to slow 150°C (300°F/Gas 2). Line an oven tray with baking paper. Mark a 20 cm (8 inch) circle on baking paper. Place egg whites in large, dry mixing bowl. Using electric beaters, beat egg whites until soft peaks form. Gradually add the sugar, beating constantly after each addition. Beat for 5–10 minutes until sugar has dissolved. Fold in cornflour and vinegar.

2 Spread meringue mixture onto marked circle. Shape evenly, running a flat-bladed knife around edge and over top of meringue. Run knife up edge of meringue mixture, all the way around, making furrows. This strengthens pavlova and gives a nice decorative finish.

3 Bake for 40 minutes or until pale and crisp. Turn off oven, cool pavlova in oven with door ajar. Top with cream and arrange fruit decoratively. Drizzle with passionfruit pulp.

ABOUT MERINGUE

■ For successful meringues, separate eggs very carefully—even the smallest amount of yolk will cause the egg foam to break down. Use only fresh, dry caster (superfine) sugar, or fine icing (confectioners) sugar, if the recipe calls for it. Make sure you clean and thoroughly dry the bowl and all the utensils you are going to use.

■ Meringues are cooked at a very low temperature—they are, in fact, dried rather than baked. Cooked meringues should lift off the tray easily and feel light and dry to the touch. (The centres can be slightly soft and chewy, or completely dry, depending on the type of dessert you are making.)

■ When spooning or piping meringue on a pie, spread the mixture to the very edges. Cover the entire filling well and evenly, as the meringue will shrink slightly during baking.

pale-coloured and when cooked and cooled, has a smooth, jelly-like texture. Raw marrow extracted from larger beef bones may be chopped and added to stuffings; cooked marrow is spread on toast as an hors d'oeuvre or cooked in dishes such as Milanese risotto.

Marrow, Vegetable A sausage-shaped vegetable belonging to the same family as the zucchini (courgette). Young marrows have the best flavour and most delicate flesh and can be cooked in the same way as zucchini. Large older marrows have a high water content and bland flavour and are best stuffed with a savoury filling and baked, or cooked gently in butter and their own juice.

Marshmallow A whipped confectionary (candy) with a springy, puffy texture made from gelatine, sugar, flavouring and colouring. It is commercially

available in bite-sized, sugar-dusted portions or can be made at home.

Marzipan A confectionary (candy) made from a sugar and water syrup, almond paste and sometimes egg

white cooked together, cooled, and then kneaded into a smooth firm paste. It is cut or moulded into small shapes which are used to decorate cakes or it is boxed as gift confectionary; it is also used as a coating under the top icing of rich fruit cakes.

Mascarpone A fresh, unripened, soft, creamy cheese, made from cow's milk cream, with a high fat content and a rich, buttery taste. It is usually served as a dessert with sweetened fruit or mixed with brandy or liqueurs.

Matzo A thin sheet of unleavened bread, usually made with wheat flour and water only. It is traditionally eaten during the Jewish Passover when only unleavened products are eaten. Matzo meal, made from ground matzo crackers, is used in place of breadcrumbs at Passover.

Mayonnaise A cold uncooked sauce made by whisking oil and egg

yolk into an emulsion. It is flavoured with lemon juice, vinegar or mustard and seasonings. Mayonnaise is served as a salad dressing and accompaniment to cold meat, fish and egg dishes; it is the basis of many other cold sauces.

Meat The flesh of animals used for food. The term often refers only

to lamb, beef, pork and some game and not to poultry, fish and seafood.

Meatballs Small balls made of minced (ground) beef, lamb, veal or pork, seasoned and bound together with beaten egg or breadcrumbs. Meatballs can be steamed, simmered, shallow-fried or deep-fried and served either as finger food (with a dipping sauce) or as a first or main course.

Meatloaf A mixture of minced (ground) beef, pork or veal (or a combination of these), seasoned, bound together with beaten egg, breadcrumbs or rice, formed into a loaf shape and baked; it can be eaten hot or cold and is usually served with sauce or gravy.

Medlar A plum-sized fruit with yellowish-brown skin and firm

MEXICAN CLASSICS

LAMB EMPANADAS

★ **Preparation time:** 1 hour
Total cooking time: 20 minutes
Serves 6

2 teaspoons olive oil
250 g (8 oz) minced lamb
½ small onion, finely
  chopped
½ medium green pepper
  (capsicum), finely
  chopped
1 small carrot, finely
  chopped
1 teaspoon ground
  cinnamon
2 teaspoons soft brown
  sugar

2 tablespoons tomato paste

Pastry
2 cups self-raising flour,
  sifted
250 g (8 oz) butter,
  chopped
1 egg
¼ cup (2 fl oz) water
30 g (1 oz) butter, extra,
  softened
1 egg yolk, extra, lightly
  beaten

1 Heat oil in medium pan; add mince and onion, cook over medium-high heat 3 minutes. Add chopped pepper, carrot, cinnamon, sugar and tomato paste. Mix well. Remove from heat, cool.
2 Preheat oven to 200°C (400°F/Gas 6). Brush a 32 x 28 cm (13 x 11 inch) oven tray with melted butter or oil. Dust with flour. Shake off excess.
3 To make Pastry: Place flour and butter in food processor. Process 30 seconds or until mixture has a fine crumbly texture. Add egg and water. Process 30 seconds or until mixture comes together. Turn dough onto a lightly floured surface. Knead until smooth. Be careful not to handle too much or the dough will become

sticky. Divide into three equal portions.
4 On a lightly floured surface, roll each portion into a 20 x 20 cm (8 x 8 inch) square. Spread two of the squares with the extra butter. Stack all three dough squares on top of each other, with the unbuttered square on top. Roll out the layers together.
5 To assemble: Cut out six 15 cm (6 inch) circles from pastry. Divide meat mixture evenly between the circles. Brush edges with egg yolk. Fold in half, pressing edges together. Place on prepared tray, brush with egg yolk and bake 15 minutes or until puffed and golden. May be served with Tomato Salsa and a green salad.

GUACAMOLE

★ **Preparation time:** 20 minutes
Total cooking time: nil
Serves 6

2 ripe avocados
1 small onion
1 medium tomato
1 tablespoon chopped
  fresh coriander

¼ cup (2 fl oz) sour
  cream
1 tablespoon lemon juice
Tabasco sauce, to taste

1 Cut avocados in half and remove the seed with the blade of a sharp knife. Peel avocados and place flesh in medium bowl. Mash well with a fork until smooth.
2 Peel and finely chop onion and tomato; mix with chopped fresh coriander. Add to avocado in bowl with remaining ingredients, mix well. Serve as a dip with corn chips or add to taco filling.

Sidebar

Melon Large fruit with a thick rind and juicy flesh. The many varieties fall into three main groups: round with netted, bark-like skin, fragrant orange flesh and a cluster of pale seeds in the centre, such as the cantaloupe (rockmelon), galia melon and Persian melon; oval and smooth-skinned with creamy-white to dark green sweet flesh and a central cluster of seeds such as the honeydew, casaba, charentais, crenshaw, ogen melon and santa claus melon; and the watermelons, larger with moist reddish flesh studded with dark seeds. Melon is eaten fresh as a fruit and added to fruit salads; some

Melba Toast Thin, crisp slices of crustless bread served with dips, pâtés and creamy soups. It was originally created for the Australian opera singer Dame Nellie Melba.

made into preserves. like flavour. It can be over-ripe, it has a wine-Asia. Edible only when tree native to central greyish flesh borne on a

---

OPPOSITE PAGE, ABOVE: LAMB EMPANADAS; BELOW: GUACAMOLE. THIS PAGE, ABOVE: BURRITOS AND TOMATO SALSA

BURRITOS

★ **Preparation time:** 15 minutes
Total cooking time: 40 minutes
Serves 4

500 g (1 lb) rump steak	1 bay leaf
1 teaspoon olive oil	2 cups (16 fl oz) beef stock
1 medium onion, finely sliced	8 x 20 cm (8 inch) tortillas
1 cinnamon stick	Tomato Salsa, to serve
4 cloves	

1 Trim meat of excess fat; cut into 2 cm (¾ inch) cubes. Heat oil in a medium pan, add onion. Cook until golden brown.

2 Add meat, cinnamon stick, cloves, bay leaf and beef stock. Bring to boil. Reduce heat, simmer covered for 30 minutes or until meat is soft and liquid is almost absorbed. Remove and discard the cinnamon stick, cloves and bay leaf.

3 Shred meat with two forks. Serve rolled up in the tortillas with Tomato Salsa and salad.

TOMATO SALSA

★ **Preparation time:** 10 minutes
Total cooking time: nil
Serves 4–6

1 medium tomato, finely chopped	1 medium red onion, finely sliced
2 tablespoons chopped fresh coriander	2 teaspoons grated lemon rind
	3 tablespoons lemon juice

1 Thoroughly combine all ingredients in a medium bowl.

2 Serve as an accompaniment to Empanadas, a filling for Tacos, wrapped in a tortilla for Burritos or as a refreshing sauce with meat, chicken or seafood dishes. It tastes best when served at room temperature.

Note: Use spring onions (scallions) if a milder flavour is preferred. Or add a little finely chopped green or red chilli for zest. The size of the tomato and onion will determine the quantity that this recipe makes. It is at its best when eaten fresh, but it can be stored, covered, for up to two days in the refrigerator.

...varieties are served with ham as an hors d'oeuvre.

M

Merguez A spicy sausage of Algerian origin made from minced (ground) goat or mutton and flavoured with harissa.

Meringue A mixture of egg white and sugar, beaten into a stiff froth and then baked in a slow oven; used in various desserts such as pavlova, vacherin and baked Alaska.

Mesclun A mixture of the slightly bitter leaves and young shoots of wild plants such as endive (chicory), rocket, dandelion and chervil. It originated in the Nice region of the south of France and the name is derived from the local word mesclumo, a mixture. A similar salad from the area around Rome is called mesdassisi and is served with walnuts.

Meunière A method of cooking fish. A fillet or small whole fish is dusted with flour, then pan-fried in butter; it is served with a sauce of brown butter, lemon

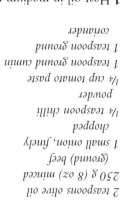

TEX MEX CHILLI CON CARNE

Preparation time: 30 minutes
Total cooking time: 40 minutes
Serves 4

1 tablespoon olive oil
2 cloves garlic, crushed
750 g (1½ lb) lean round steak, cut into 2 cm (¾ inch) cubes
1 large onion, chopped
2 bay leaves
1 cup (8 fl oz) tomato juice
440 g (14 oz) can tomatoes, crushed
470 g (15 oz) can red kidney beans, drained
½ teaspoon ground oregano
1 teaspoon ground cumin
½ teaspoon chilli powder

1 Heat olive oil and crushed garlic in a large pan. Add meat and cook in batches over medium heat until well browned.
2 Add chopped onion, bay leaves, tomato juice and crushed tomatoes. Stir and bring to the boil; reduce heat.
3 Simmer covered until meat is very soft and liquid has reduced by half. Stir in kidney beans, oregano, cumin and chilli powder and heat. Serve with Guacamole and corn chips.

OPPOSITE PAGE: OLD FASHIONED MINCE TARTS.
RIGHT: Spicy Beef and Bean Tacos.
ABOVE: Tex Mex Chilli con Carne.

SPICY BEEF AND BEAN TACOS

Preparation time: 25 minutes
Total cooking time: 15 minutes
Serves 4

2 teaspoons olive oil
250 g (8 oz) minced (ground) beef
12 taco shells
1 small onion, finely chopped
¼ teaspoon chilli powder
2 small carrots, grated
2 medium tomatoes, sliced
¼ cup tomato paste
1 teaspoon ground cumin
1 teaspoon ground coriander
440 g (14 oz) can refried beans
½ small lettuce, shredded
½ cup grated cheddar cheese

1 Heat oil in medium pan; add mince and onion. Cook over medium-high heat for 3 minutes or until well browned and almost all the liquid has evaporated.
2 Add chilli powder, tomato paste, cumin, coriander and refried beans. Mix well. Cook, stirring occasionally, for 2–3 minutes or until mixture is hot.
3 To serve, preheat oven to 180°C (350°F/Gas 4). Place taco shells over the rungs of the oven rack. This will prevent them from closing up while they are crisp. Heat for about 8 minutes until they are crisp. Alternatively, taco shells can be heated in a microwave oven. Follow instructions on the packet. Fill shells with mince mixture, cheese, carrot, tomato and lettuce. Sour cream or Guacamole can also be added if desired.

MINCEMEAT

FRUIT MINCE

★ *Preparation time:* 20 minutes
Total cooking time: nil
Makes 3½ cups

275 g (8¾ oz) finely chopped raisins	1 apple, peeled, coarsely grated
155 g (5 oz) sultanas, chopped	1 teaspoon grated lemon rind
¼ cup finely chopped dried apricots	1 teaspoon grated orange rind
2 tablespoons finely chopped glacé (candied) cherries	1 tablespoon lemon juice
2 tablespoons chopped almonds	1 teaspoon mixed spice
½ cup mixed peel	¼ teaspoon ground nutmeg
⅓ cup currants	¼ cup (2 fl oz) brandy
1 cup soft brown sugar	60 g (2 oz) butter, melted

1 Place all ingredients together in a large mixing bowl. Mix well with a wooden spoon.

2 Spoon fruit mince mixture into airtight containers or sterilised jars and seal well.

3 Keep the containers in a cool, dark place for up to three months. Stir the mixture occasionally, sealing the jars or containers well after each opening. Mixture may be frozen if desired.

TO MAKE MINCE TARTS

Place 2 cups of plain (all-purpose) flour, 185 g (6 oz) of chopped butter, 2 tablespoons of caster (superfine) sugar and 1 teaspoon of custard powder in a food processor. Process the mixture for 20 seconds or until it is fine and crumbly. Add 2 egg yolks and 1 tablespoon of water and process for 20 seconds or until mixture comes together. Turn onto a lightly floured surface. Knead gently until dough is smooth. Cover with plastic wrap and refrigerate for about 15 minutes. Roll the pastry between two sheets of baking paper until it is 2.5 mm (⅛ inch) thick. Cut pastry into circles, using a 7 cm (2¾ inch) round cutter. Ease circles into greased shallow patty tins. Spoon 1–2 teaspoonsful of fruit mince filling into each. (You will need about 1 cup fruit mince altogether.) Re-roll the pastry trimmings. Cut into shapes; use to decorate tops of the pies. Bake in a preheated moderate 180°C (350°F/Gas 4) oven 10–15 minutes or until golden. Dust with icing (confectioners) sugar.

Note: Traditionally fruit mince is made with suet (animal fat); we used butter in this recipe. Suet is sold in chunks and must be grated or melted if it is to be used in fruit mince, cakes or puddings. Mincemeat made with suet will keep for several years, if stored in a dry, dark place.

Mexican Food This has evolved from a mixture of the old Indian traditions and the food of the Spanish colonists. Chilli is the one ingredient common to all Mexican food. There are over a hundred varieties.

Large chillies are stuffed with meat and nuts: smaller varieties are ground or crushed and used to flavour almost all the country's dishes. Tortillas (flatbreads made from cornmeal) are the central part of Mexican food. They can be crisply fried and folded to make taco shells; torn into pieces and fried to use as scoops for sauces (tostaditas): stuffed with beans, cheese and sour cream and baked (enchiladas): or fried and piled up in a stack with filling in between (tostadas). Tex-mex food is what is normally experienced in the West as Mexican food. It is milder in flavour and uses more meat, cheese and sour cream than the original Tex-mex tortillas are usually made from wheat flour.

Microwave Cookery A method of cooking food using energy waves

MICROWAVE

Use your microwave oven to cook vegetables, heat milk for sauces or coffee, melt butter and chocolate, heat prepared meals and defrost raw and cooked food. Most foods normally steamed or poached can be successfully cooked in the microwave.

Microwave ovens vary a great deal and cooking times are therefore approximate. They depend on how well done you like your food and on the power rating of your microwave.

MICROWAVE COOKWARE

- Glass: Use ordinary glass dishes for short-term or low-power heating and defrosting. Ovenproof glass can be used for all microwave cooking.
- Pottery or earthenware: This should be non-porous and well-glazed with no metallic content. Use only for defrosting or low-power cooking.
- China: For reheating only. Do not use any china with a metallic trim or pattern.
- Paper: Use greaseproof (not waxed) paper, paper towels or plastic-coated paper containers for quick heating and reheating.

DEFROSTING MEAT AND POULTRY
Use a medium-low (30%) power level

Cut	Microwave Time PER 500 g (1 lb)	Standing Time
Roast beef	8-10 minutes	10-15 minutes
Steaks	4-6 minutes	5-10 minutes
Minced beef	5-8 minutes	5-10 minutes
Roast pork	8-12 minutes	5-10 minutes
Pork chops	5-8 minutes	5-10 minutes
Pork ribs	6-8 minutes	5-10 minutes
Minced pork	6-8 minutes	5-10 minutes
Roast lamb	8-10 minutes	10-15 minutes
Lamb shoulder	7-10 minutes	10-15 minutes
Lamb chops	5-8 minutes	5-10 minutes
Whole turkey	6-10 minutes	20-30 minutes
Turkey buffé	5-10 minutes	15-20 minutes
Turkey pieces	7-10 minutes	10-15 minutes
Whole chicken	5-8 minutes	10-15 minutes
Chicken pieces	5-7 minutes	10-15 minutes
Duck	8-10 minutes	10-15 minutes

DEFROSTING IN THE MICROWAVE

- Remove the food from its original wrapping or container. Many rigid plastic containers are not designed for use in a microwave. Discard any metal twists or clips. For convenience foods, follow the instructions given on the package.
- Place food, preferably on a rack, in a shallow microwave-safe dish with sides high enough to catch and hold liquids as the food thaws.
- Defrost all foods, loosely covered unless specifically stated otherwise, according to oven manufacturer's instructions.
- Where practical, large dense foods, such as joints of meat, may be turned over once or twice during defrosting to assist equal heat distribution.
- When defrost time is complete, allow to stand as required. Continue specific food preparation and microwave cooking or reheating as required.

MICROWAVING VEGETABLES

A microwave oven does really come into its own when used to cook vegetables. The vegetables should be placed in a microwave-safe dish, with water and seasonings, covered and cooked on HIGH for the stated time. The vegetables will retain their colour, crispness and nutrients.

- Aluminium foil: This can be used in small quantities to shield food (e.g. cutlet bones) from overcooking. Never cover food completely with foil or allow it to touch interior oven walls.
- Plastic: Plastic cookware and wraps that are designated microwave-safe can be used for most cooking and reheating purposes. Never use metal twist ties to secure bags and always poke holes in plastic wrap to allow steam to escape. Ordinary plastic containers and wraps should be used only for reheating or quick cooking.

Vegetables	Quantity	Preparation	Cooking Time (Minutes)
Artichokes	250 g	1/4 cup water	8-9
Asparagus, fresh	250 g	2 tablespoons water	2-4
Asparagus, frozen	250 g	2 tablespoons water	2-3
Beans, fresh	250 g	1-2 tablespoons water	3-4
Beans, frozen	250 g	1 tablespoon water	5-7
Broccoli, fresh	250 g	2 tablespoons water	3-4
Broccoli, frozen	250 g	2 tablespoons water	5-7
Brussels Sprouts, fresh	250 g	2 tablespoons water	3-4
Brussels Sprouts, frozen	250 g	2 tablespoons water	5-7
Cabbage, shredded	1/2 small	only water remaining after washing, butter	6-8
Carrots, fresh	250 g	2 tablespoons water	3-4
Carrots, frozen	250 g	2 tablespoons water	6-8
Cauliflower, fresh	1/2 head	slit stalks, 2 tablespoons water	7-8
Cauliflower, frozen	250 g	2 tablespoons water	5-7
Corn on cob, fresh	2	remove husks, dot with butter, wrap in plastic wrap	6-8
Corn on cob, frozen	250 g	dot with butter	8-10
Eggplant (aubergine), sliced	250 g	brush with oil	3-4
Leeks, whole	250 g	2 tablespoons water	5-7
Mushrooms, fresh	250 g	whole or sliced, dot with butter	3-5
Onions, sliced	250 g	1 tablespoon butter	3-4
Parsnips, sliced	250 g	2 tablespoons water	5-6
Peas, fresh	250 g	2 tablespoons water	3-5
Peas, frozen	250 g	1 tablespoon water	2-4
Potatoes, boiled	250 g	cut into quarters, 2 tablespoons water	6-8
Potatoes, jacket	250 g	pierce skin, rub with oil, turn over after 3 minutes	4-6
Pumpkin	250 g	cut into serving pieces, 2 tablespoons water	4-6
Spinach, fresh	250 g	only water remaining after washing, 1 tablespoon butter	4-5
Spinach, frozen	250 g	washing, 1 tablespoon butter, dash nutmeg and pepper	5-7
Tomatoes, halved	250 g	dot with butter and pepper	3-4
Zucchini (courgettes), sliced	250 g	1 tablespoon butter and pepper	3-4

MINT

which are absorbed by food molecules; they cause the molecules to vibrate rapidly, creating friction which provides the heat that cooks the food. Microwave cooking is much faster than conventional cooking. It is best used for foods that are usually boiled, steamed or poached and is particularly successful with vegetables, fruit and fish. The microwave oven is an excellent way to defrost or reheat food.

Mille-Feuille A pastry consisting of layers of crisp puff pastry interspersed with layers of whipped cream or crème pâtissière and jam (usually strawberry or raspberry). The top pastry layer is glazed or dusted with finely powdered sugar or glazed with icing (frosting). Savoury mille-feuille, with a filling of creamy salmon or shellfish, may be served as a first course or as a buffet or luncheon dish.

Mincemeat Finely chopped dried fruit and fresh apple, mixed with

MINTED LAMB SALAD

★ **Preparation time:** 25 minutes
Total cooking time: 10 minutes
Serves 4

500 g (1 lb) lamb fillets
1 tablespoon olive oil
1 red oak leaf lettuce
60 g (2 oz) yellow teardrop tomatoes
60 g (2 oz) cherry tomatoes
105 g (3½ oz) haloumi cheese
¼ cup (2 fl oz) olive oil, extra
½ teaspoon sugar

1 tablespoon white wine vinegar
½ teaspoon French mustard
1 tablespoon chopped fresh mint
1 tablespoon olive oil, extra

1 Trim meat of excess fat and sinew. Heat oil in a heavy-based pan; add meat. Cook on medium-high heat, turning frequently, 7–8 minutes for a medium-rare result. Do not overcook; meat should be pink in the centre. Remove to a plate, cover loosely with foil. Let cool, thinly slice diagonally.

2 Wash and dry lettuce thoroughly, and tear leaves into bite-size pieces. Arrange lettuce on individual serving plates and arrange the teardrop and cherry tomatoes and lamb slices on top. Place the oil, sugar, vinegar, mustard, and mint in a small screw-top jar and shake well.

3 Drain cheese and cut fingers about 1 cm (½ inch) thick and 4 cm (1½ inches) long. Pat dry. Add extra oil to pan, heat on moderate heat. Add cheese, cook for 2 minutes or until golden, turning

HOT MINTED POTATO SALAD

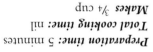

★ **Preparation time:** 30 minutes
Total cooking time: 20 minutes
Serves 8

1 kg (2 lb) tiny new potatoes
¼ cup chopped fresh parsley
5 large sprigs fresh mint
2 tablespoons chopped fresh dill
1 cup (8 fl oz) sour light cream
1 medium white onion, grated
2 tablespoons chopped chives
salt and ground pepper
2 tablespoons mayonnaise

1 Place potatoes and mint in large saucepan; add enough water to cover. Heat until boiling; reduce heat and cover. Gently simmer until potatoes are just tender, about 10–12 minutes. Drain well; discard the mint.

2 In a bowl, stir together sour cream, onion, mayonnaise, fresh herbs and seasonings to taste. Add to hot potatoes and mix well. Serve warm.

MINT SAMBAL

★ **Preparation time:** 5 minutes
Total cooking time: nil
Makes ¾ cup

1 cup fresh mint leaves
½ cup plain yoghurt
1 medium onion, peeled
1 green chilli (optional)

Chop mint and onion in a blender. Add enough yoghurt to form a smooth, creamy mixture. Add chopped chilli to taste. Serve with curries or barbecued chicken. This versatile sambal can also be used as a marinade for chicken pieces, with the addition of some chopped fresh ginger and ¼ teaspoon turmeric. Marinate overnight, then barbecue or grill (broil) the chicken.

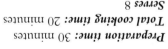

Opposite page: Vegetable couscous
Above: Minted lamb salad

Note: Haloumi is firm, salty white cheese from Cyprus. It is delicious grilled or fried, and does not melt and stick to the pan. Haloumi cheese is available from Greek or Cypriot delicatessens. You can substitute fingers of uncooked feta cheese.

occasionally. Drain on paper towels. Arrange warm cheese on top of salad, shake salad dressing again, drizzle over salad and serve immediately.

MOROCCAN CLASSICS

VEGETABLE COUSCOUS

✴ ✴ **Preparation time:** 40 minutes + overnight soaking
Total cooking time: 2 hours
Serves 6

2 cups dried chick peas (garbanzo beans)
105 g (3½ oz) small stringless beans, cut in 5 cm (2 inch) diagonal slices
2 zucchini (courgettes), unpeeled, cut in 1 cm (½ inch) rounds
1 medium, ripe tomato, cut into eight pieces
1 tablespoon chopped flat-leaf parsley
1 tablespoon chopped fresh coriander
ground pepper

Couscous
1 cup couscous (semolina)
¾ cup (6 fl oz) boiling water
2 teaspoons butter

⅓ cup (2½ fl oz) vegetable oil
1 onion, finely chopped
1 small stick cinnamon
200 g (6½ oz) eggplant (aubergine), cut into 2 cm (¾ inch) cubes
3 medium carrots, cut in 5 mm (¼ inch) rounds
3 medium new potatoes, cut into 1 cm (½ inch) cubes
155 g (5 oz) pumpkin, cut into 1 cm (½ inch) cubes
¼ teaspoon allspice
3 teaspoons harissa, or to taste
2 cups (16 fl oz) boiling water

1 Cover chick peas with cold water, soak overnight. Drain, wash well and cook in large pan, on low simmer for 1½ hours. Drain.

2 Heat oil in a large heavy-based pan and cook onion and cinnamon stick over low heat until onion softens. Add eggplant, carrot and potato. Cover and cook on low heat for 10 minutes, stirring occasionally with a wooden spoon.

3 Add pumpkin, allspice and harissa. Pour boiling water over mixture and add chick peas, beans and zucchini. Simmer, covered, for another 15 minutes. Stir in tomato just before serving. Garnish with the fresh parsley and coriander. Sprinkle with pepper.

4 **To prepare Couscous:** Pour boiling water on couscous in a bowl. Stir in the butter and allow to stand for about 10 minutes. Steam in a pan with a close-fitting lid on low heat for 5 minutes. Serve with vegetables.

HARISSA

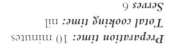

✴ **Preparation time:** 10 minutes
Total cooking time: nil
Serves 6

105 g (3½ oz) dried red chillies
6 cloves garlic, peeled
½ cup ground coriander
⅓ cup ground cumin
⅔ cup (5 fl oz) olive oil
⅓ cup salt

1 Wearing rubber or cotton gloves remove stems of chillies. Split chillies in half, remove seeds and soften chillies in hot water.

2 Process garlic, salt, ground coriander and cumin seeds, and drained red chillies to a paste, slowly adding olive oil until well combined. Serve.

---

suet or butter and sweet spices and soaked with brandy, rum or madeira; used as a filling for tarts and pies, traditionally served at Christmas.

Minestrone A hearty soup of Italian origin. Minestrone varies from region to region, but basically contains fresh vegetables and dried beans, simmered slowly in beef stock and thickened with pasta or rice.

Mint A herb with a strong fresh scent and flavour. There are many varieties. Most used in cooking is spearmint, which is made into jelly and sauce to accompany lamb, goes well with peas and boiled potatoes, is finely chopped as an ingredient in Middle Eastern salads and dips, and flavours drinks. Apple mint, lemon mint and pineapple mint are often added to fruit salads. Peppermint oil is used in the confectionery (candy) industry.

Miso A thick, salty, nutty-flavoured paste made from mashed and salted soya beans mixed with rice, barley or wheat grains, then fermented. Light or yellow miso, made with rice, is sweet and creamy

flavouring for soups and dressings; red miso, made with barley, has a strong, salty taste and is used in soups, casseroles and general cooking. When using miso in hot dishes, add just before serving and do not allow to boil.

Mixed Grill A dish consisting of several varieties of grilled (broiled) meat and vegetables, such as lamb chops, steak, sausages, kidney, liver, bacon, tomato, onion and mushroom.

Mixed Spice Also known as pudding spice, a traditional English blend of sweet spices, generally nutmeg, cinnamon, cloves and ginger, but sometimes also including allspice and coriander, used in rich fruit cakes, puddings and biscuits (cookies).

Mocha A strongly flavoured Arabian coffee bean, originally grown near the Red Sea and named after the Yemenite seaport from which it was exported. 'Mocha', in cooking, refers to food

---

B'STILLA (SHREDDED CHICKEN PIE)

★★
Preparation time: 45 minutes
Total cooking time: 2 hours 30 minutes
Serves 8 first course size

Filling
1.6 kg (3¼ lb) chicken
1 large onion, finely chopped
1 large bunch flat-leaf parsley, chopped
1 bunch fresh coriander, chopped
¼ teaspoon ground turmeric
¼ teaspoon ground saffron
2 tablespoons vegetable oil
1 teaspoon ground cinnamon

1 teaspoon ground ginger
1½ cups (12 fl oz) water
5 eggs, lightly beaten
1 cup icing (confectioners) sugar
ground cinnamon
ground pepper
500 g (1 lb) filo pastry
250 g (8 oz) unsalted (sweet) butter, melted
1 cup ground almonds
ground cinnamon, extra
1 cup icing (confectioners) sugar, extra
1 teaspoon ground cinnamon

1 Preheat oven to 180°C (350°F/Gas 4). Place chicken, onion, parsley, coriander, turmeric, saffron, oil, cinnamon, ginger and water in a roasting pan. Bake for 1½ hours. Remove chicken from pan and cool. Shred flesh, discard skin and bones.

2 Skim fat from liquid in pan and transfer liquid to medium pan. Heat until simmering, add eggs, sugar, cinnamon and pepper to taste. Cook until thick.

3 Preheat oven to 190°C (375°F/Gas 5). Grease a 20 cm (8 inch) pie dish. Place a sheet of filo in pie dish. Brush with melted butter. Place a sheet on top, brush with butter. Repeat layering and buttering with seven more sheets, sprinkling some

of the combined ground almonds, cinnamon and icing sugar on the last sheet of pastry.

4 Spread egg mixture and chicken filling on top, fold over pastry edges, brush again with butter. Butter and layer four more sheets, cut into a round, and cover pie. Butter more sheets of filo and form into rose shapes. Place on top of pie, brush with melted butter. Bake 30–45 minutes. Sprinkle with rest of combined almond mixture.

KHOBZ (WHOLEMEAL FLAT BREAD)

★★
Preparation time: 1 hour
Total cooking time: 12 minutes
Makes 16

2½ cups wholemeal plain (all-purpose) flour
½ teaspoon sweet ground paprika
1 teaspoon caster (superfine) sugar
1 teaspoon salt
7 g (¼ oz) sachet yeast
1¼ cups (10 fl oz) tepid water
⅓ cup cornmeal (maize flour)
1 tablespoon oil
1 egg, lightly beaten
2 tablespoons sesame seeds

1 Preheat oven to 180°C (350°F/Gas 4). Combine ½ cup flour, sugar, salt, yeast and water in bowl. Stand covered in a warm place until foaming.

2 Sift remaining flour, paprika and cornmeal into bowl, add oil. Stir in yeast mixture. Mix to firm dough. Knead until smooth. Stand covered in warm place 20 minutes.

3 Divide into sixteen, roll into balls, flatten into 10 cm (4 inch) rounds.

4 Place on greased baking tray. Brush with egg, sprinkle with sesame seeds. Stand, covered, until puffed. Bake 12 minutes.

MOROCCAN CLASSICS

OPPOSITE PAGE, ABOVE: B'STILLA (SHREDDED CHICKEN PIE); BELOW: KHOBZ (WHOLEMEAL BREAD). THIS PAGE, ABOVE: SAFFRON CHICKEN; RIGHT: PRESERVED LEMONS

SAFFRON CHICKEN

★ *Preparation time:* 30 minutes + overnight soaking
Total cooking time: 1¼ hours
Serves 6

12 chicken pieces	125 g (4 oz) chick peas
½ teaspoon ground sweet	(garbanzo beans),
paprika	soaked overnight
½ teaspoon ground	3 cups (24 fl oz) chicken
cumin	stock
ground pepper	⅓ cup finely chopped
90 g (3 oz) butter	flat-leaf parsley
750 g (1½ lb) red or	1 tablespoon fresh lemon
brown onions, sliced	thyme
¼ teaspoon ground	250 g (8 oz) rice, cooked
saffron or turmeric	lemon juice

1 Season chicken with paprika, cumin and pepper. Heat butter in a deep heavy-based pan, add onion and chicken, cook until chicken is golden.
2 Sprinkle chicken with saffron, add drained chick peas and chicken stock. Simmer gently, uncovered, for 1 hour or until chicken is tender.
3 Add chopped parsley and thyme to chicken just before serving. Spoon rice into heated serving dish. Place chicken pieces on top and pour over the sauce. Sprinkle with lemon juice and serve.

PRESERVED LEMONS

★ *Preparation time:* 1 hour, spread over 3 days
Preserving time: 3 weeks
Makes 16

16 thin-skinned lemons	water
coarse salt	lemon juice

1 Wash lemons well. Place in a large glass, stainless steel or plastic container. Cover with cold water and allow to soak for 3–5 days, changing water daily.
2 Drain lemons. Insert the point of a sharp knife into peel, 5 mm (¼ inch) from the bud end of each lemon and make four incisions lengthwise to within 5 mm (¼ inch) of the other end. Then cut through incisions so that lemons are cut completely through both sides, but are still held together at both ends.
3 Insert one-quarter teaspoon coarse salt into centre of each lemon, and arrange lemons in sterilised preserving jars and sprinkle with 1 tablespoon coarse salt. Add strained juice of 1 lemon to each jar and pour in enough boiling water to cover lemons. Store in a cool dry place for at least 3 weeks.
To use: Rinse well; serve with Middle Eastern fish or meat dishes. Use peel only.

(such as ice-cream or cakes) flavoured with coffee or a coffee and chocolate mixture.

Mock Cream A fresh cream substitute used as a filling for cakes and buns. It is generally made by beating together icing (confectioners) sugar and butter until stiff and fluffy.

Molasses A thick, dark syrup produced in the manufacture of cane sugar.

Monosodium Glutamate A sodium salt with little flavour of its own. It occurs naturally in many foods and is manufactured for use as an additive (mainly in Asian cooking) to enhance the natural flavour of a dish.

Monterey Jack A cheddar-style, cow's milk cheese, pale yellow in colour.

Mornay Sauce A béchamel sauce flavoured with gruyère or parmesan cheese and used to coat seafood, egg and vegetable dishes to be browned under the griller (broiler) or in the oven.

MUFFINS

Muffins are classified as quickbreads—quickly made and quick-ly eaten. They can be sweet or savoury, even high fibre and healthy. Serve them for breakfast or lunch, with morning coffee, and with soup for a light evening meal.

These muffins are surprisingly easy to make: you simply add the combined liquid ingredients to the combined dry ingredients, stirring together with a fork in a few quick strokes. The mixture will look rather lumpy but light, fine-textured muffins will be the result. Overmixing will result in a tough texture. Use deep American-style muffin tins, straight-sided, with a non-stick finish. Brush oil only over the base of tins; the un-oiled sides allow the batter to climb while baking and also help to form rounded tops.

Muffins are best eaten as soon as possible after they are made, and served warm with butter. If storage is necessary, they may be kept for up to 2 days in an airtight container and reheated in a low oven before serving. Muffins freeze well for up to 3 months and can be wrapped in foil and reheated in a moderate oven for 10–12 minutes.

BELOW, FROM TOP: BRAN, PUMPKIN AND PRUNE, CHOCOLATE, BERRY.

BASIC MUFFINS

Preheat oven to 200°C (400°F/Gas 6). Brush oil into base of 12 muffin tins. Sift 1¾ cups self-raising flour into a bowl. Add 2 tablespoons caster (superfine) sugar and 1 teaspoon baking powder. Mix together well. Melt 75 g (2½ oz) butter; place it in another bowl with 1 egg and ¾ cup (6 fl oz) milk. Beat the mixture well.

Add liquid all at once to dry ingredients and stir gently with a fork until mixture is just combined; the batter should look quite lumpy. Spoon the batter evenly into muffin tins, filling each two-thirds full. Bake for 20–25 minutes, until golden brown. Loosen muffins with a spatula and remove at once to a wire rack to cool. Serve warm.

VARIATIONS

■ BERRY: Add 1 cup of fresh blueberries or chopped strawberries to dry ingredients.

■ WHOLEMEAL: Use ¾ cup wholemeal flour and 1 cup white self-raising flour instead of all self-raising flour; add 1 teaspoon mixed spice and ½ cup sultanas to the dry ingredients.

■ SPICY APPLE: Add 1 teaspoon cinnamon, ¼ teaspoon nutmeg and 1 cup chopped, peeled and cored apples to the dry ingredients and increase the quantity of sugar to ⅓ cup.

■ CHEESE AND BACON: Cook 3 rashers of finely chopped bacon until they are quite crisp; drain. Add the bacon with 1 cup grated cheddar cheese to the dry ingredients. Reduce the quantity of sugar to 1 tablespoon.

■ ORANGE AND POPPYSEED: Add 3 teaspoons grated orange rind and 1–2 tablespoons poppy seeds to dry ingredients.

■ BANANA: Add 1 large mashed banana and ½ teaspoon mixed spice to the dry ingredients.

BRAN MUFFINS

Place 1 cup natural bran in a bowl, pour 1 cup boiling water over and leave to stand for 1 hour. Preheat oven to 200°C (400°F/Gas 6). Brush oil

into base of 12 muffin tins.

Add to bran mixture, 1 beaten egg, ⅓ cup soft brown sugar and 2 tablespoons vegetable oil. Mix well. Sift 1 cup plain (all-purpose) flour into another bowl. Add ⅓ cup milk powder, 1½ teaspoons baking powder and 1½ teaspoons bicarbonate of soda (baking soda). Mix together well. Add the bran mixture all at once; stir with a fork until just combined. Spoon mixture into muffin tins, filling each of them two-thirds full. Bake 15-20 minutes or until the muffins are golden.

VARIATIONS

■ CARROT AND PINEAPPLE: Add ½ cup shredded carrot, ½ cup well-drained canned unsweetened crushed pineapple and ½ teaspoon ground ginger at the same time as the egg is added.

■ PUMPKIN AND PRUNE: Add 1 cup cooked mashed pumpkin and ¾ cup chopped pitted prunes at the same time as the egg is added; increase brown sugar to ½ cup.

CHOCOLATE MUFFINS

Preheat the oven to 180°C (350°F/Gas 4). Brush oil into the base of 15 muffin tins.

In a mixing bowl, combine 2 cups self-rising flour, ½ cup caster (superfine) sugar, 125 g (4 oz) grated milk chocolate, 2 eggs, 2 teaspoons vanilla essence, 75 g (2 ½ oz) unsalted butter, melted, and 1 cup sour cream. Using electric beaters, beat for 1 minute on low speed, increase speed to high and beat for 1 minute more.

Spoon half the mixture into tins, place 1 square of good quality dark chocolate in centre of each muffin; add remaining mixture. Press choc bits all over the tops of the muffins. Bake for 15 minutes or until the muffins are puffed and lightly browned.

When you serve chocolate muffins warm, the chocolate centre will be runny and melted. You can, if you prefer, let them cool on a wire rack and eat them after the chocolate has had sufficient time to harden. In any case, these muffins do not keep their fresh flavour for long and should be eaten on the day they are baked.

ABOVE, FRONT ROW, LEFT TO RIGHT: Spicy Apple, Berry. SECOND ROW: Orange and Poppyseed, Berry. THIRD ROW: Berry, Chocolate, Berry. Bran.

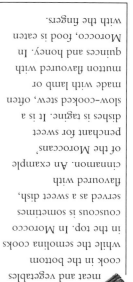

Moroccan Food

Unlike its north African neighbours Moroccan food is spiced with subtlety. Lemon is a favourite flavour and preserved lemon peel is used in many of its most famous dishes.

Cinnamon, coriander and orange-flower water are also common. The exception to this subtle flavouring is harissa, a fiery condiment used in Algeria and Tunisia as well. Its main ingredients are chillies, garlic and coriander and it is served with couscous and soups. Couscous is probably the most famous dish from north Africa. It is made from semolina and steamed over a rich stew of meat and vegetables, traditionally in a couscousier, a metal pan topped with a steamer. The meat and vegetables cook in the bottom while the semolina cooks in the top. In Morocco couscous is sometimes served as a sweet dish, flavoured with cinnamon. An example of the Moroccans' penchant for sweet dishes is tagine. It is a slow-cooked stew, often made with lamb or mutton flavoured with quinces and honey. In Morocco, food is eaten with the fingers.

MUFFINS

ENGLISH MUFFINS

★★ **Preparation time:** 20 minutes +
1 hour 40 minutes standing
Total cooking time: 16 minutes
Makes 15

7 g (¼ oz) sachet dried
4 cups plain (all-purpose)
flour
½ teaspoon sugar
yeast
1 teaspoon plain
(all-purpose) flour
¼ cup (2 fl oz) warm
water
1⅓ cups (10½ fl oz)
lukewarm milk
1 teaspoon salt
1 egg, lightly beaten
flour, extra
40 g (1⅓ oz) butter,
melted

1 Lightly dust two 32 x 28 cm (13 x 11 inch) oven trays with flour. Combine yeast, sugar, flour and water in a small bowl and blend until smooth. Stand, covered with plastic wrap, in a warm place for 10 minutes or until mixture is foamy.

2 Sift extra flour and salt into a large bowl. Make a well in centre, add milk, egg, butter and yeast mixture. Using a knife, mix to a soft dough. Turn dough onto lightly floured surface, knead for 2 minutes or until smooth. Shape dough into ball, place in large, lightly oiled bowl. Leave, covered with plastic wrap, in a warm place for 1½ hours or until dough is well risen.

3 Preheat oven to moderately hot 210°C (415°F/Gas 6–7). Knead dough again for 2 minutes or until smooth. Roll dough to 1 cm (½ inch) thickness. Cut into rounds with an 8 cm (3 inch) cutter. Place rounds on prepared oven trays. Leave, covered with plastic wrap, in warm place for 10 minutes. Bake muffins for 8 minutes, turn muffins over and bake for another 8 minutes.

Note: Muffins are easy and quick to make. They can be served for breakfast or lunch or with morning coffee or tea. They are best eaten on the day they are made. Serve warm with butter. Muffins may be frozen for up to three months.

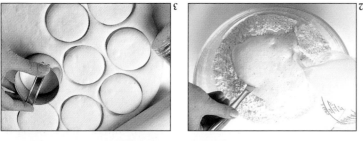

MUSHROOMS

SEASONED MUSHROOM CAPS

Preparation time: 15 minutes
Total cooking time: 20 minutes
Makes 16

16 medium mushroom caps
2 tablespoons olive oil
2 rashers bacon, finely chopped
1/2 cup soft fresh breadcrumbs
1 clove garlic, crushed

2 spring onions (scallions), finely chopped
1/4 cup grated parmesan cheese
2 tablespoons finely chopped flat-leaf parsley
1 egg, lightly beaten

1 Preheat oven to hot 240°C (475°F/Gas 9). Line a 32 x 28 cm (13 x 11 inch) oven tray with foil; grease foil. Remove mushroom stems from caps. Arrange caps on tray; chop the stems finely.

2 Heat oil in large frying pan; add bacon. Cook over medium heat for 3 minutes, stirring occasionally. Add chopped mushroom stems to pan with the bacon. Cook over high heat for 2 minutes. Remove pan from heat.

3 Transfer the mixture to a medium bowl. Add breadcrumbs, garlic, onion, cheese, parsley and egg; using wooden spoon, stir until combined.

4 Divide bacon and mushroom mixture evenly into 16 portions. Press mixture into each cap. Bake for 12 minutes or until lightly golden.

OPPOSITE PAGE: ENGLISH MUFFINS.
ABOVE: SEASONED MUSHROOM CAPS

MUSHROOMS PROVENCAL

Preparation time: 45 minutes
Total cooking time: 50 minutes
Serves 4–6

500 g (1 lb) mushrooms
1 medium leek
60 g (2 oz) butter
1 clove garlic, crushed
juice and grated rind of
1 lemon
pepper

1/2 cup chopped parsley
freshly grated nutmeg
1 1/2 cups soft wholemeal breadcrumbs
2 tablespoons olive oil
1 garlic clove

1 Wipe over mushrooms and cut into slices. Trim leek and wash well; cut into fine shreds. Preheat oven to 200°C (400°F/Gas 6), and grease a 20 cm (8 inch) ovenproof dish.

2 Melt butter in a heavy based pan, add leek and cook, stirring, for 5 minutes over a low heat. Add sliced mushrooms and toss to coat in leek and butter mixture. Cover and cook 10 minutes. Remove lid, add crushed garlic and lemon rind and cook until most of the juices have evaporated, about 15–20 minutes.

3 Pour lemon juice over, reduce and season with pepper, parsley and nutmeg. Fold through 1/2 cup of the breadcrumbs. Spoon into prepared casserole dish.

4 Heat oil in pan; add whole garlic and cook until garlic browns. Remove and discard garlic. Add remaining breadcrumbs to oil, toss to coat crumbs.

5 Sprinkle crumbs over mushroom mixture. Bake for about 20 minutes or until mixture has heated through and crumb topping is crisp.

Mortadella A large, lightly smoked sausage made of pork or mixtures of either pork and beef or veal and ham, mixed with coarsely diced pork fat, seasoned, flavoured with parsley and studded with green olives and pistachio nuts. It is served, thinly sliced, as an hors d'oeuvre, salad meat or sandwich filling.

Moussaka A baked dish consisting of eggplant (aubergine), minced (ground) lamb or beef and a topping of cheese sauce. It is popular throughout the Middle East and, despite its Arabic name, most likely originated in Greece.

Mousse A rich, light sweet or savoury dish that derives its smooth, foamy texture from whisked egg white, whipped cream, or both. It may be served hot or cold. The name comes from the French word for froth or foam.

Mousseline A mousse-like savoury dish in which meat, seafood or poultry is folded into a beaten cream and egg white mixture and cooked in small moulds.

Mozzarella A rindless, unripened curd cheese, with a soft, plastic texture and a mild, slightly sweet, milky

MUSHROOMS WITH GARLIC AND RED PEPPER (CAPSICUM) SAUCES

★★ **Preparation time:** 30 minutes +
1 hour refrigeration
Total cooking time: 2 minutes each
batch
Serves 8

700 g (1 lb 6 oz) button
   mushrooms
1/3 cup plain (all-purpose)
   flour
3 eggs
1 cup dry breadcrumbs
1 small red pepper
   (capsicum)
1 cup (8 fl oz) olive oil
2 egg yolks

1 teaspoon Dijon
   mustard
1 tablespoon lemon juice
1 small clove garlic, crushed
2 tablespoons plain
   yoghurt
2 teaspoons finely
   chopped fresh parsley
olive oil for deep-frying,
   extra

1 Wipe mushrooms with a damp cloth to remove any grit. Place flour in a large plastic bag, add mushrooms and shake until they are evenly coated in flour. Place eggs in a medium bowl and beat lightly. Dust excess flour from mushrooms. Divide mushrooms in half and coat first half well with egg. Repeat with second half.

2 Place dry breadcrumbs in a large plastic bag. Add half the egg-coated mushrooms; shake to coat mushrooms thoroughly in breadcrumbs. Place crumbed mushrooms in a large bowl. Repeat with remaining mushrooms. Cover and refrigerate for 1 hour.

3 Brush red pepper with a little of the oil. Grill (broil) pepper until skin is black, then wrap in damp tea-towel until cool. Rub off skin and place pepper in food processor or blender. Process to a smooth paste. Place egg yolks, mustard and half the lemon juice in a medium mixing bowl. Using electric beaters, beat for 1 minute. Add oil, about a teaspoon at a time, beating constantly until mixture is thick and creamy. Increase addition of oil as mayonnaise thickens. Continue beating until all oil is added; add remaining lemon juice. Divide mayonnaise between two bowls. Into one stir the garlic, yoghurt and parsley; stir pepper puree into the other half.

4 Heat the extra olive oil in a medium heavy-based pan. Gently lower batches of mushrooms into moderately hot oil. Cook over medium-high heat for 1 minute or until golden brown. Remove with a slotted spoon and drain on paper towels. To serve, arrange the mushrooms on individual serving plates. Serve the sauces in separate bowls.

ABOVE: *MUSHROOMS WITH GARLIC AND RED PEPPER SAUCES.* OPPOSITE PAGE: *CHINESE VEGETABLES WITH MUSHROOMS AND OYSTER SAUCE*

Muesli A breakfast food of mixed raw cereals,
bran, wheat germ, nuts and dried fruit eaten with milk or yoghurt.

Muffin Also known as American muffin, a light, sweet, soft bread baked in small, deep, round moulds. Basic muffins are made from a batter of egg, milk, flour and sugar. Sweet or savoury flavourings can be added.

Mulberry A juicy berry, similar in appearance to a blackberry. Mulberries may be eaten fresh dusted with sugar and accompanied by cream.

M taste. It was originally made from buffalo milk, but is now produced from cow's milk; aged for two or three days only, it should be used within a few days of purchase. Mozzarella is primarily a cooking cheese, used in pizza and pasta dishes and melted as a topping.

MUSHROOMS

CHINESE VEGETABLES WITH MUSHROOMS AND OYSTER SAUCE

★ **Preparation time:** 20 minutes
Total cooking time: 8 minutes
Serves 4

8 dried Chinese mushrooms
2 tablespoons vegetable oil
1 bunch Chinese green vegetables (bok choy, choy sum, gai lan)
2 tablespoons oyster sauce

1 Soak mushrooms in hot water. Thoroughly wash the green vegetables and drain well. Cut off thick stalks as these require longer cooking.
2 Trim stems from mushrooms, squeeze water from caps. Simmer in lightly salted water for 5 minutes; drain.
3 Bring a pan of water to the boil and plunge the vegetable stems in the water; cook for 1–2 minutes. Remove stems, drain. Briefly blanch the leafy parts and drain well.
4 Heat oil in a frying pan. Add well-drained vegetables and mushrooms and toss over moderate heat until well coated. Serve dressed with the oyster sauce.

MARINATED MUSHROOMS

★ **Preparation time:** 5 minutes
Total cooking time: 8 minutes
Serves 4

375 g (12 oz) button mushrooms
1 bay leaf
1 tablespoon chopped fresh tarragon
freshly ground black pepper
1 clove garlic, crushed
1 tablespoon lemon juice
1/4 cup (2 fl oz) olive oil
1 cup (8 fl oz) dry white wine or apple juice
1 tablespoon chopped fresh parsley

1 Wipe mushrooms with a damp cloth and trim stalks level with caps. Heat oil in a medium pan, add garlic and mushrooms and toss over high heat until mushrooms have absorbed oil.
2 Add lemon juice, white wine, bay leaf, tarragon and pepper. Bring mixture to the boil and simmer for 5 minutes. Allow mushrooms to cool in liquid. Remove bay leaf. Sprinkle mushrooms with chopped parsley.
3 Drain mushrooms and serve on cocktail sticks as a first course or serve as a salad.

Note: Two skinned and chopped tomatoes can be added at the same time as the wine if desired.

MUSHROOM SOUP

★ **Preparation time:** 15 minutes
Total cooking time: 20 minutes
Serves 4

500 g (1 lb) field mushrooms (open cap)
1 litre (4 cups) hot chicken stock
90 g (3 oz) butter
1 bay leaf
1 large onion, chopped
salt
1 clove garlic, crushed
2 tablespoons plain (all-purpose) flour
freshly ground black pepper
1/2 cup (4 fl oz) cream

1 Wipe mushrooms with a damp cloth and chop caps and stems. Melt butter in a large pan and add onion and garlic. Cook until onion is soft but not brown, add mushrooms and cook over high heat for 3 minutes while stirring.
2 Sprinkle flour over mushrooms, mix to combine, then stir in hot stock. Bring to the boil, add bay leaf and simmer for 10 minutes. Remove bay leaf and cool soup slightly.
3 Place soup in a food processor or blender and blend until smooth. (It may be necessary to do this in two batches.)
4 Return soup to rinsed pan, season with salt and pepper, heat until boiling. Stir in cream, serve.

can be pureed for sorbets and ice-cream, stewed as a pie filling or made into jam. They are not usually commercially available (the berries are easily crushed), but the tree is common in gardens and bears a copious crop each summer.

Mulligatawny
A spicy, soup-like dish of boiled rice topped with peppery, curry-flavoured chicken or meat broth. The dish dates from the days of the British Raj in India.

Münster A soft cow's milk cheese with a texture that varies from smooth and waxy to dry and crumbly. It has a distinctive pungent taste and aroma.

Mushroom Edible fungus found in a variety of shapes and sizes and ranging in taste from mild and nutty to strong and meaty. They may be eaten raw, in salads, or cooked. The most widely cultivated is the common mushroom with an umbrella-shaped cap that opens out as the mushroom grows. The youngest are sold as button mushrooms or champignons; next in size are cups (popular for stuffing); largest and with the most developed flavour are flats. The cep is a round-capped and

MUSSELS

TOMATO GARLIC MUSSELS

Preparation time: 15 minutes
Total cooking time: 15 minutes
Serves 2–3

18 large live mussels
30 g (1 oz) butter
3 cloves garlic, crushed
3 large ripe tomatoes, chopped
1 tablespoon worcestershire sauce
2 tablespoons tomato paste
1/4 cup (2 fl oz) apple juice

1 Pick over mussels; discard those with damaged shells. Remove beards from mussels; wash away any grit. Prise open shells with small knife. Meat will be attached to one half-shell; discard other half.
2 Melt butter in large pan. Add garlic; cook 1 minute or until golden. Add tomato, worcestershire sauce, tomato paste and apple juice; stir over medium heat 2 minutes. Bring to boil, reduce heat. Simmer, uncovered, 5 minutes.
3 Add mussels, cover and simmer 5 minutes or until mussels are tender.

GRILLED MUSSELS

Preparation time: 10 minutes
Total cooking time: 5–10 minutes
Serves 2–4

500 g (1 lb) mussels in shell
1 clove garlic, crushed
1 small red chilli, finely chopped
2 tablespoons lemon juice

1 Place mussels in pan of simmering water. Remove mussels as shells open; discard any that do not open.
2 Open out mussels and loosen from shells using scissors. Return mussels to half shells; discard other shells.
3 Combine lemon juice, garlic and chilli; spoon over mussels. Place on grill tray and grill under medium heat until heated through. Sprinkle mussels with parsley to serve.

ABOUT MUSSELS

■ To remove all grit from mussels, immerse in salted water with a sprinkling of oatmeal or flour for at least 1 hour. The live mussels will digest the oatmeal, become plumper and expel grit.

stalked mushroom valued for its earthy flavour. The chanterelle or girolle, an apricot-coloured, firm-fleshed, trumpet-shaped mushroom has a meaty flavour. The morel has a pointed, spongy, golden brown cap with a meaty flavour. Asian mushroom varieties include the matsutake or pine mushroom, which has a dark brown cap and a thick meaty stem and, lightly grilled, is considered a great delicacy in Japan. Also used in Japanese cooking is the enokitake or enoki, a tiny mushroom with a round cap atop a slender stem. Mild-flavoured and crisp in texture, the enokitake is used in soups and stews. The large floppy cap of the shiitake mushroom, usually sold dried, is used in Chinese and Japanese cooking.

Mussel A mollusc with a smooth almond-shaped shell. Like oysters, mussels are filter feeders, and so are subject to contamination. They should not be collected

MUSTARDS

CHICKEN DIJON

Preparation time: 10 minutes
Total cooking time: 20 minutes
Serves 6

6 single chicken breast fillets
3/4 cup whole egg mayonnaise
1/4 cup Dijon mustard
1/4 cup cream

1 Preheat oven to moderate 180°C (350°F/Gas 4). Lay a large piece of aluminium foil over an oven tray. Brush foil with melted butter or oil. Place chicken breasts side-by-side on prepared tray.

2 Combine mayonnaise, mustard and cream in small mixing bowl; stir until well combined.

3 Spoon the mayonnaise mixture over each chicken fillet.

4 Cover chicken with another large sheet of foil. Fold foil sheets together around edges until well sealed. Bake for 20 minutes or until chicken is tender. The sauce may separate a little. Disguise this by garnishing with a large sprig of fresh herbs.

HERB MUSTARD

Place 1/4 cup of white mustard seeds and 1 cup blanched almonds in a food processor and process until well ground. In a medium bowl, combine 1 cup (8 fl oz) of oil, 1 cup (8 fl oz) of white vinegar and 1/4 cup (2 fl oz) of sherry with 1 tablespoon each of chopped fresh chives, parsley and dill. Gradually pour through processor chute with the motor running. Process until mixture is thick and creamy. Spoon into sterilised jars. Seal and label the jars and store in a cool place for up to 4 weeks. This recipe makes about 2 cups of Herb Mustard.

HOT GRAIN MUSTARD

In a medium-sized heatproof bowl, combine 1/2 cup of black mustard seeds, 1/2 cup of yellow mustard seeds, 1 teaspoon of lightly crushed black peppercorns, 1 cup (8 fl oz) of oil, 1 cup (8 fl oz) of white vinegar, and 2 teaspoons chopped fresh herbs of your choice. When you have mixed the ingredients well, place the bowl over a pan of simmering water. Gradually whisk in 2 beaten egg yolks and continue whisking until mixture is thick and creamy. Remove bowl from heat. When mixture has cooled, spoon it into sterilised jars. Seal and label the jars and store in a cool place for up to two weeks. This recipe makes about 3 cups of Hot Grain Mustard.

DEVIL SAUCE

In a small bowl, mix together 1 teaspoon each of Dijon mustard, anchovy sauce, worcestershire sauce, white wine vinegar and sugar. Stir in 1 cup (8 fl oz) of whipped cream and serve with cold chicken.

M from areas where pollution is suspected. Mussels are available live in the shell or canned (cooked, smoked or in various sauces).

Mustard A pungently flavoured spice derived from the seeds of three members of the cabbage family and usually prepared as a condiment. White mustard, the mildest in flavour, is used in American mustards; brown and black mustard have more pungent seeds than white mustard. Black mustard seeds are used in Indian cooking and in pickles and chutneys. Brown and black mustard seeds (alone or in combination) are ground into mustard powder (used to make English mustard) or made into French-style mustards. Prepared mustard is made by macerating mustard seeds in a liquid (grape juice, wine, vinegar or water) and then pounding them to a paste. It is used as an accompaniment to meats, poultry and fish and as a flavouring in vinaigrettes, sauces and some hot dishes.

Mutton The meat of a mature sheep, best suited to moist cooking.

OPPOSITE PAGE: TOMATO GARLIC MUSSELS.

ABOVE: CHICKEN DIJON.

N

Naan A tear-shaped, flat leavened Indian bread, traditionally baked plastered onto the inside walls of the tandoor, an urn-shaped clay oven.

Nam Pla See Nuoc Mam.

Napoleon A small pastry consisting of three layers of puff pastry filled with crème pâtissière or sweetened whipped cream, and topped with glacé icing decorated with lines of melted chocolate.

Nashi A golden-green pear the shape and size of an apple. The translucent flesh is crisp, juicy and sweet and the fruit may be eaten on its own or served with cheese. The nashi is also known as Asian pear, apple pear and Chinese pear. It is in season in autumn and early winter.

Nasi Goreng An Indonesian dish consisting of fried rice garnished with chillies, thinly sliced meat, fried onions and slices of omelette.

NOODLES

BEEF SOUP WITH RICE NOODLES

★★

Preparation time: 30 minutes + 1 hour marinating
Total cooking time: 1 hour
Serves 4

375 g (12 oz) fillet (tenderloin) steak
1 small, thin-skinned cucumber
1.5 litres (6 cups) beef stock
2 tablespoons soft brown sugar, extra
2 tablespoons fish sauce (nuoc mam)
1 cup fresh bean sprouts
2 lettuce leaves, cut in small pieces
6 tablespoons finely chopped fresh mint leaves
½ cup roasted peanuts, finely chopped

2 teaspoons soy sauce
¼ cup (2 fl oz) coconut milk
1 tablespoon crunchy peanut butter
1 tablespoon soft brown sugar or palm sugar
2 teaspoons sambal oelek or 1 small red chilli, finely chopped
1 teaspoon oil
125 g (4 oz) rice vermicelli

1 Trim meat of any fat and sinew. Slice meat across grain evenly into thin slices. Combine with soy sauce, coconut milk, peanut butter, sugar and sambal oelek. Refrigerate, covered, for 1 hour.

2 Heat oil in pan. Brown meat in small batches over high heat for 3 minutes. Remove from heat.

3 Cut cucumber in quarters lengthways and then into thin slices. Heat stock to boiling point. When boiling, add extra sugar and fish sauce.

4 Remove tails from bean sprouts. Place a tablespoon cucumber slices in each bowl. Divide sprouts, lettuce and mint leaves evenly between bowls. Place some vermicelli and a ladle of stock in each bowl, top with slices of cooked beef. Sprinkle with peanuts, serve immediately.

NOODLES WITH PRAWNS (SHRIMPS) AND PORK

★★

Preparation time: 20 minutes
Total cooking time: 10 minutes
Serves 4

10 large cooked prawns (shrimps)
200 g (6½ oz) roast or Chinese barbecued pork
500 g (1 lb) fresh, thick noodles
¼ cup (2 fl oz) peanut oil
2 teaspoons finely chopped garlic
125 g (4 oz) fresh bean sprouts, tails removed
3 spring onions (scallions), finely sliced
¼ cup chopped fresh coriander, for garnish

1 tablespoon commercial chilli and ginger sauce, optional
1 tablespoon white vinegar
¼ cup (2 fl oz) chicken stock
1 tablespoon black bean sauce
1 tablespoon soy sauce

1 Peel and devein prawns. Cut the pork evenly into thin slices. Cook the noodles in a large pan of rapidly boiling water until just tender; drain and set aside.

2 Heat the oil in a wok or heavy-based frying pan, swirling gently to coat base and side. Add the garlic and cook, stirring, until it turns pale gold. Add the prawns and pork, stir for 1 minute. Add noodles to wok with black bean sauce, soy sauce, chilli and ginger sauce, vinegar and chicken stock. Stir-fry over high heat until the mixture has heated through and the sauce has been absorbed.

3 Add bean sprouts and spring onion and cook for 1 minute. Serve garnished with coriander.

Note: Chinese barbecued pork can be purchased from specialty Chinese stores.

ABOVE: BEEF SOUP WITH RICE NOODLES.
OPPOSITE PAGE: CRISP-FRIED THAI NOODLES

CRISP-FRIED THAI NOODLES

Preparation time: 30 minutes
Total cooking time: 20 minutes
Serves 6 as a first course

★★

125 g (4 oz) rice vermicelli
oil for deep-frying
250 g (8 oz) pork mince
8 medium green (uncooked) prawns (shrimps), peeled and deveined
125 g (4 oz) fresh bean sprouts, tails removed
2 eggs, lightly beaten
1 red chilli, seeded and finely chopped
1 teaspoon chopped garlic
1 tablespoon fish sauce (nuoc mam)
2 tablespoons fresh coriander leaves
2 tablespoons caster (superfine) sugar
2 tablespoons white vinegar

1 Heat oil in a wok. Use tongs to lower small batches of vermicelli into the oil—the strands will instantly swell. Deep-fry each batch of noodles until golden, turning to colour both sides. Drain on paper towel. Cool oil to room temperature.

2 Pour off all but 2 tablespoons oil from wok. Heat oil, add garlic and stir until golden. Add the mince. Cook over high heat for 3 minutes until meat is well browned and almost all of the liquid has evaporated. Add the prawns, stirring for another 30 seconds. Add sugar, vinegar, fish sauce and chilli. Bring to boil, stirring; add the eggs. Cook, stirring, until eggs are set.

3 Add the bean sprouts and noodles, tossing them thoroughly to combine. Scatter with coriander leaves. Serve immediately.

NOODLE SALAD

Preparation time: 10 minutes + 10 minutes standing + refrigeration
Total cooking time: 20 minutes
Serves 4

250 g (8 oz) fresh thick egg noodles
2 red peppers (capsicums), seeded, cut into quarters
2 green peppers (capsicums), seeded, cut into quarters
1 large carrot, cut into fine strips, 6 cm (2 1/2 inches) long
2 tablespoons lemon juice
1/3 cup (2 1/2 fl oz) olive oil
1 tablespoon finely chopped fresh mint
3 spring onions (scallions), chopped

1 Cook noodles in a large pan of boiling water until just tender; drain and cool.

2 Place peppers on foil-lined oven tray, skin side up. Grill at medium heat for 20 minutes or until skins blister and burn. Remove from grill, cover with clean damp tea-towel and stand 10 minutes.

3 Carefully remove skin from peppers. Cut flesh into 1 cm (1/2 inch) wide strips. Place in bowl with noodles, spring onions and carrot; toss.

4 Whisk oil, lemon and mint in small jug. Pour over salad, mix well. Cover, refrigerate several hours or overnight. Toss again just before serving.

Note: Do not attempt to speed things up by deep-frying too many of the noodles at a time—they will not crisp. If still puffed and white, they will not stay crisp when returned to the sauce.

Navarin A French term for a rich stew of lamb or mutton cooked with root vegetables, usually small onions and potatoes. It can also be the name given to a ragout garnished with turnips.

Nectarine A round, shiny, reddish-skinned fruit with fragrant juicy flesh surrounding a large stone: it is a variety of peach. Nectarines can be eaten fresh, added to fruit salads, stewed or baked; they are in season in late summer.

Nesselrode Pudding A chilled custard dessert made from chestnut purée, egg yolk, cream and sometimes glacé (candied) fruit.

Neufchâtel Cheese A fresh unripened, soft, white cow's milk cheese made from whole or partly skimmed milk. In taste and appearance it is similar to cream cheese, but is softer in texture, more moist and has a lower fat content. Neufchâtel can be eaten fresh with fruit or used for cheesecakes, mousses, icings and cake toppings.

OPPOSITE PAGE: SATAY LAMB WITH NOODLES

ABOVE: SEAFOOD NOODLE HOT POT; RIGHT: Crisp FRIED NOODLES AND CHILLI VEGETABLES.

SEAFOOD NOODLE HOT POT

Preparation time: 15 minutes
Total cooking time: 14 minutes
Serves 4–6

2 tablespoons vegetable oil
4 cm (1 1/2 inch) piece fresh ginger, peeled and grated
4 spring onions (scallions), trimmed and sliced
1/2 small cabbage, shredded
2 litres (8 cups) water or fish stock
1/4 cup (2 fl oz) soy sauce
2 tablespoons dry sherry
1 teaspoon sesame oil
200 g (6 1/2 oz) flat rice noodles
250 g (8 oz) bottled oysters, drained
250 g (8 oz) scallops
250 g (8 oz) green (uncooked) prawns (shrimps), peeled and deveined, tail intact
shredded green tops of spring onion (scallion), for garnish

1 Heat the oil in a large pan. Add the ginger, spring onion and cabbage; cook gently until the cabbage is just soft.
2 Add the water, soy sauce, sherry and sesame oil; bring to the boil, add noodles and cook for 8 minutes. Reduce to a simmer, add oysters, scallops and prawns and cook for 3–4 minutes or until the prawns are just cooked.
3 Place into a serving bowl, top with shredded spring onion and serve.

CRISP FRIED NOODLES AND CHILLI VEGETABLES

Preparation time: 25 minutes
Total cooking time: 10 minutes
Serves 4–6

100 g (3 1/2 oz) packet rice vermicelli
oil, for deep-frying
1 teaspoon oil
2 teaspoons grated fresh ginger
1 tablespoon finely chopped coriander
1 clove garlic, finely diced
1 green pepper (capsicum), cut into strips
1 red pepper (capsicum), cut into strips
410 g (13 oz) can baby corn, drained
410 g (13 oz) can straw mushrooms, drained
1/2 cup (4 fl oz) soy sauce
1/4 cup (2 fl oz) malt vinegar
2 teaspoons brown sugar
1 teaspoon preserved chopped chilli
1 onion, cut into thin wedges
1 large carrot, cut into thin strips
1/2 cup coriander leaves, for garnish

1 Deep-fry rice vermicelli in hot oil. Drain on paper towel. Place on a large serving plate and keep warm.
2 Heat teaspoon of oil in a large pan. Add ginger, coriander and garlic and cook for 2 minutes. Add onion, green and red pepper, and carrot. Stir-fry for 3 minutes. Add corn, mushrooms, combined soy sauce, vinegar, brown sugar and chilli. Stir and cook over high heat for 3 minutes.
3 Spoon vegetables over the noodles and pour over any remaining sauce. Garnish with coriander leaves and serve.

Newburg Shellfish, usually lobster, sautéed and served with a rich sauce of cream, sherry and egg yolk.

Niçoise, à la A French term for dishes which have tomato, garlic, black olives, anchovy and olive oil in the sauce. This style of cooking originated around Nice, in southern France.

Noisette A French term for dishes flavoured with or made of hazelnuts. It is also used to describe a thick slice from a boned loin of lamb, rolled and secured with a thin band of fat, like a tournedos.

Noisette Butter A sauce made by slowly heating butter until foaming and nut-brown, adding lemon juice, then immediately pouring over fish, brains, eggs or cooked vegetables.

Noodle A dough of flour and water (sometimes made with egg yolk or whole egg) cut into long, ribbon-like strips and fried or boiled. Noodles originated in Asia and also feature in the cooking of the Mediterranean, particularly Italy, and northern Europe. The name comes from the German *Nudel*.

SATAY LAMB WITH NOODLES

Serves 4

Preparation time: 15 minutes
Total cooking time: 10 minutes

750 g (1½ lb) lamb fillets
½ cup (4 fl oz) coconut milk
¼ teaspoon garam masala
105 g (3½ oz) dried egg noodles
3 teaspoons sesame oil
2 spring onions (scallions), finely chopped

¼ cup (2 fl oz) peanut oil
3 large onions, cut in thin wedges
⅓ cup crunchy peanut butter
2 tablespoons hoisin sauce

1 Trim lamb of any fat and sinew. Slice meat across grain evenly into thin slices. Heat 1 tablespoon of oil in wok or heavy-based frying pan, swirling to coat base and side. Add onion, stir-fry over high heat for 5 minutes. Remove from wok; keep warm.

2 Heat remaining oil in wok, swirling to coat base and side. Cook meat quickly in small batches over high heat until browned but not cooked through. Remove and drain on paper towel.

3 Combine peanut butter, hoisin sauce, coconut milk and garam masala in a small bowl. Add to wok, stir over medium heat until mixture boils. Return meat and onion to wok, stir until coated with sauce and just heated through.

4 Cook noodles in large pan of boiling water until just tender; drain. Toss with sesame oil and spring onion. Serve topped with satay lamb.

EGG NOODLES WITH CHICKEN AND HAM

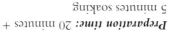

Preparation time: 20 minutes + 5 minutes soaking
Total cooking time: 5 minutes

Serves 4–6

315 g (10 oz) egg noodles, soaked in water 5 minutes
oil, for deep-frying
105 g (3½ oz) ham from the bone, cut into thin strips
¾ cup (4 fl oz) chicken stock
2 tablespoons dry sherry
1 tablespoon soy sauce

½ cooked chicken, meat removed and cut into thin strips
1 tablespoon chopped ginger
2 spring onions (scallions), chopped
315 g (10 oz) can baby corn, drained

1 Drain noodles well, dry between sheets of paper towel. Deep-fry in oil until just crisp. Drain and place onto large serving plate. Keep warm. Remove all but 2 teaspoons of oil from pan.

2 Add ginger and spring onions to pan, cook for 2 minutes. Add corn, chicken and ham. Stir in stock, sherry and soy sauce, cook for 3–4 minutes.

3 Spoon chicken and ham mixture over noodles, top with sauce. Serve.

MARINATED BEEF AND NOODLE SALAD

Preparation time: 20 minutes + 2 hours marinating
Total cooking time: 5 minutes

Serves 4–6

Salad
410 g (13 oz) rare roast beef, cut into thin strips
315 g (10 oz) fresh wheat noodles
1 cup mint leaves, roughly chopped
1 cup coriander, roughly chopped
1 butterhead (cabbage) lettuce, torn into pieces
1 cucumber, peeled, seeded and sliced
1 red onion, sliced

Marinade
¼ cup (2 fl oz) lemon juice
¼ cup (2 fl oz) fish sauce (nuoc mam)
2 tablespoons soy sauce
3 teaspoons brown sugar
2 teaspoons sambal oelek (bottled red chillies)

1 Combine marinade ingredients; pour over beef, cover and marinate for 2 hours.

2 Cook noodles in boiling water until just tender; drain. While still hot add mint and coriander, toss.

3 Place lettuce, cucumber and onion on serving plate, add noodles. Arrange meat slices on top and pour over remaining marinade.

Nougat A chewy confectionery (candy) traditionally made of honey, sugar, egg white and nuts.

Nouvelle Cuisine A style of cooking which emphasises fresh, natural ingredients and flavours, and imaginative presentation; sauces are light and based on reduced stocks and purees rather than fats and flour.

Nuoc Mam Also called nam pla, literally 'fish water', a clear, amber-coloured seasoning sauce with a pungent, salty flavour. It is used in Vietnamese and Thai cooking to bring out the flavour in other foods. Vietnamese nuoc mam is darker in colour and has a stronger fishy taste than other types.

Nut A hard-shelled seed, particularly one with an edible kernel. They are among the earliest of human foods. Nuts are at home in cakes, desserts and confectionery (candy) as well as in curries and stir fries; roasted nuts are a popular snack food.

Nutmeg A hard, brown oval seed which is ground into a pungent spice; it is most fragrant when freshly grated.

NOODLES

Most Asian noodles are shaped in long narrow strings or flat strips, their length traditionally signifying long life. Different types of flour are used. Some noodles are made with eggs, and some need to be soaked before cooking.

Both dried and fresh noodles are sold: fresh ones can be kept for 3–4 days in the refrigerator; dried noodles will keep indefinitely in a cool, dry place. In Asian cuisines, noodles are served in soups and stir-fries, and can also be deep-fried.

WHEAT FLOUR NOODLES are made with or without eggs. Egg noodles range in colour from light golden to deep yellow, while the eggless types are paler. Available fresh or dried, they are sold in compressed bundles and may be thick or thin, flat (for soups) or rounded (for frying). Cook fresh or dried varieties in a large pan of boiling water until just tender, testing frequently. When cooked, drain, run under cold running water, and drain the noodles again.

WHEAT NOODLES FROM JAPAN include: somen, very fine, thin and white, may be boiled, drained and eaten cold with a dipping sauce or simmered and served in clear, delicate soups; and udon, thick and buff-coloured, used for heartier broths. They are sold in dried form, attractively bound in bundles and (less widely) fresh or in vacuum packs.

RICE FLOUR NOODLES, made from ground rice and water, come in various widths and thicknesses, but thin rice vermicelli (*mi fun*) and the flat, dried form known as *ho fun* or rice sticks are the most common. Rice vermicelli are soaked in hot water for 10 minutes before using in soups or stir-fries. For a crispy garnish, small bundles, direct from the pack, can be deep-fried in hot oil. Thicker noodles are soaked for 30–40 minutes, then cooked in boiling water for 6–10 minutes, testing frequently, until they are just tender.

FRESH RICE NOODLES, thick and pearly white, are sold in Asian stores. Some have a light coating of oil which is removed by pouring boiling water over them. Rice noodles can also be bought in the form of large rolled sheets, which are cut crossways into ribbons. Soak noodles in boiling water for about 2 minutes until barely tender, drain well and add to stir-fries.

GROUND BUCKWHEAT plus a little wheat flour is the basis of Japanese soba noodles; usually beige coloured, some are subtly flavoured with green tea or beetroot. They can be purchased in dried form from Asian and health food stores; fresh soba noodles may be more difficult to find. Cook in boiling water until just tender, drain. Serve either hot in a broth or cold with a dipping sauce.

BEAN FLOUR NOODLES, made with soya or mung bean starch, are fine and semi-translucent. They are known as cellophane noodles or bean thread vermicelli. Soak noodles in hot water for 10 minutes or until softened, then drain well before adding to stir-fries. In small bundles (unsoaked), noodles can also be deep-fried.

CHINESE NOODLES WITHOUT EGG

CHINESE NOODLES

HARUSAME (JAPANESE BEAN NOODLES)

CELLOPHANE/BEAN THREAD NOODLES

HARUSAME (JAPANESE BEAN NOODLES)

FRESH RICE NOODLES

RICE VERMICELLI

SOMEN NOODLES

FRESH NOODLES WITHOUT EGGS

UDON NOODLES

DRIED BUCKWHEAT NOODLES

DRIED GREEN PEA BUCKWHEAT NOODLES

FRESH BUCKWHEAT NOODLES

FRESH CHINESE NOODLES

FRESH CHINESE EGG NOODLES

OCTOPUS

MARINATED BABY OCTOPUS SALAD

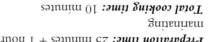

Preparation time: 25 minutes + 1 hour marinating
Total cooking time: 10 minutes
Serves 4

800 g (1 lb 10 oz) baby octopus
1/3 cup (2 1/2 fl oz) olive oil
2 cloves garlic, crushed
1 tablespoon sweet Thai chilli sauce
1 medium red pepper (capsicum), finely chopped
2 tablespoons chopped fresh coriander
2 tablespoons sweet Thai lime juice

1 Clean octopus with a small sharp knife: cut off head, or slit open, and remove gut.

2 Pick up body, push beak up with index finger; remove and discard. Clean octopus well under running water; pat dry with paper towel. Combine with oil and garlic. Cover with plastic wrap and marinate for 1–2 hours.

3 Heat barbecue grill. When very hot, cook octopus for 3–5 minutes or until tender. Drain well on paper towel. Combine chilli sauce, pepper, coriander and juice in serving bowl. Add octopus, stir. Serve warm or cold.

OCTOPUS IN RED WINE

Preparation time: 20 minutes
Total cooking time: 35 minutes
Serves 4

1 kg (2 lb) baby octopus
2 tablespoons brown vinegar
1/3 cup (2 1/2 fl oz) olive oil
1/2 teaspoon cracked black pepper
1 large onion, finely chopped
1/2 teaspoon dried oregano
2 bay leaves
2 tablespoons dry red wine

1 To clean octopus, use a small, sharp knife to slit open head; remove gut. Pick up body and use index finger to push beak up; remove and discard. Rinse octopus; pat dry with paper towel.

2 Place octopus, oil, onion and bay leaves in large heavy-based frying pan. Cook, uncovered, over medium heat for 20 minutes or until almost all the liquid is absorbed, stirring occasionally.

3 Add remaining ingredients to pan. Bring to boil, reduce heat and simmer, covered, for 15 minutes or until octopus is just tender. Serve warm or cold with Greek salad.

*ABOVE: MARINATED BABY OCTOPUS SALAD.
OPPOSITE PAGE, ABOVE: CRUMBED BRAINS;
BELOW: KIDNEYS AND BACON.*

Oat Bran The coarse outer layers of the oat, removed in the milling process. Oat bran is used in cooking and is regarded as a good source of soluble fibre. It can be added to bread, muffin and biscuit (cookie) doughs, to hamburgers, rissoles and meat loaves, and is often eaten at breakfast sprinkled on cereal or chopped fruit.

Oatcake A cake of unleavened bread made from oatmeal, water and a small amount of fat. Traditionally in northern England dollops of dough were cooked on a hot griddle until firm, then hung up until crisp and dry. In Scotland and Wales thin rounds of oatmeal paste were cooked slowly in a cool oven.

Oatmeal Ground oats, used as a breakfast cereal and in baking. Coarse and

O

OFFAL

KIDNEYS AND BACON

★ **Preparation time:** 10 minutes
Total cooking time: 10 minutes
Serves 4

4 rashers bacon
8 lamb's kidneys
1/4 cup plain (all-purpose) flour
salt and freshly ground pepper
30 g (1 oz) butter
1 tablespoon olive oil

1/2 cup (4 fl oz) veal or chicken stock
2 teaspoons Dijon mustard
2 teaspoons lemon juice
1 tablespoon chopped parsley

1 Remove rind from bacon. Cook bacon in a hot dry pan. Transfer to a heated serving plate and keep hot. Wipe pan clean with paper towel.

2 Remove skin and core from kidneys and slice kidneys across in half. Combine flour, salt and pepper and roll kidneys in flour, shaking off excess. Heat butter and oil in a heavy-based pan and cook kidneys over medium heat until browned; the inside should be faintly pink and moist. Remove from pan and keep warm.

3 Add stock, mustard, lemon juice and parsley to pan and simmer until sauce is reduced by half. Return the kidneys to the pan for a few seconds only to heat through.

4 Serve kidneys and sauce with bacon and accompany with hot buttered toast.

CRUMBED BRAINS

★ **Preparation time:** 20 minutes
Total cooking time: 12 minutes
Serves 4

4 sets lamb's brains
2 tablespoons plain (all-purpose) flour
salt and freshly ground pepper
1 egg

2 tablespoons milk
1/2 cup dried breadcrumbs
light olive oil for shallow frying
grilled bacon for serving

1 Rinse brains under cold running water and carefully remove as much of the surrounding membrane and blood vessels as possible. Place brains in a pan of lightly salted water and bring to the boil. Reduce heat and simmer for 6–7 minutes; drain. Plunge brains into a bowl of iced water to prevent further cooking; drain again, then pat dry with paper towels. If desired, cut each set of brains through centre horizontally to give two pieces.

2 Combine flour, salt and pepper on a sheet of greaseproof paper. Toss brains in seasoned flour; shake off excess. Beat egg in a small bowl; add milk and mix to combine. Dip brains into egg mixture. Coat with breadcrumbs; shake off excess. Store, covered, in the refrigerator for 30 minutes before cooking.

3 Heat oil in a heavy-based pan; fry brains until golden brown on all sides. Remove from pan; drain on paper towel. Serve brains hot with grilled bacon.

---

medium oatmeal is used for porridge (as is rolled oats) and in sausage mixtures, such as the Scottish haggis. Fine oatmeal is used in pancakes, muffins, and other baked goods.

Octopus A tender-fleshed saltwater mollusc with eight tentacles, a large head with a strong beak, a small sac-like body and no internal backbone; best for eating are the small varieties. Octopus should be either cooked slowly—simmered in wine or its own juices or stuffed and baked—or cooked rapidly over a high heat. Popular in Mediterranean countries, Asia and especially in Japan. Fresh octopus is usually sold whole and already tenderised by beating; it is also available frozen, dried and pre-cooked in cans.

Oeufs à la Neige (Eggs in the Snow) A dessert of French origin consisting of egg-sized spoonfuls of vanilla-flavoured meringue poached in sweetened milk, drained and placed on top of a rich custard sauce made from the poaching milk.

Offal Also called variety meats, the general term used to describe the edible internal organs of an animal—heart, liver, tripe, kidneys,

sweetbreads and brains—as well as the tongue, tail, feet and head.

Oil, Vegetable The clear liquid extracted from various seeds, nuts and fruit, including almond, avocado, canola, coconut, cottonseed, grapeseed, hazelnut, maize, olive, peanut, pumpkin seed, safflower, sesame seed, soy bean, sunflower seed and walnut. Fine-flavoured oils, such as olive, walnut, hazelnut, almond and pumpkin seed, are generally used to flavour cold foods (such as salads) and are added to hot foods (pasta, fish or cooked vegetables) just before serving to preserve the oil's aroma and taste. Oils used primarily for cooking include maize, peanut, coconut (high in saturated fats), cottonseed, sunflower and vegetable (a blend of oils sold as an all-purpose cooking oil).

Okra Also known as ladies' fingers, a long, rigid, five-sided, green seed pod, pointed at one end and containing numerous small white seeds. Okra has a gelatinous quality when cooked and its role in a dish is often that of a thickener. In Middle Eastern and Greek cooking the pod is

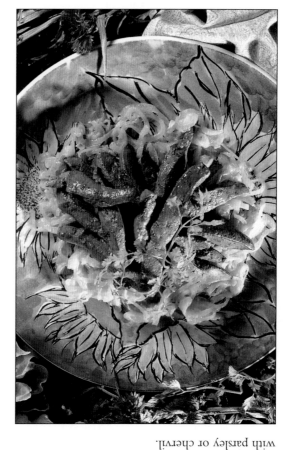

VENETIAN LIVER

Preparation time: 15 minutes
Total cooking time: 30 minutes
Serves 4

500 g (1 lb) calf's liver, trimmed
60 g (2 oz) butter
4 medium white onions, sliced
salt and freshly ground pepper
60 g (2 oz) butter, extra
parsley or chervil
¾ cup (6 fl oz) dry white wine

1 Remove all skin from liver and cut liver into very thin slices, removing tubes. Cover, set aside.

2 Heat butter in a heavy-based pan and cook onions until soft but not brown. Add wine and simmer gently, stirring occasionally, for 20 minutes or until pale golden in colour. If necessary add a little water to pan to prevent onions drying out. Add salt and pepper; remove onions to a serving dish and keep hot. Wipe pan clean with paper towel.

3 Heat extra butter in the same pan until it turns a pale brown colour. Cook liver slices over high heat for about 1 minute, turning once; the inside should be just cooked and still tender.

4 Arrange liver slices over onions and garnish with parsley or chervil.

TRIPE AND ONIONS

Preparation time: 25 minutes
Total cooking time: 2½ hours
Serves 4

1 kg (2 lb) tripe
1½ cups (12 fl oz) stock (see method)
1 small onion, chopped
salt, pepper and nutmeg to taste

45 g (1½ oz) butter
2 medium onions, chopped
¼ cup plain (all-purpose) flour
1 cup (8 fl oz) milk
2 tablespoons chopped parsley

1 To blanch tripe, wash well and place in a pan of cold water with a generous squeeze of lemon juice. Bring to the boil, pour off water and plunge tripe into cold water. Drain well.

2 Cut blanched tripe into small strips and place in a large pan with chopped onion. Add water to cover. Bring to boil, cover and simmer for about 2 hours or until tender. Drain tripe and reserve 1½ cups (12 fl oz) of liquid for stock.

3 Heat butter in a medium pan and cook extra onion until soft but not brown. Stir in flour and cook for 1 minute. Add stock and milk gradually to pan, stirring until mixture is smooth. Stir constantly over medium heat until sauce boils and thickens. Add tripe, salt, pepper, nutmeg and parsley and simmer for 5 minutes.

LEFT: VENETIAN LIVER, ABOVE: TRIPE AND ONIONS. OPPOSITE PAGE, ABOVE: CHICKEN WITH OKRA; BELOW: OKRA WITH ONIONS AND TOMATOES.

OKRA
(LADIES' FINGERS)

OKRA WITH ONIONS AND TOMATO

✴ ✴ **Preparation time:** 10 minutes + 4 hours soaking
Total cooking time: 1 hour 4 minutes
Serves 4

1 cup chick peas (garbanzo beans)	1 tablespoon lemon juice
3 cups (24 fl oz) water	2 tablespoons red wine, optional
1 tablespoon olive oil	500 g (1 lb) okra (ladies' fingers) or 2 x 375 g (12 oz) cans okra, drained
8 small pickling onions	2 cloves garlic, crushed
4 medium tomatoes, peeled and chopped	1 tablespoon chopped fresh oregano
1½ cups (12 fl oz) tomato juice	1 teaspoon ground pepper

1 Soak chick peas in water for 4 hours or overnight; drain. Heat oil in medium pan; add onions and garlic. Cook on medium-high heat for 4 minutes or until golden. Add tomatoes, chick peas, tomato juice, lemon juice and wine. Simmer, covered, for 40 minutes.

2 Add okra and simmer for another 20 minutes. If using canned okra, add to tomato mixture in last 5 minutes of cooking. Stir through oregano and pepper. Serve with rice as a main meal or as an accompaniment to a meat dish.

CHICKEN WITH OKRA
(LADIES' FINGERS)

✴ **Preparation time:** 10 minutes
Total cooking time: 55 minutes
Serves 4

8 chicken thigh cutlets	2 cloves garlic, crushed
440 g (14 oz) can tomatoes, chopped	¼ cup (2 fl oz) olive oil
¼ teaspoon ground black pepper	2 large onions, thinly sliced
750 g (1½ lb)	1 kg (2 lb) baby okra (ladies' fingers) or 4 x 375 g (12 oz) cans okra drained, not rinsed
2 tablespoons butter, melted	

1 Trim chicken of excess fat and sinew. Place chicken on a cold, lightly oiled grill (broiler) tray. Cook under medium-high heat for 12 minutes or until tender, turning once. Brush with combined butter and half the garlic several times during cooking. Remove from grill; keep warm.

2 Heat oil in a heavy-based pan. Add onions and remaining garlic. Stir over high heat for 3 minutes. Reduce heat to low, cook for another 10 minutes, stirring occasionally. Add tomatoes and pepper. Simmer, covered, for 5 minutes.

3 Preheat oven to moderately hot 210°C (415°F/Gas 6–7). Top and tail okra and add to pan. Stir gently to combine. Simmer, covered, for 10 minutes. Pour okra mixture into a shallow ovenproof dish.

4 Arrange chicken over okra. Bake 15 minutes or until just heated through. Serve warm with bread, olives and cheese.

fruit of an evergreen tree native to the Mediterranean region. Olives are picked unripe (green) and ripe (black). The flesh is treated to remove its bitterness and is then soaked in brine. Oil pressed from the ripe fruit has cosmetic and medicinal uses as well as an acclaimed culinary role. Green olives have a tart taste and come from fruit picked before fully mature. Olives are served as a finger food with drinks (a practice that goes back to Roman times), and in cooking are used in sauces, stuffings, pizzas, breads, salads and as a garnish. The olive is the oldest tree in continuous cultivation and has been

Olive The small, oval, oil-rich

usually left whole; in Cajun cooking it is cut into wheel-like discs and is often partnered with tomato. Okra is native to tropical Africa; its introduction into America dates from the slave trade days and it is the characteristic ingredient in many soups and stews in the south of the United States and the Caribbean. Okra is in season from summer to autumn and is also sold frozen, dried and in cans.

ONIONS

Onions have been revered since ancient times. This pungent member of the lily family, with its slightly sweet flavour and savoury aroma, will enhance most meat or vegetable dishes. Fried, baked or pickled, onions are also a versatile vegetable in their own right.

GOLDEN BABY ONIONS

Peel 12 small onions, leaving base intact. Heat 30 g (1 oz) butter, 1 tablespoon oil and 1/4 teaspoon ground sweet paprika in frying pan. Add onions, cook over medium heat for 5 minutes or until tender. Stir in 1/2 teaspoon soft brown sugar. Serve hot.

CURRIED ONION RINGS

Peel and slice 2 medium onions into thin rings. Heat 2 tablespoons olive oil in a frying pan. Add 2 teaspoons curry powder and onion rings. Cook for 5 minutes or until onions are tender. Stir in 1/2 teaspoon soft brown sugar. Serve hot.

GARLIC ONIONS

Peel and cut 2 medium onions into eight wedges. Heat 1 tablespoon butter and 2 tablespoons oil in a frying pan. Add 1–2 cloves crushed garlic and onions. Cook over medium heat for 5–6 minutes or until tender. Sprinkle with chopped chives. Serve hot.

SPICY ONIONS AND TOMATOES

Peel and thinly slice 2 medium red onions. Heat 1 tablespoon butter, 1 tablespoon oil, 1/2 teaspoon each ground cumin, coriander, turmeric and garam masala, cook 2–3 minutes. Stir in 2 chopped medium ripe tomatoes. Cook for 3 minutes more or until the onions are soft. Serve onions hot, sprinkled with chopped coriander.

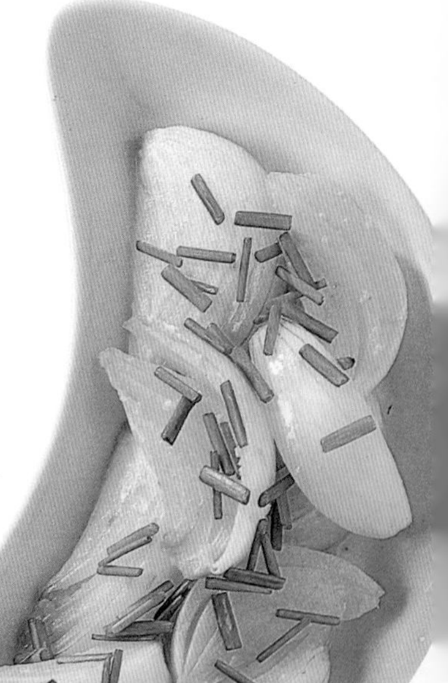

GOLDEN BABY ONIONS

GARLIC ONIONS

SPICY ONIONS AND TOMATOES

CURRIED ONION RINGS

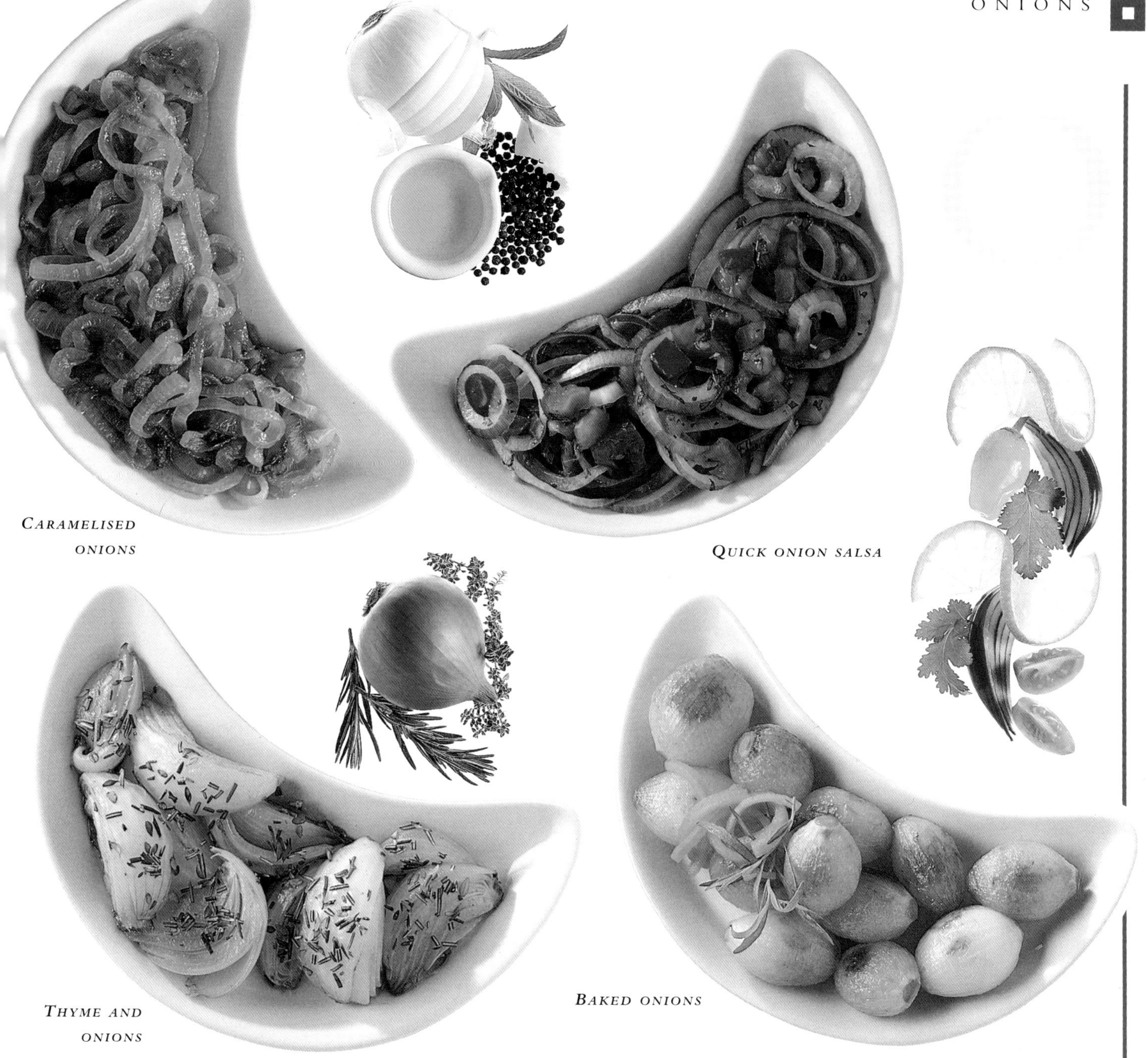

295

THYME AND ONIONS

Peel and cut 2 medium onions into eight wedges. Heat 2 teaspoons butter and 2 tablespoons oil in heavy-based frying pan. Add onions, cook over medium heat for 5 minutes or until tender and golden. Stir in 1 teaspoon each chopped fresh thyme and rosemary. Cook for 1 minute more. Drizzle with vinegar. Serve hot.

CARAMELISED ONIONS

Peel and cut 2 medium onions into thin rings. Heat 1½ tablespoons butter and 1 tablespoon oil in heavy-based frying pan. Add onions, cook over low heat for 10–12 minutes or until onions are dark golden, stirring occasionally. Serve hot.

BAKED ONIONS

Peel 8 small onions, leaving bases intact. Place in baking dish. Brush liberally with a mixture of 1 tablespoon melted butter and 1 tablespoon olive oil. Bake in moderate 180°C (350°F/Gas 4) oven for 30 minutes or until golden brown. Serve hot.

QUICK ONION SALSA

Peel and finely slice 1 large red onion. Combine in a bowl with 2 tablespoons lime juice, 1 tablespoon olive oil, 1 teaspoon soft brown sugar, 1 tablespoon chopped fresh coriander, 1 chopped tomato, and 1 finely chopped jalapena chilli. Mix well. Season to taste. Cover and set aside at room temperature 10 minutes before serving.

BAKED ONIONS

THYME AND ONIONS

QUICK ONION SALSA

CARAMELISED ONIONS

ONIONS

OLIVES

Olive Oil A pale yellow to deep green, mono-unsaturated vegetable oil pressed from the pulp of ripe olives. It has a fruity flavour and in cooking adds both flavour and nutrition to any dish in which it is an ingredient. Cold-pressed olive oil is produced by pressure only. Heat allows more oil to be extracted, but affects the flavour. Olive oil is graded according to its level of acidity: the finest, extra virgin, with less than

grown in the eastern Mediterranean for some 6,000 years. Egyptian paintings show olives being picked; ancient Crete, about 3,800 years ago, became the centre of an export trade shipping olive oil to Egypt and Asia Minor. The olive was virtually indispensable in ancient times, valued for its fruit and the multi-purpose oil it provided, as well as for its close-grained hardwood. Olives are sometimes available fresh but more usually are sold pickled whole (either loose or in jars and cans), pitted and stuffed with pimiento or almonds or salted and dried (either loose or in vacuum-sealed packs).

CHICKEN AND OLIVES

★★ *Preparation time:* 30 minutes + 1 hour standing
Total cooking time: 1 hour
Serves 6

12 chicken pieces	1 red pepper (capsicum), chopped
1 teaspoon ground cinnamon	1/4 cup fresh coriander, chopped
1 teaspoon ground ginger	1 1/2 cups (12 fl oz) chicken stock
1/2 teaspoon ground turmeric	4 strips preserved lemon rind, grated
1 teaspoon ground sweet paprika	
1/2 teaspoon ground pepper	
2 onions, chopped	
1/4 cup (2 fl oz) olive oil	
2 tablespoons lemon juice	
1 cup green olives	

1 Combine chicken with spices in large bowl. Stand, covered, for 1 hour. Heat 2 tablespoons oil in a large pan. Cook chicken until well browned, but not cooked through. Transfer to larger pan.

2 Add remaining oil to first pan. Add onion and pepper. Cook over low heat for 5 minutes, stirring. Add to chicken pieces in larger pan.

3 Add coriander and stock, juice and olives. Simmer, covered, for 40 minutes, until chicken is tender and liquid has reduced. Serve with rice.

MARINATED OLIVES

■ Whisk together olive oil, crushed garlic, finely chopped orange rind, orange juice and freshly ground pepper. Add Kalamata olives, sliced red onion and mix well. Cover and marinate for 2–3 hours before serving.

■ Crack green olives lightly with a meat mallet under a towel, or make small slits around the olive with a small sharp knife. Combine with olive oil, dry vermouth, bruised juniper berries, freshly ground black pepper. Add olives, whole blanched almonds and sliced lemons and mix well. Cover and marinate for 12 hours in refrigerator, stirring occasionally.

■ Combine olive oil, lemon juice, crushed garlic, chopped fresh oregano and a crumbled bay leaf. Add black olives, thinly shredded lemon rind, chopped celery, chopped red pepper (capsicum) and chopped flat-leaf parsley; mix well. Cover and marinate olives for 2–3 hours before serving.

■ Whisk together olive oil, crushed garlic, balsamic vinegar and freshly ground black pepper. Add some black olives, chopped sundried tomatoes, chopped fresh basil and pine nuts; mix well. Cover and marinate olives for 2–3 hours before serving.

ABOVE: CHICKEN AND OLIVES.
OPPOSITE PAGE: BLACK OLIVE AND ONION PIE

OLIVES

1 per cent acid and deep green in colour has the fullest flavour—use it drizzled on pasta, salads and vegetables; next are fine virgin olive oil (less then 1.5 per cent acidity) and virgin olive oil (less than 3 per cent). Pure olive oil, made from a blend of virgin oil and refined olive oil, has the same acid content as virgin olive oil. Refined olive oil is made by removing impurities from oils that do not meet the

standards for extra virgin or virgin olive oil: such blends have a milder flavour and are often labelled as 'light'. Spain and Italy lead in the production of fine olive oil. It is available in bottles or large cans.

Omelette A dish of beaten eggs cooked in a frying pan and often folded over a filling. Omelette can be served at breakfast or as a light luncheon or supper dish: a sweet filling transforms it into a dessert. Omelettes have been known in France since the Middle Ages.

Onion The bulb of a member of the lily family, related to garlic and leek, with pungently flavoured flesh encased in thin, close outer layers. There are many varieties, varying in colour, shape and

OLIVE AND ONION TART

✹ ✹ **Preparation time:** 1 hour + 30 minutes refrigeration
Total cooking time: 1 hour 25 minutes
Serves 8

2 cups plain (all-purpose) flour
105 g (3½ oz) butter
4–5 tablespoons iced water
1 kg (2 lb) white onions, peeled and sliced
30 g (1 oz) butter, extra
1 tablespoon French mustard
1 cup sour cream
3 eggs, lightly beaten
⅓ cup sliced black olives

1 Sift flour into bowl; add chopped butter. Rub butter into flour 1 minute or until mixture is crumbly. Add almost all the water; mix to a firm dough, adding more water if necessary. Turn onto floured surface; knead 1 minute, then roll out to fit 23 cm (9 inch) flan tin. Fit pastry in tin and refrigerate 30 minutes.

2 Preheat oven to 180°C (350°F/Gas 4). Cut a sheet of greaseproof paper to fit flan tin; place over pastry and cover with dried beans or rice. Bake 10 minutes, discard paper and beans; return pastry to oven for another 10 minutes.

3 Heat extra butter in pan. Add onions, cook on low heat 45 minutes; cool. Spread mustard over pastry. Whisk sour cream and eggs in bowl. Spread onions over mustard and pour egg mixture over. Scatter olives on top. Bake 35 minutes or until filling has set. Stand 5 minutes before cutting.

OLIVE AND ROSEMARY FOCACCIA

✹ **Preparation time:** 30 minutes + 55 minutes proving time
Total cooking time: 30 minutes
Makes 8 rolls

7 g (¼ oz) dry yeast
1 teaspoon sugar
¾ cup (6 fl oz) warm water
2¾ cups plain (all-purpose) flour
1 teaspoon salt
1 tablespoon dried rosemary
1 tablespoon olive oil
⅓ cup black olives, sliced
2 tablespoons olive oil, extra
flour

1 Combine yeast and sugar in small bowl. Stir in ¼ cup of water. Stand, covered with plastic wrap, in a warm place for 10 minutes or until foamy.

2 Sift flour and salt into large bowl. Stir in rosemary. Make well in centre; add oil, yeast mixture and remaining water. Mix to firm dough with a knife. Turn dough onto floured surface, knead 10 minutes. Shape dough into ball, place in large, lightly oiled mixing bowl. Cover, leave in warm place 45 minutes or until well risen.

3 Preheat oven to moderately hot 210°C (415°F/Gas 6–7). Brush two 32 x 28 cm (13 x 11 inch) oven trays with oil. Knead dough again until smooth. Divide into 8 pieces. Knead one portion at a time and shape into a flat 10 cm (4 inch) round. Repeat with remaining dough, press olives onto surface and brush with extra oil. Bake 30 minutes or until golden.

intensity of taste, but in general the onion is sharp in flavour when raw and mellow when cooked. Onions can be used an ingredient in salads or added as a garnish; they can be boiled, fried or baked as a vegetable; or cooked in a wide variety of

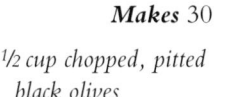

dishes. Simmered slowly in butter, they provide an almost sweet filling for the classic French onion tart and are also made into a famous French soup; onion rings dipped in batter and deep-fried are a popular first course in Indian cooking; and studded with cloves, the onion flavours sauces and casseroles. The birthplace of the ancestor of today's onion was probably central Asia. It was a food of the poor in ancient Greece and Rome and since the Middle Ages has been adopted throughout Europe.

Fresh onions are available throughout the year, but are best from early autumn to late spring; onions are also frozen and pickled. Spring

onions (scallions) are onions pulled when immature.

OLIVE AND ROSEMARY PALMIERS

★ **Preparation time:** 20 minutes
Total cooking time: 15 minutes
Makes 30

½ cup chopped, pitted black olives
⅓ cup grated parmesan cheese
1 tablespoon chopped rosemary

4 slices salami, chopped
2 tablespoons oil
2 teaspoons Dijon mustard
2 sheets ready-rolled puff pastry
oil or melted butter

1 Preheat oven to moderately hot 200°C (400°F/Gas 6). Brush two oven trays with melted butter or oil. Combine olives, cheese, rosemary, salami, oil and mustard in a blender or food processor. Process for 30 seconds or until mixture becomes a paste.
2 Place a sheet of pastry on work surface and spread evenly with half the olive paste. Fold two opposite sides over to meet edge to edge in the centre. Fold once again, then fold in half to give 8 layers of pastry.
3 Cut into 1 cm (½ inch) slices. Lay slices, cut side up, on prepared trays, allowing room for spreading. Open slices out slightly at the folded end to give a 'V' shape. Repeat with remaining pastry and olive paste. Bake for 15 minutes or until palmiers are golden brown.

CRUDITES WITH OLIVE PASTE

★ **Preparation time**: 15 minutes
Total cooking time: nil
Serves 4–6

500 g (1 lb) black olives
⅓ cup (2½ fl oz) olive oil
2 cloves garlic, peeled
¼ cup basil leaves
1 tablespoon lemon juice
freshly ground pepper

selection of fresh vegetables—snow peas (mange tout), small radishes, pieces of cucumber, whole baby mushrooms

1 Remove stones from the olives. Place the olives, olive oil, garlic cloves, basil leaves and lemon juice into blender or food processor.
2 Blend at high speed until the mixture is a coarse paste—do not over-process or the mixture will become too smooth. Season to taste with black pepper.
3 Serve olive paste in a bowl, surrounded by fresh, seasonal vegetables of your choice.

Note: Olive Paste can be made 2–3 days before it is needed and stored in the refrigerator.

ABOVE: CRUDITES WITH OLIVE PASTE; LEFT: OLIVE AND ROSEMARY PALMIERS.
OPPOSITE, ABOVE: ORANGE GELATO; BELOW: ORANGE AND SPINACH SALAD

ORANGES

ORANGE AND SPINACH SALAD

★ **Preparation time** : 15 minutes
Total cooking time: nil
Serves 4–6

4 medium oranges
10–12 spinach leaves
1 medium red onion, sliced
1/4 cup (2 fl oz) red wine vinegar
1/3 cup (2 1/2 fl oz) olive oil
1/2 cup pitted black olives
1/4 cup toasted pine nuts

1 Place each orange on a board, cut a 2 cm (3/4 inch) slice off each end to where the pulp starts. Peel, removing all white membrane. Separate segments by carefully cutting between membrane and flesh with a small sharp knife. Do this over a bowl so you don't lose the juice.
2 Tear spinach into bite-sized pieces, place into a large bowl. Add the sliced onion, orange and black olives.
3 Place the olive oil and vinegar in a small bowl. Whisk until well combined.
4 Pour dressing over salad and toss to mix well. Place into serving bowl, sprinkle with toasted pine nuts and serve the salad immediately.

ABOUT ORANGES

■ Oranges keep well for many weeks, but once the skins develop soft spots, use them quickly.
▨ Make orange juice by squeezing fruit and straining any seeds or pith. Juice can be frozen for several months: try freezing it in ice-cube trays.

ORANGE GELATO

★ **Preparation time:** 30 minutes + churning and freezing
Total cooking time: 20 minutes
Makes 1.5 litres (6 cups)

1 1/4 cups pure icing (confectioners) sugar
2 egg whites
2 tablespoons Cointreau or Grand Marnier liqueur

1 1/2 cups (12 fl oz) freshly squeezed orange juice
2 cups (16 fl oz) water
1 tablespoon lemon juice
1/4 cup icing (confectioners) sugar, extra
slices of orange to serve

1 Place icing sugar, orange juice, water and lemon juice in a large pan. Stir over medium heat for 4–5 minutes or until sugar is dissolved. Bring to boil. Reduce heat. Simmer gently for 15 minutes; remove from heat.
2 Pour mixture into a large bowl; allow to cool. Stir in liqueur.
3 Using electric beaters, beat egg whites until soft peaks form. Gradually beat in the extra icing sugar until mixture is thick and glossy.
4 Using a metal spoon, gently fold egg whites into orange mixture. Pour mixture into an ice-cream machine and churn for about 30 minutes, or freeze until just solid.
5 To make by hand, prepare up to step 3. Before adding egg whites, pour the mixture into a freezer tray and freeze until it is beginning to set around the edges.
6 Remove from freezer and beat well. Beat egg whites to soft peaks. Add extra sugar. Beat well. Fold into orange mixture. Return to tray and freeze until firm. Serve with slices of orange.

Orange A round citrus fruit with a bright orange skin and juicy, orange-coloured, segmented flesh. Orange is eaten fresh as a fruit, chopped and added to fruit salads, cooked in both sweet and savoury dishes and made into marmalade; its juice is a favourite at breakfast; and its rind is used fresh or dried to flavour desserts, cakes and savoury sauces. There are three main types of orange: sweet oranges, including the large, thick-skinned navel (named for the navel-like growth at the blossom end) and the smaller, thin-skinned Valencia, are used for juicing and as a snack and dessert fruit; bitter oranges, including the Seville, which is used to make marmalade and tangy sauces; and blood oranges, with sweet, juicy, blood-red flesh, eaten as a dessert fruit and used for juicing.

The orange originated in southern Asia and has been cultivated in China for at least 4,000 years. The fruit was known to the Romans and grew in the ancient Middle East, where bitter oranges preserved in their skins in sugar may well be the forerunner of today's marmalade. The Moors planted orange orchards

ORANGE BUN

Preparation time: 45 minutes + 1 hour 5 minutes standing
Total cooking time: 20 minutes
Makes one 23 cm (9 inch) round

2 cups plain (all-purpose) flour
7 g (1/4 oz) sachet dried yeast
1/3 cup mixed peel
2 tablespoons caster (superfine) sugar
2 teaspoons grated orange rind
1/3 cup (2 1/2 fl oz) warm milk

1 egg, lightly beaten
30 g (1 oz) butter, melted
1/3 cup (2 1/2 fl oz) orange juice

Glaze
1 tablespoon water
1 teaspoon sugar
1 teaspoon gelatine

1 Brush deep 23 cm (9 inch) round cake tin with oil or melted butter. Sift flour into a large mixing bowl. Add yeast, mixed peel, sugar and orange rind; stir until combined. Make a well in centre.

2 Combine milk, orange juice, egg and butter in small mixing bowl; add to flour mixture. Using a knife, mix to a soft dough. Turn onto lightly floured surface, knead 10 minutes or until dough is smooth and elastic. To test, press a finger into the dough. When ready, dough will spring back immediately and not be indented.

3 Place dough into a large, lightly oiled mixing bowl. Leave, covered with plastic wrap, in warm place for 45 minutes or until well risen.

4 Knead dough again for 1 minute or until smooth. Press into prepared cake tin. Leave, covered with plastic wrap, in a warm place for 20 minutes or until well risen.

5 Preheat oven to moderate 180°C (350°F/Gas 4). Cut dough into eight wedges by carefully making deep cuts with a sharp, pointed, oiled knife. Be careful not to push out the air. If dough deflates, leave for another 5 minutes or until risen.

6 Bake for 20 minutes or until bun is golden brown and cooked through—bun should sound hollow when tapped. Turn onto wire rack.

7 To make Glaze: Combine water, sugar and gelatine in small mixing bowl. Place over a pan of simmering water, heat until sugar and gelatine are dissolved. Brush over bun while still hot.

ORANGE SESAME RICE SALAD

Preparation time: 30 minutes
Total cooking time: nil
Serves 8

12 fresh asparagus spears
155 g (5 oz) small snow peas (mange tout)
2 cups long-grain rice, cooked and cooled
1 small cucumber, thinly sliced
1 large red pepper (capsicum), thinly sliced
2 large spring onions (scallions)
2 oranges
1 Spanish (large red) onion, thinly sliced

Dressing
2 tablespoons sesame oil
2/3 cup (5 fl oz) orange juice
2 teaspoons grated ginger
2 teaspoons finely grated orange rind
1 clove garlic, crushed
1 tablespoon honey

1 Plunge the asparagus spears into a bowl of boiling water. Leave for 2 minutes until the asparagus is a vibrant green and slightly tender; drain. Plunge the spears into a bowl of iced water. When cold, drain; pat dry with paper towel. Cut the asparagus into 3 cm (1 1/4 inch) pieces diagonally. Top and tail the snow peas.

2 Carefully peel the oranges, making sure you cut deep enough to remove the white membrane. Separate the segments by cutting between the membrane and the flesh.

3 Combine all the ingredients in large bowl. Pour the Dressing over and stir until well combined.

4 To make Dressing: Shake all ingredients together in small jar 30 seconds until well mixed.

ABOVE: ORANGE BUN.
OPPOSITE PAGE: OXTAIL SOUP

Oregano Also known as wild marjoram.
Oregano is a hardy perennial herb similar in appearance and related to marjoram, but with a more robust

Orange Flower Water A fragrant liquid made from neroli, an essential oil extracted from sweet-scented blossom of the bitter orange tree. Intensely flavoured, it is added sparingly to sponge cakes and confectionery (candy) and is popular in Middle Eastern cooking in pastries and syrups. Available from specialty stores.

available fresh all year round, and are also sold canned; orange juice can be bought freshly squeezed or as a concentrate; orange peel is sold dried and candied.

in Spain from the eighth century on. The Spanish planted the first oranges in America in Florida in the sixteenth century. The fruit is now grown in tropical and sub-tropical regions world-wide. Oranges are

OXTAIL SOUP

★ *Preparation time:* 10 minutes
Total cooking time: 3 hours
Makes 4 litres

1 oxtail (approximately 750 g/1½ lb)	2 sticks celery, finely chopped
30 g (1 oz) butter	1 large onion, finely chopped
1 large parsnip, peeled and finely chopped	2 tablespoons barley
1 turnip, peeled and finely chopped	4 whole cloves
2 large carrots, peeled and finely chopped	¼ cup chopped parsley
	2 litres (8 cups) beef stock
	white pepper
	salt to taste

1 Trim oxtail and cut into 2.5 cm (1 inch) pieces.

2 Melt butter in a large heavy-based pan. Add oxtail in batches. Cook until browned; remove and drain. Add parsnip, turnip, carrots, celery and onion; stir until onion becomes transparent. Return meat to pan. Add barley, cloves, parsley, stock, pepper and salt.

3 Simmer for 2½ hours, skimming the froth off the surface as it rises in the pan. Serve Oxtail Soup in individual soup bowls, accompanied by bread or toast.

ABOUT OXTAIL

■ Oxtail requires long, moist cooking to tenderise the meat and reveal its distinctive texture. It is surrounded by a rich layer of fat which should be retained as it will contribute to the fine oxtail flavour. Froth from the fat will rise throughout cooking and should be regularly skimmed off with a spoon. Alternatively, cook oxtail the day before it is needed (this will also improve its flavour), and carefully lift away the cold fat when it has solidified on top.

■ As well as the classic soup, oxtail can be cooked as a casserole. The tail can also be boned, stuffed and braised slowly.

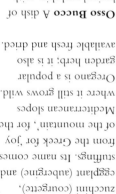

flavour. It is used to flavour pizza toppings, tomato-based sauces, zucchini (courgette), eggplant (aubergine) and stuffings. Its name comes from the Greek for 'joy of the mountain', for the Mediterranean slopes where it still grows wild. Oregano is a popular garden herb; it is also available fresh and dried.

Osso Bucco A dish of braised veal shin, with bone and marrow intact, which before serving is sprinkled with gremolata (a mixture of chopped parsley, garlic and grated lemon rind). The tasty bone marrow can be taken out with a toothpick. Osso bucco is a specialty of Milan, in northern Italy. The name means 'bone with a hole'. See VEAL for recipe.

Oven Fry To bake food in a hot oven so that it has the appearance and taste of fried food, but not the fat content. The food is brushed lightly with oil, butter or margarine or coated with seasoned flour or breadcrumbs before cooking.

Oxtail A flavoursome cut of meat consisting of the skinned tail of an ox or cow which requires long, slow cooking and is used to make soups and stews.

Oyster A marine mollusc with a soft creamy-grey to creamy-tan body, encased in rough, blue-grey, irregularly shaped hinged shell. It is found adhering to rocks in shallow tidal waters around the world. Oysters are eaten raw, with a squeeze of lemon juice, a touch of freshly grated black pepper or they can be fried, grilled (broiled) or poached or incorporated in soups, stuffings and sauces. Oysters have been gathered and eaten since the time of the earliest humans. There are ancient shell mounds on the coasts of North America (where the Native Americans seem to have always cooked them) and Australia; the shellfish was abundant along the European coastline from Scandinavia to the Mediterranean. Oysters are filter feeders, and so are subject to contamination; they

Oxtail soup is regarded as a traditional British dish, although some claim it crossed the Channel with French émigrés at the time of the Revolution.

OYSTERS

NEW ORLEANS OYSTERS

Preparation time: 10 minutes
Total cooking time: 4–6 minutes
Serves 4

24 large oysters, shell removed
1/2 cup plain (all-purpose) flour
1/2 cup (4 fl oz) vegetable oil
45 g (1 1/2 oz) unsalted (sweet) butter
lemon wedges and mayonnaise to serve

1/4 teaspoon dried basil
1/4 teaspoon white pepper
1/4 teaspoon ground black pepper
1/4 teaspoon cayenne pepper
1/4 teaspoon thyme
1/4 teaspoon oregano
1/2 teaspoon dried paprika

1 Dry oysters on paper towel. In shallow dish, mix peppers, thyme, oregano, paprika and basil ; set aside two teaspoons of the spice mix. Add the flour to remaining spice mix and stir thoroughly.

2 Thread three oysters onto eight oiled skewers (choose thin bamboo or metal skewers) and coat with spiced flour.

3 Heat the oil and butter in a wide pan. Cook the oysters until golden, turning several times, for about 6 minutes. Drain on paper towel. Sprinkle with the reserved two teaspoons of spice mix and serve with lemon wedges and dish of mayonnaise.

OYSTERS MORNAY

Heat 1 tablespoon butter in a small pan and add 2 tablespoons plain (all-purpose) flour. Stir over low heat for 2 minutes. Gradually add 1 cup (8 fl oz) milk to pan, stir until mixture is smooth. Stir over heat for 2 minutes until the mixture boils and thickens. Add 1/4 cup grated cheddar cheese, 1/2 teaspoon French mustard, 1 teaspoon lemon juice, salt and white pepper; stir until smooth. Spoon sauce over 24 oysters on the half shell, sprinkle with extra grated cheese and grill (broil) until lightly browned. Serves 2–4.

OYSTERS ROCKEFELLER

Heat 1 tablespoon butter in a medium pan and cook 1/4 cup finely chopped onion and 1 clove crushed garlic until onion is soft. Remove from heat and add 3/4 cup finely chopped cooked spinach (well drained), 3/4 cup (6 fl oz) thick sour cream, salt and freshly ground pepper. Spoon mixture over 24 oysters on the half shell. Mix 1/2 cup fine fresh breadcrumbs with 1/2 cup grated cheddar cheese and sprinkle mixture over the oysters. Grill oysters until the topping turns golden brown. Serves 2–4.

ABOVE: NEW ORLEANS OYSTERS.
OPPOSITE PAGE: SOUFFLE OYSTERS (LEFT) AND OYSTERS WITH PINE NUTS AND BACON (RIGHT)

SOUFFLE OYSTERS

✳︎✳︎ **Preparation time:** 25 minutes
Total cooking time: 20 minutes
Serves 3

18 oysters in the shell
½ cup (4 fl oz) milk
1 tablespoon butter
2 teaspoons seed mustard
1 egg, separated
1 tablespoon self-raising flour

1 Preheat oven to moderate 180°C (350°F/Gas 4). Line a 32 x 28 cm (13 x 11 inch) oven tray with foil. Place oysters on tray and remove any grit from surface of oyster flesh.

2 Heat butter in a small heavy-based pan; add the flour. Stir over low heat for 2 minutes or until the mixture is lightly golden. Add milk gradually, stirring until the mixture is smooth. Stir constantly over medium heat for 5 minutes, or until the mixture boils and thickens. Boil for 1 minute, then remove from heat and cool. Stir in the mustard and egg yolk. Transfer to a medium mixing bowl.

3 Place egg white in a small, clean dry bowl. Using electric beaters, beat until firm peaks form. Using a metal spoon, fold beaten egg white gently into sauce mixture.

4 Spoon a heaped teaspoonful of mixture onto each oyster and bake for 15 minutes or until they are slightly puffed and golden. Serve immediately.

OYSTERS WITH PINE NUTS AND BACON

✳︎ **Preparation time:** 25 minutes
Total cooking time: 20 minutes
Serves 3

18 oysters in the shell
2 rashers bacon, finely chopped
2 tablespoons pine nuts, roughly chopped
3 teaspoons worcestershire sauce
1 tablespoon finely chopped fresh chives

1 Preheat oven to moderate 180°C (350°F/Gas 4). Line a 32 x 28 cm (13 x 11 inch) oven tray with foil. Place oysters on tray. Remove any grit from the surface of oyster flesh.

2 Cook bacon in a small heavy-based pan over medium heat until browned. Add pine nuts and sauce, stir to combine well. Remove from heat.

3 Spoon onto each oyster. Sprinkle with chives. Bake 5–10 minutes. Serve immediately.

OYSTERS KILPATRICK

Combine 2 tablespoons worcestershire sauce, 2 tablespoons tomato sauce, 2 teaspoons chopped parsley, ¾ cup finely chopped bacon and freshly ground black pepper in a small bowl. Spoon mixture onto 24 oysters on the half shell and grill (broil) under hot grill until cooked. Serves 2–4.

---

should not be collected from areas where pollution is suspected. Fresh oysters are available from September to April (months with 'r' in the name) in the northern hemisphere and all year round in the southern hemisphere. They are sold unshelled, on the half shell or bottled in fresh water; oysters are also available canned, either plain or smoked.

Oyster Sauce A thick, dark brown sauce originally made from oysters fermented in brine and then ground to a paste, but now usually thickened with cornflour (cornstarch) and darkened with caramel colouring. It has a strong, salty, slightly fishy flavour and is used as an all-purpose seasoning in Chinese cooking, especially stir-fries and braised dishes. It is a popular dressing on steamed Chinese vegetables, and is often used with other sauces. Oyster sauce originated in... Canton (now Guangzhou), a seaport in south-eastern China and was traded far inland, taking the taste of the sea to towns far from the coast. It is available in bottles, jars and cans (transfer to glass jar after opening).

P

Paella A dish of Spanish origin consisting of short-grained rice, olive oil, shellfish, chicken or rabbit and vegetables, seasoned with garlic and coloured with saffron. It takes its name from *paellera*, the shallow, two-handled pan in which it is traditionally cooked. Paella originated in the Valencia region of eastern Spain.

Palm Heart See Heart of Palm.

Pancake A thin, flat cake made from a batter of flour, egg and milk cooked quickly on each side in a greased frying pan or on a griddle and then served hot, usually folded over or rolled around a filling which can be either sweet or savoury. Pancakes are similar to, but thicker than, crêpes. In North America pancakes stacked one upon the other and covered with

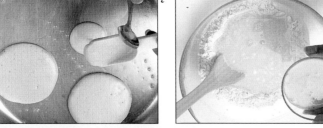

PANCAKES

PIKELETS

Preparation time: 10 minutes
Total cooking time: 15 minutes
Makes 16 pikelets

1 cup self-raising flour
2 tablespoons sugar
¼ teaspoon bicarbonate of soda (baking soda)
1 egg, lightly beaten
30 g (1 oz) butter, melted

½–¾ cup (4–6 fl oz) milk
½ teaspoon lemon juice or vinegar
extra melted butter

1 Sift flour, sugar and soda into a medium-sized mixing bowl. Add juice or vinegar to the milk to sour it; allow to stand for 5 minutes.

2 Make a well in centre of dry ingredients and add the egg, ½ cup (4 fl oz) milk and the butter; mix to form a smooth batter. If batter is too thick to pour from the spoon, add remaining milk.

3 Brush base of frying pan lightly with melted butter. Drop 1–2 tablespoons of mixture onto base of pan, about 2 cm (¾ inch) apart. Cook over medium heat for 1 minute, or until underside is golden. Turn pikelets over and cook other side. Remove from pan; repeat with remaining mixture. Serve warm with curls or pats of butter.

ABOUT PANCAKES

■ Pancake batter improves with standing but does not keep well. Make only as much batter as you need, about an hour or two before cooking.

■ Add variety to batter by using different flours—try cornmeal (maize flour), buckwheat or wholemeal flours.

■ Pancakes can be eaten with either sweet or savoury fillings. Fill with leftover casseroles, pasta sauces or mornays for a quick supper.

■ Use a soup ladle to transfer batter from bowl to pan. Ideally, pancakes are cooked on a cast-iron griddle, but a heavy-based metal frying pan will do; the cooking surface should be very hot.

BASIC PANCAKES

Preparation time: 15 minutes + 1 hour standing
Total cooking time: 5–10 minutes
Makes about 12

1 cup plain (all-purpose) flour
pinch of salt
1 egg
1¼ cups (10 fl oz) milk
oil
lemon juice and sugar to serve

1 Sift the flour and salt into a medium bowl; make a well in the centre. Add the egg and milk and whisk until smooth. Set mixture aside for 1 hour.

2 Heat a lightly oiled frying pan. Pour 3 tablespoons of mixture into the pan. Tilt pan to spread the mixture evenly. Gently lift edges with a knife. When underside of pancake is golden, turn over and cook the other side. Transfer to a plate and sprinkle with lemon juice and sugar. Roll up and serve hot.

Note: Instead of lemon juice and sugar, plain pancakes may be served hot with either cream or ice-cream. This basic recipe can be used to make a number of dishes based on sweet or savoury pancakes.

OPPOSITE PAGE: PIKELETS.
ABOVE: FLAPJACKS; RIGHT: BASIC PANCAKES

FLAPJACKS

Preparation time: 20 minutes
Total cooking time: 20 minutes
Makes about 10

2 cups self-raising flour
1/4 teaspoon baking powder
1 cup (8 fl oz) milk
2 tablespoons honey
2 eggs, lightly beaten
45 g (1½ oz) butter, melted
butter, extra
whipped butter and maple syrup to serve

1 Sift flour and baking powder into a medium bowl; make a well in the centre. Combine milk, honey, eggs and butter in a jug or separate bowl; add to flour mixture.

2 Beat mixture until combined and batter is free of lumps (mixture will be quite thick).

3 Heat a medium-sized frypan, grease with a little extra butter. Pour 2 tablespoons of the batter into pan. Cook over medium heat for 2 minutes, or until the underside is golden. Turn flapjack over; cook other side. Transfer to a plate and cover with a tea-towel. Keep warm.

4 Repeat with remaining batter, greasing the pan as necessary. Serve flapjacks topped with whipped butter and maple syrup.

5 **To make whipped butter:** Allow butter to soften to room temperature, then beat with electric beaters in a small bowl for 3–4 minutes or until light and creamy.

Notes: Flapjack batter will thicken as it stands. If you are making a large quantity of flapjacks you may need to stir in a little milk from time to time. True maple syrup is much more expensive than imitation maple syrup, but the flavour is so much better that it is worth the expense.

maple syrup are a popular breakfast dish. Pancakes were traditionally cooked and eaten on Shrove Tuesday, also known as Pancake Day, a day of revelry and merry-making before the fasting of Lent.

Pancetta Unsmoked bacon from the belly of the pig, cured with spices, salt and pepper. It is usually sold rolled into a sausage shape, and is served cut into thin slices.

Panettone A cake made from sweet yeast dough enriched with egg yolk (which gives it its colour), candied fruits and raisins. It is usually in the shape of a tall, round loaf. Panettone is a speciality of Milan, in northern Italy, where it is now made commercially for sale around the world. It is served with coffee for breakfast and is traditional Christmas fare.

Panforte A flat, very rich cake with a nougat-like texture containing nuts, honey, candied fruit and spices. It is a speciality of Siena, in Italy and, because of its energy-giving properties, is said to have been carried by the Crusaders on military expeditions.

SATAY VEGETABLE AND SPROUT PANCAKES

Preparation time: 35 minutes
Total cooking time: 15 minutes
Serves 4–6

Pancakes
250 g (8 oz) button
mushrooms, thinly sliced
1 large carrot, coarsely
grated
1 teaspoon baking powder
1¼ cups plain (all-
purpose) wholemeal flour
1 egg
1½ cups (12 fl oz) milk
1 teaspoon oil

Filling
250 g (8 oz) fresh snow
pea (mange tout) sprouts
250 g (8 oz) mung bean
sprouts
2 tablespoons lemon juice
2 teaspoons sambal oelek
6 spring onions
(scallions), finely sliced

Dressing
½ cup crunchy peanut
butter
2 tablespoons cider
vinegar
2 tablespoons lemon juice
1 cup roasted peanuts

1 To prepare Pancakes: Sift flour and baking powder into large bowl. Make a well in centre. Combine egg, milk and oil, stir into flour; mix to a smooth batter. Pour mixture into a jug.

2 Brush heated pancake pan with oil. Pour in batter to thinly cover pan base. Cook 2–3 minutes until mixture sets. Turn over with metal spatula, cook another 1–2 minutes. Remove to a plate, cover with greaseproof paper. Continue until all mixture has been used. Keep pancakes warm.

3 To make Filling: Combine vegetables and peanuts. Divide between pancakes. Fold or roll

4 To make Dressing: Combine all ingredients in a small bowl, whisking well. Pour over each pancake, place on large platter or individual serving plates.

BLINI WITH SOUR CREAM AND SMOKED SALMON

Preparation time: 15 minutes
Total cooking time: 10–15 minutes
Makes about 50

Blini
1 cup self-raising flour
2 eggs, lightly beaten
½ cup (4 fl oz) milk
1 tablespoon sour cream

Topping
½ cup (4 fl oz) sour cream
2 tablespoons mayonnaise
2 teaspoons lemon juice
1 tablespoon finely
chopped chives
1 tablespoon finely
chopped mint
125 g (4 oz) sliced
smoked salmon

1 Sift flour into bowl, make a well in centre. Add combined eggs, milk and cream; stir until batter is smooth and free of lumps. Let stand 10 minutes.

2 Heat large non-stick frying pan, brush with oil or melted butter. Drop teaspoonful of mixture into pan. When bubbles appear on surface, turn blini and cook other side. Remove from pan, set aside. Repeat with remaining mixture.

3 To make Topping: Combine sour cream, mayonnaise, lemon juice, chives, and mint. Spoon some mixture on each blini. Top with smoked salmon. Decorate with lemon peel if desired.

Pan-fry To cook food in a pan smeared with a little fat.

Pan-grill (Pan-broil) Also called dry-frying. To cook food in an ungreased pan. Fat released from the food is poured off as it accumulates. This method is used for fatty foods such as bacon or sausages and in low-fat diets.

Papaya Also known as pawpaw, a large, oval-shaped tropical fruit with smooth green to yellow skin, juicy golden flesh with a melon-like texture and a central cavity filled with small black seeds. Serve fresh and fully ripe with a sprinkle of lime juice for breakfast or as a dessert fruit, or add cubes to fruit salad (it combines especially well with passionfruit). Under-ripe papaya can be cooked as a vegetable. The fruit is native to the Americas and is thought to have been taken to Europe by Portuguese explorers; it now grows in tropical regions throughout the world. Its name comes from the Caribbean name *ababai*. Papaya is in season in early summer.

Papillote, en A French term for a cooking method in which individual portions of food—meat, fish, poultry

THAI CORN PANCAKES WITH CORIANDER MAYONNAISE

✶✶ **Preparation time:** 15 minutes
Total cooking time: 3–5 minutes each

Serves 6

440 g (14 oz) can sweet corn kernels, drained
1 tablespoon peanut oil

2 cloves garlic
1 small red chilli
2 cm (3/4 inch) piece fresh ginger
2 eggs
1/4 cup cornflour (cornstarch)
2 tablespoons fresh coriander leaves,
1/4 cup (2 fl oz) lime juice
8 spring onions (scallions), finely chopped
freshly ground black pepper, to taste

Coriander Mayonnaise
2/3 cup whole egg mayonnaise
1/3 cup coriander leaves, finely chopped
1 tablespoon sweet chilli sauce
freshly ground black pepper

1 Roughly chop garlic and ginger. Place eggs, cornflour, coriander, garlic, chilli, ginger, pepper, chilli sauce and half the corn in a food processor. Using pulse action, process for 30 seconds or until mixture is smooth. Transfer to a bowl and fold in remaining corn.

2 Heat oil in a large frying pan. Spoon two tablespoons of corn mixture into pan and cook over medium heat 2–3 minutes or until golden. Turn over and cook the second side 1–2 minutes or until cooked through. Repeat process until all mixture is used. Drain pancakes on paper towel.

3 **To make Coriander Mayonnaise:** Combine mayonnaise, lime juice, coriander and spring onions in bowl. Mix well. Add pepper to taste. Serve pancakes hot or cool with a dollop of Coriander Mayonnaise.

OPPOSITE PAGE: BLINI WITH SOUR CREAM AND SMOKED SALMON. ABOVE: THAI CORN PANCAKES WITH CORIANDER MAYONNAISE

CRAYFISH AND PRAWN (SHRIMP) CREPE STACK

✶✶ **Preparation time:** 25–30 minutes
Total cooking time: 20 minutes

Serves 4–6

250 g (8 oz) cooked crayfish meat
250 g (8 oz) cooked prawn (shrimp) meat
75 g (2½ oz) butter
2 spring onions (scallions), finely sliced
4 tablespoons plain (all-purpose) flour
1½ cups (12 fl oz) milk
3/4 cup yoghurt
1 tablespoon lemon juice
pepper
3/4 cup grated cheddar cheese

Crêpe Batter
1 cup plain (all-purpose) flour
2 teaspoons grated lemon rind
1 egg
2–2½ cups (16–20 fl oz) milk
1 tablespoon butter, melted
butter for frying

1 Flake crayfish and chop prawns into small pieces.
2 In a large saucepan melt butter. Cook spring onions for 2–3 minutes. Add flour. Cook for 1 minute. Gradually pour in milk and stir until thick . Add yoghurt, lemon juice and pepper. Mix well. Add crayfish and prawns. Set aside.

3 **To make Crêpe Batter:** Sift flour into a bowl. Add lemon rind. In a separate bowl combine egg and milk; heat lightly. Add melted butter. Gradually pour egg mixture into flour. Stir until a smooth batter is formed.
4 Melt a little butter in pan and cook crêpes. When each crêpe is cooked, remove and stack. approximately 20 cm (8 inches) in diameter.
5 Preheat oven to 150°C (300°F/Gas 2). Prepare the crêpe stack by placing one crêpe on a serving platter and spreading evenly with some of the sauce mixture. Continue alternating pancakes with sauce until crêpe stack is complete. Sprinkle top with grated cheese and place in oven for 10 minutes until cheese melts and crêpe stack is heated through.

Papillote A technique in which food—usually fish or vegetables—are wrapped in strong, greased paper or aluminium foil (often cut into a heart shape) and then baked or grilled (broiled). This technique preserves juices and flavour. Papillote is also the name of the paper frill used to decorate the bone end of a lamb or veal chop or a chicken drumstick.

Pappadam A thin, crisp water of Indian origin made from lentil, potato or rice flour. Fry in hot vegetable oil, one at a time; hold down with tongs for 3 seconds, then turn over and cook for another 3 seconds; the pappadams will swell, bubble and turn golden brown. Lift out and drain on absorbent paper. Pappadams are best served hot, as an accompaniment to Indian meals. They are sold dried in packets; varieties made especially to be microwaved are also available.

Paprika A seasoning made from the dried, ground flesh of a variety of sweet red pepper (capsicum). It is piquant, rather than hot, and is used to flavour.

PASTA

P asta is the Italian name for a dough made, in its most basic form, from flour and water. This most versatile of foods comes in a diverse range of shapes and sizes, bearing an even greater variety of names, some of which alter from one Italian region to another.

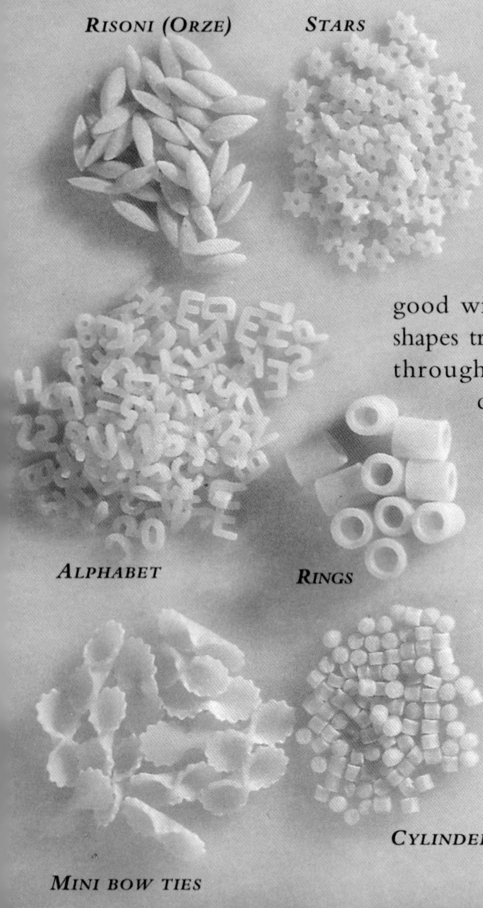

TO COOK PASTA

E ssential equipment is a large, deep pot. Allow 4 cups water for each 125 g (4 oz) pasta, add salt and a little oil, and bring water to a rapid boil. Add pasta gradually so that water does not go off the boil. When adding nests of dried pasta, unravel the pasta strands in the water with a fork. Cook uncovered for the time recommended by manufacturer, but it should be *al dente* (firm but not hard in the middle). When pasta is cooked, drain quickly, turn into a heated serving dish and toss with sauce, or return drained pasta to pan and add about 1 cup of sauce and a dash of olive oil. Mix well and serve topped with remaining sauce.

Cooking times: Start testing fresh pasta after 2 minutes for thin strips such as fettuccini, after 5 minutes for stuffed forms such as ravioli. Dry pasta takes longer—test after 5 minutes for tiny shapes, 7–8 minutes for larger shapes and 10–12 minutes for the very large shapes.

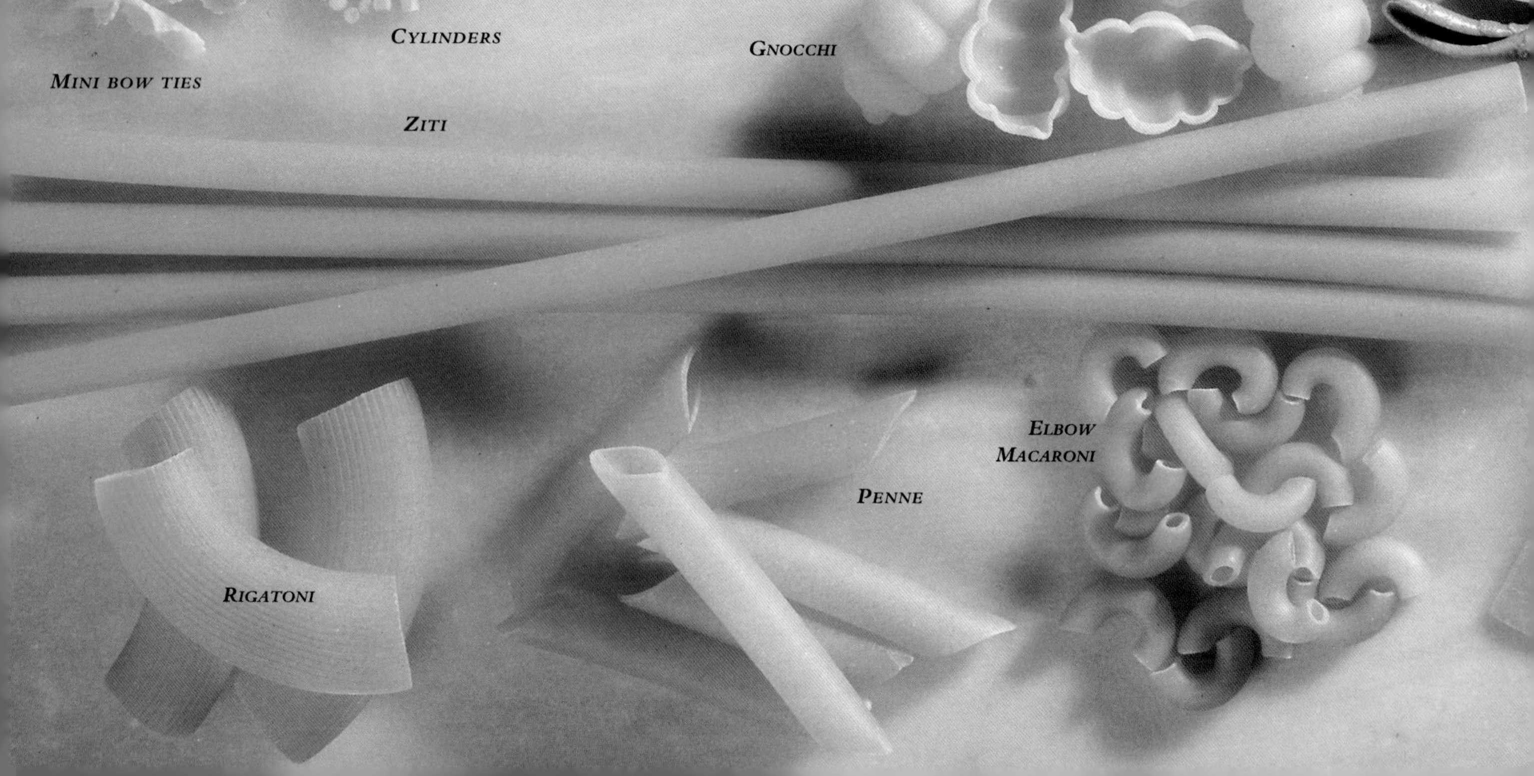

S ome pastas, both dry and fresh, are flavoured with herbs or spices, or coloured with spinach or tomato puree. Each pasta shape is ideally suited to a particular type of sauce. Spaghetti combines beautifully with rich tomato, butter and cream-based sauces which coat the strands well. Shorter pasta shapes like penne, rigatoni and fusilli are good with meaty, chunky sauces, as the pasta shapes trap the sauce and the meat is distributed throughout the dish. Vermicelli is ideal for creamy, cheese or egg sauces that cling to the thin strands. Flat, wide pasta, such as malfade are dressed with richly flavoured tomato and game sauces. Smaller shapes like macaroni add substance to soups and ragouts. Bow ties and shells are best served with other attractive ingredients such as vegetable pieces, prawns or mussels. Stuffed pasta such as ravioli and tortellini taste best when eaten with subtle sauces that do not overwhelm the main seasoning.

RIGATONI

PENNE

ELBOW MACARONI

ZITI

GNOCCHI

MINI BOW TIES

CYLINDERS

RINGS

ALPHABET

STARS

RISONI (ORZO)

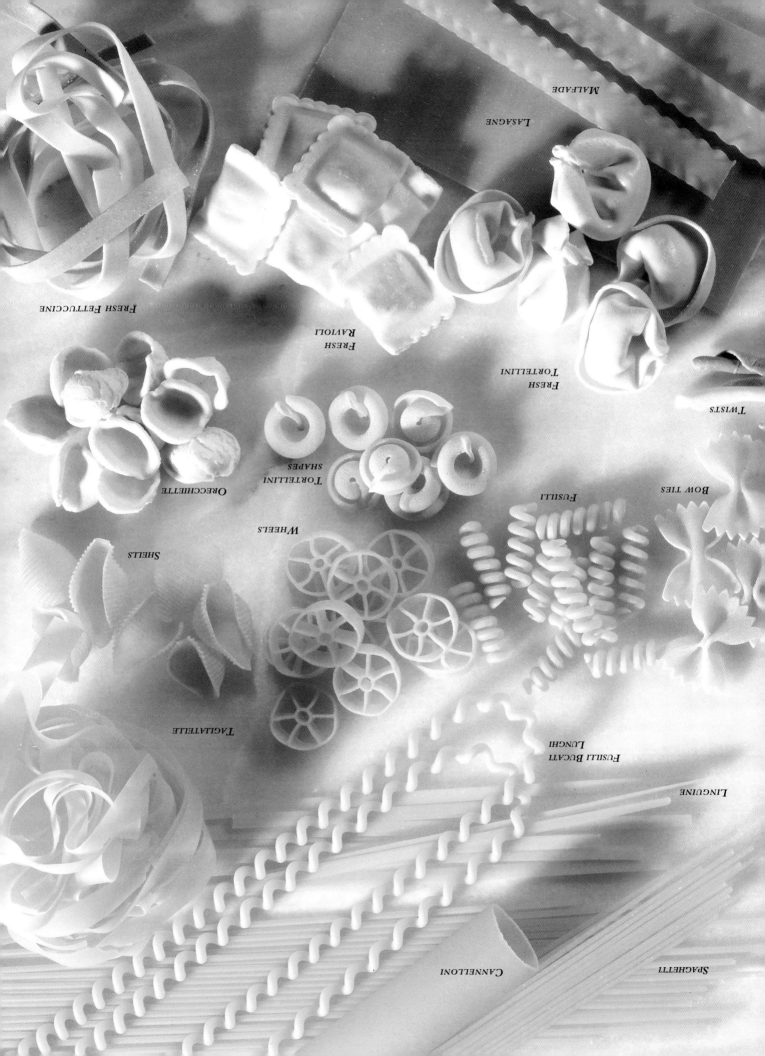

MALFADE

LASAGNE

FRESH FETTUCCINE

FRESH RAVIOLI

FRESH TORTELLINI

TWISTS

ORECCHIETTE

TORTELLINI SHAPES

FUSILLI

BOW TIES

WHEELS

SHELLS

TAGLIATELLE

FUSILLI BUCATI LUNGHI

LINGUINE

CANNELLONI

SPAGHETTI

THAI PAPAYA (PAWPAW) SALAD

★ **Preparation time:** 15 minutes
Total cooking time: nil
Serves 4–6

1 medium-sized papaya
(pawpaw), about
750 g (1½ lb)
¼ cup Chinese dried
prawns (shrimps),
soaked in boiling water
for 10 minutes
1 teaspoon mashed garlic
4–6 tablespoons lime juice
4–6 tablespoons nuoc mam
(fish sauce)
1–2 teaspoons sugar
1–4 teaspoons sweet chilli
sauce

1 Peel the papaya and cut into large cubes.
2 Grind the prawns and garlic to a paste in a food processor or mortar and add half the lime juice and half the nuoc mam. Stir into the papaya.
3 Slowly add the remaining lime juice and nuoc mam, with sugar and sweet chilli sauce to taste. The salad should have a tart-sweet taste.
4 Pile the salad into a salad dish lined with lettuce leaves and garnish with thinly sliced cucumber and sliced spring onions (scallions) if desired.

ABOUT PAPAYA (PAWPAW)

■ Ripe papaya is best cut just before serving; sprinkle with lime or lemon juice.
■ If refrigerating papaya, keep it closely covered to prevent its distinctive smell from tainting other foods, particularly dairy products.
■ Papaya contains an enzyme which is extracted and used to tenderise meat.

PAPAYAS (PAWPAWS)

SPICED PAPAYA (PAWPAW)

★ **Preparation time:** 15 minutes + overnight standing
Total cooking time: 40 minutes
Makes 1 litre (4 cups)

1 large ripe firm papaya
(pawpaw)
2 teaspoons whole allspice
1 tablespoon whole cloves
sugar
1 x 5 cm (2 inch) piece
cinnamon stick
white vinegar

1 Peel papaya, cut into halves and scrape out the seeds. Cut each half into finger length pieces. Weigh them and allow 1½ cups sugar for each 50 g (1½ oz) fruit. Put fruit into a container, sprinkle the sugar over and leave overnight.

2 Put fruit and syrup into a large saucepan or boiler and heat gently, stirring until sugar has dissolved; simmer until papaya looks transparent (do not overcook). Drain syrup from fruit, measure and allow ¾ cup (6 fl oz) vinegar for every 2½ cups (20 fl oz) syrup. Add the vinegar to the syrup with cloves, allspice and lightly crushed cinnamon stick.

3 Bring mixture to boil, cover and boil gently for 10 minutes. Set aside until cold; strain. Replace syrup in pan, add papaya and cook for 7 minutes.

4 Remove from heat, lift papaya slices out with a slotted spoon and put into sterilised jars. Bring syrup back to boil and spoon over papaya. Cool before sealing. Label and date.

goulashes, ragoûts, stuffings and sauces and is sprinkled on dips and eggs, cheese and seafood dishes. The red pepper comes from a shrub native to Central America and has been known in Europe since the time of Columbus. The form used to make paprika developed in Hungary and is smaller and more pungently flavoured than Spanish paprika, which is made from a milder red pepper. The name comes from the Hungarian word for 'sweet pepper'.

Paratha An unleavened, rich, flaky Indian bread made from a dough of wholemeal flour, ghee, salt and water, formed into a disc shape and fried on both sides; the dough can also be folded around a vegetable mixture to make a stuffed version. Parathas are usually reserved for special occasions; they are generally made at home but are sometimes available from Indian restaurants.

Parfait A chilled dessert served in a tall glass and eaten with a long-handled spoon. It usually consists of layers of custard, jelly, ice-cream and whipped cream. The term also

PARSNIPS

PARSNIP SOUP

Preparation time: 20 minutes
Total cooking time: 40 minutes
Serves 4–6

60 g (2 oz) butter
2 onions, chopped
1 kg (2 lb) small parsnips, peeled and chopped
1/2 teaspoon ground turmeric
1 teaspoon curry powder
1/2 teaspoon ground cardamom
1 litre (4 cups) vegetable stock
1 cup (8 fl oz) evaporated skim milk
croutons or chopped herbs, to garnish

1 Melt butter in a large pan. Add parsnips and onions. Cover and cook over low heat for 3–4 minutes.

2 Add curry powder, cardamom and turmeric. Stir to combine and cook for 1 minute. Pour in vegetable stock. Bring to the boil, reduce heat and simmer, covered, until the vegetables are tender (about 30 minutes).

3 Remove soup from heat. Allow to cool for 10 minutes. Blend in an electric blender or food processor until smooth. Return liquid to pan. Add evaporated milk. Stir over low heat until soup is heated through. Serve with croutons or a sprinkling of fresh, chopped herbs.

Note: Parsnips have a distinctively nutty flavour which has a sweetening effect in soups and other vegetable dishes, such as stews and casseroles. Choose parsnips which are small and firm. Larger parsnips may have a woody core—which will make them inedible.

PARSNIP CHIPS

Preparation time: 10 minutes
Total cooking time: 6 minutes
Serves 8

4 large parsnips   oil for deep-frying
2 tablespoons lemon juice

1 Peel parsnips. Cut parsnips diagonally into 2.5 mm (1/8 inch) slices. Place slices in a large bowl and cover with water. Add lemon juice to water. Set aside.

2 When ready to cook, drain parsnip slices and thoroughly dry with paper towel.

3 Heat oil in deep heavy-based pan. Gently lower a third of the parsnip slices into moderately hot oil. Cook over medium-high heat 1–2 minutes or until golden; remove with tongs. Repeat with remaining parsnip slices. Drain chips on paper towel and serve immediately.

Note: For best results when deep-frying, use peanut, corn, safflower or soybean oil. These oils have a bland flavour and a high smoking point, which means that they can be heated to a very high temperature without burning or smoking.

OPPOSITE PAGE, ABOVE: SPICED PAPAYA, BELOW: THAI PAPAYA SALAD. THIS PAGE, ABOVE: PARSNIP CHIPS; RIGHT: PARSNIP SOUP

---

refers to a frozen rich custard dessert.

Parma Ham Fine quality salt-cured ham also known as prosciutto made from the hind legs of a variety of pig raised on controlled foods in the Parma region of northern Italy and cured in the traditional manner. Hams are rubbed with salt, left in a cool place for several weeks, then washed and allowed to dry out and mature in a cool, well-ventilated atmosphere for ten to twelve months. Rosy pink, marbled with lines of white fat, and only mildly salty, parma ham sliced water thin and served with melon or fresh figs is a popular antipasto not only in Italy but around the world. Hannibal, on his way from Carthage to Rome is said to have been served salt-cured ham at a banquet in Parma in 217 BC.

Parmesan A very hard cow's milk cheese with a strong taste and grainy texture, famous as a grating cheese. Parmesan is made by the cooked curd method (the curd is 'cooked' in heated whey) and is matured for up to three

PASSIONFRUIT

PASSIONFRUIT VANILLA SLICE

Preparation time: 35 minutes
Total cooking time: 20–25 minutes
Makes 12 squares

2 sheets ready-rolled puff pastry
1/2 teaspoon vanilla essence

Custard
1/4 cup custard powder
1/4 cup caster (superfine) sugar
1 cup (8 fl oz) cream
1 1/2 cups (12 fl oz) milk

Icing
1/4 cup passionfruit pulp
25 g (3/4 oz) unsalted (sweet) butter
1 1/2 cups icing (confectioners) sugar

1 Preheat oven to moderately hot 210°C (415°F/Gas 6–7). Line two oven trays with baking paper. Place pastry sheets on prepared trays and prick all over with a fork. Bake for 10–15 minutes or until golden and crisp. Cool on wire rack.

2 **To make Custard:** Blend custard powder, sugar and cream in heavy-based pan. Gradually add milk; stir constantly over medium heat until custard boils and thickens. Remove from heat, stir in essence. Cover surface of custard with plastic wrap to prevent skin forming. Cool completely.

3 Spread one sheet of pastry evenly with custard. Top with remaining pastry sheet, upside down.

4 **To make Icing:** Combine pulp, butter and icing sugar in heatproof bowl. Stand bowl over pan of simmering water, stir until icing is smooth and glossy; remove from heat. Spread icing evenly over pastry sheet with a flat-bladed knife. Refrigerate for several hours or until pastry softens slightly. Cut into squares with a serrated knife.

PASSIONFRUIT AND PISTACHIO NUT ICE-CREAM

Preparation time: 15 minutes + overnight freezing
Total cooking time: 15 minutes
Serves 8

1/2 cup (4 fl oz) milk
1 1/2 cups (12 fl oz) cream
6 egg yolks
1 1/4 cups caster (superfine) sugar
pulp of 8 passionfruit
1/3 cup shelled pistachio nuts, chopped
passionfruit pulp for serving

1 Heat milk and cream until almost boiling.

2 Using electric beaters, beat yolks and sugar until pale and thick. Add milk and cream gradually. Return mixture to pan. Stir constantly over medium heat until lightly thickened (do not boil). Transfer to bowl, cool, stirring occasionally.

3 Reserve a quarter cup of passionfruit pulp, place remainder in pan. Warm over medium heat 1–2 minutes. Remove from heat, strain. Add passionfruit juice and reserved pulp to cream mixture. Pour into 6-cup capacity metal tray, freeze 3–4 hours or until just frozen around edges.

4 Transfer to large bowl. Beat until thick and creamy. Add nuts, mix well. Freeze overnight or until firm. Serve with passionfruit pulp.

LEFT: PASSIONFRUIT VANILLA SLICE.
ABOVE: PASSIONFRUIT AND PISTACHIO NUT ICE-CREAM.
OPPOSITE PAGE: RICOTTA-FILLED RAVIOLI WITH FRESH TOMATO SAUCE

Parsley A herb with bright green, fern-like leaves and a mild, celery-like flavour, widely used as a seasoning and a garnish. There are two main varieties—curly-leaf and the larger flat-leaf or Italian parsley. Curly-leaf is best used as a garnish, either in sprigs or sprinkled, finely chopped, on food. The more flavoursome flat-leaf is preferable for cooking; it is the main ingredient in the Middle Eastern salad tabouli. Parsley combines

years. Because of its extremely low moisture content parmesan can be stored at low temperatures almost indefinitely. It is used, grated, in cooking (it does not become stringy as most cheeses do) and as a garnish; young parmesan can also be served as a table cheese with fruit. The cheese has been made in Parma, in northern Italy, for some eight hundred years and is now made around the world by the same method. Cheese carrying the stamp 'parmigiano reggiano' comes from a select area of northern Italy. Parmesan is available in block and is best used freshly grated; it is also sold grated in vacuum-sealed packs.

PASTA

RICOTTA-FILLED RAVIOLI WITH FRESH TOMATO SAUCE

✷✷ **Preparation time:** 45 minutes +
30 minutes standing
Total cooking time: 45 minutes
Serves 4–6

Ravioli Dough
1 cup plain (all-purpose) flour
1 egg
1 tablespoon oil
1 teaspoon water

Filling
500 g (1 lb) ricotta cheese
125 g (4 oz) prosciutto, finely chopped
1 tablespoon flat-leaf parsley
1 egg yolk

Sauce
1 tablespoon oil
1 onion, chopped
2 cloves garlic, crushed
1 carrot, chopped
1 kg (2 lb) ripe tomatoes, skinned and chopped
45 g (1½ oz) tomato paste
1 teaspoon soft brown sugar
½ cup (4 fl oz) chicken stock
1 tablespoon worcestershire sauce
½ cup chopped fresh basil

1 To make Ravioli Dough: Sift the flour into a bowl. Make a well in the centre and add the egg, oil and water, gradually incorporating them into the flour to form a smooth dough. Turn dough onto a lightly floured board, knead until smooth and elastic. Cover dough and set aside for 30 minutes.

2 To make Filling: Combine ricotta, prosciutto, parsley and egg yolk. Mix well.

To make Sauce: Place oil in a large heavy-based pan. Add the onion, garlic and carrot. Cook over low heat for 5–7 minutes. Add the tomatoes, tomato paste, sugar, chicken stock, worcestershire sauce and basil. Bring mixture to the boil, reduce to simmer, cover and cook for 30 minutes. Puree the mixture in a blender and keep warm.

3 Halve dough and shape each half into a smooth ball. Roll out each portion thinly to a long rectangle. Place teaspoonful of filling in small mounds at 5 cm (2 inch) intervals, in regular lines, on one sheet of dough. Brush between the mounds of filling with water. Place the other sheet of dough carefully over the top. Press down between mounds of filling to seal. Use a pastry wheel or a sharp knife to cut into squares. Drop the ravioli into a pan of rapidly boiling water and cook for 8–10 minutes, or until tender. Remove ravioli from water using a slotted spoon and place into a heated serving dish. Cover with sauce and serve immediately with parmesan shavings.

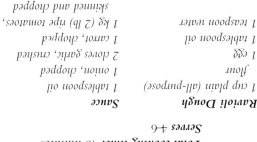

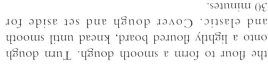

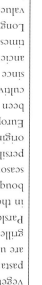

Parsnip A root vegetable with a carrot-like shape and creamy white flesh. When cooked it has a strong, slightly sweet flavour which goes well with roast meats. The parsnip originated in eastern Europe and was developed in Germany; for many centuries it was the food of the poor in Europe. The vegetable was introduced into North America in the early years of the seventeenth century.

Parsley is an ingredient in the flavouring bouquet garni and the seasonings gremolata and persillade. The herb originated in southern Europe and has been cultivated since ancient times. Long valued for its medicinal as well as its culinary properties, it is rich in vitamin C and minerals and is sometimes called the herb of health. The ancient Romans wore wreaths of parsley to ward off the effects of alcohol. Parsley is particularly well with salads, egg dishes, stews, vegetables, rice and pasta; deep-fried sprigs are used to garnish grilled meats and fish.

FETTUCCINE BOLOGNESE

★

Preparation time: 10 minutes
Total cooking time: 1 hour 40 minutes
Serves 6

2 tablespoons oil
2 medium onions, chopped
2 cloves garlic, crushed
500 g (1 lb) minced
(ground) beef
440 g (14 oz) can
tomatoes with their
liquid, crushed
½ cup tomato paste
1 tablespoon chopped
fresh oregano
1 litre (4 cups) water
500 g (1 lb) dried
fettuccine
250 g (8 oz) small
mushrooms, quartered
2 tablespoons chopped
fresh basil

1 Heat oil in heavy-based pan, add the onion and stir over medium heat for 3 minutes or until soft. Add garlic, stir for 1 minute. Add the meat and cook over high heat for 5 minutes until meat is well browned and all the liquid has evaporated. Use a fork to break up any lumps of mince as it cooks.

2 Add the mushrooms, basil, crushed tomatoes with liquid, tomato paste, oregano and water. Bring to the boil, then reduce heat to a simmer. Cook, uncovered, for 1½ hours, or until the sauce has reduced and thickened.

3 Bring a large pan of water to the boil. Add fettuccine and cook until just tender. Serve with meat sauce.

SPAGHETTI CARBONARA

★ ★

Preparation time: 20 minutes
Total cooking time: 10 minutes
Serves 6

4 cloves garlic
1 tablespoon oil
6 rashers bacon, chopped
⅓ cup (2½ fl oz) white
wine
4 eggs
¾ cup grated cheddar
cheese
500 g (1 lb) spaghetti,
cooked and kept warm
¾ cup shredded
parmesan cheese
freshly ground black
pepper to taste
¼ cup chopped parsley

1 Peel and halve garlic cloves. Heat oil in pan, add garlic, stir until lightly golden, remove garlic and discard. Add bacon to the pan and cook over medium heat until crisp and golden. Add wine and cook for another minute.

2 Whisk eggs in a bowl; add cheeses, pepper and parsley.

3 To serve, place drained spaghetti in a large bowl, add the bacon with pan juices and toss together well. Add the beaten egg and cheese mixture, mix well. Serve pasta immediately, with extra parmesan cheese, if desired.

ABOVE: FETTUCCINE BOLOGNESE.
OPPOSITE PAGE: PASTA WITH LAMB AND
VEGETABLES.

Partridge A ground-dwelling game bird related to the pheasant and native to Europe and the British Isles. Partridge is hung unplucked and uncleaned for three to four days after killing to develop its flavour and to tenderise the flesh. Young birds can be grilled (broiled) or roasted in the same way as chicken; older birds are best slowly casseroled. Allow one bird per person. Partridge is available fresh and frozen from specialist game and poultry stores.

Passionfruit Also called granadilla, the egg-shaped fruit of the passionflower vine with sharp-sweet, juicy, fragrant orange pulp studded with small black edible seeds. The leathery skin varies in colour from pale yellow-green to pink, to deep purple-brown; it is smooth and shiny when immature and deeply dimpled when ripe.

Passionfruit can be eaten fresh (scooped from the shell with a spoon) or the pulp can be added to fruit salads, yoghurt and ice-cream, mousse and dessert sauces; it is the traditional topping for pavlova. The passionfruit vine is native to tropical

Pasta A dough or paste made of wheat flour, water, salt and sometimes eggs, cooked in boiling water and served with many different sauces. Pasta is cut and shaped into a wide variety of shapes—ribbons, bows, strings, rings, tubes, spirals and shells—each one known by a particular name. It can be home-made or bought either fresh (*pasta fresca*) or dried (*pasta secca*). There are two main forms of fresh pasta: *pasta liscia* (strips of smooth or flat pasta) and *pasta ripiena* (stuffed pasta, such as tortellini).

America. It was named by Spanish Jesuit priests in South America for its large flower in whose form they saw all aspects of the Crucifixion of Christ (the three nails, the five wounds, the crown of thorns and the apostles). Passionfruit is in season in late summer but can usually be found fresh through the year; passionfruit pulp is available canned.

CHICKEN CANNELLONI WITH CHILLI TOMATO SAUCE

Preparation time: 20 minutes
Total cooking time: 45 minutes
Serves 4

1 tablespoon olive oil
1 small onion, finely minced
2 spring onions (scallions), chopped
2 teaspoons bottled crushed chilli
3 small carrots, finely diced
1/2 cup chopped parsley
800 g (1 lb 10 oz) can peeled tomatoes, chopped
1/4 cup (2 fl oz) white wine or chicken stock
1 egg, beaten

500 g (1 lb) chicken mince
2 tablespoons grated parmesan cheese
1/2 cup (4 fl oz) cream
125 g (4 oz) packet instant cannelloni tubes

Garnish
1 cup (8 fl oz) sour cream
2 medium avocados, sliced

1 Preheat oven to moderate 180°C (350°F/Gas 4). Lightly brush a 35 x 20 x 6 cm (14 x 8 x 2½ inch) shallow oblong baking dish with oil or melted butter.

2 Heat oil in a pan. Add onion, chilli and carrot, cook for 3–4 minutes or until the onion is tender. Add the parsley, tomatoes and wine or stock and bring to the boil, stirring. Reduce heat and simmer, covered, for 10 minutes—the sauce should still be quite liquid.

3 Combine egg, chicken mince, spring onion, cream and parmesan cheese, and mix well. Place mixture into a piping bag which has been fitted with a large, plain nozzle. Pipe mixture into the cannelloni tubes.

4 Spoon half the tomato mixture over base of prepared dish. Arrange filled cannelloni tubes over tomato mixture in a single layer. Top with remaining tomato mixture. Bake for 30 minutes or until pasta is tender. Serve garnished with sour cream and sliced avocado.

Note: Take care when piping filling into uncooked cannelloni tubes as they are brittle and easy to chip or shatter. For best results, stand tubes on end on a chopping board and fill to the top with chicken mixture.

PASTA WITH LAMB AND VEGETABLES

Preparation time: 15 minutes
Total cooking time: 20 minutes
Serves 4

2 tablespoons oil
1 large onion, cut into eighths
2 garlic cloves, crushed
500 g (1 lb) lamb mince
1 small red pepper (capsicum), seeded and chopped
155 g (5 oz) shelled broad beans (fava beans)

125 g (4 oz) small mushroom caps, halved
440 g (14 oz) can tomatoes
2 tablespoons tomato paste
500 g (1 lb) dried penne pasta
175 g (4 oz) feta cheese
2 tablespoons shredded fresh basil

1 Heat the oil in a large heavy-based pan, add the onion and garlic and stir-fry over medium heat for 2 minutes or until lightly browned. Add lamb mince; stir-fry over high heat for 4 minutes or until meat is well browned and all liquid has evaporated. Use a fork to break up any lumps as mince cooks.

2 Add pepper, broad beans, mushrooms, undrained, crushed tomatoes and tomato paste; bring mixture to boil, reduce heat to a simmer, cover and cook for 10 minutes or until the vegetables are tender, stir occasionally.

3 Cook the penne in a large pan of rapidly boiling water, with a little oil added, until it is just tender. Remove from heat and drain. Spoon pasta into serving bowls, top with lamb and vegetable sauce, crumble cheese over the sauce and sprinkle with basil.

and ravioli). Pasta is often regarded as the national food of Italy. Simple to make and to cook, economical, healthy and versatile, it has long been the food of rich and poor alike. Roman writer Horace was fond of a type of lasagne

seasoned with leek and chick peas (a similar dish is still made in southern Italy); medieval manuscripts have many references to macaroni, including mention of macaroni cooked with cheese; a fifteenth-century cookbook gives instructions for sun-drying vermicelli; and tagliatelle has been cooked from at least the sixteenth century. From the end of the eighteenth century street stalls selling pasta were common: pasta was cooked on the spot and eaten hot with the fingers. The first pasta factories date from the nineteenth century. Egg pasta is associated with northern Italy; pasta made with durum wheat flour is from the south.

Pastrami Lean beef, cured, spiced and rubbed with dried chilli and black peppercorns. It is deep red in colour and is

PASTA AND VEGETABLES

⭐ **Preparation time:** 20 minutes
Total cooking time: 50–55 minutes
Serves 4

1 tablespoon olive oil
1 large onion, finely chopped
1 clove garlic, crushed
3 medium zucchini (courgettes), sliced
4 button mushrooms, sliced
1 cup frozen peas
2 cups (16 fl oz) tomato pasta sauce
salt and pepper to taste
1 tablespoon oil, extra
1½ cups dried pasta (penne or spiralli)
⅓ cup grated parmesan cheese

1 Preheat oven to slow 150°C (300°F/Gas 2). Heat oil in frying pan. Add onion and garlic, cook over low heat for 4 minutes or until onion is soft. Add zucchini and mushrooms, cook for 3 minutes. Add peas and pasta sauce, cook for another 3 minutes. Season with salt and pepper. Remove from heat and set aside.
2 Bring a large pan of water to a rapid boil, add oil and pasta, cook 10–12 minutes or until pasta is just tender. Drain and add to vegetables in pan.
3 Spoon mixture into a casserole dish. Sprinkle with parmesan cheese and bake, covered, for 20–30 minutes.

ABOVE: PASTA AND VEGETABLES;
RIGHT: FETTUCCINE WITH PESTO.
OPPOSITE PAGE: BEEF LASAGNE

FETTUCCINE WITH PESTO

⭐ **Preparation time:** 20 minutes
Total cooking time: 10 minutes
Serves 4

⅓ cup pine nuts
2 cups fresh basil leaves, tightly packed
1 cup (8 fl oz) olive oil
2 cloves garlic
⅔ cup parmesan cheese
45 g (1½ oz) butter, softened
freshly ground black pepper to taste
500 g (1 lb) fettuccine, cooked

1 Place pine nuts in a dry pan, stir over moderate heat until nuts are lightly golden. Place in a food processor with basil leaves, olive oil and garlic. Blend until smooth. Transfer to a large bowl.
2 Add parmesan cheese, butter and black pepper, mix well.
3 To serve, drain cooked pasta well, add the prepared pesto and toss. Serve immediately. Sprinkle extra parmesan cheese on top before serving, if desired.

Note: Pesto sauce can be made up in larger quantities for later use. It will keep well in the refrigerator for at least a week if placed in a glass jar with a well-fitting lid. Pour a thin layer of olive oil over the surface of the sauce before replacing the lid. Pesto can also be stored in the freezer, and will retain its flavour and colour.

BEEF LASAGNE

★★ **Preparation time:** 45 minutes
Total cooking time: 1 hour 40 minutes
Serves 16

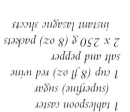
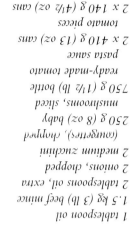

1 tablespoon oil
1.5 kg (3 lb) beef mince
2 tablespoons oil, extra
2 onions, chopped
2 medium zucchini (courgettes), chopped
250 g (8 oz) baby mushrooms, sliced
750 g (1½ lb) bottle ready-made tomato pasta sauce
2 x 410 g (13 oz) cans tomato pieces
2 x 140 g (4½ oz) cans tomato paste

Cream Sauce
125 g (4 oz) butter
⅔ cup plain (all-purpose) flour
1.5 litres (6 cups) milk
salt and pepper
155 g (5 oz) cheddar cheese, grated
¼ cup grated parmesan cheese

2 x 250 g (8 oz) packets instant lasagne sheets
salt and pepper
1 cup (8 fl oz) red wine
1 tablespoon caster (superfine) sugar

1 Preheat oven to moderate 180°C (350°F/Gas 4). Grease two 20 x 35 x 7 cm (8 x 14 x 2¾ inch) baking dishes. Heat oil in large pan, cook mince in batches until browned. Transfer to bowl. Heat extra oil in the same pan, cook onion until soft. Add zucchini and mushrooms, cook until just tender. Return meat to onion mixture, add pasta sauce, undrained tomato pieces, tomato paste, sugar, wine, and salt and pepper. Simmer, covered, for 30 minutes, stirring occasionally. Remove from heat and set aside.

2 To make Cream Sauce: Heat butter in a medium pan until melted. Add flour, cook, stirring over heat until mixture bubbles. Remove from heat, add milk gradually to pan, stirring, until smooth. Stir over heat until sauce boils and thickens. Add salt, pepper and cheese. Mix until smooth and cheese has melted.

3 To assemble lasagne, spread half a cup of tomato mixture over the base of each baking dish. Top with lasagne sheets to cover. Spread one-sixth of the cheese sauce over pasta. Spread a quarter of the tomato sauce over cheese sauce in each dish. Repeat layering with pasta, cream sauce, then tomato sauce, finishing with a pasta sheet topped with cream sauce. Sprinkle top with grated parmesan. Bake lasagne for 45 minutes, or until pasta is cooked through and the top is lightly browned.

Pastry An unleavened dough made from fat (butter, margarine or lard), flour and sometimes sugar, and bound with water. Different types of pastry result from the kind of fat used and variations in the proportions of the ingredients. Shortcrust pastry forms the containers for sweet and savoury pies, flans and tarts; crisp, filo pastry and flaky puff pastry are used for dishes ranging from sausage rolls to delicate desserts; hot-water crust pastry is used particularly for English game pies. Pastry is also a general term for sweet baked foods made with pastry dough.

Pastry Cream See Crème Pâtissière.

Pâté and Terrine Preparations of minced (ground) meat, poultry, game, fish or vegetables. In general, pâté is a fine-textured paste or spread: the name 'pâté' comes from the French *pâté en croûte*, a rich savoury meat, poultry or game mixture cooked encased in pastry; the term is also applied to mixtures that have been served sliced as a cold meat or sandwich filling.

SPAGHETTI MARINARA

★ **Preparation time:** 20 minutes
Total cooking time: 25–30 minutes
Serves 4

1 tablespoon olive oil
1 small onion, finely chopped
1 clove garlic, chopped
1 large carrot, diced
1 stalk celery, diced
800 g (1 lb 10 oz) can peeled tomatoes, pureed
1/2 cup (4 fl oz) white wine
375 g (12 oz) marinara mix (see Note)
1/4 cup (2 fl oz) cream
500 g (1 lb) spaghetti, cooked
1/4 cup chopped parsley

1 Heat the oil in a pan. Add the onion, garlic, carrot and celery. Cook until the vegetables are tender. Add the pureed tomatoes, parsley and white wine. Simmer uncovered, stirring occasionally, for 15 minutes.

2 Add marinara mix to the sauce with the cream; stir to combine ingredients and cook for two minutes.

3 To serve, combine well-drained spaghetti with sauce. Serve immediately.

Note: Marinara mix is a mixture of seafood pieces (usually including octopus, calamari, mussels and prawns/shrimps) sold by fishmongers.

FETTUCCINE ALFREDO

★ **Preparation time:** 10 minutes
Total cooking time: 5–10 minutes
Serves 4

500 g (1 lb) fresh fettuccine (plain, spinach or tomato)
1 cup (8 fl oz) cream
60 g (2 oz) butter
2/3 cup grated parmesan cheese
black pepper

1 Bring a large pan of water to the boil. Add a little salt. Drop in the fettuccine and cover the pot until the water returns to the boil—fresh fettuccine will take only a few minutes to cook. Drain in a colander.

2 Heat 2/3 cup (5 fl oz) of the cream along with the butter in a heavy casserole dish and simmer over medium heat for about 1 minute or until the cream has thickened slightly.

3 Transfer the drained fettuccine to the casserole dish, place over low heat, add remaining cream, cheese and pepper. Toss until all fettuccine is coated with sauce. Serve immediately with extra parmesan cheese if desired.

ABOVE: SPAGHETTI MARINARA.
OPPOSITE PAGE: VEGETABLE LASAGNE

Pâte Brisée A shortcrust pastry made from a dough of flour, butter, margarine or lard (or a mixture of these), sugar, egg and water. It is mixed directly on the work surface by placing the wet ingredients in a well formed in the centre of the dry ingredients and, using the fingertips, first mixing together the wet ingredients, then gradually drawing in the dry ingredients. It is called pâte brisée, literally 'broken dough', because the ingredients are 'broken' into one another. Pâte brisée is used in French cooking for both sweet and savoury dishes.

baked or sautéed, then pureed to a creamy consistency. A terrine is usually coarser in texture and is served sliced. Pâté is usually served at room temperature, either spread on bread or dry biscuits (crackers) as finger food, or cut into thick slices as a first course. A type of pâté was made in the days of ancient Rome, chiefly with pork, but sometimes including other ingredients such as spiced and marinated birds' tongues.

PASTA

casserole dish with oil or melted butter. Cut peppers into quarters. Remove seeds and membrane. Place pepper pieces skin-side up on grill tray and brush with oil. Grill (broil) for 10 minutes, or until skin is black. Cover with a damp tea-towel until cool. Peel off skin and cut pepper into long thin strips. Set aside. Slice eggplant into 1 cm (½ inch) rounds, place in a large pan of boiling water. Cook for 1 minute or until just tender; drain and pat dry with paper towel. Set aside.

2 Heat oil in a large heavy-based frying pan. Add onion, garlic and herbs. Cook over medium heat for 5 minutes or until the onion is soft. Add mushrooms and cook for 1 minute. Add tomatoes, beans, sauce, salt and pepper. Bring to boil, reduce heat. Simmer, uncovered, for 15 minutes or until sauce thickens. Remove from heat.

3 Dip lasagne sheets in hot water to soften slightly and arrange four sheets on base of prepared dish. Arrange half of each of the eggplant, spinach, basil, pepper, mushroom mixture and sun-dried tomatoes over pasta. Top with a layer of pasta and press gently. Repeat layers. Top with cheese sauce and sprinkle with combined parmesan and cheddar cheeses. Bake for 45 minutes or until pasta is soft.

4 To make Cheese Sauce: Heat butter in medium pan, add flour. Stir over medium heat for 2 minutes or until mixture is golden. Add milk gradually, stirring until mixture boils and thickens. Boil for 1 minute. Add ricotta and stir until smooth.

VEGETABLE LASAGNE

★★ *Preparation time:* 20 minutes
Total cooking time: 1 hour 15 minutes
Serves 6

3 large red peppers (capsicums)
2 large eggplants (aubergines)
2 tablespoons oil
1 large onion, finely chopped
3 cloves garlic, crushed
1 teaspoon dried mixed herbs
1 teaspoon dried oregano
500 g (1 lb) mushrooms, sliced
440 g (14 oz) can whole tomatoes, crushed
440 g (14 oz) can red kidney beans, drained
1 tablespoon sweet chilli sauce
salt and pepper, to taste

250 g (8 oz) packet instant lasagne
1 bunch English spinach, chopped
1 cup basil leaves
105 g (3½ oz) sun-dried tomatoes, sliced
¼ cup grated parmesan cheese
¼ cup grated cheddar cheese

Cheese Sauce
60 g (2 oz) butter
¼ cup plain (all purpose) flour
2 cups (16 fl oz) milk
600 g (1¼ lb) ricotta cheese

1 Preheat oven to moderate 180°C (350°F/Gas 4). Brush a 35 x 28 cm (14 x 11 inch) ovenproof

TORTELLINI WITH MUSHROOM CREAM SAUCE

★ *Preparation time:* 10 minutes
Total cooking time: 8 minutes
Serves 4

60 g (2 oz) butter
185 g (6 oz) small mushrooms, sliced
1 clove garlic, crushed
300 ml (9 fl oz) cream
1 teaspoon grated lemon rind

pinch pepper
pinch nutmeg
3 tablespoons grated parmesan cheese
500 g (1 lb) tortellini, cooked and kept warm

1 Melt butter in a pan. Add mushrooms and cook over medium heat for 30 seconds. Add garlic, cream, lemon rind, pepper and nutmeg to taste.
2 Stir over low heat for 1–2 minutes. Add parmesan and cook gently for 3 minutes.
3 To serve, combine well-drained pasta with sauce. Serve immediately.

Pâte Sucrée Literally 'sugar dough', a sweet, crisp, shortcrust pastry made from butter or margarine (lard is never used), sugar and egg yolk and used in French cooking for flan cases and tartlets. It is mixed in the same way as pâte brisée.

Paupiette A thin fillet of meat, poultry or fish spread with a stuffing mixture of finely chopped meat, herbs and seasonings and then rolled up, secured with string or toothpicks and braised. Beef paupiettes are usually referred to as beef olives.

Pavlova A dessert consisting of a meringue case filled with whipped cream and topped with fresh fruit (usually including strawberries and passionfruit pulp). The dish is attributed to Herbert Sachse, chef at a leading hotel in Perth, Western Australia, who created it in 1935 and named it in memory of the 1929 visit to the city by the ballerina Anna Pavlova.

Pawpaw See Papaya.

Peach A round, yellow to rosy pink, downy-skinned, stone fruit with pale, fragrant, sweet, juicy flesh. There are two main types: slipstone or freestone (the flesh of

PASTRY

The success of a tart, quiche or flan depends on the pastry base—it should be light, crisp and golden. Once you have mastered the techniques of good pastry-making, you will have perfect results every time. For quiches and flans, use shortcrust, filo or puff pastry. Purchased, ready-rolled pastry saves time and also gives an excellent result.

ABOUT SHORTCRUST PASTRY

Plain (all-purpose) flour is the flour generally used to make shortcrust pastry; however, adding a little self-raising flour can give a much lighter result.

Although other shortenings can be used, butter produces the best flavour. Chop it into small (pea-size) pieces and make sure it is cold when you begin. Eggs make dough crumbly (short) and rich; milk gives a softer pastry that browns well.

Whether mixing by hand or with a food processor, work quickly and lightly to avoid melting the butter. Mixing dough for too long, handling it roughly or adding too much liquid will result in tough pastry.

Once you have rubbed the butter into the flour, add ice-cold water (or other liquid) a tablespoon at a time, until the mixture just comes together in a stiff dough.

Form the dough into a ball, cover with plastic wrap and chill for at least 30 minutes before rolling out. This will make the dough more manageable and prevent the pastry from shrinking as it cooks.

ABOUT CHOUX PASTRY

This is a very different pastry from shortcrust in that the flour is mixed with boiling liquid and then the eggs are added. The result is light puffs of pastry, hollow in the middle. Choux pastry is used for éclairs, cream puffs and profiteroles. Once cooked and filled they should be eaten immediately, otherwise they become soggy.

ABOUT PUFF PASTRY

Puff pastry is probably the most difficult to make but is considered the finest of all pastries. Good-quality commercial puff pastry is widely available, in blocks as well as packs of ready-rolled puff sheets. In this book, all recipes requiring puff pastry use the commercial type.

ROLLING OUT PASTRY

Use a marble or smooth wooden rolling pin. Divide the dough in half if necessary and form each half into a ball. Roll out dough on a smooth, lightly floured surface (marble is ideal), or between two sheets of plastic wrap or baking paper. Roll dough away from you, using short, quick strokes. Turn the dough a quarter turn after each roll, being careful not to stretch it. Roll out to an even thickness, about 4 cm (1½ inches) bigger than the size of the dish to be lined.

LINING THE DISH

Wrap rolled dough loosely around the rolling pin and lift it over the pie dish or flan tin; unroll dough gently, taking care not to stretch it. Ease the dough into the tin and press it into the sides of the tin with the fingers. If using a metal dish, roll the pin over the top of the dish to cut off any excess dough. If using a ceramic dish, trim off the edges of the dough with a sharp knife.

DECORATIVE EDGES

For a decorative finish to the edges of open or closed pies, crimp or nip around the edge of the dough with fingers, mark with a fork, or cut at even intervals and fold each cut segment over.

To make a coin edge, trim dough to edge of dish and brush rim with water. From leftover dough, cut out 1.5 cm (½ inch) rounds and place, slightly overlapping, around rim, pressing gently.

Decorate open pies with plaits: make pastry for a two-crust pie, line the dish, then roll the rest into a rectangle. Cut into 9 strips. Plait 3, join next 3 and plait, then repeat with last 3 strips. Moisten edge with water, place plait on rim and press gently.

BAKING BLIND

Baking an unfilled pastry case is called 'baking blind' and gives a crisp, firm base, even if the filling is a moist one. In some dishes, if the pastry case is not baked blind, the filling will be cooked but the pastry base will be soggy.

Line pastry case with a sheet of greaseproof paper and spread a layer of raw rice or beans evenly on top (the weight prevents the pastry rising). Preheat oven to 220°C (425°F/Gas 7) and bake for 10–15 minutes. Remove paper and rice or beans and discard. Bake pastry for another 5–10 minutes or until it is light golden. The filling can now be placed in the pre-cooked pastry case.

PASTRY TIPS

■ It is important to cook pastry at the correct temperature: if your oven tends to be cooler or hotter than normal, you may need to slightly adjust the baking time. Pastry should be crisp and golden-brown and the filling properly set.

■ Ceramic and glass pie plates or quiche dishes do not conduct heat as well as metal ones do. However, they are more attractive than metal dishes. To ensure your pastry becomes brown and crisp when baked in these dishes, put a biscuit (cookie) tray made of metal in the oven when preheating it. Place the ceramic or glass pie plate on the hot tray and the pastry on the bottom will cook faster.

■ A 20 cm (8 inch) pie will give 5–6 serves; if the pie is very rich, cut it into 7–8 pieces. A 23 cm (9 inch) pie will give 6–8 pieces (more if rich), and a 25 cm (10 inch) pie can be cut into 8–12 pieces or more.

PREPARING AHEAD

Ready-to-bake, pastry-lined dishes can be stored in the refrigerator or freezer. Line the dish with pastry, cover with heavy-duty aluminium foil or plastic wrap and freeze for up to 12 weeks. Alternatively, cover with plastic wrap and store in refrigerator for up to 24 hours. Before filling an unbaked frozen pastry-lined dish, bring it to room temperature, and bake blind at 220°C (425°F/Gas 7) for 10–15 minutes. Or bake it straight from the freezer for 15–20 minutes.

PASTRY RECIPES

CHOUX PASTRY

Sift 1 cup plain (all-purpose) flour, 1 teaspoon caster (superfine) sugar and ¼ teaspoon salt onto a piece of greaseproof paper. Place 1 cup (8 fl oz) water in a pan with 90 g (3 oz) butter. Heat until the butter is melted, bring to the boil, remove from heat and add the flour mixture all at once. Stir vigorously with a wooden spoon until the mixture leaves the sides of the pan and forms a smooth ball.

Transfer the mixture to the small bowl of an electric mixer and add 3 beaten eggs, a little at a

MINI FRUIT DANISH

Using 2 ready-rolled puff pastry sheets, cut each sheet into 3 strips. Cut each strip into 3, giving 18 squares altogether.

In a small bowl, beat together 30 g (1 oz) softened butter with ¼ cup icing (confectioners) sugar until smooth. Add 1 egg yolk and ¼ cup ground almonds and beat until combined.

Spread a little filling on each pastry square. Place two canned apricot halves side-by-side diagonally on each of the squares. Bring the remaining two corners of each square over the apricots; press corners together. Preheat oven to 210°C (415°F/Gas 6–7). Place pastries on oven trays and bake for 15 minutes or until they turn golden brown; remove from oven.

In a small pan, heat together ½ cup apricot jam and 1 tablespoon water. Strain the mixture and brush as a glaze over the pastries. Allow to cool before serving.

SHORTCRUST PASTRY

This recipe uses mustard and is suitable for savoury pies and tarts. For sweet dishes, omit the mustard and add 2 tablespoons caster (superfine) sugar. Makes one 23 cm (9 inch) tart shell.

Put 2½ cups plain (all-purpose) flour and ½ teaspoon dry mustard in a food processor with 125 g (4 oz) cold butter, chopped into small pieces. Process until the mixture resembles coarse breadcrumbs. Slowly add 2 tablespoons cold water and process until the mixture comes together, adding more water if necessary. Cover dough with plastic wrap, form into a ball and chill for 30 minutes.

To make by hand: Sift the flour and mustard into a large bowl; add the butter. Using your fingertips, rub butter into flour for 3 minutes or until mixture is fine and crumbly. Add water and mix to a soft dough, adding more water if necessary. Form dough into a ball, cover with plastic wrap and refrigerate for 30 minutes.

RICH SHORTCRUST PASTRY

Use this for sweet pies and tarts. Makes one 23 cm (9 inch) tart shell.

Place 2 cups plain (all-purpose) flour into a food processor with 125 g (4 oz) cold butter, chopped into pieces, and 2 tablespoons of caster (superfine) sugar. Process until mixture resembles coarse breadcrumbs. Add 1 egg yolk and 1 tablespoon iced water and process until mixture comes together, adding more water if necessary. Wrap in plastic wrap and chill for 30 minutes.

To make by hand: Sift flour into large bowl; add butter. Rub butter into flour with the fingertips for 3 minutes or until mixture is fine and crumbly; stir in sugar. Add egg yolk and water, mix to a soft dough; press into a ball. Cover with plastic wrap and refrigerate for 30 minutes.

Chocolate Sauce (see Index for recipes).

FILLINGS FOR CHOUX PUFFS

CREAM PUFFS: Fill puffs with whipped cream and dust with icing (confectioners) sugar.
PROFITEROLES: Make smaller puffs. When cold, fill with Crème Pâtissière and serve with Chocolate Sauce (see Index for recipes).

time, beating well after each addition (the mixture should become smooth and glossy).

Place heaped teaspoonsful of mixture on a greased tray, allowing room for spreading. Bake at 220°C (425°F/Gas 7) for 10 minutes; reduce heat to 180°C (350°F/Gas 4) and bake for another 15 minutes, until puffs are crisp and golden. Turn the oven off.

Make a small slit in the side of each puff. Place puffs in the oven with the door ajar for 10 minutes to dry out the centres. Cool puffs on a rack. Just before serving, split and fill as desired.

Food processor method: Place flour, sugar and salt in a food processor bowl fitted with a metal blade and process for a few seconds to aerate. Combine water and butter in a small pan, heat until butter melts, then bring to a fast boil. With machine running, pour bubbling mixture through the feed tube onto the flour and process for a few seconds until the dough becomes thick and smooth. Allow to cool for 2 or 3 minutes. Pour beaten eggs in a slow, steady stream through the feed tube and process until the mixture is thick and glossy.

Place heaped teaspoonsful of mixture on a greased tray, allowing room for spreading. Bake for 10 minutes, reduce heat to 180°C (350°F/Gas 4) and bake for another 15 minutes until puffs are crisp and golden. Turn oven off.

Make a small slit in side of each puff. Place them in the oven with the door ajar for 10 minutes to dry out the centres. Cool puffs on a rack. Just before serving, split and fill as desired.

SAVOURY PUFFS: Omit sugar, fill with Salmon or Cheese Filling (recipes below).

Salmon Filling: Heat 60 g (2 oz) butter in a medium pan, add ¼ cup plain (all-purpose) flour. Stir over low heat for 2 minutes or until flour mixture is lightly golden. Add 1¼ cups (10 fl oz) milk gradually to pan, stirring until mixture is smooth. Stir continuously until mixture boils and thickens; boil for another minute, then remove from heat. Drain a 125 g (4 oz) can red salmon, remove the skin and bones, and flake salmon. Add to mixture in pan along with 2 teaspoons lemon juice, 1 tablespoon mayonnaise and ⅓ cup finely chopped chives; stir gently until combined.

Cheese Filling: Heat 1 tablespoon butter in a medium pan, add 125 g (4 oz) button mushrooms, thinly sliced, and cook over low heat for 3 minutes or until the mushrooms are just tender. Add ¼ cup plain (all-purpose) flour and 1 teaspoon freshly ground black pepper. Stir over low heat for 2 minutes or until the flour mixture is lightly golden. Add 1 cup (8 fl oz) milk and ¼ cup (2 fl oz) cream to the pan slowly, stirring until mixture is smooth. Stir continuously until the mixture boils and thickens; boil for another minute, then remove the pan from heat. Stir in ½ cup grated cheddar cheese and ¼ cup finely chopped parsley.

CLOCKWISE FROM TOP RIGHT: Quiche Lorraine (see recipe page 362); Mince Pie (see page 269); Choux Puffs; Blueberry-Cream Cheese Tart (see page 139); Lemon-Lime Pie (see page 254); Fruit Flan (see page 444) and Mini Apricot Danish

which separates easily from the stone), and clingstone (the flesh clings to the stone). The name comes through the French from the Latin *Persicum malum*, Persian apple. Peaches are in season from early summer to autumn; they are also available canned, in syrup.

Peanut Also called groundnut, the edible seed of a legume encased in brittle, pale-brown pods that develop and ripen below ground. Peanuts can be eaten raw, roasted and salted as a savoury snack, or coated in toffee or chocolate as a confectionery (candy). Peanuts are important in the cooking of South-East Asia as satay sauces or added whole to dishes. Peanuts are made into peanut butter and peanut oil is extracted from them.

Peanut Butter A spread made from ground, roasted peanuts and used in sandwiches (it combines well with celery, crisp bacon, raisins, honey and jam), on toast or as an ingredient in home-made satay sauce. It is available as either a smooth, creamy paste or

P A T E S

RED PEPPER (CAPSICUM) PATE

 Preparation time: 8 minutes
Total cooking time: 35 minutes
Makes 1 cup

4 large red peppers (capsicum)	150 g (4³/4 oz) butter, melted
3 cloves garlic, unpeeled	pinch sugar
2 tablespoons balsamic vinegar	2 teaspoons finely chopped parsley
1 tablespoon sweet chilli sauce	

1 Preheat oven to hot 240°C (475°F/Gas 9). Line a 32 x 28 cm (13 x 11 inch) oven tray with foil. Cut the peppers in half lengthways and remove seeds and membrane. Cut in half again. Arrange pepper pieces on oven tray with the garlic cloves. Bake for 20 minutes. Remove from oven; cover peppers with damp tea-towel until cool. Peel skins from pepper pieces and garlic cloves, discard skins.
2 Place peppers, garlic, vinegar and chilli sauce in a food processor and process until smooth. With motor running, pour in melted butter in a thin, steady stream; process until the mixture is thick and creamy.
3 Transfer mixture to a small pan. Stir over low heat for 15 minutes. Remove from heat and stir in the sugar and parsley. Serve with crackers or Melba toast. This pâté will keep in an airtight jar or container for up to three weeks.

Note: Red Pepper Pâté can be used on pizzas as a base sauce instead of tomato sauce. It is also delicious spread on blini and topped with ham, turkey or fresh herbs.

QUICK SALMON PATE

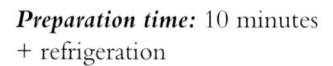

 Preparation time: 10 minutes
+ refrigeration
Total cooking time: nil
Serves 4

1 x 210 g (7 oz) can red salmon	1 tablespoon lemon juice
200 g (6½ oz) soft cream cheese	1 teaspoon wholegrain mustard
1 onion, roughly chopped	few drops Tabasco sauce
2 gherkins	freshly ground pepper, to taste
2 tablespoons cream	

1 Place all ingredients in a food processor and process until smooth.
2 Spoon the mixture into a serving dish and refrigerate for several hours. Serve with crackers or Melba toast.

OPPOSITE PAGE: RED PEPPER PATE.
ABOVE: GRAND MARNIER PATE.

GRAND MARNIER PATE

✳ **Preparation time:** 30 minutes
+ overnight refrigeration
Total cooking time: 10–15 minutes
Serves 8

500 g (1 lb) chicken livers or duck livers
125 g (4 oz) butter
1 medium onion, chopped
2 spring onions (scallions), chopped
2 cloves garlic, crushed
2–3 tablespoons Grand Marnier or cognac or port
1/2 cup (4 fl oz) cream
salt and pepper
2 teaspoons chopped fresh parsley or chives
2 teaspoons chopped fresh thyme
12 slices white or brown bread

1 Preheat oven to 180°C (350°F/Gas 4). Trim livers of sinew. Heat butter in a large heavy-based frying pan. Place livers, onion, garlic and Grand Marnier in frying pan. Stir over medium heat until the liver is just cooked and onion is soft. Bring to boil and simmer for 4–5 minutes. Remove from heat, cool slightly.

2 Place mixture in a food processor. Process for 20–30 seconds or until smooth. Add cream; process for 10 seconds. Transfer mixture to a medium bowl. Stir in herbs. Season with salt and pepper, mix well. Spoon into small ramekins, or one large ramekin dish. Refrigerate overnight or until firm. Serve pâté at room temperature accompanied by Melba toast.

3 To make Melba toast: Cut crusts from bread. Flatten slices with a rolling pin; cut each in half, or quarter diagonally. Bake 5–10 minutes or until crisp and lightly golden. Cool. Alternatively, toast sliced sandwich bread until golden, then remove the crusts. Split through the middle of the slice using a serrated knife. Cut each slice into quarters and brown the untoasted sides under a hot grill.

CHICKEN LIVER AND BRANDY PATE

✳ **Preparation time:** 30 minutes
+ overnight refrigeration
Total cooking time: 10–15 minutes
Serves 4–6

125 g (4 oz) butter
1 large onion, chopped
2 cloves garlic, crushed
2 rashers rindless bacon, chopped
250 g (8 oz) chicken livers, trimmed
1/4 teaspoon dried thyme
freshly ground black pepper
2 tablespoons cream

Topping
60 g (2 oz) butter, melted
2 tablespoons snipped chives
1 tablespoon brandy
30 g (1 oz) butter, extra, melted

1 Melt butter in a pan, add onion, garlic and bacon. Cook until onion is tender and bacon is cooked.

2 Add chicken livers and cook, stirring occasionally, for 5–10 minutes. Remove from heat. Stir in thyme, pepper, cream, brandy and melted butter.

3 Spoon mixture into a food processor or blender; process until smooth. Pour into serving dishes.

4 To make Topping: Pour melted butter over pâté. Sprinkle top with chives. Refrigerate pâté overnight. Stand at room temperature 30 minutes before serving. Serve with toast, crackers or crusty French bread.

Note: Liver-based pâtés are quite strongly flavoured and need the addition of well-balanced seasonings—onion, garlic, spices and alcohol. They improve if kept for two or three days before serving, and will keep for up to a week, covered, in the refrigerator.

Pear A tear-drop shaped fruit with yellow, green or light brown skin and juicy white flesh. It can be eaten fresh, added to both fruit salads (it blends particularly well with raspberries and blackcurrants) and savoury salads, poached in syrup or wine and used in many other desserts such as mousses, soufflés and tarts. The pear originated in Asia. It was introduced into Europe by the ancient Greeks and was a popular fruit in ancient Rome.

Peanut Oil An oil made from peanut kernels, used for frying and to make salad dressings. Mildest in flavour is the European version; it is almost flavourless and used for dressing delicately flavoured salads. American peanut oil has a more nutty taste. Asian oil is darker and more strongly flavoured. It can be heated to a very high temperature, so is good for frying.

a crunchy version containing pieces of crushed nut. Peanut butter was popularised in North America in the twentieth century.

PEACHES

POACHED PEACHES WITH MARSALA CREAM AND VANILLA FINGERS

✶✶

Preparation time: 50 minutes
Total cooking time: 30 minutes
Serves 8

4 egg yolks
1/4 cup caster (superfine)
   sugar
1/4 cup (2 fl oz) marsala
1 1/4 cups (10 fl oz)
   cream, whipped
1 cup sugar
4 cups (32 fl oz) water
8 medium peaches

Vanilla Fingers

60 g (2 oz) butter
3/4 cup icing
   (confectioners) sugar
2 egg whites
1/4 teaspoon vanilla
   essence
1/2 cup plain (all-purpose)
   flour

1 Using electric beaters, beat egg yolks and caster sugar in a medium heatproof bowl for 1 minute. Place bowl over a pan of simmering water, beat constantly until just warmed through. Add marsala gradually to egg mixture, whisking for 3 minutes or until thick and foamy. Remove from heat, continue whisking another 2 minutes or until mixture cools. Transfer to a clean bowl, fold in whipped cream. Cover and refrigerate.

2 Combine sugar and water in a large, heavy-based pan. Stir over medium heat until sugar has completely dissolved. Bring to boil, reduce heat

slightly, add whole peaches. Simmer, covered, 20 minutes, turning peaches occasionally. Using a slotted spoon, lift peaches carefully from syrup onto a plate; cool. Remove skins gently with fingers. Store, covered with plastic wrap, in the refrigerator until needed. Set aside peaches at room temperature for 15 minutes before serving.

3 To make Vanilla Fingers: Preheat oven to moderate 180°C (350°F/Gas 4). Cut two pieces of baking paper to fit two 32 x 28 cm (13 x 11 inch) biscuit (oven) trays. Using a pencil and ruler, draw parallel lines 7 cm (2³/₄ inches) apart. Brush trays with a little oil or melted butter and place paper pencil-side down. Using electric beaters, beat butter and icing sugar in a medium mixing bowl until light and creamy. Add egg whites gradually, beating thoroughly after each addition. Add essence; beat until combined. Using a metal spoon, fold in sifted flour.

4 Spoon mixture into a piping bag fitted with a 1 cm (¹/₂ inch) plain nozzle. Using drawn lines as a guide, pipe mixture into 7 cm (2³/₄ inch) lengths, leaving about 5 cm (2 inches) between each finger. Bake 7 minutes or until just lightly golden. Leave on tray until firm, then lift onto a wire rack to cool completely. To serve, arrange a peach with a large dollop of marsala cream and three Vanilla Fingers on each plate.

ABOVE: POACHED PEACHES WITH MARSALA CREAM AND VANILLA FINGERS. OPPOSITE PAGE: PÊCHE MELBA

Peas, Dried The seed of several varieties of the common garden pea grown specifically to be dried. They were an important vegetable before frozen peas became commonly available. Dried peas may be whole with wrinkled skins intact, or husked and split in two at the natural division (split peas). In India whole dried peas are roasted and spiced as a snack food; in England, where they are known as 'mushy peas', they are soaked, simmered and served either with fish and chips or poured over hot meat pies. Split peas are prepared from the green and yellow field pea varieties of the common garden pea; they are sweeter and less starchy than whole dried peas. Split peas are used for pea soup, pease pudding and in Germany they are often baked with sauerkraut and sour cream.

Peas, Green Small, round, juicy green seeds encased in a green pod, a popular vegetable throughout the world. In most varieties the pod is discarded, although it can be used to make pea soup; some varieties such as the snow pea

PECHE MELBA

Preparation time: 15 minutes
Total cooking time: 8 minutes
Serves 4

2 cups (16 fl oz) water
1/2 cup sugar
1 small vanilla bean
2 teaspoons lemon juice

4 ripe peaches (freestone)
250 g (8 oz) raspberries
1/4 cup icing (confectioners) sugar
4 scoops vanilla ice-cream

1 Place water, sugar and vanilla bean in a medium pan and heat while stirring to dissolve sugar. Simmer syrup for 2 minutes.
2 Cut peaches in halves, peel and remove stones. Poach peaches in syrup until barely tender; remove pan from heat and allow fruit to cool in syrup; chill well.
3 Puree raspberries in a food processor or electric blender with icing sugar and lemon juice. Strain and chill.
4 Place a scoop of ice-cream in each serving dish, top with two well-drained peach halves, spoon raspberry puree over the top. Serve immediately.

PEACH AND ZUCCHINI (COURGETTE) MUFFINS

Preparation time: 8 minutes +
5 minutes standing
Total cooking time: 18 minutes
Makes 15 muffins

345 g (11 oz) packet buttercake mix
1/2 cup finely chopped canned peaches in natural juice, well drained
1 egg
60 g (2 oz) unsalted (sweet) butter, melted
2 teaspoons grated lemon rind
2/3 cup coarsely grated zucchini (courgette)

1 Preheat oven to moderately hot 210°C (415°F/Gas 6-7). Brush fifteen 1/2-cup capacity muffin cups with oil or melted butter.
2 Place contents of cake mix packet, egg, lemon rind, zucchini, peaches and butter in a large bowl. Using a wooden spoon, stir until ingredients are just combined—do not overbeat.
3 Spoon the mixture into prepared muffin cups, until they are two-thirds full. Bake for 18 minutes or until muffins are puffed and lightly browned. Leave muffins in tin for 5 minutes before turning onto a wire rack to cool. Decorate with Buttercream or Cream Cheese Icing (see Index for recipes), and extra fresh or canned peach slices, if desired.

PEACHES, CREAM AND CUSTARD PARFAIT

Preparation time: 10 minutes
Total cooking time: nil
Serves 4

425 g (13 1/2 oz) can sliced peaches, drained, chopped
6 teaspoons peach schnapps liqueur
1/2 cup (4 fl oz) cream, whipped
1 1/2 cups (12 fl oz) vanilla custard
1/2 litre (2 cups) vanilla ice-cream
2 tablespoons flaked almonds, toasted

1 Place peaches and liqueur in a bowl and stand for 5 minutes.
2 Layer ice-cream, peaches and custard into four parfait glasses. Top with whipped cream and sprinkle with almonds. Serve immediately.
Note: To vary, make up a 90 g (3 oz) packet of orange jelly. When set, chop into pieces and fold through custard mixture.

A B O U T   P E A C H E S

■ Slightly under-ripe peaches are best for cooking or baking and are easier to peel.
■ To peel, immerse peaches in boiling water for 30 seconds. Remove, plunge into iced water—the skins will loosen. Halve peaches and remove the stone before peeling with a small knife. Rub the flesh with lemon juice to prevent discolouration.

(mange tout) have very tender pods that need only to be topped and tailed before cooking whole. Petits pois, a variety of tiny, sweet-tasting green peas popular in France, are shelled before use. Peas may be boiled, braised, steamed or microwaved and served hot as a vegetable or added to soups, casseroles and salads. The familiar green pea grown to be eaten fresh was developed in Italy in the seventeenth century; from there it was introduced into

France. Christopher Columbus is said to have planted the first peas in America. Fresh green peas are available for most of the year; green peas are also sold frozen and freeze-dried.

Pease Pudding Split peas, soaked, boiled, mashed and traditionally served with boiled salt pork. In bygone days butchers in the north of England sold slabs of pease pudding along with the pork for reheating at home.

Pecan Nut An elliptical, smooth-shelled nut containing a ridged kernel (similar in appearance to a walnut

VIETNAMESE CHICKEN SALAD

Preparation time: 30 minutes
Total cooking time: 5 minutes
Serves 4

1–2 tablespoons vegetable oil
1½ cups shredded white radish
1 stalk celery, shredded
1 medium onion, thinly sliced
1 large carrot, grated
3 spring onions (scallions), shredded
250 g (8 oz) cooked chicken, shredded
lettuce leaves

2 tablespoons crushed roasted peanuts
fresh herbs (mint, parsley)

Dressing
2½ tablespoons nuoc mam or thin soy sauce
3 tablespoons lime or lemon juice
3 tablespoons vegetable oil
2 teaspoons sugar
1 clove garlic, crushed

1 Heat oil in a wok or heavy-based frying pan. Add radish and celery and stir-fry over medium heat for around two minutes until vegetables are softened; add onion, cook lightly for 1 minute longer. Remove from heat; cool.
2 Combine radish, celery, onion, carrot, spring onion and chicken. Arrange on lettuce leaves and garnish with crushed peanuts and herbs.
3 To make Dressing: Combine all ingredients. Add to chicken several minutes before serving.

CHOCOLATE PEANUT BITES

Preparation time: 30 minutes
Total cooking time: nil
Makes about 20

3 cups icing (confectioners) sugar
¾ cup soft brown sugar
125 g (4 oz) butter, softened
2 cups peanut butter
1 cup unsalted peanuts (optional)
250 g (8 oz) dark (semi-sweet) chocolate
15 g (½ oz) extra butter

1 Beat together sugars and butter until blended—mixture will be crumbly. Mix in peanut butter and nuts, if using.
2 Press into an ungreased 30 x 25 cm (12 x 10 inch) tin, smoothing the surface.
3 Melt chocolate with the extra butter until smooth. Spread over peanut layer. Leave until set. Cut into 2.5 cm (1 inch) pieces.

ABOUT PEANUTS

■ Peanuts are easily shelled by hand and will keep for long periods. However, for convenience and immediate use in cooking, buy shelled raw peanuts.
■ To toast peanuts, spread out in a single layer on a baking sheet and place in a moderate oven for about 10 minutes, or place under a hot grill for around 5 minutes. Keep an eye on the nuts as they can burn quickly.

kernel) with a sweet, buttery flavour. Whole pecan kernels can be eaten as a snack (either raw or roasted and salted) and are used whole in biscuits (cookies), cakes, breads and the American favourite, pecan pie; chopped and ground nuts may be sprinkled on ice-cream, used in pastry fillings or added to confectionery (candy). The pecan tree is native to central North America. The nuts are available in the shell or shelled in airtight packs.

Pêche Melba A dessert consisting of peaches poached in vanilla syrup, chilled, then served with vanilla ice-cream and fresh raspberry puree. The dish was created for Australian diva Dame Nellie Melba by the esteemed French chef Auguste Escoffier. It was inspired by Melba's performance in the opera *Lohengrin*. The

peaches and ice-cream were originally served between the wings of an ice-carved swan and covered with spun sugar.

Pecorino A sheep's milk cheese made by the cooked curd method

PEARS

FRESH PEARS POACHED IN WHITE WINE

Preparation time: 15 minutes
Total cooking time: 20 minutes
Serves 4

4 ripe pears
2 cups (16 fl oz) water
1 cinnamon stick
1 strip lemon rind
1 cup sugar
1 cup (8 fl oz) good quality white wine

1 Peel the pears, leaving the stalks attached. Remove the core section with an apple corer, leaving pear whole.
2 Place the water, white wine, sugar, cinnamon stick and lemon rind in a large pan. Bring to the boil. Add the whole pears and poach gently for 5–10 minutes, depending on ripeness of pears. Pears should be firm but tender when tested with a skewer. Lift pears out of liquid with a slotted spoon. Set aside.
3 Boil syrup rapidly for 5–10 minutes, or until it has thickened slightly. Spoon syrup over pears. Serve warm or chilled.

OPPOSITE PAGE: VIETNAMESE CHICKEN SALAD.
ABOVE: FRESH PEARS POACHED IN WHITE WINE;
RIGHT: PEAR AND BRIE SALAD

PEAR AND BRIE SALAD

Preparation time: 15 minutes
Total cooking time: nil
Serves 4

200 g (6½ oz) brie, at room temperature
3 medium pears
1 butter or mignonette lettuce
3 tablespoons oil
1 tablespoon tarragon vinegar
1/3 cup chopped pecans

1 Cut brie into thin wedges. Cut pears into quarters and remove cores, then slice thinly—do not peel.
2 Wash and dry lettuce thoroughly. Tear into bite-size pieces and arrange on individual serving plates. Top with brie and pears.
3 Place oil and vinegar in a small screwtop jar and shake well. Drizzle dressing over salad and sprinkle with chopped pecans. Serve immediately.

ABOUT PEARS

■ There are many varieties of pear throughout the world. Some are particularly suitable for cooking (among them the Conference Pear and American Bose), and others (especially the beurre—meaning 'buttered'—varieties) are best enjoyed in their natural state.
■ When buying pears, choose specimens with their stalks intact (this helps to preserve them), and with flesh that yields slightly to pressure near the stalk end.

Pectin A natural gelling agent that occurs in some fruits. When pectin-containing fruits are cooked with sugar they set into a firm jam and jelly. Blackcurrants, redcurrants, citrus fruits, cooking apples, quinces, gooseberries and plums are high in pectin; strawberries and pears have very little. Under-ripe or just ripe fruit contains more pectin than over-ripe fruit. Commercial pectin is available in powdered form.

Pecorino cheese (curd is 'cooked' in heated whey). There are two varieties, pecorino romano, a hard, grating cheese (first made near Rome), similar in taste and texture to parmesan and used mostly in cooking; and pecorino fresco, a young, soft and mild-tasting version that can be used as a table cheese. Pecorino originated in southern Italy nearly 2,000 years ago and was traditionally made by shepherds: the name comes from the Italian word pecora, ewe.

Peperoni A sausage of Italian origin made from ground pork and beef (cured and dried during processing), added fat and flavoured with ground chilli pepper and other spices. Peperoni is ready to eat without

PEAS & POTATOES

F rozen peas are used in these recipes. Fresh peas can be substituted but will take longer to cook. When cooking potatoes twice, for example boiling them before frying in oil, or boiling and mashing before baking, boil them on the day you are finishing the dish to avoid a stale taste.

MINTED PEAS

Steam, microwave or lightly boil 2 cups frozen green peas. Toss through 1 tablespoon of finely chopped fresh mint and ¼ teaspoon of soft brown sugar. Serve hot.

MINTED PEAS

CREAMED PEAS

Steam, microwave or lightly boil 2 cups frozen green peas. Drain. Mash with a fork. Add 2 teaspoons butter and salt and freshly ground black pepper to taste. Stir to combine. Serve hot.

CREAMED PEAS

PEAS WITH BASIL AND TOMATO

Heat 2 teaspoons oil in heavy-based frying pan. Add 1 clove crushed garlic and ½ cup chopped canned tomatoes in juice. Cook for 1 minute. Add 2 cups frozen green peas and 1–2 tablespoons finely shredded basil. Cook for 2–3 minutes or until just tender. Serve hot.

PEAS WITH BASIL AND TOMATO

PEPPERED PEAS AND GARLIC

Heat 1 tablespoon oil in heavy-based frying pan. Add 2 cloves crushed garlic and 1 teaspoon cracked black pepper. Stir in 2 cups frozen green peas and ½ teaspoon sugar. Cook over medium heat 2–3 minutes or until tender. Drizzle with balsamic vinegar if desired. Serve hot.

PEPPERED PEAS AND GARLIC

POTATO CHIPS OR CURLS

DUCHESS POTATOES

HASSELBACK POTATOES

QUICK CHEESY POTATO BAKE

POTATO CHIPS OR CURLS

Peel 4 medium potatoes. Cut lengthways in 1 cm (½ inch) thick slices, then into 1 cm (½ inch) wide sticks, or peel long potato strips with a vegetable peeler. Cook in a pan of hot oil for 4–5 minutes for chips, 2–3 minutes for curls, or until crisp. Drain well on paper towels. Serve hot.

DUCHESS POTATOES

Peel and chop 4 medium potatoes. Cook in a large pan of boiling water until just tender; drain and mash. Add 3 egg yolks, 2 tablespoons cream and 2 tablespoons grated parmesan cheese. Mix thoroughly. Pipe mixture in swirls onto greased oven trays. Bake in moderately hot oven 210°C (415°F/Gas 6–7) for 20 minutes or until golden brown. Sprinkle with paprika. Serve hot.

HASSELBACK POTATOES

Peel and halve 4 medium potatoes. Place potatoes cut-side down. Use a sharp knife to make thin slices in potatoes, taking care not to cut right through. Place potatoes cut-side up in baking dish. Brush with 1 tablespoon olive oil combined with 1 tablespoon melted butter. Sprinkle with lemon pepper. Bake in moderately hot 210°C (415°F/Gas 6–7) oven for 45 minutes or until golden and slightly crisp. Serve immediately.

QUICK CHEESY POTATO BAKE

Peel and thinly slice 4 medium potatoes. Thinly slice 1 onion. Layer potato and onion slices in an ovenproof baking dish. Sprinkle grated cheddar cheese between each layer. Pour over combined ½ cup (4 fl oz) cream, ¾ cup (6 fl oz) milk and 1 teaspoon mustard powder. Sprinkle top with extra grated cheese and chopped chives. Bake in moderate oven 180°C (350°F/Gas 4) for 40 minutes or until cooked. Serve hot.

further cooking, its most common use is as a pizza topping.

Pepino Also known as the melon pear and tree melon, an apple-sized, melon-shaped vine fruit with smooth yellow-green skin streaked with purple and pale juicy flesh with a central cluster of edible seeds. Pepino can be eaten fresh in the same way as melon, diced and added to fruit salad, or lightly sautéed and served as an accompaniment to fish and meat. The fruit is native to Peru and Chile and was introduced into Florida in the late nineteenth century. It is in season from autumn to spring.

Pepper A pungent spice derived from the dried berry-like fruit (peppercorn) of a tropical climbing vine. Both white and black pepper come from the same plant, but are picked at different stages of maturity. Black pepper is picked while the berries are still unripe; white pepper comes from berries that are allowed to ripen before being harvested. They are then soaked in water to remove their skins. Black and white pepper is used to flavour all types of savoury food.

PEASE PUDDING

★ *Preparation time:* **10 minutes +** overnight soaking
Total cooking time: **2 hours**
Serves 4

500 g (1 lb) split peas, soaked overnight and drained	*30 g (1 oz) butter, softened*
1 onion, finely chopped	*1/2 teaspoon white pepper*
1 sprig fresh rosemary	*2 tablespoons malt vinegar*
salt to taste	
2 eggs, lightly beaten	

1 Preheat oven to 180°C (350°F/Gas 4). Brush a 4-cup capacity ovenproof dish with melted butter or oil.

2 Place peas, onion and rosemary sprig into a large pan. Cover with water. Place lid on saucepan and cook over low heat for 1 hour or until peas are starting to soften.

3 Drain peas in a strainer or colander. Discard rosemary. Mash peas with potato masher. Add eggs, butter, pepper, salt and vinegar. Blend until smooth.

4 Pour pudding mixture into prepared dish and stand dish in a bain-marie. Bake for 30–45 minutes or until pudding sets. Unmould to serve. Alternatively, pour into a 1.5 litre (6-cup) pudding steamer and steam for 1 hour.

DRIED PEAS

PEA AND HAM SOUP

★ *Preparation time:* **30 minutes +** overnight soaking
Total cooking time: **1 1/2 – 2 hours**
Serves 6

250 g (8 oz) split peas	*freshly ground pepper*
500 g (1 lb) bacon bones	*1 tablespoon lemon juice*
1 teaspoon chopped fresh thyme	*3–4 frankfurts, sliced (optional)*
2 medium onions, diced	*chopped parsley for serving*
2 medium carrots, diced	
1 cup sliced celery	
2 bay leaves	
2.5 litres (10 cups)	*chicken stock or water*

1 Rinse peas well and place in a medium bowl. Add sufficient water to cover and soak overnight. Drain peas and discard water.

2 Place peas in large, heavy pan with bones, onions, carrots, celery, bay leaves, stock or water, pepper and thyme. Bring to boil, cover; simmer gently for 1 1/2–2 hours. Remove bay leaves.

3 Remove bacon bones to a plate and scrape meat from them; chop meat and add to soup with lemon juice. Bring soup to the boil, add frankfurts and heat for 3 minutes.

4 Serve soup sprinkled with parsley.

ABOUT DRIED PEAS

■ Some cooking authorities maintain that split peas do not need to be soaked in water before they are cooked. However, if they are soaked in cold water for 8 hours or overnight, cooking time will be considerably reduced.

■ There are two ways to soak split peas and other pulses:

Slow soaking method: Place peas in a large bowl and cover with cold water. Pick off and discard any peas that rise to the surface. Leave to soak for 8 hours or overnight. If you plan to soak the peas for a longer time, place the bowl in the refrigerator or the peas may ferment.

Quick soaking method: Wash the peas and place in a large saucepan with plenty of cold water. Bring to the boil and boil for 2 minutes. Remove pan from heat, cover and set aside for 1–2 hours or until the peas have swelled. Drain, place peas in a large pan and cover with fresh water. Bring to the boil very slowly—boiling too fast can produce hard peas.

■ Skim any scum that rises to the top of the pan with a slotted spoon. (Although some cooks do not bother with this, skimming does produce a finer flavoured dish.)

■ Dried peas form a complete protein when eaten with a grain, such as rice.

SUGAR PEAS AND CARROTS IN LIME BUTTER

Preparation time: 10 minutes
Total cooking time: 10 minutes
Serves 4

125 g (4 oz) carrots	1 tablespoon lime juice
125 g (4 oz) sugar snap peas	1/2 teaspoon soft brown sugar
45 g (1 1/2 oz) butter	1 lime
2 cloves garlic, crushed	

1 Peel carrots and cut into thin diagonal slices. Wash and string sugar snap peas. Heat the butter in a large heavy-based frying pan. Add garlic and cook over low heat for 1 minute. Add lime juice and sugar. Cook, stirring over low heat, until the sugar has completely dissolved.

2 Add the peas and carrots and cook over medium heat for 2–3 minutes, or until the vegetables are tender but still crisp. Serve hot, garnished with lime zest.

Note: To make lime zest, peel lime rind into

long strips with a vegetable peeler. Remove pith, cut rind into thin strips with a sharp knife.

PEPPERED PEAS AND GARLIC

Heat 1 tablespoon oil in heavy-based frying pan. Add 2 cloves crushed garlic and 1 teaspoon cracked black pepper. Stir in 2 cups frozen green peas and 1/2 teaspoon sugar. Cook over medium heat 2–3 minutes or until peas are tender. Drizzle with balsamic vinegar, if desired. Serve hot.

SAUTEED PEAS AND SPRING ONIONS (SCALLIONS)

Heat 30 g (1 oz) butter in a heavy-based frying pan. Add 2 cups frozen green peas, 1 clove crushed garlic and 2 finely sliced spring onions (scallions). Stir over medium heat 2–3 minutes, or until peas and onions are just tender. Serve hot.

SWEET CORIANDER PEAS

Heat 30 g (1 oz) butter in pan. Add 1 1/2 teaspoons lemon juice, 1/2 teaspoon sugar and 2 cups frozen green peas. Cook over medium heat 2–3 minutes or until just tender. Add 2 tablespoons finely chopped fresh coriander leaves and toss well.

OPPOSITE PAGE: PEASE PUDDING.
ABOVE: SUGAR PEAS AND CARROTS IN LIME BUTTER

For the best flavour ground pepper should be added to hot dishes towards the end of cooking time; in long cooking dishes tie peppercorns in a muslin (cheesecloth) bag and remove before serving.

Green peppercorns are the berries picked while still green; they are usually preserved in brine and are used, sparingly, to flavour soups, stews, pâtés and sauces. Pink peppercorns are the soft, almost ripe,

berries of an unrelated South American tree; they are used more for their colour than their flavour. Pepper is best used freshly ground, as it goes stale very quickly.

Peppermint A herb of the mint family grown mainly for the oil distilled from its leaves and flowers. Peppermint essence it is used to flavour confectionery (candy), chocolate fillings, cake icings, and the liqueur crème de menthe. The leaves can also be made into herb tea, or chopped and sprinkled over fruit salad. Rats are said to detect peppermint.

Pepper, Sweet Also called Bell Pepper or Capsicum. A large, mostly hollow, shiny skinned fruit of a shrub native to tropical South America. Although a member of the same family as the fiery chilli pepper, its crisp, moist flesh is mild in flavour and is used as both a salad

and a cooked vegetable. Varieties include the red (the sweetest), green, yellow, orange and black. The stalk, white membrane and seeds should be removed before use. Sweet pepper is used raw and thinly sliced in salads and crudités, is cooked in casseroles, grilled (broiled) or filled with various stuffings. It is an important ingredient in the cooking of Central America, the Mediterranean, the Middle East and Asia. Sweet peppers are available fresh throughout the year; sun-dried peppers in oil are sometimes available. Paprika is the ground and dried flesh of a variety of sweet pepper.

Persimmon A smooth-skinned, tomato-shaped fruit with yellow to orange coloured flesh that is soft, sweet and jelly-like when fully ripe, but otherwise has a sharp

PECAN NUTS

COFFEE PECAN SLICE

★ Preparation time: 30 minutes
Total cooking time: 40 minutes
Makes 15

1½ cups plain (all-purpose) flour
½ cup icing (confectioners) sugar
75 g (2½ oz) unsalted (sweet) butter, melted
2 eggs, lightly beaten
1 teaspoon coffee powder

Topping
2 tablespoons cream
2 tablespoons molasses or dark corn syrup
⅓ cup soft brown sugar
150 g (4¾ oz) unsalted (sweet) butter
2 cups pecan halves

1 Preheat oven to moderate 180°C (350°F/Gas 4). Brush an 18 x 27 cm (7 x 10¾ inch) shallow rectangular tin with melted butter or oil. Line with baking paper, extending over two sides. Place flour, icing sugar and butter in food processor. Process for 1 minute or until mixture comes together. Turn out onto a lightly floured surface and knead dough gently for 30 seconds or until smooth. Press into prepared tin and bake for 15 minutes or until just golden. Cool completely in on a wire rack.

2 **To make Topping:** Combine cream, syrup, sugar, butter, eggs and coffee in a medium mixing bowl and beat with a wooden spoon until smooth. Add pecans and stir to combine.

3 Pour Topping over pastry base; bake for 25 minutes or until set. Cool completely in tin. Lift out and cut into squares, using a sharp knife.

PECAN CHICKEN

★ Preparation time: 30 minutes
Total cooking time: 10 minutes
Serves 4

4 chicken breast fillets
1 cup pecan halves
½ cup grated Gouda cheese
½ cup dry breadcrumbs
1 egg, lightly beaten
1 tablespoon water
60 g (2 oz) butter
2 tablespoons oil
springs of watercress or parsley, for garnish

freshly ground black pepper
1 teaspoon ground sage
½ cup fresh white breadcrumbs

1 Pound chicken fillets flat between sheets of plastic wrap to 1 cm (½ inch) thickness.

2 Reserve 8 pecan halves; finely chop remainder. In a shallow bowl, mix chopped pecans, cheese, breadcrumbs, sage and pepper to taste. In separate shallow bowl, beat egg and water until combined.

3 Coat fillets with half of the pecan mixture, dip them in the egg mixture, then coat with the remaining pecan mixture.

4 Heat butter and oil in large, shallow pan. Place fillets, two at a time, in pan; cook until golden brown and tender, turning once, 2–3 minutes per side. (Keep fillets warm while cooking the remainder.) Serve garnished with reserved pecans and watercress or parsley.

PEPPER

BARBECUED PEPPERED STEAKS WITH MANGO AND AVOCADO SALSA

⭐⭐ *Preparation time:* 10 minutes +
30 minutes standing

Total cooking time: 6–16 minutes

Serves 6

6 fillet (tenderloin) steaks, about 125 g (4 oz) each	*Mango and Avocado Salsa*
1–2 tablespoons whole black peppercorns	1 large ripe mango
1 tablespoon white mustard seeds	1 large ripe avocado
2 tablespoons oil	1 spring onion (scallion), finely sliced
	1 tablespoon lime juice
	dash Tabasco sauce

1 Trim meat of excess fat and sinew. Flatten steaks to an even thickness. Nick edges to prevent curling. Crush peppercorns and mustard seeds briefly in a blender until coarsely cracked; or, place in a paper bag and crush with a rolling pin. Spread on a plate.

2 Rub oil over the steaks, then press on the peppercorn mixture to coat thoroughly. Store in refrigerator, covered with plastic wrap, for about 30 minutes.

3 Place meat on a lightly oiled preheated grill or flat plate. Cook over high heat for 2 minutes each side to seal, turning once. For a rare result, cook for another minute each side. For medium and well done results, move meat to a cooler part of the barbecue, cook for another 2–3 minutes each side for medium and 4–6 minutes each side for well done. Serve with Mango and Avocado Salsa.

4 To make Mango and Avocado Salsa: Peel the mango and cut off cheeks from both sides; cut flesh into cubes. Peel avocado and cut into cubes. Combine mango, avocado, spring onion, lime juice and Tabasco in a small bowl, toss well. Cover and refrigerate until required.

OPPOSITE PAGE: COFFEE PECAN SLICE

ABOVE: BARBECUED PEPPERED STEAKS WITH MANGO AND AVOCADO SALSA

PEPPERED BEEF FILLET (TENDERLOIN)

⭐ *Preparation time:* 10 minutes

Total cooking time: 50 minutes–
1 hour 35 minutes

Serves 6

1 kg (2 lb) whole beef fillet (tenderloin) or rib eye in one piece	*Green Peppercorn Sauce*
2 tablespoons freshly cracked black peppercorns	1/2 cup (4 fl oz) chicken stock
1 tablespoon soy sauce	2 teaspoons canned green peppercorns, rinsed and drained
3 tablespoons olive oil	1/2 cup (4 fl oz) cream
	2 teaspoons brandy

1 Preheat oven to moderately hot 210°C (415°F/Gas 6–7). Tie the meat securely with string at regular intervals to retain its shape during cooking. Rub meat all over with soy sauce; roll meat in freshly cracked black peppercorns, pressing to coat surface and ends.

2 Heat oil in deep baking dish on top of stove; add meat and brown all over on high heat. Transfer baking dish to oven.

3 Roast meat 45 minutes for a rare result, 1 hour for a medium result and 1 hour 30 minutes for well done. Baste the meat occasionally with pan juices. Remove from oven. Leave in a warm place for 10 minutes, covered with foil. Remove string before slicing. Serve with Green Peppercorn Sauce.

4 To make Green Peppercorn Sauce: Add the chicken stock to juices in baking dish. Stir over low heat on top of stove until mixture is boiling; add cream and drained green peppercorns. Boil the mixture for 2 minutes, stirring constantly; add the brandy. Boil for another minute; remove dish from heat.

Pesto A thick, uncooked sauce made by blending together basil leaves, olive oil, garlic, pine nuts and parmesan cheese. Traditionally it was made with a mortar and pestle, but pesto can also be made in a food processor. It is usually served over pasta, although in Genoa, where it originated (the sauce is also known as pesto alla Genovese), it is also added to minestrone. *Pesto* is the Italian word for paste.

Petits Fours Fancy bite-sized biscuits (cookies), cakes or confectionery (candy) usually served with coffee at the end of a meal.

---

astringent taste. Ripe persimmon pulp can be eaten plain, as a fruit, added to fruit salad, mousses and custards, or used to top ice-cream; it is also made into jam. The persimmon is native to Japan and China, where it has been cultivated for more than a thousand years. Sharon fruit, a persimmon variety developed in Israel, can be eaten raw, even when firm and under-ripe. Persimmon is in season in late autumn and early winter; it is also available dried.

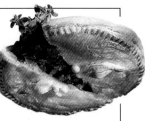

Pie A sweet or savoury mixture topped with a pastry crust and baked; quite often pies have a bottom crust as well—these completely enclosed pies are called double-crusted pies in North America. The term 'pie' is also used in North America for a bottom crust with a filling, in Britain this is usually called a tart.

Pickles and Relish Preserves made of vegetables such as onions, cucumber, cauliflower and sweet pepper, sliced if necessary, soaked in brine, then rinsed, put into jars and covered with spiced vinegar. Eggs and walnuts can also be pickled.

Pheasant A game bird with delicately flavoured white flesh, now raised commercially in many parts of the world. Young birds can be roasted (baste frequently to prevent the flesh from drying out). Pheasant can also be larded or covered with a layer of fat or bacon strips to keep the meat moist. Older birds should be casseroled or pot-roasted. Pheasant is available from specialist poultry shops.

PEPPERS (CAPSICUM)

HERB-MARINATED PEPPERS (CAPSICUM)

★

Preparation time: 20 minutes + 2 hours marinating
Total cooking time: 5 minutes
Serves 4

4 red peppers (capsicum)
1/2 cup (4 fl oz) olive oil
2 tablespoons lemon juice
1 tablespoon chopped fresh basil
1 tablespoon chopped fresh parsley
2 teaspoons chopped fresh oregano
8 rocket (arugula) leaves
8 cos (romaine) lettuce leaves
200 g (6 1/2 oz) feta cheese

1 Cut each pepper into quarters; remove seeds and stems. Place skin-side up under a preheated grill; cook until skin blisters and turns black. Cover peppers with a clean, damp tea-towel and allow to stand for 5 minutes. Peel away skin.

2 Cut pepper pieces into 2 cm (3/4 inch) strips. Combine olive oil, lemon juice, fresh basil, parsley and oregano in a small jug.

3 Place pepper strips in a small bowl, pour oil mixture over and marinate for at least 2 hours, or preferably overnight. Serve strips with rocket and cos lettuce leaves and some cubed feta cheese.

GARLIC PEPPERS (CAPSICUM)

★

Preparation time: 15 minutes
Total cooking time: 15 minutes
Makes 1 litre (4 cups)

1 green pepper (capsicum)
1 red pepper (capsicum)
2 cups (16 fl oz) white wine vinegar
2 cloves garlic, peeled and cut into slices
1/2 cup sugar
2 teaspoons salt

1 Cut peppers lengthwise into quarters. Discard core, seeds and white pith. Blanch in boiling water until softened, about 1 minute. Drain and pack snugly into a jar with sliced garlic.

2 In a pan slowly heat sugar, vinegar and salt, stirring until sugar dissolves. Heat until boiling.

3 Pour hot liquid over peppers. Cover at once with an airtight lid. Label and date. Leave for 1 week before opening.

ABOUT PEPPERS (CAPSICUM)

■ Peppers can be served either cooked or raw. The flavour is particularly complemented by tomatoes, eggplant (aubergine), garlic, onion, herbs such as thyme and oregano, and olive oil.
■ Roasting or grilling (broiling) peppers and peeling off the skin removes bitterness and intensifies the sweet flavour.

PEPPERS

CHEESY RICE-STUFFED PEPPERS (CAPSICUM)

Preparation time: 40 minutes
Total cooking time: 25 minutes
Serves 6

3 small red peppers (capsicum)
3 small green peppers (capsicum)
1 cup short-grain rice
2 cups (16 fl oz) water
315 g (10 oz) can corn kernels, drained
2 jalapeño chillies, chopped
1 small onion, chopped
1 tablespoon olive oil
1/4 teaspoon chilli powder
1/2 teaspoon ground cumin
1 teaspoon chicken stock powder
3/4 cup cheddar cheese, grated
2 tablespoons tomato paste

1 Preheat oven to 180°C (350°F/Gas 4). Cut tops off peppers and set tops aside. Carefully remove pith and seeds, taking care not to tear the pepper shells open.

2 Heat oil in a medium pan. Stir in onion, chilli powder, cumin, stock powder, tomato paste and rice. Add water. Cover with tight-fitting lid. Bring slowly to boil; stir once. Reduce heat, simmer, covered until almost all the water is absorbed. Remove from heat. Stand, covered for 5 minutes or until all the water is absorbed and rice is just tender. Stir through the corn, chillies and 1/2 cup cheese.

3 Fill each pepper with rice mixture. Sprinkle each with a little of the remaining cheese. Replace tops. Place peppers on an oven tray and bake for 15 minutes or until peppers have softened slightly. Serve peppers warm. May be accompanied by tortillas and salad.

ROASTED PEPPERS (CAPSICUM) AND OLIVE PIE

Preparation time: 20 minutes
Total cooking time: 40 minutes
Serves 4-6

2 sheets ready-rolled shortcrust pastry
1 cup pitted black olives
1 teaspoon olive oil
2 cloves garlic, crushed
1/2 teaspoon sugar
1 medium red pepper (capsicum)
1 yellow pepper (capsicum)
1 tablespoon oil, extra
1 large red onion, cut into thin wedges
2/3 cup finely grated gruyère cheese

1 Preheat oven to moderately hot 210°C (415°F/Gas 6-7). Lightly grease a 23 cm (9 inch) round fluted flan tin with melted butter or oil. Place one sheet of pastry on lightly floured surface. Brush with a little water, top with second pastry sheet. Roll pastry large enough to line prepared tin. Ease pastry into tin, trim edge with a sharp knife. Cut a sheet of baking paper large enough to cover pastry-lined tin. Spread a layer of dried beans or rice over the paper. Bake for 10 minutes, remove and discard paper and beans or rice. Cook pastry for another 10 minutes or until lightly browned.

2 Place the olives, oil, garlic and sugar in a food processor. Process until smooth. Spread mixture over the base of prepared pastry case. Cut peppers into quarters. Place skin-side up on oven tray and grill until the skin blisters and turns black. Cover peppers with a tea-towel; cool slightly. Peel away skin and cut peppers into 1 cm (1/2 inch) strips.

3 Heat extra oil in small pan, add onion and cook over medium heat until soft. Add sliced peppers, heat through. Sprinkle half the cheese over the olive mixture. Spoon pepper and onion mixture over cheese. Top with remaining cheese, bake for 10 minutes or until cheese has melted and pie is heated through.

Pilaf (Pilau) Rice lightly browned in oil or butter then cooked in spiced stock: vegetables, meat, poultry or fish may be added half way through the cooking process. The rice is served either fluffed with a fork and piled onto the plate or pressed into an oiled ring mould which is turned onto a serving plate. Pilaf can be a main dish or an

Piklet Also known as a Scottish pancake, a small, thick, sweet pancake, served warm or cold with butter and jam or honey.

Pigeon A small game bird with rich dark meat: a squab is a baby pigeon with milder flavoured meat. Commercially raised squab can be grilled (broiled) or roasted and the breast meat served rare, thinly sliced, topped with a sauce; the flesh of older birds and wild pigeon or dove tends to be tougher and long, slow cooking is best, either casseroled or roasted or stuffed with bacon fat or stuffed with bacon fat. Allow one bird per person. Pigeons have been a popular food since medieval times, when dovecotes on the top of large houses provided meat throughout winter. Pigeon is available from specialist poultry shops.

PICKLES & CHUTNEYS

P ickles and chutneys were originally made to preserve foods without the aid of refrigeration. Vegetables for chutneys are generally stewed in vinegar, sugar and spices until they are soft. Pickled vegetables are usually cooked for a shorter time and tend to retain their shape.

PICKLES

PICKLED PEARS

Place 3 firm peeled, halved and cored pears in a pan with the juice and thin strips of rind from a lemon. Cover with cold water. Bring to the boil, reduce heat and simmer until the pears are just tender when tested with a skewer.

Meanwhile, in another pan, slowly heat ½ cup of sugar, 1½ cups (12 fl oz) white vinegar, 1 stick of cinnamon and 1 teaspoon whole cloves. Stir until sugar dissolves. Heat until boiling, then remove the pan from the heat.

Carefully pack the pears tightly into a warm, sterilised jar with cinnamon and cloves. Pour the hot sugar liquid over pears to cover them completely. Seal jar immediately. When cool, label and date jar. Keep for 2 weeks before opening. Pickled pears may be stored for up to 4 months. Serve with cold turkey or ham.

PICKLED VEGETABLES

Coarsely chop ½ small cauliflower, 1 red pepper (capsicum), 2 unpeeled cucumbers, 1 carrot, 3 stalks celery and 2 onions. Place in a large bowl, cover with water and sprinkle with 315 g (10 oz) coarse salt. Set the bowl aside, covered with a dry cloth, and

T he quality of your pickles and chutneys depends upon the quality of the ingredients you use. Old limp vegetables, even when they are heavily seasoned with vinegar, spices and salt, will taste like old limp vegetables.

■ **VEGETABLES AND FRUIT:** Choose fresh, young, firm fruits and vegetables. Fruits may be pickled while they are still slightly under-ripe. Vegetables such as onions and cucumbers should be small and of even size. Wash them carefully to remove dirt and grit, which could cause bacterial action. The vegetables can be either raw or cooked, depending on the recipe. Raw fruit and vegetables are usually salted first to reduce their water content and to make the pickling process more effective.

■ **VINEGAR:** Use good quality vinegars that have an acid level of at least 5 per cent. Anything less may not preserve properly. Use malt vinegar for more strongly flavoured raw ingredients, and cider and wine vinegars for more delicate pickles, especially fruit.

■ **PICKLING SPICES:** Unless ground spices are specifically stated in the recipe, use fresh, whole spices such as cloves, small hot red chillies, peppercorns, coriander seeds and mustard seeds for pickling, as they leave no sediment. Stale spices may give a musty flavour. For pickled fruits and vegetables and for spicing chutneys, tie the spices in a little piece of muslin which can be extracted when cooking is complete.

■ **SALT:** Use coarse cooking salt or kosher salt when brining pickles: the iodine and other chemicals present in table salt may cause pickles to become cloudy and to darken in colour.

CHUTNEYS

TOMATO CHUTNEY

Peel and coarsely chop 1 kg (2 lb) ripe tomatoes, 3 onions and two green apples. Peel, halve and stone 3 peaches and chop, coarsely. Place them all in a large pan or boiler. Add 2¾ cups dark brown sugar, 2 cups white vinegar, 1 tablespoon salt and 1 teaspoon each of mixed spice and Mexican chilli powder. Bring slowly to the boil and simmer for about 2 hours, uncovered, until the mixture is thick. Stir occasionally. Remove chutney from heat and stand for 5 minutes. Spoon into warm sterilised jars; seal immediately. When cool, label and date.

VARIATIONS

■ Green tomatoes can be substituted for fully ripe ones, if preferred.
■ Add a large red or green pepper (capsicum), peeled and chopped.
■ Use dark malt vinegar instead of white vinegar.

POINTS FOR SUCCESS

■ Seal pickles and chutneys as soon as possible after cooking, with non-corrosive lids. Plastic, plastic-coated metal, cork or wax coverings are all suitable, although transparent covers which let in the light are not suitable for chutney. It is important that metal lids are plastic-coated, as the acid in the vinegar will cause oxidisation if the contents of the jar touch the lid.
■ Chutneys are best kept for at least a month after bottling in order to allow flavours to properly develop and mellow.
■ Pickles and chutneys can be stored for up to a year in a cool, dark place. It is not necessary to refrigerate until the jars have been opened.
■ Wash the jars well beforehand. Use warm, soapy water and rinse thoroughly. Dry off in a 140°C (275°F/Gas 1) oven. Use while still hot, to prevent the jars cracking when filled.

CLOCKWISE FROM ABOVE: *LIME CURRY PICKLE, TOMATO CHUTNEY, TOMATO CHUTNEY WITH GREEN PEPPER, TOMATO CHUTNEY WITH DARK MALT VINEGAR, GREEN TOMATO CHUTNEY, PICKLED PEARS AND PICKLED VEGETABLES.*

LIME CURRY PICKLE

Cut each of 12 limes into 8–10 wedges lengthways, and then cut the wedges in half crossways. In a glass bowl, layer the limes with 4 tablespoons of salt. Cover bowl with a clean cloth and let stand in a warm, dry place for 3 days, stirring occasionally. Drain and rinse the limes.
Combine, in a large pan, 1½ cups (12 fl oz) good quality olive oil, 1 tablespoon toasted and crushed yellow mustard seeds, 2 teaspoons ground cumin, 2 teaspoons ground ginger and ½ teaspoon coarsely ground pepper. Stir over low heat until hot. Add the limes with ⅓ cup (2½ fl oz) white wine vinegar, 3 crushed garlic cloves and 2 long, red chillies, seeded and chopped. Stir over moderate heat for 5 minutes; stir in 3 tablespoons of sugar and heat until dissolved. Ladle pickle into warm, sterilised jars and seal. When cool, label and date. Serve with curries.

leave to stand overnight. Drain, rinse and drain again. Combine in a large pan, 1.25 litres (5 cups) of white vinegar, 5 whole dried chillies, ½ cup of sugar, 1 teaspoon of celery seeds and 1 tablespoon of mustard seeds.
Heat slowly, stirring, until the sugar is dissolved, then bring to the boil. Simmer 3 minutes, add vegetables and boil for another 12 minutes. Remove from heat; pack vegetables into warm sterilised jars using a slotted spoon. Return liquid to heat; bring to the boil. Pour boiling liquid over vegetables and seal. When cool, label and date jars. Pickled vegetables can be used as part of an antipasto platter, or they can be finely chopped and mixed into tuna mayonnaise.

accompaniment. The dish is of Middle Eastern origin (the name is derived from a Persian word for 'boiled rice'); rice is prepared in a similar way in India and Pakistan.

Pimento Also known as allspice and Jamaica pepper, the dried and ground berries of a tree native to Jamaica. The term is sometimes also applied to the dried and ground flesh of the pimiento, a sweet pepper grown in Spain.

Pimiento A sweet pepper, long and thin in form and with mild-flavoured flesh that is cut into strips and used to add colour to a range of foods. Skinned pimiento strips are used in salads, as an accompaniment to cold meats, as a garnish and as a stuffing for pitted olives. Pimiento ranges in colour from green to red, depending upon the ripeness of the fruit when picked; it is available bottled or canned in oil or brine. Its dried and ground flesh, *pimentón*, is a spice similar to paprika, much used in Spanish cooking.

Pineapple A large, cylindrical tropical fruit with thick skin, a crown of cactus-like leaves and fragrant, sharply

---

PIES

BACON, HERB AND VEGETABLE PIE

★★ **Preparation time:** 25 minutes
Total cooking time: 55 minutes
Serves 6

30 g (1 oz) butter
1 medium onion, chopped
2 leeks, thinly sliced
1 parsnip, chopped
1 large carrot, chopped
1 clove garlic, crushed
105 g (3½ oz) button mushrooms, halved
155 g (5 oz) bacon off the bone, chopped
1 tablespoon plain (all-purpose) flour
1 tablespoon chopped fresh rosemary
1¼ cups (10 fl oz) cream
2 sheets ready-rolled puff pastry
1 egg, lightly beaten

1 Preheat oven to moderate 180°C (350°F/Gas 4). Heat butter in heavy-based pan, add garlic and onion. Cook over medium heat for 3 minutes or until golden. Add flour, stir 1 minute.

2 Add mushrooms and bacon, cook for 5 minutes. Add carrot, parsnip and leek. Gradually stir in cream and rosemary. Bring to boil, reduce heat, cover, simmer 15 minutes or until vegetables are tender.

3 Spoon mixture into 23 cm (9 inch) pie dish. Cut each pastry sheet into twelve equal strips; weave strips into tight lattice pattern, brushing with egg. Carefully lift pastry and place over pie. Trim edges with a sharp knife. Brush top of pastry with egg. Bake 25 minutes or until golden.

ABOVE: BACON, HERB AND VEGETABLE PIE
OPPOSITE: CHICKEN PIE

CHICKEN PIE

★★ **Preparation time:** 40 minutes
Total cooking time: 1 hour
Serves 6-8

Pastry
2 cups plain (all-purpose) flour
2 tablespoons plain (all-purpose) flour
½ teaspoon ground nutmeg
½ teaspoon salt
140 g (4½ oz) butter
1 teaspoon water
75 g (2½ oz) butter, melted

Filling
1 kg (2 lb) chicken thigh fillets
200 g (6½ oz) ham
2 large leeks, chopped
1 onion, thinly sliced
½ cup (4 fl oz) chicken stock
½ cup (4 fl oz) cream
1 egg, for glazing
ground pepper

1 To make Pastry: Sift flour into a bowl; add salt. Rub through the butter until mixture resembles fine breadcrumbs. Add water to form a stiff dough, knead lightly, refrigerate.

2 To make Filling: Trim fat and any bone chips from fillets, cut into 2½ cm (1 inch) pieces; cut ham into 1 cm (½ inch) strips.

3 Preheat oven to 200°C (400°F/Gas 6). Grease a large shallow ovenproof dish with melted butter. Combine pepper, flour and nutmeg in a plastic bag, toss chicken pieces in flour mixture until well coated. Shake off excess flour.

4 Place half the leek and onion in layers over the

base of prepared casserole dish. Top with half the ham and chicken pieces. Repeat layers using remaining onion, leek, ham and chicken. Drizzle melted butter over filling, add stock.

5 Knead pastry lightly, roll it out to fit dish. Cover pie with prepared pastry. Decorate edges of pastry to form a seal on the pie, glaze with beaten egg. Cut three deep slits in the pastry to allow steam to escape—cream will be added through these later. Bake for 1 hour, or until pastry is golden brown and chicken is cooked. Remove from the oven and leave to stand for 5 minutes. Pour cream into slits and allow to stand for another 10 minutes before serving.

BLACKBERRY PIE

✷ ✷ **Preparation time:** 45 minutes
Total cooking time: 45 minutes
Serves 6–8

2 cups self-raising flour
2 tablespoons icing (confectioners) sugar
2 tablespoons custard powder
250 g (8 oz) chilled butter, chopped
1 egg, lightly beaten
¼ cup (2 fl oz) water
1 egg, extra, lightly beaten
1 tablespoon raw sugar

Filling
¼ cup cornflour (cornstarch)
2 x 425 g (13½ oz) cans blackberries, drained, juice reserved
2 tablespoons caster (superfine) sugar
1 teaspoon finely grated orange rind

1 Preheat oven to moderate 180°C (350°F/Gas 4). Brush a shallow, 23 cm (9 inch) round ovenproof pie plate with melted butter or oil.

2 To make Filling: Blend the cornflour with a small amount of the reserved blackberry juice in a small bowl until smooth. Combine the remaining juice, caster sugar, orange rind and cornflour mixture in a medium pan. Stir over low heat for 5 minutes, or until mixture boils and thickens. Remove pan from heat and set aside. Allow mixture to cool.

3 Place the flour, icing sugar, custard powder and butter in a food processor. Process for 15 seconds or until mixture is a fine, crumbly texture. Add egg and water, process for 15 seconds or until the mixture comes together, adding more liquid if necessary. Turn onto well-floured surface, knead for 2 minutes or until smooth. Store, covered with plastic wrap, in refrigerator for about 15 minutes.

4 Roll two-thirds of pastry out on a well-floured surface until large enough to cover base and sides of prepared pie plate. Spread cornflour mixture evenly into pie shell, top with the blackberries. Roll remaining pastry into a circle large enough to cover top of the pie. Brush edges with extra egg to seal. Trim edges with a sharp knife. Brush the top of the pie with beaten egg. Using a fork, make a pattern around the edge. Sprinkle with the raw sugar. Bake in preheated oven for 35 minutes or until the pastry is crisp and golden. Let the pie stand for 5 minutes before cutting into wedges for serving. Serve hot with cream or ice-cream.

---

sweet, juicy, yellow flesh. Peeled, cored and sliced, pineapple can be eaten fresh, as a fruit; diced, it is added to fruit salad, savoury salad and is an ingredient in sweet and sour dishes; chopped pineapple is used in cakes; grilled (broiled) pineapple rings are a traditional accompaniment for ham

steaks (pineapple also combines well with chicken, pork and duck); puréed pineapple can be used in drinks and sorbets; and pineapple can also be made into jam. Raw pineapple contains an enzyme similar to that found in papaya (pawpaw) which means it will not set in gelatine preparations; however, the enzyme is not present in the cooked or canned fruit. Pineapple is in peak season in spring, but can usually be bought fresh throughout the year; it is also available canned, juiced and glacéed (candied). The fruit was named for its resemblance to a large pine cone.

Pine Nut The small, slender, soft, pale seed shed by the fully mature cone of certain types of pine tree.

VEGETABLE PIE

Preparation time: 40 minutes + 40 minutes refrigeration
Total cooking time: 55 minutes
Serves 4–6

Pastry
1½ cups plain (all-purpose) and chopped
wholemeal flour
nutmeg
125 g (4 oz) butter, cubed
1 tablespoon iced water
1 egg yolk, lightly beaten
2 teaspoons lemon juice

Filling
30 g (1 oz) butter
1 small onion, finely sliced
2 large, firm tomatoes, chopped
1 cup grated cheddar cheese

6 spinach leaves, washed

1 cup mashed potato (315 g/10 oz raw potato)
1 cup mashed pumpkin (200 g/6½ oz raw pumpkin)

1 To make Pastry: Sift flour into large mixing bowl. Return husks to bowl. Add butter. Using fingertips, rub butter into flour for 4 minutes or until mixture is a fine, crumbly texture. Make a well in the centre and mix in combined water, egg yolk and lemon juice until mixture clings together to form a ball. Place on lightly floured surface and knead for 1 minute. Cover with plastic wrap and refrigerate for 30 minutes.

2 Preheat oven to moderately hot 210°C (415°F/Gas 6–7). Brush a deep, 20 cm (8 inch) pie plate lightly with melted butter or oil. Roll pastry out between 2 sheets of greaseproof paper on lightly floured surface. Line prepared plate with pastry, being careful not to stretch pastry. Trim the excess from edge using large, sharp knife. Chill for 10 minutes.

3 Line the pastry with greaseproof paper, fill with rice, dried peas or beans. Bake for 12 minutes. Remove and discard paper, rice, peas or beans. Return pastry to oven and continue to bake for 15 minutes or until pastry is cooked and golden brown. Allow to cool for 5 minutes.

4 To make Filling: Melt the butter in a medium pan; add the chopped onion. Stir over medium-high heat for 2 minutes. Add the chopped spinach and nutmeg, cover and cook until the spinach is tender.

5 Spread the mashed potato over the base of the baked pie crust; top with spinach mixture, mashed pumpkin, tomato slices and cheese. Bake for about 20 minutes to heat thoroughly. Serve pie hot or cold.

FAMILY MEAT PIE

Preparation time: 20 minutes
Total cooking time: 1 hour 10 minutes
Serves 4–6.

1 tablespoon oil
1 medium onion, chopped
750 g (1½ lb) minced (ground) beef
90 g (3½ oz) button mushrooms, sliced
2 tablespoons tomato paste
2 sheets frozen shortcrust pastry, thawed
1 sheet frozen puff pastry, thawed
1 egg, lightly beaten

1 cup (8 fl oz) beef stock
2 tablespoons plain (all-purpose) flour

1 Preheat oven to very hot 240°C (475°F/Gas 9). Heat oil in a heavy-based pan; add onion and mince. Stir over medium-high heat until meat is well browned and almost all liquid has evaporated. Use a fork to break up any lumps.

2 Add the mushrooms, tomato paste and stock. Reduce heat, simmer, uncovered, for 15 minutes. Mix the flour with a little cold water to make a smooth paste. Stir into meat, bring to the boil and cook until sauce has thickened. Cool.

3 Line a 23 cm (9 inch) pie plate with shortcrust pastry, overlapping the sheets if necessary. Fill with cold meat mixture. Moisten edges with water, cover with puff pastry and press edges together. Trim excess pastry, decorate top if desired.

4 Brush top with beaten egg and cut a few steam holes. Place dish on an oven tray and bake for 10 minutes. Reduce oven temperature to moderate 180°C (350°F/Gas 4) and bake for 30 minutes or until pastry is golden.

ABOVE: FAMILY MEAT PIE
OPPOSITE PAGE: GOURMET VEGETABLE PIZZA

Pine nuts add richness to stuffings, sauces (such as pesto), salads, vegetable dishes, stews, cakes and biscuits (cookies) and are often used to garnish rice dishes.

Piroshki Tiny filled Russian savoury pastries, served hot as a finger food, as a first course or as an accompaniment to soup. They can be made with yeast dough, choux pastry, shortcrust or puff pastry, and are filled with cream cheese, smoked pork, fish, chopped vegetables, game or poultry. They can be baked or deep-fried.

Pissaladière A savoury flan with a filling of onions simmered in olive oil, garnished with anchovy fillets and black olives, then baked. Pissaladière is a specialty of the Nice region of southern France and it is similar to the Italian pizza—the cooked onions are placed on a circle of bread dough and coated with a paste made of anchovy purée, olive oil, cloves, thyme, bay leaf and pepper.

Pistachio Nut A small, oval nut with a brown shell and a green kernel with a mild, slightly sweet taste. The nuts may be eaten from the

PIZZAS

GOURMET VEGETABLE PIZZA

★★ Preparation time: 30 minutes +
30 minutes standing
Total cooking time: 1 hour
Serves 6

Pizza Dough
2 tablespoons polenta or cornmeal
1 teaspoon dried yeast
1 teaspoon sugar
1½ cups plain (all-purpose) flour
½ cup warm water
1 teaspoon salt
⅓ cup basil leaves, finely chopped
1 tablespoon olive oil

Tomato Sauce
1 tablespoon olive oil
1 small red onion, finely chopped
1 tablespoon oil

1 clove garlic, crushed
1 large tomato, chopped
1 tablespoon tomato paste
½ teaspoon dried oregano

Topping
60 g (2 oz) button mushrooms, finely sliced
100 g (3½ oz) baby corn
1½ cups grated mozzarella cheese
60 g (2 oz) spinach leaves, finely shredded
1 small red pepper (capsicum), cut into short thin strips
2 tablespoons pine nuts

1 Brush a 30 cm (12 inch) pizza tray with oil and sprinkle with polenta or cornmeal.

2 To make Pizza Dough: Combine yeast, sugar and 2 tablespoons of the flour in a small mixing bowl. Gradually add water; blend until smooth. Stand, covered with plastic wrap, in a warm place for about 10 minutes or until foamy.

3 Sift the remaining flour into a large mixing bowl. Add salt and basil, make a well in the centre. Add yeast mixture and oil. Using a knife, mix to a soft dough.

4 Turn dough onto a lightly floured surface, knead for 5 minutes or until smooth. Shape dough into a ball, place in a large, lightly oiled mixing bowl. Leave, covered with plastic wrap, in a warm place for 20 minutes or until well risen. While dough is rising, prepare sauce.

5 To make Tomato Sauce: Heat oil in a small pan, add the onion and garlic and cook over a medium heat for 3 minutes or until soft. Add tomato, reduce heat and simmer for 10 minutes, stirring occasionally. Stir in tomato paste and oregano, cook for another 3 minutes. Allow sauce to cool before using.

6 Preheat oven to moderately hot 210°C (415°F/Gas 6–7). Turn dough out onto a lightly floured surface, knead for another 5 minutes or until smooth. Roll out to fit the prepared tray.

7 Spread the sauce onto the pizza base; arrange the mushrooms and corn evenly on top. Sprinkle half the mozzarella over mushrooms and corn, followed by the spinach, pepper and remaining cheese. Sprinkle with pine nuts. Bake for 40 minutes or until crust is golden. Serve pizza, cut into wedges, immediately.

shell, salted or unsalted, as a snack; shelled pistachio nuts are added to pâtés, terrines, stuffings and spiced sausages and are used to garnish rice dishes; they are also used in confectionery (candy), ice-creams, cakes, sweet pastry fillings and biscuits (cookies). The shells are sometimes dyed red, a practice that began in the United States in the 1930s to cover blemishes. The pistachio nut is the fruit of a tree native to the Middle East which is now cultivated widely in the lands of the Mediterranean and in the south of the United States.

Piston A vegetable and pasta soup, similar to minestrone. It is seasoned just before serving with a condiment of pounded basil leaves, mixed with oil and parmesan cheese. A specialty of Provence, in southern France. piston is closely related to the minestrone served with pesto alla Genovese across the Ligurian Sea in northern Italy. The name piston is derived from the Italian word for 'pesto', and the soup is

Pizza A flat base of bread dough spread with various savoury toppings (tomato puree, cheese, salami, ham, seafood, chopped vegetables, anchovy and olives), seasoned with herbs and garlic, brushed with olive oil and baked, traditionally in a wood-

Pitta Bread A slightly leavened, soft, flat, wheat flour bread baked until puffed and hollow. Pitta can be either cut in half across the middle or slit open at the edges; either way a pocket is formed which can then be filled with hot meat (such as lamb cubes), vegetable mixtures (such as falafel) or with salad. Cut or torn into smaller portions, pitta bread is the traditional accompaniment to dips such as hummus bi tahini and baba ghannouj. It can also be used as a pizza base. Pitra is of Middle Eastern origin.

P traditionally served with the basil sauce in a mortar in the centre of the table to allow diners to season their soup to taste.

TRADITIONAL PIZZA

★★ **Preparation time:** 1 hour
Total cooking time: 45 minutes
Serves 6

Pizza Dough
1 tablespoon olive oil
2 teaspoons cornmeal (maize flour) or semolina
1 teaspoon dried yeast
1 teaspoon sugar
1 1/2 cups plain (all-purpose) flour
1/2 cup (4 fl oz) warm water
1 teaspoon salt

Tomato Sauce
1 tablespoon olive oil
1 small onion, finely chopped
1 clove garlic, crushed
1 large tomato, finely chopped
1 tablespoon tomato paste
1/2 teaspoon dried oregano

1 Preheat oven to moderately hot 210°C (415°F/Gas 6–7). Brush a 30 cm (12 inch) pizza tray with oil and sprinkle with cornmeal or semolina. Combine yeast, sugar and 2 tablespoons of flour in a small mixing bowl. Gradually add water; blend until smooth. Stand, covered with plastic wrap, in a warm place for about 10 minutes or until foamy.

2 Sift remaining flour into a large mixing bowl. Add salt and make a well in the centre. Add yeast mixture and oil. Using a knife, mix to a soft dough.

3 Turn dough onto a lightly floured surface, knead 5 minutes or until smooth. Shape dough into a ball, place in a large, lightly oiled mixing bowl. Leave, covered with plastic wrap, in a warm place 20 minutes or until well risen.

4 Turn dough out onto a lightly floured surface, knead for another 5 minutes, until smooth and elastic. Roll out to fit prepared tray, cover with topping and cook in preheated oven for 30 minutes.

5 To make Tomato Sauce: Heat oil in a small pan, add onion and garlic and cook over a medium heat 3 minutes or until soft. Add tomato, reduce heat and simmer for 10 minutes, stirring occasionally. Stir in tomato paste and oregano, cook for another 2 minutes. Set aside to cool.

VARIATIONS

■ **Napolitana:** Spread 1 quantity Tomato Sauce on a pizza base. Sprinkle with 1 cup of grated mozzarella cheese and 1 tablespoon of chopped fresh oregano. Bake in preheated oven for 30 minutes.

■ **Peperoni:** Spread 1 quantity Tomato Sauce on a pizza base. Sprinkle with 125 g (4 oz) of grated mozzarella cheese and 1 finely chopped red pepper (capsicum). Top with 125 g (4 oz) thinly sliced peperoni. Bake in preheated oven for 30 minutes.

■ **Four Seasons:** Spread 1/2 quantity of Tomato Sauce on a pizza base. Fry in oil, in separate batches, 75 g (2 1/2 oz) of sliced button mushrooms, 3 chopped bacon rashers, 1 finely sliced onion. Place each of these on one quarter of pizza. Place 5 canned anchovy fillets over onion. On remaining quarter of pizza, arrange 3 sliced small bocconcini and 1 tablespoon shredded fresh basil. Bake for 30 minutes.

ABOVE: TRADITIONAL PIZZA
OPPOSITE PAGE: GARLIC BUTTER POLENTA

POLENTA

GARLIC BUTTER POLENTA WITH ROASTED PEPPER (CAPSICUM)

Preparation time: 30 minutes + 2 hours refrigeration
Total cooking time: 10–15 minutes
Serves 2–4

1½ cups (10½ fl oz) chicken or vegetable stock	25 g (¾ oz) butter, extra, melted
1 cup (8 fl oz) water	1 tablespoon olive oil
1 cup polenta	1 clove garlic, crushed
½ cup freshly grated parmesan cheese	freshly grated parmesan cheese, extra, for serving
25 g (¾ oz) butter	fresh ricotta cheese for serving
2 large red peppers (capsicum)	

1 Place the stock and water in a medium pan and bring to boil. Add polenta, reduce heat and stir constantly for 3–6 minutes or until very thick. Remove from heat, stir in parmesan cheese and butter. Spread mixture into a foil-lined 26 x 8 x 4.5 cm (10½ x 3 x 1¾ inch) bar tin: smooth surface. Refrigerate for 2 hours.

2 Cut peppers in half. Remove seeds and membrane. Place skin-side up on a grill tray. Cook under preheated grill until skin blisters and blackens. Cover with a damp tea-towel; cool. Peel skin and discard. Cut flesh into thin strips.

3 Turn polenta out and cut into slices. Brush one side of slices with combined melted butter, oil and garlic.

4 Cook under a preheated grill for 3–4 minutes or until slices are lightly browned. Repeat process on other sides. Serve hot with pepper strips, extra grated parmesan cheese and fresh ricotta cheese.

ABOUT POLENTA

■ Polenta is finely milled cornmeal (maize flour) which is simmered slowly with water and stirred constantly to produce a thick porridge-like mixture. It is a staple of Italian cooking with a variety of uses. Although rather bland in flavour, its versatile texture makes it adaptable to many sweet or savoury dishes.

■ A popular alternative to potatoes, rice or pasta, polenta is easy to prepare and is often served with strong-tasting meats such as spicy sausages, sautéed liver or roast game, or with marinated, grilled vegetables.

■ Polenta can be enriched with milk or a soft cheese (such as chèvre), and stirred into soups or stews, or made into dumplings.

■ Alternatively, the polenta mixture can be spread over the base of a buttered baking dish. When it has cooled and set, it is cut into wedges or slices and fried or toasted. It can be eaten alone with butter or cheese, or served as an accompaniment to savoury dishes.

■ Polenta slices can be flavoured after cooking: brush with olive oil, or spread with olive paste, mashed anchovies or feta cheese.

Plum A round fruit with smooth shiny skin that ranges in

Plantain A tropical fruit closely related to the banana, but plumper and longer, with thick green skin and firmer, more fibrous flesh. Plantain is grilled (broiled), fried or barbecued and served as a vegetable, or it can be diced and added to curries, soups, casseroles and omelettes; it can become bitter if overcooked. Raw plantain is never sweet, even when fully ripe. Young leaves can be used in soups and salads.

Pizza is eaten hot, as either a first or a main course; small portions or miniature pizzas can be served as finger food. Pizza originated in Naples, in southern Italy, where nineteenth-century street vendors vied with each other to attract customers to their tasty fare—the classic Neapolitan pizza has a thin, crisp crust with a topping of tomato and mozzarella cheese. In Rome pizza is made in large, rectangular pans, cut into pieces and sold by weight. Sicily is the home of the thick-crust or pan pizza, rolled thicker than the Neapolitan original and baked in a greased pan.

OPPOSITE PAGE: PORK WITH SOY ORANGE SAUCE
RIGHT: POPPY SEED TWISTS
ABOVE: POPPY SEED LOAF

colour from deep purple to green, yellow or red, depending on the variety; it has sweet, juicy flesh and a flat stone. Raw plums can be eaten unskinned as a snack; stoned, sliced and added to fruit salad; or puréed for use in sauces, ice-creams and desserts. Plums may be stewed or poached, made into filling for pies and tarts, cooked in fruit puddings and cakes or made into jam; spicy plum sauce combines well with roast meats (especially pork) and poultry. The plum is thought to have originated in western Asia. They grew in the Hanging Gardens of Babylon; the Romans imported plum trees from Damascus and improved the quality of the fruit by grafting and cross-fertilisation. Plums are in season in summer and early autumn; they are also available canned and dried as prunes.

Plum Pudding A rich steamed or boiled pudding made with dried fruit (prunes, raisins, sultanas and glacé cherries), nuts, suet and rum or whisky. It has a dense, moist, cake-like texture. Plum pudding, decorated with holly, flamed with brandy and

---

POPPY SEEDS

POPPY SEED LOAF

★

Preparation time: 15 minutes
Total cooking time: 50 minutes
Makes 1 loaf

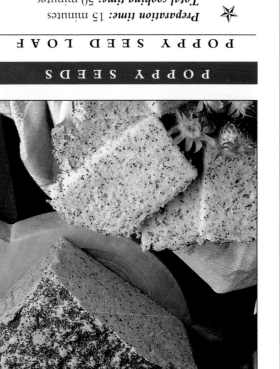

2½ cups self-raising flour
¼ cup caster (superfine) sugar
¼ cup poppy seeds
1 kg (2 lb) peeled, grated potato
185 g (6 oz) butter, melted and cooled
2 eggs, lightly beaten
1 teaspoon poppy seeds, extra

1 Preheat oven to moderate 180°C (350°F/Gas 4). Brush a 21 x 14 x 7 cm (8½ x 5½ x 2¾ inch) loaf tin with melted butter or oil. Line the base and sides with paper; grease paper.
2 Sift flour into large mixing bowl. Add sugar, poppy seeds and potato. Make a well in the centre. Add butter and eggs. Stir with a wooden spoon until just combined; do not overbeat.
3 Spoon mixture into tin; smooth surface, sprinkle with extra poppy seeds. Bake for 50 minutes or until skewer comes out clean when inserted in centre of loaf. Leave loaf in tin for 3 minutes before turning it onto a wire rack to cool.

Note: Loaf will keep, refrigerated, for 4 days, or may be frozen successfully for up to 4 weeks. Can be served as accompaniment to a cheese/fruit platter.

POPPY SEED TWISTS

★★

Preparation time: 20 minutes +
15 minutes refrigeration
Total cooking time: 15 minutes
Makes 24

½ cup plain (all-purpose) flour
1 tablespoon poppy seeds
45 g (1½ oz) butter, chopped
2 tablespoons iced water
1 egg, beaten

1 Preheat oven to moderate 180°C (350°F/Gas 4). Brush a 32 x 28 cm (13 x 11 inch) oven tray with melted butter or oil. Place flour in a medium mixing bowl, make a well in the centre and add butter. Using two knives, cut butter in a crossing motion until reduced to very small pieces. Stir in the water with a knife and mix to a firm dough. Turn out onto a lightly floured surface, knead for 1 minute or until smooth. Store, covered in plastic wrap, in refrigerator for 15 minutes.
2 On a lightly floured surface, roll pastry to a 24 x 16 cm (9½ x 6½ inch) rectangle. Sprinkle with poppy seeds and press them gently into the pastry with the back of a spoon. Fold pastry into three layers, and re-roll to a 30 x 12 cm (12 x 4¾ inch) rectangle. Cut crossways into 24 strips.
3 Hold a strip at each end, and twist ends in opposite directions. Place on prepared tray and brush lightly with beaten egg. Bake for 15 minutes or until golden. Cool on a wire rack. Serve as an appetiser or with soup.

PORK

PORK WITH SOY ORANGE SAUCE

Preparation time: 10 minutes + overnight marinating
Total cooking time: 30 minutes
Serves 8

8 pork butterfly medallions or pork chops, about 185 g (6 oz) each
2 cloves garlic, crushed
2 teaspoons dried rosemary
3/4 cup (6 fl oz) orange juice
1/4 cup (2 fl oz) soy sauce
1 tablespoon honey
1 tablespoon olive oil, extra, for frying
2 tablespoons olive oil

1 Trim meat of excess fat and sinew. Place pork steaks in a single layer in a large, shallow glass or ceramic dish. Combine orange juice, soy sauce, oil, garlic, rosemary and honey and pour over steaks. Place in refrigerator to marinate for several hours or overnight.

2 Preheat oven to slow 150°C (300°F/Gas 2). Heat oil in a large, heavy-based pan; remove steaks from marinade, reserving marinade. Add steaks to pan in batches, cook over medium heat 4–5 minutes each side. Remove from heat and drain on paper towels. Place cooked steaks on a plate and cover loosely with foil. Keep cooked steaks warm in oven.

3 Pour marinade in a pan. Stir over medium heat until mixture boils; reduce heat slightly and simmer for about 5 minutes or until reduced by half. To serve, place a steak on each plate and

Note: Pork fillets are a delicate cut with little fat visible. If not available, choose another lean cut.

BARBECUED GINGER PORK SATAYS

Preparation time: 20 minutes + 1 hour marinating
Total cooking time: 10 minutes
Serves 6

500 g (1 lb) pork fillets
2 tablespoons grated fresh ginger
1/2 teaspoon ground pepper
1 teaspoon sesame oil
1 tablespoon lemon juice
1 small onion, grated
salt and pepper, to taste

1 Cut pork into even-sized cubes. Place grated ginger, pepper, sesame oil, lemon juice, onion and salt and pepper in a bowl and mix well. Mix pork cubes with marinade and leave for 1 hour.

2 Thread pork cubes onto skewers. Cook on preheated barbecue flatplate for 5 minutes each side or until cooked to personal taste. Serve with a salad and hot bread rolls.

Note: If preferred, white fish fillets can be used as a substitute for pork in this recipe. Reduce the marinating time to a couple of hours so that the high acid content of the marinade does not break up the flesh of the fish. Reduce the cooking time as well, cooking just until flesh flakes easily.

spoon over a little of the sauce. Accompany with a steamed green vegetable such as asparagus or snow peas (mange tout).

---

served with brandy butter, is traditional Christmas fare. Ice-cream, whipped cream or custard can also accompany the pudding.

Poach To cook food by gently simmering it in liquid in a shallow pan.

Polenta Cornmeal (maize flour) cooked in water and butter until the consistency of thick porridge. It can be eaten hot, on its own, or mixed with parmesan cheese and baked, grilled (broiled) or fried and served in wedges as a vegetable dish. The mixture can be varied with the addition of chopped meat or vegetables; slices of cold polenta are often fried in butter and served topped with a tomato sauce. Polenta has been a staple food in  northern Italy since the arrival of corn from the Americas in the sixteenth century. The word comes from *puls*, the boiled grains (usually millet) fed to the early Roman soldiers.

Pomegranate A round, reddish-golden skinned fruit about the size of an orange. It is divided by walls of bitter-tasting pith into several chambers, each containing numerous

seeds embedded in sacs of sweet, deep pink, jelly-like pulp. The seeds and pulp can be scooped from the shell and eaten or may be added to fruit salad; pomegranate juice is used to make grenadine syrup (a bright red, non-alcoholic drink used as a colouring and flavouring for cocktails, ice-cream, fruit salad and other desserts). The pomegranate is of Asian origin and spread west to the African shores of the Mediterranean many thousands of years ago. It was cultivated by the ancient Hittites, Persians and Egyptians. It has long been regarded as a symbol of fertility. In Greek mythology Persephone, goddess of spring, was condemned to spend half of each year in Hades for eating six forbidden pomegranate seeds—when she emerged from the shades the land quickened with the first signs of spring and, on her return to the underworld, stilled with autumn. The pomegranate is in season in late autumn.

Popcorn A snack made by heating the kernels of a type of corn known as

ROAST LEG OF PORK

Preparation time: 30 minutes
Total cooking time: 3 hours 30 minutes
Serves 6-8

4 kg (8 lb) leg of pork
cooking salt

Apple Sauce
500 g (1 lb) green or cooking apples, peeled, cored and quartered
1/2 cup (4 fl oz) water
1 tablespoon caster (superfine) sugar

60 g (2 oz) butter, cubed

Gravy
1 tablespoon brandy or Calvados
2 tablespoons plain (all-purpose) flour
2 cups (16 fl oz) chicken stock

1 Preheat oven to very hot 260°C (500°F/Gas 10). Score pork rind with a very sharp knife at 2 cm (¾ inch) intervals. Rub in cooking salt to ensure crisp crackling. Place pork, rind side uppermost, on a roasting rack in a large baking dish. Add a little water to the dish. Cook for 30 minutes or until skin begins to crackle and bubble. Reduce heat to moderate 180°C (350°F/Gas 4) and bake pork for 2 hours 40 minutes (approximately 20 minutes per 500 g/1 lb).

2 Baste meat occasionally with pan juices; do not cover or the crackling will soften. Remove from oven. Leave in a warm place for 10 minutes covered with foil, before slicing. Serve with Apple Sauce and Gravy.

3 To make Apple Sauce: Place prepared apple and water in a small pan. Cover and simmer for 10 minutes until apple is very soft. Remove from heat, stir in the sugar and cubed butter while apple is still warm. Sauce can be pushed through a sieve if a smoother texture is desired.

To make Gravy: Reserve about 2 tablespoons meat juices in pan. Heat on top of stove; add brandy and stir mixture quickly to lift sediment from bottom of pan. Cook for 1 minute. Remove from heat and stir in flour; mix well. Return pan to heat and cook for 2 minutes, stirring mixture constantly. Gradually add chicken stock; cook, stirring occasionally, until the gravy boils and thickens. Season to taste.

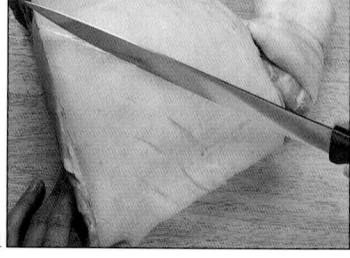

PORK WITH FENNEL

Preparation time: 35 minutes
Total cooking time: 1 hour 40 minutes
Serves 6

1 teaspoon olive oil	1 egg, lightly beaten
3 rashers bacon, finely chopped	30 g (1 oz) butter
1.4 kg (2¾ lb) pork loin, rind removed	1 tablespoon extra olive oil,
1 cup fresh white breadcrumbs	½ cup (4 fl oz) sweet sherry
1 cup finely chopped fresh fennel bulb	½ cup (4 fl oz) orange juice
1 tablespoon chopped capers	2 tablespoons red wine vinegar
2 tablespoons chopped fresh chives	1 teaspoon finely grated orange rind

1 Preheat oven to 180°C (350°F/Gas 4). Heat oil in a medium pan and add the bacon. Cook over medium-high heat for 2 minutes or until crisp. Remove from pan and drain on paper towels.

2 Trim pork of excess fat. Cut through lengthways to open out but do not cut right through. Open out, flatten with the palm of your hand.

3 Combine the bacon, breadcrumbs, fennel, capers and chives in a medium bowl; add egg and stir to combine. Press the stuffing over the opened loin. Roll up and tie securely with string.

4 Heat butter and oil in frying pan. Cook loin over medium heat 3–4 minutes until evenly browned. Remove from pan and place in a large baking dish.

5 Scrape sediment from pan. Add combined sherry, orange juice, red wine vinegar and orange rind to pan. Simmer uncovered for 2 minutes. Pour over pork. Bake 1½ hours or until cooked through.

6 Remove string from pork, slice and place on serving platter, spoon pan juices over, serve.

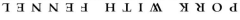

CREAMY LEMON PORK

Preparation time: 10 minutes
Total cooking time: 45–50 minutes
Serves 4

750 g (1½ lb) diced pork fillet (tenderloin)	½ cup (4 fl oz) cream
25 g (¾ oz) butter	1 tablespoon lemon juice
185 g (6 oz) button mushrooms, sliced	freshly ground black pepper to taste
1 cup (8 fl oz) chicken stock	½ small lemon, cut into small wedges
1 tablespoon plain (all-purpose) flour	finely chopped fresh parsley

1 Trim meat of excess fat and sinew. Heat butter in a heavy-based pan. Cook meat quickly, in small batches over medium-high heat until well browned; drain on paper towels.

2 Add mushrooms to pan and cook for 2 minutes. Return meat to pan with stock; bring to boil. Reduce heat to simmer, cook covered, 30 minutes or until meat is tender, stirring occasionally.

3 Mix together flour and cream. Add to pan, increase heat, stir until sauce thickens. Simmer 2 minutes. Season with juice and pepper. Serve with noodles, decorate with lemon wedges and parsley.

Popover An airy batter pudding or quick bread made from a batter of flour, egg and milk (very similar to the mixture used to make Yorkshire pudding). Popovers are baked in greased muffin tins or cups in a very hot oven so they rise quickly, forming a crisp, golden shell while the inside remains moist and mostly hollow. Popovers should be eaten hot, either with butter and jam or honey, or split open and filled with a

popping corn. The moisture in the kernel changes to steam, swelling the soft starchy interior until it bursts through the skin as a puffy white ball. Popcorn is eaten as a snack, either with melted butter and salt or with a sweet coating. Packs of popping corn for cooking on the stove-top (add to a little heated oil in a heavy lidded pan: it should start to pop in a minute or so and be ready in another minute) and a special pop-in-the-bag product for microwave ovens are available from supermarkets: cooked popcorn is sold in sealed bags or, freshly popped, in open cartons.

PORK STEAKS WITH GRAINY MUSTARD CREAM

✹ **Preparation time:** 15 minutes
Total cooking time: 12 minutes
Serves 6

6 pork butterfly steaks, about 200 g (6½ oz) each, or 6 noisettes
3 tablespoons plain (all-purpose) flour
½ teaspoon ground black pepper
1 teaspoon soy sauce
2 teaspoons seeded mustard

¾ cup (6 fl oz) orange juice
1 chicken stock cube, crumbled
¼ cup (2 fl oz) oil
1 medium onion, finely chopped
1 teaspoon cornflour (cornstarch)
⅓ cup (2½ fl oz) sour cream

1 Trim meat of excess fat and sinew. Combine flour and pepper on a sheet of greaseproof paper. Toss steaks in the seasoned flour until lightly coated; shake off excess.
2 Heat 2 tablespoons oil in a heavy-based pan; add meat. Cook over a medium heat 2–3 minutes each side or until tender, turning once. Remove from pan, drain on paper towels.

SWEET AND SOUR PORK

✹✹ **Preparation time:** 20 minutes + 20 minutes marinating
Total cooking time: 12 minutes
Serves 4–6

750 g (1½ lb) pork belly or spareribs
1 tablespoon soy sauce
1 tablespoon dry sherry
½ medium cucumber
2 tablespoons Chinese sweet mixed pickles
1 cup cornflour (cornstarch)
1.25 litres (5 cups) vegetable oil
¼ green pepper (capsicum), shredded
¼ red pepper (capsicum), shredded

1 medium onion, sliced from top to base
½ cup (4 fl oz) white vinegar
1 cup (8 fl oz) water
¼ cup (2 fl oz) tomato sauce
⅓ cup sugar
1 teaspoon powdered chicken stock
1 tablespoon cornflour (cornstarch), extra

1 Thickly slice pork, cut into 1 cm (½ inch) strips crossways so that each piece consists of layers of pork and fat. Remove small bones if using spareribs. Brush with soy and sherry, set aside for 20 minutes.
2 Peel the cucumber, cut in half and scoop out the seeds, then cut into thin slices lengthways. Finely chop the pickles or cut into fine shreds.
3 Coat the pork thickly with cornflour and shake off the excess. Fry in several batches in the oil until lightly golden, about 2 minutes. Remove and spread on a rack to drain and cool.
4 Stir-fry the peppers and onion in 3 tablespoons of oil taken from the frying pan. (Reserve the remaining hot oil.) Add the cucumber and pickles and fry briefly, add vinegar, water, sauce, sugar, chicken stock and extra cornflour. Stir until cornflour is dissolved. Bring to the boil, simmer, stirring, until thickened.
5 Reheat oil, fry pork a second time until golden and crisp, about 2 minutes. Pour on sauce, serve.

Pork The meat of the domestic pig. Pale and succulent, it has long been prized for its richness and flavour. Suckling or sucking pig is an animal slaughtered at two months of age. Top quality pork should be pale pink, smooth and finely grained with white fat and smooth, thin skin. Pork is suitable for roasting, grilling (broiling), barbecuing. Pork is available from health food shops and supermarkets.

Poppy Seed The fine grey-blue seeds of the poppy plant. Poppy seeds have a strong, nutty flavour. They are often sprinkled on bread and savoury crackers, before baking; are added to pasta and potato dishes, and are used to make the traditional Jewish poppy seed cake. The poppy seed is native to Asia. Seeds are available from health food shops and supermarkets.

savoury preparation of meat or vegetables; herbs, grated cheese or sugar may be added to the batter.

BARBECUED PORK MEDALLIONS WITH TAPENADE

★ **Preparation time:** 20 minutes
Total cooking time: 15 minutes
Serves 4

4 pork butterfly
medallions, about 200 g
(6¹/₂ oz) each or
4 pork loin medallion
steaks, about 155 g
(5 oz) each
1 clove garlic, crushed
125 g (4 oz) pitted black
olives, finely chopped
2 anchovies, finely
chopped
1 small, ripe tomato,
peeled, seeded and
chopped
2 teaspoons balsamic
vinegar
1 medium red chilli,
finely chopped
1 tablespoon chopped
fresh basil leaves

Tapenade
2 tablespoons olive oil
¹/₂ small onion, finely
chopped

2 tablespoons olive oil
(5 oz) each
1 tablespoon lemon juice
1 tablespoon fresh thyme
leaves
¹/₄ teaspoon ground black
pepper

1 If using pork loin medallion steaks, shape into
rounds by securing thinner tail end to the
medallion with toothpicks. Trim meat of excess
fat and sinew.

2 Combine oil, lemon juice, thyme and pepper,
brush over meat.

3 Place meat on lightly oiled preheated flatplate
or grill. Cook over medium heat for 5 minutes
on each side or until tender. Serve with
Tapenade.

4 To make Tapenade: Heat the oil in small
pan, add onion and garlic, stir until onion is
tender. Add olives, anchovies, tomato, vinegar,
chilli and basil, stir for 1 minute to combine.
Serve hot or cold.

Note: The pork for this recipe can be cooked
under a preheated grill. Unless it is cooked
carefully at a moderate heat, pork can become dry
and tough. Cuts such as those used in this recipe
are done when the flesh feels fairly firm to touch;
it should still be juicy and faintly pink.

To make butterfly medallions, trim meat from
the bone of pork chops. Discard the bones. Using
a sharp knife, cut meat horizontally through the
centre starting at the fatty end. Ensure that you
do not cut right through. Open the meat out and
press with your hands to flatten slightly.
Medallions are now ready to use in your recipe.

OPPOSITE PAGE, ABOVE: SWEET AND SOUR PORK;
BELOW: PORK STEAKS WITH GRAINY MUSTARD
CREAM. ABOVE: BARBECUED PORK MEDALLIONS
WITH TAPENADE

3 Heat remaining oil in pan, stir
over medium heat 3 minutes or until soft. Add
half the juice, stock cube, sauce and mustard, stir
until combined. Blend cornflour with remaining
juice until smooth; add to pan. Stir over low heat
until sauce boils and thickens. Remove from
heat; cool slightly. Add sour cream, stir until
smooth. Return meat; heat through and serve.

Pork is the main meat
in the cooking of China
and South-East Asia. In
China and Vietnam the
plump pig is a symbol of
prosperity. The animals
are also known for their
fecundity—a sow can have
up to a dozen young in a
single litter. For
centuries pork was
virtually the only meat
eaten by the peasant
communities of
Europe—nothing of the
carcass was wasted,
from the ears to the
trotters.

Nineteenth-century
gastronomic writer
Charles Monselet
described the pig as
'nothing but an immense
dish that walks'.

Pork is available fresh,
cured in brine or pickling
solution or cured and
smoked. It is
complemented by the
flavours of sage and
juniper berries.

Porridge Oatmeal or
rolled oats cooked in
water or milk until thick
and creamy. Porridge is
usually served hot with
milk and sugar, for
breakfast, but it can also
be eaten cold, with salt.
Porridge is descended
from gruel—which was a
staple of peasant diets.

It is healthiest to choose
lean cuts and trim off
excess fat.

Pork is the main meat
...

pan-frying and
casseroling; pork joints
can also be pickled.

POTATOES

CRISP POTATO SKINS WITH CHILLI CHEESE DIP

★ **Preparation time:** 30 minutes
Total cooking time: 1 hour 15 minutes
Serves 4–6

6 medium potatoes, about
1.2 kg (2¹⁄₂ lb)
oil for shallow frying

Chilli Cheese Dip
³⁄₄ cup (6 fl oz) sour cream
2 cups grated cheddar
cheese
1 tablespoon oil
1 small onion, finely
chopped

1 clove garlic, crushed
1 teaspoon mild chilli
powder

1 Preheat oven to moderately hot 210°C (415°F/Gas 6–7). Scrub potatoes and dry thoroughly; do not peel. Prick each potato twice with a fork. Bake for 1 hour, turning once, until skins are crisp and flesh is soft when pierced with a knife. Remove from oven and cool.

2 Cut potatoes in half and scoop out flesh, leaving about 5 mm (¹⁄₄ inch) of potato in the shell (save unused flesh for another use). Cut each half potato into three wedges.

3 Heat oil in a medium heavy-based pan. Gently lower batches of potato skins into moderately hot oil. Cook for 1–2 minutes or until golden and crisp. Drain on paper towels. Serve immediately with Chilli Cheese Dip.

4 To make Chilli Cheese Dip: Heat oil in a small pan. Add onion and cook over medium heat for 2 minutes or until soft. Add garlic and chilli powder; cook for 1 minute, stirring. Add sour cream and stir until mixture is warm and thinned down slightly; add cheese and stir until melted and mixture is almost smooth. Serve hot.

ABOUT POTATOES

■ Potatoes are members of the nightshade family (as are tomatoes and aubergines/eggplant). If exposed to light they can develop a greenish-tinged toxic compound under the skin which may cause illness in sensitive individuals. Unwashed potatoes will keep longer, as the soil helps keep out light. Discard potatoes which have turned green, or which have sprouting eyes.

■ Potatoes do not store well in the refrigerator—the low temperatures turn the flesh black as the starch converts to sugar. Store them in a cool, dark, dry place.

■ When deep-frying potatoes (for example when making French fries), a crisper result is obtained if the cut potatoes are soaked for about an hour beforehand in water to remove some of the starch. Dry well with paper towels before frying.

POTATOES

LAYERED POTATO AND APPLE BAKE

★ **Preparation time:** 20 minutes
Total cooking time: 45 minutes
Serves 6

2 large potatoes
3 medium green apples
1 medium onion
¹⁄₄ teaspoon ground
nutmeg

1 cup (8 fl oz) cream
¹⁄₂ cup finely grated
cheddar cheese
freshly ground black
pepper

1 Preheat oven to moderate 180°C (350°F/Gas 4). Brush a shallow 2 litre (8-cup) ovenproof dish with melted butter or oil. Peel potatoes and cut into 5 mm (¹⁄₄ inch) slices. Peel, core and quarter apples. Cut into 5 mm (¹⁄₄ inch) slices. Slice onion into very fine rings.

2 Layer potato, apple and onion in prepared dish, ending with a layer of potato. Sprinkle evenly with cheese. Pour cream over top, covering as evenly as possible.

3 Sprinkle with nutmeg and black pepper to taste. Bake for 45 minutes or until golden brown. Remove from oven and allow to stand for 5 minutes before serving.

Note: To prevent the sliced potato and apple turning brown while assembling dish, dip them in a bowl of cold water with a squeeze of lemon juice. Drain and pat dry with paper towels.

Port A rich, sweet, fortified wine used to flavour duck and game dishes, sauces (such as Cumberland sauce), pâtés, and desserts such as jellies, creams and syrups for poached fruit. True port is made from a variety of grapes grown in northern Portugal and shipped through the town of Oporto.

Port Salut A semi-soft, pasteurised cow's milk cheese with a smooth, savoury taste, a creamy texture, a reddish-orange rind and a golden interior with a few tiny holes. Port Salut (literally 'port of salvation') originated in Brittany, north-western France, created by Trappist monks who found haven in a local abbey after years of exile in Switzerland following the French Revolution. The cheese found instant popularity when it reached the markets of Paris in the 1870s. In the years following World War II the monks, unable to keep pace with demand, sold the brand name Saint Paulin to commercial dairies to produce a similar cheese. Port Salut should be served at room temperature on cheeseboards with fresh or dried fruit, as a snack cheese and in sandwiches; it is also cooked in savouries.

Potato A starchy, tuberous root vegetable with crisp white or yellow flesh and smooth brown, russet, yellow or purple skin. A remarkably versatile vegetable, it can be boiled, roasted, fried, baked or barbecued; it is the classic accompaniment to fish and meat courses or can itself form the basis of a main course. New potatoes are small, young potatoes; they have pearly, translucent skin (which need not be removed) and slightly waxy flesh and are boiled whole and served with melted butter or used for making potato salad. Old potatoes are floury and are best for boiling and mashing or for baking in their skins; they can also be used in soups and as pie topping. Slightly waxy potatoes roast well and are also made into chips and French fries. Very waxy potatoes are ideal for potato salad. The potato is native to South America and was first cultivated high in the Andes as early as 5,000 years ago. When introduced into England

BAKED POTATOES AND FILLINGS

Pierce 2 large potatoes all over with a fork; place on a rack in moderately hot 210°C (415°F/Gas 6–7) oven, bake 1 hour or until tender. Meanwhile, prepare topping. Make a deep slash or cross-cut in each cooked potato; squeeze to open and fill with topping. Serves 2.

Note: To microwave jacket potatoes, pierce them all over with a fork. Wrap each potato in a layer of paper towel and place directly on microwave turntable. Cook on high setting for 10 minutes. Leave for 2 minutes.

HOT CHILLI

Cook 250 g (8 oz) beef mince in 1 teaspoon olive oil over medium-high heat for 5 minutes or until meat is brown and almost all the liquid has evaporated. Add 1 small sliced onion, 2 cloves of crushed garlic, 1 sliced red chilli, ½ medium red pepper (capsicum), seeded and thinly sliced, 2 tablespoons of tomato puree and 1 cup (8 fl oz) of beef stock. Stir well to combine. Bring to boil, reduce heat and simmer, uncovered, for 20 minutes. Add freshly ground black pepper to taste. Make lengthways slashes in 2 baked potatoes, squeeze slightly and top with meat mixture; garnish with extra chilli slices. Serves 2.

BLACK RUSSIAN

Slash 2 baked potatoes lengthways. Top each with 30 g (1 oz) of sliced smoked salmon, half a slice of lemon and 1 tablespoon sour cream. Garnish with black caviar and serve. Serves 2.

SPICED PRAWN (SHRIMP)

Cook 250 g (8 oz) of peeled, cooked medium prawns (shrimps), a pinch of turmeric and a pinch of ground coriander in 15 g (½ oz) of butter in a pan, over medium-high heat, for 1 minute. Add pepper to taste. Slash 2 baked potatoes lengthways and fill with prawn mixture. Serves 2.

NAPOLETANA

Peel and chop 2 medium, firm, ripe tomatoes. Place in a pan with 1 tablespoon olive oil and a pinch of dried oregano. Simmer for 10 minutes. Remove from heat, add freshly ground pepper to taste. Fluff up the tops of 2 baked potatoes. Top with tomato mixture, garnish with anchovy fillets and pitted black olives. Serves 2.

GARLIC MUSHROOMS

Cook 125 g (4 oz) of quartered button mushrooms and 1 clove of crushed garlic in 45 g (1½ oz) of butter in a medium pan until tender. Add 2 teaspoons finely chopped parsley and freshly ground black pepper to taste. Spoon mixture into 2 cross-cut baked potatoes. Serves 2.

SPICY POTATO PASTRIES

Preparation time: 40 minutes
Total cooking time: 25 minutes
Makes 36

4 large potatoes (1.3 kg/2 lb 10 oz), peeled and cut into small cubes
30 g (1 oz) butter
1 clove garlic, crushed
2 teaspoons finely grated fresh ginger
1 medium onion, finely chopped
1 teaspoon turmeric
1 teaspoon garam masala
1 teaspoon ground cardamom
1 tablespoon lemon juice
1/4 cup chopped fresh coriander
1/4 cup chopped fresh mint
4 sheets ready rolled puff pastry, thawed
1 egg, lightly beaten
2 teaspoons poppy seeds

1 Preheat oven to moderate 200°C (400°F/Gas 6). Brush two 32 x 28 cm (13 x 11 inch) oven trays with melted butter or oil. Cook potato in boiling water until just tender. Drain, set aside.
2 Heat butter in pan; add garlic, ginger, onion and spices. Cook over medium high heat for 4 minutes or until onion is soft. Add potato, lemon juice, coriander and mint; stir gently to combine. Remove from heat; cool.
3 Cut each pastry sheet into 9 even squares. Brush edges with beaten egg. Place 2 teaspoons potato mixture in the centre of each square, fold over to form a triangle and press edges to seal.
4 Brush top of each triangle with egg; sprinkle with poppy seeds. Place 2.5 cm (1 inch) apart on prepared trays. Bake for 20–25 minutes.

POTATO AND CHEESE CAKES WITH APPLE

Preparation time: 25 minutes
Total cooking time: 20 minutes
Makes 18

2 cups mashed potato
125 g (4 oz) cheddar cheese, grated
2 tablespoons plain (all-purpose) flour
1 egg, lightly beaten
1/2 teaspoon ground nutmeg
2–3 tablespoons olive oil

Apple Sauce
2 large green apples, peeled and cored
2 tablespoons water
2 tablespoons chopped fresh mint
1 tablespoon white vinegar

1 Combine potato, cheese, sifted flour, egg and nutmeg in mixing bowl. Stir until the mixture is just combined; do not overbeat.
2 Heat olive oil in a medium, heavy-based pan. Spoon level tablespoonsful of prepared potato mixture into pan. Cook over medium high heat for 5 minutes. Turn over and cook for another 5 minutes or until Potato and Cheese Cakes are golden brown and cooked through. Top each Potato and Cheese Cake with a spoonful of Apple Sauce and serve immediately.
3 **To make Apple Sauce:** Cut apples into large cubes and place in a small pan. Add the water, cover and cook over low heat until apples are tender and all the water has evaporated. Mash well with a fork and add mint and vinegar. Stir until well combined.

by Sir Francis Drake in the sixteenth century it soon found favour in Ireland, where it flourished in the poor soils where other food crops failed; Sir Walter Raleigh is said to have planted the first potatoes in Ireland in 1586. Early in the eighteenth century the potato

recrossed the Atlantic to the American colonies. However, acceptance was slower in continental Europe. The French regarded it as 'unsuitable for food' and the vegetable was shunned until the work of French agronomist Auguste Parmentier in the late eighteenth century promoted it in a more favourable light — it is now a staple food in France. Fresh potatoes are available throughout the year; they are also available frozen, dehydrated and canned.

Poultry Domestic birds bred for their meat and eggs, such as chicken, duck, goose, guinea fowl and turkey. Chicken is the most widely eaten of all poultry, next is turkey. Poultry is available whole or in portions, either fresh, frozen or cooked.

Praline A confectionery (candy) made from almonds cooked in caramel, then cooled and

POTATO SOUFFLE

★ **Preparation time:** 20 minutes
Total cooking time: 1 hour
Serves 2–4

2 large potatoes
pepper and salt to taste
4 spring onions (scallions), finely chopped
1/3 cup sour cream
90 g (3 oz) cheddar cheese, grated
4 eggs, separated
pinch cream of tartar

1 Preheat oven to 180°C (350°F/Gas 4). Butter a 6-cup capacity soufflé dish.

2 Peel potatoes, cut each into 4 pieces, place in a pan, cover with water and boil until tender. Remove from heat, drain and mash (do not add butter or milk).

3 Add sour cream, grated cheese, egg yolks and pepper and salt to taste. Blend well and add spring onions.

4 Beat egg white with cream of tartar until stiff. Fold into the potato mixture and spoon into prepared dish. Bake for 45 minutes and serve hot.

POTATO AND TOMATO SOUP

★ **Preparation time:** 30 minutes
Total cooking time: 25 minutes
Serves 4–6

15 g (1/2 oz) butter
1 teaspoon finely grated lemon rind
1/2 teaspoon thyme leaves
1 clove garlic, crushed
4 medium tomatoes
2 medium potatoes (500 g/1 lb), sliced
2 medium potatoes (460 g/14 1/2 oz), peeled and sliced
2 tablespoons chopped fresh chives or spring onions (scallions)
1 tablespoon tomato paste

1 large onion, chopped
freshly ground pepper
4 cups (1 litre) chicken stock
1 bay leaf
fresh thyme sprigs, for garnish
sour cream, to serve

1 Heat the butter in large pan; add onion and garlic. Cook over medium heat until onion is soft. Add tomato, potato, chives, tomato paste, rind, thyme, bay leaf and stock.

2 Bring to the boil, reduce heat and simmer, uncovered, for about 20 minutes or until potato is tender. Remove from heat; discard bay leaf. Allow to cool.

3 Place the mixture in batches in a food processor. Process 30 seconds or until the mixture is smooth. Return to pan, season with pepper to taste; heat through. Serve topped with a little sour cream and garnished with thyme sprigs.

OPPOSITE PAGE: Spicy Potato Pastries
ABOVE: Potato and Salami Pikelets and
Potato and Tomato Soup

POTATO AND SALAMI PIKELETS

★ **Preparation time:** 25 minutes
Total cooking time: 6 minutes per batch
Makes 18–20 pikelets

1/2 cup (4 fl oz) milk
1 teaspoon white vinegar
1/2 cup self-raising flour
1 teaspoon bicarbonate of soda (baking soda)
1/2 cup mashed potato
2 eggs, lightly beaten
30 g (1 oz) butter, melted

45 g (1 1/2 oz) salami, finely chopped
30 g (1 oz) butter, extra
30 g (1 oz) sun-dried tomatoes, cut into fine strips, for garnish
fresh basil leaves, for garnish

1 Combine milk and vinegar in a small bowl and leave for 5 minutes. Sift the flour and soda into a medium mixing bowl. Make a well in the centre; add mashed potato, beaten eggs and combined milk and vinegar. Stir with a wooden spoon until well combined.

2 Add melted butter and chopped salami, stir gently until combined.

3 Heat extra butter in medium pan; spoon level tablespoonsful of the mixture into pan, about 2 cm (3/4 inch) apart.

4 Cook over medium heat 3 minutes each side or until golden. Serve warm garnished with sun-dried tomatoes and basil leaves.

PRAWNS (SHRIMPS)

SESAME PRAWNS (SHRIMPS) WITH TANGY MINT CHUTNEY

★★

Preparation time: 20 minutes
Total cooking time: 2 minutes per batch
Serves 4

24 uncooked large king prawns (shrimps)
oil for deep frying

Tangy Mint Chutney
1 cup fresh mint leaves, firmly packed
1/2 cup fruit chutney
2 tablespoons lemon juice

1/4 cup plain (all-purpose) flour
1 egg, lightly beaten
2/3 cup dried breadcrumbs
1/2 cup sesame seeds

1 Peel prawns, leaving tails intact. Cut prawns down the back, devein and flatten slightly.

2 Toss prawns in flour; shake off excess. Dip prawns in beaten egg, coat with combined breadcrumbs and sesame seeds.

3 Heat oil in a deep, heavy-based pan. Gently lower prawns into moderately hot oil. Cook over medium-high heat for 2 minutes or until golden brown. Carefully remove from oil with tongs or a slotted spoon. Drain on paper towels.

4 To make Tangy Mint Chutney: Combine mint, chutney and lemon juice in a blender or food processor. Process for 15 seconds or until smooth. Serve as a dip for prawns.

SPANISH PRAWN (SHRIMP) SALAD

★

Preparation time: 25 minutes
Total cooking time: nil
Serves 6

500 g (1 lb) medium king prawns (shrimps), cooked
2 large oranges
1/2 teaspoon finely grated orange rind
1 small mignonette or cos (romaine) lettuce
1 small red onion, finely sliced

2 tablespoons red wine vinegar
1/4 cup (2 fl oz) olive oil
1 clove garlic, crushed

1 Peel prawns, leaving the tails intact. Remove veins from back. Cut a slice off each end of orange to where flesh starts. Using a small knife, cut the skin away in a circular motion, cutting just deep enough to remove all the white membrane (reserve a little peel for grating). Separate the segments by cutting between the membrane and the flesh.

2 Wash and dry lettuce thoroughly. Arrange the leaves on individual plates or a serving platter, top with prawns, orange segments and onion rings.

3 Place the vinegar, olive oil, orange rind and garlic in a small screw-top jar and shake well. Drizzle over salad and serve immediately with crusty bread.

ABOUT PRAWNS (SHRIMPS)

■ Choose firm prawns with crisp shells and a fresh, pleasant smell; stale prawns will be limp and dry. Frozen prawns are available but should not be substituted for fresh prawns unless specified in recipes, as the thawed flesh is slightly mushy.

Pretzel A savoury snack made with a yeast-leavened dough that is formed into the shape of a loose knot, boiled in water, drained and then brushed with egg and sprinkled with coarse salt before baking. It may be either a crusty, soft-centred bread or a crunchy biscuit (cracker). The pretzel originated in the Alsace region on the German border where it was traditionally served with beer. Commercially available pretzels are sometimes also made in the form of long sticks.

Profiterole A small choux pastry puff with a sweet or savoury filling. Profiteroles are probably best known as a dessert, filled with crème pâtissière or chantilly cream and topped with chocolate, caramel or coffee sauce.

Prosciutto An Italian ham from the hind leg of the pig, rubbed with salt and other dry seasonings and matured for eight to ten months. It is deep pink, has a slight sheen and is usually served sliced wafer thin as a first course, although it may also be cooked as part of another dish. Best known varieties are

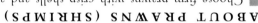

CRYSTAL PRAWNS (SHRIMPS)

★★ *Preparation time:* 15 minutes +
30 minutes marinating
Total cooking time: 20 minutes
Serves 4

750 g (1½ lb) medium
green (uncooked)
prawns (shrimps)
125 g (4 oz) sugar snap
peas or snow peas
(mange tout)
2 spring onions
(scallions), roughly
chopped
1 tablespoon oyster sauce
2 teaspoons dry sherry
1 teaspoon cornflour
(cornstarch), extra
1 teaspoon sesame oil
oil for deep-frying
½ teaspoon crushed garlic
½ teaspoon finely grated
ginger

1 small red pepper
(capsicum)
1 egg white, lightly
beaten
1 tablespoon cornflour
(cornstarch)
2 teaspoons salt

1 Peel the prawns, and devein. Place the shells, heads and the spring onion in a pan with water to cover; bring to the boil. Simmer, uncovered, for 15 minutes. Strain into a bowl. Reserve ½ cup (4 fl oz) prawn liquid. Place the prawns in a glass bowl. Add 1 teaspoon of the salt and stir briskly for a minute. Rinse under cold, running water. Repeat procedure twice more, using ½ teaspoon salt each time. Rinse prawns thoroughly the final time. Pat dry on paper towels.
2 Combine cornflour and egg white in a bowl, add prawns and marinate for 30 minutes in the refrigerator.
3 Cut the pepper into thin strips; wash and string the sugar snap peas. Combine the reserved prawn liquid, oyster sauce, sherry, extra cornflour and sesame oil in a small bowl. Heat the oil in a wok or deep heavy-based frying pan. Gently lower prawns into moderately hot oil. Cook over medium-high heat for 1–2 minutes or until lightly golden. Carefully remove prawns from oil with tongs or a slotted spoon. Drain on paper towels. Keep warm.
4 Pour off all but 2 tablespoons of the oil. Replace pan over heat and add the garlic and ginger. Stir-fry for 30 seconds, add peas and peppers, stir-fry over high heat for 2 minutes. Add the combined sauce ingredients, cook, stirring, until sauce boils and thickens. Add prawns, stir to combine. Remove from heat. Serve immediately.

OPPOSITE PAGE, ABOVE: SESAME PRAWNS WITH TANGY MINT CHUTNEY; BELOW: SPANISH PRAWN SALAD. ABOVE: CRYSTAL PRAWNS

SPAGHETTI CREOLE

Preparation time: 15 minutes
Total cooking time: 25–30 minutes
Serves 6

1 tablespoon oil
100 ml (3 fl oz) white
wine
500 g (1 lb) spaghetti
chopped fresh parsley to
garnish
425 g (13½ oz) can
peeled tomatoes, crushed

Sauce
60 g (2 oz) butter
500 g (1 lb) green
(uncooked) prawns
(shrimps), shelled and
deveined
2 teaspoons curry powder
300 ml (9 fl oz) carton
cream
2 tablespoons freshly
grated parmesan cheese

1 Bring a large pan of water, with the oil added, to boil. Slowly add spaghetti, cook for 10–12 minutes, or until firm and tender. Drain, rinse under warm water, drain thoroughly. Return spaghetti to pan. Add prawn sauce. Toss over low heat 1–2 minutes. Serve garnished with parsley.
2 **To make Sauce:** Melt butter in a frying pan. Cook prawns until just pink. Remove prawns from pan and set aside. Add wine, tomato, seasonings, cream and cheese. Simmer for 10 minutes.

Note: Freshly grated parmesan cheese is preferable to the packaged grated parmesan.

Parma ham (this particular curing process originated in Parma, in northern Italy) and San Daniele ham from the Fruili region in the north-east, reckoned by many to be the finest.

Provençale, à la. A French term for dishes, sauces and garnishes containing olive oil, garlic and tomatoes, typical of the Provence region of southern France.

Provolone A soft, yellow, cow's milk cheese with a mild to sharp taste (depending on age) and a smooth-textured interior free of holes. Provolone is made by the *pasta filata* or stretched curd method in which the curd is kneaded and manipulated under hot water or whey. The cheese originated in Campania, in southern Italy, and is descended from similar cheeses made in Roman times. Provolone can be served with fruit and on cheese boards, and is also a good cooking cheese.

Prune The dried fruit of certain varieties of plum tree. Prunes have a dark, wrinkled appearance and sweet, rich flavour. They are generally soaked and then gently stewed, and served as a dessert or with breakfast cereal or as a

filling for tarts and pastries. Prunes can be wrapped with bacon and grilled to serve as finger food or can accompany main course savoury dishes, such as pork, rabbit and game. They can also be eaten as a snack (without the need to soak first). Sun-dried prunes have been known since the times of the ancient Romans; today dehydration is usually by artificial heat. Prunes are sold (either pitted or unpitted) in vacuum-sealed packs and cans.

Pudding A hot, sweet dish, traditionally steamed or baked, eaten at the end of a meal. Puddings are many and varied

and range from the rich fruit puddings eaten on festive occasions to rice pudding and bread and butter pudding. The term originally referred to all boiled dishes, and this tradition lives on in the name of several savoury mixtures such as steak and kidney pudding and black pudding.

Puff Pastry A rich, crisp, flaky pastry used for both sweet and savoury dishes. Its airiness is achieved by

HOT AND SOUR THAI PRAWN (SHRIMP) SOUP

⭐ **Preparation time:** 10 minutes
Total cooking time: 20 minutes
Serves 4

410 g (13 oz) medium green prawns (shrimps)
1 tablespoon oil
1.5 litres (6 cups) water
1 teaspoon roughly chopped garlic
3/4 teaspoon salt
4 red chillies
1 stalk lemon grass, thick base only, roughly chopped

3 dried or fresh Kaffir lime leaves
1 tablespoon roughly chopped fresh coriander
2 spring onions (scallions), finely sliced
1 red chilli, extra, finely sliced
6 teaspoons nuoc mam (fish sauce)
2 tablespoons lime juice

1 Peel and devein prawns. Reserve heads and shells. Heat the oil in a pan and, when very hot, add the prawn shells and heads. Cook over high heat until they turn pink. Add the water, garlic, salt, chillies, lemon grass and lime leaves. Bring to the boil, reduce to a simmer and cook, uncovered, for 15 minutes.
2 Strain the stock into a clean pan through a double thickness of paper towel placed in a sieve.
3 Add prawns and heat until simmering. Continue simmering until prawns have turned pink. This will only take a few minutes. Remove from heat, add coriander, spring onion, chilli, nuoc mam and lime juice. Serve at once.

PRAWN (SHRIMP) CROUSTADE

⭐ ⭐ **Preparation time:** 45 minutes
Total cooking time: 35 minutes
Serves 6

1/2 loaf unsliced bread
1/2 cup (4 fl oz) olive oil
1 clove garlic, crushed

Filling
500 g (1 lb) green (uncooked) prawns (shrimps)
1 1/2 cups (12 fl oz) water
2 slices lemon

60 g (2 oz) butter
6 spring onions (scallions)
3 tablespoons plain (all-purpose) flour
ground pepper
1 tablespoon lemon juice
1 teaspoon dried dill
1/4 cup (2 fl oz) cream
parsley and lemon, to garnish

1 Preheat oven to 210°C (415°F/Gas 6–7). Remove crust from bread, cut into 5 cm (2 inch) thick slices. Cut each slice diagonally to form 2 triangles. Cut a 1 cm (1/2 inch) border around the bread slices, scoop out centre, taking care to leave a base. This gives a cavity in which to place prawn filling. Heat oil and garlic together in a small pan, brush all over bread cases. Bake for 10 minutes.
2 To make Filling: Shell and devein prawns and chop roughly. Place in a small pan and cover with water. Add lemon slices, simmer for 15 minutes, strain and reserve liquid.
3 Heat butter in a small pan, cook chopped spring onions until soft, add flour and pepper. Stir over low heat 2 minutes. Gradually add reserved prawn liquid. Stir constantly over medium heat for 5 minutes or until sauce boils and thickens. Add lemon juice, dill, cream and prawns and heat gently for approximately 5 minutes.
4 To serve, spoon filling into bread cases, garnish with parsley and lemon.

PRUNES

OPPOSITE PAGE, ABOVE: *HOT AND SOUR THAI PRAWN SOUP; BELOW: PRAWN CROUSTADE. THIS PAGE: PRUNE AND NUT LOAF*

BRAISED PORK MEDALLIONS WITH PRUNES

Preparation time: 15 minutes
Total cooking time: 30 minutes
Serves 4

4 pork loin medallions, about 185 g (6 oz) each
2 cloves garlic, crushed
1 tablespoon fresh thyme leaves
1 large tomato, peeled, seeded, finely chopped
½ cup (4 fl oz) cream
16 pitted prunes

2 cups (16 fl oz) chicken stock
2 tablespoons oil
1 large onion, cut into wedges

1 Trim meat of excess fat and sinew. Shape into rounds by securing a length of string around the medallions. Tie with a bow for easy removal. Place the stock in medium pan, bring to boil. Reduce heat to a simmer, cook, uncovered, for 5 minutes or until reduced to ¾ cup (6 fl oz).

2 Heat oil in a heavy-based pan, add meat. Cook over high heat 2 minutes each side to seal, turning once; drain on paper towels.

3 Add onion and garlic to pan, stir for 2 minutes. Return meat to pan with thyme, tomato and stock. Cover the pan, bring to a simmer and simmer for 10 minutes or until meat is tender, turning once. Add cream and prunes. Simmer for 5 minutes longer and serve.

PRUNE AND NUT LOAF

Preparation time: 40 minutes
Total cooking time: 1 hour
Makes 1 loaf

1 cup wholemeal plain (all-purpose) flour
1 teaspoon mixed spice
125 g (4 oz) butter, cubed
2 eggs
½ cup (4 fl oz) sour cream
¼ cup (2 fl oz) milk
1 cup chopped pitted prunes
⅓ cup walnut halves

1 cup plain (all-purpose) flour, sifted
1 cup rolled oats
½ cup caster (superfine) sugar
1 teaspoon bicarbonate of soda (baking soda)

1 Preheat oven to moderately hot 190°C (375°F/Gas 5). Place flours, oats, sugar, bicarbonate of soda and mixed spice in a large bowl and mix well. Rub in butter with fingertips until mixture resembles breadcrumbs.

2 Whisk eggs and sour cream together in a small bowl. Make a well in the centre of the flour and oat mixture. Pour in the egg mixture and milk and mix to a stiff but moist dough. Mix in the pitted prunes and walnut halves.

3 Spoon mixture into a greased 14 x 21 cm (5½ x 8½ inch) loaf tin. Smooth top and decorate with extra walnut halves if desired. Bake for about 1 hour or until cooked.

4 Cool loaf in tin for 5 minutes. Turn loaf out onto wire rack to cool completely. Store in an airtight container.

PRUNES IN PORT

Preparation time: 10 minutes
Total cooking time: 5 minutes
Makes about 1 litre (4 cups)

750 g (1½ lb) dessert prunes, stones carefully removed
rind of 1 lemon and 1 orange, cut into thin strips
2 cinnamon sticks
3 cups (24 fl oz) port
¼ cup brown sugar

1 Place prunes in a bowl. Place port, sugar, cinnamon sticks and rind in a pan. Heat until boiling point is reached.

2 Pour mixture over prunes. Cool completely. Remove cinnamon sticks.

3 Place prunes in sterilised jars. Pour the syrup over prunes to completely cover. Seal and label the jars. Store in a cool place. Leave for about a week before opening for use. When properly stored, prunes will keep for up to 12 months.

---

a lengthy procedure of repeatedly rolling and folding the dough to give it a multi-layered form. During baking the pastry rises up to four or five times its original thickness. Although its invention is widely attributed to seventeenth-century French landscape painter Claude Lorrain (who in his youth trained as a pastrycook), it seems that puff pastry was made in the fourteenth century (the Bishop of Amiens listed puff pastry cakes in 1311) and may even have been known in ancient Greece. Puff pastry is commercially available frozen in sheets.

Puffaloon Small cakes made by deep-frying rounds of a type of scone (biscuit) dough. They are served hot with butter, golden syrup or light corn syrup, or honey.

Pulses The edible seeds, usually dried, of pod-bearing plants; they include lentils, beans and peas. They are a rich source of protein, vitamins and minerals, making them important in a vegetarian diet. Pulses have been a staple food in many parts of the world for thousands of years and today.

PUMPKINS

feature in the cooking of many regions—China, the Middle East, Egypt, Africa and Central and South America.

Pumpernickel A solid, dark-coloured, strongly flavoured bread made from a mixture of rye flour, rye meal and cracked rye grains.

Pumpkin In North America called winter squash, the large, hard-skinned fruit of a trailing vine

with golden, nutty-flavoured flesh and a central cavity filled with flat, oval seeds. There are many varieties ranging from small, round golden nuggets, to bell-shaped butternuts, pear-shaped hubbards, cylindrical banana pumpkins and plump, ribbed Queensland blues. Pumpkin can be served as a vegetable—steamed, boiled (and mashed) or baked; it can be stuffed, made into soups, scones (biscuits), pancakes, sweet pies, cheesecake, bread and chutney. The fragrant, trumpet-shaped

PUMPKIN PIE

★★ **Preparation time:** 20 minutes +
30 minutes standing
Total cooking time: 55 minutes
Serves 8

1 1/4 cups plain
(all-purpose) flour
100 g (3 1/2 oz) butter,
chopped
2 teaspoons caster
(superfine) sugar
4 tablespoons water, chilled
1 egg yolk, lightly beaten
1 tablespoon milk

Filling
2 eggs, lightly beaten

3/4 cup soft brown sugar
500 g (1 lb) pumpkin,
cooked, mashed and
cooled
1/3 cup (2 1/2 fl oz) cream
1 tablespoon sherry
1 teaspoon ground
cinnamon
1/2 teaspoon ground
nutmeg
1/2 teaspoon ground
ginger

1 Preheat oven to moderate 180°C (350°F/Gas 4). Sift flour into large mixing bowl; add chopped butter. Using fingertips, rub the butter into the flour for 2 minutes or until the mixture is a fine, crumbly texture; stir in sugar. Add almost all the water, mix to a firm dough, adding more liquid if necessary. Turn onto a lightly floured surface, knead for 1 minute or until smooth. Store, covered with plastic wrap, in refrigerator for at least 30 minutes.

2 Roll out the pastry between 2 sheets of plastic wrap, large enough to cover base and sides of a 23 cm (9 inch) pie dish; reserve the pastry

trimmings. Roll out the trimmings to 2.5 mm (1/8 inch) thickness and, using a sharp knife, cut into leaf shapes of different sizes. Score vein markings onto leaves. Beat egg yolk with milk, and brush onto pastry edge. Arrange leaves around pastry edge, pressing gently to attach. Brush leaves lightly with egg mixture.

3 Cut a sheet of greaseproof paper large enough to cover the pastry-lined dish. Spread a layer of dried beans or rice evenly over paper. Bake for 10 minutes; remove from oven and discard paper and beans. Return pastry to oven for 5 minutes or until it is lightly golden. Set aside to cool.

4 To make Filling: Whisk the eggs and sugar in a large mixing bowl. Add pumpkin, cream, sherry and spices and combine thoroughly. Pour into pastry shell and bake for 40 minutes or until set. If pastry edge begins to brown too much during cooking, cover with aluminium foil. Serve at room temperature.

ABOUT PUMPKINS

■ Whole pumpkins can be stored for longer than cut pumpkin. Cover cut pieces with plastic food wrap and store in the refrigerator.

■ Covering the surface of a cut pumpkin from which the seeds have been scooped with a layer of coarse milled black pepper will help prevent it going soft.

■ Pumpkin does not freeze well.

ABOVE: PUMPKIN PIE
OPPOSITE PAGE, ABOVE: PUMPKIN SCONES;
BELOW: FRIED PUMPKIN RIBBONS

FRIED PUMPKIN RIBBONS

Peel 500 g (1lb) pumpkin. Peel pumpkin into ribbons using a vegetable peeler. Heat a medium pan half-filled with oil. Deep-fry pumpkin ribbons in batches until crisp and golden. Drain on paper towels. Sprinkle with salt and pepper to taste. Serve hot.

CURRIED PUMPKIN SOUP

★ *Preparation time:* 15 minutes
Total cooking time: 45 minutes
Serves 6

1 medium onion, chopped	750 g–1 kg (1½–2 lb) pumpkin, peeled, cubed, steamed and mashed
1 tablespoon curry powder	60 g (2 oz) butter
1 bay leaf	1 clove garlic, crushed
1 litre (4 cups) chicken stock	pinch each of sugar and nutmeg
2 cups (16 fl oz) milk (or skim milk if preferred)	
1/4 cup (2 fl oz) cream	
freshly ground black pepper and fresh chives to garnish	

1 In a large saucepan, sauté onion and garlic in butter until very soft, about 5 minutes. Add mashed pumpkin, sugar, nutmeg, curry powder and bay leaf. Season to taste. Stir in stock and heat until boiling.

2 Reduce heat and simmer gently for 30 minutes. Remove from heat. Discard bay leaf.

3 Stir in milk and heat for 2–3 minutes. Serve with a swirl of cream, pepper and chopped chives.

PUMPKIN SCONES

★ *Preparation time:* 35 minutes
Total cooking time: 12 minutes
Makes 12

30 g (1 oz) butter	1 egg, lightly beaten
2 tablespoons caster (superfine) sugar	1/2 cup (4 fl oz) milk
1/2 cup mashed pumpkin	2½ cups self-raising flour, sifted

1 Preheat oven to very hot 220°C (425°F/Gas 7). Cream butter and sugar together until light and fluffy. Mix in pumpkin, egg and milk.

2 Lightly fold in flour and mix until a soft dough is formed.

3 Turn onto a floured board (use self-raising flour). Knead lightly. Press or roll out to form a round about 2 cm (¾ inch) thick.

4 Cut into rounds using a floured plain cutter. Place on greased oven tray. Glaze with a little milk. Bake for 10–12 minutes. Serve warm with butter.

SWEET SPICED PUMPKIN

Peel 500 g (1 lb) of pumpkin. Cut into thin slices. Place on a greased foil-lined oven tray. Melt 40 g (1½ oz) of butter. Brush over pumpkin. In a bowl, place ½ teaspoon each of ground cumin, ground coriander, ground ginger and 1 teaspoon soft brown sugar. Mix well and sprinkle over the pumpkin. Bake in moderate 180°C (350°F/Gas 4) oven 35 minutes or until cooked through. Serve hot.

blossoms can be chopped into salads, fried in butter or stuffed; pumpkin seeds can be toasted, tossed in salt and eaten as a snack. Pumpkins are native to the Americas and were cultivated perhaps as early as 10,000 years ago, pre-dating by several thousands of years the domestication of corn (maize) and beans. They reached Europe in the seventeenth century, but were not widely cultivated until the eighteenth and nineteenth centuries when their properties of easy cultivation and long storage life made them valuable as winter fare.

Punch A hot or cold beverage consisting of a mixture of fruit juice, water, often carbonated liquid and sometimes alcohol. Apart from fruit juices, ingredients can include champagne, wine, spirits, lemonade, soda and mineral water.

Puree A thick, creamy liquid or paste made by processing a solid food in a blender or food processor or pushing it through a sieve.

Puri A flat, unleavened deep-fried wholemeal Indian bread. The dough is rolled thin, cut into rounds and then deep-fried until puffed and golden brown.

Quail A small game bird with mottled brown plumage found in flat open country in Europe, Asia, North America, Africa and Australia. Quail can be roasted (with a veal- or pork-based

stuffing), split, flattened and grilled (broiled), barbecued, pan-fried (with grapes), or casseroled. It has delicate flesh and care should be taken not to dry it out—cover with bacon fat, wrap in vine leaves or baste frequently to keep the flesh moist. In northern Italy quail is often marinated in wine, sage, rosemary and pepper, then simmered in the marinade and served on slices of grilled (broiled) polenta. Quail is best in autumn, when the bird is plump and the flesh full-flavoured. Serve two per person.

Quail eggs are plum-shaped, greenish-beige with dark brown markings, and about one-third the size of hen's eggs. They may be served hard-boiled in salads or in aspic, and are available pickled. Farm-raised quail

QUICHES

QUICHE LORRAINE

★ **Preparation time: 30 minutes +**
20 minutes refrigeration
Total cooking time: 1 hour 10 minutes
Serves 10–12

Pastry
1 1/2 cups plain (all-purpose) flour
105 g (3 1/2 oz) butter, chopped
1 egg
1 tablespoon water, approximately

Filling
10 thinly sliced bacon rashers
6 eggs
2/3 cup (5 fl oz) milk
1 1/4 cups (10 fl oz) thick cream
salt and pepper
1/2 cup grated cheddar cheese

1 To make Pastry: Place flour and butter in food processor. Process for 30 seconds or until mixture is fine and crumbly. Add egg and almost all the water; process for 20 seconds or until mixture just comes together when squeezed, adding more water if required. Turn onto a lightly floured board. Knead mixture gently to form a smooth dough. Refrigerate, covered with plastic wrap, for 20 minutes. Preheat oven to moderately hot 210°C (415°F/Gas 6–7).

2 Roll pastry on a floured board large enough to fit a 32 cm (13 inch) round loose-bottomed flan tin. Ease pastry into tin. Trim edge with a sharp knife. Cut a sheet of baking paper large enough to cover pastry. Place paper over pastry; spread a layer of dried beans or rice evenly over paper. Bake for 15 minutes, remove paper and beans; bake for another 10 minutes or until pastry case is lightly browned; cool. Reduce oven temperature to moderate 180°C (350°F/Gas 4).

3 To make Filling: Reserve 4 slices of bacon. Chop the remaining bacon. Heat pan, cook bacon until crisp; drain on paper towels. Combine eggs, milk, cream, salt and pepper in a jug. Whisk well. Sprinkle bacon into pastry case, pour cream mixture over. Cut reserved bacon rashers in half. Lay strips over cream mixture, sprinkle with cheese. Bake 40 minutes or until cooked through and golden. Serve hot or cold.

Note: Do not overwork dough when making pastry in a food processor or pastry will be tough.

ABOVE: QUICHE LORRAINE.
OPPOSITE PAGE: CHICKEN AND CORN QUICHE

QUICHE

QUICHE An open tart with a thin pastry shell (usually shortcrust) filled with a rich savoury egg custard.

Quenelle A small, light, savoury dumpling made from finely chopped or pureed fish, meat or poultry, bound with egg and flour, formed into an egg or sausage shape and poached. Quenelles are usually served with a rich sauce as a first course; small quenelles can also garnish soup. The name comes from the German Knödel, dumpling.

Queen of Puddings A baked dessert popular in nineteenth-century England consisting of a layer of breadcrumbs, milk and egg yolk, spread with strawberry jam, cooked and cooled, then topped with meringue made from the egg white, and returned to the oven until meringue is crisp.

Quatre Épices See Four Spices.

Quark Low fat curd cheese made in Austria and Germany. It can have a smooth consistency or be in the form of small curds, like cottage cheese.

(fresh and frozen) and quail eggs are available from specialist game and poultry stores.

CHICKEN AND CORN QUICHE

★★ **Preparation time:** 35 minutes + 20 minutes refrigeration
Total cooking time: 1 hour
Serves 4

1 cup plain (all-purpose) flour
60 g (2 oz) butter, chopped
1/2 cup grated cheddar cheese
1–2 tablespoons iced water

Filling
1/2 cup (4 fl oz) cream
1/2 cup (4 fl oz) milk
2 eggs
1/2 medium red pepper (capsicum), chopped
125 g (4 oz) can corn kernels, drained
1 egg yolk
1 1/2 cups chopped cooked chicken
25 g (3/4 oz) butter, chopped
1 medium onion, finely chopped
1/4 cup grated cheddar cheese
1 tablespoon chopped fresh chives

1 Sift flour into a large mixing bowl; add chopped butter. Using fingertips, rub butter into flour until mixture is fine and crumbly. Add egg yolk, grated cheese and enough water to mix to a firm dough. Turn onto a lightly floured surface, knead gently for 30 seconds or until smooth. Refrigerate, covered with plastic wrap, for 20 minutes.

2 Preheat oven to moderately hot 210°C (415°F/Gas 6–7). Brush a shallow 20 cm (8 inch) round cake tin with melted butter or oil. Roll out the pastry between two sheets of plastic wrap, large enough to cover base and sides of tin. Ease pastry into tin; trim edge with a sharp knife.

3 Cut a sheet of greaseproof paper large enough to cover pastry-lined tin. Line pastry with paper, spread a layer of dried beans or rice evenly over paper. Bake 10 minutes, remove from oven and discard the paper and beans. Return to oven for another 7 minutes or until lightly golden. Cool.

4 **To make Filling:** Reduce oven to moderate 180°C (350°F/Gas 4). Heat butter in small pan, cook onion until just soft; drain on paper towels. Spread onion, chicken, corn and pepper over pastry base. Combine the remaining ingredients in a large bowl; mix well. Pour into pastry case. Bake 35 minutes, or until lightly browned and set. Stand in tin for 5 minutes before cutting for serving. Serve hot or cold with a green salad.

INDIVIDUAL SEAFOOD QUICHES

★ **Preparation time:** 30 minutes
Total cooking time: 30 minutes
Serves 8

8 sheets filo pastry
60 g (2 oz) butter, melted
155 g (5 oz) small peeled cooked prawns (shrimps)
155 g (5 oz) fresh scallops, cleaned and halved
3 eggs
3/4 cup (6 fl oz) cream
1/2 cup (4 fl oz) milk
4 spring onions (scallions), chopped
1/4 cup grated cheddar cheese
2 tablespoons plain (all-purpose) flour
1 tablespoon chopped fresh lemon thyme

1 Preheat oven to moderate 180°C (350°F/Gas 4). Brush eight 8 cm (3 inch) flan tins with melted butter or oil. Layer four sheets of filo together, brushing each layer with melted butter. Cut the pastry in half, cut each half into four squares. Repeat with remaining pastry and butter. Line each flan tin with four squares of pastry placed at right angles to each other. Brush with any remaining butter.

2 Divide prawns and scallops between the prepared tins. In a large bowl combine eggs, cream, milk, chopped spring onions, cheese and flour; mix well. Pour mixture over the seafood, sprinkle with lemon thyme, bake for 30 minutes or until golden brown and set. Leave to stand in tins for 5 minutes. Serve hot with a green salad and crusty bread.

flavoured with ham, cheese, onion, leek, spinach, mushroom, asparagus or seafood. Quiche is usually served warm as a first or a light main course; miniature versions are often served as finger food; and cold quiche is a popular picnic food. The quiche originated in Nancy, in Lorraine, on the French-German border, where it has been known since the sixteenth century and was originally made with bread dough. Quiche Lorraine, with a filling of egg and ham or bacon, is a specialty of the region; true quiche Lorraine should never contain cheese, which is thought to be a Parisian addition. The name comes from the German *kuchen*, cake.

Quince A large, fragrant, yellow-skinned fruit, round to pear-shaped and usually too hard and sour to eat raw, but which when cooked has soft, pink, delicately sweet flesh with the slightly grainy texture of stewed pear. It is related to the apple and the pear. Quince is stewed slowly as a filling for pies and tarts, baked whole as a dessert, made into quince paste to serve with soft ripe cheese, roasted whole as an accompaniment for game; and, pectin-rich, is often made into jellies,

VEGETABLE QUICHE

⭐ ⭐   ***Preparation time:*** 40 minutes + 20 minutes refrigeration
Total cooking time: 50 minutes
Serves 4–6

3/4 cup plain (all-purpose) flour
1/2 cup wholemeal flour
105 g (3 1/2 oz) butter, chopped
1–2 tablespoons lemon juice

Filling
105 g (3 1/2 oz) broccoli, cut into small florets
2 small zucchini (courgettes), cut into 2 cm (3/4 inch) slices
155 g (5 oz) pumpkin, cut into 2 cm (3/4 inch) cubes

2 teaspoons oil
1 small red pepper (capsicum), cut into 2 cm (3/4 inch) squares
1 medium onion, chopped
55 g (1 1/2 oz) butter
3 tablespoons plain (all-purpose) flour
1 cup (8 fl oz) milk
2 egg yolks
1 cup finely grated cheddar cheese
freshly ground black pepper, to taste
125 g (4 oz) can corn kernels, drained

1 Sift flours into a large mixing bowl, return husks to bowl. Using fingertips, rub butter into flour for 2 minutes or until mixture is fine and crumbly. Add almost all the lemon juice, mix to a firm dough, adding more liquid if necessary. Turn onto a lightly floured surface, press together until smooth. Brush a 20 cm (8 inch) fluted flan tin with oil. Roll out pastry large enough to cover base and side of tin. Ease pastry into tin; trim. Refrigerate, covered with plastic wrap 20 minutes.

2 Preheat oven to 180°C (350°F/Gas 4). Line pastry with a sheet of greaseproof paper large enough to cover; spread a layer of dried beans or rice evenly over paper. Bake for 10 minutes, remove from oven and discard paper and beans. Return to oven for 10 minutes or until lightly golden. Set aside to cool.

3 To make Filling: Steam broccoli, zucchini and pumpkin until just tender. Drain. Heat oil in a heavy-based frying pan and cook peppers and onion over medium heat until soft. Set aside. Heat butter in a small pan; add flour. Stir over low heat 2 minutes or until mixture is just golden. Add milk gradually to pan, stirring until mixture is smooth. Stir constantly over medium heat until mixture boils and thickens; boil 1 minute and remove from heat. Beat in egg yolks until mixture is smooth; stir in cheese.

4 Place the cooked vegetables in a large bowl. Add corn and pepper. Pour hot sauce over; mix. Pour vegetable mixture into pastry shell. Bake for 20 minutes, until top is golden. Serve hot.

BLUE CHEESE QUICHE

⭐ ⭐   ***Preparation time:*** 50 minutes + 20 minutes refrigeration
Total cooking time: 50 minutes
Serves 4–6

1 cup plain (all-purpose) flour
1/2 cup ground walnuts
60 g (2 oz) butter, chopped
1–2 tablespoons water

Filling
155 g (5 oz) blue cheese
1/2 cup (4 fl oz) cream
2 eggs, lightly beaten
1 tablespoon chopped fresh parsley

1 Sift flour into a bowl; add walnuts and butter. Rub butter into flour with your fingertips until the mixture is fine and crumbly. Add 1 tablespoon water; mix to a firm dough, adding more water if necessary. Turn dough out onto a lightly floured surface and roll out large enough to cover base and side of a 20 cm (8 inch) flan tin. Ease pastry into tin; trim. Refrigerate for 20 minutes.

2 Preheat oven to moderate 180°C (350°F/Gas 4). Line pastry with a sheet of greaseproof paper large enough to cover; spread a layer of dried beans or rice evenly over paper. Bake 10 minutes, discard paper and beans, return pastry to oven for another 10 minutes or until lightly golden. Cool.

3 To make Filling: Place cheese in a mixing bowl and lightly mash. Add cream, eggs and parsley, whisking to combine. Pour into prepared pastry shell, bake for 30 minutes, until filling is puffed and golden. Serve warm.

QUINCES

TAGINE OF LAMB WITH QUINCES

Preparation time: 50 minutes
Total cooking time: 1 hour
Serves 6

1 kg (2 lb) shoulder of
lamb cut in 2 cm
(3/4 inch) cubes
2 large onions, chopped
in 2 cm (3/4 inch) cubes
1/2 teaspoon ground
pepper
1/2 teaspoon mildly hot paprika
1 bunch fresh coriander,
finely chopped

1/4 teaspoon ground
saffron
1/2 teaspoon ground
ginger
500 g (1 lb) quinces
cored, halved and
peeled
60 g (2 oz) butter
1 cup pitted prunes,
pre-soaked

1 Place cubed lamb and one of the chopped onions in a large heavy-based pan. Season to taste with pepper and paprika and cover with water.
2 Add fresh coriander, saffron and ginger. Bring to the boil, reduce heat, cover and simmer for about an hour, or until lamb is tender.
3 Cut the quinces into roughly the same sized pieces as the meat. Cook the quinces and the second onion together in butter in a pan until lightly golden.

4 Halfway through cooking time for the lamb, add cooked onion, quinces and prunes. When lamb is cooked, serve on a warmed serving dish.

Note: This is a Moroccan dish and one of the most successful combinations of meat and fruit. Substitute hot paprika if a spicier flavour is preferred. Dates can be used instead of prunes and pears instead of quinces.

QUINCE CONSERVE

Preparation time: 30 minutes
Total cooking time: 1 1/2 hours
Makes 1.5 litres (6 cups)

1.5 kg (3 lb) quinces
2.5 litres water
3/4 cup (6 fl oz) lemon
juice
2 teaspoons grated lemon
rind
5 1/2 cups sugar, warmed

1 Peel and core quinces and slice thinly. Place peel and cores in muslin (cheesecloth) and tie.
2 Combine quinces, muslin bag, water and rind in a large pan or boiler. Bring to the boil and simmer, covered, for about 50 minutes or until fruit is pulpy. Discard muslin bag. Stir in the lemon juice.
3 Add the warm sugar and stir until dissolved. Boil rapidly, uncovered, for about 40 minutes or until setting point is reached.
4 Remove cooked conserve from heat and stand for 10 minutes. Pour into warm, sterilised jars and seal immediately. When cool, label and date jars.

jams and conserves (the pectin level is highest if fruit is picked when greenish-yellow). Quinces preserved in syrup are an old-time dessert favourite in northern Italy. In Middle Eastern cooking it is often stuffed with peas, beans or minced (ground) beef and spices.

The quince originated in Asia, and reached the eastern Mediterranean in ancient times. It was popular with the ancient Greeks, who ate it hollowed out and baked with honey. As the fruit travelled north and west, so its name changed—in southern France kydonia became cydonea, in northern France, coing, and across the Channel, quince. In Greek mythology the quince was the famous golden apple awarded by Paris to Aphrodite, goddess of love. Since the time of the ancients the fruit has been a symbol of love, marriage and fertility and in medieval Europe a gift of quinces was regarded as a declaration of serious ardour.

R

Radicchio A salad vegetable with white stalks and crisp, reddish-purple, peppery flavoured leaves; the two main varieties are Verona (small and round with compact wrinkly leaves) and Treviso (long leaves). Radicchio adds an interesting bitter bite to mixed-leaf salads or it may be braised or grilled and served with meat or poultry. A variety of chicory (endive), radicchio is available fresh throughout the year.

Rabbit A small, furred animal of the hare family. Young rabbit bred for the table has lean and tender white flesh similar to chicken; wild rabbit has darker and more stringy meat. Rabbit is often marinated in wine seasoned with shallots, garlic and thyme before being sautéed, stewed or casseroled; it can also be roasted (care should be taken during cooking that the flesh does not dry out). Rabbits can be bought ready to cook, fresh or frozen, from specialist butchers.

RASPBERRIES

RASPBERRY MOUSSE CAKE

★★ *Preparation time:* 35 minutes + refrigeration
Total cooking time: 15 minutes
Serves 8

1 egg
2 tablespoons plain (all-purpose) flour
2 tablespoons self-raising flour
2 tablespoons cornflour (cornstarch)
2 eggs
1/3 cup caster (superfine) sugar

Raspberry Mousse
410 g (13 oz) fresh or frozen raspberries
1/3 cup caster (superfine) sugar
2 eggs
250 g (8 oz) packet cream cheese, softened
1 1/4 cups (10 fl oz) thickened cream
1 tablespoon gelatine
2 tablespoons water
icing (confectioners) sugar for serving

1 Preheat oven to moderate 180°C (350°F/Gas 4). Brush a 20 cm (8 inch) round springform tin with melted butter or oil.

2 Sift flours and cornflour 3 times onto greaseproof paper. Using electric beaters, beat eggs in small mixing bowl for 3 minutes or until thick and pale. Add caster sugar gradually, beating constantly until dissolved and mixture is pale yellow and glossy.

3 Transfer mixture to large mixing bowl. Using a metal spoon, fold in dry ingredients quickly and lightly. Spread mixture evenly into prepared tin. Bake for 15 minutes or until sponge is lightly golden and shrinks from side of tin. Leave sponge in tin for 3 minutes before turning onto wire rack to cool.

4 To make Raspberry Mousse: Process 315 g (10 oz) raspberries to a smooth texture in blender or food processor, pass through a fine sieve. Reserve half of the puree for serving. Using electric beaters, beat egg and sugar in small bowl until creamy. Add cream cheese, beat until smooth. In a separate bowl beat cream until soft peaks form.

5 Combine gelatine with water in small bowl, stand bowl in hot water, stir until gelatine dissolves. Using a metal spoon, fold gelatine, half of the raspberry puree and reserved whole raspberries into cream cheese mixture, then fold in cream. Cover with plastic wrap and refrigerate for 10 minutes or until mixture has thickened, stirring occasionally.

6 To assemble, cut cake in half horizontally. Place first cake layer on a board. Spread cake evenly with mousse. Top with remaining cake layer, refrigerate until the mousse has set.

7 For serving, sift icing sugar over top of the cake. Cut the cake into wedges. Place on individual serving plates and spoon reserved puree around cake.

ABOVE: RASPBERRY MOUSSE CAKE.
OPPOSITE PAGE: RASPBERRY CHICKEN SALAD

RASPBERRY AND STRAWBERRY RIPPLE

✳ ✳ **Preparation time:** 20 minutes + freezing
Total cooking time: nil
Serves 8–10

500 g (1 lb) strawberries	125 g (4 oz) raspberries
1½ cups caster (superfine) sugar	½ cup caster (superfine) sugar, extra
2 tablespoons lemon juice	raspberries and strawberries, extra, for serving
2¼ cups (18 fl oz) cream, lightly whipped	

1 Line the base and sides of a 7-cup capacity loaf tin with foil. Remove stalks from strawberries. Place in a food processor with sugar and juice. Process for 30 seconds or until quite smooth.

2 Reserve ⅓ cup whipped cream, fold remaining cream into strawberry mixture. Pour into metal freezer tray. Freeze, stirring occasionally, until thick. Do not allow mixture to freeze solid.

3 Using a food processor, blend raspberries and extra sugar. Fold into the reserved cream and mix well.

4 Spoon a layer of strawberry ice-cream over base of the prepared tin. Spoon raspberry mixture and remaining strawberry ice-cream randomly over base. Using a sharp knife or skewer, swirl mixtures together, being careful not to dig into foil. Freeze for 3–4 hours or overnight. Serve in scoops or remove from tin and cut into slices. Garnish with extra raspberries and strawberries.

RASPBERRY CHICKEN SALAD

✳ **Preparation time:** 15 minutes
Total cooking time: 10 minutes
Serves 4

2 tablespoons raspberry vinegar	4 chicken breast fillets, about 440 g (14 oz)
1 cup (8 fl oz) white wine	60 g (2 oz) curly endive (chicory)
½ teaspoon French mustard	1 red coral lettuce
salt and freshly ground black pepper, to taste	60 g (2 oz) watercress
200 g (6½ oz) raspberries	½ cup (4 fl oz) olive oil

1 Trim chicken of excess fat and sinew. Pour wine into large heavy-based frying pan and add enough water to make the liquid 2 cm (¾ inch) deep. Cover and bring to the boil. Reduce heat, add chicken to pan, cover and simmer gently for 10 minutes or until cooked through. Remove from pan. Drain, cool. Cut into slices.

2 Wash and dry endive, lettuce and watercress. Tear into bite-size pieces, discarding thicker stems of watercress. Place in a large mixing bowl.

3 Place olive oil, vinegar, mustard and seasonings in a small screw-top jar and shake well. Pour one-third of the dressing over leaves and toss lightly to combine. Place ⅓ cup of the raspberries and the remaining dressing in food processor. Process for 10 seconds or until smooth. Arrange salad leaves on serving plates, top with chicken slices and remaining raspberries. Drizzle with raspberry dressing and serve immediately.

RASPBERRY JAM

✳ **Preparation time:** 30 minutes
Total cooking time: 15 minutes
Makes 3 cups

1 kg (2 lb) raspberries	1 kg (2 lb) sugar, warmed
1 teaspoon tartaric acid	

1 Check fruit and discard hulls and any leaves. Place raspberries in a large stainless steel pan and mash fruit lightly with a potato masher to release juice. Heat fruit gently until boiling, stirring occasionally.

2 Add warmed sugar, stir until it dissolves; return mixture to boil. Cook rapidly for 3 minutes, add the tartaric acid and boil for another 5 minutes or until setting point is reached.

3 Cool jam slightly and pour into hot sterilised jars. Seal jars, and when cool label and date. Store jam in a cool dark place.

Radish A root vegetable with peppery tasting crunchy white flesh. The roots range in size, shape and skin colour from small, round and red to long, thin and white. Radish is eaten raw with dips, in salads and as a garnish; it can also be boiled or steamed as a vegetable. Daikon, a giant white radish, is an important ingredient in the cooking of Japan and China. The radish has been grown in China for more than 3000 years; it was a favourite of the ancient world. Radish is available fresh throughout the year; daikon is sold pickled.

Ragoût A French term for a stew made from cubes of meat, poultry, fish, game or vegetables cooked in a thickened, well-seasoned broth.

Raisin A grape of a sweet variety dried either naturally in the sun or artificially. Raisins are sprinkled on breakfast cereal, can be added to rice and salads, are used in fruit cakes, biscuits and puddings and can be served with cheese at the end of a meal. There are varieties with or without seeds.

Rambutan A small oval fruit encased in a thick red skin covered with soft spines. Its pale-coloured translucent flesh has a similar taste to a grape. Peeled and stoned, the rambutan is added to fruit salad, green salad or fish salad, and

can also be served on a cheese board. The rambutan is related to the lychee and longan and is available canned (in syrup).

Rapeseed Oil See Canola Oil.

Rarebit Also known as Welsh rarebit, a hot snack consisting of cheese melted with beer, seasoned with mustard or worcestershire sauce, spread on toast and browned under a griller.

Raspberry The soft, fragrant, juicy fruit of a thorny plant related to the rose. Raspberries can be served fresh, with cream or ice-cream, added to fruit salad, pureed for use in desserts and sauces or cooked as a filling in tarts. The raspberry originated in the

cold climate of northern Europe, Asia and

RASPBERRY COCONUT BISCUITS

★ ★ **Preparation time:** 40 minutes
Total cooking time: 15 minutes
Makes 28

Biscuit Pastry
60 g (2 oz) butter
1/2 cup caster (superfine) sugar
1 egg
2/3 cup plain (all-purpose) flour
2/3 cup self-raising flour

Icing
105 g (3 1/2 oz) pink marshmallows
45 g (1 1/2 oz) butter
1/4 cup icing (confectioners) sugar, sifted
1/2 cup desiccated coconut
1/3 cup raspberry jam

1 Preheat oven to moderate 180°C (350°F/Gas 4). Line two oven trays with baking paper.
2 To make Biscuit Pastry: Using electric beaters, beat butter and sugar in small mixing bowl until light and creamy. Transfer to large bowl. Add egg; beat until combined. Using a metal spoon, fold in sifted flours. Turn dough onto lightly floured surface. Knead gently for 1 minute or until smooth. Roll out dough between two sheets baking paper to 5 mm (1/4 inch) thickness. Using a knife or fluted pastry wheel, cut dough into 4.5 x 6 cm (1 3/4 x 2 1/2 inch) rectangles. Place on prepared trays, allowing room for spreading. Re-roll remaining pastry and repeat cutting. Bake for 10 minutes or until lightly golden. Transfer to wire rack when cool.
3 To make Icing: Combine marshmallows and butter in small pan. Stir over low heat until marshmallows and butter are melted and smooth. Stir in icing sugar; mix until smooth. Place coconut on sheet of greaseproof paper. Working quickly, spread about quarter teaspoon of icing along each long side of biscuit, leaving a space in the centre. Dip iced biscuit into coconut; shake off excess coconut.
4 Place jam in small pan and heat gently until thinned and warm. Spread a little jam down centre of each biscuit.

RASPBERRY SAUCE

Heat 250 g (8 oz) raspberries and 1 tablespoon caster (superfine) sugar in a small pan, stirring until the sugar is melted. Puree in a blender or food processor or push through a sieve with a wooden spoon. Set aside until cool. This can be served over ice-cream or as a sauce with rich chocolate cake or lemon tart. It is best made on the day you wish to serve it.

RIGHT: RASPBERRY COCONUT BISCUITS

America. Raspberries are available fresh from mid-summer to autumn, and can also be bought frozen.

Ratatouille A stew of summer vegetables originally from the Provence region of southern France and traditionally consisting of eggplant (aubergine), zucchini (courgette), onion, tomato and garlic. Sometimes red pepper (capsicum) is added and the mixture is simmered in olive oil.

Ravigote Sauce A seasoned, spicy sauce. Cold ravigote, a vinaigrette mixed with capers, chopped herbs and onion, is served with cold meat and fish. Hot ravigote is made by cooking chopped shallots in wine vinegar, then adding veal velouté sauce, and chopped parsley, tarragon, chives and chervil. Ravigote butter is flavoured with chopped shallots, herbs and sometimes mustard.

Ravioli Small squares of pasta dough filled with meat, cheese or vegetable mixtures then

boiled in water and served with a sauce (usually sprinkled with grated parmesan cheese) as a first course or main dish. Ravioli can be made at home or bought fresh or frozen.

RATATOUILLE SQUARES

Preparation time: 15 minutes
Total cooking time: 45 minutes
Makes 4 tarts

2 sheets ready-rolled puff pastry
1 egg, lightly beaten
1 tablespoon olive oil
1 medium onion, finely sliced
2 cloves garlic, crushed
2 medium long slender eggplant (aubergines), cut into 2 cm (3/4 inch) squares
2 medium zucchini (courgettes), cut into 1 cm (1/2 inch) slices
1 medium red pepper (capsicum), cut into 2 cm (3/4 inch) squares
1 medium green pepper (capsicum), cut into 2 cm (3/4 inch) squares
2 medium tomatoes, roughly chopped

1 Preheat oven to moderate 180°C (350°F/Gas 4). Brush one pastry sheet with egg; top with the other sheet. Cut pastry into four squares. Place on large baking tray and cook for 20 minutes until puffed and golden. Set aside to cool.
2 Heat oil in a large heavy-based frying pan, cook onion and garlic over medium heat for 5 minutes. Add eggplant, zucchini and red peppers. Cook, covered, for 10 minutes, stirring occasionally.
3 Add tomato and cook uncovered for 10 minutes, stirring occasionally, until most of the liquid has evaporated. To serve, cut an 8 cm (3 inch) round hole in the top of each of the pastry squares, and pull out the soft pastry in the centre. Fill each of the cavities with ratatouille and serve immediately.

RATATOUILLE

Preparation time: 30 minutes + 30 minutes standing
Total cooking time: 45 minutes
Serves 4–6

2 large eggplant (aubergines), salt
2 medium zucchini (courgettes), cut into 5 mm (1/4 inch) slices
1/2 cup (4 fl oz) olive oil
1 large brown onion, chopped
2 cloves garlic, crushed
2 teaspoons sugar

2 medium ripe tomatoes, peeled, seeded and chopped
1/4 cup grated parmesan cheese
1/4 cup (2 fl oz) white wine
2 tablespoons red wine vinegar
ground pepper, to taste

1 Wash eggplant and cut into 1 cm (1/2 inch) slices, sprinkle with salt and allow to stand. Lightly salt sliced zucchini and stand 30 minutes. Wash salt from eggplant and zucchini, pat dry with paper towels.
2 Heat oil in frying pan. Add onion and cook until golden brown. Add garlic and eggplant pieces and cook until brown, remove; cook zucchini slices until golden.
3 Transfer all vegetables to large pan. Sprinkle with sugar, pepper and vinegar. Add the tomato and wine. Cover and simmer for about 30 minutes.
4 Serve sprinkled with parmesan cheese.

Red Cabbage A red-leafed cabbage, similar in taste to green cabbage. Stewed with apples, bacon, sugar and nutmeg it is traditionally served with game and roast beef. It is also pickled or served raw in salads.

Redcurrant See Currant.

Reduce To boil down a sauce or gravy in order to concentrate its flavour and thicken its consistency.

Refresh To plunge lightly boiled vegetables into cold water to halt the cooking process and maintain their colour.

Rémoulade Sauce A mayonnaise-based cold sauce flavoured with chopped tarragon, chervil, parsley, gherkin, capers and sometimes anchovies. Rémoulade is served with cold poultry, fish, shellfish (particularly crab and lobster), meat and eggs.

Rendang A hot and spicy dry curry of Indonesian origin consisting of cubed beef, mutton or chicken fried with spices and then cooked slowly in coconut milk until the meat is tender and the gravy thick and paste-like.

OPPOSITE PAGE, ABOVE: RATATOUILLE; BELOW: RATATOUILLE SQUARES. ABOVE: SPICED RHUBARB AND PEAR COBBLER; RIGHT: RHUBARB FOOL

RHUBARB

SPICED RHUBARB AND PEAR COBBLER

Preparation time: 25 minutes
Total cooking time: 35 minutes
Serves 4

410 g (13 oz) rhubarb
3 large pears, peeled
1 tablespoon finely grated orange rind
1 tablespoon finely grated lemon rind
1/2 teaspoon mixed spice
1/3 cup demerara sugar
2 tablespoons marsala
2 tablespoons orange juice

Batter
1/4 cup desiccated coconut
2 tablespoons plain (all-purpose) flour
1/3 cup self-raising flour

60 g (2 oz) butter, melted
4 tablespoons desiccated or shredded coconut extra
1/2 cup demerara sugar, extra

Topping
1 cup fresh white breadcrumbs
2 tablespoons caster (superfine) sugar
2 eggs, lightly beaten
2 tablespoons milk
30 g (1 oz) butter, melted

1 Preheat oven to moderate 180°C (350°F/Gas 4). Brush a deep, 6-cup capacity rectangular ovenproof dish with melted butter or oil. Wash the rhubarb, cut stalks into 3 cm (1 1/4 inch) lengths. Cut pears into 2 cm (3/4 inch) cubes.

Combine rhubarb, pears, orange and lemon rinds, mixed spice, demerara sugar, marsala and orange juice in a large pan. Cover and simmer for 10 minutes, stirring occasionally. Remove from heat. Keep warm.
2 To make Batter: Sift the coconut, flours and sugar into a medium mixing bowl; make a well in the centre. Add combined egg, milk and butter all at once. Whisk until all liquid is incorporated and batter is smooth and free of lumps.
3 Pour hot fruit into prepared dish. Pour batter evenly over the top.
4 To make Topping: Combine breadcrumbs, sugar, coconut and butter in a small mixing bowl. Sprinkle over batter. Bake the cobbler for 25 minutes or until skewer comes out clean when inserted in centre. Serve immediately.

RHUBARB FOOL

Cut a bunch of rhubarb into 1 cm (1/2 inch) lengths, place in a colander and wash well. Place rhubarb in a pan with a little water, just enough to prevent it sticking, 3 tablespoons sugar and a pinch of ground cinnamon. Cover the pan and simmer for 15–20 minutes or until the rhubarb is very soft. Remove from heat and beat with a wooden spoon until it is smooth. Leave it to cool, then add 150 ml (5 fl oz) lightly whipped cream and stir well. Serve as a dessert or with hot croissants for breakfast.

Rennet A substance made from the stomach lining of unweaned calves. It is used to coagulate milk in the making of junket and hard cheese. Rennet is available in tablet form (often in a variety of flavours) for junket making.

Rhubarb The pink, fleshy stalks of a leafy vegetable cooked, sweetened and eaten as a dessert or breakfast dish. The trimmed stalks are cut into short lengths and stewed, poached or baked in a sugar syrup until tender; serve warm or cold or use as a filling for pies, tarts and crumbles. The leaves contain poisonous oxalic acid and must not be eaten. Rhubarb is sold fresh all year but is best in autumn and winter.

Rice The small oval grain from a semi-aquatic grass cultivated in warm climates. An important food (it is the staple of more than half the world's people); it is always eaten cooked, either hot or cold. Brown rice is the whole kernel with just the inedible husk removed; it has a chewy texture and a slightly nutty flavour.

White (polished) rice is the inner kernel. Types of rice include long-grain, with long narrow kernels; sometimes called Indian rice (it includes aromatic varieties such as basmati), this is the variety used in China and South-East Asia— when cooked the grains remain separate and it is used for plain boiled rice, rice salads and in stuffings. Medium-grain rice has plump oval kernels which when cooked are moist enough to hold together yet are still distinct; it can often be used in place of long-grain rice. Short-grain rice, also called pearl, round or pudding rice, has almost round kernels that

become sticky and cling together when cooked; it is the rice grown in Italy, and includes arborio, used to make risotto; in Spain it is used in paella. It is suitable for puddings and moulded rings and an Asian short-grained variety called glutinous or sticky rice is the preferred rice for sweet dishes in Asia. Converted rice has been parboiled and then dried; the starch content is reduced and the cooked grain is especially fluffy. Wild rice is the seed of an aquatic grass native to the Minnesota Lakes of North America.

RICE

BALINESE-STYLE FRIED RICE

★★ **Preparation time:** 30 minutes
Total cooking time: 20 minutes
Serves 6

2 teaspoons oil	5 cups cold, cooked rice
2 eggs, lightly beaten	1 tablespoon soy sauce
2 medium onions, chopped	1 tablespoon nuoc mam (fish sauce)
2 cloves garlic	1 tablespoon sambal oelek
3 tablespoons oil, extra	1 tablespoon tomato paste
1/4 teaspoon shrimp paste	6 spring onions (scallions), finely chopped
250 g (8 oz) raw prawn (shrimp) meat	spring onions (scallions), thin-skinned cucumber
125 g (4 oz) rump steak, finely sliced	and 2–3 long, red chillies, for garnish
1 cooked chicken breast, finely sliced	

1 Heat oil in a wok or deep heavy-based pan. Season eggs and add to pan. Make an omelette by pulling the cooked edges of the egg towards the centre. When set, turn onto a plate to cool. Cut into fine strips and set aside.
2 Place onions and garlic in a food processor or blender and process until finely chopped. Or, chop very finely by hand, using a sharp knife. Heat extra oil in a wok and cook the onion mixture, stirring frequently until it has reduced in volume and is translucent. Add the shrimp paste and cook for another minute.

3 Add prawn meat and sliced rump steak to the wok, stir over high heat. Add cooked chicken and rice; toss until heated through. In a bowl, combine the soy sauce, nuoc mam, sambal oelek, tomato paste and spring onion and add to the rice mixture. Toss until ingredients are mixed well. Remove wok from heat and add spring onion brushes. Transfer to a serving platter, add prepared omelette strips, cucumber garnish and chilli flowers.
4 To make Spring Onion Brushes: Take a 7 cm (2¾ inch) piece of spring onion; cut a ring of chilli. Thread spring onion through chilli. Make fine, parallel cuts from the end of the onion towards the centre. Place in iced water and leave until they open out.
5 To make Cucumber Garnish: Run the tines of a fork down the length of a cucumber and cut cucumber into thin slices.
6 To make Chilli Flowers: Using a very sharp knife, make five cuts down the length of each chilli; stopping just short of the base. Place in a bowl of iced water for 30 minutes or until the 'flower' opens.

WILD AND BROWN RICE SALAD

★ **Preparation time:** 10 minutes
Total cooking time: 40 minutes
Serves 6

1/2 cup wild rice	1 tablespoon chopped fresh basil
1 cup brown rice	
1/4 cup slivered almonds	3 tablespoons light vegetable oil
1 tablespoon chopped fresh parsley	2 teaspoons white wine vinegar
1 tablespoon chopped fresh chives	

1 Cook wild rice and brown rice separately in large pans of boiling water until just tender. Drain, rinse under cold water and drain again thoroughly. Refrigerate. Rice should be quite cold and dry before assembling salad.
2 Preheat oven to moderate 180°C (350°F/Gas 4). Spread the slivered almonds on a foil-covered oven tray; cook for 3 minutes or until golden.
3 Combine cold wild and brown rice, parsley, chives, basil, oil and white wine vinegar in a serving bowl; top with cooled almonds just before serving.

ABOVE: BALINESE-STYLE FRIED RICE. OPPOSITE PAGE, BELOW: SAVOURY RICE; ABOVE: VALENCIA STYLE RICE

RICE

ABOUT RICE

■ Rice comes in either brown or white versions and three main varieties: long-grain, medium grain and short-grain. Brown rice (rice without the bran removed) takes at least twice as long to cook as white rice.

■ To make fluffy white rice in which grains remain separate, bring 8 cups (2 litres) of water to the boil, add 1 cup of rice and boil, uncovered, for 12–15 minutes. Strain in a colander. For pearly white rice, in which the grains stick together, place 1 cup rice in pan, add water to 2.5 cm (1 inch) above rice, bring to boil, reduce heat to very low, cover with tight-fitting lid, cook 20 minutes or until water is absorbed.

■ Cooked rice can be stored in the refrigerator, covered, for a few days. It may be frozen and reheated, when required, in a microwave oven or in a colander over a pan of boiling water.

Rice Flour Also called rice powder, a flour ground from milled rice; used in Asia to make rice noodles and used commercially as a thickening agent in cakes and puddings.

Rice Paper A thin, almost transparent, edible paper made from the straw of rice. It is used to wrap sweet and savoury foods; macaroons are often baked on rice paper as it doesn't need to be removed before the cakes are served.

Rice Vinegar A mild-flavoured, pale yellow liquid distilled from fermented rice and used in Chinese and Japanese cooking, and sometimes in salad dressings. It is sold in small bottles.

Ricotta A soft, smooth, moist, white cheese with a bland, sweetish flavour. Traditionally ricotta is made from whey, which when heated coagulates in the same way as the white of an egg; sometimes skimmed or whole cow's milk is added, giving the cheese a creamier consistency and a fuller flavour. Ricotta

SAVOURY RICE

Preparation time: 10 minutes
Total cooking time: 20 minutes
Serves 4

1 tablespoon ghee or oil
1 medium onion, finely sliced
1 1/2 cups long-grain rice
3 cups (24 fl oz) boiling water
1 teaspoon salt

1 Heat ghee in a medium pan with a well-fitting lid. Add onion, cook until golden brown; remove from pan and set aside on a plate. In the ghee remaining in the pan, lightly cook the rice, stirring, for 2 minutes.
2 Add salt and boiling water and cook, uncovered, until the water has evaporated sufficiently for the surface of the rice to show. Cover tightly, reduce heat to very low and cook for 15 minutes.
3 Remove lid from pan; fluff the rice with a fork and let the steam escape. Spoon onto a serving plate and garnish with reserved onions. Serve immediately.

VALENCIA-STYLE RICE

Preparation time: 10 minutes
Total cooking time: 15 minutes
Serves 4–6

1 1/4 cups long-grain rice
1 tablespoon olive oil
15 g (1/2 oz) butter
1 medium onion, chopped
2 teaspoons finely grated orange rind
1/2 cup (4 fl oz) orange juice
1/2 cup (4 fl oz) sweet sherry
1 1/2 cups (12 fl oz) chicken stock

1 Soak rice in cold water 10 minutes, drain, rinse with cold water; drain again.
2 Heat oil and butter in a medium pan over low heat. Add onion and cook until golden brown and soft; add rice, reduce heat to low. Stir rice for 2 minutes or until lightly golden.
3 Add orange rind, juice, sherry and stock. Cover pan with tight-fitting lid. Bring to the boil; stir once. Reduce heat and simmer, covered, 8–10 minutes or until almost all liquid is absorbed. Remove pan from heat and stand, covered, 5 minutes or until all liquid is absorbed. Separate rice grains with a fork and serve.

can be served as a dessert with fruit or warm honey, used as filling for cheesecake, or mixed with a sharp-tasting soft cheese as a savoury spread or filling for cannelloni. Ricotta is bought fresh and must be used quickly.

Rigani A variety of the herb oregano which is mostly used dried rather than fresh. Much used in Greek cooking, rigani is available dried in bunches or as crumbled leaves in small packages.

Rillettes Also known as potted pork, a spread made from pork (or sometimes rabbit, goose or poultry), seasoned with garlic, onions and herbs, cooked slowly in lard and then pounded to a paste. It is served spread on bread or toast.

Risotto Short-grained rice (arborio is best) sautéed in butter or oil and then simmered gently in stock until thick and creamy. A range of ingredients (especially shellfish, chicken liver, beef marrow, savoury sausages and vegetables) can be added. Risotto with parmesan cheese and extra butter is served in Italy as an alternative to pasta. Risotto means 'little rice'.

TOMATO RICE CUPS

★★ **Preparation time:** 30 minutes
Total cooking time: 1 hour 30 minutes
Serves 4

8 large ripe tomatoes, about 1 1/2 kg (3 lb)	1/3 cup (2 1/2 fl oz) olive oil
1 cup coarsely chopped flat-leaf parsley	3 large onions, finely chopped
salt and freshly ground black pepper, to taste	2/3 cup short-grain rice
2 tablespoons olive oil, extra	1/4 cup tomato paste
	1/2 cup (4 fl oz) water

1 Arrange tomatoes on a board, base-side up. Cut bases from tomatoes with a sharp knife and set them aside. Squeeze tomatoes gently to remove excess seeds; discard seeds. Use a small spoon to scoop out flesh and remaining seeds from tomato cups; chop flesh finely. Set cups aside.

2 Heat oil in heavy-based pan. Add onion, cook over low heat 20 minutes, stirring occasionally. Add rice, stir over low heat 3 minutes. Add chopped tomato and tomato paste. Bring to boil, reduce heat and simmer, covered, for 7 minutes. Remove from heat; cool slightly. Stir in parsley and season with salt and pepper to taste.

3 Preheat oven to moderate 180°C (350°F/Gas 4). Spoon rice mixture evenly into tomato cups; use reserved bases to cover filling. Arrange tomatoes in a deep baking dish.

4 Pour water into dish. Drizzle oil over tomatoes. Cover dish with foil. Bake for 30 minutes, remove foil and bake for another 30 minutes. Baste with pan juices just before serving. Serve hot.

DOLMADES

★★ **Preparation time:** 1 hour + 1 hour standing
Total cooking time: 55 minutes
Makes about 35

250 g (8 oz) vine leaves in brine	3/4 cup (6 fl oz) olive oil
1/3 cup coarsely chopped fresh dill	2 large onions, finely chopped
1 tablespoon finely chopped fresh mint	3/4 cup short-grain rice
salt and freshly ground black pepper, to taste	6 spring onions (scallions), chopped
1 tablespoon lemon juice	1 1/2 cups (12 fl oz) water

1 Rinse vine leaves in cold water; soak in warm water 1 hour; drain. Heat 1/2 cup (4 fl oz) oil in pan. Add onion. Cook over low heat 5 minutes; remove from heat, leave covered 5 minutes.

2 Add rice, spring onions, herbs, salt and pepper to pan; mix well. Lay out a vine leaf, vein-side-up.

3 Place 3 teaspoons of mixture on centre of leaf. Fold sides over mixture, roll towards leaf tip. Repeat process with remaining filling and leaves.

4 Place five vine leaves over base of medium heavy-based pan. Arrange rolled dolmades in the pan in two layers; drizzle with remaining oil. Place a plate on top of the dolmades; cover with water. Bring to boil, reduce heat and simmer, covered, for 45 minutes. Remove plate; drizzle with lemon juice. Serve warm or cold.

LEFT: Tomato rice cups; ABOVE: Dolmades.
OPPOSITE PAGE: Kedgeree

Rissole A small ball of minced meat, poultry, fish or shellfish, coated in breadcrumbs and fried or baked.

Roast To cook food in the dry heat of an oven, a method most often used for larger cuts of meat, poultry or game. Roasting results in a browned, crunchy crust and a moist interior. Spit roasting involves rotating the food over a naked flame.

Rock Cake A small, individual cake with firm texture

and rough, rock-like appearance containing dried fruit. Rock cakes are eaten warm or cold, buttered or plain.

Rockefeller Oyster Oyster in the shell topped with a sauce of pureed spinach, onion and celery, flavoured with a dash of either pernod or Tabasco, sprinkled with breadcrumbs and cooked under a griller until the top begins to brown. The Rockefeller oyster was created at Antoine's, a famous New Orleans restaurant, and allegedly

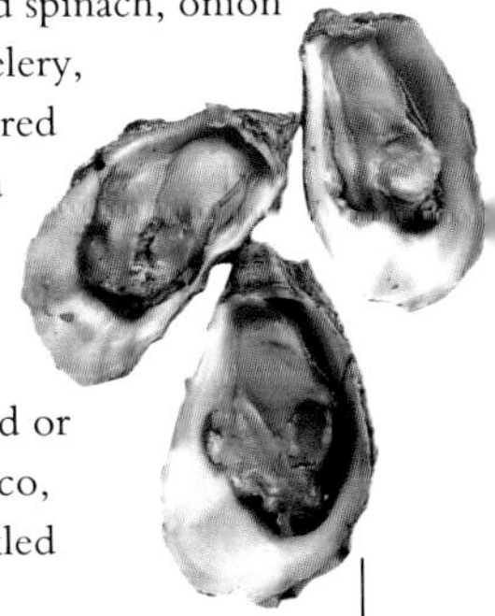

BAKED RICE CUSTARD

★ **Preparation time:** 20 minutes
Total cooking time: 1 hour
Serves 4

¼ cup short-grain rice	1–2 teaspoons grated lemon rind
2 eggs	1 teaspoon vanilla essence
¼ cup caster (superfine) sugar	½ cup (4 fl oz) cream
1½ cups (12 fl oz) milk	¼ teaspoon ground nutmeg or cinnamon
¼ cup sultanas or currants (optional)	

1 Preheat oven to moderately slow 160°C (325°F/Gas 3). Brush a deep, 20 cm (8 inch) round ovenproof dish (1.5 litre/6-cup capacity) with melted butter or oil. Cook rice in medium pan of boiling water until just tender; drain.

2 In a medium mixing bowl, whisk the eggs, sugar, milk, cream, essence and rind for about 2 minutes. Fold in the cooked rice and sultanas or currants. Pour mixture into prepared dish. Sprinkle with nutmeg or cinnamon.

3 Place filled dish into deep baking dish. Pour in water to come halfway up the sides. Bake for 50 minutes or until custard is set and a knife comes out clean when inserted in the centre. Remove dish from baking dish immediately. Allow to stand for 5 minutes before serving. Serve with cream or stewed fruits.

4 Spoon mixture into prepared dish. Dot the top of the kedgeree with butter, pour the cream over. Bake for 20 minutes. Serve with buttered toast and lemon slices.

KEDGEREE

★ **Preparation time:** 15 minutes
Total cooking time: 30 minutes
Serves 4

500 g (1 lb) smoked haddock	¼ teaspoon ground nutmeg
1 teaspoon finely grated lemon rind	pinch pepper
1 bay leaf	salt to taste
1½ cups cooked long-grain rice	1 tablespoon lemon juice
3 hard-boiled eggs, finely chopped	45 g (1½ oz) butter, chopped
	¾ cup (6 fl oz) cream

1 Preheat oven to moderate 180°C (350°F/Gas 4). Brush a shallow 6-cup capacity ovenproof dish with melted butter or oil. Cut fish into 3 cm (1¼ inch) cubes, place in large pan with lemon rind and bay leaf, cover with water and simmer until just cooked, about 6–8 minutes.

2 Using a slotted spoon, remove fish pieces from liquid. Flake fish with a fork.

3 In a large bowl, combine cooked rice, eggs, fish, nutmeg, pepper, salt and lemon juice.

WARM RICE AND DATE SALAD

★ **Preparation time:** 25 minutes
Total cooking time: 1 hour
Serves 4–6

½ cup wild rice	2 teaspoons soft brown sugar
¾ cup basmati or jasmine rice	1 teaspoon French seeded mustard
1 cup chopped fresh dates	⅓ cup toasted chopped macadamia nuts
1 banana, sliced	
	Dressing
¼ cup (2 fl oz) lemon juice	¼ cup (2 fl oz) olive oil

1 Wash and drain wild rice. Add it to 450 ml (14 fl oz) boiling water. Cover and simmer for 45 minutes or until tender.

2 Wash basmati rice well. Place in a pan with cold water to cover 1 cm (½ inch) above the level of the rice. Bring to the boil, then cover tightly and cook for 10–15 minutes, or until tender.

3 To make Dressing: Combine oil, lemon juice, brown sugar and mustard in a screw-top jar. Shake well to combine.

4 Combine rice, dates and banana. Pour dressing over rice mixture and stir gently to combine. Place on a serving plate and garnish with macadamia nuts. Serve immediately.

Rockmelon See Melon.

Roe Hard roe is the massed eggs of the female and includes sturgeon roe (better known as caviar), lumpfish roe and salmon roe. Milt or soft roe is the sperm of the male fish; soft herring roe has a creamy, smooth texture and is often fried in butter and served with lemon juice; the soft roe of cod and mullet is blended with cooked potato, olive oil and lemon juice to make the Greek dip taramasalata.

Rollmop A boned herring fillet rolled around a slice of onion or a gherkin, secured with a wooden toothpick and pickled in spiced vinegar. Rollmops are available in jars.

Rocket (Arugula) A salad green with slender deep green leaves similar in shape to radish tops. Its spicy, bitter flavour complements other leaves in a mixed green salad. The older (and larger) the leaf, the more pungent the flavour.

came by its name when a customer described the dish as being 'as rich as Rockefeller'.

CARROT PILAF

★ **Preparation time:** 15 minutes
Total cooking time: 30 minutes
Serves 4–6

2 cups long-grain rice
2 tablespoons butter
2 tablespoons olive oil
2 cups coarsely grated carrot
1 cup (8 fl oz) white wine
1 tablespoon golden syrup (light corn syrup)
2½ cups (20 fl oz) chicken stock
finely ground black pepper
½ cup chopped pistachios

1 Wash rice until water runs clear. Drain well.
2 Heat butter and oil in heavy-based pan. Add rice; fry 3–4 minutes. Add carrot and pepper; fry for 5 minutes, stirring constantly. Add golden syrup and mix thoroughly.
3 Add stock and wine. Bring to the boil, reduce heat to low, cover with tight-fitting lid and cook for 20–25 minutes or until rice is tender.
4 Place in serving bowl. Sprinkle pistachios over.

PARSLEYED BROWN RICE

Note: Rice must be washed well under cold running water when preparing a pilaf, to ensure light fluffy rice grains.

Stir 1½ cups quick-cooking brown rice into plenty of rapidly boiling water and cook according to packet directions. Drain. Toss through 1 bunch chopped parsley, 1½ tablespoons grated lemon rind and ½ teaspoon cracked black peppercorns.

RICE AND VEGETABLE PILAF

★ **Preparation time:** 20 minutes
Total cooking time: 35 minutes
Serves 4

3 medium tomatoes, chopped
1 medium onion, sliced
3 tablespoons olive oil
2 cloves garlic, crushed
2 teaspoons ground cumin
2 teaspoons paprika
½ teaspoon allspice
1½ cups long-grain rice
155 g (5 oz) button mushrooms, sliced
2 medium zucchini (courgettes), sliced
155 g (5 oz) broccoli, cut into florets
1½ cups (12 fl oz) vegetable stock
3/4 cup (6 fl oz) white wine

1 Heat oil in a large heavy-based pan. Add onion, cook for 10 minutes over medium heat until golden brown. Add garlic and spices, cook for another minute.
2 Add rice to pan, stir until well combined. Add stock, wine, tomato and mushrooms. Bring to the boil. Reduce heat to low, cover pan with a tight fitting lid. Simmer for 15 minutes. Remove pan from heat.
3 Add zucchini and broccoli to pan. Cover, cook 5–7 minutes, until just tender. Serve.

ABOVE: RICE AND VEGETABLE PILAF.
OPPOSITE PAGE, ABOVE: VEGETABLE RISOTTO;
BELOW: PORCINI MUSHROOM AND ONION RISOTTO

VEGETABLE RISOTTO

★★ ★

Preparation time: 15 minutes
Total cooking time: 30 minutes
Serves 6

1.25 litres (5 cups)
  chicken stock
2 tablespoons olive oil
1 medium onion, finely
  chopped
1 bunch asparagus, cut into
  3 cm (1¼ inch) lengths
2 medium zucchini
  (courgettes), cut into
  2 cm (¾ inch) slices
2 small tomatoes, chopped
105 g (3½ oz) snow peas
  (mange tout), cut into
  2 cm (¾ inch) lengths
1½ cups short-grain
  rice
½ cup grated parmesan
  cheese

1 Place chicken stock in a medium pan. Cover; bring to the boil. Reduce heat and simmer. Place asparagus, zucchini and snow peas in a heatproof bowl and cover with boiling water. Allow to stand for 2 minutes, then drain. Refresh with cold water, drain well.

2 Heat oil in a large heavy-based pan. Add onion, stir over medium heat until golden; add rice. Reduce heat to medium low, stir rice for 3 minutes or until lightly golden. Add a quarter of the stock to the pan, stir constantly for 7 minutes or until stock is absorbed.

3 Repeat the process until all but ½ cup (4 fl oz) of stock has been used, and rice is almost tender. Add vegetables with the remaining stock, stir 5 minutes until liquid is absorbed and vegetables are tender. Stir in parmesan. Serve.

PORCINI MUSHROOM AND ONION RISOTTO

★★ ★

Preparation time: 10 minutes +
  45 minutes soaking
Total cooking time: 30 minutes
Serves 4

15 g (½ oz) packet sliced
  dried porcini
  mushrooms
155 g (5 oz) fresh
  mushrooms, chopped
1½ cups arborio rice
2 tablespoons chopped
  parsley
¼ cup grated parmesan
  cheese
2 onions, chopped
60 g (2 oz) butter
1 litre (4 cups) chicken
  stock
1 clove garlic, crushed

1 Soak porcini mushrooms in a cup of hot water for 45 minutes; drain. Bring chicken stock to boil. Meanwhile, melt butter in pan; add onion and garlic and cook over low heat until tender and brown.

2 Add rice; stir until combined. Add 1 cup (8 fl oz) simmering stock and bring to boil. Cook until liquid has almost evaporated, stirring often. Add another cup of stock; cook until liquid has almost evaporated, stirring often. Add porcini and fresh mushrooms and continue adding stock as above. It should take about 20 minutes from the first addition to add all the stock.

3 Reduce heat to low; stir in parsley and parmesan cheese. Cover; cook 2 minutes and serve immediately.

Romaine Lettuce Also known as cos, a lettuce with long, crisp leaves: the outer leaves are dark and pungent, the inner leaves pale and mild in taste. Romaine lettuce is the favoured variety used to make Caesar salad and is valued for its crispness.

Romano A hard grating cheese, usually made from cow's milk, similar in taste and texture to parmesan. When made with sheep's milk the cheese is called pecorino romano.

Roquefort A creamy-textured, blue-vein, ewe's milk cheese with a pronounced aroma and a pungent, salty flavour. The cheese is matured for three months in the damp limestone caves of Roquefort-sur-Soulzon in south-eastern France. It is best served at room temperature.

Rose Water A liquid distilled from fragrant rose petals and used particularly in the cooking of India and the Middle East. It flavours Indian desserts such as *gulab jamun* (rich, fried dumplings soaked in rose water syrup) as well as creams, jellies and ices. Rose water essence is much stronger than rose water and should be used sparingly.

RICOTTA

RICOTTA AND PESTO PIZZAS

⭐⭐ **Preparation time:** 1 hour
Total cooking time: 15 minutes
Makes 6 individual pizzas

Pizza Dough
7 g (¼ oz) sachet dry yeast
1¾ cups (14 fl oz) warm
  water
4 cups plain (all-purpose)
  wholemeal flour
2 tablespoons olive oil

Topping
2 cloves garlic
1 cup fresh basil leaves
½ cup fresh parsley sprigs
⅓ cup walnuts
¾ cup grated parmesan
  cheese
½ cup (4 fl oz) olive oil
250 g (8 oz) ricotta
  cheese
250 g (8 oz) sun-dried
  tomatoes, sliced

1 Combine yeast and water. Stand in a warm place for 10 minutes. Sift flour into a large basin. Make a well in the centre and add yeast mixture and oil. Mix well, using a wooden spoon, until dough forms a soft ball.

2 Knead dough on a lightly floured surface until it is smooth and springs back when touched. Transfer to a lightly oiled, large basin. Cover with plastic wrap and stand in a warm position until dough has doubled in bulk. Prepare Topping while dough is proving.

3 Preheat oven to 200°C (400°F/Gas 6). Grease two oven trays.

4 To make Topping: Combine garlic, basil, parsley, walnuts and parmesan in blender or food

processor. Blend mixture at medium speed, adding oil in a thin stream until a thick paste is formed.

5 Punch dough down and divide into six equal portions. Shape each portion into a flat circle 13 cm (5 inches) in diameter. Lay each portion of dough on prepared oven trays.

6 Spread ricotta cheese on each portion. Top with the basil mixture. Arrange slices of sun-dried tomatoes over basil mixture. Bake for 15 minutes or until dough is golden brown and cooked through. Remove pizzas from trays immediately and serve with freshly made salad.

CHOCOLATE RICOTTA TORTE

⭐ **Preparation time:** 30 minutes
⭐⭐ **Total cooking time:** 40 minutes
Serves 8

Cake
125 g (4 oz) butter,
  softened
1 cup caster (superfine)
  sugar
2 eggs
1¼ cups self-raising flour
½ cup cocoa
¾ cup (6 fl oz) water

Filling
200 g (6½ oz) ricotta
  cheese
2 tablespoons caster
  (superfine) sugar

30 g (1 oz) mixed peel,
  finely chopped
30 g (1 oz) glacé cherries,
  finely chopped

Topping
2 teaspoons instant coffee
  powder
1 teaspoon hot water
300 ml (9 fl oz) cream

¼ cup (2 fl oz) brandy
¾ cup slivered almonds,
  toasted

1 Preheat oven to 180°C (350°F/ Gas 4). Combine butter, sugar, eggs, sifted flour and cocoa, and the water in small bowl. Beat with electric mixer 3 minutes or until mixture is smooth and pale.

2 Pour mixture into a greased and base-lined 23 cm (9 inch) round cake tin. Bake 40 minutes; turn onto wire rack to cool. Trim top, if necessary, to allow cake to sit flat. Cut cake horizontally into 3 layers.

3 To make Filling: Combine ricotta cheese, sugar, peel and cherries.

4 To make Topping: Dissolve coffee in water. Combine cream and coffee mixture and whip until soft peaks form.

5 Place a layer of cake on serving plate; brush with one-third of the brandy and spread with half the Filling. Top with another cake layer; brush with one-third of the brandy and spread with remaining Filling. Top with remaining cake layer. Brush with remaining brandy. Spread top and sides of cake with Topping. Sprinkle top with almonds.

OPPOSITE PAGE: RICOTTA AND PESTO PIZZAS.
ABOVE: ORANGE AND CURRANT ROCK CAKES

ROCK CAKES

ORANGE AND CURRANT ROCK CAKES

Preparation time: 8 minutes
Total cooking time: 20 minutes
Makes 9 rock cakes

1 1/2 cups self-raising flour
1/4 cup caster (superfine) sugar
1 teaspoon grated orange rind
1 egg, lightly beaten
2 tablespoons orange juice
2 teaspoons sugar
60 g (2 oz) unsalted (sweet) butter, melted
1/2 cup currants

1 Preheat oven to moderately hot 210°C (415°F/Gas 6–7). Brush a 32 x 28 cm (13 x 11 inch) oven tray with melted butter or oil, line base with paper; grease paper.
2 Sift flour into small mixing bowl; add rind and butter. Using electric beaters, beat mixture on low speed for 2 minutes.
3 Add currants, sugar and combined egg and juice. Beat on high speed for 1 minute or until the ingredients are just combined.
4 Pile mixture in portions of approximately 2 level tablespoonsful, on prepared tray, about 5 cm (2 inch), apart. Sprinkle rock cakes with sugar. Bake for 20 minutes or until golden brown. Turn onto wire rack to cool. Serve warm or cool with butter and marmalade, if desired.

ROCK CAKES

Preparation time: 30 minutes
Total cooking time: 10–15 minutes
Makes about 20

2 cups self-raising flour, sifted
90 g (3 oz) butter or margarine, cut into pieces
1 tablespoon mixed nuts (optional)
1/2 cup mixed fruit
sugar
1/2 cup caster (superfine) sugar
1 egg
1/2 teaspoon ground ginger
1/4 cup (2 fl oz) milk

1 Preheat oven to hot 200°C (400°F/Gas 6). Brush two oven trays with melted butter or oil, line the bases with paper; grease paper. Place sifted flour in a large bowl. Add pieces of butter and rub in with fingertips until mixture resembles breadcrumbs.
2 Mix in caster sugar, fruit, nuts and ginger. Whisk egg into milk and add to dry ingredients. Mix to a stiff dough.
3 Pile mixture, in portions of approximately 2 level tablespoonsful, on prepared oven trays. Bake for 10–15 minutes or until golden brown. Transfer to a wire rack to cool. Before serving, rock cakes can be split and buttered if desired.

VARIATIONS

■ Use 1 cup of wholemeal self-raising flour instead of 1 cup of the white flour.
■ Sprinkle rock cakes with cinnamon, raw sugar or coffee crystals before baking.

---

or sweet soufflé mixture baked, spread with a filling and rolled; or sponge cake wrapped around a sweet filling.

Roux A mixture of 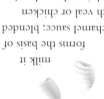 butter and flour cooked over a low heat and used to thicken many sauces. Blended with milk it forms the basis of béchamel sauce; blended with veal or chicken stock it makes it velouté sauce. Brown roux, used to thicken espagnole and demi-glace sauces, is made by cooking the flour and butter mixture until it turns brown.

Rum A spirit distilled from sugarcane and used in cooking to flavour sweet foods such as rich fruit cakes, pancake batters, dessert creams and mousses. Rum combines well with vegetables such as sweet potato and plantain.

Rum Baba See Baba au Rhum.

Rutabaga See Swede.

Rye A cereal grain used to make bread, cakes and crispbreads. Cracked rye is cooked with milk or water as a breakfast food.

Rye Bread A dark-coloured, dense-textured bread with a slightly sour taste. It is commonly served with shellfish.

Sabayon Sauce A light, foamy sauce made with whipped egg yolks, sugar and a liquid (usually dry or sweet white wine or champagne) and served warm and foaming with puddings, cakes or fruit; it is a French variation of the Italian dessert zabaglione.

Sacher Torte A dense chocolate cake with two layers separated by a thin filling of apricot jam and the whole covered with smooth chocolate. Created by Franz Sacher, chief pastrycook to the Austrian statesman Metternich during the Congress of Vienna (1814–15), the cake was later the cause of a protracted argument between Sacher's descendants and Vienna's famous Demel pâtisserie as to whether in its true form it had two layers or was simply a cake spread with jam and then iced.

Saffron A spice made from the dried, thread-like stamens of the saffron crocus. It is strongly fragrant and dark orange in colour. Saffron is very expensive—the small crocus flower

S

SALADS

CAESAR SALAD

★ *Preparation time:* 20 minutes
Total cooking time: 15 minutes
Serves 4–6

1 clove garlic
1 tablespoon olive oil
3 slices thick bread
2 rashers bacon
1 cos (romaine) lettuce
3 tablespoons olive oil, extra

1 tablespoon lemon juice
1 tablespoon sour cream
1/2 teaspoon worcestershire sauce
4 anchovies, chopped
105 g (3 1/2 oz) parmesan, thinly shaved

1 Preheat oven to moderate 180°C (350°F/Gas 4). Cut the garlic in quarters; place in a small bowl with oil. Stand for 10 minutes, stirring occasionally. Discard garlic. To make croûtons, remove crusts from bread. Brush the bread with oil; cut into small squares. Place on oven tray and bake for 10 minutes or until golden. Leave to cool.

2 Cut rind and excess fat from bacon; cut into small strips. Fry on medium heat until crisp.

3 Wash and dry lettuce thoroughly. Use larger leaves to line a serving bowl; tear remainder into bite-size pieces and place in bowl.

4 Place extra oil, juice, sour cream and sauce in small screw-top jar; shake well. Drizzle dressing over lettuce; add bacon, anchovies, croûtons and parmesan to bowl (reserve a little parmesan for garnish); toss lightly to combine. Serve immediately.

COLESLAW

★ *Preparation time:* 15 minutes
Total cooking time: nil
Serves 6

1/4 small cabbage, finely shredded
2 medium carrots, grated
1 stick celery, finely chopped
1 large white onion, finely chopped
1 small red pepper (capsicum), chopped

Dressing
1/2 cup mayonnaise
2 tablespoons white wine vinegar
1 teaspoon French mustard

1 Place vegetables in a large mixing bowl and toss to combine.

2 **To make Dressing:** In a separate bowl, place mayonnaise, vinegar and mustard. Mix well to combine. Pour onto salad and toss. Transfer to a serving bowl.

ABOVE: CAESAR SALAD. OPPOSITE PAGE, BELOW: WALDORF SALAD; ABOVE: SALAD NIÇOISE

SALAD NICOISE

Preparation time: 20 minutes
Total cooking time: nil
Serves 4–6

140 g (4½ oz) green beans
2 medium tomatoes, cut into 8 wedges
1 small red onion, cut into rings
3 hard-boiled eggs, quartered
1 clove garlic, crushed
1 tablespoon white wine vinegar
¼ cup (2 fl oz) olive oil
45 g (1½ oz) can anchovies, drained
⅔ cup black pitted olives
425 g (13½ oz) can tuna, drained
½ teaspoon French mustard

1 Top and tail beans and place into a large pan of boiling water. Stand 1 minute, drain and plunge into iced water. Drain well; cut the beans in half.
2 Arrange the beans, tomato, onion, egg, chunks of tuna, olives and anchovies on a large serving platter or shallow bowl.
3 Place the olive oil, vinegar, garlic and French mustard in a small screw-top jar and shake well. Drizzle dressing over salad. Serve immediately with crusty bread.

SEAFOOD SALAD

Preparation time: 20 minutes
Total cooking time: 2 minutes
Serves 4

200 g (6½ oz) calamari rings
500 g (1 lb) cooked medium king prawns (shrimps)
200 g (6½ oz) jar mussels
4 lettuce cups
⅓ cup (2½ fl oz) thousand island dressing
1 tablespoon cream
1 teaspoon finely chopped fresh parsley

1 Boil 3 cm (1¼ inches) water in a large pan. Add the calamari rings; simmer 2 minutes, turning once. Do not overcook or calamari will become rubbery. Remove from the pan with a slotted spoon. Set aside to cool.
2 Peel and devein the prawns. Drain mussels.
3 Arrange prepared seafood in lettuce cups. Combine thousand island dressing and cream and drizzle over seafood. Sprinkle parsley on top. Serve immediately.

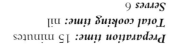

WALDORF SALAD

Preparation time: 15 minutes
Total cooking time: nil
Serves 6

3 medium red apples
2 medium green apples
2 sticks celery, sliced
¼ cup walnut halves
¼ cup mayonnaise
2 tablespoons French dressing
1 tablespoon sour cream

1 Quarter and core the apples and cut into 2 cm (¾ inch) chunks.
2 Place in a large mixing bowl with the celery and walnuts.
3 In a separate bowl combine mayonnaise, French dressing and sour cream, mix well. Add to salad and fold through. Transfer to a lettuce-lined serving bowl. Serve immediately.

---

has only three stamens and each must be plucked by hand; it takes more than 150,000 fresh flowers to produce 1 kilogram (2.2 pounds) of dried saffron. Fortunately only scant amounts are needed to impart its unique flavour and colour. Saffron is used in fish dishes, such as bouillabaisse, with rice (as in the Spanish dish, paella, and saffron rice), popular in Indian and Asian cooking), in poultry and beef stews, in curries, tomato-based sauces, sweet breads and biscuits (cookies). Saffron is best purchased as threads (to use, pound in a mortar and steep in warm liquid to bring out the flavour).

Sage A herb with grey-green aromatic leaves with a pungent, slightly bitter flavour, originally used medicinally but now used in cooking, especially in stuffings for poultry and pork and as a traditional flavouring for cottage cheese. In Italian cooking it flavours veal and other meat dishes; in Germany it is used in eel dishes; and in Greece sage tea is a popular beverage. Sage is native to the northern shores of the Mediterranean. It is available fresh or dried.

ASPARAGUS AND PROSCIUTTO SALAD

Preparation time: 20 minutes
Total cooking time: 3 minutes
Serves 4

2 bunches asparagus
(about 6 spears per
person)
3 teaspoons tarragon
vinegar
2 teaspoons poppy seeds
4 slices prosciutto
30 g (1 oz) parmesan
cheese
3 tablespoons olive oil

1 Trim any woody ends from the asparagus and place into a large pan of boiling water. Stand for 1 minute, then drain and plunge into iced water. Drain well. Arrange on individual serving plates.

2 Place the prosciutto under a hot grill for 2 minutes or until very crispy. Allow to cool.

3 Place the oil, tarragon vinegar and poppy seeds in a small screw-top jar and shake well. Drizzle dressing over asparagus and crumble the prosciutto on top. Using a vegetable peeler or sharp knife, shave strips of parmesan over the prosciutto and serve immediately.

Note: Prosciutto is an Italian smoked meat, also known as Parma ham. It is available from delicatessens, usually sliced paper thin.

ASIAN NOODLE VEGETABLE SALAD

Preparation time: 30 minutes
Total cooking time: 15 minutes
Serves 4–6

6 spring onions (scallions)
500 g (1 lb) thick rice
(or egg) noodles
1 medium carrot
4 ripe plum tomatoes
12 snow peas (mange tout)
125 g (4 oz) can baby
corn, drained and
halved (or fresh)
155 g (5 oz) fresh bean
sprouts
45 g (1½ oz) roasted
peanuts
soy sauce, optional

Dressing
2 teaspoons sesame oil
¼ cup (2 fl oz) olive oil
5 teaspoons white rice
vinegar
1¼ teaspoons sugar
salt and cracked black
pepper, to taste
1 teaspoon finely chopped
fresh red chilli
1–2 tablespoons chopped
fresh coriander

1 Trim spring onions, cut in thin diagonal slices. Cook noodles in large pan of boiling water 3–4 minutes or until just tender. Remove from heat, drain. Rinse under cold water, drain again.

2 Mark a cross on the top of each tomato. Place in boiling water 1–2 minutes; plunge into cold water; drain. Peel down skin at cross. Cut tomatoes in half, remove seeds. Cut flesh into narrow strips. Peel carrot, cut into thin matchstick lengths. Trim snow peas, cut into diagonal slices.

3 If using fresh baby corn, boil in lightly salted water 3 minutes; drain. Plunge in cold water.

4 To make Dressing: Combine oils, vinegar, sugar, salt, pepper, chilli and coriander in a screw-top jar; shake vigorously to combine.

drain and set aside. Plunge bean sprouts into boiling water 1–2 minutes; drain. Combine all vegetables and peanuts in a salad bowl. Add Dressing and mix thoroughly. Chill briefly before serving. Drizzle with soy sauce, if desired.

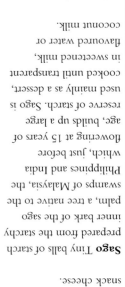

Sake A Japanese alcoholic drink made from fermented rice. A sweet sake, mirin, is an important flavouring in Japanese cooking; sweet sherry can be substituted.

Saint Paulin A pasteurised cow's milk pressed curd cheese with a semi-soft texture and a flavour ranging from buttery and slightly sweet to tangy. Now factory-made all over France, it is derived from Port Salut, a cheese first made in the early nineteenth century in the Port-du-Salut monastery in Brittany.

Sago Tiny balls of starch prepared from the starchy inner bark of the sago palm, a tree native to the swamps of Malaysia, the Philippines and India which, just before flowering at 15 years of age, builds up a large reserve of starch. Sago is used mainly as a dessert, cooked until transparent in sweetened milk, flavoured water or coconut milk.

Sage Derby A close-textured cow's milk cheese flavoured with fresh sage leaves, which give it a green hue with darker green streaks. It is a variant of the English cheese, Derby. Serve at room temperature on a cheese platter and as a snack cheese.

Salad A mixture of foods, either savoury or sweet, such as vegetables (raw or cooked) and salad greens, fresh fruits, seafood, poultry, meats, eggs, pasta and grains. Savoury salads are usually served with a dressing. In North America a green salad is often served after the first course and before the main course; in many parts of Europe it is served with the main course; in France it is served after the main course. Salads featuring green beans, corn, rice, tomato, potato or cabbage are often served as side dishes, while first and main course salads include Caesar salad, and salads of cheese, seafood, chicken, pasta and meats. Fruit such as grapefruit segments, grapes and cantaloupe (rockmelon) are added to savoury salads.

Salad Dressing A flavoured liquid used to moisten and flavour a salad; it can be a sprinkling of lemon juice, or can be a mixture of olive oil and vinegar or a cold sauce such as mayonnaise. The dressing can be served mixed through the salad or as an accompaniment.

OPPOSITE PAGE, ABOVE: ASIAN NOODLE VEGETABLE SALAD; BELOW: ASPARAGUS AND PROSCIUTTO SALAD. ABOVE: CURLY ENDIVE SALAD WITH CRISP PROSCIUTTO AND GARLIC CROUTONS

CURLY ENDIVE (CHICORY) SALAD WITH CRISP PROSCIUTTO AND GARLIC CROUTONS

★ **Preparation time:** 20 minutes
Total cooking time: 5 minutes
Serves 4–6

1 large bunch curly endive (chicory)
1/2 red oak leaf lettuce
2 red onions
4 slices white or sliced brown bread
2 large cloves garlic
55 g (1 1/2 oz) butter, softened
35 g (1 1/4 oz) feta cheese, mashed

4–6 thin slices prosciutto
1 large avocado

Dressing
2 tablespoons olive oil
1/4 cup sugar
1/4 cup (2 fl oz) spicy tomato sauce
1 tablespoon soy sauce
1/3 cup (2 1/2 fl oz) red wine vinegar

1 Rinse endive and oak leaf lettuce in cold water. Shake lightly in a tea-towel to absorb excess water. Tear endive and lettuce into pieces. Peel and slice onions; separate into onion rings. Combine endive, lettuce and onion rings in a salad bowl or wide shallow dish.

2 Toast bread one side only. Mash garlic, butter and feta cheese into a paste, spread over the untoasted side of the bread. Remove crusts; toast buttered side of bread until crisp and golden on the surface. Cut each slice into 1 cm (1/2 inch) cubes.

3 Place prosciutto under very hot grill for a few seconds until crisp. Remove and cut into 5 cm (2 inch) pieces. Set aside. Peel avocado and cut into thin wedges.

4 To make Dressing: Whisk oil, sugar, tomato sauce, soy sauce and vinegar together in small bowl. Add prosciutto and avocado to the salad and pour over half the dressing. Arrange croûtons on top and serve remaining dressing in a jug.

CHEF'S SALAD

★ **Preparation time:** 15 minutes
Total cooking time: nil
Serves 6

6 lettuce leaf cups
60 g (2 oz) Swiss cheese
4 thin slices leg ham
3 medium egg tomatoes
2 hard-boiled eggs, quartered
2 tablespoons chopped pimiento, optional

3/4 cup cooked, chopped chicken
1/2 cup (4 fl oz) French dressing

1 Wash and dry lettuce thoroughly. Cut the cheese and ham slices into evenly-sized, fine strips. Cut each tomato into 6 wedges.

2 Combine the cheese, ham, tomato wedges, chicken, pimiento and eggs in a mixing bowl. Toss to combine. Serve salad in lettuce cups. Drizzle the French dressing over, toss lightly and serve immediately.

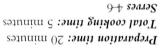

Salami A cured dry sausage made from minced (ground) pork and seasoned with garlic and other herbs and spices; it is sometimes smoked and can be flavoured with red wine. Salami is served thinly sliced as finger food, in salads and sandwiches and as a pizza topping. The sausage is thought to have originated in the ancient city of Salamis, in Cyprus, but is now commonly associated with Italy; distinctive types of salami are also made in Denmark, Hungary, Austria, Spain and Germany.

Salmon A large fish that spends most of the year in cooler ocean waters, but swims up rivers to spawn in fresh water. It has delicately flavoured, fatty pink flesh. Salmon may be grilled (broiled), baked or poached; the flesh may also be smoked or salted. It is used in many traditional dishes such as the Scandinavian gravlax (raw salmon salted and marinated with dill and pepper) and the Russian koulibiac (a fish and vegetable pie). Smoked salmon is served cold, thinly sliced, with lemon and capers, or

CHAR-GRILLED BEEF AND EGGPLANT (AUBERGINE) SALAD

★ **Preparation time:** 25 minutes + 30 minutes marinating
Total cooking time: 20 minutes
Serves 4

2 medium eggplant (aubergine)	2 medium onions
1/4 cup (2 fl oz) olive oil	2 medium red peppers (capsicum)
1 tablespoon lemon juice	3 medium zucchini (courgettes)
750 g (1 1/2 lb) sirloin or rump steak	2 tablespoons salt
45 g (1 1/2 oz) snow pea sprouts (mange tout)	105 g (3 1/2 oz) button mushrooms
1/4 cup shredded fresh basil	

1 Cut eggplant in half lengthways, lay cut side down and cut into long 1 cm (1/2 inch) slices. Spread out in a single layer on a plate and sprinkle with salt. Set aside for 15 minutes, place in a colander and rinse under cold water. Pat dry thoroughly with paper towels.

2 Cut the zucchini into 2 cm (3/4 inch) pieces. Slice the peppers into 2 cm (3/4 inch) strips. Cut the mushrooms in half. Slice the onions thickly. Combine all the vegetables with oil and lemon juice in a large bowl. Cover with plastic wrap and leave to marinate for 30 minutes at room temperature.

3 Remove excess fat and sinew from steak. Place the steak on a preheated lightly greased grill or flatplate barbecue. Cook on high heat for 2 minutes each side to seal, turning once. Move meat to a cooler part of the barbecue, continue to cook for another 2 minutes each side for a medium-rare result. Transfer meat to a plate, cover loosely with foil. Allow to cool, then slice thinly with a sharp knife.

4 Using a slotted spoon, remove the vegetables from the marinade. Cook in two batches on the barbecue for about 5 minutes each batch until vegetables are just tender and lightly browned. Allow to cool.

5 Arrange a pile of snow pea sprouts on individual serving plates. Top with sliced meat and cooled vegetables. Garnish with shredded fresh basil. Serve immediately, at room temperature.

Note: Eggplant (aubergine), especially more mature ones, can contain bitter juices. When sprinkled with salt, as in this recipe, juices are drawn out and the bitterness reduced. This salting process also reduces the amount of fat which is absorbed by the eggplant during cooking. Make sure you dry well before cooking.

ABOVE: CHAR-GRILLED BEEF AND EGGPLANT SALAD. OPPOSITE PAGE: TUNA SALAD WITH GARLIC MAYONNAISE.

TUNA SALAD WITH GARLIC MAYONNAISE

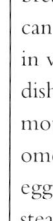

Preparation time: 25 minutes
Total cooking time: 15 minutes
Serves 6

6 small red potatoes, peeled	**Garlic Mayonnaise**
155 g (5 oz) snow peas (mange tout)	3 egg yolks
1 bunch asparagus	1 clove garlic, crushed
250 g (8 oz) cherry tomatoes	½ teaspoon French mustard
2 x 425 g (13½ oz) cans tuna, drained	2 tablespoons lemon juice
	1 cup (8 fl oz) olive oil

1 Cut the potatoes into 2 cm (¾ inch) cubes and cook in a large pan of boiling water until just tender. Drain and set aside. Place snow peas in a pan of boiling water, stand one minute, drain and plunge into iced water. Drain and set aside. Trim woody ends from asparagus, and repeat process as for snow peas. Cut asparagus into 5 cm lengths.
2 To make Garlic Mayonnaise: Place the yolks, garlic, mustard and juice in a medium mixing bowl. Using electric beaters, beat ingredients together for 1 minute. Add oil, about 1 teaspoon at a time, beating constantly until mixture is thick and creamy. Increase the addition of oil as the mayonnaise thickens. Continue beating until all the oil is added.
3 Arrange the potatoes, snow peas, asparagus, tomatoes and chunks of tuna on individual plates. Place spoonfuls of mayonnaise on each plate or pass around in a bowl. Serve immediately.

FRAGRANT RICE SALAD

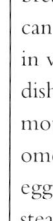

Preparation time: 25 minutes
Total cooking time: 15 minutes
Serves 4

1 cup Basmati or Thai fragrant rice	2 spring onions (scallions), sliced
2 medium carrots, sliced diagonally	155 g (5 oz) Chinese barbecued pork, thinly sliced
1 medium green pepper (capsicum), cut into short, thin strips	2 tablespoons peanut oil
200 g (6½ oz) can baby corn, cut into 2 cm (¾ inch) lengths	1 tablespoon sesame oil
	2 teaspoons lime juice
	2 teaspoons soy sauce

1 Bring a large pan of water to the boil. Add rice gradually and cook for 12–15 minutes until just tender. Drain, rinse under cold water, drain again thoroughly.
2 Place rice, carrot, pepper, baby corn, spring onion and pork in a serving bowl. Toss to combine.
3 Place peanut and sesame oils, lime juice and soy sauce in a small screw-top jar and shake well. Drizzle over the salad and toss lightly to combine. Serve immediately.

Note: Barbecued pork is available from Chinese food stores.

TURKEY SALAD WITH CRANBERRY DRESSING

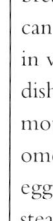

Preparation time: 15 minutes
Total cooking time: nil
Serves 4

125 g (4 oz) watercress	1 tablespoon oil
500 g (1 lb) sliced cooked turkey	1 teaspoon white wine vinegar
2 small oranges	2 tablespoons chopped pistachio nuts
2 tablespoons cranberry sauce	

1 Wash and dry the watercress thoroughly. Break into large sprigs, discarding any thick stems. Arrange on a serving platter.
2 Arrange turkey slices in the centre of the watercress. Using a sharp knife, peel the oranges, removing all white pith, cut into slices and arrange around the turkey.
3 Place the cranberry sauce, oil and vinegar in a small bowl. Whisk until combined. Spoon dressing over the turkey. Sprinkle with chopped pistachios and serve immediately.

with cream cheese or horseradish sauce, and often accompanied by bread, toast or blinis; it can also be incorporated in various hot and cold dishes, including mousses, dips, crêpes, omelettes and scrambled eggs, and tossed through steaming pasta.

Salmon was once abundant in northern Atlantic waters; it was the most commonly eaten fish in medieval Europe and by the seventeenth century the fish was still so plentiful in Scottish streams that employers were forbidden by law from feeding it to their servants more than three times a week. Salmon is now farmed in many parts of the world. Fresh salmon can be bought whole, or as cutlets or fillets; it is also available smoked and in cans.

Salsa A highly seasoned, chunky sauce based on tomato, chilli, garlic and onion, served as an accompaniment to Mexican and Tex-Mex dishes. Salsas can be fresh or cooked and range in flavour from mild to fiery. Commercially made varieties are available from supermarkets and specialist food stores.

MEDITERRANEAN SALAD

★ Preparation time: 40 minutes
Total cooking time: 2 minutes
Serves 8

1 medium eggplant (aubergine)	250 g (8 oz) cherry tomatoes, halved
salt	2 small cucumbers, sliced
2 tablespoons oil	1 red onion, very thinly sliced

Dressing
1/3 cup (2 1/2 fl oz) olive oil
1 tablespoon balsamic vinegar
1 clove garlic, crushed
1 tablespoon chopped fresh oregano leaves

250 g (8 oz) feta cheese sliced
2/3 cup pitted black olives

1-2 tablespoons chopped fresh basil leaves

1 Cut eggplant into 2.5 cm (1 inch) cubes and spread out on a plate. Sprinkle with a little salt and let stand for 30 minutes. Rinse under cold water, pat dry with paper towels.

2 Heat oil in a shallow pan, add eggplant. Stir over medium heat for 2 minutes or until eggplant is lightly browned and tender; drain on paper towels, cool. Toss eggplant in a bowl with tomato, cucumber, onion, cheese, olives and basil.

3 **To make Dressing:** Place all ingredients in a small screw-top jar. Shake vigorously for 10 seconds or until combined. Add to salad, toss until mixed well.

SMOKED SALMON SALAD

★ Preparation time: 20 minutes
Total cooking time: nil
Serves 4

60 g (2 oz) watercress	1 small onion, finely sliced into rings
200 g (6 1/2 oz) smoked salmon slices	1 medium avocado, sliced lengthways
1 tablespoon lemon juice	2 tablespoons cream
1/3 cup (2 1/2 fl oz) olive oil	1 tablespoon chopped fresh dill
1/3 cup soft cream cheese	1 stick celery

1 Wash and dry the watercress thoroughly. Break into large sprigs. Arrange the sprigs on individual plates or a serving platter. Arrange salmon, avocado and onion over sprigs. Cut the celery into 5 cm (2 inch) lengths, then into long strips. Scatter over salad.

2 Combine olive oil, lemon juice and cream cheese in a food processor or blender and process until smooth. Stir in cream and chopped dill. Drizzle dressing over salad and serve immediately with crusty breadsticks.

CITRUS WALNUT SALAD

★ Preparation time: 20 minutes
Total cooking time: nil
Serves 8

2 oranges
2 grapefruit

Walnut Dressing
2 tablespoons walnut oil
2 tablespoons oil
2 teaspoons tarragon vinegar
2 teaspoons seeded mustard
1 teaspoon sweet chilli sauce

125 g (4 oz) sugar snap peas
1/2 bunch rocket (arugula), leaves torn
1/2 bunch oak leaf lettuce, shredded
1 large cucumber, sliced
1/3 cup walnut pieces

1 Using a sharp knife, peel oranges and grapefruit. Separate fruit into segments, remove seeds. Cover sugar snap peas with boiling water; stand for 2 minutes. Plunge immediately into iced water. Drain and pat dry with paper towels. Combine fruit, sugar snap peas, rocket, shredded lettuce, cucumber and walnut pieces in a large bowl.

2 **To make Walnut Dressing:** Combine oils, vinegar, mustard and chilli sauce in a screw-top jar and shake well.

3 Pour dressing over salad ingredients and toss lightly until combined.

Salsa is now often used as a generic word for sauce.

Salsify A long, thin root vegetable with a delicate, oyster-like flavour. The most common variety has pale, almost white, flesh and light brown skin. A black-skinned variety, known also as scorzonera, has cream-coloured flesh. Salsify is usually boiled or sautéed and served in butter and parsley or with a béchamel or cream sauce.

Salt A white odourless and sharp-tasting crystalline powder, sodium chloride, used as a seasoning and preserving agent. Salt can be mined from seams of rock salt trapped underground (it is then boiled down and crystallised) or obtained through the evaporation of sea water or from inland salt pans.

Table salt is finely ground rock salt with additives to make it free-flowing. Kosher salt is an evaporated salt with large, irregularly shaped crystals free from additives and iodine. Bay and sea salt, in the form of small, brittle chunks and flakes, is produced by evaporation and has an intensely salty taste; it should be crushed in a mortar or mill before use. In North America 'rock salt' refers to non-edible salt used for ice-cream machines.

Saltimbocca A dish consisting of thin slices of veal sautéed in butter, then topped with ham or prosciutto and sage and gently braised in white wine (rolled up or left flat, either way secured with a toothpick).

Sambal An accompaniment to an Indonesian curry or rice meal. Sambals are made with chilli peppers, minced onion, oil and lime juice and they are often varied by the addition of other ingredients such as shrimp paste or tomato.

Sambal Oelek A hot chilli relish used in Indonesian cooking. Sambal oelek is commercially available; it can also be made at home in a food processor by blending about 20 fresh red chillies, roughly chopped, with 1–2 tablespoons vinegar. Place in a sterilised jar and store in the refrigerator for up to one month. You can use it to replace fresh chillies in almost any dish. Take care when handling chillies—wear plastic gloves and keep hands away from the eyes.

TRI-COLOUR PASTA SALAD

✦ **Preparation time:** 20 minutes + 1 hour standing
Total cooking time: 10 minutes
Serves 6

2 tablespoons olive oil
2 tablespoons white wine vinegar
1 small garlic clove, halved
375 g (12 oz) tri-colour pasta spirals
1 tablespoon olive oil, extra

3/4 cup sun-dried tomatoes in oil, drained
1/2 cup pitted black olives
105 g (3 1/2 oz) parmesan cheese
1 cup quartered artichoke hearts
1/2 cup shredded fresh basil leaves

1 Combine olive oil, vinegar and garlic in a small screw-top jar. Shake well to mix and allow to stand for 1 hour.
2 Bring a large pan of water to the boil. Slowly add the pasta spirals and cook until just tender. Drain in a colander and toss with extra olive oil while still hot. Allow to cool completely.
3 Cut sun-dried tomatoes into fine strips and cut olives in half. Cut parmesan cheese into paper-thin slices.
4 Place pasta, tomato, olives, cheese, artichokes and basil in a large serving bowl. Remove garlic, pour dressing over. Toss gently to combine.

OPPOSITE PAGE: MEDITERRANEAN SALAD.
ABOVE: TRI-COLOUR PASTA SALAD

GARDEN SALAD

✦ **Preparation time:** 15 minutes
Total cooking time: nil
Serves 8

200 g (6 1/2 oz) mixed green lettuce leaves
125 g (4 oz) red cabbage
1 medium carrot
1 large stick celery
1 small green pepper (capsicum)
1/4 cup (2 fl oz) French dressing

1 Wash and dry lettuce leaves thoroughly; tear into bite-size pieces.
2 Finely shred cabbage; grate carrot and finely slice celery and pepper. Combine in a large serving bowl, add the dressing and toss lightly to combine. Serve immediately.

RED LEAF SALAD

✦ **Preparation time:** 15 minutes
Total cooking time: nil
Serves 6

155 g (5 oz) mixed red lettuce leaves
105 g (3 1/2 oz) fennel bulb, finely sliced

1 small red onion, sliced
2 tablespoons olive oil
1 tablespoon balsamic vinegar

1 Wash and dry lettuce leaves thoroughly, and tear into bite-size pieces.
2 Combine lettuce, fennel and onion in serving bowl. Drizzle oil onto salad, then vinegar. Toss lightly.

Samosa A small savoury snack of Indian origin consisting of a spiced and seasoned mixture of minced (ground) meat and chopped vegetables encased in a semi-circle of pastry and fried in ghee or oil. Samosas should be served hot, accompanied by mint or coriander chutney.

Sandwich In its simplest form a sandwich is a savoury or sweet filling or spread contained between two slices of bread to make an eat-in-the-hand meal. There are many variations, including Danish or open sandwiches, with substantial toppings piled high; rolled sandwiches, with the bread rolled around a filling; ribbon sandwiches made from three layers of bread (alternate slices of white and brown); the club sandwich, also made with three slices of bread; and sandwiches with hot fillings (bacon, roast beef,

grilled steak). In France the name has been adopted for a length of crusty baguette, split open and filled with pâté, ham or cheese. The

---

THAI POTATO SALAD

Preparation time: 15 minutes
Total cooking time: 5 minutes
Serves 8

1 kg (2 lb) baby potatoes
2 tablespoons chopped fresh coriander

Dressing
1 clove garlic
1/4 cup (2 fl oz) lime juice
2 tablespoons oil
2 tablespoons chopped fresh mint
1 tablespoon nam pla (see Note)
2 teaspoons sweet Thai chilli sauce
1 teaspoon sugar

1 Scrub potatoes under cold water. Cut potatoes in half and cook in boiling water for 5 minutes or until just tender. Drain, rinse under cold water and allow to cool.

2 To make Dressing: Crush clove of garlic into a bowl. Add lime juice, oil, chopped fresh mint and coriander, nam pla, chilli sauce and sugar; stir until well combined.

3 Pour mixture into a small screw-top jar; shake for 30 seconds until well mixed. Place potatoes in a bowl, pour dressing over and toss until well combined.

Note: Nam pla is the Thai version of fish sauce. It is available in specialist delicatessens.

BEAN SALAD

Preparation time: 10 minutes
Total cooking time: nil
Serves 6

155 g (5 oz) green beans
315 g (10 oz) can broad (lima) beans
315 g (10 oz) can butter beans
440 g (14 oz) can red kidney beans
1 small red onion, finely sliced
2 tablespoons chopped fresh parsley
2 tablespoons French dressing

1 Top and tail green beans. Cut into 4 cm (1 1/2 inch) lengths and place in a small pan of boiling water. Allow to stand for 1 minute, drain and plunge into iced water. Drain well.

2 Drain canned beans in a colander; rinse well under running water. Leave to drain. Combine beans, onion and parsley in a serving bowl. Pour dressing over; stir to combine.

Note: Any combination of beans can be used for this salad; look for a good contrast in colour and size.

ABOVE: THAI POTATO SALAD, OPPOSITE PAGE, BELOW: QUICK CHICKEN SALAD; ABOVE: CORIANDER SALAD

QUICK CHICKEN SALAD

★ *Preparation time:* 20 minutes
Total cooking time: nil
Serves 4

1 red oak leaf or coral lettuce
1 barbecued chicken
1 medium avocado, thinly sliced
2 sticks celery, cut into 1 cm (1/2 inch) slices
1/4 cup bottled mayonnaise
1/4 cup (2 fl oz) buttermilk
2 teaspoons tarragon vinegar
1/3 cup chopped pecans or walnuts

1 Wash and dry the lettuce thoroughly. Tear into bite-size pieces and arrange on a serving platter or individual plates. Divide the barbecued chicken into pieces, leaving skin on where possible and cutting larger sections so that the pieces are roughly uniform.

2 Arrange half the chicken pieces on the lettuce, top with half the avocado. Repeat with remaining chicken and avocado; scatter celery slices over the top.

3 Place mayonnaise, buttermilk and tarragon vinegar in a small screw-top jar and shake until well combined. Drizzle over salad. Garnish with chopped pecans or walnuts. Serve salad immediately with hot wholemeal bread rolls or crunchy French bread.

CORIANDER SALAD

★ *Preparation time:* 15 minutes +
20 minutes soaking
Total cooking time: 1 minute
Serves 6

1/3 cup burghul (cracked wheat)
2 tablespoons balsamic vinegar
1/2 cup (4 fl oz) orange juice
1 cup fresh coriander leaves
200 g (6 1/2 oz) red cabbage, finely sliced
1 small red onion, finely sliced
1/2 teaspoon honey
1 small clove garlic, crushed
1/4 teaspoon Dijon mustard

1 Place burghul in a small mixing bowl. Heat orange juice in small pan until hot; pour over burghul. Allow to stand for 20 minutes or until all juice is absorbed.

2 Place burghul, coriander, cabbage and onion in a large bowl; mix well.

3 Place honey, vinegar, oil, garlic and mustard in a small jar. Screw lid on tightly and shake vigorously until well combined.

4 Pour dressing over salad, and toss well to coat. Transfer to serving bowl. May be served with grilled or barbecued meat, chicken or fish.

Sapodilla A round fruit with thin, leathery green to brown skin and pale, sweet flesh with a custard-like texture tasting somewhat like soft brown sugar. It can be eaten scooped from the shell, chopped into fruit salad or puréed and added to ice-cream. The sapodilla tree is native to central America and the Caribbean and was taken to the Philippines by the Spanish. A milky latex obtained from its bark is used as the basis for chewing gum.

Sapote A tropical fruit from Central America. The black sapote, also known as the chocolate pudding fruit, is similar in size and shape to a persimmon. It has green skin and soft, sweet, dark brown flesh. It can be eaten scooped straight from the skin, puréed as a sauce or added to ice-cream. The white sapote, also green-skinned, has pale yellow, buttery-textured sweet flesh.

sandwich takes its name from the Earl of Sandwich (1718-92) who, during a long gambling session, asked his man-servant to keep him supplied with sliced beef between two pieces of bread.

SALAD DRESSINGS

A salad dressing is the making of a salad—even a bowl of torn lettuce leaves can taste delicious when tossed with the right dressing. The addition of extra ingredients to a basic vinaigrette or mayonnaise gives the dressings their distinctive flavour and aroma.

The dressing should enhance the flavour of a salad without overpowering its other components. The success of a dressing depends very much on the quality of the ingredients and the subtle balance between them.

■ A good olive oil, not too fruity, is the basis.

■ Vegetable or nut oils can be used in conjunction with olive oil; the distinctive taste of sesame or chilli oil enhances a salad with Asian ingredients.

■ Wine vinegars are made from both red and white wine; herb-flavoured vinegars are delicious when used in moderation, as are fruit vinegars such as raspberry vinegar.

■ Lemon juice can be used in place of some or all of the vinegar.

■ Rice vinegars from China and Japan are sweet and mild and go well with cabbage and carrots.

■ Add dressing to salad just before serving so that leaves don't wilt. Don't drown salads—use just enough dressing to moisten leaves.

VINAIGRETTE

BASIC VINAIGRETTE

In a small screw-top jar, place ¼ cup (2 fl oz) oil, 2 tablespoons white wine vinegar, 1 teaspoon seeded mustard and some freshly ground black pepper to taste. Shake well until evenly mixed. Alternatively, mix in a bowl with a fork or small whisk. Use immediately. This will make ½ cup (4 fl oz) dressing.

VARIATIONS

■ The sharp taste of vinaigrette can be reduced by the addition of ½ teaspoon sugar, if desired.

■ Use freshly squeezed citrus juice instead of vinegar. This is particularly good in poultry or game salads.

■ Add 1 tablespoon of finely chopped fresh herbs such as chives, parsley, marjoram, thyme.

■ As a dressing for shredded raw, green vegetables such as cabbage or spinach, add 1 tablespoon of freshly grated parmesan cheese.

■ The addition of the finely chopped white and sieved yolk of a hard-boiled egg will give the vinaigrette a smoother and thicker texture.

MAYONNAISE

BASIC MAYONNAISE

Place 2 egg yolks, 2–3 teaspoons white vinegar and white pepper to taste in food processor or blender. Process for 15 seconds or until blended. With motor running, add 1 cup (8 fl oz) olive oil slowly in a thin steady stream and blend until mixture is thick and creamy. Adjust the flavour with more vinegar if you wish. If mixture is too thick, lighten its texture by adding a little hot water. This recipe makes approximately 1¼ cups (10 fl oz).

MAYONNAISE SAUCES

Variations to mayonnaise are often used as sauces, particularly with fish dishes, rather than as salad dressings.

AIOLI

Aioli is a Mediterranean sauce which is served with fish soups or vegetables. Combine egg yolks with 3 cloves crushed garlic and 1/2 teaspoon salt in a blender, then proceed as with basic recipe; after oil has been added, adjust flavour with 3–4 teaspoons lemon juice rather than vinegar.

SAUCE TARTARE

Place 1 cup basic mayonnaise in a bowl and stir in 4 tablespoons finely chopped capers, 6 tablespoons chopped gherkins, 2 tablespoons chopped fresh parsley and 2 tablespoons cream or sour cream. Adjust flavour with salt and pepper to taste. Serve with fried or grilled fish.

VARIATIONS

■ A lighter sauce can be made using equal quantities of olive oil and a good vegetable oil.

■ Add the mashed pulp of 1 avocado and fold it gently through the mayonnaise.

■ To make a less rich mayonnaise, add 2–3 tablespoons of natural yoghurt.

■ Add 2 tablespoons tomato paste and 1 tablespoon chopped fresh basil.

■ Mix 2/3 cup thick cream with 2 tablespoons mayonnaise. Serve with salads containing fruit.

THOUSAND ISLAND DRESSING

Thousand Island Dressing is usually served on lettuce leaves. Place mayonnaise in a bowl and stir in 2 teaspoons tomato puree, 1 teaspoon French mustard, a pinch cayenne pepper, 1–2 teaspoons worcestershire sauce, 1 tablespoon finely chopped celery, 1 tablespoon sweet pickle, 1 teaspoon chopped capers, 1 chopped hard-boiled egg, salt and freshly ground black pepper to taste.

SAUCE VERTE

Sauce Verte goes particularly well with fish such as salmon and trout, and with cold egg dishes. Blanch 10 sprigs of watercress in boiling water. With 1 cup basic mayonnaise, blend 1/4 cup cooked spinach leaves, strained and finely chopped, watercress and 4 sprigs each of fresh tarragon and parsley.

GREEN GODDESS DRESSING

Green Goddess Dressing often accompanies shellfish. Make the basic mayonnaise and place in a bowl. Stir in 3–4 chopped anchovy fillets, 1 clove finely chopped garlic, 1/4 cup (2 fl oz) sour cream and 1/4 cup (2 fl oz) chopped fresh mixed herbs.

FROM LEFT: SAUCE TARTARE, RASPBERRY VINEGAR, VIRGIN OLIVE OIL, FRESH HERB VINAIGRETTE, CITRUS VINAIGRETTE, TARRAGON OIL.

Sardine A small, silvery, saltwater fish with tender, strong-flavoured, dark, oily flesh. Fresh sardines are best grilled (broiled) or dusted with flour, quickly pan-fried and served hot with boiled potatoes and a wedge of lemon. The sardine is a member of the herring family. From ancient times in southern Europe it was salted for use in inland areas. In medieval France, sardines were packed into earthenware jars for distribution in areas far from the sea. The fish is named after the Mediterranean island of Sardinia, once centre of a fishing industry based on this small fish. Sardines are available fresh, frozen and canned.

sardines

Sashimi A dish of Japanese origin consisting of slices of raw, very fresh fish cut into small cubes (tuna or salmon) or sliced paper thin (flounder and sea bream), garnished with grated daikon (giant white radish), shredded lettuce.

SALMON

POACHED SALMON CUTLETS

Preparation time: 5 minutes
Total cooking time: 15 minutes
Serves 4

1/4 cup fresh parsley
1/2 cup (4 fl oz) dry white wine
1 1/2 cups (12 fl oz) fish stock
1/2 teaspoon salt
1/2 teaspoon cracked black pepper
pinch ground nutmeg
2 spring onions (scallions), finely chopped
4 salmon cutlets, tail end
2 tablespoons finely chopped fresh parsley, extra

1 Finely chop the fresh parsley.
2 Combine fish stock, salt, pepper, nutmeg, wine and spring onions in a shallow medium pan. Bring ingredients in pan slowly to the boil; boil for 1 minute.
3 Place salmon cutlets in stock in a single layer. Simmer, covered, for 10 minutes. Remove salmon cutlets to serving plates with a slotted spoon; keep warm.
4 Boil the stock for another minute; add chopped fresh parsley. Spoon liquid over the salmon and serve immediately.

SALMON WITH DILL MAYONNAISE

Preparation time: 30 minutes
Total cooking time: 15–20 minutes
Serves 4

1.5 kg (3 lb) whole salmon
2 tablespoons finely chopped fresh dill
2 cups (16 fl oz) fish stock
pepper
1 cup home-made mayonnaise

1 Scale, wash and trim salmon. Place in a fish kettle or large pan. Pour the fish stock over the salmon. Poach till flesh flakes, approximately 15 minutes. Do not turn.
2 Remove salmon and chill well.
3 Place mayonnaise, fresh dill and pepper in a mixing bowl and stir until combined. Transfer mixture to a serving bowl and garnish with a sprig of fresh dill.
4 Skin salmon on one side and serve from each side of the backbone with a spoon and fork.

Note: Use a pair of heavy-duty kitchen scissors to trim away the fins and tail of fish.

ABOVE: POACHED SALMON CUTLETS. OPPOSITE PAGE: SALMON AND CAMEMBERT CROQUETTES

SALMON AND CAMEMBERT CROQUETTES

Preparation time: 40 minutes + 3 hours standing
Total cooking time: 30–35 minutes
Makes 16

3 large potatoes, about 1 kg (2 lb), peeled and chopped	1 tablespoon vinegar
1 small onion, finely chopped	1 egg, lightly beaten
2 x 215 g (7 oz) cans pink salmon, drained and flaked	freshly ground pepper
1 tablespoon chopped fresh parsley	60 g (2 oz) camembert cheese, cubed
2 teaspoons finely grated lemon rind	1/4 cup plain (all-purpose) flour
1/4 cup (2 fl oz) lemon juice	2 eggs, lightly beaten, extra
	ground pepper, extra
	1 1/2 cups fresh white breadcrumbs
	oil, for deep-frying

1 Cook potato in large pan of boiling water until just tender; drain and mash. Transfer to a large mixing bowl. Add onion, salmon, parsley, lemon rind and juice, vinegar, egg and pepper to taste. Stir to combine. Divide mixture into 16 evenly sized portions. Form each portion into a sausage shape about 7 cm (2¾ inches) long, working a

piece of camembert in the centre of each, making sure the camembert is well enclosed.

2 Combine flour and pepper on a sheet of greaseproof paper. Toss the croquettes in the seasoned flour; shake off the excess. Dip in beaten egg, then press into the crumbs to coat them evenly; shake off excess. Store, covered, in the refrigerator for 3 hours.

3 Heat oil in deep, heavy-based pan. Gently lower a few croquettes at a time into moderately hot oil. Cook over medium-high heat for 5 minutes or until golden brown. Carefully remove from oil with tongs. Drain on paper towels and keep warm. Repeat with remaining croquettes. Serve as a first course, an accompaniment or as a main meal with vegetables or salad.

ABOUT SALMON

■ Fresh salmon is available whole, cut into cutlets or fillets. It has a deep pink flesh and is prized for its delectable flavour.

■ Whole salmon is wonderful if poached or baked and can be served hot or cold.

■ Fresh salmon is ideal for marinating and serving raw. Use fresh ginger and herbs to flavour.

■ Pâtés made from salmon look attractive because of the pretty colour. The taste is superb.

■ Canned salmon is very popular for use in cookery and as a sandwich filling.

Sauce A hot or cold seasoned liquid served with a dish to add flavour to it. A sauce may be thick or thin, strained or chunky. Classic French sauces may be based on a roux of butter and flour (béchamel, brown sauce), on a butter emulsion (béarnaise, hollandaise), or on a cold emulsion of oil and egg yolks (mayonnaise); all can be varied with the addition of a great variety of other ingredients. Other sauces are based on pureed vegetables or fruit (coulis), ground

Satay Small morsels of marinated beef, lamb, pork, poultry or seafood, threaded on bamboo or wooden skewers and grilled. Satays are served hot, accompanied by peanut sauce and cubes of cucumber as a first course. Satays are found in the cooking of South-East Asia, especially Indonesia, Malaysia and Singapore, where they are often cooked on small charcoal braziers by street vendors.

cucumber, thin strips of carrot or finely chopped ginger and accompanied by a dipping sauce of wasabi (a pungent horseradish sauce), dark soy sauce and sweet cooking wine. Sashimi is generally served as a first course.

SALMON CUTLETS WITH ORIENTAL MAYONNAISE

✱ **Preparation time:** 10 minutes
Total cooking time: 5 minutes
Serves 4

Oriental Mayonnaise
1 cup home made (or good quality) mayonnaise
2 tablespoons chopped fresh coriander leaves
2 teaspoons finely grated fresh ginger
2 teaspoons honey, warmed

1 teaspoon soy sauce
½ teaspoon sesame oil
3 tablespoons vegetable oil
2 teaspoons balsamic vinegar
freshly ground pepper
4 x 160 g (5¼ oz) salmon cutlets

1 To make Oriental Mayonnaise: Prepare 30 minutes in advance. Place mayonnaise in a small bowl, add remaining ingredients; mix well.

2 Whisk vegetable oil, vinegar and pepper in a shallow dish, add salmon and turn to coat fish.

3 Heat a heavy-based pan until very hot and cook cutlets over high heat for 2–3 minutes each side. Salmon should still be slightly pink and moist in the centre. Serve with Oriental Mayonnaise.

SALMON AND NOODLE BAKE

✱ **Preparation time:** 10 minutes
Total cooking time: 45–50 minutes
Serves 4–5

250 g (8 oz) dried wheat flour noodles
200 g (6½ oz) can red salmon, undrained
1 tomato, peeled and finely chopped
2 teaspoons finely chopped fresh dill
1 tablespoon lemon juice
1 cup finely chopped broccoli
2 eggs, lightly beaten
200 g (6½ oz) ricotta cheese, sieved
3 spring onions (scallions), finely chopped
⅔ cup grated cheddar cheese

1 Cook noodles in large pan of boiling water until just tender; drain; cool. Preheat oven to moderate 180°C (350°F/Gas 4). Remove bones from salmon, mash salmon in bowl using a fork. Add tomato, dill, juice and broccoli; mix well.

2 Combine noodles with eggs, ricotta and onions until well coated. Press half noodle mixture over base of paper-lined and greased 20 cm (8 inch) springform pan. Press salmon mixture over noodles, smooth over with back of spoon. Top with remaining noodle mixture. Sprinkle with cheese, bake for 35 minutes or until golden.

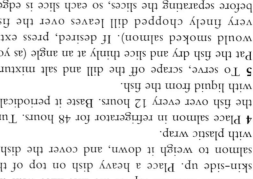

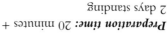

GRAVLAX

✱ **Preparation time:** 20 minutes + 2 days standing
Total cooking time: nil
Serves 8

2 salmon fillets, each about 315–500 g (10–16 oz)
1½ tablespoons sugar
1 teaspoon white pepper
1 cup roughly chopped fresh dill, with stems
3 tablespoons sea salt

1 Wash fillets thoroughly. Do not skin.

2 In a bowl combine salt, sugar and pepper. Mix well. Thoroughly rub salt mixture into each flesh side of the fillets.

3 In a shallow dish place one of the salmon fillets skin-side down. Sprinkle the dill over it. Place the other fillet on top of the first fillet with the skin-side up. Place a heavy dish on top of the salmon to weigh it down, and cover the dishes with plastic wrap.

4 Place salmon in refrigerator for 48 hours. Turn the fish over every 12 hours. Baste it periodically with liquid from the fish.

5 To serve, scrape off the dill and salt mixture. Pat the fish dry and slice thinly at an angle (as you would smoked salmon). If desired, press extra very finely chopped dill leaves over the fish before separating the slices, so each slice is edged with dill. May be served with a mustard sauce, freshly made toast and a green salad.

---

nuts (satay sauce), cooked tomato (ketchup), cream, yoghurt, cream cheeses and oils. Sweet sauces include custards, rich cream sauces and fruit purees. Many sauces are commercially available, either bottled, canned or dry in packets, to be mixed with water, milk or stock.

Sauerbraten A dish of German origin consisting of beef or pork marinated (for one to three days) in a spiced vinegar or red wine mixture, then cooked slowly in the mixture. It is served hot and thinly sliced, traditionally accompanied by the thickened marinade, dumplings and red cabbage.

Sauerkraut White cabbage, sliced water-thin, salted to draw out moisture then fermented in brine for four to six weeks. Braised or stewed (sometimes with additional ingredients such as sliced apple, onion or juniper berries) sauerkraut is the classic accompaniment to roast goose, boiled pork, frankfurter and smoked sausage. Fermented cabbage was eaten by workers on the Great Wall of China more than 2,000 years ago. In

SANDWICHES

OPEN SANDWICH FILLINGS

Open sandwiches must be eaten with a knife and fork (they're much too messy to be eaten with the hands). Because of this they are usually piled high with ingredients and garnished with herbs or nuts.

■ Spread slices of rye or pumpernickel bread with butter. Combine equal quantities of mayonnaise and thick sour cream and add chopped hard-boiled eggs. Pile mixture on bread, top with slices of smoked salmon and a spoonful of salmon roe or black caviar. Garnish with a sprig or two of dill.

■ Spread wholemeal bread with butter and top with lettuce and slices of rare roast beef. Add sliced mango or ripe pawpaw (papaya), a generous spoonful of grain mustard and garnish with watercress or alfalfa.

■ Spread sliced bagels or croissants with butter and top with rocket (arugula) leaves. Mix chopped cooked chicken with mayonnaise, chopped apple, celery and green spring onions (scallions) and pile on top of rocket. Top with pecans before serving.

■ Spread rye or pumpernickel bread with butter, add a lettuce leaf and pile smoked trout on top.

Add a spoonful of horseradish cream and garnish with a tiny slice of lemon and a parsley sprig.

■ Spread rye bread with butter and top with lettuce leaves, sliced tomato and thinly sliced cucumber. Add whole peeled prawns (shrimps), finely sliced red onion rings and a spoonful of tartare sauce.

■ Slice a French baguette diagonally and spread with butter. Top with watercress, lightly coloured green asparagus spears, thinly sliced prosciutto and sliced hard-boiled egg. Add a spoonful of mayonnaise and sprinkle with paprika.

■ Spread wholemeal bread thickly with cottage cheese and top with grated carrot, slices of pastrami or corned beef, sliced pickled dill cucumbers and sliced red pepper (capsicum).

■ Spread split horseshoe rolls with butter and top with lettuce leaves. Top with sliced avocado, sliced tomato and crisply cooked bacon.

■ Spread walnut or cracked wheat bread generously with cream cheese or ricotta cheese and add some sliced fresh pear, sliced fresh figs and finely chopped glacé ginger. Top with a walnut half or two.

■ Spread rye or pumpernickel bread with creamy blue cheese and top with sliced apple and chopped celery. Scatter with chopped spring onions (scallions).

■ Spread rye crispbread with butter and top with shredded lettuce leaves. Add slices of ham, sliced Swiss cheese and sliced tomato. Scatter chopped green spring onions (scallions) on top.

OPPOSITE PAGE: GRAVLAX.
ABOVE: OPEN SANDWICH FILLINGS

---

ancient Gaul, food, including cabbage, was salted for the winter and by medieval times salted, fermented cabbage was a staple throughout central and Eastern Europe.

Sausage Minced meat or poultry, seasoned and mixed with a little ground cereal or crumbed bread and usually stuffed into a tube like casing. Sausages are an ancient way of making sure that every edible part of the carcass was used (including the cleaned intestine, traditionally used as casing). The mixture was often preserved by salting—the word 'sausage' comes from the Latin *salsus*, salted.

Sausage Roll A roll of minced meat, seasoned with herbs and spices, encased in puff or flaky pastry and baked. Sausage rolls are eaten hot as a snack or finger food. They originated as a way of using up leftovers.

Sauté To cook food in a frying pan in a small amount of hot butter or oil until brown.

Scallop A mollusc with a distinctive, ribbed, fan–shaped. hinged shell. It propels itself by using a

Scald To heat a liquid, especially milk, to the temperature when tiny bubbles appear at the edge of the pan. The term also means to plunge fruit or vegetables into boiling water to remove impurities or make peeling easier.

Savory, Summer and Winter Two similar aromatic herbs with a delicate, peppery flavour slightly reminiscent of sage and mint. They are used in stuffings and often added to cooked broad beans. Summer savory, an annual, has silvery green leaves and a sweeter taste. Winter savory is a perennial with stiffer leaves.

Saveloy A small, plump sausage made with pork, seasoned with pepper and garlic and sometimes smoked.

Savarin A large ring–shaped cake made of baba dough without raisins. After cooking, it is soaked with rum–flavoured syrup and the centre filled with crème pâtissière (confectioners custard) or Chantilly cream and fruit.

SARDINES

SARDINES WITH TOMATO SAUCE

Preparation time: 30 minutes
Total cooking time: 15 minutes
Serves 4–6

500 g (1 lb) small fresh sardines
1/2 cup plain (all-purpose) flour
1/2 teaspoon ground pepper
1/3 cup (2 1/2 fl oz) olive oil
lemon and lime wedges for serving, optional

Tomato Sauce
1 tablespoon olive oil
2 cloves garlic, crushed
440 g (14 oz) can tomatoes, crushed
1/4 cup (2 fl oz) white wine
2 tablespoons tomato paste
1/4 cup chopped fresh basil

1 **To make Tomato Sauce:** Heat oil in medium pan; add garlic. Cook over low heat for 2 minutes. Add tomato, white wine, tomato paste and basil. Simmer, uncovered, for 10 minutes.

2 Cut heads from sardines and discard. Clean and rinse body under cold running water, pat dry.

3 Combine flour and pepper in bowl. Toss sardines lightly in seasoned flour. Shake off excess. Heat oil in a medium pan; add sardines. Cook over medium heat for 2 minutes each side. Drain on paper towels.

4 Place sardines on large serving plate, top with Tomato Sauce and serve immediately with lemon and lime wedges if desired.

FRIED SARDINES WITH SAMBUCA

Preparation time: 15 minutes
Total cooking time: 3 minutes
Serves 4

8 large sardines
2 tablespoons grated parmesan cheese
plain (all-purpose) flour for dusting
2 eggs, lightly beaten
2 tablespoons sambuca
freshly ground black pepper
60 g (2 oz) butter
lemon wedges
fresh parsley

1 Cut heads from sardines. Cut along underside of fish, open out, press flat. With skin side up, press along backbone, pull backbone away. Wash, drain.
2 Dust sardines with flour. Combine eggs, sambuca, parsley, cheese and pepper. Add fish; toss to coat.
3 Melt butter in frying pan and add sardines in a single layer. Fry on both sides for 1 minute or until lightly browned. Drain on paper towels. Serve with lemon wedges.

Note: Sambuca is an Italian liqueur with the taste of aniseed. It is usually drunk with two coffee beans floating in the glass.

ABOVE: SARDINES WITH TOMATO SAUCE.
OPPOSITE PAGE, BELOW: COCONUT LAMB SATAYS; ABOVE: PORK SATAYS.

HERBED SARDINES

Preparation time: 10 minutes
Total cooking time: 5 minutes
Serves 2–4

2 x 105 g (3 1/2 oz) cans sardines
60 g (2 oz) butter
2 teaspoons lemon juice
1 clove garlic, crushed
2 tablespoons chopped mixed fresh herbs (parsley, chervil, lemon thyme, chives)
4 large slices brioche, French or Italian bread
freshly ground pepper

1 Drain sardines well and pat gently with paper towels to remove excess oil.
2 Beat butter in a small bowl until very soft and add chopped mixed herbs, garlic, lemon juice and pepper.
3 Toast brioche or bread slices on one side until golden. Arrange sardines on untoasted side. Carefully spread butter mixture over sardines and grill until butter is melted and sardines are hot. Serve immediately.

PORK SATAYS

★ **Preparation time:** 30 minutes +
overnight marinating
Total cooking time: 8 minutes
Makes 8 satays

750 g (1½ lb) pork fillets
1 large onion, roughly
   chopped
2 cloves garlic
1 stick lemongrass, thick
   base only, chopped, or
2 strips lemon rind
2 thick slices galangal,
   optional
1 teaspoon chopped fresh
   ginger

1 teaspoon ground cumin
½ teaspoon ground fennel
1 tablespoon ground
   coriander
1 teaspoon turmeric
½ teaspoon salt
1 tablespoon soft dark
   brown sugar
1 tablespoon lemon juice,
   malt vinegar or
   tamarind liquid

1 Place pork fillets in freezer for about 30 minutes or until fillets are firm enough to make slicing easy. Trim meat of any fat and sinew. Slice pork across the grain into very thin, even strips. Place the onion in a food processor or blender and process until smooth. Add garlic cloves and lemongrass. Process until smooth, adding a little water, if necessary. Transfer onion mixture to a large bowl.
2 Stir in the galangal, ginger, cumin, fennel, coriander, turmeric, salt, sugar and lemon juice. Add meat, stir well to combine. Store, covered, in the refrigerator overnight, turning occasionally. Drain, reserving marinade.

COCONUT LAMB SATAYS

★ **Preparation time:** 10 minutes +
2 hours standing
Total cooking time: 3 minutes
Serves 4

4 lamb leg chops, about
   800 g (1 lb 10 oz)
1 small onion
1 clove garlic, crushed
¼ cup desiccated coconut
2 tablespoons oil
1 teaspoon sesame oil

1 tablespoon light soy
   sauce
1 teaspoon sambal oelek
1 tablespoon tamarind
   sauce
1 tablespoon vinegar

1 Remove fat and bones from lamb chops and cut meat into 2 cm (¾ inch) cubes.
2 Chop onion. Place in a bowl and combine with lamb cubes, garlic, tamarind sauce, soy sauce, sambal oelek and coconut. Cover and leave to marinate in refrigerator for 2 hours or overnight.
3 Thread lamb onto skewers, brush with combined oils and cook under a preheated grill for 3 minutes, turning occasionally.

3 Thread the meat on long bamboo skewers. Cover the ends with foil to prevent burning. Place skewers on a cold, lightly oiled grill. Cook under medium-high heat until tender. Turn skewers occasionally, basting with reserved marinade several times.

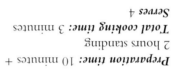

Scaloppine A small thin slice of boneless veal cut across the grain and flattened (in France known as escalope, in Germany as Schnitzel, used in the famous dish Wienerschnitzel). The term 'scaloppine' is often extended to include a dish of northern Italian origin in which the slices are coated in flour, fried in butter or oil and served with a tomato or wine sauce.

Scampi The Italian name for a large marine prawn (shrimp) with long, thin claws. When cooked they have delicately flavoured white flesh and are often served cooked in butter, garlic, white wine and herbs or fried in batter (scampi fritti). The French name is langoustine.

large muscle to successively open and shut its shell; it is this muscle, creamy-white to creamy-pink in colour, that is eaten—the pinky-orange roe, also edible, is sometimes discarded. Scallops are generally cooked and served on the shell. Cold poached scallops can feature in a seafood salad.

CLASSIC SAUCES

Sauces are used to flavour, coat or accompany a dish; some are used to bind the ingredients together. A fine, smooth, well-flavoured sauce will improve both the taste and appearance of the dish with which it is served.

Here are six basic sauces. Once the techniques of preparation are mastered, the range of variations is almost endless.

BASIC WHITE SAUCE

Melt 30 g (1 oz) unsalted (sweet) butter in a small heavy-based pan, blend in 30 g (1 oz) plain (all-purpose) flour and cook mixture gently for 1 minute, whisking continuously. Remove pan from heat; gradually whisk in 300 ml (9 fl oz) of lukewarm milk. Bring the mixture slowly to the boil and continue cooking gently, whisking all the time, until the sauce comes to the boil and thickens. Simmer the sauce very gently for another 2–3 minutes. Season sauce with salt and white ground pepper. Makes 300 ml (9 fl oz). Serve over vegetables, such as cauliflower and broccoli, or with fish, shellfish, or corned beef.

VARIATIONS

■ **MORNAY (CHEESE) SAUCE:** Follow the basic recipe but before seasoning, stir in 60 g (2 oz) finely grated gruyère or cheddar, 1 teaspoon Dijon mustard and a pinch of cayenne pepper.

■ **CAPER SAUCE:** Follow basic recipe, using half milk and half meat stock. Before seasoning, add 1 tablespoon capers and 1–2 teaspoons lemon juice. Reheat gently.

■ **BÉCHAMEL SAUCE:** For this classic French sauce, place the milk in a pan with a slice of onion, ½ stick celery and ½ carrot, both chopped, a bay leaf and 3 black peppercorns. Bring slowly to the boil, remove from heat, cover and set aside to infuse for 30 minutes. Strain, reserving the milk, and proceed as for basic recipe.

BÉARNAISE SAUCE

Put into a pan 4 tablespoons white wine vinegar, 2 finely chopped spring onions (scallions) and a few chopped tarragon sprigs. Boil gently until liquid has reduced by one-third. Set aside to cool, then strain into a heatproof bowl or the top of a double boiler. Add 2 egg yolks to vinegar and heat over gently simmering water. Whisk until thick and smooth. Gradually add 125 g (4 oz) softened butter, a small piece at a time, whisking until each piece has been absorbed and sauce has thickened. Season. Serve warm. Makes 200 ml (6 fl oz). Serve with steak, chicken, or fried fish.

HOLLANDAISE SAUCE

Melt 185 g (6 oz) unsalted (sweet) butter in a small pan. Skim froth from top and discard. Allow melted butter to cool, but not re-set. Combine 2 tablespoons water and 4 egg yolks in a small, heavy-based pan; whisk 30 seconds or until pale and creamy. Place pan over low heat and continue whisking for 3 minutes, until mixture is thick. Remove from heat and add cooled butter a little at a time, whisking after each addition. (Discard whey in bottom of the pan.) Stir in 2 tablespoons lemon juice, season to taste. Serve warm. Makes 250 ml (8 fl oz). Serve with asparagus, broccoli, poached eggs (Eggs Benedict), poached or grilled fish.

VARIATIONS

■ **MOUSSELINE:** Stir 3 tablespoons thick cream into sauce just before serving.
■ **LIGHTER HOLLANDAISE:** Just before serving, fold in 2 stiffly beaten egg whites.
■ **SAUCE MALTAISE:** Stir in grated rind of 1 orange and 4 tablespoons of orange juice in place of lemon juice.

BEURRE BLANC

Place 1 cup (8 fl oz) white wine and 1 tablespoon finely chopped spring onions (scallions) in small heavy-based pan. Boil to reduce to 2 tablespoons. Remove from heat. Cut 250 g (8 oz) chilled butter into small cubes. Add 2 cubes to wine mixture, whisk in vigorously. Return pan to low heat and continue whisking in butter, a piece at a time. The sauce will thicken to the consistency of runny cream. Remove from heat. Makes 250 ml (8 fl oz). Serve with grilled fish or asparagus.

RICH TOMATO SAUCE

Heat 2 tablespoons olive oil in a heavy-based pan, add 1 finely chopped onion and cook over medium heat for 5 minutes, until onion is lightly golden, stirring occasionally. Add 2 cloves crushed garlic and cook for 1 minute. Add 1 tablespoon red wine vinegar and 1 kg (2 lb) large ripe tomatoes which have been peeled and chopped; bring to boil. Reduce heat to low and simmer, uncovered, for 25 minutes, stirring occasionally. Add ¼ cup (2 fl oz) tomato paste, 1 teaspoon sugar, 1 teaspoon dried basil leaves and 1 teaspoon dried oregano leaves. Simmer 15 minutes, stirring often. Use as a topping for pizza or a sauce with pasta, or serve warm with sausages or steak. Makes 1½ cups (12 fl oz).

SAUCE ESPAGNOLE

Melt 125 g (4 oz) butter in large pan. Add 60 g (2 oz) each finely chopped celery, carrot, onion and bacon. Stir over medium heat 10 minutes or until well browned. Add 2 tablespoons plain (all-purpose) flour. Stir over low heat 8–10 minutes or until browned. Remove from heat; blend in 2 litres (8 cups) beef stock and 2–3 tablespoons tomato paste. Add a bouquet garni. Simmer, partially covered, over low heat for 1½ hours, skimming off surface regularly, or until liquid has reduced by about half. Remove from heat. Add salt and pepper to taste. Strain and reheat. Makes 2 cups (16 fl oz). Serve with grilled steak, cutlets, roasted game or vegetables. To make a richer sauce, stir in 1 tablespoon of sherry or Madeira.

CLOCKWISE FROM TOP LEFT: BEARNAISE SAUCE, RICH TOMATO SAUCE, BECHAMEL SAUCE, SAUCE MALTAISE, HOLLANDAISE SAUCE. CENTRE: SAUCE ESPAGNOLE

Schnitzel See Scaloppine.

Scone A small plain cake made from a simple flour and milk dough raised with baking powder or bicarbonate of soda (baking soda); in North America such a cake is known by the term 'biscuit', and the term 'scone' refers to a plain or sweet quick bread made from a richer dough that usually contains egg. Scones are served freshly baked, split in half, with butter or cream and jam or honey as a light mid-morning or mid-afternoon meal; scones with clotted cream and strawberry jam are the basis of Devonshire tea. Dried fruit can be added to the dough or, for a savoury scone, flavourings can include onion, cheese or herbs. In North America scones (biscuits) are often served as an accompaniment to a meal or may be split open to sandwich fillings such as smoked turkey and ham. Scones originated in Scotland and were originally cooked on a griddle (a thick flat iron with a handle).

Score To make small incisions on the outer

SAUCES SWEET

CARAMEL SAUCE

Bring 1 cup (8 fl oz) water to boil in medium pan. Add 1 cup sugar and stir until dissolved. Return pan to heat and bring to the boil. Cook rapidly (without stirring) until golden brown, occasionally brushing sugar crystals from inside of pan with a pastry brush dipped in cold water. Place pan in a sink and, with hand covered with a towel, add ½ cup (4 fl oz) water to pan. (Mixture will splatter.) Return pan to heat and stir until caramel is dissolved. Chill sauce before serving.

VANILLA CREAM SAUCE

Heat 1 cup (8 fl oz) cream and ½ cup (4 fl oz) milk in a medium pan until almost boiling. Using electric beaters beat 3 egg yolks, 1 teaspoon cornflour (cornstarch) and 2 tablespoons caster (superfine) sugar in a small bowl and pour hot cream mixture over yolks while beating. Return mixture to pan and heat gently while stirring to a smooth sauce. (Do not boil.) Strain sauce into a cold bowl; add ½ teaspoon vanilla essence, chill.

RUM OR BRANDY SAUCE

Using electric beaters beat 1 egg yolk and 2 tablespoons caster (superfine) sugar in a small bowl until light in colour. Stir in 2 tablespoons rum or brandy and ½ cup (4 fl oz) lightly whipped cream. Fold in 1 stiffly beaten egg white. Serve within 30 minutes of preparing.

HOT FUDGE SAUCE

Break 105 g (3½ oz) dark (semi-sweet) chocolate into pieces and place in a small pan with 30 g (1 oz) butter, 2 tablespoons corn syrup, ½ cup soft brown sugar and ½ cup (4 fl oz) cream. Stir over low heat until ingredients have melted. Bring to boil and remove from heat. Serve warm or hot.

STRAWBERRY SAUCE

Place 250 g (8 oz) hulled strawberries in a blender with 2 tablespoons caster (superfine) sugar and 1 tablespoon lemon or orange juice. Blend until smooth; strain if desired. Chill before serving.

HARD SAUCE

Beat 125 g (4 oz) unsalted (sweet) butter in a bowl until soft. Gradually add 2 cups sifted icing (confectioners) sugar and beat until mixture is light and creamy. Beat in 1 tablespoon brandy, whisky or rum. Cover, refrigerate until firm.

BUTTERSCOTCH SAUCE

Place 60 g (2 oz) butter in a medium pan with 1 cup soft brown sugar, 1 cup (8 fl oz) cream and 2 tablespoons golden syrup (light corn syrup). Heat gently while stirring until smooth. Bring to the boil and simmer sauce for 1 minute. Cool.

ABOVE: ICE-CREAM SUNDAE WITH STRAWBERRY SAUCE. OPPOSITE: BLACK PUDDING WITH CABBAGE AND APPLE

Scottish Food

Scottish Food Scotland is popularly identified with the uncomplicated and sustaining foods needed before facing its bracing air. Steaming porridge, warming broths, oatmeal cakes and haggis—traditional fare of Highland crofting communities—are a response to the climate which, although inhospitable in so many ways, is ideal for growing oats. The region is also the home of some exceptionally fine food, based on high quality local ingredients and in its preparation showing the influence of the old alliance between Scotland and France—for centuries the kitchens of

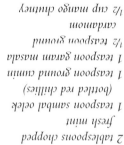

surface of a food in order to decorate it, to allow the penetration of a marinade, or in the case of some fruits (such as an apple) to prevent the skin from splitting during baking.

Scotch Egg A hard-boiled egg, shelled and encased in sausage mince, coated with breadcrumbs and deep-fried. Scotch eggs may be eaten hot or cold.

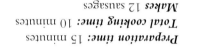

BARBECUED BEEF AND MINT SAUSAGES

★ *Preparation time:* 15 minutes
Total cooking time: 10 minutes
Makes 12 sausages

750 g (1½ lb) beef mince
250 g (8 oz) sausage mince
2 tablespoons cornflour (cornstarch)
1 egg, lightly beaten
1 medium onion, finely chopped
2 cloves garlic, crushed
2 tablespoons chopped fresh mint
1 teaspoon sambal oelek (bottled red chillies)
1 teaspoon ground cumin
1 teaspoon garam masala
½ teaspoon ground cardamom
½ cup mango chutney

1 Combine minced beef and sausage mince in a bowl. Add cornflour, egg, onion, garlic, mint, sambal oelek, cumin, garam masala and cardamom; mix well.
2 Divide mixture into 12 even-sized portions. Using wet hands, mould each portion into sausage shapes.
3 Place sausages on lightly oiled preheated grill or flatplate. Cook on medium heat for 10 minutes or until cooked through, turning occasionally during cooking. Serve with mango chutney, and peas and mashed potato if desired.

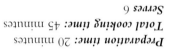

SPICY SAUSAGE AND BACON PAELLA

★ *Preparation time:* 20 minutes
Total cooking time: 45 minutes
Serves 6

4 chorizo or other spicy sausages, sliced
4 rashers bacon, chopped diagonally
1 medium onion, sliced
1 medium green capsicum (pepper), sliced
1 clove garlic, crushed
black pepper to taste
1 teaspoon turmeric
¾ cup chicken stock
440 g (14 oz) canned tomatoes
1½ cups long-grain rice

1 Cook the sausages and bacon in a large pan until they are quite well browned (this should take about 5 minutes). Remove them from the pan and drain on paper towels.
2 Add the onion, capsicum, garlic and rice to the pan. Cook over medium heat, stirring, for 3 minutes.
3 Add the canned tomatoes with their juice and stir well. Add the stock, turmeric and pepper and stir to combine. Carefully cover the pan with a tight-fitting lid.
4 Bring slowly to the boil; stir once. Reduce the heat and simmer, covered, for 25 minutes or until the liquid is almost absorbed and the rice is tender. Add the sausage and bacon mixture and heat through. Season with salt and pepper.

BLACK PUDDING WITH CABBAGE AND APPLE

★ *Preparation time:* 15 minutes
Total cooking time: 20–25 minutes
Serves 4

2 rashers bacon
500 g (1 lb) black pudding, peeled and sliced
2 tart green apples, peeled and sliced
2 tablespoons stock
30 g (1 oz) butter
1 small onion, diced
3 cups shredded cabbage
ground pepper
buttered toast, to serve

1 Remove the rind from the bacon and cut into strips. Skin black pudding and cut diagonally into 1.5 cm (⅝ inch) thick slices.
2 Heat butter in pan. Add bacon, cook for 2–3 minutes and remove. Add black pudding to pan, cook for 5 minutes, remove and keep warm.
3 Cook diced onion for 1 minute, add bacon, cabbage, apple, stock and pepper. Cover and cook gently for about 10–15 minutes.
4 Arrange cabbage mixture over base of a serving plate. Top with warm black pudding and serve with toast.

soup, may be served over a boiled potato as the main course) and fish (such as meat

it is a thick broth or a includes soup (which, if at midday and usually meal of the day is taken or coffee. The main with marmalade and tea oatcakes or warm baps milk), followed by toast, and delicious poached in the north-eastern coast finnan haddie (smoked haddock, a specialty of kippers or perhaps fish, ham and eggs, or fresh without sugar), fried (traditionally eaten oatmeal porridge cooked breakfast of begins with a nourishing In Scotland the day

cakes.
North America) and known as biscuits in buns, scones (small cakes are delicious breads, more widely used, there flour has always been Edinburgh, where wheat cities of Glasgow and Lowlands and the

In the venison and hare. the forests and fields heaths supply grouse and salmon and trout, the estate streams teem with rich sauces and pastries; game braised in wine, such as cream soups, have produced dishes Highland landed gentry

PORK SAUSAGE BURGER WITH MUSTARD CREAM

★ **Preparation time:** 20 minutes
Total cooking time: 10 minutes

Serves 6

1 kg (2 lb) pork mince	**Mustard Cream**
1 small onion, finely chopped	1/2 cup (4 fl oz) sour cream
1 cup fresh breadcrumbs	1 tablespoon wholegrain mustard
2 cloves garlic, crushed	2 teaspoons lemon juice
1 egg, lightly beaten	
1 teaspoon dried sage	
6 long crusty bread rolls	

1 Prepare and heat barbecue. Place mince in large mixing bowl. Add onion, breadcrumbs, garlic, egg and sage. Using hands, mix to combine thoroughly. Divide the mixture into 6 equal portions; shape into sausage shapes about 16 cm (6½ inches) long.

2 Place burgers on hot, lightly oiled barbecue flatplate or grill. Barbecue for 5–10 minutes, turning occasionally.

3 Place burgers on a long crusty roll with Mustard Cream. Garnish with chives and serve with a salad, if desired.

4 To make Mustard Cream: Place sour cream, wholegrain mustard and juice in a small bowl and stir to combine.

CHICKEN AND CORN SAUSAGES WITH SALSA CRUDA

★ **Preparation time:** 20 minutes + refrigeration
Total cooking time: 35 minutes

Makes 12

800 g (1 lb 10 oz) chicken mince	**Salsa Cruda**
1 cup fresh breadcrumbs	2 large tomatoes, finely chopped
125 g (4 oz) can creamed corn	1 medium onion, finely chopped
1 tablespoon fresh chives, finely chopped	1 clove garlic, crushed
1/4 cup cornmeal	2 tablespoons fresh coriander, finely chopped
	1 tablespoon orange juice

1 Preheat oven to moderate 180°C (350°F/Gas 4). Line an oven tray with aluminium foil and brush lightly with oil. Place mince, breadcrumbs, corn, chives and cornmeal in a large mixing bowl and combine thoroughly. Divide into 12 equal portions and shape into sausages about 13 cm (5 inches) long. Mixture will be quite moist.

2 To make Salsa Cruda: Combine all ingredients in a bowl; refrigerate for at least 1 hour. Serve at room temperature.

3 Place sausages on prepared tray; bake 35 minutes, turning occasionally. Serve with Salsa Cruda.

HERBED SCALLOP KEBABS

Serves 8
Preparation time: 1 hour
Total cooking time: 5–10 minutes

24 scallops
6 large spring onions (scallions), green part only
2 zucchini (courgettes)
2 medium carrots
15 g (1 oz) butter, melted
2 teaspoons lemon juice
1 tablespoon white wine
2 teaspoons mixed dried herbs
1/4 teaspoon onion powder

1 Wash scallops and remove vein; pat dry with paper towels. Cut spring onion greens in half lengthways, then into 8 cm (3 inch) lengths. Line an oven tray with aluminium foil. Using a vegetable peeler, slice zucchini and carrots lengthways into thin ribbons. Plunge vegetable strips into a bowl of boiling water; leave 2 minutes; drain, then plunge in bowl of ice water. When cold, drain. Pat dry with paper towels.

2 Roll a scallop in a strip of onion, carrot and zucchini and secure with a small skewer. Repeat this process with remaining scallops and vegetables. Cover exposed ends of skewers with foil to prevent burning.

OPPOSITE PAGE, ABOVE: PORK SAUSAGE BURGER WITH MUSTARD CREAM; BELOW: CHICKEN AND CORN SAUSAGES WITH SALSA CRUDA.
ABOVE: HERBED SCALLOP KEBABS

SCALLOP SALAD WITH LIME AND GINGER

Serves 4
Preparation time: 20 minutes
Total cooking time: 2 minutes

410 g (13 oz) scallops
1/2 teaspoon honey
3 medium zucchini (courgettes), cut into matchsticks
1 tablespoon peanut oil
1/4 cup (2 fl oz) peanut oil, extra
1 tablespoon lime juice
2 medium carrots, cut into matchsticks
1 teaspoon grated fresh ginger
2 spring onions (scallions), cut in 1 cm (1/2 inch) diagonal slices
1 tablespoon chopped fresh coriander

1 Wash scallops and remove brown vein. Pat dry with paper towels. Heat oil in heavy-based pan, add scallops. Cook on high heat 2 minutes or until golden, turning once. Remove from pan and keep warm.

2 Place extra peanut oil, lime juice, ginger, coriander and honey in a small screw-top jar. Shake well.

3 Arrange a bed of vegetables on a serving platter or individual plates. Pile scallops on top, pour dressing over and serve immediately.

3 Combine butter, juice and wine in a small mixing bowl. Brush over the scallops. Sprinkle with combined herbs and onion powder. Place under hot grill 5–10 minutes or until scallops are tender and cooked through.

---

trout, salmon, haddock, halibut or cod), meat (beef or lamb), game or meats prepared in sausages (such as haggis), pies or black puddings. Steamed and baked puddings or fruit tarts (especially berry) complete the meal. A light supper, called 'high tea', of foods such as cold meats, shepherd's pie, fish and chips or bacon and eggs is eaten in the evening. Cakes, scones, buns and biscuits (cookies) are always on hand, and specialties include butter-rich shortbread and the almond encrusted Dundee cake. The national drink, of course, is whisky.

Seafood A collective term for edible fish and shellfish. A mixture of seafood, usually including squid (calamari), peeled prawns (shrimp), crab meat and baby octopus is often sold under the name 'marinara mix' and is used for adding to a tomato sauce for spaghetti marinara or to make a seafood pizza. A mixture of two or three types of seafood is often served accompanied by a mayonnaise-based sauce and bread and butter.

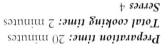
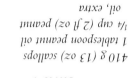

CHIVE SCONES (BISCUITS) WITH BACON BUTTER

★ *Preparation time:* 12 minutes + 30 minutes standing
Total cooking time: 25 minutes
Makes 32

Bacon Butter
90 g (3 oz) butter, softened
2 teaspoons bacon chips

Chive and Onion Scones
3 cups self-raising flour
40 g (1 1/3 oz) sachet French onion soup mix
60 g (2 oz) butter
1 cup (8 fl oz) milk
1 egg yolk
2 tablespoons freshly chopped chives
2 tablespoons milk, extra

1 To make Bacon Butter: Combine butter and bacon chips in a bowl; mix well. Store, covered with plastic wrap in refrigerator, for 30 minutes.
2 Preheat oven to hot 240°C (475°F/Gas 9). Line a 32 x 28 cm (13 x 11 inch) oven tray with baking paper. Place flour, soup mix and butter in food processor. Using pulse action, press button for 15 seconds. Add milk, yolk and chives to bowl, process 5 seconds or until mixture almost forms a dough.
3 Turn dough onto a lightly floured surface; knead for 30 seconds. Press mixture evenly into a floured shallow 30 x 20 cm (12 x 8 inch) rectangular tin. Turn out onto a floured board. Using a sharp knife, cut dough into 32 pieces. Brush tops with extra milk.
4 Arrange pieces spaced evenly apart on prepared oven tray. Bake for 10 minutes. Reduce

temperature to moderately hot 210°C (415°F/Gas 6-7), and bake for another 15 minutes, or until scones are well risen and browned. Serve warm with chilled bacon butter.

DEVONSHIRE SCONES (BISCUITS)

★ *Preparation time:* 15 minutes
Total cooking time: 15-20 minutes
Makes 15

3 cups self-raising flour
1 cup (8 fl oz) milk
2 tablespoons sugar
beaten egg, for glaze
55 g (1 3/4 oz) butter, chopped
strawberry jam and whipped cream, to serve

1 Preheat oven to moderately hot 210°C (415°F/Gas 6-7). Brush a baking tray with oil. Sift flour into mixing bowl, add sugar. Using your fingertips, rub in butter until mixture resembles breadcrumbs. Make a well in the centre and pour in milk, mix to form a soft, slightly sticky dough.
2 Turn onto a floured surface and knead lightly. Pat or roll to a thickness of 2 cm (3/4 inch). Cut into 6 cm (2 1/2 inch) rounds with a cutter and place close together on prepared tray.
3 Brush scones with beaten egg. Bake for 15-20 minutes. Serve hot, with jam and cream.

LEFT: DEVONSHIRE SCONES
ABOVE: CITRUS ROUND
OPPOSITE PAGE: POTATO SCONES

404

Sear To quickly brown the surface of a food, usually meat, using a very high heat. It is done to seal in the juices.

Seasoning An ingredient added to a food to heighten its natural flavour.

Sea Urchin A marine animal with a soft body encased in a hard, spherical shell with radiating needle-sharp spines; it is an echinoderm, not a mollusc. The edible part is the bright red-orange roe, which has a salty taste and the consistency of raw egg.

Semolina A food made by coarsely grinding hard durum wheat. Semolina is used to make milk puddings, cakes, custards and biscuits (cookies). Semolina flour, milled from the heart of durum wheat, is used to make pasta.

Sesame Oil A strongly flavoured amber-coloured oil pressed from roasted sesame seeds. It is used in Chinese cooking, mainly as a flavouring; in Japan sesame oil is blended with other oils to fry tempura. When heated sesame oil loses

CITRUS ROUND

★

Preparation time: 20 minutes
Total cooking time: 20 minutes
Makes 8 wedges

2 cups self-raising flour
2 teaspoons grated lemon rind
60 g (2 oz) butter
2 tablespoons chopped mixed peel
1 tablespoon caster (superfine) sugar
1 egg, beaten lightly
1/3 cup wheatgerm
1 tablespoon lemon juice
3 tablespoons milk

1 Preheat oven to very hot 220°C (425°F/Gas 7). Sift flour into a large bowl, add butter and rub in lightly with fingertips. Mix in mixed peel, sugar, lemon rind and wheatgerm.

2 Combine egg, lemon juice and milk. Make a well in the centre of the flour and pour in liquid all at once. Mix quickly to form a soft dough. Turn onto floured surface (use self-raising flour) and knead lightly.

3 Shape dough into a round approximately 20 cm (8 inches) in diameter and place on a greased tray. With a floured knife, cut completely through to the bottom to form eight wedges. Glaze top with a little milk.

4 Bake round for 20 minutes. Cool on a wire rack for 5 minutes and serve with butter and marmalade.

POTATO SCONES (BISCUITS)

★

Preparation time: 20 minutes
Total cooking time: 15–20 minutes
Makes 8 large scones

1 1/2 cups self-raising flour
3/4–1 cup (6–8 fl oz) milk
1 cup cold, mashed potato
1/2 cup coarsely grated tasty cheese
30 g (1 oz) butter

1 Preheat oven to 200°C (400°F/Gas 6). Grease an oven tray with melted butter or margarine; dust with flour. Sift flour into a bowl. Add the mashed potato and stir to combine. Add the butter and milk and mix to form a soft dough. Turn onto a lightly floured surface.

2 Knead dough lightly. Divide into eight portions. Roll each portion into a thin roll approximately 25 cm (10 inches) long. Shape the rolls into knots. Place on prepared tray.

3 Brush the tops of the knots with the remaining milk and sprinkle with the grated cheese. Bake 15–20 minutes until scones are golden and cooked through. Serve scones warm, spread with butter.

Note: Potato scones are delicious served with a hearty casserole.

much of its flavour. Cleopatra is said to have used it as a skin oil; thirteenth-century Venetian traveller Marco Polo praised it as the best oil he tasted during his journeys. Sesame oil is available from supermarkets and Asian food stores.

Sesame Seeds Also known as benne seeds, the small oval seeds of a semi-tropical plant. Lightly toasted seeds can be tossed through salads, vegetable dishes, stuffings and stews; raw seeds are often sprinkled on bread, buns and biscuits (cookies) before baking. In the Middle East ground sesame seeds are used to make the confectionery (candy) halva and the dressing tahini. In Africa the seeds are roasted and eaten like peanuts and are also ground into a flour. In Japan and Korea freshly roasted then lightly crushed seeds are added to dips and dressings; in China whole roasted seeds are used as a garnish and are ground into a brown and nutty flavoured paste.

Shallot A small onion, similar in shape to a clove of garlic, with a reddish-brown skin and purple-tinged white flesh and with a mild flavour. Shallot bulbs and leaves are used raw, finely

...chopped in salads, and are cooked; they are widely used in the cooking of northern France to flavour sauces and casseroles.

Shashlik The Russian name for cubes of mutton or lamb marinated in vinegar and oil flavoured with thyme, nutmeg, onion and bay leaf, then grilled (broiled). Shashlik is similar to the Middle-Eastern kebab.

Shellfish An edible water animal with a shell or carapace. There are three main classes: crustaceans, including lobsters, crabs, prawns and (shrimps) crayfish; molluscs, including oysters, scallops, mussels, clams and whelks; and cephalopods (with a reduced internal shell and technically classed as molluscs) namely, squid, cuttlefish and octopus.

Shepherd's Pie A dish consisting of finely chopped or minced (ground) cooked lamb, seasoned with worcestershire sauce, thickened with flour and fried onion and stock, simmered; the mixture is transferred to a pie dish, topped with mashed potato and then browned under a grill.

SCOTTISH CLASSICS

SCOTCH BROTH

★ *Preparation time:* 25 minutes + overnight soaking
Total cooking time: 2 hours
Serves 4–6

1/4 cup dried peas (blue boilers)	1 large carrot, cut into 1 cm (1/2 inch) cubes
2 tablespoons pearl barley	1 stick celery, sliced
6 lamb neck chops, (750 g/1 1/2 lb)	2 cups shredded cabbage
1.5 litres (6 cups) water	salt, pepper
1 leek, cut into 2 cm (3/4 inch) pieces	1/4 cup chopped fresh parsley
1 turnip, cut into 1 cm (1/2 inch) cubes	

1 Place whole dried peas (blue boilers) in a large bowl. Cover with warm water; stand, uncovered, overnight. Rinse peas twice and drain thoroughly.

2 Place peas, barley, chops and water in a large heavy-based pan. Bring to boil, skim froth from the top. Add leek and turnip. Reduce heat to low and simmer, covered, for 1 1/2 hours.

3 Add carrot and celery to pan. Simmer, uncovered, for another 30 minutes.

4 Add cabbage. Stir until cabbage is just heated through and tender. Season to taste. Stir in parsley just before serving.

OATCAKES

★ *Preparation time:* 5 minutes
Total cooking time: 25 minutes
Makes 25

1 cup fine oatmeal	1 teaspoon caster (superfine) sugar
1 cup medium oatmeal	1/2 teaspoon baking powder
1/2 teaspoon salt	60 g (2 oz) lard, melted
	1/2 cup (4 fl oz) warm water
	extra oatmeal

1 Preheat oven to moderate 180°C (350°F/Gas 4). Line two 32 x 28 cm (13 x 11 inch) oven trays with baking paper. Combine oatmeals, baking powder, salt and sugar in a large mixing bowl. Make a well in the centre; add lard and water.

2 Using a flat-bladed knife, work mixture into a firm dough. Turn dough out onto a surface lightly sprinkled with fine oatmeal; press into a flattish square.

3 Roll out to a 30 x 30 cm (12 x 12 inch) square, about 2.5 mm (1/8 inch) thick, sprinkling with extra oatmeal if necessary. Cut into 6 cm (2 1/2 inch) diamonds. Repeat with leftover dough.

4 Place oatcakes on trays about 5 mm (1/4 inch) apart; bake 25 minutes. Allow to cool on trays. Serve warm with butter.

LEFT: SCOTCH BROTH. ABOVE: OATCAKES
OPPOSITE PAGE, ABOVE: HOTCH POTCH;
BELOW: CRUMBED TROUT WITH PARSLEY BUTTER

CRUMBED TROUT WITH PARSLEY BUTTER

★ **Preparation time:** 15 minutes +
20 minutes refrigeration
Total cooking time: 4 minutes
Serves 6–8

2 large trout fillets (about	3 teaspoons lemon juice
500 g/1 lb), skin	1/4 teaspoon cracked black
removed	peppercorns
2 teaspoons milk	1 spring onion (scallion),
1/4 cup fine oatmeal	finely chopped
1/4 cup (2 fl oz) oil	1 tablespoon finely
	chopped fresh parsley

Parsley Butter
60 g (2 oz) butter,
softened

1 Cut each trout fillet evenly into four pieces. Brush each with milk, then coat with oatmeal. Repeat process with remaining fillets, milk and oatmeal. Arrange coated trout on a tray. Cover with plastic wrap and refrigerate for 20 minutes.
2 To make Parsley Butter: Place butter in small bowl; mash with a fork. Gradually mix in lemon juice and peppercorns. Add spring onion and parsley; mix well. Serve in dollops or form into a log shape and cut into rounds.
3 Heat oil in medium non-stick frying pan; add trout pieces. Cook over medium heat for 2 minutes on each side or until lightly golden. Serve with parsley butter.

HOTCH POTCH (LAMB STEW)

★ **Preparation time:** 25 minutes
Total cooking time: 1 hour 45 minutes
Serves 4–6

1 tablespoon oil	315 g (10 oz)
3 lamb shanks, about	cauliflower, chopped
1 kg (2 lb)	2 carrots, chopped
1 large onion, chopped	1 cup frozen peas,
1 large turnip, chopped	thawed
1 stick celery, chopped	2 cups shredded lettuce
1 litre (4 cups) water	2 tablespoons finely
2 teaspoons salt	chopped fresh parsley
1 teaspoon cracked black	
pepper	

1 Heat oil in a large heavy-based pan; add lamb. Cook over medium heat for 10 minutes or until well browned. Add onion, turnip, celery, water, salt and pepper. Bring to boil, reduce heat to low; simmer, covered, for 1 hour, stirring occasionally.
2 Add cauliflower, carrots and peas to pan. Simmer, uncovered, for 30 minutes.
3 Carefully transfer lamb from pan to chopping board with slotted spoon or tongs; cool slightly. Remove all flesh from bones and chop coarsely. Discard the bones.
4 Return lamb to pan with lettuce and parsley. Stir over low heat for 3 minutes, or until just heated through.

Sherbet A smooth, iced dessert consisting of milk, sugar, sometimes gelatine or egg white and a sharp-tasting, usually citrus, fruit flavouring. Sherbet is softer and less rich than ice-cream and although similar, lacks the biting fruity tang of sorbet (which does not include milk). It can be served topped with a few spoonfuls of champagne or liqueur and accompanied by sliced fresh fruit. Both sherbet and sorbet have their origins in ancient Persia—the word 'sherbet' comes from *sharbia*, the Arabic word for 'drink'. Sherbet is commercially available or can be made at home.

Sherry A fortified wine produced in Spain and usually taken as a pre-dinner drink. Both dry sherry and sweet sherry are used in the cooking of savoury dishes (especially sauces, game stews and chicken dishes—usually added just before serving), and in sweet dishes (such as trifle and other cold desserts).

Sherry was imported into England from the sixteenth century from the Spanish port of Jerez de la Frontera—the name sherry derives from attempts to render *jerez* into English.

Shish Kebab See Kebab.

Shortbread A rich, buttery, slightly sweet, thick biscuit (cookie) made from flour, sugar and butter only. Shortbread originated in Scotland; it is usually baked in a round pan, scored into segments before baking but can also be cut into rectangular fingers. In Britain it is traditional Christmas fare.

Shortcake A cake made from a dough similar to that used for scones (biscuits) but enriched with butter, sugar and milk or cream. Sponge cake can also be used. Shortcake is usually served as a dessert, split horizontally and filled with

QUEEN MARY'S TART

★
Preparation time: 8 minutes +
20 minutes refrigeration
Total cooking time: 45 minutes
Makes 22 cm (8¾ inch) round

250 g (8 oz) packet puff
    pastry
4 eggs, lightly beaten
2 tablespoons apricot jam
½ cup dried mixed peel
¼ cup sultanas
3 teaspoons self-raising
    flour, sifted
90 g (3 oz) butter
⅓ cup caster (superfine)
    sugar

1 Preheat oven to hot 240°C (475°F/Gas 9). Brush a deep 22 cm (8¾ inch) flan tin with melted butter. Roll out pastry to line the base and side of prepared tin; trim edges. Refrigerate for 20 minutes. Prick pastry evenly with a fork; bake for 10 minutes. Remove from oven; spread base with jam.

2 Using electric beaters, beat butter and sugar in a small mixing bowl until light and creamy. Add eggs gradually, beating thoroughly after each addition—mixture will appear curdled. Add mixed peel, sultanas and flour; beat on low speed for 20 seconds until ingredients are just combined.

3 Pour mixture into cooled pastry case; bake for 10 minutes. Reduce temperature to moderately hot 210°C (415°F/Gas 6–7), bake tart for another 25 minutes, or until skewer comes out clean when inserted into filling. Serve warm or cold.

ATHOLL BROSE

★
Preparation time: 5 minutes +
30 minutes standing
Total cooking time: nil
Makes 1 litre (4 cups)

¾ cup fine oatmeal
1 cup (8 fl oz) warm
    water
2 teaspoons honey
½ cup (4 fl oz)
    Drambuie
½ cup (4 fl oz) thick
    pure cream

1 Place the oatmeal into a medium mixing bowl. Make a well in the centre. Gradually add the water, stirring with a wooden spoon. Set aside, covered with a tea-towel, for 30 minutes.

2 Place oatmeal mixture into a coarse strainer and push the liquid through into a clean jug, pressing until oatmeal is dry; discard the oatmeal. Reserve liquid and strain it a second time through a fine strainer into a clean jug.

3 Add honey, Drambuie and cream. Whisk thoroughly. Pour into sterilised jars or bottles, and shake well. Store, sealed, in a cool dark cupboard until ready to use. Always shake before using.

Note: Atholl Brose is a drink traditionally offered at Christmas, Hogmanay and Burns Night.

ABOVE: QUEEN MARY'S TART
OPPOSITE PAGE: SEAFOOD MORNAY CASSEROLE

SEAFOOD

SEAFOOD MORNAY CASSEROLE

★ *Preparation time:* 25 minutes
Total cooking time: 40 minutes
Serves 4–6

3 medium white fish fillets
250 g (8 oz) medium green prawns (shrimps)
200 g (6½ oz) scallops
410 g (13 oz) mussels
1 small onion, cut in half
2 bay leaves
½ lemon, sliced
½ cup (4 fl oz) good quality white wine

Sauce
45 g (1½ oz) butter
1 stick celery, chopped
1 large carrot, finely chopped

6 teaspoons plain (all-purpose) flour
1½ cups (12 fl oz) milk
125 g (4 oz) gruyère cheese, grated
1 cup frozen peas

Topping
1 cup fresh white breadcrumbs
½ cup flaked almonds
2 teaspoons finely grated lemon rind
½ teaspoon freshly ground black pepper
60 g (2 oz) butter, chopped

1 Preheat oven to moderate 180°C (350°F/Gas 4). Remove skin and bones from fish fillets; cut fish into 3 cm (1¼ inch) cubes. Peel and devein prawns. Wash scallops, remove brown vein. Remove beards from mussels and wash away any grit. Prise open shells, remove mussels; discard shells. Place fish, prawns, scallops and mussels in pan. Cover with cold water; add onion, bay leaves, lemon and wine. Bring slowly to the boil. Cover; reduce heat to low and simmer for 3–4 minutes. Remove seafood from cooking liquid. Place in lightly greased casserole dish.

2 **To make Sauce:** Heat butter in medium pan; add celery and carrot. Cook for 1 minute; add flour. Stir over low heat for 2 minutes or until flour mixture is lightly golden. Add milk gradually, stirring until mixture is smooth. Stir constantly over medium heat for 3 minutes, or until mixture boils and thickens. Boil for another minute, remove from heat. Cool.

3 Add cheese and peas to sauce and stir. Pour sauce over mixed seafood; toss gently to combine.

4 **To make Topping:** Combine breadcrumbs, almonds, lemon rind and pepper in bowl, mix well. Spread evenly over top of seafood mixture. Dot with butter. Bake for 20 minutes or until casserole is heated through and topping golden brown. Serve garnished with a sprig of dill.

VARIATIONS

■ Use fresh white fish only and omit shellfish for an economical version of this dish. For special occasions, add shelled lobster and fresh oysters.

■ Use a mixture of cornflake crumbs and parmesan cheese to make topping.

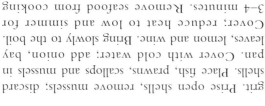

409

sweetened whipped cream and sliced fruit (usually strawberries, but also blueberries or peaches); the top is also spread with cream and fruit. Shortcake is American in origin and gets its name from the 'short' (rich and crumbly) dough used in its preparation.

Shortcrust Pastry A simple, rich, crumbly pastry made by rubbing fat (butter, margarine or lard) into flour, then stirring in just enough liquid—usually water—to hold the mixture together; the dough should be chilled before use. Shortcrust is used for pie crusts and tart bases. It can be sweetened with sugar, enriched with egg or made into a savoury crust by the addition of herbs or grated cheese. Ready-made frozen shortcrust pastry is available from supermarkets.

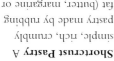

Shortening A fat used for frying and baking, usually made from vegetable oils although animal fat is sometimes added. Shortening is used in doughs, pastries (especially to make crisp shortcrust pie crusts), breads and cakes.

Short Soup Also known as wonton soup, a Chinese soup

SEAFOOD SALAD

Preparation time: 50 minutes
Total cooking time: 10 minutes
★
Serves 4

500 g (1 lb) uncooked
king prawns (shrimps),
peeled and deveined
1 small cooked crayfish
250 g (8 oz) scallops
2 tablespoons lemon juice
2 medium firm-fleshed
white fish fillets
1 cos (romaine) lettuce
1 avocado, peeled and
sliced
2 hard-boiled eggs, 1
chopped, 1 left whole

salt
¼ teaspoon dried chilli
flakes
freshly ground pepper

Dressing
5 tablespoons olive oil
1 tablespoon lemon juice
2 tablespoons finely
chopped parsley

1 Bring a large pan of salted water to the boil, add the prawns and cook for about 3 minutes, or until they turn pink. Remove immediately and plunge into a bowl of iced water.
2 Cut the crayfish in half, remove flesh from shells and cut flesh into small pieces.
3 Poach scallops in water with lemon juice added for a minute or two until tender; drain. Poach fish in the same water for 5 minutes or until tender. Drain and flake into large pieces.
4 To make Dressing: Mix together in a large bowl the oil, lemon juice, salt, chilli flakes and pepper. Add the drained seafood and toss gently until well coated.
5 Tear lettuce into rough pieces and line the bottom of a large china or glass salad bowl. Remove seafood from bowl with a slotted spoon to drain away dressing and place a layer of seafood on top of lettuce, followed by avocado slices and some of the chopped egg. Continue layering in this way, ending with a layer of seafood.
6 Sieve the yolk of the remaining hard boiled egg and mix it with the parsley. Discard the white, or chop and add it to the salad if desired.
7 Sprinkle the salad with egg and parsley mixture and serve with Green Goddess Dressing (see Index for recipe).

Note: The layered arrangement of this dish makes it look spectacular when served in a glass bowl. However, it can also be served simply with all ingredients mixed together and spread on a large platter, over a bed of lettuce or with bowls of lettuce served separately. Alternatively, pile salad into halved and hollowed out avocados.

ABOVE: SEAFOOD WITH NOODLES
OPPOSITE PAGE: SEAFOOD BAKE

SEAFOOD WITH NOODLES

Preparation time: 35 minutes
Total cooking time: 30 minutes
★
Serves 4-6

500 g (1 lb) green king
prawns (shrimps)
2 boneless fish fillets,
about 250 g (8 oz)
4 small squid hoods
2 tablespoons olive oil
3 cloves garlic, crushed
1 teaspoon ground sweet
paprika
1 teaspoon chopped red
chilli

chilli
3 small ripe tomatoes,
peeled and chopped
2 tablespoons tomato
paste
1 cup (8 fl oz) fish stock
1 cup (8 fl oz) red wine
1 teaspoon soft brown
sugar
500 g (1 lb) pasta

1 Shell and devein prawns, leaving tails intact. Cut fish into 3 cm (1¼ inch) pieces. Using a sharp knife, cut squid into thin rings. Set aside.
2 Heat oil in wok or pan; add garlic, paprika and chilli. Cook on medium-high heat for 2 minutes. Add prawns, fish and squid and toss over high heat for 3-4 minutes. Remove and set aside.
3 Add tomato, tomato paste, fish stock, red wine and brown sugar to pan. Bring slowly to the boil, reduce heat and simmer, uncovered, for 10 minutes. Return seafood to pan and mix well.
4 Cook pasta in a large quantity of boiling water until just tender. Drain well. Combine seafood mixture with pasta and serve immediately.

consisting of chicken stock, noodle dumplings filled with minced (ground) meat mixtures and sometimes garnished with chopped spring onion (scallion).

Shrimp A small prawn; pink shrimps are found on the Atlantic coasts of northern Europe as well as the west coast of North America; grey shrimps are caught off Britain and northern France. Both are used in bisques and salads. In North America the term is used for all prawns, whatever the size.

Shrimp Paste An extremely pungent seasoning paste made from sun-dried, salted prawns (shrimps). In the cooking of South-East Asia it flavours curries and dipping sauces; use sparingly.

Siena Cake See Panforte.

Silver Beet Also known as Swiss chard, a leaf vegetable with large, bubble-textured, spinach-flavoured leaves and fleshy white celery-like stems. The green leaves are cooked and eaten like spinach, or, finely.

SEAFOOD BAKE

★ **Preparation time:** 25 minutes
Total cooking time: 25 minutes
Serves 10–12

30 g (1 oz) butter
2 tablespoons plain all-purpose) flour
500 g (1 lb) scallops
1 kg (2 lb) boneless white fish fillets
2 cups croutons
1 cup grated Swiss cheese
2 tablespoons flaked almonds

1 kg (2 lb) uncooked prawns (shrimps)
2 tablespoons dry white wine
1 tablespoon lemon juice
1 tablespoon tomato paste
1 cup cream
2 teaspoons seeded mustard
1/2 teaspoon cracked black peppercorns

1 Preheat oven to moderately hot 210°C (415°F/Gas 6–7). Heat butter in pan; add flour. Stir over low heat for 1 minute or until flour mixture is golden. Add combined wine, juice and tomato paste to pan, stir until smooth. Add cream, stirring over medium heat for 3 minutes or until mixture boils and thickens. Remove from heat, stir in mustard and peppercorns; cool.

2 Peel and devein prawns; rinse and drain well. Rinse scallops and remove coral, leaving coral intact; drain well. Cut the fish fillets into 3 cm (1 1/4 inch) cubes. Combine seafood, sauce, 1 1/2 cups of the croutons and 1/4 cup of the cheese in a large mixing bowl; mix well.

3 Spoon the mixture into a shallow ovenproof dish; sprinkle with the remaining croutons, remaining cheese and the almonds. Bake for 20 minutes or until top is golden and seafood is just cooked through.

Note: Croûtons are crisp toasted cubes of bread, available packaged in supermarkets or delicatessens. To make your own, you will need six slices of thick toasting bread. Cut off crusts and discard. Cut remaining bread into 1.5 cm (1/2 inch) cubes. Scatter on a foil-lined tray and bake in a moderate oven for 15 minutes or until golden, turning occasionally. Cool on tray.

ABOUT SEAFOOD

■ Fresh scallops should be white and firm to the touch with a bright orange coral and fresh smell. Do not freeze—when thawed they often shrink, become waterlogged and develop a stale odour.

■ The cooked flesh of the lobster has a slightly sweet yet salty flavour. They are best cooked quickly (by frying, baking, boiling, steaming, poaching or barbecuing) to retain moisture. Place live lobsters in the freezer for at least six hours before cooking to stun them.

■ Mussels should have tightly closed shells when bought fresh. They can be stored, wrapped in a damp cloth, in the refrigerator for one day. Remove from cooking liquid as soon as the shells open; discard any unopened shells.

---

chopped, may be added to salads.

Silverside A large cut of beef, the boneless outer part of the top of the hindleg (butt). Silverside is usually prepared as corned beef, but fresh cuts can be roasted or pot roasted.

Simmer To cook food in a liquid that is just below boiling point. When a liquid is simmering bubbles form but usually burst before they reach the surface.

Simnel Cake A rich fruit cake sandwiched and coated with almond paste and now traditionally associated with Easter, although it was originally made for Mothering Sunday, in May.

Sirloin A cut of beef from between the rump and the ribs. Sirloin, porterhouse and T-bone steaks are taken from it; it may also be divided into roasting pieces.

Smørrebrød See Danish Open Sandwich.

Snail A small, soft-bodied, land-dwelling mollusc. Some snails are prized as food, especially in Europe. They are usually cooked with garlic butter and

served in the shell. Snails are commercially raised, often on a diet of cabbage, wheat or oats. Most highly regarded in France is the Burgundy vine leaves from the Burgundy vineyards. The Romans were probably the first to farm snails. Snails are available canned; the shells are sold separately. Snails are called escargots in France.

Snow Peas (Mange Tout) and Sugar Snap Peas Bright green varieties of pea with sweet, delicately flavoured pods, that are eaten whole. Snow peas are harvested when the peas are still immature; sugar peas are fully mature but the pod is so tender that they can be cooked and eaten unshelled. Both can be added, raw, to salads. To prepare either pea, break off the stalk end and remove any string; lightly boil or steam and serve while still crisp. Snow peas are popular in Asian cooking.

Soda Bread A bread in which the leavening agent is a combination of bicarbonate of soda (baking soda) and buttermilk (or some other acid ingredient), which react together to

---

SEAFOOD STEW

✷ *Preparation time:* 20 minutes
Total cooking time: 50 minutes
Serves 4–6

315 g (10 oz) uncooked
  prawns (shrimps)
¼ cup (2 fl oz) olive oil
2 medium onions, finely
  chopped
2 medium carrots, chopped
2 sticks celery, finely
  chopped
2 cloves garlic, crushed
6 medium tomatoes,
  about 1 kg (2 lb),
  peeled and chopped
¼ cup (2 fl oz) good
  quality white wine
1 kg (2 lb) boneless fish
  fillets, cut into 3 cm
  (1¼ inch) pieces
salt and pepper
12 mussels, beards
  removed
¼ cup (2 fl oz) good
  quality white wine, extra
2 tablespoons chopped
  parsley
1 tablespoon fresh thyme
  leaves
2 tablespoons tomato
  paste

1 Peel and devein prawns, leaving tails intact. Heat oil in a pan. Cook onion for 10 minutes. Add carrots, celery and garlic. Cook, stirring, for 10 minutes.

2 Add tomatoes and wine. Bring to boil, reduce heat and simmer, covered, for 20 minutes. Stir in tomato paste. Add prawns. Cover and simmer for another 3 minutes. Add fish, salt and pepper, simmer for 2 minutes more.

3 Place mussels in a large pan, add extra wine and herbs. Cover, cook over medium heat for 2–3 minutes until mussels open. Strain liquid from mussels into tomato mixture and combine. Arrange mussels on top.

SEAFOOD WITH MANGO SALSA

✷✷ *Preparation time:* 30 minutes + 1 hour refrigeration
Total cooking time: 3 minutes
Serves 6

1 dozen oysters on the
  shell
2 medium tubes calamari,
  about 315 g (10 oz)
15 g (½ oz) butter
1 tablespoon lemon juice
1 tablespoon chopped
  fresh parsley
12 cooked prawns
  (shrimps), unpeeled

Mango Salsa
1 large ripe mango
1 small fresh red chilli
1 stalk lemongrass
1 teaspoon finely chopped
  coriander
1 teaspoon finely grated
  fresh ginger
2 teaspoons finely
  chopped fresh dill
2 teaspoons honey
salt and white pepper, to
  taste

Dill Vinaigrette
2 tablespoons white wine
  vinegar
1 tablespoon lemon juice
½ cup (4 fl oz) oil
1 teaspoon Dijon
  mustard

1 Remove any grit from the surface of oyster flesh. Slice the calamari tubes into rings about 1 cm (½ inch) wide. Melt butter in a medium frying pan, add calamari and lemon juice and stir over medium heat for about 3 minutes, or until calamari is opaque. Add parsley and stir. Remove mixture from the pan and set aside to cool. Refrigerate, along with the prawns and oysters, until required.

2 To make Mango Salsa: Peel the mango, remove the seed and cut the flesh into small cubes. Cut the chilli in half lengthways, remove the seeds and slice finely. Cut a 2 cm (¾ inch) piece of the white part from the lemongrass stalk and chop finely. Mix together the mango, chilli, lemongrass, coriander and ginger in a small bowl and refrigerate for 1 hour. Allow salsa to stand at room temperature for 10 minutes before serving.

3 To make Dill Vinaigrette: Place the vinegar, oil, mustard, dill and honey in a small jar. Shake vigorously for 1 minute or until all ingredients are well combined. Add salt and pepper to taste.

4 To serve, divide the oysters, calamari and prawns evenly between individual serving plates. Add a tablespoon of Mango Salsa to each plate. Pour Dill Vinaigrette into bowls to accompany each plate, or pass a small jug of dressing around separately for guests to help themselves.

ABOVE: SEAFOOD STEW
OPPOSITE PAGE: TRADITIONAL SHORTBREAD

SHORTBREAD

TRADITIONAL SHORTBREAD

Preparation time: 20 minutes
Total cooking time: 40 minutes
Makes about 8 wedges

250 g (8 oz) butter, softened	1²/₃ cups plain (all-purpose) flour
½ cup icing (confectioners) sugar, sifted	¼ cup rice flour

1 Beat butter and icing sugar in a bowl with an electric mixer until light and fluffy. Sift in flours; and combine well with a wooden spoon. Press dough into a ball; knead lightly until smooth. Pat dough into a greased 23 cm (9 inch) round tin, or shape into a 23 cm (9 inch) round, about 1 cm (½ inch) thick, on greased baking tray.
2 Pinch a decorative edge to shortbread round, using floured fingers as shown.

3 Score top of round into even fingers or wedges. Pierce all over with a fork. Bake at 140°C (275°F/Gas 1) for 35–40 minutes, or until shortbread is set and browned. Cool on trays for 2–3 minutes. Transfer to a wire rack. When shortbread is almost cool, cut through score marks into neat pieces (use a bread knife and cut with a sawing motion). Cool shortbread completely. Store in an airtight container.

ABOUT SHORTBREAD

■ There are many variations on the shortbread theme. Traditional Scottish tea favourites include petticoat tails (round shortbreads inspired by the petticoat hoops worn by nineteenth century women), Ayrshire shortbread (made with cream) and oatmeal shortbread. All use very fresh, high quality ingredients for the best results.
■ Handle shortbread dough lightly—overworking will give a tough, chewy product.
■ Candied peel and almonds are popular traditional decorations for shortbread.

generate bubbles of carbon dioxide. Traditional Irish soda bread contains only local wholemeal flour, buttermilk, bicarbonate of soda

(baking soda) and salt; it is scored with a deep cross for even baking.

Sorbet A smooth, sharp-tasting iced dessert which consists of sugar syrup and fruit juice or sometimes a liqueur (such as Calvados) or champagne.

Sorbets can be served in a tall glass or shallow dish, and. topped with a few spoonfuls of liqueur or champagne, garnished with frosted fruits or accompanied by a pureed fruit sauce. Sometimes a small scoop is served between courses to refresh the palate; a savoury sorbet (such as thyme, rosemary, avocado or olive) can be served

1

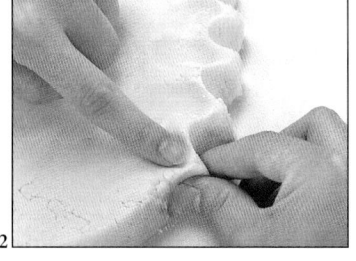
2

3

GINGER SHORTBREAD CREAMS

✦

Preparation time: 25 minutes
Total cooking time: 15 minutes
Makes 22

1/2 cup plain (all-purpose)
flour
60 g (2 oz) unsalted
(sweet) butter
1/2 cup self-raising flour
2 tablespoons cornflour
(cornstarch)
1/3 cup icing (confectioners)
sugar

Filling
105 g (3 1/2 oz) unsalted
(sweet) butter, chopped
1 tablespoon finely
chopped glacé ginger
2 tablespoons soft brown
sugar

1 Preheat oven to moderate 180°C (350°F/Gas 4). Line two 32 x 28 cm (13 x 11 inch) trays with baking paper. Place flours, butter and sugar in food processor. Process for 30 seconds or until mixture comes together. Turn onto a lightly floured surface, knead for 20 seconds.
2 Roll level teaspoons of mixture into balls. Place on trays, press with a fork in a criss-cross pattern. Bake 15 minutes, until just golden. Transfer to a wire rack to cool before filling.
3 To make Filling: Beat butter and sugar until light and creamy; add ginger, beat well. Spread half biscuits with filling, sandwich with others.

GREEK SHORTBREAD

✦

Preparation time: 20 minutes
Total cooking time: 15 minutes
Makes about 38

200 g (6 1/2 oz) butter
1 cup icing (confectioners)
sugar, sifted
1 teaspoon finely grated
orange rind
1 egg
1 egg yolk
2 1/2 cups plain (all-
purpose) flour

1 1/2 teaspoons baking
powder
1 teaspoon ground
cinnamon
250 g (8 oz) blanched
almonds, toasted,
finely chopped
icing (confectioners) sugar,
extra

1 Preheat oven to moderately slow 160°C (325°F/Gas 3). Line an oven tray with baking paper. Using electric beaters, beat butter, sugar and rind in a small mixing bowl until light and creamy. Add egg and egg yolk, beating in thoroughly.
2 Transfer mixture to large mixing bowl. Using a metal spoon, fold in sifted flour, baking powder, cinnamon and almonds; mix until well combined.
3 Shape level tablespoons of mixture into crescent shapes. Place on prepared trays. Bake 15 minutes or until lightly golden. Stand 5 minutes before transferring biscuits to wire rack to cool. While still warm, dust with icing sugar. Just before serving, dust heavily again with icing sugar.

ABOVE: GREEK SHORTBREAD
RIGHT: GINGER SHORTBREAD CREAMS
Opposite page: CHOCOLATE HEDGEHOG SLICE

---

as an accompaniment to a meat course.

Both sorbet and sherbet reached Europe through ancient Persia— the word sherbet comes from *sharbia*, the Arabic word for 'drink'— although iced fruit drinks may have originated in ancient China. 'Sorbet' is the French version of the word.

Sorghum A cereal which is a staple food in parts of Africa and Asia where it is cooked like rice, or ground into a flour and made into porridge and flat cakes. A fermented drink is also made from its seeds. Ground sorghum is available from health food or Asian grocery shops for use in stews or as a porridge.

Sorrel A green, leafy plant with a bitter, slightly lemony flavour. Sorrel is usually cooked, like

spinach; it can be pureed as an omelette filling or made into a soup; very young and tender leaves can be added (sparingly) to a green salad; and it is often used as a stuffing for fish.

Sorrel is native to Europe; in ancient times it was eaten to offset the richness of some foods. It is especially popular in the cooking of Provence, in southern France. The name is

SLICES (BARS)

CHOCOLATE HEDGEHOG SLICE

✳ **Preparation time:** 30 minutes + 30 minutes refrigeration
Total cooking time: 5–10 minutes
Makes 50

250 g (8 oz) chocolate cream biscuits, crushed
1/2 cup desiccated coconut
1 cup pecans, roughly chopped
1 tablespoon cocoa powder, sifted
105 g (3 1/2 oz) dark (semi-sweet) chocolate, chopped
80 g (2 2/3 oz) unsalted (sweet) butter
1 tablespoon golden syrup (light corn syrup)

Icing
105 g (3 1/2 oz) dark (semi-sweet) chocolate, chopped
45 g (1 1/2 oz) unsalted (sweet) butter

1 egg, lightly beaten
extra pecans, for decoration
60 g (2 oz) dark (semi-sweet) chocolate melts, extra

1 Line base and sides of shallow 30 x 20 cm (12 x 8 inch) rectangular tin with foil. Combine biscuit crumbs, coconut, pecans and cocoa in medium mixing bowl. Make a well in the centre.

2 Combine chocolate, butter and syrup in small heavy-based pan. Stir over low heat until chocolate and butter have melted and mixture is smooth. Remove from heat. Pour with egg onto dry ingredients. Combine well with wooden spoon. Press into tin. Refrigerate for 30 minutes.

COCONUT JAM SLICE

✳ **Preparation time:** 20 minutes
Total cooking time: 35 minutes
Makes 25 squares

1 1/2 cups plain (all-purpose) flour
1/3 cup caster (superfine) sugar
155 g (5 oz) unsalted (sweet) butter

Topping
2 eggs
1/2 cup icing (confectioners') sugar
2 cups desiccated coconut
1/3 cup blackberry jam

1 Preheat oven to moderate 180°C (350°F/Gas 4). Brush a 23 cm (9 inch) square cake tin with oil or melted butter. Line with baking paper, extending over two sides. Place flour, butter and sugar into food processor. Press pulse button for 30 seconds or until mixture comes together. Turn onto lightly floured surface, knead 20 seconds or until smooth. Press into tin; refrigerate 10 minutes. Bake 15 minutes or until golden; cool.

2 To make Topping: Whisk sugar and eggs in bowl until combined. Stir in coconut.

3 Spread jam over cooled base. Spread topping over jam, pressing down with back of spoon. Bake for 20 minutes, until lightly golden. Cut into 25 squares when cool.

3 To make Icing: Stir chocolate and butter in small bowl over pan of simmering water until melted and smooth; cool. Spread over slice. Refrigerate. When set, cut into squares. Top with pecans dipped in extra melted chocolate.

Soufflé A light and fluffy egg dish, either savoury or sweet. There are two types: hot and cold. The airy texture of a hot soufflé is achieved by folding stiffly whisked egg whites through a warm sauce or purée; air trapped in the white causes the soufflé to rise when baked. Hot soufflé must be served immediately. A cold soufflé is a mousse-like mixture lightened with whipped egg whites; it is set in a mould with sides extended by foil.

Soup A liquid food made from meat, poultry or fish, usually with vegetables, or from one or more vegetables and usually served hot. A soup course is often served at the start of a meal, or, if thick and hearty, may be a meal in itself. The wide range of

soups includes clear consommés, pureed vegetables with cream, meat and vegetable mixtures thickened with a roux and cold soups.

Sour Cream Cream to which a special culture has been added to give it a sharp, slightly sour taste. It is thicker than pure fresh cream. Sour cream is used in

soups, savoury dips and salad dressings; as a filling for jacket potatoes and in cheesecake. It is used particularly in eastern European cooking.

Sourdough Fermented dough, saved when making a batch of bread and used instead of yeast as a starter when making the next batch.

Soursop Also called prickly custard apple, the green-skinned, heart-shaped fruit of a small tree native to tropical America.

Soy Bean An oval bean, about the size of the common pea, borne in hairy pods on a bush native to China. Most common

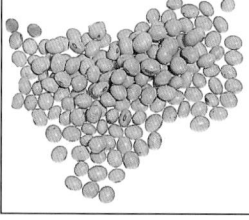

CHOCOLATE CARAMEL SLICE

★★ ***Preparation time:*** 15 minutes
Total cooking time: 20 minutes
Makes 24 triangles

125 g (4 oz) plain sweet biscuits, crushed
80 g (2²⁄₃ oz) unsalted (sweet) butter, melted
2 tablespoons desiccated coconut
410 g (13 oz) can sweetened condensed milk

125 g (4 oz) butter
¹⁄₃ cup caster (superfine) sugar
¹⁄₃ cup golden syrup (light corn syrup)
250 g (8 oz) milk chocolate melts
1 tablespoon vegetable oil

1 Brush a shallow 30 x 20 cm (12 x 8 inch) rectangular cake tin with oil or melted butter. Line base and sides with aluminium foil; grease foil. Combine biscuit, melted butter and coconut in a medium mixing bowl. Press mixture evenly into prepared pan; smooth surface.
2 Combine condensed milk, butter, sugar and syrup in small pan. Stir over low heat 15 minutes or until sugar has dissolved and mixture is smooth and thick. Remove from heat; cool slightly. Pour over biscuit base; smooth surface.
3 Place milk chocolate melts and oil in small heatproof bowl. Stand bowl over a pan of simmering water, stir until chocolate has melted and mixture is smooth. Spread chocolate mixture over caramel. Allow to partially set before marking into 24 triangles. Refrigerate until firm.

WALNUT BROWNIES

★ ***Preparation time:*** 10 minutes + 20 minutes standing
Total cooking time: 35 minutes
Makes 20 diamonds

105 g (3¹⁄₂ oz) unsalted (sweet) butter
²⁄₃ cup soft brown sugar
³⁄₄ cup (6 fl oz) water
¹⁄₄ cup sultanas, chopped
1 cup self-raising flour
1 cup plain (all-purpose) flour
1 teaspoon ground cinnamon
1 tablespoon cocoa powder
¹⁄₂ cup chopped walnuts

¹⁄₄ cup choc bits (chocolate chips)
20 walnut halves

Icing
60 g (2 oz) unsalted (sweet) butter
³⁄₄ cup icing (confectioners) sugar
1 tablespoon cocoa powder
1 tablespoon milk

1 Preheat oven to moderate 180°C (350°F/Gas 4). Brush shallow 27 x 18 cm (10³⁄₄ x 7 inch) rectangular tin with oil. Cover base with baking paper, extending over two longer sides; grease paper. Combine butter, sugar, water and sultanas in pan. Stir over low heat 5 minutes until butter melts and sugar dissolves; remove from heat.
2 Sift flours, cinnamon and cocoa into a bowl; add nuts and choc bits. Make a well in centre. Add butter mixture. Stir until just combined.

ABOVE: CHOCOLATE CARAMEL SLICE
OPPOSITE PAGE: MOIST CHOCOLATE BROWNIES

Spoon into tin. Bake 30 minutes or until skewer comes out clean when inserted in centre. Stand 20 minutes before turning onto a wire rack to cool. **3 To make Icing:** Beat butter until light and creamy; add sugar, cocoa and milk. Beat until smooth. Spread over brownie. Cut into diamonds, top each with a walnut half.

MOIST CHOCOLATE BROWNIES

★★

Preparation time: 20 minutes
Total cooking time: 45 minutes
Makes 36 squares

1½ cups plain (all-purpose) flour
¼ cup cocoa powder
1 teaspoon baking powder
½ teaspoon bicarbonate of soda (baking soda)
½ cup chopped macadamia nuts
125 g (4 oz) unsalted (sweet) butter
200 g (6½ oz) dark (semi-sweet) cooking chocolate, chopped
1 cup caster (superfine) sugar
2 eggs, lightly beaten
⅓ cup (2½ fl oz) sour cream
⅓ cup chopped macadamia nuts, extra

Chocolate Cream Topping
155 g (5 oz) dark (semi-sweet) cooking chocolate, chopped
½ cup (4 fl oz) sour cream

1 Preheat oven to moderate 180°C (350°F/Gas 4). Brush a shallow, 23 cm (9 inch) square cake tin with oil or melted butter. Line the base and sides with paper; grease paper. Sift flour with cocoa, baking powder and bicarbonate of soda into a large mixing bowl; add the nuts. Make a well in the centre.

2 Place the butter and chocolate in a medium heatproof bowl. Stand the bowl over a pan of simmering water and stir until the chocolate and butter have melted and the mixture is smooth. Remove from heat; add the sugar, eggs and cream. Beat with a wire whisk until all ingredients are well combined and the mixture is thick and smooth. Add chocolate mixture to the dry ingredients. Using a wooden spoon, stir until well combined—do not overbeat. Spread mixture into the prepared tin. Bake for 40 minutes or until a skewer comes out clean when inserted in the centre of the slice. Leave to cool in the tin.

3 To make Chocolate Cream Topping: Place the chopped cooking chocolate in a medium heatproof bowl. Stand the bowl over a pan of simmering water and stir until all the chocolate has melted. Remove from heat and leave for 2 minutes. Add cream to the chocolate and beat with a wire whisk until the mixture is thick and glossy. While the mixture is still warm, spread Chocolate Cream Topping over the cooled slice and sprinkle with nuts. Allow the Topping to set before cutting the slice evenly into 4 cm (1½ inch) squares.

is the creamy-yellow variety, but they can also be red, purple, brown or black. Soy beans are valued for their high vegetable protein content and can be eaten in a number of ways: fresh, dried, sprouting, ground and as bean curd and soy-bean milk. Miso, widely used in the cooking of Japan, is a paste of fermented, salted soy bean. Dried soy beans are used in soups, stews and casseroles.

Soy Sauce A dark, salty sauce of Chinese origin made from fermented roasted soy beans, another grain (usually wheat) and brine; the mixture is aged for up to two years, then filtered and bottled. Dark soy sauce is aged longer and towards the end of processing is tinted and flavoured with molasses. Soy sauce is indispensable in Asian cooking; it is used as a seasoning and marinade and adds flavour and colour to many dishes. Chinese cooking uses both dark and light soy sauce; light is used with seafood, chicken, vegetables, soups and in dipping sauces; dark soy sauce is used in red meat dishes. Japanese soy sauce, *shoyu*, is usually sweeter and less salty than the Chinese variety; in Indonesia, *kecap manis*, a thick, dark, sweetened soy sauce, is often used. A seasoning made

SLICES

Spanish Food Spain shares with its Mediterranean neighbours access to a myriad of fish and shellfish, the use of aromatic hillside herbs and the Roman legacy of olives. From the Phoenicians came the chickpea (garbanzo bean) and the salting of fish. However what makes Spanish

Spaghetti Pasta in the form of long strands, made from a flour and water dough. It is best with oil-based sauces that allow the strings to remain slippery and separate. Spaghetti has been made in southern Italy for many hundreds of years; commercially made spaghetti is available in dried or fresh, in refrigerated and frozen forms.

from fermented soy beans, known as *shih*, was in use in China more than 2000 years ago. A strained sauce similar to the version in use today has been made since the sixth century. Soy sauce is available from supermarkets and Asian food stores.

BRANDY ALEXANDER SLICE

★
Preparation time: 20 minutes + 3 hours refrigeration
Total cooking time: 5 minutes
Makes 12 bars

90 g (3 oz) unsalted (sweet) butter, chopped
60 g (2 oz) dark (semi-sweet) cooking chocolate, chopped
1/2 cup grated milk
1 tablespoon brandy
1 tablespoon crème de cacao liqueur
1/2 teaspoon ground nutmeg
60 g (2 oz) dark (semi-sweet) chocolate melts

1/3 cup icing (confectioners) sugar, sifted
250 g (8 oz) packet plain chocolate biscuits, crushed
310 g (10 oz) ricotta cheese
1/4 cup (2 fl oz) cream

1 Brush a shallow 30 x 20 cm (12 x 8 inch) tin with oil. Line the base and sides with baking paper. Place butter and chocolate in a small heatproof bowl. Stand bowl over a pan of simmering water. Stir until chocolate has melted and mixture is smooth. Remove from heat. Place biscuit crumbs in a small bowl, add chocolate mixture and stir, using a flat-bladed knife. Press biscuit mixture evenly over base of prepared tin; set aside.

2 Using electric beaters, beat cheese, cream and sugar in small mixing bowl on medium speed for 3 minutes or until mixture is light and creamy. Add chocolate, brandy and liqueur. Beat on low speed for another minute.

3 Spread cheese mixture over prepared base; sprinkle with nutmeg. Refrigerate several hours or overnight. Cut into 12 bars. Place chocolate melts in small heatproof bowl and stand over simmering water until chocolate has melted. Use to pipe a design on top of each bar.

PRUNE AND CREAM CHEESE SCROLLS

★ ★
Preparation time: 30 minutes + 30 minutes refrigeration
Total cooking time: 15 minutes
Makes 20

1 1/2 cups plain (all-purpose) flour
90 g (3 oz) unsalted (sweet) butter
1 tablespoon custard powder
1/3 cup caster (superfine) sugar
250 g (4 oz) cream cheese

Prune Filling
1/4 cup caster (superfine) sugar
2 teaspoons grated lemon rind
1 cup chopped, pitted prunes
1 egg yolk
2–3 tablespoons milk

1 Brush two 32 x 28 cm (13 x 11 inch) biscuit (oven) trays with oil or melted butter. Place flour, custard powder, butter and sugar in food processor. Using pulse action, press button for

ABOVE: BRANDY ALEXANDER SLICE
OPPOSITE PAGE: CHOCOLATE CARROT SLICE

Spanish cooking sidebar

cuisine distinct is the Muslim/Arab influence of the Moors, who ruled the country from the eighth to the fifteenth century. From this period comes the emphasis on spices and seasonings, with an array introduced including nutmeg, cloves, saffron, cumin, cinnamon, turmeric and vanilla. The Moors were keen agriculturalists; they built irrigation systems to open up farming lands and planted citrus groves, especially the orange, throughout Spain; they also introduced eggplant (aubergine) and

asparagus, apricots and pomegranates, almonds and pistachios, rice and sugar. Arab culinary influence is also seen in Spain's syrup-soaked pastries.

The next major strand in the development of Spanish cuisine was the introduction of new foods from the Americas— sweet pepper (capsicum), chilli and tomato, all now firmly identified with national dishes, and potato and chocolate (chocolate drinks were long favoured in Spain as a daily energiser before coffee became widely available). Regardless of all these influences, Spanish cooking is still

CHOC RUM SLICE

Preparation time: 15 minutes + 1 hour refrigeration
Total cooking time: 3 minutes
Makes 19 cm (7 1/2 inch) square slice

250 g (8 oz) plain chocolate biscuits, crushed
1 teaspoon ground cinnamon
2 tablespoons rum
1 cup mixed fruit or sultanas
1/2 cup walnuts, chopped
125 g (4 oz) dark (semi-sweet) chocolate, chopped
125 g (4 oz) butter
1/2 cup (4 fl oz) condensed milk
1 egg

1 Brush a deep 19 cm (7 1/2 inch) square cake tin with oil or melted butter. Line base and sides with aluminium foil; grease foil. Combine biscuit crumbs, fruit and walnuts in a large mixing bowl. Make a well in the centre.

2 Combine butter and milk in a small pan. Stir over low heat until butter has melted; remove from heat, whisk in egg, cinnamon and rum.

3 Add butter mixture to dry ingredients. Stir with a wooden spoon until well combined. Press mixture evenly into prepared tin.

4 Place chocolate in glass bowl. Stir over barely simmering water until melted; remove from heat. Spread chocolate evenly over slice using a flat-bladed knife. Mark into slices. Refrigerate, covered, until firm. Cut into slices to serve (slice will cut better if cold).

CHOCOLATE CARROT SLICE

Preparation time: 15 minutes
Total cooking time: 30 minutes
Makes 32

1 cup self-raising flour
1 teaspoon ground cinnamon
3/4 cup caster (superfine) sugar
1/2 cup finely grated carrot
1 cup mixed dried fruit
1/2 cup choc bits (chocolate chips)
1/3 cup desiccated coconut
2 eggs, lightly beaten
90 g (3 oz) unsalted (sweet) butter, melted

Cream Cheese Frosting
125 g (4 oz) cream cheese
30 g (1 oz) unsalted (sweet) butter
1 1/2 cups icing (confectioners) sugar, sifted
1 teaspoon hot water
1/3 cup chopped walnuts

1 Preheat oven to moderate 180°C (350°F/Gas 4). Brush a shallow 23 cm (9 inch) square cake tin with oil or melted butter; line the base and sides with baking paper. Sift flour and cinnamon into large bowl. Add sugar, carrot, mixed fruit, choc bits and coconut; stir until just combined. Add beaten eggs and butter, stir until just combined.

2 Spread mixture evenly into prepared tin; smooth surface. Bake for 30 minutes or until golden. Cool in tin; turn onto a flat surface.

3 To make Cream Cheese Frosting: Using electric beaters, beat cream cheese and butter in a small bowl until smooth. Add icing sugar and beat for 2 minutes or until mixture is light and fluffy. Add water, beat until combined. Spread slice with frosting, using a flat-bladed knife. Cut into 16 squares, then sprinkle with walnuts. Cut into squares, then cut each square into triangles.

15 seconds or until mixture is fine and crumbly. Add egg yolk and milk; process for 15 seconds or until mixture comes together. Turn onto a lightly floured surface; knead for 1 minute or until smooth. Roll out dough on baking paper to form a 30 x 28 cm (12 x 11 inch) rectangle.

2 To make Prune Filling: Beat cream cheese, sugar and rind in small bowl until light and creamy. Spread over dough. Top with prunes.

3 Roll dough from one long side into the centre. Roll dough from opposite side to meet in centre. Refrigerate 30 minutes or until firm. Heat oven to moderate 180°C (350°F/Gas 4). Cut roll into 1.5 cm (5/8 inch) slices. Place onto trays, allowing room for spreading. Bake 15 minutes or until lightly golden. Transfer to wire racks to cool.

SOUFFLES

Baked soufflés are made by combining a rich sauce or purée with stiffly beaten egg whites, and baking them in special deep, straight-sided ovenproof dishes. They emerge dramatically from the oven, puffed and golden, and must be served at once, before they begin to sink.

Savoury or sweet, soufflés can be baked in one large dish or in small ones for individual servings. When buying dishes for soufflés, choose attractive ones because hot soufflés are usually served in the same dish they are cooked in. For successful soufflés it is important to beat the egg whites just before cooking. If you let them stand before folding them into the sauce or if you let the soufflé stand before baking, the egg whites will sink and become watery. Hot soufflés are best served with a simple salad. Sweet soufflés are delicious when served with vanilla ice-cream or freshly whipped cream.

THIS PAGE, CENTRE ROW, FROM LEFT: COFFEE; BLUEBERRY; SPINACH; BOTTOM: HERB. OPPOSITE PAGE, TOP: CHOCOLATE; CENTRE ROW, FROM LEFT: RASPBERRY, MOCHA, CHEESE; BOTTOM: SALMON

CHEESE SOUFFLE

Preheat oven to 180°C (350°F/Gas 4). Grease one 18 cm (7 inch) soufflé dish or four small (1-cup) dishes generously with butter, then dust with fine, dry breadcrumbs. Melt 125 g (4 oz) butter in a pan and add 1 cup plain (all-purpose) flour. Stir well to combine and cook over low heat, stirring, for 1 minute. Remove pan from heat, add 1 cup (8 fl oz) warm milk, stir or whisk until smooth, then return to the heat and stir until mixture boils and thickens. Remove pan from heat. Beat 4 egg yolks until very well mixed, add to the sauce, stirring constantly, until well combined. Add 125 g (4 oz) grated cheddar cheese, salt, pepper and 1/2 teaspoon Dijon mustard. Allow sauce to cool slightly. Beat the 4 egg whites until stiff peaks form. Fold one-third of the egg white into the cooked sauce, using a metal spoon, then add the rest, folding very gently. Pour the mixture gently but without delay, into the prepared dish, filling it to within 1 cm (1/2 inch) of the rim. Sprinkle with a tablespoon freshly grated parmesan cheese. Bake soufflé for 40–45 minutes for a large soufflé, 25–30 minutes for individual dishes. Serve immediately.

VARIATIONS

■ **HERB SOUFFLÉ:** Add 1 finely chopped spring onion (scallion) and 1 tablespoon finely chopped fresh herbs (chervil, parsley, marjoram or chives) at the same time as the cheese.

■ **SPINACH SOUFFLÉ:** Replace cheddar cheese with 1/2 cup cooked spinach, finely chopped (after chopping, squeeze with your hands to remove as much moisture as possible), a pinch of grated nutmeg, 1 tablespoon grated parmesan cheese and 2 tablespoons grated Swiss cheese. Add these to the cooked sauce before adding the egg white.

■ **SALMON SOUFFLÉ:** Replace cheddar cheese with a 250 g (8 oz) can of red salmon, drained and flaked, and 2 tablespoons finely chopped fresh chives. Stir these into the cooked sauce before adding the egg white.

BASIC SWEET SOUFFLE

Preheat oven to 190°C (375°F/Gas 5). Grease a 20 cm (8 inch) soufflé dish and dust with caster (superfine) sugar. Melt 45 g (1½ oz) butter in a small pan, add 45 g (1½ oz) plain (all-purpose) flour and stir over low heat for 1 minute or until smooth. Remove pan from heat and gradually add 1 cup (8 fl oz) warm milk, stirring constantly. Add ¼ teaspoon salt, ½ cup sugar and 1 teaspoon vanilla essence, return pan to heat and stir continuously until mixture becomes thick and smooth. Set sauce aside to cool. Beat 4 egg yolks and add them gradually to the cooled sauce, stirring well between each addition. Beat 5 egg whites until stiff and then fold them gently into the sauce using a metal spoon. Pour the mixture carefully into the prepared soufflé dish filling to within 1 cm (½ inch) of the rim. Stand the soufflé in a deep baking dish that is half filled with hot water. Bake in preheated oven for 15 minutes, then reduce temperature to 180°C (350°F/Gas 4) and bake for another 25 minutes. Serve immediately.

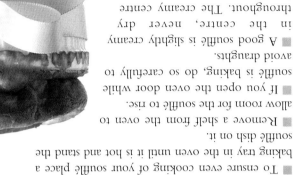
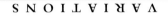

V A R I A T I O N S

■ COFFEE SOUFFLE: Substitute ½ cup strong black coffee for half the milk.

■ CHOCOLATE SOUFFLE: Melt 60 g (2 oz) dark (semi-sweet) chocolate over hot water and stir into the sauce before you add the egg yolks.

■ BLUEBERRY SOUFFLE: Puree 200 g (6½ oz) fresh blueberries in a food processor until smooth. Fold into the sauce with the egg yolks.

■ RASPBERRY SOUFFLE: Puree 250 g (8 oz) raspberries in a food processor. Strain to remove seeds. Fold into sauce with the egg yolks.

■ MOCHA SOUFFLE: Dissolve 1–2 tablespoons of instant coffee in 1 tablespoon of hot water. Melt 60 g (2 oz) dark (semi-sweet) chocolate over hot water, mix with the coffee. Allow to cool and fold into sauce before adding the egg yolks.

P O I N T S   F O R   S U C C E S S

■ Fold flavourings into the basic sauce before adding beaten egg whites.

■ Eggs should be at room temperature.

■ To beat egg whites successfully, they must be free of any trace of yolk. The bowl and beaters must be dry and free of any trace of grease. If any of the egg yolk slips into the white during separation, carefully remove it with half an egg shell or a teaspoon.

■ For best results, hand beat the egg whites with a wire whisk rather than using electric beaters.

■ Egg whites should be beaten only until the moment that stiff peaks form. When ready, the mixture should stay in a peak when you hold the whisk upright. Do not over-beat egg white as it will break up when you fold it through the sauce and the soufflé will not rise properly.

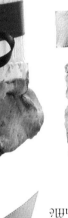

■ Fold the beaten whites lightly and quickly into the warm sauce.

■ To ensure even cooking of your soufflé place a baking tray in the oven until it is hot and stand the soufflé dish on it.

■ Remove a shelf from the oven to allow room for the soufflé to rise.

■ If you open the oven door while soufflé is baking, do so carefully to avoid draughts.

■ A good soufflé is slightly creamy in the centre, never dry throughout. The creamy centre becomes a sauce. Serve everyone some of the thoroughly cooked soufflé and a little of the creamy, soft centre.

STIR-FRIED BEEF AND SNOW PEAS (MANGE TOUT)

★ *Preparation time:* 10 minutes
Total cooking time: 5 minutes
Serves 4

410 g (13 oz) rump steak, finely sliced	1½ teaspoons cornflour (cornstarch)
2 tablespoons soy sauce	½ cup (4 fl oz) beef stock
½ teaspoon grated ginger	1 teaspoon soy sauce
2 tablespoons peanut oil	¼ teaspoon sesame oil extra
200 g (6½ oz) snow peas (mange tout), topped and tailed	

1 Place meat in a dish. Combine soy sauce and ginger, sprinkle over meat and stir to coat well. Heat oil in a wok or heavy-based frying pan, swirling gently to coat base and side.

2 Add the beef and snow peas and stir-fry over high heat for 2 minutes, or until the meat changes colour.

3 Dissolve cornflour in a little stock. Add to wok with remaining stock, extra soy sauce and sesame oil. Stir until sauce boils and thickens. Serve with steamed rice.

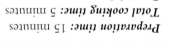

SNOW PEA (MANGE TOUT) AND ASPARAGUS SALAD

★ *Preparation time:* 15 minutes
Total cooking time: 5 minutes
Serves 4–6

200 g (6½ oz) snow peas (mange tout)	3 teaspoons sesame oil
1 bunch asparagus spears	3 teaspoons rice vinegar or red wine vinegar
	½ teaspoon sugar

Dressing
1 tablespoon sesame seeds
2 tablespoons peanut oil

1 Top and tail snow peas. Trim any woody ends from asparagus. Cut spears diagonally in half. Place in a pan of boiling water. Leave for 1 minute, then drain asparagus and plunge into iced water. Drain well.

2 To make Dressing: Place oils, vinegar and sugar in a small screw-top jar and shake well. Place asparagus and snow peas in a serving bowl. Pour dressing over; toss to combine.

3 Place sesame seeds in a dry frying pan. Cook over medium heat for 1–2 minutes until lightly golden. Sprinkle over salad, serve immediately.

ABOVE: Snow Pea and Asparagus Salad
OPPOSITE PAGE: Cock-a-leekie

SNOW PEAS (MANGE TOUT)

SNOW PEA (MANGE TOUT) SALAD

★ *Preparation time:* 20 minutes
Total cooking time: 5 minutes
Serves 8

200 g (6½ oz) snow peas (mange tout)	**Garlic Croûtons**
1 large red pepper (capsicum), sliced	3 slices white bread
4 leaves oak leaf lettuce	¼ cup (2 fl oz) olive oil
5 leaves white coral lettuce	1 clove garlic, crushed
250 g (8 oz) cherry tomatoes	**Dressing**
60 g (2 oz) watercress sprigs	2 tablespoons olive oil
parmesan cheese, to serve	1 tablespoon mayonnaise
	1 tablespoon sour cream
	2 tablespoons lemon juice
	1 teaspoon brown sugar
	cracked pepper, to taste

1 Wash lettuces and tomatoes. Combine snow peas, red pepper, lettuces, tomatoes and watercress in a large mixing bowl.

2 To make Garlic Croûtons: Remove crusts from bread slices. Cut bread into 1 cm (½ inch) squares. Heat oil in a small, heavy-based pan, add garlic. Stir in bread. Cook until golden and crisp. Remove from heat; drain on paper towel.

3 To make Dressing: Whisk all ingredients in a small mixing bowl for 2 minutes. Just before serving, pour Dressing over salad, toss. Top with garlic croûtons and shavings of parmesan cheese.

---

fairly basic, relying on quality fresh produce and natural flavouring—garlic, onion, pepper (capsicum), olive oil, saffron and cumin—rather than complicated techniques. Pork is the common meat of the region.

The traditional start to the day is a breakfast of churros (sugared twists of fried pastry) with coffee or thick, chocolate-flavoured milk. At midday most Spaniards meet friends in cafés, pick at tapas (platters of finger food that can include olives, pickled vegetables, fried and marinated seafoods and savoury pastries) before taking the main meal of the day (comida), a leisurely affair that can stretch over several hours. The Spanish traditionally begin a meal with a green salad, a habit which seems to date from the time of Moorish rule. In the early evening the cafés again fill and the tapas ritual is repeated.

Spareribs Pork spareribs are cut from the belly area and consist of long narrow strips with small bones and layers of fat and tasty lean meat. The term is also used for breast ribs after the outer cuts have been removed.

(available in sets or as individual slices), valued for the sweet, nutty flavour of the meat that clings to them.

Spatchcock A small chicken or game bird that has been split down the back and flattened, then often threaded onto a pair of skewers before being grilled (broiled) or roasted.

Spearmint The most commonly used member of the mint family. It is used in mint sauce to accompany lamb, adds flavour to boiled peas and potatoes and is also an important ingredient in Thai cooking. Mint leaves dry well, keeping their colour and smell.

Speck The fatty top part of a leg of bacon, usually smoked and salted. It is available in small pieces and can be sliced as a cold snack or cut into small cubes and used to add flavour to cooked dishes. It is Austrian in origin.

Speculaas Thin, crisp biscuits (cookies) spiced with ginger, cinnamon and allspice and topped with slivered almonds, often made in the shape of legendary and traditional characters. Speculaas are popular in the Netherlands and southern Germany—from where they originated.

SOUPS

MULLIGATAWNY

Preparation time: 30 minutes
Total cooking time: 1 hour 10 minutes
Serves 6

1 kg (2 lb) chicken pieces, such as thighs, drumsticks, breasts
2 tablespoons plain (all-purpose) flour
2 teaspoons curry powder
1 teaspoon turmeric
1/2 teaspoon ground ginger
60 g (2 oz) butter
6 cloves

12 peppercorns
1 large apple, peeled and diced
1.5 litres (6 cups) chicken stock
2 tablespoons lemon juice
1/2 cup (4 fl oz) fresh cream
boiled rice and chutney to serve

1 Wipe chicken pieces with paper towels. Combine flour, curry powder, turmeric and ginger; rub mixture all over chicken pieces.
2 Heat butter in a heavy-based pan and lightly brown chicken on all sides. Add cloves, peppercorns, apple and stock; bring to the boil, and simmer, covered, for 1 hour.
3 Remove chicken pieces from pan and discard peppercorns and cloves. Skin chicken and cut flesh into small dice. Return to soup with the lemon juice and cream; gently reheat.
4 Serve in heated bowls, accompanied by hot boiled rice and chutney offered separately for

COCK-A-LEEKIE

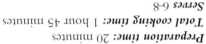

Preparation time: 20 minutes
Total cooking time: 1 hour 45 minutes
Serves 6-8

1.2 kg (2 1/2 lb) chicken
1 small bunch parsley
2 large leeks, chopped
2 teaspoons salt
1 teaspoon cracked black pepper
12 pitted prunes

1 teaspoon fresh thyme leaves
1 bay leaf
1.5 litres (6 cups) water

1 Rinse the chicken thoroughly, both inside and out, under cold running water; drain well and pat dry with paper towels. Trim off excess fat and cut chicken in half.
2 Place chicken, leeks, water, herbs and salt in a large heavy-based pan. Bring slowly to the boil; reduce heat to low. Simmer, uncovered, for 1 1/2 hours, skimming froth from the top occasionally. Discard bay leaf and parsley.
3 Carefully remove chicken halves from the pan; cool slightly. Shred flesh coarsely, discarding the skin and bones.
4 Return chicken flesh to pan with pepper and prunes; stir until just heated through.

stirring into soup, if desired. Other accompaniments, such as coconut, sultanas or chopped peanuts, can also be offered.

VICHYSSOISE

Preparation time: 25 minutes + 1 hour refrigeration
Total cooking time: 30 minutes
Serves 6

2 large leeks, chopped
2 medium potatoes, about 460 g (14½ oz), peeled and chopped
1 cup (8 fl oz) milk
½ cup (4 fl oz) cream
2 tablespoons chopped fresh chives
grated nutmeg
3 cups (24 fl oz) chicken stock

1 Place leek, potato, chives and stock in a large pan. Bring to the boil, reduce heat. Simmer, covered, until vegetables are tender, about 30 minutes. Add milk. Allow to cool.

2 Place soup in food processor. Process 30 seconds or until smooth. Transfer to large bowl; stir in cream. Cover and refrigerate for 1 hour or overnight. Serve sprinkled with nutmeg.

Note: Traditionally served chilled, this soup can, however, be gently reheated and served hot.

WATERCRESS SOUP

Preparation time: 40 minutes
Total cooking time: 15 minutes
Serves 8

1 large onion
4 spring onions (scallions)
470 g (15 oz) watercress
90 g (3 oz) butter
⅓ cup plain (all-purpose) flour
2¼ cups (20 fl oz) chicken stock
2 cups (16 fl oz) water
sour cream, to serve

1 Roughly chop onion, spring onions and watercress. Heat butter in a large heavy-based pan; add onions and watercress. Stir over low heat for 3 minutes or until vegetables have softened. Add flour; stir until well combined.

2 Add combined stock and water gradually to...

BEEF CONSOMME

Preparation time: 45 minutes
Total cooking time: 4–5 hours
Serves 6

1 large carrot, chopped
1 large brown onion, chopped
3 stalks celery, chopped
2 kg (4 lb) sawn beef and veal bones
500 g (1 lb) shin of beef or gravy beef, chopped
3 litres cold water
2 teaspoons salt
bouquet garni
10 peppercorns
2 egg whites
crushed shells of the eggs
¼ cup (2 fl oz) dry sherry

1 Place carrot, onion and celery in a large baking pan; scatter bones and meat on top. Roast in a moderate oven 180°C (350°F/Gas 4), turning occasionally, for 1 hour or until meat and vegetables are well browned but not dark.

2 Transfer meat and vegetables to a large stock pot and cover with cold water. Add salt, bouquet garni and peppercorns and bring slowly to boil, skimming surface well. Simmer stock gently, half-covered, for 3–4 hours, skimming surface occasionally. Strain stock through a colander lined with muslin (cheesecloth) or a fine sieve. Cool stock, then refrigerate until jellied. Remove all fat from surface.

3 To clarify, place de-fatted stock in a large clean pan with egg whites and crushed egg shells. Bring to boil slowly, whisking occasionally with a wire whisk when liquid gradually rises in pan. Simmer gently for 20 minutes. Strain stock through a muslin-lined colander or sieve.

4 Place in a clean pan and reheat gently; add sherry. Serve consommé in heated soup bowls.

Spice The aromatic seeds, fruit, bark, roots or flowers of trees and shrubs, almost always dried, used to flavour both sweet and savoury preparations. Most spices grow in tropical and semi-tropical climates, especially in India and South-East Asia (the Moluccas, a group of islands off Indonesia and original home of the clove and nutmeg trees, were long known as the Spice Islands). For thousands of years spices reached Europe along trading routes through south-western Asia. Among the first to reach the Mediterranean were pepper and cinnamon. Spices were rare and expensive; they were used in innumerable dishes and sauces, both sweet and savoury. For centuries the lucrative trade was monopolised by Venetian merchants. It was the desire to find the source of the spices that launched the fleets of Dutch and Portuguese ships. These voyages of discovery not only found their goal, the fabled Spice Islands of South-East Asia, but also

CHICKEN NOODLE MUSHROOM SOUP

★ **Preparation time:** 15 minutes +
15 minutes soaking
Total cooking time: 20 minutes
Serves 4–6

2 teaspoons sesame oil
2 teaspoons vegetable oil
3 half chicken breast
fillets, cut into cubes
1.25 litres (5 cups)
chicken stock
2 tablespoons soy sauce
1 slice fresh root ginger

½ cup sliced dried
mushrooms, soaked 15
minutes in hot water
105 g (3½ oz) cellophane
noodles, soaked in
water for 15 minutes
⅓ cup snipped chives, for
garnish

1 Heat oils in large pan, add chicken and cook until golden brown. Remove from pan; pour out any remaining oil from pan.
2 Return chicken to pan, add stock, soy sauce, ginger and mushrooms. Bring to the boil and simmer, uncovered, for 10 minutes. Add well drained noodles and simmer for 5 minutes longer. Remove the slice of ginger.
3 Pour into a large serving bowl. Garnish with chives. Serve immediately.

Note: Cellophane noodles are made from soy or mung bean flour and are also known as bean thread vermicelli. They can be found in Asian food stores and most large supermarkets.

RISONI (ORZO) SEAFOOD SOUP

★ **Preparation time:** 20 minutes
Total cooking time: 20 minutes
Serves 4–6

¼ cup (2 fl oz) olive oil
1 onion, chopped
2 cloves garlic, crushed
2 tablespoons chopped
parsley
1 cup (8 fl oz) red wine
1 cup (8 fl oz) tomato
puree
2 cups (16 fl oz) water
2 tablespoons tomato
paste

¾ cup risoni (orzo)
315 g (10 oz) seafood
mix
ground black pepper

Bread Slices
1 small Vienna loaf,
sliced thinly
⅓ cup (2½ fl oz) olive oil
extra 2 cloves garlic,
crushed

1 Heat oil in a large pan, add onion and garlic, and cook until golden. Add parsley and wine. Add tomato puree, water and tomato paste. Bring to the boil, sprinkle in risoni and gently boil until risoni is just tender.
2 Stir in seafood mix and cook for 3 minutes. Serve with crisp Bread Slices.
3 **To make Bread Slices:** Place slices of bread on baking tray. Combine oil and garlic and brush over each bread slice. Bake at 200°C (400°F/Gas 6) until crisp and golden brown.

OPPOSITE PAGE: WATERCRESS SOUP
LEFT: CHICKEN NOODLE MUSHROOM SOUP
ABOVE: RISONI SEAFOOD SOUP

reached the shores of the Americas.

Spices are available whole or ground. Because ground spices lose flavour quickly it is best to grind in small quantities as needed or regularly replace commercially ground spices.

Spinach Also called English spinach, a vegetable with dark green leaves. It is often served with butter and a sprinkle of nutmeg, as an accompaniment to poultry and veal; used in stuffings, soufflés and quiches; and raw leaves may be added to salads.

It probably originated in south-western Asia and was taken by the Moors to Spain in the eleventh or twelfth century. Spinach grows best in cool climates. It is available fresh most of the year and can also be bought frozen, preserved in glass jars or canned.

Split Pea The dried pea, yellow or green in colour and with husks removed, split in two at the natural division. Split peas are used to make pea and ham soup and pease pudding. In India yellow split peas are made into dhal.

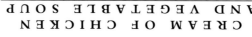

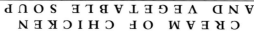

Sponge Cake A fluffy, light-textured cake which achieves its airiness from stiffly beaten egg white. There are several distinct types. Sponge cakes may be flavoured with vanilla, grated citrus peel, cocoa or orange flower water; after baking, the cake may be moistened with a liqueur or

thin syrup. Sponges are often used for layer cakes, filled with jam and cream and topped with a dusting of icing (confectioners) sugar.

Sponge Fingers Airy finger-shaped biscuits (cookies) made using sponge cake mixture; they are firm on the outside and soft in the centre. The tops are dusted with icing (confectioners) sugar before baking. Sponge fingers are served with chilled cream desserts, ice-cream and fruit purees and can be used as a border for cold charlottes.

Spotted Dick A steamed or boiled suet pudding studded with currants, sultanas or other dried fruit, usually served hot; a traditional English dessert.

Spring Onion Also known as scallion and

CREAM OF CHICKEN AND VEGETABLE SOUP

☆☆ ***Preparation time:*** 20 minutes
Total cooking time: 1 hour 45 minutes
Serves 6

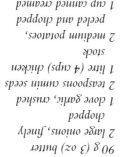

Stock
1 kg (2 lb) chicken
1.5 litres (6 cups) water
1/2 stick celery, chopped
6 peppercorns
1 bay leaf
1 clove garlic, sliced
1 small onion, chopped

Soup
1 medium carrot
1 tablespoon oil
1 medium onion, sliced
200 g (6 1/2 oz) button mushrooms, sliced
1/4 cup plain (all-purpose) flour
2/3 cup (5 fl oz) milk
1 cup (8 fl oz) cream
105 g (3 1/2 oz) snow peas (mange tout), thinly sliced
3 medium tomatoes, peeled, seeded, chopped
1 tablespoon soy sauce
salt and freshly ground black pepper, to taste

1 To make Stock: Wipe chicken and dry with paper towel.Cut chicken into breasts, thighs, legs and wings. Place in large heavy-based pan with water, celery, peppercorns, bay leaf, garlic and onion. Bring to boil; reduce heat and simmer, covered, for 1 1/4 hours. Remove from heat; cool slightly. Strain, reserving chicken and 1.25 litres (5 cups) stock; discard onion mixture.
2 To make Soup: Cut carrot into matchstick strips. Heat oil in large heavy-based pan, add onion, carrot and mushrooms. Cook, stirring, over low heat until onion is tender. Stir in stock, and blended flour and milk. Bring to boil. Reduce heat and simmer, stirring, until slightly thickened.
3 Cut reserved chicken into thin strips. Add chicken, cream, snow peas, tomato and soy sauce to soup. Stir until heated through. Season to taste. Serve hot.

CORN AND CHEESE CHOWDER

☆ ***Preparation time:*** 15 minutes
Total cooking time: 30 minutes
Serves 8

90 g (3 oz) butter
2 large onions, finely chopped
1 clove garlic, crushed
2 teaspoons cumin seeds
1 litre (4 cups) chicken stock
2 medium potatoes, peeled and chopped
1 cup canned creamed corn
2 cups fresh corn kernels
1/4 cup chopped fresh parsley
1 cup grated cheddar cheese
salt and freshly ground black pepper to taste
1/4 cup (2 fl oz) cream, optional
2 tablespoons chopped fresh chives, to garnish

1 Heat butter in a large heavy-based pan. Add onion and cook over medium-high heat for 5 minutes or until golden. Add garlic and cumin seeds and cook for 1 minute, stirring constantly. Add chicken stock. Bring to boil. Add potato; reduce heat and simmer, uncovered, for 10 minutes.
2 Add creamed corn, corn kernels and parsley. Bring to boil, reduce heat and simmer for 10 minutes more.
3 Stir in cheese, salt and pepper to taste, and cream. Heat gently until cheese melts. Serve immediately, sprinkled with chopped chives.

SPANISH CLASSICS

GAZPACHO

★ **Preparation time:** 15 minutes +
1–2 hours refrigeration
Total cooking time: nil

Serves 4–6

3 slices white bread, crusts removed	2 tablespoons olive oil
8 large ripe tomatoes, peeled, seeded and chopped	1–2 cups (8–16 fl oz) iced water
1 cucumber, peeled, seeded and chopped	**Garnish**
1 small onion, chopped	1 medium red pepper (capsicum), cut into thin strips
1 small green pepper (capsicum), chopped	1 medium onion, thinly sliced
1/3 cup chopped fresh mint	1 small cucumber, peeled, seeded and chopped
2 cloves garlic, crushed	2 hard-boiled eggs, seeded and chopped, chopped
2 tablespoons red wine vinegar	1/2 cup sliced green olives
2 tablespoons tomato paste	

1 Combine all ingredients for soup, except iced water, in a large bowl. Cover with plastic wrap and set aside for 20 minutes.

2 Divide mixture into thirds. Place one-third into food processor. Using pulse action, press button for 30 seconds or until smooth. Pour mixture into a large bowl; repeat with remaining two

batches. Thin the mixture to desired consistency using iced water. Cover with plastic wrap and refrigerate for at least one hour.

3 **To Garnish:** Serve individual soup bowls half-filled with small ice cubes. Place garnishes in small bowls and pass around for guests to add to soup as desired.

POTATO AND ONION OMELETTE

★ **Preparation time:** 15 minutes
Total cooking time: 20 minutes

Serves 4–6

2 tablespoons olive oil	1/4 teaspoon ground sweet paprika
2 large potatoes, cut into small cubes	1 tablespoon olive oil, extra
2 medium onions, chopped	4 eggs

1 Heat oil in a medium heavy-based pan; add potato and onion. Cook over medium-high heat until golden brown and well coated with oil. Reduce heat, cover pan and cook for 5–6 minutes, stirring occasionally, until potato is cooked.

2 Remove potato and onion from pan. Drain on paper towel. Beat eggs and paprika in a medium bowl until frothy; gently stir in potato and onion mixture.

3 Heat extra oil in a clean pan. Add egg mixture and cook, covered, over medium heat for 15–20 minutes or until mixture is firm. Place under a hot grill (broiler) until golden brown.

4 Serve omelette hot or cold, cut into wedges, with a simple salad.

OPPOSITE PAGE, ABOVE: CHICKEN AND VEGETABLE SOUP, BELOW: CORN AND CHEESE CHOWDER THIS PAGE, ABOVE: GAZPACHO, BELOW: POTATO AND ONION OMELETTE

Sprout A grain, seed or pulse, germinated to grow as a plant and used as a food. Sprouts most commonly used include mung beans, soy beans and alfalfa. Small and crunchy, sprouts can be added to salads and are often an ingredient in

green onion, a variety of onion with small, white, mild-flavoured bulbs and long, green, grass-like leaves. They are eaten raw and finely sliced in salads. The name comes from Scallion, a port in ancient Palestine.

Spring Roll A layer of thin dough wrapped around a filling of cooked vegetables and meats, rolled up and deep-fried until crisp and golden. Spring rolls are usually served with a dipping sauce, as finger food or a first course. Variations are eaten throughout South-East Asia. They are traditionally served during Lunar New Year celebrations.

Spring Roll Wrapper Pliable, paper-thin sheet of white rice flour dough usually sold frozen in packs of 20–30. When using, keep wrappers covered with a cloth.

Sprouts (continued)

Chinese stir-fries. If sprouting seeds at home use dried seeds sold as food (seeds sold for gardening have often been treated with fungicides). Sprouts are also available fresh or canned.

Spumone An Italian frozen dessert consisting of ice-cream layers assembled in a mould and then frozen. Spumone usually has a layer of chocolate ice-cream, a strawberry or raspberry ice-cream layer and a green layer of pistachio ice-cream; the inner layers can also consist of whipped cream or liqueur-soaked fruits. The dessert is served sliced.

Spun Sugar Also known as angel's hair, gossamer-fine threads of sugar made from syrup boiled to a light caramel. Spun sugar is used as a decoration or garnish for ice-creams, special desserts and festive cakes. Croquembouche, the traditional French wedding cake, is a high pile of choux pastry puffs glazed with spun sugar.

Squab A small, young pigeon, about four weeks old. Its dark, sweet, succulent flesh, which is served rare, can be grilled (broiled) or roasted. Care should be taken not to overcook it.

MIXED VEGETABLES WITH GARLIC MAYONNAISE

⭐ *Preparation time:* 30 minutes
Total cooking time: 15 minutes
Serves 4–6

Garlic Mayonnaise
2 egg yolks
4 cloves garlic, crushed
1 cup (8 fl oz) olive oil
pinch pepper
2 tablespoons lemon juice

Vegetables
4 small eggplants (aubergines)
4 medium red peppers (capsicum)
4 medium firm tomatoes
4 small onions
1/3 cup (2 1/2 fl oz) olive oil
1/3 cup chopped fresh parsley
1 clove garlic, crushed
1/4 teaspoon ground pepper

1 To make Garlic Mayonnaise: Place egg yolks and garlic into a medium mixing bowl. Whisk together for 1 minute. Add oil, about a teaspoon at a time, whisking constantly until mixture is thick and creamy; increase the speed at which oil is added as mayonnaise thickens. Stir in pepper and lemon juice. Set aside.

2 Place whole unpeeled vegetables onto a lightly oiled grill tray. Cook under a hot grill (broiler) for 6–8 minutes, turning once, until vegetables are black all over. Remove, cover with a clean wet tea-towel, and allow to cool slightly. Peel blackened skin from vegetables and cut into 2 cm (3/4 inch) cubes. Arrange in a serving dish.

3 Combine the olive oil, parsley, garlic and pepper in a small bowl and pour over vegetables. Serve, warm, as a single course, with Garlic Mayonnaise and bread.

ABOVE: MIXED VEGETABLES WITH GARLIC MAYONNAISE
OPPOSITE PAGE, ABOVE: ORANGE AND CARAMEL CUSTARD; BELOW: CHICKEN SPANISH STYLE

PAELLA

⭐⭐ *Preparation time:* 25 minutes
Total cooking time: 50 minutes
Serves 4–6

1 tablespoon olive oil
4 boned chicken thighs, each cut into 4 pieces
1 large red pepper (capsicum), chopped
1 tablespoon chopped parsley
425 g (13 1/2 oz) marinara mix
2 cups long-grain rice
1 tablespoon olive oil, extra

2 cloves garlic, crushed
1 medium onion, sliced, top to base
1/2 teaspoon ground turmeric
1 litre (4 cups) chicken stock
1 cup frozen peas
125 g (4 oz) salami, thinly sliced
1 lemon, cut into 6 wedges

1 Heat oil in large heavy-based pan, add chicken pieces. Cook over medium-high heat for 2–3 minutes or until golden brown, turning once. Remove from pan, drain on paper towel. Add pepper, parsley and marinara mix to pan and stir for 1 minute over medium-high heat. Remove mixture and set aside.

2 Soak the rice in cold water for 10 minutes; drain, rinse under cold running water and drain again.

3 Heat extra oil in a pan, add garlic and onion, cook on medium heat for 1 minute or until golden. Add rice and stir well, making sure grains are well coated with oil. Stir in turmeric and stock and cover pan with a tight-fitting lid.

4 Bring the rice and stock mixture slowly to the boil, stirring once. Reduce heat and simmer, covered for 8–10 minutes. Place chicken on top of the rice, cover and cook over low heat for another 10 minutes.

5 Add pepper and marinara mix, peas and salami. Cover and cook over low heat for 8–10 minutes or until almost all the liquid has been absorbed.

6 Remove from heat and set aside, covered, for 5 minutes or until all the liquid has been absorbed and the rice is just tender. Separate the rice grains with a fork just before serving on a large platter garnished with lemon wedges.

CHICKEN SPANISH STYLE

✳ **Preparation time:** 30 minutes
Total cooking time: 35 minutes
Serves 4–6

6 chicken breast fillets
6 thin slices leg ham
toothpicks, to secure fillets
60 g (2 oz) butter
1 small onion, chopped
1 small carrot, finely chopped
1/4 teaspoon ground pepper
1/4 teaspoon ground nutmeg
1 tablespoon plain (all-purpose) flour
1 1/2 cups (12 fl oz) chicken stock
1 cup (8 fl oz) apple cider

1 Preheat oven to moderate 180°C (350°F/Gas 4). Using a sharp knife, make a deep incision into the thickest section of each breast. Insert a slice of ham, secure with toothpicks. Cover with plastic wrap and refrigerate until required.

2 Heat butter in pan, add onion and carrot. Cook 4 minutes over low heat until onion and carrot are soft. Add flour, stir over low heat until lightly golden. Add combined stock and cider gradually to pan, stirring until mixture is smooth. Add pepper and nutmeg. Stir constantly over medium heat 3 minutes or until sauce boils and thickens; boil for 1 minute more. Remove from heat.

3 Place chicken in a single layer in a shallow ovenproof dish. Pour sauce over, cover and bake for 20–25 minutes.

4 Remove toothpicks from chicken and serve with a spoonful of sauce.

ORANGE AND CARAMEL CUSTARD

✳ **Preparation time:** 30 minutes + 8 hours refrigeration
Total cooking time: 55 minutes
Serves 4–6

Caramel
1 cup (8 fl oz) cream
1/2 cup (4 fl oz) water
1 teaspoon finely grated orange rind
1 cup caster (superfine) sugar

Custard
1 cup (8 fl oz) milk
3 eggs
3 egg yolks
1/3 cup caster (superfine) sugar

1 Preheat oven to moderately slow 160°C (325°F/Gas 3). Brush a deep 20 cm (8 inch) round tin or ovenproof dish with melted butter.

2 **To make Caramel:** Combine water and sugar in small pan. Stir constantly over low heat until sugar dissolves, then bring to boil. Reduce heat; simmer, uncovered, without stirring, 3–4 minutes or until golden brown. Pour into dish.

3 **To make Custard:** Heat milk, cream and rind in small pan until almost boiling. Cool and strain. Beat eggs, yolks and sugar with electric beaters until thick and pale. Add milk gradually to egg mixture, beating constantly.

4 Pour through fine strainer over caramel in dish. Stand dish in deep baking dish. Pour in hot water to come halfway up sides. Bake 45 minutes or until set. Remove dish from hot water bath. Cool; refrigerate for at least 8 hours. Serve.

Squid Also known as calamari, a saltwater mollusc with a long cylindrical body and ten tentacles surrounding a parrot-like beak. It is prized for its delicately flavoured, firm, white flesh. Squid is found in temperate waters throughout the world. It has long been an important ingredient in the cooking of Asia and the Mediterranean.

Squash A general term for edible members of the gourd family, native to the Americas. They are usually divided into summer squash and winter squash. Summer squash, soft-skinned and quick-growing, are picked young and include zucchini (courgette), patty pan squash, scalloped squash, baby marrows and custard squash; small summer squash may be steamed or boiled. Winter squash are the larger, slow-growing, hard-skinned varieties, such as pumpkin.

Star Anise The dried, star-shaped fruit of a tree native to southern China, used as a spice. It has a strong aniseed flavour. Star anise has long been used in Asian cooking to flavour meat and poultry dishes and is one of the components of five spice powder; it has been known in Europe since the early seventeenth century. It is available whole or ground.

Star Fruit See Carambola.

Steak A slice of meat, usually beef, taken from between the rump and the rib. Steak cuts include T-bone, porterhouse and sirloin; fillet or tenderloin (the most tender) comes from beneath the lower backbone. Steak can be grilled (broiled), barbecued or pan-fried, and is usually served with a sauce.

Steam To cook food by using the concentrated moist heat of steam given off by steadily boiling water. Steaming can be done in a double saucepan the top half of which has a perforated base; in a covered basin set in a pot of boiling

---

MEXICAN-STYLE BEEF SPARERIBS

✳ *Preparation time:* 15 minutes
Total cooking time: 1 hour
Serves 4

1.5 kg (3 lb) beef spareribs
2 bay leaves
1 1/2 cups (12 fl oz) water
1/4 cup soft brown sugar
1 clove garlic, crushed
1 tablespoon Mexican style chilli powder, or to taste
1 teaspoon dried oregano
1 teaspoon ground cumin
bottled hot pepper sauce to taste

Sauce
1 tablespoon vegetable oil
1/2 cup chopped onion
1 clove garlic, crushed
1 tablespoon white sugar
2 tablespoons cider vinegar
425 g (13 1/2 oz) can tomato puree

1 Place spareribs and bay leaves in a large pan. Combine water, brown sugar and garlic, pour over ribs. Heat until boiling, reduce heat and cover. Gently simmer, turning ribs occasionally, until tender, about 30–45 minutes.

2 To make Sauce: Heat oil in small pan, add onion and garlic; cook until soft. Stir in sugar, vinegar, puree, chilli powder, oregano, cumin and sauce. Heat until boiling, reduce heat. Simmer, stirring occasionally, 5 minutes. Cover, keep warm.

3 Drain ribs, pat dry on paper towels. Grill (broil) about 13 cm (5 inches) above glowing coals, turning and basting frequendy with sauce, about 10–15 minutes. Serve with remaining sauce.

BARBECUED PORK SPARERIBS

✳ *Preparation time:* 5 minutes +
2 hours marinating
Total cooking time: 20 minutes
Serves 6–8

1 kg (2 lb) pork spareribs
1/4 cup (2 fl oz) lemon juice
2 tablespoons tomato paste
2 tablespoons hoisin sauce
2 tablespoons chilli sauce
1/4 cup honey
2 tablespoons sesame seeds, toasted

1 Remove rind from the spareribs. Trim off any excess fat. In a bowl or jug, combine tomato paste, hoisin sauce, chilli sauce, lemon juice and honey. Place spareribs in a large, shallow dish and pour the marinade over. Store in refrigerator, covered with plastic wrap, for 2 hours or overnight, turning occasionally.

2 Drain meat, reserving the marinade. Place the spareribs on a lightly oiled preheated grill or flatplate. Cook over a medium heat for 20 minutes or until tender, turning occasionally.

3 Heat the remaining marinade in a small pan over low heat; do not boil. Pour over the ribs just before serving.

4 Sprinkle ribs with the toasted sesame seeds. May be served with boiled or fried rice and steamed green vegetables.

ABOVE: BARBECUED PORK SPARERIBS. OPPOSITE PAGE, BELOW: SPINACH FRITTERS WITH WALNUT SAUCE; ABOVE: SPINACH AND AVOCADO SALAD.

SPINACH FRITTERS WITH WALNUT SAUCE

★ Preparation time: 20 minutes
Total cooking time: 6–8 minutes
Serves 6

12 spinach leaves, stalks removed
1/3 cup (2 1/2 fl oz) oil

Sauce
2 eggs
2 cups wholemeal breadcrumbs
1 cup walnuts, ground
4 drops Tabasco sauce
1/2 cup toasted ground walnuts
1 cup plain yoghurt
pinch of ground saffron

1 Wash spinach under cold running water. Chop roughly and place in a pan. Cover, cook until spinach is tender. Drain; cool. Using hands, squeeze spinach to remove excess moisture. Chop finely.

2 Place spinach in a bowl, add lightly beaten eggs, breadcrumbs, ground walnuts and Tabasco sauce. Mix well to combine. Divide mixture into twelve equal portions. Shape each into a round. Heat oil in shallow pan. Add fritters and cook over a medium heat, turning once, until fritters are golden brown on both sides.

3 While fritters are cooking, prepare sauce by combining walnuts, yoghurt and saffron. Stir well to mix. Serve fritters with walnut sauce.

Note: If fresh spinach is not available substitute a 250 g (8 oz) packet of frozen spinach. Thaw, remove excess moisture using paper towels.

SPINACH AND AVOCADO SALAD

★ Preparation time: 15 minutes
Total cooking time: nil
Serves 6

12 large spinach leaves
75 g (2 1/2 oz) walnuts, chopped
1 medium avocado, sliced
2 tablespoons walnut oil
3 teaspoons white wine vinegar

1 Wash and dry spinach thoroughly. Place in a serving bowl with the walnuts and avocado.

2 Place oil and vinegar in a small screw-top jar and shake well. Pour over salad ingredients; toss lightly. Serve immediately.

CREAMED SPINACH

Tear 1 bunch spinach into pieces. Heat 15 g (1/2 oz) butter in heavy-based frying pan. Add 1 finely sliced small onion. Cook 2–3 minutes or until onion is soft. Add spinach, cook 1 minute. Stir in 1/4 cup (2 fl oz) cream, heat through. Sprinkle with nutmeg and grated cheddar cheese. Serve hot.

SHREDDED SPINACH AND BACON

Finely shred 1 bunch spinach. Cut 2 bacon rashers in thin strips. Heat 2 teaspoons olive oil in frying pan. Add bacon, fry on medium-high heat until almost crisp. Add spinach, toss through until just wilted. Serve hot.

water; or, as in China and South-East Asia, in multi-layered metal or bamboo steamers.

Steamboat A Chinese meal consisting of small portions of meat and seafood cooked at the table in simmering stock. Each diner uses chopsticks or a long-handled small wire basket to add or retrieve food, when cooked, each portion is dipped in sauce and eaten. Meat is cooked first, then seafood, then vegetables. As a final course, noodles are cooked in the remaining broth and served with it as soup. The dish is traditionally cooked in a Mongolian fire pot, a table-top cooking device which has a moat (for the stock) around a chimney-like funnel and is set over glowing coals; a fondue set or saucepan and gas ring may be substituted. This style of cooking is believed to have originated with the nomadic Mongolians of northern China.

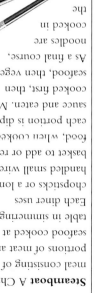

Steamed Pudding A British specialty, the steamed pudding is cooked in a deep covered basin over boiling water. The basic pudding mixture usually consists of flour, fat, sugar and eggs; dried or fresh fruits, spices and flavourings such as coffee, vanilla and

chocolate, may be added. Steamed puddings range from the dense and fruit-rich plum (or Christmas) pudding to light, cake-like, soufflé puddings. Steamed ginger pudding, a warming winter favourite which probably evolved as a less expensive version of the traditional plum pudding, is made with a layer of honey or

golden syrup (light corn syrup can be substituted) at the bottom of the basin; this soaks into the batter and forms a syrupy topping sauce when the pudding is unmoulded.

Stew A selection of meat, poultry or fish and vegetables, with herbs and seasonings added, which is cooked slowly with liquid in a covered container (either on the cook-top or in the oven) until the meat and vegetables are tender. Many less expensive, tougher cuts of meat are suitable for stewing.

SPINACH AND SALMON TERRINE

✳ ✳
Preparation time: 35 minutes
Total cooking time: 10 minutes
Serves 8

2 packets frozen chopped spinach
30 g (1 oz) butter
1/2 cup chopped spring onions (scallions)
1 tablespoon chopped fresh dill
nutmeg and pepper to taste
6 eggs
1 tablespoon cornflour (cornstarch)
1 tablespoon lime juice

Filling
1/4 cup chopped spring onions (scallions)
1 teaspoon chopped fresh dill
1 tablespoon lime juice
1 tablespoon horseradish
250 g (8 oz) Neufchâtel cheese
200 g (6 1/2 oz) sliced smoked salmon

1 Preheat oven to moderate 180°C (350°F/Gas 4). Brush a shallow 30 x 25 cm (12 x 10 inch) Swiss roll (jelly roll) tin with melted butter or oil. Line base and sides with baking paper, extending 5 cm (2 inch) extra at ends. Thaw spinach and squeeze out excess moisture using paper towels. Heat butter in medium pan. Add onion and dill, stir over medium heat 1 minute. Add spinach, heat through. Season with nutmeg and pepper. Remove from heat.

2 Beat eggs in medium bowl. Blend cornflour and juice in small bowl until smooth. Combine with eggs and spinach mixture. Pour into prepared tin. Bake 7 minutes or until firm to touch. Turn onto a damp tea-towel covered with sheet of baking paper and sprinkled with cheese. Cover with a cloth and leave to cool.

3 **To make Filling:** Place onion, dill, juice, horseradish and cheese in food processor. Process 30 seconds or until smooth.

4 Cut spinach base into three strips. Place one strip on board. Spread with a layer of Filling, top with one-third of the smoked salmon slices. Spread second strip with a thin layer of Filling. Place cheese-side down on salmon. Repeat procedure with next layer. Decorate with rolled smoked salmon slices. Cut the terrine into 2 cm (3/4 inch) slices to serve. Serve cool as a first course, with light salad as an accompaniment.

BASIL SPINACH SALAD

Tear 1 bunch of spinach into pieces. Combine in a large bowl with 1/4 cup of shredded basil leaves and 2 tablespoons of toasted pine nuts. Finely slice 1 rasher of bacon. Cook bacon in a small pan until crisp. Remove from pan and drain on paper towels. In a small bowl, combine 2 tablespoons oil, 1 tablespoon white wine vinegar, 1/2 teaspoon sugar and 1 tablespoon sour cream. Mix well and drizzle over salad. Top with bacon and parmesan cheese.

ABOVE: SPINACH AND SALMON TERRINE.
OPPOSITE PAGE: VEGETARIAN MINI SPRING ROLLS

432

VEGETARIAN MINI SPRING ROLLS

★ *Preparation time:* 55 minutes + 30 minutes standing
Total cooking time: 20 minutes
Makes 20

4 dried Chinese mushrooms	³/₄ teaspoon finely grated ginger
155 g (5 oz) fried bean curd	6 spring onions (scallions), finely chopped
3 cups shredded Chinese cabbage	1 tablespoon oil
1 large carrot, grated	1 teaspoon crushed garlic
1 tablespoon soy sauce	
5 large spring roll wrappers	
oil, extra, for deep-frying	

1 Place mushrooms in a bowl and cover with hot water. Leave for 30 minutes. Drain, squeeze to remove excess liquid. Remove stems; chop caps finely. Cut bean curd into small cubes and set aside. Heat oil in wok or heavy-based frying pan, swirling gently to coat base and side. Add spring onion, garlic, ginger, cabbage, carrot, mushrooms and bean curd. Stir-fry for 5 minutes over a moderate to high heat until vegetables are softened. Add the soy; stir to combine. Allow to cool.

2 Cut each spring roll wrapper into four squares. Work with one square at a time, keeping the remainder covered with a clean, damp tea-towel. Place 2 teaspoonsful of the filling on the wrapper and fold one point over. Fold in the two side points, then roll up towards the last point, forming a log shape. Seal point with a little flour and water paste. Repeat process with remaining wrappers and filling.

3 Heat the extra oil in a wok; deep-fry the rolls, four at a time, until golden, for about 3 minutes. Remove rolls from oil with a slotted spoon; drain on paper towels. Serve warm.

Stilton A creamy-textured, blue-veined, semi-firm cow's milk cheese. It is creamy-white to amber in colour and has a strong aroma reminiscent of pears. Stilton dates from the seventeenth century, when it was sold to coach passengers who stopped at the Bell Inn in the village of Stilton, in eastern England. The cheese should be served at room temperature at the end of a meal.

Stir-fry To rapidly and uniformly cook chopped food (vegetables, meat, poultry or seafood) in a little hot oil, in either a wok or a frying pan (skillet), over a high heat, all the time turning the mixture with a spatula. Stir-frying seals in flavours and the food also retains its crispness.

Stock A thin, clear, flavoured liquid obtained by simmering vegetables, herbs and spices with meat, poultry or seafood. The liquid is then strained and chilled so that any fat which rises to the top can be removed. Stock is used to enrich soups, casseroles and sauces. Stock can be home-made but is also available in cans and long-life cartons, as a powder and as a moist cube.

SQUID (CALAMARI)

GREEK STYLE SQUID (CALAMARI)

★
Preparation time: 30 minutes
Total cooking time: 35 minutes
Serves 6–8

1 kg (2 lb) medium tubes calamari
1½ cups cooked rice
1 egg, lightly beaten

Stuffing
1 tablespoon olive oil
2 spring onions (scallions), chopped
⅓ cup pine nuts
½ cup currants
2 tablespoons chopped fresh parsley
2 teaspoons finely grated lemon rind

Sauce
1 tablespoon olive oil
1 onion, finely chopped
1 clove garlic, crushed
4 large ripe tomatoes, peeled and chopped
¼ cup (2 fl oz) good quality red wine
1 tablespoon chopped oregano

1 Preheat oven to moderately slow 160°C (325°F/Gas 3). Wash and dry calamari tubes. Combine oil, onion, pine nuts, currants, parsley, lemon rind and rice in a bowl. Mix well. Add enough egg to moisten all ingredients.

2 Three-quarters fill each tube. Secure end with a toothpick or skewer. Place in single layer in a casserole dish.

3 **To make Sauce:** Heat oil in pan; add onion and garlic and cook over low heat 2 minutes or until onion is soft. Add tomato, wine and oregano. Cover; cook over low heat 10 minutes.

4 Pour sauce over calamari; cover and bake 20 minutes or until tender. Remove toothpicks; slice thickly. Spoon sauce over just before serving.

FRIED SQUID (CALAMARI) WITH TARTARE SAUCE

★ ★
Preparation time: 20 minutes
Total cooking time: 1 minute per batch
Serves 4

500 g (1 lb) small, cleaned calamari tubes
2 tablespoons cornflour (cornstarch)
2 eggs, lightly beaten
2 cloves garlic, crushed
2 teaspoons grated lemon rind
1 cup dried breadcrumbs
oil for deep frying

Tartare Sauce
1 cup mayonnaise
2 tablespoons chopped fresh chives
2 tablespoons chopped pickled onions
1 tablespoon seeded mustard

1 Slice calamari thinly. Place cornflour on a plate. Combine eggs, garlic and rind in a bowl. Place breadcrumbs on another plate. Toss calamari in cornflour; shake off excess. Dip in egg mixture. Coat with breadcrumbs; shake off excess.

2 Heat oil in a deep heavy-based pan. Gently lower small batches of calamari into moderately hot oil. Cook over medium-high heat for 1 minute or until just heated through and lightly browned. Carefully remove from oil with a slotted spoon. Drain on paper towels, keep warm. Repeat with remaining calamari.

3 **To make Tartare Sauce:** Combine mayonnaise, chives, pickled onions and mustard. Mix well. Serve as a dip.

Stollen A German yeast cake made with dried fruits, candied peel and almonds, and sprinkled with sugar before baking. It is traditionally eaten at Christmas.

Strawberry The red, heart-shaped, juicy berry of a ground-hugging plant related to the rose, now cultivated throughout the world. Strawberries can be added to fruit and savoury salads, eaten with a little cream or a dusting of sugar and a squeeze of lemon juice, and used whole or sliced to garnish a range of cakes and desserts. They are puréed for use in ice-cream and sorbets, and cooked as jams, jellies, preserves and fillings for tarts and pies.

Strawberries have been cultivated in Europe since the thirteenth century. At the beginning of the eighteenth century the scarlet Virginia strawberry reached France from North America—it is the ancestor of the large varieties commercially available today. The wild strawberry has a more intense flavour.

Stroganoff A traditional Russian dish consisting of strips of fillet beef, lightly sautéed and coated with a sauce of sour cream; it sometimes

STEAK DIANE

> **Preparation time:** 5 minutes
> **Total cooking time:** 15–20 minutes
> **Serves** 6

6 fillet steaks, about 125 g (4 oz) each	4 cloves garlic, crushed
½ teaspoon ground black pepper	2 tablespoons worcestershire sauce
45 g (1½ oz) butter	1 tablespoon brandy
15 g (½ oz) butter, extra	½ cup (4 fl oz) cream
2 spring onions (scallions), finely chopped	2 tablespoons finely chopped fresh parsley

1 Trim meat of excess fat and sinew. Flatten steaks to an even thickness. Nick edges to prevent curling. Sprinkle each steak with pepper. Heat butter in pan; add steaks. Cook over high heat 2 minutes each side to seal, turning once. For a rare result, cook for another minute each side. For medium and well-done results, reduce heat to medium, cook for another 2–3 minutes each side for medium and 4–6 minutes each side for well done. Remove from pan, drain on paper towels.
2 Heat extra butter in pan. Add chopped spring onion and garlic; cook for 3 minutes. Add worcestershire sauce and brandy and stir to dislodge crusty pieces from the bottom of pan.

OPPOSITE PAGE, ABOVE: FRIED SQUID; BELOW: GREEK STYLE SQUID. THIS PAGE, ABOVE: STEAK DIANE; RIGHT: STEAK WITH CORIANDER BUTTER

Stir in the cream; simmer for 5 minutes. Return steaks to the pan with parsley and heat through.

STEAK WITH CORIANDER BUTTER

> **Preparation time:** 20 minutes
> **Total cooking time:** 5–15 minutes
> **Serves** 8

8 x 185 g (6 oz) scotch fillet steaks	1 tablespoon finely chopped fresh mint
	1 teaspoon grated orange rind
Coriander Butter	2 teaspoons finely grated ginger
155 g (5 oz) butter, softened	
2 tablespoons finely chopped fresh coriander	

1 Trim meat of excess fat and sinew. Secure meat with string or toothpicks.
2 To make Coriander Butter: Beat butter in small bowl until creamy. Add coriander, mint, rind and ginger. Beat until combined. Place in log shape on piece of foil. Roll up, refrigerate until firm.
3 Place steaks on oiled, preheated grill or flatplate. Cook over high heat for 2 minutes each side to seal, turning once. For a rare result, cook for another minute each side. For medium and well-done results, move meat to cooler part of flatplate, cook another 2–3 minutes each side for medium and 4–6 minutes each side for well done. Slice Coriander Butter into 1 cm (½ inch) thick rounds. Place on top of hot steaks to serve.

---

contains mushrooms and onions. Stroganoff is often served over noodles. It has been known since the eighteenth century and is said to have been created for a member of the Stroganov family, wealthy

merchants originally from Novgorod.

Strudel A dessert or savoury dish consisting of a wafer-thin pastry dough wrapped around a filling, then baked (traditionally bent into a crescent or horseshoe shape). It is usually served warm. Sweet fillings can include apple, sour cherry, and cream cheese mixtures. Savoury strudels with fillings such as chopped, boiled beef with bacon

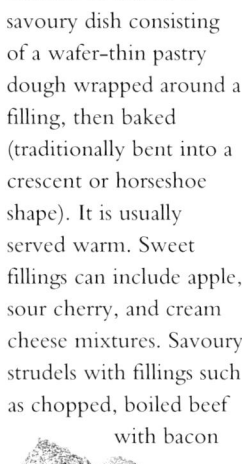

and onions are popular in Austria.

Stuffing A savoury mixture of breadcrumbs, rice, minced meat, poultry or fish, with chopped fruit or vegetables, herbs, spices and other flavourings, which is bound with milk or egg and used to add bulk and flavour to meat, fish, poultry and vegetables. Stuffing often serves the dual purpose

of filling a cavity created by the removal of innards or seeds, and so preserving the shape of the food. Any leftover stuffing can be cooked separately on a greased baking dish.

Succotash A dish of North American origin consisting of a mixture of corn kernels and lima beans. It is served as an accompaniment to meat or poultry. Succotash descends from the

misickquatash of the Narraganset Indians, made with corn and kidney beans cooked in bear fat.

Suckling Pig Also known as sucking pig, a young pig slaughtered when no more than eight weeks old, prized for its sweet, rich, succulent meat. Suckling pig may be spit-roasted whole over a barbecue or oven-roasted.

Suet The white fat which lies around lamb and beef kidneys. It is firm, dry and non-greasy to handle and is used as fat in the cooking of pastries and rich boiled

STEAK AND KIDNEY PUDDING

⭐
⭐⭐
Preparation time: 30 minutes
Total cooking time: 4 hours 10 minutes
Serves 4

500 g (1 lb) round or rump steak	½ cup (4 fl oz) red wine
200 g (6½ oz) lamb kidneys	1 cup (8 fl oz) beef stock
2 tablespoons plain (all-purpose) flour	2 tablespoons chopped fresh parsley
30 g (1 oz) butter	1 bay leaf
1 tablespoon oil	
1 medium onion, sliced	**Suet Pastry**
1 clove garlic, crushed	1½ cups self-raising flour
125 g (4 oz) button mushrooms, quartered	90 g (3 oz) suet, skinned, finely grated
	½ cup (4 fl oz) water, approximately

1 Trim meat of excess fat and sinew. Cut meat evenly into 3 cm (1¼ inch) cubes. Peel skin from kidneys, cut kidneys into quarters, trim off any excess fat and sinew. Place flour in a plastic bag, add meat and kidneys and toss to coat. Shake off any excess flour.
2 Heat the butter and oil in a heavy-based pan. Add onion and garlic, stirring until soft, remove. Add the meat and kidneys in small batches, cooking quickly over a medium-high heat until well browned on all sides; drain on paper towels.

3 Return the onion, garlic, meat and kidneys to pan. Add the mushrooms, wine, stock, parsley and bay leaf; bring to the boil. Reduce heat to a simmer, cook, covered, for 1 hour or until the meat is tender, stirring occasionally. Allow mixture to cool.
4 To make Suet Pastry: Sift flour into a bowl, stir in the grated suet. Add sufficient water to mix to a firm dough. Knead on a lightly floured surface until smooth. Roll two-thirds of suet pastry to fit the base and side of an 8-cup pudding basin; brush the top edge with water.
5 Spoon cooled meat filling into pastry. Roll remaining pastry to cover basin, press edges of pastry firmly together to seal. Grease a sheet of greaseproof paper large enough to cover the top of the basin plus about 5 cm (2 inches) all round. Place the paper over top of pudding.
6 Place a sheet of foil over the top of the paper, secure tightly with string. Place basin on a trivet in a large pan. Add enough water to come halfway up side of basin. Bring to boil, reduce heat to a simmer and cook, covered, 3 hours. Turn out onto a plate, cut into wedges to serve.

STEAK TARTARE

⭐
Preparation time: 15 minutes
Total cooking time: nil
Serves 4

500 g (1 lb) eye fillet of beef	2 tablespoons chopped capers
salt and pepper	2 tablespoons chopped fresh parsley
4 egg yolks	
1 medium white onion, finely chopped	pumpernickel bread or toast triangles for serving

1 Trim meat so that no sinew or fat is evident. Chop or mince beef finely in a meat mincer or food processor; it should not become pulp. Season meat well with salt and pepper.
2 Divide mixture into four portions, shape each into a round cake and place on serving plates. Using the back of a soup spoon, make a shallow impression in the top of each cake and slide in a whole egg yolk.
3 Serve each steak with a small mound of onion, capers and parsley on the side and accompany with pumpernickel bread or toast triangles.

Note: Some people like to serve Steak Tartare with Tabasco or chilli sauce.

ABOVE: STEAK AND KIDNEY PUDDING
OPPOSITE PAGE: STRAWBERRY SHORTCAKE

STRAWBERRIES

STRAWBERRY SHORTCAKE

✳

Preparation time: 20 minutes
Total cooking time: 12–15 minutes

Makes one 20 cm (8 inch) round cake

280 g (9 oz) plain (all-purpose) flour	*¾ cup (6 fl oz) milk*
4 teaspoons baking powder	*1½ cups (12 fl oz) strawberries, halved, or other sliced fresh fruit*
1 teaspoon salt	
1½ tablespoons sugar	

1 Preheat oven to 220ºC (425ºF/Gas 7). Brush a 20 cm (8 inch) round cake tin with butter or oil. Coat base and side evenly with flour; shake off excess. Place flour, baking powder, salt and sugar in a large bowl.

2 Slowly stir in milk, using just enough to combine dough. Turn out onto a floured board and knead for 1–2 minutes. Place dough in prepared cake tin. Bake for 12–15 minutes. Turn cake out onto wire rack to cool.

3 Split cake horizontally using two forks. Spread cut side of bottom half with half of the whipped cream. Place most of the halved strawberries or other sliced fresh fruit over the cream. Top with other half of cake. Spread remaining cream on top and decorate with remaining strawberries or fruit.

STRAWBERRY CONSERVE

✳

Preparation time: 15 minutes + overnight soaking
Total cooking time: 30–40 minutes

Makes 1½ cups

500 g (1 lb) strawberries	*1½ cups sugar*

1 Wash and drain fruit; remove stalks. Cover fruit with ½ cup sugar and leave to stand overnight.

2 Strain liquid from strawberries. Place liquid in pan, add remaining sugar and stir over low heat for 10 minutes. Do not allow to boil.

3 Add fruit, cooking until setting point is reached, about 20–30 minutes. Ladle into warm, sterilised jars. When cool, seal and label jars.

STRAWBERRY SUNSET

Freeze ¼ cup (2 fl oz) of concentrated orange juice until icy cold but not frozen. Soften 1 litre (4 cups) of rich vanilla ice-cream. Place ice-cream in refrigerator for about 30 minutes. Fold in orange concentrate and 2 tablespoons of orange liqueur (for example, Grand Marnier). Arrange hulled strawberries in four stemmed glasses and spoon over orange cream and fruit. Sprinkle with ground cinnamon and serve immediately.

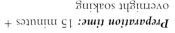

Sugar A sweet-tasting food used mainly as a flavouring. It is extracted from many plants, principally sugar cane (in tropical regions) and sugar beet (in cooler climates); lesser quantities are obtained from certain maple and palm trees and the sorghum plant. To process sugar from cane the juice is extracted and boiled until it crystallises (candies); centrifugal machines are used to separate the raw sugar crystals from the liquid molasses. For beet sugar the juice is extracted from the root. There are various types of sugar. Brown sugar is soft and moist with a characteristic flavour that comes from a film of molasses surrounding each crystal; it is used especially in baking chewy biscuits (cookies) and dark cakes. Raw sugar, made directly from the clarified juice of sugar cane, has coarse, straw-coloured crystals. White or granulated sugar, with medium-

Suet is available in solid form from butchers or can be bought packaged, shredded and ready for use from the supermarket. It is used to make puddings. Suet is

STRAWBERRY TRIFLE

Preparation time: 35 minutes + refrigeration
Total cooking time: 10–15 minutes
Serves 4–6

425 g (13½ oz) can peach slices
2 tablespoons custard powder
2 tablespoons sugar
2 cups (16 fl oz) milk
1¼ cups (10 fl oz) cream, whipped
250 g (8 oz) strawberries, halved
¼ cup walnut halves, toasted

1 jam Swiss roll (jelly roll)
90 g (3 oz) packet raspberry jelly crystals
1 cup (8 fl oz) boiling water
¼ cup (2 fl oz) sweet sherry

1 Drain peach slices and reserve syrup. Cut the Swiss roll in 1 cm (½ inch) slices. Arrange over base and around the sides of a serving bowl.

2 Combine sherry and two tablespoons of reserved peach syrup. Arrange peach slices over base. Pour sherry and syrup mixture over. Cover, refrigerate.

3 Dissolve jelly crystals in water. Pour into shallow 17 cm (6¾ inch) square tin. Refrigerate until set. When set, cut into cubes.

4 Blend the custard powder and sugar with a little of the milk until smooth; add remaining milk. Stir over low heat until mixture boils and thickens. Cover surface with plastic wrap. Allow to cool completely.

5 Place jelly cubes over peach slices. Spoon over custard. Decorate with whipped cream, strawberry halves and walnuts. Serve.

STRAWBERRY AND MARSHMALLOW PARFAIT

Preparation time: 15 minutes + 3 hours refrigeration
Total cooking time: nil
Serves 6

90 g (3 oz) packet vanilla ice-cream
strawberry flavoured jelly crystals
105 g (3½ oz) white or pink marshmallows, halved
2 cups (16 fl oz) boiling water
250 g (8 oz) strawberries, chopped
whipped cream for decoration
6 whole strawberries, extra

1 Stir jelly crystals in water in bowl until sugar crystals have dissolved; refrigerate until set.

2 Process half the strawberries in food processor for 30 seconds.

3 Layer ice-cream, jelly, remaining chopped strawberries, marshmallows and strawberry puree into six parfait glasses. Decorate with whipped cream and strawberries.

STRAWBERRY MALLOW

Place ½ cup of chopped marshmallows in a medium bowl and stir in 1 cup of plain yoghurt. (Use wet scissors to chop marshmallows easily.) Add 250 g (8 oz) sliced fresh strawberries and mix well. Cover and refrigerate for 1 hour. Spoon mixture into 4 dessert dishes and sprinkle with toasted flaked almonds before serving.

Malaysian and Indonesian dishes.

Sugar cane, a perennial grass, probably originated in southern India. The plant spread from there south to Malaysia and Indonesia, and north and west to ancient Persia. The 'sweet reed' and crystals that could be obtained from its juice, were also known to the Greeks and Romans. Sugar reached Europe with the Crusaders returning from south-western Asia in the thirteenth century but it did not displace honey as a general sweetener until the eighteenth century, when it inspired the development of elaborate French confectioneries (candies) and pâtisseries.

sized crystals, is refined from sugar cane and is used as a general sweetener. Caster (superfine) sugar has finer crystals and dissolves more quickly than white sugar and so is best for meringues, and some cakes and puddings. Powdered or icing (confectioners) sugar is granulated sugar milled to a fine powder. Palm sugar, or jaggery, is extracted from a species of low-branched palm tree and has a strong, treacle-like flavour: it gives deep colour and rich flavour to a number of sweet and savoury Indian,

Sukiyaki A stew-like dish of Japanese origin consisting of finely sliced meat (usually beef, but pork, chicken and seafood can also be used) and vegetables, soy sauce and sake cooked at the table (this can be done in an electric frying pan). Traditionally each diner breaks a raw egg into an individual bowl, beats it with chopsticks and then dips the hot food into it before eating.

Sultana The dried fruit of a white grape, softer and sweeter than both the raisin and currant. Sultanas are baked in cakes, biscuits (cookies), puddings and slices, added to stuffings, casseroles and curries, sprinkled on breakfast cereals

or tossed through salads. They originated in Crete, where in ancient times sweet, seedless grapes were sun-dried and exported throughout the Aegean.

Summer Pudding A cold dessert made by lining a basin with slices of bread, filling it with a lightly poached soft fruit (such as raspberries, redcurrants).

STROGANOFF

BEEF STROGANOFF

 Preparation time: 25 minutes
Total cooking time: 15 minutes
Serves 6

1 kg (2 lb) piece fillet steak
1/3 cup plain (all-purpose) flour
1/4 teaspoon freshly ground black pepper
1/2 cup (4 fl oz) good quality dry white wine
1/4 cup (2 fl oz) chicken stock
3/4 cup (6 fl oz) sour cream
1 tablespoon finely chopped fresh parsley

1 tablespoon tomato paste
2 teaspoons French mustard
sweet paprika
1 tablespoon ground sweet paprika
500 g (1 lb) small mushrooms
1 large onion, chopped
1/4 cup (2 fl oz) olive oil
pepper

1 Trim meat of excess fat and sinew. Slice meat across the grain evenly into short, thin pieces. Combine flour and pepper on a sheet of greaseproof paper. Toss meat in seasoned flour; shake off excess.
2 Heat 2 tablespoons oil in a heavy-based pan. Cook meat quickly, in small batches, stirring over medium-high heat until well browned; drain on paper towels.
3 Add remaining oil to pan. Add the onion, cook over a medium heat for 3 minutes or until soft.

Add mushrooms, stir over medium heat 5 minutes. Add the paprika, tomato paste, mustard, wine and stock to pan, bring to the boil. Reduce heat and simmer for 5 minutes, uncovered, stirring occasionally.
4 Return meat to pan. Add sour cream, stir until combined and just heated through. Sprinkle with parsley just before serving.

CHICKEN STROGANOFF

 Preparation time: 20 minutes
Total cooking time: 15 minutes
Serves 6

30 g (1 oz) butter
2 tablespoons oil
2 onions, thinly sliced
2 cloves garlic, crushed
8 chicken thigh fillets, sliced
freshly ground black pepper
1 cup (8 fl oz) sour cream
2 teaspoons sweet paprika
1/4 cup (2 fl oz) tomato paste

250 g (8 oz) mushrooms, sliced
2 tablespoons chopped fresh parsley

1 Heat butter and oil together in a large frying pan. Add onion and garlic and cook over a medium heat 3 minutes or until onion is soft.
2 Add chicken slices. Cook, stirring, until chicken is tender. Stir in mushrooms and paprika. Cook until mushrooms are tender.
3 In a bowl, combine sour cream, tomato paste and pepper. Stir into pan. Simmer gently until heated through. Sprinkle with chopped parsley. Serve with boiled rice or pasta.

STRUDELS

CREAMY CHICKEN STRUDEL

Preparation time: 30 minutes
Total cooking time: 40 minutes
★ ★
Serves 4

1 tablespoon oil	10 sheets filo pastry
1 large onion, chopped	90 g (3 oz) butter, melted
2 garlic cloves, crushed	1 stick of celery, finely chopped
250 g (8 oz) chicken mince	1 small red pepper (capsicum), finely chopped
1 tablespoon curry powder	1 small avocado, sliced
1/3 cup ricotta cheese	1 tablespoon sesame seeds
1/4 cup (2 fl oz) sour cream	

1 Preheat oven to moderate 180°C (350°F/Gas 4). Brush an oven tray with melted butter or oil. Heat oil in heavy-based pan, add onion and garlic, cook over medium heat for 2 minutes or until lightly browned. Add chicken mince, cook over high heat 4 minutes or until chicken is browned and all liquid has evaporated. Use a fork to break up any lumps of mince as it cooks. Add curry powder, cook 1 minute, remove pan from heat; cool mixture. Combine chicken mixture with ricotta cheese and sour cream.

2 Cover filo pastry with a damp tea-towel. Remove one sheet of pastry, place on work surface, brush all over with melted butter. Place another sheet on top, brush with butter. Repeat with remaining pastry and most of the butter.

3 Spoon chicken mixture along the long side of the pastry. Top with celery, pepper and avocado.

4 Roll up, tucking in ends. Place, seam-side down, on prepared tray, brush with butter, sprinkle with sesame seeds. Bake for 30 minutes or until pastry is golden brown. Serve sliced.

CREAM CHEESE STRUDEL

Preparation time: 15 minutes
Total cooking time: 25 minutes
★ ★
Serves 6

250 g (8 oz) cream cheese, softened	1/3 cup sultanas
2 sheets ready-rolled puff pastry	1/4 cup plain (all-purpose) flour
1 tablespoon lemon juice	1 tablespoon caster (superfine) sugar, extra
3 tablespoons caster (superfine) sugar	
2 tablespoons milk	

1 Preheat oven to moderate 180°C (350°F/Gas 4). Beat the cream cheese, lemon juice and caster sugar together until smooth. Lightly stir in the sifted flour and sultanas.

2 Place pastry sheets on a work surface. Place half the cheese mixture along one side of each pastry sheet, about 5 cm (2 inches) in from the edge. Roll up as for a Swiss roll (jelly roll). Press ends together to seal.

3 Place on a greased baking sheet. Brush with milk; sprinkle with extra caster sugar. Bake the strudels for 25 minutes, or until golden brown.

---

blackcurrants, loganberries and blackberries; then chilling it overnight, until the juice soaks into the bread, flavouring and colouring it. The whole is turned out and served with whipped cream. Summer pudding is a traditional English dessert.

Sundae A dessert or sweet snack consisting of ice-cream topped with a flavoured syrup and sometimes fruit, often sprinkled with crushed nuts and whipped cream and served in a long, shallow glass dish. It originated in the United States in the nineteenth century where it was a special Sunday treat.

Sunflower Seed Small, flat, oval seed from the yellow flowerhead of the centre of the huge sunflower plant. The seeds can be used raw in soups, stir-fries, pasta and rice dishes. Roasted, they add crunch to salads and cooked vegetables; boiled, they can be added to cakes, biscuits (cookies) and puddings. Sunflower seeds are often used as bird feed.

A flour ground from the roasted seeds is available from healthfood stores. Oil pressed from the seeds is used in cooking, and in salad dressings, margarines and shortenings. The sunflower plant is believed to have originated in Central America. It was taken to Spain in the sixteenth century and spread throughout Europe.

Supreme of Chicken The breast and wing of a chicken, removed and cooked in one piece, and often served with a rich cream sauce.

Sushi A dish of Japanese origin consisting of small rolls of seaweed containing cooked rice and savoury fillings such as a thin slice of raw fish (usually tuna) or omelette, or a vegetable. Other shapes are also made. Sushi featuring seaweed is called *maki*, that made with fish or seafood, *nigri*, and with omelette, *fukusa*. In Japan sushi is sold in small specialty restaurants or at a separate counter in larger restaurants. Sushi is served cold, with wafer-thin slices of pickled ginger, and is usually eaten with the fingers. The dish originated as a fisherman's snack.

APPLE STRUDEL

Preparation time: 20 minutes
Total cooking time: 30 minutes
Serves 8

½ cup ground walnuts
1 tablespoon soft brown sugar
1 teaspoon ground cinnamon

6 sheets filo pastry
60 g (2 oz) butter, melted
470 g (15 oz) can pie apple
½ cup sultanas

1 Preheat oven to moderately hot 210°C (415°F/Gas 6-7). Combine the walnuts, sugar and cinnamon.

2 Work with one sheet of filo at a time, keeping remainder covered with a damp tea-towel to prevent drying out. Brush first pastry sheet with a little melted butter; sprinkle 2 teaspoonsful of walnut mixture over the pastry. Repeat procedure with remaining pastry sheets, layering the buttered sheets one on top of the other and sprinkling all but the last layer with walnut mixture.

3 Combine the apple and sultanas. Spread mixture down the centre of pastry. Fold in the narrow ends to meet; fold over the long ends to make an envelope. Place seam-side down on a lightly greased baking tray. Brush the top and sides with butter. Make diagonal slits across the top at 3 cm (1¼ inch) intervals.

4 Bake strudel for 15 minutes. Reduce the heat to moderate 180°C (350°F/Gas 4) and cook for another 15 minutes or until crisp and golden. Serve warm.

CHERRY STRUDEL

Drain a 470 g (15 oz) can of cherries. Stone and halve cherries; set aside in a colander to drain. Combine ¾ cup of very finely chopped walnuts, ½ cup of sugar, 1 tablespoon of grated lemon rind and 1 teaspoon each of ground cinnamon and ground allspice in a large bowl. In another bowl, combine ¾ cup of soft, white breadcrumbs with 60 g (2 oz) of melted butter. Add crumb mixture to nut mixture; stir well.

Lay a sheet of puff pastry on a work surface and brush with a little melted butter. Spread with nut mixture, followed by cherries, leaving a 5 cm (2 inch) margin on each side. Fold over lengthways and press edges together firmly. Tuck in short ends. Brush all over with melted butter, sprinkle with poppy seeds, if desired, and place on a greased oven tray. Bake for 10 minutes in a hot 200°C (400°F/Gas 6) oven, reduce heat to 180°C (350°F/Gas 4): bake for another 25-30 minutes or until golden. Serve warm with whipped cream.

MUSHROOM STRUDEL

Preparation time: 20 minutes
Total cooking time: 25 minutes
Serves 4-6

15 g (½ oz) butter
1 clove garlic, crushed
2 teaspoons lemon juice
500 g (1 lb) medium mushroom caps, sliced
2 teaspoons finely grated lemon rind
freshly ground pepper

8 sheets filo pastry
90 g (3 oz) butter, extra, melted
½ cup grated pecorino cheese
6 spring onions (scallions), sliced
2 teaspoons poppy seeds

1 Melt butter in a medium-sized pan. Add garlic and lemon juice and cook over a low heat for 2 minutes. Add mushrooms, rind and pepper. Cook until mushrooms are just tender; cool.

2 Cover filo pastry with a damp tea-towel. Remove one sheet of pastry, place on work surface, brush all over with melted butter. Place another sheet on top, brush with butter. Repeat with remaining pastry and most of the butter.

3 Place cooled filling along the centre, parallel with long sides of pastry. Sprinkle with cheese and spring onion. Roll up pastry, tucking in the ends. Place on a well-oiled tray, with the seam underneath. Brush top and sides with butter, sprinkle with poppy seeds.

4 Bake at 200°C (400°F/Gas 6) for 8 minutes. Reduce heat to 180°C (350°F/Gas 4) and cook for another 15 minutes.

Opposite page: CREAM CHEESE STRUDEL
Above: MUSHROOM STRUDEL

442

SWEET POTATOES

TWO-POTATO HASH BROWNS

★ **Preparation time:** 20 minutes
Total cooking time: 25 minutes
Serves 4–6

3 rashers bacon, finely chopped (optional)	2 tablespoons olive oil
500 g (1 lb) potatoes, peeled	salt and freshly ground black pepper, to taste
250 g (8 oz) orange sweet potato, peeled	sour cream
1 large onion, finely chopped	2 tablespoons chopped fresh chives

1 Preheat oven to moderate 180°C (350°F/Gas 4). Brush an oven tray with melted butter or oil. Grease an egg ring to use as a mould. Place bacon in small pan. Cook over medium-high heat for 3 minutes. Drain on paper towels. Cut potato and sweet potato in half. Cook in boiling water for 10 minutes, or until just starting to soften. Drain well and grate them both.

2 Place potatoes, onion, bacon, oil, salt and pepper in a bowl. Toss well to ensure even mixing. Press spoonsful of mixture in egg ring on oven tray. Level the top surface. Remove ring and repeat with remaining mixture.

3 Bake for 20 minutes or until crisp and golden. Serve immediately, topped with sour cream and chopped fresh chives.

CHILLI SWEET POTATO AND EGGPLANT (AUBERGINE) CRISPS

★ **Preparation time:** 5 minutes
Total cooking time: 20 minutes
Serves 4–6

1 orange sweet potato, about 315 g (10 oz)	1/4 teaspoon ground chilli powder
1 slender eggplant (aubergine), about 375 g (12 oz)	1/4 teaspoon ground coriander
oil for deep frying	1 teaspoon chicken salt

1 Peel sweet potato. Cut sweet potato and eggplant into long thin strips of similar size. Place in a large bowl, mix.

2 Heat oil in a deep heavy-based pan. Gently lower half the combined sweet potato and eggplant into the moderately hot oil. Cook over medium-high heat for 10 minutes or until golden and crisp. Carefully remove the crisps from the oil with tongs or slotted spoon. Drain on paper towels. Repeat cooking process with remaining sweet potato and eggplant.

3 Combine chilli powder, coriander and salt in a small bowl. Sprinkle all the mixture over hot crisps. Toss until well coated. Serve immediately.

ABOUT SWEET POTATOES

■ Sweet potatoes have either orange, white or yellow flesh and have a sweet flavour.

■ If cut into chips and deep-fried, sweet potatoes make an interesting alternative to potatoes.

Sweet and Sour Sauce A sauce of Chinese origin which combines sweet and tart ingredients, such as sugar and vinegar, usually thickened with cornflour (cornstarch) and often also containing pineapple fruit juice, pieces or sweet pepper (capsicum). It is available ready made in jars.

Sweetbread Classed as offal or variety meat; sweetbreads can be either the thymus gland (in the throat) or the pancreas (near the stomach) of calves and lambs. They are valued for their delicate flavour. Sweetbreads must be soaked in several changes of water then blanched before use. They may be poached, sautéed, braised, grilled (broiled) and served with a sauce.

Sweet Corn See Corn.

Sweet Pepper See Peppers, Sweet.

Sweet Potato A starchy tuber, no relation to the potato. There are three

Swede Also known as rutabaga, a fleshy root vegetable, larger than a turnip and with a stronger, cabbage-like, flavour. Swedes can be boiled, baked or roasted with meat and are often pureed for use in savoury puddings and pies.

SWISS ROLLS

CHOCOLATE RASPBERRY SWISS ROLL

★★

Preparation time: 25 minutes
Total cooking time: 12–15 minutes
Makes one Swiss roll (jelly roll)

1/2 cup self-raising flour
1/4 cup cocoa powder
3 eggs
1/2 cup caster (superfine) sugar
1/4 cup grated dark chocolate (semi-sweet)

1 tablespoon hot water
1 tablespoon caster (superfine) sugar, extra
1 1/4 cups (10 fl oz) cream, softly whipped
1 packet frozen raspberries

1 Preheat oven to moderate 180°C (350°F/Gas 4). Brush a 30 x 25 x 2 cm (12 x 10 x 3/4 inch) Swiss roll (jelly roll) tin with oil. Line base and sides with paper; grease paper. Sift flour and cocoa three times onto greaseproof paper. Using electric beaters, beat eggs in bowl for 4–5 minutes or until thick and pale. Add sugar gradually, beating constantly until mixture is pale yellow and glossy.

2 Transfer mixture to large bowl. Using a metal spoon, fold in sifted flour, cocoa, chocolate and water quickly and lightly. Spread mixture evenly into tin; smooth surface. Bake 12–15 minutes, until lightly golden and springy.

3 Place sheet of greaseproof paper on a dry tea-towel. Sprinkle with extra sugar. Turn cake onto paper; stand 2 minutes. Carefully roll cake up with paper; allow to stand for 5 minutes. Unroll cake, discard paper. Spread with whipped cream and raspberries; re-roll. Trim ends of roll.

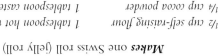

ABOUT SWISS ROLLS

■ When the cake base is cooked it will have shrunk a little from the sides of the tin. If you are not sure that it has cooked through, push a skewer into the centre of the cake: if it comes out clean, the cake is cooked. The skewer method should only be tried at the very end of the cooking time. Making a hole in a partially cooked sponge cake can cause it to collapse.

■ A Swiss roll is rolled up with its paper while still warm because if it cools before being rolled it will crack. The paper prevents the layers of cake from sticking together and makes it easy to unroll for filling. It can be filled with jam while still hot (and therefore not require the preliminary rolling with paper), but if you attempt to fill a hot cake with cream, the cream will become oily.

OPPOSITE PAGE, ABOVE: TWO-POTATO HASH BROWNS; BELOW: CHILLI SWEET POTATO AND EGGPLANT CRISPS. THIS PAGE: CHOCOLATE RASPBERRY SWISS ROLL.

---

main varieties which differ in colour: white, orange (also known as kumara) and red. All are cooked in the same way as the potato, although sugar is sometimes added to emphasise their natural sweetness.

Swiss Chard See Silver Beet.

Swiss Roll A thin sheet of sponge cake spread with a sweet filling, then rolled up. The finished cake is sprinkled with icing (confectioners) sugar and sliced.

Syrup A sweet liquid, usually a solution of sugar and a liquid. Corn syrup is the liquid form of sugar refined from corn. Light corn syrup is less sweet than sugar; dark corn syrup has caramel colouring and flavouring added and tastes similar to molasses. See also Golden Syrup and Maple Syrup.

Szechwan Pepper Also known as Chinese pepper, a fragrant, intensely flavoured (but not fiery hot) spice made from the dried berries of the Chinese prickly ash.

T

Tabasco A thin, red, fiery-tasting sauce made by fermenting chilli peppers with salt in oak barrels for four years, then straining it and adding vinegar. Tabasco sauce is used sparingly to add a hot flavour to sauces, salad dressings, tomato juice, meat, crab and lobster dishes, and is an essential ingredient in Cajun cooking. It was first made in Louisiana in 1868 and is named for the Tabasco region in Mexico, original home of the chilli peppers used. The sauce is sold around the world in distinctive, small bottles.

Tabouli A salad of Middle Eastern origin made with burghul (cracked wheat), finely chopped fresh flat-leaf parsley, diced tomato, olive oil, mint and lemon juice. Traditionally wrapped in cos (romaine) lettuce

T A R T S

FRUIT FLAN

⭐ *Preparation time:* 40 minutes + refrigeration
Total cooking time: 30 minutes
Makes 2 x 23 cm (9 inch) flans

2½ cups plain (all-purpose) flour
½ cup caster (superfine) sugar
185 g (6 oz) butter, chopped
1 egg
1 egg yolk
1 tablespoon water

Custard
2½ cups (20 fl oz) milk
3 eggs
2 tablespoons plain (all-purpose) flour
2 tablespoons cornflour (cornstarch)
¼ cup sugar
2 teaspoons vanilla essence

Topping
2 kiwi fruit (Chinese gooseberries), sliced
425 g (13½ oz) can peach halves, sliced
14 black grapes
250 g (8 oz) strawberries, halved
½ cup strawberry jam
1 tablespoon brandy

1 Place flour, sugar and butter in food processor. Using pulse action, process for 30 seconds or until mixture is fine and crumbly. Add egg, egg yolk and water and process for 20 seconds or until mixture just comes together when squeezed.

2 Preheat oven to moderately hot 210°C (415°F/Gas 6–7). Halve pastry, wrap one portion in plastic wrap and set aside. On floured board, roll other half to fit a 23 cm (9 inch) round loose-bottomed flan tin. Ease pastry into tin, trim edge with a sharp knife. Repeat with remaining half of pastry and a second flan tin. Cut a sheet of baking paper to cover each pastry-lined tin. Place paper into each tin, spread a layer of dried beans or rice evenly on top. Bake for 10 minutes. Remove paper and rice or beans, bake for another 10 minutes or until lightly browned; cool.

3 To make Custard: Whisk ½ cup (4 fl oz) milk with eggs, sifted flours and sugar in medium bowl. Heat remaining milk in a pan until warm, remove from heat. Gradually whisk into egg mixture. Return mixture to pan, whisk over heat until custard boils and thickens. Simmer for 3 minutes. Stir in essence. Remove from heat and cool. Spread into pastry case.

4 To make Topping: Arrange fruit decoratively over custard. Heat jam and brandy together in pan, then strain through a sieve; brush over fruit. Refrigerate flan before serving.

ABOVE: FRUIT FLAN
OPPOSITE PAGE: PASSIONFRUIT RICOTTA TART

PASSIONFRUIT RICOTTA TART

★★
Preparation time: 30 minutes + 1 hour 20 minutes refrigeration
Total cooking time: 20 minutes
Serves 6

1 1/4 cups plain (all-purpose) flour
90 g (3 oz) butter, chopped
1/4 cup caster (superfine) sugar
2 tablespoons iced water

Filling
1 1/2 cups ricotta cheese
1/2 cup sugar
3 eggs
1/2 cup (4 fl oz) cream
3 passionfruit
2 teaspoons icing (confectioners) sugar

1 Sift flour into large mixing bowl, add butter. Using fingertips, rub butter into flour for 2 minutes or until mixture is fine and crumbly; stir in sugar. Add almost all the water, mix to a firm dough, adding more water if necessary. Turn onto a lightly floured surface, press together until smooth. Roll out and line a 20 cm (8 inch) deep round flan tin. Cover with plastic wrap and refrigerate for 20 minutes.

2 Preheat oven to moderate 180°C (350°F/Gas 4). Cut a sheet of greaseproof paper large enough to cover pastry-lined tin. Place over pastry and spread a layer of dried beans or rice evenly over paper. Bake for 10 minutes then remove from oven and discard paper and beans. Return to oven for 10 minutes, or until pastry is lightly golden. Allow to cool.

3 To make Filling: Place the ricotta, sugar, eggs and cream in food processor. Using pulse action, press button for 20 seconds or until mixture is smooth. Add passionfruit pulp and process for 5 seconds. Pour into pastry shell and bake for 1 hour or until set and lightly golden. Cool and refrigerate for 1 hour. Dust with icing sugar before serving.

APPLE AND SOUR CREAM FLAN

★★
Preparation time: 35 minutes + 30 minutes refrigeration
Total cooking time: 45 minutes

Serves 4–6
1 cup plain (all-purpose) flour
1/4 cup caster (superfine) sugar
2 tablespoons cornflour (cornstarch)
1 teaspoon vanilla essence
3/4 cup (6 fl oz) sour cream
30 g (1 oz) butter, melted
2 tablespoons apricot jam, warmed and sieved
1/4 cup finely grated cheddar cheese

Filling
2 small green apples
30 g (1 oz) butter, chopped
1–2 tablespoons iced water
1 egg, lightly beaten

1 Place flour, cheese and butter in a food processor. Using the pulse action, press button for 20 seconds or until mixture is fine and crumbly. Add almost all the water and process for another 15 seconds or until mixture comes together. Turn onto a lightly floured board and knead lightly. Brush a 20 cm (8 inch) round flan tin with oil or melted butter. Roll out pastry large enough to cover base and side of tin. Ease pastry into tin; trim. Cover with plastic wrap; refrigerate for 30 minutes.

2 Preheat oven to moderate 180°C (350°F/Gas 4). Cut a sheet of greaseproof paper large enough to cover pastry-lined tin. Place over pastry and spread a layer of dried beans or rice evenly over paper. Bake for 10 minutes, remove from oven and discard the paper and beans. Return to the oven for another 10 minutes or until the pastry is lightly golden. Set aside to cool before filling.

3 To make Filling: Peel apples; remove core and slice thinly. In a medium mixing bowl, combine egg, sugar, cornflour, essence and sour cream until smooth. Pour mixture into pastry base and arrange apple slices on top; brush with melted butter. Bake for 25 minutes or until apples are lightly golden. Brush tart with apricot jam while warm. Serve warm or cold.

---

leaves and eaten with the hands, tabbouli is often served as an accompaniment to grilled meat and poultry.

Taco A tortilla which has been folded and fried until crisp and which is traditionally served with a spicy meat filling; re-fried beans, grated cheese, chopped tomato, shredded lettuce and chilli-based sauce may be added. Ready-made taco shells are available from supermarkets.

Taffy A confectionery (candy) made from boiled syrup which is pulled and worked into long strands (this incorporates air and gives taffy its characteristic light and creamy texture) then twisted and cut into bite-sized pieces and wrapped for storage. Taffy is popular in North America; saltwater taffy, a feature of New Jersey seaside resorts, has a little added salt (not saltwater).

Tagine A highly spiced Moroccan stew of meat, vegetables or fruit, often served at banquets.

Tagliatelle Long, flat ribbon pasta, often coloured and flavoured with spinach or tomato, boiled in water and served with a sauce. It is a specialty of northern and central Italy and is said to have been

CARAMEL NUT TARTLETS

★ ★ **Preparation time:** 30 minutes
Total cooking time: 40 minutes
Makes about 18

¹/₂ cup plain (all-purpose) flour
1 tablespoon caster (superfine) sugar
45 g (1¹/₂ oz) butter
¹/₄ cup (2 fl oz) water
1 tablespoon milk
¹/₄ cup (2 fl oz) cream

Filling
250 g (8 oz) unsalted whole nut mix
¹/₂ cup sugar
¹/₄ cup (2 fl oz) water

1 Preheat oven to moderate 180°C (350°F/Gas 4). Sift flour into a medium bowl; add sugar. Add butter and rub into flour with fingertips for 2 minutes or until mixture is fine and crumbly. Add milk, mix to a soft dough. Knead on lightly floured surface 1 minute or until smooth.

2 Roll pastry out thinly; cut into circles using a 6 cm (2¹/₂ inch) fluted cutter. Press into greased shallow patty tins, prick evenly with fork. Bake 10 minutes or until lightly golden.

3 To make Filling: Spread nuts on an oven tray. Bake 10 minutes or until they are lightly golden. Combine sugar and water in a medium pan. Stir constantly over low heat until sugar has dissolved. Bring to boil. Reduce heat; simmer, uncovered, without stirring, for 10 minutes or until mixture turns golden brown. Remove from heat, add cream and stir. (If syrup sets in lumps when the cream is added, return pan to heat for 1 minute or until the mixture is smooth.) Add nuts and stir. Spoon into pastry shells; cool before serving.

INDIVIDUAL HERB TARTS

★ **Preparation time:** 15 minutes
Total cooking time: 35 minutes
Makes 18

18 slices white bread, crusts removed
40 g (1¹/₂ oz) butter, softened
1 teaspoon chopped fresh dill
1 teaspoon chopped fresh thyme
1 tablespoon chopped fresh parsley
2 teaspoons chopped fresh chives

Filling
2 eggs
2 tablespoons milk
¹/₂ cup (4 fl oz) cream
2 tablespoons grated parmesan cheese

1 Preheat oven to moderately hot 210°C (415°F/Gas 6–7). Brush two muffin or patty pans with melted butter or oil. Cut bread into rounds using an 8 cm (3 inch) plain biscuit (cookie) cutter. Flatten out each round with a rolling pin. Spread both sides of each bread round with butter and gently press them into the muffin pans. Bake for 10 minutes, or until bread rounds are lightly browned and crisp. Take care not to overcook rounds or they will be brittle.

2 To make Filling: Reduce heat to moderate 180°C (350°F/Gas 4). Combine eggs, milk, herbs and cream in a bowl; mix well. Pour the egg mixture into prepared bread cases and sprinkle with parmesan cheese. Bake for 25 minutes or until the tart filling is lightly browned and set. Serve immediately.

inspired by the flaxen hair of Lucrezia Borgia.

Tahini A thick, smooth, paste of roasted, ground sesame seeds. In the Middle East it is mixed with lemon juice, garlic and chick peas (garbanzo beans) to make a dip served with flat bread. Tahini is also used in cakes, biscuits (cookies) and the confectionery (candy) halva; it is available in jars from supermarkets.

Tamale A sweet or savoury cornmeal cake steamed inside a corn husk. A Mexican specialty, it is often served hot as a first course. The tamale is made by spreading a dough of ground dried corn and water (called *masa*) on a corn husk, adding a sweet or savoury filling, then wrapping it up and steaming until cooked. Banana leaf or cooking foil may be substituted for the corn husk. Tamales are a traditional festival food and were once considered to be a gift from the gods.

Tamarillo An egg-shaped fruit with glossy, deep red skin and soft, tart-tasting flesh with tiny seeds. The bitter skin is removed by blanching; the flesh can

T E R R I N E S

RED PEPPER (CAPSICUM) TERRINE

⭐ ⭐ **Preparation time:** 30 minutes +
45 minutes standing
Total cooking time: 1 hour 15 minutes
Serves 8

3 large red peppers (capsicum)	salt
	⅓ cup (2½ fl oz) oil
750 g (1½ lb) eggplant (aubergine)	500 g (1 lb) spinach
	⅓ cup pesto

1 Preheat oven to moderate 180°C (350°F/Gas 4). Cut peppers in half and remove seeds. Place peppers cut side down on an oven tray. Bake for 30 minutes or until skin blisters and browns. Cover with damp tea-towel, cool; peel off skins.
2 Cut eggplant into 5 mm (¼ inch) slices. Sprinkle with salt, set aside for 45 minutes. Rinse under cold water, drain and dry with paper towel.
3 Heat 1 tablespoon of the oil in a pan, add a layer of eggplant slices. Cook over medium heat for 2 minutes each side until lightly browned. Drain. Repeat with remaining oil and eggplant.
4 Remove stalks from spinach leaves, place leaves in medium bowl, cover with hot water. Stand for 1 minute, then drain and rinse under cold water. Line a 31 x 12 cm (12½ x 4¾ inch) loaf tin with

a double layer of spinach leaves, allowing leaves to drape over sides of tin.
5 Place a quarter of the eggplant in overlapping slices along base of tin. Top with a third of the peppers, spread with a quarter of the pesto. Repeat layering with remaining eggplant, pepper and pesto.
6 Enclose filling completely with spinach leaves. Bake for 30 minutes or until terrine is tender; set aside to cool. Store terrine, covered with plastic wrap, in the refrigerator. Turn out of tin to serve.

PORK AND VEAL TERRINE

⭐ ⭐ **Preparation time:** 30 minutes
Total cooking time: 2 hours
Serves 6

500 g (1 lb) pork, minced	1 cup (8 fl oz) dry white wine
500 g (1 lb) veal, minced	salt and freshly ground pepper
2 eggs, beaten	
1 onion, finely chopped	½ teaspoon chopped fresh thyme
1 clove garlic, finely chopped	½ teaspoon ground mace
2 tablespoons melted lard	6 rashers rindless bacon

1 Preheat oven to slow 150°C (300°F/Gas 2). In a large bowl, mix together minced pork and veal. Add beaten eggs, onion, garlic, lard, wine, salt, pepper, thyme and mace.
2 Line base and sides of a terrine or 21 x 14 cm (8½ x 5½ inch) loaf tin with bacon rashers. Spoon prepared mixture into the tin and fold the ends of the bacon rashers over to cover the top.
3 Cover tin with a lid or foil and place in a roasting pan half-filled with water. Bake terrine for 2 hours. Remove from oven, cool and refrigerate.
4 When the terrine is cold, turn it out of the tin and cut into slices. Serve at room temperature with crusty bread or a crisp salad.

ABOUT TERRINES

■ Traditionally terrines are baked in a special earthenware mould (called a terrine) with a tight-fitting lid. Some versions are baked uncovered, cooled, then pressed with a weight to compact the mixture for slicing.
■ Pork has long been the favoured ingredient for both terrines and pâtés. Nowadays there are many recipes, including vegetable and fish terrines, which use less fatty mixtures.
■ Terrines with interesting layers or textures, or colourful ingredients, look very attractive when sliced. Serve with crackers, toast or fresh bread.

OPPOSITE PAGE: CARAMEL NUT TARTLETS
ABOVE: RED PEPPER TERRINE

be added to sweet and savoury salads or sweetened and cooked for use in tarts and hot puddings. The tamarillo is native to Peru; There are also yellow varieties.

Tamarind Sour-sweet pulp from the seed pods of a tropical tree, used to give a bite to curries, stews and chutneys and as an

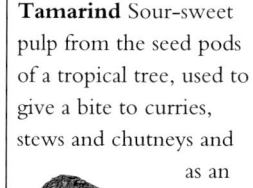

ingredient in worcestershire sauce. It is available from Asian food stores in the form of dried pulp or a paste.

Tandoori A traditional Indian method of cooking in which chicken or lamb is marinated in a spicy red paste, threaded onto long skewers and cooked in a tandoor or clay oven. Tandoori paste is available from specialist food stores.

Tangelo A citrus fruit which has pale, yellow to orange, sharp-tasting, juicy flesh. The fruit has orange-coloured peel that is easily removed. It is produced by crossing the grapefruit with the tangerine (or mandarin).

Glossary

Tangerine Also called mandarin, a small, loose-skinned variety of orange with sweet, juicy, easily separated segments. The fruit is named after the seaport of Tangier in Morocco, where it has long been grown.

Tapas Platters of hot or cold bite-sized savoury snacks—olives, nuts, pickles, stuffed or grilled (broiled) vegetables, sliced meats and dry sausages—eaten with drinks, especially sherry. Tapas originated in Spain.

Tapenade A savoury spread made by puréeing pitted black olives with anchovies, capers, garlic, lemon juice and olive oil. It is served with crusty bread, or can be diluted with olive oil and

used as a dressing for grilled sweet pepper (capsicum) or eggplant (aubergine). Tapenade originated in Provence in southern France and the name derives from the local word tapeno, capers.

Tapioca Tiny balls of starch prepared from the tuberous root of the cassava plant (grown in tropical America, the Pacific Islands, Indonesia, the Philippines and Africa). It is cooked in sweetened milk or water as a dessert or used to thicken soups and stews.

DEEP-FRIED SPICED TOFU

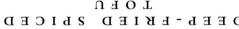

★
Preparation time: 10 minutes
Total cooking time: 10 minutes
Serves 4

375 g (12 oz) block firm tofu
1 teaspoon ground cardamom
1 clove garlic, crushed
1/2 cup rice flour
2 teaspoons ground coriander
1/2 cup (4 fl oz) water
oil, for deep frying

1 Drain tofu, cut into 1 cm (1/2 inch) thick slices.
2 Combine the flour, coriander, cardamom and garlic in a bowl. Add water and stir until smooth.
3 Heat oil in a pan. Dip tofu slices into the spice mixture, coating thickly.
4 Lower tofu slices into heated oil, three at a time, and cook over medium heat for 1 minute on each side, or until slices are crisp and golden brown; drain on paper towel. Repeat with remaining slices. Serve hot with a tomato-chilli dipping sauce.

ABOUT TOFU

■ Tofu is sometimes also called bean curd or soy cheese. Like tempeh (made from cooked and fermented soy bean paste), it is a protein food used in many recipes instead of meat.
■ Tofu should be kept in the refrigerator, covered with water, and will keep fresh for up to a week if the water is changed regularly.
■ Tofu is available in different textures; firmer varieties hold their shape better for stir-fried dishes or salads. It is also sold fried and baked.

TOFU

ASIAN-STYLE TOFU SALAD

★
Preparation time: 20 minutes + 1 hour marinating
Total cooking time: nil
Serves 4

2 teaspoons Thai sweet chilli sauce
1/2 teaspoon grated ginger
1 clove garlic, crushed
2 teaspoons soy sauce
2 tablespoons oil
250 g (8 oz) firm tofu
105 g (3 1/2 oz) snow peas (mange tout), cut into 3 cm (1 1/4 inch) lengths
2 small carrots, cut into matchsticks
105 g (3 1/2 oz) red cabbage, finely shredded
2 tablespoons chopped peanuts

1 Place chilli sauce, ginger, garlic, soy and oil in a small screw-top jar and shake well. Cut tofu into 2 cm (3/4 inch) cubes. Place tofu in a medium bowl, pour marinade over and stir. Cover with plastic wrap and refrigerate for 1 hour.
2 Place snow peas in small pan, pour boiling water over and leave to stand for 1 minute, then drain and plunge into iced water. Drain well.
3 Add snow peas, carrots and cabbage to tofu and toss lightly to combine. Transfer to a serving bowl or individual plates, sprinkle with nuts and serve immediately.

OPPOSITE PAGE, ABOVE: ASIAN-STYLE TOFU SALAD
BELOW: DEEP-FRIED SPICED TOFU
ABOVE: WARM TOMATO AND HERB SALAD

TOMATOES

WARM TOMATO AND HERB SALAD

✷ *Preparation time:* 20 minutes
Total cooking time: 15 minutes
Serves 6

1 clove garlic, crushed
1 tablespoon olive oil
12 slices French bread,
 cut 2 cm (³/₄ inch) thick
1 tablespoon olive oil,
 extra
250 g (8 oz) cherry
 tomatoes
250 g (8 oz) yellow pear
 tomatoes
¼ cup shredded basil
 leaves
1 tablespoon chopped
 fresh tarragon
¼ cup chopped fresh
 parsley
salt and freshly ground
 black pepper, to taste

1 Preheat oven to moderate 180°C (350°F/Gas 4). Combine garlic and oil in a small bowl. Brush mixture lightly on one side of bread slices; place on a baking tray, bake for 7 minutes. Turn bread over, brush other side and bake for another 5 minutes. Set aside to cool.

PESTO-TOPPED CHERRY TOMATOES

✷ *Preparation time:* 35 minutes
Total cooking time: nil
Makes about 50

1 cup chopped fresh
 parsley, firmly packed
15 g (½ oz) butter at
 room temperature
2 cloves garlic
2 tablespoons pine nuts
¼ cup (2 fl oz) olive oil
⅔ cup grated parmesan
 cheese
500 g (1 lb) cherry
 tomatoes

¼ cup fresh basil leaves

1 Place parsley, garlic, pine nuts and oil in a food processor or blender and process until mixture forms a puree.

2 Add remaining ingredients, except tomatoes. Process until well combined.

3 Slice tops from tomatoes. Spoon a small mound of pesto mixture on top of each tomato. (A small amount of flesh may be scooped out to allow for more pesto filling.) Refrigerate until required.

2 Heat extra oil in frying pan. Add tomatoes and stir over medium heat 2 minutes, until just soft.

3 Add herb, salt and pepper, stir-fry for 1 minute more until combined. Serve warm with croutons.

Taramasalata A creamy dip made by pureeing *tarama*, the dried, salted and pressed roe of mullet, with bread, garlic, onion, olive oil and lemon juice. A Greek and Turkish specialty, taramasalata is served chilled on thin toast or pitta bread. Tarama is available in jars and cans from gourmet stores.

Taro The starchy tuber of a tropical plant with rough, brown, hairy skin and firm, pale flesh. It is widely used in the cooking of the Pacific and South-East Asia, either boiled or baked and served as a vegetable, or steamed and sweetened and made into a pudding.

Tarragon A herb with a subtle liquorice-like flavour. It combines well with chicken and is mixed with chervil, chives and parsley to make the classic *fines herbes* blend. Tarragon vinegar is an important ingredient in béarnaise sauce and mayonnaise. French tarragon has the most intense flavour and aroma. Russian tarragon, is inferior in flavour. The dried form of the herb loses its flavour quickly.

ABOVE: GRILLED TOMATOES WITH BRUSCHETTA

BELOW: TOMATO AND OLIVE CRISPBREAD STEW; OPPOSITE PAGE, ABOVE: TOMATO AND PEPPER

FRESH TOMATO RELISH

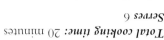

Preparation time: 20 minutes
Total cooking time: 20 minutes
Serves 6

1 tablespoon olive oil
1 small red onion, finely chopped
3 ripe tomatoes, peeled and chopped
1/2 cup (4 fl oz) red wine vinegar
2 teaspoons soft brown sugar
2 zucchini (courgettes), chopped
1 green pepper (capsicum), chopped
1/2 cup black olives, pitted, chopped
1 tablespoon capers
2 tablespoons pine nuts
2 tablespoons finely chopped flat-leafed parsley

1 Heat oil in a large pan, add the onion, cover and cook over low heat for 1 minute. Add tomato, cover and cook over low heat until tomato is soft. Add the vinegar and brown sugar and simmer, uncovered, for about 10 minutes or until the sauce has reduced and thickened.

2 Add zucchini and pepper; cover and cook until the vegetables are just tender. Cool for 10 minutes. Add the olives, capers, pine nuts and parsley and mix well.

GRILLED TOMATOES WITH BRUSCHETTA

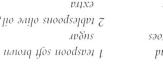

Preparation time: 15 minutes
Total cooking time: 35 minutes
Serves 4

1 loaf Italian bread
4 large ripe tomatoes
1/2 teaspoon dried marjoram leaves
salt and freshly ground black pepper, to taste
2 tablespoons olive oil
2 tablespoons red wine vinegar
1 teaspoon soft brown sugar
2 tablespoons olive oil, extra
1 clove garlic, cut in half
1/2 cup chopped marinated artichokes, drained
1 tablespoon finely chopped flat-leaf parsley

1 Cut bread into thick slices. Preheat grill. Cut tomatoes in half and gently squeeze out seeds. Place tomatoes cut-side up in a shallow ovenproof dish. Place marjoram, salt and pepper, oil, vinegar and sugar in a small screw-top jar and shake well. Pour dressing over tomatoes.

2 Cook tomatoes under hot grill for 30 minutes; turn halfway through cooking. Remove from heat; keep warm.

3 Brush bread slices liberally with oil on both sides; toast until golden. Rub cut surface of garlic over bread. Place the cooked tomatoes onto the bread slices, top with artichokes and sprinkle with parsley. Serve immediately.

cultivation is thought to have originated in China some 5000 years ago. Herb teas or tisanes are infusions made with fresh or dried leaves or blossoms and include mint, rose hip, hyssop, sage and camomile.

Teacake A light cake eaten warm, sliced and buttered. The traditional English teacake is a round, yeast dough bun, split open and grilled or toasted, then served hot with butter; other versions are sprinkled with sugar and spices or other toppings.

Tempura A Japanese dish consisting of pieces of seafood and vegetables dipped in batter and deep-fried. Tempura is served hot with soy sauce for dipping.

Tenderloin See Fillet.

Teriyaki A Japanese dish of meat, poultry or fish marinated in mirin and soy sauce then grilled (broiled) or barbecued. Teriyaki sauce is sold in bottles.

Terrine A preparation of minced (ground) meat, poultry, game, fish or vegetables cooked in a deep, straight-sided earthenware container lined with thinly sliced pork fat to keep the mixture moist, and sealed with a tight-fitting lid. Terrine is served at room

TOMATO AND BROWN LENTIL SOUP

★ *Preparation time:* 10 minutes
Total cooking time: 40 minutes
Serves 4

1 large onion	*¼ cup (2 fl oz) olive oil*
1 cup brown lentils	*1 clove garlic, crushed*
1 bay leaf	*1 litre (4 cups) water*
2 small dried chillies	*¼ cup tomato paste*
	salt and freshly ground black pepper, to taste

1 Finely chop onion. Rinse lentils in cold water; drain well.

2 Heat oil in a large heavy-based pan. Add the onion and garlic and stir over low heat for 10 minutes.

3 Add tomato paste, chillies, bay leaf, lentils and water; bring to boil. Reduce heat and simmer, covered, for 30 minutes or until the lentils are soft.

4 Remove chillies and bay leaf and discard. Add salt and pepper to taste. Serve soup with fresh, crusty bread.

ABOVE: TOMATO AND BROWN LENTIL SOUP
LEFT: STUFFED TOMATOES
OPPOSITE PAGE, ABOVE: CHEESY SUN-DRIED TOMATO HOT BREAD; BELOW: TOMATO PASTA SALAD

STUFFED TOMATOES

★ *Preparation time:* 20 minutes +
15 minutes standing
Total cooking time: 40 minutes
Serves 6

¼ cup burghul (cracked wheat)	*2 tablespoons tomato paste*
⅓ cup (2½ fl oz) hot water	*1 tablespoon barbecue sauce*
1 tablespoon oil	*1 teaspoon dried oregano*
1 small onion, finely chopped	*1 tablespoon finely chopped parsley*
500 g (1 lb) beef mince	*6 large firm tomatoes*
60 g (2 oz) sun-dried tomatoes, finely sliced	*2 teaspoons olive oil*

1 Preheat oven to 180°C (350°F/Gas 4). Brush a deep baking dish with oil. Place burghul in a small bowl and add hot water. Set aside for 15 minutes. Squeeze excess moisture from burghul. Heat oil in a heavy-based frypan; add onion and mince, cook for 5 minutes. Use a fork to break up any lumps as mince cooks. Remove from heat and drain excess liquid. Transfer to mixing bowl.

2 Add burghul, sun-dried tomato, tomato paste, barbecue sauce and herbs to mince mixture.

3 Cut a 2 cm (¾ inch) slice from the base of each tomato, and scoop out seeds and membrane. Fill cavity with mince mixture and replace tops.

4 Brush each tomato all over with olive oil and place about 3 cm (1¼ inch) apart in prepared dish. Bake for 35 minutes.

---

temperature (chilling dulls the flavour), cut into slices and accompanied by gherkins and pickled onions, usually as a first course.

Thai Food The

cooking of Thailand is characterised by subtle blending of hot, sweet, salty, bitter and sour flavours. It shows influences from China (especially in the use of ingredients), from India, Java, Cambodia and Sri Lanka. The chilli pepper, native to the Americas, did not reach Thailand until the sixteenth century when it was introduced by the Portuguese; now, with mint, basil, spring onion (scallion), coriander and coconut milk, it is one of the central flavours of Thai cuisine. A traditional Thai meal consists of a variety of dishes (usually a soup, a curry, a steamed dish, a fried one and a salad) selected for a balance of flavours, textures and colours. All are served at the same time and eaten warm or at room temperature, using a spoon and fork; rice is always served. The main meal is followed by fresh tropical fruits and cakes and desserts made of mung bean

onion

basil, spring onion (scallion), coriander

mung bean

TOMATO PASTA SALAD

Preparation time: 20 minutes
Total cooking time: 12 minutes
Serves 10

1/2 cup oil-packed sun-dried tomatoes, drained
250 g (8 oz) cherry tomatoes
250 g (8 oz) yellow pear tomatoes
1 tablespoon balsamic vinegar
2 tablespoons oil, from sun-dried tomatoes
1/3 cup chopped flat-leaf parsley
salt, pepper
fresh basil leaves, to garnish

500 g (1 lb) pasta bows
1/2 cup (4 fl oz) olive oil
1–2 cloves garlic, crushed
1 bunch fresh asparagus

1 Combine sun-dried tomatoes, garlic, vinegar and oils in food processor. Process for 20 seconds or until all ingredients are combined.

2 Cook the pasta in a large pan of boiling, salted water for 12 minutes or until just tender; drain.

3 Plunge asparagus spears into a bowl of boiling water. Leave them for 2 minutes until they turn a vibrant green colour and are slightly tender. Drain spears, then plunge into a bowl of ice water. When cold, drain and pat dry with paper towels. Cut into 3 cm (1 1/4 inch) lengths. Cut cherry tomatoes and pear tomatoes in half, lengthways.

4 Assemble salad while pasta is still warm: combine pasta, tomatoes, asparagus and parsley in a large serving bowl; mix in tomato dressing. Add salt and pepper, to taste. Garnish with basil leaves and serve.

CHEESY SUN-DRIED TOMATO HOT BREAD

Preparation time: 15 minutes
Total cooking time: 15 minutes
Serves 10

60 g (2 oz) butter, softened
1/3 cup grated parmesan cheese
2 French bread sticks

1 tablespoon chopped basil
2 tablespoons sun-dried tomato paste

1 Preheat oven to moderately hot 210°C (415°F/Gas 6–7). Combine butter, cheese, sun-dried tomato paste and basil in a small mixing bowl.

2 Slice bread almost through at 1.5 cm (5/8 inch) intervals, leaving base intact. Spread butter mixture between the slices, then press back into loaf shape.

3 Wrap bread in foil. Bake for 10 minutes, open foil and bake for another 5 minutes or until bread is crisp.

Note: Bread sticks can be assembled several hours ahead and baked just before serving. Prepared unbaked bread sticks can be frozen for up to 2 months. Sun-dried tomato paste is available from most delicatessens.

Thyme A fragrant herb with small, oval, greyish-green leaves that have a strong aroma and a pungent, clove-like taste. Thyme is used in marinades for lamb, beef and poultry; with bay leaf and parsley, it is part of a bouquet garni; it is added to stuffings and tomato-based sauces, and combines well with rabbit. Thyme leaves can be bought fresh, dried or ground.

Tilsit A smooth, semi-hard, cow's milk cheese, pale yellow in colour, with a fruity, mild to medium-sharp flavour. It is a good snack cheese, teaming well with fruit and salad vegetables, can also be used in sandwiches and on cheese boards, and melts well for use in sauces.

Timbale A custardy mixture of meat, poultry, seafood or vegetables cooked in individual moulds and usually served with a sauce as a first course. Timbales are named after the deep, round moulds in which they are cooked.

Tipsy Cake A dessert, similar to trifle, consisting of sponge cake liberally sprinkled with sherry, brandy or sweet

flour, rice, coconut, palm sugar and eggs. Water and tea accompany the meal.

Tiramisù A rich Italian dessert consisting of sponge fingers (lady fingers) dipped in marsala or brandy and topped with layers of zabaglione, coffee-flavoured mascarpone cheese and whipped cream; it is served chilled. Tiramisù was created in Siena, where it was called *zuppa del Duca*, the Duke's soup; because of its popularity with the expatriate English in nineteenth-century Florence it became *zuppa inglese*, English soup; tiramisù—pick me up—is a relatively recent name.

Tisane A herbal tea, usually drunk for its medicinal properties. Tisanes include angelica (to help digestion), camomile (for an upset stomach and to aid sleep), lemon balm (to calm the nerves and aid digestion), peppermint tea (believed to ward off colds) and rose petals and violets with honey (for soothing a cough).

Toast To brown or crisp food by exposing it to dry heat. Toasting will develop a fuller flavour in nuts and seeds. The term also refers to a slice of bread exposed to heat

TROUT

TROUT WITH ALMONDS

★ *Preparation time:* 15 minutes
Total cooking time: 15 minutes
Serves 4

4 trout, approximately 200 g (6½ oz) each, gutted and scaled	90 g (3 oz) butter
5 tablespoons lemon juice	½ cup (4 fl oz) dry white wine
½ cup blanched halved almonds	lemon slices, to garnish
¼ cup plain (all-purpose) flour	dill or parsley sprigs, to garnish
ground pepper, to taste	
½ teaspoon dried dill leaves	
¼ teaspoon mustard powder	

1 Using scissors, remove fins from trout, trim tail; wipe over surface of fish with damp paper towel to remove any loose scales. Season flour with pepper, dill and mustard powder.

2 Brush surface of fish with lemon juice and reserve any excess. Coat whole trout in seasoned flour to form a crust. Shake off excess flour.

3 Heat butter in a large pan, add the almonds and cook, stirring, until golden. Remove from heat. Drain almonds on paper towel. Add trout to pan and cook over medium-high heat until tender, turning once and taking care not to break them. Remove trout from the pan and drain well on paper towel.

4 Add remaining lemon juice and the wine to pan; simmer, uncovered, over high heat until liquid has reduced by half. Add reserved almonds and pour over fish. Serve immediately, garnished with lemon slices and dill or parsley sprigs.

SMOKED TROUT WITH KIWI FRUIT SALAD

★ *Preparation time:* 20 minutes
Total cooking time: nil
Serves 4

3 whole plate-sized smoked trout	2 tablespoons hazelnut oil
2 kiwi fruit (Chinese gooseberries)	1 large ripe avocado
assorted lettuce (butter, mignonette, cos/romaine, endive/chicory)	juice and rind of 1 lime
1 tablespoon white wine vinegar	¼ cup hazelnuts, finely chopped

1 Skin trout. Gently remove the fillets from each side. Cut each fillet into two pieces. Peel and slice kiwi fruit and avocado.

2 Combine lime juice, rind, vinegar and oil.

3 Wash lettuce and arrange on either one large platter or individual serving plates.

4 Arrange smoked trout fillets, kiwi fruit and avocado on top of lettuce and lightly pour over the lime dressing. Sprinkle with hazelnuts and serve immediately.

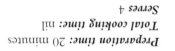

MOROCCAN-STYLE TROUT WITH DATES

★ **Preparation time:** 30 minutes
Total cooking time: 20 minutes
Serves 2

2 medium trout	30 g (1 oz) butter, melted
1 cup chopped dates	¼ teaspoon ground
¼ cup cooked rice	pepper
1 onion, finely chopped	¼ teaspoon ground ginger
¼ cup chopped almonds	1 teaspoon caster
2 tablespoons chopped	(superfine) sugar
fresh coriander	¼ teaspoon ground
½ teaspoon ground	cinnamon
cinnamon	

1 Preheat oven to 160°C (325°F/Gas 3). Clean trout, rinse under cold water. Dry with paper towel.
2 Combine dates, rice, onion, almonds, coriander and cinnamon in a bowl.
3 Spoon seasoning mixture into fish cavities; close opening with metal skewers. Place on oven tray.
4 Brush fish with melted butter, sprinkle with combined pepper, ginger and sugar. Bake for 20 minutes, or until golden. Sprinkle fish with cinnamon before serving.

OPPOSITE PAGE: TROUT WITH ALMONDS
ABOVE: MOROCCAN-STYLE TROUT WITH DATES

ABOUT TROUT

■ Trout has a very delicate taste which can be easily overwhelmed by stronger flavours. It is usually cooked whole. The flesh is slightly dry and should not be overcooked.
■ The colour of trout (and salmon) flesh is influenced by what the fish eats; it can be varied in farmed trout by a controlled diet.
■ It is usual to remove the skin from trout before eating. The flesh comes away very easily from the backbone, which can be removed, once half the fish has been eaten.
■ One of the simplest and most delicious ways to serve trout is to fry it in olive oil. Make sure the fish is absolutely fresh. Rinse inside and out under cold running water and dry well with paper towel. Cut off all the fins with scissors or a sharp knife. Dip trout in plain (all-purpose) flour seasoned with salt and pepper; shake off any excess. Cover the base of a pan large enough to comfortably hold the trout with a shallow layer of olive oil. Heat the oil and add trout. Cook over high heat to sear the outside, then lower the heat slightly. After about 3 minutes, turn the trout over. Increase the heat again to sear the skin, then reduce it and cook the trout for another 3 minutes, or until the fish is cooked through. Remove and drain on a dish lined with paper towel. Serve with lemon wedges and a mayonnaise and sour cream mixture.

so that its surfaces become brown and dry. Toasted bread, spread with butter or other spreads, is served at breakfast, or used to make toasted sandwiches.

Toffee A rich, sticky, usually brown confectionery (candy) which is made by adding butter to a boiled mixture of sugar and water. It can be soft and chewy or hard and crunchy, depending on cooking time and temperature.

Tofu Soybean curd, a white to cream coloured, smooth-textured and bland-flavoured food made by adding a setting agent to a thin liquid of ground boiled soya beans and water. It is valued for its high vegetable protein content and is widely used in the cooking of China, Japan and South East Asia. Tofu absorbs the flavours of foods cooked with it. Tofu, either soft ('silken') or firm, is available fresh and in long-life packs.

Tomato A round, smooth-skinned, juicy, seed-filled fruit with a rich, slightly sweet flavour, used as a

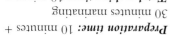

TUNA

TUNA STEAKS WITH OLIVE PASTE

✻ **Preparation time:** 15 minutes +
1 hour marinating
Total cooking time: 4 minutes
Serves 6

Marinade
1/3 cup (2 1/2 fl oz) olive oil
2 tablespoons dry white wine
2 tablespoons lemon juice
6 tuna steaks, about 200 g (6 1/2 oz) each

Olive Paste
1 cup pitted black olives
2 teaspoons capers
1 clove garlic, crushed
1 tablespoon olive oil
1 tablespoon finely chopped parsley
6 teaspoons sour cream

1 Combine olive oil, white wine and lemon juice in a small screw-top jar and shake vigorously for 30 seconds. Place tuna steaks in a single layer in a shallow ceramic or glass dish. Pour marinade over and refrigerate for 1 hour, turning tuna over halfway through marinating time.

2 To make Olive Paste: Combine olives, capers, garlic and oil in food processor and, using pulse action, process for 30 seconds or until well combined. Refrigerate until required.

3 Remove tuna steaks from dish, reserve marinade. To barbecue, place tuna on a preheated lightly greased chargrill or flat plate. Cook over high heat for 2–3 minutes on each side, basting occasionally with marinade. Alternatively, cook steaks on a foil-lined grill pan under high heat for 2–3 minutes each side, basting occasionally with marinade. Stir chopped parsley into Olive Paste and set aside for 10 minutes at room temperature.

4 To serve, place one tuna steak on each plate, top with a level tablespoon of Olive Paste and a teaspoon of sour cream. Serve immediately.

TUNA TERIYAKI

✻ **Preparation time:** 10 minutes +
30 minutes marinating
Total cooking time: 10 minutes
Serves 4

500 g (1 lb) tuna fillet

Teriyaki Marinade
2 tablespoons soy sauce
1 tablespoon lemon juice
2 tablespoons dry sherry
2 cm (3/4 inch) piece green ginger, finely grated
1/2 cup (4 fl oz) fish stock

1 Remove any skin from tuna fillet. Cut into four even pieces.
2 In a shallow dish, combine all the marinade ingredients.
3 Place tuna fillets into the marinade and allow to stand for at least 30 minutes. Turn tuna during marinating time.
4 Place tuna on a foil-lined grill pan and cook until flesh flakes—approximately 2–3 minutes each side. Baste during cooking, using all the marinade. Serve immediately.

vegetable. It is eaten raw as a salad vegetable, or cooked in a variety of sauces and dishes, or made into juice. Types include the common tomato, used in salads; plum tomatoes, with dense, flavoursome flesh, good for soups and sauces; the tiny cherry tomato, used whole in salads and as a garnish; and pear-shaped yellow tomatoes, noted for low acidity and used in salads and preserves.

Tongue Classed as offal usually beef, but lamb's tongue is also eaten. Tongue is poached in court bouillon and served hot with a brown or fruit sauce. Cold, pressed tongue is served sliced accompanied by pickles and chutney.

Torte A rich, dense-textured cake, often layered with custard, fruit, whipped cream and ground nuts.

Tortellini Small rings of pasta, usually stuffed with finely chopped seasoned meat, often served with a cream or tomato sauce.

Tortilla A paper-thin Mexican flatbread made from corn or wheat flour quickly cooked (but not

BALSAMIC VINEGAR

ABOVE: FRESH TUNA WITH HERBS AND BALSAMIC VINEGAR

OPPOSITE PAGE: TUNA STEAKS WITH OLIVE PASTE

FRESH TUNA WITH HERBS AND BALSAMIC VINEGAR

✳

Preparation time: 5 minutes
Total cooking time: 10 minutes
Serves 4

2 tablespoons olive oil
4 tuna steaks
1 tablespoon chopped parsley
1 tablespoon chopped basil
2 tablespoons balsamic vinegar

1 Heat the oil in a large frying pan. Add tuna steaks to the pan in a single layer and cook on both sides over medium heat for about 10 minutes, or until the fish is cooked through. (Cooking time will depend on the thickness of tuna steaks.)

2 Transfer tuna steaks to a serving plate. Sprinkle with chopped parsley and basil and drizzle with balsamic vinegar.

Note: Tuna is an oily fish and should be eaten as fresh as possible. Tuna steaks are usually cooked with the skin on.

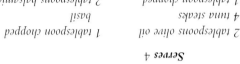

FRESH TUNA FETTUCCINE

✳ ✳

Preparation time: 15 minutes
Total cooking time: 15–20 minutes
Serves 6

750 g (1½ lb) fettuccine
2 large, ripe tomatoes
125 g (4 oz) fresh asparagus, cut into 3 cm (1¼ inch) lengths
½ cup (4 fl oz) olive oil
500 g (1 lb) tuna steaks
3 cloves garlic, crushed
2 onions, sliced
¼ cup finely sliced basil leaves
¼ cup chopped capers

1 Cook fettuccine in a large pan of rapidly boiling salted water until just tender; drain and toss with a little oil to keep strands separate.

2 Peel tomatoes and chop. Cook asparagus in a small pan of rapidly boiling water for 2 minutes or until just tender; drain, rinse under cold water and drain again.

3 Heat 1 tablespoon of the oil in a large frying pan. Add tuna steaks and cook for 2 minutes on each side or until golden brown on the outside but still moist on the inside; remove from pan. Using a fork, shred tuna and remove any bones; set aside.

4 Heat remaining oil in pan. Add the garlic and onion, stir over medium heat for 3 minutes or until onion is tender. Add cooked fettuccine, asparagus, tuna, chopped tomato, basil and chopped capers; stir over medium heat until all ingredients are combined and heated through.

FRESH TUNA RISSOLES

✳

Preparation time: 20 minutes
Total cooking time: 10–15 minutes
Serves 4

500 g (1 lb) fresh tuna fillet
1 medium onion, finely chopped
1½ cups mashed potato
1 tablespoon finely chopped pimiento
pepper
2 tablespoons finely chopped parsley
seasoned plain (all-purpose) flour
1 egg, beaten
dry breadcrumbs
oil for shallow frying

1 Skin tuna fillet. Cut into small pieces. Mince in a food processor or chop very finely.

2 Put tuna meat into a bowl. Add onion, potato, pimiento, pepper and parsley. Mix well. Mould spoonfuls of the mixture into rissoles.

3 Coat rissoles with flour. Dip in beaten egg and roll in breadcrumbs.

4 Lower a few rissoles at a time into hot oil. Shallow-fry until golden, turning once. Drain on paper towels and serve.

---

browned) on a griddle or in a pan. Tortillas may serve as a wrapper for fillings, or as an edible scoop or plate.

Tournedos Also known as filet mignon, a small, round, thick steak cut from a fillet of beef. Usually pan-fried and served on a round of fried bread accompanied by a rich sauce.

Treacle A thick, dark, strong-tasting syrup, a by-product of cane sugar refining. It is used in baking and in the production of confectionery (candy).

Trifle A traditional English dessert consisting of layers of sponge cake sprinkled with sweet sherry, interspersed with fruit or fruit jam, cream, rich egg custard and crushed nuts.

Tripe The stomach lining of cattle, ranging from quite smooth-textured to deeply honeycombed. Tripe is blanched, then boiled in water and milk. It can be served with onions in a parsley sauce, or sautéed with onions.

Trout A freshwater fish of the salmon family with delicately flavoured flesh, available fresh, frozen and smoked.

RIGHT: *SEASONED TURKEY WITH SOUR CHERRY SAUCE*

SEASONED TURKEY WITH SOUR CHERRY SAUCE

★ *Preparation time:* 20 minutes
Total cooking time: 2 hours 55 minutes

Serves 8–10

4 kg (8 lb) self-basting turkey
45 g (1½ oz) butter
1 large onion, finely chopped
250 g (8 oz) can water chestnuts, drained, chopped
2 tablespoons chopped blanched almonds
1 medium apple, peeled, chopped
2 spring onions (scallions), chopped
2 tablespoons finely chopped flat-leaf parsley

1 egg
1 cup cooked long-grain rice
2 cups (16 fl oz) water
salt, pepper

Sour Cherry Sauce
670 g (1 lb 7 oz) jar pitted morello cherries
¼ cup redcurrant jelly
2 teaspoons balsamic vinegar
2 cups (16 fl oz) pan juices, strained
salt, pepper
¼ cup cornflour (cornstarch)
⅓ cup (2½ fl oz) water

1 Preheat oven to moderate 180°C (350°F/Gas 4). Trim excess fat from turkey, rinse well. Pat inside and out with paper towel. Tuck wing tips to underside. Place turkey, breast side up, on rack in a deep baking dish. Melt butter in pan; add onion. Stir over low heat for 5 minutes or until onion is soft. Add water chestnuts and almonds, cook for 5 minutes, stirring occasionally. Add apple and spring onion; stir until heated through. Remove from heat, add salt and pepper, parsley, egg and rice; mix well. Spoon into turkey cavity; secure with string or skewer. Pack remaining mixture in neck cavity; secure. Add water to pan.

2 Bake turkey for 2 hours, basting occasionally with pan juices. Prick all over with a fork, bake another 30 minutes. Remove from oven, reserve pan juices. Rest turkey for 15 minutes. Carve and serve with seasoning and Sour Cherry Sauce.

3 To make Sour Cherry Sauce: Drain cherry juice into a heavy-based pan; reserve cherries. Add jelly, vinegar and juices to pan. Stir over medium heat for 10 minutes or until mixture boils and reduces slightly. Add cherries, boil for 2 minutes; season. Blend cornflour with water in a bowl to form a smooth paste and add to pan. Stir over medium heat until sauce boils and thickens.

Truffle, Chocolate A small, very rich confectionery (candy) made from chocolate, butter, cream and liqueur, formed into small balls and rolled in cocoa powder or chopped nuts. Truffles are usually served with

coffee. They are named for their similarity in appearance to the fungi, black truffle.

Truffle, Fungi An edible fungus that grows underground in forests in France and Italy. Truffles are prized for their musky fragrance and delicate flavour; they are used in pâtés, tossed through pasta and as a filling for omelettes. There are two types of truffle: the black truffle, available fresh (in France), bottled or canned; and the white truffle, found in Italy.

Truss To secure the legs, wings and front opening of poultry, before roasting, to maintain the bird's shape and prevent the loss of stuffing during cooking.

Tuile A thin, curved, crisp biscuit (cookie) made of sugar, slivered almonds, butter and eggs.

shaped by draping the hot, pliable biscuit over a rolling pin.

Tuna A large saltwater fish with dark, compact meat which turns pink when cooked and has a rich, gamey flavour. Fresh tuna may be poached, baked, grilled (broiled) or barbecued; it is also served raw—diced or sliced water thin as in the Japanese dish sashimi. In ancient times the fish was a favourite of the sea-faring Phoenicians, who smoked and salted it; in ancient Greece and Rome it was roasted

sprinkled with salt and oil; pickled tuna was common in medieval times. Tuna is available fresh and frozen, usually as boneless steaks, also as cutlets and fillets, and cooked and canned.

Turkey A large, heavy-bodied domestic fowl native to the Americas and now bred throughout the world. It is valued for its plump breast, which provides a higher proportion of white to dark meat than other poultry. Whole turkey can be stuffed and roasted; it is also available as boneless roasts, rolled, tied and ready to cook; as breast slices and steaks (which can be sautéed like a veal escalope); and thighs, drumsticks and wings. The meat can be prepared as turkey

REDCURRANT-GLAZED ROAST TURKEY

★★ **Preparation time:** 15 minutes
Total cooking time: 1 hour 20 minutes
Serves 8

3 kg (6 lb) turkey breast (bone-in)
1/4 cup redcurrant jelly
2 tablespoons golden syrup (light corn syrup)
1/4 cup brown sugar
40 g (1 1/3 oz) butter, melted
1 cup (8 fl oz) water

Gravy
2 tablespoons plain (all-purpose) flour
3/4 cup (6 fl oz) chicken stock

Apple Stuffing
20 g (2/3 oz) butter
1 medium onion, finely chopped
1 large green apple, finely chopped
2 spring onions (scallions), finely chopped
4 slices dry bread, grated
1 tablespoon chopped chives
2 teaspoons lemon juice

1 Preheat oven to 180°C (350°F/Gas 4). Trim turkey of excess fat. Combine jelly, syrup and sugar in small mixing bowl. Stir until smooth. Brush turkey all over with melted butter; place on a roasting rack in a deep baking dish. Pour water into base of dish. Cover with foil and bake for 40 minutes. Remove from oven; brush liberally with jelly mixture. Bake uncovered for another 20 minutes. Repeat process, baking for 20 minutes more. Remove turkey from oven, transfer to carving board. Leave, covered with foil, in warm place for 15 minutes before slicing.

2 **To make Gravy:** Sprinkle flour evenly over an oven tray. Place under hot grill until flour is golden. Add flour to pan juices, stir over low heat for 2 minutes. Add stock gradually to pan, stirring until mixture is smooth. Stir constantly over medium heat for 5 minutes or until mixture boils and thickens; boil for one minute more, then remove from heat. Serve hot with turkey.

3 **To make Apple Stuffing:** Heat butter in heavy-based pan. Add onion and apple, stir over medium heat until golden brown. Add remaining ingredients, combine well. Serve hot with turkey.

DEVILLED TURKEY STIR-FRY

★ **Preparation time:** 10 minutes
Total cooking time: 7 minutes
Serves 4–6

2 tablespoons bottled mango chutney
1 tablespoon worcestershire sauce
2 tablespoons peanut oil
4 cups coarsely chopped cooked turkey
1 red pepper (capsicum)
1 green pepper (capsicum)
1 celery stick
1 carrot
1 tablespoon Dijon mustard

1 Cut each pepper in half, remove seeds and membrane. Cut into thin strips. Slice celery diagonally, cut carrot into thin slices. Heat oil in a frying pan. Add peppers, celery and carrot. Stir-fry over medium-high heat for 5 minutes.
2 Add turkey to pan and toss for 1 minute.
3 Combine chutney, worcestershire sauce and mustard in a bowl; add to pan. Cook, stirring, for 1 minute until ingredients are well coated and heated through. Serve with rice or noodles.

---

pastrami, turkey salami, turkey ham and smoked turkey sausage. In the United States roast turkey with cornbread stuffing is traditionally eaten on Thanksgiving Day (the last Thursday in November).

Turkish Delight A confectionery (candy) with a firm, smooth texture made by thickening a sugar and lemon juice syrup with cornflour (cornstarch) and flavouring it with rose water or peppermint. When cool the mixture is cut into cubes and coated with icing (confectioners') sugar. Its Turkish name is *rahat lokum*, giving a rest to the mouth.

Turmeric A bright yellow powdered spice ground from the dried roots of a tropical plant related to ginger. It has a mild, bitter-sweet flavour. Turmeric is an essential ingredient in curry powders and pastes and is used in pickles, chutneys and prepared mustard.

Turnip A globe-shaped, white-fleshed root vegetable with a

TURNIPS

TURNIP AND BACON SOUP

Preparation time: 20 minutes
Total cooking time: 1 hour 25 minutes
Serves 4–6

1 tablespoon dripping
3 large brown onions, peeled and thinly sliced
750 g (1½ lb) turnips, peeled, cut into 1 cm (½ inch) cubes
250 g (8 oz) bacon, rind removed cut into 1 cm (½ inch) squares
1.5 litres (6 cups) chicken stock
ground pepper
ground nutmeg
chopped parsley, for garnish
2 medium potatoes, cut into 1 cm (½ inch) cubes

1 Heat dripping in a large pan, cook onion until transparent. Add bacon, continue cooking for about 10 minutes, or until bacon is crisp.
2 Add potatoes and turnips, stir. Cover pan, reduce heat and cook slowly for 10 minutes.

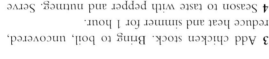

3 Add chicken stock. Bring to boil, uncovered, reduce heat and simmer for 1 hour.
4 Season to taste with pepper and nutmeg. Serve in a heated soup tureen, garnished with parsley.

HONEYED BABY TURNIPS WITH LEMON THYME

Preparation time: 10 minutes
Total cooking time: 7 minutes
Serves 4

500 g (1 lb) baby turnips
45 g (1½ oz) butter
¼ cup honey
3 teaspoons lemon juice
½ teaspoon grated lemon rind
3 teaspoons chopped fresh lemon thyme leaves

1 Rinse and lightly scrub turnips under water. Trim tips and stalks. Cook in boiling water for 1 minute. Drain; rinse under cold water, drain.
2 Heat butter in pan; add honey. Bring to boil, add juice and rind. Boil over high heat for 3 minutes. Add turnips to mixture. Cook over high heat for 3 minutes or until turnips are almost tender and well glazed (test with a skewer).
3 Add the lemon thyme. Remove pan from heat and toss until the turnips are well coated with honey mixture. Serve warm.

---

distinctive flavour used in soups, stews and casseroles. In Italy caramelised sliced turnip is served as a dessert.

Turnover A square or circle of pastry turned over a filling, sealed and baked or deep-fried. Turnovers can be large or individual-sized, sweet or savoury and may be eaten hot or cold as a finger food, snack or main meal.

Tzatziki A tangy yoghurt and cucumber dip of Greek origin. It is served as finger food or a first course with toasted pieces of flat bread, or

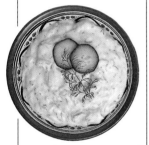

crudités (thinly sliced raw vegetables); as a salad dressing; or as an accompaniment to fried or grilled fish or barbecued meat.

Upside-down Cake A fruit-topped cake popular as a dessert. A layer of poached fruit (traditionally pineapple rings, but also peaches, apricots, apples, pears or cherries) and sometimes nuts is arranged in the bottom of a cake pan, covered with a butter and sugar syrup, topped with cake batter and baked. The cooked cake is inverted and served warm with cream.

V

Vanilla The fragrant, slender seed pod, called a 'bean', of a climbing orchid. Vanilla is used to flavour creams and ice-creams, sweet sauces, custards, syrups, cakes and drinks (especially milk-based chocolate drinks). Vanilla beans can be used more than once—they are infused in hot liquid until the desired strength of flavour is reached, then rinsed and dried for further use.

Vanilla sugar is made by burying a vanilla bean in a

Vacherin A cold dessert consisting of a ring or basket of meringue filled with layers of softened ice-cream and fruit (usually fresh, such as strawberries or peaches, but crystallised (candied) fruits and chestnut purée may also be used), and topped with sweetened whipped cream. Sometimes ice-creams of various flavours are used as the filling instead of fruit.

VEAL

VEAL SCHNITZEL

Preparation time: 20 minutes + 30 minutes refrigeration
Total cooking time: 8 minutes
Serves 4

4 veal escalopes
¼ cup plain (all-purpose) flour
freshly ground pepper
1 egg, beaten
1 cup fresh breadcrumbs
light olive oil for frying
4 slices lemon
2 teaspoons capers
chopped fresh parsley

1 To flatten veal, place escalopes between two sheets of plastic wrap and gently flatten with a rolling pin, taking care not to break meat. Make small nicks about every 5 cm (2 inches) around edge of each escalope with scissors to prevent veal from curling during cooking.

2 Combine flour and pepper on greaseproof paper. Coat veal with flour; shake off excess. Dip in beaten egg. Coat with breadcrumbs, pressing crumbs firmly onto meat. Place veal on a flat tray and refrigerate for 30 minutes before cooking.

3 Heat oil in a heavy-based pan. Add two escalopes and cook for about 2 minutes each side, until golden brown. Remove from pan, drain on paper towels and keep hot. Cook remaining escalopes.

4 Serve veal escalopes hot, topped with a slice of lemon, a few capers and a sprinkling of chopped fresh parsley.

VEAL WITH WINE AND MUSTARD SAUCE

Preparation time: 10 minutes
Total cooking time: 20 minutes
Serves 6

6 veal steaks, about 140 g (4½ oz) each
½ cup plain (all-purpose) flour
1 teaspoon ground mustard seeds
45 g (1½ oz) butter
2 teaspoons oil
1 cup (8 fl oz) good quality white wine
⅔ cup (5 fl oz) chicken stock
3 teaspoons seed mustard

1 Trim meat of fat and sinew. Combine flour and ground mustard seeds on a sheet of greaseproof paper. Toss meat in seasoned flour; shake off excess. Reserve 3 teaspoons of seasoned flour.

2 Heat butter and oil in a large heavy-based frying pan. Add steaks to pan. (Unless you have a very large pan you will have to cook them in batches.) Cook meat over medium-high heat 3 or 4 minutes each side. Remove from pan; drain on paper towels and keep warm. Repeat with remaining steaks.

3 Add combined wine, stock, mustard and reserved seasoned flour to pan, stirring to incorporate any browned bits from the bottom of the pan. Stir until mixture boils and thickens. Place veal on serving plates and pour sauce over.

*ABOVE: VEAL WITH WINE AND MUSTARD SAUCE
OPPOSITE PAGE: VEAL MARSALA*

VEAL MARSALA

Preparation time: 10 minutes
Total cooking time: 10 minutes
Serves 4

4 veal steaks, about	1/3 cup (2 1/2 fl oz)
185 g (6 oz) each	chicken stock
2 tablespoons plain	1 tablespoon soy sauce
(all-purpose) flour	2 teaspoons plum
2 tablespoons oil	conserve
1/3 cup (2 1/2 fl oz)	1 spring onion (scallion),
marsala	finely chopped

1 Trim meat of excess fat and sinew. Place veal steaks between two sheets of plastic wrap and gently flatten to an even thickness with a rolling pin, taking care not to break the meat. Spread the flour on a sheet of greaseproof paper. Toss veal lightly in flour; shake off excess.

2 Heat the oil in a heavy-based pan; add meat. Cook over a medium heat for 2–3 minutes each side, turning once. Remove meat from pan, drain on paper towels. Leave, covered with aluminium foil, in a warm place.

3 Add marsala and chicken stock to pan and bring to the boil. Boil mixture for 1 minute, uncovered, stirring constantly. Add the soy sauce and plum conserve, stir until combined and heated through. Return veal steaks to pan, heat through in the sauce for about 1 minute. Serve immediately, sprinkled with chopped spring onion. May be served with boiled new potatoes.

VEAL AND MUSHROOM CASSEROLE

Preparation time: 20 minutes
Total cooking time: 2 hours
Serves 4

750 g (1 1/2 lb) veal steaks	1/4 cup plain (all-purpose)
1/2 cup (4 fl oz) good	flour
quality white wine	30 g (1 oz) butter
1 tablespoon chopped	1 clove garlic, crushed
fresh thyme	1 tablespoon Dijon
1 cup (8 fl oz) chicken	mustard
stock	1 cup (8 fl oz) cream
375 g (12 oz) button	
mushrooms, halved	

1 Trim meat of excess fat and sinew. Cut into 1 cm (1/2 inch) strips. Toss meat with flour in plastic bag, shake off excess flour. Heat butter and garlic in heavy-based pan. Add meat and cook quickly in small batches over medium heat until well browned. Drain on paper towels.

2 Return meat to pan. Add mustard, cream, white wine, thyme and stock. Bring mixture to boil, reduce heat. Simmer, covered, 1 1/2 hours, stirring occasionally.

3 Add mushrooms; cook for another 15 minutes or until meat is tender. May be served with pasta and steamed julienned vegetables.

Note: Seeded mustard or hot English mustard may be used instead of the Dijon mustard. This recipe may be made one day ahead and kept in an airtight container in refrigerator. Reheat gently.

jar of sugar—the longer it is left, the stronger the flavour becomes.

The vanilla orchid is native to Central America. The pods are gathered, drenched repeatedly in hot water, and left in the sun to sweat and then dry out. They shrivel, darken and produce a coating of vanillin, the strongly scented crystalline substance which gives vanilla its distinctive aroma and flavour. The finest beans are deep-brown, pliable and covered with a frosting of vanillin. Vanilla essence (a liquid made from the bean which is very powerful and should be used sparingly) and vanilla sugar are also available; imitation vanilla essence is a chemical attempt to synthesise the flavour of true vanilla.

Variety Meats See Offal.

Veal The meat of a young calf, unweaned or just weaned, reared for slaughter. The meat of milk-fed veal is very pale pink and delicately grained, with a little satiny white fat; meat from animals that have started to eat grass is darker and coarser, but lacks the rich flavour of beef. Veal is a lean, tender meat; it has little natural fat and is best cooked slowly. Braising

VEAL

and moist heat cooking methods are ideal: roasting and grilling (broiling) should be at a lower heat than for other meats. Like chicken, veal has no strong flavour of its own but absorbs those of the vegetables and herbs cooked with it. It is also good with tangy sauces. Thin slices of veal cut across the grain (in France known as *escalope*, in Italy, *scaloppine* and in Germany, *Schnitzel*) can be fried in butter and served with various sauces or garnishes; rolled around a flavoursome filling and braised; or, with sage and prosciutto, cooked in butter and white wine as in the Italian dish saltimbocca.

Vegetable Any edible part of a plant—leaf, stem, bud, flower, seed, root, bulb or tuber—cultivated as a food. Some fruits are used as vegetables, including the tomato, eggplant (aubergine) and sweet pepper (capsicum). Seed and pod vegetables include peas, beans and lentils; spinach, lettuce and cabbage are leaf vegetables; celery is a stem; carrots, turnips and parsnips are fleshy roots;

Above: OSSO BUCCO; LEFT: ITALIAN VEAL POT ROAST. Opposite: VEAL BIRDS IN TOMATO SAUCE

ITALIAN VEAL POT ROAST

Preparation time: 30 minutes ✷✷
Total cooking time: 1 hour 50 minutes
Serves 4–6

1.5 kg (3 lb) fillet of veal, pocketed
1 tablespoon chutney
1 tablespoon olive oil
1 egg yolk

1 onion, grated
1 clove garlic, crushed
1/2 small red chilli, chopped finely
1 large carrot, grated
1/2 cup ground almonds
1/4 cup pine nuts
1/3 cup chopped raisins

1 tablespoon olive oil, extra
2 cups (16 fl oz) good quality red wine
1 cup (8 fl oz) beef stock
whole baby potatoes and onions, cooked, for garnish (optional)

1 Remove any excess fat or sinew from meat. Heat olive oil in pan, add onion, garlic and chilli and fry for 2–3 minutes. Add grated carrot and cook for 2 minutes longer, stirring to combine. Remove pan from heat; add ground almonds, pine nuts and chopped raisins. Allow the mixture to cool slightly and add combined egg yolk and chutney. Mix well to combine.

2 Place stuffing mixture in pocket of meat, pushing in firmly with back of spoon. Secure with string.

3 Heat extra oil in large pan. Add meat and cook until well browned all over. Add wine and stock, bring to the boil and then reduce heat. Simmer covered until meat is tender, about 1½ hours.

4 Remove meat from the pot. Bring liquid to the boil and simmer gently until sauce has reduced and thickened. Serve meat in slices with sauce spooned over.

OSSO BUCCO

Preparation time: 30 minutes ✷
Total cooking time: 2 hours
Serves 6

1.8 osso bucco (2 kg) (veal shanks, cut into 4 cm pieces)
2¼ cups plain (all-purpose) flour
1/4 cup (2 fl oz) olive oil
1 large onion, chopped
1 large carrot, sliced
2 cloves garlic, crushed

2/3 cup (5½ fl oz) dry white wine
2/3 cup (5½ fl oz) beef stock
440 g (14 oz) canned tomatoes, chopped
1/4 cup tomato paste
1/2 teaspoon caster sugar

1 Preheat oven to moderate 180°C (350°F/Gas 4). Toss osso bucco in seasoned flour; shake off excess.

2 Heat a little of the oil in a heavy-based pan. Cook the meat on both sides over medium-high heat until well browned; drain on paper towels. Transfer the meat to a large baking dish.

3 Add the onion, garlic and carrots to pan, stir until onion is soft. Add the wine, stock, undrained tomatoes, tomato paste and sugar. Bring to the boil; reduce the heat and simmer 5 minutes.

4 Spoon sauce over meat. Cover dish with foil, bake 1¾ hours or until veal is tender. Serve sprinkled with 1 tablespoon chopped parsley, 2 teaspoons grated lemon rind and 1 clove chopped garlic. (This mixture is called Gremolata.)

VEAL BIRDS IN TOMATO SAUCE

✷✷ **Preparation time:** 12 minutes
Total cooking time: 40 minutes
Serves 6

6 veal steaks, about
105 g (3½ oz) each
12 thin slices prosciutto
1 cup grated mozzarella
cheese
2 x 45 g (1½ oz) cans
anchovies in oil,
drained
2 tablespoons plain
(all-purpose) flour
¼ teaspoon ground black
pepper

2 tablespoons oil
⅓ cup (2½ fl oz) dry
white wine
⅓ cup (2½ fl oz)
chicken stock
½ cup bottled chunky
tomato sauce
1 teaspoon capers
1 tablespoon chopped
fresh parsley

1 Preheat oven to moderate 180°C (350°F/Gas 4). Place steaks between two sheets of plastic wrap and gently flatten to an even thickness of about 2.5 mm (⅛ inch) with a rolling pin, taking care not to break the meat. Place 2 slices of prosciutto over each steak. Sprinkle 2 tablespoons cheese over the prosciutto and top with 3 anchovies.

2 Roll up the steaks and tie securely with string at regular intervals to retain their shape during cooking. Combine flour and pepper on greaseproof paper. Toss the meat lightly in seasoned flour; shake off excess.

3 Heat oil in heavy-based pan. Cook meat quickly over medium heat until well browned all over. Arrange in a single layer over the base of a shallow casserole dish. Add the white wine, stock, tomato sauce and capers to pan; bring to the boil. Pour sauce over the meat. Cover dish, transfer to oven, cook for 35 minutes. Remove string just before serving. Serve sprinkled with chopped parsley.

ABOUT VEAL

Veal does not have a strong flavour of its own so is often teamed with foods such as anchovies or capers. Sauces featuring lemon, wine, marsala or tomato and a variety of herbs help keep the veal moist and enhance its flavour.

---

yams and potatoes are tubers; bulbs include onions, shallots and fennel; and broccoli and cauliflower are heads of tightly massed flower buds. Mushrooms and other fungi are generally included with vegetables. Vegetables are eaten raw as salads, and cooked either

Vegetable Marrow A sausage-shaped vegetable belonging to the same family as the zucchini (courgette). Young marrows have the best flavour and most delicate flesh and can be cooked in the same way as zucchini. Large older marrows have a high water content and a bland flavour.

Velouté Sauce A basic white sauce made with lightly browned roux and a well-flavoured, reduced veal, chicken or fish stock. The name comes from the French word for velvety.

Venison Meat from any kind of deer; it is a dark red, very lean meat with a fine grain. Farm-raised venison is milder in flavour and more tender than the game version. Game venison should be

ASIAN VEGETABLES

The wide and exotic range of vegetables found in Asian food stores and supermarkets sometimes can be daunting. Many already have a place in Western cuisines, while others have yet to be discovered. Here is a brief introduction to these vegetables and ways to enjoy them.

BEAN SPROUTS (NGA CHOY)

Crisp, white, short sprouts are the most tender but are highly perishable: use within 3 days of purchase. Rinse and remove any sprouts that are limp or brown; traditionally the root and growing tip are trimmed, but the tip contains most nutrients. Serve raw in salads, lightly steamed and seasoned with sesame oil or soy sauce, or add to stir-fries.

BITTER MELON OR CUCUMBER (FOO GWA)

Yellow-green melon which looks like a small, warty cucumber. To prepare: rinse well, cut in half lengthways, remove and discard seeds, slice melon crossways. Blanch melon pieces for 3 minutes, drain and use in stir-fries with a Chinese sauce, black beans or garlic. As the name suggests, it does have a bitter flavour, and is definitely an acquired taste. However, cooked with beans or meat, the bitterness can be somewhat mitigated.

BOK CHOY (CHINESE CHARD, PAK CHOY)

Use the crisp olive green leaves and the thick white celery-like stems (sliced) in meat or seafood stir-fries or soups. Or steam rinsed bundles briefly to retain texture, and serve with oyster sauce. The stalks have a mild, slightly sweet, flavour and the leaves are tangy.

CHILLIES, RED AND GREEN

Highly flavoured and very spicy; the smaller and redder the chilli, the hotter it is. Used as a spice, rather than as a vegetable, they are rarely eaten whole. For a milder chilli flavour, add a washed whole chilli to the dish and remove it just before serving, or slit the chilli open and remove the seeds and membrane (which are the hottest parts). When chopping chillies, wear plastic gloves to avoid skin irritation. If you cook with chillies often, it is best to keep a board aside especially for chopping them.

CHINESE CABBAGE (WONG BOK, CELERY CABBAGE)

Elongated in shape, with pale green leaves and slight mustard flavour, it is used extensively in the cooking of northern China and Japan. Rinse the leaves and finely shred or tear into bite-size pieces. Steam until barely tender or braise with other vegetables in oyster sauce or add to stir-fries. Blanch whole leaves, fill with savoury filling and roll up. Also used to make kimchi, the fiery Korean pickle.

CHINESE VEGETABLE MARROW (CHIT KOU, FUZZY MELON)

Small 15 cm (6 inch) melon with dark green furry skin. Before use, peel melon and remove stem end. Slice or shred as desired. Steam, boil or stir-fry; complements sweet and sour dishes and readily absorbs other flavours.

CHOY SUM (FLOWERING CHINESE CABBAGE)

Tender fleshy white stems, bright green leaves (similar to bok choy) but harvested when the bright yellow flowers appear. All these parts are eaten, but cook stems for longer; steam or blanch and serve with oyster or mushroom sauce, or as an accompaniment to meat dishes.

GAI LAN (CHINESE BROCCOLI, CHINESE KALE)

Fleshy stems, dull green leaves and small white flower heads are all eaten. Regarded as a gourmet vegetable, it is similar in flavour to Western broccoli but has a slightly earthier taste. In Chinese restaurants it is most often lightly steamed and served with oyster sauce. It can also be blanched and used in stir-fries, especially with pork or in mixed vegetable dishes.

DAIKON (JAPANESE RADISH, LOH BOK, CHINESE WHITE TURNIP)

This large white cylindrical radish is mostly eaten raw in salads. Peel and finely slice, cut into matchsticks or grate. In Japan, it is often served with fried foods such as tempura. In Chinese dishes it is sliced or cubed and braised with meat, which it helps tenderise. Daikon can be pickled in white vinegar or brine and is sometimes dried.

CHRYSANTHEMUM LEAVES (SHUNGIKU, TONG HO)

A close relative of the Mother's Day variety, but the aromatic dark green leaves are entirely edible. In Japanese and Chinese cooking, they are usually parboiled and tossed in sesame oil or used as a pot herb when cooking meat. In Chinese cooking, they are stir-fried and are popular in steamboats. The leaves must be rinsed very well to rid them of excess sand.

WATERCRESS (SAI YEUNG CHOY)

At its prime when leaves are dark green-purple colour, stems crisp with no unpleasant smell. To prepare, rinse well, then chop entire plant or just snip off leaves and discard stalks. In Asian cuisine it is usually blanched in boiling water, then refreshed in cold water and served with a dressing such as soy sauce or sesame oil. Can be pureed with vegetable stock to make a cool, refreshing, peppery soup or steamed with other vegetables. A useful garnish.

TARO ROOT (WOO TOW, DASHEEN)

Large tan-coloured bulb with tough outer skin marked by rings, and white flesh. Store in a cool dark place (not in refrigerator). Peel, slice and steam or boil until tender before adding to rich or fatty meat stews. Like potatoes, it can be boiled, mashed, baked or sautéed with garlic. When cooked, the flesh is greyish.

SPRING ONION (TSUNG, SCALLION)

Mostly sold in bunches with roots intact. To prepare, remove root and base of stem and any damaged parts of leaves; wash well; slice diagonally into even-sized pieces. Most flavour is in the white stem. They add colour and subtle onion flavour to salads, stir-fries or soups. They need little cooking.

SNOW PEA (HO LAN DOW, SUGAR PEA, MANGE TOUT)

Bright green, crisp pods are blanched and used whole in salads, stir-fries and soups. To prepare, soak in cold water, pull off stem end and any string from edge of pod. Add to dishes only at the last moment.

SNAKE BEAN (DOH GOK, ASPARAGUS BEAN)

These stringless beans which grow up to 30 cm (12 inches) are cut into 5 cm (2 inch) lengths and used in stir-fries, curries and soups. They can also be cooked in the same ways as other types of green beans, but have less flavour.

VEGETABLES

SWEET VEGETABLE CURRY

★ **Preparation time:** 20 minutes
Total cooking time: 40 minutes
Serves 4

2 medium carrots
1 medium parsnip
1 medium potato
2 tablespoons oil
2 medium onions, chopped
1 teaspoon ground cardamom
1/4 teaspoon ground cloves
1 1/2 teaspoons ground cumin seeds
1 teaspoon ground coriander
1 teaspoon turmeric
1 teaspoon brown mustard seeds
1/2 teaspoon chilli powder

2 teaspoons grated fresh ginger
1 1/3 cups (10 1/2 fl oz) vegetable stock
3/4 cup (6 fl oz) apricot nectar (juice)
2 tablespoons fruit chutney
1 medium green pepper (capsicum), cut into 2 cm (3/4 inch) squares
200 g (6 1/2 oz) small button mushrooms
315 g (10 oz) cauliflower, cut into small florets
1/4 cup ground almonds

1 Cut carrots, parsnip and potato into 2 cm (3/4 inch) pieces. Heat oil in large heavy-based pan. Add onion, cook over medium heat for 4 minutes or until just soft. Add cardamom, cloves, cumin seeds, coriander, turmeric, mustard seeds, chilli powder and grated ginger; cook, stirring, 1 minute or until aromatic.

2 Add carrot, parsnip, potato, stock, nectar and chutney. Cook, covered, over medium heat, stirring occasionally, for 25 minutes.

3 Stir in pepper, mushrooms and cauliflower. Simmer for another 10 minutes or until vegetables are tender. Stir in ground almonds. Serve.

Note: Any vegetables may be used in this curry. For example, broccoli, zucchini (courgette), red pepper (capsicum) or orange sweet potato would be suitable. May be served with steamed rice. Add one can of chick peas (garbanzo beans) to make this a complete meal.

WHITE WINTER VEGETABLE CASSEROLE

★ **Preparation time:** 5 minutes
Total cooking time: 1 hour 20 minutes
Serves 4

8 baby potatoes, halved
2 medium swedes, peeled and sliced
4 baby onions, halved
200 g (6 1/2 oz) cauliflower, cut into florets
60 g (2 oz) butter
1/3 cup plain (all-purpose) flour
425 g (13 1/2 oz) can chicken consommé
1 1/2 cups (12 fl oz) milk
1/2 cup freshly grated parmesan cheese

larded before roasting; it can also be braised and casseroled. Farm venison can be roasted, pan-fried or grilled—allow to rest for 5–10 minutes before serving—added to stir-fries, or made into kebabs and barbecued. Care should be taken not to overcook venison, as it will dry out. Forequarter cuts are best slowly simmered to make casseroles, curries and ragoûts.

Vermicelli Italian vermicelli—long, thin strands of pasta dough, sometimes coiled into nests—is boiled and served with a sauce or broken into short lengths and added to soup. In Chinese cooking, vermicelli made with soya bean flour is boiled or fried for use in soups and vegetable dishes and fine strands of pearly white rice flour vermicelli are added to soups or fried in oil for use as a garnish. The name comes from the Italian for 'little worms'.

Vermouth A wine used as an aperitif or as a cocktail ingredient, made by infusing a base wine (red or white) with herbs, spices, barks or peels, then fortifying the result with distilled spirits. It can be used to flavour stuffings, sauces and poaching stock, and in place of wine in some chicken dishes.

MEDITERRANEAN-STYLE VEGETABLES

Preparation time: 30 minutes +
1 hour 15 minutes standing
Total cooking time: 15 minutes
Serves 6

1 large eggplant (aubergine)	1 small green pepper (capsicum), chopped
1 tablespoon salt	90 g (3 oz) button mushrooms, halved
250 g (8 oz) cherry tomatoes	1 medium red pepper (capsicum), halved
1 tablespoon olive oil	1/3 cup fresh basil leaves
2 tablespoons chopped fresh oregano leaves	2 medium zucchini (courgettes), sliced
2 tablespoons balsamic vinegar	
1 tablespoon olive oil, extra	

1 Preheat oven to moderate 180°C (350°F/Gas 4). Place the potato, swede, onion and cauliflower in a greased 6-cup capacity casserole dish.

2 Heat butter in a medium pan; add flour. Stir over low heat 2 minutes or until flour mixture is lightly golden in colour.

3 Add chicken consommé and milk gradually to pan, stirring until mixture is smooth. Stir constantly over medium heat for 2 minutes or until sauce boils and thickens.

4 Pour sauce over vegetables. Cover and bake for 1 hour. Sprinkle with parmesan cheese and bake, uncovered, for 10 minutes, or until cheese is golden and vegetables are soft.

1 Preheat oven to moderate 180°C (350°F/Gas 4). Brush an oven tray with oil. Cut eggplant lengthways into thin slices, spread out in a single layer on a board; sprinkle with salt. Set aside for 15 minutes; rinse and dry thoroughly. Place eggplant slices in a single layer on tray.

2 Score a small cross on each tomato, place on tray with eggplant. Brush eggplant and tomatoes with oil; bake for 10 minutes. Remove from oven and allow to cool. Cut eggplant into strips.

3 Remove seeds from red pepper; brush skin with oil. Grill until skin is black, then wrap in a damp tea-towel until cool. Rub off skin, and slice. Shred fresh basil leaves. Place zucchini in a small heatproof bowl. Cover with boiling water, stand for 1 minute, drain and plunge into cold water, drain well.

4 Combine all vegetables and herbs in a large mixing bowl. Sprinkle balsamic vinegar and oil over vegetables and toss well to combine. Allow to stand for 1 hour for flavours to combine, then serve at room temperature.

Note: Salting eggplant reduces the bitterness and the amount of fat absorbed during cooking. Scoring tomatoes prevents them from bursting when baked. This dish teams well with baked lamb and beef. You can change the flavour by varying the herbs or adding a clove of crushed garlic when adding oil.

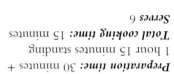

OPPOSITE PAGE: SWEET VEGETABLE CURRY
ABOVE: MEDITERRANEAN-STYLE VEGETABLES

Vinaigrette A thin oil and vinegar dressing, often containing herbs, spices, mustard or finely chopped onion. Vinaigrette is served especially with green salads, and can also be used to dress some vegetable, meat, poultry and fish dishes.

Victoria Sponge A sponge cake used as the base for queen cakes, jam sandwich cake and castle pudding. The sponge is named after Queen Victoria, who spent part of each year on the Isle of Wight, where the cake was served regularly at tea parties.

Vichyssoise A soup made by cooking potatoes and the white part of leeks in chicken stock, puréeing the mixture and adding cream. It is usually served chilled, topped with chives. The soup was created in the early 1900s at New York's Ritz-Carlton Hotel.

Verte, Sauce Literally 'green sauce', a mayonnaise containing a blend of finely chopped herbs and leaf vegetables (such as spinach, watercress, tarragon, parsley and chervil). Sauce verte is served with cold fish, eggs and vegetable dishes.

Vinegar A sharp-tasting liquid obtained when the alcohol in wine, or alcoholic solutions from grains, apples and other sources, is changed by fermentation into acetic acid. Wine vinegar is fermented from fresh wine; cider vinegar from apple cider, malt vinegar from malt liquor and sweet-sour vinegars from rice wine; the quality of the vinegar depends upon the quality of the wine or of the other alcohol from which it has been made. Vinegar is used in salad dressings, mayonnaise, mustards, mint and horseradish.

Vine Leaf The leaf of the grape vine, much used in Greek and Middle Eastern cooking; it has a slightly bitter flavour which is lessened by blanching. Leaves for cooking should be medium-light green and not too young; they are used to wrap fish and small game birds before braising (imparting a slightly lemony taste), and are probably best known for their use in dolmades, small cylindrical packages of rice, minced lamb, finely chopped onion, nuts and seasonings. Vine leaves are available fresh or preserved in brine.

GRILLED VEGETABLES WITH GARLIC MAYONNAISE

★★ *Preparation time: 30 minutes*
Total cooking time: 15 minutes
Serves 8

2 medium eggplants (aubergines), cut into thin slices lengthways
salt
4 small leeks, halved lengthways
2 medium red peppers (capsicum), cut into eighths
4 small zucchini (courgettes), halved lengthways
8 large flat mushrooms

Dressing
1 tablespoon balsamic vinegar
2 tablespoons Dijon mustard
2 teaspoons dried oregano
1 cup (8 fl oz) olive oil

Garlic Mayonnaise
2 egg yolks
1 tablespoon lemon juice
2 cloves garlic, crushed
1 cup (8 fl oz) olive oil
1 tablespoon chopped fresh chives
1 tablespoon chopped fresh parsley
1 tablespoon water

1 Sprinkle eggplant slices with salt, allow to stand 30 minutes. Rinse under cold water, pat dry with paper towel. Place eggplant, leek, peppers and zucchini in a single layer on a flat grill tray, brush with dressing.
2 Cook, under pre-heated grill, on high for 5 minutes, turning once; brush occasionally with dressing. Add mushrooms, cap side up, to grill tray, brush with dressing. Continue to cook vegetables for 10 minutes or until tender, turning mushrooms only once. Brush vegetables with dressing during cooking. Serve with Garlic Mayonnaise.
3 To make Dressing: Combine vinegar, mustard and oregano in a small bowl; gradually whisk in oil.
4 To make Garlic Mayonnaise: Place egg yolks, lemon juice and garlic in a food processor or blender, blend for 5 seconds until combined. With motor constantly operating, add oil slowly in a thin, steady stream until all oil is added and mayonnaise is thick and creamy. Add chives, parsley and water, blend for 3 seconds until combined.

FILO VEGETABLE POUCHES

★ *Preparation time: 45 minutes*
Total cooking time: 35–40 minutes
Makes 12

Filling
235 g (7½ oz) can water chestnuts, sliced
3 cups grated carrot
2 large onions, finely chopped
1 tablespoon grated ginger
1 tablespoon finely chopped fresh coriander
1 tablespoon miso
¼ cup tahini paste
pepper, to taste
8 sheets filo pastry
125 g (4 oz) butter, melted
1 cup (8 fl oz) water

AND VEGETABLE CASSEROLE

OPPOSITE PAGE: GRILLED VEGETABLES WITH GARLIC MAYONNAISE. THIS PAGE, ABOVE: FILO VEGETABLE POUCHES; RIGHT: SPICY CHICK PEA AND VEGETABLE CASSEROLE

1 To make Filling: Combine carrot, onion, ginger, coriander and water in large pan. Cover. cook over low heat 20 minutes. Uncover, cook for another 5 minutes or until all liquid has evaporated. Remove from heat, cool slightly. Stir in water chestnuts, miso and tahini paste. Season with pepper.

2 Preheat oven to moderate 180°C (350°F/Gas 4). Brush two oven trays with melted butter or oil. Cover filo pastry with a damp tea-towel to prevent drying out. Remove one sheet of filo and place on work surface. Brush lightly with butter. Top with another three pastry sheets, brushing each layer with butter. Cut filo into six even squares. Repeat process with remaining pastry, giving 12 squares in total.

3 Divide filling evenly between the squares, placing filling in the centre. Bring edges together and pinch to form a pouch. Brush the lower portion of each pouch with butter. Place on prepared trays. Bake for 10–12 minutes or until golden brown and crisp. Serve hot with sweet chilli sauce, if desired.

Note: Tahini paste is an oily paste made from sesame seeds. It may separate on standing. If this should occur, stir well before using.

SPICY CHICK PEA (GARBANZO BEAN) AND VEGETABLE CASSEROLE

✳ **Preparation time:** 25 minutes + overnight soaking
Total cooking time: 1 hour 30 minutes
Serves 4

1½ cups dried chick peas (garbanzo beans)
2 tablespoons oil
1 large onion, chopped
1 clove garlic, crushed
3 teaspoons ground cumin
½ teaspoon chilli powder
½ teaspoon allspice
425 g (13½ oz) can peeled tomatoes, crushed
1½ cups (12 fl oz) vegetable stock

315 g (10 oz) pumpkin, cut into 2 cm (¾ inch) cubes
155 g (5 oz) green beans, topped and tailed
200 g (6½ oz) button squash, quartered
2 tablespoons tomato paste
1 teaspoon dried oregano

1 Place chick peas in a large bowl, cover with cold water and soak overnight; drain in a colander. Heat oil in a large pan, add onion and garlic; stir-fry for 2 minutes or until tender. Add cumin, chilli and allspice and stir-fry 1 minute.
2 Add chickpeas, tomato and stock to pan. Bring to boil, reduce heat and simmer, covered, for 1 hour, stirring occasionally.
3 Add cubed pumpkin, green beans, button squash, tomato paste and oregano. Stir to combine. Simmer, covered, for another 15 minutes. Remove lid from pan and simmer uncovered for another 10 minutes to reduce and thicken sauce slightly.

sauces, and in marinades; to add bite to soups, sauces and stews, and for pickling and preserving. Flavoured vinegars, which have herbs or fruits added, are also available, or can be made at home. Red wine vinegars are used to make demi-glace sauces for game, beef and lamb dishes, and in vinaigrette; white wine vinegars can be made into dressings for fish dishes and used in vinaigrette, mayonnaise and hollandaise sauce, and as a base for herbed vinegars. Raspberry vinegar can be used in vinaigrette, teamed with cream to dress fruit, or used in place of lemon when cooking veal or chicken. Lemon balm vinegar can be used in salad dressings. Tarragon vinegar is an essential ingredient of bearnaise sauce. It is also used in mayonnaise and in marinades for chicken, fish and seafoods. Rosemary vinegar is good in lamb stew and in sauces for fish and shellfish. Dill vinegar is used in sauces for fish, in sour cream and yoghurt sauces and dressings, and for pickling cucumbers. Sherry vinegar, smooth, rich and slightly tart, makes flavoursome gravies and combines well with nut oils in vinaigrette. Balsamic vinegar, made from the

Juice of the sweet Trebbiano grape and aged in aromatic hardwood casks, is deep-coloured and mellow-flavoured; it is used to dress berries, to deglaze roasting pans for gravy, and as a salad dressing.

Cider vinegar, slightly sweet and with a faint apple flavour, is used to make sauces for roast pork and roast duck, in vinaigrettes, and can be substituted for rice vinegar in Chinese cooking. Malt vinegar, dark-coloured and too strongly flavoured for use in salad dressings, is used as a condiment on fish and chips, is an ingredient in worcestershire sauce, and is used for pickling onions and walnuts. White or distilled vinegar (usually distilled malt vinegar) is colourless and sharp-flavoured; it is used in the pickling of gherkins and cocktail onions and in the manufacture of sauces and chutneys. Spirit vinegar, the strongest of all vinegars, differs from distilled vinegar in that it contains a small amount of alcohol; it is used for pickling. White rice vinegar, mild-flavoured, pale and clear, is distilled from fermented rice; it is used to flavour the rice in the Japanese dish sushi and can be used as a dressing for raw vegetables such as cabbage and carrots, in vinaigrettes and as a

VEGETABLE FRITTERS WITH TOMATO SAUCE

Preparation time: 30 minutes
Total cooking time: 40 minutes
Makes 12

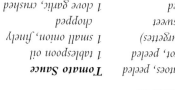

2 medium potatoes, peeled
1 medium carrot, peeled
2 zucchini (courgettes)
125 g (4 oz) sweet potato, peeled
1 small leek
2 tablespoons plain (all-purpose) flour
3 eggs, lightly beaten
oil for frying

Tomato Sauce
2 medium tomatoes, peeled
1 tablespoon oil
1 small onion, finely chopped
1 clove garlic, crushed
1/2 teaspoon ground paprika
3 ripe medium tomatoes, finely chopped
1/4 cup finely shredded fresh basil

1 Grate potatoes, carrot, zucchini and sweet potato. Using hands squeeze out as much moisture as possible from the vegetables. Slice leek finely, add to grated vegetables and combine.
2 Sprinkle flour over vegetables; stir. Add eggs; mix well. Heat 5 mm (1/4 inch) of oil in a pan; drop in 1/4 cup of mixture. Form mixture into a 10 cm (4 inch) round. Fry 2–3 at a time 3 minutes each side over medium heat until crispy. Drain; keep warm. Repeat with remaining mixture.
3 **To make Tomato Sauce:** Heat oil in pan. Add onion, garlic and paprika; cook over medium heat 3 minutes or until soft. Add tomato, reduce heat; cook 10 minutes, stirring occasionally. Stir in basil.

MUSHROOMS EN CROUTE

Preparation time: 40 minutes
Total cooking time: 20–25 minutes
Makes 48

8 slices white bread
1 tablespoon dry sherry
2 teaspoons cornflour (cornstarch)
75 g (2 1/2 oz) butter, melted
1/3 cup (2 1/2 fl oz) sour cream
1 tablespoon olive oil
1 clove garlic, crushed
1/2 small onion, finely chopped
375 g (12 oz) small button mushrooms, finely sliced
salt and pepper, to taste
1 tablespoon finely chopped fresh parsley
1 teaspoon finely chopped fresh thyme
1/4 cup shredded parmesan cheese

1 Preheat oven to moderate 180°C (350°F/Gas 4). Cut the crusts from the bread. Brush both sides of bread with the melted butter. Cut each slice into 6 small rectangles or squares. Place bread croûtes on a foil-lined tray. Bake 5–10 minutes or until golden and crisp.
2 Heat the oil in a large frying pan; add the garlic and onion. Cook, stirring over low heat, until onion is soft. Add the mushrooms and cook over medium heat for 5 minutes or until tender. Season with salt and pepper.

ABOVE: VEGETABLE FRITTERS WITH TOMATO SAUCE. OPPOSITE PAGE: RICE AND RATATOUILLE WITH CHEESE CRUST.

3 Pour in the sherry. Blend the cornflour and sour cream, add to mushroom mixture and stir until mixture boils and thickens. Remove pan from heat and stir in the parsley and thyme. Set aside to cool.

4 Spread mushroom mixture on each croûte. Top with parmesan. Place on a baking tray and bake for 5 minutes or until croûtes are heated through.

RICE AND RATATOUILLE WITH CHEESE CRUST

★ **Preparation time:** 45 minutes
Total cooking time: 55–60 minutes
Serves 4–6

2 large eggplants (aubergines)	2 zucchini (courgettes), about 500 g (1 lb), cut in 2 cm (³/4 inch) slices
1 teaspoon salt	1 teaspoon sugar
750 g (1½ lb) tomatoes	1 cup (8 fl oz) water
⅓ cup (2½ fl oz) olive oil	1 cup (8 fl oz) tomato juice
6 cloves garlic, peeled, chopped	½ cup long-grain rice
2 large onions, cut in 2 cm (³/4 inch) cubes	**Topping**
salt and pepper to taste	3 eggs
2 large red peppers (capsicums), cut into 2 cm (³/4 inch) squares	½ cup (4 fl oz) cream
	2 teaspoons French mustard
1 large green pepper (capsicum), cut in 2 cm (³/4 inch) squares	1 cup grated cheddar cheese
	salt and pepper

1 Preheat oven to moderate 180°C (350°F/Gas 4). Peel eggplant, cut into 3 cm (1¼ inch) cubes. Place in a colander. Sprinkle well with salt and leave to stand for 15 minutes. Rinse under cold water; drain. Pat dry with paper towels. Score a small cross on each tomato. Place in boiling water for 1–2 minutes and then immediately in cold water. Remove, peel down skin from cross. Cut tomatoes in quarters.

2 Heat oil in large heavy-based pan. Add eggplant, garlic and onion, cook over medium heat 5 minutes. Season with salt and pepper. Add red and green peppers, sliced zucchini, tomato quarters and sugar, cook for another 5 minutes. Remove from heat.

3 Add water, tomato juice and rice, mix well. Transfer mixture to an 8-cup capacity ovenproof dish. Cover and bake for 20–30 minutes or until rice has absorbed the liquid and is tender.

4 To make Topping: Whisk eggs, cream and French mustard in a large jug. Stir in cheddar cheese and season with salt and pepper. Pour Topping over cooked vegetables and rice. Return to oven and bake for 15 minutes or until Topping is set. Leave casserole to stand for 5 minutes before serving.

Note: The cheese topping in this recipe is a bit like a thin custard which sets on top of the dish. For added flavour, you can add 1 tablespoon chopped fresh oregano or marjoram and a little freshly grated parmesan cheeses.

Walnut A nut encased in a hard, round shell and consisting of two deeply ridged lobes of creamy-white, mild-flavoured flesh. Walnuts can be eaten as a snack, chopped and added to stuffing and savoury salads or used in cakes, biscuits (cookies) and confectionery (candy). They are available in the shell, shelled (in packs or cans) and pickled.

Waldorf Salad A salad made with chopped apples, celery and walnuts or pecans, with a mayonnaise dressing, usually served on lettuce as a side dish. It was created at the Waldorf-Astoria Hotel.

Waffle A flat, crisp-surfaced cake made by cooking batter in a special hinged iron with a honeycomb-patterned grid. Waffles are served hot, topped with jam, honey or maple syrup, and cream or ice-cream.

Wafer A small, thin, crisp biscuit (cookie), often served with ice-creams; while hot, they are sometimes shaped into rolls or cones.

WALNUTS

WALNUT BISCUITS

★ ★
Preparation time: 10 minutes
Total cooking time: 15–20 minutes
Makes 28

200 g (6½ oz) butter, softened
½ cup caster (superfine) sugar
2 tablespoons orange flower water
2 cups plain (all-purpose) flour, sifted

Walnut Filling
½ cup walnuts, chopped
¼ cup caster (superfine) sugar
1 teaspoon ground cinnamon

1 Preheat oven to 160°C (325°F/Gas 3). Brush a 32 x 28 cm (13 x 11 inch) oven tray with melted butter or oil, line the base with paper; grease paper. Beat butter and sugar in small mixing bowl until light and creamy.

2 Transfer the mixture to a large bowl. Using a metal spoon, fold in orange flower water and sifted flour until well combined. Press with your hands until mixture comes together to make a stiff dough.

3 **To make Walnut Filling:** Mix walnuts, sugar and cinnamon in a medium bowl.

4 Roll heaped tablespoonsful of dough into balls. Press a hollow in the centre with your thumb. Place 1 teaspoon of Filling into each hollow.

Place on trays, flatten slightly without folding dough over filling. Bake 15–20 minutes or until biscuits are golden. Cool on a wire rack.

WALNUT AND HERB SALAD

★
Preparation time: 15 minutes
Total cooking time: nil
Serves 4–6

1 butter lettuce
½ bunch watercress
1 bunch fresh oregano
1 bunch fresh basil
½ bunch fresh mint
½ bunch fresh coriander
1 cup walnut halves

Dressing
¼ cup (2 fl oz) tarragon vinegar
2 tablespoons walnut oil
½ teaspoon freshly ground pepper

1 Wash lettuces and watercress; dry thoroughly. Prepare herbs by breaking into sprigs or removing leaves from tough stalks. Wash and dry thoroughly.

2 Arrange lettuce, watercress and herbs in a large salad bowl. Add walnuts and toss to combine.

3 **To make Dressing:** Combine vinegar, oil and pepper in a small bowl and whisk to combine.

4 Pour dressing over salad just prior to serving.

ABOVE: WALNUT BISCUITS
OPPOSITE PAGE, ABOVE: SWEET AND SPICY WALNUTS; BELOW: WALNUT AND HERB SALAD

WALNUTS

CHERRY, DATE AND WALNUT ROLL

✳ **Preparation time:** 20 minutes +
15 minutes standing
Total cooking time: 50 minutes
Makes one roll

75 g (2½ oz) finely	½ cup chopped walnuts
chopped fresh dates	¼ cup chopped glacé
2 tablespoons currants	cherries
⅓ cup (2½ fl oz) water	½ teaspoon ground
⅓ cup soft brown sugar	nutmeg
45 g (1½ oz) butter	1 egg, lightly beaten
½ teaspoon bicarbonate	¾ cup self-raising flour,
of soda (baking soda)	sifted

1 Preheat oven to moderate 180°C (350°F/Gas 4). Brush a nut roll tin (4-cup capacity) with melted butter or oil. Line inside with paper; grease paper. Place dates, currants, water, sugar and butter in small pan. Stir over low heat 5 minutes or until butter has melted and mixture boils. Remove pan from heat, cool slightly. Add soda to pan; stir. Allow to cool.

2 Place walnuts, cherries, nutmeg, egg, cooled date mixture and flour in a large mixing bowl. Stir with a wooden spoon until just combined.

3 Spoon mixture into prepared tin; close open end of tin with lid. Lay tin on its side in oven, bake for 45 minutes. Leave cake in tin 15 minutes before transferring to wire rack to cool.

SWEET AND SPICY WALNUTS

✳ **Preparation time:** 5 minutes
Total cooking time: 10 minutes
Serves 8

60 g (2 oz) butter	2 cups walnut halves
1 teaspoon ground	¼ cup caster (superfine)
cinnamon	sugar
1 teaspoon ground	
cardamom	

1 Preheat oven to moderately hot 200°C (400°F/Gas 6). Melt butter in a medium pan; remove from heat. Add cinnamon and cardamom to pan; stir until combined.

2 Add the walnuts and stir until well coated in spice mixture. Spread walnuts in a single layer on an oven tray. Bake for 8 minutes or until lightly browned; remove from oven.

3 Place caster sugar in a medium bowl. Add the hot walnuts and stir until well coated. Serve hot or cold as a snack.

ABOUT WALNUTS

■ Store walnuts in an airtight container. Shelled walnuts will keep for about 6 months in the refrigerator and can be frozen for about 12 months.

■ If you buy 500 g (1 lb) unshelled walnuts the yield will be about 250 g (½ lb).

■ Walnuts are excellent for use in cakes, biscuits (cookies) and salads.

Walnut Oil A fragrant, clear, pale golden oil pressed from walnut kernels and used mainly in dressings for salads and cooked vegetables.

Wasabi A pungent, powerfully flavoured root, not unlike the horseradish root, used in Japanese cooking as an ingredient in sushi and, mixed with soy sauce, as an accompaniment to sashimi. Wasabi is available in powdered form (to be reconstituted with a little sake or cold water), or as a pale green paste in tubes; the fresh root can sometimes be bought from stores which specialise in Japanese food.

Water Chestnut A crisp, white-fleshed, delicately flavoured root vegetable valued as an ingredient in Chinese cooking because it remains crunchy after it is cooked. Water chestnuts can be bought fresh, from Asian food stores, and sometimes canned.

Watercress A plant with small, deep green, peppery-tasting leaves and stems which are used in salads and soups, and as a garnish. Watercress is available fresh throughout the year.

WONTONS

WONTONS WITH CHILLI DIP

★★ **Preparation time:** 40 minutes
Total cooking time: 10–15 minutes

Makes 48

250 g (8 oz) lean pork	1 tablespoon chopped fresh coriander
105 g (3½ oz) green (uncooked) prawns (shrimps), peeled	48 round egg pastry wonton wrappers oil for deep frying
60 g (2 oz) bamboo shoots, drained	

Chilli Dip

3 spring onions (scallions), chopped	¼ cup honey
1 cm (½ inch) piece fresh ginger, peeled	¼ cup (2 fl oz) sweet chilli sauce
salt and white pepper	1 teaspoon chopped fresh ginger
¼ cup chopped unsalted peanuts	1 teaspoon rice vinegar
½ teaspoon sugar	

1 Trim pork of excess fat and sinew. Cut into cubes. Process pork, prawns, bamboo shoots, onion and ginger in food processor for 20–30 seconds. Add salt, pepper, peanuts, sugar and coriander.

2 Place 1 teaspoon of mixture in centre of each wrapper. Brush edges with water. Bring wrapper edges together to form pouches; squeeze to secure.

3 Heat oil in deep, heavy-based pan. Lower wonton pouches into moderately hot oil. Cook in batches over medium heat for 1 minute or until golden, crisp and cooked through. Remove from oil with slotted spoon, drain on paper towels.

4 To make Chilli Dip: Combine honey, sauce, ginger and vinegar in a bowl. Mix well.

STEAMED PRAWN (SHRIMP) WONTONS

★★ **Preparation time:** 40 minutes
Total cooking time: 20–30 minutes

Makes 12

8 large prawns (shrimps)	1 tablespoon Chinese soy sauce
250 g (8 oz) minced (ground) pork	1 tablespoon Chinese rice wine or dry sherry
45 g (1½ oz) can water chestnuts, drained, finely chopped	1 tablespoon sesame oil
45 g (1½ oz) can bamboo shoots, drained, finely chopped	1 egg white, lightly whisked
1 tablespoon oyster sauce	1 tablespoon rice flour or cornflour (cornstarch)
1 tablespoon hoisin sauce	12 wonton wrappers

1 Peel the prawns and chop very finely. Combine with minced pork, water chestnuts, bamboo shoots, oyster sauce, hoisin sauce, soy sauce, rice wine or sherry, sesame oil, egg white and rice flour or cornflour.

2 Place 1 teaspoon of mixture in the centre of each wrapper. Brush edges with a little water. Bring the wrapper edges together to form pouches and squeeze gently to secure.

3 Lay a piece of aluminium foil on the base of a steamer; brush with oil, and place wontons on top. Steam for 20–30 minutes until cooked. Serve wontons from the steamer accompanied by a piquant sauce.

*ABOVE: WONTONS WITH CHILLI DIP
OPPOSITE PAGE: VEGETABLE WONTONS WITH CHILLI SAUCE*

Watermelon A large melon with a hard, smooth, mottled-green skin and sweet, juicy, reddish flesh studded with dark seeds; it is eaten fresh as a fruit and added to fruit salads. Watermelons grow on a trailing vine and are available for most of the year.

Waterzooi A stew made with chicken or fish; the liquid is sometimes served separately as a soup and the solids served over rice.

Welsh Rarebit See Rarebit.

Wheat A cereal grain, staple for half the world's population. It is ground into flour and used to make bread, pasta, cakes and biscuits (cookies), and as a breakfast cereal.

Whitebait Tiny, matchstick-length silvery fish (the young of several species), generally cooked whole, dusted with flour and deep-fried, as a first course.

White Sauce A sauce based on a roux of butter and flour with milk (béchamel sauce) or chicken, veal or fish stock (velouté sauce).

Wholemeal A coarse-textured flour ground from the entire wheat kernel and used to make bread, cakes, biscuits (cookies) and pasta.

VEGETABLE WONTONS WITH CHILLI SAUCE

★★ **Preparation time:** 40 minutes +
30 minutes soaking
Total cooking time: 20 minutes
Makes 25

8 dried Chinese
  mushrooms
1 tablespoon peanut oil
200 g (6½ oz) packet
  wonton wrappers
oil for deep frying
1 tablespoon soy sauce

1 teaspoon sesame oil
1 teaspoon grated ginger
2 spring onions
  (scallions), finely
  chopped
1 medium carrot, finely
  chopped
1 medium parsnip, finely
  chopped
90 g (3 oz) broccoli, cut
  into small florets
2 tablespoons breadcrumbs

Chilli Sauce
1 tablespoon peanut oil
1 clove garlic, crushed
¼ cup (2 fl oz) sweet
  chilli sauce
2 tablespoons soy sauce
2 tablespoons sherry
1 tablespoon lemon juice

1 Soak mushrooms in hot water 30 minutes. Drain, squeeze out liquid. Discard stems. Slice caps finely.

2 Heat oils in wok or heavy-based frying pan. Add ginger and spring onions. Cook 1 minute over medium heat. Add mushrooms, carrot, parsnip and broccoli; stir-fry 3 minutes or until vegetables are just softened. Stir in breadcrumbs, soy sauce and water. Remove from heat; cool.

3 Place a heaped teaspoonful of the vegetable mixture in the centre of each wrapper. Brush edges of pastry with water and pinch edges together to seal. Heat oil in a wok or deep-fryer. Cook wontons in batches (no more than four at a time), for 2 minutes or until golden. Remove with a slotted spoon. Drain on paper towels. Serve with Chilli Sauce.

4 **To make Chilli Sauce:** Heat oil in a pan, add garlic. Cook until golden. Add chilli and soy sauces, sherry and juice, stir until heated.

Note: If wrappers are not used immediately, cover unused ones with a damp tea-towel.

Wild Rice The long, dark-brown, nutty-flavoured grain of an aquatic grass which grows in the Minnesota lakes of North America. Wild rice is boiled or steamed and served with poultry or fish; sautéed onions, mush-rooms or nuts are sometimes added for flavouring. Because it is expensive, it is often extended with cooked brown or white rice.

Wine The fermented juice of grapes, used in cooking to add flavour to both savoury and sweet dishes.

Witloof See Chicory.

Wonton A Chinese snack made of a savoury filling inside a small square of paper-thin dough. Wontons can be steamed or deep-fried. Wrappers can be made like pasta and rolled out until almost transparent; they are also sold fresh in packs of about 30 at Asian food stores.

Worcestershire Sauce A thin, brown-black, piquant sauce made from vinegar, molasses, soy sauce, anchovy sauce, thought to contain soy a secret recipe but ginger, tamarind, shallots and garlic.

Y

Yabby Freshwater crayfish found in creeks, rivers, waterholes and dams across Australia and related to similar species native to France (écrevisse) and North America (crawfish). Its cooked meat (mostly in the tail and claws) is white, sweet, moist and delicately flavoured; it is best served with a mild-flavoured sauce or just a splash of extra virgin olive oil, freshly grated

black pepper and a squeeze of lemon juice. Yabbies are farmed commercially in Australia and are exported live around the world. Yabbies are best cooked live. Stun them first for 20 minutes in the freezer. They are available live or cooked from fish markets and specialist fish shops.

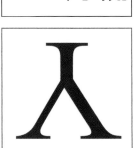

Yakitori A Japanese dish consisting of small pieces of chicken threaded on bamboo skewers and grilled (broiled) over glowing coals while being basted with a soy sauce-based marinade.

YEAST COOKERY

SAVOURY PIZZA SNAILS

★ ★

Preparation time: 1½ hours,
Total cooking time: 40 minutes
Makes about 35

1 tablespoon olive oil
1 onion, finely chopped
½ cup finely chopped
green pepper (capsicum)
¼ cup finely chopped
black olives
30 g (1 oz) compressed
yeast, crumbled
1 teaspoon sugar
½ cup wholemeal plain
(all-purpose) flour

1¼ cups (10 fl oz)
warm water
2¼ cups plain (all-purpose) flour
½ cup rye flour
1 teaspoon salt
¼ cup tomato paste
2 teaspoons dried sweet
basil leaves
1 cup grated cheddar
cheese

1 Heat oil in a pan. Add onion and peppers and cook over low heat for about 8 minutes or until soft. Add olives to pan and cook for 2 minutes. Remove from heat and leave to cool.

2 Combine yeast with sugar and wholemeal flour in a bowl. Gradually add water, blend until smooth. Cover bowl with plastic wrap, leave in warm place 10 minutes or until mixture is foamy.

3 Sift remaining flours into a large mixing bowl and add salt. Make a well in the centre and add yeast mixture. Using a knife, mix to a soft dough.

4 Turn onto a lightly floured surface. Knead for 5 minutes or until dough is smooth. Shape into a ball, place in a large, clean, lightly oiled bowl. Leave, covered with plastic wrap, in a warm place for about 30 minutes or until dough is well-risen.

5 Knead dough again for about 3 minutes or until smooth. Roll out onto a lightly floured surface to a 30 x 45 cm (12 x 18 inch) rectangle. Spread dough evenly with tomato paste. Top with the cooled vegetable mixture. Sprinkle with basil and grated cheese.

6 Roll up tightly across the rectangle, to make a long roll. Using a sharp knife, cut through roll to base at 1 cm (½ inch) intervals. Arrange 'snails' on lightly oiled tray about 8 cm (3 inches) apart. Cover with plastic wrap and leave in a warm place for 20 minutes or until snails are well-risen.

7 Bake at 200°C (400°F/Gas 6) for 15 minutes. Reduce heat to 180°C (350°F/Gas 4) and bake another 15 minutes or until golden and crisp. Leave snails on trays for 5 minutes before transferring to a wire rack to cool.

DOUGHNUTS

★ ★

Preparation time: 1½ hours,
Total cooking time: 15 minutes
Makes 25

4 cups plain (all-purpose)
unbleached or bakers
flour
105 g (3½ oz) butter,
melted
2 x 7 g (¼ oz) sachets
dry yeast
2 tablespoons caster
(superfine) sugar
1½ cups (10 fl oz)
warm milk
1 teaspoon salt
1 egg, beaten
½ cup caster (superfine)
sugar, extra
1 teaspoon cinnamon
light olive oil for frying

1 Combine flour, yeast, sugar and salt in a medium mixing bowl. Combine egg, milk and butter and gradually add to flour mixture; mix to a soft dough. Turn dough onto a lightly floured surface and knead for 10 minutes, until dough is smooth and elastic. Shape dough into a ball and place in a large, lightly oiled mixing bowl. Leave, covered with plastic wrap, in a warm place for 45 minutes or until ball has doubled in volume.

2 Knead dough for 1 minute until smooth; rest dough for 5 minutes. Roll out to 5 mm (¼ inch) thickness and cut into circles with a doughnut cutter, or use an 8 cm (3 inch) and a 4 cm (1½ inch) round cutter to make doughnut rings. Place doughnuts on lightly floured baking trays, cover; leave in a warm place for 20 minutes to rise.

3 Heat oil to a depth of 6 cm (2½ inches) and fry doughnuts for 1–2 minutes on each side until golden brown and cooked through. Drain on paper towels.

4 Combine sugar and cinnamon and toss doughnuts through mixture.

RUM BABA

★★ **Preparation time:** 1½ hours
Total cooking time: 25 minutes
Serves 8

2 cups plain (all-purpose) flour	7 g (¼ oz) sachet dry yeast
3 eggs, beaten	2 tablespoons caster (superfine) sugar
60 g (2 oz) butter, melted	½ teaspoon salt
½ cup chopped raisins	½ cup (4 fl oz) lukewarm milk
Syrup	
1½ cups (12 fl oz) water	
1 cup sugar	
½ cup (4 fl oz) rum	

1 Brush a deep 23 cm (9 inch), 1.25 litre (5-cup) capacity baba or savarin tin with melted butter. Combine flour, salt, sugar and yeast in a medium mixing bowl; make a well in the centre. Add milk, eggs and butter and mix to a thick batter.

2 Using your hand, beat and slap the mixture against the side of the bowl for 6 minutes or until it is still quite tacky but smooth and glossy. Scrape down from side of bowl during this process. Leave, covered with plastic wrap, in a warm place for about 1 hour or until the mixture has doubled in volume.

3 Preheat the oven to moderately hot 210°C (415°F/Gas 6–7). Add raisins and stir dough to incorporate fruit. Spoon into prepared tin. Leave, covered with plastic wrap, in a warm place for about 30 minutes, until dough has doubled in size. Bake for 20 minutes, until well browned and cooked through.

4 Turn baba immediately onto a wire rack placed over a shallow oven tray. Prick well with a fork or skewer; spoon hot syrup liberally over baba until it is well soaked.

5 To make Syrup: Place water and sugar in a pan and stir over moderate heat until sugar has dissolved. Bring to the boil and simmer for 5 minutes. Remove from heat and add rum.

Note: For best results, use unbleached or bakers flour for this recipe.

ABOUT YEAST

■ Fresh (compressed) yeast loses its effectiveness with age. It should be stored in the refrigerator for no longer than two weeks, or can be frozen for up to two months. Dry yeast can be stored for longer, in a cool, dry place.

■ Test compressed yeast for freshness by dissolving it in warm water with a teaspoon of sugar—within 10 minutes it should be frothing.

■ Yeast depends for its action on the temperature of the dough. If it is too cold, yeast activity will be slowed, while high temperatures will kill the yeast organisms.

Yam The starchy tuber of a tropical vine which originated in China and is now found throughout the Pacific, Africa and the Caribbean. Yams have brownish skin and yellow to white flesh and can be baked (whole in the skin), boiled or fried. Cooked yam has a taste similar to cooked potato.

Yarrow A member of the daisy family that grows wild in Britain and Europe. Its slightly bitter leaves can be steamed or braised and eaten as a vegetable, made into soup, or chopped finely and added to salads.

Yeast A tiny, single-celled organism that multiplies rapidly in warm and moist environments. Bakers yeast is used as the raising agent in various kinds of dough, where it ferments the sugar in the dough to produce the bubbles of carbon dioxide gas which make the mixture rise. Yeast has been used in bread-making since its accidental discovery more than 4000 years ago. It is available in two forms: compressed (fresh) yeast which is partially dried and formed into a cake, and dried or granular yeast. Yeast is also used in brewing and wine-making.

Yoghurt A thick, creamy, tangy-tasting milk product made by coagulating milk with a bacterial product. Yoghurt can feature in all parts of a meal. It is the base of a number of Middle Eastern dips and is used to thicken and enrich soups, stews and curries. Yoghurt has a cooling effect on the palate and is often served with chopped cucumber as an accompaniment to a spicy meal; it is also used in salad dressings and in sauces for hot cooked vegetables. Tenderising yoghurt marinades are used in many Indian dishes, particularly in tandoori dishes and korma curries. As a dessert, yoghurt can be sweetened with honey or mixed fresh or stewed fruit, or it can be baked in cakes, cheesecakes and biscuits (cookies). Natural yoghurt containing cultures such as *Lactobacillus acidophilus* and *Bifidobacteria bacterium* is considered to have beneficial effects on the digestive system. These cultures are believed to help restore a healthy balance in the intestines by re-establishing bacteria which are normally present but may

HOT CROSS BUNS

Preparation time: 2 hours
Total cooking time: 30–35 minutes
Makes 12

4 cups plain (all-purpose) flour
1 1/2 teaspoons mixed spice
2 x 7 g (1/4 oz) sachets dry yeast
1/2 cup caster (superfine) sugar
60 g (2 oz) butter, melted
60 g (2 oz) eggs, beaten
1 1/4 cups (10 fl oz) warm milk
1 cup dried mixed fruit

1 Place flour, spice, yeast and sugar in food processor and process for 1–2 minutes. Combine butter, egg and milk in small bowl. With motor running, add liquid to dry ingredients, process until combined. Turn mixture onto floured board, knead in dried fruit, then knead for 10–15 minutes, until dough is smooth and elastic.
2 Place in greased bowl, cover with cloth. Leave in a warm place 1 hour or until doubled in bulk.
3 Brush 30 x 20 x 3 cm (12 x 8 x 1 1/4 inch) tin with oil or melted butter. Divide dough into 12 round buns. Arrange in tin, 2 cm (3/4 inch) apart. Cover with cloth and allow to rise 45 minutes.
4 Preheat oven to moderately hot 210°C (415°F/Gas 6–7). Pipe a cross on each bun. Bake 30–35 minutes, or until golden brown. If necessary, cover with foil to prevent over-browning. Brush glaze over buns while still hot.

ABOVE: HOT CROSS BUNS. OPPOSITE PAGE, ABOVE: CURRIED YOGHURT CHICKEN; BELOW: YOGHURT CAKE WITH LEMON SYRUP

PANETTONE

Preparation time: 1 hour 40 minutes
Total cooking time: 1 hour 15 minutes
Makes one 20 cm (8 inch) loaf

3/4 cup mixed fruit
2 tablespoons mixed peel
2 tablespoons orange juice
45 g (1 1/2 oz) fresh yeast
1 teaspoon sugar
2 tablespoons lukewarm water
3 cups plain (all-purpose) flour
60 g (2 oz) butter,
3 eggs, lightly beaten
2 tablespoons caster (superfine) sugar
1/2 cup (4 fl oz) lukewarm milk
extra milk for glazing

1 Brush a 20 cm (8 inch) charlotte tin with oil or melted butter. Combine fruit, peel and orange juice in a small bowl and set aside while preparing the rest of the cake.
2 Combine yeast, sugar and water in a bowl; blend until smooth. Leave, covered with plastic wrap, in warm place 10 minutes or until foamy.
3 Sift flour into large mixing bowl, add butter. Rub butter into flour with fingertips for 2 minutes or until mixture is fine and crumbly. Add fruit mixture, stir until well mixed.
4 Combine eggs, caster sugar and milk; stir in yeast mixture. Make a well in centre of flour, add liquid. Mix to a soft, wet dough with a knife.
5 Using your hand, vigorously beat dough for 5 minutes or until it becomes slightly stringy, smooth and glossy. Scrape mixture down side of bowl. Leave, covered with plastic wrap, in a warm place for 30 minutes or until well risen.
6 Repeat beating for another 5 minutes; turn dough onto lightly floured surface, knead 10 minutes or until it is not sticky. Place in tin, leave, covered with plastic wrap, in a warm place for 30 minutes or until well risen.
7 Preheat oven to moderately hot 210°C (415°F/Gas 6–7). Brush dough with extra milk, bake 15 minutes; reduce heat to moderate 180°C (350°F/Gas 4), bake 1 hour more or until well browned and cooked through—it will sound hollow when tapped.

Note: For crosses, fill a piping bag with a mixture made from 1/4 cup self-raising flour and 1/4 cup (2 fl oz) water. Glaze: Stir 1/4 teaspoon gelatine, 2 teaspoons honey and 1 tablespoon water in a small pan over low heat until dissolved.

YOGHURT

CURRIED YOGHURT CHICKEN

Preparation time: 20 minutes + marinating
Total cooking time: 40–45 minutes
Serves 6

1 cup plain yoghurt
1/2 cup (4 fl oz) coconut cream
1/4 cup fresh coriander, chopped
1 onion, finely chopped
1 clove garlic, crushed
1 tablespoon lime juice

1 teaspoon finely grated lime rind
1 tablespoon curry powder
freshly ground black pepper
1 kg (2 lb) chicken pieces
1 cup plain yoghurt, extra

1 Combine yoghurt, coconut cream, chopped coriander, onion, garlic, lime juice and rind, curry powder and pepper in a large, shallow glass or ceramic dish. Add the chicken pieces. Mix to coat completely.

2 Cover dish with plastic wrap. Marinate the chicken for several hours, or overnight, in the refrigerator.

3 Remove chicken from marinade. Place chicken in a shallow baking pan. Bake in a moderate oven 180°C (350°F/Gas 4) for 40–45 minutes.

4 Garnish with fresh coriander leaves and serve with extra yoghurt and rice or salad.

YOGHURT CAKE WITH LEMON SYRUP

Preparation time: 20 minutes
Total cooking time: 1 hour 10 minutes
Serves 8–10

2 1/2 cups self-raising flour, sifted
1/2 teaspoon baking powder
1 cup caster (superfine) sugar
1 cup plain yoghurt
1 cup (8 fl oz) milk
2 eggs, lightly beaten
lemon rind, extra, cut into thin strips, to serve
whipped cream, to serve

Lemon Syrup
1 1/4 cups caster (superfine) sugar
3/4 cup (6 fl oz) water
rind of 1 lemon cut into thin strips
1/4 cup (2 fl oz) lemon juice

1 Preheat oven to 180°C (350°F/Gas 4). Brush a deep 23 cm (9 inch) round cake tin with oil or melted butter. Line base with paper; grease paper. Place flour, baking powder and sugar into bowl. Pour over combined yoghurt, milk and eggs. Beat with electric beaters on low speed for 2 minutes, then on high speed 5 minutes.

2 Spoon into tin. Bake 1 hour or until skewer comes out clean when inserted into centre. Pour half of prepared Lemon Syrup over top immediately; leave for 10 minutes. Serve with extra lemon strips, extra syrup and cream.

3 **To make Lemon Syrup:** Stir all ingredients in pan over low heat until sugar dissolves; do not boil. Simmer 7 minutes or until thick. Keep warm. Remove lemon strips before serving.

---

have been destroyed by infections or drugs such as penicillin. Yoghurt has been used in the Middle East for many thousands of years, and its therapeutic properties are often cited as the reason for the famed longevity of the people of the Caucasus. Commercially available yoghurt may be made from fat-free, reduced fat or full-cream milk, and may be either natural, flavoured with vanilla or other sweeteners, or mixed with fruit. Flavoured frozen yoghurt and drinking yoghurt are also available.

Yorkshire Pudding A light, crisp baked batter served with roast beef. In Yorkshire, in the north of England, where it originated, the pudding is traditionally served before the meat.

Youngberries A sweet, purple fruit which is a cross between several types of blackberry.

Yule Log Also called *Bûche de Noël,* a traditional French Christmas cake with a number of popular variations in other countries. A rolled sponge is filled and coated with chocolate butter cream and the surface decorated to resemble bark.

YOGHURT & FRESH CHEESES

Yoghurt and soft, fresh, cottage-style cheeses are easy to make and nutritious. The fat content depends on the kind of milk used. Milk powder (whole or skim) can be added to home-made yoghurt to increase the protein and calcium content and improve texture.

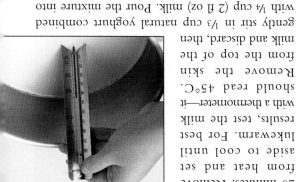

FROM LEFT TO RIGHT, BELOW: BLUEBERRY SWIRL, CREME FRAICHE, LASSI, HERB CHEESE ROLL, SOFT CHEESE

YOGHURT

Yoghurt is eaten with many combinations of fresh or stewed fruits or chopped nuts. It can be used as a tenderising marinade for meats and poultry, to thicken and enrich casseroles, stews and some soups, and as a sauce with hot vegetable dishes.

Natural yoghurt containing the 'friendly' bacteria *Lactobacillus acidophilus* and *Bifidobacteria bacterium* is thought to assist the functioning of the digestive system by supplementing the body's natural bacteria.

THICK CREAMY YOGHURT

Combine 2¾ cups (22 fl oz) milk with ⅓ cup full-cream milk powder in a saucepan and heat gently to boiling point until froth rises. Reduce the heat and allow the milk to simmer very gently for

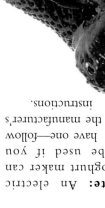
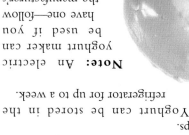
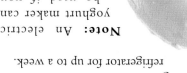

20 minutes. Remove from heat and set aside to cool until lukewarm. For best results, test the milk with a thermometer—it should read 45°C. Remove the skin from the top of the milk and discard, then gently stir in ⅓ cup natural yoghurt combined with ¼ cup (2 fl oz) milk. Pour the mixture into sterilised jars and seal. Stand the jars in a saucepan and fill the saucepan with hot tap water. Wrap a blanket around the saucepan to keep in the warmth and set aside for at least 6 hours. Chill the yoghurt well for 3–4 hours before using it. Makes 2 cups.

Yoghurt can be stored in the refrigerator for up to a week.

Note: An electric yoghurt maker can be used if you have one—follow the manufacturer's instructions.

FRESH CHEESES

HERB CHEESE ROLL

Using electric beaters, beat 500 g (1 lb) cream cheese until smooth and creamy. Add 200 g (6½ oz) fresh ricotta cheese; beat well. Spread evenly over a sheet of baking paper into a 25 cm (10 inch) square. Combine 2 tablespoons finely chopped chives, 1 tablespoon each finely chopped lemon thyme and oregano, 1–2 teaspoons grated lemon rind and 2–3 tablespoons finely grated fresh parmesan cheese. Sprinkle mixture on top of cheese square, then slide square and baking paper onto a flat tray. Cover and refrigerate 2–3 hours. Using baking paper as a guide, carefully roll cheese mixture, Swiss roll (jelly roll) style. Lift roll onto plastic wrap. Wrap up tightly and refrigerate overnight. Roll in ground toasted almonds or walnuts. Serve sliced or in a log with crackers or breads.

SOFT CHEESE

Press 250 g (8 oz) cottage cheese and ½ cup (4 fl oz) sour cream through a fine sieve. Gradually beat in 2 teaspoons chopped chives, 2 teaspoons chopped parsley and 2 cloves crushed garlic. Add salt and freshly ground black pepper. Pack into a muslin (cheesecloth)-lined sieve or draining mould over a bowl. Fold muslin over cheese, place small weight on top and refrigerate 24 hours. Unmould and serve with capers, salad greens and Melba toast.

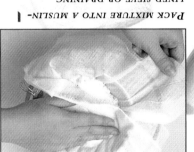

TO MAKE SOFT CHEESE: PRESS CHEESE AND SOUR CREAM THROUGH SIEVE UNTIL SMOOTH

PACK MIXTURE INTO A MUSLIN-LINED SIEVE OR DRAINING MOULD; FOLD MUSLIN OVER

BLUEBERRY SWIRL

Puree 200 g (6½ oz) fresh blueberries in a food processor until smooth. Taste, and if necessary add 1–2 teaspoons of caster (superfine) sugar. Place a dollop of plain yoghurt in a tall glass and, tilting the glass, fill with alternating spoonfuls of blueberry puree and yoghurt, ending with blueberries. Makes 4 glasses.

CREME FRAICHE

Crème Fraîche is the rich, slightly tart cream used with fresh seasonal fruits, fish, and some soups, sauces and savoury dishes. It is available commercially, but can be made at home easily. Combine equal quantities of fresh cream and cultured sour cream in a bowl. Cover the bowl and set it aside to stand at room temperature until the cream mixture has thickened—this will take 1–2 days. Cover and refrigerate before using. Crème Fraîche will keep in the refrigerator for up to a week.

MINT LASSI

In a large bowl or jug, whisk together ⅓ cup plain yoghurt, 3–4 teaspoons of sugar and 1 tablespoon chopped fresh mint. Gradually add 2⅓ cups (18½ fl oz) iced water or soda water and whisk again until well combined. Pour over ice cubes into a tall glass. To vary, add ⅓ cup (2⅓ fl oz) mango puree and omit the mint, if desired. Serves 4 as a refreshing drink.

Zabaglione A foamy Italian dessert sauce made with whole eggs, egg yolk, sugar and marsala. These are whisked together over gentle heat in the top of a double boiler. Zabaglione can be served warm with sweet, crisp biscuits (cookies) or spooned over strawberries, or

chilled. It is an ingredient in some versions of the rich dessert tiramisu. Zabaglione can also be made with other dessert wines or liqueurs; in Spain it is made with sherry, and in France a similar sauce made with sweet white wine or champagne is known as *sabayon*. The name zabaglione is derived from a Neapolitan dialect word which means 'to foam'.

Zest The thin, coloured, outside rind of a citrus fruit. It contains volatile oils that add fragrance and concentrated flavour to both sweet and savoury foods.

Zucchini Also known as courgette. A small, slender vegetable marrow, botanically a

ZUCCHINI (COURGETTES)

ZUCCHINI (COURGETTE), APPLE AND APRICOT SLICE

★★ **Preparation time:** 20 minutes + 10 minutes standing
Total cooking time: 1 hour
Serves 8

125 g (4 oz) butter
1/2 cup soft brown sugar
2 egg yolks
1 cup wholemeal self-raising flour
1/4 cup wheatgerm
1/4 cup finely chopped dried apricots
1/4 cup (2 fl oz) boiling water

425 g (13 1/2 oz) can pie-pack apple
1 small zucchini (courgette), grated
1/2 cup rolled oats
1/2 cup desiccated coconut
2 tablespoons honey
2 egg whites, stiffly beaten

1 Preheat oven to 180°C (350°F/Gas 4). Brush a 20 x 30 cm (8 x 12 inch) shallow rectangular pan with oil or melted butter. Line base and sides with greaseproof paper; grease paper.
2 Beat butter and sugar in a small bowl with an electric mixer until light and fluffy. Add egg yolks, beat until combined. Using a metal spoon, fold in sifted flour, including husks, and wheatgerm. Press evenly over base of pan.
3 Soak apricots in boiling water 10 minutes or until plump and almost all liquid is absorbed.
4 Spread apple over prepared base. In a bowl, combine undrained apricots with zucchini, oats, coconut and honey. Fold in egg whites with a metal spoon.

5 Spoon mixture over apple and smooth the surface. Bake slice for 1 hour or until golden and cooked through. Leave slice to cool in pan. Serve with flavoured yoghurt, if desired.

ZUCCHINI (COURGETTE) WITH CUMIN CREAM

★ **Preparation time:** 5 minutes
Total cooking time: 12 minutes
Serves 4–6

1 lemon
1/2 teaspoon cumin seeds
4 large zucchini (courgettes)
1/2 cup (4 fl oz) cream
salt and freshly ground black pepper, to taste
30 g (1 oz) butter
1 tablespoon oil

1 Grate rind from lemon to make 1/2 teaspoonful and squeeze 2 teaspoons lemon juice. Set aside. Cut zucchini into 5 mm (1/4 inch) thick diagonal slices. Heat butter and oil in a large frying pan and add half the zucchini slices. Cook over medium-high heat for 2 minutes on each side or until golden. Remove from pan; drain on paper towel; keep warm. Repeat with remaining zucchini slices.
2 Add cumin seeds to pan, stir over low heat for 1 minute. Add lemon rind and juice; bring to boil. Add cream to the pan and boil for 2 minutes or until sauce thickens slightly; season to taste. Do not boil sauce for too long as it may curdle.
3 Return zucchini slices to pan. Stir over low heat for 1 minute or until just heated through. Serve warm or cold.

fruit but used as a vegetable. It has thin skin (green or yellow) and pale flesh with a central cluster of small, soft edible seeds. Very young zucchini are the sweetest and most tender. Zucchini can be eaten raw in salads or cut into lengths and served with dips; they are steamed, braised or boiled and served as a vegetable, and can be stuffed and baked. Zucchini combines particularly well with tomato. The male flower can be picked while still firmly closed and used in cooking, usually stuffed then dipped in batter and fried, or stuffed and baked (the female flower, recognisable by its thicker stem, is left to mature into the vegetable). The zucchini was developed in Italy from seeds brought back from the Americas by Christopher Columbus. It is available fresh throughout the year.

Zwieback A rusk made from slightly sweetened yeast dough (sometimes flavoured with lemon or cinnamon) baked then cut into thin slices and returned to a slow oven until crisp and golden.

Until slices are crisp and brown. Cool on trays.

ZUCCHINI (COURGETTE) AND CHEESE PIE

✳ *Preparation time:* 30 minutes
Total cooking time: 30 minutes
Serves 4–6

---

4 large zucchini (courgettes), coarsely grated
2 tablespoons chopped mint
250 g (8 oz) feta cheese
8 sheets filo pastry
250 g (8 oz) ricotta cheese
2 tablespoons olive oil
2 tablespoons poppy seeds

---

1 Preheat oven to 200°C (400°F/Gas 6). Combine zucchini with cheeses and mint. Mix together using a wooden spoon.
2 Brush each sheet of filo pastry with oil and fold in half to form a smaller rectangle. Place one folded sheet in a well-oiled 23 cm (9 inch) pie plate, brush with oil, then top with a second sheet. Spread one-third of the filling on top. Repeat until all of the pastry and filling have been used, finishing with a sheet of folded pastry. Brush top with oil and sprinkle with poppy seeds.
3 Bake for 10 minutes, then reduce heat to 180°C (350°F/Gas 4) and cook for another 20 minutes, or until pastry is crisp and golden. Cut into wedges and serve.

OPPOSITE PAGE: *ZUCCHINI WITH CUMIN CREAM*
ABOVE: *ZUCCHINI AND CHEESE PIE*
LEFT: *ZUCCHINI SWIRLS*

ZUCCHINI (COURGETTE) SWIRLS

✳ *Preparation time:* 12 minutes +
1 hour refrigeration
Total cooking time: 15 minutes
Makes 25

---

2 medium zucchini (courgettes), coarsely grated
1/2 cup grated fresh parmesan cheese
60 g (2 oz) salami, finely chopped
1 clove garlic, crushed
4 sheets filo pastry
1 small onion, grated
60 g (2 oz) butter, melted
1/3 cup dried packaged breadcrumbs

---

1 Brush two 32 x 28 cm (13 x 11 inch) oven trays with oil or melted butter. Combine zucchini, onion, salami, garlic and parmesan in a medium mixing bowl.
2 Lightly brush each pastry sheet with butter and layer them on top of each other. Spread zucchini mixture over pastry sheets leaving a 5 cm (2 inch) border along one long side; sprinkle breadcrumbs evenly over zucchini mixture.
3 Roll pastry up tightly over filling towards side with border. Brush roll all over with remaining butter; cover with plastic wrap, refrigerate 1 hour. Preheat oven to moderately hot 210°C (415°F/Gas 6–7). Using a sharp knife, cut roll into 25 slices; arrange on prepared trays. Bake 15 minutes or

INDEX

Page numbers in **bold** indicate main entries, including recipes and illustrations; *italics* indicate other illustrations; ***bold italics*** refer to dictionary (marginal) entries.

A

abalone, **8**
abbacchio, **8–9**
Aberdeen sausage, **9**
acidulated water, **9**
agar-agar, **9**
Aïoli, **9**, 391
à la, **9–10**
al dente, **10**
alfalfa sprouts, **10**
allemande, à l', **10**
allspice, **10–11**
almond paste, **12**
almonds, **8-11**, **11–12**
  about, 8
  Apricot & Almond Vacherin, 263, *263*
  Flaked Almond Decoration, 83
  Flaked Almond Tuiles, 50
  Trout with Almonds, 454, *454*
alum, **12–13**
Amaretti, **13**, 56
ambrosia, **13**
Américaine, à l', **13–14**
American food, **12-14**, *14–15*
  see also hamburgers; hot dogs
anchovies, **15**, *15*, **18**
  about, 15
  Bagna Cauda, **29–30**, 175, *175*
  Green Goddess Dressing, **198**, 391
  Olive, Pepper & Anchovy Focaccia, 61
  Pissaladière, 15, *15*, **342**
Angel Food Cake, **18**, 76, *76*
angelica, **18–19**
angels on horseback, **19**
anglaise, à l', **19**
anise, **20**
  see also star anise
antipasto, **16-17**, **20–1**
  see also appetisers; finger food; hors d'oeuvres
Anzac Biscuits, **21**, 56, 57
appetisers, **21**
  Poppy Seed Twists, 346, *346*
  see also antipasto; finger food; hors d'oeuvres
apples, **18-19**, **21–3**
  about, 18
  Apple & Sour Cream Flan, 445
  Apple Sauce, 18, 348, 354
  Apple Strudel, 441
  Apple Stuffing, 460
  Apple, Tomato & Mint Chutney, 110, *110*
  Black Pudding with Cabbage & Apples, 401, *401*
  Charoseth, 237
  Deep Dish Apple Pie, 14, *14*
  Fruit Bread & Apple Pudding, 131, *131*
  Ginger Apple Marmalade, 193
  Layered Potato & Apple Bake, 352
  Rosemary, Tomato & Apple Jelly, 233, *233*
  Spicy Apple Muffins, 276, 277
  Zucchini, Apple & Apricot Slice, 484
apricots, **20-1**, **23**
  about, 20
  Apricot & Almond Vacherin, 263, *263*
  Apricot Betty, 133
  Mini Apricot Danish, *323*
  Zucchini, Apple & Apricot Slice, 484
arborio rice, **23**
arrowroot, **23–4**
arroz con pollo, **24**
artichokes, **22-3**, **24–5**
  about, 22
  Goats Cheese & Artichoke Tarts, 166, *166*
  Marinated Artichokes, 17, *17*
  microwaving of, 271
  Pompeii Focaccia, 176, *176*
arugula *see* rocket
asafoetida, **25–6**
asparagus, **24-5**, *26*
  about, 25
  Artichoke & Asparagus Salad, 22, *22*
  Asparagus & Prosciutto Salad, 382, *382*
  Asparagus Strudel, 165
  Chicken & Asparagus Fritatta, 181, *181*
  Copenhagen Focaccia, 176, *177*
  microwaving of, 271
  Snow Pea & Asparagus Salad, 422, *422*
asparagus beans *see* snake beans
aspic, **26–7**, 190
aubergines *see* eggplants
avgolemono, **27**
avocados, **26-7**, *27*
  Avocado Aspic Mousse, 190
  Avocado Dip, 143
  Avocado Sauce, 257
  Guacamole, 140, **200**, 266, *266*
  Mango & Avocado Salsa, 335, *335*
  Spinach & Avocado Salad, 431, *431*

B

Baba (au Rhum), **28**
  see also Rum Baba
babaco, **28**
Baba Ghannouj, **28**, 246, *246*
bacon, **28**, **28–9**
  about, 28
  Bacon Butter, 404
  Bacon, Herb & Vegetable Pie, 340, *341*
  Broccoli with Bacon & Pine Nuts, 41, *41*
  Cauliflower with Bacon, 65, *65*
  Cheese & Bacon Focaccia, 61
  Cheese & Bacon Muffins, 276
  Cheese, Bacon & Chive Loaf, 60
  Corn & Bacon Hotpot, 118, *118*
  Dublin Coddle, 223, *223*
  freezing of, 183
  Hearty Bacon & Bean Stewpot, 38, *38*
  Irish Stew, 224, *224*
  Kidneys & Bacon, 291, *291*
  Oysters with Pine Nuts & Bacon, 303, *303*
  Quails with Tarragon & Pancetta, 187, *187*
  Quiche Lorraine, 362, *362*
  Shredded Spinach & Bacon, 431
  Spicy Sausage & Bacon Paella, 401
  Spaghetti Carbonara, 314
  Turnip & Bacon Soup, 461
  see also angels on horseback; devil on horseback; ham; pork
bagels, **29**, 237
Bagna Cauda, **29–30**, 175, *175*

baguette, **30**
Baked Beans, Boston, 13
baked puddings, **129-30**
baking blind, **30**
baking powder, **30**
baking soda *see* bicarbonate of soda
Baklava, **31**, 201, *201*
balsamic vinegar, **31**
bamboo shoots, **32**
bananas, **29-30**, **32–3**
  about, 29
  Banana Bran Muffins, 58
  Banana Date Chutney, 110, *110*
  Banana Ice-cream, 220
  Banana Muffins, 276
Banbury tart, **33**
bannocks, **33**
baps, **33**
barbecue cookery, **31-34**, *33–4*
  about, 31
  Barbecued Beef & Mint Sausages, 401
  Barbecued Honey Chicken Wings, 101, *101*
  Barbecued Honey Seafood, 211, *211*
  Barbecued Lobster Tails, 257, *257*
  Barbecued Pork Spare Ribs, 32, *32*, 430, *430*
  Barbecued Trout, 213, *213*
  Fish Barbecued with Fennel, 161
barley, **34**
barley sugar, **34–5**
barley water, **34**
barquettes, **35**
basil, **35**, *35*, 202, *202*
  about, 35
  Basil Spinach Salad, 432
  Peas with Basil & Tomato, 330, *330*
  see also pesto
basmati, **35**
basting, **35**
batters, **36**
Bavarois, 36
bay, **36–7**, 202, *202*
bean curd, **36**, *37*
  about, 36
  see also tofu
bean flour noodles, 288
beans, dried, **38-9**, *38–9*
  about, 38
  Bean Salad, 388
  Black Bean Sauce, 46
  Boston Baked Beans, 13
  microwaving of, 271
  Spicy Beef & Bean Tacos, 268, *268*
  see also under individual beans eg lima beans
beans, green, **40**
  Gingered Green Beans, 193
bean sprouts, **37**, 466, *466*

baguette, **30**
Béarnaise Sauce, **39**, **41**, 45, 398
Béchamel Sauce, **42**, 398
beef, **42–3**, *42-7*
  Barbecued Beef & Mint Sausages, 401
  Beef & Asparagus, 24, *24*
  Beef & Pimiento Loaf, 261
  Beef Bourguignon, 179, *179*
  Beef Burgers with Caramelised Onions, 207, *207*
  Beef Consomme, 424
  Beef Curry with Potatoes, 123
  Beef Goulash, 149, *149*
  Beef Lasagne, 317, *317*
  Beef Rendang, 218, *218*
  Beef Samosas, 214, *215*
  Beef Soup, 284, *284*
  Beef Stroganoff, 439, *439*
  Beef Vindaloo, 215
  Borscht, 48, **54**
  Burritos, **61–2**, 267, *267*
  Carbonnade de Boeuf, **76–7**
  Carpaccio, **78**, 225, *225*
  Carpetbag Burgers, 208, *208*
  carving, 87
  Char-grilled Beef, 384, *384*
  Corned Beef Hash, 12
  defrosting of, 270
  Fettuccine Bolognese, 314, *314*
  Guinness Beef Stew, 223, *223*
  Hot Chilli Filling, 353
  Marinated Beef & Noodle Salad, 287, *287*
  Mexican-Style Beef Spareribs, 430
  Moussaka, 201, **279**
  Peppered Beef Fillet, 335
  Peppered Steaks, 335, *335*
  Roast Brisket of Beef, 236
  roasting, 42
  Spicy Beef & Bean Tacos, 268, *268*
  Steak & Kidney Pudding, 436, *436*
  Steak Diane, 435, *435*
  Steak Tartare, 436
  Steak with Coriander Butter, 435, *435*
  Steak with Speedy Barbecue Marinade, 31, *31*
  Stir-fried Beef & Snow Peas, 422
  Teriyaki Beef Kebabs, 238
  Teriyaki Steaks, 34, *34*
  Tex Mex Chilli con Carne, **101**, 268, *268*
  see also corned beef
beef stock, 43
beef tea, **43**
beer, **44**
beer bread, **44**
beetroot, **44–5**, **48**
  Borscht, 48, **54**
beignet soufflé, **45**
Belgian endive, **156**

bell peppers *see* peppers, sweet
bel paese, **45**
besan flour, **45–6**
beurre manie, **46**
beverages *see* drinks
bicarbonate of soda, **46**
binding, **46**
biryani, **46**
biscuits, **46–7**, **48–57**
  about, 49
  Anzac Biscuits, **21**, *56*, 57
  Chocolate Lemon Swirls, 251, *251*
  Coffee Hazelnut Biscuits, 209, *209*
  Florentines, 51, *51*, **169**
  freezing, 183
  Herbed Cheese Crackers, 90, *90*
  Honey Peanut Butter Cookies, 212
  Raspberry Coconut Biscuits, 368, *368–9*
  savoury, **47**
  Walnut Biscuits, 474, *474*
  see also macaroons; scones; shortbread
bisque, **47**
bitter melon, **48**, 466, *466*
Black Bean Sauce, 46, 120
blackberries, **48**
  Blackberry Ice-cream, 220
  Blackberry Pie, 341
  Blackberry Sorbet, *220*, 221
black bread *see* rye bread
blackcurrants, **48**, 125
black-eyed peas/beans, 38
Black Forest Cake, **48**, 78, *78*
black pudding, **49**
  Black Pudding with Cabbage & Apple, 401, *401*
blanching, **49**
blancmange, **49**
blanquette, **49**
blending, **49**
blini, **50**
  Blini with Sour Cream & Smoked Salmon, 306, *306*
  see also pancakes
blintz, **50**
blood sausage *see* black pudding
blueberries, **50**
  Blueberry & Strawberry Cheesecake, 92, *92*
  Blueberry Cheese Tart, 139, *139*
  Blueberry-Cream Cheese Tart, *322*
  Blueberry Soufflé, *420*, 421
  Blueberry Swirl, *482*, 483
blue vein cheese, **50–1**
  Blue Cheese Quiche, 364
  Teriyaki Steaks with Blue Cheese & Herb Butter, 34, *34*
bok choy, **51**, 466, *466*

bolognaise sauce, **51–2**
Bombay duck, **52**
bombes, **52**, 137
borage, **52–3**
bordelaise, à la, **53**
börek, **53**
borlotti beans, 38, **53**
Borscht, 48, **54**
bouchée, **54**
bouillabaisse, **54**
bouillon, **54–5**
bouquet garni, **55**
bourguignonne, à la, **55**
bourride, **55**
bow ties, 308, *308*, *309*
boysenberries, **55**
brains, **55–6**
  Crumbed Brains, 291, *291*
  see also offal
bran, **56**, 58
  Bran Muffins, 276–7, *276*, 277
brandade, **56**
brandy, **56**
  Brandy Alexander, 144
  Brandy Alexander Punch, 145
  Brandy Alexander Slice, 418, *418*
  Brandy Butter, 134
  Brandy Sauce, 400
  Brandy Snaps with Coffee Liqueur Cream, 56
brawn, **56–7**
Brazil nuts, 57
  Brazil Nut Cheese Cake, 92, *92*
bread, **57–8**, **59–63**
  Almond, 11
  Brown Soda, 222, *222*, **225**
  Cheesy Sun-dried Tomato Hot, 453, *453*
  Corn, 13, *13*, **117**
  freezing, 183
  Garlic, 189
  Herb & Garlic Cornbread Slices, 188, *188*
  Khobz, 274, *274*
  Poppy Seed, 346, *346*
  see also damper; focaccia
bread puddings
  Bread & Butter Pudding, 131, *132–3*
  Fruit Bread & Apple Pudding, 131, *131*
brie, **58**
  Pear & Brie Salad, 329, *329*
brine, **58**
brioche, **58**
broad beans, **59**
  see also beans
broccoli, **41**, **59**
  microwaving, 271
  see also Chinese broccoli
broiling *see* grilling
broth, **60**, 406, *406*
brownies, **60**

brown sauce, **60**
  see also Sauce Espagnole
brussels sprouts, **60**, 271
bubble & squeak, **60**
buckwheat, **60–1**
buckwheat noodles, 288, *289*
buns, **61**
  Chelsea, **96**, 157, *157*
  Hot Cross, 61, 62, **212**, 480, *480*
  Orange, 300, *300*
burgers *see* hamburgers
burghul, **61**
Burritos, **61–2**, 267, *267*
butter, **62–3**
butter beans *see* lima beans
buttercreams, 80–1
buttermilk, **63**
  Buttermilk Nutmeg Tart, 139, *139*
butternut pumpkin, **63**
butter of Provence *see* Aïoli
butters
  Bacon, 404
  Blue Cheese & Herb, 34
  Brandy, 134
  Coriander, 435
  Herb & Garlic, 188
  Lemon, **247**, 250, *250*
  Parsley, 407
  Sage, 195
  Whipped, 305
butterscotch, **63**
  Butterscotch Sauce, 29, 400
  Butterscotch Self-saucing Pudding, 129, *129*

C

cabanossi, **66**
cabbage, **64**, **66–7**
  Black Pudding with Cabbage & Apple, 401, *401*
  Coleslaw, 380
  microwaving, 271
  see also Chinese cabbage
cabecou, **67**
cabinet pudding, **67**
Caerphilly, **67**
Caesar Salad, **67–8**, 380, *380*
café au lait, **68**, 113
café frappé *see* Granita di Caffè
caffè latte, **68**, 112, 113
caffè macchiato, 113, *113*
Cajun food, **66–8**, **68–9**
  see also Roux
cake decorating, 70, 80–3
  Frosted Grapes, 198
  see also icing
cakes, **69–70**, 80
  about, 70, 75
  angel food, **18**, 75–6
  Banana Peanut Butter, 30
  Banana Spice Loaf, 29
  Black Forest, **48**, 78, *78*
  Bran & Fruit Loaf, 58, *58*

butter, **69–70**
Carrot, 85, *85*
celebration, **77–8**
Cherry, Date & Walnut, 475
chocolate, **71–2**
Chocolate Raspberry Swiss Roll, 443, *443*
Chocolate Sponge, 75
Date & Walnut Loaf, 128
cooling, 80, *80*
Dundee, 74, *74*, **148**
Eccles, **150**, 159, *159*
freezing, 183
fruit & nut, **73–4**
Hazelnut Chocolate Rolls, 210, *210*
Honey Date, 212, *212*
Madeira, 70, **259**
Marble, 69, **262**
Orange & Currant Rock, 379, *379*
Panforte, 71, *71*, **305**
Raspberry Mousse, 366, *366*
Rock, 379
Semolina, 251, *251*
sponge, 75–6
teacakes, 79
Yoghurt, 481, *481*
  see also Gingerbread; short-cake; slices; Swiss rolls
calamari, **70**
  see also squid
camembert, **71**
  Salmon & Camembert Croquettes, 393, *393*
camomile, **71**
canapés, **72**, 84, *84*
Candied Rind, 254, *254*
candy *see* confectionery
cannellini beans, 38, **72**
  see also beans
cannelloni, **72**, 309
  Chicken Cannelloni, 315
canola oil, **73**
cantaloupes, **73**
  see also melons
Cape gooseberries, **73–4**
capers, **74**
  Caper Sauce, 398
capons, **74**
cappuccino, **74**, 112, *112*
capsicums *see* peppers, sweet
carambola, **75**
caramel, **75–6**
  Caramel Nut Tartlets, 446, *446*
  Caramel Sauce, 400
  Caramel Toffee Fondue, 175
  Chocolate Caramel Slice, 416, *416*
  Crème Caramel, **121**, 127, *127*
  Hot Caramel Mango, 258, *258*
  Orange & Caramel Custard, 429, *429*

caramels, 114, *116*
caraway, **76**
  Caraway Dumplings, 149, *149*
carbonnade de boeuf, **76–7**
cardamom, **77**
  Yoghurt Cardamom Cream, 185
cardoon, **77**
carob, **77–8**
Carpaccio, 78, 225, *225*
carpetbag steak, **78**
carrots, **78–9**, 85
  about, 85
  Carrot & Pineapple Muffins, 277
  Carrot Parsnip Frittata, 152, *152*
  Carrot Pilaf, 376
  Chocolate Carrot Slice, 419, *419*
  microwaving, 271
  Sugar Peas & Carrots in Lime Butter, 333, *333*
carving, **86–7**
cashew nuts, **79**
cassata, **84**
cassava, 44, **84**
casseroles, **84–5**
  freezing, 183
  Seafood Mornay, 409, *409*
  Spicy Chick Pea & Vegetable, 471, *471*
  Veal & Mushroom, 463
  White Winter Vegetable, 468–9
Cassoulet, **85**, 178, *178*
cauliflower, **65**, **85**, 88
  microwaving, 271
caviar, **85–6**
  Caviar Oysters, 167, *167*
cayenne pepper, **88**
celeriac, **88**
celery, **88–9**, *89*
celery cabbage *see* Chinese cabbage
ceps, **89**
cereals, **89–90**
  see also couscous
Ceviche, **90**, 255, *255*
champignon, **90**
Chapattis, **90**, 215
charlottes, **91**
  Apple Charlottes, 19, *19*
chateaubriand, **91**
chayote *see* chokos
cheddar cheese, **91**, 94
cheese, **90–1**, **94–5**
  Bacon & Cheese Burger, 28
  Beef & Pimiento Loaf with Cheese, 261
  Cheese & Bacon Focaccia, 61
  Cheese & Bacon Muffins, 276
  Cheese & Chive Focaccia, 61

cheese (continued)
Cheese, Bacon & Chive Loaf, 60
Cheese Choux Puffs, 323
Cheese Fondue, 175, *175*
Cheese Sauce, 201
Cheese Soufflé, 420, *421*
Cheese Triangles, 200, *200*
Cheesy Rice-stuffed Peppers, 337, *337*
Cheesy Sun-dried Tomato Hot Bread, 453, *453*
Chilli Cheese Dip, 352, *352*
Corn & Cheese Chowder, 426, *426*
Grapes with Cheese, 198
Herb & Cheese Scroll, 59
Herb Cheese Roll, 483, *483*
Mornay Sauce, 398
Potato & Cheese Cakes, 354
Quick Cheesy Potato Bake, 331, *331*
Rice & Ratatouille with Cheese Crust, 473, *473*
Soft Cheese, **483**
Zucchini & Cheese Pie, 485, *485*
Zucchini Cheese Dumplings, 148
see also under individual cheese eg cheddar cheese
cheesecakes, **92-3**, **95-6**
see also cream cheese
cherimoya see custard apples
cherries, **94**, *96*
Berry Cherry Crumble, *132,* 133
Cherry Chocolates, 116, *116*
Cherry, Date & Walnut Roll, 475
Cherry Strudel, 441
Cherry Teacake, 79, *79*
Sour Cherry Sauce, 458, *458*
chervil, **96-7**
Cheshire cheese, **97**
chestnuts, **95**, **97-8**
about, 95
chèvre, **98**
chicken, **96-101**, **98-9**
about, 99
B' Stilla, 274, *274*
Cassoulet, **85**, *178, 178*
Chicken & Asparagus Frittata, 181, *181*
Chicken & Corn Quiche, 363, *363*
Chicken & Corn Sausages with Salsa Cruda, 402, *402*
Chicken & Olives, 296, *296*
Chicken & Smoked Ham Jambalaya, 68, *68*
Chicken Burgers, 207, *207*
Chicken Cacciatore, 98, *98*
Chicken Cannelloni, 315
Chicken Chow Mein, 101
Chicken Curry, 258, *258*
Chicken Dijon, 283, *283*

Chicken Kiev, **99-100**
Chicken Liver & Brandy Pâté, 325
Chicken Noodle Mushroom Soup, 425, *425*
Chicken Pie, 340-1, *340*
Chicken Provençale, 102, *102*
Chicken Satay, 33, *33*
Chicken Soup with Matzo Balls, 235, *235*
Chicken Spanish Style, 429, *429*
Chicken Stroganoff, 439
Chicken Teriyaki, 232, *232*
Chicken with Okra, 293, *293*
Chinese Chicken & Noodles, 37, *37*
Chinese Lemon Chicken, 250, *250*
Coq au Vin, 97, *97*, **116**
Cream of Chicken & Vegetable Soup, 426, *426*
Creamy Chicken Strudel, 440
Crunchy Fried Chicken, 12, *12*
Curried Chicken Apple & Celery Salad, 89
Curried Yoghurt Chicken, 481, *481*
defrosting, 270
Egg Noodles with Chicken & Ham, 287, *287*
freezing, 182, 183
Garlic Chicken Kebabs, 239, *239*
Ginger-Chilli Drumsticks, 192, *192*
Honey Mint Roasted Chicken, 211, *211*
Indonesian Chicken in Coconut Milk, 219
livers, **103**
Nasi Goreng, 218, *218*, **284**
Padang Chicken, 217, *217*
Paella, **304**, 428
Pecan Chicken, 340-1, *340*
pre-cooked, **102**
Quick Chicken Dumplings, 148, *148*
Quick Chicken Salad, 389, *389*
Raspberry Chicken Salad, 367, *367*
Saffron Chicken, 275, *275*
Smoked Chicken Salad, 102
Soup with Chicken Dumplings, 148, *148*
Tandoori Chicken Kebabs, 216, *216*
Vietnamese Chicken Salad, 328, *328*
Yakitori, 167, *167*, **478**
chick peas, 38, **98**, **160**
Falafel, 246, *246*
Hummus, 140, 208, **213**, 245, *245*

Spicy Chick Pea & Vegetable Casserole, 471, *471*
chicory, **100**
chillies, **100-1**, 466, *466*
Chilli Cheese Dip, 352, *352*
Chilli Crab & Soft Noodles, 121, *121*
Chilli Dip, **101**, 476, *476*
Chilli Flowers, 372
Chilli Sauce, 477
Chilli Sweet Potato & Eggplant Crisps, 442, *442*
Crisp Fried Noodles & Chilli Vegetables, 286, *286*
Ginger-Chilli Drumsticks, 192, *192*
Hot Chilli Cauliflower, 65, *65*
Hot Chilli Corn, 118, *118*
Hot Chilli Filling, 353
Tex Mex Chilli con Carne, 268, *268*
chilli powder, **101**
chimichanga see Burritos
Chinese beans, 39
Chinese broccoli, **102**, 467, *467*
Chinese cabbage, 466, *466*
Chinese chard, 466
Chinese food, **102-3**, **104-6**
Chinese Chicken & Noodles, 37
Chinese Lemon Chicken, 250, *250*
Chinese Vegetables, 281, *281*
Chow Mein, 101, *106*
see also wontons
Chinese gooseberry see kiwi fruit
Chinese kale see Chinese broccoli
Chinese noodles, 288, 289
Chinese parsley see coriander
Chinese white cabbage see bok choy
Chinese white turnip see daikon
Chinese zucchini, 466, *466*
chipolatas, **103**
chips
Fish & Chips, 168, *168*
Parsnip Chips, 311, *311*
Potato Chips, 331, *331*
chit kou see Chinese zucchini
chives, **103-4**, 202, *202*
Chive Scones with Bacon Butter, 404
chocolate, **104-5**, **107-9**
Black Forest Cake, **48**, 78, *78*
Cherry Chocolates, 116, *116*
Choc-Mint Swirls, 55, *55*
Chocolate Caramel Slice, 416, *416*
Chocolate Carrot Slice, 419, *419*
Chocolate Chestnut Mousse, 95, *95*

Chocolate Chip Cookies, 54, *54*
Chocolate Chip Ice-cream, 220
Chocolate Glacé Apricots, 21, *21*
Chocolate Glacé Icing, 81
Chocolate Hedgehog Slice, 415, *415*
Chocolate Lemon Swirls, 251, *251*
Chocolate Mock Cream, 78
Chocolate Muffins, 276, 277, *277*
Chocolate Peanut Bites, 328
Chocolate Raspberry Swiss Roll, 443, *443*
Chocolate Ricotta Torte, 378
Chocolate Sauce, 107, 134
Chocolate Soufflé, 421, *421*
Chocolate Sponge, 75
Chocolate Truffles, 109, *109*, **458**
Choc Rum Slice, 419
Coconut Macaroons, 111, *111*
Dark Chocolate Pudding with Mocha Sauce, 140, *140*
decorations, 82-3, *82*
Easy Chocolate Cake, 71
Ginger Chocolates, 192, *192*
Hazelnut Chocolate Roll, 210, *210*
melting, 72, 83, *83*
Moist Chocolate Brownies, 417, *417*
Mud Cake, 72, *72*
Panforte, 71, *71*, **305**
Rich Chocolate Gelato, 221, *221*
chokos, **105**
Chop Suey, **105**
chorizo, **105**
choux pastry, **105-6**, 320, 322-3, *323*
chowder, **106**
see also soups
Chow mein, 101, **106**
choy sum, 466, *466*
Christmas food
Frosted Cake, 77, 77
Ice-cream Pudding, 134, *134*
Steamed Pudding, 134
chrysanthemum leaves, 467, *467*
churro, **106**
chutney, **106-7**, **110**, **338-9**
Apple, 18
Mint Chutney Dip, 214
Tangy Mint, 356, *356*
see also pickles; relishes
cider, **107**
cilantro see coriander
cinnamon, **107**
cinnamon sugar, **107**
citron, **108**
citrus fruit, **108**
Citrus Round, *404*, 405
Citrus Walnut Salad, 386

Passionfruit & Citrus Flummery, 138, *138*
pectin content of, 228, 229
see also under individual fruit eg oranges
clams, **108**
clarifying, **109**
cloves, **109**
cobblers, **133**
Cock-a-Leekie, **109**, 423, *423*
cocktails, **110**
Brandy Alexander, 144
Frozen Strawberry Daiquiri, 144, *144*
Japanese Slipper, 144, *144*
Long Island Iced Tea, 144
Margarita, 144, *144*
Martini, 144
Pina Colada, 144, *144*
see also fruit cocktail
cocoa, **110**
coconut, **110-11**, *111*
about, 111
Coconut Ice-cream, 220
Coconut Jam Slice, 415
Coconut Lamb Satays, 397, *397*
Fragrant Coconut Dip, 143
Honey & Chocolate Cake, 79, *79*
Kiwi Fruit & Coconut Cheesecake, 92, *93*
Raspberry Coconut Biscuits, 368, *368-9*
coconut cream, **111**
coconut milk, **111**, 219
cod, **111**
coddling, **111**
coeur à la crème, **114**
coffee, **112-13**, *114*
Coffee Glacé Icing, 81, 209
Coffee Hazelnut Biscuits, 209, *209*
Coffee Ice-cream, 220
Coffee Liqueur Cream, 56
Coffee Pecan Slice, 334, *334*
Coffee Soufflé, 420, *421*
Coffee Sponge, 75
Iced Coffee, **216**, 113, *113*
Irish Coffee, **222**, 113
see also under individual coffee eg cappuccino
colby cheese, **114**
Colcannon, 114, **115**, 222, *222*
Coleslaw, 64, *64*, 380
compotes, **115**
confectioners sugar see icing sugar
confectionery, **114-16**
Chocolate Peanut Bites, 328
Easy Chocolate Fudge, 107, *107*
Ginger Chocolates, 192, *192*
Turkish Delight, 115, *115*, **460**
see also fruit leather
confits, **115**
conserves, **115**
Quince, 365, *365*

Strawberry, 437
consommés, *116*
see also soups
cookies *see* biscuits
Coq au Vin, 97, *97*, **116**
Coquilles St Jacques, **116**
coriander, **116**, **117**, 202, *202*
about, 117
Coriander Butter, 435
Coriander Mayonnaise, 307
Coriander Salad, 389, *389*
Eggplant & Coriander Salad, 156, *156*
Sweet Coriander Peas, 333
corn, *117*, **118**
Chicken & Corn Quiche, 363, *363*
Chicken & Corn Sausages with Salsa Cruda, 402, *402*
Chicken & Corn Soup, 97
Corn & Cheese Chowder, 426, *426*
Corn Bread, 13, *13*, **117**
Corn Fritters, 167, *167*
Fish Cakes in Corn Husks, 34
Herb & Garlic Cornbread Slices, 188, *188*
microwaving, 271
Thai Corn Pancakes, 307, *307*
corned beef, *117*, **119**
about, 119
Corned Beef Hash, 12
cornflower, *117*
Cornish hen, *118*
Cornish Pasties, *118*, 157
cornmeal, *118*
see also polenta
cornstarch *see* cornflour
corn syrup *see* syrups
cottage cheese, *118*
Cottage Cheese Blintzes, 237, *237*
Liverwurst Cottage Dip, 142
cottage pie *see* Shepherd's Pie
coulibiac, *119*
coulis, *119*
courgette *see* zucchini
court bouillon, *119*
couscous, *119*, 273, *273*, 278
crab, 119, **120–1**
about, 120
Corn & Crabmeat Soup, 118
crabapples, *120*
cracked wheat, *120*
see also burghul
cranberries, *120*
Cranberry Dressing, 385
crayfish, *120*
Crayfish & Prawn Crepe Stack, 307
cream, *120–1*
cream cheese, *121*
Bagels & Lox, 237
Blueberry Cheese Tart, 139, *139*
Blueberry-Cream Cheese Tart, *322*

Cream Cheese Frosting, 419
Cream Cheese Strudel, 440, *440*
Cream Cheese Icing, 79, 81
Prune & Cream Cheese Scrolls, 418–19
Salmon & Cheese Squares, *166*, 167
cream of tartar, *121*
Cream Puffs, 323
Crème Brûlée, *121*, 126, *126*
Crème Caramel, *121*, 127, *127*
Crème Chantilly, *121*, 130
Crème Fraîche, *121–2*, *482*, 483
Crème Pâtissière, *122*, 126
crêpes, *122*
Crayfish & Prawn Stack, 307
Smoked Salmon & Dill, 173, *173*
Suzette, 180, *180*
see also pancakes
cress, *122*
croissants, *122–3*, 183
croquembouche, *123*
croque monsieur, *123*
croquettes, *123*
Ham & Mushroom, 206
Salmon & Camembert, 393, *393*
crostini, *123*
croustades, *123–4*
croûte, en, *124*
croutes, *124*
Crisp Bread, 84
croûtons, *124*, 411
crown roast, *124*
crudités, *124*
with Olive Paste, 298, *298*
with Sun-dried Tomato Dip, 142, *142*
crumbles, *133*
crystallised cake decorations, 83
cucumber, *122*, *124*
Cucumber Yoghurt, 192
Sunomono, 230, *230*
Yoghurt & Cucumber Raita, 215
Cumberland Sauce, *125*
cumin, *125*
Fish & Cumin Kebabs, 238, *238*
cumquats, *125*
currants, *125*
Redcurrant-glazed Roast Turkey, 460, *460*
see also blackcurrants
currants, dried, *125–6*
Orange & Currant Rock Cakes, 379, *379*
curries, **123-4**, *126*
accompaniments to, 123
Almond & Coconut Lamb, 8, 8–9
Chicken, 258, *258*
Coconut Fish, 111, *111*
Curried Chicken Apple & Celery Salad, 89

Curried Onion Rings, 294, *294*
Curried Pumpkin Soup, 361
Curried Yoghurt Chicken, 481, *481*
Curry Mayonnaise, 89
Eggs Vindaloo, 152, *152*
freezing, 183
Green Chicken, 99
Lime Curry Pickle, 339, *339*
Roghan Josh, 244, *244*
Sweet Vegetable, 468, *468*
curry leaves, *126*
curry paste & curry powder, *126–7*
custard, **125-7**, *127*
about, 125
Baked Rice, 375, *375*
Orange & Caramel, 429, *429*
Peaches, Cream & Custard Parfait, 327
Quick Brandy, 162, *162*
Sweet Custard Rolls, 164, *164*
custard apples, *127*
see also soursop
cuttlefish, *127*

D

daikon, *128*, 467, *467*
daiquiri, *128*
Frozen Strawberry Daiquiri, 144, *144*
damper, *129*
Olive Damper, 63, *63*
damsons, *129*
dandelions, *130*
Danish blue cheese, 51, *130*
Danish Open Sandwich, *130–1*
Danish pastry, *131*
freezing, 183
Mini Apricot, 323
Mini Fruit, 322
dariole, *131*
dasheen *see* taro
dashi, *132*
dates, *128*, *132–3*
Banana Date Chutney, 110, *110*
Cherry, Date & Walnut Roll, 475
Date & Chocolate Fudge Slice, 108
Honey Date Cake, 212, *212*
Moroccan-style Trout with Dates, 455, *455*
Warm Rice & Date Salad, 375
daube, en, *133*
deep frying, *133*
deglazing, *134*
dégorger, *134*
demerara sugar, *134*
demi-glacé, *134*
desserts, *135*
baked puddings, **129-30**
bread puddings, **131**
Christmas, **134**

crumbles, crisps & cobblers, **133**
fruit, **135-6**
ice-creams, **137**
jellies, **138**
mousses, **138**
steamed puddings, **140-1**
tarts, **139**
see also cheesecakes; fondues; pies; soufflés; strudels
dessert wine, *136*
devilled, *136*
devilled butter, *136*
devil on horseback, *136*
Devonshire Scones/Tea, *137*, 404, *404*
dhal, *137*, 140
diable, *137*
diba, *138*
dibs Roman, *138*
dijonnaise, *138*
dill, *139*, 202, *202*
Cucumber & Fennel with Dill, 122
Dill Vinaigrette, 412
Smoked Salmon & Dill Crêpes, 173, *173*
dim sims, *139*
dips, *140*, **142-3**
Chilli Cheese, 352, *352*
Chilli, 476, *476*
Guacamole, 140, *200*, 266, *266*
Mint Chutney, 214
see also Baba Ghannouj
doh gok, 467
Dolmades, *141*, 374, *374*
doner kebabs, *141–2*
double Gloucester cheese, *142*
dough, *143*
Doughnuts, **143-4**, 478
drambuie, *144*
dredging, *144*
Dresden sauce, *144*
dressings, *144*, 390–1
Citrus, 27
Cranberry, 385
Green Goddess, *198*, 391
Sweet & Sour, 102
Thai, 25
Thousand Island, 391
Walnut, 386
see also marinades; mayonnaises; salad dressings; sauces; vinaigrettes
dried beans, 38, *38*
see also beans
dried fruit *see* fruit, dried
drinks
Athol Brose, 408
Banana & Passionfruit Smoothie, 30
Banana Smoothie, 30
beef tea, *43*
cocktails, *144*
Fruit Cocktail, *181*, *184*
fruit cups & punches, *145*

Iced Coffee, 113, *113*, **216**
Lemonade, 250
Mint Lassi, *482–3*, 483
dripping, *144–5*
dry-frying *see* pan-grilling
duchess potatoes, *145*
duck, *145–7*, *146–7*
carving, 87
defrosting, 270
Peking Duck, 104–5, *105*
dumplings, *147*, **148-9**
see also gnocchi
Dundee Cake, 74, *74*, *148*
durian, *148–9*
durum wheat, *149*
duxelles, *149*

E

Eccles Cakes, *150*, 159, *159*
eclairs, *150*
edam cheese, *150–1*
eels, *151*
egg noodles, *154*, 288, *289*
see also noodles
eggplants, *154–5*, **156**
about, 156
Baba Ghannouj, *28*, 246, *246*
Char-grilled Beef & Eggplant Salad, 384, *384*
Chilli Sweet Potato & Eggplant Crisps, 442, *442*
Mediterranean Medley Focaccia, 176, *177*
microwaving, 271
Moussaka, 201, *279*
Veal Scaloppine with Eggplant, 225
eggs, **150-5**, *151–4*
about, 150
Eggs Benedict, 153, *155*
Eggs Florentine, 151, *155*
Huevos Rancheros, 151, *213*
poaching, 151
Scotch Eggs, 153, *153*, *401*
scrambling, 151
see also coddling; frittatas; soufflés
emmenthal, *155*
empanada, *155*
enchilada, *156*
endive, Belgian, *156*
endive, curly, *156–7*
Curly Endive Salad, 383, *383*
Grape & Endive Salad, 198, *198*
English food, **157–8**, *157-9*
Banbury tart, *33*
Bangers and Mash, 158, *158*
Chelsea Buns, *96*, 157, *157*
Cornish Pasties, *118*, 157
Devonshire Scones/Tea, *137*, 404, *404*
Eccles Cakes, *150*, 159, *159*
English Muffins, *158*, 278, *278*

English food *(continued)*
Lancashire Hot Pot, **241**,
243, *243*
Queen of Puddings, 363
Shepherd's Pie, 158, *158*,
406–7
Spotted Dick, 159, **426**
Summer Pudding, 135, *135*,
439–40
English spinach *see* spinach
entrecôte, **158**
entrée, **158**
escabèche, **159**
escalope, **159**
escargot, **159**
see also snails
escarole, **159**
espresso coffee, 112, **159**
estouffade, **159**

F
Fairy Cakes, 70, *70*
falafel, **160**, 246, *246*
feijoa, **160**
fennel, **160–1**, *160–1*
Cucumber & Fennel with
Dill, 122
Pork with Fennel, 349, *349*
fenugreek, **161**
feta cheese, **161**
fettuccini, **161–2**
Alfredo, 318
& Tuna, 174
Bolognese, 314, *314*
Fresh Tuna, 457
with Pesto, 316, *316*
figs, **162–3**, *162–3*
about, 162
filé powder, **163**
filet mignon, **163**
fillets, **163**
filo pastry, **163–4**, *164–5*
about, 164
fines herbes, **164**
finger food, **164**, *166–7*
see also antipasto; appetisers;
hors d'oeuvres; Yakitori
finnan haddie, **164–5**
fish, **165**, *168*
canned, **174**
fresh, **168–71**
smoked, **172–3**
see also under individual fish eg
tuna
fish sauce *see* nuoc mam
five spice powder, **168**
flambé, **168**
flans, **168**
Apple & Sour Cream, 445
Avocado, Tomato & Ham, 27
Fruit, 322, 444, *444*
Smoked Fish, 172
see also tarts
Flapjacks, **169**, 305, *305*
fleuron, **169**
florentine, à la, **170**

Florentines, 51, *51*, **169**
flour, **170**
flowers, edible, **170–1**
flummeries, **171**
Passionfruit & Citrus, 138, *138*
focaccia, 61, *61*, **171–2**, *176–7*
Olive & Rosemary, 297
foie gras, **172**
fondant, **172**
fondues, **172–3**, **175**
about, 175
Bagna Cauda, **29–30**, *175*, 175
foo gwa *see* bitter melon
fools, **173**
Rhubarb, 371, *371*
forcemeat, **173**
four spices, **173**
frankfurters, **173–4**
see also hot dogs
frappé, **174**
freezing, **174**, *182–3*
French bread *see* baguette
French dressing, **174**
French food, **174–5**, *178*,
178–80
Cassoulet, **85**, 178, *178*
Classic French Omelette,
154, *154–5*
French fries, **178**
French toast, **178**
fricassée, **178**
frikadeller, **178**
frittatas, **179**, *181*
about, 181
Carrot Parsnip, 152, *152*
fritters, **179**, *184*
Cauliflowers, 88
Corn, 167, *167*
Onion, 184, *186*
Spinach, 431, *431*
Vegetable, 472, *472*
fritto misto, **179**
fromage blanc, **179–80**
frosting, **180**
fruit, **180**, 183
Citrus Genoise Sponge, 76
Spiced Fruit & Nut Bars,
116, *116*
Fruit & Nut Bread, 62, *62*
Fruit Flan, 322, 444, *444*
Fruit Mince Pudding with
Citrus Sauce, 141, *141*
Fruits in Chardonnay Jelly,
190, *190*
Ice-cream Fruit Bombe, 137
for pickles & chutneys, 338
Spotted Dick, 159, **426**
Summer Pudding, 135, *135*,
439–40
Trifle, 136, *136*
see also under individual fruit eg
lemons
fruit cake, **181**
about, 73
Bran & Fruit Loaf, 58, *58*
Dundee, 74, *74*, **148**
Festive, 74

Wholemeal Fruit & Nut, 73,
73
fruit cocktail, **181**, *184*
fruit cups, **184**
see also punches & fruit cups
fruit, dried, **180–1**, **185**
fruit leather, **184**
fruit mince *see* mincemeat
fruit salad, **184–5**
Dried, 185, *185*
Moroccan Style, 135, *135*
Pavlova with Fruit Salad
Topping, 264, *265*
with Port, 136
frying, **185**
fudge, **185**
Date & Chocolate Slice, 108
Easy Chocolate, 107, *107*
Hot Fudge Sauce, 400
Tipsy, 114, *115*
fusilli, 308, *309*
fuzzy melons *see* Chinese
zucchini

G
Gado Gado, **186**, 219, *219*
gai lan *see* Chinese broccoli
galangal, **186**
game, **186–7**, *186–7*
see also under individual game eg
grouse
gammon, **187**
garam masala, **187**
garbanzo beans *see* chick peas
garlic, **187–8**, *188–9*, 202, *202*
about, 188
Aïoli, *9*, 391
Garlic Butter Polenta, 345, *345*
Garlic Chicken Kebabs, 239,
239
Garlic Focaccia, 61, *61*
Garlic Mayonnaise, 385,
385, 428, *428*, 470
Garlic Mushroom Filling, 353
Garlic Onions, 294, *294*
Garlic Peppers, 336
Lamb Shanks with Roasted
Garlic, 244, *244*
Mushrooms with Garlic &
Red Pepper Sauces, 280, *280*
Peppered Peas & Garlic, 330,
330, 333
Tomato Garlic Mussels, 282,
282
garlic chives, 202, *202*
garnish, **188**
gâteau, **188–9**
Gazpacho, **189**, 427, *427*
Gefilte Fish, **189**, 236, *236*
gelatine, **189–90**, *190–1*
about, 191
gelato, **190**
Chocolate, 221, *221*
Orange, 299, *299*
Genoise cake, **190**
ghee, **190**

gherkins, **191**
giblets, **191**
ginger, **191**, *192–3*
about, 193
Ginger Pork Satays, 347
Ginger Shortbread Creams,
414, *414*
Ginger Syrup, 262
Scallop Salad with Lime &
Ginger, 403, *403*
Steamed Fish with Ginger,
171, *171*
gingerbeer, **191**
Gingerbread, **191**, 193, *193*
Gingerbread Families, 52,
52–3
Gingernuts, 55
glacé, **192**
glacé fruit, **192**
glacé icing, 81, 209
glazes, **192**
globe artichokes *see* artichokes
Gloucester cheese, double, 142
gnocchi, **193**, *194–5*, 308
goats cheese
Goats Cheese & Artichoke
Tarts, 166, *166*
Warm Goat Cheese Salad,
91, *91*
see also chèvre
goats milk, **193**
golden berries *see* Cape
gooseberries
golden syrup, 130, **193**
goose, **194**, *196*
about, 196
gooseberries, **194**
gorgonzola cheese, 51, **194**
gouda cheese, **195**
gougère, **195**
goulash, **195**
Beef, 149, *149*
granadilla *see* passionfruit
Grand Marnier Pâte, 325, *325*
granita, **195**
Granita di Caffè, 113
grapefruit, **196**, *197*
about, 197
grapes, **195–6**, *198*
gratin, **196**
gravlax, **196–7**
gravy, **197**, 348
grecque, à la, **197**
Greek food, **197–8**, *199–201*
Baklava, **31**, 201, *201*
Greek Lamb Kebabs, 239, *239*
Greek Shortbread, 414, *414*
Greek Style Squid, 434, *434*
Moussaka, 201, **279**
Taramasalata, 140, 167, *167*,
199, *199*, **449**
Tzatziki, 199, *199*, **461**
green beans, **38–9**
see also beans
greengages, **198**
Green Goddess Dressing, **198**,
391

green peppers *see* peppers, sweet
gremolata, **198–9**
grenadine molasses *see* dibs
Roman
gribichi sauce, **199**
griddle cakes, **199**
grilling, **199**
grissini, 142, *142*, **199**
ground cherries *see* Cape
gooseberries
groundnuts *see* peanuts
grouse, **199–200**
gruel, **200**
gruyère cheese, **200**
Guacamole, 140, **200**, 266, *266*
guava, **201**, 233, *233*
gugelhopf, **201**
Guinness, **225**
Guinness Beef Stew, 223, *223*
gumbo, **201**

H
haddock, **204**
Kedgeree, **238**, 375, *375*
Smoked Haddock, 172, *172*
haggis, **204**
haloumi, **264–5**
halva, **205**
ham, **204–6**, *205*
about, 204
Avocado, Tomato & Ham
Flan, 27
carving, 87
Chicken & Ham Pie, 100, *100*
Chicken & Smoked Ham
Jambalaya, 68, *68*
Egg Noodles with Chicken
& Ham, 287, *287*
Eggs Benedict, 153
freezing, 182
Pea & Ham Soup, 332
hamburgers, **206**, *207–8*
Bacon & Cheese Burger, 28
Pork Sausage Burger, 402, *402*
hares, **206**
haricot beans, 38, **206**
see also beans
Harissa, **206**, 273
hash, **207**
havarti, **207**
hazelnuts, **207**, *209–10*
about, 209
head cheese *see* brawn
hearts, **207**
hearts of palms, **207**
herbs, *202–3*, **207–8**
freezing, 183
Herb & Cheese Scroll, 59
Herb & Garlic Butter, 188
Herb & Garlic Cornbread
Slices, 188, *188*
Herb Cheese Roll, 483, *483*
Herb Dumplings, 148
Herbed Cheese Crackers, 90,
90
Herbed Sardines, 396

Herbed Scallop Kebabs, 403, *403*
Herb-marinated Peppers, 336, *336*
Herb Meatballs with Rich Tomato Sauce, 259, *259*
Herb Mustard, 283
Herb Soufflé, 420, *420*
Individual Herb Tarts, 446
Olive & Herb Rolls, 59
Warm Tomato & Herb Salad, 449, *449*
Walnut & Herb Salad, 474, *475*
see also bouquet garni
herrings, **208**
Hoisin Marinade, 257
Hoisin Sauce, **208**
ho lan dow *see* snow peas
Hollandaise Sauce, 24, 153, **208–9**, 399
hominy, **209**
honey, **209–10**, **211–12**
about, 211
Barbecued Honey Chicken Wings, 101, *101*
Honey & Coconut Cake, 79, *79*
Honey & Cream Cheese Icing, 79, *79*, 81
Honeyed Baby Turnips with Lemon Thyme, 461, *461*
Honeycomb, 115, *115*, **210**
honeydew melons, **210–11**
hors d'oeuvres, **211**
see also antipasto; appetisers; finger food
horseradish, **211**, **213**
about, 213
Horseradish Cream, 119, 208, 213
Hot Cross Buns, 61, 62, **212**, 480, *480*
hot dogs, **212**
hotwater pastry, **212–13**
huckleberries *see* blueberries
Huevos Rancheros, 151, **213**
Hummus, 140, 208, **213**, 245, *245*
Hushpuppies, 68, *68*, **213**

I

ice-cream, **214–15**, **220–1**
Christmas Pudding, 134, *134*
Fruit Bombe, 137
Mango, 137, *137*
Passionfruit & Pistachio Nut, 312, *312*
Sundae, *400*
see also gelato
Iced Coffee, 113, *113*, **216**
Iced Tea, 144, **216**
icing, 80–83, **217**
cream cheese, 81
decorations for, 82-3, *82*, 83

Honey & Cream Cheese, 79
Pink, 79, *79*
Royal, 77, *77*
see also buttercreams; glacé icing
icing sugar, **217**
Ile Flottante, **217**
Indian food, **214-16**, **217–19**
see also Chapattis; dhal; pappadums
Indonesian food, **217-19**, *219*, **222**
Balinese-style Fried Rice, 372, *372*
Gado Gado, **186**, 219, *219*
Nasi Goreng, 218, *218*, *284*
Irish Coffee, **222**, 113
Irish food, **222-4**, **222–5**
Cheese Pudding, 91, *91*
Colcannon, 114, **115**, 222, *222*
Italian food, **225-7**, **226–7**
Carpaccio, *78*, 225, *225*
Italian Veal Pot Roast, 464, *464*
Minestrone, 225, **273**
see also antipasto; gelato; pasta

J

jackfruit, **230**
jalapeño chilli, **230**
jalousie, **231**
Jamaica pepper *see* allspice
jambalaya, 68, *68*, **232**
Jam Pudding, Steamed, 141
jams & marmalades, **228–9**, **231–2**
Apricot & Lemon, 20
Black Cherry, 94
Ginger Apple Marmalade, 193
Grapefruit Marmalade, 197, *197*
Raspberry, 367
see also conserves
Japanese food, **230-2**, **232–3**
Japanese noodles, 288, *288*
Japanese radishes *see* daikon
Japanese Slipper, 144, *144*
jarlsberg cheese, **233–4**
jellies, **233-4**, *234*
Fruits in Chardonnay, 190, *190*
jerky, **234**
Jerusalem artichokes *see* artichokes
Jewish food, **235-6**, **235-7**
blintz, 50
Gefilte Fish, **189**, 236, *236*
Johnny cakes, **236**
jsung *see* spring onions
julienne, **236**
juniper berries, **236–7**
junket, **237**
jus, au, **237**

K

kale, **238**
kangaroo, **238**
kasha, **238**
kebabs, **238**, **238-9**
Herbed Scallop, 403, *403*
Tandoori Chicken, 216, *216*
Kedgeree, **238**, 375, *375*
kibbi, **238**
kidney beans, **239**
kidneys, **238-9**
Kidneys & Bacon, 291, *291*
Steak & Kidney Pudding, 436, *436*
kippers, **239**
kiwi fruit, **239**
Kiwi Fruit & Coconut Cheesecake, 92, *93*
Smoked Trout with Kiwi Fruit Salad, 454
kofta, **239**
korma, **239**
kumara *see* sweet potatoes

L

Ladies' Fingers, **240**, 245, *245*
lamb, **240-1**, **240-4**
about, 240
Almond & Coconut Lamb Curry, 8, *8–9*
Cassoulet, *85*, 178, *178*
Coconut Lamb Satays, 397, *397*
defrosting, 270
Greek Lamb Kebabs, 239, *239*
Hotch Potch, 407, *407*
Irish Stew, 224, *224*
Ladies' Fingers, 245, *245*
Lamb Empanados, 266, *266*
Lamb Korma, 216
Lamb Stew, 407, *407*
Minted Lamb Salad, 272, *272*
Mongolian Lamb, 242, *242*
Pasta with Lamb & Vegetables, 315, *315*
Satay Lamb, 287, *287*
Scotch Broth, 406, *406*
Shepherds Pie, 158, *158*, **406-7**
Souvlakia, 200, *200*
Spicy Coriander Lamb, 117
Spicy Lamb in Pitta Bread, 247, *247*
Tagine of Lamb, 365, *365*
lamingtons, **241**
Lancashire Hot Pot, **241**, 243, *243*
langue de chat, **242**
lard, **242**
larding, **242**
lasagne, **242–3**
Beef, 317, *317*
Vegetable, 319, *319*
Lassi, **243**, 482, *482–3*

Lebanese food, **243–4**, **245-7**
Baba Ghannouj, *28*, 246, *246*
Tabouli, 247, *247*, **444–5**
Lebkuchen, 57, *57*
leeks, **244–5**, **248**
microwaving, 271
legumes, **245**
see also under individual legume eg peas
Leicester cheese, **245–6**
lemon balm, **246–7**
Lemon Butter, **247**, 250, *250*
lemon grass, 202, *202*, **247–8**
lemons, **246**, **249-52**
about, 249
Apricot & Lemon Jam, 20
Cold Lemon Soufflé, 191, *191*
Creamy Lemon Pork, 349
Lemon Butter, **247**, 250, *250*
Lemon Cream Cheese Icing, 81
Lemon Curd Filling, 76
Lemon Glacé Icing, 81
Lemon-Lime Pie, 254, *254*, *322*
Lemon Meringue Pie, 252, *252*
Lemon Sauce, 213
Lemon Sorbet, **220**, 221
Lemon Sponge, 75
Lemon Syrup, 251, 481
Lemon Zabaglione, 227, *227*
Preserved Lemons, 275, *275*
Veal Chops with Sage & Lemon, 227
lentils, **248**, **253**
about, 253
Tomato & Brown Lentil Soup, 452, *452*
see also dhal
lettuce, **249–50**
Leyden cheese, **250**
lima beans, 38, **250**
limburger cheese, **250–1**
limes, **251–2**, **254-5**
about, 255
Ceviche, *90*, 255, *255*
Crème Brûlée with Plums in Lime, 126, *126*
Lime Curry Pickle, 339, *339*
Scallop Salad with Lime & Ginger, 403, *403*
linzer torte, **252**
liqueurs, **252–3**
liver, **253**
Chicken Liver & Brandy Pâté, 325
Chopped Liver, 235, *235*
Pasta with Chicken Livers, 103
Venetian Liver, 292, *292*
see also foie gras
liverwurst, **253–4**
Liverwurst Cottage Dip, 142
lobster, **254-5**, **256-7**, 411
loganberries, **255**
loh bok *see* daikon
longan, **255–6**
Long Island Iced Tea, 144

loquats, **256**
lotus lilies, **256–7**
lychees, **257**
lyonnaise, à la, **257**

M

macadamia nuts, **258**
Macadamia Nut Ice-cream, 220
macaroni, **258**, 308, *308*
macaroons, **258**
Almond, 11, *11*
Coconut, 111, *111*
mace, **258–9**
mackerel, **259**
Madeira Cake, 70, **259**
madeleine, **259**
madrilène, **259**
maître d' hôtel butter, **259**
maize *see* corn
malfade, 308
malt, **260**
mandarins, **260**
mange tout *see* snow peas
mangoes, **258**, **260–1**
about, 258
Mango & Avocado Salsa, 335, *335*
Mango Cheesecake, 92, *92*
Mango Ice-cream, 137, *137*
Mango Salsa, 412
mangosteen, **261**
manioc *see* cassava
maple syrup, **261**
marachino, **262**
Marble Cake, 69, **262**
marengo, **262**
margarine, **262**
Margarita, 144, *144*
marinades
Barbecue, 31
Hoisin, 257
Teriyaki, 456
marjoram, 202, *202*, **263**
marmalade, **263**
see also jams & marmalades
marrow, bone, **263–4**
marrow, vegetable, **264**
marshmallow, **264**
see also desserts
Martini, 144
marzipan, **11**, **12**, **264–5**
mascarpone cheese, **265**
Date & Mascarpone Tart, 128
matzo, 235, *235*, **265**
mayonnaises, **265–6**
Aïoli, *9*, 391
Basic, 390–1
Coriander, 307
Curry, 89
Garlic, 385, *385*, 428, *428*, 470
Oriental, 394
Tarragon, 23
see also dressings; marinades; vinaigrettes

meat, *266*, 270
  Family Meat Pie, 342, *342*
  see also under individual meats
meatballs, 259–60, *266*
meatloaves, 261, *266*
medlars, *266–7*
Melba toast, *267*
melons, 262, *267–8*
  about, 262
  Melon with Proscuitto, 16, *16*
  Prawn & Melon Skewers, 166, *166*
  see also bitter melon
meringues, *263–5*, *268*
  about, 264
  Lemon Meringue Pie, 252, *252*
mesclun, *268*
meunière, *268–9*
Mexican food, 266–8, *269*
  arroz con pollo, *24*
  Burritos, *61–2*, 267, *267*
  enchilada, *156*
  Mexican-style Beef Spareribs, 430
  tamale, *446*
microwave cookery, *269*, *270–1*, *272*
mille-feuille, *272*
mincemeat, *269*, *272–3*
  Mince Pies, *323*
Minestrone, 225, *273*
mint, 203, *203*, *272*, *273*
  Apple, Tomato & Mint Chutney, 110, *110*
  Barbecued Beef & Mint Sausages, 401
  Honey Mint Roasted Chicken, 211, *211*
  Mint & Yoghurt Raita, 258
  Mint Chutney Dip, 214
  Minted Peas, 330, *330*
  Mint Jelly, 234, *234*
  Mint Lassi, *482–3*, 483
  Onion & Mint in Yoghurt, 216
  Tangy Mint Chutney, 356, *356*
  Tomato-Mint Sauce, 242
miso, 230, *273–4*
mixed grills, *274*
mixed spice, *274*
mocha, *274–5*
  Hot Mocha Java, 113
  Mocha Sauce, 140
  Mocha Soufflé, 421, *421*
mock cream, *275*
molasses, *275*
monosodium glutamate, *275*
Mongolian Lamb, 242, *242*
Monterey Jack, *275*
Mornay Sauce, *275*, 398
  see also lobster; oysters
Moroccan food, *273–5*, *278*
  Harissa, *206*, 273
  Moroccan Fish with Fresh Tomato Sauce, 169, *169*

Moroccan-style Fish with Dates, 455, *455*
Moroccan-style Fresh Fruit Salad, 135, *135*
mortadella, *279*
Moussaka, 201, *279*
mousseline, *279*, 399
mousses, *279*
  Avocado Aspic, 190
  Chocolate Chestnut, 95, *95*
  Classic Chocolate, 107, *107*
  Easy Orange, 138, *138*
  Raspberry, 366, *366*
  Smoked Trout, 173
mozzarella, *279–80*
  Mozzarella, Basil & Tomato Salad, 35, *35*
muesli, *280*
muffins, *276–8*, *280*
  Banana Bran, 58
  English, *158*, 278, *278*
  Peach & Zucchini, 327
mulberries, *280–1*
Mulligatawny, *281*, 423
mung beans, 38
münster cheese, *281*
mushrooms, 271, *279–81*, *281–2*
  Broccoli & Mushrooms, 41, *41*
  Chicken Noodle Mushroom Soup, 425, *425*
  Garlic Mushroom Filling, 353
  Ham & Mushroom Croquettes, 206
  Mushrooms en Croûte, 472–3
  Mushroom Strudel, 441, *441*
  Porcini Mushroom & Onion Risotto, 377, *377*
  Tortellini with Mushroom Cream Sauce, 319
  Veal & Mushroom Casserole, 463
mushy peas, 326
mussels, *282*, *282–3*, 411
  about, 282
mustards, *283*, *283*
  Grainy Mustard Cream, 207, 350–1, *350*
  Mustard Cream, 205, 402
  Rabbit with Dijon Mustard, 186, 187
mutton, *283*

N

naan, *284*
nam pla *see* nuoc mam
Napoleons, *284*
Napoletana Filling, 353
nashis, *284*
Nasi Goreng, 218, *218*, *284*
navarin, *285*
  Lamb Navarin with Vegetables, 241, *241*
nectarines, *285*

nesselrode pudding, *285*
neufchâtel cheese, *285*
newburg, *286*
nga choy *see* bean sprouts
niçoise, à la, *286*
noisette, *286*
noisette butter, *286*
noodles, *284–9*, *286*, 288–9
  Asian Noodle Vegetable Salad, 382, *382*
  Chicken Noodle Mushroom Soup, 425, *425*
  Chilli Crab & Soft Noodles, 121, *121*
  Chinese Chicken & Noodles, 37, *37*
  Salmon & Noodle Bake, 394
  Seafood with Noodles, 410, *410*
nougat, *287*
nouvelle cuisine, *287*
nuoc mam, *287*
nutmeg, *287*
nuts, *287*
  Caramel Nut Tartlets, 446, *446*
  Fruit & Nut Bread, 62, *62*
  Nut Sponge, 75
  Spiced Fruit & Nut Bars, 116, *116*
  Wholemeal Fruit & Nut Cake, 73, *73*
  see also under individual nuts eg almonds

O

oat bran, *290*
oatcakes, *290*, *401*, 406, *406*
oatmeal, *290–1*
octopus, *290*, *291*
  Chilli-Garlic Octopus, 17, *17*
oeufs à la neige, *291*
offal, *291–2*, *291–2*
  freezing, 182
  see also brains; kidneys; liver; tripe
oil, vegetable, *292*, 390
okra, *292–3*, *293*
olive oil, *296–7*, 390, *390*
olives, *293*, *296*, *296–8*
  Olive & Herb Rolls, 59
  Olive & Onion Flat Bread, 61
  Olive Damper, 63, *63*
  Olive Paste, 298, *298*, 456
  Olive, Pepper & Anchovy Focaccia, 61
  Pompeii Focaccia, 176, *176*
  Roasted Peppers & Olive Pie, 337
  Sherried Duck with Olives & Walnuts, 147
  Tomato & Olive Crispbread, 450, *450*
omelettes, *297*
  Classic French, 154, *154–5*
  Classic Soufflé, 154, *154–5*

Potato & Onion, 427, *427*
  see also frittatas
onions, *294–5*, *297–8*
  Black Olive & Onion Pie, 297, *297*
  Broccoli & Onion Stir-fry, 41, *41*
  Caramelised Onions, 207, *207*, 295, *295*
  Chive & Onion Scones, 404
  French Onion Soup, 178–9, *179*
  microwaving, 271
  Okra with Onions & Tomato, 293, *293*
  Olive & Onion Flat Bread, 61
  Onion & Mint in Yoghurt, 216
  Onion Fritters, 184, *184*
  Porcini Mushroom & Onion Risotto, 377, *377*
  Potato & Onion Omelette, 427, *427*
  Ricotta & Onion Boats, 167, *167*
  Tripe & Onions, 292, *292*
orange flower water, *300*
oranges, *299–300*, *299–300*
  about, 300
  Easy Orange Mousse, 138, *138*
  Orange & Caramel Custard, 429, *429*
  Orange & Currant Rock Cakes, 379, *379*
  Orange & Poppyseed Muffins, 276, *277*
  Orange Cream Cheese Icing, 81
  Orange Dumplings, 148
  Orange Glacé Icing, 81
  Orange Glazed Ham, 205, *205*
  Orange Sponge, 75, *75*
  Spiced Figs & Oranges, 163
oregano, 203, *203*, *300–1*
orzo *see* risoni
Osso Bucco, *301*, 464, *464*
oven frying, *301*
oxtail, *301*, *301–2*
  about, 301
oysters, *302–3*, *302–3*
  Caviar Oysters, 167, *167*
  Rockefeller Oysters, 302, *375–6*
  see also carpetbag steak
oyster sauce, *303*

P

Paella, *304*, 428
  Spicy Sausage and Bacon Paella, 401
pak choy *see* bok choy
Pakoras, Vegetable, 214–15, *215*
palm hearts *see* hearts of palm
pancakes, *304–5*, *304–7*, 305
  about, 304

Cottage Cheese Blintzes, 237, *237*
Flapjacks, *169*, 305, *305*
Mandarin, 104–5, *105*
  see also blini; crêpes; pikelets
pancetta, *305*
  see also bacon
Panettone, 305, 480
Panforte, 71, *71*, *305*
pan-frying, *306*
pan-grilling, *306*
papayas, *306*, 310
papillote, en, *306*
pappadums, 123, *307*
paprika, *307*, 310
paratha, *310*
parfaits, *310–11*
  Peaches, Cream & Custard, 327
  Strawberry & Marshmallow, 438
parma ham, *311*
parmesan cheese, *311–12*
  Baked Fennel Parmesan, 161, *161*
  Fresh Pears & Parmesan, 16, *16*
  Parmesan Cauliflower, 65, *65*
  Sunflower & Parmesan Biscuits, 49, *49*
parsley, 203, *203*, *312–13*
  Parsley Butter, 407
  Parsleyed Brown Rice, 376
parsnips, *311*, *313*
  Carrot Parsnip Frittata, 152, *152*
  microwaving, 271
partridge, *314*
passionfruit, *312*, *314–15*
  Passionfruit & Citrus Flummery, 138, *138*
  Passionfruit Cream Cheese Icing, 81
  Passionfruit Glacé Icing, 81
  Passionfruit Ice-cream, 220
  Passionfruit Ricotta Tart, 445, *445*
  Pineapple & Passionfruit Punch, 145, *145*
pasta, *308–9*, *313–19*
  about, 308
  Pasta with Chicken Livers, 103
  Risoni Seafood Soup, 425, *425*
  Tomato Pasta Salad, 453, *453*
  Tri-colour Pasta Salad, 387, *387*
  see also cannelloni; fettucine; lasagne, noodles; penne; ravioli; spaghetti; tortellini
pastes
  Olive, 298, *298*, 456
  Roasted Garlic, 189
pastrami, *316–17*
pastry, *317*, *320–3*
  see also under individual pastry
  pastry cream *see* Créme Pâtissière

pâte brisée, *318*
pâtés, 317-18, **324–5**
  Port & Pepper, 103, *103*
pâte-sucrée, *319*
paupiette, *319*
pavlovas, 264, *265*, *319*
pawpaw *see* papayas
peaches, *319*, *324*, **326–7**
  about, 327
peanut butter, **324–5**
peanut oil, *325*
peanuts, *324*, **328**
  about, 328
  Honey Peanut Butter Cookies, 212
  Peanut Brittle, 114, *114*
  Peanut Sauce, 219, *219*
pearl barley, *34*
pears, *325*, **329**
  about, 332
  Almond & Pear Tart, 10, *10*
  Fresh Pears & Parmesan, 16, *16*
  Pickled Pears, 338, *338*
  Spiced Rhubarb & Pear Cobbler, 371, *371*
peas, dried, *326*, **332**
  about, 332
  Pease Pudding, *327*, **332**, *332*
peas, green, **326–7**, **330**, **333**
  microwave cookery of, 271
pecan nuts, **327–8**, **334**
  Pecan Pie, 13
  Steamed Date & Pecan Pudding, 128, *128*
Pêche Melba, *327*, *327*, *328*
pecorino, **328–9**
pectin, 228, **329**
penne, 308, *308*
  with Artichoke Hearts, 22, *22*
peperoni, *329*, *332*
  Peperoni Pizza, 344
pepinos, *332*
pepper, **332–3**, *335*
  Peppered Peas & Garlic, 330, *330*
peppermint, *333*
peppers, sweet, *334*, **336–7**
  about, 336
  Char-grilled Pepper, 17, *17*
  Creamy Eggs with Red Pepper, 151, *151*
  Garlic Butter Polenta with Roasted Pepper, 345, *345*
  Huevos Rancheros, 151
  Mediterranean Medley Focaccia, 176, *177*
  Mushrooms with Garlic & Red Pepper Sauces, 280, *280*
  Olive, Pepper & Anchovy Focaccia, 61
  Pompeii Focaccia, 176, *177*
  Red Pepper Pâté, 324, *324*
  Red Pepper Terrine, 447, *447*
  Tomato & Pepper Stew, 450, *450*

persimmons, **334–5**
pesto, 35, *335*
  Fettuccine with Pesto, 316, *316*
  Pesto-topped Cherry Tomatoes, 449
  Ricotta & Pesto Pizzas, 378, *378*
petits fours, *335*
pheasants, *336*
pickles, *336*, **338–9**
  see also chutneys; relishes
pies, **340-2**, *366*
  Apricot, 21, *21*
  Black Olive & Onion, 297, *297*
  B' Stilla, 274, *274*
  Chicken & Ham, 100, *100*
  Deep Dish Apple, 14, *14*
  Egg, Salmon & Rice, 150, *150*
  Fish, 170, *170*
  Key Lime, 255
  Lemon-Lime, 254, *254*, *323*
  Lemon Meringue, 252, *252*
  Mince, 323
  Pecan, 13
  Pumpkin, 360, *360*
  Roasted Peppers & Olive, 337
  Shepherd's, 158, *158*, **406–7**
  Steak, Onion & Tomato, 45, *45*
  Venison, 186, *186*
  Zucchini & Cheese, 485, *485*
pigeons, *337*
pikelets, 304, *304*, *337*
  Potato & Salami, 355, *355*
pilaf, *337*, *340*
  Carrot, 376
  Rice & Vegetable, 376, *376*
pimento, *340*
pimiento, *340*
  Beef & Pimiento Loaf, 261
Pina Colada, 144, *144*
pineapple, **340–1**
  Carrot & Pineapple Muffins, 277
  Pineapple & Passionfruit Punch, 145, *145*
  Pineapple Upside down Pudding, 129, *129*
pine nuts, **341–2**
  Oysters with Pine Nuts & Bacon, 303, *303*
  Rocket & Pine Nut Dip, 143, *143*
piping bags, 81, *81*
piroshki, *342*
Pissaladière, 15, *15*, *342*
pistachio nuts, **342–3**
  Passionfruit & Pistachio Nut Ice-cream, 312, *312*
  Pistachio Nut Ice-cream, 220
  Pistachio Praline Truffles, 109, *109*
pistou, **343–4**
pitta bread, *344*

Spicy Lamb in Pitta Bread, 247, *247*
pizzas, *226*, **343–4**, **344–5**
  Ricotta & Pesto, 378, *378*
  Savoury Pizza Snails, 478, *478*
  Traditional Crispy, *226*, *226*
  Wedges, 167, *167*
plantains, *345*
plum pudding, **346–7**
plums, **345–6**
  Plums in Lime, 126, *126*
polenta, *345*, *347*
  about, 345
pomegranates, **347–8**
popcorn, **348–9**
popovers, **349–50**
poppy seeds, *346*, *350*
pork, **347-51**, **350–1**
  Barbecued Pork Spare Ribs, 32, *32*, *430*
  Braised Pork Medallions, 359
  Cassoulet, **85**, *178*, *178*
  Coppa & Salami, 17, *17*
  Crisp-fried Thai Noodles, 285, *285*
  microwave defrosting of, 271
  Noodles with Prawns & Pork, 284
  Pork & Bean Soup, 39
  Pork & Veal Terrine, 447
  Pork Satays, 397, *397*
  Skewered Ginger Pork, 31
  Wonton Frills, 166, *166*
  Wontons with Chilli Dip, 476, *476*
  see also bacon; ham
porridge, *351*
port, *352*
  Fruit Salad with Port, 136
  Port & Pepper Pâté, 103, *103*
  Prunes in Port, 359
port salut, *352*
potatoes, **331**, **352-5**, **353–4**
  about, 352
  Bangers & Mash, 158, *158*
  Cabbage & Potato Cakes, 64, *64*
  Colcannon, 114, **115**, 222, *222*
  fillings for, 353, *353*
  Hot Minted Potato Salad, 272
  Latkes, 236, *236*
  microwave cookery of, 271
  Potato & Coriander Salad, 117
  Potato & Onion Omelette, 427, *427*
  Potato Gnocchi, 194, *194*
  Potato Scones, 405, *405*
  Shepherd's Pie, 158, *158*, **406–7**
  Thai Potato Salad, 388, *388*
poultry, *354*
  microwave defrosting of, 270
  see also under poultry eg chicken

praline, **354–5**
  Pistachio Praline Truffles, 109, *109*
prawns, *355*, **356-8**
  about, 356
  Avocado & Prawn Salad, 27
  Crayfish & Prawn Crêpe Stack, 307
  Creamy Prawn Curry, 124, *124*
  Garlic King Prawns, 32, *32*
  Nasi Goreng, 218, *218*, *284*
  Noodles with Prawns & Pork, 284
  Prawn & Melon Skewers, 166, *166*
  Prawn Gumbo, 67, *67*
  Spiced Prawn Filling, 353
  Steamed Prawn Wontons, 476
  Sunomono, 230, *230*
  Wontons, 476, *476*
pretzels, 49, *356*
profiteroles, *323*, *356*
prosciutto, **356–7**
  Asparagus & Prosciutto Salad, 382, *382*
  Curly Endive Salad with Crisp Prosciutto, 383, *383*
  Fig & Prosciutto Salad, 163
provençale, à la, *357*
provolone, **357–8**
prune plums *see* damsons
prunes, **357–8**, *359*
  devil on horseback, **136**
  Prune & Cream Cheese Scrolls, 418–19
  Pumpkin & Prune Muffins, 276, 277
puddings, *358*
  see also black pudding; desserts; Yorkshire Pudding
puff pastry, *320*, **358–9**
puftaloons, *359*
pulses, **359–60**
  see also under individual pulse eg lentils
pumpernickel, *360*
pumpkins, **360–1**, **360–1**
  about, 360
  microwave cookery of, 271
  Pumpkin & Prune Muffins, 276, 277
  Pumpkin Gnocchi, 195, *195*
punches & fruit cups, 145, *145*, **361**
purees, *361*
puri, *361*

quails, **362–3**
  Quails with Tarragon & Pancetta, 187, *187*
quark, 363
quatre épices *see* four spices
Queen of Puddings, *363*
quenelle, *363*

quiches, **362-4**, **363–4**
quinces, **364–5**, *365*

rabbit, *366*
  Rabbit with Dijon Mustard, *186*, 187
radicchio, *366*
radishes, *367*
  see also daikon
ragoûts, *367*
ragù *see* bolognaise sauce
raisins, *367*
raita
  Mint & Yoghurt, 258
  Yoghurt & Cucumber, 215
rambutan, *368*
rapeseed *see* canola oil
rarebit, *368*
raspberries, **366-9**, **368–9**
  Chocolate & Creamy Berry Roulade, 109, *109*
  Chocolate Raspberry Swiss Roll, 443, *443*
  Raspberry Ice-cream, 220
  Raspberry Sorbet, 221, *221*
  Raspberry Soufflé, 421, *421*
ratatouille, *369*, *370*
  Rice & Ratatouille, 473, *473*
ravigote sauce, *369*
ravioli, 308, *309*, *369*
  Ricotta-filled, 313, *313*
red cabbage, *370*
  Sweet Red Cabbage, 64, *64*
redcurrants *see* currants
red kidney beans, 38
  see also beans
reducing, *370*
refreshing, *370*
relishes, *336*
  Cucumber, 122
  Fresh Tomato, 451
  Tomato, 88, 246
  see also chutneys; pickles
rémoulade sauce, *370*
rendang, *370*
  Beef Rendang, 218, *218*
rennet, *371*
rhubarb, *371*, *371*
rice, **371–2**, **372-7**
  about, 373
  Cheesy Rice-stuffed Peppers, 337, *337*
  Dirty Rice, 67
  Egg, Salmon & Rice Pie, 150, *150*
  Fragrant Rice Salad, 385
  Fried Rice, 106, *106*
  Kedgeree, **238**, 375, *375*
  Orange Sesame Rice Salad, 300
  Rice & Ratatouille, 473, *473*
  Sushi Rolls, 231, *231*
  Warm Lentil & Rice Salad, 253, *253*
rice flour, *373*

rice noodles, 288, *288*
rice paper, **373**
rice vinegar, **373**
ricotta, **373–4**, **378**
 Figs with Ricotta, 163
 Passionfruit Ricotta Tart, 445, *445*
 Ricotta & Onion Boats, 167, *167*
 Ricotta-filled Ravioli, 313, *313*
rigani, **374**
rigatoni, 308
rillettes, **374**
risoni, 308
 see also pasta
risotto, **374**
 see also rice
rissoles, **375**
 Fresh Tuna Rissoles, 457
rock cakes, **375**, **379**
Rockefeller Oysters, **375–6**
rocket, **376**
 Rocket & Pine Nut Dip, 143, *143*
 Rocket Express Focaccia, 176, *177*
rockmelons *see* cantaloupes; melons
roe, **376**
Rollmops, 170, **376**
romaine lettuce, **377**
romano, **377**
roquefort cheese, 51, **377**
rosemary, 203, *203*, **378**
 Olive & Rosemary Focaccia, 297
 Olive & Rosemary Palmiers, 298, *298*
 Rosemary Stuffing, 240, *240*
 Rosemary, Tomato & Apple Jelly, 233, *233*
rosewater, **377**
rough puff pastry, **378**
rouille, **378**
roulades, **378–9**
 Chocolate & Creamy Berry Roulade, 109, *109*
Roux, 66, **379**
Royal Icing, 77, *77*
rum, **379**
 Choc Rum Slice, 419
 Rum Sauce, 400
 Rum Baba, 479, *479*
 see also Baba (au Rhum)
runner beans, 39
rutabagas *see* swedes
rye, **379**
rye bread, **379**
 Wholemeal Rye Sourdough Bread, 63, *63*

S

sabayon sauce, **380**
sacher torte, **380**
saffron, **380–1**
 Saffron Chicken, 275, *275*

sage, 203, *203*, **381**
 Roast Leg of Lamb with Sage & Tarragon, 241, *241*
 Sage Butter, 195
 Sage Jelly, 234, *234*
 Veal Chops with Sage & Lemon, 227
sage derby, **382**
sago, **382**
saint paulin, **382**
sai yeung choy, 467
sake, **382**
salad dressings, **383**, **390–1**
 see also dressings; marinades; mayonnaises; vinaigrettes
salads, **380–9**, *383*
 see also dressings; marinades; mayonnaises; vinaigrettes
 Artichoke & Asparagus, 22, *22*
 Asian-style Tofu, 448, *448*
 Avocado & Prawn, 27
 Basil Spinach, 432
 Bean & Walnut, 40, *40*
 Beetroot, 48
 Caesar, **67–8**, 380, *380*
 Country Bean, 39, *39*
 Crunchy Fennel, 160, *160*
 Eggplant & Coriander, 156, *156*
 Fig & Prosciutto, 163
 Gado Gado, **186**, 219, *219*
 Grape & Endive, 198, *198*
 Grapefruit Watercress, 197, *197*
 Grated Carrot, 85
 Ham, 206, *206*
 Hot Avocado, 26, *26*
 Hot Minted Potato, 272
 Marinated Octopus, 290, *290*
 Marinated Beef & Noodle, 287, *287*
 Minted Lamb, 272, *272*
 Mozzarella, Basil & Tomato , 35, *35*
 Noodle, 285
 Orange & Spinach, 299, *299*
 Orange Sesame Rice, 300
 Pear & Brie, 329, *329*
 Potato & Coriander, 117
 Raspberry Chicken, 367, *367*
 Roast Tomato, 450
 Scallop, 403
 Seafood, 381, 410
 Smoked Chicken, 102
 Snow Pea & Asparagus, 422, *422*
 Snow Pea, 422
 Spanish Prawn, 356, *356*
 Spinach & Avocado, 431, *431*
 Summer Melon, 262
 Sunomono, 230, *230*
 Sweet Bean, 38
 Tabouli, 247, *247*, **444–5**
 Thai Papaya, 310, *310*
 Tomato Pasta, 453, *453*
 Tomato antipasto, 17, *17*

Vietnamese Chicken, 328, *328*
 Waldorf, 381, *381*, **474**
 Walnut & Herb, 474, *474*
 Warm Chicken, 102
 Warm Duck, 147, *147*
 Warm Goat Cheese, 91, *91*
 Warm Lentil & Rice, 253, *253*
 Warm Rice & Date, 375
 Warm Tomato & Herb, 449, *449*
 Wild & Brown Rice, 372
 see also coleslaw
salami, **384**
 Coppa & Salami antipasto, 17, *17*
 Potato & Salami Pikelets, 355, *355*
salmon, **384–5**, **392–4**
 about, 393
 Black Russian Filling, 353
 Blini with Sour Cream & Smoked Salmon, 306, *306*
 Copenhagen Focaccia, 176, *177*
 Egg, Salmon & Rice Pie, 150, *150*
 Quick Salmon Pâté, 324
 Salmon & Cheese Squares, 166, *167*
 Salmon Choux Puffs, 323
 Salmon Dip, 142
 Salmon Patties, 174, *174*
 Salmon Soufflé, 420, *421*
 Smoked Salmon & Dill Crêpes, 173, *173*
 Smoked Salmon Dip, 143
 Smoked Salmon Salad, 386
 Spinach & Salmon Terrine, 432, *432*
salsas, **385–6**
 Mango & Avocado, 335, *335*
 Mango, 412
 Quick Onion, 295, *295*
 Cruda, 402
 Tomato, 267, *267*
salsify, **386**
salt, **386**
 for pickling, 338
saltimbocca, **387**
sambal oelek, **387**
sambals, **387**
 Mint, 272
Sambuca, Fried Sardines with, 396
samosas, **388**
 Beef, 214, *214*
sandwiches, **388–9**, **395**
 Bacon, Lettuce & Tomato, 28, *28*
 Danish open, **130–1**
 Finger, 166, *166*
 freezing, 183
sapodilla, **389**
sapote, **389**
sardines, **392**, **396**
 Rollmops, 170, **376**
sashimi, **392–3**

satays, **393**, **397**
 Chicken, 33, *33*
 Ginger Pork, 347
sauces, **393–4**, **398–9**
 Apple, 18, 348, 354
 Béarnaise, **39**, **41**, 398
 Béchamel, **42**, 398
 Bigarade, **46**
 Black Bean, 46, 120
 Cheese, 201
 Chilli, 477
 Crème, 130
 Devil, 283
 Dipping, 232
 Easy Béarnaise, 45
 Espagnole, **159**, 399
 Fresh Tomato, 169, 313
 Garlic & Red Pepper, 280
 Green Peppercorn, 335
 Hollandaise, 24, **208–9**, 399
 Lemon, 25, 213, 250
 Mandarin, 146
 Meat, 201
 Mornay, **275**, 398
 Mousseline, **279**, 399
 Mushroom Cream, 319
 Onion, 119
 Peanut, 33, 219, *219*
 Quick Hollandaise, 153
 Rich Tomato, 194, 259, *259*, 399
 Sour Cherry, 458, *458*
 Soy Orange, 347, *347*
 Spicy Grape, 198
 Spicy Vinegar, 169
 Strawberry, 184
 Suzette, 180
 Tartare, **390**, 391, 434
 Tomato Cream, 261
 Tomato Mint, 242
 Tomato, 396, 472
 Verte, 391, **469**
 Walnut & Garlic, 189
 Walnut, 431
 Whiskey, 204, *204*
 Wine & Mustard, 462
 Yoghurt Cardamom Cream, 185
 Yoghurt, 245
 see also chutneys; dressings; marinades; mayonnaises; salad dressings; salsas; vinaigrettes
sauces, sweet, **400**
 Butterscotch, 29, 400
 Caramel, 400
 Chocolate, 107, 134
 Cinnamon Coconut, 30
 Citrus, 141
 Golden Syrup, 130
 Mocha, 140
 Raspberry, 368
sauerbraten, **394**
sapote, **389**
sauerkraut, **394–5**
sausage rolls, **395**
sausages, **395**, **401–2**
 Bangers & Mash, 158, *158*

Dublin Coddle, 223, *223*
 see also black pudding; salami
sauté, **395**
savarin, **396**
saveloys, **396**
savory, **396**
scalding, **396**
scallions *see* spring onions
scallops, **396–7**, **403**, 411
scaloppine, **397**
 Veal, 225
scampi, **397**
schnitzel, Veal, 462
scones, **400**, **404–5**
 Pumpkin, 361, *361*
scoring, **400–1**
Scotch Eggs, 153, *153*, **401**
Scottish food, **401–3**, **406–8**
 bannocks & baps, **33**
 Cock-a-Leekie, **109**, 423, *423*
 Dundee Cake, 74, *74*, **148**
 haggis, **204**
Scottish pancakes *see* pikelets
seafood, **403–4**, **409–12**
 about, 411
 Baked Fish with Spices, 171
 Barbecued Honey Seafood, 211, *211*
 Blackened Fish, 66, *66*
 Ceviche, **90**, 255, *255*
 Coconut Fish Curry, 111, *111*
 Fish & Chips, 168, *168*
 Fish & Cumin Kebabs, 238, *238*
 Fish Barbecued with Fennel, 161
 Fish Cakes in Corn Husks, 34
 Fish Pie, 170, *170*
 Gefilte Fish, **189**, 236, *236*
 Gravlax, 394, *394*
 Kedgeree, **238**, 375, *375*
 Moroccan Fish, 169, *169*
 Pan Fried Fish, 169
 Pissaladière, 15, *15*, **342**
 Risoni Seafood Soup, 425, *425*
 Seafood Laksa, 217, *217*
 Seafood Noodle Hot Pot, 286, *286*
 Seafood Parcels, 165, *165*
 Seafood Quiches, 363
 Seafood Salad, 381, 410
 Smoked Fish Flan, 172
 Spaghetti Creole, 357
 Spaghetti Marinara, 318, *318*
 Steamed Fish with Ginger, 171, *171*
 Sunomono, 230, *230*
 Sushi Rolls, 231, *231*
 see also under individual seafood eg crab
seasoning, **404**
sea urchins, **404**
semolina, **404**
sesame
 Orange Sesame Rice Salad, 299, *299*
 Sesame Prawns, 356, *356*

sesame oil, *404–5*
sesame seeds, *405*
shallots, *405–6*
shaslik, *406*
shellfish, *406*
shells, pasta, 308, *309*
Shepherd's Pie, 158, *158*, *406–7*
sherbet, *407*
sherry, *407–8*
  Meatballs in Sherry Sauce, 260, *260*
  see also trifle
shish kebabs *see* kebabs
shortbread, *408*, *413–14*
  about, 413
  Hazelnut, 210, *210*
shortcake, *408–9*
  Strawberry, 437, *437*
shortcrust pastry, 320, 322, *409*
shortening, *409*
short soup, *409–10*
  see also Wonton Soup
shrimp paste, *410*
shrimps, *410*
  see also prawns
shungiku *see* snake beans
Siena Cake *see* Panforte
silver beet, *410–11*
silverside, *411*
  see also corned beef
simmering, *411*
simnel cake, *411*
sirloin, *411*
skewers, food on
  about skewers, 31
  Ginger Pork, 31
  Oriental Veal, 239
  Prawn & Melon, 166, *166*
  Souvlakia, 200, *200*
  Yakitori, 167, *167*, 478
  see also kebabs; satays
slices, *415–19*
  Coffee Pecan, 334, *334*
  Date & Chocolate Fudge, 108
  Passionfruit Vanilla, 312, *312*
  Sour Cream & Chocolate, 108, *108*
  Zucchini Apple & Apricot, 484
smoked fish, *165*, *168*
  see also haddock; salmon; seafood; trout
smørrebrød *see* Danish Open Sandwich
snails, *411–12*
snake beans, 39, 467, *467*
snow peas, *326–7*, *412*, *422*, 467, *467*
  Satay Vegetable & Sprout Pancakes, 306
soda bread, *412–13*
  Brown, 222, *222*, *225*
  Soft Cheese, 483, *483*
sorbets, *220–1*, *413–14*
sorghum, *414*

sorrel, 203, *203*, *414–15*
soufflés, *415*, *420–1*
  Classic Omelette, 154, *154–5*
  Cold Lemon, 191, *191*
  Potato, 355
soups, *415–16*, *423–6*
  Beef, 284, *284*
  Borscht, 48, *54*
  Carrot, 85
  Cauliflower, 88
  Chicken & Corn, 97
  Chicken Dumpling, 148, *148*
  Cock-a-Leekie, *109*, 423, *423*
  Corn & Crabmeat, 118
  Creamed Fennel, 160, *160*
  Creamy Asparagus, 25, *25*
  Curried Pumpkin, 361
  freezing of, 183
  French Onion, 178–9, *179*
  Garlic, 189, *189*
  Gazpacho, *189*, 427, *427*
  Hot & Sour Thai Prawn, 358, *358*
  Minestrone, 225, *273*
  Misoshiru, 230
  Miso, 230
  Mulligatawny, *281*, 423
  Mushroom, 281
  Oxtail, 301, *301*
  Parsnip, 311, *311*
  Pea & Ham, 332
  Pork & Bean, 39
  Potato & Tomato, 355
  Split Pea, 259, *259*
  Tomato & Brown Lentil, 452, *452*
  Turnip & Bacon, 461
  Vichyssoise, 424, *469*
  Wonton, 106, *106*
  see also broth; chowder; short soup
sour cream, *416*
sourdough, 143, *416*
soursop, *416*
soy beans, *416–17*
  see also bean curd; Hoisin Sauce; tofu
soy sauce, *417–18*
spaghetti, 308, *309*, *418*
  & Meatballs, 260, *260*
  Carbonara, 314
  Creole, 357
  Marinara, 318, *318*
  Puttanesca, 226, *226*
Spanish food, *418–19*, *422*, *427–9*
  arroz con pollo, *24*
  empanada, *155*
  Gazpacho, *189*, 427, *427*
  Paella, *304*, 428
  Spanish Prawn Salad, 356, *356*
spareribs, *422–3*, *430*
  Barbecued Pork, 32, *32*, 430, *430*
spatchcocks, *423*
  Sweet & Spicy, 33

spearmint, *423*
speck, *423*
speculaas, *423*
spices, *424–5*
spinach, *425*, *431–2*
  microwave cookery of, 271
  Orange & Spinach Salad, 299, *299*
  Spinach Frittata, 181, *181*
  Spinach Gnocchi, 194
  Spinach Soufflé, 420, *420*
split peas, *326*, *425*
  Pease Pudding, *327*, 332, *332*
  Split Pea Soup, 259, *259*
sponge cakes, 75–6, *75*, *76*, *426*
  see also cakes
sponge fingers, *426*
Spotted Dick, 159, *426*
spring onions, 467, *467*, *426–7*
  Sauteed Peas & Spring Onions, 333
  Spring Onion brushes, 372
  see also duxelles
spring rolls, *427*, *433*
  Mini, 104, *104*
sprouts, *427–8*
spumone, *428*
spun sugar, 83, *428*
squabs, *428*
squash, *429*
squid, *429*, *434*
star anise, *430*
star fruit *see* carambola
steak, *430*, *435–6*
  see also beef
steamboat, *431*
steamed pudding, *431–2*
  Dark Chocolate Pudding, 140, *140*
  Fruit Mince Pudding, 141, *141*
  Steamed Jam Pudding, 141
steaming, *430–1*
stews, *432*
  freezing, 183
  Guinness Beef, 223, *223*
  Irish, 224, *224*, *226*
  Lancashire Hot Pot, *241*, *243*, *243*
  Seafood, 412, *412*
  Tomato & Pepper, 450, *450*
stilton cheese, 51, *433*
stir-fries, *433*
  Broccoli & Onion, 41, *41*
  Devilled Turkey, 460, *460*
  Stir-fried Beef & Snow Peas, 422
stock, *433*
  Beef, 43
  bouillon, *54–5*
  Chicken, 97
  see also court bouillon; dashi
stollen, *434*
strawberries, *434*, *437–8*
  Blueberry & Strawberry Cheesecake, 92, *92*

Meringue Nests with Kahlua Cream & Strawberries, 263, *264*
  Raspberry & Strawberry Ripple, 367
  Strawberry Ice-cream, 220
  Strawberry Sauce, 184, 400, *400*
strawberry tomatoes *see* Cape gooseberries
stroganoff, *434–5*, *439*
strudels, *435*, *440–1*
  Asparagus, 165
stuffing, *435–6*
  Apple, 460
  Breadcrumb, 96
  Chestnut, 95
  Roast Duck, 146
  Rosemary, 240
succotash, *436*
suckling pig, *436*
suet, *436–7*
  Suet Pastry, 436
sugar, *437–8*
sugar peas *see* snow peas
sugar snap peas, *412*
sukiyaki, *439*
sultanas, *439*
Summer Pudding, 135, *135*, *439–40*
sundaes, *440*
  with Strawberry Sauce, 400
sunflower seeds, *440–1*
supreme of chicken, *441*
sushi, 231, *231*, *441–2*
swedes, *442*
sweet & sour sauce, *442*
sweetbreads, *442*
sweet corn *see* corn
sweet peppers *see* peppers, sweet
sweet potatoes, *442*, *442–3*
  about, 442
Swiss chard *see* silver beet
Swiss rolls, *443*, *443*
  about, 443
syrups, *443*
  Ginger, 262
  golden, 130, *193*
  Lemon, 251, 481
  maple, *261*
Szechwan pepper, *443*

T

tabasco, *444*
Tabouli, 247, *247*, *444–5*
tacos, *445*
  Spicy Beef & Bean, 268, *268*
taffy, *445*
tagine, *445*
  Lamb with Quinces, 365, *365*
tagliatelle, 309, *445–6*
tahini, *446*
tamale, *446*
tamarillo, *446–7*
tamarind, *447*

tandoori, *447*
  Chicken Kebabs, 216, *216*
tangelo, *447*
tangerines, *448*
tapas, *448*
Tapenade, 351, *448*
tapioca, *448*
Taramasalata, 140, 167, *167*, 199, *199*, *449*
taro, 467, *467*, *449*
tarragon, 203, *203*, *449*
  Roast Leg of Lamb with Sage & Tarragon, 241, *241*
Tartare, Sauce, 390, 391, 434, *450*
tarte tatin, *450*
tarts, *444–6*, *450*
  Almond & Pear, 10, *10*
  Blueberry Cheese, 139, *139*
  Blueberry Cream, 323
  Buttermilk Nutmeg, 139, *139*
  Custard, 127
  Date & Mascarpone, 128
  Frozen Lemon, 249, *249*
  Goats Cheese & Artichoke, 166, *166*
  Leek, 248, *248*
  Mince, 268, *269*
  Queen Mary's, 408, *408*
  see also flans
tea, 144, *216*, *450–1*
teacakes, 79, *79*, *451*
tempura, *451*
  Vegetable, 232, *232*
tenderloin, *163*, *451*
teriyaki, *451*
  see also beef; chicken; tuna
terrines, 317–18, *447*, *451–2*
  about, 447
  Spinach & Salmon, 432, *432*
Thai food, *452–3*
  Crisp-fried Thai Noodles, 285, *285*
  Hot & Sour Prawn Soup, 358, *358*
  Thai Corn Pancakes, 307, *307*
  Thai Dressing, 25
  Thai Papaya Salad, 310, *310*
  Thai Potato Salad, 388, *388*
Thousand Island Dressing, 391
thyme, 203, *203*, *453*
  Honeyed Baby Turnips with Lemon Thyme, 461, *461*
  Thyme & Onions, 295, *295*
tilsit, *453*
timbale, *453*
tipsy cake, *453–4*
tiramisù, *454*
tisanes, *454*
toast, *454–5*
toffee, *455*
tofu, *448*, *455*
  about, 448
  see also bean curd
tomatoes, *449–53*, *455–6*
  Apple, Tomato & Mint Chutney, 110, *110*

tomatoes *(continued)*
Fresh Tomato Sauce, 169
microwave cookery of, 271
Minted Tomato & Beans, 40, *40*
Napoli Focaccia, 176, *177*
Okra with Onions & Tomato, 293, *293*
Peas with Basil & Tomato, 330, *330*
Potato & Tomato Soup, 355
Rich Tomato Sauce, 194, 259, *259*, 399
Ricotta-filled Ravioli with Fresh Tomato Sauce, 313, *313*
Rosemary, Tomato & Apple Jelly, 233, *233*
Spicy Onions & Tomatoes, 294, *294*
Stuffed Tomatoes, 452, *452*
Sun-dried Tomato Dip with Grissini & Crudités, 142, *142*
Tomato Chutney, 339, *339*
Tomato Cream Sauce, 261
Tomato Garlic Mussels, 282, *282*
Tomato-Mint Sauce, 242
Tomato Relish, 88, 246
Tomato Rice Cups, 374, *374*
Tomato Salad, 17, *17*
Tomato Salsa, 267, *267*
Tomato Sauce, 396, 472
tong ho *see* chrysanthemum leaves
tongue, **456**
tortellini, 308, *309*, **456**
with Mushroom Cream Sauce, 319
tortes, **456**
see also cakes
tortilla, 117, *117*, **456–7**
tournedos, **457**
treacle, **457**
trifle, 136, *136*, **457**
Strawberry, 438, *438*
tripe, **457**
Tripe & Onions, 292, *292*
trout, **454–5**, **457**
about, 455
Barbecued Trout with Horseradish Cream & Lemon Sauce, 213, *213*

Smoked Trout Mousse, 173
Trout with Parsley Butter, 407, *407*
truffles, chocolate, **458**
truffles (fungi), **458**
trussing, **458**
tuiles, **458–9**
see also biscuits
tuna, **456–7**, *459*
Fettuccine & Tuna with Capers, 174
Tuna Mornay, 174
Tuna Salad, 385, *385*
turkey, **458–60**, *459–60*
carving, 86
microwave defrosting of, 270
Turkey Salad with Cranberry Dressing, 385
Turkish coffee, 113
Turkish Delight, 115, *115*, **460**
turmeric, **460**
turnips, **460–1**, *461*
turnovers, **461**
Tzatziki, 199, *199*, **461**

U

upside-down cake, **461**

V

vacherin, **462**
Apricot & Almond, 263, *263*
vanilla, **462–3**
Baked Vanilla Custard, 125, *125*
Basic Vanilla Ice-cream, 220, *221*
Passionfruit Vanilla Slice, 312, *312*
Vanilla Buttercream Icing, 81
Vanilla Cream Sauce, 400
Vanilla Fingers, 326, *326*
variety meats *see* offal
veal, **462–5**, *463–4*
about, 465
Apricot Veal Birds, 20, *20*
Oriental Veal Sticks, 239
Osso Bucco, **301**, 464, *464*
Pork & Veal Terrine, 447

Veal Chops with Sage & Lemon, 227
Wonton Frills, 166, *166*
see also scaloppine; schnitzel
vegetable marrows, **465**
vegetables, *464–5*, **468–73**
Asian Noodle Vegetable Salad, 382, *382*
Asian vegetables, **466–7**
Cajun Vegetables, 66
Chinese Vegetables with Mushrooms & Oyster Sauce, 281, *281*
Crisp Fried Noodles with Chilli Vegetables, 286, *286*
freezing, 183
Gourmet Vegetable Pizza, 343, *343*
Honey-braised Vegetables with Bean Curd, 36, *36*
microwave cookery of, 270-1
Mixed Vegetables with Garlic Mayonnaise, 428, *428*
Pasta & Vegetables, 316, *316*
pickled, 338–9, *338*, *339*
Rice & Vegetable Pilaf, 376, *376*
Vegeburger with Chick Pea Sauce, 208
Vegetable & Sprout Pancakes, 306
Vegetable Couscous, 273, *273*
Vegetable Curry, 124, *124*
Vegetable Lasagna, 319, *319*
Vegetable Pakoras, 214–15, *215*
Vegetable Pie, 342
Vegetable Quiche, 364, *364*
Vegetable Risotto, 377, *377*
Vegetable Tempura, 232, *232*
Vegetable Wontons, 477, *477*
Vegetarian Mini Spring Rolls, 433, *433*
see also under individual vegetables eg tomatoes
velouté sauce, **465**
venison, **465–6**
Venison Pie, 186, *186*
vermicelli, 288, *288*, 308, *468*
vermouth, *468*

Vichyssoise, 424, *469*
Victoria sponge, *469*
Vienna Coffee, Spiced, 113
Vietnamese Chicken Salad, 328, *328*
vinaigrettes, *469*
Avocado, 27
Basic, 390
Dill, 412
see also dressings; marinades; mayonnaises
vinegars, *470–3*
for pickles & chutneys, 338
for salad dressings, 390
vine leaves, *470*
vol-au-vent, *473*

W

wafers, *474*
waffles, *474*
Waldorf Salad, 381, *381*, *474*
walnut oil, *475*
walnuts, *474*, *474–5*
Bean & Walnut Salad, 40, *40*
Citrus Walnut Salad, 386
Date & Walnut Loaf, 128
Prune & Nut Loaf, 359, *359*
Sherried Duck with Olives & Walnuts, 147
Walnut & Garlic Sauce, 189
Walnut Brownies, 416–17
Walnut Dressing, 386
Walnut Sauce, 431
wasabi, *475*
water chestnuts, *475*
watercress, 467, *467*, *475*
Grapefruit Watercress Salad, 197, *197*
Watercress Soup, 424, *424*
watermelons, *476*
waterzooi, *476*
Welsh rarebit *see* rarebit
wheat, *476*
see also durum wheat
wheat noodles, 288
whitebait, *476*
white sauce, *476*
see also Béchamel Sauce
wholemeal, *476*
see also bread; muffins
wild rice, *477*

wine, *477*
Octopus in Red Wine, 290
Pears Poached in White Wine, 329, *329*
see also port; sherry
winter cherries *see* Cape gooseberries
witloof *see* chicory
wong bok *see* Chinese cabbage
wontons, *476–7*, *477*
Frills, 166, *166*
Soup, 106, *106*
see also short soup
woo tow, 467
worcestershire sauce, *477*

Y

yabbies, *478*
Yakitori, 167, *167*, *478*
yams, *479*
yarrow, *479*
yeast, *478–80*, *479*
about, 479
yellow wax beans, 39
yoghurt, *480–1*, *481–3*
Cucumber Yoghurt, 192
Lassi, *243*
Mint & Yoghurt Raita, 258
Onion & Mint in Yoghurt, 216
Yoghurt & Cucumber Raita, 215
Yoghurt Cardamom Cream, 185
Yoghurt Sauce, 245
Yorkshire Pudding, 42, *42*, *481*
youngberries, *481*
yule log, *481*

Z

zabaglione, 227, *227*, *484*
zest, *484*
ziti pasta, 308
zucchini, *484–5*, *484–5*
microwave cookery of, 271
Peach & Zucchini Muffins, 327
Zucchini Cheese Dumplings, 148
see also Chinese zucchini
zwieback, *485*

ACKNOWLEDGEMENTS

HOME ECONOMISTS: Tracy Rutherford, Tracey Port, Jo Forrest, Maria Sampsonis, Melanie McDermott, Dimitra Stais, Donna Hay, Jodie Vassallo, Jo Kennedy, Kerrie Carr, Cherise Koch, Denise Munro, Voula Mantzouridis, Anna Paola Boyd, Christine Sheppard
PHOTOGRAPHY: Luis Martin (special features), Andre Martin (cover), Reg Morrison, Jon Bader, Joe Filshie, Peter Scott, Andrew Furlong, Ray Joyce, Phil Haley, Hans Schlupp
STYLISTS: Mary Harris (special features), Carolyn Fienberg (cover),

Rosemary De Santis, Suzie Smith, Wendy Berecry, Anna Phillips, Georgina Dolling
ARTISTS: Jackie Richards, Wing Ping Tong, Joanne Morris, Southida Vongsaphay

Sydney Market Authority, The Sharp Home Library of Microwave Cooking (for microwave information)
For props: Pacific East India Co.; Barbara's Storehouse